1991-1992 BASKETBALL ALMANAC

Contributing Writers
Matt Marsom
Marty Strasen
Nick Rousso
Michael Bradley
Morgan Hughes
Bob Sakamoto
Bruce Martin
Pete Palmer
David Korus
Tom Owens

PUBLICATIONS INTERNATIONAL, LTD.

Matt Marsom is managing editor of *Basketball Weekly,* where he also serves as a writer of both pro and college basketball. Marsom is a contributing writer for *Street & Smith* magazines.

Marty Strasen is assistant editor of *Basketball Weekly* and covers both pro and college basketball. He has also written for several major newspapers, including the *Detroit Free Press.*

Nick Rousso is the editor of *Dick Vitale's Basketball* and *Don Heinrich's College Football,* and is an associate editor for *Bill Mazeroski's Baseball, The Show,* and *Don Heinrich's Pro Review.*

Michael Bradley is a freelance writer whose work has appeared in *The Sporting News, The Philadelphia Inquirer,* and a variety of national sports publications.

Morgan Hughes is the former editor of *Grandslam Baseball* and *Hockey Stars and Hockey Heroes* and is currently editor of *Tennis Midwest.* He is also a freelance writer who has contributed to *The Sporting News, Sport, Village Voice,* and *Hockey Scene.*

Bob Sakamoto is a sports reporter for the *Chicago Tribune,* covering the Chicago Bears. He formerly covered the Chicago Bulls and is the author of *Michael "Air" Jordan: MVP & NBA Champ.* He is a regular contributor to *Basketball Weekly.*

Bruce Martin has covered the Charlotte Hornets for *The Gazette* in Gastonia, North Carolina, since the team's inception in 1987. He is a freelance writer who contributes to *Basketball Weekly, Courtside, Beckett Basketball Monthly,* and *Street & Smith's Pro Basketball.*

Pete Palmer edited both *Total Baseball* and *The Hidden Game of Baseball* with John Thorn. Palmer, a renowned sports statistician, is a member of the Society for American Baseball Research (SABR).

David Korus is a freelance statistician who lives in Massachusetts.

Tom Owens is the author of *Greatest Baseball Players of All Time, Collecting Sports Autographs,* and the *1991 Official Baseball Card Price Guide.* He is a former editor of *Sports Collectors Digest.*

CONTENTS

CONTENTS
5

CONTENTS

CONTENTS 7

NBA Veterans And Rookies

In this section, you'll find scouting reports on 300 NBA veterans and 60 NBA rookies (plus a recap of the 1991 college draft on page 309). Considering that the NBA will tip off the 1991-92 season with exactly 324 players, this section is sure to include virtually every NBA player—and then some.

Each player's scouting report begins with his vital stats: team, position, height, weight, etc. Next comes a four-part evaluation of the player. "Background" reviews the player's career, starting with college and continuing up through the 1990-91 season. "Strengths" examines his best assets, including things like character and leadership.

"Weaknesses" assesses the player's significant flaws, including things like attitude and off-court behavior. And "analysis" tries to put the player's game into perspective. Is he on the way up or on the way down? How does he fit in with his team's system? What can be expected of him in 1991-92? These are some of the questions that are explored.

For a quick run-down on each player, you'll find a "player summary" box. The box also includes a "fantasy value" figure, which suggests a draft price for any of the fantasy basketball games that have mushroomed throughout the country. The price range is a guide based on $260 for a 15-player roster. No player can be worth more than $100 (though Michael Jordan comes pretty close).

Finally, the box contains a "card value" figure, which is a suggested buying price for a mint 1991-92 basketball card of that player. The price does not take into account any error, variation, or specialty cards.

The scouting reports of the NBA veterans include their college and NBA statistics. The college stats include games (G), field goal percentage (FGP), free throw percentage (FTP), rebounds per game (RPG), and points per game (PPG). The veterans' NBA stats include the following:

- games (G)
- minutes (MIN)
- field goals made (FGs/FG)
- field goal percentage (FGs/PCT)
- 3-point field goals made (3-PT FGs/FG)
- 3-point field goal percentage (3-PT FGs/PCT)
- free throws made (FTs/FT)
- free throw percentage (FTs/PCT)
- offensive rebounds (Rebounds/OFF)
- total rebounds (Rebounds/TOT)
- assists (AST)
- steals (STL)
- blocked shots (BLK)
- points (PTS)
- points per game (PPG)

The statistics of rookie players are treated a little differently. Their college statistics are expanded to include most of the same categories listed immediately above. For rookies, you'll also find a list of their college achievements, such as All-America and all-conference honors.

ALAA ABDELNABY

Team: Portland Trail Blazers
Position: Forward
Height: 6'10" **Weight:** 240
Birthdate: June 24, 1968
NBA Experience: 1 year

College: Duke
Acquired: 1st-round pick in
1990 draft (25th overall)

Background: Abdelnaby, who was born in Egypt and moved to the United States in 1971, led Duke to three Final Four appearances and established a school record for career field goal percentage (.599). His limited playing time as a rookie can be attributed to the stockpile of talent in Portland, but he did show progress during the second half of the 1990-91 season.

Strengths: Abdelnaby is not a prolific rebounder, scorer, or defender, but he does all three well enough to warrant a chance. He displays good hands. Portland has been impressed with his maturity, work ethic, and smarts. He has low-post offensive potential but is unpolished.

Weaknesses: A former college center, Abdelnaby must learn how to play power forward while facing the basket. Without a refined offensive game by NBA standards, Abdelnaby must develop more confidence in his medium-range jump shot. Free throw shooting is another area of concern.

Analysis: Abdelnaby showed tremendous improvement late in his college career and elevated himself to a first-round draft choice with his progress at the various all-star camps. However, that growth has been slowed by having to spend most of his time on the bench of a team loaded with standout big men. With increased minutes, Abdelnaby could develop into a steady contributor.

PLAYER SUMMARY	
Will	improve
Can't	dribble
Expect	nothing fancy
Don't Expect	many minutes
Fantasy Value	$1-2
Card Value	10¢

COLLEGE STATISTICS

		G	FGP	FTP	RPG	PPG
86-87	DUKE	29	.580	.522	1.7	3.7
87-88	DUKE	34	.496	.698	2.0	4.9
88-89	DUKE	33	.634	.701	3.8	8.9
89-90	DUKE	38	.620	.775	6.6	15.1
Totals		134	.599	.728	3.7	8.5

NBA REGULAR-SEASON STATISTICS

		G	MIN	FGs FG	FGs PCT	3-PT FGs FG	3-PT FGs PCT	FTs FT	FTs PCT	Rebounds OFF	Rebounds TOT	AST	STL	BLK	PTS	PPG
90-91	POR	43	290	55	.474	0	.000	25	.568	27	89	12	4	12	135	3.1
Totals		43	290	55	.474	0	.000	25	.568	27	89	12	4	12	135	3.1

MARK ACRES

Team: Orlando Magic
Position: Forward/Center
Height: 6'11" **Weight:** 225
Birthdate: November 15, 1962
NBA Experience: 4 years

College: Oral Roberts
Acquired: Selected from Celtics in
1989 expansion draft

Background: Acres set school records at Oral Roberts in field goal percentage and blocked shots. He played in Europe for two seasons and then joined the Celtics for two years as a bench player. After being selected by Orlando in the 1989 expansion draft, Acres had his best season as a pro, recording career highs in points, rebounds, and assists.

Strengths: Acres uses his big body effectively inside and is a smart frontcourt player. He grabs the rebounds he's supposed to get and makes few mistakes. Acres is an unselfish role player, content to contribute starting or coming off the bench.

Weaknesses: His lack of quickness hurts him in a league where speed is commonplace. He has no inside scoring moves and he can't shoot either. Position defense is why he's on the floor, but he's hardly a scare to opposing centers. Acres blocks few shots and commits many fouls.

Analysis: Acres is a No. 3 center who has moved to the No. 2 spot on the talent-poor Magic (remember, Greg Kite is Orlando's starting center). Acres will hang on in the league because he's a role player who has a good attitude and does the job he's assigned to do. Still, he has very little talent.

PLAYER SUMMARY

Will..rebound
Can't...........................average 20 points
Expect......................low-profile minutes
Don't Expect.............inside domination
Fantasy Value..................................$1-2
Card Value..5¢

COLLEGE STATISTICS

		G	FGP	FTP	RPG	PPG
81-82	OR	22	.586	.727	8.1	14.6
82-83	OR	28	.552	.719	9.6	18.8
83-84	OR	31	.552	.717	10.5	20.8
84-85	OR	29	.582	.626	9.7	18.8
Totals		110	.564	.696	9.6	18.5

NBA REGULAR-SEASON STATISTICS

			FGs		3-PT FGs		FTs		Rebounds						
		G	MIN	FG	PCT	FG	PCT	FT	PCT	OFF	TOT	AST	STL	BLK	PTS	PPG
87-88	BOS	79	1151| 108	.532	0	.000	71	.640	105	270	42	29	27	287	3.6
88-89	BOS	62	632	55	.482	1	1.000| 26	.542	59	146	19	19	6	137	2.2
89-90	ORL	80	1691| 138	.484	3	.750	83	.692	154	431	67	36	25	362	4.5
90-91	ORL	68	1313| 109	.509	1	.333	66	.653	140	359	25	25	25	285	4.2
Totals		289	4787	410	.502	5	.625	246	.647	458	1206	153	109	83	1071	3.7

MICHAEL ADAMS

Team: Washington Bullets
Position: Guard
Height: 5'10" **Weight:** 165
Birthdate: January 19, 1963
NBA Experience: 6 years

College: Boston College
Acquired: Traded from Nuggets for a
1991 first-round pick, 6/91

Background: Adams was named second-team All-Big East three straight years at Boston College. The former CBA Rookie of the Year (1986) holds or has held numerous NBA records for 3-point shots attempted and made. He enjoyed his most productive season in 1990-91, leading the Nuggets in scoring, assists, and steals while becoming the NBA's all-time leader in 3-pointers with 658. Denver dealt him to Washington in June.

Strengths: Adams's main weapon is his quickness, which explains his high-scoring 1990-91 campaign under the run-and-gun system of Nuggets coach Paul Westhead. He races the ball up-court and can penetrate nearly at will. When he heats up with his long-range heaves, few players can put points on the board as quickly. He shares the NBA record of nine 3-pointers in a game with Dale Ellis.

Weaknesses: At times, Adams goes too fast for his own good. Despite good ball-handling skills, his reckless style results in a lot of turnovers and his teammates are not always able to keep up with him. Although Adams launches more than eight 3-point shots per game, he converts less than 30 percent.

Analysis: Because of his quickness, Adams is one of the most difficult players in the league to defend. He creates huge match-up problems. However, Adams occasionally becomes his own best defender by playing out of control and taking ill-advised shots. Washington coach Wes Unseld will certainly limit Adams's creative freedom this year.

PLAYER SUMMARY

Will ....set tempo
Can't ....slow down
Expect 3-pointers
Don't Expect ....high FG pct.
Fantasy Value $27-30
Card Value..................................5¢

COLLEGE STATISTICS

		G	FGP	FTP	RPG	PPG
81-82	BC	26	.495	.590	1.2	5.3
82-83	BC	32	.481	.809	2.7	16.2
83-84	BC	30	.455	.756	3.4	17.3
84-85	BC	31	.467	.748	3.3	15.3
Totals		119	.470	.750	2.7	13.9

NBA REGULAR-SEASON STATISTICS

				FGs		3-PT FGs		FTs		Rebounds						
		G	MIN	FG	PCT	FG	PCT	FT	PCT	OFF	TOT	AST	STL	BLK	PTS	PPG
85-86	SAC	18	139	16	.364	0	.000	8	.667	2	6	22	9	1	40	2.2
86-87	WAS	63	1303	160	.407	28	.275	105	.847	38	123	244	85	6	453	7.2
87-88	DEN	82	2778	416	.449	139	.367	166	.834	40	223	503	168	16	1137	13.9
88-89	DEN	77	2787	468	.433	166	.356	322	.819	71	283	490	166	11	1424	18.5
89-90	DEN	79	2690	398	.402	158	.366	267	.850	49	225	495	121	3	1221	15.5
90-91	DEN	66	2346	560	.394	167	.296	465	.879	58	256	693	147	6	1752	26.5
Totals		385	12043	2018	.416	658	.338	1333	.849	258	1116	2447	696	43	6027	15.7

MARK AGUIRRE

Team: Detroit Pistons
Position: Forward
Height: 6'6" **Weight:** 232
Birthdate: December 10, 1959
NBA Experience: 10 years

College: DePaul
Acquired: Traded from Mavericks for Adrian Dantley and a 1991 1st-round pick, 2/89

Background: Aguirre is credited with putting DePaul on the big-time NCAA basketball map. He made the 1980 U.S. Olympic team and, in 1981, was *The Sporting News* College Player of the Year. Aguirre was the No. 1 pick in the 1981 draft and was a mainstay with the Mavericks for almost eight years, averaging at least 22.6 PPG for six seasons. He eventually wore out coach John MacLeod with his petulant outbursts.

Strengths: Aguirre is a scorer, period. When the Pistons needed instant offense off the bench, they called on Aguirre. He can can the jumper, nail the 3-pointer, or post up on his man and beat him to the hoop.

Weaknesses: The biggest one is his mouth. His career has been held back by a penchant for complaining and stirring up dissension on a ballclub. Aguirre is not much of a rebounder, and his passive defense cost him playing time in Detroit.

Analysis: Aguirre began wearing out his welcome in the Motor City despite the presence of good friend Isiah Thomas, and he's expected to be wearing a new uniform this season. He can still carry a team in stretches with his offensive skills.

PLAYER SUMMARY
Will ....score inside and out
Can't ....find happiness
Expect ....scoring binges
Don't Expect.................strong defense
Fantasy Value $12-15
Card Value...8¢

COLLEGE STATISTICS

		G	FGP	FTP	RPG	PPG
78-79	DeP	32	.520	.765	7.6	24.0
79-80	DeP	28	.540	.766	7.6	26.8
80-81	DeP	29	.582	.774	8.6	23.0
Totals		89	.546	.768	7.9	24.5

NBA REGULAR-SEASON STATISTICS

		G	MIN	FG	PCT	FG	PCT	FT	PCT	OFF	TOT	AST	STL	BLK	PTS	PPG
81-82	DAL	51	1468	381	.465	25	.352	168	.680	89	249	164	37	22	955	18.7
82-83	DAL	81	2784	767	.483	16	.211	429	.728	191	508	332	80	26	1979	24.4
83-84	DAL	79	2900	925	.524	15	.268	465	.749	161	469	358	80	22	2330	29.5
84-85	DAL	80	2699	794	.506	27	.318	440	.759	188	477	249	60	24	2055	25.7
85-86	DAL	74	2501	668	.503	16	.286	318	.705	177	445	339	62	14	1670	22.6
86-87	DAL	80	2663	787	.495	53	.353	429	.770	181	427	254	84	30	2056	25.7
87-88	DAL	77	2610	746	.475	52	.302	388	.770	182	434	278	70	57	1932	25.1
88-89	DAL/DET	80	2597	586	.461	51	.293	288	.733	146	386	278	45	36	1511	18.9
89-90	DET	78	2005	438	.488	31	.333	192	.756	117	305	145	34	19	1099	14.1
90-91	DET	78	2006	420	.462	24	.308	240	.757	134	374	139	47	20	1104	14.2
Totals		758	24233	6512	.489	310	.307	3357	.744	1566	4074	2536	599	270	16691	22.0

DANNY AINGE

Team: Portland Trail Blazers
Position: Guard
Height: 6'5" **Weight:** 185
Birthdate: March 17, 1959
NBA Experience: 10 years

College: Brigham Young
Aquired: Traded from Kings for Byron Irvin, a 1991 1st-round pick, a 1992 2nd-round pick, and cash, 8/90

Background: Ainge was a multi-sport star at Brigham Young and played two years of professional baseball with the Toronto Blue Jays, primarily as an infielder. He batted .220. He has enjoyed much better success in the NBA, where he was an All-Star in 1988 and won two championship rings with the Boston Celtics. Ainge spent 1990-91 as Portland's third guard.

Strengths: Ainge is a fierce competitor with championship experience, a knack for leadership, and uncanny court sense. Not only does he bury his long-range shots with consistency, but he is not afraid to launch them in crucial situations. When the game is up for grabs, Ainge can win it.

Weaknesses: Those boos that follow Ainge to opposing arenas serve as a reminder that his temper has gotten the best of him in the past. Although he's not nearly the antagonist he once was, Ainge has always played with an emotional fire that sometimes works against him. Defense and quickness have never been his favorite subjects.

Analysis: What Ainge lacks in raw talent, he makes up for in effort and intensity. He accepted his bench role in Portland after a season as the superstar in Sacramento. His shooting touch and mere presence on the floor made the 1990-91 Trail Blazers a better team than they were the previous year.

PLAYER SUMMARY

Will ....mix it up
Can't...........................shake reputation
Expect ....instant offense
Don't Expect...........................fan clubs
Fantasy Value $15-17
Card Value...............................10¢

COLLEGE STATISTICS

		G	FGP	FTP	RPG	PPG
77-78	BYU	30	.514	.864	5.8	21.1
78-79	BYU	27	.548	.768	3.8	18.4
79-80	BYU	29	.533	.782	3.9	19.1
80-81	BYU	32	.518	.824	4.8	24.4
Totals		118	.526	.816	4.6	20.9

NBA REGULAR-SEASON STATISTICS

		G	MIN	FG	PCT	FG	PCT	FT	PCT	OFF	TOT	AST	STL	BLK	PTS	PPG
81-82	BOS	53	564	79	.357	5	.294	56	.862	25	56	87	37	3	219	4.1
82-83	BOS	80	2048	357	.496	5	.172	72	.742	83	214	251	109	6	791	9.9
83-84	BOS	71	1154	166	.460	6	.273	46	.821	29	116	162	41	4	384	5.4
84-85	BOS	75	2564	419	.529	15	.268	118	.868	76	268	399	122	6	971	12.9
85-86	BOS	80	2407	353	.504	26	.356	123	.904	47	235	405	94	7	855	10.7
86-87	BOS	71	2499	410	.486	85	.443	148	.897	49	242	400	101	14	1053	14.8
87-88	BOS	81	3018	482	.491	148	.415	158	.878	59	249	503	115	17	1270	15.7
88-89	BOS/SAC	73	2377	480	.457	116	.380	205	.854	71	255	402	93	8	1281	17.5
89-90	SAC	75	2727	506	.438	108	.374	222	.831	69	326	453	113	18	1342	17.9
90-91	POR	80	1710	337	.472	102	.406	114	.826	45	205	285	63	13	890	11.1
Totals		739	21068	3589	.476	616	.387	1262	.853	553	2166	3347	888	96	9056	12.3

MARK ALARIE

Team: Washington Bullets
Position: Forward
Height: 6'8" **Weight:** 225
Birthdate: December 11, 1963
NBA Experience: 5 years

College: Duke
Acquired: Traded from Nuggets with Darrell Walker for Jay Vincent and Michael Adams, 11/87

Background: Alarie was a mainstay on three of Duke's NCAA tournament teams, and he was named first-team All-ACC as a senior. He came into the NBA with a reputation as a hard-nosed, physical, smart player. Alarie had his breakthrough season in 1989-90 when he averaged in double figures for the first time. He missed an extended period of time in 1990-91 because of tendinitis in his knee.

Strengths: Alarie's aggressiveness on the backboards and sound fundamentals make him a valuable role player. He's also a darn good outside shooter, with range up to 20 feet. Though right-handed, Alarie is a better dribbler left-handed.

Weaknesses: He is not really big enough to bang with the true power forwards and not quick enough to stay with the true small forwards. Though a good shooter, Alarie doesn't have the quickness to create his own shots.

Analysis: Alarie is a good team player with limitations that can be covered up in certain systems. The Bullets can use him defensively to bang against certain forwards. His surprisingly good outside shot is another perk.

PLAYER SUMMARY	
Will	clean boards
Can't	blow by anyone
Expect	quality bench minutes
Don't Expect	acrobatic moves
Fantasy Value	$1-2
Card Value	5¢

COLLEGE STATISTICS

		G	FGP	FTP	RPG	PPG
82-83	DUKE	28	.494	.813	6.5	13.0
83-84	DUKE	34	.575	.761	7.2	17.5
84-85	DUKE	31	.585	.792	5.1	15.9
85-86	DUKE	40	.535	.822	6.2	17.1
Totals		133	.550	.797	6.3	16.1

NBA REGULAR-SEASON STATISTICS

		G	MIN	FGs FG	FGs PCT	3-PT FGs FG	3-PT FGs PCT	FTs FT	FTs PCT	Rebounds OFF	Rebounds TOT	AST	STL	BLK	PTS	PPG
86-87	DEN	64	1110	217	.490	2	.222	67	.663	73	214	74	22	28	503	7.9
87-88	WAS	63	769	144	.480	4	.222	35	.714	70	160	39	10	12	327	5.2
88-89	WAS	74	1141	206	.478	13	.342	73	.839	103	255	63	25	22	498	6.7
89-90	WAS	82	1893	371	.473	10	.204	108	.812	151	374	142	60	39	860	10.5
90-91	WAS	42	587	99	.440	5	.238	41	.854	41	117	45	15	8	244	5.8
Totals		325	5500	1037	.475	34	.252	324	.775	438	1120	363	132	109	2432	7.5

GREG ANDERSON

Team: Denver Nuggets
Position: Forward/Center
Height: 6'10" **Weight:** 230
Birthdate: June 22, 1964
NBA Experience: 4 years
College: Houston

Acquired: Traded from Nets with a future first-round pick via the Trail Blazers; Nuggets sent Walter Davis to Blazers, and Blazers sent Drazen Petrovic and Terry Mills to Nets, 1/91

Background: Anderson played behind Akeem Olajuwon as a freshman at the University of Houston before starting his final three years and emerging as one of the top rebounders in Southwest Conference history. He was named to the NBA All-Rookie Team with San Antonio and played two promising years there. Since he underwent knee surgery in 1989, however, he has been a journeyman of sorts. He concluded 1990-91 with Denver and finished last on the team in scoring.

Strengths: Anderson is a skilled rebounder and an adept inside scorer when at the top of his game, but he has done nothing consistently since the knee injury. He runs the floor well for a big man and has a cool nickname—"Cadillac."

Weaknesses: It would be too simple to blame Anderson's demise on an injury, because he is capable of contributing far more than he does. There are legitimate questions about his desire to excel. In addition to his struggles in every other category, Anderson's shooting has eroded. His offensive range is limited and he does not handle the ball well at all.

Analysis: At this stage, Anderson has to be considered a huge question mark. He obviously possesses sufficient skills to play pro basketball. The challenge will be for him to put the past couple of years behind and regain some of his San Antonio form. Anderson may already have reached his peak.

PLAYER SUMMARY

Will..rebound
Can't.............................handle the ball
Expect.................................more trades
Don't Expect....................consistency
Fantasy Value.............................$1-2
Card Value.......................................5¢

COLLEGE STATISTICS

		G	FGP	FTP	RPG	PPG
83-84	HOU	35	.485	.528	3.5	3.3
84-85	HOU	30	.573	.535	8.1	15.4
85-86	HOU	28	.572	.586	12.9	19.1
86-87	HOU	30	.526	.604	10.6	18.2
Totals		123	.550	.576	8.5	13.5

NBA REGULAR-SEASON STATISTICS

				FGs		3-PT FGs		FTs		Rebounds						
		G	MIN	FG	PCT	FG	PCT	FT	PCT	OFF	TOT	AST	STL	BLK	PTS	PPG
87-88	SA	82	1984	379	.501	1	.200	198	.604	161	513	79	54	122	957	11.7
88-89	SA	82	2401	460	.503	0	.000	207	.514	255	676	61	102	103	1127	13.7
89-90	MIL	60	1291	219	.507	0	.000	91	.535	112	373	24	32	54	529	8.8
90-91	MIL/NJ/DEN															
		68	924	116	.430	0	.000	60	.522	97	318	16	35	45	292	4.3
Totals		292	6600	1174	.495	1	.111	556	.547	625	1880	180	223	324	2905	9.9

NICK ANDERSON

Team: Orlando Magic
Position: Forward/Guard
Height: 6'6" **Weight:** 205
Birthdate: January 20, 1968

NBA Experience: 2 years
College: Illinois
Acquired: 1st-round pick in 1989 draft
(11th overall)

Background: Anderson was a starter on the "Flying Illini" Final Four team of 1988-89, and he was a unanimous All-Big Ten selection that year. In his rookie season with Orlando, he played in 81 games and reached double figures in scoring. He finished fourth on the club in that department in 1990-91.

Strengths: Anderson's game is scoring. He's not an exceptional shooter, but he knows how to take it to the hole. He's strong, quick, and can really sky. He can beat his man, slam it home, and draw the foul.

Weaknesses: Though listed at 6'6", he's probably an inch or two shorter than that. Anderson plays the game like a small forward but is too small to play the position. And he doesn't have the consistent outside shot to be a two guard. Though he goes to the line, his free throw shooting is weak, especially for a guard. He has struggled defensively in the NBA. He's not a great ball-handler.

Analysis: Anderson is a strong NBA talent who will only get better. If he steadily improves his jumper, his free throw shooting, and his defense, then he'll really be a keeper. His in-between size, though, will always be a problem.

PLAYER SUMMARY	
Will	improve with experience
Can't	match up with forwards
Expect	athletic moves
Don't Expect	a lot of assists
Fantasy Value	$11-13
Card Value	15¢

COLLEGE STATISTICS

		G	FGP	FTP	RPG	PPG
87-88	ILL	33	.572	.642	6.6	15.9
88-89	ILL	36	.538	.669	7.9	18.0
Totals		69	.553	.657	7.3	17.0

NBA REGULAR-SEASON STATISTICS

		G	MIN	FGs FG	FGs PCT	3-PT FGs FG	3-PT FGs PCT	FTs FT	FTs PCT	Rebounds OFF	Rebounds TOT	AST	STL	BLK	PTS	PPG
89-90	ORL	81	1785	372	.494	1	.059	186	.705	107	316	124	69	34	931	11.5
90-91	ORL	70	1971	400	.467	17	.293	173	.668	92	386	106	74	44	990	14.1
Totals		151	3756	772	.480	18	.240	359	.686	199	702	230	143	78	1921	12.7

RON ANDERSON

Team: Philadelphia 76ers
Position: Forward
Height: 6'7" **Weight:** 215
Birthdate: October 15, 1958
NBA Experience: 7 years

College: Santa Barbara City; Fresno St.
Acquired: Traded from Pacers for draft rights to Everette Stephens, 10/88

Background: This is the classic case of an overachiever success story. Anderson didn't play high school ball and was discovered on a playground. He was a supermarket stock manager at the time and was persuaded to play junior college ball. He advanced to Fresno State where he led his team in scoring both years. In the last three years, he has developed into the 76ers' most consistent bench scorer.

Strengths: Anderson has the ability to slither free, and his smooth, soft jumper is a deadly one. It never looks like he is expending himself, yet the numbers are always there on the final stat sheet. He's in outstanding physical shape.

Weaknesses: Anderson is basically just an outside jump-shooter; if he's cold, you have to take him out. He's not much of a factor on either board, doesn't create his own shots, and is no scare defensively. He isn't a threat from 3-point range either.

Analysis: Anderson comes in at shooting guard or small forward and, more often than not, fills it up. He's a one-dimensional player, but the Sixers need his scoring off the bench. When on, Anderson is one of the better sixth men in the league.

PLAYER SUMMARY	
Will	hit the jumper
Can't	play in the paint
Expect	perimeter points
Don't Expect	much else
Fantasy Value	$4-5
Card Value	5¢

COLLEGE STATISTICS

		G	FGP	FTP	RPG	PPG
80-81	SBC	33	.502	.747	9.9	11.8
81-82	SBC	32	.652	.786	10.6	20.3
82-83	FSU	35	.549	.813	5.8	16.3
83-84	FSU	33	.570	.788	6.1	17.6
Totals		133	.573	.788	8.1	16.5

NBA REGULAR-SEASON STATISTICS

				FGs		3-PT FGs		FTs		Rebounds						
		G	MIN	FG	PCT	FG	PCT	FT	PCT	OFF	TOT	AST	STL	BLK	PTS	PPG
84-85	CLE	36	520	84	.431	1	.500	41	.820	39	88	34	9	7	210	5.8
85-86	CLE/IND	77	1676	310	.494	2	.222	85	.669	130	274	144	56	6	707	9.2
86-87	IND	63	721	139	.473	0	.000	85	.787	73	151	54	31	3	363	5.8
87-88	IND	74	1097	217	.498	0	.000	108	.766	89	216	78	41	6	542	7.3
88-89	PHI	82	2618	566	.491	2	.182	196	.856	167	406	139	71	23	1330	16.2
89-90	PHI	78	2089	379	.451	3	.143	165	.838	81	295	143	72	13	926	11.9
90-91	PHI	82	2340	512	.485	9	.209	165	.833	103	367	115	65	13	1198	14.6
Totals		492	11061	2207	.480	17	.183	845	.805	682	1797	707	345	71	5276	10.7

WILLIE ANDERSON

Team: San Antonio Spurs
Position: Guard/Forward
Height: 6'8" **Weight:** 185
Birthdate: January 8, 1967
NBA Experience: 3 years

College: Georgia
Acquired: 1st-round pick in 1988 draft
(10th overall)

Background: During his college days at Georgia, Anderson also found time to make a name for himself on the international level. He competed on the United States Olympic team in 1988 and played in the 1987 Pan-American Games. His scoring average has declined since his stellar rookie year, but mostly as a result of a better supporting cast.

Strengths: Anderson, quite simply, is a scorer. His versatility allows him to play either guard or small forward and his lateral quickness allows him to penetrate against bigger defenders. If there were any questions about the durability of his lean frame, he answered them by missing just one game in his first two seasons.

Weaknesses: For a big guard, which is where he spends most of his time, Anderson is not an especially gifted jump-shooter. His field goal percentage in 1990-91 was the lowest of his young career. Anderson also has trouble keeping possession of his dribble against smaller guards.

Analysis: Even though his scoring average has decreased in each of his first three years, Anderson remains an emerging star. When the Spurs needed him to score a lot of points as a rookie, he began drawing comparisons to former NBA scoring king George Gervin. Since then, he has given up some of those points (and comparisons) for a more talented Spurs team which has won two straight Midwest Division titles.

PLAYER SUMMARY

Will ....score
Can't............................hit 3-pointers
Expect.....................................versatility
Don't Expect............................10 APG
Fantasy Value $20-23
Card Value................................10¢

COLLEGE STATISTICS

		G	FGP	FTP	RPG	PPG
84-85	GA	13	.487	.625	1.5	3.3
85-86	GA	29	.503	.787	3.4	8.5
86-87	GA	30	.500	.794	4.1	15.9
87-88	GA	35	.500	.784	5.1	16.7
Totals		107	.500	.784	3.9	12.6

NBA REGULAR-SEASON STATISTICS

				FGs		3-PT FGs		FTs		Rebounds						
		G	MIN	FG	PCT	FG	PCT	FT	PCT	OFF	TOT	AST	STL	BLK	PTS	PPG
88-89	SA	81	2738	640	.498	4	.190	224	.775	152	417	372	150	62	1508	18.6
89-90	SA	82	2788	532	.492	7	.269	217	.748	115	372	364	111	58	1288	15.7
90-91	SA	75	2592	453	.457	7	.200	170	.798	68	351	358	79	46	1083	14.4
Totals		238	8118	1625	.484	18	.220	611	.771	335	1140	1094	340	166	3879	16.3

MICHAEL ANSLEY

Team: Orlando Magic
Position: Forward
Height: 6'7" **Weight:** 225
Birthdate: February 8, 1967
NBA Experience: 2 years

College: Alabama
Acquired: 2nd-round pick in 1989 draft (37th overall)

Background: Ansley finished his college career as Alabama's No. 1 career scorer and rebounder and shot a career .577 from the field. He led Orlando in field goal percentage in each of his first two seasons, although his scoring, minutes, and rebounding all decreased in 1990-91. Orlando did not re-sign Ansley after the season.

Strengths: One would be hard-pressed to find a player who hustles more than Ansley. He seems to come up with every loose ball and can outrebound bigger players through effort alone. He demonstrates impressive inside scoring ability for a player his size.

Weaknesses: Judging solely on the basis of talent, Ansley does not stack up well against most NBA players. He is a power forward in the body of a small forward. He lacks the outside shooting ability and quickness to play on the perimeter yet is too small to be effective in the paint. Ansley is especially vulnerable when trying to defend seven-foot power forwards near the basket.

Analysis: If not for his desire to do all the little things like pouncing on loose balls, boxing out, and setting picks, Ansley might be playing in the CBA. Others with his size and similar perimeter deficiencies would never stick with an NBA club. Because of his work ethic, Ansley is the exception.

PLAYER SUMMARY

Will ....overachieve
Can't.......................shoot from outside
Expect...............................all-out effort
Don't Expect...................ball-handling
Fantasy Value................................$1-3
Card Value...10¢

COLLEGE STATISTICS

		G	FGP	FTP	RPG	PPG
85-86	ALA	33	.604	.538	4.2	5.9
86-87	ALA	33	.597	.670	7.8	11.0
87-88	ALA	31	.560	.731	9.2	18.1
88-89	ALA	31	.572	.768	9.2	20.3
Totals		128	.577	.713	7.6	13.7

NBA REGULAR-SEASON STATISTICS

		G	MIN	FGs FG	FGs PCT	3-PT FGs FG	3-PT FGs PCT	FTs FT	FTs PCT	Rebounds OFF	Rebounds TOT	AST	STL	BLK	PTS	PPG
89-90	ORL	72	1221	231	.497	0	.000	164	.722	187	362	40	24	17	626	8.7
90-91	ORL	67	877	144	.548	0	.000	91	.717	122	253	25	27	7	379	5.7
Totals		139	2098	375	.515	0	.000	255	.720	309	615	65	51	24	1005	7.2

B.J. ARMSTRONG

Team: Chicago Bulls
Position: Guard
Height: 6'2" **Weight:** 175
Birthdate: September 9, 1967
NBA Experience: 2 years

College: Iowa
Acquired: 1st-round pick in 1989 draft
(18th overall)

Background: After becoming Iowa's all-time leader in assists, Armstrong was plucked by the Bulls in the 1989 draft. Though he had the look of a 15-year-old, B.J. was playing alongside Michael Jordan in his rookie year. The biggest improvements he made in 1990-91 were better outside shooting and the confidence to take it to the hole. He may have been the Bulls' top bench player last season.

Strengths: Armstrong possesses the quickness to guard the Kevin Johnsons and is built for the Bulls' speed game. He's a bright kid who works hard. He's an outstanding free throw shooter and he hit half of his 3-pointers last year (plus a big one against Detroit in the Eastern Conference finals).

Weaknesses: His lack of muscle makes him susceptible to being posted by bigger, stronger guards. He also needs to improve some on his decision-making.

Analysis: Isiah Thomas took him to school in the 1990 playoffs, but he had little left to teach him in '91. The Bulls consider Armstrong the point guard of the future, eventually replacing John Paxson. If he makes the same big strides next year as he did this past season, he'll become a fixture in Chicago.

PLAYER SUMMARY	
Will	handle the ball
Can't	muscle anyone
Expect	quickness, penetration
Don't Expect	post-up moves
Fantasy Value	$8-10
Card Value	15¢

COLLEGE STATISTICS

		G	FGP	FTP	RPG	PPG
85-86	IOWA	29	.485	.905	0.6	2.9
86-87	IOWA	35	.519	.794	2.5	12.4
87-88	IOWA	34	.482	.849	2.2	17.4
88-89	IOWA	32	.484	.833	2.5	18.6
Totals		130	.492	.831	2.0	13.1

NBA REGULAR-SEASON STATISTICS

		G	MIN	FGs FG	FGs PCT	3-PT FGs FG	3-PT FGs PCT	FTs FT	FTs PCT	Rebounds OFF	Rebounds TOT	AST	STL	BLK	PTS	PPG
89-90	CHI	81	1291	190	.485	3	.500	69	.885	19	102	199	46	6	452	5.6
90-91	CHI	82	1731	304	.481	15	.500	97	.874	25	149	301	70	4	720	8.8
Totals		163	3022	494	.482	18	.500	166	.878	44	251	500	116	10	1172	7.2

THURL BAILEY

Team: Utah Jazz
Position: Forward
Height: 6'11" **Weight:** 232
Birthdate: April 7, 1961
NBA Experience: 8 years

College: North Carolina St.
Acquired: 1st-round pick in 1983 draft (7th overall)

Background: Bailey starred for the 1983 North Carolina State national championship team and hit the critical shot vs. UNLV to send the Wolfpack to the Final Four. He has averaged double figures in scoring in every pro season except his rookie year. He twice finished second in the voting for the NBA's Sixth Man Award and was the Jazz's fourth-leading scorer in 1990-91.

Strengths: No one in the league has an unkind word to say about Bailey, a soft-spoken and unselfish leader. His willingness to come off the bench even though he has long been one of Utah's five best players is admirable. He is a well schooled low-post scorer and a quick turnaround shooter. Bailey has played in 347 consecutive games and is an invaluable teacher as Utah's co-captain.

Weaknesses: Bailey is not always as aggressive as he needs to be in the paint, which may have something to do with his peaceful personality. Coaches would like to see him play with more intensity and power on a consistent basis.

Analysis: Bailey may finish his career as one of the most overlooked players in the league. Other top reserves have received Sixth Man Awards for their efforts off the bench; Bailey has finished second. The fact that he is not bothered by that typifies his unselfishness. He always puts in an honest day's work and will likely continue in a reserve role.

PLAYER SUMMARY

Will	score in post
Can't	attain stardom
Expect	leadership
Don't Expect	many starts
Fantasy Value	$7-9
Card Value	8¢

COLLEGE STATISTICS

		G	FGP	FTP	RPG	PPG
79-80	NCST	28	.436	.673	3.6	4.5
80-81	NCST	27	.525	.736	6.1	12.3
81-82	NCST	32	.548	.814	6.8	13.7
82-83	NCST	36	.501	.717	7.7	16.7
Totals		123	.513	.745	6.2	12.2

NBA REGULAR-SEASON STATISTICS

		G	MIN	FGs FG	FGs PCT	3-PT FGs FG	3-PT FGs PCT	FTs FT	FTs PCT	Rebounds OFF	Rebounds TOT	AST	STL	BLK	PTS	PPG
83-84	UTA	81	2009	302	.512	0	.000	88	.752	115	464	129	38	122	692	8.5
84-85	UTA	80	2481	507	.490	1	1.000	197	.842	153	525	138	51	105	1212	15.1
85-86	UTA	82	2358	483	.448	0	.000	230	.830	148	493	153	42	114	1196	14.6
86-87	UTA	81	2155	463	.447	0	.000	190	.805	145	432	102	38	88	1116	13.8
87-88	UTA	82	2804	633	.492	1	.333	337	.826	134	531	158	49	125	1604	19.6
88-89	UTA	82	2777	615	.483	2	.400	363	.825	115	447	138	48	91	1595	19.5
89-90	UTA	82	2583	470	.481	0	.000	222	.779	116	410	137	32	100	1162	14.2
90-91	UTA	82	2486	399	.458	0	.000	219	.808	101	407	124	53	91	1017	12.4
Totals		652	19653	3872	.475	4	.138	1846	.814	1027	3709	1079	351	836	9594	14.7

CHARLES BARKLEY

Team: Philadelphia 76ers
Position: Forward
Height: 6'6" **Weight:** 250
Birthdate: February 20, 1963
NBA Experience: 7 years

College: Auburn
Acquired: 1st-round pick in 1984 draft
(5th overall)

Background: Barkley was known as the "Round Mound of Rebound" at Auburn, where he played at nearly 270 pounds. He was named SEC Player of the Year as a junior and then entered the NBA draft. In just his second season, he developed into a 20-PPG, 12-RPG player. He had an MVP-calibre year this past season, and MVP Michael Jordan said Barkley deserved the award.

Strengths: Inch-per-inch, Barkley is perhaps the best rebounder in the NBA. His mass and muscle allow him to create incredible position. And despite his bulky frame, he can jump, has soft hands, has a nice outside touch, and can drive coast-to-coast on court-length dashes. His strength and demeanor make him an intimidating factor.

Weaknesses: His major flaws have nothing to do with basketball ability. Barkley sometimes is too quick to criticize teammates, has a hot temper, and perennially leads the league in technical fouls. His free throw shooting is below average, and he fires up too many 3's.

Analysis: If the frustration of not becoming an NBA title contender doesn't get to him, Barkley will become one of the greatest forwards to ever play the game. He and David Robinson are the next in line to approach the Magic-Bird-Michael level of superstardom.

PLAYER SUMMARY

Will..........................score and rebound
Can't....................restrain his emotions
Expect..........................25 PPG, 12 RPG
Don't Expect .."please" & "thank you"
Fantasy Value.............................$89-92
Card Value..25¢

COLLEGE STATISTICS

		G	FGP	FTP	RPG	PPG
81-82	AUB	28	.595	.636	9.8	12.7
82-83	AUB	28	.644	.631	9.5	14.4
83-84	AUB	28	.638	.683	9.5	15.1
Totals		84	.626	.652	9.6	14.1

NBA REGULAR-SEASON STATISTICS

				FGs		3-PT FGs		FTs		Rebounds						
		G	MIN	FG	PCT	FG	PCT	FT	PCT	OFF	TOT	AST	STL	BLK	PTS	PPG
84-85	PHI	82	2347	427	.545	1	.167	293	.733	266	703	155	95	80	1148	14.0
85-86	PHI	80	2952	595	.572	17	.227	396	.685	354	1026	312	173	125	1603	20.0
86-87	PHI	68	2740	557	.594	21	.202	429	.761	390	994	331	119	104	1564	23.0
87-88	PHI	80	3170	753	.587	44	.280	714	.751	385	951	254	100	103	2264	28.3
88-89	PHI	79	3088	700	.579	35	.216	602	.753	403	986	325	126	67	2037	25.8
89-90	PHI	70	3085	706	.600	20	.217	557	.749	361	909	307	148	50	1989	28.4
90-91	PHI	67	2498	665	.570	44	.284	475	.722	258	680	284	110	33	1849	27.6
Totals		526	19880	4403	.580	182	.242	3466	.738	2417	6249	1968	871	562	12454	23.7

DANA BARROS

Team: Seattle SuperSonics
Position: Guard
Height: 5'11" **Weight:** 165
Birthdate: April 13, 1967
NBA Experience: 2 years

College: Boston College
Acquired: 1st-round pick in 1989 draft (16th overall)

Background: Barros, the all-time scoring leader at Boston College, became the first player in Big East history to lead the conference in scoring in consecutive years. He started every game the Golden Eagles played during his four seasons there. He has not been as fortunate as a pro, having started 25 games as a rookie but none in 1990-91.

Strengths: The diminutive Barros was an explosive college scorer, largely because of his sheer quickness. He has proven he can score on the NBA level as well, having averaged 16.2 points in the 25 games he has started. His 3-point range and ability to penetrate make him a promising offensive player.

Weaknesses: Barros often tries too hard to prove he deserves more playing time. He made no secret of his displeasure with his decreased minutes in 1990-91, after playing in 81 games as a rookie. He is not as polished a passer as most point guards, too often trying to finish his own play creations. Barros is very susceptible on the defensive end, especially when backed into the post.

Analysis: With an assurance of steady playing time, Barros could develop into a fine NBA point guard. He guided Seattle to a 14-11 mark as a rookie starter. However, he must develop more of a passing mentality, choose his shots more wisely, and improve his defense dramatically. He also must perfect the art of playing within himself.

PLAYER SUMMARY

Will.....................................create shots
Can't.................................play defense
Expect....................offensive mind-set
Don't Expect..................physical play
Fantasy Value...............................$4-7
Card Value...15¢

COLLEGE STATISTICS

		G	FGP	FTP	RPG	PPG
85-86	BC	28	.479	.791	2.8	13.7
86-87	BC	29	.458	.850	2.9	18.7
87-88	BC	33	.480	.850	3.4	21.9
88-89	BC	29	.475	.857	3.6	23.9
Totals		119	.473	.841	3.2	19.7

NBA REGULAR-SEASON STATISTICS

			G	MIN	FG	PCT	FG	PCT	FT	PCT	OFF	TOT	AST	STL	BLK	PTS	PPG
89-90	SEA		81	1630	299	.405	95	.399	89	.809	35	132	205	53	1	782	9.7
90-91	SEA		66	750	154	.495	32	.395	78	.918	17	71	111	23	1	418	6.3
Totals			147	2380	453	.432	127	.398	167	.856	52	203	316	76	2	1200	8.2

JOHN BATTLE

Team: Cleveland Cavaliers
Position: Guard
Height: 6'2" **Weight:** 175
Birthdate: November 9, 1962
NBA Experience: 6 years

College: Rutgers
Acquired: Signed as a free agent, 7/91

Background: Battle led the Atlantic 10 in scoring in his last two years at Rutgers. He came into the league known for his shooting and scoring ability, and he has demonstrated those skills on a consistent basis with the Hawks. His field goal percentage has almost always been at 45 or 46 percent. He had his best year in Atlanta in 1990-91, finishing third on the team in scoring. He signed as a free agent with Cleveland in July.

Strengths: Not only is he a good medium-range shooter, but Battle is a strong leaper who likes to shoot in the paint. He is also known as a rugged one-on-one defensive player—and a real nice guy too.

Weaknesses: Battle has two-guard skills, but he has the body of a point guard—yet he doesn't have point-guard skills. Battle also has a fragile psyche and he has been known to suffer from a lack of confidence.

Analysis: Battle isn't big enough or a deadly enough shooter to be a starting shooting guard, but he's a sound enough scorer to be a legitimate back-up. He is the kind of role player an NBA contender might covet—someone who is happy contributing with limited playing time. He'll stabilize Cleveland's uncertain backcourt.

PLAYER SUMMARY

Will ....score in the paint
Can't ....lead team in assists
Expect ....quality reserve minutes
Don't Expect.................a starting spot
Fantasy Value $2-4
Card Value.......................................8¢

COLLEGE STATISTICS

		G	FGP	FTP	RPG	PPG
81-82	RUT	29	.433	.429	1.0	2.4
82-83	RUT	31	.489	.725	1.5	5.9
83-84	RUT	25	.493	.725	3.1	21.0
84-85	RUT	29	.491	.729	4.0	21.0
Totals		114	.488	.707	2.4	12.1

NBA REGULAR-SEASON STATISTICS

		G	MIN	FG	PCT	FG	PCT	FT	PCT	OFF	TOT	AST	STL	BLK	PTS	PPG
85-86	ATL	64	639	101	.455	0	.000	75	.728	12	62	74	23	3	277	4.3
86-87	ATL	64	804	144	.457	0	.000	93	.738	16	60	124	29	5	381	6.0
87-88	ATL	67	1227	278	.454	16	.390	141	.750	26	113	158	31	5	713	10.6
88-89	ATL	82	1672	287	.457	11	.324	194	.815	30	140	197	42	9	779	9.5
89-90	ATL	60	1477	275	.506	2	.154	102	.756	27	99	154	28	3	654	10.9
90-91	ATL	79	1863	397	.461	14	.286	270	.854	34	159	217	45	6	1078	13.6
Totals		416	7682	1482	.465	43	.279	875	.791	145	633	924	198	31	3882	9.3

KENNY BATTLE

Team: Denver Nuggets
Position: Forward
Height: 6'6" **Weight:** 210
Birthdate: October 10, 1964
NBA Experience: 2 years

College: Northern Illinois; Illinois
Acquired: Claimed off waivers, 1/91

Background: Battle helped guide Illinois to the Final Four in 1989, leading the Fighting Illini in steals as a junior and senior. He began his college career at Northern Illinois, where he led major-college freshmen in scoring. Battle was drafted by Detroit but has played for Phoenix and Denver in his two NBA seasons. His scoring average was identical (6.1 PPG) for both the Suns and Nuggets in 1990-91. Denver did not re-sign him after the season.

Strengths: Battle runs the floor like a guard and is an exciting finisher on the fast break, as evidenced by his participation in the NBA Slam Dunk Contest as a rookie. He is a gifted athlete who plays at top speed. He can blanket his man and create turnovers, and his leaping ability helps him on the boards.

Weaknesses: For his size, Battle cannot boast of consistent perimeter skills. He needs to develop a medium-range jumper to keep defenders from backing off him and cutting off his penetration to the hoop. Although his reckless approach can force other teams into turnovers, it also results in many of his own.

Analysis: The drop-off in Battle's shooting percentage can be directly attributed to the way he is played defensively. When no one paid him much respect as a rookie, he got most of his points on dunks. Now that he is being forced to shoot from outside, improving that part of his game is his biggest challenge.

PLAYER SUMMARY

Will	slam it home
Can't	stick jumpers
Expect	turnovers
Don't Expect	control
Fantasy Value	$3-5
Card Value	12¢

COLLEGE STATISTICS

		G	FGP	FTP	RPG	PPG
84-85	NILL	27	.528	.658	6.2	20.1
85-86	NILL	27	.568	.653	6.5	19.6
87-88	ILL	33	.578	.682	5.5	15.6
88-89	ILL	36	.604	.755	4.8	16.6
Totals		123	.569	.686	5.7	17.8

NBA REGULAR-SEASON STATISTICS

				FGs		3-PT FGs		FTs		Rebounds						
		G	MIN	FG	PCT	FG	PCT	FT	PCT	OFF	TOT	AST	STL	BLK	PTS	PPG
89-90	PHO	59	729	93	.547	1	.250	55	.671	44	124	38	35	11	242	4.1
90-91	PHO/DEN	56	945	133	.472	3	.125	70	.753	83	176	62	60	18	339	6.1
Totals		115	1674	226	.500	4	.143	125	.714	127	300	100	95	29	581	5.1

WILLIAM BEDFORD

Team: Detroit Pistons
Position: Center
Height: 7'1" **Weight:** 235
Birthdate: December 14, 1963
NBA Experience: 4 years

College: Memphis St.
Acquired: Traded from Suns for a
1988 1st-round pick, 6/87

Background: Bedford was a dominant player at Memphis State, where he led the team in scoring, rebounding, and blocks as a senior. Phoenix made him the No. 6 pick in the 1986 draft and envisioned a strong and nimble seven-footer who could shoot. However, Bedford got mixed up in a drugs scandal that forced the Suns to clean house. He was dealt to Detroit, where he has been a career back-up and a major disappointment.

Strengths: William interests GMs with his height, agility, and ability to block shots on occasion. At times, he shows a fine outside shot. He also runs the court well for a big man.

Weaknesses: Bedford hasn't perfected a go-to move down low, something he can score with consistently. His defense is soft and, on a team full of lions, he has the tenacity of a kitten. There are also lingering questions about his character and background.

Analysis: Bedford has the physical tools to be an effective NBA center, but he needs to mature and develop his game. With Detroit centers Bill Laimbeer and James Edwards growing old, Bedford will get his chance with the Pistons.

PLAYER SUMMARY

Will	get more chances
Can't	post consistently
Expect	more minutes
Don't Expect	a team leader
Fantasy Value	$1-2
Card Value	8¢

COLLEGE STATISTICS

		G	FGP	FTP	RPG	PPG
83-84	MSU	26	.578	.536	5.3	9.5
84-85	MSU	35	.542	.673	7.6	12.2
85-86	MSU	32	.584	.628	8.5	17.3
Totals		93	.567	.626	7.3	13.2

NBA REGULAR-SEASON STATISTICS

				FGs		3-PT FGs		FTs		Rebounds						
		G	MIN	FG	PCT	FG	PCT	FT	PCT	OFF	TOT	AST	STL	BLK	PTS	PPG
86-87	PHO	50	979	142	.397	0	.000	50	.581	79	246	57	18	37	334	6.7
87-88	DET	38	298	44	.436	0	.000	13	.565	27	65	4	8	17	101	2.7
89-90	DET	42	246	54	.432	1	.167	9	.409	15	58	4	3	17	118	2.8
90-91	DET	60	562	106	.438	5	.385	55	.705	55	131	32	2	36	272	4.5
Totals		190	2085	346	.419	6	.300	127	.608	176	500	97	31	107	825	4.3

BENOIT BENJAMIN

Team: Seattle SuperSonics
Position: Center
Height: 7'0" **Weight:** 250
Birthdate: November 22, 1964
NBA Experience: 6 years

College: Creighton
Acquired: Traded from Clippers for Olden Polynice; SuperSonics also received the option to exchange 1991 and 1993 1st-round picks, 2/91

Background: Benjamin played for Creighton and led the nation in blocked shots (5.1 BPG) as a junior. He gave up his final year of college eligibility to enter the NBA draft and is ranked in a number of Los Angeles Clipper career leader categories. While playing for the Clippers and Seattle in 1990-91, Benjamin recorded the highest rebounding average of his enigmatic career.

Strengths: Benjamin can rebound and block shots as well as just about anyone in the NBA, assuming his head is in the game. His size, strength, soft touch, and sharp passing skills give him potential to become a dominating center. He has improved his focus somewhat but is not nearly where he should be.

Weaknesses: The biggest void in Benjamin's game has always been psychological. For reasons mostly unknown to those who have coached him, Benjamin has never displayed the dedication or consistency required to raise his game to the next level. Too often, he takes the night off without any warning. Another side effect of his lack of concentration is frequent foul trouble.

Analysis: Benjamin's 1990-91 performance improved after he was dealt to Seattle midway through the season, but he still has a long way to go if he hopes to overcome his reputation as an underachiever. He will never rank among the best centers in the game, but he should be a far more dominating player than he is. The road to improvement starts in Benjamin's head.

PLAYER SUMMARY

Will	block shots
Can't	stay focused
Expect	erratic games
Don't Expect	a quick fix
Fantasy Value	$27-30
Card Value	12-15¢

COLLEGE STATISTICS

		G	FGP	FTP	RPG	PPG
82-83	CRE	27	.555	.655	9.6	14.8
83-84	CRE	30	.543	.743	9.8	16.2
84-85	CRE	32	.582	.738	14.1	21.5
Totals		89	.562	.720	11.3	17.7

NBA REGULAR-SEASON STATISTICS

		G	MIN	FGs FG	FGs PCT	3-PT FGs FG	3-PT FGs PCT	FTs FT	FTs PCT	Rebounds OF	Rebounds TOT	AST	STL	BLK	PTS	PPG
85-86	LAC	79	2088	324	.490	1	.333	229	.746	161	600	79	64	206	878	11.1
86-87	LAC	72	2230	320	.449	0	.000	188	.715	134	586	135	60	187	828	11.5
87-88	LAC	66	2171	340	.491	0	.000	180	.706	112	530	172	50	225	860	13.0
88-89	LAC	79	2585	491	.541	0	.000	317	.744	164	696	157	57	221	1299	16.4
89-90	LAC	71	2313	362	.526	0	.000	235	.732	156	657	159	59	187	959	13.5
90-91	LAC/SEA	70	2236	386	.496	0	.000	210	.712	157	723	119	54	145	982	14.0
Totals		437	13623	2223	.501	1	.063	1359	.728	884	3792	821	344	1171	5806	13.3

WINSTON BENNETT

Team: Cleveland Cavaliers
Position: Forward
Height: 6'7" **Weight:** 210
Birthdate: February 9, 1965
NBA Experience: 2 years

College: Kentucky
Acquired: 3rd-round pick in 1988 draft
(64th overall)

Background: Bennett missed his senior year at Kentucky with a serious knee injury, but he came back in his redshirt season to help the Wildcats to the SEC title. He finished as the school's ninth career rebounder. Bennett spent one season in the CBA and one in Europe before catching on with the Cavaliers.

Strengths: There's plenty of perseverance here, as Bennett kept plugging away when others may have given up. He plays with heart and hustle and is pretty good on the glass.

Weaknesses: The knee injury will forever mar a promising career. It reduces his mobility and prevents him from being the kind of player he showed signs of becoming back in high school. On top of that, Bennett has always been known as a poor outside shooter. His .374 shooting in 1990-91 only underlined that notion. Defenders can sag on Bennett and double up on others.

Analysis: If he's lucky, Bennett will hang on as a role player. With the annual influx of top collegiate talent into the NBA each season, plus the importing of top European and Soviet players, his NBA career is uncertain. He will be one of the first to be released in favor of a hotshot rookie.

```
PLAYER SUMMARY
Will ........................................hang tough
Can't.........demand long-term contract
Expect ...........................limited minutes
Don't Expect ...................NBA "tenure"
Fantasy Value ..............................$1-2
Card Value.......................................10¢
```

COLLEGE STATISTICS

		G	FGP	FTP	RPG	PPG
83-84	KEN	34	.429	.698	3.8	6.5
84-85	KEN	30	.429	.675	5.3	7.2
85-86	KEN	36	.506	.728	7.0	12.7
87-88	KEN	33	.513	.729	7.8	15.3
Totals		133	.484	.713	6.0	10.5

NBA REGULAR-SEASON STATISTICS

			FGs		3-PT FGs		FTs		Rebounds						
		G	MIN	FG	PCT	FG	PCT	FT	PCT	OFF	TOT	AST	STL	BLK	PTS	PPG
89-90	CLE	55	990	137	.479	0	.000	64	.667	84	188	54	23	10	338	6.1
90-91	CLE	27	334	40	.374	0	.000	35	.745	30	64	28	8	2	115	4.3
Totals		82	1324	177	.450	0	.000	99	.692	114	252	82	31	12	453	5.5

LARRY BIRD

Team: Boston Celtics
Position: Forward
Height: 6'9" **Weight:** 220
Birthdate: December 7, 1956

NBA Experience: 12 years
College: Indiana St.
Acquired: 1st-round pick in 1978 draft
(6th overall)

Background: Boston's living legend almost played for Bobby Knight, but he dropped out of Indiana, began pumping gas, and wound up at Indiana State. There, he averaged 30 PPG and led the Sycamores to the 1979 NCAA championship game. The 1979 College Player of the Year is a three-time NBA MVP. He's led the Celtics to three world titles.

Strengths: Bird maximizes his athletic talent more than anyone. He has an uncanny sixth sense for making pin-point passes, and his sense of teamwork and unselfishness elevates his teammates to a higher level. Bird in his prime was a fearsome outside shooter. He's still deadly from 3 and at the line.

Weaknesses: Bird isn't a leaper and doesn't have the quickness to keep up with some of the swifter small forwards in the league. Age and injuries to both of his heels have defused his overall effectiveness.

Analysis: This future Hall of Famer is in the twilight of a brilliant career. Injuries are taking their toll and he is no longer the dominant player he once was. Bird has said of his imminent departure: "I'll just hop in my truck, head back home to French Lick, Indiana, and watch the fumes in my rearview mirror."

PLAYER SUMMARY

Will ....do everything
Can't ....hog the ball
Expect ....points, rebound, assists
Don't Expect......less than 100 percent
Fantasy Value..............................$74-77
Card Value ....35-50¢

COLLEGE STATISTICS

		G	FGP	FTP	RPG	PPG
76-77	ISU	28	.544	.840	13.3	32.8
77-78	ISU	32	.524	.793	11.5	30.0
78-79	ISU	34	.532	.831	14.9	28.6
Totals		94	.533	.822	13.3	30.3

NBA REGULAR-SEASON STATISTICS

				FGs		3-PT FGs		FTs		Rebounds						
		G	MIN	FG	PCT	FG	PCT	FT	PCT	OFF	TOT	AST	STL	BLK	PTS	PPG
79-80	BOS	82	2955	693	.474	58	.406	301	.836	216	852	370	143	53	1745	21.3
80-81	BOS	82	3239	719	.478	20	.270	283	.863	191	895	451	161	63	1741	21.2
81-82	BOS	77	2923	711	.503	11	.212	328	.863	200	837	447	143	66	1761	22.9
82-83	BOS	79	2982	747	.504	22	.286	351	.840	193	870	458	148	71	1867	23.6
83-84	BOS	79	3028	758	.492	18	.247	374	.888	181	796	520	144	69	1908	24.2
84-85	BOS	80	3161	918	.522	56	.427	403	.882	164	842	531	129	98	2295	28.7
85-86	BOS	82	3113	796	.496	82	.423	441	.896	190	805	557	166	51	2115	25.8
86-87	BOS	74	3005	786	.525	90	.400	414	.910	124	682	566	135	70	2076	28.1
87-88	BOS	76	2965	881	.527	98	.414	415	.916	108	703	467	125	57	2275	29.9
88-89	BOS	6	189	49	.471	0	.000	18	.947	1	37	29	6	5	116	19.3
89-90	BOS	75	2944	718	.473	65	.333	319	.930	90	712	562	106	61	1820	24.3
90-91	BOS	60	2277	462	.454	77	.389	163	.891	53	509	431	108	58	1164	19.4
Totals		852	32781	8238	.497	597	.373	3810	.884	1711	8540	5389	1514	722	20883	24.5

ROLANDO BLACKMAN

Team: Dallas Mavericks
Position: Guard
Height: 6'6" **Weight:** 206
Birthdate: February 26, 1959

NBA Experience: 10 years
College: Kansas St.
Acquired: 1st-round pick in 1981 draft
(9th overall)

Background: Blackman earned All-America recognition at Kansas State and was named to the Big Eight All-Decade Team for the 1980s. His pro career has included four All-Star appearances and ten consecutive seasons in which he has scored 1,000 points or more. He is Dallas' all-time leader in points, field goals, starts, and minutes. He paced the Mavericks in scoring and minutes in 1990-91.

Strengths: Blackman is one of the best clutch performers in the league. He has won countless games with fourth-quarter heroics, always wanting to take the key shots. Blackman has 3-point range and a quick release yet is big enough to score inside. He also excels at defense. He is a well respected leader.

Weaknesses: About the only dimension Blackman does not bring to the shooting guard position is raw speed, which he once possessed. Still, he always seems to be in the right place at the right time.

Analysis: Detroit coach Chuck Daly once said he was going to make a videotape of Blackman to show his own guard, Joe Dumars, some of the little things that make Blackman perhaps the most clever player in the NBA. The veteran Maverick is a unique blend of offense, defense, and pure class.

PLAYER SUMMARY	
Will	do it all
Can't	pass up big shots
Expect	leadership
Don't Expect	inconsistency
Fantasy Value	$9-12
Card Value	12¢

COLLEGE STATISTICS

		G	FGP	FTP	RPG	PPG
77-78	KSU	29	.472	.656	6.4	10.9
78-79	KSU	28	.510	.735	3.9	17.3
79-80	KSU	31	.539	.690	4.7	17.8
80-81	KSU	33	.532	.783	5.0	15.0
Totals		121	.517	.717	5.0	15.2

NBA REGULAR-SEASON STATISTICS

				FGs		3-PT FGs		FTs		Rebounds						
		G	MIN	FG	PCT	FG	PCT	FT	PCT	OFF	TOT	AST	STL	BLK	PTS	PPG
81-82	DAL	82	1979	439	.513	1	.250	212	.768	97	254	105	46	30	1091	13.3
82-83	DAL	75	2349	513	.492	3	.200	297	.780	108	293	185	37	29	1326	17.7
83-84	DAL	81	3025	721	.546	1	.091	372	.812	124	373	288	56	37	1815	22.4
84-85	DAL	81	2834	625	.508	6	.300	342	.828	107	300	289	16	16	1598	19.7
85-86	DAL	82	2787	677	.514	4	.138	404	.836	88	291	271	79	25	1762	21.5
86-87	DAL	80	2758	626	.495	5	.333	419	.884	96	278	266	64	21	1676	21.0
87-88	DAL	71	2580	497	.473	0	.000	331	.873	82	246	262	64	18	1325	18.7
88-89	DAL	78	2946	594	.476	30	.353	316	.854	70	273	288	65	20	1534	19.7
89-90	DAL	80	2934	626	.498	13	.302	287	.844	88	280	289	77	21	1552	19.4
90-91	DAL	80	2965	634	.482	40	.351	282	.865	63	256	301	69	19	1590	19.9
Totals		790	27157	5952	.500	103	.302	3262	.836	923	2844	2544	573	236	15269	19.3

LANCE BLANKS

Team: Detroit Pistons
Position: Guard
Height: 6'4" **Weight:** 195
Birthdate: September 9, 1966
NBA Experience: 1 year

College: Virginia; Texas
Acquired: 1st-round pick in 1990 draft (26th overall)

Background: Blanks transferred from Virginia to Texas after his sophomore year and became part of the Longhorns' famed and feared outside-shooting, high-scoring attack. He is the son of ex-Oilers and Patriots running back Sid Blanks and the cousin of ex-Rangers infielder Larvell Blanks. He rarely left the bench during his rookie year with the Pistons.

Strengths: Blanks is fairly quick for his size and is a dangerous long-range shooter when he is on a roll. In two years at Texas, he launched 432 3-pointers. He has good hands on defense.

Weaknesses: Outside of shooting, Blanks needs to work on all parts of his NBA game. He has the athletic ability to improve; unfortunately, he spent last year getting rusty on the Detroit bench, as the Pistons went with the three-guard rotation of Isiah Thomas, Joe Dumars, and Vinnie Johnson. Blanks wishes the NBA 3-point line was a little shorter.

Analysis: Detroit has a lot of age in its backcourt, which means Blanks could get more of a chance with the Pistons. If he steadily develops his overall game, he could become a starting shooting guard. However, he'll probably become a guy who'll give you instant offense off the bench.

PLAYER SUMMARY

Will..put it up
Can't...........................be the playmaker
Expect...................perimeter accuracy
Don't Expect ....lots of assists
Fantasy Value $1-2
Card Value..10¢

COLLEGE STATISTICS

		G	FGP	FTP	RPG	PPG
85-86	VA	14	.438	.500	1.1	2.4
86-87	VA	24	.520	.286	0.8	1.2
88-89	TEX	34	.450	.684	5.6	19.7
89-90	TEX	32	.402	.797	4.3	20.3
Totals		104	.429	.729	3.5	13.3

NBA REGULAR-SEASON STATISTICS

			FGs		3-PT FGs		FTs		Rebounds						
	G	MIN	FG	PCT	FG	PCT	FT	PCT	OFF	TOT	AST	STL	BLK	PTS	PPG
90-91 DET	38	214	26	.426	2	.125	10	.714	4	20	26	9	2	64	1.7
Totals	38	214	26	.426	2	.125	10	.714	4	20	26	9	2	64	1.7

MOOKIE BLAYLOCK

Team: New Jersey Nets
Position: Guard
Height: 6'1" **Weight:** 185
Birthdate: March 20, 1967
NBA Experience: 2 years

College: Midland; Oklahoma
Acquired: 1st-round pick in 1989 draft
(12th overall)

Background: Mookie, born Daron Oshay Blaylock, earned All-America recognition in 1989 on a powerhouse Oklahoma team. He was the first NCAA player to collect 200 assists and 100 steals in back-to-back seasons. Blaylock was selected 12th by New Jersey in the 1989 draft, bit he struggled through 37-percent shooting his rookie year.

Strengths: There aren't a lot of players in the NBA who can match Blaylock's quickness—he finished sixth in the league in steals in 1990-91. He is a prototypical point guard who can also bomb away from outside. He has a flair for pushing the ball up-court, and he's known as a tough competitor.

Weaknesses: The jury is still out on his shot selection, as evidenced by his poor field goal and 3-point shooting percentages. Mookie needs to cool the trigger finger and concentrate more on his playmaking responsibilities. He can get careless at times.

Analysis: Blaylock is helping Nets fans forget about the fiasco of Pearl Washington, the previous playmaker. Still, he needs to tighten his game if he's to become a quality point guard. The fact that the Nets drafted super playmaker Kenny Anderson doesn't bode well for Mookie.

PLAYER SUMMARY

Will ....take his shots
Can't ....do it alone
Expect.........................up-tempo game
Don't Expect.............tons of rebounds
Fantasy Value $4-7
Card Value....................................20¢

COLLEGE STATISTICS

		G	FGP	FTP	RPG	PPG
85-86	MID	34	.566	.738	3.2	16.8
86-87	MID	33	.516	.723	4.2	19.6
87-88	OKLA	39	.460	.684	4.2	16.4
88-89	OKLA	35	.455	.650	4.7	20.0
Totals		141	.495	.696	4.1	18.1

NBA REGULAR-SEASON STATISTICS

	G	MIN	FGs FG	FGs PCT	3-PT FGs FG	3-PT FGs PCT	FTs FT	FTs PCT	Rebounds OFF	Rebounds TOT	AST	STL	BLK	PTS	PPG
89-90 NJ	50	1267	212	.371	18	.225	63	.778	42	140	210	82	14	505	10.1
90-91 NJ	72	2585	432	.416	14	.154	139	.790	67	249	441	169	40	1017	14.1
Totals	122	3852	644	.400	32	.187	202	.786	109	389	651	251	54	1522	12.5

MUGGSY BOGUES

Team: Charlotte Hornets
Position: Guard
Height: 5'3" **Weight:** 140
Birthdate: January 9, 1965
NBA Experience: 4 years

College: Wake Forest
Acquired: Selected from Bullets in
1988 expansion draft

Background: Bogues learned the game at the famed Dunbar High School in
Baltimore, where he teamed with Reggie Lewis and Reggie Williams. At Wake
Forest, Tyrone terrorized ACC guards with his intimidating quickness, and he set
ACC career records for assists and steals. His pro career really took off after
Charlotte plucked him in the expansion draft. He was fourth in the NBA in assists
in 1989-90.

Strengths: Bogues is a pesky pressing guard who makes it difficult for point
guards to run an offense. Even those playmakers considered quick seem slow
when Bogues is buzzing around. Twice, Bogues has led the NBA in turnover-to-
assist ratio, and he also finishes high in steals.

Weaknesses: Guards can easily post up on Bogues and they can also shoot
over him. His outside shot is still suspect, and he's not very good at jump-balls.

Analysis: He will always have a place with an up-tempo team because of his
tremendous ball-handling and blistering speed. It's best to use him as a pack of
dynamo to bring off the bench. Bogues is one of the most entertaining and
popular players in the NBA.

PLAYER SUMMARY

Will	lead the break
Can't	win the tip
Expect	pressing defense
Don't Expect	post-up points
Fantasy Value	$20-23
Card Value	15-25¢

COLLEGE STATISTICS

		G	FGP	FTP	RPG	PPG
83-84	WF	32	.304	.692	0.7	1.2
84-85	WF	29	.500	.682	2.4	6.6
85-86	WF	29	.455	.730	3.1	11.3
86-87	WF	29	.500	.806	3.8	14.8
Totals		119	.473	.749	2.4	8.3

NBA REGULAR-SEASON STATISTICS

				FGs		3-PT FGs		FTs		Rebounds						
		G	MIN	FG	PCT	FG	PCT	FT	PCT	OFF	TOT	AST	STL	BLK	PTS	PPG
87-88	WAS	79	1628	166	.390	3	.188	58	.784	35	136	404	127	3	393	5.0
88-89	CHA	79	1755	178	.426	1	.077	66	.750	53	165	620	111	7	423	5.4
89-90	CHA	81	2743	326	.491	5	.192	106	.791	48	207	867	166	3	763	9.4
90-91	CHA	81	2299	241	.460	0	.000	86	.796	58	216	669	137	3	568	7.0
Totals		320	8425	911	.448	9	.134	316	.782	194	724	2560	541	16	2147	6.7

MANUTE BOL

Team: Philadelphia 76ers
Position: Center
Height: 7'7" **Weight:** 225
Birthdate: October 16, 1962
NBA Experience: 6 years

College: Bridgeport
Acquired: Traded from Warriors for a
1991 1st-round pick, 8/90

Background: Bol is perhaps the most fascinating player in a league full of characters. A member of the Dinka Tribe, he was discovered in the Sudan and imported to Bridgeport College, where he was a novelty more than anything. He is a quick study, as evidence by the four languages he speaks. He is known for blocking shots and for killing a lion with a spear during one of his tribal rituals in Africa.

Strengths: The "Dinka Discourager," the tallest man in NBA history, is an intimidating shot-blocker, leading the NBA in 1986 and '89 despite limited minutes. He was named to the second-team All-Defensive Team in 1986. His presence forces even the best shooters to make adjustments.

Weaknesses: Everything else. Bol can't shoot at all and he hasn't developed any kind of post move. He can't handle the ball, and the only thing he can do on offense is grab the garbage and stuff it in.

Analysis: Bol is one of the most popular players in the league and has engaged in hilarious locker room high jinks with Charles Barkley and Rick Mahorn. He will be a career back-up center, someone who can come off the bench and impact the game with his shot-blocking.

PLAYER SUMMARY

Will...........................distort the offense
Can't...............................muscle inside
Expect ....blocked shots
Don't Expect ....acrobatic moves
Fantasy Value $6-8
Card Value....................................10-15¢

COLLEGE STATISTICS

		G	FGP	FTP	RPG	PPG
84-85	BPT	31	.611	.595	13.5	22.5
Totals		31	.611	.595	13.5	22.5

NBA REGULAR-SEASON STATISTICS

		G	MIN	FG	PCT	FG	PCT	FT	PCT	OFF	TOT	AST	STL	BLK	PTS	PPG
85-86	WAS	80	2090	128	.460	0	.000	42	.488	123	477	23	28	397	298	3.7
86-87	WAS	82	1552	103	.446	0	.000	45	.672	84	362	11	20	302	251	3.1
87-88	WAS	77	1136	75	.455	0	.000	26	.531	72	275	13	11	208	176	2.3
88-89	GS	80	1769	127	.369	20	.220	40	.606	116	462	27	11	345	314	3.9
89-90	GS	75	1310	56	.331	9	.188	25	.510	33	276	36	13	238	146	1.9
90-91	PHI	82	1522	65	.396	1	.071	24	.585	66	350	20	16	247	155	1.9
Totals		476	9379	554	.410	30	.192	202	.564	494	2202	130	99	1737	1340	2.8

ANTHONY BONNER

Team: Sacramento Kings
Position: Forward
Height: 6'8" **Weight:** 225
Birthdate: June 8, 1968
NBA Experience: 1 year

College: St. Louis
Acquired: 1st-round pick in 1990 draft
(23rd overall)

Background: Bonner led all Division I players in rebounding as a senior at St. Louis University. He finished as the school's career leader in points, rebounds, steals, and games played. His rookie season in Sacramento saw him start six games, appear in 34, and average one point every three minutes.

Strengths: Bonner is a bruising rebounder who is willing to sacrifice his body in match-ups with bigger players. He displays flashes of promise both offensively and defensively and is most comfortable on the blocks.

Weaknesses: As a rookie, Bonner learned the hard way that the offensive moves that worked for him in college do not necessarily work against larger and stronger NBA players. Small by power-forward standards, Bonner must learn to pull his game away from the basket to be a legitimate pro scorer. That will require a better short-range jump shot. His defense also needs work.

Analysis: Few expected Bonner to step into the league and become an instant contributor, so his first-year inconsistency came as no surprise. His willingness to bang the boards should allow him to increase his minutes even if his offensive game may not yet rank as NBA-caliber. There is plenty of time to learn.

PLAYER SUMMARY	
Will	bang the boards
Can't	play outside
Expect	refinement
Don't Expect	high FG pct.
Fantasy Value	$3-5
Card Value	10¢

COLLEGE STATISTICS

		G	FGP	FTP	RPG	PPG
86-87	STL	35	.592	.661	9.6	10.3
87-88	STL	28	.537	.597	8.8	13.8
88-89	STL	37	.560	.582	10.4	15.5
89-90	STL	33	.500	.693	13.8	19.8
Totals		133	.539	.634	10.7	14.8

NBA REGULAR-SEASON STATISTICS

				FGs		3-PT FGs		FTs		Rebounds						
		G	MIN	FG	PCT	FG	PCT	FT	PCT	OFF	TOT	AST	STL	BLK	PTS	PPG
90-91	SAC	34	750	103	.448	0	.000	44	.579	59	161	49	39	5	250	7.4
Totals		34	750	103	.448	0	.000	44	.579	59	161	49	39	5	250	7.4

SAM BOWIE

Team: New Jersey Nets
Position: Center
Height: 7'1" **Weight:** 240
Birthdate: March 17, 1961
NBA Experience: 6 years

College: Kentucky
Acquired: Traded from Trail Blazers with a 1989 1st-round pick for Buck Williams, 6/89

Background: Bowie and Ralph Sampson came out of high school the same year as perhaps the most heralded tandem of big men ever. Bowie was on his way to becoming a dominant collegian at Kentucky when serious leg injuries forced him to sit out two seasons. Portland drafted him anyway, ahead of Michael Jordan, and will never live that down. His career has been crippled by injuries. He would've been a favorite for Comeback Player of the Year in 1989-90 if that award hadn't been discontinued.

Strengths: Bowie is a polished pivot player and does all the right things. He's a strong rebounder, both on the offensive and defensive boards, and, despite his leg injuries, can still get up to block the shot. He is always a threat to score down low and is a very good passer.

Weaknesses: His health is always a question. In his seven years in the league, he has yet to play a full season. He could be a little meaner inside.

Analysis: When healthy, Bowie is a legitimate NBA starting center with the potential to become a bit dominant, especially given the dearth of quality pivot men in the league. He can't carry a team a la Patrick Ewing or Hakeem Olajuwon, but he can provide some considerable support.

PLAYER SUMMARY	
Will	score and rebound
Can't	stay healthy
Expect	consistent play
Don't Expect	82 games
Fantasy Value	$7-9
Card Value	12¢

COLLEGE STATISTICS

		G	FGP	FTP	RPG	PPG
79-80	KEN	34	.531	.764	8.1	12.9
80-81	KEN	28	.520	.720	9.1	17.4
83-84	KEN	34	.516	.722	9.2	10.5
Totals		96	.522	.735	8.8	13.4

NBA REGULAR-SEASON STATISTICS

				FGs		3-PT FGs		FTs		Rebounds						
		G	MIN	FG	PCT	FG	PCT	FT	PCT	OFF	TOT	AST	STL	BLK	PTS	PPG
84-85	POR	76	2216	299	.537	0	.000	160	.711	207	656	215	55	203	758	10.0
85-86	POR	38	1132	167	.484	0	.000	114	.708	93	327	99	21	96	448	11.8
86-87	POR	5	163	30	.455	0	.000	20	.667	14	33	9	1	10	80	16.0
88-89	POR	20	412	69	.451	5	.714	28	.571	36	106	36	7	33	171	8.6
89-90	NJ	68	2207	347	.416	10	.323	294	.776	206	690	91	38	121	998	14.7
90-91	NJ	62	1916	314	.434	4	.182	169	.732	176	480	147	43	90	801	12.9
Totals		269	8046	1226	.458	19	.317	785	.730	732	2292	597	165	553	3256	12.1

RANDY BREUER

Team: Minnesota Timberwolves
Position: Center
Height: 7'3" **Weight:** 258
Birthdate: October 11, 1960
NBA Experience: 8 years

College: Minnesota
Acquired: Traded from Bucks with a conditional exchange of 1991 or 1992 second-round picks for Brad Lohaus, 1/90

Background: Breuer led the Big Ten in scoring and blocked shots as a senior at the University of Minnesota, but entered the NBA as a project. He enjoyed his best season in 1987-88 with Milwaukee, with career bests in nine statistical categories. His role with the Timberwolves was reduced in 1990-91 because of the addition of rookie Felton Spencer.

Strengths: Shot-blocking has long been the most legitimate talent claimed by Breuer, who hovers above all but a handful of NBA post players. He has blocked 100 or more shots in three seasons. Breuer has improved his hook shot and is now a decent halfcourt scorer.

Weaknesses: Breuer has always been mechanical offensively and his shooting range is limited to the paint, although he has improved his scoring ability over the years. Every free throw is an adventure for him. He is extremely slow on his feet, lacks court sense, and gets outrebounded by much smaller players. His defense is soft, to say the least.

Analysis: Breuer has proven he can contribute offensively, despite his reputation as just another tall body. His skills have improved gradually, although he appears to have reached the limits of his marginal athletic ability. Unless he lands with a team with very little height, he will continue to be a role player.

PLAYER SUMMARY

Will..shoot hooks
Can't..jump
Expect ....role playing
Don't Expect......................................10 PPG
Fantasy Value................................$2-4
Card Value..5¢

COLLEGE STATISTICS

		G	FGP	FTP	RPG	PPG
79-80	MINN	31	.558	.649	3.2	7.7
80-81	MINN	30	.575	.688	5.5	15.2
81-82	MINN	29	.554	.756	7.2	16.8
82-83	MINN	29	.586	.769	8.9	20.4
Totals		119	.570	.729	6.1	14.9

NBA REGULAR-SEASON STATISTICS

		G	MIN	FGs FG	FGs PCT	3-PT FGs FG	3-PT FGs PCT	FTs FT	FTs PCT	Rebounds OFF	Rebounds TOT	AST	STL	BLK	PTS	PPG
83-84	MIL	57	472	68	.384	0	.000	32	.696	48	109	17	11	38	168	2.9
84-85	MIL	78	1083	162	.511	0	.000	89	.701	92	256	40	21	82	413	5.3
85-86	MIL	82	1792	272	.477	0	.000	141	.712	159	458	114	50	116	685	8.4
86-87	MIL	76	1467	241	.485	0	.000	118	.584	129	350	47	56	61	600	7.9
87-88	MIL	81	2258	390	.495	0	.000	188	.657	191	551	103	46	107	968	12.0
88-89	MIL	48	513	86	.480	0	.000	28	.549	51	135	22	9	37	200	4.2
89-90	MIL-MIN	81	1879	298	.428	0	.000	126	.653	154	417	97	42	108	722	8.9
90-91	MIN	73	1505	197	.453	0	.000	35	.443	114	345	73	35	80	429	5.9
Totals		576	10969	1714	.468	0	.000	757	.640	938	2621	513	270	629	4185	7.3

FRANK BRICKOWSKI

Team: Milwaukee Bucks
Position: Forward/Center
Height: 6'10" **Weight:** 240
Birthdate: August 15, 1959

NBA Experience: 7 years
College: Penn St.
Acquired: Traded from Spurs for Paul Pressey, 8/90

Background: Brickowski led Penn State in scoring his junior and senior years. After being drafted in the third round by the Knicks, he played overseas for three years in Italy, France, and Israel. Brickowski was part of the deal that brought Mychal Thompson to the Lakers from the Spurs. He was the Bucks' fourth-leading scorer last season and third-leading rebounder.

Strengths: Brickowski has developed some surprisingly effective moves near the basket and often fools defenders with a quickness that belies his big body. He is an effective shooter when open and can also bang inside. His 80-percent free throw percentage is a plus for an inside player like him.

Weaknesses: He doesn't possess the all-out speed to keep up with some of the league's swifter power forwards, such as Chicago's Horace Grant or Detroit's John Salley. Brickowski could also pursue offensive rebounds with a bit more vigor, and his passing ability isn't so strong. Brickowski also had turnover tendencies, finishing second to guard Alvin Robertson in that category last year.

Analysis: At 32 years of age, his game isn't going to get much better. Last year, he started for the Bucks alongside Danny Schayes and Fred Roberts on the NBA's most unathletic-looking front line; he would be a role player on many other teams. Brickowski is the kind of player that Bucks coach Del Harris likes to mold into his system.

PLAYER SUMMARY

Will....................................run the court
Can't.............................pass effectively
Expect ....consistent effort
Don't Expect....................ball-handling
Fantasy Value................................$3-5
Card Value..8¢

COLLEGE STATISTICS

		G	FGP	FTP	RPG	PPG
77-78	PSU	25	.457	.840	2.6	3.8
78-79	PSU	24	.495	.792	4.5	5.7
79-80	PSU	27	.521	.781	7.5	11.3
80-81	PSU	24	.601	.778	6.3	13.0
Totals		100	.537	.788	5.3	8.5

NBA REGULAR-SEASON STATISTICS

			FGs		3-PT FGs		FTs		Rebounds						
	G	MIN	FG	PCT	FG	PCT	FT	PCT	OFF	TOT	AST	STL	BLK	PTS	PPG
84-85 SEA	78	1115	150	.492	0	.000	85	.669	76	260	100	34	15	385	4.9
85-86 SEA	40	311	30	.517	0	.000	18	.667	16	54	21	11	7	78	2.0
86-87 LAL/SA	44	487	63	.508	0	.000	50	.714	48	116	17	20	6	176	4.0
87-88 SA	70	2227	425	.528	1	.200	268	.768	167	483	266	74	36	1119	16.0
88-89 SA	64	1822	337	.515	0	.000	201	.715	148	406	131	102	35	875	13.7
89-90 SA	78	1438	211	.545	0	.000	95	.674	89	327	105	66	37	517	6.6
90-91 MIL	75	1912	372	.527	0	.000	198	.798	129	426	131	86	43	942	12.6
Totals	449	9312	1588	.523	1	.053	915	.736	673	2072	771	393	179	4092	9.1

SCOTT BROOKS

Team: Minnesota Timberwolves
Position: Guard
Height: 5'11" **Weight:** 165
Birthdate: July 31, 1965
NBA Experience: 3 years

College: Texas Christian; San Joaquin Delta; Cal.-Irvine
Acquired: Traded from 76ers for a 1990 2nd-round pick, 6/90

Background: Brooks divided his college career among Texas Christian, San Joaquin Delta Junior College, and finally Cal.-Irvine, where he led the Pacific Coast Athletic Association in scoring, steals, and free throw percentage in 1986-87. Despite being passed up in the NBA draft, he emerged from the CBA and appeared in 154 games in two years with Philadelphia. Brooks led Minnesota in 3-pointers in 1990-91.

Strengths: Brooks is a tireless worker who loves to pressure the ball from one end of the court to the other. His quickness, great hands, and ability to handle the ball make him a consummate point guard, although he has been used at off guard as well. His assist-to-turnover ratio is a dazzling four-to-one.

Weaknesses: Although he led Minnesota from the 3-point line, Brooks does not shoot the ball consistently enough to be considered a scoring threat. His size works against him in a halfcourt set, allowing the opposition to exploit him in the low post. He also has trouble seeing the whole court on offense.

Analysis: Brooks covers up many of his flaws with all-out hustle. He is a valuable defensive weapon and handles the ball brilliantly. As an all-around player, however, Brooks is not able to provide consistent scoring to force opposing defenses to account for him. His greatest value is as a defensive specialist off the bench.

PLAYER SUMMARY

Will	hound the ball
Can't	rebound
Expect	hustle
Don't Expect	much scoring
Fantasy Value	$1-3
Card Value	5¢

COLLEGE STATISTICS

		G	FGP	FTP	RPG	PPG
83-84	TCU	27	.529	.714	1.2	3.8
84-85	SJD	31	.525	.882	1.5	13.1
85-86	C-I	30	.448	.886	2.3	10.3
86-87	C-I	28	.478	.845	1.8	23.8
Totals		116	.489	.860	1.7	12.8

NBA REGULAR-SEASON STATISTICS

				FGs		3-PT FGs		FTs		Rebounds						
		G	MIN	FG	PCT	FG	PCT	FT	PCT	OFF	TOT	AST	STL	BLK	PTS	PPG
88-89	PHI	82	1372	156	.420	55	.359	61	.884	19	94	306	69	3	428	5.2
89-90	PHI	72	975	119	.431	31	.392	50	.877	15	64	207	47	0	319	4.4
90-91	MIN	80	980	159	.430	45	.333	61	.847	28	72	204	53	5	424	5.3
Totals		234	3327	434	.427	131	.357	172	.869	62	230	717	169	8	1171	5.0

CHUCKY BROWN

Team: Cleveland Cavaliers
Position: Forward
Height: 6'8" **Weight:** 214
Birthdate: February 29, 1968
NBA Experience: 2 years

College: North Carolina St.
Acquired: 2nd-round pick in 1989 draft (43rd overall)

Background: Brown was an All-Atlantic Coast Conference first-team selection after his senior season, in which he averaged 16.4 PPG and 8.8 RPG. He's second on North Carolina State's all-time field goal-percentage list. Although he was drafted 43rd overall in the 1989 draft, Brown was one of three rookies to make the Cavaliers' roster. Last season, he came off the bench to average 8.5 PPG. His .524 shooting percentage tied for tops on the team.

Strengths: This guy would have made the ultimate Laker or Celtic because he was born to run. That's when he's at his best, racing up and down an open court ready to launch a jumper at a moment's notice. He can also be a force on the backboards from his small-forward position. He has an upbeat attitude.

Weaknesses: Brown has difficulty when teams force him to play a halfcourt game. He's not a good ball-handler and he can't create his own shot. He doesn't have 3-point shooting range and, last year, turned the ball over too often.

Analysis: This is a young package of potential that could find stardom in the right situation. He is definitely better suited for a running team. He has shown flashes of someday becoming a bona fide starter, and he possesses the athleticism to be a scorer in the NBA. Considering that he was a second-round draft choice, Brown is more than living up to expectations.

PLAYER SUMMARY	
Will	fill the break
Can't	shoot the 3
Expect	lots of movement
Don't Expect	patience
Fantasy Value	$3-5
Card Value	15¢

COLLEGE STATISTICS

		G	FGP	FTP	RPG	PPG
85-86	NCST	31	.475	.618	2.2	3.1
86-87	NCST	34	.587	.762	4.3	6.6
87-88	NCST	32	.572	.636	6.0	16.6
88-89	NCST	31	.548	.648	8.8	16.4
Totals		128	.557	.667	5.3	10.6

NBA REGULAR-SEASON STATISTICS

		G	MIN	FGs FG	FGs PCT	3-PT FGs FG	3-PT FGs PCT	FTs FT	FTs PCT	Rebounds OFF	Rebounds TOT	AST	STL	BLK	PTS	PPG
89-90	CLE	75	1339	210	.470	0	.000	125	.762	83	231	50	33	26	545	7.3
90-91	CLE	74	1485	263	.524	0	.000	101	.701	78	213	80	26	24	627	8.5
Totals		149	2824	473	.498	0	.000	226	.734	161	444	130	59	50	1172	7.9

DEE BROWN

Team: Boston Celtics
Position: Guard
Height: 6'1" **Weight:** 161
Birthdate: November 29, 1968
NBA Experience: 1 year

College: Jacksonville
Acquired: 1st-round pick in 1990 draft
(19th overall)

Background: Brown was Jacksonville's main man as a junior, leading the Dolphins in scoring, rebounding, and steals while splitting time between big guard and small forward. He set the school mark for career 3-pointers with 87. His real name is DeCovan Kadell Brown, but he was nicknamed "Dee-lightful" by his Jacksonville teammates. He helped solidify the Celtics' backcourt in his rookie season.

Strengths: Brown has a tremendous vertical leap for someone just 6'1", as evidenced by his winning the NBA's Slam Dunk Contest in Charlotte during the All-Star Weekend. He has lightning-quick speed and is dangerous on the fastbreak. Brown is considered one of the fastest players in the league. He's also a very good free throw shooter.

Weaknesses: Brown had trouble hitting the outside shot last year. He converted just 46.4 percent of his shots from the field, and that figure includes the numerous fastbreak lay-ups he accumulated. He was only hit 7-of-34 from beyond the 3-point arc, as his adjustment from the college boundary of 19'9" to the pros' 23'9" didn't go smoothly.

Analysis: Dee was just what the aging Celtics needed—a youthful shot in the arm. Along with steady Brian Shaw and Reggie Lewis, Boston won't get beat up and down the court. If Brown can find a way to capitalize on his leaping ability and develop a consistent outside shot, he could one day rank among the league's better point guards.

PLAYER SUMMARY

Will	run and jump
Can't	sit still
Expect	steals
Don't Expect	rebounds
Fantasy Value	$6-8
Card Value	15-25¢

COLLEGE STATISTICS

		G	FGP	FTP	RPG	PPG
86-87	JACK	21	.431	.591	1.3	3.4
87-88	JACK	28	.452	.818	4.5	10.1
88-89	JACK	30	.490	.824	7.6	19.6
89-90	JACK	29	.496	.683	6.6	19.3
Totals		108	.482	.762	5.3	13.9

NBA REGULAR-SEASON STATISTICS

		G	MIN	FGs FG	FGs PCT	3-PT FGs FG	3-PT FGs PCT	FTs FT	FTs PCT	Rebounds OFF	Rebounds TOT	AST	STL	BLK	PTS	PPG
90-91	BOS	82	1945	284	.464	7	.206	137	.873	41	182	344	83	14	712	8.7
Totals		82	1945	284	.464	7	.206	137	.873	41	182	344	83	14	712	8.7

MIKE BROWN

Team: Utah Jazz
Position: Forward/Center
Height: 6'9" **Weight:** 260
Birthdate: July 19, 1963
NBA Experience: 5 years

College: George Washington
Acquired: Traded from Hornets for
Kelly Tripucka, 6/88

Background: Brown went from Atlantic 10 Freshman of the Year to George Washington University's second all-time leading scorer and rebounder, despite being hampered by a toe injury as a senior. He started his pro career in Italy before playing for Chicago and Utah. His best year came with the Jazz in 1989-90. He has appeared in 82 games in each of the last two seasons.

Strengths: Rebounding and versatility have made Brown an important ingredient in Utah's success. He is able to play both forward and center and his defense has improved greatly since he came to the NBA. He can be a solid inside shooter, though he dropped off after his best shooting season in 1989-90.

Weaknesses: Brown's bulk can work against him by allowing quicker players to beat him to the spot. He has trouble locating open men when he finds himself in traffic and is not a confident ball-handler. More than anything, he could use more consistency.

Analysis: A lot of teams could use a player like Brown to provide relief for their big men. Like many reserves, however, Brown is prone to having his good and bad games. He played very well for the Jazz in the 1991 playoffs. When he gets off to a quick start, he can string together productive minutes.

PLAYER SUMMARY
Will.................................plug the lane
Can't...............................pass the ball
Expect.................................versatility
Don't Expect.............................finesse
Fantasy Value.............................$2-4
Card Value....................................8¢

COLLEGE STATISTICS

		G	FGP	FTP	RPG	PPG
81-82	GW	27	.497	.518	8.5	15.6
82-83	GW	29	.520	.655	10.3	17.1
83-84	GW	29	.535	.730	12.1	19.6
84-85	GW	26	.480	.649	11.0	16.6
Totals		111	.509	.653	10.5	17.3

NBA REGULAR-SEASON STATISTICS

		G	MIN	FG	PCT	FG	PCT	FT	PCT	OFF	TOT	AST	STL	BLK	PTS	PPG
86-87	CHI	62	818	106	.527	0	.000	46	.639	71	214	24	20	7	258	4.2
87-88	CHI	46	591	78	.448	0	.000	41	.577	66	159	28	11	4	197	4.3
88-89	UTA	66	1051	104	.419	0	.000	92	.708	92	258	41	25	17	300	4.5
89-90	UTA	82	1397	177	.515	1	.500	157	.789	111	373	47	32	28	512	6.2
90-91	UTA	82	1391	129	.454	0	.000	132	.742	109	337	49	29	24	390	4.8
Totals		338	5248	594	.475	1	.333	468	.720	449	1341	189	117	80	1657	4.9

MARK BRYANT

Team: Portland Trail Blazers
Position: Forward
Height: 6'9" **Weight:** 245
Birthdate: April 25, 1965
NBA Experience: 3 years

College: Seton Hall
Acquired: 1st-round pick in 1988 draft
(21st overall)

Background: Bryant helped push Seton Hall into its first-ever NCAA tournament as a senior and was an All-Big East selection. He started 32 of his first 34 games as a pro, struggled, and has since been plagued by injury problems. His rookie year was cut more than a month short when he fractured his thumb in a fight with Joe Kleine. In 1990-91, he broke his toe and was sidelined for 27 games late in the year.

Strengths: Bryant has impressive physical ability and is not shy about throwing his weight around. He is an aggressive rebounder and has shown signs of becoming a decent inside scorer when he holds his ground near the basket.

Weaknesses: In his first two years, Bryant tended to get caught up in the mind games of many of his opponents. He has improved in that respect but can be easily distracted at times. His physical approach also catches the eyes of NBA officials, resulting in foul trouble. Bryant does not have great shooting range and should stay inside on offense.

Analysis: Just when he seemed to be overcoming some of the bad habits that held him down during his first two seasons, a toe injury cost Bryant 27 games of what could have been his best year by far. He has raised his field goal percentage and learned to play more intelligently. If he can stay healthy for a full season, Bryant will continue to earn respect around the league.

PLAYER SUMMARY

Will	use his muscle
Can't	avoid fouls
Expect	more floor time
Don't Expect	a starting job
Fantasy Value	$1-2
Card Value	5¢

COLLEGE STATISTICS

		G	FGP	FTP	RPG	PPG
84-85	SH	26	.475	.649	6.8	12.2
85-86	SH	30	.523	.678	7.5	14.0
86-87	SH	28	.496	.706	7.1	16.8
87-88	SH	34	.564	.748	9.1	20.5
Totals		118	.521	.705	7.7	16.2

NBA REGULAR-SEASON STATISTICS

		G	MIN	FGs FG	FGs PCT	3-PT FGs FG	3-PT FGs PCT	FTs FT	FTs PCT	Rebounds OFF	Rebounds TOT	AST	STL	BLK	PTS	PPG
88-89	POR	56	803	120	.486	0	.000	40	.580	65	179	33	20	7	280	5.0
89-90	POR	58	562	70	.458	0	.000	28	.560	54	146	13	18	9	168	2.9
90-91	POR	53	781	99	.488	0	.000	74	.733	65	190	27	15	12	272	5.1
Totals		167	2146	289	.479	0	.000	142	.645	184	515	73	53	28	720	4.3

JUD BUECHLER

Team: New Jersey Nets
Position: Forward
Height: 6'6" **Weight:** 220
Birthdate: June 19, 1968
NBA Experience: 1 year

College: Arizona
Acquired: 2nd-round pick in 1990 draft (38th overall); drafted by the SuperSonics for the Nets on a pre-draft agreement

Background: Buechler was Arizona's scoring and rebounding leader as a senior and was always a top marksman, finishing his career with a blazing 54.7 shooting percentage. Buechler was All-Pac-10 his senior year before being drafted by Seattle for New Jersey in the second round. (Seattle agreed to draft Buechler for the Nets providing that they passed on Gary Payton in the first round.) As a rookie, Buechler appeared in 74 games, although he finished 13th on the Nets in scoring.

Strengths: Buechler is a disciplined player who only fouled out three times in his four years of college ball. Although there is nothing special in his game, he is a fundamentally sound role player who won't hurt you while he's spelling a regular. He was also an outstanding amateur volleyball player.

Weaknesses: Jud isn't particularly fast, nor does he possess a great deal of hang time. There is nothing flashy about his game, and his field goal percentage suffered in his rookie year. He won't get many rebounds.

Analysis: Buechler is a smart player who can occupy somebody's bench and do an adequate job when called upon. He will never lead anyone to an NBA title. He is the kind of heady forward you like to mix in with a squad of naturally talented athletes.... On the other hand, he may get more playing time on the Professional Beach Volleyball circuit.

PLAYER SUMMARY

Will .... not make mistakes
Can't .... dazzle a crowd
Expect .... steady bench play
Don't Expect .... a scoring threat
Fantasy Value $2-4
Card Value .... 12¢

COLLEGE STATISTICS

		G	FGP	FTP	RPG	PPG
86-87	ARIZ	30	.486	.571	2.3	4.5
87-88	ARIZ	36	.516	.655	2.4	4.7
88-89	ARIZ	33	.607	.816	6.6	11.0
89-90	ARIZ	32	.538	.765	8.3	14.9
Totals		131	.547	.743	4.9	8.7

NBA REGULAR-SEASON STATISTICS

			FGs		3-PT FGs		FTs		Rebounds						
	G	MIN	FG	PCT	FG	PCT	FT	PCT	OFF	TOT	AST	STL	BLK	PTS	PPG
90-91 NJ	74	859	94	.416	1	.250	43	.652	61	141	51	33	15	232	3.1
Totals	74	859	94	.416	1	.250	43	.652	61	141	51	33	15	232	3.1

WILLIE BURTON

Team: Miami Heat
Position: Guard/Forward
Height: 6'7" **Weight:** 219
Birthdate: May 26, 1968
NBA Experience: 1 year

College: Minnesota
Acquired: 1st-round pick in 1990 draft
(9th overall)

Background: A four-sport athlete in high school, Burton became the University of Minnesota's second all-time leading scorer (behind Mychal Thompson). As a senior, Burton led the Gophers into the NCAA Southeast Regional finals with a career-high 36 points in a win over Northern Iowa. He was named first-team All-Big Ten as a senior. Miami chose him ninth overall in the 1990 draft, and he played nearly 2,000 minutes as a rookie.

Strengths: Burton has the versatility and ability to play either big guard or small forward. He can hurt you from outside or going to the basket, and he goes to the glass well on the offensive end. He has shown flashes of developing into a clutch player.

Weaknesses: Though a 3-point threat in college, he has yet to develop a long-ball shot in the pros. His rebounding prowess at Minnesota—ninth best in Gopher history—has yet to surface in the NBA. Burton is perhaps a tweener, too small for a forward but not slick enough for a guard. Miami coach Ron Rothstein was disappointed with his ball-handling.

Analysis: Burton is in the right situation with Miami—a young prospect with a new team. He was the Heat's fifth-leading scorer as a rookie, ranking behind youngsters Sherman Douglas, Glen Rice, Rony Seikaly, and Kevin Edwards. He needs to work on his ball-handling and develop more of a scoring touch if he's to become a legitimate NBA starter.

PLAYER SUMMARY	
Will	hustle
Can't	bury the 3
Expect	versatility
Don't Expect	blocked shots
Fantasy Value	$7-9
Card Value	15-25¢

COLLEGE STATISTICS

		G	FGP	FTP	RPG	PPG
86-87	MINN	28	.455	.649	4.2	8.7
87-88	MINN	28	.516	.713	5.6	13.7
88-89	MINN	30	.529	.797	7.5	18.6
89-90	MINN	32	.519	.770	6.4	19.3
Totals		118	.511	.749	6.0	15.3

NBA REGULAR-SEASON STATISTICS

			FGs		3-PT FGs		FTs		Rebounds						
	G	MIN	FG	PCT	FG	PCT	FT	PCT	OFF	TOT	AST	STL	BLK	PTS	PPG
90-91 MIA	76	1928	341	.441	4	.133	229	.782	111	262	107	72	24	915	12.0
Totals	76	1928	341	.441	4	.133	229	.782	111	262	107	72	24	915	12.0

MICHAEL CAGE

Team: Seattle SuperSonics   **College:** San Diego St.
Position: Forward   **Acquired:** Traded from Clippers for
Height: 6'9" **Weight:** 230   draft rights to Gary Grant and a 1989
Birthdate: January 28, 1962   1st-round pick, 6/88
NBA Experience: 7 years

Background: Cage was voted Western Athletic Conference Player of the Year as a senior at San Diego State and finished as the school's career leader in scoring, rebounding, and games played. He won the NBA rebounding title with the Los Angeles Clippers in 1987-88, grabbing 30 boards on the final night of the season to clinch it. The 1990-91 season was his lowest scoring year as a pro.

Strengths: The muscular Cage has made his living off the backboard. He finished among the league's top ten rebounders four consecutive years from 1986-90, the last of which he spent out of position at center. Cage is no offensive slouch either, having shot better than 50 percent during his career. He has good touch near the basket and can drive.

Weaknesses: Largely by no fault of his own, Cage has become a less productive inside scorer. Seattle was using the power forward as a center and has since brought Cage off the bench. His moves can be predictable. Cage is also capable of defensive lapses.

Analysis: When in the proper position, Cage can hoard all-important rebounds and provide his share of scoring. He is able to wear down opposing players and has an admirable work ethic. When forced to play the pivot, however, Cage gets worn down himself. His best days may be behind him.

PLAYER SUMMARY	
Will	go to the glass
Can't	play center
Expect	5,000 career boards
Don't Expect	10 PPG
Fantasy Value	$6-8
Card Value	5¢

COLLEGE STATISTICS

		G	FGP	FTP	RPG	PPG
80-81	SDS	27	.558	.756	13.1	10.9
81-82	SDS	29	.488	.661	8.8	11.0
82-83	SDS	28	.570	.747	12.6	19.5
83-84	SDS	28	.562	.741	12.6	24.5
Totals		112	.548	.732	11.8	16.5

NBA REGULAR-SEASON STATISTICS

		G	MIN	FGs FG	FGs PCT	3-PT FGs FG	3-PT FGs PCT	FTs FT	FTs PCT	Rebounds OFF	Rebounds TOT	AST	STL	BLK	PTS	PPG
84-85	LAC	75	1610	216	.543	0	.000	101	.737	126	392	51	41	32	533	7.1
85-86	LAC	78	1566	204	.479	0	.000	113	.649	168	417	81	62	34	521	6.7
86-87	LAC	80	2922	457	.521	0	.000	341	.730	354	922	131	99	67	1255	15.7
87-88	LAC	72	2660	360	.470	0	.000	326	.688	371	938	110	91	58	1046	14.5
88-89	SEA	80	2536	314	.498	0	.000	197	.743	276	765	126	92	52	825	10.3
89-90	SEA	82	2595	325	.504	0	.000	148	.698	306	821	70	79	45	798	9.7
90-91	SEA	82	2141	226	.508	0	.000	70	.625	177	558	89	85	58	522	6.4
Totals		549	16030	2102	.502	0	.000	1296	.704	1778	4813	658	549	346	5500	10.0

ADRIAN CALDWELL

Team: Houston Rockets
Position: Forward
Height: 6'8" **Weight:** 266
Birthdate: July 4, 1966
NBA Experience: 2 years

College: Southern Methodist; Lamar
Acquired: Signed as a free agent, 8/89

Background: After transferring from SMU, Caldwell led Lamar in scoring, rebounding, and field goal percentage in his only season at the school. He was bypassed in the 1989 draft but made Houston's roster as a free agent. Of his 42 rookie field goals, 14 were dunks, and the 1990-91 season featured more of the same.

Strengths: Caldwell's strength is his athletic build. He is a gifted leaper for a big man and has all the muscle required to carve out a living as a rebounder. The Rockets were impressed by his play in the California Summer Pro League.

Weaknesses: You name it, and chances are it's a potential weakness for the untested Caldwell. He is not blessed with any kind of court sense, mainly because he only played one year of Division I college ball as a regular. He struggles with his outside shooting and is frighteningly poor from the free throw line. In his brief minutes, he has displayed a penchant for fouling, especially as a rookie.

Analysis: No team thought highly enough of Caldwell to make him as much as a second-round draft choice, yet he has played in the league for two years. In that regard, his career is off to a successful start. Impressing the coaches in summer league play is one thing, but Caldwell now must play with confidence when given his rare chances during the season. The Rockets are loaded with big men, which will make his road to playing time a rocky one.

PLAYER SUMMARY

Will ....crash boards
Can't.................................shoot jumpers
Expect ....mistakes
Don't Expect ....early emergence
Fantasy Value $1-2
Card Value..5¢

COLLEGE STATISTICS

		G	.FGP	FTP	RPG	PPG
86-87	SMU	28	.489	.341	2.4	2.1
88-89	LAM	26	.568	.449	10.0	14.7
Totals		54	.556	.428	6.1	8.2

NBA REGULAR-SEASON STATISTICS

		G	MIN	FGs FG	FGs PCT	3-PT FGs FG	3-PT FGs PCT	FTs FT	FTs PCT	Rebounds OFF	Rebounds TOT	AST	STL	BLK	PTS	PPG
89-90	HOU	51	331	42	.553	0	.000	13	.464	36	109	7	11	18	97	1.9
90-91	HOU	42	343	35	.422	0	.000	7	.412	43	100	8	19	10	77	1.8
Totals		93	674	77	.484	0	.000	20	.444	79	209	15	30	28	174	1.9

ELDEN CAMPBELL

Team: Los Angeles Lakers
Position: Forward/Center
Height: 6'11" **Weight:** 215
Birthdate: July 23, 1968
NBA Experience: 1 year

College: Clemson
Acquired: 1st-round pick in 1990 draft
(27th overall)

Background: Campbell led the Atlantic Coast Conference in blocked shots three straight years and became Clemson's career scoring leader. As an NBA rookie in 1990-91, Campbell saw limited action in 52 regular-season games but played some key stretches during the playoffs. He scored 21 points in game five of the NBA Finals.

Strengths: Campbell is an athletic shot-blocker with a long wingspan and a nose for the ball. He goes after nearly every opposing shot. His athletic ability and quickness also make him a strong finisher on the fastbreak and a promising rebounder.

Weaknesses: As athletic as he is, Campbell is by no means a polished big man. His instincts help him on defense, but offensively he lacks refined moves in the post. The same goes for his rebounding fundamentals, like boxing out. His college field goal percentage was beefed up with slam dunks and lay-ups; it's not that easy in the NBA.

Analysis: Watching Campbell swat shots and run the floor makes one wonder what kind of player he could become if given more of a chance to play. If he can sharpen his fundamentals, learn a handful of low-post moves, and develop a consistent short-range jump shot, Campbell has the potential to emerge as an exciting and versatile player. Right now, his talent is raw.

PLAYER SUMMARY

Will ....block shots
Can't ....create own shots
Expect ....thrills
Don't Expect ....polish
Fantasy Value $1-2
Card Value ....10¢

COLLEGE STATISTICS

		G	FGP	FTP	RPG	PPG
86-87	CLEM	31	.554	.702	4.1	8.8
87-88	CLEM	28	.629	.619	7.4	18.8
88-89	CLEM	29	.550	.688	7.7	17.5
89-90	CLEM	35	.522	.599	8.0	16.4
Totals		123	.562	.641	6.8	15.3

NBA REGULAR-SEASON STATISTICS

			FGs		3-PT FGs		FTs		Rebounds						
	G	MIN	FG	PCT	FG	PCT	FT	PCT	OFF	TOT	AST	STL	BLK	PTS	PPG
90-91 LAL	52	380	56	.455	0	.000	32	.653	40	96	10	11	38	144	2.8
Totals	52	380	56	.455	0	.000	32	.653	40	96	10	11	38	144	2.8

TONY CAMPBELL

Team: Minnesota Timberwolves
Position: Guard/Forward
Height: 6'7" **Weight:** 215
Birthdate: May 7, 1962
NBA Experience: 7 years

College: Ohio St.
Acquired: Signed as a free agent, 9/89

Background: Campbell was selected Big Ten Player of the Year after leading Ohio State in four statistical categories as a senior. His pro career started slowly on the Detroit bench and in the CBA, but he exploded onto the scene with the Lakers when Byron Scott and Magic Johnson suffered injuries in the 1989 playoffs. Since then, he has emerged as Minnesota's two-time leading scorer.

Strengths: Putting the ball in the basket is Campbell's specialty. He gets to the hoop, draws fouls, and is not afraid to take the big shots. He is versatile enough to play small forward or big guard. Confidence may be Campbell's greatest asset. When given his chance, he stepped forward.

Weaknesses: Campbell still has not mastered the art of defense, which was the biggest reason he rode the pines early in his career. His shot selection could stand some improvement, although he has not been surrounded by many proven scorers during his two years in Minnesota. Campbell also is not a solid enough ball-handler to play big guard full-time.

Analysis: Campbell will soon come to a crossroads. Will he adjust his game and become less selfish when surrounded by better scorers, or will he continue to take things upon himself? He seems most comfortable in a situation where he is the focal point of the offense.

PLAYER SUMMARY

Will	draw fouls
Can't	pass up a shot
Expect	20 PPG
Don't Expect	10 APG
Fantasy Value	$30-33
Card Value	15¢

COLLEGE STATISTICS

		G	FGP	FTP	RPG	PPG
80-81	OSU	14	.417	.500	0.6	1.6
81-82	OSU	31	.424	.798	5.0	12.8
82-83	OSU	30	.503	.799	8.3	19.0
83-84	OSU	29	.513	.807	7.4	18.6
Totals		104	.482	.798	6.0	14.7

NBA REGULAR-SEASON STATISTICS

				FGs		3-PT FGs		FTs		Rebounds						
		G	MIN	FG	PCT	FG	PCT	FT	PCT	OFF	TOT	AST	STL	BLK	PTS	PPG
84-85	DET	56	625	130	.496	0	.000	56	.800	41	89	24	28	3	316	5.6
85-86	DET	82	1292	294	.484	2	.222	58	.795	83	236	45	62	7	648	7.9
86-87	DET	40	332	57	.393	0	.000	24	.615	21	58	19	12	1	138	3.5
87-88	LAL	13	242	57	.564	1	.333	28	.718	8	27	15	11	2	143	11.0
88-89	LAL	63	787	158	.458	2	.095	70	.843	53	130	47	37	6	388	6.2
89-90	MIN	82	3164	723	.457	9	.167	448	.787	209	451	213	111	31	1903	23.2
90-91	MIN	77	2893	652	.434	16	.262	358	.803	161	346	214	121	48	1678	21.8
Totals		413	9335	2071	.456	30	.197	1042	.790	576	1337	577	382	98	5214	12.6

ANTOINE CARR

Team: Sacramento Kings
Position: Forward
Height: 6'9" **Weight:** 265
Birthdate: July 23, 1961
NBA Experience: 7 years

College: Wichita St.
Acquired: Traded from Hawks with Sedric Toney for Kenny Smith and Michael Williams, 2/90

Background: Carr played with Cliff Levingston and Xavier McDaniel at Wichita State, where his No. 35 was retired after an All-America career. He played 5 1/2 years in Atlanta with varying degrees of success before becoming more of a scoring factor in Sacramento. The 1990-91 season was by far Carr's best. He led the Kings in scoring and field goal percentage.

Strengths: Carr is an offensive minded power forward with strong low-post moves. He holds his position well in the lane, is not afraid to put a body on opposing players, and always looks to score. He is also a fierce finisher, once shattering a backboard in warm-ups while with the Hawks.

Weaknesses: When pushed out of the paint, Carr becomes largely ineffective. His jump-shooting is poor and most of his rebounds are a result of inside positioning. Carr also has struggled to keep his weight down and, in related developments, often has found himself in foul trouble.

Analysis: Carr underachieved during most of his time in Atlanta. He was not pleased with the number of minutes he was playing and wanted to score more than the offense would allow. He has since become a primary offensive weapon. If he can keep his weight down, improve his rebounding, and avoid making stupid fouls, Carr's best days could await.

PLAYER SUMMARY

Will ....work inside
Can't...shoot
Expect.....................................20 PPG
Don't Expect..........................10 RPG
Fantasy Value $9-11
Card Value.....................................10¢

COLLEGE STATISTICS

		G	FGP	FTP	RPG	PPG
79-80	WSU	29	.501	.667	5.9	15.2
80-81	WSU	33	.586	.765	7.3	15.8
81-82	WSU	28	.566	.791	7.0	16.0
82-83	WSU	22	.575	.765	7.6	22.6
Totals		112	.557	.746	6.9	17.1

NBA REGULAR-SEASON STATISTICS

		G	MIN	FGs FG	FGs PCT	3-PT FGs FG	3-PT FGs PCT	FTs FT	FTs PCT	Rebounds OFF	Rebounds TOT	AST	STL	BLK	PTS	PPG
84-85	ATL	62	1195	198	.528	2	.333	101	.789	79	232	80	29	78	499	8.0
85-86	ATL	17	258	49	.527	0	.000	18	.667	16	52	14	7	15	116	6.8
86-87	ATL	65	695	134	.506	1	.333	73	.709	60	156	34	14	48	342	5.3
87-88	ATL	80	1483	281	.544	1	.250	142	.780	94	289	103	38	83	705	8.8
88-89	ATL	78	1488	226	.480	0	.000	130	.855	106	274	91	31	62	582	7.5
89-90	ATL/SAC	77	1727	356	.494	0	.000	237	.795	115	322	119	30	68	949	12.3
90-91	SAC	77	2527	628	.511	0	.000	295	.758	163	420	191	45	101	1551	20.1
Totals		456	9373	1872	.510	4	.167	996	.779	633	1745	632	194	455	4744	10.4

JOE BARRY CARROLL

Team: Phoenix Suns
Position: Center
Height: 7'1" **Weight:** 255
Birthdate: July 24, 1958
NBA Experience: 10 years

College: Purdue
Acquired: Signed as a free agent, 1/91

Background: Carroll was an All-America center at Purdue and the No. 1 overall draft choice by Golden State in 1980. Since spending his first six-plus years with the Warriors, Carroll has played for five NBA clubs and put in a 25-game stint in Italy. He was recovering from a leg injury when picked up by Phoenix and played only 96 minutes in 1990-91.

Strengths: Carroll knows how to score in the pivot, having amassed more than 12,000 points in his pro career. When healthy, he can also rebound adequately. Ten years of experience have to count for something.

Weaknesses: Even when he was in his prime, many questioned Carroll's desire. Now that he has been slowed by years and injuries, one must question his ability to become a significant contributor again. He is not able to run the floor and his skills in every area have slipped. He has not shot better than 45 percent from the field since 1986-87.

Analysis: Carroll has been in the league long enough to know the players and how to play them. However, his body can no longer do what his mind tells it to. If he stays healthy for a full season, Carroll may be able to contribute as a reserve.

PLAYER SUMMARY

Will ....warm bench
Can't...run
Expect.....................................injuries
Don't Expect..................return to form
Fantasy Value $1-2
Card Value...5¢

COLLEGE STATISTICS

		G	FGP	FTP	RPG	PPG
76-77	PURD	28	.497	.630	7.4	7.9
77-78	PURD	27	.522	.664	10.7	15.6
78-79	PURD	35	.583	.640	10.1	22.8
79-80	PURD	33	.539	.660	9.2	22.3
Totals		123	.546	.651	9.3	17.7

NBA REGULAR-SEASON STATISTICS

		G	MIN	FG	PCT	FG	PCT	FT	PCT	OFF	TOT	AST	STL	BLK	PTS	PPG
80-81	GS	82	2919	616	.491	0	.000	315	.716	274	759	117	50	121	1547	18.9
81-82	GS	76	2627	527	.519	0	.000	235	.728	210	633	64	64	127	1289	17.0
82-83	GS	79	2988	785	.513	0	.000	337	.719	220	688	169	108	155	1907	24.1
83-84	GS	80	2962	663	.477	0	.000	313	.723	235	636	198	103	142	1639	20.5
85-86	GS	79	2801	650	.463	0	.000	377	.752	193	670	176	101	144	1677	21.2
86-87	GS	81	2724	690	.472	0	.000	340	.787	173	589	214	92	123	1720	21.2
87-88	GS/HOU	77	2004	402	.435	0	.000	172	.764	131	489	113	50	106	976	12.7
88-89	NJ	64	1996	363	.448	0	.000	176	.800	118	473	105	71	81	902	14.1
89-90	NJ/DEN	76	1721	312	.411	0	.000	137	.774	133	443	97	47	115	761	10.0
90-91	PHO	11	96	13	.361	0	.000	11	.917	3	24	11	1	8	37	3.4
Totals		705	22838	5021	.474	0		2413	.747	1690	5404	1264	687	1122	12455	17.7

BILL CARTWRIGHT

Team: Chicago Bulls
Position: Center
Height: 7'1" **Weight:** 245
Birthdate: July 30, 1957
NBA Experience: 11 years

College: San Francisco
Acquired: Traded from Knicks with 1988 1st- and 3rd-round picks for Charles Oakley and 1988 1st- and 3rd-round picks, 6/88

Background: Cartwright was Mr. All-American at San Francisco, and the Knicks chose him third overall in the 1979 draft. He had an up-and-down career in the Big Apple, twice averaging 20-plus PPG but then languishing because of chronic foot problems. He was nicknamed "Medical Bill" and "Billy Idle" by the New York press. Cartwright caught his second wind when he arrived in Chicago.

Strengths: He's from the old school—an old-fashioned low-post scorer who will use his power to post up. He'll then launch one of those gangly-looking, high-over-the-head shots that somehow goes in. He is a better-than-average defensive center and matches up well with most NBA pivot men—ex-teammate Patrick Ewing in particular.

Weaknesses: Cartwright has never had the greatest pair of hands in the world. He's not very mobile, is a mediocre rebounder, and blocks few shots.

Analysis: Cartwright is nearing the end of a checkered career. There are still two more effective years left and, with the shortage of quality centers who can post up, he becomes somewhat of a valuable commodity. The Bulls can, if they choose, elongate his career by playing back-up Will Perdue more often.

PLAYER SUMMARY

Will ....muscle inside
Can't ....run the court
Expect.........................low-post scoring
Don't Expect ....blocked shots
Fantasy Value $2-4
Card Value...............................5¢

COLLEGE STATISTICS

		G	FGP	FTP	RPG	PPG
75-76	SF	30	.530	.735	6.9	12.5
76-77	SF	31	.566	.733	8.5	19.4
77-78	SF	21	.667	.733	10.1	20.6
78-79	SF	29	.605	.734	15.7	24.5
Totals		111	.589	.734	10.2	19.1

NBA REGULAR-SEASON STATISTICS

		G	MIN	FG	PCT	FG	PCT	FT	PCT	OFF	TOT	AST	STL	BLK	PTS	PPG
79-80	NY	82	3150	665	.547	0	.000	451	.797	194	726	165	48	101	1781	21.7
80-81	NY	82	2925	619	.554	0	.000	408	.788	161	613	111	48	83	1646	20.1
81-82	NY	72	2060	390	.562	0	.000	257	.763	116	421	87	48	65	1037	14.4
82-83	NY	82	2468	455	.566	0	.000	380	.744	185	590	136	41	127	1290	15.7
83-84	NY	77	2487	453	.561	0	.000	404	.805	195	649	107	44	97	1310	17.0
85-86	NY	2	36	3	.429	0	.000	6	.600	2	10	5	1	1	12	6.0
86-87	NY	58	1989	335	.531	0	.000	346	.790	132	445	96	40	26	1016	17.5
87-88	NY	82	1676	287	.544	0	.000	340	.798	127	384	85	43	43	914	11.1
88-89	CHI	78	2333	365	.475	0	.000	236	.766	152	521	90	21	41	966	12.4
89-90	CHI	71	2160	292	.488	0	.000	227	.811	137	465	145	38	34	811	11.4
90-91	CHI	79	2273	318	.490	0	.000	124	.697	167	486	126	32	15	760	9.6
Totals		765	23557	4182	.535	0	.000	3179	.780	1568	5310	1153	404	633	11543	15.1

TERRY CATLEDGE

Team: Orlando Magic
Position: Forward
Height: 6'8" **Weight:** 230
Birthdate: August 22, 1963
NBA Experience: 6 years

College: South Alabama
Acquired: Selected from Bullets in 1989 expansion draft

Background: Catledge led the nation in rebounding and finished fifth in scoring as a senior at South Alabama. After his rookie campaign with Philadelphia, he became a double-figure scorer in Washington and led Orlando in his first year with the Magic. Catledge played fewer minutes and scored fewer points during the 1990-91 season.

Strengths: Catledge is a tough, physical player who will mix it up inside. His rebounding numbers have never been what they were on the college level but he hits the glass relentlessly, especially the offensive boards. His defense is adequate if unspectacular.

Weaknesses: Once Catledge gets the ball, a shot almost always follows. His career average is less than one assist per game. He does not qualify as a potent shooter either. Although his power moves near the hoop can be effective, he does not have much range and struggles against bigger players. He is woeful from the foul line.

Analysis: Catledge has a power forward's mentality but his frame is better suited for a small-forward role. Without a great repertoire of perimeter offense, he specializes in power moves and short jumpers. His selfishness was a big reason for his decreased playing time just one year after his impressive Orlando debut.

PLAYER SUMMARY

Will..exert force
Can't...hit FTs
Expect.........................numerous shots
Don't Expect...................many assists
Fantasy Value..........................$15-17
Card Value...8¢

COLLEGE STATISTICS

		G	FGP	FTP	RPG	PPG
82-83	SALA	28	.558	.696	9.9	19.7
83-84	SALA	30	.590	.717	11.1	19.9
84-85	SALA	28	.532	.592	11.5	25.6
Totals		86	.556	.663	10.8	21.7

NBA REGULAR-SEASON STATISTICS

				FGs		3-PT FGs		FTs		Rebounds						
		G	MIN	FG	PCT	FG	PCT	FT	PCT	OFF	TOT	AST	STL	BLK	PTS	PPG
85-86	PHI	64	1092	202	.469	0	.000	90	.647	107	272	21	31	8	494	7.7
86-87	WAS	78	2149	413	.495	0	.000	199	.594	248	560	56	43	14	1025	13.1
87-88	WAS	70	1610	296	.506	0	.000	154	.655	180	397	63	33	9	746	10.7
88-89	WAS	79	2077	334	.490	1	.200	153	.602	230	572	75	46	25	822	10.4
89-90	ORL	74	2462	546	.474	2	.250	341	.702	271	563	72	36	17	1435	19.4
90-91	ORL	51	1459	292	.462	0	.000	161	.624	168	355	58	34	9	745	14.6
Totals		416	10849	2083	.483	3	.107	1098	.643	1204	2719	345	223	82	5267	12.7

DUANE CAUSWELL

Team: Sacramento Kings
Position: Center
Height: 7'0" **Weight:** 240
Birthdate: May 31, 1968
NBA Experience: 1 year

College: Temple
Acquired: 1st-round pick in 1990 draft
(18th overall)

Background: Causwell's college career at Temple was cut a semester short because of academic ineligibility, but he finished second in the nation in blocked shots as a junior (4.1 BPG). Projected as a back-up by most observers, Causwell started 55 games as a rookie and finished 15th in the league in blocks.

Strengths: Shot-blocking and rebounding were the primary reasons Sacramento drafted Causwell in the first round. Besides ranking on the league's shot-swatting charts, he finished fifth among rookies in rebounding average.

Weaknesses: Causwell is very mechanical offensively and in most other facets of the game. In fact, blocking shots is about the only aspect which comes easily to him. That includes rebounding, and explains why he was considered a project. To his credit, few would have predicted that he would shoot above 50 percent in his rookie year, which he did.

Analysis: Yes, Causwell is a project. But if his rookie year is any indication, he is one who could pan out. His offense needs much more work but has improved already. With his shot-blocking ability, defensive play is not as grave a concern. Many rookies struggle when forced into action too early; Causwell handled it better than most would have guessed.

PLAYER SUMMARY

Will	block shots
Can't	create offense
Expect	much improvement
Don't Expect	15 PPG
Fantasy Value	$2-4
Card Value	20¢

COLLEGE STATISTICS

		G	FGP	FTP	RPG	PPG
87-88	TEMP	33	.491	.433	2.6	2.0
88-89	TEMP	30	.514	.683	8.9	11.3
89-90	TEMP	12	.486	.596	8.3	11.3
Totals		75	.504	.624	6.0	7.2

NBA REGULAR-SEASON STATISTICS

			FGs		3-PT FGs		FTs		Rebounds						
	G	MIN	FG	PCT	FG	PCT	FT	PCT	OFF	TOT	AST	STL	BLK	PTS	PPG
90-91 SAC	76	1719	210	.508	0	.000	105	.636	141	391	69	49	148	525	6.9
Totals	76	1719	210	.508	0	.000	105	.636	141	391	69	49	148	525	6.9

CEDRIC CEBALLOS

Team: Phoenix Suns
Position: Forward
Height: 6'6" **Weight:** 210
Birthdate: August 2, 1969
NBA Experience: 1 year

College: Cal. St. Fullerton
Acquired: 2nd-round pick in 1990 draft (48th overall)

Background: Ceballos, a Maui, Hawaii, native, played just one year of varsity basketball in high school before going on to lead the Big West in scoring as a junior and senior at Cal. State Fullerton. He finished in the nation's top ten in rebounding as a senior. His rookie season in the NBA came as a pleasant surprise to the Suns, as he averaged a point every 1.4 minutes.

Strengths: The athletic Ceballos has wide shoulders and long arms, allowing him to gain inside position and play above the rim. Despite the fact he is still learning the game, his scoring instincts are sophisticated. He had a 34-point game as a rookie.

Weaknesses: His inability to sink the medium-range jump shot is a concern Ceballos began to address in earnest as a college senior. He still lacks consistency from the 15-foot range. Considering his leaping ability and wingspan, he should be a better defender than his five blocked shots would indicate.

Analysis: Ceballos's play as a rookie was more than one expects from a late second-round draft choice. If the 1990 draft were held again now, someone would snag him early in the first round. He is an exciting scorer who battles big men and runs the floor. His ability to develop an all-around game will determine how high his star rises.

PLAYER SUMMARY

Will ....attack the hoop
Can't.......................shoot consistently
Expect............................explosiveness
Don't Expect ....much passing
Fantasy Value $6-8
Card Value..25¢

COLLEGE STATISTICS

		G	FGP	FTP	RPG	PPG
88-89	CSF	29	.442	.672	8.8	21.2
89-90	CSF	29	.485	.670	12.5	23.1
Totals		58	.463	.671	10.7	22.1

NBA REGULAR-SEASON STATISTICS

			FGs		3-PT FGs		FTs		Rebounds						
	G	MIN	FG	PCT	FG	PCT	FT	PCT	OFF	TOT	AST	STL	BLK	PTS	PPG
90-91 PHO	63	730	204	.487	1	.167	110	.663	77	150	35	22	5	519	8.2
Totals	63	730	204	.487	1	.167	110	.663	77	150	35	22	5	519	8.2

TOM CHAMBERS

Team: Phoenix Suns
Position: Forward
Height: 6'10" **Weight:** 230
Birthdate: June 21, 1959

NBA Experience: 10 years
College: Utah
Acquired: Signed as a free agent, 7/88

Background: Chambers earned All-America recognition at Utah before moving on to become one of the NBA's most productive scorers. He has played in four All-Star Games, including an MVP performance in 1987. He came to Phoenix in 1988 as the first unrestricted free agent in NBA history. The 1990-91 season was his third in Phoenix, where he holds the team's season scoring record.

Strengths: Chambers is tough to defend because he can score in so many ways. He is equally adept at shooting from long range or driving to the hoop and scoring with either hand. He runs the floor, works the pick-and-roll to near perfection, and is deadly from the foul line. He poses match-up problems because he is too big for small forwards and too elusive for power forwards.

Weaknesses: Defense has never been a strong suit, but Chambers is not asked to excel on that end. He often releases early to get easy points on the break. A physical defense can sometimes limit his production.

Analysis: Chambers is paid to score, and he does it as well as any forward in the league. In fact, not many forwards in NBA history have put points on the board like he has. If he can overcome back spasms which slowed him near the end of 1990-91, expect him to burn the nets for a few more seasons.

PLAYER SUMMARY

Will	score
Can't	focus on defense
Expect	20 PPG
Don't Expect	10 APG
Fantasy Value	$31-34
Card Value	12¢

COLLEGE STATISTICS

		G	FGP	FTP	RPG	PPG
77-78	UTA	28	.496	.625	3.7	6.4
78-79	UTA	30	.544	.543	8.9	16.0
79-80	UTA	28	.543	.713	8.7	17.2
80-81	UTA	30	.594	.742	8.7	18.6
Totals		116	.553	.665	7.6	14.6

NBA REGULAR-SEASON STATISTICS

		G	MIN	FG	PCT	FG	PCT	FT	PCT	OFF	TOT	AST	STL	BLK	PTS	PPG
81-82	SD	81	2682	554	.525	0	.000	284	.620	211	561	146	58	46	1392	17.2
82-83	SD	79	2665	519	.472	0	.000	353	.723	218	519	192	79	57	1391	17.6
83-84	SEA	82	2570	554	.499	0	.000	375	.800	219	532	133	47	51	1483	18.1
84-85	SEA	81	2923	629	.483	6	.273	475	.832	164	579	209	70	57	1739	21.5
85-86	SEA	66	2019	432	.466	13	.271	346	.836	126	431	132	55	37	1223	18.5
86-87	SEA	82	3018	660	.456	54	.372	535	.849	163	545	245	81	50	1909	23.3
87-88	SEA	82	2680	611	.448	33	.303	419	.807	135	490	212	87	53	1674	20.4
88-89	PHO	81	3002	774	.471	28	.326	509	.851	143	684	231	87	55	2085	25.7
89-90	PHO	81	3046	810	.501	24	.279	557	.861	121	571	190	88	47	2201	27.2
90-91	PHO	76	2475	556	.437	20	.274	379	.826	104	490	194	65	52	1511	19.9
Totals		791	27080	6099	.475	178	.301	4232	.806	1604	5402	1884	717	505	16608	21.0

REX CHAPMAN

Team: Charlotte Hornets
Position: Guard
Height: 6'4" **Weight:** 195
Birthdate: October 5, 1967
NBA Experience: 3 years

College: Kentucky
Acquired: 1st-round pick in 1988 draft (8th overall)

Background: At Kentucky, Chapman became the first freshman to lead the Wildcats in scoring. He also became only the third Kentucky player to score 1,000 points in his first two years, placing him in the company of Dan Issel and Cotton Nash. However, Chapman left school after his sophomore year. In each of his first two years as a pro, he finished second on the Hornets in scoring.

Strengths: Though you wouldn't know it by looking at him, Chapman can really get up in the air. He has unlimited athletic ability and, if you play off him fearing the drive, he'll burn you from outside. He is developing into a good 3-point shooter. His 42-inch vertical leap allows him to make moves that not many can match.

Weaknesses: From the neck up, Chapman needs help. His shot selection is among the worst in the league, although one must remember that he's still a rather inexperienced player. Maybe the smarts will come. His passing leaves much to be desired—especially the entry passes. His defense has improved but it still needs work.

Analysis: There have been occasional trade rumors, but Chapman would be a worthy gamble for any team. His unquestioned athletic talent will always intrigue general managers. He possesses that rare quality of being able to dunk in your face or sit outside and bomb away from the perimeter. If he picks up some court savvy, he will have a long and memorable career.

PLAYER SUMMARY	
Will	score plenty
Can't	play the point
Expect	hang time
Don't Expect	leadership
Fantasy Value	$8-10
Card Value	12¢

COLLEGE STATISTICS

		G	FGP	FTP	RPG	PPG
86-87	KEN	29	.444	.735	2.3	16.0
87-88	KEN	32	.501	.794	2.9	19.0
Totals		61	.475	.771	2.6	17.6

NBA REGULAR-SEASON STATISTICS

		G	MIN	FG	PCT	FG	PCT	FT	PCT	OFF	TOT	AST	STL	BLK	PTS	PPG
				FGs		3-PT FGs		FTs		Rebounds						
88-89	CHA	75	2219	526	.414	60	.314	155	.795	74	187	176	70	25	1267	16.9
89-90	CHA	54	1762	377	.408	47	.331	144	.750	52	179	132	46	6	945	17.5
90-91	CHA	70	2100	410	.445	48	.324	234	.830	45	191	250	73	16	1102	15.7
Totals		199	6081	1313	.421	155	.322	533	.797	171	557	558	189	47	3314	16.7

MAURICE CHEEKS

Team: New York Knicks
Position: Guard
Height: 6'1" **Weight:** 180
Birthdate: September 8, 1956

NBA Experience: 13 years
College: West Texas St.
Acquired: Traded from Spurs for Rod Strickland, 2/90

Background: Cheeks was a three-time All-Missouri Valley Conference selection. He was the point guard on all those great Philadelphia 76ers teams of the early 1980s, but was traded to San Antonio in 1989 and to New York in 1990. He is the NBA's all-time leader in steals and is fifth in assists.

Strengths: Even at age 35, Cheeks is quicker than many guards in the league. He is next to impossible to rattle in a pressure situation and he can still pick your pocket. Not only is he one of the greatest assist men in history, but he can both penetrate and hit the outside shot. His field goal percentage is outstanding.

Weaknesses: Age, of course, is the big factor, as Cheeks slowly but surely slows down. He's also been criticized for being too quiet—he's not the stir-'em-up leader you'd want from a point guard.

Analysis: Though Cheeks can't always blow by defenders like he did five years ago, he compensates with a world of smarts. He is one of the best clutch performers in the game; his playoff scoring average is three points higher than his regular-season mark. Cheeks is an asset starting or coming off the bench.

PLAYER SUMMARY

Will ....pick your pocket
Can't ....be rattled
Expect ....poise, savvy
Don't Expect..........................turnovers
Fantasy Value $3-5
Card Value...8¢

COLLEGE STATISTICS

		G	FGP	FTP	RPG	PPG
74-75	WTS	26	.467	.585	2.2	3.9
75-76	WTS	23	.600	.619	4.0	11.1
76-77	WTS	30	.606	.704	4.0	13.9
77-78	WTS	27	.545	.714	5.6	16.8
Totals		106	.568	.678	3.9	11.6

NBA REGULAR-SEASON STATISTICS

				FGs		3-PT FGs		FTs		Rebounds							
		G	MIN	FG	PCT	FG	PCT	FT	PCT	OFF	TOT	AST	STL	BLK	PTS	PPG
78-79	PHI	82	2409	292	.510	0	.000	101	.721	63	254	431	174	12	685	8.4
79-80	PHI	79	2623	357	.540	4	.444	180	.779	75	274	556	183	32	898	11.4
80-81	PHI	81	2415	310	.534	3	.375	140	.787	67	245	560	193	39	763	9.4
81-82	PHI	79	2498	352	.521	6	.273	171	.777	51	248	667	209	33	881	11.2
82-83	PHI	79	2465	404	.542	1	.167	181	.754	53	209	543	184	31	990	12.5
83-84	PHI	75	2494	386	.550	8	.400	170	.733	44	205	478	171	20	950	12.7
84-85	PHI	78	2616	422	.570	6	.231	175	.879	54	217	497	169	24	1025	13.1
85-86	PHI	82	3270	490	.537	4	.235	282	.842	55	235	753	207	27	1266	15.4
86-87	PHI	68	2624	415	.527	4	.235	227	.777	47	215	538	180	15	1061	15.6
87-88	PHI	79	2871	428	.495	3	.136	227	.825	59	253	635	167	22	1086	13.7
88-89	PHI	71	2298	336	.483	1	.077	151	.774	39	183	554	105	17	824	11.6
89-90	SA/NY	81	2519	307	.504	4	.250	171	.847	50	240	453	124	10	789	9.7
90-91	NY	76	2147	241	.499	5	.250	105	.814	22	173	435	128	10	592	7.8
Totals		1010	33249	4740	.525	49	.250	2281	.795	679	2951	7100	2194	292	11810	11.7

DERRICK COLEMAN

Team: New Jersey Nets
Position: Forward
Height: 6'10" **Weight:** 230
Birthdate: June 21, 1967

NBA Experience: 1 year
College: Syracuse
Acquired: 1st-round pick in 1990 draft
(1st overall)

Background: Coleman teamed with Billy Owens and Sherman Douglas to give Syracuse one of its most talented squads ever. In his senior year, Coleman averaged 17.9 PPG and 12.1 RPG and earned several College Player of the Year awards. New Jersey selected him as the No. 1 pick in the 1990 draft, and he lived up to his reputation by winning the Rookie of the Year Award last season. He led the Nets in rebounding and finished second in scoring and blocked shots. He was one of just six NBA players to average 18 points and ten rebounds a game last year.

Strengths: Coleman can kill you with his medium-range shot, and he has the makings of becoming a dominant inside scorer. He finished tenth in the league in rebounding last year, and he also handles the ball extremely well for someone his size. He is learning to become a force on defense and could one day be an intimidating shot-blocker. One NBA personnel chief likened him to a young Karl Malone.

Weaknesses: Coleman could raise his field goal percentage from 46.7 percent, which isn't too hot for an inside player. He was third on the Nets in fouls, which isn't good for your franchise player.

Analysis: The sky's the limit for this fast, agile, talented big man. Playing in the Meadowlands could stunt his career, although the nearby New York media will certainly let the world know of his many exploits. He has the potential to become one of the top forwards in the game—if he isn't already.

PLAYER SUMMARY

Will	score and rebound
Can't	win games alone
Expect	big numbers all over
Don't Expect	sophomore jinx
Fantasy Value	$13-15
Card Value	25¢

COLLEGE STATISTICS

		G	FGP	FTP	RPG	PPG
86-87	SYR	38	.560	.686	8.8	11.9
87-88	SYR	35	.587	.630	11.0	13.5
88-89	SYR	37	.575	.692	11.4	16.9
89-90	SYR	33	.551	.715	12.1	17.9
Totals		143	.568	.684	10.7	15.0

NBA REGULAR-SEASON STATISTICS

			FGs		3-PT FGs		FTs		Rebounds						
	G	MIN	FG	PCT	FG	PCT	FT	PCT	OFF	TOT	AST	STL	BLK	PTS	PPG
90-91 NJ	74	2602	514	.467	13	.342	323	.731	269	759	163	71	99	1364	18.4
Totals	74	2602	514	.467	13	.342	323	.731	269	759	163	71	99	1364	18.4

BIMBO COLES

Team: Miami Heat
Position: Guard
Height: 6'1" **Weight:** 182
Birthdate: April 22, 1968
NBA Experience: 1 year

College: Virginia Tech
Acquired: Draft rights traded from Kings for Rory Sparrow, 6/90

Background: Coles is the all-time leading scorer in Virginia Tech and Metro Conference history, as he became the first to lead the league in scoring three straight years. He also holds the Virginia Tech record for assists and was a member of the 1988 bronze-medal Olympic team. However, Coles had a poor senior year, hitting just 40.4 percent of his field goals and only 30.7 percent of his 3-point attempts. As a rookie with the Heat in 1990-91, he appeared in all 82 games.

Strengths: Coles has the speed to take it to the hole, and he led all Heat reserves in steals with 65. He rebounds very well for a 6'1" guard and was third on the Heat in assists, despite ranking only eighth in minutes.

Weaknesses: Bimbo's outside shooting may be what keeps him on the narrow precipice that separates the NBA from the CBA. He hit only 41 percent of his shots last season, and that's a no-no for a pro guard. He played in all 82 games but averaged just 4.9 points a game. Though he fired up 3-pointers at will in college, he's shown that he can't hit the long bomb in the NBA.

Analysis: If he doesn't improve his outside shooting, Coles could wind up in the CBA alongside another fast ball-handler with no outside touch, Ennis Whatley. At his current level, Coles doesn't offer much to an NBA team. He's okay as a fill-in point guard who gives the starter a rest.

PLAYER SUMMARY

Will.................................push the ball
Can't.............................hit from outside
Expect ....assists
Don't Expect.......................3-pointers
Fantasy Value................................$1-3
Card Value..10¢

COLLEGE STATISTICS

		G	FGP	FTP	RPG	PPG
86-87	VT	28	.412	.716	3.0	10.0
87-88	VT	29	.443	.741	3.6	24.2
88-89	VT	27	.455	.785	4.1	26.6
89-90	VT	31	.404	.738	4.7	25.3
Totals		115	.429	.748	3.9	21.6

NBA REGULAR-SEASON STATISTICS

				FGs		3-PT FGs		FTs		Rebounds						
	G	MIN	FG	PCT	FG	PCT	FT	PCT	OFF	TOT	AST	STL	BLK	PTS	PPG
90-91 MIA	82	1355	162	.412	6	.176	71	.747	56	153	232	65	12	401	4.9
Totals	82	1355	162	.412	6	.176	71	.747	56	153	232	65	12	401	4.9

LESTER CONNER

Team: Milwaukee Bucks
Position: Guard
Height: 6'4" **Weight:** 213
Birthdate: September 17, 1965
NBA Experience: 8 years

College: Los Medanos; Chabot; Oregon St.
Acquired: Traded from Nets for Greg Anderson, 1/91

Background: Conner led Oregon State to a 52-6 record his junior and senior years. He finished his collegiate career as a consensus All-American, leading the Pac-10 in steals and assists as a senior. After four years at Golden State (and one in the CBA), he caught on with Houston and then the Nets, where he started 61 games in 1989-90. He was a back-up guard with the Bucks last season, finishing 11th on the team in scoring.

Strengths: Conner is known as a good defensive player. He was fourth on the Bucks in steals last year despite being tenth in minutes played. He is also careful with the ball, with a history of committing few turnovers. He has the size and strength to match up defensively with most big guards and can also cover playmakers as well.

Weaknesses: His outside shot has been inconsistent throughout his career, and he has never been a serious threat to put up big numbers on the scoreboard. Although he has been used as a point guard, his ball-handling and playmaking skills are rather weak.

Analysis: Conner is best used as a defensive role player. He'll work hard on defense, will harass opposing guards, and will often come up with a steal. However, he doesn't have any strong offensive skills and shouldn't be used for extended minutes. He won't find much playing time with Milwaukee.

PLAYER SUMMARY

Will ....play tough defense
Can't.....................shoot from outside
Expect ....steals
Don't Expect................................points
Fantasy Value $1-2
Card Value..5¢

COLLEGE STATISTICS

		G	FGP	FTP	RPG	PPG
78-79	LM	31	—	—	—	25.2
79-80	CHAB	35	.581	.728	6.1	22.7
80-81	OSU	28	.482	.670	4.3	7.0
81-82	OSU	30	.517	.745	5.4	14.9
Totals		124	.548	.724	4.0	17.9

NBA REGULAR-SEASON STATISTICS

		G	MIN	FG	FGs PCT	FG	3-PT FGs PCT	FT	FTs PCT	OFF	Rebounds TOT	AST	STL	BLK	PTS	PPG
82-83	GS	75	1416	145	.479	0	.000	79	.699	69	221	253	116	7	369	4.9
83-84	GS	82	2573	360	.493	1	.167	186	.718	132	305	401	162	12	907	11.1
84-85	GS	79	2258	246	.451	4	.200	144	.750	87	246	369	161	13	640	8.1
85-86	GS	36	413	51	.375	2	.286	40	.741	25	62	43	24	1	144	4.0
87-88	HOU	52	399	50	.463	0	.000	32	.780	20	38	59	38	1	132	2.5
88-89	NJ	82	2532	309	.457	13	.351	212	.788	100	355	604	181	5	843	10.3
89-90	NJ	82	2355	237	.414	2	.154	172	.804	90	265	385	172	8	648	7.9
90-91	NJ/MIL	74	1008	96	.464	0	.000	68	.723	21	112	165	85	2	260	3.5
Totals		562	12954	1494	.456	22	.222	933	.755	544	1604	2279	939	49	3943	7.0

ANTHONY COOK

Team: Denver Nuggets
Position: Forward/Center
Height: 6'9" **Weight:** 215
Birthdate: March 19, 1967
NBA Experience: 1 year

College: Arizona
Acquired: Draft rights traded from Pistons for a 1992 2nd-round pick, 9/90

Background: Cook finished his college career at Arizona as the top shot-blocker in Pac-10 history and ranked among the Wildcats' career leaders in points and rebounds. He was acquired by Detroit from Phoenix on 1989 draft day but spent his first pro season in Greece. His return in 1990-91 saw him start 25 games for Denver; he shot poorly but contributed rebounds and blocked shots.

Strengths: Cook is a well schooled shot-blocker with good defensive timing. He is not a physical player, but he can score when close to the hoop and is a strong finisher on the break.

Weaknesses: The Pistons had the right idea when they suggested Cook spend a year in Europe to bulk up and develop his game. Unfortunately, Cook is still a string bean and lacks consistency in just about everything but shot-blocking. His offensive skills are not NBA-caliber and his free throw shooting is especially poor. Added strength would assist him greatly.

Analysis: Cook is still a raw talent and will get a chance to become a complete player thanks to his shot-blocking proficiency. The year in Greece was probably good for him, but he did not add much bulk and gets tossed around in the lane. Considering his lack of a perimeter game, those are not encouraging characteristics. If he keeps his current physique, Cook will have to demonstrate an ability to move his game away from the hoop to be successful.

PLAYER SUMMARY

Will ....block shots
Can't.................................bury jumpers
Expect.........................defensive effort
Don't Expect ....50-percent shooting
Fantasy Value $2-4
Card Value.......................................10¢

COLLEGE STATISTICS

		G	FGP	FTP	RPG	PPG
85-86	ARIZ	32	.500	.658	4.3	6.1
86-87	ARIZ	30	.480	.540	7.2	9.7
87-88	ARIZ	38	.618	.716	7.1	13.9
88-89	ARIZ	33	.629	.627	7.2	17.5
Totals		133	.575	.645	6.5	12.0

NBA REGULAR-SEASON STATISTICS

			FGs		3-PT FGs		FTs		Rebounds						
	G	MIN	FG	PCT	FG	PCT	FT	PCT	OFF	TOT	AST	STL	BLK	PTS	PPG
90-91 DEN	58	1121	118	.417	0	.000	71	.550	134	326	26	35	72	307	5.3
Totals	58	1121	118	.417	0	.000	71	.550	134	326	26	35	72	307	5.3

WAYNE COOPER

Team: Portland Trail Blazers
Position: Center
Height: 6'10" **Weight:** 220
Birthdate: November 16, 1956

NBA Experience: 13 years
College: New Orleans
Acquired: Signed as a free agent, 7/89

Background: Cooper led the University of New Orleans to the Sun Belt Conference championship as a senior under coach Butch Van Breda Kolff. He has played with six different NBA teams in his 13-year career and this is his second stint with Portland. Although Cooper had his least productive scoring year in 1990-91, he finished third on the team in blocked shots.

Strengths: Cooper specializes in defense, especially shot-blocking. Two of his seasons have resulted in 200-plus blocks and he has swatted 100 or more in five other campaigns. Cooper is not a bad shooter when facing the basket within 15 feet, although he has never scored much.

Weaknesses: If offense were the sole criterion for judging centers, Cooper would not rank highly. He rarely looks to score and has virtually no low-post moves when not facing the basket. Cooper has also been bothered by nagging back problems throughout his career.

Analysis: Cooper's interior defense has been a constant wherever he has played. He used to provide as many minutes of solid defense and shot-blocking as his coach would ask of him; now he can give about 12 minutes a game.

PLAYER SUMMARY
Will............................play post defense
Can't..score
Expect ....blocked shots
Don't Expect............many more years
Fantasy Value $1-2
Card Value..5¢

COLLEGE STATISTICS

		G	FGP	FTP	RPG	PPG
74-75	NO	17	.485	.750	3.1	2.1
75-76	NO	26	.504	.723	9.4	12.1
76-77	NO	28	.451	.691	10.1	13.2
77-78	NO	27	.536	.775	12.7	18.1
Totals		98	.496	.742	9.4	12.3

NBA REGULAR-SEASON STATISTICS

		G	MIN	FG	FG PCT	3-PT FG	3-PT PCT	FT	FT PCT	OFF	TOT	AST	STL	BLK	PTS	PPG
78-79	GS	65	795	128	.437	0	.000	41	.672	90	280	21	7	44	297	4.6
79-80	GS	79	1781	367	.489	1	.250	136	.751	202	507	42	20	79	871	11.0
80-81	UTA	71	1420	213	.452	1	.333	62	.689	166	440	52	18	51	489	6.9
81-82	DAL	76	1818	282	.422	1	.125	119	.744	200	550	115	37	106	682	9.0
82-83	POR	80	2099	320	.443	0	.000	135	.685	214	611	116	27	136	775	9.7
83-84	POR	91	1662	304	.459	0	.000	185	.804	176	476	76	26	106	793	8.7
84-85	DEN	80	2031	404	.472	0	.000	161	.685	229	631	86	28	197	969	12.1
85-86	DEN	78	2112	422	.466	3	.429	174	.795	190	610	81	42	227	1021	13.1
86-87	DEN	69	1561	235	.448	0	.000	79	.725	162	473	68	13	101	549	8.0
87-88	DEN	45	865	118	.437	0	.000	50	.746	98	270	30	12	94	286	6.4
88-89	DEN	79	1864	220	.495	1	.250	79	.745	212	619	78	36	211	520	6.6
89-90	POR	79	1176	138	.454	0	.000	25	.641	118	339	44	18	95	301	3.8
90-91	POR	67	746	57	.393	0	.000	33	.786	54	188	22	7	61	147	2.2
Totals		959	19930	3208	.457	7	.146	1279	.737	2111	5994	831	291	1508	7700	8.0

TYRONE CORBIN

Team: Minnesota Timberwolves
Position: Forward
Height: 6'6" **Weight:** 222
Birthdate: December 31, 1962
NBA Experience: 6 years

College: DePaul
Acquired: Selected from Phoenix in 1989 expansion draft

Background: Corbin led DePaul in both scoring and rebounding as a junior and senior. He made his NBA debut with San Antonio and played for Cleveland and Phoenix before landing in Minnesota via the 1989 expansion draft. He has played in all 164 Timberwolves games over two years. Corbin led the team in rebounds in 1989-90 and in steals both seasons. He started all 82 games in 1990-91.

Strengths: Corbin has earned a reputation as a hard worker and a physical inside player. He fights for rebounds, comes up with steals and loose balls, and plays solid defense on men his size or bigger. What one might never guess from those credentials is that Corbin also has a nice touch around the basket.

Weaknesses: For a small forward, Corbin's perimeter play is limited. He is not a steady jump-shooter and would prefer to grind out his points underneath. His field goal percentage dipped in 1990-91 after a team-leading mark the year before.

Analysis: Corbin will probably remain underrated because his game is not as flashy as those of other NBA small forwards. However, every team needs a player who will get on the floor for the ball and put in a full night's work on defense and in the middle. Corbin is that player.

PLAYER SUMMARY
Will ....hustle on defense
Can't ....stay outside
Expect...........................garbage points
Don't Expect.................................grace
Fantasy Value $7-9
Card Value.......................................8¢

COLLEGE STATISTICS

		G	FGP	FTP	RPG	PPG
81-82	DeP	28	.417	.718	6.1	5.1
82-83	DeP	33	.471	.773	7.9	10.6
83-84	DeP	30	.525	.744	7.4	14.2
84-85	DeP	29	.534	.814	8.1	15.9
Totals		120	.504	.764	7.4	11.5

NBA REGULAR-SEASON STATISTICS

		G	MIN	FG	PCT	FG	PCT	FT	PCT	OFF	TOT	AST	STL	BLK	PTS	PPG
85-86	SA	16	174	27	.422	0	.000	10	.714	11	25	11	11	2	64	4.0
86-87	SA/CLE	63	1170	156	.409	1	.250	91	.734	88	215	97	55	5	404	6.4
87-88	CLE/PHO	84	1739	257	.490	1	.167	110	.797	127	350	115	72	18	625	7.4
88-89	PHO	77	1655	245	.540	0	.000	141	.788	176	398	118	82	13	631	8.2
89-90	MIN	82	3011	521	.481	0	.000	161	.770	219	604	216	175	41	1203	14.7
90-91	MIN	82	3196	587	.448	2	.200	296	.798	185	589	347	162	53	1472	18.0
Totals		404	10945	1793	.470	4	.118	809	.782	806	2181	904	557	132	4399	10.9

TERRY CUMMINGS

Team: San Antonio Spurs
Position: Forward
Height: 6'9" **Weight:** 235
Birthdate: March 15, 1961
NBA Experience: 9 years

College: DePaul
Acquired: Traded from Bucks for Alvin Robertson and Greg Anderson, 5/89

Background: Cummings led DePaul in rebounding each of his three seasons before turning pro a year early. He was originally drafted second overall by San Diego in 1982 and became the first rookie since Kareem Abdul-Jabbar to rank in the top ten in scoring and rebounding. Cummings played in two All-Star Games in five stellar seasons as a Milwaukee Buck. He finished second to David Robinson in scoring and rebounding in each of his past two years in San Antonio.

Strengths: Cummings can score and rebound with the best of forwards and is a nightmare for opposing coaches. He can post up small forwards for turnaround jumpers, drive past bigger players, or unload from the perimeter. Cummings runs the floor well yet is smart enough to know when to apply the brakes. He is solid with both hands and a physical rebounder.

Weaknesses: Perhaps Cummings could be more dominant on defense, but that's about the only flaw in his game.

Analysis: It is not surprising that the Spurs won 35 more games in Cummings's first year with the team than they did the season before. He brings experience, scoring, rebounding, and a physical style of play that tells opposing teams they are in for a war. When one talks about the best power forwards to play in the NBA, the name Terry Cummings deserves mention.

PLAYER SUMMARY

Will ....score, rebound
Can't..........................be checked easily
Expect....................................leadership
Don't Expect ....softness with age
Fantasy Value $47-50
Card Value...10¢

COLLEGE STATISTICS

		G	FGP	FTP	RPG	PPG
79-80	DeP	28	.508	.832	9.4	14.2
80-81	DeP	29	.498	.750	9.0	13.0
81-82	DeP	28	.567	.756	11.9	22.3
Totals		85	.530	.775	10.1	16.4

NBA REGULAR-SEASON STATISTICS

		G	MIN	FGs FG	FGs PCT	3-PT FGs FG	3-PT FGs PCT	FTs FT	FTs PCT	Rebounds OFF	Rebounds TOT	AST	STL	BLK	PTS	PPG
82-83	SD	70	2531	684	.523	0	.000	292	.709	303	744	177	129	62	1660	23.7
83-84	SD	81	2907	737	.494	0	.000	380	.720	323	777	139	92	57	1854	22.9
84-85	MIL	79	2722	759	.495	0	.000	343	.741	244	716	228	117	67	1861	23.6
85-86	MIL	82	2669	681	.474	0	.000	265	.656	222	694	193	121	51	1627	19.8
86-87	MIL	82	2770	729	.511	0	.000	249	.662	214	700	229	129	81	1707	20.8
87-88	MIL	76	2629	675	.485	1	.333	270	.665	184	553	181	78	46	1621	21.3
88-89	MIL	80	2824	730	.467	7	.467	362	.787	281	650	198	106	72	1829	22.9
89-90	SA	81	2821	728	.475	19	.322	343	.780	226	677	219	110	52	1818	22.4
90-91	SA	67	2195	503	.484	7	.212	164	.683	194	521	157	61	30	1177	17.6
Totals		698	24068	6226	.489	34	.283	2668	.715	2191	6032	1721	943	518	15154	21.7

DELL CURRY

Team: Charlotte Hornets
Position: Guard
Height: 6'5" **Weight:** 200
Birthdate: June 25, 1964
NBA Experience: 5 years

College: Virginia Tech
Acquired: Selected from Cavaliers in 1988 expansion draft

Background: The Metro Conference's Player of the Year as a senior, Curry became the league's second-leading career scorer behind Keith Lee. He was a successful pitcher in college (he featured a 95-mph fastball) and was drafted by the Baltimore Orioles on the 14th round. Curry was drafted by Utah, was traded to Cleveland, and was picked up by Charlotte in the expansion draft. He has averaged in double figures the last four years.

Strengths: Curry has the ability to light up a scoreboard in a hurry with a dangerous outside shot, particularly from 3-point land. Former Timberwolves coach Bill Musselman once described him as one of the five best pure shooters in the NBA. Powerful wrists help him release shots from long distances with relative ease.

Weaknesses: He hasn't always played the kind of defense coaches would like and his attitude has gotten him into trouble at times. Ideally, you would use him exclusively in a zone defense because he can't stay with anyone in a man-to-man scheme. He has the mentality all great shooters must have, which sometimes creates ego problems.

Analysis: In a league where shooting is the highest priority, Curry will always find employment. With more and more teams disguising zone defenses and packing it in, zone-breakers like Curry will be in demand. He still has to scrap for playing time with the Hornets, who have a bunch of talented, young guards.

PLAYER SUMMARY

Will..light it up
Can't ....earn full-time job
Expect 3-pointers
Don't Expect ....no-look passes
Fantasy Value..............................$8-10
Card Value...5¢

COLLEGE STATISTICS

		G	FGP	FTP	RPG	PPG
82-83	VT	32	.475	.850	3.0	14.5
83-84	VT	35	.522	.759	4.1	19.3
84-85	VT	29	.482	.758	5.8	18.2
85-86	VT	30	.529	.789	6.8	24.1
Totals		126	.505	.785	4.8	19.0

NBA REGULAR-SEASON STATISTICS

			MIN	FGs FG	FGs PCT	3-PT FGs FG	3-PT FGs PCT	FTs FT	FTs PCT	Rebounds OFF	Rebounds TOT	AST	STL	BLK	PTS	PPG
86-87	UTA	67	636	139	.426	17	.283	30	.789	30	78	58	27	4	325	4.9
87-88	CLE	79	1499	340	.458	28	.346	79	.782	43	166	149	94	22	787	10.0
88-89	CHA	48	813	256	.491	19	.345	40	.870	26	104	50	42	4	571	11.9
89-90	CHA	67	1860	461	.466	52	.354	96	.923	31	168	159	98	26	1070	16.0
90-91	CHA	76	1515	337	.471	32	.372	96	.842	47	199	166	75	25	802	10.6
Totals		337	6323	1533	.465	148	.345	341	.846	177	715	582	336	81	3555	10.5

QUINTIN DAILEY

Team: Seattle SuperSonics
Position: Guard
Height: 6'3" **Weight:** 207
Birthdate: January 22, 1961
NBA Experience: 9 years

College: San Francisco
Acquired: Signed as a free agent, 2/90

Background: Dailey left the University of San Francisco after an All-America junior year and made the NBA All-Rookie Team in his first season with Chicago. He was a potent scorer with the Bulls but encountered drug problems that would plague him for much of the early part of his career. Dailey has since undergone rehab and held assignments with the L.A. Clippers, Sioux Falls of the CBA, and most recently Seattle, where he played in 30 games in 1990-91.

Strengths: Dailey knows how to score in the NBA, and for that reason has been able to hang on in the league. He has good size and can play both guard positions.

Weaknesses: Selflessness has never been a good characterization of Dailey's game. He looks to shoot before all else, yet is not a great pure shooter. In fact, his career shooting average is less than 46 percent. Dailey has slowed considerably since he first entered the league and is a liability on defense.

Analysis: Essentially, Dailey is capable of filling an NBA roster spot, but not much more. Although his talents have deteriorated to the CBA level in many areas, he will continue to shoot the ball often. Dailey's drug problem is apparently behind him; his NBA career soon will be also.

PLAYER SUMMARY

Will ....shoot jumpers
Can't ....help defensively
Expect ....a fourth-guard role
Don't Expect...............................passing
Fantasy Value $1-2
Card Value...5¢

COLLEGE STATISTICS

		G	FGP	FTP	RPG	PPG
79-80	SF	29	.527	.634	3.7	13.6
80-81	SF	31	.572	.772	5.5	22.4
81-82	SF	30	.546	.789	5.2	25.2
Totals		90	.551	.747	4.8	20.5

NBA REGULAR-SEASON STATISTICS

		G	MIN	FG	PCT	FG	PCT	FT	PCT	OFF	TOT	AST	STL	BLK	PTS	PPG
				|FGs		|3-PT FGs		|FTs		|Rebounds						
82-83	CHI	76	2081	470	.466	5	.200	206	.730	87	260	280	72	10	1151	15.1
83-84	CHI	82	2449	583	.474	4	.125	321	.811	61	235	254	109	11	1491	18.2
84-85	CHI	79	2101	525	.473	7	.233	205	.817	57	208	191	71	5	1262	16.0
85-86	CHI	35	723	203	.432	0	.000	163	.823	20	68	67	22	5	569	16.3
86-87	LAC	49	924	200	.407	1	.100	119	.768	34	83	79	43	8	520	10.6
87-88	LAC	67	1282	328	.434	2	.167	243	.776	62	154	109	69	4	901	13.4
88-89	LAC	69	1722	448	.465	1	.111	217	.759	69	204	154	90	6	1114	16.1
89-90	SEA	30	491	97	.404	1	.200	52	.788	18	51	34	12	0	247	8.2
90-91	SEA	30	299	73	.471	0	.000	38	.613	11	32	16	7	1	184	6.1
Totals		517	12072	2927	.456	21	.159	1564	.778	419	1295	1184	495	50	7439	14.4

ADRIAN DANTLEY

Team: Milwaukee Bucks
Position: Forward
Height: 6'5"　**Weight:** 210
Birthdate: February 28, 1956

NBA Experience: 15 years
College: Notre Dame
Acquired: Signed as a free agent, 4/91

Background: Dantley was a two-time All-American at Notre Dame. He was the NBA's Rookie of the Year with Buffalo and, after stints with the Pacers and Lakers, became a scoring champion with Utah (1981 and '84). Detroit and Dallas acquired him for his scoring punch, but dumped him because of his sour attitude. Dantley played in ten games with Milwaukee last season.

Strengths: A.D. may be the best 6'5" post player to ever play the game. Coaches are amazed at his ability to score down low consistently, while giving away five inches to an opponent. He also has an accurate outside shot.

Weaknesses: Dantley is no good for teams who like to run. The complaint from the Pistons was that Dantley sometimes slowed things up so he could operate in a halfcourt attack. Some of his skills have deteriorated because of age.

Analysis: This is probably Dantley's last hurrah. The era of the dominant low-post scorer has given way to today's high-tech forwards, who can slash to the basket, shoot outside, and run. It is probably time for Dantley to call it a career.

PLAYER SUMMARY	
Will	score inside
Can't.	fill the break
Expect	bench points
Don't Expect	transition points
Fantasy Value	$12-15
Card Value	8¢

COLLEGE STATISTICS

		G	FGP	FTP	RPG	PPG
73-74	ND	28	.558	.826	9.1	18.3
74-75	ND	29	.542	.806	10.2	30.4
75-76	ND	29	.588	.779	10.1	28.6
Totals		86	.562	.800	9.8	25.8

NBA REGULAR-SEASON STATISTICS

		G	MIN	FG	PCT	FG	PCT	FT	PCT	OFF	TOT	AST	STL	BLK	PTS	PPG
				|FGs|		|3-PT FGs|		|FTs|		|Rebounds|						
76-77	BUF	77	2816	544	.520	0	.000	476	.818	251	587	144	91	15	1564	20.3
77-78	IND/LAL	79	2933	578	.512	0	.000	541	.796	265	620	253	118	24	1697	21.5
78-79	LAL	60	1775	374	.510	0	.000	292	.854	131	342	138	63	12	1040	17.3
79-80	UTA	68	2674	730	.576	0	.000	443	.842	183	516	191	96	14	1903	28.0
80-81	UTA	80	3417	909	.559	2	.286	632	.806	192	509	322	109	18	2452	30.6
81-82	UTA	81	3222	904	.570	1	.333	648	.792	231	514	324	95	14	2457	30.3
82-83	UTA	22	887	233	.580	0	.000	210	.847	58	140	105	20	0	676	30.7
83-84	UTA	79	2984	802	.558	1	.250	813	.859	179	448	310	61	4	2418	30.6
84-85	UTA	55	1971	512	.531	0	.000	438	.804	148	323	186	57	8	1462	26.6
85-86	UTA	76	2744	818	.563	1	.091	630	.791	178	395	264	64	4	2267	29.8
86-87	DET	81	2736	601	.534	1	.167	539	.812	104	332	162	63	7	1742	21.5
87-88	DET	69	2144	444	.514	0	.000	492	.860	84	227	171	39	10	1380	20.0
88-89	DET/DAL	73	2422	470	.493	0	.000	460	.810	117	317	171	43	13	1400	19.2
89-90	DAL	45	1300	231	.477	0	.000	200	.787	78	172	80	20	7	662	14.7
90-91	MIL	10	126	19	.380	1	.333	18	.692	8	13	9	5	0	57	5.7
Totals		955	34151	8169	.540	7	.171	6832	.818	2207	5455	2830	944	150	23177	24.3

BRAD DAUGHERTY

Team: Cleveland Cavaliers
Position: Center
Height: 7'0" **Weight:** 263
Birthdate: October 19, 1965
NBA Experience: 5 years

College: North Carolina
Acquired: 1st-round pick in 1986 draft (1st overall)

Background: Daugherty has always been ahead of his time, performing in the McDonald's High School All-Star Game as a 16-year-old senior. At North Carolina, he led the Atlantic Coast Conference in rebounding as a junior and led the country in field goal percentage as a senior. He has appeared in the NBA All-Star Game in three of the last four years. In 1990-91, he finished 16th in the league in scoring and sixth in rebounding.

Strengths: Daugherty can hurt you inside or out. He has the power to muscle underneath for baskets and also has the touch to make precision passes from the high post. Rivals have called him the best passing center in the league. Of his many varied shots, the best is a jump hook. His field goal percentage is usually high.

Weaknesses: He won't block as many shots as you'd like from a seven-foot center. Daugherty was criticized early in his career for playing soft underneath, but that hasn't been borne out with the Cavaliers.

Analysis: Many consider him one of the four best centers in the NBA, alongside Patrick Ewing, Hakeem Olajuwon, and David Robinson. He is a complete player with one of the best attitudes you'll find among pro athletes. Daugherty is the kind of center a team can win a championship with. He won't necessarily carry a club, but he will fill the middle quite nicely.

PLAYER SUMMARY	
Will	score in different ways
Can't	block lots of shots
Expect	solid numbers
Don't Expect	a franchise player
Fantasy Value	$17-20
Card Value	10¢

COLLEGE STATISTICS

		G	FGP	FTP	RPG	PPG
82-83	NC	35	.558	.663	5.2	8.2
83-84	NC	30	.610	.678	5.6	10.5
84-85	NC	36	.625	.742	9.7	17.3
85-86	NC	34	.648	.684	9.0	20.2
Totals		135	.620	.700	7.4	14.2

NBA REGULAR-SEASON STATISTICS

		G	MIN	FGs FG	FGs PCT	3-PT FGs FG	3-PT FGs PCT	FTs FT	FTs PCT	Rebounds OFF	Rebounds TOT	AST	STL	BLK	PTS	PPG
86-87	CLE	80	2695	487	.538	0	.000	279	.696	152	647	304	49	63	1253	15.7
87-88	CLE	79	2957	551	.510	0	.000	378	.716	151	665	333	48	56	1480	18.7
88-89	CLE	78	2821	544	.538	1	.333	386	.737	167	718	285	63	40	1475	18.9
89-90	CLE	41	1438	244	.479	0	.000	202	.704	77	373	130	29	22	690	16.8
90-91	CLE	76	2946	605	.524	0	.000	435	.751	177	830	253	74	46	1645	21.6
Totals		354	12857	2431	.521	1	.100	1680	.724	724	3233	1305	263	227	6543	18.5

BRAD DAVIS

Team: Dallas Mavericks
Position: Guard
Height: 6'3" **Weight:** 183
Birthdate: December 17, 1955

NBA Experience: 14 years
College: Maryland
Acquired: Signed as a free agent, 12/80

Background: Davis helped Maryland to a 69-15 record over three years, then left school a year early. He started with the Lakers, Indiana, and Utah, and played for Anchorage of the CBA before signing on with the 1980-81 Dallas Mavericks charter team. He is the only remaining Maverick from that team.

Strengths: Teammate Derek Harper calls Davis the hardest working player in the NBA. Davis can still bury his jump shots when left open and finds the open men on the court. He knows the Mavericks' system better than anyone.

Weaknesses: Davis has lost the quickness that once made him an effective penetrator. Now he struggles when checked by quick guards. He also is of little help on defense because he lacks both the size to stop bigger guards and the speed to stay with smaller ones. His shooting percentage has plummeted.

Analysis: Davis will always be a fan favorite in Dallas and has earned great respect around the league for his work ethic and commitment. However, he is past the point where he can be of great help to any NBA team.

PLAYER SUMMARY

Will...............................sink open shots
Can't.........................play quick guards
Expect ....supreme effort
Don't Expect ....past results
Fantasy Value $1-3
Card Value.............................5¢

COLLEGE STATISTICS

		G	FGP	FTP	RPG	PPG
74-75	MD	29	.580	.820	3.3	12.6
75-76	MD	28	.513	.793	2.6	11.6
76-77	MD	27	.512	.784	3.5	12.4
Totals		84	.535	.799	3.1	12.2

NBA REGULAR-SEASON STATISTICS

		G	MIN	FG	PCT	FG	PCT	FT	PCT	OFF	TOT	AST	STL	BLK	PTS	PPG
77-78	LAL	33	334	30	.417	0	.000	22	.759	4	35	83	15	2	82	2.5
78-79	LAL/IND	27	298	31	.564	0	.000	16	.696	1	17	52	16	2	78	2.9
79-80	IND/UTA	18	268	35	.556	0	.000	13	.813	4	17	50	13	1	83	4.6
80-81	DAL	56	1686	230	.561	3	.176	163	.799	29	151	385	52	11	626	11.2
81-82	DAL	82	2614	397	.515	14	.286	185	.804	35	226	509	73	6	993	12.1
82-83	DAL	79	2323	359	.572	11	.256	186	.845	34	198	565	80	11	915	11.6
83-84	DAL	81	2665	345	.530	7	.184	199	.836	41	187	561	94	13	896	11.1
84-85	DAL	82	2539	310	.505	47	.409	158	.888	39	193	581	91	10	825	10.1
85-86	DAL	82	1971	267	.532	32	.360	198	.868	26	146	467	57	15	764	9.3
86-87	DAL	82	1582	199	.456	32	.302	147	.860	27	114	373	63	10	577	7.0
87-88	DAL	71	1480	208	.501	30	.405	91	.843	18	102	303	51	18	537	7.2
88-89	DAL	78	1395	183	.483	32	.314	99	.805	14	108	242	48	18	497	6.4
89-90	DAL	73	1292	179	.490	35	.337	77	.770	12	93	242	47	9	470	6.4
90-91	DAL	80	1426	159	.426	22	.259	91	.771	13	118	230	45	17	431	5.4
Totals		928	21873	2932	.511	265	.322	1645	.828	297	1705	4643	745	143	7774	8.4

TERRY DAVIS

Team: Dallas Mavericks
Position: Forward
Height: 6'9" **Weight:** 236
Birthdate: June 17, 1967
NBA Experience: 2 years

College: Virginia Union
Acquired: Signed as a free agent, 8/91

Background: From tiny Virginia Union, the alma mater of the Knicks' Charles Oakley, Davis made headlines as a two-time Central Intercollegiate Athletic Association Player of the Year. He was also a third-team All-American in 1988. As a senior, he shot a blazing 62 percent from the floor. Though he wasn't drafted, he signed with Miami as a free agent in 1989. He was a bench player for the Heat for two years before signing with Dallas in August.

Strengths: Davis has good agility for a big man and has proven to be quite adept on the offensive boards. He is actually contributing more than one would expect from an undrafted free agent. He is tall enough to play some back-up center and has a nice, soft shooting touch from the perimeter.

Weaknesses: He doesn't possess the strength to bang with the musclebound power forwards and centers in the NBA. Talented, experienced big men can blow by him and take him to school. His free throw shooting was atrocious last year.

Analysis: At times, Davis has flashed major-league potential. For instance, in a five-game stretch in March 1990, he averaged 11 points and nine rebounds while shooting 60.5 percent. Nevertheless, he is still pretty much a raw, unpolished player who has yet to establish himself in any particular area. The Mavericks are hurting at forward, so he should get a chance to develop in Dallas.

PLAYER SUMMARY	
Will	clean offensive boards
Can't	block shots
Expect	a soft touch
Don't Expect	overnight stardom
Fantasy Value	$1-3
Card Value	5¢

COLLEGE STATISTICS

		G	FGP	FTP	RPG	PPG
85-86	VU	27	.462	.605	4.3	4.1
86-87	VU	32	.521	.690	11.3	11.5
87-88	VU	31	.566	.715	10.9	22.7
88-89	VU	31	.615	.682	11.9	22.3
Totals		121	.567	.692	9.8	15.5

NBA REGULAR-SEASON STATISTICS

				FGs		3-PT FGs		FTs		Rebounds						
		G	MIN	FG	PCT	FG	PCT	FT	PCT	OFF	TOT	AST	STL	BLK	PTS	PPG
89-90	MIA	63	884	122	.466	0	.000	54	.621	93	229	25	25	28	298	4.7
90-91	MIA	55	996	115	.487	1	.500	69	.556	107	266	39	18	28	300	5.5
Totals		118	1880	237	.476	1	.333	123	.583	200	495	64	43	56	598	5.1

WALTER DAVIS

Team: Portland Trail Blazers
Position: Guard
Height: 6'6" **Weight:** 200
Birthdate: September 9, 1954
NBA Experience: 14 years
College: North Carolina

Acquired: Traded from Nuggets via the Nets; Nets sent Greg Anderson and a future first-round pick to Nuggets, and Trail Blazers sent Drazen Petrovic and Terry Mills to Nets, 1/91

Background: Davis helped carry North Carolina to the 1977 NCAA title game. His NBA career started with a Rookie of the Year season in Phoenix, where he remains the team's career scoring leader, and has gone on to include six All-Star showings. He was picked up by Portland (from Denver) during 1990-91.

Strengths: Davis owns one of the prettiest jump shots the NBA has ever seen, and it remains a very effective weapon. Even at age 37, there is no question he can fill the bucket. He can play both big guard and small forward.

Weaknesses: Davis is a liability on defense (always has been) and his overall game has diminished with age. He is not always able to create shots for himself and his 1990-91 field goal percentage was the worst of his 14-year career.

Analysis: Davis does not have much longer to display those textbook jump shots with perfect release and rotation. He can provide instant offense and outstanding free throw shooting off the bench, but not much else besides experience.

PLAYER SUMMARY

Will	launch jumpers
Can't	play defense
Expect	a quality reserve
Don't Expect	15 PPG
Fantasy Value	$4-5
Card Value	8¢

COLLEGE STATISTICS

		G	FGP	FTP	RPG	PPG
73-74	NC	27	.500	.793	4.7	14.3
74-75	NC	31	.505	.754	6.3	16.1
75-76	NC	29	.541	.777	5.7	16.6
76-77	NC	32	.578	.778	5.7	15.5
Totals		119	.531	.773	5.6	15.7

NBA REGULAR-SEASON STATISTICS

		G	MIN	FGs FG	FGs PCT	3-PT FGs FG	3-PT FGs PCT	FTs FT	FTs PCT	Rebounds OFF	Rebounds TOT	AST	STL	BLK	PTS	PPG
77-78	PHO	81	2590	786	.526	0	.000	387	.830	158	484	273	113	20	1959	24.2
78-79	PHO	79	2437	764	.561	0	.000	340	.831	111	373	339	147	26	1868	23.6
79-80	PHO	75	2309	657	.563	0	.000	299	.819	75	272	337	114	19	1613	21.5
80-81	PHO	78	2182	593	.539	7	.412	209	.836	63	200	302	97	12	1402	18.0
81-82	PHO	55	1182	350	.523	3	.188	91	.820	21	103	162	46	3	794	14.4
82-83	PHO	80	2491	665	.516	7	.304	184	.818	63	197	397	117	12	1521	19.0
83-84	PHO	78	2546	652	.512	20	.230	233	.863	38	202	429	107	12	1557	20.0
84-85	PHO	23	570	139	.450	3	.300	64	.877	6	35	98	18	0	345	15.0
85-86	PHO	70	2239	624	.485	18	.237	257	.843	54	203	361	99	3	1523	21.8
86-87	PHO	79	2646	779	.514	21	.259	288	.862	90	244	364	96	5	1867	23.6
87-88	PHO	68	1951	488	.473	36	.375	205	.887	32	159	278	86	3	1217	17.9
88-89	DEN	81	1857	536	.498	20	.290	175	.879	41	151	190	72	5	1267	15.6
89-90	DEN	69	1635	497	.481	6	.130	207	.912	46	179	155	59	9	1207	17.5
90-91	DEN/POR	71	1483	403	.468	11	.306	107	.915	71	181	125	80	3	924	13.0
Totals		987	28118	7933	.513	152	.271	3046	.850	869	2983	3810	1251	132	19064	19.3

JOHNNY DAWKINS

Team: Philadelphia 76ers
Position: Guard
Height: 6'2" **Weight:** 170
Birthdate: September 28, 1963
NBA Experience: 5 years

College: Duke
Acquired: Traded from Spurs with Jay Vincent for Maurice Cheeks, Chris Welp, and David Wingate, 8/89

Background: A superstar in college, Dawkins finished as Duke's all-time leading scorer and the ACC's No. 2 career scorer. He was the first ACC player to collect 2,000 points, 500 assists, and 500 rebounds. San Antonio selected him with the No. 10 pick in the first round of the 1987 draft. He missed most of 1988-89 with a leg injury and was traded to Philadelphia after the season. Dawkins sat out virtually the entire 1990-91 season because of a torn anterior cruciate ligament.

Strengths: Dawkins is a skittering waterbug with outstanding quickness and turbo propulsion to the basket. He also jumps very well for a 6'2" guard and is learning when and where to deliver the ball. Before his recent injury, he was developing into a fine all-around point guard. He's an excellent free throw shooter.

Weaknesses: Dawkins came into the league as a shooting guard trapped inside a point guard's body. He originally had difficulty making the transition, although he improved in Philly. His quickness helps him on defense, but bigger guards can plow through him. Last year's injury may curtail some of his quickness.

Analysis: Even if he's 100 percent after coming back from his injury, Dawkins still has a little ways to go before reaching the upper echelon of playmakers. As his outside shot drops more and more often, it will enhance his ability to blow by defenders for lay-ups and easy scoop shots.

PLAYER SUMMARY

Will ....score quickly
Can't....................................stay healthy
Expect................points from the point
Don't Expect ....a slow pace
Fantasy Value............................$14-16
Card Value...15¢

COLLEGE STATISTICS

		G	FGP	FTP	RPG	PPG
82-83	DUKE	28	.500	.682	4.1	18.1
83-84	DUKE	34	.481	.831	4.1	19.4
84-85	DUKE	31	.495	.795	4.5	18.8
85-86	DUKE	40	.549	.812	3.6	20.2
Totals		133	.508	.790	4.0	19.2

NBA REGULAR-SEASON STATISTICS

				FGs		3-PT FGs		FTs		Rebounds						
		G	MIN	FG	PCT	FG	PCT	FT	PCT	OFF	TOT	AST	STL	BLK	PTS	PPG
86-87	SA	81	1682	334	.437	14	.298	153	.801	56	169	290	67	3	835	10.3
87-88	SA	65	2179	405	.485	19	.311	198	.896	66	204	480	88	2	1027	15.8
88-89	SA	32	1083	177	.443	0	.000	100	.893	32	101	224	55	0	454	14.2
89-90	PHI	81	2865	465	.489	22	.333	210	.861	48	247	601	121	9	1162	14.3
90-91	PHI	4	124	26	.634	1	.250	10	.909	0	16	28	3	0	63	15.8
Totals		263	7933	1407	.471	56	.308	671	.861	202	737	1623	334	14	3541	13.5

VLADE DIVAC

Team: Los Angeles Lakers
Position: Center
Height: 7'1" **Weight:** 240
Birthdate: February 2, 1968
NBA Experience: 2 years

College: None
Acquired: 1st-round pick in 1989 draft
(26th overall)

Background: Divac was a national sports hero in Yugoslavia before being drafted by the Lakers in 1989. In fact, his wedding four days after the draft was televised nationally. He led Partizan to the European club championship in 1988, and averaged approximately 20 points and 11 rebounds in his three years there. He was named to the 1989-90 NBA All-Rookie Team. Divac started 81 of 82 games in 1990-91 and improved in virtually all areas.

Strengths: Divac is a gifted passer and ball-handler for a big man, and is especially dangerous when dishing off from the high post. His low-post offense is not overly physical but can be effective. He shoots well, with good range for his size, and runs the floor. Divac is a talented shot-blocker and rebounder with frightening potential.

Weaknesses: Like many Europeans, Divac can rely too much on finesse when he has the ball in the paint. The Lakers would like him to be consistently aggressive on both ends of the court, although he has come a long way in that regard. He tends to fall down a lot on defense, often in an effort to draw fouls.

Analysis: Somewhat unexpectedly, Divac appears to have answered the Lakers' desperate call for a center to replace Kareem Abdul-Jabbar. He is young, versatile, has good hands and feet, and has the ability to do just about all that is asked of him. Divac will only get better as he learns to become more of an enforcer.

PLAYER SUMMARY	
Will	find open men
Can't	stick to power game
Expect	high FG pct.
Don't Expect	20 PPG
Fantasy Value	$10-12
Card Value	20¢

COLLEGE STATISTICS
—DID NOT PLAY—

NBA REGULAR-SEASON STATISTICS

		G	MIN	FG	PCT	FG	PCT	FT	PCT	OFF	TOT	AST	STL	BLK	PTS	PPG
89-90	LAL	82	1611	274	.499	0	.000	153	.708	167	512	75	79	114	701	8.5
90-91	LAL	82	2310	360	.565	5	.357	196	.703	205	666	92	106	127	921	11.2
Totals		164	3921	634	.535	5	.263	349	.705	372	1178	167	185	241	1622	9.9

JAMES DONALDSON

Team: Dallas Mavericks
Position: Center
Height: 7'2" **Weight:** 280
Birthdate: August 16, 1957

NBA Experience: 11 years
College: Washington St.
Acquired: Traded from Clippers for
Kurt Nimphius, 11/85

Background: Donaldson was a second-team All-Pac-10 selection at Washington State. He was taken in the fourth round of the 1980 draft by Seattle. Donaldson was playing perhaps the best ball of his pro career for Dallas when a serious knee injury in March 1989 shelved him for the remainder of the season. He started all 82 games for Dallas in 1990-91.

Strengths: Donaldson is powerful and has excellent touch around the basket. His hook shot and turnaround jumper have been effective for years, and he has recently added a pretty consistent mid-range shot to his arsenal. He is a good rebounder and his beef makes opposing players leery of entering the lane.

Weaknesses: Injuries and age have slowed Donaldson considerably, and he was never fleet-footed from the start. This limits him when trying to defend centers with quick low-post moves and leaves him lagging behind most fast breaks. He is not an aggressive scorer despite his high shooting percentage.

Analysis: Donaldson will never be seen as one of the NBA's great centers. However, he has to qualify as one of the most underrated. Few men his size possess the kind of offensive touch he has mastered. His role will diminish in upcoming years but, when healthy, Donaldson should become a key reserve.

PLAYER SUMMARY

Will	rebound
Can't	run, jump
Expect	inside touch
Don't Expect	healthy knees
Fantasy Value	$3-6
Card Value	5¢

COLLEGE STATISTICS

		G	FGP	FTP	RPG	PPG
75-76	WSU	9	.571	.667	1.9	1.1
76-77	WSU	22	.576	.316	3.4	3.4
77-78	WSU	27	.522	.653	11.3	12.6
78-79	WSU	26	.556	.541	10.8	11.3
Totals		84	.542	.581	8.1	8.5

NBA REGULAR-SEASON STATISTICS

			MIN	FGs FG	PCT	3-PT FGs FG	PCT	FTs FT	PCT	Rebounds OFF	TOT	AST	STL	BLK	PTS	PPG
80-81	SEA	68	980	129	.542	0	.000	101	.594	107	309	42	8	74	359	5.3
81-82	SEA	82	1710	255	.609	0	.000	151	.629	138	490	51	27	139	661	8.1
82-83	SEA	82	1789	289	.583	0	.000	150	.688	131	501	97	19	101	728	8.9
83-84	SD	82	2525	360	.596	0	.000	249	.761	165	649	90	40	139	969	11.8
84-85	LAC	82	2392	351	.637	0	.000	227	.749	168	668	48	28	130	929	11.3
85-86	LAC/DAL	83	2682	256	.558	0	.000	204	.803	171	795	96	28	139	716	8.6
86-87	DAL	82	3028	311	.586	0	.000	267	.812	295	973	63	51	136	889	10.8
87-88	DAL	81	2523	212	.558	0	.000	147	.778	247	755	66	40	104	571	7.0
88-89	DAL	53	1746	193	.573	0	.000	95	.766	158	570	38	24	81	481	9.1
89-90	DAL	73	2265	258	.539	0	.000	149	.700	155	630	57	22	47	665	9.1
90-91	DAL	82	2800	327	.532	0	.000	165	.721	201	727	69	34	93	819	10.0
Totals		850	24440	2941	.576	0	.000	1905	.734	1936	7067	717	321	1183	7787	9.2

SHERMAN DOUGLAS

Team: Miami Heat
Position: Guard
Height: 6'0 **Weight:** 180
Birthdate: September 15, 1966
NBA Experience: 2 years

College: Syracuse
Acquired: 2nd-round pick in 1989 draft (28th overall)

Background: Douglas was the catalyst in Syracuse's "Clockwork Orange" triumvirate that included Billy Owens and Derrick Coleman. He is the all-time NCAA career assists leader and was a first-team All-American his senior year, when he became the first Big East player to lead the league in assists three straight years. Despite all that, he was drafted in only the second round. He proved GMs wrong by making the NBA All-Rookie Team.

Strengths: Douglas is a great ball-handler and passer with breakaway speed. He doesn't commit many turnovers and he constantly sets up teammates for makeable shots. Douglas is a tremendous penetrator and has taken over the leadership role at an early age. He led the Heat in scoring last season.

Weaknesses: Like many younger players, Douglas needs to work on his defense. He has a tendency to sag off his man too much, perhaps still thinking about his days in college when he played zone defense. With his quickness, he should be recording more steals.

Analysis: Douglas is developing into the prototype NBA point guard with his great passing and penetrating skills. His shooting accuracy (50.4 percent) forces defenses to play him honest, though his free throw percentage of 68.6 percent is low for a guard. With modest improvements, Douglas will be on his way to NBA stardom.

PLAYER SUMMARY	
Will	penetrate
Can't	hit FTs
Expect	a future All-Star
Don't Expect	any let-up
Fantasy Value	$15-17
Card Value	40¢

COLLEGE STATISTICS

		G	FGP	FTP	RPG	PPG
85-86	SYR	27	.613	.727	1.2	5.4
86-87	SYR	38	.531	.744	2.6	17.3
87-88	SYR	35	.519	.693	2.2	16.1
88-89	SYR	38	.546	.632	2.4	18.2
Totals		138	.538	.695	2.2	14.9

NBA REGULAR-SEASON STATISTICS

		G	MIN	FGs FG	FGs PCT	3-PT FGs FG	3-PT FGs PCT	FTs FT	FTs PCT	Rebounds OFF	Rebounds TOT	AST	STL	BLK	PTS	PPG
89-90	MIA	81	2470	463	.494	5	.161	224	.687	70	206	619	145	10	1155	14.3
90-91	MIA	73	2562	532	.504	4	.129	284	.686	78	209	624	121	5	1352	18.5
Totals		154	5032	995	.499	9	.145	508	.686	148	415	1243	266	15	2507	16.3

GREG DREILING

Team: Indiana Pacers
Position: Center
Height: 7'1" **Weight:** 250
Birthdate: November 7, 1963
NBA Experience: 5 years

College: Wichita St.; Kansas
Acquired: 2nd-round pick in 1986
draft (26th overall)

Background: Dreiling was the center on Kansas' Final Four team in 1986. In four years as a collegian, his teams were a combined 106-29. He shot 60.6 percent as a senior. Dreiling was drafted early in the second round of the 1986 draft, but he was just a bit player with Indiana for four years. He was promoted to back-up center last season. He averaged just 3.5 points per game but shot 50.5 percent from the floor.

Strengths: This guy has a big body and can be a physical player at times. He is the kind of player who comes into a game knowing his role and doesn't try to play beyond his limitations.

Weaknesses: Dreiling isn't much of a scoring threat and his lack of speed hurts him against teams that thrive on a running game. He is an adequate rebounder coming off the bench, but he isn't a threat to do much else. He blocked only 29 shots in the 73 games he played in last season, and his 60-percent free throw shooting wasn't too pretty either.

Analysis: There always seems to be room on NBA rosters for guys like Dreiling. He doesn't do anything spectacular, but he does play his role and doesn't hurt you when he's out there. His size, 7'1" and 250 pounds, always seems to intrigue coaches, as if perhaps someday he will develop into a force in the middle. It says here that the best he'll be is an adequate career back-up.

PLAYER SUMMARY

Will ....be a back-up
Can't ....score big numbers
Expect ....limited minutes
Don't Expect ....a late bloomer
Fantasy Value $1-2
Card Value.....................................10¢

COLLEGE STATISTICS

		G	FGP	FTP	RPG	PPG
81-82	WSU	29	.543	.753	4.2	8.1
83-84	KAN	32	.531	.742	4.8	9.7
84-85	KAN	34	.577	.727	6.9	13.1
85-86	KAN	39	.600	.711	6.7	11.6
Totals		134	.568	.731	5.8	10.8

NBA REGULAR-SEASON STATISTICS

		G	MIN	FG	PCT	FG	PCT	FT	PCT	OFF	TOT	AST	STL	BLK	PTS	PPG
86-87	IND	24	128	16	.432	0	.000	10	.833	12	43	7	2	2	42	1.8
87-88	IND	20	74	8	.471	0	.000	18	.692	3	17	5	2	4	34	1.7
88-89	IND	53	396	43	.558	0	.000	43	.672	39	92	18	5	11	129	2.4
89-90	IND	49	307	20	.377	0	.000	25	.735	21	87	8	4	14	65	1.3
90-91	IND	73	1031	98	.505	0	.000	63	.600	66	255	51	24	29	259	3.5
Totals		219	1936	185	.489	0	.000	159	.660	141	494	89	37	60	529	2.4

LARRY DREW

Team: Los Angeles Lakers
Position: Guard
Height: 6'2" **Weight:** 190
Birthdate: April 2, 1958

NBA Experience: 10 years
College: Missouri
Acquired: Signed as a free agent, 8/89

Background: Drew closed his college career as Missouri's all-time assists king and No. 2 career scorer. He played his rookie year with Detroit but was traded to Kansas City. Drew was a proficient scorer and assists man with the Kings for five seasons and with the L.A. Clippers for two before spending 1988-89 in the Italian League. The Lakers picked him up in 1989 and Drew has played the last two years primarily in a reserve role to Magic Johnson.

Strengths: Drew handles the ball well, which is mostly what a club needs from a reserve point guard. He can be a good shooter but is streaky, which allows defenders to leave him to double-team others. He can play both guard positions.

Weaknesses: The quickness that used to help Drew flash past opposing guards no longer exists. He still can run the floor and penetrate, but nothing like his earlier seasons. Drew has a history of questionable decision-making with the ball and sometimes lapses into those habits again.

Analysis: Drew provided much-needed relief for Magic in his first season with the Lakers but his role was greatly reduced in 1990-91. The advantages to having Drew on the roster are his experience and ability to fill both guard positions. That should allow him to hang on with someone.

PLAYER SUMMARY

Will..................................handle the ball
Can't.........................score consistently
Expect ....fewer minutes
Don't Expect..............................10 PPG
Fantasy Value $1-2
Card Value...5¢

COLLEGE STATISTICS

		G	FGP	FTP	RPG	PPG
76-77	MO	28	.429	.746	2.8	6.9
77-78	MO	30	.436	.762	3.0	12.7
78-79	MO	28	.495	.640	2.6	15.2
79-80	MO	31	.541	.818	2.9	12.9
Totals		117	.479	.745	2.8	12.0

NBA REGULAR-SEASON STATISTICS

				FGs		3-PT FGs		FTs		Rebounds						
		G	MIN	FG	PCT	FG	PCT	FT	PCT	OFF	TOT	AST	STL	BLK	PTS	PPG
80-81	DET	76	1581	197	.407	4	.235	106	.797	24	120	249	88	7	504	6.6
81-82	KC	81	1973	358	.473	8	.296	150	.794	30	149	419	110	1	874	10.8
82-83	KC	75	2690	599	.492	2	.125	310	.820	44	207	610	126	10	1510	20.1
83-84	KC	73	2363	474	.462	3	.300	243	.776	33	146	558	121	10	1194	16.4
84-85	KC	72	2373	457	.501	7	.250	154	.794	39	164	484	93	8	1075	14.9
85-86	SAC	75	1971	376	.485	10	.323	128	.795	25	125	338	66	2	890	11.9
86-87	LAC	60	1566	295	.432	12	.167	139	.837	26	103	326	60	2	741	12.4
87-88	LAC	74	2024	328	.456	26	.289	83	.769	21	119	383	65	0	765	10.3
89-90	LAL	80	1333	170	.444	32	.395	46	.767	12	98	217	47	4	418	5.2
90-91	LAL	48	496	54	.432	14	.424	17	.773	5	34	118	15	1	139	2.9
Totals		714	18370	3308	.467	118	.291	1376	.798	259	1265	3702	791	45	8110	11.4

CLYDE DREXLER

Team: Portland Trail Blazers
Position: Guard
Height: 6'7" **Weight:** 222
Birthdate: June 22, 1962

NBA Experience: 8 years
College: Houston
Acquired: 1st-round pick in 1983 draft
(14th overall)

Background: Drexler gained notoriety at the University of Houston (where he played in two Final Fours) for his breathtaking slam dunks. He has maintained that reputation as a pro and has led Portland in scoring each of the past four years. Drexler is the Blazers' all-time leader in games played, minutes, scoring, offensive rebounds, and steals. He started all 82 games of the 1990-91 campaign and made his fifth All-Star appearance.

Strengths: Phenomenal leaping ability and hang time have helped "Clyde the Glide" establish himself as a superstar player. Few can make things happen in the open court or finish a break like he can. Drexler has become a reliable shooter with 3-point range. His post-up moves give small guards fits. He rebounds well and gets the ball to open men better than he ever has.

Weaknesses: Drexler will not be a candidate for the All-Defensive Team, preferring to save his focus for offense until the game is on the line and Portland really needs a stop. He is not a snazzy ball-handler.

Analysis: The No. 1 knock on Drexler has been his inability to come through in the playoffs, but that has changed over the past couple of seasons. He is no longer vulnerable in halfcourt games because of his improved long-range shot and better decision-making. Drexler can not be viewed as a one-dimensional superstar any more.

PLAYER SUMMARY	
Will	soar to hoop
Can't	use left hand
Expect	20 PPG
Don't Expect	more playoff flops
Fantasy Value	$69-73
Card Value	20¢

COLLEGE STATISTICS

		G	FGP	FTP	RPG	PPG
80-81	HOU	30	.505	.588	10.5	11.9
81-82	HOU	32	.569	.608	10.5	15.2
82-83	HOU	34	.536	.737	8.8	15.9
Totals		96	.538	.643	9.9	14.4

NBA REGULAR-SEASON STATISTICS

		G	MIN	FGs FG	FGs PCT	3-PT FGs FG	3-PT FGs PCT	FTs FT	FTs PCT	Rebounds OFF	Rebounds TOT	AST	STL	BLK	PTS	PPG
83-84	POR	82	1408	252	.451	1	.250	123	.728	112	235	153	107	29	628	7.7
84-85	POR	80	2555	573	.494	8	.216	223	.759	217	476	441	177	68	1377	17.2
85-86	POR	75	2576	542	.475	12	.200	293	.769	171	421	600	197	46	1389	18.5
86-87	POR	82	3114	707	.502	11	.234	357	.760	227	518	566	204	71	1782	21.7
87-88	POR	81	3060	849	.506	11	.212	476	.811	261	533	467	203	52	2185	27.0
88-89	POR	78	3064	829	.496	27	.260	438	.799	289	615	450	213	54	2123	27.2
89-90	POR	73	2683	670	.494	30	.283	333	.774	208	507	432	145	51	1703	23.3
90-91	POR	82	2852	645	.482	61	.319	416	.794	212	546	493	144	60	1767	21.5
Totals		633	21312	5067	.491	161	.268	2659	.781	1697	3851	3602	1390	431	12954	20.5

KEVIN DUCKWORTH

Team: Portland Trail Blazers
Position: Center
Height: 7'0" **Weight:** 275
Birthdate: April 1, 1964
NBA Experience: 5 years

College: Eastern Illinois
Acquired: Traded from Spurs for
Walter Berry, 12/86

Background: Duckworth established a career rebounding record at Eastern Illinois, where his .631 field goal percentage as a senior placed him sixth in the nation. His pro career started slowly in San Antonio but he was voted the NBA's Most Improved Player for 1987-88 with Portland, after raising his scoring average from 5.4 to 21.4 in his last 46 games as a starter. He played in the 1988-89 All-Star Game and ranked third on the Blazers in scoring and rebounding during 1990-91.

Strengths: Duckworth is amazingly agile and possesses great touch for his mass. His offensive game is potent, featuring accurate hooks and soft turnaround jumpers. His range is pretty good for a big man and he passes the ball with precision. Duckworth is quicker than he appears and gets good post position.

Weaknesses: Weight and foul problems have followed Duckworth, who is not a great rebounder or shot-blocker. The main problem is he can't get off the ground. His defensive decision-making could be better, which would help him avoid fouling.

Analysis: Say what you will about his bulk, but Duckworth is one of the more talented and reliable centers in the NBA, especially offensively. When his team needs two points, he usually touches the ball near the paint. Duckworth compensates for his athletic deficiencies with crafty moves that get results.

PLAYER SUMMARY
Will ....score inside
Can't ....jump
Expect ....soft touch
Don't Expect.............................10 RPG
Fantasy Value $8-10
Card Value...10¢

COLLEGE STATISTICS

		G	FGP	FTP	RPG	PPG
82-83	EILL	30	.528	.674	6.0	9.6
83-84	EILL	28	.597	.685	6.8	11.6
84-85	EILL	28	.516	.657	7.5	19.0
85-86	EILL	32	.631	.762	9.1	19.5
Totals		118	.577	.705	7.4	15.0

NBA REGULAR-SEASON STATISTICS

				FGs		3-PT FGs		FTs		Rebounds						
		G	MIN	FG	PCT	FG	PCT	FT	PCT	OFF	TOT	AST	STL	BLK	PTS	PPG
86-87	SA/POR	65	875	130	.476	0	.000	92	.687	76	223	29	21	21	352	5.4
87-88	POR	78	2223	450	.496	0	.000	331	.770	224	576	66	31	32	1231	15.8
88-89	POR	79	2662	554	.477	0	.000	324	.757	246	635	60	56	49	1432	18.1
89-90	POR	82	2462	548	.478	0	.000	231	.740	184	509	91	36	34	1327	16.2
90-91	POR	81	2511	521	.481	0	.000	240	.772	177	531	89	33	34	1282	15.8
Totals		385	10733	2203	.482	0	.000	1218	.754	907	2474	335	177	170	5624	14.6

CHRIS DUDLEY

Team: New Jersey Nets
Position: Center
Height: 6'11" **Weight:** 240
Birthdate: February 22, 1965
NBA Experience: 4 years

College: Yale
Acquired: Traded from Cavaliers for two future 2nd-round picks, 2/90

Background: What's a Yale graduate doing in the NBA? Talk about playing with smarts. The three-time All-Ivy League big man was second in the nation in rebounding as a senior. Cleveland drafted him in 1987, but it banished him to New Jersey in 1989-90. Last year, Dudley came off the bench for the Nets to average 7.1 PPG. Despite limited minutes, he pulled down 511 rebounds—third on the team behind Derrick Coleman and Chris Morris.

Strengths: Dudley's claim to fame is the way he attacks the glass. He knows how to use his large frame inside to wall off opponents from the backboards. He also has an aggressive, forceful approach to rebounding. He is a smart, tough defender.

Weaknesses: Dudley has proven that brains have nothing to do with free throw shooting. Two years ago, he hit just .319 from the line, making him the George Brett of the NBA. Last season, he improved to just 53.4 percent. In one game in 1989-90, he connected on just 1-of-19 free throws. His field goal shooting has also been poor.

Analysis: For a guy chosen in the fourth round of the draft, Dudley hasn't had a bad career. He's a role player whose one specialty is rebounding. He's especially good on the offensive glass but, unfortunately, often gets fouled going back up and...well, you know the rest. NBA teams do like to have one big guy on their roster who doesn't mind sacrificing his body.

PLAYER SUMMARY	
Will	rebound
Can't	shoot FTs
Expect	physical play
Don't Expect	a well-rounded game
Fantasy Value	$1-2
Card Value	5¢

COLLEGE STATISTICS

		G	FGP	FTP	RPG	PPG
83-84	YALE	26	.464	.467	5.1	4.5
84-85	YALE	26	.446	.533	10.2	12.6
85-86	YALE	26	.539	.482	9.8	16.2
86-87	YALE	24	.569	.542	13.3	17.8
Totals		102	.513	.512	9.5	12.7

NBA REGULAR-SEASON STATISTICS

		G	MIN	FGs FG	FGs PCT	3-PT FGs FG	3-PT FGs PCT	FTs FT	FTs PCT	Rebounds OFF	Rebounds TOT	AST	STL	BLK	PTS	PPG
87-88	CLE	55	513	65	.474	0	.000	40	.563	74	144	23	13	19	170	3.1
88-89	CLE	61	544	73	.435	0	.000	39	.364	72	157	21	9	23	185	3.0
89-90	CLE/NJ	64	1356	146	.411	0	.000	58	.319	174	423	39	41	72	350	5.5
90-91	NJ	61	1560	170	.408	0	.000	94	.534	229	511	37	39	153	434	7.1
Totals		241	3973	454	.422	0	.000	231	.431	549	1235	120	102	267	1139	4.7

JOE DUMARS

Team: Detroit Pistons
Position: Guard
Height: 6'3" **Weight:** 195
Birthdate: May 23, 1963
NBA Experience: 6 years

College: McNeese St.
Acquired: 1st-round pick in 1985 draft (18th overall)

Background: At McNeese State, Dumars led the Southland Conference in scoring three times and averaged 26.4 PPG his junior year. He still ranks in the top 20 among the NCAA's all-time leading scorers. But in Detroit, he got pegged early as all-defense, no-offense. He has increased his scoring average every season and now scores 20 PPG. Dumars was named the MVP of the 1989 NBA Finals and has been first- or second-team all-defense the last three years.

Strengths: Dumars is a great one-on-one defender, one of the very few who can keep up with Michael Jordan. This modest, unassuming athlete is also a deadly shooter who can penetrate and pass like a point guard. He is one of the top clutch shooters in the game. A complete, all-around player and also one of the nicest guys in the league.

Weaknesses: There aren't many. His 189 turnovers last season were a bit on the high side. Also, he's a poor defensive rebounder for an off guard.

Analysis: Dumars is known as the quiet assassin, and with good reason. While the rest of his teammates shout and pout, Dumars quietly sticks the dagger in your heart. Time and again, while teams are busy trying to contain Isiah Thomas or cool off Vinnie Johnson, it's Dumars who buries the most critical shot or comes up with the key defensive play. At the moment, he and Jordan are probably the two best two guards in the East.

PLAYER SUMMARY

Will ....do everything
Can't ....create controversy
Expect ....great defense
Don't Expect........................selfishness
Fantasy Value...............................$14-16
Card Value.......................................15¢

COLLEGE STATISTICS

		G	FGP	FTP	RPG	PPG
81-82	MSU	29	.444	.719	2.2	18.2
82-83	MSU	29	.435	.711	4.4	19.6
83-84	MSU	31	.471	.824	5.3	26.4
84-85	MSU	27	.495	.852	4.9	25.8
Totals		116	.462	.788	4.2	22.5

NBA REGULAR-SEASON STATISTICS

				FGs		3-PT FGs		FTs		Rebounds						
		G	MIN	FG	PCT	FG	PCT	FT	PCT	OFF	TOT	AST	STL	BLK	PTS	PPG
85-86	DET	82	1957	287	.481	5	.313	190	.798	60	119	390	66	11	769	9.4
86-87	DET	79	2439	369	.493	9	.409	184	.748	50	167	352	83	5	931	11.8
87-88	DET	82	2732	453	.472	4	.211	251	.815	63	200	387	87	15	1161	14.2
88-89	DET	69	2408	456	.505	14	.483	260	.850	57	172	390	63	5	1186	17.2
89-90	DET	75	2578	508	.480	22	.400	297	.900	60	212	368	63	2	1335	17.8
90-91	DET	80	3046	622	.481	14	.311	371	.890	62	187	443	89	7	1629	20.4
Totals		467	15160	2695	.485	68	.366	1553	.842	352	1057	2330	451	45	7011	15.0

LEDELL EACKLES

Team: Washington Bullets
Position: Guard
Height: 6'5" **Weight:** 215
Birthdate: November 24, 1966
NBA Experience: 3 years

College: San Jacinto; New Orleans
Acquired: 2nd-round pick in 1988 draft (36th overall)

Background: The man with the unusual name was a big-time scorer at New Orleans, leading the American South Conference with 23.4 PPG as a senior, good enough to rank 22nd in the nation. He developed his game at the noted San Jacinto Junior College in Texas. He was named MVP of the NJCAA tournament while leading the Ravens to a 37-0 record. Though a second-round draft pick, Eackles has averaged in double figures in each of his three seasons with Washington.

Strengths: Ledell knows how to use his 6'5", 215-pound body to bull past scrawnier backcourt players, while still maintaining a soft shooting touch. He is a natural scorer who has a knack for drawing fouls and getting to the line.

Weaknesses: One of the biggest is his weight. He has a tendency to balloon up and that affects his speed. Eackles is a streak shooter who must develop consistency. He can stick with his man defensively when guarding the ball, but he loses concentration when his player is moving without the ball. He is weak on the boards.

Analysis: You could call him a second-round steal for the Bullets. Despite his drawbacks, he was third on the team in scoring last season. His field goal percentage of 45.3 last season will rise when he becomes more selective in his shots. Basically, Eackles is a talented scorer who needs more consistency to become a star.

PLAYER SUMMARY

Will ....score
Can't ....rebound
Expect...........................inconsistency
Don't Expect ....assists
Fantasy Value $3-5
Card Value..............................8¢

COLLEGE STATISTICS

		G	FGP	FTP	RPG	PPG
84-85	SJ	29	.550	.730	5.4	19.0
85-86	SJ	37	.583	.755	6.4	27.2
86-87	NO	28	.456	.724	4.1	22.6
87-88	NO	31	.508	.802	4.9	23.4
Totals		125	.529	.758	5.3	23.3

NBA REGULAR-SEASON STATISTICS

				FGs		3-PT FGs		FTs		Rebounds						
		G	MIN	FG	PCT	FG	PCT	FT	PCT	OFF	TOT	AST	STL	BLK	PTS	PPG
88-89	WAS	80	1459	318	.434	9	.225	272	.786	100	180	123	41	5	917	11.5
89-90	WAS	78	1696	413	.439	19	.322	210	.750	74	175	182	50	4	1055	13.5
90-91	WAS	67	1616	345	.453	14	.237	164	.739	47	128	136	47	10	868	13.0
Totals		225	4771	1076	.442	42	.266	646	.762	221	483	441	138	19	2840	12.6

MARK EATON

Team: Utah Jazz
Position: Center
Height: 7'4" **Weight:** 290
Birthdate: January 24, 1957

NBA Experience: 9 years
College: Cypress; UCLA
Acquired: 4th-round pick in 1982 draft (72nd overall)

Background: Eaton was 22 years old and fixing cars when he was found by an assistant coach at Cypress (California) Junior College. After two years at Cypress he attended UCLA, where he played just 196 minutes in two seasons. In nine pro campaigns, Eaton has never finished lower than seventh in blocked shots and set a league record with 456 in 1984-85. He was the league's Defensive Player of the Year in 1984 and 1989. The 1990-91 season was his worst shot-blocking year, the first time he swatted less than 200.

Strengths: Eaton remains one of the most intimidating shot-blockers in history. He is an ever-present deterrent who forces the opposition to take its attack outside. He can neutralize even the best of centers by applying his bulk.

Weaknesses: Everything but shot-blocking can be considered a weakness for Eaton. Although his hook has improved, his only truly reliable offensive weapon is the dunk. Eaton is as slow as they come, which limits his ability to defend when pulled away from the hoop and makes him an underachieving rebounder.

Analysis: Despite his many drawbacks, Eaton is an impact player. His shot-blocking is a dimension that forces opposing teams to alter their game plans and attack in different ways. He may be the most valuable one-dimensional player ever. As his number of blocks shrinks, so will his playing time.

PLAYER SUMMARY

Will ....block shots
Can't ....do much else
Expect........................less playing time
Don't Expect ....any offense
Fantasy Value $2-4
Card Value..5¢

COLLEGE STATISTICS

		G	FGP	FTP	RPG	PPG
78-79	CYP	35	.633	.667	10.9	13.8
79-80	CYP	25	.578	.482	8.7	15.0
80-81	UCLA	19	.459	.294	2.6	2.1
81-82	UCLA	11	.417	.800	2.0	1.3
Totals		90	.595	.572	7.4	10.1

NBA REGULAR-SEASON STATISTICS

		G	MIN	FGs FG	FGs PCT	3-PT FGs FG	3-PT FGs PCT	FTs FT	FTs PCT	Rebounds OFF	Rebounds TOT	AST	STL	BLK	PTS	PPG
82-83	UTA	81	1528	146	.414	0	.000	59	.656	86	462	112	24	275	351	4.3
83-84	UTA	82	2139	194	.466	0	.000	73	.593	148	595	113	25	351	461	5.6
84-85	UTA	82	2813	302	.449	0	.000	190	.712	207	927	124	36	456	794	9.7
85-86	UTA	80	2551	277	.470	0	.000	122	.604	172	675	101	33	369	676	8.4
86-87	UTA	79	2505	234	.400	0	.000	140	.657	211	697	105	43	321	608	7.7
87-88	UTA	82	2731	226	.418	0	.000	119	.623	230	717	55	41	304	571	7.0
88-89	UTA	82	2914	188	.462	0	.000	132	.660	227	843	83	40	315	508	6.2
89-90	UTA	82	2281	158	.527	0	.000	79	.669	171	601	39	33	201	395	4.8
90-91	UTA	80	2580	169	.579	0	.000	71	.634	182	667	51	39	188	409	5.1
Totals		730	22042	1894	.456	0	.000	985	.650	1634	6184	783	314	2780	4773	6.5

BLUE EDWARDS

Team: Utah Jazz
Position: Guard
Height: 6'5" **Weight:** 200
Birthdate: October 31, 1965
NBA Experience: 2 years

College: Louisburg; East Carolina
Acquired: 1st-round pick in 1989 draft (21st overall)

Background: Edwards was a junior college All-American before his two-year career at East Carolina. As a senior, he led the Pirates in scoring, rebounds, steals, assists, blocked shots, 3-point percentage, and field goals. He has improved steadily in two years as a pro, although a late-season ankle sprain in 1990-91 reduced his playing time. Of his 62 games played, he started 56.

Strengths: Edwards is a combination of speed and strength who usually plays small forward but can also fill in at big guard. His athletic prowess is most noticeable in two areas: dunks and defense. His drives to the hoop are explosive and tough for one defender to stop and he finishes the break with flair. He will outrebound his man.

Weaknesses: Although they have improved, Edwards's outside shots still need more consistency to bring defenders closer and open lanes to the basket. His ball-handling skills are below average for a perimeter player and he does not always recognize when to shoot and when to dish off.

Analysis: Edwards is a rising star with loads of potential and plenty of time to develop. His quickness and athletic ability already have earned him respect as a challenging match-up for opposing forwards. He pushes himself defensively and, on offense, needs only to continue improving his ball-handling and shooting.

PLAYER SUMMARY	
Will	finish the break
Can't	dribble in traffic
Expect	drives to the hoop
Don't Expect	high 3-point pct.
Fantasy Value	$3-5
Card Value	5¢

COLLEGE STATISTICS

		G	FGP	FTP	RPG	PPG
84-85	LOU	29	.636	.645	6.1	17.8
85-86	LOU	31	.700	.658	6.0	22.3
86-87	ECAR	28	.561	.739	5.6	14.4
88-89	ECAR	29	.551	.755	6.9	26.7
Totals		117	.612	.701	6.2	20.4

NBA REGULAR-SEASON STATISTICS

			FGs		3-PT FGs		FTs		Rebounds						
	G	MIN	FG	PCT	FG	PCT	FT	PCT	OFF	TOT	AST	STL	BLK	PTS	PPG
89-90 UTA	82	1889	286	.507	9	.300	146	.719	69	251	145	76	36	727	8.9
90-91 UTA	62	1611	244	.526	6	.250	82	.701	51	201	108	57	29	576	9.3
Totals	144	3500	530	.516	15	.278	228	.712	120	452	253	133	65	1303	9.0

JAMES EDWARDS

Team: Los Angeles Clippers
Position: Forward/Center
Height: 7'1" **Weight:** 252
Birthdate: November 22, 1955

NBA Experience: 14 years
College: Washington
Acquired: Traded from Pistons for Jeff Martin, 8/91

Background: "Buddha" was an All-Pac-10 performer at Washington, finishing as the school's No. 2 all-time scorer. Edwards was drafted by the Lakers and was quickly dealt to Indiana. He has also played for Cleveland, Phoenix, and Detroit, posting double-figure scoring totals every year but one. He was dealt to the Clippers in August.

Strengths: Edwards is one of the most fearsome scorers down low—he loves to hit the fadeaway jumper. He was often the first option in the Pistons offense early in the game as Detroit strived to establish dominance inside.

Weaknesses: Buddha doesn't rebound like a 7'1", 250-pound inside scorer should. In fact, 6'2" guard Vinnie Johnson had three more boards than Edwards last season. Edwards also doesn't block many shots and has definitely seen his best days. He disappeared in the 1991 playoffs against the Bulls.

Analysis: Edwards didn't want to go to the Clippers and was contemplating retirement instead. L.A., deep at forward, would use Edwards at center.

PLAYER SUMMARY

Will ....hit the fadeaway
Can't..................intimidate defensively
Expect ....13 PPG
Don't Expect.............many more years
Fantasy Value $2-4
Card Value......................................5¢

COLLEGE STATISTICS

		G	FGP	FTP	RPG	PPG
73-74	WASH	25	.425	.548	4.6	6.8
74-75	WASH	26	.473	.543	7.6	12.3
75-76	WASH	28	.523	.606	7.1	17.6
76-77	WASH	27	.552	.647	10.4	20.9
Totals		106	.509	.598	7.5	14.6

NBA REGULAR-SEASON STATISTICS

		G	MIN	FGs FG	FGs PCT	3-PT FGs FG	3-PT FGs PCT	FTs FT	FTs PCT	Rebounds OFF	Rebounds TOT	AST	STL	BLK	PTS	PPG
77-78	LAL/IND	83	2405	495	.453	0	.000	272	.646	197	615	85	53	78	1262	15.2
78-79	IND	82	2546	534	.501	0	.000	298	.676	179	693	92	60	109	1366	16.7
79-80	IND	82	2314	528	.512	0	.000	231	.681	179	578	127	55	104	1287	15.7
80-81	IND	81	2375	511	.509	0	.000	244	.703	191	571	212	32	128	1266	15.6
81-82	CLE	77	2539	528	.511	0	.000	232	.684	189	581	123	24	117	1288	16.7
82-83	CLE/PHO	31	667	128	.487	0	.000	69	.639	56	155	40	12	19	325	10.5
83-84	PHO	72	1897	438	.536	0	.000	183	.720	108	348	184	23	30	1059	14.7
84-85	PHO	70	1787	384	.501	0	.000	276	.746	95	387	153	26	52	1044	14.9
85-86	PHO	52	1314	318	.542	0	.000	212	.702	79	301	74	23	29	848	16.3
86-87	PHO	14	304	57	.518	0	.000	54	.771	20	60	19	6	7	168	12.0
87-88	PHO/DET	69	1705	302	.470	0	.000	210	.654	119	412	78	16	37	814	11.8
88-89	DET	76	1254	211	.500	0	.000	133	.686	68	231	49	11	31	555	7.3
89-90	DET	82	2283	462	.498	0	.000	265	.749	112	345	63	23	37	1189	14.5
90-91	DET	72	1903	383	.484	1	.500	215	.729	91	277	65	12	30	982	13.6
Totals		943	25293	5279	.500	1	.050	2894	.697	1683	5554	1364	376	808	13453	14.3

KEVIN EDWARDS

Team: Miami Heat
Position: Guard
Height: 6'3" **Weight:** 197
Birthdate: October 30, 1965
NBA Experience: 3 years

College: Lakewood; DePaul
Acquired: 1st-round pick in 1988 draft (20th overall)

Background: Edwards was one of the bright stars that was supposed to return DePaul to its glory years. He finished his two-year career with the best shooting percentage (53.4) ever by a DePaul guard. He also had 64 dunks in those two seasons. In three years with the Heat, he has played in nearly every game, averaging in double figures each year. Last season, he finished second on the team in assists and first in steals.

Strengths: Edwards is strong going to the basket and isn't bashful about putting it up. He had a knack for scoring critical baskets in college, although that hasn't carried over to the pros. He puts out a good effort on the defensive end, as evidenced by his steals totals.

Weaknesses: His jump shot has been missing in action for most of the last two season, as he's shot just 41 percent from the floor. That's pretty bad when your position is shooting guard. Edwards is not a playmaker and he's had a history of being turnover prone.

Analysis: The jury is still out on whether the Heat made a wise choice with their 20th pick in the '88 draft. A shooting guard is no good if he can't shoot. Edwards is bound to lose some serious playing time this year. First, the Heat moved small forward Glen Rice to off guard late last year and he seemed more comfortable in the position. Second, Miami drafted shooting guard Steve Smith high in the first round. Neither move bodes well for Edwards.

PLAYER SUMMARY

Will...put it up
Can't.............................can his jumpers
Expect.....................up-and-down play
Don't Expect ....leadership
Fantasy Value.................................$2-4
Card Value..5¢

COLLEGE STATISTICS

		G	FGP	FTP	RPG	PPG
84-85	LAKE	33	.589	.715	5.4	18.6
85-86	LAKE	32	.626	.761	7.5	24.1
86-87	DeP	31	.536	.808	5.0	14.4
87-88	DeP	30	.533	.783	5.3	18.3
Totals		126	.576	.760	5.8	18.9

NBA REGULAR-SEASON STATISTICS

				FGs		3-PT FGs		FTs		Rebounds						
		G	MIN	FG	PCT	FG	PCT	FT	PCT	OFF	TOT	AST	STL	BLK	PTS	PPG
88-89	MIA	79	2349	470	.425	10	.270	144	.746	85	262	349	139	27	1094	13.8
89-90	MIA	78	2211	395	.412	9	.300	139	.760	77	282	252	125	33	938	12.0
90-91	MIA	79	2000	380	.410	24	.286	171	.803	80	205	240	130	46	955	12.1
Totals		236	6560	1245	.416	43	.285	454	.771	242	749	841	394	106	2987	12.7

CRAIG EHLO

Team: Cleveland Cavaliers
Position: Guard/Forward
Height: 6'7" **Weight:** 205
Birthdate: August 11, 1961

NBA Experience: 8 years
College: Odessa; Washington St.
Acquired: Signed as a free agent, 1/87

Background: Ehlo set a Pac-10 record for assists as a senior at Washington State. He was a reserve for Houston before spending some time in the CBA. Since joining Cleveland, he has become a valuable role player. He played in all 82 games last season, averaging 10.1 points and becoming a starter after the injury to star guard Mark Price.

Strengths: His size allows him to play either guard or forward, and that versatility is a valuable commodity. He is a tough defender who is underrated as a shooter and a scorer. Coaches and players realize his abilities. Ehlo led the Cavaliers in steals last year and was third in rebounds.

Weaknesses: Though he's a gritty defender, Ehlo doesn't have the quickness to always stay with the faster guards in the league. No one will ever forget how Michael Jordan slipped away from him to hit the dramatic last-second, game-winning shot that eliminated Cleveland from the 1989 playoffs and sent the franchise tumbling backwards.

Analysis: Ehlo would be a valuable reserve for just about any NBA team. His size gives him flexibility and he is becoming a respected 3-point shooter. In Price's absence last year, he also led the Cavs in assists and proved he could perhaps be a legitimate starter on some clubs. He is the type of player title-contending teams covet.

PLAYER SUMMARY

Will ....play all over
Can't ....specialize
Expect.....................steals and assists
Don't Expect ....hang time
Fantasy Value $5-7
Card Value....................................5¢

COLLEGE STATISTICS

		G	FGP	FTP	RPG	PPG
79-80	ODES	28	.487	.714	5.1	12.6
80-81	ODES	30	.500	.772	6.8	20.7
81-82	WSU	30	.479	.600	2.2	5.1
82-83	WSU	30	.547	.633	3.2	12.0
Totals		**118**	**.505**	**.701**	**4.3**	**12.6**

NBA REGULAR-SEASON STATISTICS

		G	MIN	FGs FG	FGs PCT	3-PT FGs FG	3-PT FGs PCT	FTs FT	FTs PCT	Rebounds OFF	Rebounds TOT	AST	STL	BLK	PTS	PPG
83-84	HOU	7	63	11	.407	0	.000	1	1.000	4	9	6	3	0	23	3.3
84-85	HOU	45	189	34	.493	0	.000	19	.633	8	25	26	11	3	87	1.9
85-86	HOU	36	199	36	.429	3	.333	23	.793	17	46	29	11	4	98	2.7
86-87	CLE	44	890	99	.414	5	.172	55	.707	55	161	92	40	30	273	6.2
87-88	CLE	79	1709	226	.466	22	.344	89	.674	86	274	206	82	30	563	7.1
88-89	CLE	82	1867	249	.475	39	.390	71	.607	100	295	266	110	19	608	7.4
89-90	CLE	81	2894	436	.464	104	.419	126	.681	147	439	371	126	23	1102	13.6
90-91	CLE	82	2766	344	.445	49	.329	95	.679	142	388	376	121	34	832	10.1
Totals		**456**	**10577**	**1435**	**.457**	**222**	**.369**	**494**	**.674**	**559**	**1637**	**1372**	**504**	**143**	**3586**	**7.9**

MARIO ELIE

Team: Golden State Warriors
Position: Guard
Height: 6'5" **Weight:** 210
Birthdate: November 26, 1963
NBA Experience: 1 year

College: American International
Acquired: Signed as a free agent, 2/91

Background: A world traveler, Elie played in Portugal, Argentina, Ireland, and Miami (of the USBL) after his college career at American International. He speaks four languages. He was drafted by Milwaukee in 1985 but was released before the season. He joined Albany of the CBA during 1989-90 and saw his first NBA action for Philadelphia (three games) in 1990-91. The Warriors picked him up in February and Elie became a regular off the bench.

Strengths: Versatility is Elie's main strength. He does a lot of things well, but none exceptionally other than free throw shooting. He scores in spurts, has good range, and sees the court well because of his size. He is willing to adapt to whatever role he is given.

Weaknesses: Elie is not an especially gifted ball-handler and a much less talented defender. He is a step slow and struggles when checking quicker players. His skills in all areas are not refined, largely because he has not played against NBA competition.

Analysis: Finally, Elie found himself in the right place at the right time and was of big help to Golden State in the 1991 playoffs. He is talented enough to hold down a roster spot but is not strong enough in any one area to ever excel on the NBA level. After all his travels, a roster spot should suit Elie just fine.

PLAYER SUMMARY

Will	....contribute
Can't	.....................check small guards
Expect	......................solid FT shooting
Don't Expect	.........an NBA starting job
Fantasy Value	..................................$1-3
Card Value	....5¢

COLLEGE STATISTICS

		G	FGP	FTP	RPG	PPG
81-82	AI	25	.586	.742	8.3	15.4
82-83	AI	31	.527	.739	7.7	15.9
83-84	AI	31	.565	.794	8.6	18.9
84-85	AI	33	.549	.777	9.0	20.1
Totals		120	.555	.767	8.4	17.7

NBA REGULAR-SEASON STATISTICS

		G	MIN	FGs FG	FGs PCT	3-PT FGs FG	3-PT FGs PCT	FTs FT	FTs PCT	Rebounds OFF	Rebounds TOT	AST	STL	BLK	PTS	PPG
90-91	WAS/GS	33	644	79	.497	4	.400	75	.843	46	110	45	19	10	237	7.2
Totals		33	644	79	.497	4	.400	75	.843	46	110	45	19	10	237	7.2

SEAN ELLIOTT

Team: San Antonio Spurs
Position: Forward
Height: 6'8" **Weight:** 205
Birthdate: February 2, 1968
NBA Experience: 2 years

College: Arizona
Acquired: 1st-round pick in 1989 draft
(3rd overall)

Background: Elliott was college basketball's 1989 Player of the Year at Arizona, where he broke Lew Alcindor's Pac-10 record with 2,555 career points. He started 69 of 81 games as a rookie for San Antonio and followed that up with 82 consecutive starts in 1990-91, leading the Spurs in 3-pointers and ranking third on the team in scoring and rebounding.

Strengths: Elliott owns a huge offensive arsenal. He can shoot from the perimeter, drive to the hoop, and make crisp passes. Despite his lack of bulk, he is a better-than-expected rebounder. His versatility allows him to play big guard in addition to small forward. Pre-draft questions about his knee have been answered by his play in 163 of 164 games.

Weaknesses: There are not many flaws in Elliott's game. He is not a physical defender and gets tossed around by bigger players, but he makes up for those deficiencies with quickness.

Analysis: Elliott's second year proved that he has fully adjusted to the NBA. He was San Antonio's best perimeter shooter and has extended his range past the 3-point circle, which makes his quick move to the bucket even more devastating. There is no reason to believe his scoring average, shooting percentage, and rebounding totals will not continue to rise—a frightening thought for opponents.

PLAYER SUMMARY

Will	get to the hoop
Can't	outmuscle big men
Expect	steady shooting
Don't Expect	any letdown
Fantasy Value	$9-11
Card Value	25¢

COLLEGE STATISTICS

		G	FGP	FTP	RPG	PPG
85-86	ARIZ	32	.486	.749	5.3	15.6
86-87	ARIZ	30	.510	.770	6.0	19.3
87-88	ARIZ	38	.570	.793	5.8	19.6
88-89	ARIZ	33	.480	.841	7.2	22.3
Totals		133	.512	.793	6.1	19.2

NBA REGULAR-SEASON STATISTICS

				FGs		3-PT FGs		FTs		Rebounds						
		G	MIN	FG	PCT	FG	PCT	FT	PCT	OFF	TOT	AST	STL	BLK	PTS	PPG
89-90	SA	81	2032	311	.481	1	.111	187	.866	127	297	154	45	14	810	10.0
90-91	SA	82	3044	478	.490	20	.313	325	.808	142	456	238	69	33	1301	15.9
Totals		163	5076	789	.486	21	.288	512	.828	269	753	392	114	47	2111	13.0

DALE ELLIS

Team: Milwaukee Bucks
Position: Guard
Height: 6'7" **Weight:** 213
Birthdate: August 8, 1960

NBA Experience: 8 years
College: Tennessee
Acquired: Traded from SuperSonics for Ricky Pierce, 2/91

Background: Ellis was an All-American at Tennessee, where his shooting accuracy enabled him to average 22.6 PPG his senior year and 21.2 as a junior. He was a faceless reserve for Dallas for three years, but the infamous trade for Al Wood brought him to Seattle and NBA stardom. He missed part of the 1989-90 season when he broke three ribs in a car accident. In 1990-91, Ellis was dealt to Milwaukee, but he ended the season on the injured list. Dale holds the league record for most minutes played in a game (69).

Strengths: This guy has one of the prettiest jumpers in the league, and one of the deadliest. He is particularly effective coming off screens or shooting from 3-point land. The scoring totals he put up with Seattle proved that he was one of basketball's greatest offensive weapons.

Weaknesses: Ellis doesn't dedicate himself to defense, and his ball-handling has always been sub-standard. Passing is not one of his strong points, but most coaches would rather have him just put it up anyway.

Analysis: Coming over during the season, Ellis didn't have time to adjust to the Bucks' system. He was relegated to the Milwaukee bench, as Alvin Robertson and Jay Humphries started in the backcourt. If he can handle the change of assignments, he will be a valuable part of the Bucks' offense.

PLAYER SUMMARY

Will................................shoot from afar
Can't................................pile up assists
Expect...20 PPG
Don't Expect ....suffocating defense
Fantasy Value.............................$27-30
Card Value..8¢

COLLEGE STATISTICS

		G	FGP	FTP	RPG	PPG
79-80	TENN	27	.445	.775	3.6	7.1
80-81	TENN	29	.597	.748	6.4	17.7
81-82	TENN	30	.654	.796	6.3	21.2
82-83	TENN	21	.601	.751	10.0	22.6
Totals		107	.595	.765	6.3	17.5

NBA REGULAR-SEASON STATISTICS

				FGs		3-PT FGs		FTs		Rebounds						
		G	MIN	FG	PCT	FG	PCT	FT	PCT	OFF	TOT	AST	STL	BLK	PTS	PPG
83-84	DAL	67	1059	225	.456	12	.414	87	.719	106	250	56	41	9	549	8.2
84-85	DAL	72	1314	274	.454	42	.385	77	.740	100	238	56	46	7	667	9.3
85-86	DAL	72	1086	193	.411	63	.364	59	.720	86	168	37	40	9	508	7.1
86-87	SEA	82	3073	785	.516	86	.358	385	.787	187	447	238	104	32	2041	24.9
87-88	SEA	75	2790	764	.503	107	.413	303	.767	167	340	197	74	11	1938	25.8
88-89	SEA	82	3190	857	.501	162	.478	377	.816	156	342	164	108	22	2253	27.5
89-90	SEA	55	2033	502	.497	96	.375	193	.818	90	238	110	59	7	1293	23.5
90-91	SEA/MIL	51	1424	340	.474	57	.363	120	.723	66	173	95	49	8	857	16.8
Totals		556	15969	3940	.490	625	.400	1601	.779	958	2196	953	521	105	10106	18.2

PERVIS ELLISON

Team: Washington Bullets
Position: Forward/Center
Height: 6'10" **Weight:** 225
Birthdate: April 3, 1967
NBA Experience: 2 years

College: Louisville
Acquired: Traded from Kings via the Jazz; Jazz sent Eric Leckner and Bob Hansen to Kings, and Bullets sent Jeff Malone to Jazz, 6/90

Background: Ellison was a star at such an early age, he was nicknamed "Never Nervous Pervis" for being so accustomed to big games. He was the MVP of the 1986 NCAA tournament as a freshman at Louisville after his 25 points and 11 rebounds lifted the Cardinals past Duke in the title game. He's the only Louisville player to record 2,000 points and 1,000 rebounds and he is third on the NCAA career list in blocked shots. After a year in Sacramento, he was traded to Washington.

Strengths: This guy can leap. He reportedly skied up to the 12'6" mark on the backboard one day, just six inches short of the top. He is an excellent shot-blocker and defensive player who led the Bullets in rebounding last season.

Weaknesses: Pervis had a disappointing rookie season with Sacramento, where he was slowed by injuries. He didn't have much range on his shot, although last season he improved his percentage from 44.2 to 51.3. He needs to develop offensive moves and take better care of the ball. He was third on the team in turnovers last season. At 6'9", he is a little too short to play center.

Analysis: Everyone was comparing him to Bill Russell coming out of college, but Russell gave up on him in Sacramento and traded him east. There are doubts whether he is a true center. On a contender, he would be ideal as the rebounding, shot-blocking, tough-defense power forward. He's young, and there's still time for him to develop some post-up moves.

PLAYER SUMMARY	
Will	block shots
Can't	shoot from outside
Expect	good defense
Don't Expect	slashing moves
Fantasy Value	$2-4
Card Value	15¢

COLLEGE STATISTICS

		G	FGP	FTP	RPG	PPG
85-86	LOU	39	.554	.682	8.2	13.1
86-87	LOU	31	.533	.719	8.7	15.2
87-88	LOU	35	.601	.692	8.3	17.6
88-89	LOU	31	.615	.652	8.7	17.6
Totals		136	.577	.687	8.4	15.8

NBA REGULAR-SEASON STATISTICS

				FGs		3-PT FGs		FTs		Rebounds						
		G	MIN	FG	PCT	FG	PCT	FT	PCT	OFF	TOT	AST	STL	BLK	PTS	PPG
89-90	SAC	34	866	111	.442	0	.000	49	.628	64	196	65	16	57	271	8.0
90-91	WAS	76	1942	326	.513	0	.000	139	.650	224	585	102	49	157	791	10.4
Totals		110	2808	437	.493	0	.000	188	.644	288	781	167	65	214	1062	9.7

A.J. ENGLISH

Team: Washington Bullets
Position: Guard
Height: 6'3" **Weight:** 180
Birthdate: July 11, 1967
NBA Experience: 1 year

College: Virginia Union
Acquired: 2nd-round pick in 1990 draft (37th overall)

Background: English gained prominence as the NCAA Division II Player of the Year as a senior at Virginia Union. That year, he averaged 33.4 PPG to lead all Division II players. He impressed NBA scouts by averaging 32.7 PPG in his first three games at the Portsmouth Invitational. He played in 70 games as a Bullet rookie last season and averaged 8.8 points per game, sixth on the team.

Strengths: English is a pure scorer, one of those players that always finds a way to get the ball to the basket. He has shown signs that, with experience, he could become a team leader. Despite his scoring heroics in college, he's shown an ability to pass and work within a team concept.

Weaknesses: For such a prolific shooter and scorer in college, he had trouble finding the range from the NBA's 3-point arc, making just 3-of-31 attempts. His 114 turnovers were fairly high for the minutes he played. Since he loves to shoot, he'll need to improve on his field goal percentage, which was 43.9 last year. His free throw shooting could also use some work.

Analysis: For a second-round pick, English was a steal. If he raises his shooting percentages, he could become a dangerous sixth man. It's always a gamble selecting a player with gaudy numbers who didn't play top-level competition, but in this case, it looks like the Bullets may have hit a small jackpot.

PLAYER SUMMARY

Will ....shoot
Can't...............................steal the ball
Expect.................solid bench minutes
Don't Expect 3-pointers
Fantasy Value $1-3
Card Value..20¢

COLLEGE STATISTICS

		G	FGP	FTP	RPG	PPG
86-87	VU	31	.447	.758	2.9	9.8
87-88	VU	29	.471	.714	4.7	16.3
88-89	VU	30	.504	.812	4.0	20.5
89-90	VU	30	.496	.792	5.1	33.4
Totals		120	.485	.778	4.2	20.0

NBA REGULAR-SEASON STATISTICS

			FGs		3-PT FGs		FTs		Rebounds						
	G	MIN	FG	PCT	FG	PCT	FT	PCT	OFF	TOT	AST	STL	BLK	PTS	PPG
90-91 WAS	70	1443	251	.439	3	.097	111	.707	66	147	177	25	15	616	8.8
Totals	70	1443	251	.439	3	.097	111	.707	66	147	177	25	15	616	8.8

PATRICK EWING

Team: New York Knicks
Position: Center
Height: 7'0" **Weight:** 240
Birthdate: August 5, 1962

NBA Experience: 6 years
College: Georgetown
Acquired: 1st-round pick in 1985 draft
(1st overall)

Background: "Hoya Paranoia" really got started when Ewing registered at Georgetown. He led the Hoyas to three NCAA finals, including the championship in 1984. He was the consensus Player of the Year as a senior while setting records across the board. He is one of the greatest defensive players in NCAA history, and he starred on the 1984 gold-medal Olympic team. In New York, he was Rookie of the Year in 1986 and All-NBA First Team in 1990. Last year, he finished fifth in the league in scoring and rebounding and third in blocked shots.

Strengths: He is an intimidator on defense; his 7'0", 240-pound body seems to be everywhere swatting away shots. His post moves on offense are virtually unstoppable by a single defender, and he has developed a dangerous medium-range jump shot. Ewing is quick for a center and is a franchise player.

Weaknesses: Patrick led the Eastern Conference in turnovers last season with 291. Though in fairness, Ewing touches the ball far more than most pivot men.

Analysis: Along with Hakeem Olajuwon and David Robinson, Ewing is one of the top three centers in the NBA. He is the kind of player you can build a championship team around, and perhaps the Knicks are headed in that direction with the hiring of Pat Riley as coach. One thing Ewing does need is a competent point guard to get him the ball. Mark Jackson did that as a rookie, but his game has tailed off.

PLAYER SUMMARY	
Will	dominate inside
Can't	shoot 3-pointers
Expect	MVP-type performance
Don't Expect	great ball-handling
Fantasy Value	$85-90
Card Value	30¢

COLLEGE STATISTICS

		G	FGP	FTP	RPG	PPG
81-82	GEOR	37	.631	.617	7.5	12.7
82-83	GEOR	32	.570	.629	10.2	17.7
83-84	GEOR	37	.658	.656	10.0	16.4
84-85	GEOR	37	.625	.637	9.2	14.6
Totals		143	.620	.635	9.2	15.3

NBA REGULAR-SEASON STATISTICS

				FGs		3-PT FGs		FTs		Rebounds						
		G	MIN	FG	PCT	FG	PCT	FT	PCT	OFF	TOT	AST	STL	BLK	PTS	PPG
85-86	NY	50	1771	386	.474	0	.000	226	.739	124	451	102	54	103	998	20.0
86-87	NY	63	2206	530	.503	0	.000	296	.713	157	555	104	89	147	1356	21.5
87-88	NY	82	2546	656	.555	0	.000	341	.716	245	676	125	104	245	1653	20.2
88-89	NY	80	2896	727	.567	0	.000	361	.746	213	740	188	117	281	1815	22.7
89-90	NY	82	3165	922	.551	1	.250	502	.775	235	893	182	78	327	2347	28.6
90-91	NY	81	3104	845	.514	0	.000	464	.745	194	905	244	80	258	2154	26.6
Totals		438	15688	4066	.532	1	.032	2190	.742	1168	4220	945	522	1361	10323	23.6

DUANE FERRELL

Team: Atlanta Hawks
Position: Forward
Height: 6'7" **Weight:** 210
Birthdate: February 28, 1965
NBA Experience: 3 years

College: Georgia Tech
Acquired: Signed as a free agent, 8/90

Background: Ferrell enjoyed a productive four-year career at Georgia Tech, pumping in more than 1,800 points. Although he averaged 18.6 PPG his senior year, he wasn't drafted by an NBA team. After college, he signed with the Hawks as a free agent, was cut after one year, and then re-signed with them four months later. In 1990-91, his third season in Atlanta, he played in 78 games as a reserve.

Strengths: Ferrell is a versatile 6'7" forward who shot an impressive 48.9 percent last year coming off the bench. He's pretty good at taking it to the hole. Despite his limited playing time, he was fifth on the Hawks in offensive rebounds. He has developed into an 80-percent free throw shooter and has a good attitude.

Weaknesses: Ferrell isn't an exceptional talent, and there's a big drop-off when the Hawks take out Dominique Wilkins and bring in Ferrell. Duane isn't a real threat from outside and he's not a big assists man. His assist-to-turnover ratio (55-to-78) was terrible last year. As a defensive rebounder, he was little better than 5'7" teammate Spud Webb.

Analysis: After being passed over in the NBA draft and cut by the Hawks twice, Ferrell is just glad to be in the league. He won't get many minutes playing behind Wilkins and, if Dominique went down with an injury, he wouldn't be the man to fill in. Ferrell had to sweat on draft day when the Hawks signed small forward Stacey Augmon with the No. 9 pick.

PLAYER SUMMARY

Will ....struggle in the NBA
Can't..start
Expect ....bench scoring
Don't Expect ....assists
Fantasy Value $2-4
Card Value...5¢

COLLEGE STATISTICS

		G	FGP	FTP	RPG	PPG
84-85	GT	32	.504	.571	4.1	9.1
85-86	GT	34	.595	.758	4.9	12.1
86-87	GT	29	.519	.812	5.9	17.9
87-88	GT	32	.532	.749	6.6	18.6
Totals		127	.537	.733	5.4	14.3

NBA REGULAR-SEASON STATISTICS

			FGs		3-PT FGs		FTs		Rebounds						
		G	MIN	FG	PCT	FG	PCT	FT	PCT	OFF	TOT	AST	STL	BLK	PTS	PPG
88-89	ATL	41	231	35	.422	0	.000	30	.682	19	41	10	7	6	100	2.4
89-90	ATL	14	29	5	.357	0	.000	2	.333	3	7	2	1	0	12	0.9
90-91	ATL	78	1165	174	.489	2	.667	125	.801	97	179	55	33	27	475	6.1
Totals		133	1425	214	.472	2	.500	157	.762	119	227	67	41	33	587	4.4

DANNY FERRY

Team: Cleveland Cavaliers
Position: Forward
Height: 6'10" **Weight:** 230
Birthdate: October 17, 1966
NBA Experience: 1 year
College: Duke

Acquired: Draft rights traded from Clippers with Reggie Williams for Ron Harper, 1990 and 1992 1st-round picks, and a 1991 2nd-round pick, 11/89

Background: After an illustrious career at Duke, in which he was named the nation's Player of the Year as a senior, Ferry snubbed the NBA and spent a year in Italy to avoid playing with the moribund L.A. Clippers. When his rights were traded to Cleveland for Ron Harper, he came home and was a big disappointment, averaging just 8.6 PPG last season coming off the bench.

Strengths: Ferry knows how to use his 6'10", 230-pound body, which is fairly mobile. He has all the court intelligence and instincts you'd want, having grown up the son of former NBA player Bob Ferry. If he lives up to his potential, Danny would be the kind of player who could score inside, hit the outside jumper, or make the set-up pass for an easy basket.

Weaknesses: His lack of quickness hurts him when he goes against the swifter forwards. He shot just 42.8 percent from the floor as he readjusted to the higher level of play in the NBA. His 120 turnovers were fairly high for the minutes he played.

Analysis: This will be the season of reckoning for Ferry. Having had a year to make the transition, he should now be making an impact on the league—if he is indeed the player everyone thought he was. Should he live up to expectations, the Cavaliers would have a potential All-Star forward for years to come. If he doesn't, they may long dread the day they traded Ron Harper.

PLAYER SUMMARY

Will......................score inside and out
Can't............................live up to billing
Expect............................improved play
Don't Expect ....a savior
Fantasy Value.............................$8-10
Card Value ....25¢

COLLEGE STATISTICS

		G	FGP	FTP	RPG	PPG
85-86	DUKE	40	.460	.628	5.5	5.9
86-87	DUKE	33	.449	.844	7.8	14.0
87-88	DUKE	35	.476	.828	7.6	19.1
88-89	DUKE	35	.522	.756	7.4	22.6
Totals		143	.484	.775	7.0	15.1

NBA REGULAR-SEASON STATISTICS

			FGs		3-PT FGs		FTs		Rebounds						
	G	MIN	FG	PCT	FG	PCT	FT	PCT	OFF	TOT	AST	STL	BLK	PTS	PPG
90-91 CLE	81	1661	275	.428	23	.299	124	.816	99	286	142	43	25	697	8.6
Totals	81	1661	275	.428	23	.299	124	.816	99	286	142	43	25	697	8.6

VERN FLEMING

Team: Indiana Pacers   **NBA Experience:** 7 years
Position: Guard   **College:** Georgia
Height: 6'5" **Weight:** 185   **Acquired:** 1st-round pick in 1984 draft
Birthdate: February 4, 1961   (18th overall)

Background: Fleming teamed with Dominique Wilkins at Georgia and, as a senior, led the Southeastern Conference in scoring. He played on the 1984 Olympic team and was credited by Michael Jordan as providing his toughest defense in practices. In his seven years with the Pacers, he has averaged in double figures every year while make the transition from shooting guard to point guard.

Strengths: Fleming has the advantage of being able to think like a shooting guard while running the Pacers' offense. At 6'5", he has a height advantage over most playmakers, and while Indiana annually looks for a better point guard, he's been it for a number of years. Fleming is the Pacers' all-time assist leader, and he makes very few mistakes. He canned 53.1 percent of his shots last season.

Weaknesses: Vern isn't the most creative point guard, and sometimes it seems like the Pacers are playing with two shooting guards. His range is limited from outside and he's not spectacular at anything.

Analysis: On a title contender, he would be the ideal third guard, one who could fill in at either the point or the off-guard spot. With his perchance for not making mistakes, he could enter a game and not hurt a team. Also, his size allows him to match up defensively with bigger guards. Among starting playmakers, however, Fleming is rather average.

PLAYER SUMMARY	
Will	play tough defense
Can't	make All-Star moves
Expect	selective shooting
Don't Expect	turnovers
Fantasy Value	$6-9
Card Value	5¢

COLLEGE STATISTICS

		G	FGP	FTP	RPG	PPG
80-81	GEOR	30	.480	.697	2.7	10.0
81-82	GEOR	31	.496	.640	3.9	9.9
82-83	GEOR	34	.535	.716	4.6	16.9
83-84	GEOR	30	.503	.754	4.0	19.8
Totals		125	.508	.705	3.8	14.2

NBA REGULAR-SEASON STATISTICS

		G	MIN	FGs FG	FGs PCT	3-PT FGs FG	3-PT FGs PCT	FTs FT	FTs PCT	Rebounds OFF	Rebounds TOT	AST	STL	BLK	PTS	PPG
84-85	IND	80	2486	433	.470	0	.000	260	.767	148	323	247	99	8	1126	14.1
85-86	IND	80	2870	436	.506	1	.167	263	.745	102	386	505	131	5	1136	14.2
86-87	IND	82	2549	370	.509	2	.200	238	.788	109	334	473	109	18	980	12.0
87-88	IND	80	2733	442	.523	0	.000	227	.802	106	364	568	115	11	1111	13.9
88-89	IND	76	2552	419	.515	3	.130	243	.799	85	310	494	77	12	1084	14.3
89-90	IND	82	2876	467	.508	12	.353	230	.782	118	322	610	92	10	1176	14.3
90-91	IND	69	1929	356	.531	4	.222	161	.729	83	214	369	76	13	877	12.7
Totals		549	17995	2923	.507	22	.204	1622	.774	751	2253	3266	699	77	7490	13.6

SLEEPY FLOYD

Team: Houston Rockets
Position: Guard
Height: 6'3" **Weight:** 183
Birthdate: March 6, 1960
NBA Experience: 9 years

College: Georgetown
Acquired: Traded from Warriors with Joe Barry Carroll for Ralph Sampson and Steve Harris, 12/87

Background: Floyd was a college All-American at Georgetown, leading the Hoyas in scoring all four years and to the NCAA championship game in 1982. He was an All-Star in 1986-87, when he set a Golden State season assist record with 848. He played in all 82 games for Houston in 1990-91, but he made a career-low four starts and suffered his worst shooting season.

Strengths: Floyd is an elusive penetrator with many moves to the bucket. He makes things happen. A streak shooter, he has 3-point range and excels on the fast break. Defensively, he takes chances and often comes up with steals.

Weaknesses: The knock on Floyd has always been inconsistency. He can carry a team when he's on a shooting tear, but those times are becoming less frequent. He does not possess the passing mentality of a classic point guard (never has), and he turns the ball over by trying to do too much by himself.

Analysis: Although Floyd struggled in his first season as a reserve since early in his career, he may become more comfortable in that role. He never was a true point guard anyway, and he has the scoring ability to come off the bench and ignite a team. He also has that great penetrating ability which gives a team an explosive dimension, even if he does lack consistency.

PLAYER SUMMARY	
Will	penetrate
Can't	play consistently
Expect	production
Don't Expect	high FG pct.
Fantasy Value	$10-13
Card Value	8¢

COLLEGE STATISTICS

		G	FGP	FTP	RPG	PPG
78-79	GEOR	29	.456	.813	4.1	16.6
79-80	GEOR	32	.554	.757	3.1	18.7
80-81	GEOR	32	.467	.806	4.2	19.0
81-82	GEOR	37	.504	.720	3.4	16.7
Totals		130	.496	.774	3.7	17.7

NBA REGULAR-SEASON STATISTICS

		G	MIN	FGs FG	FGs PCT	3-PT FGs FG	3-PT FGs PCT	FTs FT	FTs PCT	Rebounds OFF	Rebounds TOT	AST	STL	BLK	PTS	PPG
82-83	NJ/GS	76	1248	226	.429	10	.400	150	.833	56	137	138	58	17	612	8.1
83-84	GS	77	2555	484	.463	8	.178	315	.816	87	271	269	103	31	1291	16.8
84-85	GS	82	2873	610	.445	42	.294	336	.810	62	202	406	134	41	1598	19.5
85-86	GS	82	2764	510	.506	39	.328	351	.796	76	297	746	157	16	1410	17.2
86-87	GS	82	3064	503	.488	73	.384	462	.860	56	268	848	146	18	1541	18.8
87-88	GS/HOU	77	2514	420	.433	14	.194	301	.850	77	296	544	95	12	1155	15.0
88-89	HOU	82	2788	396	.443	109	.373	261	.845	48	306	709	124	11	1162	14.2
89-90	HOU	82	2630	362	.451	89	.380	187	.806	46	198	600	94	11	1000	12.2
90-91	HOU	82	1850	386	.411	48	.273	185	.752	52	159	317	95	17	1005	12.3
Totals		722	22286	3897	.454	432	.333	2548	.822	560	2134	4577	1006	174	10774	14.9

GREG FOSTER

Team: Washington Bullets
Position: Center
Height: 6'11" **Weight:** 240
Birthdate: September 3, 1968
NBA Experience: 1 year

College: UCLA; Texas-El Paso
Acquired: 2nd-round pick in 1990 draft (35th overall)

Background: Foster was the big man for the University of Texas-El Paso, helping the Miners to two consecutive NCAA tournament appearances. As a senior, he was named the MVP of the Western Athletic Conference tournament. Foster once shattered a backboard after a dunk in UTEP's Memorial Gym. Though only a second-round pick in 1990, he earned a job with the Bullets. Used sparingly his rookie season, he averaged 4.4 PPG.

Strengths: His biggest plus is his 6'11", 240-pound body. The Bullets have been desperate for help inside and are hoping that they can turn this project into a player. He enjoys physical contact and could one day fill the role of NBA banger. He has said that if he wasn't in the NBA, he'd would be playing football because he loves to hit people.

Weaknesses: In this day and age of the mobile, fast center, Foster is dragging his feet. He is definitely suited for a halfcourt offense; mobility and athleticism are foreign concepts to him. He doesn't have any range on his shot. Even close-in, he hit on only 46 percent of his shots last year.

Analysis: Big guys like him seem to hang around the NBA forever, usually drifting from one team to the next. If he takes on the Rick Mahorn-Scott Hastings-type role, as a physical player who will sacrifice his body, some NBA team will always have a spot for him. He doesn't exhibit any signs of developing into a scorer. In fact, even his college numbers were rather paltry.

PLAYER SUMMARY

Will	make contact
Can't	shoot
Expect	bruises
Don't Expect	a starting job
Fantasy Value	$1-3
Card Value	10¢

COLLEGE STATISTICS

		G	FGP	FTP	RPG	PPG
86-87	UCLA	31	.500	.500	2.5	3.3
87-88	UCLA	11	.527	.432	5.5	8.5
88-89	UTEP	26	.483	.651	7.3	11.1
89-90	UTEP	32	.465	.811	6.2	10.6
Totals		100	.483	.661	5.2	8.2

NBA REGULAR-SEASON STATISTICS

			FGs		3-PT FGs		FTs		Rebounds						
	G	MIN	FG	PCT	FG	PCT	FT	PCT	OFF	TOT	AST	STL	BLK	PTS	PPG
90-91 WAS	54	606	97	.460	0	.000	42	.689	52	151	37	12	22	236	4.4
Totals	54	606	97	.460	0	.000	42	.689	52	151	37	12	22	236	4.4

KEVIN GAMBLE

Team: Boston Celtics
Position: Guard/Forward
Height: 6'5" **Weight:** 210
Birthdate: November 13, 1965
NBA Experience: 4 years

College: Lincoln; Iowa
Acquired: Signed as a free agent, 12/88

Background: Gamble's story is the kind coaches and kids love to hear. After an unspectacular college career at Lincoln College and Iowa, he was drafted by Portland in the third round. He didn't make it with the Trail Blazers and he wound up playing in the CBA and the Philippines. Gamble was given one last NBA chance with a rebuilding Celtic team. He proved to be a valuable reserve and, last season, was fourth on the team in scoring. He averaged more than Robert Parish.

Strengths: Gamble is a scrappy, hungry ballplayer who appreciates where he is and how he got there, and will fight dearly to remain there. He is a flashy, exciting player who can get out on the break and also show some athletic moves. Last year, he was third on the Celtics in steals, fourth in assists, and was second on the club in field goal percentage at 58.7, which was third-best in the league.

Weaknesses: He still has streaks where he'll play erratically, and that's when Boston coach Chris Ford has to either settle him down or yank him. He turned the ball over 148 times last year and he missed all seven of his 3-point attempts last season.

Analysis: What a find. From nowhere, Gamble has emerged as a viable contributor and, at age 25, gives the Celtics the youth they so desperately need. There was some concern whether he would be just a temporary flash, but those doubts were answered last season.

PLAYER SUMMARY

Will ....hit his shots
Can't ....shoot 3's
Expect.................exciting bench play
Don't Expect ....floor leadership
Fantasy Value................................$6-8
Card Value ....35¢

COLLEGE STATISTICS

		G	FGP	FTP	RPG	PPG
83-84	LINC	30	.559	.777	9.2	21.3
84-85	LINC	31	.579	.817	9.7	20.5
85-86	IOWA	30	.474	.700	1.7	2.6
86-87	IOWA	35	.544	.697	4.5	11.9
Totals		126	.558	.768	6.2	14.1

NBA REGULAR-SEASON STATISTICS

				FGs		3-PT FGs		FTs		Rebounds						
		G	MIN	FG	PCT	FG	PCT	FT	PCT	OFF	TOT	AST	STL	BLK	PTS	PPG
87-88	POR	9	19	0	.000	0	.000	0	.000	2	3	1	2	0	0	0.0
88-89	BOS	44	375	75	.551	2	.182	35	.636	11	42	34	14	3	187	4.3
89-90	BOS	71	990	137	.455	3	.167	85	.794	42	112	119	28	8	362	5.1
90-91	BOS	82	2706	548	.587	0	.000	185	.815	85	267	256	100	34	1281	15.6
Totals		206	4090	760	.554	5	.135	305	.784	140	424	410	144	45	1830	8.9

WINSTON GARLAND

Team: Denver Nuggets
Position: Guard
Height: 6'2" **Weight:** 175
Birthdate: December 19, 1964
NBA Experience: 4 years

College: Southeastern;
S.W. Missouri St.
Acquired: Traded from Clippers for a
1996 or 1997 2nd-round pick, 6/91

Background: Garland guided Southwest Missouri State to its first NCAA tournament appearance as a senior in 1987 and was named Player of the Year in the Association of Mid-Continent Universities. He led Golden State in assists and steals each of his first two NBA seasons, but he was traded to the Clippers in 1989-90. Garland replaced Gary Grant as the Clips' starter near the end of 1990-91. After the season, he was dealt to Denver.

Strengths: Garland performs under control and can play both guard spots, although he has played the point for most of his young career. He is not afraid to take big shots and has good range.

Weaknesses: For a point guard, Garland is rather slow and has limited penetrating ability. He prefers to keep it outside and take shots himself rather than creating. In that regard, Garland is better suited for playing off guard rather than the point. However, his field goal percentage has never been above .439 and he lacks the height required to shoot over most two guards.

Analysis: Garland has been in the right place at the right time, playing with the Warriors before they drafted All-Star Tim Hardaway and then the guard-thin Clippers. Now he goes to Denver, which is talented but inexperienced at guard. With the Nuggets, Garland will back up a backcourt that features rookie Mark Macon and sophomore Chris Jackson.

PLAYER SUMMARY

Will ....work for shots
Can't.....................blow past defenders
Expect ....controlled play
Don't Expect.........enough penetration
Fantasy Value $1-2
Card Value..5¢

COLLEGE STATISTICS

		G	FGP	FTP	RPG	PPG
83-84	SE	34	.518	.836	4.4	17.0
84-85	SE	30	.516	.853	3.6	18.2
85-86	SMS	32	.461	.771	3.6	16.5
86-87	SMS	34	.503	.752	2.5	21.2
Totals		130	.499	.802	3.5	18.3

NBA REGULAR-SEASON STATISTICS

		G	MIN	FGs FG	FGs PCT	3-PT FGs FG	3-PT FGs PCT	FTs FT	FTs PCT	Rebounds OFF	Rebounds TOT	AST	STL	BLK	PTS	PPG
87-88	GS	67	2122	340	.439	13	.333	138	.879	68	227	429	116	7	831	12.4
88-89	GS	79	2661	466	.434	10	.233	203	.809	101	328	505	175	14	1145	14.5
89-90	GS/LAC	79	1762	230	.401	12	.333	102	.836	51	214	303	78	10	574	7.3
90-91	LAC	69	1702	221	.426	4	.154	118	.752	46	198	317	97	10	564	8.2
Totals		294	8247	1257	.427	39	.271	561	.817	266	967	1554	466	41	3114	10.6

KENNY GATTISON

Team: Charlotte Hornets
Position: Forward.
Height: 6'8" **Weight:** 252
Birthdate: May 23, 1964
NBA Experience: 4 years

College: Old Dominion
Acquired: Signed as a free agent,
12/89

Background: The Sun Belt Conference Player of the Year in 1986, Gattison wound up as the league's all-time leading rebounder. He also garnered All-America consideration as a senior at Old Dominion. In his senior year, he ranked third nationally in field goal percentage with a mark of 63.7. Gattison played with Phoenix for a year before tearing the anterior cruciate ligament in his left knee. He played part of 1988-89 in Italy and signed with Charlotte in 1989-90. The Hornets cut him in preseason that year but signed him up again in December.

Strengths: Gattison is the kind of player who will do whatever is asked, no matter the consequences. If you need someone to set screens, block out, bang the boards, Gattison's your man. He is a physically gifted player who can perform a number of functions. He can even score inside.

Weaknesses: He doesn't have much of a touch from outside and he needs to improve on his free throw shooting (66.1 percent last year). With his reckless style of play, he wound up with 211 fouls last season, third-highest on the team. Though an inside player, he's only 6'8".

Analysis: With his "do-what-it-takes" attitude, Gattison is a great complement for any team. He will fit into whatever is needed by his club, making him an ideal bench player. Though not an outside threat, his field goal percentage is always high. Given enough playing time, his athleticism will come through.

PLAYER SUMMARY	
Will	sacrifice his body
Can't	shoot FTs
Expect	hustling minutes
Don't Expect	fancy passes
Fantasy Value	$3-5
Card Value	10¢

COLLEGE STATISTICS

		G	FGP	FTP	RPG	PPG
82-83	OD	29	.503	.705	7.5	8.4
83-84	OD	31	.494	.650	7.1	11.1
84-85	OD	31	.538	.610	9.2	16.1
85-86	OD	31	.637	.673	7.8	17.4
Totals		122	.552	.650	7.9	13.3

NBA REGULAR-SEASON STATISTICS

		G	MIN	FGs FG	FGs PCT	3-PT FGs FG	3-PT FGs PCT	FTs FT	FTs PCT	Rebounds OFF	Rebounds TOT	AST	STL	BLK	PTS	PPG
86-87	PHO	77	1104	148	.476	0	.000	108	.632	87	270	36	24	33	404	5.2
88-89	PHO	2	9	0	.000	0	.000	1	.500	0	1	0	0	0	1	0.5
89-90	CHA	63	941	148	.550	1	1.000	75	.682	75	197	39	35	31	372	5.9
90-91	CHA	72	1552	243	.532	0	.000	164	.661	136	379	44	48	67	650	9.0
Totals		214	3606	539	.519	1	.167	348	.655	298	847	119	107	131	1427	6.7

TATE GEORGE

Team: New Jersey Nets
Position: Guard
Height: 6'5" **Weight:** 190
Birthdate: May 29, 1968
NBA Experience: 1 year

College: Connecticut
Acquired: 1st-round pick in 1990 draft
(22nd overall)

Background: George is Connecticut's all-time leader in assists and steals. In the 1990 NCAA tournament, he hit a dramatic game-winning shot at the buzzer to beat Clemson 71-70 in the third round. George became the first Connecticut player to be selected in the first round when the Nets took him 22nd last year. In his rookie season, he played just 594 minutes.

Strengths: George's attitude is his biggest plus so far. The Nets said they drafted him because he was always happy and the team needed an infusion of cheeriness. He does have point-guard skills and plays good defense. His good size allows him to play both guard positions and match up defensively with the bigger guards in the league.

Weaknesses: For a first-round pick by a weak team, George had a rather disappointing year, playing in just 56 games and averaging just 3.4 PPG. He shot 41.5 percent from the field and never made the kind of impact that No. 1 draft choices are expected to make.

Analysis: George doesn't appear to possess the offensive skills to be a regular contributor, so he may have to make his mark defensively. At best, he could develop into a decent third guard, providing solid minutes at both the point and shooting positions. At worst, he could continue to languish on the New Jersey bench...and nothing could be worse than that.

PLAYER SUMMARY

Will ....play defense
Can't..score
Expect.........................solid floor game
Don't Expect ....outside shooting
Fantasy Value..................................$1-2
Card Value..20¢

COLLEGE STATISTICS

		G	FGP	FTP	RPG	PPG
86-87	CONN	26	.368	.775	3.6	10.0
87-88	CONN	34	.500	.831	2.9	9.9
88-89	CONN	31	.433	.758	3.4	7.3
89-90	CONN	37	.479	.727	3.5	11.5
Totals		128	.448	.773	3.3	9.7

NBA REGULAR-SEASON STATISTICS

	G	MIN	FG	PCT	3-PT FG	3-PT PCT	FT	PCT	OFF	TOT	AST	STL	BLK	PTS	PPG
90-91 NJ	56	594	80	.415	0	.000	32	.800	19	47	104	25	5	192	3.4
Totals	56	594	80	.415	0	.000	32	.800	19	47	104	25	5	192	3.4

DERRICK GERVIN

Team: New Jersey Nets
Position: Forward/Guard
Height: 6'8" **Weight:** 215
Birthdate: March 28, 1963
NBA Experience: 2 years

College: Texas-San Antonio
Acquired: Signed as a free agent, 2/90

Background: Derrick is the younger brother of George "The Iceman" Gervin, the former NBA scoring machine. Derrick starred at Texas-San Antonio, where he scored 25.6 PPG his junior year. Philadelphia drafted him after his junior season, but he ended up playing in the CBA in 1985-86. He didn't play ball at all in 1986-87, spent 1987-88 and 1988-89 in European leagues, and went back to the CBA in 1989-90 (where he averaged 31.7 PPG). New Jersey signed him in February 1990, although it did not re-sign him after 1990-91.

Strengths: As you would guess from his bloodline, Derrick loves to shoot. Like his older brother, this Gervin also has a way of getting to the basket. He will never put up the prolific numbers that the three-time scoring champion George did, but shooting is his specialty.

Weaknesses: The Gervin family motto is, "Have ball, will shoot." Two years ago, Gervin took 197 shots while handing out a total of eight assists. Last season, he put up 394 shots and posted 30 assists. His field goal percentage was low last year, and he was no threat from 3-point land. His defense needs work.

Analysis: Used in certain stretches of a game, Gervin can be effective. The problem is, for all the points he scores, he is likely to give them right back defensively. He can score in a hurry but only concentrates on that part of the game. He will be a career role player who can come off the bench for temporary instant offense.

PLAYER SUMMARY

Will ....shoot often
Can't...................................play defense
Expect ....a gunner
Don't Expect............................a passer
Fantasy Value $1-3
Card Value..12¢

COLLEGE STATISTICS

		G	FGP	FTP	RPG	PPG
82-83	TSA	25	.522	.728	7.1	13.9
83-84	TSA	27	.546	.763	8.9	23.2
84-85	TSA	28	.563	.817	9.6	25.6
Totals		80	.548	.780	8.6	21.1

NBA REGULAR-SEASON STATISTICS

				FGs		3-PT FGs		FTs		Rebounds						
		G	MIN	FG	PCT	FG	PCT	FT	PCT	OFF	TOT	AST	STL	BLK	PTS	PPG
89-90	NJ	21	339	93	.472	0	.000	65	.730	29	65	8	20	7	251	12.0
90-91	NJ	56	743	164	.416	7	.250	90	.789	40	110	30	19	19	425	7.6
Totals		77	1082	257	.435	7	.226	155	.764	69	175	38	39	26	676	8.8

KENDALL GILL

Team: Charlotte Hornets
Position: Guard
Height: 6'5" **Weight:** 200
Birthdate: May 25, 1968
NBA Experience: 1 year

College: Illinois
Acquired: 1st-round pick in 1990 draft (5th overall)

Background: At Illinois, Gill was considered one of the top guards in the country. As a junior, he canned 38-of-83 3-point attempts and helped his team to the Final Four. As a senior, he was a first-team All-Big Ten selection and a UPI first-team All-American. In his final season, he became the first Illini to lead the Big Ten in scoring since 1943. Gill played in all 82 games as a rookie and finished fourth on the Hornets in scoring.

Strengths: Gill is a great leaper, and that allows him to play a little bit bigger than his 6'5" height. He is accurate from long range, although he only hit 2-of-14 from 3-point land as a rookie. The scouting report labels him as a well-rounded athlete, classy and intelligent. His size and lateral movement allow him to play tough defense. He was second on the Hornets in assists and steals, and he proved to be a strong free throw shooter.

Weaknesses: Making the typical rookie adjustments wasn't easy for Gill—especially the longer 3-point shots. Gill was second on the club in turnovers. He was the fifth player taken in the 1990 draft, and he didn't quite live up to such high expectations.

Analysis: Gill has all the physical tools to become a top guard. When he begins to play with more confidence, his normally dependable outside shot will begin dropping with increasing frequency. Coaches around the league recognize his potential and have him figured for a star.

PLAYER SUMMARY

Will ....take it inside
Can't......................................hit 3's yet
Expect ....a complete game
Don't Expect ....a gunner
Fantasy Value.............................$10-12
Card Value..25¢

COLLEGE STATISTICS

		G	FGP	FTP	RPG	PPG
86-87	ILL	31	.482	.642	1.4	3.7
87-88	ILL	33	.471	.753	2.2	10.4
88-89	ILL	24	.542	.793	2.9	15.4
89-90	ILL	29	.500	.777	4.9	20.0
Totals		117	.501	.755	2.8	12.0

NBA REGULAR-SEASON STATISTICS

			FGs		3-PT FGs		FTs		Rebounds						
	G	MIN	FG	PCT	FG	PCT	FT	PCT	OFF	TOT	AST	STL	BLK	PTS	PPG
90-91 CHA	82	1944	376	.450	2	.143	152	.835	105	263	303	104	39	906	11.0
Totals	82	1944	376	.450	2	.143	152	.835	105	263	303	104	39	906	11.0

ARMON GILLIAM

Team: Philadelphia 76ers
Position: Forward
Height: 6'9" **Weight:** 245
Birthdate: May 28, 1964
NBA Experience: 4 years

College: Independence; UNLV
Acquired: Traded from Hornets with Dave Hoppen for Mike Gminski, 1/91

Background: As a college senior, Gilliam was a consensus second-team All-American while leading the UNLV Runnin' Rebels to a Final Four appearance. That year, he averaged 23.2 points and 9.3 rebounds per game. Phoenix selected him No. 2 in the 1987 draft, and he responded by making the NBA All-Rookie Team. Despite strong scoring numbers, he has been traded twice in the last two years, first to Charlotte and then to Philadelphia.

Strengths: Gilliam is nearly unstoppable when he gets the ball in the low post, beating opponents with hook shots and turnaround jumpers. He's a feisty, physical, powerful player, as evidenced by the practice fight he got into with Tom Chambers in Phoenix. He will wear opponents down with his 6'9", 245-pound body.

Weaknesses: Despite his size and strength, he doesn't rebound as well as he should. He's a poor ball-handler, is no better a passer, and doesn't run the court well. You must slow the game down to make him effective. Gilliam is a notoriously weak defensive player.

Analysis: Teams are always searching for accomplished low-post scorers, and Gilliam is one of the few who fit that bill. However, his passive defensive play has frustrated both coaches and teammates. Teammate Charles Barkley was steamed in the playoffs last year when Chicago continually burned Armon inside. He needs to buckle down.

PLAYER SUMMARY	
Will	score down low
Can't	run the court
Expect	double-digit PPG
Don't Expect	strong defense
Fantasy Value	$9-12
Card Value	8¢

COLLEGE STATISTICS

		G	FGP	FTP	RPG	PPG
82-83	IND	38	.621	.632	8.3	16.9
84-85	UNLV	31	.621	.653	6.8	11.9
85-86	UNLV	37	.529	.737	8.5	15.7
86-87	UNLV	39	.600	.728	9.3	23.2
Totals		145	.590	.693	8.3	17.2

NBA REGULAR-SEASON STATISTICS

				FGs		3-PT FGs		FTs		Rebounds						
		G	MIN	FG	PCT	FG	PCT	FT	PCT	OFF	TOT	AST	STL	BLK	PTS	PPG
87-88	PHO	55	1807	342	.475	0	.000	131	.679	134	434	72	58	29	815	14.8
88-89	PHO	74	2120	468	.503	0	.000	240	.743	165	541	52	54	27	1176	15.9
89-90	PHO/CHA	76	2426	484	.515	0	.000	303	.723	211	599	99	69	51	1271	16.7
90-91	CHA/PHI	75	2644	487	.487	0	.000	268	.815	220	598	105	69	53	1242	16.6
Totals		280	8997	1781	.496	0	.000	942	.745	730	2172	328	250	160	4504	16.1

GERALD GLASS

Team: Minnesota Timberwolves
Position: Guard/Forward
Height: 6'6" **Weight:** 221
Birthdate: November 12, 1967
NBA Experience: 1 year

College: Delta St.; Mississippi
Acquired: 1st-round pick in 1990 draft
(20th overall)

Background: Glass began his college career at Division II Delta State before transferring to Ole Miss and becoming the school's sixth-place career scorer in just two seasons. As an NBA rookie in 1990-91, he scored 32 points against the Lakers and led Minnesota in scoring three straight games on a December road trip, averaging 27.7 points during that stretch. His playing time diminished at the end of the year. Glass saw just 20 minutes of action in the final 22 games.

Strengths: Glass is a scorer; witness his team-leading average of 27.9 points per 48 minutes. He can back defenders in and hit fadeaway jumpers with regularity. He pounds the defensive boards and can play two positions: small forward and big guard.

Weaknesses: The biggest concern about Glass is his laid-back style. He looks like he is just going through the motions at times and needs to become more aggressive. Glass does not possess great quickness, which hurts him most at the defensive end of the court. Though considered a fine shooter, Glass has not shown the ability to knock down NBA 3-pointers consistently (2-of-17 as a rookie).

Analysis: Glass regressed during his senior year of college and had a lot to prove in the pros. He did display great scoring ability when given the opportunity, but he could not shine consistently enough to earn playing time down the stretch. He must improve his work ethic, keep his weight down, and approach the game with more intensity if he wants a chance.

PLAYER SUMMARY

Will	sink fadeaways
Can't	stay aggressive
Expect	points in bunches
Don't Expect	quickness
Fantasy Value	$3-5
Card Value	15¢

COLLEGE STATISTICS

		G	FGP	FTP	RPG	PPG
85-86	DELT	31	.554	.722	6.5	12.5
86-87	DELT	33	.605	.702	12.5	26.1
88-89	MISS	30	.532	.736	8.5	28.0
89-90	MISS	30	.490	.736	7.6	24.1
Totals		124	.544	.724	8.9	22.7

NBA REGULAR-SEASON STATISTICS

			FGs		3-PT FGs		FTs		Rebounds						
	G	MIN	FG	PCT	FG	PCT	FT	PCT	OFF	TOT	AST	STL	BLK	PTS	PPG
90-91 MIN	51	606	149	.438	2	.118	52	.684	54	102	42	28	9	352	6.9
Totals	51	606	149	.438	2	.118	52	.684	54	102	42	28	9	352	6.9

MIKE GMINSKI

Team: Charlotte Hornets
Position: Center
Height: 6'11" **Weight:** 260
Birthdate: August 3, 1959

NBA Experience: 11 years
College: Duke
Acquired: Traded from 76ers for
Armon Gilliam and Dave Hoppen, 1/91

Background: Gminski has been an NBA mainstay ever since leaving Duke as the school's all-time leading rebounder and second-leading scorer. He was the ACC Player of the Year as a junior and an All-American as a senior. He spent seven years in New Jersey and three in Philadelphia before being traded to Charlotte.

Strengths: Gminski has a tremendous outside shooting touch for a big man, which forces opponents to play him away from the basket and opens lanes for teammates to penetrate. Defensively, he keeps players such as Hakeem Olajuwon below their scoring averages. Gminski is a smart, classy player and quite unselfish. He's an excellent free throw shooter.

Weaknesses: Gminski is not a shot-blocking center and will never alter or distort an offensive game plan. He has to work hard to keep pace with the faster centers. Despite his outside touch, he isn't a 3-point threat.

Analysis: Gminski gave the Hornets instant credibility in the middle, as he ranked among the more effective pivot men in the league. He is the kind of center that, when surrounded by the right personnel, can help a team to the NBA Finals. He makes very few mistakes and enhances the play of those around him.

PLAYER SUMMARY	
Will	hit from outside
Can't	dominate a game
Expect	smart team play
Don't Expect	slashing moves
Fantasy Value	$9-12
Card Value	8¢

COLLEGE STATISTICS

		G	FGP	FTP	RPG	PPG
76-77	DUKE	27	.515	.703	10.7	15.3
77-78	DUKE	32	.547	.841	10.0	20.0
78-79	DUKE	30	.519	.729	9.2	18.8
79-80	DUKE	33	.538	.841	10.9	21.3
Totals		122	.531	.792	10.2	19.0

NBA REGULAR-SEASON STATISTICS

				FGs		3-PT FGs		FTs		Rebounds						
		G	MIN	FG	PCT	FG	PCT	FT	PCT	OFF	TOT	AST	STL	BLK	PTS	PPG
80-81	NJ	56	1579	291	.423	0	.000	155	.767	137	419	72	54	100	737	13.2
81-82	NJ	74	740	119	.441	0	.000	97	.822	70	186	41	17	48	335	4.5
82-83	NJ	80	1255	213	.500	0	.000	175	.778	154	382	61	35	116	601	7.5
83-84	NJ	82	1655	237	.513	0	.000	147	.799	161	433	92	37	70	621	7.6
84-85	NJ	81	2418	380	.465	0	.000	276	.841	229	633	158	38	92	1036	12.8
85-86	NJ	81	2525	491	.517	0	.000	351	.893	206	668	133	56	71	1333	16.5
86-87	NJ	72	2272	433	.457	0	.000	313	.846	192	630	99	52	69	1179	16.4
87-88	NJ/PHI	81	2961	505	.448	0	.000	355	.906	245	814	139	64	118	1365	16.9
88-89	PHI	82	2739	556	.477	0	.000	297	.871	213	769	138	46	106	1409	17.2
89-90	PHI	81	2659	458	.457	3	.176	193	.821	196	687	128	43	102	1112	13.7
90-91	PHI/CHA	80	2196	357	.442	2	.143	128	.810	186	582	93	40	56	844	10.6
Totals		850	22999	4040	.466	5	.109	2487	.844	1989	6203	1154	482	948	10572	12.4

GARY GRANT

Team: Los Angeles Clippers
Position: Guard
Height: 6'3" **Weight:** 195
Birthdate: April 21, 1965
NBA Experience: 3 years

College: Michigan
Acquired: Draft rights traded from SuperSonics with a 1991 1st-round pick for Michael Cage, 6/88

Background: Grant was a consensus All-American at Michigan, where he concluded his career as the school's all-time leader in assists and earned Big Ten Defensive Player of the Year honors as a junior. As a pro, his career has not been as lauded. He led all rookies in steals and assists but has been in and out of a starting job over the past two seasons, partly because of injuries. In 1990-91, he failed to average double figures in scoring for the first time.

Strengths: Grant has good size and speed (despite ankle surgery in 1990 and knee surgery in 1991) and is able to drive past defenders. He racks up a lot of assists because of his constant eye for the open man. Grant is a leader who craves the ball.

Weaknesses: Costly turnovers and poor judgment have earned Grant a reputation as a crunch-time choker. His shot selection down the stretch is beyond questionable. He tries to do too much and often finds himself flying to the hoop without an outlet. He is not blessed with great ability as a shooter, which magnifies his troubles when playing out of control.

Analysis: Unless he settles down and eliminates some of the erratic elements of his game, Grant will always be more style than substance. He tries to make routine plays look difficult, while the great ones make difficult plays look routine. If the Clippers cannot afford to keep him in the starting lineup, who can?

PLAYER SUMMARY

Will..penetrate
Can't ....avoid turnovers
Expect ....fewer starts
Don't Expect ....a steady hand
Fantasy Value.................................$5-7
Card Value..5¢

COLLEGE STATISTICS

		G	FGP	FTP	RPG	PPG
84-85	MICH	30	.550	.817	2.5	12.9
85-86	MICH	33	.494	.744	3.2	12.2
86-87	MICH	32	·.537	.782	5.0	22.4
87-88	MICH	34	.530	.808	3.4	21.1
Totals		129	.528	.790	3.5	17.2

NBA REGULAR-SEASON STATISTICS

				FGs		3-PT FGs		FTs		Rebounds						
		G	MIN	FG	PCT	FG	PCT	FT	PCT	OFF	TOT	AST	STL	BLK	PTS	PPG
88-89	LAC	71	1924	361	.435	5	.227	119	.735	80	238	506	144	9	846	11.9
89-90	LAC	44	1529	241	.466	5	.238	88	.779	59	195	442	108	5	575	13.1
90-91	LAC	68	2105	265	.451	9	.231	51	.689	69	209	587	103	12	590	8.7
Totals		183	5558	867	.448	19	.232	258	.739	208	642	1535	355	26	2011	11.0

HARVEY GRANT

Team: Washington Bullets
Position: Forward
Height: 6'9" **Weight:** 215
Birthdate: July 4, 1965
NBA Experience: 3 years

College: Clemson; Independence; Oklahoma
Acquired: 1st-round pick in 1988 draft (12th overall)

Background: Harvey is the identical twin brother of the Bulls' Horace Grant. The two actually enrolled together at Clemson, but when it became apparent that they were competing for the same spot, Harvey transferred to Oklahoma. There, he led the Sooners to the NCAA title game in 1988 and was the tournament's top rebounder. He was a disappointment with Washington his first two seasons, but he came on strong at the end of his second year. Last season, he was the Bullets' second-leading scorer and second-leading rebounder.

Strengths: Grant possesses a good outside shot, and his lean, wiry body is made to run the court. His athleticism needs a little fine-tuning and his defense will improve when he puts on a little weight and muscle. He led the Bullets in steals last year and was third in blocked shots.

Weaknesses: Harvey isn't as effective inside as you'd like from a guy his height. Again, his lack of muscle hurts him. Grant has been accused of being too passive and tentative at times—a criticism occasionally leveled at his twin brother.

Analysis: If he doesn't bulk up, perhaps Grant will settle in to the small-forward position. That's the kind of body and game he has—more finesse than power. If he becomes a small forward, he won't have to go man-to-man with Horace, which both dislike. Harvey will do better with an open-court, transition team.

PLAYER SUMMARY	
Will	hit from outside
Can't	put on muscle
Expect	finesse
Don't Expect	post-up baskets
Fantasy Value	$13-16
Card Value	15¢

COLLEGE STATISTICS

		G	FGP	FTP	RPG	PPG
84-85	CLEM	28	.496	.585	4.5	5.1
85-86	IND	33	.586	.707	11.8	22.4
86-87	OKLA	34	.534	.730	9.9	16.9
87-88	OKLA	39	.547	.729	9.4	20.9
Totals		134	.553	.712	9.1	17.0

NBA REGULAR-SEASON STATISTICS

			FGs		3-PT FGs		FTs		Rebounds						
	G	MIN	FG	PCT	FG	PCT	FT	PCT	OFF	TOT	AST	STL	BLK	PTS	PPG
88-89 WAS	71	1193	181	.464	0	.000	34	.596	75	163	79	35	29	396	5.6
89-90 WAS	81	1846	284	.473	0	.000	96	.701	138	342	131	52	43	664	8.2
90-91 WAS	77	2842	609	.498	2	.133	185	.743	179	557	204	91	61	1405	18.2
Totals	229	5881	1074	.485	2	.083	315	.711	392	1062	414	178	133	2465	10.8

HORACE GRANT

Team: Chicago Bulls
Position: Forward
Height: 6'10" **Weight:** 220
Birthdate: July 4, 1965
NBA Experience: 4 years

College: Clemson
Acquired: 1st-round pick in 1987 draft
(10th overall)

Background: Grant was the ACC Player of the Year his senior year after averaging 21.0 PPG at Clemson. The Bulls were fortunate in getting Scottie Pippen (fifth) and Grant (tenth) together in the 1987 draft. Grant really emerged in the 1990 Eastern Conference finals against Detroit, and last season was the Bulls' leading rebounder and third-leading scorer.

Strengths: Horace is one of the most athletic power forwards in the game. He's a quick leaper who can outrun most power forwards while still hold his own in the strength department. He's in his element in the open court, although last season he exhibited some post moves. His passing game is improving.

Weaknesses: Grant still needs to work on his halfcourt game, and he occasionally needs to be motivated by coach Phil Jackson. Ex-Bulls coach Doug Collins used to call him "Harvey" (the name of Horace's less-talented twin brother) until he performed up to Collins's expectations. He could still use a little more muscle.

Analysis: Grant could well be the prototype of the future power forward—someone with a lively body who's fast and agile. It's not easy for heavier, slower power forwards to keep up with this jumping jack. The Bulls once considered trading Grant because he had become, they thought, too close to Pippen, and that tight friendship was proving distracting. That's the best move the Bulls never made.

PLAYER SUMMARY

Will.....................................run the court
Can't................................muscle inside
Expect ....offensive rebounds
Don't Expect ....banging
Fantasy Value $12-15
Card Value.......................................12¢

COLLEGE STATISTICS

		G	FGP	FTP	RPG	PPG
83-84	CLEM	28	.533	.744	4.6	5.7
84-85	CLEM	29	.555	.637	6.8	11.3
85-86	CLEM	34	.584	.725	10.5	16.4
86-87	CLEM	31	.656	.708	9.6	21.0
Totals		122	.598	.704	8.0	13.9

NBA REGULAR-SEASON STATISTICS

			FGs		3-PT FGs		FTs		Rebounds						
	G	MIN	FG	PCT	FG	PCT	FT	PCT	OFF	TOT	AST	STL	BLK	PTS	PPG
87-88 CHI	81	1827	254	.501	0	.000	114	.626	155	447	89	51	53	622	7.7
88-89 CHI	79	2809	405	.519	0	.000	140	.704	240	681	168	86	62	950	12.0
89-90 CHI	80	2753	446	.523	0	.000	179	.699	236	629	227	92	84	1071	13.4
90-91 CHI	78	2641	401	.547	1	.167	197	.711	266	659	178	95	69	1000	12.8
Totals	318	10030	1506	.524	1	.077	630	.689	897	2416	662	324	268	3643	11.5

JEFF GRAYER

Team: Milwaukee Bucks
Position: Guard/Forward
Height: 6'5" **Weight:** 213
Birthdate: December 17, 1965
NBA Experience: 3 years

College: Iowa St.
Acquired: 1st-round pick in 1988 draft
(13th overall)

Background: This second-team All-American led Iowa State into the NCAA tournament his senior year. He wound up his career as the Cyclones' all-time leading scorer, and he played on the 1988 Olympic team that came away with a bronze medal. Milwaukee drafted Grayer in the middle of the first round in 1988, but he missed most of his first year with a knee injury. He has struggled to make his mark during the last two seasons.

Strengths: Grayer knows how to shake free and go to the hole with a variety of moves. He's also a decent ball-handler and passer. He needs more playing time to blossom.

Weaknesses: Is this 6'5" athlete a guard or a forward? He has trouble going against small forwards, but he can't find playing time at guard with the Bucks. He has had trouble canning his shots, both from the field and at the line. Defensively, he still has a ways to go. The knee injury from his rookie year forced him to sit almost an entire season and retarded his development. The injury may have reduced his overall quickness.

Analysis: He is probably better off playing guard, but where is the opportunity when the Bucks already have Alvin Robertson, Jay Humphries, and Dale Ellis? Grayer is a role player who could become a scorer in the right situation. If the Bucks can't use him, some other team will give him a chance.

PLAYER SUMMARY	
Will	display athleticism
Can't	get untracked
Expect	versatility
Don't Expect	PT as a Buck
Fantasy Value	$2-4
Card Value	10¢

COLLEGE STATISTICS

		G	FGP	FTP	RPG	PPG
84-85	ISU	33	.529	.653	6.5	12.2
85-86	ISU	33	.547	.629	6.3	20.7
86-87	ISU	27	.504	.740	7.0	22.4
87-88	ISU	32	.523	.711	9.4	25.3
Totals		125	.526	.686	7.3	20.0

NBA REGULAR-SEASON STATISTICS

			FGs		3-PT FGs		FTs		Rebounds						
		G	MIN	FG	PCT	FG	PCT	FT	PCT	OFF	TOT	AST	STL	BLK	PTS	PPG
88-89	MIL	11	200	32	.438	0	.000	17	.850	14	35	22	10	1	81	7.4
89-90	MIL	71	1427	224	.460	1	.125	99	.651	94	217	107	48	10	548	7.7
90-91	MIL	82	1422	210	.433	0	.000	101	.687	111	246	123	48	9	521	6.4
Totals		164	3049	466	.446	1	.077	217	.680	219	498	252	106	20	1150	7.0

A.C. GREEN

Team: Los Angeles Lakers
Position: Forward
Height: 6'9" **Weight:** 224
Birthdate: October 4, 1963
NBA Experience: 6 years

College: Oregon St.
Acquired: 1st-round pick in 1985 draft (23rd overall)

Background: Green was named Pac-10 Player of the Year as a junior at Oregon State and wound up his career as the school's second-leading rebounder and third-leading scorer. He has been dependable as both a starter and a reserve for the Lakers, leading the team in rebounding four straight years from 1986-90. He was voted a starter in the 1989-90 All-Star Game ahead of Utah's Karl Malone. The 1990-91 campaign was his lowest scoring season since his rookie year.

Strengths: Green is a hard-working rebounder who attacks the glass. Although not a primary scoring threat, he is dangerous when left alone and not afraid to go inside. He is an aggressive defender, runs the floor, and gives the Lakers durability. He has played all 82 games in five of his six seasons.

Weaknesses: Green is an average shooter and his effectiveness on the boards can largely be attributed to the fact that opponents are more concerned about his teammates. He's better at running the floor than banging inside with big men.

Analysis: The 1990-91 season proved what Karl Malone fans were all saying the year before: Green is no All-Star starter. That's not to say he is not a valuable player, however. He crashes the glass (especially on offense) and is a potent finisher on the fast break. He would qualify as a full-time starter on most NBA teams.

PLAYER SUMMARY

Will ....attack the glass
Can't ....be a bruiser
Expect........................offensive boards
Don't Expect..............................15 PPG
Fantasy Value $8-11
Card Value...8¢

COLLEGE STATISTICS

		G	FGP	FTP	RPG	PPG
81-82	OSU	30	.615	.610	5.3	8.6
82-83	OSU	31	.559	.689	7.6	14.0
83-84	OSU	23	.657	.770	8.7	17.8
84-85	OSU	31	.599	.680	9.2	19.1
Totals		115	.602	.696	7.7	14.7

NBA REGULAR-SEASON STATISTICS

				FGs		3-PT FGs		FTs		Rebounds						
		G	MIN	FG	PCT	FG	PCT	FT	PCT	OFF	TOT	AST	STL	BLK	PTS	PPG
85-86	LAL	82	1542	209	.539	1	.167	102	.611	160	381	54	49	49	521	6.4
86-87	LAL	79	2240	316	.538	0	.000	220	.780	210	615	84	70	80	852	10.8
87-88	LAL	82	2636	322	.503	0	.000	293	.773	245	710	93	87	45	937	11.4
88-89	LAL	82	2510	401	.529	4	.235	282	.786	258	739	103	94	55	1088	13.3
89-90	LAL	82	2709	385	.478	13	.283	278	.751	262	712	90	66	50	1061	12.9
90-91	LAL	82	2164	258	.476	11	.200	223	.738	201	516	71	59	23	750	9.1
Totals		489	13801	1891	.508	29	.221	1398	.752	1336	3673	495	425	302	5209	10.7

RICKEY GREEN

Team: Philadelphia 76ers
Position: Guard
Height: 6'0" **Weight:** 172
Birthdate: August 18, 1954

NBA Experience: 13 years
College: Vincennes; Michigan
Acquired: Signed as a free agent, 10/90

Background: In 1976, Green led Michigan to the NCAA championship game. As a senior, he was runner-up to Marques Johnson for Player of the Year honors. His NBA career started slowly in Golden State and Detroit, then picked up with Utah, where he was a big assists and steals man for much of his eight seasons there. He has played for four more teams in the last three years.

Strengths: One of the quickest players to ever play the game, Green led the NBA in steals in 1984 and still skitters along at age 37. His youthful body allowed him to average 10.0 PPG for the Sixers last season. He replaced the injured Johnny Dawkins in the starting lineup and wound up leading the team in assists.

Weaknesses: He sometimes goes too fast for his teammates, and his 3-point percentage leaves something to be desired. His age is bound to catch up with him soon. He no longer pilfers the ball like he used to, and his field goal percentage has also fallen off.

Analysis: Green was the stop-gap for the Sixers when Dawkins got injured. Rickey will go back to his bench role this season. He's a crafty veteran who can get by on guile, and he can still be a valuable reserve on a contending team.

<table>
<tr><td colspan="2">PLAYER SUMMARY</td></tr>
<tr><td>Will</td><td>run the show</td></tr>
<tr><td>Can't</td><td>turn back the clock</td></tr>
<tr><td>Expect</td><td>assists</td></tr>
<tr><td>Don't Expect</td><td>physical play</td></tr>
<tr><td>Fantasy Value</td><td>$3-5</td></tr>
<tr><td>Card Value</td><td>5¢</td></tr>
</table>

COLLEGE STATISTICS

		G	FGP	FTP	RPG	PPG
73-74	VINC	36	.401	.699	6.6	17.3
74-75	VINC	32	.503	.657	6.5	21.0
75-76	MICH	32	.491	.785	3.7	19.9
76-77	MICH	28	.483	.766	2.9	19.5
Totals		128	.467	.729	5.0	19.4

NBA REGULAR-SEASON STATISTICS

		G	MIN	FGs FG	FGs PCT	3-PT FGs FG	3-PT FGs PCT	FTs FT	FTs PCT	Rebounds OFF	Rebounds TOT	AST	STL	BLK	PTS	PPG
77-78	GS	76	1098	143	.381	0	.000	54	.600	49	116	149	58	1	340	4.5
78-79	DET	27	431	67	.379	0	.000	45	.672	15	40	63	25	1	179	6.6
80-81	UTA	47	1307	176	.481	0	.000	70	.722	30	116	235	75	1	422	9.0
81-82	UTA	81	2822	500	.493	0	.000	202	.765	85	243	630	185	9	1202	14.8
82-83	UTA	78	2783	464	.493	2	.154	185	.797	62	223	697	220	4	1115	14.3
83-84	UTA	81	2768	439	.486	2	.118	192	.821	56	230	748	215	13	1072	13.2
84-85	UTA	77	2431	381	.477	6	.300	232	.869	37	189	597	132	3	1000	13.0
85-86	UTA	80	2012	357	.471	5	.172	213	.852	32	135	411	106	6	932	11.6
86-87	UTA	81	2090	301	.467	7	.368	172	.827	38	163	541	110	2	781	9.6
87-88	UTA	81	1116	157	.424	4	.211	75	.904	14	80	300	57	1	393	4.9
88-89	CHA/MIL	63	871	129	.489	3	.273	30	.909	11	69	187	40	2	291	4.6
89-90	IND	69	927	100	.433	1	.091	43	.843	9	54	182	51	1	244	3.5
90-91	PHI	79	2248	334	.463	8	.222	117	.830	33	137	413	57	6	793	10.0
Totals		920	22904	3548	.469	38	.207	1630	.808	471	1795	5153	1331	50	8764	9.5

SIDNEY GREEN

Team: San Antonio Spurs
Position: Forward
Height: 6'9" **Weight:** 230
Birthdate: January 4, 1961
NBA Experience: 8 years

College: UNLV
Acquired: Traded from Magic for Mark McNamara and a 1991 1st-round pick, 10/90

Background: Green finished his college days as the top rebounder and second-leading scorer in UNLV history. Green has established himself as a productive board-crasher in Chicago, Detroit, New York, and Orlando (where he led the Magic in rebounding in 1989-90) before his most recent stop in San Antonio. He was a key reserve at power forward for the Spurs in 1990-91.

Strengths: Rebounding, especially pounding the offensive boards, is what Green does best. His muscular frame and willingness to fight for position causes pain around the league. Green also has developed a decent jump hook and can score inside. His low-post defense is aided by his physical nature.

Weaknesses: Green becomes much less effective when pushed away from the post. He is not blessed with great range on his jump shot and, although he has decent moves, has never been a scorer on the NBA level. Green lacks the quickness required to defend on the perimeter.

Analysis: Green's value is directly proportional to his rebounding ability and physical play. On a thin Orlando squad in 1989-90, he led the team on the boards. For the vastly superior Spurs in 1990-91, he was a role player off the bench. In any scenario, you know what you're getting in Green, and scoring is not a big part of it.

PLAYER SUMMARY

Will.....................................apply bruises
Can't ....play on perimeter
Expect ....fierce rebounding
Don't Expect...................much scoring
Fantasy Value $4-7
Card Value...5¢

COLLEGE STATISTICS

		G	FGP	FTP	RPG	PPG
79-80	UNLV	32	.518	.727	11.1	15.6
80-81	UNLV	26	.515	.708	10.9	15.0
81-82	UNLV	30	.535	.769	9.0	16.7
82-83	UNLV	31	.548	.700	11.9	22.1
Totals		119	.531	.723	10.7	17.4

NBA REGULAR-SEASON STATISTICS

				FGs		3-PT FGs		FTs		Rebounds						
		G	MIN	FG	PCT	FG	PCT	FT	PCT	OFF	TOT	AST	STL	BLK	PTS	PPG
83-84	CHI	49	667	100	.439	0	.000	55	.714	58	174	25	18	17	255	5.2
84-85	CHI	48	740	108	.432	0	.000	79	.806	72	246	29	11	11	295	6.1
85-86	CHI	80	2307	407	.465	0	.000	262	.782	208	658	139	70	37	1076	13.4
86-87	DET	80	1792	256	.472	0	.000	119	.672	196	653	62	41	50	631	7.9
87-88	NY	82	2049	258	.441	0	.000	126	.663	221	642	93	65	32	642	7.8
88-89	NY	82	1277	194	.460	0	.000	129	.759	157	394	76	47	18	517	6.3
89-90	ORL	73	1860	312	.468	1	.333	136	.651	166	588	99	50	26	761	10.4
90-91	SA	66	1099	177	.461	0	.000	89	.848	98	313	52	32	13	443	6.7
Totals		560	11791	1812	.458	1	.040	995	.731	1176	3668	575	334	204	4620	8.3

DARRELL GRIFFITH

Team: Utah Jazz
Position: Guard
Height: 6'4" **Weight:** 195
Birthdate: June 16, 1958

NBA Experience: 10 years
College: Louisville
Acquired: 1st-round pick in 1980 draft
(2nd overall)

Background: Dubbed "Dr. Dunkenstein" for his high-flying days at Louisville, Griffith led the Cardinals to the 1980 NCAA championship and was named MVP of the finals. He also won the Wooden Award as college basketball's outstanding player. Griffith has spent his entire pro career with Utah, where he was Rookie of the Year in 1980-81. He enjoyed his best year in 1984-85 but missed the entire 1985-86 season with a broken ankle. He posted a career-low 5.7 PPG last year.

Strengths: Griffith loves unleashing his high-arching, long-range jumper at crucial times and still hits from 3-point country with regularity. Pressure means nothing to him. He can heat up quickly off the bench.

Weaknesses: Griffith does not handle the ball well for a guard, nor does he pass well or play great defense. He is a scorer, period. Injuries have stripped him of his once-limitless athletic ability and made it difficult for him to keep up on defense. His shooting plummeted to 39.1 percent in 1990-91.

Analysis: The Dr. Dunkenstein days are long gone for Griffith, whose role now is to provide instant offense as a reserve. At the rate he is shooting, however, those days are numbered as well. Griffith no longer does anything else well enough to warrant a roster spot should his rainbow jumper abandon him.

PLAYER SUMMARY

Will......................shoot from anywhere
Can't..........................penetrate/pass
Expect.....................clutch 3-pointers
Don't Expect............effective defense
Fantasy Value...............................$1-2
Card Value...5¢

COLLEGE STATISTICS

		G	FGP	FTP	RPG	PPG
76-77	LOU	28	.502	.634	3.9	12.8
77-78	LOU	20	.522	.709	8.1	27.9
78-79	LOU	32	.497	.709	4.4	18.5
79-80	LOU	36	.553	.713	4.8	22.9
Totals		116	.523	.697	5.0	20.1

NBA REGULAR-SEASON STATISTICS

				FGs		3-PT FGs		FTs		Rebounds						
		G	MIN	FG	PCT	FG	PCT	FT	PCT	OFF	TOT	AST	STL	BLK	PTS	PPG
80-81	UTA	81	2867	716	.464	10	.192	229	.716	79	288	194	106	40	1671	20.6
81-82	UTA	80	2597	689	.482	15	.288	189	.697	128	305	187	95	34	1582	19.8
82-83	UTA	77	2787	752	.484	38	.288	167	.679	100	304	270	138	33	1709	22.2
83-84	UTA	82	2650	697	.490	91	.361	151	.696	95	338	283	114	23	1636	20.0
84-85	UTA	78	2776	728	.457	92	.358	216	.725	124	344	243	133	30	1764	22.6
86-87	UTA	76	1843	463	.446	67	.335	149	.703	81	227	129	97	29	1142	15.0
87-88	UTA	52	1052	251	.429	28	.275	59	.641	36	127	91	52	5	589	11.3
88-89	UTA	82	2382	466	.446	61	.311	142	.780	77	330	130	86	22	1135	13.8
89-90	UTA	82	1444	301	.464	80	.372	51	.654	43	166	63	68	19	733	8.9
90-91	UTA	75	1005	174	.391	48	.348	34	.756	17	90	37	42	7	430	5.7
Totals		765	21403	5237	.463	530	.332	1387	.707	780	2519	1627	931	242	12391	16.2

JACK HALEY

Team: New Jersey Nets
Position: Forward
Height: 6'10" **Weight:** 240
Birthdate: January 27, 1964

NBA Experience: 3 years
College: ULCA
Aquired: Claimed off waivers, 12/89

Background: Haley started for UCLA as a senior. There, his most notable accomplishment was dating and eventually marrying a beautiful cheerleader named Stacy, who is now an actress. Haley and his Hollywood good looks have appeared in five national commercials and in an Aerosmith music video. His sister has served as the press secretary for First Lady Barbara Bush. Haley has the same name as the actor who played the Tinman in *The Wizard of Oz*. With his poor shooting, Jack has also earned that nickname.

Strengths: Haley throws his 6'10", 240-pound body around with reckless abandon and is afraid of nothing. He's also a noted cheerleader, and his most familiar pose while playing for the Bulls was as a towel-waving, crowd-inciting benchman. This tough guy once picked a fight with Charles Barkley.

Weaknesses: After grabbing a rebound, at which he is fairly proficient, he has problems putting it back in. There isn't much of a shot to speak of. Haley picks up fouls easily, but in his limited role, it doesn't matter.

Analysis: He's the kind of guy coaches love as their 12th man, since he'll hustle and bang and play tough defense and do all the dirty work with nary a complaint. Players with such limited basketball ability seldom last long in this league of thoroughbreds, but Haley's infectious rah-rah attitude and willingness to bang may keep him around.

PLAYER SUMMARY

Will	slam his body
Can't	shoot
Expect	bruises
Don't Expect	anything fancy
Fantasy Value	$1-2
Card Value	10¢

COLLEGE STATISTICS

		G	FGP	FTP	RPG	PPG
84-85	UCLA	25	.409	.412	1.7	1.0
85-86	UCLA	29	.380	.721	6.3	4.3
86-87	UCLA	32	.467	.619	4.7	5.2
Totals		86	.425	.636	4.4	3.7

NBA REGULAR-SEASON STATISTICS

				FGs		3-PT FGs		FTs		Rebounds						
		G	MIN	FG	PCT	FG	PCT	FT	PCT	OFF	TOT	AST	STL	BLK	PTS	PPG
88-89	CHI	51	289	37	.474	0	.000	36	.783	21	71	10	11	0	110	2.2
89-90	CHI/NJ	67	1084	138	.398	0	.000	85	.680	115	300	26	18	12	361	5.4
90-91	NJ	78	1178	161	.469	0	.000	112	.619	140	356	31	20	21	434	5.6
Totals		196	2551	336	.438	0	.000	233	.662	276	727	67	49	33	905	4.6

TOM HAMMONDS

Team: Washington Bullets
Position: Forward
Height: 6'9" **Weight:** 225
Birthdate: March 27, 1967
NBA Experience: 2 years

College: Georgia Tech
Acquired: 1st-round pick in 1989 draft (9th overall)

Background: Hammonds was a third-team All-American as a senior at Georgia Tech and was described by rival Duke coach Mike Krzyzewski as "one of the best players to come out during my nine years in the league (ACC). I love Tom Hammonds." Though drafted No. 9 in the 1989 draft, Hammonds has played sparingly with the Bullets and has done little in his two years.

Strengths: Hammonds is known for his incessant work ethic and his penchant for getting along well with teammates. He has shown flashes of an ability to score, if given enough playing time.

Weaknesses: Hammonds is not wide and strong enough to play power forward, so the Bullets have him playing facing the basket. That adjustment isn't working—he doesn't have the perimeter game to play that way—and he has become a huge disappointment. He averaged only 5.2 PPG last year and blocked just seven shots in 70 games. His 58 offensive rebounds were only seven more than point guard Haywoode Workman.

Analysis: The strength, size, and quickness of NBA frontcourt players is having a debilitating effect on Hammonds, who was used to simply shooting over the shorter, slower forwards in college. Scouts have said his slow adjustment reminds them of Kenny Walker's early years with the Knicks. He might be better off bulking up and trying to make it as a power forward, where his lack of an outside shot wouldn't be as damaging.

PLAYER SUMMARY

Will.............................be a team player
Can't ....block shots
Expect............................more struggles
Don't Expect.............a perimeter game
Fantasy Value $1-2
Card Value....................................10¢

COLLEGE STATISTICS

		G	FGP	FTP	RPG	PPG
85-86	GT	34	.609	.816	6.4	12.2
86-87	GT	29	.569	.797	7.2	16.2
87-88	GT	30	.568	.826	7.2	18.9
88-89	GT	30	.538	.773	8.1	20.9
Totals		123	.566	.801	7.2	16.9

NBA REGULAR-SEASON STATISTICS

			FGs		3-PT FGs		FTs		Rebounds						
	G	MIN	FG	PCT	FG	PCT	FT	PCT	OFF	TOT	AST	STL	BLK	PTS	PPG
89-90 WAS	61	805	129	.437	0	.000	63	.643	61	168	51	11	14	321	5.3
90-91 WAS	70	1023	155	.461	0	.000	57	.722	58	206	43	15	7	367	5.2
Totals	131	1828	284	.450	0	.000	120	.678	119	374	94	26	21	688	5.3

BOB HANSEN

Team: Sacramento Kings
Position: Guard
Height: 6'6" **Weight:** 190
Birthdate: January 18, 1961
NBA Experience: 8 years

College: Iowa
Acquired: Traded from Jazz with Eric Leckner via the Bullets; Bullets sent Jeff Malone to Jazz, and Kings sent Pervis Ellison to Bullets, 6/90

Background: Hansen was All-Big Ten as a senior at Iowa, where he saw NCAA tournament action all four years. In seven years with Utah, he never averaged double figures in scoring but was a key contributor defensively and became a full-time starter. Hansen's 1990-91 season, his first in Sacramento, was soured by injury. He played in 36 games, starting 24, and had his worst shooting year.

Strengths: Hansen's weapons are defense and perimeter shooting, although his .375 field goal percentage does not speak well for the latter. Still, he can be productive when left open. He defends the league's dangerous shooting guards better than most and is rarely caught out of position.

Weaknesses: Scoring has never been a priority with Hansen and he is basically a catch-and-shoot guy. He does not create. He plays conservatively at times and his recent injuries can only serve to slow him more. His foul shooting is poor.

Analysis: Hansen was acquired by the Kings to provide perimeter punch and steady defense. But his shooting was horrendous and even his ability as a stopper must be questioned because of his injury woes. Hansen's ability to contribute is already limited because he lacks a complete offensive repertoire. Unless he returns to form, he risks becoming strictly a role player.

PLAYER SUMMARY

Will ....play defense
Can't ....shoot FTs
Expect ....streak shooting
Don't Expect ....10 PPG
Fantasy Value $1-2
Card Value..5¢

COLLEGE STATISTICS

		G	FGP	FTP	RPG	PPG
79-80	IOWA	33	.425	.589	2.0	5.6
80-81	IOWA	22	.449	.849	3.4	8.4
81-82	IOWA	25	.494	.699	4.1	12.0
82-83	IOWA	31	.487	.760	5.4	15.4
Totals		111	.471	.721	3.7	10.3

NBA REGULAR-SEASON STATISTICS

		G	MIN	FGs FG	FGs PCT	3-PT FGs FG	3-PT FGs PCT	FTs FT	FTs PCT	Rebounds OFF	Rebounds TOT	AST	STL	BLK	PTS	PPG
83-84	UTA	55	419	65	.448	0	.000	18	.643	13	48	44	15	4	148	2.7
84-85	UTA	54	646	110	.489	1	.143	40	.556	20	70	75	25	1	261	4.8
85-86	UTA	82	2032	299	.476	17	.340	95	.720	82	244	193	74	9	710	8.7
86-87	UTA	72	1453	272	.453	16	.356	136	.760	84	203	102	44	6	696	9.7
87-88	UTA	81	1796	316	.517	32	.330	113	.743	64	187	175	65	5	777	9.6
88-89	UTA	46	964	140	.467	19	.352	42	.560	29	128	50	37	6	341	7.4
89-90	UTA	81	2174	265	.467	54	.351	33	.516	66	229	149	52	11	617	7.6
90-91	SAC	36	811	96	.375	19	.275	18	.500	33	96	90	20	5	229	6.4
Totals		507	10295	1563	.469	158	.326	495	.671	391	1205	878	332	47	3779	7.5

TIM HARDAWAY

Team: Golden State Warriors
Position: Guard
Height: 6'0" **Weight:** 175
Birthdate: September 12, 1966
NBA Experience: 2 years

College: Texas-El Paso
Acquired: 1st-round pick in 1989 draft (14th overall)

Background: Hardaway surpassed Nate Archibald as the all-time scoring leader at the University of Texas-El Paso. In 1989-90, he led all rookies in assists and steals while directing the high-powered Golden State offense. Hardaway topped those numbers in 1990-91, earned a trip to the All-Star Game, and led the Warriors to a first-round playoff upset of San Antonio.

Strengths: Few can handle the ball like Hardaway. His between-the-legs crossover dribble, dubbed the "UTEP two-step," mesmerizes even the best of defenders and usually opens a clear lane to the basket. His long-range shot is unorthodox but effective, as evidenced by his spot in the Long Distance Shootout on All-Star Weekend. Hardaway is a quick, effective floor leader who gets the ball into the right hands.

Weaknesses: Hardaway's small frame makes him vulnerable against bigger guards, especially on the defensive end of the court. His perimeter defense is good, but he can get backed into the post. Shot selection could be questioned if he played for a team other than Golden State (or perhaps Denver).

Analysis: Hardaway looks like a future superstar, especially with big-name point guards like Magic Johnson and Isiah Thomas now in their 30s. He has all the skills to become another player of that magnitude. All Hardaway needs to show is the ability to lift a team to a higher level. His career is off to a flying start.

PLAYER SUMMARY	
Will	penetrate
Can't	defend in post
Expect	20 PPG, 10 APG
Don't Expect	a slow pace
Fantasy Value	$50-53
Card Value	75¢-$1

COLLEGE STATISTICS

		G	FGP	FTP	RPG	PPG
85-86	UTEP	28	.521	.651	1.3	4.1
86-87	UTEP	31	.490	.663	2.0	10.0
87-88	UTEP	32	.449	.754	2.9	13.6
88-89	UTEP	33	.501	.741	4.0	22.0
Totals		124	.484	.718	2.6	12.8

NBA REGULAR-SEASON STATISTICS

			FGs		3-PT FGs		FTs		Rebounds						
	G	MIN	FG	PCT	FG	PCT	FT	PCT	OFF	TOT	AST	STL	BLK	PTS	PPG
89-90 GS	79	2663	464	.471	23	.274	211	.764	57	310	689	165	12	1162	14.7
90-91 GS	82	3215	739	.476	97	.385	306	.803	87	332	793	214	12	1881	22.9
Totals	161	5878	1203	.474	120	.357	517	.787	144	642	1482	379	24	3043	18.9

DEREK HARPER

Team: Dallas Mavericks
Position: Guard
Height: 6'4" **Weight:** 200
Birthdate: October 13, 1961

NBA Experience: 8 years
College: Illinois
Acquired: 1st-round pick in 1983 draft
(11th overall)

Background: Harper led the Big Ten in steals two straight years, then declared for the NBA draft after his junior season. He is the first player in league history to improve his scoring average in each of his first eight years (and counting). Harper is the Mavs' all-time leader in steals and has topped the 100 mark seven straight seasons. He finished fourth in scoring among point guards in 1990-91.

Strengths: Not only has Harper's scoring average continued to climb, but he has firmly established himself as one of the NBA's premier defensive guards. His quickness, great reach, and willingness to play belly-up defense all over the court have helped earn him that reputation. On offense, he can bury the 3-pointer or create shots closer to the bucket from his point-guard slot. Harper is truly a multi-dimensional standout and a fine leader.

Weaknesses: Originally a two guard, Harper will not amass staggering assist totals. He would just as soon finish his own plays, although his passing ability and court sense have improved with experience at the point.

Analysis: Scoring is not the only area in which Harper has improved for eight straight seasons, although it certainly is the most amazing. He has developed better playmaking ability and has continued to deserve his reputation as one of the NBA's most gifted and inspired defenders.

PLAYER SUMMARY

Will......................shut down opponents
Can't ....live on passing
Expect.................points from the point
Don't Expect...............................10 APG
Fantasy Value $29-33
Card Value ....15-25¢

COLLEGE STATISTICS

		G	FGP	FTP	RPG	PPG
80-81	ILL	29	.413	.717	2.6	8.3
81-82	ILL	29	.457	.756	4.6	8.4
82-83	ILL	32	.537	.675	3.5	15.4
Totals		90	.478	.701	3.6	10.9

NBA REGULAR-SEASON STATISTICS

				FGs		3-PT FGs		FTs		Rebounds						
		G	MIN	FG	PCT	FG	PCT	FT	PCT	OFF	TOT	AST	STL	BLK	PTS	PPG
83-84	DAL	82	1712	200	.443	3	.115	66	.673	53	172	239	95	21	469	5.7
84-85	DAL	82	2218	329	.520	21	.344	111	.721	47	199	360	144	37	790	9.6
85-86	DAL	79	2150	390	.534	12	.235	171	.747	75	226	416	153	23	963	12.2
86-87	DAL	77	2556	497	.501	76	.358	160	.684	51	199	609	167	25	1230	16.0
87-88	DAL	82	3032	536	.459	60	.313	261	.759	71	246	634	168	35	1393	17.0
88-89	DAL	81	2968	538	.477	99	.356	229	.806	46	228	570	172	41	1404	17.3
89-90	DAL	82	3007	567	.488	89	.371	250	.794	54	244	609	187	26	1473	18.0
90-91	DAL	77	2879	572	.467	89	.362	286	.731	59	233	548	147	14	1519	19.7
Totals		642	20522	3629	.485	449	.344	1534	.749	456	1747	3985	1233	222	9241	14.4

RON HARPER

Team: Los Angeles Clippers
Position: Guard/Forward
Height: 6'6" **Weight:** 198
Birthdate: January 20, 1964
NBA Experience: 5 years
College: Miami (OH)

Acquired: Traded from Cavaliers with 1990 and 1992 1st-round picks and a 1991 2nd-round pick for Reggie Williams and draft rights to Danny Ferry, 11/89

Background: Harper left Miami of Ohio with the all-time Mid-American Conference scoring record. He quickly established himself as a marquee player in Cleveland, finishing second in the Rookie of the Year voting. He was traded to the Clippers in November 1989, but his first campaign there was cut short when he tore the anterior cruciate ligament in his right knee. Harper returned more than a year later for the final 39 games of the 1990-91 season. He showed few ill-effects and finished second on the Clippers in scoring average.

Strengths: Harper is a dominating open-court player with slashing moves to the hoop and tremendous leaping and finishing ability. He is a nifty passer and natural leader with supreme confidence. He rebounds and blocks shots better than most guards and can be a defensive whiz when pushed.

Weaknesses: Besides the knee, Harper's only major weakness is his lack of jump-shooting skill. His shots are flat and inconsistent.

Analysis: Harper boosted the Clippers when he first arrived and again when he returned from his injury. That's the kind of player he is—one who helps a team win. He is one of the top one-on-one scorers in the league and loves having the ball in his hands. Assuming his knee holds up as well as it has so far, Harper will continue to command All-Star attention.

PLAYER SUMMARY

Will.................................create offense
Can't.......................shoot consistently
Expect.........................great leadership
Don't Expect....................a slow tempo
Fantasy Value..............................$9-12
Card Value.......................................8¢

COLLEGE STATISTICS

		G	FGP	FTP	RPG	PPG
82-83	MIA	28	.497	.674	7.0	12.9
83-84	MIA	30	.537	.570	7.6	14.9
84-85	MIA	31	.541	.661	10.7	24.9
85-86	MIA	31	.545	.665	11.7	24.4
Totals		120	.534	.642	9.3	19.5

NBA REGULAR-SEASON STATISTICS

				FGs		3-PT FGs		FTs		Rebounds						
		G	MIN	FG	PCT	FG	PCT	FT	PCT	OFF	TOT	AST	STL	BLK	PTS	PPG
86-87	CLE	82	3064	734	.455	20	.213	386	.684	169	392	394	209	84	1874	22.9
87-88	CLE	57	1830	340	.464	3	.150	196	.705	64	223	281	122	52	879	15.4
88-89	CLE	82	2851	587	.511	29	.250	323	.751	122	409	434	185	74	1526	18.6
89-90	CLE/LAC	35	1367	301	.473	14	.275	182	.788	74	206	182	81	41	798	22.8
90-91	LAC	39	1383	285	.391	48	.324	145	.668	58	188	209	66	35	763	19.6
Totals		295	10495	2247	.462	114	.266	1232	.716	487	1418	1500	663	286	5840	19.8

SCOTT HASTINGS

Team: Denver Nuggets   **NBA Experience:** 9 years
Position: Forward   **College:** Arkansas
Height: 6'10" **Weight:** 245   **Acquired:** Traded from Pistons for
Birthdate: June 3, 1960   Orlando Woolridge, 8/91

Background: It's a bit hard to believe that this NBA hackman was Arkansas' second-leading career scorer behind Sidney Moncrief. In nine NBA seasons—with New York, Atlanta, Miami, and Detroit—he's never averaged more than 5.1 PPG. In five of those seasons, he scored no more than 2.0 PPG. He was dealt to Denver in August.

Strengths: Hastings's primary duty with the Pistons was to bang, incite opposing players, and just generally typify the team's bad-boy image. He was good at getting tangled up with opposing players and being a general nuisance to them. He was Bill Laimbeer without a shot, as well as the club's top practical joker. He is also a lifetime 80-percent free throw shooter.

Weaknesses: Though he has nice range, Hastings has never proven he could score in the NBA. He isn't fast and his defense consists mainly of grabbing and bumping. He had more fouls (23) than baskets (16) last season and had goose eggs under the columns for blocks and steals. He is not a skilled rebounder.

Analysis: See Jack Haley. Or Greg Dreiling. Hastings belongs to that fraternity of NBA big bangers whose roles are simply to get physical during limited minutes and peacefully occupy a spot near the end of the bench. He has made a career of this, hanging around the pros for nine years, so it can't be all bad.

PLAYER SUMMARY

Will ....bang
Can't ....board
Expect ....hands-on approach
Don't Expect ....amazing grace
Fantasy Value $1-2
Card Value...8¢

COLLEGE STATISTICS

		G	FGP	FTP	RPG	PPG
78-79	ARK	30	.508	.730	4.6	8.3
79-80	ARK	29	.534	.781	6.7	16.2
80-81	ARK	32	.563	.735	5.4	16.3
81-82	ARK	29	.553	.740	6.0	18.6
Totals		120	.544	.748	5.7	14.8

NBA REGULAR-SEASON STATISTICS

		G	MIN	FGs FG	FGs PCT	3-PT FGs FG	3-PT FGs PCT	FTs FT	FTs PCT	Rebounds OFF	Rebounds TOT	AST	STL	BLK	PTS	PPG
82-83	NY/ATL	31	140	13	.342	0	.000	11	.550	15	41	3	6	1	37	1.2
83-84	ATL	68	1135	111	.468	1	.250	82	.788	96	270	46	40	36	305	4.5
84-85	ATL	64	825	89	.473	0	.000	63	.778	59	159	46	24	23	241	3.8
85-86	ATL	62	650	65	.409	3	.750	60	.857	44	124	26	14	8	193	3.1
86-87	ATL	40	256	23	.338	2	.167	23	.793	16	70	13	10	7	71	1.8
87-88	ATL	55	403	40	.488	5	.417	25	.926	27	97	16	8	10	110	2.0
88-89	MIA	75	1206	143	.436	9	.321	91	.850	72	231	59	32	42	386	5.1
89-90	DET	40	166	10	.303	3	.250	19	.864	7	32	8	3	3	42	1.0
90-91	DET	27	113	16	.571	3	.750	13	1.000	14	28	7	0	0	48	1.8
Totals		462	4894	510	.439	26	.329	387	.818	350	1052	224	137	130	1433	3.1

HERSEY HAWKINS

Team: Philadelphia 76ers
Position: Guard
Height: 6'3" **Weight:** 190
Birthdate: September 29, 1965
NBA Experience: 3 years

College: Bradley
Acquired: Draft rights traded from
Clippers with a 1989 1st-round pick for
draft rights to Charles Smith, 6/88

Background: Hawkins went from being a 6'3", all-city center at Westinghouse High School in Chicago to an outside gunner at Bradley. As a senior, Hawkins led the nation in scoring and was named a consensus All-American and the nation's Player of the Year. He left college as the fourth-leading scorer in NCAA history. Since arriving in Philly, his scoring average has steadily climbed, and he finished 14th in the league in 1990-91.

Strengths: This guy can absolutely scorch you when his shot is on. His outside gunning eases the pressure on Charles Barkley and his fellow front-liners. Hawkins has emerged as one of the more dangerous 3-point shooters in the league and, despite his scorer's mentality, still plays creditable defense. He was eighth in the NBA in steals last year. His 87.1 percent mark at the free throw line was among the league's best.

Weaknesses: He committed over 200 turnovers last year, which was pretty high for a shooting guard. Still, his ball-handling and passing aren't bad.

Analysis: There will always be a place in the NBA for someone who shoots like Hawkins. The bonus is, this guy is actually an unselfish player who would rather set up a big guy inside with a higher percentage shot. From his younger days as a center, he knows how to post and score inside, when necessary, and he takes his defense seriously. The steady improvement indicates that he's headed for big-time stardom.

PLAYER SUMMARY	
Will	hit from long range
Can't	hog the ball
Expect	3-pointers
Don't Expect	lazy defense
Fantasy Value	$11-13
Card Value	15¢

COLLEGE STATISTICS

		G	FGP	FTP	RPG	PPG
84-85	BRAD	30	.581	.771	6.1	14.6
85-86	BRAD	35	.542	.768	5.7	18.7
86-87	BRAD	29	.533	.793	6.7	27.2
87-88	BRAD	31	.524	.848	7.8	36.3
Totals		125	.539	.806	6.5	24.1

NBA REGULAR-SEASON STATISTICS

				FGs		3-PT FGs		FTs		Rebounds						
		G	MIN	FG	PCT	FG	PCT	FT	PCT	OFF	TOT	AST	STL	BLK	PTS	PPG
88-89	PHI	79	2577	442	.455	71	.428	241	.831	51	225	239	120	37	1196	15.1
89-90	PHI	82	2856	522	.460	84	.420	387	.888	85	304	261	130	28	1515	18.5
90-91	PHI	80	3110	590	.472	108	.400	479	.871	48	310	299	178	39	1767	22.1
Totals		241	8543	1554	.463	263	.414	1107	.868	184	839	799	428	104	4478	18.6

STEVE HENSON

Team: Milwaukee Bucks
Position: Guard
Height: 5'11" **Weight:** 177
Birthdate: February 2, 1968
NBA Experience: 1 year

College: Kansas St.
Acquired: 2nd-round pick in 1990 draft (44th overall)

Background: Henson is the only player in Kansas State history to lead the Wildcats in scoring and assists two straight seasons. He was the only Big Eight player to rank in the top ten in six different statistical categories as a senior. Though drafted late in the 1990 draft, Henson made the Bucks and played in 68 games.

Strengths: Henson is an excellent ball-handler and is adept at setting up teammates with crisp passes. Smart and heady, he already appeared able to run the Bucks' offense when starting point guard Jay Humphries needed a breather. He rarely misses free throws, hitting 38-of-42 last season (90.5 percent). He converted 92.5 percent as a sophomore, tops in the nation. He is also a 3-point threat.

Weaknesses: His tiny size is a drawback in a league where guards are getting bigger and stronger all the time. Henson's 41.8 field goal percentage was the worst he shot since his freshman year at Kansas State. The jury is still out on whether he can defend against the quicker point guards.

Analysis: He could become the ideal back-up point guard with his excellent assist-to-turnovers ratio, 3-point shooting, and court savvy. The thing he has to be wary of are mismatches and getting caught in screens. If he can raise his field goal percentage, he'll be around the NBA for a while. He'll have a tough time getting a chance with the Bucks, though, as they already have three outstanding guards.

PLAYER SUMMARY

Will ....pile up assists
Can't ....guard quick guards
Expect....................................smart play
Don't Expect......................slam dunks
Fantasy Value $1-2
Card Value..5¢

COLLEGE STATISTICS

		G	FGP	FTP	RPG	PPG
86-87	KSU	31	.395	.826	2.0	7.5
87-88	KSU	34	.429	.925	2.4	9.1
88-89	KSU	30	.465	.920	2.7	18.5
89-90	KSU	32	.446	.902	2.7	17.4
Totals		127	.442	.900	2.4	13.0

NBA REGULAR-SEASON STATISTICS

			FGs		3-PT FGs		FTs		Rebounds						
	G	MIN	FG	PCT	FG	PCT	FT	PCT	OFF	TOT	AST	STL	BLK	PTS	PPG
90-91 MIL	68	690	79	.418	18	.333	38	.905	14	51	131	32	0	214	3.1
Totals	68	690	79	.418	18	.333	38	.905	14	51	131	32	0	214	3.1

ROD HIGGINS

Team: Golden State Warriors
Position: Forward
Height: 6'7" **Weight:** 205
Birthdate: January 31, 1960

NBA Experience: 9 years
College: Fresno St.
Acquired: Signed as a free agent, 10/86

Background: Higgins led Fresno State to consecutive conference championships, pacing the team in scoring in each of his final three years. He has overcome his journeyman label in the NBA (he was with four different teams in 1985-86) by playing for five years and 187 straight games with Golden State. Higgins was fourth on the Warriors in minutes in 1990-91 at 24.7 per game.

Strengths: Though he plays both forward spots and sometimes center for undersized Golden State, Higgins is at his best from 3-point land. He is the Warriors' career leader in 3-pointers made (228) and attempted (637), for a mark of .358. Higgins's ability to ably fill three positions cannot be overlooked.

Weaknesses: Higgins is not much of a threat off the dribble, preferring to catch and shoot. Although his long arms allow him to block shots, Higgins's defensive aptitude declines when he is matched up with bigger power forwards and centers.

Analysis: Higgins is a team player who is willing to fill any role that is asked of him. His 3-point shooting can turn games around, and he will not hurt his club defensively unless he is dwarfed by his match-up. He knows his limitations and plays within them.

PLAYER SUMMARY

Will	hit 3-pointers
Can't	create off dribble
Expect	versatility
Don't Expect	a power game
Fantasy Value	$3-5
Card Value	8¢

COLLEGE STATISTICS

		G	FGP	FTP	RPG	PPG
78-79	FSU	22	.516	.742	5.8	9.4
79-80	FSU	24	.506	.837	5.7	12.9
80-81	FSU	29	.558	.852	5.4	15.4
81-82	FSU	29	.531	.771	6.3	15.1
Totals		104	.532	.805	5.8	13.5

NBA REGULAR-SEASON STATISTICS

		G	MIN	FGs FG	FGs PCT	3-PT FGs FG	3-PT FGs PCT	FTs FT	FTs PCT	Rebounds OFF	Rebounds TOT	AST	STL	BLK	PTS	PPG
82-83	CHI	82	2196	313	.448	13	.317	209	.792	159	366	175	66	65	848	10.3
83-84	CHI	78	1577	193	.447	1	.045	113	.724	87	206	116	49	29	500	6.4
84-85	CHI	68	942	119	.441	10	.270	60	.667	55	147	73	21	13	308	4.5
85-86	SEA/SA/NJ/CHI															
		30	332	39	.368	1	.111	19	.704	14	51	24	9	11	98	3.3
86-87	GS	73	1497	214	.519	3	.176	200	.833	72	237	96	40	21	631	8.6
87-88	GS	68	2188	381	.526	19	.487	273	.848	94	293	188	70	31	1054	15.5
88-89	GS	81	1887	301	.476	66	.393	188	.821	111	376	160	39	42	856	10.6
89-90	GS	82	1993	304	.481	67	.347	234	.821	120	422	129	47	53	909	11.1
90-91	GS	82	2024	259	.463	73	.332	185	.819	109	354	113	52	37	776	9.5
Totals		644	14636	2123	.475	253	.339	1481	.805	821	2452	1074	393	302	5980	9.3

SEAN HIGGINS

Team: San Antonio Spurs
Position: Forward
Height: 6'9" **Weight:** 195
Birthdate: December 30, 1968
NBA Experience: 1 year

College: Michigan
Acquired: 2nd-round pick in 1990 draft (54th overall)

Background: Higgins helped Michigan win the 1989 NCAA championship and shot better than 42 percent from 3-point range as a junior. He entered the draft a year early and was selected with the final pick. Higgins saw action in 50 games as a rookie and once tallied 22 points.

Strengths: Higgins was a dead-eye college shooter with great range and showed glimpses of that ability as a pro. His size makes it possible for him to play big guard or small forward.

Weaknesses: Higgins has trouble creating his own shots and does not play enough defense to warrant evaluation. Most questioned his early-entry decision because of his lack of maturity on the court. For a gunner, Higgins's rookie shooting numbers were disappointing (3-of-19 3-pointers).

Analysis: One-dimensional players rarely stick in the NBA, especially long-range shooters who struggle to make 3's. However, Higgins showed better court sense and made better decisions than expected and likely earned himself another chance to let his perimeter game shine. He will have to develop in other areas and show a willingness to defend if he hopes to play steady minutes for a contender.

PLAYER SUMMARY

Will ....spot up from outside
Can't.................................play defense
Expect ....better shooting
Don't Expect ....leadership skills
Fantasy Value $1-3
Card Value...8¢

COLLEGE STATISTICS

		G	FGP	FTP	RPG	PPG
87-88	MICH	12	.500	.786	3.2	9.8
88-89	MICH	34	.506	.771	3.1	12.4
89-90	MICH	26	.470	.804	3.6	14.0
Totals		72	.490	.785	3.3	12.5

NBA REGULAR-SEASON STATISTICS

			FGs		3-PT FGs		FTs		Rebounds						
	G	MIN	FG	PCT	FG	PCT	FT	PCT	OFF	TOT	AST	STL	BLK	PTS	PPG
90-91 SA	50	464	97	.458	3	.158	28	.848	18	63	35	8	1	225	4.5
Totals	50	464	97	.458	3	.158	28	.848	18	63	35	8	1	225	4.5

TYRONE HILL

Team: Golden State Warriors
Position: Forward
Height: 6'9" **Weight:** 243
Birthdate: March 17, 1968
NBA Experience: 1 year

College: Xavier (OH)
Acquired: 1st-round pick in 1990 draft
(11th overall)

Background: Hill joined an exclusive group of 62 college players to score 2,000 points and grab 1,000 rebounds in a career. He ranked third in the NCAA in rebounding as a senior at Xavier and second as a junior. His rookie season saw him average one rebound for every 3.1 minutes, ranking among the league leaders in productivity. He led Golden State with 157 offensive caroms.

Strengths: Hard work and rebounding are the fortes of Hill. He has a muscular body and uses it to get good inside position. His quick feet help him play perimeter defense and he has fine leaping ability. Hill runs the court better than most big forwards.

Weaknesses: Hill is mechanical offensively and must improve his moves to the basket. He often played with his back to the hoop in college and the release on his jump shot is not pretty. He is an underachieving shot-blocker considering his size and athletic ability.

Analysis: Hill has the potential to become a big-time rebounder, although not the dominant board-getter he was in college. He has a good deal to learn offensively, but his work ethic and desire to excel at the pro level will help him develop those skills.

PLAYER SUMMARY

Will...rebound
Can't.......................shoot from outside
Expect..........................great work ethic
Don't Expect.............................15 PPG
Fantasy Value.................................$4-7
Card Value..25¢

COLLEGE STATISTICS

		G	FGP	FTP	RPG	PPG
86-87	XAV	31	.552	.672	8.4	8.8
87-88	XAV	30	.557	.745	10.5	15.3
88-89	XAV	33	.606	.701	12.2	18.9
89-90	XAV	32	.581	.658	12.6	20.2
Totals		126	.579	.692	11.0	15.9

NBA REGULAR-SEASON STATISTICS

			MIN	FGs		3-PT FGs		FTs		Rebounds		AST	STL	BLK	PTS	PPG
		G	MIN	FG	PCT	FG	PCT	FT	PCT	OFF	TOT	AST	STL	BLK	PTS	PPG
90-91	GS	74	1192	147	.492	0	.000	96	.632	157	383	19	33	30	390	5.3
Totals		74	1192	147	.492	0	.000	96	.632	157	383	19	33	30	390	5.3

CRAIG HODGES

Team: Chicago Bulls
Position: Guard
Height: 6'2" **Weight:** 190
Birthdate: June 27, 1960
NBA Experience: 9 years

College: Long Beach St.
Acquired: Traded from Suns for Ed Nealy and a 1989 2nd-round pick, 12/88

Background: Hodges starred at Fresno State for Tex Winter and then became a role player for the Clippers, Bucks, and Suns. Always a noted outside gunner, he led the NBA in 3-point percentage in 1986 and 1988. Phoenix traded him to hometown Chicago in 1988.

Strengths: Like Colonel Sanders, Hodges knows how to do one thing—but he does it right. What he does is shoot 3-pointers, good enough to win the Long Distance Shootout at the last two All-Star Games. He's virtually a sure thing at the free throw line, hitting 26-of-27 last season.

Weaknesses: Although he tries, his defense leaves something to be desired. Hodges really doesn't have the size to play extended minutes at off guard, and he isn't the passer and ball-handler to play the point. Since he rarely penetrates or goes to the basket, he doesn't draw many fouls, which is a shame because he is deadly from the line.

Analysis: As long as he stays in Chicago and hangs out with Michael Jordan, he'll be fine. With Jordan penetrating, drawing triple teams, and creating a magic all his own, Hodges can sit on the cusp of the 3-point arc patiently waiting for his Airness to dish off. He seems to have found a home in Chicago.

PLAYER SUMMARY

Will .... bury the 3
Can't .... play physical
Expect .... free throw accuracy
Don't Expect .... versatility
Fantasy Value $2-4
Card Value .... 8¢

COLLEGE STATISTICS

		G	FGP	FTP	RPG	PPG
78-79	LBS	28	.521	.776	2.0	10.1
79-80	LBS	33	.499	.838	2.1	12.6
80-81	LBS	26	.462	.600	2.6	11.0
81-82	LBS	28	.475	.739	3.2	17.5
Totals		115	.487	.742	2.5	12.8

NBA REGULAR-SEASON STATISTICS

		G	MIN	FGs FG	FGs PCT	3-PT FGs FG	3-PT FGs PCT	FTs FT	FTs PCT	Rebounds OFF	Rebounds TOT	AST	STL	BLK	PTS	PPG
82-83	SD	76	2022	318	.452	20	.222	94	.723	53	122	275	82	4	750	9.9
83-84	SD	76	1571	258	.450	10	.217	66	.750	22	86	116	58	1	592	7.8
84-85	MIL	82	2496	359	.490	47	.348	106	.815	74	186	349	96	1	871	10.6
85-86	MIL	66	1739	284	.500	73	.451	75	.872	39	117	229	74	2	716	10.8
86-87	MIL	78	2147	315	.462	85	.373	131	.891	48	140	240	76	7	846	10.8
87-88	MIL/PHO	66	1445	242	.463	86	.491	59	.831	19	78	153	46	2	629	9.5
88-89	PHO/CHI	59	1204	203	.472	75	.417	48	.842	23	89	146	43	4	529	9.0
89-90	CHI	63	1055	145	.438	87	.481	30	.909	11	53	110	30	2	407	6.5
90-91	CHI	73	843	146	.424	44	.383	26	.963	10	42	97	34	2	362	5.0
Totals		639	14522	2270	.464	527	.402	635	.826	299	913	1715	539	25	5702	8.9

DENNIS HOPSON

Team: Chicago Bulls
Position: Guard
Height: 6'5" **Weight:** 195
Birthdate: April 22, 1965
NBA Experience: 4 years

College: Ohio St.
Acquired: Traded from Nets for a 1990 1st-round pick and 1991 and 1992 2nd-round picks, 6/90

Background: Hopson was a superstar at Ohio State his senior year, averaging 29 PPG to lead the Big Ten and being named a first-team All-American by *The Sporting News.* His incredible scoring exploits with the Buckeyes prompted the Nets to select him with their third pick of the 1987 draft. It turned out to be a horrible decision.

Strengths: Dennis hasn't demonstrated too many in three disappointing years with the Nets and one with the Bulls. In his third season at New Jersey, he did average 15.8 PPG and he came up with 100 steals.

Weaknesses: Where do we start? In four years, he has never shot above 43 percent and he can't create his own shot. He's been labeled as "soft," as a variety of minor injuries have seemingly taken away his confidence. Hopson's ball-handling is questionable and he hasn't demonstrated a willingness to play tough defense. He averaged just 4.3 PPG last year as he slowly sank to the end of the bench, behind even undrafted forward Scott Williams.

Analysis: Hopson was brought in to be Michael Jordan's back-up, but that project has failed. There is talk that the Bulls will get rid of Hopson before his value depreciates even further. When he plays, he looks like someone who has lost all confidence in a game that was superb in college. His best chance might be with one of the recent expansion teams, where he would have opportunities to put his game back together.

PLAYER SUMMARY

Will.............................warm the bench
Can't..........................create own shot
Expect ....limited minutes
Don't Expect ....another Jordan
Fantasy Value................................$5-7
Card Value...8¢

COLLEGE STATISTICS

		G	FGP	FTP	RPG	PPG
83-84	OSU	29	.474	.829	3.7	5.3
84-85	OSU	30	.494	.736	4.7	9.8
85-86	OSU	33	.545	.778	5.8	20.9
86-87	OSU	33	.518	.814	8.2	29.0
Totals		125	.519	.793	5.7	16.8

NBA REGULAR-SEASON STATISTICS

				FGs		3-PT FGs		FTs		Rebounds						
		G	MIN	FG	PCT	FG	PCT	FT	PCT	OFF	TOT	AST	STL	BLK	PTS	PPG
87-88	NJ	61	1365	222	.404	12	.267	131	.740	63	143	118	57	25	587	9.6
88-89	NJ	62	1551	299	.419	4	.148	186	.849	91	202	103	70	30	788	12.7
89-90	NJ	79	2551	474	.434	32	.317	271	.792	113	279	151	100	51	1251	15.8
90-91	CHI	61	728	104	.426	1	.200	55	.663	49	109	65	25	14	264	4.3
Totals		263	6195	1099	.423	49	.275	643	.783	316	733	437	252	120	2890	11.0

JEFF HORNACEK

Team: Phoenix Suns
Position: Guard
Height: 6'4" **Weight:** 190
Birthdate: May 3, 1963
NBA Experience: 5 years

College: Iowa St.
Acquired: 2nd-round pick in 1986 draft (46th overall)

Background: Hornacek walked on at Iowa State, earned a scholarship, and wound up setting a Big Eight career assist record with 665. His pro career has evolved in a similar pattern—from unheralded to highly respected. He increased his scoring average each year through 1989-90, when he peaked at 17.6 and led all NBA guards in field goal percentage (.536). In 1990-91, he finished third in the league in 3-point shooting percentage (.418).

Strengths: Hornacek is a dead-eye gunner who will kill you if you leave him open from anywhere on the court. He makes few mistakes, is good with both hands, and approaches each game with a great work ethic. Hornacek plays hard-nosed defense and can easily slide over to point guard.

Weaknesses: If Hornacek has an obvious weakness, it's that he is not exceptionally fast. Still, he runs the floor well and can get to the hoop off the dribble.

Analysis: He may look like your neighborhood paper boy, but Hornacek plays basketball on a high level every night. A coach's son, he has a thorough understanding of the game. He locates the seams in opposing defenses and exploits them with accurate long-range bombs. He was underrated early in his career, but everyone around the NBA knows and respects him now.

PLAYER SUMMARY

Will ....nail 3-pointers
Can't ....be left alone
Expect..........................hard-nosed play
Don't Expect ....mistakes
Fantasy Value $17-20
Card Value...8¢

COLLEGE STATISTICS

		G	FGP	FTP	RPG	PPG
82-83	ISU	27	.422	.711	2.3	5.4
83-84	ISU	29	.500	.790	3.5	10.0
84-85	ISU	34	.521	.844	3.6	12.5
85-86	ISU	33	.478	.776	3.8	13.7
Totals		123	.489	.790	3.3	10.7

NBA REGULAR-SEASON STATISTICS

		G	MIN	FGs FG	FGs PCT	3-PT FGs FG	3-PT FGs PCT	FTs FT	FTs PCT	Rebounds OFF	Rebounds TOT	AST	STL	BLK	PTS	PPG
86-87	PHO	80	1561	159	.454	12	.279	94	.777	41	184	361	70	5	424	5.3
87-88	PHO	82	2243	306	.506	17	.293	152	.822	71	262	540	107	10	781	9.5
88-89	PHO	78	2487	440	.495	27	.333	147	.826	75	266	465	129	8	1054	13.5
89-90	PHO	67	2278	483	.536	40	.408	173	.856	86	313	337	117	14	1179	17.6
90-91	PHO	80	2733	544	.518	61	.418	201	.897	74	321	409	111	16	1350	16.9
Totals		387	11302	1932	.509	157	.369	767	.843	347	1346	2112	534	53	4788	12.4

JAY HUMPHRIES

Team: Milwaukee Bucks
Position: Guard
Height: 6'3" **Weight:** 185
Birthdate: October 17, 1962
NBA Experience: 7 years

College: Colorado
Acquired: Traded from Suns for Craig Hodges and a 1988 2nd-round pick, 2/88

Background: Humphries was an All-Big Eight selection as a senior at Colorado. He set 16 school records, including career assists, steals, and games played. He was originally drafted by Phoenix, where he started all 82 games in his second and third seasons before a 1988 trade brought him to Milwaukee. He has led the Bucks in assists and minutes each of the last two years and was second in scoring and steals in 1990-91.

Strengths: Humphries does a little bit of everything from the point. He shoots the ball well, finds open men off penetration, dribbles well with both hands, and plays hard-nosed defense. Humphries was ninth in the league in assist-to-turnover ratio (3.56) in 1990-91. He has also added the 3-pointer to his arsenal.

Weaknesses: There are few noticeable flaws in Humphries's game beyond his occasional attempt to make the brilliant play on offense. He lacks the creativity of the league's more spectacular playmakers.

Analysis: Humphries defines the solid point guard. He shoots for a high percentage, scores in double figures, records many more assists than turnovers, and plays hard at both ends of the floor. Humphries does not rank among the big-name point men of the NBA, but his consistent contributions do not go unnoticed in Milwaukee.

PLAYER SUMMARY

Will....................................play both ends
Can't.................................gain stardom
Expect ....steady contributions
Don't Expect ....many turnovers
Fantasy Value $12-15
Card Value..10¢

COLLEGE STATISTICS

		G	FGP	FTP	RPG	PPG
80-81	COLO	28	.517	.660	2.1	6.4
81-82	COLO	27	.467	.639	2.6	10.3
82-83	COLO	28	.501	.632	3.3	14.3
83-84	COLO	29	.509	.788	3.2	15.4
Totals		112	.498	.696	2.8	11.7

NBA REGULAR-SEASON STATISTICS

		G	MIN	FGs FG	PCT	3-PT FGs FG	PCT	FTs FT	PCT	Rebounds OFF	TOT	AST	STL	BLK	PTS	PPG
84-85	PHO	80	2062	279	.446	4	.200	141	.829	32	164	350	107	8	703	8.8
85-86	PHO	82	2733	352	.479	4	.138	197	.767	56	260	526	132	9	905	11.0
86-87	PHO	82	2579	359	.477	5	.185	200	.769	62	260	632	112	9	923	11.3
87-88	PHO/MIL	68	1809	284	.528	3	.167	112	.732	49	174	395	81	5	683	10.0
88-89	MIL	73	2220	345	.483	25	.266	129	.816	70	189	405	142	5	844	11.6
89-90	MIL	81	2818	496	.494	21	.300	224	.786	80	269	472	156	11	1237	15.3
90-91	MIL	80	2726	482	.502	60	.373	191	.799	57	220	538	129	7	1215	15.2
Totals		546	16947	2597	.487	122	.291	1194	.784	406	1536	3318	859	54	6510	11.9

BYRON IRVIN

Team: Washington Bullets
Position: Guard
Height: 6'5" **Weight:** 190
Birthdate: December 2, 1966
NBA Experience: 2 years

College: Arkansas; Missouri
Acquired: Traded from Kings for
Steve Colter, 10/90

Background: Irvin averaged more than 16 PPG over his two-year stay at Missouri, where he transferred after beginning his college career at Arkansas. A first-round draft choice of Portland, he saw limited action as a rookie in 1989-90 and played even less with Washington during the 1990-91 season. His scoring average has been an identical 5.2 PPG each year. He's a cousin of Atlanta's Doc Rivers.

Strengths: Irvin is a good perimeter shooter with range a few feet inside the 3-point line. His offensive arsenal is best-suited for coming off screens, but he can create his own shot as well. He runs the floor and is an above-average rebounder for his position. His free throw shooting is reliable.

Weaknesses: Although his ball-handling skills are decent, Irvin often turns the ball over while trying to push it up-court against poor numbers. He needs to pick his spots to run. Irvin creates very little for teammates and his one-on-one defensive achievements are not much to brag about.

Analysis: Irvin's all-around skills are enough to earn him occasional minutes, but he lacks any one outstanding talent that would keep him on the floor for longer stretches. With Portland, he played behind Clyde Drexler. In Washington, there is no such excuse for his home on the bench. First-rounders should be playing by now.

PLAYER SUMMARY	
Will	run the court
Can't	earn steady minutes
Expect	good shooting
Don't Expect	3-pointers
Fantasy Value	$1-3
Card Value	8¢

COLLEGE STATISTICS

		G	FGP	FTP	RPG	PPG
84-85	ARK	33	.477	.577	1.8	5.4
85-86	ARK	28	.448	.708	2.8	9.9
87-88	MO	30	.514	.718	3.5	12.9
88-89	MO	36	.532	.826	4.7	19.7
Totals		127	.501	.756	3.2	12.2

NBA REGULAR-SEASON STATISTICS

		G	MIN	FGs FG	FGs PCT	3-PT FGs FG	3-PT FGs PCT	FTs FT	FTs PCT	Rebounds OFF	Rebounds TOT	AST	STL	BLK	PTS	PPG
89-90	POR	50	488	96	.473	5	.357	61	.670	30	74	47	28	1	258	5.2
90-91	WAS	33	316	60	.465	1	.200	50	.820	24	45	24	15	2	171	5.2
Totals		83	804	156	.470	6	.316	111	.730	54	119	71	43	3	429	5.2

CHRIS JACKSON

Team: Denver Nuggets
Position: Guard
Height: 6'1" **Weight:** 168
Birthdate: March 9, 1969
NBA Experience: 1 year

College: Louisiana St.
Acquired: 1st-round pick in 1990 draft
(3rd overall)

Background: In two seasons at LSU, Jackson accomplished things most four-year players will never approach. He broke three NCAA freshman records: most points in a game against a Division I opponent (55), most in a season (965), and highest scoring average (30.2). In two years, he broke the 50-point mark four times. Jackson's first pro season was cut short by foot surgery, but he played 67 games, finished third on the Nuggets in scoring, and once tallied 35 points.

Strengths: He does not use strings, but it seems the ball is attached to Jackson's hand. He handles it well at full speed, has a nifty crossover dribble, and can create his own shots. Jackson, extremely quick, is hard to defend in the open court and can bury jumpers when hot.

Weaknesses: The much-publicized problem with Jackson is that he is a two guard in a point guard's body. He was rarely asked to pass in college. The same goes for playing defense. As for his 3-point range, Jackson hit just 24 percent from behind the arc last year.

Analysis: Jackson, who has a neurological disorder called Tourette's Syndrome, showed signs of becoming a great weapon. His ball-handling skills and lightning quickness make him a promising point man if he can further refine his passing. The scoring will be there.

PLAYER SUMMARY

Will.....................................look to score
Can't.................................slow the pace
Expect.....................................15 PPG
Don't Expect........Magic-style passing
Fantasy Value.............................$15-18
Card Value.......................................25¢

COLLEGE STATISTICS

		G	FGP	FTP	RPG	PPG
88-89	LSU	32	.486	.815	3.4	30.2
89-90	LSU	32	.461	.910	2.5	27.8
Totals		64	.474	.863	3.0	29.0

NBA REGULAR-SEASON STATISTICS

		G	MIN	FGs FG	FGs PCT	3-PT FGs FG	3-PT FGs PCT	FTs FT	FTs PCT	Rebounds OFF	Rebounds TOT	AST	STL	BLK	PTS	PPG
90-91	DEN	67	1505	417	.413	24	.240	84	.857	34	121	206	55	4	942	14.1
Totals		67	1505	417	.413	24	.240	84	.857	34	121	206	55	4	942	14.1

MARK JACKSON

Team: New York Knicks
Position: Guard
Height: 6'3" **Weight:** 205
Birthdate: April 1, 1965

NBA Experience: 4 years
College: St. John's
Acquired: 1st-round pick in 1987 draft (18th overall)

Background: Jackson was a second-team All-American as a senior at St. John's and finished his career with the school's all-time assists record. He exploded onto the NBA scene, earning the unanimous vote for Rookie of the Year in 1987-88 and a trip to the All-Star Game the following season. In a dismal 1989-90, however, he lost his starting job and the support of Knicks fans. He began 1990-91 as a starter, lost that role by mid-season, and was dealt a four-game suspension by the team for "detrimental conduct." He finished the year as a productive reserve.

Strengths: Jackson can be an explosive playmaker, largely because of his ability to penetrate. He cuts through the lane and can either find the open man or make acrobatic shots in traffic. He already ranks fifth on the Knicks' all-time assists list.

Weaknesses: It seems the biggest problem with Jackson is mental. His play deteriorated when the fans got on him and his 1990-91 suspension was for constant criticism of the organization. When his head is not right, his game gets worse. He tends to showboat on offense and is a defensive liability.

Analysis: Just when many thought Jackson was on his way out, he was named Knick of the Month for April. It just goes to show that there is a considerable amount he can contribute when in the right frame of mind. The next couple of seasons will determine whether Jackson is New York's point guard of the future or excess baggage.

PLAYER SUMMARY

Will..............................penetrate
Can't ....avoid controversy
Expect.................flashes of greatness
Don't Expect.....................consistency
Fantasy Value...........................$12-15
Card Value.....................................8¢

COLLEGE STATISTICS

		G	FGP	FTP	RPG	PPG
83-84	STJ	30	.575	.688	2.0	5.8
84-85	STJ	35	.564	.725	1.3	5.1
85-86	STJ	36	.478	.739	3.5	11.3
86-87	STJ	30	.504	.806	3.7	18.9
Totals		131	.510	.751	2.6	10.1

NBA REGULAR-SEASON STATISTICS

				FGs		3-PT FGs		FTs		Rebounds							
		G	MIN	FG	PCT	FG	PCT	FT	PCT	OFF	TOT	AST	STL	BLK	PTS	PPG
87-88	NY	82	3249	438	.432	32	.254	206	.774	120	396	868	205	6	1114	13.6
88-89	NY	72	2477	479	.467	81	.338	180	.698	106	341	619	139	7	1219	16.9
89-90	NY	82	2428	327	.437	35	.267	120	.727	106	318	604	109	4	809	9.9
90-91	NY	72	1595	250	.492	13	.255	117	.731	62	197	452	60	9	630	8.8
Totals		308	9749	1494	.453	161	.294	623	.734	394	1252	2543	513	26	3772	12.2

DAVE JAMERSON

Team: Houston Rockets
Position: Guard
Height: 6'5" **Weight:** 192
Birthdate: August 13, 1967
NBA Experience: 1 year

College: Ohio
Acquired: Draft rights traded from Heat with draft rights to Carl Herrera for draft rights to Alec Kessler, 6/90

Background: Jamerson led the nation in 3-pointers made per game (4.7) as a senior at Ohio University, where he was voted Mid-American Conference Player of the Year. He increased his draft stock by winning MVP honors at the Portsmouth Invitational all-star camp. He spent the majority of his first pro season on the Houston bench and shot just 38.1 percent from the field.

Strengths: His shooting was expected to earn Jamerson playing time, but it turned out that his biggest strength was his hard-nosed approach. He refuses to back down and plays better defense than expected. Still, Jamerson's future is his quick-release jumper and great range. He is good-sized for a guard.

Weaknesses: Jamerson is not a great ball-handler and thus cannot be relied upon to create his own shot. While he hustles and works hard, he does not possess above-average athletic ability. The biggest knock on him (other than 5-of-19 3-point shooting as a rookie) is that he is strictly a gunner.

Analysis: The very first minute of Jamerson's rookie year set the tone—he made two turnovers. He must play better with the ball in his hands to earn more minutes. Perhaps the biggest thing Jamerson has in his favor is his motivation. He vows to work hard in the off-season to prove he is worthy of his first-round draft status and to avoid another campaign like his first.

PLAYER SUMMARY

Will	release ball quickly
Can't	handle it well
Expect	much better shooting
Don't Expect	effective drives
Fantasy Value	$3-5
Card Value	8¢

COLLEGE STATISTICS

		G	FGP	FTP	RPG	PPG
85-86	OHIO	28	.575	.831	3.0	14.0
87-88	OHIO	30	.476	.851	3.8	17.3
88-89	OHIO	29	.484	.860	4.7	19.0
89-90	OHIO	28	.459	.842	6.4	31.2
Totals		115	.488	.846	4.5	20.3

NBA REGULAR-SEASON STATISTICS

			FGs		3-PT FGs		FTs		Rebounds						
	G	MIN	FG	PCT	FG	PCT	FT	PCT	OFF	TOT	AST	STL	BLK	PTS	PPG
90-91 HOU	37	202	43	.381	5	.263	22	.815	9	30	27	6	1	113	3.1
Totals	37	202	43	.381	5	.263	22	.815	9	30	27	6	1	113	3.1

HENRY JAMES

Team: Cleveland Cavaliers
Position: Forward
Height: 6'9" **Weight:** 220
Birthdate: July 29, 1965
NBA Experience: 1 year

College: St. Mary's (TX)
Acquired: Signed as a free agent, 9/90

Background: James played his college career in relative obscurity at St. Mary's in San Antonio, then labored in the CBA before earning his first NBA stint in 1990-91. He was averaging 21.8 points and 7.8 rebounds per game for Wichita Falls before making an immediate impact with injury-torn Cleveland. James scored 25 points in his third NBA game and started the last four contests of the season.

Strengths: James is an adept scorer with a nice touch and 3-point range. He hit 40 percent (24-of-60) from behind the arc. His size allows him to shoot over defenders and he can score in big spurts when he heats up. James lit up the Pistons for 13 points in the second quarter in his second NBA game.

Weaknesses: Like most CBA scorers, James sputters on defense. He is no shot-blocking threat and has not yet learned how to force the NBA's high-scoring forwards to work for their points. He also has not proven to be the rebounder he was at the CBA level. He could use some added bulk to help his inside game at both ends of the court.

Analysis: There is no doubt James was a bright spot in an otherwise dreary year in Cleveland. He came out of nowhere to provide much-needed points. He averaged 14 PPG in his four starts and the Cavs went 4-0. James would not be a starter on many clubs (including a healthy Cleveland squad), but plenty of teams could use his offensive prowess off the bench.

PLAYER SUMMARY

Will ....score in spurts
Can't ....shine on defense
Expect ....more NBA minutes
Don't Expect ....many NBA starts
Fantasy Value $4-6
Card Value..5¢

COLLEGE STATISTICS

		G	FGP	FTP	RPG	PPG
88-89	SM	26	.551	.861	7.6	23.3
Totals		26	.551	.861	7.6	23.3

NBA REGULAR-SEASON STATISTICS

			FGs		3-PT FGs		FTs		Rebounds						
	G	MIN	FG	PCT	FG	PCT	FT	PCT	OFF	TOT	AST	STL	BLK	PTS	PPG
90-91 CLE	37	505	112	.441	24	.400	52	.722	26	79	32	15	5	300	8.1
Totals	37	505	112	.441	24	.400	52	.722	26	79	32	15	5	300	8.1

AVERY JOHNSON

Team: San Antonio Spurs
Position: Guard
Height: 5'11" **Weight:** 175
Birthdate: March 25, 1965
NBA Experience: 3 years

College: Cameron; Southern
Acquired: Signed as a free agent,
1/91

Background: Johnson led the nation in assists as a junior and senior at Southern University, where he was a two-time Southwestern Athletic Conference Player of the Year. He was not drafted, but he made Seattle as a free agent and played two-plus years there before joining San Antonio in 1990-91. Johnson started ten games for the Spurs and enjoyed his best season in virtually every statistical category.

Strengths: A pure point guard, Johnson covers the court like a pinball. His quickness allows him to penetrate and show off his crafty passing skills in the open court. For his small stature, Johnson displays the toughness and leadership coaches love.

Weaknesses: Unlike his older brother Vinnie, the younger Johnson has not proven he can be a consistent scorer at the NBA level. His outside shooting ability is suspect, although he followed up two straight seasons of sub-40-percent shooting by hitting better than 48 percent from the field in 47 games with the Spurs. If that continues, Johnson will stick. His defensive deficiencies would then become the next topic.

Analysis: Avery has the quickness and the point guard know-how, but Vinnie needs to work with him on his outside shot. His perimeter skills, though, are getting better. NBA people like his approach to the game and will give him every chance.

PLAYER SUMMARY

Will.............................create for others
Can't..................shoot like big brother
Expect ....toughness
Don't Expect.............................10 PPG
Fantasy Value $2-4
Card Value..5¢

COLLEGE STATISTICS

		G	FGP	FTP	RPG	PPG
84-85	CAM	33	.509	.618	0.9	4.3
86-87	SU	31	.439	.615	2.4	7.1
87-88	SU	30	.537	.688	2.8	11.4
Totals		94	.497	.641	2.0	7.5

NBA REGULAR-SEASON STATISTICS

				FGs		3-PT FGs		FTs		Rebounds						
		G	MIN	FG	PCT	FG	PCT	FT	PCT	OFF	TOT	AST	STL	BLK	PTS	PPG
88-89	SEA	43	291	29	.349	1	.111	9	.563	11	24	73	21	3	68	1.6
89-90	SEA	53	575	55	.387	1	.250	29	.725	21	43	162	26	1	140	2.6
90-91	DEN/SA	68	959	130	.469	1	.111	59	.678	22	77	230	47	4	320	4.7
Totals		164	1825	214	.426	3	.136	97	.678	54	144	465	94	8	528	3.2

BUCK JOHNSON

Team: Houston Rockets
Position: Forward
Height: 6'7" **Weight:** 206
Birthdate: January 3, 1964
NBA Experience: 5 years

College: Alabama
Acquired: 1st-round pick in 1986 draft (20th overall)

Background: Although he plays small forward in the NBA, Johnson was once a center at Alabama, where he paced the Crimson Tide in scoring and rebounding as a junior and senior. His pro career has been spent exclusively with Houston. He has been a full-time starter and double-digit scorer each of the past two years and is the only forward in Rockets history to record 60-plus blocks and 100-plus steals in a season.

Strengths: Johnson is recognized as a hard worker, which enhances his already impressive athletic ability. He loves dunking and runs the floor well enough to do a lot of it. He has improved his offensive game considerably and plays solid one-on-one defense.

Weaknesses: Although he has come a long way, Johnson is still not the scorer that most NBA small forwards are. Very simply, he does not shoot well from the perimeter. He also lacks the good dribbling and passing ability that the top small forwards possess.

Analysis: Johnson has tried to be more offensive minded, but it looks like he's peaked in the low teens. That's fine with Houston, which now needs more consistency from him. Johnson will never rank among the name small forwards, but he puts forth his best effort and does a decent job of holding better players in check.

PLAYER SUMMARY

Will	run the floor
Can't	shoot 3's
Expect	all-out effort
Don't Expect	20 PPG
Fantasy Value	$11-13
Card Value	8¢

COLLEGE STATISTICS

		G	FGP	FTP	RPG	PPG
82-83	ALA	32	.479	.636	4.5	8.3
83-84	ALA	28	.514	.730	8.5	17.0
84-85	ALA	33	.560	.712	9.4	16.0
85-86	ALA	29	.577	.832	8.3	20.7
Totals		122	.540	.739	7.6	15.3

NBA REGULAR-SEASON STATISTICS

				FGs		3-PT FGs		FTs		Rebounds						
		G	MIN	FG	PCT	FG	PCT	FT	PCT	OFF	TOT	AST	STL	BLK	PTS	PPG
86-87	HOU	60	520	94	.468	0	.000	40	.690	38	88	40	17	15	228	3.8
87-88	HOU	70	879	155	.520	1	.125	67	.736	77	168	49	30	26	378	5.4
88-89	HOU	67	1850	270	.524	1	.111	101	.754	114	286	126	64	35	642	9.6
89-90	HOU	82	2832	504	.495	2	.118	205	.759	113	381	252	104	62	1215	14.8
90-91	HOU	73	2279	416	.477	2	.133	157	.727	108	330	142	81	47	991	13.6
Totals		352	8360	1439	.495	6	.120	570	.741	450	1253	609	296	185	3454	9.8

EDDIE JOHNSON

Team: Seattle SuperSonics
Position: Forward
Height: 6'7" **Weight:** 215
Birthdate: May 1, 1959
NBA Experience: 10 years

College: Illinois
Acquired: Traded from Suns with 1st-round picks in 1991 and either 1993 or 1994 for Xavier McDaniel, 12/90

Background: Johnson set Illinois career records for scoring, rebounding, and field goals. He still ranks among the leaders in a number of categories for Sacramento, where he starred before taking a reserve role with Phoenix. He won the NBA's Sixth Man Award in 1988-89. Johnson was traded to Seattle in the 1990-91 season. He made 27 starts and finished third on the team in scoring.

Strengths: Johnson remains one of the best pure shooters in the league. He releases the ball quickly and possesses great range. He is most dangerous when coming off a pick behind the 3-point line. He also is a deadly free throw shooter.

Weaknesses: Traditionally a poor playoff performer, Johnson struggles when his jump shot is taken away in such settings. He does not go to the hoop with confidence and is not known for his passing skills. Johnson is a liability on defense and prefers to release on the break rather than go to the boards.

Analysis: Johnson is adept at what he does—shoot quick jumpers from long distance. He is best suited for a reserve role because of his defensive and rebounding deficiencies, but his scoring ability could make it difficult for the Sonics to keep him off the floor.

PLAYER SUMMARY

Will....................unload from anywhere
Can't.................................rebound
Expect........................offensive punch
Don't Expect.........................a stopper
Fantasy Value..............................$7-9
Card Value.....................................10¢

COLLEGE STATISTICS

		G	FGP	FTP	RPG	PPG
77-78	ILL	27	.427	.741	3.1	8.1
78-79	ILL	30	.415	.531	5.7	12.1
79-80	ILL	35	.462	.655	8.9	17.4
80-81	ILL	29	.494	.756	9.2	17.2
Totals		121	.454	.671	6.9	14.0

NBA REGULAR-SEASON STATISTICS

		G	MIN	FG	PCT	FG	PCT	FT	PCT	OFF	TOT	AST	STL	BLK	PTS	PPG
				FGs		3-PT FGs		FTs		Rebounds						
81-82	KC	74	1517	295	.459	1	.091	99	.664	128	322	109	50	14	690	9.3
82-83	KC	82	2933	677	.494	20	.282	247	.779	191	501	216	70	20	1621	19.8
83-84	KC	82	2920	753	.485	20	.313	268	.810	165	455	296	76	21	1794	21.9
84-85	KC	82	3029	769	.491	13	.241	325	.871	151	407	273	83	22	1876	22.9
85-86	SAC	82	2514	623	.475	4	.200	280	.816	173	419	214	54	17	1530	18.7
86-87	SAC	81	2457	606	.463	37	.314	267	.829	146	353	251	42	19	1516	18.7
87-88	PHO	73	2177	533	.480	24	.255	204	.850	121	318	180	33	9	1294	17.7
88-89	PHO	70	2043	608	.497	71	.413	217	.868	91	306	162	47	7	1504	21.5
89-90	PHO	64	1811	411	.453	70	.380	188	.917	69	246	107	32	10	1080	16.9
90-91	PHO/SEA	81	2085	543	.484	39	.325	229	.891	107	271	111	58	9	1354	16.7
Totals		771	23486	5818	.480	299	.329	2324	.834	1342	3598	1919	545	148	14259	18.5

KEVIN JOHNSON

Team: Phoenix Suns
Position: Guard
Height: 6'1" **Weight:** 190
Birthdate: March 4, 1966
NBA Experience: 4 years
College: California

Acquired: Traded from Cavaliers with Mark West, Tyrone Corbin, 1988 1st- and 2nd-round picks, and a 1989 2nd-round pick for Larry Nance, Mike Sanders, and a 1988 2nd-round pick, 2/88

Background: Johnson concluded his college career as California's all-time leader in scoring, assists, and steals. He recorded the first triple-double in Pac-10 history and was a two-time all-conference selection. Johnson has averaged more than 20 points and ten assists per game in each of his three full seasons with Phoenix. He won the league's Most Improved Player Award in 1988-89. Johnson led the Suns in scoring, assists, and steals in 1990-91, played in his second straight All-Star Game, and won the J. Walter Kennedy Citizenship Award.

Strengths: One frightening gift runs through everything Johnson does: unbelievable quickness. Because of it, there is virtually no one capable of stopping his one-on-one penetration. Leave him open from outside and he will bury jumpers up to 20 feet. His passing skills are made more devastating because he draws multiple defenders every time he goes to the hoop.

Weaknesses: Johnson does not possess consistent 3-point range. And who needs it when you can penetrate like Johnson and have teammates named Jeff Hornacek and Tom Chambers?

Analysis: His lightning quickness not only opens scoring chances for himself, but it makes everyone around him a notch better. Coming off the best shooting season of his pro career, Johnson is well on his way to solidifying his status as one of the most dangerous players—at any position—in the NBA.

PLAYER SUMMARY

Will	drive and dish
Can't	be contained
Expect	20 PPG, 10 APG
Don't Expect	many 3's
Fantasy Value	$48-51
Card Value	40¢

COLLEGE STATISTICS

		G	FGP	FTP	RPG	PPG
83-84	CAL	28	.510	.721	3.0	9.7
84-85	CAL	27	.450	.662	3.9	12.9
85-86	CAL	29	.490	.815	3.6	15.6
86-87	CAL	34	.471	.819	3.9	17.2
Totals		118	.477	.757	3.6	14.0

NBA REGULAR-SEASON STATISTICS

			FGs		3-PT FGs		FTs		Rebounds						
	G	MIN	FG	PCT	FG	PCT	FT	PCT	OFF	TOT	AST	STL	BLK	PTS	PPG
87-88 CLE/PHO	80	1917	275	.461	5	.208	177	.839	36	191	437	103	24	732	9.1
88-89 PHO	81	3179	570	.505	2	.091	508	.882	46	340	991	135	24	1650	20.4
89-90 PHO	74	2782	578	.499	8	.195	501	.838	42	270	846	95	14	1665	22.5
90-91 PHO	77	2772	591	.516	9	.205	519	.843	54	271	781	163	11	1710	22.2
Totals	312	10650	2014	.500	24	.183	1705	.852	178	1072	3055	496	73	5757	18.5

MAGIC JOHNSON

Team: Los Angeles Lakers
Position: Guard
Height: 6'9" **Weight:** 220
Birthdate: August 14, 1959

NBA Experience: 12 years
College: Michigan St.
Acquired: 1st-round pick in 1979 draft
(1st overall)

Background: Magic Johnson, one of the greatest players to ever play the game, guided Michigan State to the 1979 NCAA title and has led the Lakers to five NBA championships. He was the first rookie to be named MVP of the NBA Finals and he has gone on to amass three league MVP Awards. Johnson surpassed Oscar Robertson as the all-time assists king in 1990-91.

Strengths: Magic does just about everything at its highest level. He is an unparalleled passer with superb vision and great penetration moves. He has become a good outside shooter with 3-point range and knows when to score and when to feed others. His almost routine triple-doubles are a statement about his rebounding ability. He is also a 90-plus-percent free throw shooter.

Weaknesses: Johnson is not able to defend quicker guards like he once could. He has lost a step, but still runs the court with great precision.

Analysis: What can be said about the Magic man that is not better expressed by his continued brilliant play? He has re-invented the point-guard position and breathed life into a league that was struggling. What's frightening is that, while he has slowed down, he continues to improve in other areas.

PLAYER SUMMARY	
Will	do whatever it takes
Can't	run like he used to
Expect	early Hall induction
Don't Expect	complacency
Fantasy Value	$85-87
Card Value	30¢

COLLEGE STATISTICS

		G	FGP	FTP	RPG	PPG
77-78	MSU	30	.458	.785	7.9	17.0
78-79	MSU	32	.468	.842	7.3	17.1
Totals		62	.463	.816	7.6	17.1

NBA REGULAR-SEASON STATISTICS

		G	MIN	FGs FG	FGs PCT	3-PT FGs FG	3-PT FGs PCT	FTs FT	FTs PCT	Rebounds OFF	Rebounds TOT	AST	STL	BLK	PTS	PPG
79-80	LAL	77	2795	503	.530	7	.226	374	.810	166	596	563	187	41	1387	18.0
80-81	LAL	37	1371	312	.532	3	.176	171	.760	101	320	317	127	27	798	21.6
81-82	LAL	78	2991	556	.537	6	.207	329	.760	252	751	743	208	34	1447	18.6
82-83	LAL	79	2907	511	.548	0	.000	304	.800	214	683	829	176	47	1326	16.8
83-84	LAL	67	2567	441	.565	6	.207	290	.810	99	491	875	150	49	1178	17.6
84-85	LAL	77	2781	504	.561	7	.189	391	.843	90	476	968	113	25	1406	18.3
85-86	LAL	72	2578	483	.526	10	.233	378	.871	85	426	907	113	16	1354	18.8
86-87	LAL	80	2904	683	.522	8	.205	535	.848	122	504	977	138	36	1909	23.9
87-88	LAL	72	2637	490	.492	11	.196	417	.853	88	449	858	114	13	1408	19.6
88-89	LAL	77	2886	579	.509	59	.314	513	.911	111	607	988	138	22	1730	22.5
89-90	LAL	79	2937	546	.480	106	.384	567	.890	128	522	907	132	34	1765	22.3
90-91	LAL	79	2933	466	.477	80	.320	519	.906	105	551	989	102	17	1531	19.4
Totals		874	32287	6074	.521	303	.298	4788	.848	1561	6376	9921	1698	361	17239	19.7

VINNIE JOHNSON

Team: Detroit Pistons
Position: Guard
Height: 6'2" **Weight:** 200
Birthdate: September 1, 1956

NBA Experience: 12 years
College: McLennan; Baylor
Acquired: Traded from SuperSonics for Greg Kelser, 11/81

Background: Johnson led the Southwest Conference in scoring as a senior at Baylor, where he was chosen second-team All-America. After starting his pro career with Seattle, he has been one of the NBA's premier bench scorers as a Detroit Piston. He was runner-up for the Sixth Man Award in 1986-87 and hit the winning shot in the deciding game of the Pistons' 1990 NBA Finals victory. In a surprise move, Detroit waived Johnson in September.

Strengths: His nickname says it all; "The Microwave" can heat up in a hurry. When he does, he is almost impossible to stop. No one gets his shots like Johnson does, with his twisting jumpers in traffic that he seems to like more than wide-open opportunities. His playground game is lethal.

Weaknesses: Age is catching up with Johnson. The past two seasons have been his worst shooting campaigns since his rookie year. When he is cold, he can be ice cold. Those nights are becoming more frequent.

Analysis: Though Detroit gave Vinnie the boot, he will surely latch on with another team. As long as he continues to get his shot at will and finds those grooves in which everything falls, a team will gladly accept the "off" nights.

PLAYER SUMMARY

Will.....................................get his shots
Can't.......................regain consistency
Expect.........................15-point quarters
Don't Expect ....high FG pct.
Fantasy Value.................................$3-5
Card Value..8¢

COLLEGE STATISTICS

		G	FGP	FTP	RPG	PPG
75-76	McL	35	—	—	—	27.6
76-77	McL	31	—	—	—	29.5
77-78	BAY	25	.501	.660	5.6	23.0
78-79	BAY	26	.522	.776	4.9	25.2
Totals		117	—	—	—	26.6

NBA REGULAR-SEASON STATISTICS

				FGs		3-PT FGs		FTs		Rebounds						
		G	MIN	FG	PCT	FG	PCT	FT	PCT	OFF	TOT	AST	STL	BLK	PTS	PPG
79-80	SEA	38	325	45	.391	0	.000	31	.795	19	55	54	19	4	121	3.2
80-81	SEA	81	2311	419	.534	1	.200	214	.793	193	366	341	78	20	1053	13.0
81-82	SEA/DET	74	1295	217	.489	3	.250	107	.754	82	159	171	56	25	544	7.4
82-83	DET	82	2511	520	.513	11	.275	245	.778	167	353	301	93	49	1296	15.8
83-84	DET	82	1909	426	.473	4	.211	207	.753	130	237	271	44	19	1063	13.0
84-85	DET	82	2093	428	.454	5	.185	190	.769	134	252	325	71	20	1051	12.8
85-86	DET	79	1978	465	.467	2	.154	165	.771	119	226	269	80	23	1097	13.9
86-87	DET	78	2166	533	.462	4	.286	158	.786	123	257	300	92	16	1228	15.7
87-88	DET	82	1935	425	.443	5	.208	147	.677	90	231	267	58	18	1002	12.2
88-89	DET	82	2073	462	.464	13	.295	193	.734	109	255	242	74	17	1130	13.8
89-90	DET	82	1972	334	.431	5	.147	131	.668	108	256	255	71	13	804	9.8
90-91	DET	82	2390	406	.434	11	.324	135	.646	110	280	271	75	15	958	11.7
Totals		924	22958	4680	.467	64	.240	1923	.743	1384	2927	3067	811	239	11347	12.3

CHARLES JONES

Team: Washington Bullets
Position: Forward
Height: 6'9" **Weight:** 225
Birthdate: April 3, 1957

NBA Experience: 8 years
College: Albany St.
Acquired: Signed as a free agent, 2/85

Background: Jones was a standout shot-blocker and rebounder while at Albany State, averaging 15 boards per game as a senior. He spent four seasons in the CBA and two overseas. Washington was the seventh NBA team to sign Jones and he led the Bullets in blocked shots in 1988-89 and 1989-90. He missed the final 19 games of 1990-91 with a pulled groin. Brothers Caldwell, Will, and Major are former NBA players.

Strengths: Jones is in the NBA for one reason: defense. He used to block shots solely because of his height, but he has perfected his timing to become one of the more skilled shot-swatters in the league. His 2.00 blocks per game ranked 12th in the league in 1990-91.

Weaknesses: As his career scoring average indicates, Jones is pretty much a non-factor on offense. He possesses no jump shot and his back-to-the-bucket moves are nearly as invisible. He never looks for opportunities, hence they never come. Though he blocks shots, Jones's rail-thin frame works against him when he is asked to defend big men on the blocks.

Analysis: Jones is the definitive journeyman who does one thing well: block shots. However, he does that one thing well enough to have played eight years in the NBA. As a back-up defensive specialist, he may have another year or two remaining at the NBA level.

PLAYER SUMMARY

Will ....block shots
Can't ....score
Expect ....a role player
Don't Expect ....10 PPG
Fantasy Value $2-4
Card Value ....5¢

COLLEGE STATISTICS

		G	FGP	FTP	RPG	PPG
75-76	ASU	24	.515	.457	8.3	9.5
76-77	ASU	27	.479	.464	13.9	11.5
77-78	ASU	27	.536	.680	13.6	13.5
78-79	ASU	29	.517	.680	15.1	14.8
Totals		107	.512	.598	12.9	12.5

NBA REGULAR-SEASON STATISTICS

		G	MIN	FGs FG	FGs PCT	3-PT FGs FG	3-PT FGs PCT	FTs FT	FTs PCT	Rebounds OFF	Rebounds TOT	AST	STL	BLK	PTS	PPG
83-84	PHI	1	3	0	.000	0	.000	1	.250	0	0	0	0	0	1	1.0
84-85	CHI/WAS	31	667	67	.528	0	.000	40	.690	71	184	26	22	79	174	5.6
85-86	WAS	81	1609	129	.508	0	.000	54	.628	122	321	76	57	133	312	3.9
86-87	WAS	79	1609	118	.474	0	.000	48	.632	144	356	80	67	165	284	3.6
87-88	WAS	69	1313	72	.407	0	.000	53	.707	106	325	59	53	113	197	2.9
88-89	WAS	53	1154	60	.480	0	.000	16	.640	77	257	42	39	76	136	2.6
89-90	WAS	81	2240	94	.508	0	.000	68	.648	145	504	139	50	197	256	3.2
90-91	WAS	62	1499	67	.540	0	.000	29	.580	119	359	48	51	124	163	2.6
Totals		457	10094	607	.488	0	.000	309	.645	784	2306	470	339	887	1523	3.3

MICHAEL JORDAN

Team: Chicago Bulls
Position: Guard
Height: 6'6" **Weight:** 198
Birthdate: February 17, 1963

NBA Experience: 7 years
College: North Carolina
Acquired: 1st-round pick in 1984 draft
(3rd overall)

Background: At North Carolina, Jordan hit the winning basket as a freshman in the 1982 NCAA championship game and went on to earn consensus All-America recognition and a 1984 Olympic gold medal. After entering the NBA a year early, he earned Rookie of the Year honors in 1984-85 and has been voted an All-Star starter in each of his seven years in the league. In 1990-91, Jordan copped his second league MVP Award and fifth straight scoring title, then earned NBA Finals MVP honors by leading the Bulls to their first NBA title.

Strengths: Jordan plays virtually every aspect of the game on its highest level. Sometimes overshadowed by his gravity-defying jams and huge scoring games are his passing, ball-handling, rebounding, and defensive talents. Last season, Jordan answered the critics who said he does not make his teammates better, as he averaged more than ten assists in a championship crushing of the Lakers.

Weaknesses: This is a reach, but Jordan has criticized teammates from time to time over the past two seasons. However, it's tough to argue with the results.

Analysis: Jordan may well be the most gifted player to ever pick up a basketball. His career scoring average is the highest in ABA/NBA history, he has a title to his credit, and he excels in every other aspect of the game. Magic Johnson and Larry Bird, both in their 30s, have been forced to make way for the NBA's undeniable feature attraction, Air Jordan.

PLAYER SUMMARY

Will........................dominate all phases
Can't...............be checked by one man
Expect...........................more title bids
Don't Expect.............less than 30 PPG
Fantasy Value..........................$95-100
Card Value.................................$1-1.50

COLLEGE STATISTICS

		G	FGP	FTP	RPG	PPG
81-82	NC	34	.534	.722	4.4	13.5
82-83	NC	36	.345	.737	5.5	20.0
83-84	NC	31	.551	.779	5.3	19.6
Totals		101	.465	.748	5.0	17.7

NBA REGULAR-SEASON STATISTICS

			FGs		3-PT FGs		FTs		Rebounds						
		G	MIN	FG	PCT	FG	PCT	FT	PCT	OFF	TOT	AST	STL	BLK	PTS	PPG
84-85	CHI	82	3144	837	.515	9	.173	630	.845	167	534	481	196	69	2313	28.2
85-86	CHI	18	451	150	.457	3	.167	105	.840	23	64	53	37	21	408	22.7
86-87	CHI	82	3281	1098	.482	12	.182	833	.857	166	430	377	236	125	3041	37.1
87-88	CHI	82	3311	1069	.535	7	.132	723	.841	139	449	485	259	131	2868	35.0
88-89	CHI	81	3255	966	.538	27	.276	674	.850	149	652	650	234	65	2633	32.5
89-90	CHI	82	3197	1034	.526	92	.376	593	.848	143	565	519	227	54	2753	33.6
90-91	CHI	82	3034	990	.539	29	.312	571	.851	118	492	453	223	83	2580	31.5
Totals		509	19673	6144	.520	179	.286	4129	.849	905	3186	3018	1412	548	16596	32.6

SHAWN KEMP

Team: Seattle SuperSonics
Position: Forward
Height: 6'10" **Weight:** 245
Birthdate: November 26, 1969
NBA Experience: 2 years

College: None
Acquired: 1st-round pick in 1989 draft (17th overall)

Background: Kemp never played a minute of college basketball before entering the NBA draft. He was a Proposition 48 casualty at Kentucky, transferred to Trinity Junior College amid scrutiny, then opted for the draft. His athletic dunks caught immediate attention as a rookie and he became a starter for the Sonics in his second year (1990-91), when Xavier McDaniel was traded. Kemp more than doubled his scoring and shot over 50 percent from the field.

Strengths: One Kemp dunk is enough for one to see that this youngster is blessed with dominating physical ability. He is strong, has a great vertical leap, and knows his way around the court. His quickness to the hoop and powerful finishes are awe-inspiring. Kemp's defense has come a long way and he is not afraid to challenge. He has impressed coaches with his hard work in practice.

Weaknesses: Perimeter shooting is still fairly new to Kemp, and he is not consistent enough with the jump shot to pull defenders outside. His free throw touch could also stand some improvement.

Analysis: Some questioned the drafting of an untested 19-year-old in the first round, but Seattle obviously got a bargain. Kemp is a legitimate superstar who will only get better. He finished fourth in the NBA Slam Dunk Contest as a rookie and second in 1990-91. He is worth the price of admission and has a great future.

PLAYER SUMMARY	
Will	attack the hoop
Can't	shoot with range
Expect	heads to turn
Don't Expect	slow development
Fantasy Value	$18-21
Card Value	25¢

COLLEGE STATISTICS

—DID NOT PLAY—

NBA REGULAR-SEASON STATISTICS

	G	MIN	FGs FG	FGs PCT	3-PT FGs FG	3-PT FGs PCT	FTs FT	FTs PCT	Rebounds OFF	Rebounds TOT	AST	STL	BLK	PTS	PPG
89-90 SEA	81	1120	203	.479	2	.167	117	.736	146	346	26	47	70	525	6.5
90-91 SEA	81	2442	462	.508	2	.167	288	.661	267	679	144	77	123	1214	15.0
Totals	162	3562	665	.499	4	.167	405	.681	413	1025	170	124	193	1739	10.7

STEVE KERR

Team: Cleveland Cavaliers
Position: Guard
Height: 6'3" **Weight:** 180
Birthdate: September 27, 1965
NBA Experience: 3 years

College: Arizona
Acquired: Traded from Suns for a 1993 2nd-round pick, 9/89

Background: Kerr was a second-team All-American as a senior at Arizona, where he set a Pac-10 mark in 1987-88 by shooting .573 from 3-point range. He is the NBA's all-time leader in 3-point field goal percentage at .489, although he has served mostly in a reserve role with Phoenix and Cleveland. He made his third four-point play in 1990-91 vs. Indiana.

Strengths: Kerr can flat-out shoot the ball. In 1989-90, he became one of two players in NBA history to shoot better than 50 percent from 3-point range (Jon Sundvold's record is .522). He is consistently around 85 percent from the free throw line. He works hard and plays with smarts.

Weaknesses: Yes, he can shoot. But can he get his own shot? In most cases, the answer is no. Kerr does very little off the dribble, largely because he is a step slower than the average NBA point guard. He does not create much for teammates either. He makes sacrifices defensively but again is limited by his lack of foot speed.

Analysis: Leave him open, and Kerr can tear you apart. Get in his face, however, and his game takes a serious plunge. Kerr is a coach's player. He is a dead-eye shooter and has solid ball skills, but he is best used in a reserve role when his team needs an offensive lift. As a starting point man, he is neither quick nor creative enough to generate much off the dribble.

PLAYER SUMMARY	
Will	hit 3's
Can't	create own shots
Expect	hard work
Don't Expect	drives and dishes
Fantasy Value	$2-4
Card Value	8¢

COLLEGE STATISTICS

		G	FGP	FTP	RPG	PPG
83-84	ARIZ	28	.516	.692	1.2	7.1
84-85	ARIZ	31	.568	.803	2.4	10.0
85-86	ARIZ	32	.540	.899	3.2	14.4
87-88	ARIZ	38	.559	.824	2.0	12.6
Totals		129	.548	.815	2.2	11.2

NBA REGULAR-SEASON STATISTICS

		G	MIN	FGs FG	FGs PCT	3-PT FGs FG	3-PT FGs PCT	FTs FT	FTs PCT	Rebounds OFF	Rebounds TOT	AST	STL	BLK	PTS	PPG
88-89	PHO	26	157	20	.435	8	.471	6	.667	3	17	24	7	0	54	2.1
89-90	CLE	78	1664	192	.444	73	.507	63	.863	12	98	248	45	7	520	6.7
90-91	CLE	57	905	99	.444	28	.452	45	.849	5	37	131	29	4	271	4.8
Totals		161	2726	311	.444	109	.489	114	.844	20	152	403	81	11	845	5.2

JEROME KERSEY

Team: Portland Trail Blazers
Position: Forward
Height: 6'7" **Weight:** 225
Birthdate: June 26, 1962
NBA Experience: 7 years

College: Longwood College
Acquired: 2nd-round pick in 1984
draft (46th overall)

Background: Kersey rewrote the record books at NAIA Longwood College, where he is the all-time leader in points, rebounds, steals, and blocked shots. He started his pro career modestly before receiving consideration for the Most Improved Player Award in 1987-88. Since then, he has been an explosive scorer and rebounder for Portland. In the last 17 games of the 1990-91 season, he averaged nearly 17 points and shot 51.1 percent from the field.

Strengths: Running the floor and finishing the break stand out most with Kersey. He is athletic and drives to the hoop aggressively. He is one of the better rebounders among small forwards and rarely gets outworked by anyone. He possesses above-average defensive skills.

Weaknesses: Kersey sometimes plays out of control, and he is a much better finisher than he is a creator for his teammates. He is not a pure shooter and is prone to big slumps from the floor and the free throw line.

Analysis: The knock on Kersey has been his inability to hit from outside, but he has changed that to become one of the name forwards in the NBA. No, he is not to be confused with a jump-shooter. But he can no longer be left alone from 15 feet, and that enhances those high-flying drives.

PLAYER SUMMARY

Will....................................finish breaks
Can't........................pose as playmaker
Expect..........................relentless effort
Don't Expect.......................great range
Fantasy Value..............................$6-8
Card Value...10¢

COLLEGE STATISTICS

		G	FGP	FTP	RPG	PPG
80-81	LONG	28	.629	.586	8.9	16.9
81-82	LONG	23	.585	.633	11.3	17.0
82-83	LONG	25	.560	.608	10.8	14.6
83-84	LONG	27	.521	.606	14.2	19.6
Totals		103	.570	.607	11.3	17.0

NBA REGULAR-SEASON STATISTICS

		G	MIN	FGs FG	FGs PCT	3-PT FGs FG	3-PT FGs PCT	FTs FT	FTs PCT	Rebounds OFF	Rebounds TOT	AST	STL	BLK	PTS	PPG
84-85	POR	77	958	178	.478	0	.000	117	.646	95	206	63	49	29	473	6.1
85-86	POR	79	1217	258	.549	0	.000	156	.681	137	293	83	85	32	672	8.5
86-87	POR	82	2088	373	.509	1	.043	262	.720	201	496	194	122	77	1009	12.3
87-88	POR	79	2888	611	.499	3	.200	291	.735	211	657	243	127	65	1516	19.2
88-89	POR	76	2716	533	.469	6	.286	258	.694	246	629	243	137	84	1330	17.5
89-90	POR	82	2843	519	.478	3	.150	269	.690	251	690	188	121	63	1310	16.0
90-91	POR	73	2359	424	.478	4	.308	232	.709	169	481	227	101	76	1084	14.8
Totals		548	15069	2896	.490	17	.168	1585	.702	1310	3452	1241	742	426	7394	13.5

ALEC KESSLER

Team: Miami Heat
Position: Forward/Center
Height: 6'11" **Weight:** 245
Birthdate: January 13, 1967
NBA Experience: 1 year

College: Georgia
Acquired: Draft rights traded from Rockets for draft rights to Dave Jamerson and Carl Herrera, 6/90

Background: Kessler left Georgia as the school's all-time leading scorer and third-leading rebounder, having paced the Bulldogs in both categories as a senior. He was named Scholar-Athlete of the Year by the USBWA in 1989 and 1990. Kessler appeared in 78 games as a rookie with Miami and started 18, even though he missed all of training camp and the preseason with a stress fracture in his left tibia.

Strengths: Kessler has a nice jump shot from 20 feet and in, has good hands, and possesses the potential to become a solid NBA rebounder. He displays great work habits and has a tremendous head on his shoulders, as evidenced by his honors degree in microbiology. He plays within his limitations.

Weaknesses: The word most often used to describe Kessler's low-post game is mechanical. Perhaps he thinks too much for his own good when he catches the ball in the paint. He must develop a "go-to" move, then master it so it becomes automatic. He possesses below-average speed and can be defended straight-up. Slow feet hurt him on defense as well.

Analysis: Kessler looks like a solid—though unspectacular—player who could carve out a pretty nice career for himself. There are many areas in which he needs to improve, but he shows a willingness to learn that new Heat coach Kevin Loughery will love. Kessler prefers the high post and does a decent job there.

PLAYER SUMMARY

Will	stick the jumper
Can't	live in the paint
Expect	coachability
Don't Expect	the spectacular
Fantasy Value	$4-6
Card Value	12¢

COLLEGE STATISTICS

		G	FGP	FTP	RPG	PPG
86-87	GA	28	.618	.714	3.4	5.0
87-88	GA	35	.492	.787	5.6	12.6
88-89	GA	31	.487	.759	9.7	19.2
89-90	GA	29	.491	.757	10.3	21.0
Totals		123	.499	.762	7.3	14.5

NBA REGULAR-SEASON STATISTICS

				FGs		3-PT FGs		FTs		Rebounds						
		G	MIN	FG	PCT	FG	PCT	FT	PCT	OFF	TOT	AST	STL	BLK	PTS	PPG
90-91	MIA	78	1259	199	.425	0	.000	88	.672	115	336	31	17	26	486	6.2
Totals		78	1259	199	.425	0	.000	88	.672	115	336	31	17	26	486	6.2

BO KIMBLE

Team: Los Angeles Clippers
Position: Guard
Height: 6'5" **Weight:** 190
Birthdate: April 9, 1966
NBA Experience: 1 year

College: Southern Cal.; Loyola Marymount
Acquired: 1st-round pick in 1990 draft (8th overall)

Background: Kimble's college career at Loyola Marymount was highly publicized, largely because of his friendship with Hank Gathers, who collapsed in a game and died of a heart ailment. Kimble led the nation in scoring as a senior and steered LMU into the NCAA round of eight. He started 22 of his first 23 games as a rookie before being benched. He finished the year on a down note.

Strengths: Kimble has great range from the perimeter and knows how to get his shots. He runs the floor well and is a dangerous pull-up man when he gets it going. He displays maturity beyond his years.

Weaknesses: Quite simply, Kimble shot the ball poorly in his first NBA season and did not make solid decisions. He totaled more turnovers than assists (by one), a sure way to play oneself onto the bench. His defense was also not up to expectations.

Analysis: What started out as a season of promise ended in frustration for the former college scoring champ. Until he starts to bury those long-range shots that earned him acclaim at LMU, he will not warrant much playing time in the NBA. He sat out 11 games due to coach's decision. When your job is to score, 38-percent shooting is not going to earn a living. The verdict is still out.

PLAYER SUMMARY

Will..launch bombs
Can't..distribute
Expect.........................improved FG pct.
Don't Expect...........................surrender
Fantasy Value...............................$4-6
Card Value...30¢

COLLEGE STATISTICS

		G	FGP	FTP	RPG	PPG
85-86	USC	28	.465	.771	3.6	12.1
87-88	LOY	26	.439	.786	3.1	22.2
88-89	LOY	18	.459	.756	4.2	16.8
89-90	LOY	32	.529	.862	7.7	35.3
Totals		104	.484	.822	4.9	22.6

NBA REGULAR-SEASON STATISTICS

			MIN	FGs		3-PT FGs		FTs		Rebounds						
		G	MIN	FG	PCT	FG	PCT	FT	PCT	OFF	TOT	AST	STL	BLK	PTS	PPG
90-91	LAC	62	1004	159	.380	19	.292	92	.773	42	119	76	30	8	429	6.9
Totals		62	1004	159	.380	19	.292	92	.773	42	119	76	30	8	429	6.9

BERNARD KING

Team: Washington Bullets
Position: Forward
Height: 6'7" **Weight:** 205
Birthdate: December 4, 1956

NBA Experience: 13 years
College: Tennessee
Acquired: Signed as a free agent, 10/87

Background: King was a consensus All-American at Tennessee before leaving after his junior year for the NBA. He won the NBA scoring title with the Knicks in 1984-85 and led his hometown team in scoring for three years. A career-threatening knee injury in 1985 kept King out the entire 1985-86 season and all but six games of 1986-87 before he made his return with Washington in 1987-88. He made his fourth All-Star appearance in 1991 and finished third in the league in scoring. A sore lower back sidelined him for 16 of the last 19 games.

Strengths: King can still score with the best of them. He may have lost a step, but his post-up moves remain highly effective and his repertoire from the wing keeps defenders guessing. King simply knows how to put the ball in the hole.

Weaknesses: On defense, the effects of age and injury are obvious. King generally tries to better his man by outscoring him, not by stopping him.

Analysis: King's comeback over the last few seasons has been one of basketball's most compelling stories. He ranks sixth on the all-time NBA list for 50-point games with eight, and two of those have come after his return from the injury. The sore back may be a bad sign at age 34.

PLAYER SUMMARY

Will .... get his points
Can't .... regain quickness
Expect .... 20 PPG
Don't Expect .... a defensive stopper
Fantasy Value $10-12
Card Value .... 10-20¢

COLLEGE STATISTICS

		G	FGP	FTP	RPG	PPG
74-75	TENN	25	.622	.782	12.3	26.4
75-76	TENN	25	.573	.669	13.0	25.2
76-77	TENN	26	.578	.712	14.3	25.8
Totals		76	.590	.719	13.2	25.8

NBA REGULAR-SEASON STATISTICS

				FGs		3-PT FGs		FTs		Rebounds						
		G	MIN	FG	PCT	FG	PCT	FT	PCT	OFF	TOT	AST	STL	BLK	PTS	PPG
77-78	NJ	79	3092	798	.479	0	.000	313	.677	265	751	193	122	36	1909	24.2
78-79	NJ	82	2859	710	.522	0	.000	349	.564	251	669	295	118	39	1769	21.6
79-80	UTA	19	419	71	.518	0	.000	34	.540	24	88	52	7	4	176	9.3
80-81	GS	87	2914	731	.588	2	.333	307	.703	178	551	287	72	34	1771	20.4
81-82	GS	79	2861	740	.566	1	.200	352	.705	140	469	282	78	23	1833	23.2
82-83	NY	68	2207	603	.528	0	.000	280	.722	99	326	195	90	13	1486	21.9
83-84	NY	77	2667	795	.572	0	.000	437	.779	123	394	164	75	17	2027	26.3
84-85	NY	55	2063	691	.530	1	.100	426	.772	114	317	204	71	15	1809	32.9
86-87	NY	6	214	52	.495	0	.000	32	.744	13	32	19	2	0	136	22.7
87-88	WAS	69	2044	470	.501	1	.167	247	.762	86	280	192	49	10	1188	17.2
88-89	WAS	81	2559	654	.477	5	.167	361	.819	133	384	294	64	13	1674	20.7
89-90	WAS	82	2687	711	.487	3	.130	412	.803	129	404	376	51	7	1837	22.4
90-91	WAS	64	2401	713	.472	8	.216	383	.790	114	319	292	56	16	1817	28.4
Totals		848	28987	7739	.518	21	.165	3933	.730	1669	4984	2845	855	227	19432	22.9

STACEY KING

Team: Chicago Bulls
Position: Forward/Center
Height: 6'11" **Weight:** 230
Birthdate: January 29, 1967
NBA Experience: 2 years

College: Oklahoma
Acquired: 1st-round pick in 1989 draft
(6th overall)

Background: King earned All-America and Big Eight Player of the Year status as a senior at Oklahoma, where he led the conference in scoring and rebounding as a senior. He was named second-team All-Rookie with Chicago in 1989-90, steadily improving his numbers through the season. In 1990-91, however, his playing time decreased and he was suspended for a game in April for walking out of a practice.

Strengths: King runs the floor well for a big man and has shown some promise offensively. Although his jumper is nothing to speak of, he possesses a decent hook shot and has had some fine scoring games. The athletic ability is there.

Weaknesses: Although he will wear a championship ring because of it, the 1990-91 season in many ways was one King might like to forget. He complained about his playing time, earned the suspension, then rarely was called off the bench in the playoffs. His main problem is a lack of aggressiveness. Though nearly seven-feet tall, he gets murdered on the defensive boards and often makes poor decisions with the ball.

Analysis: The Bulls were thrilled to get King with the sixth pick in 1989; now they seemingly have no use for him. Much less heralded players (Will Perdue, Scott Williams) contributed in his place during the 1991 playoffs and will likely see more action. King will get another chance somewhere—perhaps even in Chicago—and will have to use it wisely. His 1991 training camp could be crucial.

PLAYER SUMMARY

Will.....................................run the court
Can't ....bang the boards
Expect..........................another chance
Don't Expect...............reliable shooting
Fantasy Value................................$3-5
Card Value.....................................10¢

COLLEGE STATISTICS

		G	FGP	FTP	RPG	PPG
85-86	OKLA	14	.388	.744	3.8	6.0
86-87	OKLA	28	.438	.621	3.9	7.0
87-88	OKLA	39	.543	.675	8.5	22.3
88-89	OKLA	33	.524	.718	10.1	26.0
Totals		114	.516	.690	7.2	17.6

NBA REGULAR-SEASON STATISTICS

				FGs		3-PT FGs		FTs		Rebounds						
		G	MIN	FG	PCT	FG	PCT	FT	PCT	OFF	TOT	AST	STL	BLK	PTS	PPG
89-90	CHI	82	1777	267	.504	0	.000	194	.727	169	384	87	38	58	728	8.9
90-91	CHI	76	1198	156	.467	0	.000	107	.704	72	208	65	24	42	419	5.5
Totals		158	2975	423	.490	0	.000	301	.718	241	592	152	62	100	1147	7.3

GREG KITE

Team: Orlando Magic
Position: Center
Height: 6'11" **Weight:** 260
Birthdate: August 5, 1961
NBA Experience: 8 years

College: Brigham Young
Acquired: Signed as a free agent, 8/90

Background: Kite helped Danny Ainge rally BYU into the 1981 NCAA East Regional finals and finished his career ranked third on the school's rebounding charts. He was mostly a reserve center with Boston, the L.A. Clippers, and Charlotte before Sacramento picked him up in 1989-90. He started 47 games for the Kings that year, then all 82 for Orlando in 1990-91.

Strengths: Kite is a physical defender who gets under the skin of other centers. Some call him dirty. He bangs the body defensively, takes hard fouls, and knows his limitations on offense.

Weaknesses: Although he started all 82 games for the Magic, Kite could not be an offensive force in an empty gym. His 4.8-point scoring average was a career best. He has worked to improve his inside moves but was the least-dangerous starting center in basketball in 1990-91. He cannot handle the ball, find open men, or sink free throws.

Analysis: Any team forced to start Kite has huge problems. He is a reserve center at best, capable of frustrating better players for limited minutes. Because he plays within the boundaries of his limited game, he can stick in that kind of role. He is not an ideal starter.

PLAYER SUMMARY

Will ....irritate opponents
Can't...score
Expect........................physical defense
Don't Expect ....any offense
Fantasy Value $2-4
Card Value...5¢

COLLEGE STATISTICS

		G	FGP	FTP	RPG	PPG
79-80	BYU	21	.292	.480	4.1	1.9
80-81	BYU	32	.489	.495	8.5	8.3
81-82	BYU	30	.467	.446	7.8	6.2
82-83	BYU	29	.437	.571	8.8	7.7
Totals		112	.452	.504	7.6	6.4

NBA REGULAR-SEASON STATISTICS

				FGs		3-PT FGs		FTs		Rebounds						
		G	MIN	FG	PCT	FG	PCT	FT	PCT	OFF	TOT	AST	STL	BLK	PTS	PPG
83-84	BOS	35	197	30	.455	0	.000	5	.313	27	62	7	1	5	65	1.9
84-85	BOS	55	424	33	.375	0	.000	22	.688	38	89	17	3	10	88	1.6
85-86	BOS	64	464	34	.374	0	.000	15	.385	35	128	17	3	28	83	1.3
86-87	BOS	74	745	47	.427	0	.000	29	.382	61	169	27	17	46	123	1.7
87-88	BOS/LAC	53	1063	92	.449	0	.000	40	.506	85	264	47	19	58	224	4.2
88-89	LAC/CHA	70	942	65	.430	0	.000	20	.488	81	243	36	27	54	150	2.1
89-90	SAC	71	1515	101	.432	1	1.000	27	.500	131	377	76	31	51	230	3.2
90-91	ORL	82	2225	166	.491	0	.000	63	.512	189	588	59	25	81	395	4.8
Totals		504	7575	568	.443	1	.250	221	.480	647	1920	286	126	333	1358	2.7

JOE KLEINE

Team: Boston Celtics
Position: Center
Height: 7'0" **Weight:** 271
Birthdate: January 4, 1962
NBA Experience: 6 years

College: Notre Dame; Arkansas
Acquired: Traded from Kings with Ed Pinckney for Danny Ainge and Brad Lohaus, 2/89

Background: Kleine, who transferred to Arkansas after a year at Notre Dame, led the Razorbacks in scoring as a junior and senior and was a member of the gold medal-winning 1984 U.S. Olympic team. He started 60 games and averaged nearly ten points a game with Sacramento in 1987-88, his best statistical year as a pro. He has served as back-up center to Robert Parish in his two full years with Boston.

Strengths: Kleine uses his huge body to put the hurt on Celtic opponents. He rebounds, sets hard picks, and plays some of the most physical defense in the league. An intimidator, his fouls usually result in bruises. Kleine can hit the occasional short jumper or hook shot if left open. His work ethic is exemplary, making him a fan favorite.

Weaknesses: Finesse has no place in Kleine's game. He possesses poor hands, should be forbidden to dribble the ball, and is a below-average passer. His only real role in the offense is as a screen-setter and rebounder. Foul trouble would be a problem if he would ever earn more minutes.

Analysis: As a back-up center, Kleine does all that is asked of him. He gets the most out of his fouls, rebounds, plays defense, and throws his weight around. He can enter the game for eight or nine minutes at a time and not hurt the club. His offensive skills would have a long way to go if the Celtics—or anyone—were to consider promoting him to starter.

PLAYER SUMMARY

Will ....cause bruises
Can't............................play with finesse
Expect.........................physical defense
Don't Expect...............................10 PPG
Fantasy Value $2-4
Card Value..5¢

COLLEGE STATISTICS

		G	FGP	FTP	RPG	PPG
80-81	ND	29	.640	.750	2.4	2.6
82-83	ARK	30	.537	.633	7.3	13.3
83-84	ARK	32	.595	.773	9.2	18.2
84-85	ARK	35	.607	.720	8.4	22.1
Totals		126	.587	.723	7.0	14.5

NBA REGULAR-SEASON STATISTICS

		G	MIN	FGs FG	FGs PCT	3-PT FGs FG	3-PT FGs PCT	FTs FT	FTs PCT	Rebounds OFF	Rebounds TOT	AST	STL	BLK	PTS	PPG
85-86	SAC	80	1180	160	.465	0	.000	94	.723	113	373	46	24	34	414	5.2
86-87	SAC	79	1658	256	.471	0	.000	110	.786	173	483	71	35	30	622	7.9
87-88	SAC	82	1999	324	.472	0	.000	153	.814	179	579	93	28	59	801	9.8
88-89	SAC BOS	75	1411	175	.405	0	.000	134	.882	124	378	67	33	23	484	6.5
89-90	BOS	81	1365	176	.480	0	.000	83	.830	117	355	46	15	27	435	5.4
90-91	BOS	72	850	102	.468	0	.000	54	.783	71	244	21	15	14	258	3.6
Totals		469	8463	1193	.461	0	.000	628	.806	777	2412	344	150	187	3014	6.4

NEGELE KNIGHT

Team: Phoenix Suns
Position: Guard
Height: 6'1" **Weight:** 182
Birthdate: March 6, 1967
NBA Experience: 1 year

College: Dayton
Acquired: 2nd-round pick in 1990
draft (31st overall)

Background: Knight is Dayton's all-time assists leader and climbed his way to sixth on the school's career scoring list. As a rookie, he emerged as a reliable back-up to Kevin Johnson at the point. In five April starts when K.J. was injured, Knight scored 23.6 points and dished out 11 assists per outing.

Strengths: Penetration and passing come naturally to Knight, although he is an accomplished scoring threat as well. He pushes the ball up-court quickly and makes good decisions at high speed. He is confident with the ball and a hard-nosed defender who will not back down.

Weaknesses: Knight had college 3-point range but has yet to prove he can hit consistently from behind the NBA line. Youth and inexperience are about the only other weaknesses that became evident in his rookie season. Knight is talented but could stand some polish that comes only with more playing time.

Analysis: Had anyone known Knight would step forward and play so well as a rookie, he would have been snatched up in the first round. Instead, Phoenix has a back-up point guard being pursued by many teams as a potential starter. He could very well become one, and in the mean time is learning behind one of the best in the league. Knight went from second-rounder to valuable commodity in a flash.

PLAYER SUMMARY

Will..penetrate
Can't ....displace K.J.
Expect ....solid minutes
Don't Expect ....soft defense
Fantasy Value................................$1-3
Card Value...10¢

COLLEGE STATISTICS

		G	FGP	FTP	RPG	PPG
85-86	DAY	30	.379	.670	2.1	7.1
87-88	DAY	31	.472	.713	3.2	14.8
88-89	DAY	29	.366	.735	3.3	13.9
89-90	DAY	32	.503	.800	3.8	22.8
Totals		122	.440	.746	3.1	14.8

NBA REGULAR-SEASON STATISTICS

			FGs		3-PT FGs		FTs		Rebounds						
	G	MIN	FG	PCT	FG	PCT	FT	PCT	OFF	TOT	AST	STL	BLK	PTS	PPG
90-91 PHO	64	792	131	.425	6	.240	71	.602	20	71	191	20	7	339	5.3
Totals	64	792	131	.425	6	.240	71	.602	20	71	191	20	7	339	5.3

JON KONCAK

Team: Atlanta Hawks
Position: Center
Height: 7'0" **Weight:** 260
Birthdate: May 17, 1963
NBA Experience: 6 years

College: Southern Methodist
Acquired: 1st-round pick in 1985 draft
(5th overall)

Background: Koncak concluded his career at Southern Methodist as the school's all-time leader in rebounds, blocked shots, and field goal percentage and played for the gold medal-winning U.S. Olympic team in 1984. Most of his first five seasons with Atlanta were spent as a reserve, including an injury-plagued 1989-90 campaign. Before that season, he signed a six-year, $13.2 million contract. He started 61 games in 1990-91.

Strengths: The reason the Hawks were forced to match Detroit's huge contract offer two years ago is Koncak's value at the defensive end of the court. He bangs, can block shots, and plays sound position defense. Although no great athlete, he boxes his man out for rebounds.

Weaknesses: Looking at his offense alone, Koncak is a big-league bust. He never has been a capable scorer on the NBA level, but that aspect of his game seems to be getting worse. Last year, he scored just 4.1 PPG and recorded the worst field goal percentage of his career, despite his starting role. He is a poor foul shooter and does not handle the ball well.

Analysis: Koncak has not responded well since signing the huge contract. He started primarily out of necessity, lost that job for a seven-game stretch in March, and was nearly matched in minutes by 36-year-old Moses Malone. He must become at least passable offensively if he hopes to truly earn his keep.

PLAYER SUMMARY

Will ....play defense
Can't.............................become a scorer
Expect.............................big paychecks
Don't Expect.....................big numbers
Fantasy Value $1-2
Card Value...................................5¢

COLLEGE STATISTICS

		G	FGP	FTP	RPG	PPG
81-82	SMU	27	.461	.620	5.7	10.0
82-83	SMU	30	.527	.691	9.4	14.6
83-84	SMU	33	.621	.607	11.5	15.5
84-85	SMU	33	.592	.667	10.7	17.2
Totals		123	.559	.649	9.5	14.5

NBA REGULAR-SEASON STATISTICS

				FGs		3-PT FGs		FTs		Rebounds						
		G	MIN	FG	PCT	FG	PCT	FT	PCT	OFF	TOT	AST	STL	BLK	PTS	PPG
85-86	ATL	82	1695	263	.507	0	.000	156	.607	171	467	55	37	69	682	8.3
86-87	ATL	82	1684	169	.480	0	.000	125	.654	153	493	31	52	76	463	5.6
87-88	ATL	49	1073	98	.483	0	.000	83	.610	103	333	19	36	56	279	5.7
88-89	ATL	74	1531	141	.524	0	.000	63	.553	147	453	56	54	98	345	4.7
89-90	ATL	54	977	78	.614	0	.000	42	.532	58	226	23	38	34	198	3.7
90-91	ATL	77	1931	140	.436	1	.125	32	.593	101	375	124	74	76	313	4.1
Totals		418	8891	889	.496	1	.063	501	.603	733	2347	308	291	409	2280	5.5

LARRY KRYSTKOWIAK

Team: Milwaukee Bucks
Position: Forward
Height: 6'10" **Weight:** 240
Birthdate: September 23, 1964
NBA Experience: 5 years

College: Montana
Acquired: Traded from Spurs for Charles Davis and a 1989 2nd-round pick, 11/87

Background: Krystkowiak was named Big Sky Conference MVP three times and Academic All-American twice at Montana, finishing his career as the school's all-time scoring leader. He played his rookie year with San Antonio and became a starter in his second year with Milwaukee, but a knee injury in the 1989 playoffs slowed his progress. After ten months of rehab, he played 16 of the last 20 games of 1989-90, then missed all of the 1990-91 regular season after reconstructive surgery. He saw limited action in the 1991 playoffs.

Strengths: Krystkowiak's game is founded on heart and hustle. He is not afraid to sacrifice his body, playing aggressively in all phases. His work ethic during his grueling rehab mirrors his style on the court. He is a decent medium-range shooter who was improving steadily before the injury.

Weaknesses: The condition of his left knee remains the major concern with Krystkowiak. Speed was never a strong point in the first place. He lacks finesse both offensively and defensively. You'd have a hard time finding an NBA forward who blocks fewer shots than Krystkowiak.

Analysis: His recovery from a potentially career-ending knee injury speaks volumes for the kind of player and person Krystkowiak is. Hard work is second nature to him. If his knee holds up as the Milwaukee insiders expect it to, that same determination will continue to show in his game.

PLAYER SUMMARY

Will .... work relentlessly
Can't .... play with finesse
Expect .... a return to health
Don't Expect .... great speed
Fantasy Value $2-4
Card Value .... 8¢

COLLEGE STATISTICS

		G	FGP	FTP	RPG	PPG
82-83	MONT	28	.433	.688	4.3	4.9
83-84	MONT	30	.547	.805	10.5	18.0
84-85	MONT	30	.585	.840	10.2	21.1
85-86	MONT	32	.578	.760	11.4	22.2
Totals		120	.561	.790	9.2	16.8

NBA REGULAR-SEASON STATISTICS

				FGs		3-PT FGs		FTs		Rebounds						
		G	MIN	FG	PCT	FG	PCT	FT	PCT	OFF	TOT	AST	STL	BLK	PTS	PPG
86-87	SA	68	1004	170	.456	1	.083	110	.743	77	239	85	22	12	451	6.6
87-88	MIL	50	1050	128	.481	0	.000	103	.811	88	231	50	18	8	359	7.2
88-89	MIL	80	2472	362	.473	4	.333	289	.823	198	610	107	93	9	1017	12.7
89-90	MIL	16	381	43	.364	0	.000	26	.788	16	76	25	10	2	112	7.0
Totals		214	4907	703	.462	5	.172	528	.801	379	1156	267	143	31	1939	9.1

BILL LAIMBEER

Team: Detroit Pistons
Position: Center
Height: 6'11" **Weight:** 260
Birthdate: May 19, 1957
NBA Experience: 11 years

College: Notre Dame
Acquired: Traded from Cavaliers with Kenny Carr for Phil Hubbard, Paul Mokeski, and 1982 1st- and 2nd-round picks, 2/82

Background: Laimbeer helped Notre Dame to the school's only Final Four appearance in 1977. He spent his first pro season in Italy before spending a year and a half with Cleveland. Since joining Detroit, he has started 765 of the 766 games he has played, made four All-Star appearances, and won two NBA championships. The 1990-91 season was the worst shooting year of his career.

Strengths: Laimbeer is a proven winner. He works hard and demands the same from teammates. Although just about everyone outside of Detroit calls him dirty, he plays smart defense, draws charges (often with "flops"), sets screens, and pounds the boards. He became Detroit's all-time rebounding leader in 1990-91. When hot, Laimbeer remains one of the NBA's best-shooting big men.

Weaknesses: In 1990-91, Laimbeer lost the long-range bomb that had made him such a difficult center to defend. He has never enjoyed the low post. Laimbeer lacks the athletic skills like speed and jumping ability.

Analysis: There were whispers during the 1990-91 campaign of an impending retirement, but as long as there is a chance to win a title, the most hated player in the NBA will be loved in Detroit. Although not the weapon he was just a couple of years ago, Laimbeer still forces teammates to give it their all, as he does.

PLAYER SUMMARY

Will....................make teammates work
Can't............................score in low post
Expect.....................physical defense
Don't Expect..........national popularity
Fantasy Value.............................$7-10
Card Value.......................................10¢

COLLEGE STATISTICS

		G	FGP	FTP	RPG	PPG
75-76	ND	10	.492	.783	7.9	8.2
77-78	ND	29	.554	.677	6.6	8.1
78-79	ND	30	.538	.700	5.5	6.4
Totals		69	.538	.704	6.3	7.4

NBA REGULAR-SEASON STATISTICS

		G	MIN	FG (FGs)	PCT	FG (3-PT FGs)	PCT	FT (FTs)	PCT	OFF (Rebounds)	TOT	AST	STL	BLK	PTS	PPG
80-81	CLE	81	2460	337	.503	0	.000	117	.765	266	693	216	56	78	791	9.8
81-82	CLE/DET	80	1829	265	.494	4	.308	184	.793	234	617	100	39	64	718	9.0
82-83	DET	82	2871	436	.497	2	.154	245	.790	282	993	263	51	118	1119	13.6
83-84	DET	82	2864	553	.530	0	.000	316	.866	329	1003	149	49	84	1422	17.3
84-85	DET	82	2892	595	.506	4	.222	244	.797	295	1013	154	69	71	1438	17.5
85-86	DET	82	2891	545	.492	4	.286	266	.834	305	1075	146	59	65	1360	16.6
86-87	DET	82	2854	506	.501	6	.286	245	.894	243	955	151	72	69	1263	15.4
87-88	DET	82	2897	455	.493	13	.333	187	.874	199	832	199	66	78	1110	13.5
88-89	DET	81	2640	449	.499	30	.349	178	.776	138	776	177	51	100	1106	13.7
89-90	DET	82	2675	380	.484	57	.361	164	.854	166	780	171	57	84	981	12.1
90-91	DET	82	2668	372	.478	37	.296	123	.837	173	737	157	38	56	904	11.0
Totals		897	29541	4893	.499	157	.315	2269	.833	2596	9474	1883	607	867	12212	13.6

JEROME LANE

Team: Denver Nuggets
Position: Forward
Height: 6'6" **Weight:** 232
Birthdate: December 4, 1966
NBA Experience: 3 years

College: Pittsburgh
Acquired: 1st-round pick in 1988 draft
(23rd overall)

Background: Lane led the nation in rebounding as a sophomore at Pitt. Although he entered the NBA draft after his junior year, he left the school ranked third on the all-time rebounding list. Lane has been tabbed an underachiever, but he came closest to filling his potential in 1990-91 despite two stints on the injured list. He set Denver records with 280 offensive rebounds in a season, 25 boards in a game, and 13 offensive rebounds in a game.

Strengths: Lane is a big-time rebounder when he wants to be, especially on the offensive boards, and has improved his carom totals every year. He finished second on the Nuggets (to Blair Rasmussen) in 1990-91. He is a great leaper with a nose for the ball. A natural forward, Lane once started a college game at point guard and displays above-average passing skills.

Weaknesses: Lane is terribly inconsistent and has been known to carry too much weight. His perimeter shooting is awful, and he could build his new dream house with all of the bricks he throws up at the free throw line. For those reasons, having him in the game during crucial stretches is dangerous. He rarely concentrates for a full game and is prone to disappearing for long periods.

Analysis: For Lane to shake the many negative labels which have quite rightfully stuck, he must develop an outside shot and some touch at the charity stripe. Until then, he can only be played sparingly. Lane remains a player with huge potential but light years to travel if he hopes to reach it.

PLAYER SUMMARY

Will...rebound
Can't.................................shoot the ball
Expect.............................mental lapses
Don't Expect..............fulfilled potential
Fantasy Value.................................$2-4
Card Value...5¢

COLLEGE STATISTICS

		G	FGP	FTP	RPG	PPG
85-86	PITT	29	.470	.655	5.1	9.1
86-87	PITT	33	.568	.603	13.5	15.8
87-88	PITT	31	.513	.615	12.2	13.9
Totals		93	.525	.618	10.4	13.1

NBA REGULAR-SEASON STATISTICS

			FGs		3-PT FGs		FTs		Rebounds						
	G	MIN	FG	PCT	FG	PCT	FT	PCT	OFF	TOT	AST	STL	BLK	PTS	PPG
88-89 DEN	54	550	109	.426	0	.000	43	.384	87	200	60	20	4	261	4.8
89-90 DEN	67	956	145	.469	0	.000	44	.367	144	361	105	53	17	334	5.0
90-91 DEN	62	1383	202	.438	1	.250	58	.411	280	578	123	51	14	463	7.5
Totals	183	2889	456	.444	1	.063	145	.389	511	1139	288	124	35	1058	5.8

ANDREW LANG

Team: Phoenix Suns
Position: Center
Height: 6'11" **Weight:** 250
Birthdate: June 28, 1966
NBA Experience: 3 years

College: Arkansas
Acquired: 2nd-round pick in 1988 draft (28th overall)

Background: Lang completed his collegiate career at Arkansas as the school's all-time leader in blocked shots and its fourth-leading rebounder. His playing time has increased in each of his three years with Phoenix. Lang has emerged as a dominating shot-blocker as a professional, trailing only Manute Bol and Mark Eaton on the all-time list of blocks per minute played (one for every 8.7). He started 18 games in 1990-91 and improved his shooting and scoring numbers.

Strengths: Lang is a defensive force. He swats shots like few others and is more than capable on the defensive glass. His instincts and work ethic are first-rate, so much so that Phoenix coach Cotton Fitzsimmons experimented with him as a starter for a few weeks of the 1990-91 campaign. He runs the floor well for a big man.

Weaknesses: Offensively, Lang's skills are not NBA caliber despite his high shooting percentage. Most of his points come from within a few feet of the hoop. He does not handle the ball well, even in the post, and struggles when tightly covered. He has improved his free throw shooting but still needs work.

Analysis: Few centers (and even fewer back-up centers) play defense the way Lang does. That alone is enough to earn him valuable minutes off the bench. His offensive skills are improving but he will never be one of the high-scoring big men in the league. He is an outstanding reserve, but probably would make a decent starter on a less talented team in need of frontcourt defense.

PLAYER SUMMARY

Will ....block shots
Can't...score
Expect ....post defense
Don't Expect.............................10 PPG
Fantasy Value.................................$1-2
Card Value..5¢

COLLEGE STATISTICS

		G	FGP	FTP	RPG	PPG
84-85	ARK	33	.405	.563	2.0	2.6
85-86	ARK	26	.466	.607	6.5	8.2
86-87	ARK	32	.500	.644	7.5	8.1
87-88	ARK	30	.527	.450	7.3	9.3
Totals		121	.489	.575	5.7	6.9

NBA REGULAR-SEASON STATISTICS

				FGs		3-PT FGs		FTs		Rebounds						
		G	MIN	FG	PCT	FG	PCT	FT	PCT	OFF	TOT	AST	STL	BLK	PTS	PPG
88-89	PHO	62	526	60	.513	0	.000	39	.650	54	147	9	17	48	159	2.6
89-90	PHO	74	1011	97	.557	0	.000	64	.653	83	271	21	22	133	258	3.5
90-91	PHO	63	1152	109	.577	0	.000	93	.715	113	303	27	17	127	311	4.9
Totals		199	2689	266	.554	0	.000	196	.681	250	721	57	56	308	728	3.7

ERIC LECKNER

Team: Charlotte Hornets
Position: Center
Height: 6'11" **Weight:** 265
Birthdate: May 27, 1966
NBA Experience: 3 years

College: Wyoming
Acquired: Traded from Kings for a
1995 2nd-round pick and future
considerations, 2/91

Background: Leckner was named MVP of the Western Conference Athletic
Conference tournament for three straight years at Wyoming, where he ranked
among the NCAA leaders in field goal percentage as a senior. He spent his first
two pro years as a little-used reserve in Utah before spending 1990-91 in
Sacramento and Charlotte. As a back-up center with the Hornets, he averaged
15.6 minutes per game.

Strengths: Leckner possesses a deft touch for a big man and has good hands
and moves around the basket. Although his shooting percentage was way down
in 1990-91, he is considered a decent offensive center. He has worked himself
into shape and is determined to improve.

Weaknesses: An all-around talent Leckner is not. He is not blessed with good
athletic ability, a fact that shows up most clearly on the defensive end. He has
trouble moving his feet and ends up reaching with his hands, drawing fouls.
Because his offensive skills are his strength, Leckner's 56-percent free throw
shooting in 1990-91 is a huge concern.

Analysis: While Leckner's minutes have increased since he left Utah, his
shooting numbers have fallen. That's not a good sign for a big man who
specializes in offense. However, two new teams in one year can cause such
drop-offs. With his work ethic, significant improvement can be expected.

PLAYER SUMMARY

Will....................................look to score
Can't.................................play defense
Expect ....better shooting
Don't Expect ....athletic ability
Fantasy Value $1-3
Card Value...8¢

COLLEGE STATISTICS

		G	FGP	FTP	RPG	PPG
84-85	WYO	29	.583	.615	3.9	8.4
85-86	WYO	36	.582	.612	5.8	15.8
86-87	WYO	34	.631	.706	7.2	18.6
87-88	WYO	32	.644	.756	6.6	15.4
Totals		131	.612	.681	5.9	14.8

NBA REGULAR-SEASON STATISTICS

		G	MIN	FGs FG	FGs PCT	3-PT FGs FG	3-PT FGs PCT	FTs FT	FTs PCT	Rebounds OFF	Rebounds TOT	AST	STL	BLK	PTS	PPG
88-89	UTA	75	779	120	.545	0	.000	79	.699	48	199	16	8	22	319	4.3
89-90	UTA	77	764	125	.563	0	.000	81	.743	48	192	19	15	23	331	4.3
90-91	SAC/CHA	72	1122	131	.446	0	.000	62	.559	82	295	39	14	22	324	4.5
Totals		224	2665	376	.511	0	.000	222	.667	178	686	74	37	67	974	4.3

JIM LES

Team: Sacramento Kings
Position: Guard
Height: 5'11" **Weight:** 165
Birthdate: August 18, 1963
NBA Experience: 3 years

College: Cleveland St.; Bradley
Acquired: Signed as a free agent, 1/91

Background: Les played with Hersey Hawkins at Bradley and finished as the school's all-time assists leader. After being cut by Atlanta and Philadelphia (twice), he played his first pro ball in the CBA. Les finally landed an NBA job in 1988-89, playing all 82 games as back-up to John Stockton in Utah. He spent the 1989-90 season with the Jazz, Clippers, and back in the CBA. He was snared by Sacramento in 1990-91 and promptly led the NBA in 3-point shooting (.461).

Strengths: The 3-point shot has become Les's ticket to the show, although he had converted only one NBA trey before 1990-91. His accuracy from behind the stripe was more than 40 points better than that of second-place Trent Tucker. Les also ranked among league leaders in assist-to-turnover ratio (3.99). He makes few mistakes, hits his free throws, and handles the ball well.

Weaknesses: Les does not possess great speed and struggles to contain quicker point men. Bigger guards exploit him too by working the ball down low and posting him up. Les is too small to shoot over people as an off guard and is not much help on the boards. Although he hands out a lot of assists, he is not a great creator.

Analysis: Talk about being in the right place. Les would not have earned the chance he did with most clubs, yet he came out of nowhere with the Kings. His 3-point shooting was, incredibly enough, better than his field goal shooting. Expect him to stick around (perhaps in a reserve role) if he continues his torrid shooting, but it will surely be tougher as a known commodity.

PLAYER SUMMARY

Will	shoot from downtown
Can't	defend quickness
Expect	cautious playmaking
Don't Expect	turnovers
Fantasy Value	$1-2
Card Value	5¢

COLLEGE STATISTICS

		G	FGP	FTP	RPG	PPG
81-82	CSU	27	.467	.773	2.5	7.1
83-84	BRAD	22	.412	.707	2.1	6.3
84-85	BRAD	30	.498	.855	3.3	9.5
85-86	BRAD	35	.485	.756	3.4	14.2
Totals		114	.475	.775	2.9	9.8

NBA REGULAR-SEASON STATISTICS

				FGs		3-PT FGs		FTs		Rebounds						
		G	MIN	FG	PCT	FG	PCT	FT	PCT	OFF	TOT	AST	STL	BLK	PTS	PPG
88-89	UTA	82	781	40	.301	1	.071	57	.781	23	87	215	27	5	138	1.7
89-90	UTA/LAC	7	92	5	.357	0	.000	13	.765	3	7	21	3	0	23	3.3
90-91	SAC	55	1399	119	.444	71	.461	86	.835	18	111	299	57	4	395	7.2
Totals		144	2272	164	.395	72	.426	156	.808	44	205	535	87	9	556	3.9

LAFAYETTE LEVER

Team: Dallas Mavericks
Position: Guard
Height: 6'3" **Weight:** 175
Birthdate: August 18, 1960

NBA Experience: 9 years
College: Arizona St.
Acquired: Traded from Nuggets for 1990 and 1991 1st-round picks, 6/90

Background: Lever led Arizona State in scoring, assists, and steals as a senior and once totaled 38 points, 13 rebounds, six assists, and seven steals in a game. He has emerged as one of the top rebounding guards in NBA history; only Oscar Robertson, Tom Gola, and Magic Johnson have grabbed more boards in a season than Lever's 734 in 1989-90. The two-time All-Star underwent arthroscopic knee surgery four games into the 1990-91 campaign, his first with Dallas, and was out the remainder of the year.

Strengths: When healthy, Lever is one of the league's best and most complete guards. He rebounds extremely well, scores, handles the ball, and plays hard-nosed defense. He can play the point in addition to his natural off-guard slot. There are those who own more natural ability, but few who work harder and approach the game with the professionalism of Fat Lever.

Weaknesses: Lever is not known as a natural shooter, but his 3-point percentage soared to .414 in 1989-90. After the extended layoff, he will have to reassert his perimeter game.

Analysis: Dallas expected to have one of the best (if not *the* best) guard trios in the NBA when Lever joined Derek Harper and Rolando Blackman. If Lever can return 100 percent in 1991-92, the Mavericks still might have just that. Lever is not flashy, but he plays at a consistently high level.

PLAYER SUMMARY

Will...rebound
Can't ....give less than his all
Expect......................................leadership
Don't Expect........................flashy play
Fantasy Value.............................$34-37
Card Value...9¢

COLLEGE STATISTICS

		G	FGP	FTP	RPG	PPG
78-79	ASU	29	.413	.737	1.5	3.6
79-80	ASU	29	.445	.699	4.3	9.2
80-81	ASU	28	.463	.724	4.9	11.6
81-82	ASU	27	.454	.818	5.4	16.3
Totals		113	.450	.753	4.0	10.1

NBA REGULAR-SEASON STATISTICS

		G	MIN	FGs FG	FGs PCT	3-PT FGs FG	3-PT FGs PCT	FTs FT	FTs PCT	Rebounds OFF	Rebounds TOT	AST	STL	BLK	PTS	PPG
82-83	POR	81	2020	256	.431	5	.333	116	.730	85	225	426	153	15	633	7.8
83-84	POR	81	2010	313	.447	3	.200	159	.743	96	218	372	135	31	788	9.7
84-85	DEN	82	2559	424	.430	6	.250	197	.770	147	411	613	202	30	1051	12.8
85-86	DEN	78	2616	468	.441	12	.316	132	.725	136	420	584	178	15	1080	13.8
86-87	DEN	82	3054	643	.469	22	.239	244	.782	216	729	654	201	34	1552	18.9
87-88	DEN	82	3061	643	.473	12	.211	248	.785	203	665	639	223	21	1546	18.9
88-89	DEN	71	2745	558	.457	23	.348	270	.785	187	662	559	195	20	1409	19.8
89-90	DEN	79	2832	568	.443	36	.414	271	.804	230	734	517	168	13	1443	18.3
90-91	DAL	4	86	9	.391	0	.000	11	.786	3	15	12	6	3	29	7.3
Totals		640	20983	3882	.452	119	.300	1648	.772	1303	4079	4376	1461	182	9531	14.9

CLIFF LEVINGSTON

Team: Chicago Bulls
Position: Forward
Height: 6'8" **Weight:** 210
Birthdate: January 4, 1961

NBA Experience: 9 years
College: Wichita St.
Acquired: Signed as a free agent, 10/90

Background: Levingston led Wichita State in rebounding in each of his three years, and he set single-game records for rebounds (30) and blocks (15) before turning pro a year early. He spent two years with Detroit and six with Atlanta, his best coming in 1987-88 with the Hawks (10.0 PPG, .557 from the field). He saw limited action in his first year in Chicago, 1990-91, before emerging as a key contributor in the Bulls' title run through the playoffs.

Strengths: Levingston has great athletic skills and has earned his reputation as a tough defender. He can block shots and stay in front of high-scoring small forwards because of his quickness. He runs the floor well and finishes with the best of them. Levingston loves the alley-oop.

Weaknesses: The reason he was considered somewhat of a bust through the 1990-91 regular season is his tendency to disappear when he is not focused. He is a poor outside shooter and his field goal percentage has dropped in each of the last three seasons. His rebounding has also suffered.

Analysis: The 1991 playoffs were a showcase of what Levingston can do when his head is in the game. He gave the Bulls more than defense, hitting some crucial buckets that helped pave the way to an NBA title. It remains to be seen whether he can continue to excel as a role player over a full season.

PLAYER SUMMARY

Will ....finish the break
Can't.......................shoot from outside
Expect ....tough defense
Don't Expect...............................10 PPG
Fantasy Value $2-4
Card Value..8¢

COLLEGE STATISTICS

		G	FGP	FTP	RPG	PPG
79-80	WSU	29	.546	.622	10.1	15.8
80-81	WSU	33	.544	.619	11.4	18.5
81-82	WSU	29	.519	.624	10.2	13.9
Totals		91	.538	.621	10.6	16.2

NBA REGULAR-SEASON STATISTICS

				FGs		3-PT FGs		FTs		Rebounds						
		G	MIN	FG	PCT	FG	PCT	FT	PCT	OFF	TOT	AST	STL	BLK	PTS	PPG
82-83	DET	62	879	131	.485	0	.000	84	.571	104	232	52	23	36	346	5.6
83-84	DET	80	1746	229	.525	0	.000	125	.672	234	545	109	44	78	583	7.3
84-85	ATL	74	2017	291	.527	0	.000	145	.653	230	566	104	70	69	727	9.8
85-86	ATL	81	1945	294	.534	0	.000	164	.678	193	534	72	76	39	752	9.3
86-87	ATL	82	1848	251	.506	0	.000	155	.731	219	533	40	48	68	657	8.0
87-88	ATL	82	2135	314	.557	1	.500	190	.772	228	504	71	52	84	819	10.0
88-89	ATL	80	2184	300	.528	1	.200	133	.696	194	498	75	97	70	734	9.2
89-90	ATL	75	1706	216	.509	1	.200	83	.680	113	319	80	55	41	516	6.9
90-91	CHI	78	1013	127	.450	1	.250	59	.648	99	225	56	29	43	314	4.0
Totals		694	15473	2153	.520	4	.154	1138	.686	1614	3956	659	494	528	5448	7.9

REGGIE LEWIS

Team: Boston Celtics
Position: Guard/Forward
Height: 6'7" **Weight:** 195
Birthdate: November 21, 1965
NBA Experience: 4 years

College: Northeastern
Acquired: 1st-round pick in 1987 draft
(22nd overall)

Background: Lewis became Northeastern's all-time leading scorer and shot-blocker and the first three-time East Coast Athletic Conference Player of the Year. He rarely got off the bench as a rookie with Boston, but he finished second in the NBA's Most Improved Player voting in 1988-89 and has since become a starter and key scorer. He posted his best campaign in 1990-91, scoring more points than any other Celtic and finishing second to Larry Bird in scoring average.

Strengths: Lewis is a prime-time scorer who runs the court, finishes with style, can get his shots off the dribble, and is lethal when taking the ball to the hoop. A natural small forward and truly gifted athlete, he has developed a nice 18-foot jump shot while playing off guard with the Celtics. He has improved his free throw shooting from adequate to excellent.

Weaknesses: Although his ball-handling is vastly improved, Lewis can still have trouble with pressure. Another drawback to his playing the backcourt is his inability to hit the 3-pointer (1-of-13 in 1990-91). He can be outmuscled by stronger opponents.

Analysis: You know Lewis has reached the big-time because of his endorsement contract with a major shoe company. You can also tell by his continued improvement on the court. He has become one of the league's best backcourt scorers and would do just as well from the small-forward spot. When Boston's elder statesmen step down, Lewis will enter the spotlight.

PLAYER SUMMARY	
Will	get his points
Can't	shoot 3's
Expect	20 PPG
Don't Expect	a slow pace
Fantasy Value	$12-15
Card Value	15¢

COLLEGE STATISTICS

		G	FGP	FTP	RPG	PPG
83-84	NE	32	.528	.688	6.2	17.8
84-85	NE	31	.503	.746	7.8	24.1
85-86	NE	30	.474	.803	9.3	23.8
86-87	NE	29	.489	.761	8.5	23.3
Totals		122	.497	.756	7.9	22.2

NBA REGULAR-SEASON STATISTICS

				FGs		3-PT FGs		FTs		Rebounds						
		G	MIN	FG	PCT	FG	PCT	FT	PCT	OFF	TOT	AST	STL	BLK	PTS	PPG
87-88	BOS	49	405	90	.466	0	.000	40	.702	28	63	26	16	15	220	4.5
88-89	BOS	81	2657	604	.486	3	.136	284	.787	116	377	218	124	72	1495	18.5
89-90	BOS	79	2522	540	.496	4	.267	256	.808	109	347	225	88	63	1340	17.0
90-91	BOS	79	2878	598	.491	1	.077	281	.826	119	410	201	98	85	1478	18.7
Totals		288	8462	1832	.489	8	.148	861	.801	372	1197	670	326	235	4533	15.7

MARCUS LIBERTY

Team: Denver Nuggets
Position: Forward
Height: 6'8" **Weight:** 205
Birthdate: October 27, 1968
NBA Experience: 1 year

College: Illinois
Acquired: 2nd-round pick in 1990 draft (42nd overall)

Background: High school basketball's most coveted recruit in 1987, Liberty sat out his freshman year at Illinois under Proposition 48 and did not live up to his lofty reputation until his junior year. He then entered the draft as an underclassman and played in a team-high 76 games as a Denver rookie. He averaged 12.9 points and 5.2 rebounds in the 18 games he started.

Strengths: Liberty excels in the open court with his boundless leaping and finishing ability. He is a natural scorer and promising rebounder who can put the ball on the floor. He is versatile enough to fill in at big forward or big guard in addition to his usual small-forward position.

Weaknesses: Liberty earned an underachiever label in college, much of which has to do with his laid-back approach. He is invisible on defense and not consistently aggressive on the boards. Liberty's outside shooting must improve dramatically for him to be effective in the pros, where he will be judged on the perimeter. He played primarily in the paint in college.

Analysis: All things considered, the Nuggets may have gotten a steal in the second round. Liberty's open-court game is well suited to their style and he is not lacking in natural ability. However, his work ethic, jump shot, and defense have a long way to go.

PLAYER SUMMARY

Will ....get out on break
Can't...................................play defense
Expect ....exciting spurts
Don't Expect.....................consistency
Fantasy Value.................................$1-3
Card Value..10¢

COLLEGE STATISTICS

		G	FGP	FTP	RPG	PPG
88-89	ILL	36	.476	.781	3.9	8.4
89-90	ILL	29	.507	.763	7.1	17.8
Totals		65	.495	.769	5.3	12.6

NBA REGULAR-SEASON STATISTICS

				FGs		3-PT FGs		FTs		Rebounds						
		G	MIN	FG	PCT	FG	PCT	FT	PCT	OFF	TOT	AST	STL	BLK	PTS	PPG
90-91	DEN	76	1171	216	.421	17	.298	58	.630	117	221	64	48	19	507	6.7
Totals		76	1171	216	.421	17	.298	58	.630	117	221	64	48	19	507	6.7

TODD LICHTI

Team: Denver Nuggets
Position: Guard
Height: 6'4" **Weight:** 205
Birthdate: January 8, 1967
NBA Experience: 2 years

College: Stanford
Acquired: 1st-round pick in 1989 draft (15th overall)

Background: At Stanford, Lichti became the third player in league history to be named All-Pac-10 four consecutive seasons. He left as the school's career leader in points, games, and minutes. Lichti posted better numbers in 1989-90 than any Denver rookie since David Thompson, but his second season was sliced 53 games short because of injuries. He underwent arthroscopic surgery on his left knee January 28 and missed the remainder of the season.

Strengths: Lichti is a fearless penetrator from the two guard spot with great finishing ability. He is strong with either hand and can hit shots in traffic. His perimeter shooting is adequate and he has pushed his range past the 3-point line. Lichti is a hustling defender and competitor with good athletic skills.

Weaknesses: Though he improved his range, Lichti's field goal percentage took a nosedive under Paul Westhead's run-and-gun system. He needs to take better shots. The biggest concern is medical. Lichti's dangerous drive would become much less effective with a bum knee.

Analysis: With his work ethic, Lichti should be able to return from knee surgery and continue his rise to prominence. Perhaps the best gauge of his ability is the fact that the Nuggets traded their All-Star shooting guard, Fat Lever, before the 1990-91 season and made Lichti a starter.

PLAYER SUMMARY

Will ....use both hands
Can't ....be kept outside
Expect.........................points off drives
Don't Expect ....backing down
Fantasy Value $6-8
Card Value...........................15¢

COLLEGE STATISTICS

		G	FGP	FTP	RPG	PPG
85-86	STAN	30	.533	.814	4.7	17.2
86-87	STAN	28	.517	.809	5.7	17.6
87-88	STAN	33	.547	.879	5.6	20.1
88-89	STAN	33	.549	.850	5.0	20.1
Totals		124	.538	.840	5.3	18.8

NBA REGULAR-SEASON STATISTICS

				FGs		3-PT FGs		FTs		Rebounds						
		G	MIN	FG	PCT	FG	PCT	FT	PCT	OFF	TOT	AST	STL	BLK	PTS	PPG
89-90	DEN	79	1326	250	.486	0	.000	130	.747	49	151	116	55	13	630	8.0
90-91	DEN	29	860	166	.439	14	.298	59	.855	49	112	72	46	8	405	14.0
Totals		108	2186	416	.466	14	.230	189	.778	98	263	188	101	21	1035	9.6

ALTON LISTER

Team: Golden State Warriors
Position: Center/Forward
Height: 7'0" **Weight:** 240
Birthdate: October 1, 1958

NBA Experience: 10 years
College: San Jacinto; Arizona St.
Acquired: Traded from SuperSonics
for a 1990 1st-round pick, 8/89

Background: Lister completed his three-year career at Arizona State ranked first in career blocks and sixth in rebounding average. He is one of only three players in NBA history to record 100 or more blocks in his first eight seasons. Lister is Milwaukee's all-time leader in blocked shots. He missed all but three games of the 1989-90 season with a ruptured Achilles tendon, but he returned to lead Golden State in blocks and rebounds in 1990-91.

Strengths: For Golden State, Lister's biggest strengths are his large size and small ego. He blocks his quota of shots, gets his rebounds, and does not mind yielding to others in the scoring column. Lister is a big help defensively and still runs the floor pretty well for a big man.

Weaknesses: While Lister can provide strong interior defense, he also gets into foul trouble. He has fouled out of double-digit games in three seasons, although his recent record has been better. He is not much of a threat with the ball.

Analysis: When someone asked Don Nelson how much Lister meant to the Warriors, he responded, "Everything." His rebounding helps Golden State get out on the break and his interior defense is an ingredient the team lacked before he arrived. Lister gives way offensively to scorers like Chris Mullin, Tim Hardaway, and Mitch Richmond, and does so without complaint.

PLAYER SUMMARY

Will ....block shots
Can't ....light it up
Expect............................interior defense
Don't Expect............................a big ego
Fantasy Value $2-4
Card Value..5¢

COLLEGE STATISTICS

		G	FGP	FTP	RPG	PPG
76-77	SJ	40	—	—	16.0	17.0
78-79	ASU	29	.498	.560	6.7	8.8
79-80	ASU	27	.504	.558	8.6	12.0
80-81	ASU	26	.560	.691	9.7	15.4
Totals		122	.523	.611	10.8	13.6

NBA REGULAR-SEASON STATISTICS

				FGs		3-PT FGs		FTs		Rebounds						
		G	MIN	FG	PCT	FG	PCT	FT	PCT	OFF	TOT	AST	STL	BLK	PTS	PPG
81-82	MIL	80	1186	149	.519	0	.000	64	.520	108	387	84	18	118	362	4.5
82-83	MIL	80	1885	272	.529	0	.000	130	.537	168	568	111	50	177	674	8.4
83-84	MIL	82	1955	256	.500	0	.000	114	.626	156	603	110	41	140	626	7.6
84-85	MIL	81	2091	322	.538	0	.000	154	.588	219	647	127	49	167	798	9.9
85-86	MIL	81	1812	318	.551	0	.000	160	.602	199	592	101	49	142	796	9.8
86-87	SEA	75	2288	346	.504	0	.000	179	.675	223	705	110	32	180	871	11.6
87-88	SEA	82	1812	173	.504	1	.500	114	.606	200	627	58	27	140	461	5.6
88-89	SEA	82	1806	271	.499	0	.000	115	.646	207	545	54	28	180	657	8.0
89-90	GS	3	40	4	.500	0	.000	4	.571	5	8	2	1	0	12	4.0
90-91	GS	77	1552	188	.478	0	.000	115	.569	121	483	93	20	90	491	6.4
Totals		723	16427	2299	.515	1	.125	1149	.600	1606	5165	850	315	1334	5748	8.0

BRAD LOHAUS

Team: Milwaukee Bucks
Position: Forward/Center
Height: 6'11" **Weight:** 235
Birthdate: September 29, 1964
NBA Experience: 4 years

College: Iowa
Acquired: Traded from Timberwolves for Randy Breuer and a conditional exchange of 1991 or 1992 2nd-round picks, 1/90

Background: Lohaus increased his scoring average nearly eight points per game in his senior year at Iowa and shot 54 percent from the field as a senior. He has played with four NBA teams in as many years, his best numbers coming with expansion Minnesota in 1989. Lohaus was traded to Milwaukee in the middle of 1989-90. Although he endured a sub-par 1990-91, he shot 49 percent in the last 22 outings.

Strengths: Lohaus shoots with unlimited range and a quick release. He buried 15 of his final 34 3-point attempts (44 percent) of the 1990-91 season. Lohaus runs the floor as well as any seven-footer and uses his quickness on defense as well. He led the Bucks in blocked shots.

Weaknesses: Despite his height, Lohaus possesses virtually no inside game. His back-to-the-basket skills are forgettable. He is also prone to cold spells from the outside and does not create his own shots as well as he catches and fires. Lohaus loses any match-up in the paint that turns physical.

Analysis: Lohaus ranks among the most unconventional players in the NBA. Though seven feet tall, he is far more dangerous from behind the 3-point line than he is in the paint. His size is that of a center or power forward; his game is pure perimeter, especially on offense. When his shots aren't falling, his value drops greatly.

PLAYER SUMMARY

Will ....shoot 3's
Can't.......................bang with big men
Expect ....perimeter play
Don't Expect..............low-post offense
Fantasy Value $1-2
Card Value...5¢

COLLEGE STATISTICS

		G	FGP	FTP	RPG	PPG
82-83	IOWA	20	.310	.538	0.6	1.3
83-84	IOWA	28	.404	.673	5.2	6.8
85-86	IOWA	32	.431	.794	3.2	3.6
86-87	IOWA	35	.540	.692	7.7	11.3
Totals		115	.467	.695	4.6	6.3

NBA REGULAR-SEASON STATISTICS

		G	MIN	FG	PCT	FG	PCT	FT	PCT	OFF	TOT	AST	STL	BLK	PTS	PPG
87-88	BOS	70	718	122	.496	3	.231	50	.806	46	138	49	20	41	297	4.2
88-89	BOS/SAC	77	1214	210	.432	1	.091	81	.786	84	256	66	30	56	502	6.5
89-90	MIN/MIL	80	1943	305	.460	47	.343	75	.728	98	398	168	58	88	732	9.1
90-91	MIL	81	1219	179	.431	33	.277	37	.685	59	217	75	50	74	428	5.3
Totals		308	5094	816	.451	84	.300	243	.755	287	1009	358	158	259	1959	6.4

GRANT LONG

Team: Miami Heat
Position: Forward
Height: 6'8" **Weight:** 230
Birthdate: March 12, 1966
NBA Experience: 3 years

College: Eastern Michigan
Acquired: 2nd-round pick in 1988
draft (33rd overall)

Background: Long was named Mid-American Conference Player of the Year and MVP of the MAC tournament as a senior at Eastern Michigan. He was the only player to see action in all 82 games of Miami's inaugural season in the NBA and approached the league lead in disqualifications in each of his first two years (13 and 11). He became a full-time starter in December of the 1990-91 campaign and enjoyed career-best averages from the field and the free throw line. He was second on the Heat in rebounding.

Strengths: Long is a hard-working player who attacks the boards and runs the floor for most of his points. Coaches love his attitude and his willingness to give 100 percent every night. He has become a decent shooter from medium range and his passing skills have improved with experience.

Weaknesses: Although his number of fouls and disqualifications in 1990-91 were career lows, fouling out of ten games is nothing to boast about. Although he hustles relentlessly on defense, he is usually checking bigger players. He also sets a lot of moving picks. He lacks offensive polish.

Analysis: Long's basketball skills are borderline for an NBA forward. His heart, however, has been enough to earn him a starting job, albeit with an expansion team. He does all the little things like setting screens, boxing out, and bellying up on people. If he can learn to do those things without drawing so many whistles, his stock would rise.

PLAYER SUMMARY

Will ....crash the boards
Can't ....avoid foul trouble
Expect.................................all-out effort
Don't Expect............an offensive force
Fantasy Value $5-7
Card Value..8¢

COLLEGE STATISTICS

		G	FGP	FTP	RPG	PPG
84-85	EMU	28	.564	.609	4.0	4.1
85-86	EMU	27	.526	.644	6.6	8.6
86-87	EMU	29	.549	.725	9.0	14.9
87-88	EMU	30	.555	.765	10.4	23.0
Totals		114	.549	.725	7.6	12.9

NBA REGULAR-SEASON STATISTICS

		G	MIN	FGs FG	FGs PCT	3-PT FGs FG	3-PT FGs PCT	FTs FT	FTs PCT	Rebounds OFF	Rebounds TOT	AST	STL	BLK	PTS	PPG
88-89	MIA	82	2435	336	.486	0	.000	304	.749	240	546	149	122	48	976	11.9
89-90	MIA	81	1856	257	.483	0	.000	172	.714	156	402	96	91	38	686	8.5
90-91	MIA	80	2514	276	.492	1	.167	181	.787	225	568	176	119	43	734	9.2
Totals		243	6805	869	.487	1	.071	657	.749	621	1516	421	332	129	2396	9.9

DAN MAJERLE

Team: Phoenix Suns
Position: Guard/Forward
Height: 6'6" **Weight:** 220
Birthdate: September 9, 1965
NBA Experience: 3 years

College: Central Michigan
Acquired: 1st-round pick in 1988 draft
(14th overall)

Background: Majerle was a three-time All-Mid-American Conference selection at Central Michigan, where he ranked second on the all-time scoring, steals, and field goal percentage lists. He totaled 27 points and six steals in his pro debut and has since emerged as one of the NBA's premier all-around players. He finished second (to Detlef Schrempf) by one vote for the 1990-91 Sixth Man Award after his best season.

Strengths: Majerle can, quite literally, do it all. He handles the ball with confidence, rebounds well, plays relentless defense, and can score from both inside and outside when called upon. He possesses tremendous leaping ability and uses it to his full advantage. There is no downplaying the emotional lift his work ethic, all-out hustle, and physical style provide for his teammates.

Weaknesses: About the only flaw in Majerle's game has been his pure shooting ability, although he hoisted his field goal percentage from .424 in 1989-90 to .484 in 1990-91. Still, defenders are best advised to keep him on the perimeter rather than allowing him to drive.

Analysis: If he continues to play at his current level, one of the premier reserves in the league will soon be recognized as one of the game's truly outstanding players, regardless of role. Majerle plays every minute as if a championship were at stake. His ability to shut down opposing players at virtually every position makes him an invaluable asset.

PLAYER SUMMARY	
Will	stifle opponents
Can't	play at half speed
Expect	all-out effort
Don't Expect	20 PPG
Fantasy Value	$14-16
Card Value	12¢

COLLEGE STATISTICS

		G	FGP	FTP	RPG	PPG
84-85	CMU	12	.568	.582	6.7	18.6
85-86	CMU	27	.527	.718	7.9	21.4
86-87	CMU	23	.555	.552	8.5	21.1
87-88	CMU	32	.521	.645	10.8	23.7
Totals		94	.536	.631	8.9	21.8

NBA REGULAR-SEASON STATISTICS

				FGs		3-PT FGs		FTs		Rebounds						
		G	MIN	FG	PCT	FG	PCT	FT	PCT	OFF	TOT	AST	STL	BLK	PTS	PPG
88-89	PHO	54	1354	181	.419	27	.329	78	.614	62	209	130	63	14	467	8.6
89-90	PHO	73	2244	296	.424	19	.237	198	.762	144	430	188	100	32	809	11.1
90-91	PHO	77	2281	397	.484	30	.349	227	.762	168	418	216	106	40	1051	13.6
Totals		204	5879	874	.448	76	.306	503	.734	374	1057	534	269	86	2327	11.4

JEFF MALONE

Team: Utah Jazz
Position: Guard
Height: 6'4" **Weight:** 205
Birthdate: June 28, 1961
NBA Experience: 8 years

College: Mississippi St.
Acquired: Traded from Bullets via the Kings; Jazz sent Eric Leckner and Bob Hansen to Kings, and Kings sent Pervis Ellison to Bullets, 6/90

Background: Malone broke Bailey Howell's career scoring record as a four-year starter at Mississippi State and finished fifth on the all-time SEC scoring list. He spent his first seven NBA seasons with the Washington Bullets, played in two All-Star Games, and is the team's all-time leader in free throw percentage at 86.9. In his first season with Utah in 1990-91, Malone joined the exclusive 90-50 club by shooting better than 90 percent from the foul line and 50 percent from the field.

Strengths: Utah obtained Malone for one reason: the man can shoot. Whether off the dribble or from behind a screen, Malone can fill the basket from anywhere inside the 3-point line. He is a determined competitor and unafraid of pressure. Free throws are automatic.

Weaknesses: Amazingly, the sweet-shooting Malone does not possess 3-point range. He was 1-of-6 from behind the arc each of the last two seasons. Malone does not run the floor well for a guard, nor does he create for teammates. His defense would be adequate if he spent more energy rebounding.

Analysis: Stuck on a bad team for most of his career, Malone finally got some overdue playoff exposure with the Jazz. Although he did not earn an All-Star trip, 1990-91 may have been his best season. Malone's only problem now is that a teammate with the same last name steals the headlines.

PLAYER SUMMARY

Will ....score from perimeter
Can't..............................shoot 3's
Expect ....90-pct. FT shooting
Don't Expect.....................many assists
Fantasy Value $23-26
Card Value.......................................8¢

COLLEGE STATISTICS

		G	FGP	FTP	RPG	PPG
79-80	MSU	27	.459	.824	3.3	11.9
80-81	MSU	27	.490	.820	4.2	20.1
81-82	MSU	27	.549	.743	4.1	18.6
82-83	MSU	29	.531	.824	3.7	26.8
Totals		110	.512	.809	3.8	19.5

NBA REGULAR-SEASON STATISTICS

		G	MIN	FGs FG	FGs PCT	3-PT FGs FG	3-PT FGs PCT	FTs FT	FTs PCT	Rebounds OFF	Rebounds TOT	AST	STL	BLK	PTS	PPG
83-84	WAS	81	1976	408	.444	24	.324	142	.826	57	155	151	23	13	982	12.1
84-85	WAS	76	2613	605	.499	15	.208	211	.844	60	206	184	52	9	1436	18.9
85-86	WAS	80	2992	735	.483	3	.176	322	.868	66	288	191	70	12	1795	22.4
86-87	WAS	80	2763	689	.457	4	.154	376	.885	50	218	298	75	13	1758	22.0
87-88	WAS	80	2655	648	.476	10	.417	335	.882	44	206	237	51	13	1641	20.5
88-89	WAS	76	2418	677	.480	1	.053	296	.871	55	179	219	39	14	1651	21.7
89-90	WAS	75	2567	781	.491	1	.167	257	.877	54	206	243	48	6	1820	24.3
90-91	UTA	69	2466	525	.508	1	.167	231	.917	36	206	143	50	6	1282	18.6
Totals		617	20450	5068	.480	59	.242	2170	.874	422	1664	1666	408	86	12365	20.0

KARL MALONE

Team: Utah Jazz
Position: Forward
Height: 6'9" **Weight:** 256
Birthdate: July 24, 1963

NBA Experience: 6 years
College: Louisiana Tech
Acquired: 1st-round pick in 1985 draft (13th overall)

Background: Malone finished his college career third on the all-time scoring list and sixth in career rebounding at Louisiana Tech despite declaring for the NBA draft after his junior year. In six years with Utah, he has missed only three games. Malone finished third in the voting for 1986 Rookie of the Year and has gone on to appear in four All-Star Games, winning MVP honors in the 1989 contest. In 1990-91, he led the Jazz in scoring (second in the league), rebounding (fourth in the league), and minutes.

Strengths: Nicknamed "The Mailman" because he delivers, Malone is virtually impossible for one man to stop. He is big, quick, and incredibly strong. His low-post game features lightning moves to the hoop, impossible-to-block hooks, and a steady turnaround. He has even added a 3-pointer to his repertoire. If Malone fails to score, he almost always draws a foul. He has gone to the line more than anyone in the NBA for three straight years. He runs the floor, plays sound defense, and owns the boards.

Weaknesses: Malone makes more turnovers than the average forward, largely because defenders swarm him and he does not always dish to the open men. He prefers to go one-on-three, but it's tough to argue with the results.

Analysis: After Malone was snubbed in the fan voting as a starter in the 1990 All-Star Game, he went out and scored 61 points against Milwaukee. Suffice it to say, he will not be overlooked again any time soon. The Mailman is the premier power forward in the league and continues to improve.

PLAYER SUMMARY

Will......................................get to the line
Can't............................be stopped inside
Expect ....points, rebounds
Don't Expect..............pinpoint passing
Fantasy Value $72-75
Card Value...25¢

COLLEGE STATISTICS

		G	FGP	FTP	RPG	PPG
82-83	LAT	28	.582	.623	10.3	20.9
83-84	LAT	32	.576	.682	8.8	18.8
84-85	LAT	32	.541	.571	9.0	16.5
Totals		92	.566	.631	9.3	18.7

NBA REGULAR-SEASON STATISTICS

		G	MIN	FG	FGs PCT	FG	3-PT FGs PCT	FT	FTs PCT	OFF	Rebounds TOT	AST	STL	BLK	PTS	PPG
85-86	UTA	81	2475	504	.496	0	.000	195	.481	174	718	236	105	44	1203	14.9
86-87	UTA	82	2857	728	.512	0	.000	323	.598	278	855	158	104	60	1779	21.7
87-88	UTA	82	3198	858	.520	0	.000	552	.700	277	986	199	117	50	2268	27.7
88-89	UTA	80	3126	809	.519	5	.313	703	.766	259	853	219	144	70	2326	29.1
89-90	UTA	82	3122	914	.562	16	.372	696	.762	232	911	226	121	50	2540	31.0
90-91	UTA	82	3302	847	.527	4	.286	684	.770	236	967	270	89	79	2382	29.0
Totals		489	18080	4660	.525	25	.287	3153	.708	1456	5290	1308	680	353	12498	25.6

MOSES MALONE

Team: Milwaukee Bucks
Position: Center
Height: 6'10" **Weight:** 255
Birthdate: March 23, 1955

NBA Experience: 15 years
College: None
Acquired: Signed as a free agent, 7/91

Background: Malone, who jumped straight from high school to the NBA, was voted the league's MVP in 1979 and 1982 with Houston, and again in 1983 with Philadelphia. He led the 76ers to the 1982-83 NBA title and played in 12 consecutive All-Star Games from 1978-89. In 1990-91 with Atlanta, he surpassed the 25,000-point and 15,000-rebound plateus. He signed with Milwaukee in July.

Strengths: Malone is one of the greatest rebounders and low-post scorers in NBA history. He is especially productive on the offensive end, where his all-business approach has helped him set the NBA's career record for offensive caroms. Malone still gets his points one way or another.

Weaknesses: Defense has never been a strong suit, and that holds especially true now that he's 36 years old. He has become slow on his feet.

Analysis: In his 15th year in the league, Malone proved he can still contribute. In addition, he increased his value by showing an unexpected willingness to accept a back-up role with the Hawks. With Milwaukee, he'll get significant minutes in the Bucks' frontcourt rotation.

PLAYER SUMMARY

Will ....work relentlessly
Can't ....move like he used to
Expect ....offensive rebounds
Don't Expect..............many more years
Fantasy Value $23-27
Card Value.......................................10¢

COLLEGE STATISTICS

—DID NOT PLAY—

NBA REGULAR-SEASON STATISTICS

		G	MIN	FG	FG PCT	3-PT FG	3-PT PCT	FT	FT PCT	OFF	TOT	AST	STL	BLK	PTS	PPG
76-77	BUF/HOU	82	2506	389	.480	0	.000	305	.693	437	1072	89	67	181	1083	13.2
77-78	HOU	59	2107	413	.499	0	.000	318	.718	380	886	31	48	76	1144	19.4
78-79	HOU	82	3390	716	.540	0	.000	599	.739	587	1444	147	79	119	2031	24.8
79-80	HOU	82	3140	778	.502	0	.000	563	.719	573	1190	147	80	107	2119	25.8
80-81	HOU	80	3245	806	.522	1	.333	609	.757	474	1180	141	83	150	2222	27.8
81-82	HOU	81	3398	945	.519	0	.000	630	.762	558	1188	142	76	125	2520	31.1
82-83	PHI	78	2922	654	.501	0	.000	600	.761	445	1194	101	89	157	1908	24.5
83-84	PHI	71	2613	532	.483	0	.000	545	.750	352	950	96	71	110	1609	22.7
84-85	PHI	79	2957	602	.469	0	.000	737	.815	385	1031	130	67	123	1941	24.6
85-86	PHI	74	2706	571	.458	0	.000	617	.787	339	872	90	67	71	1759	23.8
86-87	WAS	73	2488	595	.454	0	.000	570	.824	340	824	120	59	92	1760	24.1
87-88	WAS	79	2692	531	.487	2	.286	543	.788	372	884	112	59	72	1607	20.3
88-89	ATL	81	2878	538	.491	0	.000	561	.789	386	956	112	79	100	1637	20.2
89-90	ATL	81	2735	517	.480	1	.111	493	.781	364	812	130	47	84	1528	18.9
90-91	ATL	82	1912	280	.468	0	.000	309	.831	271	667	68	30	74	869	10.6
Totals		1164	41689	8867	.493	4	.058	7999	.769	6263	15150	1656	1001	1641	25737	22.1

DANNY MANNING

Team: Los Angeles Clippers
Position: Forward
Height: 6'10" **Weight:** 235
Birthdate: May 17, 1966
NBA Experience: 3 years

College: Kansas
Acquired: 1st-round pick in 1988 draft
(1st overall)

Background: Manning was voted college Player of the Year in 1988, when he led Kansas to the NCAA championship. He ended his college career with more than three dozen school, conference, and NCAA records. His early NBA years have been slowed by a tear of the anterior cruciate in his right knee in January 1989, which caused him to miss most of his rookie year and the early part of 1989-90. In his first "full" season (1990-91), Manning started 47 games and finished fourth on the Clippers in scoring.

Strengths: Manning has been called a point guard in the body of a forward, a tribute to his passing skills. He makes those around him better and is superb with the ball in his hands. He owns an effective half-hook in the post and can shoot the medium-range jumper. He goes to the boards and starts the break with crisp outlet passes. Manning knows how to win.

Weaknesses: The knee injury has limited Manning's effectiveness on defense, particularly when matched up with quick forwards. He does not move well enough laterally to cut off their moves to the hoop.

Analysis: Manning is the kind of player who excels on a good team, because he brings out the best in those around him. With the Clippers, those talents often go unnoticed. He could score more points, but Manning prefers to do the little things that help win games. His best days are still ahead of him.

PLAYER SUMMARY

Will	play unselfishly
Can't	move well laterally
Expect	a proven winner
Don't Expect	20 PPG
Fantasy Value	$16-18
Card Value	10¢

COLLEGE STATISTICS

		G	FGP	FTP	RPG	PPG
84-85	KAN	34	.566	.765	7.6	14.6
85-86	KAN	39	.600	.748	6.3	16.7
86-87	KAN	36	.617	.730	9.5	23.9
87-88	KAN	38	.583	.734	9.0	24.8
Totals		147	.593	.740	8.1	20.1

NBA REGULAR-SEASON STATISTICS

			FGs		3-PT FGs		FTs		Rebounds						
		G	MIN	FG	PCT	FG	PCT	FT	PCT	OFF	TOT	AST	STL	BLK	PTS	PPG
88-89	LAC	26	950	177	.494	1	.200	79	.767	70	171	81	44	25	434	16.7
89-90	LAC	71	2269	440	.533	0	.000	274	.741	142	422	187	91	39	1154	16.3
90-91	LAC	73	2197	470	.519	0	.000	219	.716	169	426	196	117	62	1159	15.9
Totals		170	5416	1087	.520	1	.077	572	.734	381	1019	464	252	126	2747	16.2

SARUNAS MARCIULIONIS

Team: Golden State Warriors
Position: Guard
Height: 6'5" **Weight:** 200
Birthdate: June 13, 1964
NBA Experience: 2 years

College: Vilnius, Lithuania
Acquired: Signed as a free agent, 6/89

Background: The Lithuanian Marciulionis was the leading scorer on the Soviet Union's 1988 Olympic gold medal-winning team in Seoul, South Korea. He became the first Soviet player to join the NBA when he signed in 1989, and he finished sixth among all rookies in scoring in 1989-90. His numbers were down in 1990-91, largely because of a knee injury suffered in January. He spent two terms on the injured list and played in just 50 games.

Strengths: Although he plays left-handed, Marciulionis is ambidextrous. Anyone unconvinced should watch him handle the ball. He has an accurate jumper with 3-point range, but prefers driving to the bucket and uses his strength well inside. Many smaller defenders clear out of his path. He is a talented passer.

Weaknesses: Marciulionis does not look to shoot as often as his coaches would like. He makes turnovers not because he is a poor passer, but because he looks to dish too often. He also has a lot to learn about defending NBA players, although the effort and intensity are clearly there.

Analysis: Any talk about Marciulionis would be incomplete without mention of the fine adjustment he has made to a new culture, especially in overcoming the language barrier. He has fit in well, and he showed his mettle by fighting back from injury to help the Warriors in the playoffs. Among the foreign imports of 1989-90, he and Vlade Divac have been the big contributors.

PLAYER SUMMARY

Will ....use either hand
Can't.........................avoid urge to pass
Expect ....steady shooting
Don't Expect.......................selfish play
Fantasy Value $11-13
Card Value...20¢

COLLEGE STATISTICS

—DID NOT PLAY—

NBA REGULAR-SEASON STATISTICS

| | | | FGs | | 3-PT FGs | | FTs | | Rebounds | | | | | | |
	G	MIN	FG	PCT	FG	PCT	FT	PCT	OFF	TOT	AST	STL	BLK	PTS	PPG
89-90 GS	75	1695	289	.519	10	.256	317	.787	84	221	121	94	7	905	12.1
90-91 GS	50	987	183	.501	1	.167	178	.724	51	118	85	62	4	545	10.9
Totals	125	2682	472	.512	11	.244	495	.763	135	339	206	156	11	1450	11.6

JEFF MARTIN

Team: Detroit Pistons
Position: Guard
Height: 6'5" **Weight:** 195
Birthdate: January 14, 1967
NBA Experience: 2 years

College: Murray St.
Acquired: Traded from Clippers for James Edwards, 8/91

Background: Martin earned Ohio Valley Player of the Year honors after his senior year at Murray State and finished with 12 school records, including career scoring and blocked shots. He started 23 games as a rookie when the Clippers were hit with injuries in the backcourt and, on the year, posted 19 double-figure scoring games. Martin started 26 times in 1990-91 and once scored 25 points in a game against Utah. He was dealt to Detroit over the summer.

Strengths: A small forward in college, Martin has played mostly big guard as a pro and brings good size to the backcourt. He is a slashing penetrator with good athletic skills and loads of enthusiasm. He is above average both defensively and fundamentally for a young player.

Weaknesses: Martin must develop more consistency on his jumper if he expects to see extended minutes at shooting guard. He is pretty reliable when left open but much less so when he has to create his own shot or let one fly with a hand in his face. His ball-handling skills are not up to standards for an NBA guard, especially a part-time starter.

Analysis: All in all, Martin has done well for a relative unknown thrust into early action at a fairly new position. Most of his problems stem from his lack of experience in the backcourt, and he seems willing to work at shoring up those areas. He should become the third guard with the Pistons.

PLAYER SUMMARY

Will ....go to the hoop
Can't ....ball-handle as a guard
Expect............................solid defense
Don't Expect...............50-pct. shooting
Fantasy Value $2-4
Card Value...10¢

COLLEGE STATISTICS

		G	FGP	FTP	RPG	PPG
85-86	MSU	29	.472	.675	5.4	11.7
86-87	MSU	28	.523	.778	5.6	21.2
87-88	MSU	31	.558	.784	6.6	26.0
88-89	MSU	29	.510	.796	5.2	25.7
Totals		117	.522	.766	5.7	21.2

NBA REGULAR-SEASON STATISTICS

			FGs		3-PT FGs		FTs		Rebounds						
		G	MIN	FG	PCT	FG	PCT	FT	PCT	OFF	TOT	AST	STL	BLK	PTS	PPG
89-90	LAC	69	1351	170	.411	2	.133	91	.705	78	159	44	41	16	433	6.3
90-91	LAC	74	1334	214	.422	27	.307	68	.680	53	131	65	37	31	523	7.1
Totals		143	2685	384	.417	29	.282	159	.694	131	290	109	78	47	956	6.7

VERNON MAXWELL

Team: Houston Rockets
Position: Guard
Height: 6'4" **Weight:** 190
Birthdate: September 12, 1965
NBA Experience: 3 years

College: Florida
Acquired: Traded from Spurs for cash, 2/90

Background: Maxwell's past is cluttered with accomplishment and controversy. He broke Florida's all-time scoring record and finished as the SEC's No. 2 career scorer behind Pete Maravich. But Maxwell later admitted to using cocaine and accepting cash payments. He has been in and out of trouble as a pro as well, but since San Antonio sold his rights to Houston, he has proven he can contribute to success. No one made more 3-pointers in 1990-91.

Strengths: Maxwell is one of the better athletes in the league and has always thrown his weight around on defense. He can match up effectively with big guards and smaller point men. Maxwell is strong, quick, and a great finisher. He can get his shot whenever he wants it.

Weaknesses: Most of Maxwell's problems have stemmed from his off-court behavior. Although he led the league in 3-pointers made, only Michael Adams launched more. His percentage from inside the arc is not great either. Maxwell must learn to play a more controlled floor game.

Analysis: Maxwell looks to have found a home in Houston, where he started 79 games, played in all 82, and was a huge part of the Rockets' impressive late-season run at the Midwest Division title. He has won the right to launch bombs almost at will. Now he needs to increase his percentage and stay out of trouble.

PLAYER SUMMARY

Will ....launch 3's
Can't.............................wipe slate clean
Expect............................tough defense
Don't Expect ....high FG pct.
Fantasy Value $8-10
Card Value...10¢

COLLEGE STATISTICS

		G	FGP	FTP	RPG	PPG
84-85	FLA	30	.445	.686	2.4	13.3
85-86	FLA	33	.463	.701	4.5	19.6
86-87	FLA	34	.485	.742	3.7	21.7
87-88	FLA	33	.447	.715	4.2	20.2
Totals		130	.462	.715	3.7	18.8

NBA REGULAR-SEASON STATISTICS

				FGs		3-PT FGs		FTs		Rebounds						
		G	MIN	FG	PCT	FG	PCT	FT	PCT	OFF	TOT	AST	STL	BLK	PTS	PPG
88-89	SA	79	2065	357	.432	32	.248	181	.745	49	202	301	86	8	927	11.7
89-90	SA/HOU	79	1987	275	.439	28	.267	136	.645	50	228	296	84	10	714	9.0
90-91	HOU	82	2870	504	.404	172	.337	217	.733	41	238	303	127	15	1397	17.0
Totals		240	6922	1136	.421	232	.312	534	.712	140	668	900	297	33	3038	12.7

TRAVIS MAYS

Team: Atlanta Hawks
Position: Guard
Height: 6'2" **Weight:** 190
Birthdate: June 19, 1968
NBA Experience: 1 year

College: Texas
Acquired: Traded from Kings for Spud Webb and 1994 2nd-round pick, 7/91

Background: Mays surpassed Terry Teagle as the top scorer in Southwest Conference history while at Texas. He was named SWC Player of the Year as a junior and senior (the only player to ever win twice) and set conference records for 3-pointers made and attempted. The only rookies to average more points than Mays in 1990-91 were Derrick Coleman, Lionel Simmons, and Dennis Scott. He was among NBA leaders in 3-point percentage and once scored 36 points against Denver. He was traded to Atlanta in July.

Strengths: Mays is a perimeter scorer with great range and a fast trigger. His quick move to the hoop keeps defenders honest. What made him a sure-fire NBA success, though, is his willingness to assert himself at both ends of the court. He plays smart, aggressive defense.

Weaknesses: Mays is small for an off guard but lacks the distributing skills to be effective at the point. He is not as adept at creating for others as he is at getting his own shot. He also needs to improve his shot selection, as his poor rookie field goal percentage would indicate.

Analysis: Mays's rookie year was only slightly above average for a player of his ability. He did, however, display a great knowledge of how to score and will continue to burn the nets. When he stays healthy for a full season (he missed action with an ankle sprain, back spasms, and sore tendon in his foot in 1990-91), Mays should prove to be one of the top finds of the 1990 draft. The Hawks have traded away guards Doc Rivers and Spud Webb, so Mays will get plenty of PT in Atlanta.

PLAYER SUMMARY

Will	get his shots
Can't	star at point
Expect	defensive hustle
Don't Expect	50-pct. shooting
Fantasy Value	$13-15
Card Value	20¢

COLLEGE STATISTICS

		G	FGP	FTP	RPG	PPG
86-87	TEX	30	.423	.595	3.7	8.6
87-88	TEX	28	.459	.771	5.5	18.1
88-89	TEX	34	.449	.710	4.7	21.9
89-90	TEX	32	.433	.811	5.1	24.1
Totals		124	.442	.746	4.8	18.4

NBA REGULAR-SEASON STATISTICS

				FGs		3-PT FGs		FTs		Rebounds						
		G	MIN	FG	PCT	FG	PCT	FT	PCT	OFF	TOT	AST	STL	BLK	PTS	PPG
90-91	SAC	64	2145	294	.406	72	.365	255	.770	54	178	253	81	11	915	14.3
Totals		64	2145	294	.406	72	.365	255	.770	54	178	253	81	11	915	14.3

GEORGE McCLOUD

Team: Indiana Pacers
Position: Guard/Forward
Height: 6'8" **Weight:** 215
Birthdate: May 27, 1967
NBA Experience: 2 years

College: Florida St.
Acquired: 1st-round pick in 1989 draft
(7th overall)

Background: McCloud was named Metro Conference Player of the Year as a senior at Florida State, where he finished his career ranked third on the career scoring list. He played in just 44 games in a disappointing rookie year with Indiana. Although he more than doubled his minutes and shot 34.7 percent from 3-point range in 1990-91, his overall numbers were again sub-par.

Strengths: Indiana drafted McCloud with the seventh overall choice because of his perimeter shooting and 3-point range. His accuracy from behind the arc nearly matches his regular field goal percentage, a stat that actually belongs in the "weakness" category. McCloud is also a fine passer.

Weaknesses: As alluded to above, McCloud's field goal percentage is disastrous. He has yet to approach 40 percent for a season, which will assure a player of a spot near the end of an NBA bench. He does not penetrate or handle the ball well enough to play point and has yet to prove he can score in an off-guard role. Moreover, he is a defensive liability. He plays passively.

Analysis: McCloud's horrendous rookie year could be passed off as a result of not playing enough. His follow-up campaign, however, clearly puts this lottery pick on the verge of being a major bust, if he is not already there. Pooh Richardson, Tim Hardaway, and B.J. Armstrong were drafted with later picks in 1989. McCloud can hit 3-pointers, but can he refine the rest of his game?

PLAYER SUMMARY

Will ....shoot with range
Can't.................................play defense
Expect ....much tutoring
Don't Expect ....high FG pct.
Fantasy Value $1-2
Card Value...12¢

COLLEGE STATISTICS

		G	FGP	FTP	RPG	PPG
85-86	FSU	27	.483	.633	1.8	4.3
86-87	FSU	30	.442	.618	4.2	7.7
87-88	FSU	30	.479	.786	3.7	18.2
88-89	FSU	30	.448	.875	3.6	22.8
Totals		117	.460	.778	3.4	13.5

NBA REGULAR-SEASON STATISTICS

			FGs		3-PT FGs		FTs		Rebounds						
	G	MIN	FG	PCT	FG	PCT	FT	PCT	OFF	TOT	AST	STL	BLK	PTS	PPG
89-90 IND	44	413	45	.313	13	.325	15	.789	12	42	45	19	3	118	2.7
90-91 IND	74	1070	131	.373	43	.347	38	.776	35	118	150	40	11	343	4.6
Totals	118	1483	176	.356	56	.341	53	.779	47	160	195	59	14	461	3.9

TIM McCORMICK

Team: Atlanta Hawks
Position: Center
Height: 7'0" **Weight:** 240
Birthdate: March 10, 1962
NBA Experience: 7 years

College: Michigan
Acquired: Traded from Rockets with John Lucas for Kenny Smith and Roy Marble, 9/90

Background: As a senior at Michigan, McCormick led the Wolverines to the NIT championship, earning tournament MVP honors. Before he ever played an NBA game, he was a member of three different teams through trades. He has since seen action with five clubs, his best campaign coming with Philadelphia in 1986-87. In 1990-91, his first year with Atlanta, McCormick avoided the knee injuries that plagued him a year earlier but still saw limited action.

Strengths: McCormick is a smart player whose best basketball assets are his jump shot and his passing ability. He stays within his limitations and gets the ball in the right hands. He can back up at either power forward or center and plays good position defense.

Weaknesses: Although teams have tried to develop his inside offense, McCormick is still most comfortable when facing the hoop. He lacks quickness and jumping ability but cannot be considered a banger either. Of course, McCormick's chronic knee injuries will remain a concern.

Analysis: McCormick has shown flashes of promise, but those moments have become more rare since the knee surgeries two years ago. He lacks the refined skills to earn a steady diet of playing time; he played just 689 minutes last year. If his knees hold up, he has the smarts to retain a back-up job somewhere.

PLAYER SUMMARY

Will ....make sound decisions
Can't......................earn many minutes
Expect ....nothing spectacular
Don't Expect............................10 PPG
Fantasy Value $1-2
Card Value...5¢

COLLEGE STATISTICS

		G	FGP	FTP	RPG	PPG
80-81	MICH	30	.509	.783	3.5	5.2
82-83	MICH	28	.555	.813	6.4	12.6
83-84	MICH	32	.580	.667	5.9	12.1
Totals		90	.556	.737	5.3	9.9

NBA REGULAR-SEASON STATISTICS

				FGs		3-PT FGs		FTs		Rebounds						
		G	MIN	FG	PCT	FG	PCT	FT	PCT	OFF	TOT	AST	STL	BLK	PTS	PPG
84-85	SEA	78	1584	269	.557	0	.000	188	.715	146	398	78	18	33	726	9.3
85-86	SEA	77	1705	253	.570	1	.500	174	.713	140	403	83	19	28	681	8.8
86-87	PHI	81	2817	391	.545	0	.000	251	.719	180	611	114	36	64	1033	12.8
87-88	PHI/NJ	70	2114	348	.537	0	.000	145	.674	146	467	118	32	23	841	12.0
88-89	HOU	81	1257	169	.481	0	.000	87	.674	87	261	54	18	24	425	5.2
89-90	HOU	18	116	10	.345	0	.000	10	.526	8	27	3	3	1	30	1.7
90-91	ATL	56	689	93	.497	0	.000	66	.733	56	165	32	11	14	252	4.5
Totals		461	10282	1533	.536	1	.063	921	.704	763	2332	482	137	187	3988	8.7

RODNEY McCRAY

Team: Dallas Mavericks
Position: Forward
Height: 6'8" **Weight:** 235
Birthdate: August 29, 1961
NBA Experience: 8 years

College: Louisville
Acquired: Traded from Kings with 1990 and 1991 2nd-round picks for Bill Wennington and two 1990 1st-round picks, 6/90

Background: McCray helped lead Louisville to the 1980 NCAA title and played in three Final Fours during his college career. As a pro, he made the All-Defensive Team with Houston in 1987-88 and led the league in minutes with Sacramento in 1989-90. In his first season in Dallas, McCray finished fifth on the team in scoring and second in rebounding.

Strengths: McCray is a fine all-around talent who especially shines on the break. He has deceiving speed and loves to run the floor. He rebounds, plays shutdown defense, and is versatile. A first-rate small forward, McCray can pass well enough to play the perimeter and posts up well enough to line up at power forward. He is unselfish, a consummate pro.

Weaknesses: McCray is not a picture-perfect jump-shooter by any means, but he has improved both his range and his consistency. He can occasionally sneak to the background on offense.

Analysis: Check this stat to size up McCray's value: Dallas was 1-7 in games he missed during the 1990-91 season. Critics said he did not assert himself offensively early in his career, but there are few who question him now. His all-around game and aptitude for the open court have silenced the doubters. And there was never any doubt about McCray's defense.

PLAYER SUMMARY

Will .... run the floor
Can't .... play selfishly
Expect .... a defensive stopper
Don't Expect .... 20 PPG
Fantasy Value $12-14
Card Value .... 8¢

COLLEGE STATISTICS

		G	FGP	FTP	RPG	PPG
79-80	LOU	36	.543	.647	7.5	7.8
80-81	LOU	30	.588	.667	7.4	9.6
81-82	LOU	33	.571	.702	7.1	8.6
82-83	LOU	36	.587	.742	8.4	11.0
Totals		135	.573	.693	7.6	9.2

NBA REGULAR-SEASON STATISTICS

				FGs		3-PT FGs		FTs		Rebounds						
		G	MIN	FG	PCT	FG	PCT	FT	PCT	OFF	TOT	AST	STL	BLK	PTS	PPG
83-84	HOU	79	2081	335	.499	1	.250	182	.731	173	450	176	53	54	853	10.8
84-85	HOU	82	3001	476	.535	0	.000	231	.738	201	539	355	90	75	1183	14.4
85-86	HOU	82	2610	338	.537	0	.000	171	.770	159	520	292	50	58	847	10.3
86-87	HOU	81	3136	432	.552	0	.000	306	.779	190	578	434	88	53	1170	14.4
87-88	HOU	81	2689	359	.481	0	.000	288	.785	232	631	264	57	51	1006	12.4
88-89	SAC	68	2435	340	.466	5	.227	169	.722	143	514	293	57	36	854	12.6
89-90	SAC	82	3238	537	.515	11	.262	273	.784	192	669	377	60	70	1358	16.6
90-91	DAL	74	2561	336	.495	13	.333	159	.803	153	560	259	70	51	844	11.4
Totals		629	21751	3153	.511	30	.233	1779	.765	1443	4461	2450	525	448	8115	12.9

XAVIER McDANIEL

Team: Phoenix Suns
Position: Forward
Height: 6'7" **Weight:** 205
Birthdate: June 4, 1963
NBA Experience: 6 years

College: Wichita St.
Acquired: Traded from SuperSonics
for Eddie Johnson and 1st-round picks
in 1991 and either 1993 or 1994, 12/90

Background: McDaniel led Wichita State in scoring, rebounding, and field goal percentage as a junior and senior, and he was an All-American in 1985. He earned NBA All-Rookie honors with Seattle and went on to score more than 20 PPG in each of his next four years, making the All-Star Game in 1988. He was traded to Phoenix 15 games into the 1990-91 season and wound up third on the Suns in scoring and second in rebounding.

Strengths: McDaniel is everything you look for in a small forward, and then some. He puts points on the board with a deadly turnaround jump shot and his field goal percentage is consistently around .500. He rebounds, finishes the break, and plays physical—if unpolished—defense. McDaniel thrives as an intimidator, backing down from no one.

Weaknesses: Although a potent scorer, McDaniel is not a smooth driver or a pretty perimeter shooter. His range has improved, but he is at his best when backing in. Not a schooled ball-handler, he will account for about as many turnovers as assists.

Analysis: "X-Man" is one of the most respected small forwards in the league because he does so much more than score points. Few can match his competitive fire and physical approach. He gave up some points in the move to Phoenix, but his play remains All-Star caliber and very consistent.

PLAYER SUMMARY

Will ....mix it up
Can't ....handle the ball
Expect ....turnaround jumpers
Don't Expect..............pinpoint passing
Fantasy Value $15-17
Card Value..10¢

COLLEGE STATISTICS

		G	FGP	FTP	RPG	PPG
81-82	WSU	28	.504	.628	3.7	5.8
82-83	WSU	28	.593	.541	14.4	18.8
83-84	WSU	30	.564	.680	13.1	20.6
84-85	WSU	31	.559	.634	14.8	27.2
Totals		117	.564	.624	11.6	18.4

NBA REGULAR-SEASON STATISTICS

		G	MIN	FGs FG	PCT	3-PT FGs FG	PCT	FTs FT	PCT	Rebounds OFF	TOT	AST	STL	BLK	PTS	PPG
85-86	SEA	82	2706	576	.490	2	.200	250	.687	307	655	193	101	37	1404	17.1
86-87	SEA	82	3031	806	.509	3	.214	275	.696	338	705	207	115	52	1890	23.0
87-88	SEA	78	2803	687	.488	14	.280	281	.715	206	518	263	96	52	1669	21.4
88-89	SEA	82	2385	677	.489	11	.306	312	.732	177	433	134	84	40	1677	20.5
89-90	SEA	69	2432	611	.496	5	.294	244	.733	165	447	171	73	36	1471	21.3
90-91	SEA/PHO	81	2634	590	.497	0	.000	193	.723	173	557	187	76	46	1373	17.0
Totals		474	15991	3947	.495	35	.259	1555	.714	1366	3315	1155	545	263	9484	20.0

KEVIN McHALE

Team: Boston Celtics
Position: Forward/Center
Height: 6'10" **Weight:** 225
Birthdate: December 19, 1957

NBA Experience: 11 years
College: Minnesota
Acquired: 1st-round pick in 1980 draft
(3rd overall)

Background: McHale was All-Big Ten as a senior at Minnesota, graduating as the school's second-leading all-time scorer and rebounder. In his 11 seasons with Boston, he has made the NBA's All-Defensive Team three times, earned the Sixth Man Award twice, and won three championship rings. He surpassed the 15,000-career point barrier in 1990-91 and played in his seventh All-Star Game.

Strengths: McHale is one of the premier low-post scorers in NBA history. His long legs and patented pivot moves continue to befuddle defenders, while his turnaround jumper and variety of other crafty shots remain virtually unstoppable. After making one 3-pointer in his first nine years, McHale has made 38-of-106 (.358) over the last two seasons. That's a tribute to his work ethic.

Weaknesses: While his deficiencies in areas like foot speed and raw athletic ability can be overlooked, his recent bouts with injuries are of mild concern. His left ankle caused him the most trouble during 1990-91.

Analysis: McHale is a future Hall of Famer whose offensive abilities continue to amaze after 11 years in the league. One would think his low-post moves would have been solved by now, but that is not the case. The addition of the 3-point shot to his arsenal proves that old dogs can learn new tricks.

PLAYER SUMMARY

Will ....score inside and out
Can't ....be stopped in paint
Expect ....high FG percentage
Don't Expect ....blinding speed
Fantasy Value $31-33
Card Value...10¢

COLLEGE STATISTICS

		G	FGP	FTP	RPG	PPG
76-77	MINN	27	.552	.753	8.1	12.0
77-78	MINN	26	.591	.701	7.4	13.1
78-79	MINN	27	.517	.823	9.6	17.9
79-80	MINN	32	.567	.794	8.8	17.4
Totals		112	.553	.773	8.5	15.2

NBA REGULAR-SEASON STATISTICS

		G	MIN	FGs FG	FGs PCT	3-PT FGs FG	3-PT FGs PCT	FTs FT	FTs PCT	Rebounds OFF	Rebounds TOT	AST	STL	BLK	PTS	PPG
80-81	BOS	82	1645	355	.533	0	.000	108	.679	155	359	55	27	151	818	10.0
81-82	BOS	82	2332	465	.531	0	.000	187	.754	191	556	91	30	185	1117	13.6
82-83	BOS	82	2345	483	.541	0	.000	193	.717	215	553	104	34	192	1159	14.1
83-84	BOS	82	2577	587	.556	1	.333	336	.765	208	610	104	23	126	1511	18.4
84-85	BOS	79	2653	605	.570	0	.000	355	.760	229	712	141	28	120	1565	19.8
85-86	BOS	68	2397	561	.574	0	.000	326	.776	171	551	181	29	134	1448	21.3
86-87	BOS	77	3060	790	.604	0	.000	428	.836	247	763	198	38	172	2008	26.1
87-88	BOS	64	2390	550	.604	0	.000	346	.797	159	536	171	27	92	1446	22.6
88-89	BOS	78	2876	661	.546	0	.000	436	.818	223	637	172	26	97	1758	22.5
89-90	BOS	82	2722	648	.549	23	.333	393	.893	201	677	172	30	157	1712	20.9
90-91	BOS	68	2067	504	.553	15	.405	228	.829	145	480	126	25	146	1251	18.4
Totals		844	27064	6209	.562	39	.310	3336	.795	2144	6434	1515	317	1572	15793	18.7

DERRICK McKEY

Team: Seattle SuperSonics
Position: Forward
Height: 6'9" **Weight:** 210
Birthdate: October 10, 1966
NBA Experience: 4 years

College: Alabama
Acquired: 1st-round pick in 1987 draft
(9th overall)

Background: McKey earned Southeastern Conference Player of the Year accolades after leading Alabama to a conference title as a junior. He entered the draft a year early, was named to the 1987-88 All-Rookie Team, and became a starter the next season. McKey has averaged about 15 PPG and hit around 50 percent from the field every season since. He finished fourth on the Sonics in scoring in 1990-91, shooting at a career-high clip.

Strengths: McKey is blessed with superb athletic skills and court sense. His leaping ability makes him a great finisher and he handles the ball like a big guard. He drives to the hoop for scores, passes well, and uses both hands effectively. He is a pure scorer yet plays sound defense.

Weaknesses: About the only flaw in the physical ability of McKey is that he does not shoot the jumper with consistency. The biggest problem, however, is his laid-back approach. Unselfish to a fault, McKey does not know how to play with intensity on a nightly basis.

Analysis: McKey established himself as one of the NBA's budding superstars after his first two years. However, his game has stalled at that second-year level. Although he possesses all the physical tools necessary to be a big-time player, he seems content to score his 15 points and wait for someone else to take charge.

PLAYER SUMMARY

Will	finish breaks
Can't	sustain intensity
Expect	15 PPG
Don't Expect	an All-Star trip
Fantasy Value	$10-12
Card Value	8¢

COLLEGE STATISTICS

		G	FGP	FTP	RPG	PPG
84-85	ALA	33	.477	.606	4.1	5.1
85-86	ALA	33	.636	.786	7.9	13.6
86-87	ALA	33	.581	.862	7.5	18.6
Totals		99	.580	.797	6.5	12.4

NBA REGULAR-SEASON STATISTICS

				FGs		3-PT FGs		FTs		Rebounds						
		G	MIN	FG	PCT	FG	PCT	FT	PCT	OFF	TOT	AST	STL	BLK	PTS	PPG
87-88	SEA	82	1706	255	.491	11	.367	173	.772	115	328	107	70	63	694	8.5
88-89	SEA	82	2804	487	.502	30	.337	301	.803	167	464	219	105	70	1305	15.9
89-90	SEA	80	2748	468	.493	3	.130	315	.782	170	489	187	87	81	1254	15.7
90-91	SEA	73	2503	438	.517	4	.211	235	.845	172	423	169	91	56	1115	15.3
Totals		317	9761	1648	.502	48	.298	1024	.800	624	1704	682	353	270	4368	13.8

NATE McMILLAN

Team: Seattle SuperSonics
Position: Guard/Forward
Height: 6'5" **Weight:** 190
Birthdate: August 3, 1964
NBA Experience: 5 years

College: Chowan; North Carolina St.
Acquired: 2nd-round pick in 1986
draft (30th overall)

Background: McMillan was a junior college All-American before transferring to North Carolina State and averaging nearly seven assists per game as a senior. As a pro, he finished among the NBA's top ten in assists each of his first three years. He has never averaged more than eight points a game but always ranks among the top rebounding guards. He saw his fewest minutes during the 1990-91 campaign.

Strengths: McMillan is known for his defense and rebounding. His good size, deceiving quickness, and relentless effort help him shut down opponents ranging from point guards to small forwards. McMillan is strong on both offensive and defensive boards and passes well.

Weaknesses: If you want scoring, McMillan is not your man. He possesses virtually no jump shot and does not compensate for it with potent moves to the hoop. Although he has improved his 3-point percentage, his poor free throw shooting over the years says a lot.

Analysis: While McMillan can help a team in important areas like defense and rebounding, his lack of offensive punch overrides all. Opposing teams can sag off him and double his teammates. He was relegated to a bench role in 1990-91 and will likely see fewer and fewer minutes as rookie Gary Payton develops.

PLAYER SUMMARY

Will..rebound
Can't..score
Expect ....limited minutes
Don't Expect.............................10 PPG
Fantasy Value $4-6
Card Value..5¢

COLLEGE STATISTICS

		G	FGP	FTP	RPG	PPG
82-83	CHOW	27	.580	.696	5.0	9.9
83-84	CHOW	35	.544	.769	9.8	13.1
84-85	NCST	33	.454	.674	5.7	7.6
85-86	NCST	34	.485	.733	4.6	9.4
Totals		129	.515	.722	6.4	10.1

NBA REGULAR-SEASON STATISTICS

				FGs		3-PT FGs		FTs		Rebounds						
		G	MIN	FG	PCT	FG	PCT	FT	PCT	OFF	TOT	AST	STL	BLK	PTS	PPG
86-87	SEA	71	1972	143	.475	0	.000	87	.617	101	331	583	125	45	373	5.3
87-88	SEA	82	2453	235	.474	9	.375	145	.707	117	338	702	169	47	624	7.6
88-89	SEA	75	2341	199	.410	15	.214	119	.630	143	388	696	156	42	532	7.1
89-90	SEA	82	2338	207	.473	11	.355	98	.641	127	403	598	140	37	523	6.4
90-91	SEA	78	1434	132	.433	17	.354	57	.613	71	251	371	104	20	338	4.3
Totals		388	10538	916	.452	52	.289	506	.648	559	1711	2950	694	191	2390	6.2

REGGIE MILLER

Team: Indiana Pacers
Position: Guard
Height: 6'7" **Weight:** 185
Birthdate: August 24, 1965
NBA Experience: 4 years

College: UCLA
Acquired: 1st-round pick in 1987 draft (11th overall)

Background: Miller was an All-Pac-10 selection as a senior and left UCLA ranked second to Lew Alcindor on the school's career scoring list. He established himself as a 3-point shooter during his first two years with Indiana before an improved all-around game earned him a trip to the All-Star Game in 1989-90. Miller's 91.8-percent free throw accuracy led the NBA in 1990-91 and he ranked 12th in the league in scoring.

Strengths: It became clear early in his career that Miller would be one of the NBA's best pure shooters, and he is. He is automatic from the line and deadly from long-range. In the last two years, he has elevated his play to the star level, as he has improved his ability to create his own shots and get to the basket. He has also improved defensively—he uses his long arms well. Miller works diligently on his game and is tougher than he looks.

Weaknesses: Miller could stand to add a few pounds of muscle, which would probably help him rebound more like a 6'7" player should. His ball-handling and playmaking abilities do not stack up with those of most guards, but then, Miller does not play the point.

Analysis: Miller has the makings of an annual All-Star. He is clearly among the best pure shooters in the league and now must be counted among its top scorers as well. There were questions about his frame, but he has proven he can absorb the pounding of an NBA season while performing at a high level. Miller is nearly a franchise player.

PLAYER SUMMARY

Will......................score from anywhere
Can't.....................push people around
Expect..............................20-plus PPG
Don't Expect...................many boards
Fantasy Value...........................$34-37
Card Value..15¢

COLLEGE STATISTICS

		G	FGP	FTP	RPG	PPG
83-84	UCLA	28	.509	.643	1.5	4.6
84-85	UCLA	33	.553	.804	4.3	15.2
85-86	UCLA	29	.556	.882	5.3	25.9
86-87	UCLA	32	.543	.832	5.4	22.3
Totals		122	.547	.836	4.2	17.2

NBA REGULAR-SEASON STATISTICS

		G	MIN	FG	PCT	FG	PCT	FT	PCT	OFF	TOT	AST	STL	BLK	PTS	PPG
87-88	IND	82	1840	306	.488	61	.355	149	.801	95	190	132	53	19	822	10.0
88-89	IND	74	2536	398	.479	98	.402	287	.844	73	292	227	93	29	1181	16.0
89-90	IND	82	3192	661	.514	150	.414	544	.868	95	295	311	110	18	2016	24.6
90-91	IND	82	2972	596	.512	112	.348	551	.918	81	281	331	109	13	1855	22.6
Totals		320	10540	1961	.502	421	.383	1531	.873	344	1058	1001	365	79	5874	18.4

TERRY MILLS

Team: New Jersey Nets
Position: Forward
Height: 6'10" **Weight:** 230
Birthdate: December 21, 1967
NBA Experience: 1 year
College: Michigan

Acquired: Traded from Trail Blazers with Drazen Petrovic via the Nuggets; Nuggets sent Walter Davis to Blazers, and Nets sent Greg Anderson and a future 1st-round pick to Nuggets, 1/91

Background: Mills helped lead Michigan to the 1989 NCAA championship as a junior, then earned honorable mention All-America status as a senior, when he was the Wolverines' second-leading scorer and rebounder. He was drafted by Milwaukee, traded, and spent his rookie year with Denver and New Jersey. He played in 55 games, starting two with the Nets, and scored a season-high 20 points against New York on March 30.

Strengths: Mills possesses loads of offensive potential. For a big man, he has extraordinary touch and pretty good range on his jumper. He is also a creative passer, especially from the high post. Mills knows how to play the game and does it with a lot of finesse.

Weaknesses: Despite Mills's loftier name, there were plenty of reasons Michigan teammate Loy Vaught was chosen higher in the first round. Mills does not play aggressively on a consistent basis. He has lapses in which he seems uninterested. Better off-season conditioning would be a good place to start. Mills has trouble on defense with both bigger centers and quicker forwards.

Analysis: This remains the book on Mills: He can be as good as he wants to be. It is hard to judge a rookie on what he does in 14 minutes per game, and Mills's 20-point outburst near the end of the season may or may not have been a glimpse of things to come. The potential is certainly there for a double-figure scoring average. Commitment is the next step.

PLAYER SUMMARY

Will ....display soft touch
Can't ....stay focused
Expect......................more playing time
Don't Expect ....any guarantees
Fantasy Value $2-4
Card Value...8¢

COLLEGE STATISTICS

		G	FGP	FTP	RPG	PPG
87-88	MICH	34	.531	.729	6.4	12.1
88-89	MICH	37	.564	.769	5.9	11.6
89-90	MICH	31	.585	.759	8.0	18.1
Totals		102	.562	.755	6.7	13.8

NBA REGULAR-SEASON STATISTICS

				FGs		3-PT FGs		FTs		Rebounds						
		G	MIN	FG	PCT	FG	PCT	FT	PCT	OFF	TOT	AST	STL	BLK	PTS	PPG
90-91	DEN/NJ	55	819	134	.465	0	.000	47	.712	82	229	33	35	29	315	5.7
Totals		55	819	134	.465	0	.000	47	.712	82	229	33	35	29	315	5.7

SAM MITCHELL

Team: Minnesota Timberwolves
Position: Forward
Height: 6'7" **Weight:** 210
Birthdate: September 2, 1963
NBA Experience: 2 years

College: Mercer
Acquired: Signed as a free agent, 7/89

Background: Mitchell, the all-time leading scorer at Mercer, got a late start as a pro. After being drafted and cut by Houston in 1985, he began a teaching career. His hoop comeback took him to the USBL, to the CBA, and on a two-year stint in France before he became the NBA's oldest rookie (at 26) in 1989-90. Mitchell has been a double-figure scorer for two seasons in Minnesota and was fourth on the team in 1990-91.

Strengths: On offense, Mitchell owns a decent medium-range jumper and is willing to go hard to the basket and draw fouls. He was second on the Timberwolves in free throws attempted and made. On defense, Mitchell plays with toughness, intensity, and a fine work ethic.

Weaknesses: For a small forward, Mitchell is below average when it comes to running the floor and handling the ball. He is above average in fouling, as he led the league by drawing 338 whistles. While he does a lot of things fairly well, he does few things well enough (except fouling) to stand out.

Analysis: From France to double-figure scorer in the NBA is a big jump, but Mitchell was able to pull it off with hard work and commitment. He is not a star in a league loaded with standout forwards, but he earned 60 starts in 1990-91. His story is an inspiring one.

PLAYER SUMMARY

Will	play defense
Can't	avoid fouling
Expect	all-out effort
Don't Expect	headlines
Fantasy Value	$7-9
Card Value	15¢

COLLEGE STATISTICS

		G	FGP	FTP	RPG	PPG
81-82	MER	27	.497	.717	3.7	7.1
82-83	MER	28	.519	.784	5.9	16.5
83-84	MER	26	.507	.781	7.1	21.5
84-85	MER	31	.516	.750	8.2	25.0
Totals		112	.512	.763	6.3	17.7

NBA REGULAR-SEASON STATISTICS

		G	MIN	FGs FG	FGs PCT	3-PT FGs FG	3-PT FGs PCT	FTs FT	FTs PCT	Rebounds OFF	Rebounds TOT	AST	STL	BLK	PTS	PPG
89-90	MIN	80	2414	372	.446	0	.000	268	.768	180	462	89	66	54	1012	12.6
90-91	MIN	82	3121	445	.441	0	.000	307	.775	188	520	133	66	57	1197	14.6
Totals		162	5535	817	.443	0	.000	575	.772	368	982	222	132	111	2209	13.6

SIDNEY MONCRIEF

Team: Atlanta Hawks
Position: Guard
Height: 6'3" **Weight:** 181
Birthdate: September 21, 1957

NBA Experience: 11 years
College: Arkansas
Acquired: Signed as a free agent, 8/90

Background: Moncrief was a college All-American and finished his career as Arkansas' all-time leading scorer and rebounder. During his storied ten-year stay with Milwaukee, he guided the Bucks to ten straight winning seasons, made five All-Star appearances, and earned Defensive Player of the Year honors in 1983 and '84. He retired from the NBA after the 1988-89 season before returning to the league with Atlanta in 1990-91 and filling in at both guard slots.

Strengths: At one time, Moncrief could do just about everything well. He was the best defensive guard in the league for many years and could score in countless ways. Now, his best attributes are versatility and leadership. He knows the league, brings out the best in his teammates, and is a great stabilizer.

Weaknesses: Moncrief has lost the explosiveness that once made him a dangerous offensive player. While he can fill in and hit a crucial shot every now and then, he cannot thrive as a primary scorer. It is strange to see opponents able to beat him off the dribble.

Analysis: Moncrief proved to be a valuable addition for the Hawks. His experience certainly helped them win a few more ballgames, including one against the Pistons in the 1991 playoffs. Many teams could use such leadership.

PLAYER SUMMARY

Will	play within himself
Can't	regain All-Star form
Expect	veteran leadership
Don't Expect	explosive offense
Fantasy Value	$2-4
Card Value	8¢

COLLEGE STATISTICS

		G	FGP	FTP	RPG	PPG
75-76	ARK	28	.665	.727	7.6	12.6
76-77	ARK	28	.649	.684	8.4	15.4
77-78	ARK	36	.590	.793	7.7	17.3
78-79	ARK	30	.560	.855	9.6	22.0
Totals		122	.606	.782	8.3	16.9

NBA REGULAR-SEASON STATISTICS

				FGs		3-PT FGs		FTs		Rebounds						
		G	MIN	FG	PCT	FG	PCT	FT	PCT	OFF	TOT	AST	STL	BLK	PTS	PPG
79-80	MIL	77	1557	211	.468	0	.000	232	.795	154	338	133	72	16	654	8.5
80-81	MIL	80	2417	400	.541	2	.222	320	.804	186	406	264	90	37	1122	14.0
81-82	MIL	80	2980	556	.523	1	.071	468	.817	221	534	382	138	22	1581	19.8
82-83	MIL	76	2710	606	.524	1	.100	499	.826	192	437	300	113	23	1712	22.5
83-84	MIL	79	3075	560	.498	5	.278	529	.848	215	528	358	108	27	1654	20.9
84-85	MIL	73	2734	561	.483	9	.273	454	.828	149	391	382	117	39	1585	21.7
85-86	MIL	73	2567	470	.489	33	.320	498	.859	115	334	357	103	18	1471	20.2
86-87	MIL	39	992	158	.488	8	.258	136	.840	57	127	121	27	10	460	11.8
87-88	MIL	56	1428	217	.489	5	.161	164	.837	58	180	204	41	12	603	10.8
88-89	MIL	62	1594	261	.491	25	.342	205	.865	46	172	188	65	13	752	12.1
90-91	ATL	72	1096	117	.488	21	.328	82	.781	31	128	104	50	9	337	4.7
Totals		767	23150	4117	.502	110	.284	3587	.831	1424	3575	2793	924	226	11931	15.6

CHRIS MORRIS

Team: New Jersey Nets
Position: Forward
Height: 6'8" **Weight:** 210
Birthdate: January 20, 1966
NBA Experience: 3 years

College: Auburn
Acquired: 1st-round pick in 1988 draft (4th overall)

Background: Following in the footsteps of past Auburn greats Charles Barkley and Chuck Person, Morris was the fourth player selected in the entire 1988 NBA draft. After season No. 1, the Nets looked like geniuses for taking him when they did. An All-Rookie second-team selection, Morris was New Jersey's best all-around performer. Since then, his game has regressed. He shot a miserable .422 from the field in 1989-90 and .425 last year.

Strengths: Equipped with plenty of natural ability, Morris is as athletic as any small forward in the NBA. He can put the ball on the floor and drive to the hoop or fire away from 3-point range. Morris gets good position under the offensive boards.

Weaknesses: Morris is an immature player. One quarter you'd swear he's an All-Star and the next you're calling him a bum. Morris allegedly feels sorry for himself on occasion because he plays for the lowly Nets. Poor guy! He often seems like he's just going through the motions.

Analysis: It's no secret around the league that coach Bill Fitch and Morris do not get along. If the Nets can convince another team to take a chance on their potential problem child, they'd probably dump him in a New York minute. He's worth the chance.

PLAYER SUMMARY

Will ....become trade bait
Can't ....stay focused
Expect.................problems with coach
Don't Expect ....mature attitude
Fantasy Value $6-8
Card Value...10¢

COLLEGE STATISTICS

		G	FGP	FTP	RPG	PPG
84-85	AUB	34	.477	.620	5.0	10.4
85-86	AUB	33	.500	.670	5.2	9.8
86-87	AUB	31	.559	.711	7.3	13.5
87-88	AUB	30	.481	.795	9.8	20.7
Totals		128	.501	.712	6.7	13.4

NBA REGULAR-SEASON STATISTICS

				FGs		3-PT FGs		FTs		Rebounds						
		G	MIN	FG	PCT	FG	PCT	FT	PCT	OFF	TOT	AST	STL	BLK	PTS	PPG
88-89	NJ	76	2096	414	.457	64	.366	182	.717	188	397	119	102	60	1074	14.1
89-90	NJ	80	2449	449	.422	61	.316	228	.722	194	422	143	130	79	1187	14.8
90-91	NJ	79	2553	409	.425	45	.251	179	.734	210	521	220	138	96	1042	13.2
Totals		235	7098	1272	.434	170	.311	589	.724	592	1340	482	370	235	3303	14.1

JOHN MORTON

Team: Cleveland Cavaliers
Position: Guard
Height: 6'3 **Weight:** 183
Birthdate: May 18, 1967
NBA Experience: 2 years

College: Seton Hall
Acquired: 1st-round pick in 1989 draft
(25th overall)

Background: His best college game was also his last—a 35-point outburst in Seton Hall's 1989 NCAA title-game loss to Michigan. Drafted late in round No. 1 by Cleveland, Morton was plagued early on by a strained hamstring. It took him months to fully recover and by season's end he had shot an embarrassing .298 from the field. Morton's numbers improved across the board last season. He shot .438 from the floor and finished third on the Cavs in assists per game.

Strengths: Morton's not a natural shooter, but he is creative enough to know how to score. He's proven over time that he can handle himself at either backcourt post. With coach Lenny Wilkens's tutelage, Morton's made himself into a darn good passer.

Weaknesses: A decent enough penetrator, finishing plays is his major problem. Defensively, Morton's coming along slower than expected. He takes way too many chances and one day he'll have to realize you don't defend Spud Webb like you would Michael Jordan.

Analysis: Although Morton played much better in his second season, things are going to get a bit crowded in the Cleveland backcourt when Mark Price returns. Someone's going to be left out and that could be Morton, particularly if his game at all resembles what he did (or didn't do) in 1989-90.

PLAYER SUMMARY

Will ....play both guard spots
Can't........................ play NBA defense
Expect....................crowded backcourt
Don't Expect ....as many minutes
Fantasy Value $1-2
Card Value...12¢

COLLEGE STATISTICS

		G	FGP	FTP	RPG	PPG
85-86	SH	31	.441	.636	1.5	7.5
86-87	SH	27	.452	.730	2.6	10.4
87-88	SH	35	.486	.841	1.9	12.8
88-89	SH	38	.436	.820	3.4	17.3
Totals		131	.453	.771	2.4	12.4

NBA REGULAR-SEASON STATISTICS

				FGs		3-PT FGs		FTs		Rebounds						
		G	MIN	FG	PCT	FG	PCT	FT	PCT	OFF	TOT	AST	STL	BLK	PTS	PPG
89-90	CLE	37	402	48	.298	7	.233	43	.694	7	32	67	18	4	146	3.9
90-91	CLE	66	1207	120	.438	4	.333	113	.813	41	103	243	61	18	357	5.4
Totals		103	1609	168	.386	11	.262	156	.776	48	135	310	79	22	503	4.9

CHRIS MULLIN

Team: Golden State Warriors
Position: Forward
Height: 6'7" **Weight:** 215
Birthdate: July 30, 1963
NBA Experience: 6 years

College: St. John's
Acquired: 1st-round pick in 1985 draft
(7th overall)

Background: Mullin's college career at St. John's was highly celebrated, as he made every All-America team as a senior and virtually every one as a junior. He graduated as the Big East's all-time scoring leader. His pro career began with two good seasons, but since he voluntarily entered an alcohol rehab program in 1987-88, he has made three All-Star Games and has never averaged below 20 PPG. He started all 82 games for Golden State in 1990-91, led the league in minutes, and topped the Warriors in scoring for the fourth straight year.

Strengths: There is not much Mullin is unable to do. He shoots with great touch and 3-point range, and he can kill you even with a hand or two in his face. He is a superb passer, an above-average rebounder, and plays heads-up defense. Mullin is a well-respected leader with a great feel for the game.

Weaknesses: Mullin will never win any awards for his athletic ability, but he is actually quicker than he looks. He uses the ability he does have to its fullest.

Analysis: Mullin was likened to Larry Bird coming out of college, and after a so-so start he has more than lived up to such a high billing. He is not just one of the premier scorers in the NBA, but one of its premier players. His court sense is uncanny and his perimeter game remarkably consistent.

PLAYER SUMMARY

Will ....hit from anywhere
Can't ....win dunk contest
Expect ....20 PPG
Don't Expect ....inconsistency
Fantasy Value $68-71
Card Value.......................................15¢

COLLEGE STATISTICS

		G	FGP	FTP	RPG	PPG
81-82	STJ	30	.534	.791	3.2	16.6
82-83	STJ	33	.577	.878	3.7	19.1
83-84	STJ	27	.571	.904	4.4	22.9
84-85	STJ	35	.521	.824	4.8	19.8
Totals		125	.550	.848	4.1	19.5

NBA REGULAR-SEASON STATISTICS

				FGs		3-PT FGs		FTs		Rebounds						
		G	MIN	FG	PCT	FG	PCT	FT	PCT	OFF	TOT	AST	STL	BLK	PTS	PPG
85-86	GS	55	1391	287	.463	5	.185	189	.896	42	115	105	70	23	768	14.0
86-87	GS	82	2377	477	.514	19	.302	269	.825	39	181	261	98	36	1242	15.1
87-88	GS	60	2033	470	.508	34	.351	239	.885	58	205	290	113	32	1213	20.2
88-89	GS	82	3093	830	.509	23	.230	493	.892	152	483	415	176	39	2176	26.5
89-90	GS	78	2830	682	.536	87	.372	505	.889	130	463	319	123	45	1956	25.1
90-91	GS	82	3315	777	.536	40	.301	513	.884	141	443	329	173	63	2107	25.7
Totals		439	15039	3523	.516	208	.318	2208	.880	562	1890	1719	753	238	9462	21.6

TOD MURPHY

Team: Minnesota Timberwolves
Position: Forward
Height: 6'10" **Weight:** 220
Birthdate: December 24, 1963
NBA Experience: 3 years

College: California-Irvine
Acquired: Signed as a free agent, 8/89

Background: Murphy completed his career at Cal.-Irvine as the school's all-time leading scorer and second-leading rebounder. He was cut by Seattle in 1986 and played briefly in Italy before playing one game with the L.A. Clippers in 1987. Upon being released, Murphy played for Albany of the CBA and spent 1988-89 in Spain. He led Minnesota in 3-point shooting during 1989-90 but was plagued by injuries in 1990-91.

Strengths: Hard work lifted Murphy to his NBA roster spot and remains his biggest asset. He battles for rebounds, shows good shooting range, and plays physical defense. Tell him what to do and he gives it his all.

Weaknesses: Murphy lacks big-time athletic skills and is not a picture of precision on the court. He is slow, uncoordinated, and is unable to put the ball on the floor or make crisp passes. Recurring back spasms sidelined him for two months of the 1990-91 season.

Analysis: Murphy overachieved in 1989-90. After returning from back problems in 1991, though, he shot just 35.4 percent from the field. For the year, the Wolves' 1989-90 3-point leader made only one of his 17 attempts from downtown. As long as he stays healthy and with an expansion club, Murphy will work his way into playing time.

PLAYER SUMMARY

Will	play post defense
Can't	handle the ball
Expect	role playing
Don't Expect	10 PPG
Fantasy Value	$1-3
Card Value	8¢

COLLEGE STATISTICS

		G	FGP	FTP	RPG	PPG
82-83	C-I	28	.517	.710	5.4	8.7
83-84	C-I	29	.575	.815	7.0	14.4
84-85	C-I	30	.559	.850	8.9	17.0
85-86	C-I	30	.558	.746	7.2	20.2
Totals		117	.556	.781	7.2	15.2

NBA REGULAR-SEASON STATISTICS

				FGs		3-PT FGs		FTs		Rebounds						
		G	MIN	FG	PCT	FG	PCT	FT	PCT	OFF	TOT	AST	STL	BLK	PTS	PPG
87-88	LAC	1	19	1	1.000	0	.000	3	.750	1	2	2	1	0	5	5.0
89-90	MIN	82	2493	260	.471	16	.372	144	.709	207	564	106	76	60	680	8.3
90-91	MIN	52	1063	90	.396	1	.059	70	.667	92	255	60	25	20	251	4.8
Totals		135	3575	351	.450	17	.283	217	.696	300	821	168	102	80	936	6.9

JERROD MUSTAF

Team: New York Knicks
Position: Forward
Height: 6'10" **Weight:** 244
Birthdate: October 28, 1969
NBA Experience: 1 year

College: Maryland
Acquired: 1st-round pick in 1990 draft (17th overall)

Background: He was playing high school ball four short years ago at famed DeMatha High in Washington D.C. After being criticized by some for leaving the University of Maryland after only two seasons, Mustaf proved to be a key contributor at small forward as a Knicks rookie. He played nearly 15 minutes per night and started five games in December. Tendinitis in his knee sidelined Mustaf for almost the entire month of March.

Strengths: Although he's got the size to hold his own at power forward, Mustaf has a small forward's mentality. He can put the ball on the floor, shoot from the wing, and guard most of the league's small forwards. Young and eager to learn, he's got a refreshing attitude.

Weaknesses: Forget about the fact that he's 6'10", 244 pounds. Mustaf is a finesse player. His weight doesn't include a lot of muscle. Still a kid, his body is soft in a lot of areas. He was inconsistent when the season began and just as inconsistent when it ended.

Analysis: Mustaf handled himself quite well last season for a 21-year-old with such limited experience. A fundamentally sound player, now it's just a matter of continuing to improve each season. There's no reason to believe he won't. Many scouts figured he'd be one of the top three or four picks in this coming year's draft had he stayed in school.

PLAYER SUMMARY

Will ....take time to develop
Can't...............................muscle inside
Expect ....more minutes
Don't Expect...........................10 PPG
Fantasy Value $2-4
Card Value...10¢

COLLEGE STATISTICS

		G	FGP	FTP	RPG	PPG
88-89	MD	26	.520	.716	7.8	14.3
89-90	MD	33	.529	.774	7.7	18.5
Totals		59	.525	.756	7.7	16.6

NBA REGULAR-SEASON STATISTICS

			FGs		3-PT FGs		FTs		Rebounds						
	G	MIN	FG	PCT	FG	PCT	FT	PCT	OFF	TOT	AST	STL	BLK	PTS	PPG
90-91 NY	62	825	106	.465	0	.000	56	.644	51	169	36	15	14	268	4.3
Totals	62	825	106	.465	0	.000	56	.644	51	169	36	15	14	268	4.3

LARRY NANCE

Team: Cleveland Cavaliers
Position: Forward/Center
Height: 6'10" **Weight:** 235
Birthdate: February 12, 1959
NBA Experience: 10 years
College: Clemson

Acquired: Traded from Suns with Mike Sanders and a 1988 1st-round pick for Tyrone Corbin, Kevin Johnson, Mark West, 1988 1st- and 2nd-round picks, and a 1989 2nd-round pick, 2/88

Background: Clemson's leading rebounder for three consecutive seasons, Nance joined the Suns ten years ago. Between 1982-83 and 1986-87, Nance paced Phoenix in scoring with nearly 20 per game. His trade to the Cavs for Kevin Johnson and others was the biggest in Suns history. A two-time NBA All-Star, Nance was named to the NBA All-Defensive Team in 1989. In 1990-91, he finished second on the Cavs in scoring and rebounding.

Strengths: He blocked more shots last year than any other forward in the league. He's a very good passer who can score via a wide variety of low-post moves. Nance is still too quick for a lot of opposing forwards.

Weaknesses: Seemingly always bothered by nagging injuries, Nance hasn't played a full 82-game slate since 1983-84. Though quite consistent throughout his career, he's been pegged as a player who doesn't show up in big games.

Analysis: Today's most successful NBA teams have a big, tough guy throwing his weight around at power forward. Nance is anything but. He's always been a finesse player who gets by with size, quickness, and great anticipation.

PLAYER SUMMARY

Will ....block shots
Can't............................avoid injury bug
Expect....................same finesse game
Don't Expect..............smaller numbers
Fantasy Value $35-38
Card Value...8¢

COLLEGE STATISTICS

		G	FGP	FTP	RPG	PPG
77-78	CLEM	25	.467	.471	3.1	3.1
78-79	CLEM	29	.519	.636	7.2	11.1
79-80	CLEM	32	.515	.598	8.1	13.9
80-81	CLEM	31	.575	.690	7.6	15.9
Totals		117	.533	.628	6.7	11.5

NBA REGULAR-SEASON STATISTICS

		G	MIN	FGs FG	FGs PCT	3-PT FGs FG	3-PT FGs PCT	FTs FT	FTs PCT	Rebounds OFF	Rebounds TOT	AST	STL	BLK	PTS	PPG
81-82	PHO	80	1186	227	.521	0	.000	75	.641	95	256	82	42	71	529	6.6
82-83	PHO	82	2914	588	.550	1	.333	193	.672	239	710	197	99	217	1370	16.7
83-84	PHO	82	2899	601	.576	0	.000	249	.707	227	678	214	86	174	1451	17.7
84-85	PHO	61	2202	515	.587	1	.500	180	.709	195	536	159	88	104	1211	19.9
85-86	PHO	73	2484	582	.581	0	.000	310	.698	169	618	240	70	130	1474	20.2
86-87	PHO	69	2569	585	.551	1	.200	381	.773	188	599	233	86	148	1552	22.5
87-88	PHO/CLE	67	2383	487	.529	2	.333	304	.779	193	607	207	63	159	1280	19.1
88-89	CLE	73	2526	496	.539	0	.000	267	.799	156	581	159	57	206	1259	17.2
89-90	CLE	62	2065	412	.511	1	1.000	186	.778	162	516	161	54	122	1011	16.3
90-91	CLE	80	2927	635	.524	2	.250	265	.803	201	686	237	66	200	1537	19.2
Totals		729	24155	5128	.549	8	.178	2410	.744	1825	5787	1889	711	1531	12674	17.4

ED NEALY

Team: Phoenix Suns
Position: Forward
Height: 6'7" **Weight:** 240
Birthdate: February 19, 1960
NBA Experience: 8 years

College: Kansas St.
Acquired: Signed as a free agent, 7/90

Background: Nealy was named All-Big Eight and Academic All-American as a senior at Kansas State, where he finished as the school's career leader in rebounds and led the conference in that category three times. He has spent eight NBA seasons on four different teams, including two stints with Phoenix. He played in 55 games for the Suns in 1990-91.

Strengths: The box score is not a good place to look for the contributions Nealy makes. He'll have big rebounding numbers every so often, but his main strength is as a physical defender and pick-setter. He throws his bulk around and takes opponents out of their games. He makes few mistakes.

Weaknesses: Nealy is slow, has trouble getting off his feet, and has never had much of an offensive repertoire. His game is power forward all the way, meaning he looks up at most of his match-ups. He must be wide open to get his shot off.

Analysis: Nealy is one of the best at what he does, but then, there is not much competition. Few could earn a living in the NBA with his offensive non-production, but Nealy thrives on his role as an enforcer who can play a few key minutes without hurting his team. When on the floor, he causes problems that have nothing to do with scoring.

PLAYER SUMMARY

Will............................pound the boards
Can't...................................create shots
Expect.....................bumps and bruises
Don't Expect ....scoring
Fantasy Value................................$1-2
Card Value......................................5¢

COLLEGE STATISTICS

		G	FGP	FTP	RPG	PPG
78-79	KSU	28	.432	.789	8.2	10.2
79-80	KSU	31	.471	.724	8.8	9.8
80-81	KSU	33	.526	.720	9.1	11.0
81-82	KSU	31	.568	.615	8.6	11.3
Totals		123	.499	.700	8.7	10.6

NBA REGULAR-SEASON STATISTICS

				FGs		3-PT FGs		FTs		Rebounds						
		G	MIN	FG	PCT	FG	PCT	FT	PCT	OFF	TOT	AST	STL	BLK	PTS	PPG
82-83	KC	82	1643	147	.595	0	.000	70	.614	170	485	62	68	12	364	4.4
83-84	KC	71	960	63	.500	0	.000	48	.800	73	222	50	41	9	174	2.5
84-85	KC	22	225	26	.591	0	.000	10	.526	15	44	18	3	1	62	2.8
86-87	SA	60	980	84	.438	4	.129	51	.739	96	284	83	40	11	223	3.7
87-88	SA	68	837	50	.459	1	.500	41	.651	82	222	49	29	5	142	2.1
88-89	CHI/PHO	43	258	13	.361	0	.000	4	.444	22	78	14	7	1	30	0.7
89-90	CHI	46	503	37	.529	0	.000	30	.732	46	138	28	16	4	104	2.3
90-91	PHO	55	573	45	.464	5	.313	28	.737	44	151	36	24	4	123	2.2
Totals		447	5979	465	.505	10	.189	282	.683	548	1624	340	228	47	1222	2.7

JOHNNY NEWMAN

Team: Charlotte Hornets
Position: Forward
Height: 6'7" **Weight:** 190
Birthdate: November 28, 1963
NBA Experience: 5 years

College: Richmond
Acquired: Signed as a free agent, 7/90

Background: Richmond's all-time leading scorer, Newman spent one season playing big guard for the Cavs before being waived. The Knicks picked him up and immediately moved him to small forward. He thrived under coach Rick Pitino and New York's up-tempo game. Signed by the Hornets as a restricted free agent two summers ago, Newman enjoyed his best pro season in Charlotte in 1990-91. He led the Hornets in scoring and minutes, and he logged career highs in nearly every offensive category.

Strengths: Newman's the top scorer on a team that desperately needs offense. When he's in sync, he's fun to watch. He gives it his all defensively. Despite his frail build, Newman isn't afraid to stick his nose into the low-post fray. He's the best all-around athlete on the team.

Weaknesses: He's a streaky player who'll perform like an All-Star one night and disappear the next. Newman does a poor job on the offensive glass and his shooting range is suspect at best. He doesn't pass well on the move.

Analysis: As Newman goes, so go the Hornets, a team that's much more dependent on his offense than the Knicks were. Good teams don't make inconsistent players like Newman their go-to guy. Charlotte's not a good team.

PLAYER SUMMARY	
Will	take the most shots
Can't	remain as go-to guy
Expect	more streaky play
Don't Expect	enough rebounds
Fantasy Value	$5-7
Card Value	10¢

COLLEGE STATISTICS

		G	FGP	FTP	RPG	PPG
82-83	RICH	28	.529	.719	3.1	12.3
83-84	RICH	32	.528	.787	6.1	21.9
84-85	RICH	32	.551	.773	5.2	21.3
85-86	RICH	30	.517	.890	7.3	22.0
Totals		122	.532	.800	5.5	19.5

NBA REGULAR-SEASON STATISTICS

				FGs		3-PT FGs		FTs		Rebounds						
		G	MIN	FG	PCT	FG	PCT	FT	PCT	OFF	TOT	AST	STL	BLK	PTS	PPG
86-87	CLE	59	630	113	.411	1	.045	66	.868	36	70	27	20	7	293	5.0
87-88	NY	77	1589	270	.435	26	.280	207	.841	87	159	62	72	11	773	10.0
88-89	NY	81	2336	455	.475	97	.338	286	.815	93	206	162	111	23	1293	16.0
89-90	NY	80	2277	374	.476	45	.317	239	.799	60	191	180	95	22	1032	12.9
90-91	CHA	81	2477	478	.470	30	.357	385	.809	94	254	188	100	17	1371	16.9
Totals		378	9309	1690	.462	199	.317	1183	.817	370	880	619	398	80	4762	12.6

KEN NORMAN

Team: Los Angeles Clippers
Position: Forward
Height: 6'8 **Weight:** 219
Birthdate: September 5, 1964
NBA Experience: 4 years

College: Wabash Valley; Illinois
Acquired: 1st-round pick in 1987 draft
(19th overall)

Background: Norman was a two-time All-Big Ten selection at Illinois, where he set a school record for field goal percentage and finished his three-year career seventh on the all-time scoring list. He became a starter for the Clippers late in his rookie season, then increased his scoring average by nearly ten points in 1988-89. He has not improved on that season since, but he finished third on the Clippers in scoring and rebounding in 1990-91.

Strengths: Norman thrives in the open court, where his finishing ability can ignite a team. Offensively, he scores well with his back to the basket and gets inside for easy buckets. He is an above-average rebounder and can play defense when he sets his mind to it.

Weaknesses: Norman's shaky outside shooting can be seen in what he does from the free throw line, where he is consistently in the low 60s. He does not handle the ball well, especially when moved from small forward to off guard. Sustaining intensity is another area of concern.

Analysis: Although he has posted solid seasons, more was expected of Norman after his banner second year. If he could become a better outside shooter and play with a team-first, 48-minutes-a-night attitude, his athletic ability may still earn him the recognition many thought would be his by now.

PLAYER SUMMARY

Will ....finish breaks
Can't ....shoot FTs
Expect ....inside offense
Don't Expect ....sustained focus
Fantasy Value $10-12
Card Value...10¢

COLLEGE STATISTICS

		G	FGP	FTP	RPG	PPG
82-83	WAB	35	.605	.673	10.3	20.4
84-85	ILL	29	.632	.663	3.7	7.8
85-86	ILL	32	.641	.802	7.1	16.4
86-87	ILL	31	.578	.727	9.8	20.7
Totals		127	.608	.717	7.9	16.6

NBA REGULAR-SEASON STATISTICS

				FGs		3-PT FGs		FTs		Rebounds						
		G	MIN	FG	PCT	FG	PCT	FT	PCT	OFF	TOT	AST	STL	BLK	PTS	PPG
87-88	LAC	66	1435	241	.482	0	.000	87	.512	100	263	78	44	34	569	8.6
88-89	LAC	80	3020	638	.502	4	.190	170	.630	245	667	277	106	66	1450	18.1
89-90	LAC	70	2334	484	.510	7	.438	153	.632	143	470	160	78	59	1128	16.1
90-91	LAC	70	2309	520	.501	6	.188	173	.629	177	497	159	63	63	1219	17.4
Totals		286	9098	1883	.501	17	.215	583	.609	665	1897	674	291	222	4366	15.3

CHARLES OAKLEY

Team: New York Knicks
Position: Forward
Height: 6'9" **Weight:** 245
Birthdate: December 18, 1963
NBA Experience: 6 years

College: Virginia Union
Acquired: Traded from Bulls with 1988 1st- and 3rd-round picks for Bill Cartwright and 1988 1st- and 3rd-round picks, 6/88

Background: The top Division II rebounder in the country in 1984-85, Oakley grabbed more than 17 per game at tiny Virginia Union. He made the NBA All-Rookie Team with Chicago the following season. A chronic complainer, he was shipped to New York in 1988 in exchange for Bill Cartwright. After finishing second in the NBA in rebounding in 1986-87 and 1987-88, Oakley finished third last season. Nagging injuries affected his play in March and April. He missed the final month of the 1989-90 season with a broken hand.

Strengths: Rebounding. The NBA's "Chairman of the Boards," Oakley is one of only five active players to average more than 11 RPG in his career. He uses his wide body to its full advantage at both ends of the floor.

Weaknesses: Although he shot 52 percent from the field last year, he scored his fewest points since his rookie season. Oakley thinks he's a better offensive player than he really is. He doesn't jump well, relying instead on positioning and brute strength for many of his rebounds.

Analysis: Although he promises a lot of changes, Pat Riley certainly won't touch Oakley or Patrick Ewing, perhaps the premier power forward-center combo in the league. He'll wisely build his team around them. If Oakley played a little smarter offensively, he'd be an NBA All-Star.

PLAYER SUMMARY

Will ....play blue-collar ball
Can't ....block shots
Expect..........................a glass cleaner
Don't Expect...................offensive skill
Fantasy Value $22-25
Card Value......................................10¢

COLLEGE STATISTICS

		G	FGP	FTP	RPG	PPG
81-82	VU	28	.620	.610	12.5	15.9
82-83	VU	28	.582	.588	13.0	19.3
83-84	VU	30	.612	.621	13.1	21.7
84-85	VU	31	.625	.669	17.3	24.0
Totals		117	.611	.626	14.0	20.3

NBA REGULAR-SEASON STATISTICS

			FGs		3-PT FGs		FTs		Rebounds						
		G	MIN	FG	PCT	FG	PCT	FT	PCT	OFF	TOT	AST	STL	BLK	PTS	PPG
85-86	CHI	77	1772	281	.519	0	.000	178	.662	255	664	133	68	30	740	9.6
86-87	CHI	82	2980	468	.445	11	.367	245	.686	299	1074	296	85	36	1192	14.5
87-88	CHI	82	2816	375	.483	3	.250	261	.727	326	1066	248	68	28	1014	12.4
88-89	NY	82	2604	426	.510	12	.250	197	.773	343	861	187	104	14	1061	12.9
89-90	NY	61	2196	336	.524	0	.000	217	.761	258	727	146	64	16	889	14.6
90-91	NY	76	2739	307	.516	0	.000	239	.784	305	920	204	62	17	853	11.2
Totals		460	15107	2193	.494	26	.265	1337	.731	1786	5312	1214	451	141	5749	12.5

HAKEEM OLAJUWON

Team: Houston Rockets
Position: Center
Height: 7'0" **Weight:** 258
Birthdate: January 21, 1963

NBA Experience: 7 years
College: Houston
Acquired: 1st-round pick in 1984 draft (1st overall)

Background: Selected Southwest Conference Player of the 1980s by media and coaches, Olajuwon led Houston to the NCAA Final Four three consecutive years. As a senior, he led the nation in rebounding and field goal accuracy. The former soccer goalie in Nigeria continued to improve his game as a pro, making All-Star trips in his first six years. Olajuwon won the NBA shot-blocking title for the second straight year in 1990-91 and would have captured the rebounding crown for the third straight time had he not missed 26 games with a fractured eye socket.

Strengths: Olajuwon is one of the most versatile centers ever. He scores, rebounds, and blocks shots as well as anyone, but there are overlooked talents as well. He has an amazing touch for a center and his defensive game includes great anticipation for steals. Few play with the intensity of Olajuwon. In 1990-91, he showed his unselfishness by offering to come off the bench after returning from his eye injury.

Weaknesses: The closest thing to a weakness in Olajuwon's game has been foul trouble, but—as with every other area—he has improved greatly.

Analysis: Olajuwon might be the best center in the NBA. His numbers certainly support that claim. For someone who took up basketball in 1978, he has learned how to dominate like few can. He added an "H" to his first name in 1991, but there is little left to add to his Hall of Fame game.

PLAYER SUMMARY

Will ....do it all
Can't ....go through motions
Expect ....domination
Don't Expect............unbroken records
Fantasy Value $85-88
Card Value ....10-15¢

COLLEGE STATISTICS

		G	FGP	FTP	RPG	PPG
81-82	HOU	29	.607	.563	6.2	8.3
82-83	HOU	34	.611	.595	11.4	13.9
83-84	HOU	37	.675	.526	13.5	16.8
Totals		100	.639	.555	10.7	13.3

NBA REGULAR-SEASON STATISTICS

				FGs		3-PT FGs		FTs		Rebounds						
		G	MIN	FG	PCT	FG	PCT	FT	PCT	OFF	TOT	AST	STL	BLK	PTS	PPG
84-85	HOU	82	2914	677	.538	0	.000	338	.613	440	974	111	99	220	1692	20.6
85-86	HOU	68	2467	625	.526	0	.000	347	.645	333	781	137	134	231	1597	23.5
86-87	HOU	75	2760	677	.508	1	.200	400	.702	315	858	220	140	254	1755	23.4
87-88	HOU	79	2825	712	.514	0	.000	381	.695	302	959	163	162	214	1805	22.8
88-89	HOU	82	3024	790	.508	0	.000	454	.696	338	1105	149	213	282	2034	24.8
89-90	HOU	82	3124	806	.501	1	.167	382	.713	299	1149	234	174	376	1995	24.3
90-91	HOU	56	2062	487	.508	0	.000	213	.769	219	770	131	121	221	1187	21.2
Totals		524	19176	4774	.514	2	.069	2515	.685	2246	6596	1145	1043	1798	12065	23.0

BRIAN OLIVER

Team: Philadelphia 76ers
Position: Guard
Height: 6'4" **Weight:** 210
Birthdate: June 1, 1968
NBA Experience: 1 year

College: Georgia Tech
Acquired: 2nd-round pick in 1990
draft (32nd overall)

Background: A member of Georgia Tech's "Lethal Weapon 3" along with Dennis Scott and Kenny Anderson, Oliver helped lead the Yellow Jackets to the 1990 Final Four while quietly averaging more than 21 PPG. A painful stress fracture in his foot adversely affected his post-season play and his draft stock. Oliver played about ten minutes a game as a Sixers rookie behind Hersey Hawkins and Rickey Green. He scored a career-high 19 at Denver in early January.

Strengths: Oliver salvaged a terrible rookie debut offensively with some inspired defense. A scrappy player who won't back down against anyone, he shows flashes of being a pretty decent defensive rebounder. Oliver's versatile enough to play either guard position, although he's naturally more of a two guard.

Weaknesses: He couldn't shoot worth a darn last season. The harder he tried, the worse he got. Eventually, he focused much of his energy on contributing without the ball. His shot appears flawed and he doesn't get a lot of height on his jumper.

Analysis: Although it's not entirely fair to judge a player after just one season, Oliver's future could be in jeopardy if he doesn't do a better job offensively. A fast start to the 1991-92 season may be just what he needs.

PLAYER SUMMARY	
Will	play tough defense
Can't	shoot comfortably
Expect	all-around improvement
Don't Expect	pretty jumpers
Fantasy Value	$1-2
Card Value	10¢

COLLEGE STATISTICS

		G	FGP	FTP	RPG	PPG
86-87	GT	29	.456	.720	3.1	7.1
87-88	GT	32	.506	.745	4.3	12.6
88-89	GT	32	.554	.785	5.6	16.1
89-90	GT	34	.516	.721	6.0	21.3
Totals		127	.516	.742	4.8	14.6

NBA REGULAR-SEASON STATISTICS

				FGs		3-PT FGs		FTs		Rebounds						
		G	MIN	FG	PCT	FG	PCT	FT	PCT	OFF	TOT	AST	STL	BLK	PTS	PPG
90-91	PHI	73	800	111	.408	5	.278	52	.732	18	80	88	34	4	279	3.8
Totals		73	800	111	.408	5	.278	52	.732	18	80	88	34	4	279	3.8

ROBERT PARISH

Team: Boston Celtics
Position: Center
Height: 7'0" **Weight:** 230
Birthdate: August 30, 1953
NBA Experience: 15 years

College: Centenary
Acquired: Traded from Warriors with a 1980 1st-round pick for two 1980 1st-round picks, 6/80

Background: The best player in Centenary history, "Chief" enjoyed four solid seasons with Golden State before his career really blossomed in Boston. He played on championship Celtic teams in 1981, '84, and '86. Last year, Parish shot a blistering 60 percent from the field (No. 2 in the league) and paced the Celts in rebounding. He is the oldest active player in the NBA (38).

Strengths: Parish's numbers are as solid as they were in the mid-1980s. Scoring certainly isn't a problem and he's a terrific rebounder at both ends. Still a fine defender, rarely does an opposing center light Parish up for a big night.

Weaknesses: He doesn't block as many shots and he can't get up and down the court as he once did. Passing never has been his strong suit.

Analysis: Parish readily admits this could be his final season. The only other NBA center who was able to play so consistently for so long was Kareem Abdul-Jabbar. Although he spent most of his career playing in Abdul-Jabbar's long shadow, Parish will enter the Hall of Fame the first year he's eligible.

PLAYER SUMMARY

Will .... contemplate retirement
Can't .... block as many shots
Expect .... Hall of Fame induction
Don't Expect .... as many minutes
Fantasy Value $13-17
Card Value .... 10¢

COLLEGE STATISTICS

		G	FGP	FTP	RPG	PPG
72-73	CENT	27	.579	.610	18.7	23.0
73-74	CENT	25	.523	.628	15.3	19.9
74-75	CENT	29	.560	.661	15.4	18.9
75-76	CENT	27	.589	.694	18.0	24.8
Totals		108	.564	.655	16.9	21.6

NBA REGULAR-SEASON STATISTICS

		G	MIN	FGs		3-PT FGs		FTs		Rebounds		AST	STL	BLK	PTS	PPG
				FG	PCT	FG	PCT	FT	PCT	OFF	TOT					
76-77	GS	77	1384	288	.503	0	.000	121	.708	201	543	74	55	94	697	9.1
77-78	GS	82	1969	430	.472	0	.000	165	.625	211	679	95	79	123	1025	12.5
78-79	GS	76	2411	554	.499	0	.000	196	.698	265	916	115	100	217	1304	17.2
79-80	GS	72	2119	510	.507	0	.000	203	.715	257	793	122	58	115	1223	17.0
80-81	BOS	82	2298	635	.545	0	.000	282	.710	245	777	144	81	214	1552	18.9
81-82	BOS	80	2534	669	.542	0	.000	252	.710	288	866	140	68	192	1590	19.9
82-83	BOS	78	2459	619	.550	0	.000	271	.698	260	827	141	79	148	1509	19.3
83-84	BOS	80	2867	623	.542	0	.000	274	.745	243	857	139	55	116	1520	19.0
84-85	BOS	79	2850	551	.542	0	.000	292	.743	263	840	125	56	101	1394	17.6
85-86	BOS	81	2567	530	.549	0	.000	245	.731	246	770	145	65	116	1305	16.1
86-87	BOS	80	2995	588	.556	0	.000	227	.735	254	851	173	64	144	1403	17.5
87-88	BOS	74	2312	442	.589	0	.000	177	.734	173	628	115	55	84	1061	14.3
88-89	BOS	80	2840	596	.570	0	.000	294	.719	342	996	175	79	116	1486	18.6
89-90	BOS	79	2396	505	.580	0	.000	233	.747	259	796	103	38	69	1243	15.7
90-91	BOS	81	2441	485	.598	0	.000	237	.767	271	856	66	66	103	1207	14.9
Totals		1181	36442	8025	.543	0	.000	3469	.720	3778	11995	1872	998	1952	19519	16.5

JOHN PAXSON

Team: Chicago Bulls
Position: Guard
Height: 6'2" **Weight:** 185
Birthdate: September 29, 1960

NBA Experience: 8 years
College: Notre Dame
Acquired: Signed as a free agent, 10/85

Background: Drafted out of Notre Dame by San Antonio in 1983, Paxson was nothing more than a fringe player until he hooked up with Michael Jordan in Chicago. Last year's 55-percent accuracy from the field ranked No. 1 among NBA guards and tenth overall; he also shot .438 from 3. One of the heroes of Chicago's NBA Finals rout of the Lakers, Paxson's uncanny game-five shooting had to send shivers down your spine. His middle name is MacBeth.

Strengths: Paxson nails the open perimeter jumper as well as any guard in the NBA. If he hits his first couple of shots, he's usually in for a big night. Paxson's an unselfish team player who compensates for a lack of athletic ability with loads of court smarts and savvy. He draws a lot of charges defensively.

Weaknesses: He can be a little too unselfish at times as he tries to get everyone involved at the expense of passing up good shots. Hardly a bona fide point guard, Paxson is a tad bit conservative with the ball. Defensively, he doesn't match up well with some of the league's speedier guards.

Analysis: The perfect complement to a guy like Jordan, Paxson showed just how effective he can be during the 1991 NBA Finals. He may not be the quickest or most athletic lead guard in the league, but he certainly knows how to play with Jordan. Although B.J. Armstrong will be Chicago's point man of the future, Jordan is far more comfortable with Paxson.

PLAYER SUMMARY

Will .... increase his FG attempts
Can't .... match up defensively
Expect .... more of the same
Don't Expect .... an inflated ego
Fantasy Value $2-4
Card Value .... 5¢

COLLEGE STATISTICS

		G	FGP	FTP	RPG	PPG
79-80	ND	27	.483	.745	1.3	4.6
80-81	ND	29	.518	.685	1.8	9.9
81-82	ND	27	.535	.774	2.0	16.4
82-83	ND	29	.533	.740	2.2	17.7
Totals		112	.526	.736	1.8	12.2

NBA REGULAR-SEASON STATISTICS

				FGs		3-PT FGs		FTs		Rebounds						
		G	MIN	FG	PCT	FG	PCT	FT	PCT	OFF	TOT	AST	STL	BLK	PTS	PPG
83-84	SA	49	458	61	.445	4	.182	16	.615	4	33	149	10	2	142	2.9
84-85	SA	78	1259	196	.509	10	.294	84	.840	19	68	215	45	3	486	6.2
85-86	CHI	75	1570	153	.466	15	.294	74	.804	18	94	274	55	2	395	5.3
86-87	CHI	82	2689	386	.487	52	.371	106	.809	22	139	467	66	8	930	11.3
87-88	CHI	81	1888	287	.493	33	.347	33	.733	16	104	303	49	1	640	7.9
88-89	CHI	78	1738	246	.480	44	.331	31	.861	13	94	308	53	6	567	7.3
89-90	CHI	82	2365	365	.516	33	.359	56	.824	27	119	335	83	6	819	10.0
90-91	CHI	82	1971	317	.548	42	.438	34	.829	15	91	297	62	3	710	8.7
Totals		607	13938	2011	.500	233	.351	434	.805	134	742	2348	423	31	4689	7.7

KENNY PAYNE

Team: Philadelphia 76ers
Position: Forward
Height: 6'8" **Weight:** 220
Birthdate: November 25, 1966
NBA Experience: 2 years

College: Louisville
Acquired: 1st-round pick in 1989 draft
(19th overall)

Background: Payne was Louisville's second-leading scorer and rebounder behind Pervis Ellison in 1988-89. The Cardinals' top 3-point threat, he garnered second-team All-Metro Conference honors. A surprising first-round pick by the Sixers two years ago, Payne's done nothing to prove he belongs in the NBA. A sprained left ankle ended his 1990-91 season a couple weeks early. He averaged almost ten minutes per game.

Strengths: Shooting free throws, cheering on his teammates from the bench, and playing hard in practice are about the only things Payne does well. Actually, even though he can't rebound, he's not a bad defender close to the basket and he can run the floor.

Weaknesses: Drafted because his jumper had unlimited range, Payne's shot went into hiding last winter. He shot 36 percent from the field and 22 percent from behind the 3-point arc. Really! Unless his jumper's falling, there's not much point in having him in the game.

Analysis: Using the 19th pick in the first round on Payne was a big mistake. It conjures up memories of other Philadelphia first-round flops in recent years, like Christian Welp ('87), Tom Sewell ('84), and Leo Rautins ('83). With veteran Ron Anderson already coming off the bench at small forward, the 76ers don't even need Payne.

PLAYER SUMMARY

Will ....get one more chance
Can't................find his shooting range
Expect.............another wasted season
Don't Expect ....any sympathy
Fantasy Value $1-2
Card Value...5¢

COLLEGE STATISTICS

		G	FGP	FTP	RPG	PPG
85-86	LOU	34	.437	.773	1.7	3.6
86-87	LOU	26	.350	.696	2.5	4.2
87-88	LOU	35	.480	.763	4.7	10.7
88-89	LOU	33	.508	.840	5.7	14.5
Totals		128	.469	.782	3.7	8.5

NBA REGULAR-SEASON STATISTICS

			FGs		3-PT FGs		FTs		Rebounds						
	G	MIN	FG	PCT	FG	PCT	FT	PCT	OFF	TOT	AST	STL	BLK	PTS	PPG
89-90 PHI	35	216	47	.435	4	.400	16	.889	11	26	10	7	6	114	3.3
90-91 PHI	47	444	68	.360	4	.222	26	.897	17	66	16	10	6	166	3.5
Totals	82	660	115	.387	8	.286	42	.894	28	92	26	17	12	280	3.4

GARY PAYTON

Team: Seattle SuperSonics
Position: Guard
Height: 6'4" **Weight:** 190
Birthdate: July 23, 1968
NBA Experience: 1 year

College: Oregon St.
Acquired: 1st-round pick in 1990 draft (2nd overall)

Background: Payton was an All-American as a senior at Oregon State, where he set a school scoring record, ended his career second on the NCAA assists list, and set a Pac-10 record with 100 steals in his final season. He started all 82 games of his first pro campaign and led Seattle in steals and assists. He was named second-team All-Rookie after the 1990-91 season.

Strengths: Payton has earned and lived up to his reputation for his in-your-face approach to defense. He hounds the ball and makes his opponent work for everything he gets. He stands tall at the point, where he handles the ball well, gets good penetration, and dishes to the open men. He is a pure point guard.

Weaknesses: A trash talker, Payton can get too involved emotionally for the good of himself and his team. Opponents generally want to cram the ball down his throat. Payton is not a great shooter off the dribble, although he can stick jumpers when left open. He does not have NBA 3-point range.

Analysis: Payton is a natural point guard who prefers to penetrate, hit open teammates with crisp passes, handle the ball, and shut down his man on defense than score himself. He talks a big game, but he also plays one. With a little more polish and self-control, Payton could become a standout.

PLAYER SUMMARY

Will	play defense
Can't	shoot 3's
Expect	a pure point guard
Don't Expect	to shut him up
Fantasy Value	$3-5
Card Value	20¢

COLLEGE STATISTICS

		G	FGP	FTP	RPG	PPG
86-87	OSU	30	.459	.671	4.0	12.5
87-88	OSU	31	.489	.699	3.3	14.5
88-89	OSU	30	.475	.677	4.1	20.1
89-90	OSU	29	.504	.690	4.7	25.7
Totals		120	.485	.684	4.0	18.1

NBA REGULAR-SEASON STATISTICS

			FGs		3-PT FGs		FTs		Rebounds						
	G	MIN	FG	PCT	FG	PCT	FT	PCT	OFF	TOT	AST	STL	BLK	PTS	PPG
90-91 SEA	82	2244	259	.450	1	.077	69	.711	108	243	528	165	15	588	7.2
Totals	82	2244	259	.450	1	.077	69	.711	108	243	528	165	15	588	7.2

WILL PERDUE

Team: Chicago Bulls
Position: Center
Height: 7'0" **Weight:** 240
Birthdate: August 29, 1965
NBA Experience: 3 years

College: Vanderbilt
Acquired: 1st-round pick in 1988 draft
(11th overall)

Background: Named SEC Player of the Year as a senior at Vanderbilt, Perdue led the league in rebounding. Drafted by the Bulls in 1988, he played less than any other first-round pick as a rookie. His statistics have improved each year since. Perdue backed up Bill Cartwright in the middle for ten-to-15 minutes per game last season. He led the Bulls in rebounding nine times and enjoyed a productive post-season. He's got the biggest feet in the league.

Strengths: Phil Jackson finally had enough confidence in Perdue to occasionally use him during crunch time last season. In the past, he'd always be nailed to the bench. Although he's a mediocre shooter, Perdue has become more active offensively. He's a better passer than Cartwright.

Weaknesses: He doesn't jump well and he's even worse at anticipating the ball. Clumsy and slow, Perdue has his problems defensively, particularly on the glass. His shot's flat and he has trouble with free throws.

Analysis: A fan favorite in Chicago, Perdue's physical limitations will prevent him from ever being more than a back-up pivot man in the league. He's not the guy who'll one day take over for Cartwright as the Bulls' starting center. Perdue's a lot like Orlando's Greg Kite with a Southern accent.

PLAYER SUMMARY

Will ....pass to open man
Can't...........................get off the ground
Expect ....minimal improvement
Don't Expect ....future starter
Fantasy Value $1-2
Card Value...8¢

COLLEGE STATISTICS

		G	FGP	FTP	RPG	PPG
83-84	VAND	17	.467	.444	2.2	2.7
85-86	VAND	22	.585	.438	2.8	3.5
86-87	VAND	34	.599	.618	8.7	17.4
87-88	VAND	31	.634	.673	10.1	18.3
Totals		104	.606	.620	6.8	12.3

NBA REGULAR-SEASON STATISTICS

			FGs		3-PT FGs		FTs		Rebounds						
		G	MIN	FG	PCT	FG	PCT	FT	PCT	OFF	TOT	AST	STL	BLK	PTS	PPG
88-89	CHI	30	190	29	.403	0	.000	8	.571	18	45	11	4	6	66	2.2
89-90	CHI	77	884	111	.414	0	.000	72	.692	88	214	46	19	26	294	3.8
90-91	CHI	74	972	116	.494	0	.000	75	.670	122	336	47	23	57	307	4.1
Totals		181	2046	256	.445	0	.000	155	.674	228	595	104	46	89	667	3.7

SAM PERKINS

Team: Los Angeles Lakers
Position: Forward/Center
Height: 6'9" **Weight:** 250
Birthdate: June 14, 1961

NBA Experience: 7 years
College: North Carolina
Acquired: Signed as a free agent, 8/90

Background: Perkins was a three-time All-American at North Carolina, where he earned an NCAA title in 1982, reached the finals in 1981, and won the Lapchick Award as the nation's outstanding senior in 1984. In six years with Dallas, he became the club's all-time leader in rebounds and ranked third in blocked shots, fifth in assists, and fifth in scoring. He was signed by the Lakers before the 1990-91 season and finished fourth on the team in scoring.

Strengths: Perkins is a versatile front-liner who can play either forward spot and even center. Offensively, he is at his best when facing the basket, thanks to his nice touch, range of 18 feet, and nifty left-handed hook. On defense, he goes to the boards and his long arms help him block shots.

Weaknesses: Perkins has been slapped with an underachiever's label, although there are many forwards who would love to put up his numbers. He often sneaks to the background offensively and can get beaten on the boards by smaller players who work harder.

Analysis: As if to answer those who doubted his offensive game, Perkins has shot nearly 50 percent in each of the last two seasons. The Lakers did not expect a franchise player when they signed him (they already had one named Magic), but they did expect a well-schooled and versatile big man who plays defense. They got him.

PLAYER SUMMARY

Will ....play defense
Can't............................shake reputation
Expect ....soft touch
Don't Expect...............................20 PPG
Fantasy Value $6-8
Card Value...12¢

COLLEGE STATISTICS

		G	FGP	FTP	RPG	PPG
80-81	NC	37	.626	.741	7.8	14.9
81-82	NC	32	.578	.768	7.8	14.3
82-83	NC	35	.527	.819	9.4	16.9
83-84	NC	31	.589	.856	9.6	17.6
Totals		135	.576	.796	8.6	15.9

NBA REGULAR-SEASON STATISTICS

				FGs		3-PT FGs		FTs		Rebounds						
		G	MIN	FG	PCT	FG	PCT	FT	PCT	OFF	TOT	AST	STL	BLK	PTS	PPG
84-85	DAL	82	2317	347	.471	9	.250	200	.820	189	605	135	63	63	903	11.0
85-86	DAL	80	2626	458	.503	11	.333	307	.814	195	685	153	75	94	1234	15.4
86-87	DAL	80	2687	461	.482	19	.352	245	.828	197	616	146	109	77	1186	14.8
87-88	DAL	75	2499	394	.450	5	.167	273	.822	201	601	118	74	54	1066	14.2
88-89	DAL	78	2860	445	.464	7	.184	274	.833	235	688	127	76	92	1171	15.0
89-90	DAL	76	2668	435	.493	6	.214	330	.778	209	572	175	88	64	1206	15.9
90-91	LAL	73	2504	368	.495	18	.281	229	.821	167	538	108	64	78	983	13.5
Totals		544	18161	2908	.479	75	.265	1858	.815	1393	4305	962	549	522	7749	14.2

TIM PERRY

Team: Phoenix Suns
Position: Forward
Height: 6'9" **Weight:** 220
Birthdate: June 4, 1965
NBA Experience: 3 years

College: Temple
Acquired: 1st-round pick in 1988 draft (7th overall)

Background: Perry was named Atlantic 10 Player of the Year as a senior at Temple, where he led the Owls to a top ranking for much of the season and finished as the school's career leader in blocked shots. Although he was the seventh player taken in the 1988 draft, he has spent his three pro seasons coming off the bench. He played in a career-low 46 games in 1990-91, missing 14 with tendinitis in his left knee.

Strengths: Perry runs the floor and can get off his feet. His defense is solid and instinctual, especially his shot-blocking. He rises above defenders to get his shots off and can sky over opponents for rebounds.

Weaknesses: Perry will not be mistaken for an offensive force. Although his turnaround jumper has improved, he does not have confidence as a scorer—which is not surprising since he played the post in college. Perry is a poor ball-handler, passer, and free throw shooter with much left to learn.

Analysis: Because of his size, the Suns knew Perry would have to give up his post game and play small forward as a pro. That explains why a high first-rounder is still trying to carve his niche on an NBA team. Perry can provide a lift with his defense, but he will not earn many starts until he becomes more confident and capable offensively.

PLAYER SUMMARY

Will ....block shots
Can't ....handle the ball
Expect ....defensive punch
Don't Expect ....scoring
Fantasy Value $1-3
Card Value..8¢

COLLEGE STATISTICS

		G	FGP	FTP	RPG	PPG
84-85	TEMP	30	.414	.500	3.9	2.3
85-86	TEMP	31	.566	.575	9.5	11.6
86-87	TEMP	36	.514	.620	8.6	12.9
87-88	TEMP	33	.585	.637	8.0	14.5
Totals		130	.544	.605	7.6	10.5

NBA REGULAR-SEASON STATISTICS

				FGs		3-PT FGs		FTs		Rebounds						
		G	MIN	FG	PCT	FG	PCT	FT	PCT	OFF	TOT	AST	STL	BLK	PTS	PPG
88-89	PHO	62	614	108	.537	1	.250	40	.615	61	132	18	19	32	257	4.1
89-90	PHO	60	612	100	.513	1	1.000	53	.589	79	152	17	21	22	254	4.2
90-91	PHO	46	587	75	.521	0	.000	43	.614	53	126	27	23	43	193	4.2
Totals		168	1813	283	.524	2	.200	136	.604	193	410	62	63	97	704	4.2

CHUCK PERSON

Team: Indiana Pacers
Position: Forward
Height: 6'8" **Weight:** 225
Birthdate: June 27, 1964
NBA Experience: 5 years

College: Auburn
Acquired: 1st-round pick in 1986 draft
(4th overall)

Background: The all-time leading scorer in Auburn history when he graduated from college, Person immediately made his mark on the NBA with a Rookie of the Year season in 1986-87. His most productive all-around season came two years later. He played brilliantly in last spring's playoffs and shot better from the field during the regular season than ever before.

Strengths: An outstanding perimeter shooter, Person is Indiana's go-to guy when the game's on the line. And more often than not, he delivers. A very emotional and sensitive player, Person finally began to sacrifice his personal game for the benefit of the team last season. He always resisted such advice in the past. When he wants to make the effort, he plays sound defense.

Weaknesses: Some nights, you can just tell by looking at him that he's not the least bit interested in being at the arena. And that's how he plays. Such erratic behavior isn't normal for a five-year pro. He isn't the rebounder he could be.

Analysis: When Person's individual numbers are down, the Pacers are a better basketball team. A selfish, moody player who didn't always get along with his teammates early in his career, Person has grown up a lot in the past 12 months. Some of the Pacers actually like him. He still has a way to go and he knows it.

PLAYER SUMMARY

Will....................be team's No. 2 scorer
Can't...............sulk about reduced role
Expect...........................added maturity
Don't Expect............100-percent effort
Fantasy Value.............................$17-20
Card Value...10¢

COLLEGE STATISTICS

		G	FGP	FTP	RPG	PPG
82-83	AUB	28	.541	.758	4.6	9.3
83-84	AUB	31	.543	.728	8.0	19.1
84-85	AUB	34	.544	.738	8.9	22.0
85-86	AUB	33	.519	.804	7.9	21.5
Totals		126	.536	.757	7.5	18.3

NBA REGULAR-SEASON STATISTICS

				FGs		3-PT FGs		FTs		Rebounds						
		G	MIN	FG	PCT	FG	PCT	FT	PCT	OFF	TOT	AST	STL	BLK	PTS	PPG
86-87	IND	82	2956	635	.468	49	.355	222	.747	168	677	295	90	16	1541	18.8
87-88	IND	79	2807	575	.459	59	.333	132	.670	171	536	309	73	8	1341	17.0
88-89	IND	80	3012	711	.489	63	.307	243	.792	144	516	289	83	18	1728	21.6
89-90	IND	77	2714	605	.487	94	.372	211	.781	126	445	230	53	20	1515	19.7
90-91	IND	80	2566	620	.504	69	.340	165	.721	121	417	238	56	17	1474	18.4
Totals		398	14055	3146	.481	334	.342	973	.748	730	2591	1361	355	79	7599	19.1

JIM PETERSEN

Team: Golden State Warriors
Position: Forward/Center
Height: 6'10" **Weight:** 235
Birthdate: February 22, 1962
NBA Experience: 7 years

College: Minnesota
Acquired: Traded from Kings for
Ralph Sampson, 9/89

Background: Petersen led the Big Ten in field goal percentage as a senior at Minnesota. After playing behind Ralph Sampson with Houston early in his pro career, he was later traded from Sacramento to Golden State for the declining Sampson. Knee surgery in 1989 limited Petersen in his first season with the Warriors, but he was a 21-game starter in 1990-91 and helped provide a physical presence.

Strengths: Petersen is not afraid to throw his body around in the paint—an invaluable asset for an undersized team. He plays tough defense against centers and power forwards and is a fundamentally sound rebounder. He can stick medium-range jumpers when his number is called.

Weaknesses: Offensively, Petersen's points come primarily because someone else is being doubled. He is not a creator or ball-handler by any stretch, and most men his size have at least a semblance of a low-post game. Petersen does not.

Analysis: Returning from knee surgery was a struggle for Petersen, who had to play his way into shape over the last two seasons. Finally, near the end of the 1990-91 campaign, he was again able to contribute. Shedding a few pounds helped. Though he will not stand out, Petersen sets picks, plays sound defense, and knows his role.

PLAYER SUMMARY

Will	bang inside
Can't	score from post
Expect	physical defense
Don't Expect	10 PPG
Fantasy Value	$1-2
Card Value	5¢

COLLEGE STATISTICS

		G	FGP	FTP	RPG	PPG
80-81	MINN	22	.500	.250	1.0	1.2
81-82	MINN	21	.462	.636	2.0	3.0
82-83	MINN	29	.550	.643	5.3	6.3
83-84	MINN	24	.639	.722	6.9	11.2
Totals		96	.575	.667	4.0	5.6

NBA REGULAR-SEASON STATISTICS

				FGs		3-PT FGs		FTs		Rebounds						
		G	MIN	FG	PCT	FG	PCT	FT	PCT	OFF	TOT	AST	STL	BLK	PTS	PPG
84-85	HOU	60	714	70	.486	0	.000	50	.758	44	147	29	14	32	190	3.2
85-86	HOU	82	1664	196	.477	0	.000	113	.706	149	396	85	38	54	505	6.2
86-87	HOU	82	2403	386	.511	0	.000	152	.727	177	557	127	43	102	924	11.3
87-88	HOU	69	1793	249	.510	1	.167	114	.745	145	436	106	36	40	613	8.9
88-89	SAC	66	1633	278	.459	0	.000	115	.747	121	413	81	47	68	671	10.2
89-90	GS	43	592	60	.426	0	.000	52	.712	49	160	23	17	20	172	4.0
90-91	GS	62	834	114	.483	1	.250	50	.658	69	200	27	13	41	279	4.5
Totals		464	9633	1353	.487	2	.077	646	.725	754	2309	478	208	357	3354	7.2

DRAZEN PETROVIC

Team: New Jersey Nets
Position: Guard
Height: 6'5" **Weight:** 195
Birthdate: October 22, 1964
NBA Experience: 2 years
College: Zagreb

Acquired: Traded from Trail Blazers with Terry Mills via the Nuggets; Nuggets sent Walter Davis to Blazers, and Nets sent Greg Anderson and a future 1st-round pick to Nuggets, 1/91

Background: Recognized for years as one of Europe's most talented guards, Petrovic played for the Yugoslavian National Team and Real Madrid in the Spanish League. Preseason back surgery limited his contributions as a rookie with Portland. Last year, he was traded to New Jersey in late January, where he got more minutes and shot a very respectable 50 percent from the floor. Recruited heavily by Notre Dame in the mid-1980s, Petrovic studied law in college.

Strengths: A pure shooter who is paid to put the ball in the basket, Petrovic can also pass and handle the ball fairly well. Although he's slow afoot, he's deceivingly strong and determined enough to take the ball inside on occasion. He's the best free throw shooter on the team.

Weaknesses: Petrovic learned real fast how difficult it is to get off a shot in the NBA. Too slow to create his own shot, he's very dependent on his teammates for picks and screens. Although he works very hard to stay with his man, Petrovic's terrible foot speed makes him a defensive liability.

Analysis: Always desperate for more points, New Jersey made a wise move in acquiring Petrovic for a future draft pick. A bit upset about not getting more minutes in Portland, he's perfectly content with his reserve role in New Jersey.

PLAYER SUMMARY

Will.................drain perimeter jumpers
Can't.......................create his own shot
Expect........... designated-shooter role
Don't Expect ....much defense
Fantasy Value $3-5
Card Value......................................15¢

COLLEGE STATISTICS

—DID NOT PLAY—

NBA REGULAR-SEASON STATISTICS

			FGs		3-PT FGs		FTs		Rebounds						
		G	MIN	FG	PCT	FG	PCT	FT	PCT	OFF	TOT	AST	STL	BLK	PTS	PPG
89-90	POR	77	967	207	.485	34	.459	135	.844	50	111	116	23	2	583	7.6
90-91	POR/NJ	61	1015	243	.493	23	.354	114	.832	51	110	86	43	1	623	10.2
Totals		138	1982	450	.489	57	.410	249	.838	101	221	202	66	3	1206	8.7

RICKY PIERCE

Team: Seattle SuperSonics
Position: Guard
Height: 6'4" **Weight:** 222
Birthdate: August 19, 1959

NBA Experience: 9 years
College: Rice
Acquired: Traded from Bucks for Dale Ellis, 2/91

Background: Pierce led Rice in scoring and rebounding for three straight years. He played single seasons in Detroit and San Diego, then became one of the NBA's most celebrated bench players in Milwaukee. He won the Sixth Man Award in 1986-87 and 1989-90. Pierce served the same reserve role in Seattle after a trade in 1990-91, finishing second on the Sonics in scoring and fourth in the league in free throw accuracy. He played in his first All-Star Game.

Strengths: Everyone already knew Pierce as one of the best pure shooters in the NBA, but over the past two seasons he has added the 3-pointer to his bag of tricks. He can score coming off picks or with defenders draped over him. His strong upper body helps him draw fouls on his way to the hoop, and he can recover to hit the shots. Pierce is a great clutch scorer.

Weaknesses: Since there are virtually none offensively, any talk of holes in Pierce's game start and end with defense. He lacks the great lateral quickness and often the interest required to be a standout perimeter defender.

Analysis: Pierce probably deserved his 1991 All-Star selection even more a year earlier, but it was a fitting tribute to a great scorer who willingly comes off the bench and can take over single-handedly. What he lacks in speed, he makes up for with strength and persistence. Pierce ruins defensive game plans with his one-on-one ability.

PLAYER SUMMARY

Will ....hit from anywhere
Can't ....focus on defense
Expect ....20 PPG off bench
Don't Expect ....blinding speed
Fantasy Value $18-20
Card Value...10¢

COLLEGE STATISTICS

		G	FGP	FTP	RPG	PPG
79-80	RICE	26	.480	.718	8.2	19.2
80-81	RICE	26	.518	.706	7.0	20.9
81-82	RICE	30	.511	.794	7.5	26.8
Totals		82	.504	.751	7.6	22.5

NBA REGULAR-SEASON STATISTICS

		G	MIN	FGs FG	FGs PCT	3-PT FGs FG	3-PT FGs PCT	FTs FT	FTs PCT	Rebounds OFF	Rebounds TOT	AST	STL	BLK	PTS	PPG
82-83	DET	39	265	33	.375	1	.143	18	.563	15	35	14	8	4	85	2.2
83-84	SD	69	1280	268	.470	0	.000	149	.861	59	135	60	27	13	685	9.9
84-85	MIL	44	882	165	.537	1	.250	102	.823	49	117	94	34	5	433	9.8
85-86	MIL	81	2147	429	.538	3	.130	266	.858	94	231	177	83	6	1127	13.9
86-87	MIL	79	2505	575	.534	3	.107	387	.880	117	266	144	64	24	1540	19.5
87-88	MIL	37	965	248	.510	3	.214	107	.877	30	83	73	21	7	606	16.4
88-89	MIL	75	2078	527	.518	8	.222	255	.859	82	197	156	77	19	1317	17.6
89-90	MIL	59	1709	503	.510	46	.346	307	.839	64	167	133	50	7	1359	23.0
90-91	MIL/SEA	78	2167	561	.485	46	.397	430	.913	67	191	168	60	13	1598	20.5
Totals		561	13998	3309	.510	111	.300	2021	.866	577	1422	1019	424	98	8750	15.6

ED PINCKNEY

Team: Boston Celtics
Position: Forward
Height: 6'9" **Weight:** 215
Birthdate: March 27, 1963
NBA Experience: 6 years

College: Villanova
Acquired: Traded from Kings with Joe Kleine for Danny Ainge and Brad Lohaus, 2/89

Background: The highlight of his basketball career was leading Villanova to a national title in 1985 and being named tourney MVP. Pinckney shot 60 percent from the field during his four-year Wildcat career. A member of the Suns and the Kings before Boston acquired him in 1989, Pinckney's best NBA season came with Phoenix in 1986-87. His play improved slightly as the 1990-91 season progressed. Permanently stuck to the bench before Christmas, Pinckney moved into the starting lineup for a brief spell in April.

Strengths: Pinckney goes hard to the glass and is a nice finisher the few times Boston does run. He's a decent passer and a good jumper, and he never forces his shot. Pinckney was the Celtics' premier foul shooter last season (90 percent).

Weaknesses: Best suited to zoom up and down the floor, Pinckney appears absolutely lost in Boston's halfcourt set. He's an average shooter and he never has taken the time to learn many inside moves. He's got the physical attributes to play defense, but not the mental.

Analysis: Pinckney's only chance to really contribute at the NBA level will come with a transition team like Denver, Golden State, or Portland. He's wasting his time in Beantown and he's steadily losing his confidence. He'd welcome a trade if anyone's interested.

PLAYER SUMMARY

Will ....run the floor
Can't ....play halfcourt game
Expect ....more bench time
Don't Expect ....a future in Boston
Fantasy Value $1-2
Card Value..5¢

COLLEGE STATISTICS

		G	FGP	FTP	RPG	PPG
81-82	VILL	32	.640	.714	7.8	14.2
82-83	VILL	31	.568	.760	9.7	12.5
83-84	VILL	31	.604	.694	7.9	15.4
84-85	VILL	35	.600	.730	8.9	15.6
Totals		129	.604	.723	8.6	14.5

NBA REGULAR-SEASON STATISTICS

				FGs		3-PT FGs		FTs		Rebounds						
		G	MIN	FG	PCT	FG	PCT	FT	PCT	OFF	TOT	AST	STL	BLK	PTS	PPG
85-86	PHO	80	1602	255	.558	0	.000	171	.673	95	308	90	71	37	681	8.5
86-87	PHO	80	2250	290	.584	0	.000	257	.739	179	837	116	86	54	837	10.5
87-88	SAC	79	1177	179	.522	0	.000	133	.747	94	230	66	39	32	491	6.2
88-89	SAC/BOS	80	2012	319	.513	0	.000	280	.800	166	449	118	83	66	918	11.5
89-90	BOS	77	1082	135	.542	0	.000	92	.773	93	225	68	34	42	362	4.7
90-91	BOS	70	1165	131	.539	0	.000	104	.897	155	341	45	61	43	366	5.2
Totals		466	9288	1309	.543	0	.000	1037	.760	782	2133	503	374	274	3655	7.8

SCOTTIE PIPPEN

Team: Chicago Bulls
Position: Forward
Height: 6'7" **Weight:** 210
Birthdate: September 25, 1965
NBA Experience: 4 years
College: Central Arkansas

Acquired: Draft rights traded from SuperSonics for draft rights to Olden Polynice, a 1988 or 1989 2nd-round pick, and the option to exchange 1988 or 1989 1st-round picks, 6/87

Background: An NAIA All-American as a senior at Central Arkansas, Pippen arrived in Chicago in the 1987 draft. He's improved his all-around game every year he's been in the league, highlighted by last year's awesome drive to the NBA championship. Pippen ranked second on the team in scoring, rebounding, and steals. He played in the 1989-90 NBA All-Star Game.

Strengths: Nearly as acrobatic as Michael Jordan, Pippen has about a zillion different moves to the basket. In the open court, he's an electrifying finisher. His long arms and quick hands regularly rank him among the league leaders in steals. After blaming headaches and other assorted injuries for lousy performances in big games in past seasons, Pippen finally proved that he could perform in the clutch. He's a better perimeter jump-shooter than people realize.

Weaknesses: Pippen takes a few too many chances defensively. Rather than prevent his man from getting the ball, he positions himself for the steal. Over an entire season, some may question the consistency of his shot.

Analysis: He became a household name across the country last spring and rightfully so. Between 1990 and '91, Pippen went from being one of the game's top young forwards to a bona fide superstar. There's only one Chicago player who deserves more credit for last year's championship than Scottie Pippen.

PLAYER SUMMARY

Will	play above the rim
Can't	rest on his laurels
Expect	'92 All-Star invite
Don't Expect	more migraines
Fantasy Value	$30-33
Card Value	20¢

COLLEGE STATISTICS

		G	FGP	FTP	RPG	PPG
83-84	CARK	20	.456	.684	3.0	4.3
84-85	CARK	19	.564	.676	9.2	18.5
85-86	CARK	29	.556	.686	9.2	19.8
86-87	CARK	25	.592	.719	10.0	23.6
Totals		93	.563	.695	8.1	17.2

NBA REGULAR-SEASON STATISTICS

		G	MIN	FGs FG	FGs PCT	3-PT FGs FG	3-PT FGs PCT	FTs FT	FTs PCT	Rebounds OFF	Rebounds TOT	AST	STL	BLK	PTS	PPG
87-88	CHI	79	1650	261	.463	4	.174	99	.576	115	298	169	91	52	625	7.9
88-89	CHI	73	2413	413	.476	21	.273	201	.668	138	445	256	139	61	1048	14.4
89-90	CHI	82	3148	562	.489	28	.250	199	.675	150	547	444	211	101	1351	16.5
90-91	CHI	82	3014	600	.520	21	.309	240	.706	163	595	511	193	93	1461	17.8
Totals		316	10225	1836	.492	74	.264	739	.667	566	1885	1380	634	307	4485	14.2

OLDEN POLYNICE

Team: Los Angeles Clippers
Position: Center
Height: 7'0" **Weight:** 242
Birthdate: November 21, 1964
NBA Experience: 4 years

College: Virginia
Acquired: Traded from SuperSonics for Benoit Benjamin; SuperSonics also received the option to exchange 1991 and 1993 1st-round picks, 2/91

Background: Polynice led Virginia in scoring and rebounding for two seasons and was a three-year leader in field goal accuracy. He played in all 82 Seattle games as a rookie. Polynice was a back-up center with the Sonics until a trade with the L.A. Clippers in 1990-91 allowed him to start 30 games. He amassed his best numbers across the board, averaging double-figure points and nine rebounds in 31 games with the Clippers.

Strengths: Defense and hard work are what have earned Polynice respect. He can bang with big men yet is quick enough to get out and harass smaller players on the perimeter. Polynice knows his offensive limitations and plays within them. He does not mind setting hard picks to free up teammates.

Weaknesses: Polynice is not a "go-to guy." In fact, his offensive game is limited to mini-hook shots and a couple of low-post moves that force defenders to at least remember he's there. He is a poor ball-handler and has no outside shot, which becomes evident when he goes to the line.

Analysis: The Clippers are one of the few teams for which Polynice could have started with his slim offensive skills, and he enjoyed his best season. Still, he will never be a big point-getter on the pro level. His forte is defense, and that suits him better for a reserve role with most clubs.

PLAYER SUMMARY	
Will	play defense
Can't	shoot FTs
Expect	hard work
Don't Expect	much offense
Fantasy Value	$2-4
Card Value	8¢

COLLEGE STATISTICS

		G	FGP	FTP	RPG	PPG
83-84	VA	33	.551	.588	5.6	7.7
84-85	VA	32	.603	.599	7.6	13.0
85-86	VA	30	.572	.637	8.0	16.1
Totals		95	.578	.612	7.0	12.1

NBA REGULAR-SEASON STATISTICS

		G	MIN	FGs FG	FGs PCT	3-PT FGs FG	3-PT FGs PCT	FTs FT	FTs PCT	Rebounds OFF	Rebounds TOT	AST	STL	BLK	PTS	PPG
87-88	SEA	82	1080	118	.465	0	.000	101	.639	122	330	33	32	26	337	4.1
88-89	SEA	80	835	91	.506	0	.000	51	.593	98	206	21	37	30	233	2.9
89-90	SEA	79	1085	156	.540	1	.500	47	.475	128	300	15	25	21	360	4.6
90-91	SEA/LAC	79	2092	316	.560	0	.000	146	.579	220	553	42	43	32	778	9.8
Totals		320	5092	681	.529	1	.143	345	.580	568	1389	111	137	109	1708	5.3

TERRY PORTER

Team: Portland Trail Blazers
Position: Guard
Height: 6'3" **Weight:** 195
Birthdate: April 8, 1963
NBA Experience: 6 years

College: Wisconsin-Stevens Point
Acquired: 1st-round pick in 1985 draft
(24th overall)

Background: Porter was an NAIA All-American as a junior and senior at Wisconsin-Stevens Point, where his shooting accuracy was remarkable for a guard. He had improved his scoring average in each of his pro seasons before peaking in 1989-90, when he led the Blazers to the NBA Finals. Portland's all-time assists king, Porter again topped the team in dishes in 1990-91 and ranked second in scoring and minutes.

Strengths: A converted point guard, Porter is a fine penetrator and passer in addition to his deadly shooting skills and unlimited range. His 3-point percentage was fourth in the league in 1990-91. He loves taking the clutch shot and can stick it off the dribble. He is good with both hands and uses his strength well on penetration moves and defense.

Weaknesses: Porter does not possess blinding speed, although he compensates for it by running a smart fastbreak. Where it hurts him is on the defensive end, where quick guards give him trouble.

Analysis: Porter, often overlooked when Portland was run-of-the-mill, has emerged as one of the game's finest point guards. Although the Blazers' recent success has had much to do with that, so has Porter's long-range artillery and ability to make things happen off penetration. He is a tough competitor who has raised his level of play and developed outstanding leadership traits.

PLAYER SUMMARY

Will	stick 3's
Can't	defend quickness
Expect	leadership
Don't Expect	a high profile
Fantasy Value	$37-40
Card Value	10¢

COLLEGE STATISTICS

		G	FGP	FTP	RPG	PPG
81-82	WSP	25	.368	.692	0.5	2.0
82-83	WSP	30	.611	.697	3.9	11.4
83-84	WSP	32	.622	.830	5.2	18.8
84-85	WSP	30	.575	.834	5.2	19.7
Totals		117	.589	.796	3.8	13.5

NBA REGULAR-SEASON STATISTICS

		G	MIN	FGs FG	FGs PCT	3-PT FGs FG	3-PT FGs PCT	FTs FT	FTs PCT	Rebounds OFF	Rebounds TOT	AST	STL	BLK	PTS	PPG
85-86	POR	79	1214	212	.474	13	.310	125	.806	35	117	198	81	1	562	7.1
86-87	POR	80	2714	376	.488	13	.217	280	.838	70	337	715	159	9	1045	13.1
87-88	POR	82	2991	462	.519	24	.348	274	.846	65	378	831	150	16	1222	14.9
88-89	POR	81	3102	540	.471	79	.361	272	.840	85	367	770	146	8	1431	17.7
89-90	POR	80	2781	448	.462	89	.374	421	.892	59	272	726	151	4	1406	17.6
90-91	POR	81	2665	486	.515	130	.415	279	.823	52	282	649	158	12	1381	17.0
Totals		483	15467	2524	.489	348	.370	1651	.848	366	1753	3889	845	50	7047	14.6

PAUL PRESSEY

Team: San Antonio Spurs
Position: Guard/Forward
Height: 6'5" **Weight:** 203
Birthdate: December 24, 1958
NBA Experience: 9 years

College: Western Texas; Tulsa
Acquired: Traded from Bucks for Frank Brickowski, 8/90

Background: Pressey led Western Texas Junior College to a national title before transferring to Tulsa, where he was named Missouri Valley Conference Player of the Year as a senior. In eight years with Milwaukee, he was named to the NBA All-Defensive Team twice and climbed to second on the Bucks' all-time steals list. He started 18 games for San Antonio in 1990-91, when Rod Strickland was out with a broken hand.

Strengths: Versatility and defense sum up Pressey's game. He can shut down opponents ranging from point guards to small forwards thanks to his long wingspan and good anticipation. His size allows him to post up smaller point guards.

Weaknesses: Pressey has lost a step and becomes less effective defensively against quicker guards. He is not a sizzling jump-shooter and the shots he does take are often of the off-balance variety. He does not work the break like he once did and is susceptible to turnovers when trying to do too much.

Analysis: Pressey turned out to be a valuable acquisition for the Spurs when Strickland went down. Although the club was not the same without its starter, Pressey provided solid minutes and his numbers were not bad. His starting and starring days in Milwaukee are long gone, but he still shines on defense.

PLAYER SUMMARY

Will ....work defensively
Can't ....regain speed
Expect ....reserve minutes
Don't Expect...............................10 PPG
Fantasy Value $3-5
Card Value..................................8¢

COLLEGE STATISTICS

		G	FGP	FTP	RPG	PPG
78-79	WTEX	33	.668	.757	7.9	13.9
79-80	WTEX	37	.651	.762	7.9	14.0
80-81	TULS	33	.476	.579	5.4	10.3
81-82	TULS	30	.560	.664	6.4	13.2
Totals		133	.591	.689	6.9	12.9

NBA REGULAR-SEASON STATISTICS

				FGs		3-PT FGs		FTs		Rebounds						
		G	MIN	FG	PCT	FG	PCT	FT	PCT	OFF	TOT	AST	STL	BLK	PTS	PPG
82-83	MIL	79	1528	213	.457	1	.111	105	.597	83	281	207	99	47	532	6.7
83-84	MIL	81	1730	276	.523	2	.222	120	.600	102	282	252	86	50	674	8.3
84-85	MIL	80	2876	480	.517	7	.350	317	.758	149	429	543	129	56	1284	16.0
85-86	MIL	80	2704	411	.488	8	.182	316	.806	127	399	623	168	71	1146	14.3
86-87	MIL	61	2057	294	.477	16	.291	242	.738	98	296	441	110	47	846	13.9
87-88	MIL	75	2484	345	.491	8	.205	285	.798	130	375	523	112	34	983	13.1
88-89	MIL	67	2170	307	.474	12	.218	187	.776	73	262	439	119	44	813	12.1
89-90	MIL	57	1400	239	.472	6	.140	144	.758	59	172	244	71	23	628	11.0
90-91	SA	70	1683	201	.472	16	.281	110	.827	50	176	271	63	32	528	7.5
Totals		650	18632	2766	.488	76	.230	1826	.750	871	2672	3543	957	404	7434	11.4

MARK PRICE

Team: Cleveland Cavaliers
Position: Guard
Height: 6'0" **Weight:** 178
Birthdate: February 16, 1964
NBA Experience: 5 years

College: Georgia Tech
Acquired: Draft rights traded from Mavericks for a 1989 2nd-round pick and cash, 6/86

Background: Georgia Tech's second all-time leading scorer when he graduated in 1986, Price was drafted by Dallas and immediately traded to the Cavs. An emergency appendectomy cut short his rookie season, but he went on to become an NBA All-Star two years later. He's one of the leading 3-point shooters in NBA history. After leading the Cavs in scoring, assists, and free throw percentage in 1989-90, his career came to a crashing halt 16 games into the 1990-91 season when he tore the anterior cruciate ligament in his knee. He hosts a weekly Christian radio show in Akron, Ohio.

Strengths: Before the injury, he could score inside or out, off the dribble or spotting up. Defensively, he surprises opponents with his quickness and anticipation. He plays as if he has eyes in the back of his head.

Weaknesses: Price's left knee. Unless it fully comes around, it could make a potentially great player very average. Price's decision-making on the break is lacking at times. He doesn't put much effort into defensive rebounding.

Analysis: No one knows for sure what kind of player Price will be when he returns. While the injury shouldn't affect his sharpshooting from the perimeter, it's bound to detract from his defense and his ability to drive the lane. Until last November, he was truly one of the elite point guards in the NBA.

PLAYER SUMMARY

Will ....bury 3's forever
Can't ....rebound
Expect ....a long road back
Don't Expect ....full recovery
Fantasy Value $25-27
Card Value..10¢

COLLEGE STATISTICS

		G	FGP	FTP	RPG	PPG
82-83	GT	28	.435	.877	3.8	20.3
83-84	GT	29	.509	.824	2.1	15.6
84-85	GT	35	.483	.840	2.0	16.7
85-86	GT	34	.528	.855	2.8	17.4
Totals		126	.487	.850	2.6	17.4

NBA REGULAR-SEASON STATISTICS

		G	MIN	FGs FG	FGs PCT	3-PT FGs FG	3-PT FGs PCT	FTs FT	FTs PCT	Rebounds OFF	Rebounds TOT	AST	STL	BLK	PTS	PPG
86-87	CLE	67	1217	173	.408	23	.329	95	.833	33	117	202	43	4	464	6.9
87-88	CLE	80	2626	493	.506	72	.486	221	.877	54	180	480	99	12	1279	16.0
88-89	CLE	75	2728	529	.526	93	.441	263	.901	48	226	631	115	7	1414	18.9
89-90	CLE	73	2706	489	.459	152	.406	300	.888	66	251	666	114	5	1430	19.6
90-91	CLE	16	571	97	.497	18	.340	59	.952	8	45	166	42	2	271	16.9
Totals		311	9848	1781	.486	358	.418	938	.887	209	819	2145	413	30	4858	15.6

KEVIN PRITCHARD

Team: San Antonio Spurs
Position: Guard
Height: 6'3" **Weight:** 185
Birthdate: July 18, 1967
NBA Experience: 1 year

College: Kansas
Acquired: Traded from Warriors for future considerations, 5/91

Background: Pritchard started on a national championship team at Kansas as a sophomore in 1988, and went on to set a school record with 154 career 3-pointers. He graduated as the Jayhawks' fifth-leading all-time scorer and was ranked third in assists and steals. Pritchard's rookie year with Golden State was plagued by poor shooting, and he was traded to San Antonio in May.

Strengths: Pritchard stunned the Warriors in training camp with his athletic ability; his vertical leap is 39 inches. He is a blue-collar worker who uses his head. He handles the ball well and will not make many bad passes or costly turnovers.

Weaknesses: Despite his athletic ability, Pritchard is not quick enough to create. He has trouble getting his own shot off the dribble and does not make things happen for teammates. He plays conservatively. While Pritchard hustles defensively and is willing to sacrifice his body, he struggles against quicker players.

Analysis: Pritchard will get a chance with the Spurs because of his work ethic and refusal to throw the ball away. However, that conservative style is also the reason Pritchard will have trouble finding a large supply of minutes. He does not create well enough to be a dangerous point man and he has not proven he can shoot like an NBA two guard. Pritchard has the makings of a hard-working reserve who will not hurt his club.

PLAYER SUMMARY

Will ....hustle
Can't ....create offense
Expect ....conservative play
Don't Expect ....many minutes
Fantasy Value...................................$1-2
Card Value..8¢

COLLEGE STATISTICS

		G	FGP	FTP	RPG	PPG
86-87	KAN	36	.456	.759	2.1	9.6
87-88	KAN	37	.486	.739	2.6	10.6
88-89	KAN	31	.507	.769	2.5	14.5
89-90	KAN	35	.525	.815	2.5	14.5
Totals		139	.495	.774	2.4	12.2

NBA REGULAR-SEASON STATISTICS

		FGs		3-PT FGs		FTs		Rebounds						
	G	MIN	FG	PCT	FG	PCT	FT	PCT	OFF	TOT	AST	STL	BLK	PTS	PPG
90-91 GS	62	773	88	.384	5	.161	62	.805	16	65	81	30	8	243	3.9
Totals	62	773	88	.384	5	.161	62	.805	16	65	81	30	8	243	3.9

BRIAN QUINNETT

Team: New York Knicks
Position: Forward
Height: 6'8" **Weight:** 236
Birthdate: May 30, 1966
NBA Experience: 2 years

College: Washington St.
Acquired: 2nd-round pick in 1989
draft (50th overall)

Background: Quinnett's college career at Washington State was slowed when he broke his foot prior to his junior season. Influenced largely by ex-coach Stu Jackson, the Knicks used the 50th pick in the 1989 draft to acquire him. (Jackson had recruited him to play for the Cougars when he was a WSU assistant.) Glued to the Knicks bench for much of his rookie season, Quinnett received five times as many minutes last year in twice as many games.

Strengths: He possesses 3-point range and a decent complement of inside moves too. Quinnett's an above-average passer who has good hands and runs the floor well. He shows a lot of tenacity and a willingness to sit and learn until his time comes (if it comes).

Weaknesses: A tweener, Quinnett isn't physical enough to bang with the power forwards inside and he doesn't display enough lateral quickness to guard small forwards on the perimeter. His rebounding has been a disappointment.

Analysis: Just making the Knicks team is Quinnett's No. 1 priority. New coach Pat Riley will no doubt want to make some changes and Quinnett could be one of the fringe players sent packing. His perimeter jumper coupled with a good attitude and hard work are the only things that will keep him in the league.

PLAYER SUMMARY

Will ....shoot from outside
Can't ....defend small forwards
Expect ....brief NBA career
Don't Expect...........increased minutes
Fantasy Value.................................$1-2
Card Value...5¢

COLLEGE STATISTICS

		G	FGP	FTP	RPG	PPG
84-85	WSU	24	.474	.762	3.2	5.9
85-86	WSU	31	.488	.592	4.5	8.8
86-87	WSU	28	.499	.707	5.2	16.5
87-88	WSU	1	.375	.750	8.0	15.0
88-89	WSU	28	.481	.724	5.9	18.4
Totals		112	.486	.697	4.8	12.6

NBA REGULAR-SEASON STATISTICS

			FGs		3-PT FGs		FTs		Rebounds						
		G	FG	PCT	FG	PCT	FT	PCT	OFF	TOT	AST	STL	BLK	PTS	PPG
89-90 NY		31	193	19	.328	0	.000	2	.667	9	28	11	3	4	40	1.3
90-91 NY		68	1011| 139	.459	15	.349	26	.722	65	145	53	22	13	319	4.7
Totals		99	1204| 158	.438	15	.333	28	.718	74	173	64	25	17	359	3.6

KURT RAMBIS

Team: Phoenix Suns
Position: Forward
Height: 6'8" **Weight:** 213
Birthdate: February 25, 1958
NBA Experience: 10 years

College: Santa Clara
Acquired: Traded from Hornets for Armon Gilliam and two future 2nd-round picks, 12/89

Background: Rambis was named West Coast Athletic Conference Player of the Year as a senior at Santa Clara before being drafted and waived by the Knicks in 1980. After a short stint in Greece, he signed as a free agent with the Lakers and was a member of four championship teams. With Charlotte in 1988-89, Rambis averaged double-digit points. He made 17 starts for Phoenix in 1990-91.

Strengths: Rambis is the ultimate hard worker who does not mind a job of setting picks, diving for loose balls, pounding the boards, and playing physical defense. He has gained a cult following for his dedication to doing the little things that help win games. He will stick the medium-range jumper every now and then, but his biggest offensive strength is his unselfishness.

Weaknesses: If you need a power forward who scores points, do not look for the one wearing glasses. His offensive game is nothing to speak of. He is not fast, athletic, or anything close to graceful, but somehow he gets the job done.

Analysis: Rambis approaches the game in workman-like fashion. He is perfect for a team with plenty of firepower, because he does everything he can to free up his teammates and does not expect to have the ball in his hands. He did not earn those four championship rings on the bench.

PLAYER SUMMARY

Will ....do the dirty work
Can't......................................look flashy
Expect...........................relentless effort
Don't Expect.............................10 PPG
Fantasy Value $3-5
Card Value...8¢

COLLEGE STATISTICS

		G	FGP	FTP	RPG	PPG
76-77	SC	27	.527	.560	11.6	15.0
77-78	SC	27	.507	.692	8.6	13.7
78-79	SC	27	.512	.716	8.4	15.6
79-80	SC	27	.534	.637	9.9	19.6
Totals		108	.521	.650	9.6	16.0

NBA REGULAR-SEASON STATISTICS

		G	MIN	FGs FG	FGs PCT	3-PT FGs FG	3-PT FGs PCT	FTs FT	FTs PCT	Rebounds OFF	Rebounds TOT	AST	STL	BLK	PTS	PPG
81-82	LAL	64	1131	118	.518	0	.000	59	.504	116	348	56	60	76	295	4.6
82-83	LAL	78	1806	235	.569	0	.000	114	.687	164	531	90	105	63	584	7.5
83-84	LAL	47	743	63	.558	0	.000	42	.636	82	266	34	30	14	168	3.6
84-85	LAL	82	1617	181	.554	0	.000	68	.660	164	528	69	82	47	430	5.2
85-86	LAL	74	1573	160	.595	0	.000	88	.721	156	517	69	66	33	408	5.5
86-87	LAL	78	1514	163	.521	0	.000	120	.764	159	453	63	74	41	446	5.7
87-88	LAL	70	845	102	.548	0	.000	73	.785	103	268	54	39	13	277	4.0
88-89	CHA	75	2233	325	.518	0	.000	182	.734	269	703	159	100	57	832	11.1
89-90	CHA/PHO	74	1904	190	.509	0	.000	82	.646	156	525	135	100	37	462	6.2
90-91	PHO	62	900	83	.497	0	.000	60	.706	77	266	64	25	11	226	3.6
Totals		704	14266	1620	.537	0	.000	888	.692	1446	4405	793	681	392	4128	5.9

BLAIR RASMUSSEN

Team: Atlanta Hawks
Position: Center
Height: 7'0" **Weight:** 260
Birthdate: November 13, 1962

NBA Experience: 6 years
College: Oregon
Acquired: Traded from Nuggets for draft rights to Anthony Avent, 7/91

Background: Rasmussen started all 114 games in which he played at Oregon, and he finished fourth on the school's all-time scoring list. His highest scoring year as a pro came in 1987-88, when he helped Denver to a Midwest Division title. Rasmussen led the last-place Nuggets in rebounding and blocked shots in 1990-91, ranking in the NBA's top 20 in both categories. He missed the last seven games to undergo surgery on his right shoulder and was traded to Atlanta in July.

Strengths: Rasmussen is one of the softest shooting big men in the league, with range up to 18 feet from the hoop. He has learned how to chase the ball off the board and now challenges shots on defense. His improvement is a testament to his work ethic.

Weaknesses: There are players much smaller in build that play more physically than Rasmussen. He blocks shots, but his defense remains soft otherwise. He does not possess good speed and he often gets left behind on breaks. While he buries jumpers when open, Rasmussen cannot put the ball on the floor and get to the hoop.

Analysis: Just when you thought you could write off Rasmussen's defense and rebounding, he refines his game in both areas. He has become a decent center who could be a starter with Atlanta. He is a hard worker who wants to improve. Learning to play physical defense would be a good place to start.

PLAYER SUMMARY

Will	pull game outside
Can't	put ball on floor
Expect	improvement
Don't Expect	an intimidator
Fantasy Value	$5-7
Card Value	10¢

COLLEGE STATISTICS

		G	FGP	FTP	RPG	PPG
81-82	ORE	27	.475	.736	4.8	6.4
82-83	ORE	27	.541	.690	5.4	14.8
83-84	ORE	29	.520	.804	6.1	16.6
84-85	ORE	31	.512	.722	7.2	16.1
Totals		114	.517	.736	5.9	13.6

NBA REGULAR-SEASON STATISTICS

				FGs		3-PT FGs		FTs		Rebounds						
		G	MIN	FG	PCT	FG	PCT	FT	PCT	OFF	TOT	AST	STL	BLK	PTS	PPG
85-86	DEN	48	330	61	.407	0	.000	31	.795	37	97	16	3	10	153	3.2
86-87	DEN	74	1421	268	.470	0	.000	169	.732	183	465	60	24	58	705	9.5
87-88	DEN	79	1779	435	.492	0	.000	132	.776	130	437	78	22	81	1002	12.7
88-89	DEN	77	1308	257	.445	0	.000	69	.852	105	287	49	29	41	583	7.6
89-90	DEN	81	1995	445	.497	0	.000	111	.828	174	594	82	40	104	1001	12.4
90-91	DEN	70	2325	405	.458	2	.400	63	.677	170	678	70	52	132	875	12.5
Totals		429	9158	1871	.472	2	.333	575	.769	799	2558	355	170	426	4319	10.1

J.R. REID

Team: Charlotte Hornets
Position: Forward/Center
Height: 6'9" **Weight:** 256
Birthdate: March 31, 1968
NBA Experience: 2 years

College: North Carolina
Acquired: 1st-round pick in 1989 draft (5th overall)

Background: Coming out of high school in 1986, Reid was the No. 1-ranked player in America. A 1988 U.S. Olympian, Reid was a consensus All-American as a sophomore at North Carolina. He was forced to play out of position at center in all 82 games as a Charlotte rookie and was named to the NBA All-Rookie second team. Moved to forward halfway through the 1990-91 season, Reid finished second on the club in rebounds.

Strengths: More comfortable facing the basket at forward, Reid possesses a nice shooting touch from 12 feet and in. Whereas he couldn't match up physically with some of the league's taller centers, he uses his size, strength, and speed to his advantage at power forward. Reid displays a lot of raw athletic ability.

Weaknesses: Reid lacks individual moves and is frequently called for steps. He stands around a lot on defense and commits way too many fouls. Even after two years in the league, he still has a lot to learn about the nuances of the pro game. Simply put, he's not a center and never will be.

Analysis: Don't write J.R. off just yet. Although he'll never be the can't-miss superstar everyone predicted six years ago, he should enjoy a solid but unspectacular NBA career at power forward for the next eight to ten seasons.

PLAYER SUMMARY

Will.........................stand tall at forward
Can't ....play center
Expect....................more polished play
Don't Expect ....an All-Star
Fantasy Value $3-5
Card Value...15¢

COLLEGE STATISTICS

		G	FGP	FTP	RPG	PPG
86-87	NC	36	.584	.653	7.4	14.7
87-88	NC	33	.607	.680	8.9	18.0
88-89	NC	27	.614	.669	6.3	15.9
Totals		96	.601	.668	7.6	16.2

NBA REGULAR-SEASON STATISTICS

			FGs		3-PT FGs		FTs		Rebounds						
	G	MIN	FG	PCT	FG	PCT	FT	PCT	OFF	TOT	AST	STL	BLK	PTS	PPG
89-90 CHA	82	2757	358	.440	0	.000	192	.664	199	691	101	92	54	908	11.1
90-91 CHA	80	2467	360	.466	0	.000	182	.703	154	502	89	87	47	902	11.3
Totals	162	5224	718	.452	0	.000	374	.682	353	1193	190	179	101	1810	11.2

JERRY REYNOLDS

Team: Orlando Magic
Position: Forward/Guard
Height: 6'8" **Weight:** 206
Birthdate: December 23, 1962

NBA Experience: 6 years
College: Louisiana St.
Acquired: Selected from SuperSonics in 1989 expansion draft

Background: Reynolds played four positions at LSU, where he was the ninth player in school history to total more than 1,000 points and 500 rebounds. He entered the draft after his junior year and was a reserve in Milwaukee and Seattle before Orlando plucked him in the 1989 expansion draft. He started 40 games in 1989-90 but was used mostly off the bench in 1990-91, when he led the club in steals and topped his career high in scoring.

Strengths: "Ice" Reynolds is especially cool in the open court, where his exciting finishes bring crowds to their feet. He can create shots in traffic, often drawing fouls (he led the Magic in free throws attempted and made in 1990-91). His anticipation allows him to come up with steals, and he makes nifty passes when he wants to.

Weaknesses: Reynolds is not a steady outside shooter, but that has never stopped him from firing away. He tends to force things with defenders all over him. He is a better finisher than starter because he often turns the ball over when pressured.

Analysis: Reynolds is a playground-type player who either lights it up with defenders in his face or looks bad trying. He is effective coming off the bench when his team needs offense. When you live with his slashing drives, however, you must also accept his questionable shot selection and tendency to play above his capabilities.

PLAYER SUMMARY

Will....................................get to the line
Can't.........................stay under control
Expect................................driving shots
Don't Expect..............50-pct. shooting
Fantasy Value.............................$2-4
Card Value...8¢

COLLEGE STATISTICS

		G	FGP	FTP	RPG	PPG
82-83	LSU	32	.534	.620	6.2	10.6
83-84	LSU	29	.528	.538	8.2	14.1
84-85	LSU	29	.502	.598	6.1	11.0
Totals		90	.521	.582	6.8	11.9

NBA REGULAR-SEASON STATISTICS

		G	MIN	FGs FG	FGs PCT	3-PT FGs FG	3-PT FGs PCT	FTs FT	FTs PCT	Rebounds OFF	Rebounds TOT	AST	STL	BLK	PTS	PPG
85-86	MIL	55	508	72	.444	1	.500	58	.558	37	80	86	43	19	203	3.7
86-87	MIL	58	963	140	.393	6	.333	118	.641	72	173	106	50	30	404	7.0
87-88	MIL	62	1161	188	.449	3	.429	119	.773	70	160	104	74	32	498	8.0
88-89	SEA	56	737	149	.417	3	.200	127	.760	49	100	62	53	26	428	7.6
89-90	ORL	67	1817	309	.417	1	.071	239	.742	91	323	180	93	64	858	12.8
90-91	ORL	80	1843	344	.434	10	.294	336	.802	88	299	203	95	56	1034	12.9
Totals		378	7029	1202	.425	24	.267	997	.739	407	1135	741	408	227	3425	9.1

GLEN RICE

Team: Miami Heat
Position: Guard/Forward
Height: 6'7" **Weight:** 220
Birthdate: May 28, 1967
NBA Experience: 2 years

College: Michigan
Acquired: 1st-round pick in 1989 draft (4th overall)

Background: The all-time leading scorer in Big Ten history, he led Michigan to a national title in 1989 while averaging nearly 31 PPG in NCAA tourney play. A second-team NBA All-Rookie selection, Rice moved to shooting guard early last December and started there for the rest of the 1990-91 season. He significantly improved his scoring, rebounding, field goal percentage, and 3-point percentage, while leading Miami in minutes played.

Strengths: He can play small forward or big guard, although the latter makes more sense because of his ability to hit from long range. When he gets in a groove, Rice is one of the deadliest pure shooters in the NBA. His accuracy ranked him among the top ten 3-point specialists in the league.

Weaknesses: He has a hard time reading defense and he still doesn't put the ball on the floor as well as a guard should. Rice doesn't shoot well when covered closely and his overall decision-making has been questioned by some.

Analysis: After a miserable rookie season that saw him out of shape and overweight, Rice was a new man last year. He seemed much more comfortable at shooting guard. If he can build upon last year's success with a little more consistency, this promising young prospect will become a solid pro.

PLAYER SUMMARY

Will ....approach 20 PPG
Can't................................score in traffic
Expect ....defensive shortcomings
Don't Expect.............return to '89 form
Fantasy Value $5-7
Card Value.......................................12¢

COLLEGE STATISTICS

		G	FGP	FTP	RPG	PPG
85-86	MICH	32	.550	.600	3.0	7.0
86-87	MICH	32	.562	.787	9.2	16.9
87-88	MICH	33	.571	.806	7.2	22.1
88-89	MICH	37	.577	.832	6.3	25.6
Totals		134	.569	.797	6.4	18.2

NBA REGULAR-SEASON STATISTICS

				FGs		3-PT FGs		FTs		Rebounds						
		G	MIN	FG	PCT	FG	PCT	FT	PCT	OFF	TOT	AST	STL	BLK	PTS	PPG
89-90	MIA	77	2311	470	.439	17	.246	91	.734	100	352	138	67	27	1048	13.6
90-91	MIA	77	2646	550	.461	71	.386	171	.818	85	381	189	101	26	1342	17.4
Totals		154	4957	1020	.451	88	.348	262	.787	185	733	327	168	53	2390	15.5

POOH RICHARDSON

Team: Minnesota Timberwolves
Position: Guard
Height: 6'1" **Weight:** 180
Birthdate: May 14, 1966

NBA Experience: 2 years
College: UCLA
Acquired: 1st-round pick in 1989 draft (10th overall)

Background: Richardson was a four-year starter and three-time All-Pac-10 star at UCLA, where he set a conference record for assists. He started the last half of his rookie season with Minnesota, guiding the club to a 17-31 finish after its 5-29 start. He started all 82 games in 1990-91, improving his scoring average by nearly six points and ranking third in the NBA in assist-to-turnover ratio (4.22). He was fifth in the league in minutes at 38.5 per game.

Strengths: Richardson is a pure point guard with the skills to emerge as one of the league's best. He penetrates and hits open men with crisp passes. After a rookie year in which he always looked for outlets, he now finishes his own plays. His shooting is respectable, considering that that was the big question mark coming out of college. He runs a potent break and can trigger it with steals in transition.

Weaknesses: One gaping hole in Richardson's game is his foul shooting. He converts less than 60 percent from the line, a disgraceful figure for a penetrating point guard who can get to the stripe often. He could also stand more consistent intensity on defense.

Analysis: Minnesota snared a good one in Richardson. Though still developing, he already displays fine leadership and a knack for getting the ball into the right hands, even if it means taking more shots himself. He makes those around him better, which is not always easy on an expansion team. As he becomes surrounded by better players, his game will improve.

PLAYER SUMMARY

Will.................................drive and dish
Can't ....shoot FTs
Expect...........................points, assists
Don't Expect.............much bench time
Fantasy Value............................$12-15
Card Value..15¢

COLLEGE STATISTICS

		G	FGP	FTP	RPG	PPG
85-86	UCLA	29	.492	.689	4.5	10.6
86-87	UCLA	32	.527	.582	5.1	10.5
87-88	UCLA	30	.470	.667	5.1	11.6
88-89	UCLA	31	.555	.562	3.8	15.2
Totals		122	.513	.624	4.6	12.0

NBA REGULAR-SEASON STATISTICS

				FGs		3-PT FGs		FTs		Rebounds						
		G	MIN	FG	PCT	FG	PCT	FT	PCT	OFF	TOT	AST	STL	BLK	PTS	PPG
89-90	MIN	82	2581	426	.461	23	.277	63	.589	55	217	554	133	25	938	11.4
90-91	MIN	82	3154	635	.470	42	.328	89	.539	82	286	734	131	13	1401	17.1
Totals		164	5735	1061	.466	65	.308	152	.559	137	503	1288	264	38	2339	14.3

MITCH RICHMOND

Team: Golden State Warriors
Position: Guard
Height: 6'5" **Weight:** 215
Birthdate: June 30, 1965
NBA Experience: 3 years

College: Moberly Area; Kansas St.
Acquired: 1st-round pick in 1988 draft (5th overall)

Background: Richmond was a junior college All-American before two years at Kansas State, where he set a single-season record for points as a senior. He was a near-unanimous choice for Rookie of the Year in 1989, when he became the third Golden State rookie to average more than 20 points. He has improved his scoring average in each of the two years since. He ranked second on the Warriors and tenth in the league in scoring in 1990-91.

Strengths: Look up "pure scorer" in the dictionary and it should mention Richmond. He nails jumpers, has 3-point range, and drives through traffic without fear. When he sets his muscular frame in the post, he is almost impossible for smaller defenders to stop. He runs the floor, uses his strength well on defense, and goes to the glass.

Weaknesses: Richmond is not a great drive-and-dish player, but who needs to be when you play alongside Tim Hardaway? He does not possess blinding speed.

Analysis: There are two reasons for Richmond being overlooked for the 1991 All-Star Game—Tim Hardaway and Chris Mullin. Although just as deserving as his two teammates, Richmond was the odd man out. It would be too much to ask for continued improvement in the scoring department, but rest assured that Richmond will be making an All-Star trip in the near future.

PLAYER SUMMARY

Will .... score from anywhere
Can't .... be pushed around
Expect .... 20 PPG
Don't Expect .... many assists
Fantasy Value $22-25
Card Value .... 15-25¢

COLLEGE STATISTICS

		G	FGP	FTP	RPG	PPG
84-85	MA	40	.480	.647	4.6	10.4
85-86	MA	38	.478	.689	6.6	16.0
86-87	KSU	30	.447	.761	5.7	18.6
87-88	KSU	34	.514	.775	6.3	22.6
Totals		142	.481	.732	5.8	16.5

NBA REGULAR-SEASON STATISTICS

				FGs		3-PT FGs		FTs		Rebounds						
		G	MIN	FG	PCT	FG	PCT	FT	PCT	OFF	TOT	AST	STL	BLK	PTS	PPG
88-89	GS	79	2717	649	.468	33	.367	410	.810	158	468	334	82	13	1741	22.0
89-90	GS	78	2799	640	.497	34	.358	406	.866	98	360	223	98	24	1720	22.1
90-91	GS	77	3027	703	.494	40	.348	394	.847	147	452	238	126	34	1840	23.9
Totals		234	8543	1992	.486	107	.357	1210	.840	403	1280	795	306	71	5301	22.7

DOC RIVERS

Team: Los Angeles Clippers
Position: Guard
Height: 6'4" **Weight:** 185
Birthdate: October 13, 1961
NBA Experience: 8 years

College: Marquette
Acquired: Traded from Hawks for a 1991 1st-round pick and 1993 and 1994 2nd-round picks, 6/91

Background: A Marquette product, Rivers spent eight years with Atlanta before being traded to the Clippers on draft day, 1991. Rivers was an NBA All-Star in 1988-89, though a herniated disk caused him to miss 34 games in 1989-90. Healthy for a compete season for the first time in three years, Rivers finished second on the Hawks last year in scoring and assists and was first in steals. He is Atlanta's all-time assists and steals leader.

Strengths: One of the league's most gifted penetrators, Rivers also provided the Hawks with in-your-face defense and steady leadership. He can play either guard position and his quickness and leaping ability makes him a factor on the defensive glass.

Weaknesses: Although he produced a career high in points, Rivers shot a career low from the field last season. Dating all the way back to his high school days in Chicago, he's never been what you'd call a pure shooter. Rivers often disappears in must-win situations.

Analysis: On the verge of greatness three years ago, back problems prevented Rivers from taking his game to the next level. He's recognized as a class act by his teammates and opposing players and coaches. He'll provide the leadership from the point that the Clippers so desperately need.

PLAYER SUMMARY

Will.................................improve FG pct.
Can't ....produce in big games
Expect ....top-notch defense
Don't Expect ....lack of respect
Fantasy Value $7-10
Card Value..8¢

COLLEGE STATISTICS

		G	FGP	FTP	RPG	PPG
80-81	MARQ	31	.553	.588	3.2	14.0
81-82	MARQ	29	.453	.648	3.4	14.3
82-83	MARQ	29	.437	.611	3.2	13.2
Totals		89	.478	.615	3.3	13.9

NBA REGULAR-SEASON STATISTICS

		G	MIN	FG	FG PCT	3-PT FG	3-PT PCT	FT	FT PCT	OFF	TOT	AST	STL	BLK	PTS	PPG
83-84	ATL	81	1938	250	.462	2	.167	255	.785	72	220	314	127	30	757	9.3
84-85	ATL	69	2126	334	.476	15	.417	291	.770	66	214	410	163	53	974	14.1
85-86	ATL	53	1571	220	.474	0	.000	172	.608	49	162	443	120	13	612	11.5
86-87	ATL	82	2590	342	.451	4	.190	365	.828	83	299	823	171	30	1053	12.8
87-88	ATL	80	2502	403	.453	9	.273	319	.758	83	366	747	140	41	1134	14.2
88-89	ATL	76	2462	371	.455	43	.347	247	.861	89	286	525	181	40	1032	13.6
89-90	ATL	48	1526	218	.454	24	.364	138	.812	47	200	264	116	22	598	12.5
90-91	ATL	79	2586	444	.435	88	.336	221	.844	47	253	340	148	47	1197	15.2
Totals		568	17301	2582	.455	185	.325	2008	.782	536	2000	3866	1166	276	7357	13.0

FRED ROBERTS

Team: Milwaukee Bucks
Position: Forward
Height: 6'10" **Weight:** 245
Birthdate: August 14, 1960
NBA Experience: 8 years

College: Brigham Young
Acquired: Traded from Heat for a
1989 2nd-round pick, 6/88

Background: Roberts concluded his collegiate career at BYU as the Cougars' second all-time leading scorer. Originally drafted by the Bucks in 1982, he bounced around between Italy, San Antonio, Utah, and Boston before Milwaukee finally got him back in '88. The only Bucks player to start every game last year, Roberts logged career highs in points and offensive rebounds. He averaged more than 20 PPG and shot 60 percent from the field over the final 11 games.

Strengths: He moves well without the ball and rarely puts up a bad shot (.533 field goal percentage last year). Roberts can handle the ball and he passes surprisingly well. A true team player, his presence helps keep harmony in the locker room.

Weaknesses: Roberts will score points (34 vs. New Jersey last April), but he's yet to show any consistency. Slow and not as strong as the Milwaukee coaching staff would like, he's an average defender who doesn't rebound well.

Analysis: Roberts has quietly developed into one of the Bucks' key players. He replaced Larry Krystkowiak in the starting lineup, after Krysko blew out his knee in the 1989 playoffs, and hasn't sat down since. Roberts's defensive limitations make him more suited for a reserve role.

PLAYER SUMMARY

Will..........................look to score more
Can't..................................rebound
Expect..........................so-so defense
Don't Expect.................low-pct. shots
Fantasy Value..............................$2-4
Card Value.......................................10¢

COLLEGE STATISTICS

		G	FGP	FTP	RPG	PPG
78-79	BYU	28	.543	.783	6.8	14.3
79-80	BYU	29	.588	.724	6.1	12.9
80-81	BYU	32	.579	.777	8.0	18.8
81-82	BYU	30	.479	.798	7.2	15.5
Totals		119	.546	.776	7.0	15.5

NBA REGULAR-SEASON STATISTICS

		G	MIN	FGs FG	FGs PCT	3-PT FGs FG	3-PT FGs PCT	FTs FT	FTs PCT	Rebounds OFF	Rebounds TOT	AST	STL	BLK	PTS	PPG
83-84	SA	79	1531	214	.536	1	.250	144	.837	102	304	98	52	38	573	7.3
84-85	SA/UTA	74	1178	208	.498	1	1.000	150	.824	78	186	87	28	22	567	7.7
85-86	UTA	58	469	74	.443	1	.500	67	.770	31	80	27	8	6	216	3.7
86-87	BOS	73	1079	139	.515	0	.000	124	.810	54	190	62	22	20	402	5.5
87-88	BOS	74	1032	161	.488	0	.000	128	.776	60	162	81	16	15	450	6.1
88-89	MIL	71	1251	155	.486	3	.214	104	.806	68	209	66	36	23	417	5.9
89-90	MIL	82	2235	330	.495	2	.182	195	.783	107	311	147	56	25	857	10.5
90-91	MIL	82	2114	357	.533	4	.160	170	.813	107	281	135	63	29	888	10.8
Totals		593	10889	1638	.506	12	.182	1082	.804	607	1723	703	281	178	4370	7.4

ALVIN ROBERTSON

Team: Milwaukee Bucks
Position: Guard
Height: 6'4" **Weight:** 202
Birthdate: July 22, 1962
NBA Experience: 7 years

College: Crowder; Arkansas
Acquired: Traded from Spurs with Greg Anderson and a 1989 2nd-round pick for Terry Cummings, 5/89

Background: Following a memorable career at Arkansas, Robertson was a member of the 1984 U.S. Olympic Team. A four-time NBA All-Star (including last season), Robertson was named NBA Defensive Player of the Year in 1986. He spent five seasons with San Antonio before being traded to the Bucks in 1989. Robertson led all NBA guards in offensive rebounds in 1989-90. For the third time in his career, he topped the NBA in steals last season with more than three per game.

Strengths: Robertson creates offense with some of the best defense you'll see from a two guard. His on-the-ball defense is second to none. A professional thief, he's got very quick hands. Extraordinarily strong and speedy, Robertson slashes his way inside for a lot of his points and rebounds.

Weaknesses: He's a very mediocre perimeter jump-shooter. Opposing guards give him little respect outside of 15 feet. He seems to have lost a half-step in the transition game and he doesn't handle the ball with as much confidence as he did two years ago.

Analysis: Untypically mistake prone in his final year with the Spurs (1988-89), Robertson has raised his game to its previous All-Star level since joining Milwaukee. He's one of those special players who plays so well so often that he's taken for granted.

PLAYER SUMMARY

Will...............make All-Defensive Team
Can't.................nail perimeter jumpers
Expect ....league best in steals
Don't Expect................uninspired play
Fantasy Value.............................$12-14
Card Value...8¢

COLLEGE STATISTICS

		G	FGP	FTP	RPG	PPG
80-81	CJC	34	.572	.652	8.4	18.0
81-82	ARK	28	.528	.603	2.2	7.3
82-83	ARK	28	.548	.661	4.9	14.2
83-84	ARK	32	.499	.670	5.5	15.5
Totals		122	.540	.655	5.4	14.0

NBA REGULAR-SEASON STATISTICS

		G	MIN	FGs FG	FGs PCT	3-PT FGs FG	3-PT FGs PCT	FTs FT	FTs PCT	Rebounds OFF	Rebounds TOT	AST	STL	BLK	PTS	PPG
84-85	SA	79	1685	299	.498	4	.364	124	.734	116	265	275	127	24	726	9.2
85-86	SA	82	2878	562	.514	8	.276	260	.795	184	516	448	301	40	1392	17.0
86-87	SA	81	2697	589	.466	13	.271	244	.753	186	424	421	260	35	1435	17.7
87-88	SA	82	2978	655	.465	27	.284	273	.748	165	498	557	243	69	1610	19.6
88-89	SA	65	2287	465	.483	9	.200	183	.723	157	384	393	197	36	1122	17.3
89-90	MIL	81	2599	476	.503	4	.154	197	.741	230	559	445	207	17	1153	14.2
90-91	MIL	81	2598	438	.485	23	.365	199	.757	191	459	444	246	16	1098	13.6
Totals		551	17722	3484	.485	88	.278	1480	.752	1229	3105	2983	1581	237	8536	15.5

CLIFF ROBINSON

Team: Portland Trail Blazers
Position: Forward
Height: 6'10" **Weight:** 225
Birthdate: December 16, 1966
NBA Experience: 2 years

College: Connecticut
Acquired: 2nd-round pick in 1989 draft (36th overall)

Background: Robinson led Connecticut in scoring for three consecutive seasons and was third in the Big East as a senior. Bypassed until the second round of the 1989 draft, he played all 82 games of his rookie year and provided solid minutes in the 1990 playoffs. He was Portland's top scorer off the bench in 1990-91, significantly improving his field goal accuracy and again playing in 82 games.

Strengths: Versatility makes Robinson an invaluable reserve. He can play just about any position but the point, although he is at his best when facing the basket. He is an elusive driver who can put the ball on the floor and get to the hoop for finishes. He is a tremendous open-court player and an underrated defender with explosive shot-blocking skills.

Weaknesses: Although he has good range and has improved his shooting accuracy, Robinson is streaky from the perimeter and does not know how to pass up a bad shot. He is a below-average passer who does not have a great team concept on offense. He commits too many turnovers.

Analysis: His game lacks a layer of finish, but Robinson has the raw skills of a big-time NBA scorer. He can fill the nets from inside and outside and is willing to play hard at both ends. With better decision-making and continued improvement on his jumper, Robinson could make it tough—even for a good team—to keep him out of the lineup for extended minutes.

PLAYER SUMMARY

Will....................................finish with flair
Can't ....pass up shots
Expect.......................................versatility
Don't Expect..................slack defense
Fantasy Value $2-4
Card Value...12¢

COLLEGE STATISTICS

		G	FGP	FTP	RPG	PPG
85-86	CONN	28	.366	.610	3.1	5.6
86-87	CONN	16	.420	.570	7.4	18.1
87-88	CONN	34	.479	.655	6.9	17.6
88-89	CONN	31	.470	.684	7.4	20.0
Totals		109	.452	.644	6.1	15.3

NBA REGULAR-SEASON STATISTICS

				FGs		3-PT FGs		FTs		Rebounds						
		G	MIN	FG	PCT	FG	PCT	FT	PCT	OFF	TOT	AST	STL	BLK	PTS	PPG
89-90	POR	82	1565	298	.397	12	.273	138	.550	110	308	72	53	53	746	9.1
90-91	POR	82	1940	373	.463	6	.316	205	.653	123	349	151	78	76	957	11.7
Totals		164	3505	671	.431	18	.286	343	.607	233	657	223	131	129	1703	10.4

DAVID ROBINSON

Team: San Antonio Spurs
Position: Center
Height: 7'1" **Weight:** 235
Birthdate: August 6, 1965

NBA Experience: 2 years
College: Navy
Acquired: 1st-round pick in 1987 draft
(1st overall)

Background: As a senior at Navy, Robinson led the nation in blocked shots and won the Wooden Award as the top college player. He set NCAA records for blocks in a game, season, and career. After a two-year stint in the Navy, he exploded onto the pro scene in 1989-90, winning Rookie of the Year honors by a unanimous vote and finishing among the NBA leaders in five categories. He continued his All-Star play in 1990-91, winning the NBA rebounding crown and finishing in the top ten in scoring, blocked shots, and field goal accuracy.

Strengths: Where do you start? Robinson is simply dominant in most aspects of the game. His quickness allows him to explode to the hoop with unstoppable low-post spin moves. He can also stick jumpers up to about 16 feet or swing the ball back outside for his teammates. He challenges shots, clears the boards, and runs the break as well as any big man (not to mention most smaller ones as well).

Weaknesses: Robinson dominates in spurts, meaning there is room for more consistency. He also must refrain from forcing outside jumpers, which he can get any time he wants.

Analysis: Some are already calling Mr. Robinson the best center in the league. He is clearly among the top three and is younger than Patrick Ewing and Hakeem Olajuwon. He is gifted with a physique that few big men can dream of, and he has used it to become an instant power in the NBA. In time, Robinson will undisputedly become the game's premier big man, and perhaps one of the best ever.

PLAYER SUMMARY

Will..............................simply dominate
Can't ....be contained
Expect ....Hall of Fame career
Don't Expect...........................a drop-off
Fantasy Value $69-74
Card Value $1.00-1.50

COLLEGE STATISTICS

		G	FGP	FTP	RPG	PPG
83-84	NAVY	28	.623	.575	4.0	7.6
84-85	NAVY	32	.644	.626	11.6	23.6
85-86	NAVY	35	.607	.628	13.0	22.7
86-87	NAVY	32	.591	.637	11.8	28.2
Totals		127	.613	.627	10.3	21.0

NBA REGULAR-SEASON STATISTICS

		G	MIN	FGs FG	FGs PCT	3-PT FGs FG	3-PT FGs PCT	FTs FT	FTs PCT	Rebounds OFF	Rebounds TOT	AST	STL	BLK	PTS	PPG
89-90	SA	82	3002	690	.531	0	.000	613	.732	303	983	164	138	319	1993	24.3
90-91	SA	82	3095	754	.552	1	.143	592	.762	335	1063	208	127	320	2101	25.6
Totals		164	6097	1444	.542	1	.111	1205	.747	638	2046	372	265	639	4094	25.0

RUMEAL ROBINSON

Team: Atlanta Hawks
Position: Guard
Height: 6'2" **Weight:** 195
Birthdate: November 13, 1966
NBA Experience: 1 year

College: Michigan
Acquired: 1st-round pick in 1990 draft (10th overall)

Background: The hero of Michigan's 1989 NCAA championship as a junior, Robinson made a forgettable NBA debut in Atlanta. Replaced as a starter during the throes of a nine-game losing streak in November, he moved further and further down the Atlanta bench as the season wore on. He missed seven games with a sprained knee and 22 more because of coach Bob Weiss's decision. A fine student, Robinson took graduate classes last summer at Harvard.

Strengths: Strong and physical, Robinson has an NBA body. He's a fierce competitor who comes to play every night. He's dangerous in the open court and he plays better defense than the Atlanta coaching staff expected.

Weaknesses: Robinson turns the ball over at an embarrassing rate. He has to learn that he can't challenge defenders like he did so often in college. Robinson's a combination guard who isn't a good enough playmaker to exclusively play the point in the pros. He's not a good enough perimeter shooter to see much action at two guard.

Analysis: After such a disastrous season, the typical rookie's confidence would have been destroyed. But not Robinson's. He's too tough a kid. A new season and a fresh start is just what he needs. His rookie season was a bad dream and now he must wake up. He'll learn from his mistakes.

PLAYER SUMMARY

Will ....get better in time
Can't.......................shoot from outside
Expect ....more minutes
Don't Expect ....1990-91 repeat
Fantasy Value..................................$1-2
Card Value..10¢

COLLEGE STATISTICS

		G	FGP	FTP	RPG	PPG
87-88	MICH	33	.553	.667	3.1	9.7
88-89	MICH	37	.557	.656	3.4	14.9
89-90	MICH	30	.490	.676	4.2	19.2
Totals		100	.528	.666	3.5	14.5

NBA REGULAR-SEASON STATISTICS

			FGs		3-PT FGs		FTs		Rebounds						
	G	MIN	FG	PCT	FG	PCT	FT	PCT	OFF	TOT	AST	STL	BLK	PTS	PPG
90-91 ATL	47	674	108	.446	2	.182	47	.587	20	71	132	32	8	265	5.6
Totals	47	674	108	.446	2	.182	47	.587	20	71	132	32	8	265	5.6

DENNIS RODMAN

Team: Detroit Pistons
Position: Forward
Height: 6'8" **Weight:** 210
Birthdate: May 13, 1961
NBA Experience: 5 years

College: Cooke County;
S.E. Oklahoma St.
Acquired: 2nd-round pick in 1986
draft (27th overall)

Background: Standing only 5'11' as a high school senior, Rodman went to work for a few years as an airport laborer. An incredible nine-inch growth spurt finally convinced Rodman to give basketball a try. A three-time NAIA All-American at S.E. Oklahoma State, Dennis was drafted by Detroit in the second round in 1986. Rodman was a 1989-90 NBA All-Star and the NBA's Defensive Player of the Year each of the two past seasons. He finished the 1990-91 season as the NBA's second-leading rebounder.

Strengths: No 6'8" forward in modern-day NBA history has been as dominant defensively as Rodman. He's so versatile, he can cover centers or point guards. He smothers opponents with quickness, speed, and strength. An extraordinary leaper, Rodman's the top defensive rebounding forward in the league.

Weaknesses: Offensively, he doesn't even belong in the league. He shows little touch, he rushes his shot, and, frankly, he could care less about scoring. Almost all of the points he does score are either put-backs off the offensive glass or dunks and lay-ups on the break. He's a career 60-percent shooter from the line.

Analysis: No other NBA player works any harder than Dennis Rodman. He does things defensively that even he sometimes can't believe. Even without any semblance of an offensive game, he's one of the most coveted players in the game today.

PLAYER SUMMARY	
Will	shut down any player
Can't	score in an empty gym
Expect	NBA's top defender
Don't Expect	a lack of effort
Fantasy Value	$6-8
Card Value	10¢

COLLEGE STATISTICS

		G	FGP	FTP	RPG	PPG
82-83	CCJ	16	.616	.582	13.3	17.6
83-84	SOS	30	.618	.655	13.1	26.0
84-85	SOS	32	.648	.566	15.9	26.8
85-86	SOS	34	.645	.655	17.8	24.4
Totals		112	.635	.620	15.3	24.5

NBA REGULAR-SEASON STATISTICS

				FGs		3-PT FGs		FTs		Rebounds						
		G	MIN	FG	PCT	FG	PCT	FT	PCT	OFF	TOT	AST	STL	BLK	PTS	PPG
86-87	DET	77	1155	213	.545	0	.000	74	.587	163	332	56	38	48	500	6.5
87-88	DET	82	2147	398	.561	5	.294	152	.535	318	715	110	75	45	953	11.6
88-89	DET	82	2208	316	.595	6	.231	97	.626	327	772	99	55	76	735	9.0
89-90	DET	82	2377	288	.581	1	.111	142	.654	336	792	72	52	60	719	8.8
90-91	DET	82	2747	276	.493	6	.200	111	.631	361	1026	85	65	55	669	8.2
Totals		405	10634	1491	.555	18	.217	576	.601	1505	3637	422	285	284	3576	8.8

DELANEY RUDD

Team: Utah Jazz
Position: Guard
Height: 6'2" **Weight:** 195
Birthdate: November 8, 1962
NBA Experience: 2 years

College: Wake Forest
Acquired: Signed as a free agent,
11/90

Background: Rudd played with fellow NBA players Muggsy Bogues and Danny Young at Wake Forest, where he finished as the school's 12th-leading scorer of all time. After a brief stint in the CBA and two seasons in Greece, he has served primarily as a back-up to John Stockton in his two seasons with Utah. He played in all 82 games of the 1990-91 season, finishing third on the Jazz in assists and ninth in scoring.

Strengths: Rudd, who played shooting guard in college, has a scorer's mentality. He can hit from 3-point range, is not shy with the jump shot, and can pass off his penetration moves. He plays smart defense.

Weaknesses: Rudd's lack of quickness makes his point-guard skills pale in comparison to those of Stockton. While he is confident with the ball and can run a controlled tempo, he does not make those around him much better. His shooting percentage is not high enough to keep defenders from giving him a few steps.

Analysis: Rudd fills a role, and is happy to do so for an NBA club. He can score occasionally and is not afraid to take the big shot when given the chance, but his greatest value is as a steady hand who can come off the bench and not make mistakes. He might be worth a better look at two guard if he can manage to get his shooting percentage closer to 50 than 40.

PLAYER SUMMARY

Will	use his head
Can't	shoot consistently
Expect	controlled tempo
Don't Expect	offensive punch
Fantasy Value	$1-3
Card Value	8¢

COLLEGE STATISTICS

		G	FGP	FTP	RPG	PPG
81-82	WF	22	.333	.500	0.2	1.1
82-83	WF	32	.528	.768	2.0	12.8
83-84	WF	31	.518	.859	1.8	13.3
84-85	WF	29	.465	.818	2.6	16.7
Totals		114	.495	.805	1.7	11.7

NBA REGULAR-SEASON STATISTICS

				FGs		3-PT FGs		FTs		Rebounds						
		G	MIN	FG	PCT	FG	PCT	FT	PCT	OFF	TOT	AST	STL	BLK	PTS	PPG
89-90	UTA	77	850	111	.429	16	.286	35	.660	12	55	177	22	1	273	3.5
90-91	UTA	82	874	124	.435	17	.279	59	.831	14	66	216	36	2	324	4.0
Totals		159	1724	235	.432	33	.282	94	.758	26	121	393	58	3	597	3.8

JOHN SALLEY

Team: Detroit Pistons
Position: Forward/Center
Height: 6'11" **Weight:** 244
Birthdate: May 16, 1964
NBA Experience: 5 years

College: Georgia Tech
Acquired: 1st-round pick in 1986 draft
(11th overall)

Background: Georgia Tech's all-time leader in blocked shots, "Spider" got off to a slow start as a Piston rookie. Talented but inconsistent for much of his career, he's at his best during the post-season. The Pistons have advanced to the NBA Finals three times in his five seasons. Salley led the Pistons in blocks last year while backing up James Edwards at power forward.

Strengths: One of the premier shot-blocking forwards in the league, Salley's size and quick feet make him tough to shoot around. His unusual quickness allows him to guard big people away from the basket. He gets down court on the break faster than any of his teammates.

Weaknesses: Offensively, he's as inconsistent as any big forward in the league. A very mediocre shooter, he rarely takes the ball hard to the basket. Always in foul trouble, Salley takes too many chances and picks up way too many frustration fouls. He puts the ball on the floor when he doesn't have to.

Analysis: An aspiring comedian who is very proud of the fact that he hangs out with guys like Spike Lee and Eddie Murphy, Salley never has been willing to focus his full attention on basketball. There are too many other things in the world that interest him. As a result, he'll never be as talented a player as he should be.

PLAYER SUMMARY

Will ....block a ton of shots
Can't........................score consistently
Expect ....career in show biz
Don't Expect.........dedication to game
Fantasy Value..............................$9-11
Card Value..8¢

COLLEGE STATISTICS

		G	FGP	FTP	RPG	PPG
82-83	GT	27	.502	.637	5.7	11.5
83-84	GT	29	.589	.674	5.8	11.8
84-85	GT	35	.627	.636	7.1	14.0
85-86	GT	34	.606	.594	6.7	13.1
Totals		125	.587	.633	6.4	12.7

NBA REGULAR-SEASON STATISTICS

			MIN	FGs		3-PT FGs		FTs		Rebounds						
		G		FG	PCT	FG	PCT	FT	PCT	OFF	TOT	AST	STL	BLK	PTS	PPG
86-87	DET	82	1463	163	.562	0	.000	105	.614	108	296	54	44	125	431	5.3
87-88	DET	82	2003	258	.566	0	.000	185	.709	166	402	113	53	137	701	8.5
88-89	DET	67	1458	166	.498	0	.000	135	.692	134	335	75	40	72	467	7.0
89-90	DET	82	1914	209	.512	1	.250	174	.713	154	439	67	51	153	593	7.2
90-91	DET	74	1649	179	.475	0	.000	186	.727	137	327	70	52	112	544	7.4
Totals		387	8487	975	.523	1	.125	785	.697	699	1799	379	240	599	2736	7.1

RALPH SAMPSON

Team: Sacramento Kings
Position: Center
Height: 7'4" **Weight:** 250
Birthdate: April 7, 1960

NBA Experience: 8 years
College: Virginia
Acquired: Traded from Warriors for Jim Petersen, 9/89

Background: One of the greatest college players of all-time, Sampson joined Oscar Robertson and Bill Walton as the only three-time Player of the Year winners. He set Virginia records for all-time field goal accuracy, rebounds, and blocked shots. He was a unanimous Rookie of the Year choice in 1983-84 with Houston and earned All-Star MVP honors in 1985. In 1986-87, he missed 39 games with injuries and had knee surgery to remove lateral cartilage. He was traded the next year to Golden State and has never returned to form. He has had three knee surgeries and played just 25 games for Sacramento in 1990-91.

Strengths: Sampson could once do just about everything, but now he is limited to the advantages of height. He sees the court well, can get a few rebounds, and knows the game.

Weaknesses: The once-dominant scorer is a liability on offense, where he has shot less than 40 percent each of the past two years. His legs are not sturdy enough to support his low-post moves of old. He is also a liability on defense. Quick players eat him alive on both ends.

Analysis: Sampson's story is a sad one. He made four starts in 1990-91 with the Kings, who had hoped his presence would at least deter opposing teams from taking the ball inside. On the contrary, teams saw Sampson as the weak spot on a poor team. How much longer can there be a market for his deteriorated skills?

PLAYER SUMMARY

Will ....ride the bench
Can't.......................................regain form
Expect ....an offensive liability
Don't Expect.............many more years
Fantasy Value $1-2
Card Value...8¢

COLLEGE STATISTICS

		G	FGP	FTP	RPG	PPG
79-80	VA	34	.547	.702	11.2	14.9
80-81	VA	33	.557	.631	11.5	17.7
81-82	VA	32	.561	.615	11.4	15.8
82-83	VA	33	.604	.704	11.7	19.1
Totals		132	.568	.657	11.4	16.9

NBA REGULAR-SEASON STATISTICS

		G	MIN	FGs FG	FGs PCT	3-PT FGs FG	3-PT FGs PCT	FTs FT	FTs PCT	Rebounds OFF	Rebounds TOT	AST	STL	BLK	PTS	PPG
83-84	HOU	82	2693	716	.523	1	.250	287	.661	293	913	163	70	197	1720	21.0
84-85	HOU	82	3086	753	.502	0	.000	303	.676	227	853	224	81	168	1809	22.1
85-86	HOU	79	2864	624	.488	2	.133	241	.641	258	879	283	99	129	1491	18.9
86-87	HOU	43	1326	277	.489	0	.000	118	.624	88	372	120	40	58	672	15.6
87-88	HOU/GS	48	1663	299	.438	2	.182	149	.760	140	462	122	41	88	749	15.6
88-89	GS	61	1086	164	.449	3	.375	62	.653	105	307	77	31	65	393	6.4
89-90	SAC	26	417	48	.372	1	.250	12	.522	11	84	28	14	22	109	4.2
90-91	SAC	25	348	34	.366	1	.200	5	.263	41	111	17	11	17	74	3.0
Totals		446	13483	2915	.487	10	.179	1177	.661	1163	3981	1034	387	744	7017	15.7

MIKE SANDERS

Team: Indiana Pacers
Position: Forward
Height: 6'6" **Weight:** 215
Birthdate: May 7, 1960

NBA Experience: 9 years
College: UCLA
Acquired: Signed as a free agent, 9/89

Background: Sanders was an All-Pac-10 selection at UCLA before being drafted in the fourth round by Kansas City. After being waived by the Kings and the Spurs and playing in the CBA, his career blossomed during his four-plus years in Phoenix. Involved in the blockbuster Kevin Johnson-for-Larry Nance swap, he was traded to Cleveland in 1988. Sanders signed with Indiana as a free agent prior to the 1989-90 season. His 1990-91 scoring average was the second-lowest of his nine-year career.

Strengths: A bona fide defensive stopper, Sanders has enjoyed a lot of success against the likes of Bernard King, Scottie Pippen, and Mark Aguirre, to name just a few. An expert at the art of setting an effective pick, Sanders is selfless, he hustles, and he never complains about minutes.

Weaknesses: Even when he has the opportunity, Sanders rarely looks to score. When he did shoot last year, he converted a career-low 42 percent of his attempts. Despite his defensive prowess, Sanders doesn't rebound real well.

Analysis: Until someone better comes along, the Pacers are counting on Sanders to come off the bench every night for 15-to-20 minutes of solid blue-collar play as Chuck Person's back-up at small forward. A true team player, he's far more valuable than his numbers indicate.

PLAYER SUMMARY

Will	never stop hustling
Can't	rebound
Expect	air-tight defense
Don't Expect	10 PPG
Fantasy Value	$1-3
Card Value	5¢

COLLEGE STATISTICS

		G	FGP	FTP	RPG	PPG
78-79	UCLA	23	.421	.688	1.5	1.9
79-80	UCLA	32	.573	.792	5.9	11.3
80-81	UCLA	27	.561	.766	6.6	15.4
81-82	UCLA	27	.502	.776	6.4	14.4
Totals		109	.538	.773	5.3	11.1

NBA REGULAR-SEASON STATISTICS

		G	MIN	FGs FG	FGs PCT	3-PT FGs FG	3-PT FGs PCT	FTs FT	FTs PCT	Rebounds OFF	Rebounds TOT	AST	STL	BLK	PTS	PPG
82-83	SA	26	393	76	.484	0	.000	31	.721	31	94	19	18	6	183	7.0
83-84	PHO	50	586	97	.478	0	.000	29	.690	40	103	44	23	12	223	4.5
84-85	PHO	21	418	85	.486	3	.200	45	.763	38	89	29	23	4	215	10.2
85-86	PHO	82	1644	347	.513	0	.000	208	.809	104	273	150	76	31	905	11.0
86-87	PHO	82	1655	357	.494	2	.118	143	.781	101	271	126	61	23	859	10.5
87-88	PHO CLE	59	883	153	.505	0	.000	59	.776	38	109	56	31	9	365	6.2
88-89	CLE	82	2102	332	.453	3	.300	97	.719	98	307	133	89	32	764	9.3
89-90	IND	82	1531	225	.470	5	.357	55	.733	78	230	89	43	23	510	6.2
90-91	IND	80	1357	206	.417	4	.200	47	.825	73	185	106	37	26	463	5.8
Totals		564	10569	1878	.476	17	.215	714	.770	601	1661	752	401	166	4487	8.0

DANNY SCHAYES

Team: Milwaukee Bucks
Position: Center
Height: 6'11" **Weight:** 250
Birthdate: May 10, 1959

NBA Experience: 10 years
College: Syracuse
Acquired: Traded from Nuggets for draft rights to Terry Mills, 8/90

Background: The son of Hall of Famer Dolph Schayes, Danny was a late bloomer at Syracuse and didn't even start until his senior season. He was drafted by Utah but moved on to Denver the following year. Schayes spent seven-plus seasons with the Nuggets before joining the Bucks in August 1990. He led the Nuggets in field goal percentage three times in the late 1980s. Schayes split time with Jack Sikma in the middle last year and paced Milwaukee in rebounds.

Strengths: Play center in the league for ten seasons and you learn more than a few tricks of the trade. Let's just say Schayes knows how to get away with murder. Only three NBA centers made a higher percentage of free throws. He's a banger who knows how to go get defensive rebounds. Schayes is a 50-percent shooter from the field for his career.

Weaknesses: He's prone to foul trouble, especially against centers he can't handle. Schayes doesn't have good hands and he can't jump over the free throw line. He's been plagued by bad ankles throughout his career.

Analysis: As it turned out, the Bucks stole Schayes from Denver. The change of scenery did him wonders. He's much more comfortable in a structured offense which runs a lot of halfcourt sets. When compared to the other 50 or so centers around the league, Schayes is in the top 60 percentile.

PLAYER SUMMARY

Will ....bang on defense
Can't.........................jump over people
Expect.....................more playing time
Don't Expect.............................15 PPG
Fantasy Value $2-4
Card Value...5¢

COLLEGE STATISTICS

		G	FGP	FTP	RPG	PPG
77-78	SYR	24	.565	.756	4.0	4.7
78-79	SYR	29	.530	.833	4.2	6.2
79-80	SYR	30	.509	.769	4.5	5.9
80-81	SYR	34	.579	.822	8.4	14.6
Totals		117	.554	.806	5.4	8.2

NBA REGULAR-SEASON STATISTICS

		G	MIN	FG	PCT	FG	PCT	FT	PCT	OFF	TOT	AST	STL	BLK	PTS	PPG
81-82	UTA	82	1623	252	.481	0	.000	140	.757	131	427	146	46	72	644	7.9
82-83	UTA/DEN	82	2284	342	.457	0	.000	228	.773	200	635	205	54	98	912	11.1
83-84	DEN	82	1420	183	.493	0	.000	215	.790	145	433	91	32	60	581	7.1
84-85	DEN	56	542	60	.465	0	.000	79	.814	48	144	38	20	25	199	3.6
85-86	DEN	80	1654	221	.502	0	.000	216	.777	154	439	79	42	63	658	8.2
86-87	DEN	76	1556	210	.519	0	.000	229	.779	120	380	85	20	74	649	8.5
87-88	DEN	81	2166	361	.540	0	.000	407	.836	200	662	106	62	92	1129	13.9
88-89	DEN	76	1918	317	.522	3	.333	332	.826	142	500	105	42	81	969	12.8
89-90	DEN	53	1194	163	.494	0	.000	225	.852	117	342	61	41	45	551	10.4
90-91	MIL	82	2228	298	.499	0	.000	274	.835	174	535	98	55	61	870	10.6
Totals		750	16585	2407	.499	3	.120	2345	.808	1431	4497	1014	414	671	7162	9.5

DWAYNE SCHINTZIUS

Team: San Antonio Spurs
Position: Center
Height: 7'1" **Weight:** 260
Birthdate: October 14, 1968
NBA Experience: 1 year

College: Florida
Acquired: 1st-round pick in 1990 draft
(24th overall)

Background: Schintzius renounced his scholarship 11 games into his senior year at Florida because of a disagreement with coach Don DeVoe. Despite his All-Southeastern Conference play as a junior, pro scouts were leery because he reported to pre-draft camps out of shape. He played in 42 games and made seven starts as a rookie in 1990-91, but he injured his back late in the season.

Strengths: Schintzius is a deft passer who sees the whole court and owns a nice touch for his massive size. His bulk helps him establish rebounding position and set screens. Surprisingly, he has shown a harmless off-court demeanor and fits in well.

Weaknesses: Certain athletic skills like running and jumping seem tedious when performed by Schintzius, who lacks grace. He does not run the floor well and still struggles with his timing. Remember, he was away from competitive basketball for the better part of a year. He is not consistently focused.

Analysis: No one could have predicted how well Schintzius has blended in with his teammates. Perhaps David Robinson, a former roommate at the 1988 Olympic trials, has rubbed off. Schintzius will never match Robinson's play in the pivot, but he shows promise as a back-up. Time is on his side.

PLAYER SUMMARY

Will	rebound
Can't	stay intense
Expect	improved timing
Don't Expect	a starting job
Fantasy Value	$1-3
Card Value	10¢

COLLEGE STATISTICS

		G	FGP	FTP	RPG	PPG
86-87	FLA	34	.440	.738	6.1	10.9
87-88	FLA	35	.491	.730	6.5	14.4
88-89	FLA	30	.521	.707	9.7	18.0
89-90	FLA	11	.552	.789	9.5	19.1
Totals		110	.494	.729	7.5	14.8

NBA REGULAR-SEASON STATISTICS

			FGs		3-PT FGs		FTs		Rebounds						
	G	MIN	FG	PCT	FG	PCT	FT	PCT	OFF	TOT	AST	STL	BLK	PTS	PPG
90-91 SA	42	398	68	.439	0	.000	22	.550	28	121	17	2	29	158	3.8
Totals	42	398	68	.439	0	.000	22	.550	28	121	17	2	29	158	3.8

DETLEF SCHREMPF

Team: Indiana Pacers
Position: Forward
Height: 6'10" **Weight:** 230
Birthdate: January 21, 1963
NBA Experience: 6 years

College: Washington
Acquired: Traded from Mavericks with a future 2nd-round pick for Herb Williams, 2/89

Background: A graduate of the University of Washington, Schrempf spent the first three-plus years of his NBA career in Dallas. Traded to the Pacers in 1989, his game began to flourish. He established career highs in points, rebounds, assists, free throw shooting, and field goal percentage in 1989-90. He's got the top field goal mark in team history. Schrempf won the Sixth Man Award last season (he was runner-up in 1989-90). Second on the team in minutes last year, he paced Indiana in rebounds and 3-point field goal accuracy.

Strengths: One of the league's most versatile 6'10" players, Schrempf can and does play three different positions. A superb ball-handler and shooter, he can drive the lane or move back behind the 3-point stripe. You can't find anything wrong with his low-post defense.

Weaknesses: He doesn't block many shots and he throws a lot of errant passes on the break. Immature at times, he's easily annoyed by blown calls and his teammates' mistakes.

Analysis: Schrempf's a hot commodity off the bench who 26 other teams covet. He kept telling everyone in Dallas that all he needed was minutes. He was right. So long, Ricky Pierce. So long, Kevin McHale. Schrempf's now in a class of his own when it comes to sixth men.

PLAYER SUMMARY

Will.....................reign as top sixth man
Can't ....block shots
Expect ....greater maturity
Don't Expect ....a starting berth
Fantasy Value $10-12
Card Value.......................................10¢

COLLEGE STATISTICS

		G	FGP	FTP	RPG	PPG
81-82	WASH	28	.452	.553	2.0	3.3
82-83	WASH	31	.466	.717	6.8	10.6
83-84	WASH	31	.539	.736	7.4	16.8
84-85	WASH	32	.558	.714	8.0	15.8
Totals		122	.521	.708	6.2	11.9

NBA REGULAR-SEASON STATISTICS

		G	MIN	FGs FG	FGs PCT	3-PT FGs FG	3-PT FGs PCT	FTs FT	FTs PCT	Rebounds OFF	Rebounds TOT	AST	STL	BLK	PTS	PPG
85-86	DAL	64	969	142	.451	3	.429	110	.724	70	198	88	23	10	397	6.2
86-87	DAL	81	1711	265	.472	33	.478	193	.742	87	303	161	50	16	756	9.3
87-88	DAL	82	1587	246	.456	5	.156	201	.756	102	279	159	42	32	698	8.5
88-89	DAL/IND	69	1850	274	.474	7	.200	273	.780	126	395	179	53	19	828	12.0
89-90	IND	78	2573	424	.516	17	.354	402	.820	149	620	247	59	16	1267	16.2
90-91	IND	82	2632	432	.520	15	.375	441	.818	178	660	301	58	22	1320	16.1
Totals		456	11322	1783	.489	80	.346	1620	.788	712	2455	1135	285	115	5266	11.5

BYRON SCOTT

Team: Los Angeles Lakers
Position: Guard
Height: 6'4" **Weight:** 193
Birthdate: March 28, 1961
NBA Experience: 8 years

College: Arizona St.
Acquired: Traded from Clippers with Swen Nater for Norm Nixon, Eddie Jordan, and 1986 and 1987 2nd-round picks, 10/83

Background: In just three years, Scott became Arizona State's career scoring leader and was an All-Pac-10 selection as a senior. He worked his way into the Lakers' starting lineup as a rookie and is just four 3-pointers away from Michael Cooper's team record. He helped the Lakers to three NBA championships in the 1980s. After struggling with injuries in 1989-90, Scott played all 82 games in 1990-91 and finished third on the team in scoring.

Strengths: There are not many who shoot the 3-point shot better than Scott. He is a classic spot-up shooter who loves to launch jumpers off the fastbreak. He does not mind taking the pressure shot and has made plenty during his career. He moves well without the ball.

Weaknesses: Scott is not as adept at creating his own shot as he is coming off a screen or finding an open seam. He has never been asked to handle the ball much and tends to release rather than go to the defensive glass. His shooting has become more and more inconsistent.

Analysis: While Scott is not the player he was a few years ago (injuries can do that to you), he remains a potent offensive weapon who can burn a team from long range. With a penetrator like Magic Johnson drawing attention, the Lakers need Scott's perimeter punch.

PLAYER SUMMARY

Will ....hit pressure 3's
Can't...create
Expect ....spot-up jumpers
Don't Expect.........improving numbers
Fantasy Value $7-10
Card Value..8¢

COLLEGE STATISTICS

		G	FGP	FTP	RPG	PPG
79-80	ASU	29	.500	.733	2.7	13.6
80-81	ASU	28	.505	.693	3.8	16.6
82-83	ASU	33	.513	.782	5.4	21.6
Totals		90	.507	.747	4.0	17.5

NBA REGULAR-SEASON STATISTICS

				FGs		3-PT FGs		FTs		Rebounds							
		G	MIN	FG	PCT	FG	PCT	FT	PCT	OFF	TOT	AST	STL	BLK	PTS	PPG
83-84	LAL	74	1637	334	.484	8	.235	112	.806	50	164	177	81	19	788	10.6
84-85	LAL	81	2305	541	.539	26	.433	187	.820	57	210	244	100	17	1295	16.0
85-86	LAL	76	2190	507	.513	22	.361	138	.784	55	189	164	85	15	1174	15.4
86-87	LAL	82	2729	554	.489	65	.436	224	.892	63	286	281	125	18	1397	17.0
87-88	LAL	81	3048	710	.527	62	.346	272	.858	76	333	335	155	27	1754	21.7
88-89	LAL	74	2605	588	.491	77	.399	195	.863	72	302	231	114	27	1448	19.6
89-90	LAL	77	2593	472	.470	93	.423	160	.766	51	242	274	77	31	1197	15.5
90-91	LAL	82	2630	501	.477	71	.324	118	.797	54	246	177	95	21	1191	14.5
Totals		627	19737	4207	.500	424	.380	1406	.830	478	1972	1883	832	175	10244	16.3

DENNIS SCOTT

Team: Orlando Magic
Position: Guard/Forward
Height: 6'8" **Weight:** 232
Birthdate: September 5, 1968
NBA Experience: 1 year

College: Georgia Tech
Acquired: 1st-round pick in 1990 draft
(4th overall)

Background: Scott led Georgia Tech to the NCAA Final Four as a senior, when he recorded the highest single-season point total in Atlantic Coast Conference history, was named ACC Player of the Year, and topped the 30-point mark 18 times. He earned All-Rookie honors in 1990-91, posting the third-highest scoring average among first-year players and setting an NBA rookie record for 3-pointers.

Strengths: Scott is, quite literally, a shooting star. He has range even beyond the 3-point line and boasts one of the sweetest strokes in the game. His size serves him well on the perimeter and in the post, and there are indications he will become a good rebounder.

Weaknesses: Defense is not a specialty of Scott, who has considerable trouble against quicker perimeter players. Offensively, his only polished skill is the jump shot. He coughs up the ball nearly as many times as he finds open teammates for assists.

Analysis: Scott was a can't-miss prospect. Not many players (and far fewer rookies) have ever been able to shoot with his range. He went through a week in February in which he averaged 30 points and shot 54 percent from the field, earning the vote as NBA Player of the Week. With more consistency, a number of offensive records could fall.

PLAYER SUMMARY

Will ....hit from 25 feet
Can't ....defend quickness
Expect ....3-point records
Don't Expect ....many assists
Fantasy Value $14-17
Card Value.......................................25¢

COLLEGE STATISTICS

		G	FGP	FTP	RPG	PPG
87-88	GT	32	.440	.655	5.0	15.5
88-89	GT	32	.443	.814	4.1	20.3
89-90	GT	35	.465	.793	6.6	27.7
Totals		99	.452	.777	5.3	21.4

NBA REGULAR-SEASON STATISTICS

			FGs		3-PT FGs		FTs		Rebounds						
	G	MIN	FG	PCT	FG	PCT	FT	PCT	OFF	TOT	AST	STL	BLK	PTS	PPG
90-91 ORL	82	2336	503	.425	125	.374	153	.750	62	235	134	62	25	1284	15.7
Totals	82	2336	503	.425	125	.374	153	.750	62	235	134	62	25	1284	15.7

RONY SEIKALY

Team: Miami Heat
Position: Center
Height: 6'11" **Weight:** 252
Birthdate: May 10, 1965
NBA Experience: 3 years

College: Syracuse
Acquired: 1st-round pick in 1988 draft
(9th overall)

Background: A native of Greece, Seikaly was one of Syracuse's all-time great big men. Drafted by the Heat in 1988, he had his moments as a rookie but was inconsistent. After making significant strides in nearly every statistical category, Seikaly was named the NBA's Most Improved Player in 1989-90. Last year, he sprained ligaments in his knee two days after Christmas. He was sidelined for more than a month.

Strengths: Seikaly displays an abundance of quickness, speed, jumping ability, and inner confidence. He became more of a power player last year and in the process drew more fouls. A much-improved defensive rebounder, Seikaly's entire defensive game has improved dramatically since his rookie season.

Weaknesses: For some reason, he still insists on putting the ball on the floor. Result? Defenders usually swat it away. With a supporting cast that isn't exactly up for any awards (24-58 finish), Seikaly often tries to do too much himself. He's a below-average passer.

Analysis: Instead of spending last summer learning how to box, he should have been in a gymnasium polishing his basketball skills. Seikaly never truly regained his 1989-90 form after the knee injury. If he stays focused, he's got the ability to become a star.

PLAYER SUMMARY

Will.............................grab 10-plus RPG
Can't ....resist dribbling
Expect.....................greater discipline
Don't Expect ....an All-Star, yet
Fantasy Value $29-32
Card Value...12¢

COLLEGE STATISTICS

		G	FGP	FTP	RPG	PPG
84-85	SYR	31	.542	.558	6.4	8.1
85-86	SYR	32	.547	.563	7.8	10.1
86-87	SYR	38	.568	.600	8.2	15.1
87-88	SYR	35	.566	.568	9.6	16.3
Totals		136	.560	.576	8.0	12.6

NBA REGULAR-SEASON STATISTICS

		G	MIN	FGs FG	FGs PCT	3-PT FGs FG	3-PT FGs PCT	FTs FT	FTs PCT	Rebounds OFF	Rebounds TOT	AST	STL	BLK	PTS	PPG
88-89	MIA	78	1962	333	.448	1	.250	181	.511	204	549	55	46	96	848	10.9
89-90	MIA	74	2409	486	.502	0	.000	256	.594	253	766	78	78	124	1228	16.6
90-91	MIA	64	2171	395	.481	2	.333	258	.619	207	709	95	51	86	1050	16.4
Totals		216	6542	1214	.479	3	.273	695	.578	664	2024	228	175	306	3126	14.5

CHARLES SHACKLEFORD

Team: Philadelphia 76ers
Position: Center/Forward
Height: 6'10" **Weight:** 225
Birthdate: April 22, 1966

College: North Carolina St.
Acquired: Signed as a free agent, 7/91

Background: Shackleford, the youngest of 14 children, was a loose cannon at N.C. State. He was one of the key figures in the demise of former coach Jim Valvano, and last year was targeted as a game-fixer during his career with the Wolfpack. Shackleford, facing academic suspension, was an early entry into the 1988 NBA draft. He was selected in the second round by New Jersey, played two seasons for the Nets, then played last season in Italy. He signed a three-year contract with the 76ers in July.

Strengths: Shackleford is a terrific athlete. He is quick, can run the floor, and is a leaper. He has great hands catching the ball and on tips and put-backs. He is an outstanding rebounder, especially off the defensive glass. He has a good repertoire of post-up moves.

Weaknesses: Shackleford is immature and selfish and lacks a good feel for the game. He can't block shots, is turnover prone, is a poor passer, and is a terrible free throw shooter. He has very limited shooting range, never having hit a 3-pointer in college or the NBA.

Analysis: Philadelphia, desperate for a rebounder since trading Mike Gminski to Charlotte last season, will pay Shackleford in excess of $1 million per season to crash the boards. Philadelphia drafted center Alvaro Teheran, but he signed to play in Spain. Shackleford likely will beat out Manute Bol for the starting center spot.

PLAYER SUMMARY

Will...rebound
Can't...................................score outside
Expect.............................a rocky season
Don't Expect.................a model citizen
Fantasy Value.............................$10-12
Card Value ....35-50¢

COLLEGE STATISTICS

		G	FGP	FTP	RPG	PPG
85-86	NCST	29	.525	.618	6.1	10.3
86-87	NCST	34	.476	.520	7.6	13.9
87-88	NCST	31	.538	.591	9.6	16.6
Totals		94	.511	.568	7.8	13.7

NBA REGULAR-SEASON STATISTICS

		G	MIN	FGs FG	FGs PCT	3-PT FGs FG	3-PT FGs PCT	FTs FT	FTs PCT	Rebounds OFF	Rebounds TOT	AST	STL	BLK	PTS	PPG
88-89	NJ	60	484	83	.494	0	.000	21	.500	50	153	21	15	18	187	3.1
89-90	NJ	70	1557	247	.442	0	.000	79	.687	180	479	56	40	35	573	8.2
Totals		130	2041	330	.469	0	.000	100	.637	230	632	77	55	53	760	5.8

BRIAN SHAW

Team: Boston Celtics
Position: Guard
Height: 6'6" **Weight:** 190
Birthdate: March 22, 1966
NBA Experience: 2 years

College: St. Mary's (CA);
Cal.-Santa Barbara
Acquired: 1st-round pick in 1988 draft
(24th overall)

Background: The Pacific Coast Athletic Association Player of the Year as a senior at Cal.-Santa Barbara, Shaw was an NBA All-Rookie second-team performer with the Celtics in 1988-89. He tied for the team lead in assists. He spent the 1989-90 season with Il Messaggero Roma in the Italian League. Shaw picked up right where he left off with Boston last season. He ranked 14th in the NBA in assists. Reggie Lewis was the only Celtic to play more minutes.

Strengths: Being a 6'6" point guard certainly has its advantages. He's at his best in transition, something the Celtics don't have the personnel to do as often as Shaw would like. His speed and agility allows him to match up with smaller, quicker guards. Shaw rebounds well at both ends and he's very good from the line.

Weaknesses: In a halfcourt set, Shaw's not nearly as effective. He doesn't shoot real well from the perimeter, he gets careless with the ball, and he doesn't create a lot of scoring opportunities for his teammates. Defensively, he doesn't make many steals.

Analysis: If the Celtics would run more often and if Shaw could hit more consistently from long range, he'd be an All-Star. Give him time. He's only 25. Shaw's talents would be best utilized on a team that pushes the ball up the floor.

PLAYER SUMMARY

Will......................................run the floor
Can't..................adapt to halfcourt set
Expect.....................increased numbers
Don't Expect ....return to Italy
Fantasy Value.............................$12-14
Card Value..12¢

COLLEGE STATISTICS

		G	FGP	FTP	RPG	PPG
83-84	SM	14	.361	.737	0.9	2.9
84-85	SM	27	.402	.724	5.3	9.4
86-87	CSB	29	.434	.712	7.7	10.9
87-88	CSB	30	.466	.740	8.7	13.3
Totals		100	.434	.728	6.4	10.1

NBA REGULAR-SEASON STATISTICS

			FGs		3-PT FGs		FTs		Rebounds						
		G	MIN	FG	PCT	FG	PCT	FT	PCT	OFF	TOT	AST	STL	BLK	PTS	PPG
88-89	BOS	82	2301	297	.433	0	.000	109	.826	119	376	472	78	27	703	8.6
90-91	BOS	79	2772	442	.469	3	.111	204	.819	104	370	602	105	34	1091	13.8
Totals		161	5073	739	.454	3	.075	313	.822	223	746	1074	183	61	1794	11.1

LIONEL SIMMONS

Team: Sacramento Kings
Position: Forward
Height: 6'7" **Weight:** 210
Birthdate: November 14, 1968
NBA Experience: 1 year

College: La Salle
Acquired: 1st-round pick in 1990 draft (7th overall)

Background: Simmons won the Wooden Award in 1990 as college Player of the Year, finishing his career at La Salle ranked third on the all-time NCAA scoring list. He remains the only player in college history to amass more than 3,000 points and 1,100 rebounds. He finished second to Derrick Coleman in the 1990-91 Rookie of the Year balloting after a torrid second half of the season. He averaged 22 points and nearly ten rebounds per game after the All-Star break.

Strengths: Simmons provides versatility at the forward position. He rebounds well, gets close to the hoop for scores, and is a smooth passer from the wing. Only Gary Payton, a point guard, ranked higher in assists among rookies. Simmons is a dedicated worker who understands the game and makes teammates better.

Weaknesses: While Simmons is a scorer, he is not a shooter. His jump shot is unreliable (note the shooting percentage) and he does not have great range (only 11 3-point attempts). As with most scorers and rookies, he could stand more defensive work, although he is a promising shot-blocker.

Analysis: Despite his college credentials, there were those who wondered whether Simmons could score at the pro level, given his lack of a steady jump shot. He has answered the critics. During a Player of the Week stretch in February, Simmons averaged 33.3 points, 11.7 rebounds, and 4.7 assists while shooting 56.3 percent. Enough said.

PLAYER SUMMARY

Will...........................find ways to score
Can't...............................rely on jumper
Expect....................unselfish approach
Don't Expect 3-pointers
Fantasy Value $16-18
Card Value...15¢

COLLEGE STATISTICS

		G	FGP	FTP	RPG	PPG
86-87	LaS	33	.526	.763	9.8	20.3
87-88	LaS	34	.485	.757	11.4	23.3
88-89	LaS	32	.487	.711	11.4	28.4
89-90	LaS	32	.513	.661	11.1	26.5
Totals		131	.501	.722	10.9	24.6

NBA REGULAR-SEASON STATISTICS

		G	MIN	FGs FG	FGs PCT	3-PT FGs FG	3-PT FGs PCT	FTs FT	FTs PCT	Rebounds OFF	Rebounds TOT	AST	STL	BLK	PTS	PPG
90-91	SAC	79	2978	549	.422	3	.273	320	.736	193	697	315	113	85	1421	18.0
Totals		79	2978	549	.422	3	.273	320	.736	193	697	315	113	85	1421	18.0

SCOTT SKILES

Team: Orlando Magic
Position: Guard
Height: 6'1" **Weight:** 180
Birthdate: March 5, 1964
NBA Experience: 5 years

College: Michigan St.
Acquired: Selected from Indiana in 1989 expansion draft

Background: Skiles was an All-America performer as a senior at Michigan State, finishing second in the nation in scoring and setting school records for points, assists, steals, and free throw accuracy. However, he also earned a reputation for off-court trouble. He was an NBA back-up for four years before coming into his own with Orlando in 1990-91. One of the most improved players in the NBA, he increased his scoring average by 9.5 PPG and set a league record with 30 assists against Denver.

Strengths: They do not come any more competitive than Skiles, who simply despises losing. He knows how to run an offense and bring out the best in his teammates. He penetrates and passes with precision, and he has proven himself as a deadly 3-point shooter (fifth in the league in 1990-91).

Weaknesses: Skiles has not improved defensively as much as he has on the other end of the court. Although he is aggressive, he lacks the speed required to keep opposing point guards from driving and is not big enough to keep from being posted up. His temper used to get the best of him, but he has toned down his act.

Analysis: In one season, Skiles went from wandering back-up to star point guard. Actually, all he really needed was a chance. Anyone with his understanding of the game and desire to win deserves a shot to play. In the process, Orlando discovered it had an offensive force on its roster.

PLAYER SUMMARY

Will...distribute
Can't ....stand losing
Expect ....3-point accuracy
Don't Expect ....great defense
Fantasy Value $13-16
Card Value...10¢

COLLEGE STATISTICS

		G	FGP	FTP	RPG	PPG
82-83	MSU	30	.493	.831	2.1	12.5
83-84	MSU	28	.480	.832	2.2	14.5
84-85	MSU	29	.505	.789	3.2	17.7
85-86	MSU	31	.554	.900	4.4	27.4
Totals		118	.516	.850	3.0	18.2

NBA REGULAR-SEASON STATISTICS

		G	MIN	FGs FG	FGs PCT	3-PT FGs FG	3-PT FGs PCT	FTs FT	FTs PCT	Rebounds OFF	Rebounds TOT	AST	STL	BLK	PTS	PPG
86-87	MIL	13	205	18	.290	3	.214	10	.833	6	26	45	5	1	49	3.8
87-88	IND	51	760	86	.411	6	.300	45	.833	11	66	180	22	3	223	4.4
88-89	IND	80	1571	198	.448	20	.267	130	.903	21	149	390	64	2	546	6.8
89-90	ORL	70	1460	190	.409	52	.394	104	.874	23	159	334	36	4	536	7.7
90-91	ORL	79	2714	462	.445	93	.408	340	.902	57	270	660	89	4	1357	17.2
Totals		293	6710	954	.431	174	.371	629	.891	118	670	1609	216	14	2711	9.3

CHARLES SMITH

Team: Los Angeles Clippers
Position: Forward
Height: 6'10" **Weight:** 230
Birthdate: July 16, 1965
NBA Experience: 3 years

College: Pittsburgh
Acquired: Draft rights traded from
76ers for draft rights to Hersey
Hawkins and a 1989 1st-round pick,
6/88

Background: Smith was named Big East Player of the Year and left Pitt with the school's career records for points and blocked shots. He earned All-Rookie honors with the Clippers in 1988-89 and has ranked among the league leaders in scoring, rebounding, and blocked shots ever since. He finished among the top 25 in each of those categories in 1990-91, leading his team in each.

Strengths: Smith has emerged as quite an all-around talent. He plays bigger than his size in the paint, yet runs the floor and can handle the ball like a smaller man. He is a combination of power and finesse on offense, with range beyond 18 feet. Smith's great reach helps him on the boards and on defense, where he has improved steadily (14th in the league in blocked shots).

Weaknesses: Not all has improved since Smith's rookie year. His scoring average and shooting percentage were down in 1990-91, largely because he has not yet learned to pass out of a double-team. Smith tends to force the action in situations where he has little chance of scoring. He needs to find open shooters.

Analysis: Despite a slight drop-off, Smith remains a promising and productive young player with All-Star written all over him. There are a few areas to work on, but the basics (scoring, rebounding, and defense) are there. As for his importance: The 1990-91 Clippers were 1-8 in games he missed.

PLAYER SUMMARY

Will ....score, rebound
Can't ....pass out of trouble
Expect ....20 PPG
Don't Expect ....stagnation
Fantasy Value $14-17
Card Value...12¢

COLLEGE STATISTICS

		G	FGP	FTP	RPG	PPG
84-85	PITT	29	.502	.760	8.0	15.0
85-86	PITT	29	.404	.762	8.1	15.9
86-87	PITT	33	.550	.735	8.5	17.0
87-88	PITT	31	.558	.764	7.7	18.9
Totals		122	.500	.753	8.1	16.8

NBA REGULAR-SEASON STATISTICS

				FGs		3-PT FGs		FTs		Rebounds						
		G	MIN	FG	PCT	FG	PCT	FT	PCT	OFF	TOT	AST	STL	BLK	PTS	PPG
88-89	LAC	71	2161	435	.495	0	.000	285	.725	173	465	103	68	89	1155	16.3
89-90	LAC	78	2732	595	.520	1	.083	454	.794	177	524	114	86	119	1645	21.1
90-91	LAC	74	2703	548	.469	0	.000	384	.793	216	608	134	81	145	1480	20.0
Totals		223	7596	1578	.495	1	.045	1123	.775	566	1597	351	235	353	4280	19.2

DEREK SMITH

Team: Boston Celtics
Position: Guard/Forward
Height: 6'6" **Weight:** 218
Birthdate: November 1, 1961

NBA Experience: 9 years
College: Louisville
Acquired: Signed as a free agent, 12/90

Background: A sophomore on Louisville's 1980 national championship team, Smith enjoyed two more impressive years with the Cards before being drafted by Golden State in 1982. In 1984-85, he was a rising superstar for the Clippers, averaging 22.1 PPG. But after knee surgery, he was never the same. He spent five injury-riddled years with the Clippers, Kings, and 76ers, and then signed as a free agent with Boston last season. His 1990-91 campaign amounted to two games, 16 minutes, and five points. Since 1985, he's had eight operations.

Strengths: Although he doesn't possess nearly the speed or quickness he had before all the injuries, he can still hold his own defensively. As multi-talented as ever, he can play big guard or either forward slot. Smith can shoot, pass, and handle the ball well enough to get by.

Weaknesses: Obviously, his health is a major concern. Injuries have made him a skeleton of the player he once was. Other than defense, his game has slipped in almost every area. Even when healthy, Smith never was much of a free throw shooter.

Analysis: It's likely that Smith's career is one more injury away from extinction. He's a hard worker who knows how difficult it can be to rehabilitate an injured knee, hip, eye, etc. But at some point, it may no longer be worth all the effort.

PLAYER SUMMARY

Will	have to retire soon
Can't	move well laterally
Expect	very limited role
Don't Expect	shades of 1984-85
Fantasy Value	$1-2
Card Value	5¢

COLLEGE STATISTICS

		G	FGP	FTP	RPG	PPG
78-79	LOU	32	.632	.642	4.8	9.8
79-80	LOU	36	.573	.700	8.3	14.8
80-81	LOU	30	.540	.659	7.8	15.5
81-82	LOU	33	.590	.673	6.0	15.7
Totals		131	.577	.670	6.7	13.9

NBA REGULAR-SEASON STATISTICS

				FGs		3-PT FGs		FTs		Rebounds						
		G	MIN	FG	PCT	FG	PCT	FT	PCT	OFF	TOT	AST	STL	BLK	PTS	PPG
82-83	GS	27	154	21	.412	0	.000	17	.680	10	38	2	0	4	59	2.2
83-84	SD	61	1297	238	.546	1	.167	123	.755	54	170	82	33	22	600	9.8
84-85	LAC	80	2762	682	.537	3	.158	400	.794	174	427	216	77	52	1767	22.1
85-86	LAC	11	339	100	.552	1	.500	58	.690	20	41	31	9	13	259	23.5
86-87	SAC	52	1658	338	.446	9	.273	178	.781	60	182	204	46	23	863	16.6
87-88	SAC	35	899	174	.478	8	.348	87	.770	35	103	89	21	17	443	12.7
88-89	SAC/PHI	65	1295	216	.435	7	.226	129	.686	61	167	128	43	23	568	8.7
89-90	PHI	75	1405	261	.508	16	.444	130	.699	62	172	109	35	20	668	8.9
90-91	BOS	2	16	1	.250	0	.000	3	.750	0	0	5	1	1	5	2.5
Totals		408	9825	2031	.499	45	.294	1125	.753	476	1300	866	265	175	5232	12.8

KENNY SMITH

Team: Houston Rockets
Position: Guard
Height: 6'3" **Weight:** 170
Birthdate: March 8, 1965
NBA Experience: 4 years

College: North Carolina
Acquired: Traded from Hawks with Roy Marble for Tim McCormick and John Lucas, 9/90

Background: Smith established all-time school records for assists and steals at North Carolina, where he was named All-Atlantic Coast Conference as a senior. He averaged double figures in scoring in his first three NBA seasons with Sacramento and Atlanta, but he did not truly shine until a trade brought him to Houston before the 1990-91 campaign. Smith led the Rockets in assists, was second (to Hakeem Olajuwon) in scoring, and helped steer the club to a 52-30 record.

Strengths: Smith answered a lot of doubters while running the Rockets. Foremost, he proved he was a point guard—a cat-quick penetrator who gets the ball into the right hands. He displayed consistency with his jumper for the first time in his career, even from 3-point range. Smith is a good free throw shooter and his leadership was just what the Rockets needed.

Weaknesses: Considering his speed and quick hands, Smith still comes up short in the steals department (third among Rockets). Truth is, he does not put as much effort into defense as he does offense.

Analysis: Smith has to qualify as one of the most improved players in the NBA. He had been called all sorts of things by critics in Sacramento and Atlanta, most having to do with his inability to reach his potential. All that changed in Houston, where Smith finally lived up to his billing.

PLAYER SUMMARY

Will..penetrate
Can't.............................shine on defense
Expect.................................leadership
Don't Expect......................more critics
Fantasy Value............................$17-20
Card Value..8¢

COLLEGE STATISTICS

		G	FGP	FTP	RPG	PPG
83-84	NC	23	.519	.800	1.7	9.1
84-85	NC	36	.518	.860	2.6	12.3
85-86	NC	34	.516	.808	2.2	12.0
86-87	NC	34	.502	.807	2.2	16.9
Totals		127	.512	.823	2.2	12.9

NBA REGULAR-SEASON STATISTICS

		G	MIN	FGs FG	FGs PCT	3-PT FGs FG	3-PT FGs PCT	FTs FT	FTs PCT	Rebounds OFF	Rebounds TOT	AST	STL	BLK	PTS	PPG
87-88	SAC	61	2170	331	.477	12	.308	167	.819	40	138	434	92	8	841	13.8
88-89	SAC	81	3145	547	.462	46	.359	263	.737	49	226	621	102	7	1403	17.3
89-90	SAC/ATL	79	2421	378	.466	26	.313	161	.821	18	157	445	79	8	943	11.9
90-91	HOU	78	2699	522	.520	49	.363	287	.844	36	163	554	106	11	1380	17.7
Totals		299	10435	1778	.482	133	.345	878	.800	143	684	2054	379	34	4567	15.3

LARRY SMITH

Team: Houston Rockets
Position: Forward/Center
Height: 6'8" **Weight:** 251
Birthdate: January 18, 1958

NBA Experience: 11 years
College: Alcorn St.
Acquired: Signed as a free agent, 7/89

Background: Smith won the 1979-80 Division I rebounding crown at Alcorn State. He played nine seasons in Golden State, where he was an All-Rookie selection and became the Warriors' third-leading career rebounder. He once grabbed 31 boards in a game. In his second year with Houston in 1990-91, Smith started 28 games and finished 18th in the league in rebounding.

Strengths: Smith does two things well—rebound and play defense. His commitment to those aspects of the game is what earned him a starting spot during his years with the Warriors. He boxes out, plays physically, and shoves people out of the low post. He grabbed a season-high 25 rebounds twice in 1990-91.

Weaknesses: Offensively, Smith is only a factor on the glass. He does not profess to be any kind of scorer, and he isn't. Only once in his career has he averaged double figures. You would be hard-pressed to find a more dismal free throw shooter than Smith, who hit 24 percent from the stripe in 1990-91.

Analysis: Smith, nicknamed "Mr. Mean," was called into starting duty when Hakeem Olajuwon was injured and he filled in nicely. He knows his offensive deficiencies and concentrates his efforts elsewhere. Only Smith can make 20-rebound games seem routine. For defense, he remains an ideal role player.

PLAYER SUMMARY

Will	rebound relentlessly
Can't	shoot FTs
Expect	interior defense
Don't Expect	any offense
Fantasy Value	$2-4
Card Value	5¢

COLLEGE STATISTICS

		G	FGP	FTP	RPG	PPG
76-77	ASU	34	.527	.597	6.5	14.6
77-78	ASU	22	.593	.608	10.1	14.5
78-79	ASU	29	.600	.570	13.7	17.7
79-80	ASU	26	.579	.692	15.1	20.1
Totals		111	.572	.625	11.1	16.7

NBA REGULAR-SEASON STATISTICS

		G	MIN	FGs FG	PCT	3-PT FGs FG	PCT	FTs FT	PCT	Rebounds OFF	TOT	AST	STL	BLK	PTS	PPG
80-81	GS	82	2578	304	.512	0	.000	177	.588	433	994	93	70	63	785	9.6
81-82	GS	74	2213	220	.534	0	.000	88	.553	279	813	83	65	54	528	7.1
82-83	GS	49	1433	180	.588	0	.000	53	.535	209	485	46	36	20	413	8.4
83-84	GS	75	2091	244	.560	0	.000	94	.560	282	672	72	61	22	582	7.8
84-85	GS	80	2497	366	.530	0	.000	155	.605	405	869	96	78	54	887	11.1
85-86	GS	77	2441	314	.536	0	.000	112	.493	384	856	95	62	50	740	9.6
86-87	GS	80	2374	297	.546	0	.000	113	.574	366	917	95	71	56	707	8.8
87-88	GS	20	499	58	.472	0	.000	11	.407	79	182	25	12	11	127	6.3
88-89	GS	80	1897	219	.552	0	.000	18	.310	272	652	118	61	54	456	5.7
89-90	HOU	74	1300	101	.474	0	.000	20	.364	180	452	69	56	28	222	3.0
90-91	HOU	81	1923	128	.487	0	.000	12	.240	302	709	88	83	22	268	3.3
Totals		772	21246	2431	.533	0	.000	853	.534	3191	7601	880	655	434	5715	7.4

MICHAEL SMITH

Team: Boston Celtics
Position: Forward
Height: 6'10" **Weight:** 225
Birthdate: May 19, 1965
NBA Experience: 2 years

College: Brigham Young
Acquired: 1st-round pick in 1989 draft
(13th overall)

Background: A three-time All-WAC performer at BYU, Smith's collegiate career was interrupted by a two-year Mormon mission in Argentina. Boston's top draft choice in 1989, he never did live up to his pre-NBA billing as a rookie. Not even involved in the Celtics' regular nine-man rotation last year, Smith didn't even make it off the bench 35 times. A 23-point outburst vs. Orlando was the highlight of an otherwise dismal season.

Strengths: A skilled passer, Smith does a nice job of finding the open man. He's almost automatic from the line. When he finds his groove, he can be a dangerous shooter from all over the floor. He's yet to find his groove.

Weaknesses: Although he can be a good shooter, he needs time and space to get his shot off, a luxury in the NBA these days. The Celtics knew he couldn't play defense when they drafted him, but they figured he'd learn. He hasn't. Smith's not quick enough to check small forwards on the wing and he's not strong enough to defend big forwards in the paint.

Analysis: Until he learns how to play some defense, Smith will never be a regular on a Chris Ford-coached team. The Celtics have openly admitted they probably made a mistake in drafting him. This will be a pivotal year for Smith. He either proves that he really belongs in the NBA, or he returns home to California wondering what might have been.

PLAYER SUMMARY

Will ....continue to struggle
Can't......................fight through picks
Expect...........................more DNP-CDs
Don't Expect.................better defense
Fantasy Value $3-5
Card Value.........................12¢

COLLEGE STATISTICS

		G	FGP	FTP	RPG	PPG
83-84	BYU	29	.454	.756	5.3	8.0
86-87	BYU	32	.509	.904	8.5	20.1
87-88	BYU	32	.507	.843	7.8	21.2
88-89	BYU	29	.525	.925	8.6	26.4
Totals		122	.507	.878	7.6	19.0

NBA REGULAR-SEASON STATISTICS

			FGs		3-PT FGs		FTs		Rebounds						
		G	MIN	FG	PCT	FG	PCT	FT	PCT	OFF	TOT	AST	STL	BLK	PTS	PPG
89-90	BOS	65	620	136	.476	2	.071	53	.828	40	100	79	9	1	327	5.0
90-91	BOS	47	389	95	.475	6	.250	22	.815	21	56	43	6	2	218	4.6
Totals		112	1009	231	.475	8	.154	75	.824	61	156	122	15	3	545	4.9

OTIS SMITH

Team: Orlando Magic
Position: Guard/Forward
Height: 6'5" **Weight:** 210
Birthdate: January 30, 1964
NBA Experience: 5 years

College: Jacksonville
Acquired: Selected from Warriors in 1989 expansion draft

Background: Smith was a four-time All-Sun Belt Conference honoree at Jacksonville, finishing among that league's career top seven in steals, blocks, rebounding, and scoring. He has divided his pro years among Denver, Golden State, and Orlando, having started 35 and 39 games for the Magic over the last two seasons, respectively. He was the team's fifth-leading scorer in 1990-91 and averaged 16 points and 5.9 rebounds in games he started.

Strengths: A great athlete, Smith provides versatility in that he can play small forward or big guard. He is quick to the hoop and accents many of his drives with breathtaking slam dunks. He handles the ball well (especially against forwards) and can score in spurts (33 points against Seattle). He gets to the line.

Weaknesses: Smith is not a steady perimeter shooter, especially for a two guard. He gets most of his points on moves to the basket. When lined up at forward, he is a defensive liability in the post. He does not possess the size or strength to prevent the league's high-scoring forwards from having their way.

Analysis: Smith's effectiveness is directly related to his position. At guard, he has the size and leaping ability to shoot over defenders but has yet to develop consistency. At forward, he is quick to the hoop but struggles on defense. He contributes in the scoring column and will earn his minutes one way or another.

PLAYER SUMMARY

Will ....use the dribble
Can't ....defend forwards
Expect ....exciting finishes
Don't Expect..........a steady jump shot
Fantasy Value...............................$2-4
Card Value..8¢

COLLEGE STATISTICS

		G	FGP	FTP	RPG	PPG
82-83	JACK	29	.472	.686	8.7	14.3
83-84	JACK	28	.488	.725	7.7	16.2
84-85	JACK	29	.482	.737	6.8	12.9
85-86	JACK	31	.465	.758	8.0	15.3
Totals		117	.477	.730	7.8	14.7

NBA REGULAR-SEASON STATISTICS

		G	MIN	FG	PCT	FG	PCT	FT	PCT	OFF	TOT	AST	STL	BLK	PTS	PPG
86-87	DEN	28	168	33	.418	0	.000	12	.571	17	34	22	1	1	78	2.8
87-88	DEN/GS	72	1549	325	.491	13	.317	178	.777	126	247	155	91	42	841	11.7
88-89	GS	80	1597	311	.435	7	.189	174	.798	128	330	140	88	40	803	10.0
89-90	ORL	65	1644	348	.492	10	.250	169	.761	117	300	147	76	57	875	13.5
90-91	ORL	75	1885	407	.451	9	.196	221	.734	176	389	169	85	35	1044	13.9
Totals		320	6843	1424	.464	39	.235	754	.761	564	1300	633	341	175	3641	11.4

TONY SMITH

Team: Los Angeles Lakers
Position: Guard
Height: 6'4" **Weight:** 195
Birthdate: June 14, 1968
NBA Experience: 1 year

College: Marquette
Acquired: 2nd-round pick in 1990
draft (51st overall)

Background: Smith set Marquette single-season records for points and scoring average as a senior, earning All-Midwestern Collegiate Conference honors. He climbed to second on the all-time school assists list and finished third in scoring. He saw action in 64 games as a rookie, primarily as back-up point guard to Magic Johnson. In game five of the NBA finals, Smith filled in for an injured Byron Scott, scored 12 points on 5-of-6 shooting, and played tight defense.

Strengths: Smith is a multi-faceted guard who looks to score in addition to penetrating and passing. He has good speed and quickness and is able to free himself for shots. He accepted his limited role and played within himself when his chances came.

Weaknesses: The fact that Smith has a scorer's mentality is a source of some concern. Is he a true point guard? He played there out of necessity as a college senior and has more trouble defending point guards than less-mobile off guards. His outside shooting is hot-and-cold and he missed all seven of his 3-point attempts in 1990-91.

Analysis: Smith saw more action than he was expected to see and did a decent job filling in for the best point guard in basketball. He displayed maturity beyond his years and served notice that, despite the doubters, he can play the point on the NBA level. Whether he continues to excel in a greater role is a question that may not be answered until Magic stops dominating.

PLAYER SUMMARY

Will..............................run the offense
Can't............................beat out Magic
Expect ....a capable reserve
Don't Expect............................10 PPG
Fantasy Value.................................$2-4
Card Value..8¢

COLLEGE STATISTICS

		G	FGP	FTP	RPG	PPG
86-87	MARQ	29	.534	.753	3.3	8.1
87-88	MARQ	28	.523	.739	4.5	13.1
88-89	MARQ	28	.556	.730	3.9	14.2
89-90	MARQ	29	.495	.856	4.7	23.8
Totals		114	.521	.785	4.1	14.8

NBA REGULAR-SEASON STATISTICS

		FGs		3-PT FGs		FTs		Rebounds						
	G	MIN	FG	PCT	FG	PCT	FT	PCT	OFF	TOT	AST	STL	BLK	PTS	PPG
90-91 LAL	64	695	97	.441	0	.000	40	.702	24	71	135	28	12	234	3.7
Totals	64	695	97	.441	0	.000	40	.702	24	71	135	28	12	234	3.7

RIK SMITS

Team: Indiana Pacers
Position: Center
Height: 7'4" **Weight:** 265
Birthdate: August 23, 1966
NBA Experience: 3 years

College: Marist
Acquired: 1st-round pick in 1988 draft (2nd overall)

Background: A two-time East Coast Athletic Conference Player of the Year at Marist, Smits was the second overall selection in the 1988 draft. He was named to the NBA All-Rookie first team. He led the NBA in disqualifications his first two years and ranked among the league leaders in field goal percentage. An injured right elbow plagued him for some of the 1990-91 season. He played far fewer minutes last year than he did in the previous two.

Strengths: There's never been another seven-footer in the NBA who possesses such a delicate shooting touch. At 7'4", 265 pounds, Smits amazingly has the coordination and mobility of a small forward. He can shoot from 15 feet and in. His height and ability to anticipate enables him to reject a lot of shots.

Weaknesses: Until he makes the effort to increase his upper-body strength, he'll continue to be pushed around inside. His offensive rebounding totals are an embarrassment for a player his size. He needs to develop a greater variety of low-post shots and foul less.

Analysis: A good, solid player, Smits doesn't appear to have the drive, determination, or athletic ability to develop into the All-Star many thought he'd become. Or does he? The only thing standing in his way is himself.

PLAYER SUMMARY

Will ....block a lot of shots
Can't.......................rebound on offense
Expect...........................steady progress
Don't Expect ....great commitment
Fantasy Value $9-11
Card Value...8¢

COLLEGE STATISTICS

		G	FGP	FTP	RPG	PPG
84-85	MAR	29	.567	.577	5.6	11.2
85-86	MAR	30	.622	.681	8.1	17.7
86-87	MAR	21	.609	.722	8.1	20.1
87-88	MAR	27	.623	.735	8.7	24.7
Totals		107	.609	.693	7.6	18.2

NBA REGULAR-SEASON STATISTICS

				FGs		3-PT FGs		FTs		Rebounds						
		G	MIN	FG	PCT	FG	PCT	FT	PCT	OFF	TOT	AST	STL	BLK	PTS	PPG
88-89	IND	82	2041	386	.517	0	.000	184	.722	185	500	70	37	151	956	11.7
89-90	IND	82	2404	515	.533	0	.000	241	.811	135	512	142	45	169	1271	15.5
90-91	IND	76	1690	342	.485	0	.000	144	.762	116	357	84	24	111	828	10.9
Totals		240	6135	1243	.514	0	.000	569	.768	436	1369	296	106	431	3055	12.7

RORY SPARROW

Team: Sacramento Kings
Position: Guard
Height: 6'2" **Weight:** 175
Birthdate: June 12, 1958

NBA Experience: 11 years
College: Villanova
Acquired: Traded from Heat for draft rights to Bimbo Coles, 6/90

Background: Sparrow broke Chris Ford's Villanova record for all-time assists. His 11-year NBA career has seen him play for six clubs, but his best days were with the Knicks during the mid-1980s. Sparrow produced consecutive 500-assist seasons in 1983-84 and 1984-85 and was New York's leading playmaker from 1983-86. He made 74 starts with Sacramento in 1990-91, led the Kings in assists, and enjoyed his best shooting year since 1984-85.

Strengths: A veteran who knows the league, Sparrow plays with his head and helps teammates do the same. He leads by example. His playmaking skills are unspectacular but reliable, his defense is solid, and his pull-up jumper is as accurate as it has been in years.

Weaknesses: Sparrow is not nearly the distributor he used to be. He makes the passes that present themselves, but he creates very little on his own. He goes to the basket less frequently, preferring to do his damage from the perimeter.

Analysis: Sparrow is making the most of his final years. He has played in at least 80 games over the last three seasons and has even improved in some areas. His 1990-91 3-point shooting was the best of his career. No longer as effective at creating, he must continue to shoot well.

PLAYER SUMMARY

Will ....play defense
Can't.....................create as he used to
Expect.....................veteran leadership
Don't Expect ....three more years
Fantasy Value $3-5
Card Value..8¢

COLLEGE STATISTICS

		G	FGP	FTP	RPG	PPG
76-77	VILL	33	.513	.810	2.1	7.0
77-78	VILL	32	.512	.722	2.3	8.6
78-79	VILL	28	.514	.820	2.1	12.1
79-80	VILL	31	.560	.831	2.4	10.8
Totals		124	.525	.792	2.2	9.5

NBA REGULAR-SEASON STATISTICS

		G	MIN	FG	PCT	FG	PCT	FT	PCT	OFF	TOT	AST	STL	BLK	PTS	PPG
80-81	NJ	15	212	22	.349	0	.000	12	.750	7	18	32	13	3	56	3.7
81-82	ATL	82	2610	366	.501	1	.067	124	.838	53	224	424	87	13	857	10.5
82-83	ATL/NY	81	2428	392	.484	5	.227	147	.739	61	230	397	107	5	936	11.6
83-84	NY	79	2436	350	.474	10	.256	108	.824	48	189	539	100	8	818	10.4
84-85	NY	79	2292	326	.492	7	.226	122.	.865	38	169	557	81	9	781	9.9
85-86	NY	74	2344	345	.477	5	.250	101	.795	50	170	472	85	14	796	10.8
86-87	NY	80	1951	263	.446	11	.262	71	.798	29	115	432	67	6	608	7.6
87-88	NY/CHI	58	1044	117	.399	2	.154	24	.727	15	72	167	41	3	260	4.5
88-89	MIA	80	2613	444	.452	18	.243	94	.879	55	216	429	103	17	1000	12.5
89-90	MIA	82	1756	210	.412	8	.200	59	.766	37	138	298	49	4	487	5.9
90-91	SAC	80	2375	371	.491	31	.397	58	.699	45	186	362	83	16	831	10.4
Totals		790	22061	3206	.468	98	.262	920	.799	438	1727	4109	816	98	7430	9.4

FELTON SPENCER

Team: Minnesota Timberwolves
Position: Center
Height: 7'0" **Weight:** 265
Birthdate: January 5, 1968
NBA Experience: 1 year

College: Louisville
Acquired: 1st-round pick in 1990 draft
(6th overall)

Background: Spencer ended his career at Louisville as the school's all-time field goal percentage leader and ranked third in the nation in that category in 1989-90. He moved into the starting lineup as a senior and was one of college basketball's most improved players. Spencer earned NBA All-Rookie honors in 1990-91 with Minnesota after making 46 starts and setting club records for rebounds and blocks.

Strengths: Spencer has legitimate size for an NBA center and is willing to work hard to improve his game. He is strong on the boards (seventh in the league in offensive caroms) and has emerged as a better-than-expected shot-blocker. He knows his range on offense and stays within it. Most importantly, Spencer continues to develop.

Weaknesses: Offensively, Spencer's game is somewhat mechanical and limited to the paint. He needs to develop a handful of low-post moves and learn how to find open perimeter players when nothing is there. Spencer is slow on his feet, though he manages to get up and down the floor pretty well.

Analysis: With his size and work ethic, Spencer has a promising NBA future. He has good coordination and simply needs to refine his offensive repertoire and court sense to become a more complete player. He will not rest on his laurels; Randy Breuer started the last 13 games of the 1990-91 season at center.

PLAYER SUMMARY

Will...rebound
Can't..pass
Expect ....development
Don't Expect.................................speed
Fantasy Value.............................$2-4
Card Value.......................................10¢

COLLEGE STATISTICS

		G	FGP	FTP	RPG	PPG
86-87	LOU	31	.551	.492	2.7	3.8
87-88	LOU	35	.592	.640	4.2	7.4
88-89	LOU	33	.607	.733	5.1	8.2
89-90	LOU	35	.681	.716	8.5	14.9
Totals		134	.628	.676	5.2	8.7

NBA REGULAR-SEASON STATISTICS

			FGs		3-PT FGs		FTs		Rebounds						
	G	MIN	FG	PCT	FG	PCT	FT	PCT	OFF	TOT	AST	STL	BLK	PTS	PPG
90-91 MIN	81	2099	195	.512	0	.000	182	.722	272	641	25	48	121	572	7.1
Totals	81	2099	195	.512	0	.000	182	.722	272	641	25	48	121	572	7.1

JOHN STARKS

Team: New York Knicks
Position: Guard
Height: 6'5" **Weight:** 180
Birthdate: August 10, 1965
NBA Experience: 1 year

College: Northern Oklahoma; Oklahoma St.
Acquired: Signed as a free agent, 10/90

Background: A product of four colleges in four years, including Oklahoma State as a senior (1987-88), Starks signed on with Golden State as a free agent. A back injury ended his rookie season prematurely. After the Warriors cut him loose, he became a CBA All-Star with Cedar Rapids. He also played for Memphis in the WBL before reporting to the Knicks' camp in 1990. After missing the first month of the season with a sprained knee, Starks developed into a dependable backcourt reserve.

Strengths: He jump-starts the team off the bench with his hustle and determination. An underrated shooter, he averaged ten PPG in his ten starting assignments. He's strong and quick enough to penetrate the lane. Defensively, he's in constant motion.

Weaknesses: Starks has to avoid the four- and five-minute spurts where he loses control. He gets overanxious and makes plays he normally wouldn't. He'd get more shot opportunities if he moved better without the ball. When his shot's not falling, it hurts his entire game.

Analysis: A bona fide sparkplug off the bench, Starks's frenetic style is most effective when he's on the court for limited periods of time. His efforts may not show up in the box score, but they do in the win-loss columns. He wants to remain in the NBA very badly.

PLAYER SUMMARY

Will..................................... fire up team
Can't........................play long minutes
Expect.................hustle, hustle, hustle
Don't Expect.....................passive play
Fantasy Value $1-3
Card Value...5¢

COLLEGE STATISTICS

		G	FGP	FTP	RPG	PPG
84-85	NOK	14	.463	.774	2.4	11.1
87-88	OSU	30	.497	.838	4.7	15.4
Totals		44	.487	.820	4.0	14.0

NBA REGULAR-SEASON STATISTICS

				FGs		3-PT FGs		FTs		Rebounds						
		G	MIN	FG	PCT	FG	PCT	FT	PCT	OFF	TOT	AST	STL	BLK	PTS	PPG
88-89	GS	36	316	51	.408	10	.385	34	.654	15	41	27	23	3	146	4.1
90-91	NY	61	1173	180	.439	27	.290	79	.752	30	131	204	59	17	466	7.6
Totals		97	1489	231	.432	37	.311	113	.720	45	172	231	82	20	612	6.3

JOHN STOCKTON

Team: Utah Jazz
Position: Guard
Height: 6'1" **Weight:** 175
Birthdate: March 26, 1962

NBA Experience: 7 years
College: Gonzaga
Acquired: 1st-round pick in 1984 draft
(16th overall)

Background: Stockton led the West Coast Athletic Conference in points as a senior at Gonzaga, and in assists and steals as a sophomore, junior, and senior. After holding a back-up spot during his first two years with Utah, he broke into the starting lineup in 1986-87 and began shattering NBA assist records. He became the first player in history to record four straight seasons of 1,000 or more assists when he broke his own single-season mark in 1990-91. He also played in his third straight All-Star Game.

Strengths: Stockton is the best pure playmaker in basketball. He is quick and masterful with the ball in his hands, with an uncanny ability to take it to the hole and create easy shots for teammates. Somehow, he gets into the lane for his own scores as well. He is a deadly shooter whose scoring contributions are underrated because he looks first to pass. He hits the 3-pointer, plays defense, and makes few mistakes.

Weaknesses: About the only thing Stockton does not do is crash the boards, and why would he? Also, larger opponents can shoot over him.

Analysis: Stockton is not only one of the best guards in the league, but he is one of the smartest and most coachable. There is not much more he needs to learn about the game, especially in the area of playmaking. He makes everyone on his team look better, and he has made himself look pretty good along the way.

PLAYER SUMMARY

Will..........................make others better
Can't.........................look first to score
Expect ....more assist records
Don't Expect................................an ego
Fantasy Value.............................$58-61
Card Value.......................................20¢

COLLEGE STATISTICS

		G	FGP	FTP	RPG	PPG
80-81	GONZ	25	.578	.743	0.4	3.1
81-82	GONZ	27	.576	.676	2.5	11.2
82-83	GONZ	27	.518	.791	3.2	13.9
83-84	GONZ	28	.577	.692	2.4	20.9
Totals		107	.559	.719	2.2	12.5

NBA REGULAR-SEASON STATISTICS

		G	MIN	FGs FG	FGs PCT	3-PT FGs FG	3-PT FGs PCT	FTs FT	FTs PCT	Rebounds OFF	Rebounds TOT	AST	STL	BLK	PTS	PPG
84-85	UTA	82	1490	157	.471	2	.182	142	.736	26	105	415	109	11	458	5.6
85-86	UTA	82	1935	228	.489	2	.133	172	.839	33	179	610	157	10	630	7.7
86-87	UTA	82	1858	231	.499	7	.184	179	.782	32	151	670	177	14	648	7.9
87-88	UTA	82	2842	454	.574	24	.358	272	.840	54	237	1128	242	16	1204	14.7
88-89	UTA	82	3171	497	.538	16	.242	390	.863	83	248	1118	263	14	1400	17.1
89-90	UTA	78	2915	472	.514	47	.416	354	.819	57	206	1134	207	18	1345	17.2
90-91	UTA	82	3103	496	.507	58	.345	363	.836	46	237	1164	234	16	1413	17.2
Totals		570	17314	2535	.520	156	.326	1872	.825	331	1363	6239	1389	99	7098	12.5

ROD STRICKLAND

Team: San Antonio Spurs
Position: Guard
Height: 6'3" **Weight:** 175
Birthdate: July 11, 1966
NBA Experience: 3 years

College: DePaul
Acquired: Traded from Knicks for
Maurice Cheeks, 2/90

Background: Strickland left DePaul for the pros a year early, but not before he led the Blue Demons in scoring, assists, and steals as a junior and climbed among the school's career leaders in each category. He was a back-up point guard with New York as a rookie before a trade for Maurice Cheeks made him a starter in San Antonio. He led the Spurs in assists in 1990-91 despite missing 24 games due to injury.

Strengths: Few players penetrate with the ease and frequency of Strickland, whose nifty ball-handling and great quickness allow him to get past even the best defenders. He hits acrobatic shots off his drives and is a fine passer on the move. Strickland is outstanding in transition and employs his quickness on defense.

Weaknesses: Strickland has yet to show the maturity many feel is required to steer the ship of a title contender. During the 1990-91 season, he broke his hand in a nightclub altercation and later was accused of indecently exposing himself to a woman in a Seattle hotel. On the court, his game has a lot of playground in it and he needs to polish his pull-up jumper.

Analysis: Strickland is young and has the potential to take a place among the very best point guards in the NBA. His scoring and passing abilities complement one another and his quickness adds an extra dimension. With more maturity, Strickland could hold the key to a championship run.

PLAYER SUMMARY
Will.......................................penetrate
Can't ....avoid controversy
Expect.................................creativity
Don't Expect ....standstill shooting
Fantasy Value $8-10
Card Value...10¢

COLLEGE STATISTICS

		G	FGP	FTP	RPG	PPG
85-86	DeP	31	.497	.675	2.7	14.1
86-87	DeP	30	.582	.606	3.8	16.3
87-88	DeP	26	.528	.606	3.8	20.0
Totals		87	.534	.626	3.4	16.6

NBA REGULAR-SEASON STATISTICS

		G	MIN	FGs FG	PCT	3-PT FGs FG	PCT	FTs FT	PCT	Rebounds OFF	TOT	AST	STL	BLK	PTS	PPG
88-89	NY	81	1358	265	.467	19	.322	172	.745	51	160	319	98	3	721	8.9
89-90	NY/SA	82	2140	343	.454	8	.267	174	.626	90	259	468	127	14	868	10.6
90-91	SA	58	2076	314	.482	11	.333	161	.763	57	219	463	117	11	800	13.8
Totals		221	5574	922	.467	38	.311	507	.704	198	638	1250	342	28	2389	10.8

JON SUNDVOLD

Team: Miami Heat
Position: Guard
Height: 6'2" **Weight:** 175
Birthdate: July 2, 1961

NBA Experience: 8 years
College: Missouri
Acquired: Selected from Spurs in 1988 expansion draft

Background: After teaming up with Steve Stipanovich during a solid four-year stay at Missouri, Sundvold began his NBA stretch in Seattle. Following a three-year career in San Antonio, he was left unprotected in the 1988 expansion draft. Sundvold competed in the NBA's 1989 long-distance shootout. His .522 mark from 3-point territory in 1988-89 was an NBA record. A serious bout with pneumonia ended his 1990-91 season at the All-Star break.

Strengths: He doesn't try to do things he can't, which encompasses nearly everything but shooting treys. When Sundvold spots up and finds his range, look out. He's a pleasure to watch. He makes up for his lack of athletic ability with court smarts and savvy.

Weaknesses: He can't put the ball on the floor, spot the open man, or go to the boards. Sundvold's such a liability defensively (short and slow), that he can only be on the floor for short intervals. The closer he gets to the basket, the worse he shoots.

Analysis: The only reason Sundvold's even in the league is because he can drill 3-pointers. Or at least he could. Since setting the NBA record for 3-point accuracy, his numbers have decreased steadily. If he continues to shoot blanks from long range, financial consulting won't just be his off-season job.

PLAYER SUMMARY

Will ....attempt plenty of 3's
Can't ....do much else
Expect ....little job security
Don't Expect..........awards for defense
Fantasy Value $1-2
Card Value..5¢

COLLEGE STATISTICS

		G	FGP	FTP	RPG	PPG
79-80	MO	31	.450	.746	1.7	6.3
80-81	MO	32	.509	.859	1.7	13.8
81-82	MO	31	.485	.871	2.1	12.2
82-83	MO	34	.503	.868	2.4	17.1
Totals		128	.493	.848	2.0	12.5

NBA REGULAR-SEASON STATISTICS

		G	MIN	FG	PCT	FG	PCT	FT	PCT	OFF	TOT	AST	STL	BLK	PTS	PPG
				FGs		3-PT FGs		FTs		Rebounds						
83-84	SEA	73	1284	217	.445	9	.243	64	.889	23	91	239	29	1	507	6.9
84-85	SEA	73	1150	170	.425	12	.316	48	.814	17	70	206	36	1	400	5.5
85-86	SA	70	1150	220	.462	21	.350	39	.813	22	80	261	34	0	500	7.1
86-87	SA	76	1765	365	.486	50	.336	70	.833	20	98	315	35	0	850	11.2
87-88	SA	52	1024	176	.464	26	.406	43	.896	14	48	183	27	2	421	8.1
88-89	MIA	68	1338	307	.455	48	.522	47	.825	18	87	137	27	1	709	10.4
89-90	MIA	63	867	148	.408	44	.440	44	.846	15	71	102	25	0	384	6.1
90-91	MIA	24	225	43	.402	15	.429	11	1.000	3	9	24	7	0	112	4.7
Totals		499	8803	1646	.452	225	.391	366	.849	132	554	1467	220	5	3883	7.8

ROY TARPLEY

Team: Dallas Mavericks
Position: Forward
Height: 6'11" **Weight:** 250
Birthdate: November 28, 1964

NBA Experience: 5 years
College: Michigan
Acquired: 1st-round pick in 1986 draft
(7th overall)

Background: Tarpley powered Michigan to back-to-back Big Ten titles, earning the unanimous vote for conference Player of the Year as a junior and gaining All-America recognition as a junior and senior. The winner of the 1987-88 Sixth Man Award is a two-time offender of the league drug policy, the second strike coming when he violated his aftercare program in 1988-89. He missed all but five games of 1990-91 with a torn anterior cruciate ligament in his right knee, and on April 5 was suspended indefinitely by the ASAP Family Treatment Program for another violation of his aftercare program.

Strengths: On the court, Tarpley is a force. He is a great rebounder, potentially one of the best in the game. He possesses good range on his jump shot and runs the floor like a small forward. He averaged 20 points and 11 rebounds in his five 1990-91 games.

Weaknesses: Tarpley has a history of not showing up for practices and finding trouble away from the arenas. If he is allowed to play again, one has to wonder how long he can avoid his third strike. Working on his low-post moves and defensive intensity are concerns that pale in comparison.

Analysis: No one is sure whether Tarpley's most recent violation for alleged drinking and driving will keep him out of the league for an extended period of time, perhaps life. The only sure thing is that if anyone gives Tarpley another chance, there is a huge risk involved. Potentially a franchise player, he has been a major disappointment.

PLAYER SUMMARY

Will......................dominate the boards
Can't.................................keep clean
Expect..............................legal battles
Don't Expect..........................reliability
Fantasy Value...........................$18-20
Card Value..................................8¢

COLLEGE STATISTICS

		G	FGP	FTP	RPG	PPG
82-83	MICH	26	.407	.579	3.2	3.5
83-84	MICH	33	.527	.794	8.1	12.5
84-85	MICH	30	.525	.775	10.4	19.0
85-86	MICH	33	.541	.811	8.8	15.9
Totals		122	.522	.774	7.8	13.1

NBA REGULAR-SEASON STATISTICS

				FGs		3-PT FGs		FTs		Rebounds						
		G	MIN	FG	PCT	FG	PCT	FT	PCT	OFF	TOT	AST	STL	BLK	PTS	PPG
86-87	DAL	75	1405	233	.467	1	.333	94	.676	180	533	52	56	79	561	7.5
87-88	DAL	81	2307	444	.500	0	.000	205	.740	360	959	86	103	86	1093	13.5
88-89	DAL	19	591	131	.541	0	.000	66	.688	77	218	17	28	30	328	17.3
89-90	DAL	45	1648	314	.451	0	.000	130	.756	189	589	67	79	70	758	16.8
90-91	DAL	5	171	43	.544	0	.000	16	.889	16	55	12	6	9	102	20.4
Totals		225	6122	1165	.485	1	.063	511	.728	822	2354	234	272	274	2842	12.6

TERRY TEAGLE

Team: Los Angeles Lakers
Position: Guard/Forward
Height: 6'5 **Weight:** 195
Birthdate: April 10, 1960

NBA Experience: 9 years
College: Baylor
Acquired: Traded from Warriors for a
1991 1st-round pick, 9/90

Background: Teagle set a Southwest Conference career scoring record at Baylor, where he led the team in scoring and rebounding each of his last three years. He played in Houston and Detroit, then spent most of his pro career with Golden State before the Lakers acquired him for the 1990-91 season. Teagle came off the bench in all 82 games and finished sixth on the team in scoring. He finished the year by averaging 17.2 points in the last 11 games.

Strengths: Teagle is a scorer, plain and simple. He provides points off the bench, usually in bunches. When he heats up, nobody can contain him. He can bury jumpers despite being off-balance or among traffic. He plays with toughness on both ends and has good leaping ability.

Weaknesses: Teagle goes through cold spells in which he cannot buy a basket, yet continues taking difficult shots. His 1990-91 shooting percentage was his worst since his rookie campaign. He is a poor ball-handler who rarely played guard for Golden State, although it is his natural position.

Analysis: Teagle started slowly in 1990-91, then began to show near the end of the season why the Lakers wanted him: scoring punch off the bench. He is inconsistent with his shooting, but when he finds his touch he can be a one-man offensive show.

PLAYER SUMMARY

Will............................launch his shots
Can't.................................hit 3-pointers
Expect.........................streak shooting
Don't Expect...................ball-handling
Fantasy Value.............................$1-2
Card Value...5¢

COLLEGE STATISTICS

		G	FGP	FTP	RPG	PPG
78-79	BAY	28	.529	.708	6.5	14.6
79-80	BAY	27	.543	.830	8.2	23.0
80-81	BAY	27	.536	.735	7.0	20.0
81-82	BAY	28	.541	.722	7.5	22.2
Totals		110	.538	.755	7.3	19.9

NBA REGULAR-SEASON STATISTICS

		G	MIN	FGs FG	FGs PCT	3-PT FGs FG	3-PT FGs PCT	FTs FT	FTs PCT	Rebounds OFF	Rebounds TOT	AST	STL	BLK	PTS	PPG
82-83	HOU	73	1708	332	.428	10	.345	87	.696	74	194	150	53	18	761	10.4
83-84	HOU	68	616	148	.470	7	.259	37	.841	28	78	63	13	4	340	5.0
84-85	DET/GS	21	349	74	.540	2	.500	25	.714	22	43	14	13	5	175	8.3
85-86	GS	82	2158	475	.496	4	.160	211	.796	96	235	115	71	34	1165	14.2
86-87	GS	82	1650	370	.458	0	.000	182	.778	68	175	105	68	13	922	11.2
87-88	GS	47	958	248	.454	1	.111	97	.802	41	81	61	32	4	594	12.6
88-89	GS	66	1569	409	.476	2	.167	182	.809	110	263	96	79	17	1002	15.2
89-90	GS	82	2376	538	.480	3	.214	244	.830	114	367	155	91	15	1323	16.1
90-91	LAL	82	1498	335	.443	0	.000	145	.819	82	181	82	31	8	815	9.9
Totals		603	12882	2929	.467	29	.209	1210	.796	635	1617	841	451	118	7097	11.8

ISIAH THOMAS

Team: Detroit Pistons
Position: Guard
Height: 6'1" **Weight:** 182
Birthdate: April 30, 1961

NBA Experience: 10 years
College: Indiana
Acquired: 1st-round pick in 1981 draft
(2nd overall)

Background: The leader of Indiana's 1981 national championship team as a sophomore, Thomas declared for the draft as an underclassman and was selected by Detroit with the second overall pick. Voted to the NBA All-Star team every year he's been in the league, Thomas captured All-Star MVP honors in 1984 and '86. He guided the Pistons to back-to-back world championships in 1989 and '90. He's one of the NBA's all-time leaders in assists and steals. Thomas missed 34 games last season after breaking his right wrist.

Strengths: There's not another 6'1" player in all of basketball who can take over a game down the stretch like Thomas can. He raises his game to another level. An outstanding ball-handler and passer, Thomas jets through the lane as well as any guard in the league. He's also added a perimeter jumper to his repertoire.

Weaknesses: Thomas turns the ball over a lot (led the league in 1989-90) and he's been known to take plenty of ill-advised shots. A real streaky scorer, he doesn't shoot as well as you'd like. He takes too many chances to be considered a real good defender.

Analysis: A can't-miss Hall of Famer, Thomas is truly one of the greatest guards in NBA history. Forget about his few flaws. More than anything else, he's a winner. When the game's on the line, you want the ball in Isiah's hands.

PLAYER SUMMARY

Will	win one more title
Can't	score like he once did
Expect	late-game heroics
Don't Expect	a lack of focus
Fantasy Value	$22-25
Card Value	20¢

COLLEGE STATISTICS

		G	FGP	FTP	RPG	PPG
79-80	IND	29	.510	.772	4.0	14.6
80-81	IND	34	.554	.742	3.1	16.0
Totals		63	.534	.756	3.5	15.4

NBA REGULAR-SEASON STATISTICS

				FGs		3-PT FGs		FTs		Rebounds						
		G	MIN	FG	PCT	FG	PCT	FT	PCT	OFF	TOT	AST	STL	BLK	PTS	PPG
81-82	DET	72	2433	453	.424	17	.288	302	.704	57	209	565	150	17	1225	17.0
82-83	DET	81	3093	725	.472	36	.288	368	.710	105	328	634	199	29	1854	22.9
83-84	DET	82	3007	669	.462	22	.338	388	.733	103	327	914	204	33	1748	21.3
84-85	DET	81	3089	646	.458	29	.257	399	.809	114	361	1123	187	25	1720	21.2
85-86	DET	77	2790	609	.488	26	.310	365	.790	83	277	830	171	20	1609	20.9
86-87	DET	81	3013	626	.463	19	.194	400	.768	82	319	813	153	20	1671	20.6
87-88	DET	81	2927	621	.463	30	.309	305	.774	64	278	678	141	17	1577	19.5
88-89	DET	80	2924	569	.464	33	.273	287	.818	49	273	663	133	20	1458	18.2
89-90	DET	81	2993	579	.438	42	.309	292	.775	74	308	765	139	19	1492	18.4
90-91	DET	48	1657	289	.435	19	.292	179	.782	35	160	446	75	10	776	16.2
Totals		764	27926	5786	.459	273	.283	3285	.763	766	2840	7431	1552	210	15130	19.8

BILLY THOMPSON

Team: Miami Heat
Position: Forward
Height: 6'7" **Weight:** 217
Birthdate: December 1, 1963
NBA Experience: 5 years

College: Louisville
Acquired: Selected from Lakers in 1988 expansion draft

Background: After leading Louisville to the 1986 national title, Thompson was drafted by Atlanta and immediately traded to the Lakers. The following spring, he became the fourth man to play for an NCAA champion and an NBA champion in back-to-back years. Thompson also earned a championship ring with L.A. in 1987-88. Sent to Miami in the expansion draft, he paced the Heat in rebounding and shot-blocking during their inaugural season. A part-time starter last year, Thompson was not re-signed by Miami after the season.

Strengths: An incredible leaper with unusually long arms, he blocks as many shots as any small forward in the league. Thompson also grabs his share of rebounds, particularly off the offensive glass. He's less casual than he was earlier in his career.

Weaknesses: Thompson no longer looks to generate as much offense as he once did. Instead of knifing his way through the lane from either wing, he frequently passes the ball back out top. On defense, Thompson often gets burned off the dribble. He's below average from the line.

Analysis: He's a nice reserve to have on your team at both forward positions. Thompson won't hurt you during the 20 minutes per night he's on the floor. Just because he doesn't score a lot of points doesn't mean he's not a valuable role player.

PLAYER SUMMARY

Will......................block shots, rebound
Can't ....stay with his man
Expect..............20 consistent minutes
Don't Expect..................much scoring
Fantasy Value................................$1-3
Card Value...8¢

COLLEGE STATISTICS

		G	FGP	FTP	RPG	PPG
82-83	LOU	36	.488	.654	3.9	7.3
83-84	LOU	31	.507	.735	5.6	9.2
84-85	LOU	37	.515	.747	8.4	15.1
85-86	LOU	39	.576	.714	7.8	14.9
Totals		143	.528	.719	6.5	11.8

NBA REGULAR-SEASON STATISTICS

				FGs		3-PT FGs		FTs		Rebounds						
		G	MIN	FG	PCT	FG	PCT	FT	PCT	OFF	TOT	AST	STL	BLK	PTS	PPG
86-87	LAL	59	762	142	.544	0	.000	48	.649	69	171	60	15	30	332	5.6
87-88	LAL	9	38	3	.231	0	.000	8	.800	2	9	1	1	0	14	1.6
88-89	MIA	79	2273	349	.487	0	.000	156	.696	241	572	176	56	105	854	10.8
89-90	MIA	79	2142	375	.516	2	.500	115	.622	238	551	166	54	89	867	11.0
90-91	MIA	73	1481	205	.499	0	.000	89	.718	120	312	111	32	48	499	6.8
Totals		299	6696	1074	.505	2	.154	416	.674	670	1615	514	158	272	2566	8.6

LaSALLE THOMPSON

Team: Indiana Pacers
Position: Forward/Center
Height: 6'10" **Weight:** 260
Birthdate: June 23, 1961
NBA Experience: 9 years

College: Texas
Acquired: Traded from Kings with Randy Wittman for Wayman Tisdale and a future 2nd-round pick, 2/89

Background: Drafted No. 5 overall as a junior in 1982 by Kansas City, this University of Texas product spent more than six seasons with the Kings in K.C. and Sacramento. He ranks among the franchise's all-time leaders in games, rebounds, blocked shots, and field goal percentage. Thompson arrived in Indiana via the Wayman Tisdale deal in 1989. The Pacers' second-leading rebounder in each of the past two seasons, he grabbed 20-plus boards twice last year.

Strengths: While Thompson passes as well as any 6'10" player in the Eastern Conference, his primary strength is crashing the boards. Ever since he led the nation in rebounding at Texas ten years ago, it's been his forte. He boxes out well, possesses superb timing, and uses his big hands to their full advantage.

Weaknesses: On a team that scores a lot of points, Thompson rarely reaches double figures. Conditioned to set picks or pass the ball whenever it comes his way, he doesn't even look for his shot. He accumulated more fouls than any other Pacer last season. He doesn't jump well and he lacks quickness.

Analysis: As long as Thompson continues to rebound like he does, he'll be a valuable commodity. He's a capable enough scorer to shoot more than he does. Don't be surprised if he becomes more assertive when the ball goes his way in the future.

PLAYER SUMMARY

Will ....crash the boards
Can't.............outjump many forwards
Expect.................more scoring output
Don't Expect....................gentle picks
Fantasy Value $1-3
Card Value...5¢

COLLEGE STATISTICS

		G	FGP	FTP	RPG	PPG
79-80	TEX	30	.558	.748	9.7	12.8
80-81	TEX	30	.572	.728	12.3	19.2
81-82	TEX	27	.528	.677	13.5	18.6
Totals		87	.553	.713	11.8	16.8

NBA REGULAR-SEASON STATISTICS

				FGs		3-PT FGs		FTs		Rebounds						
		G	MIN	FG	PCT	FG	PCT	FT	PCT	OFF	TOT	AST	STL	BLK	PTS	PPG
82-83	KC	71	987	147	.512	0	.000	89	.650	133	375	33	40	61	383	5.4
83-84	KC	80	1915	333	.523	0	.000	160	.717	260	709	86	71	145	826	10.3
84-85	KC	82	2458	369	.531	0	.000	227	.721	274	854	130	98	128	965	11.8
85-86	SAC	80	2377	411	.518	0	.000	202	.732	252	770	168	71	109	1024	12.8
86-87	SAC	80	2166	362	.481	0	.000	188	.737	237	687	122	69	126	912	11.1
87-88	SAC	69	1257	215	.471	2	.400	118	.720	138	427	68	54	73	550	8.0
88-89	SAC/IND	76	2329	416	.489	0	.000	227	.808	224	718	81	79	94	1059	13.9
89-90	IND	82	2126	223	.473	1	.200	107	.799	175	630	106	65	71	554	6.8
90-91	IND	82	1946	276	.488	1	.200	72	.692	154	563	147	63	63	625	7.6
Totals		704	17561	2752	.500	4	.174	1390	.736	1847	5733	941	610	870	6898	9.8

MYCHAL THOMPSON

Team: Los Angeles Lakers
Position: Center/Forward
Height: 6'10" **Weight:** 235
Birthdate: January 30, 1955
NBA Experience: 12 years

College: Minnesota
Acquired: Traded from Spurs for Frank Brickowski, Petur Gudmundsson, a 1987 1st-round pick, a 1990 2nd-round pick, and cash, 2/87

Background: Thompson was a two-time All-American at Minnesota. Portland made him the top selection in the 1978 draft and he earned All-Rookie honors. He sat out his second season with a broken leg, but he went on to become the Blazers' career leader in minutes and rebounds in seven seasons. After a brief stint in San Antonio in 1986-87, Thompson took a reserve role with the Lakers. He backed up Vlade Divac in 1990-91, averaging 15 minutes per game.

Strengths: At this late stage in his career, his best trait is his willingness to enjoy life as a back-up. His easy-going personality livens up the locker room. He can still rebound, hit the occasional shot, and play effective post defense.

Weaknesses: Aging legs have made it increasingly difficult for him to keep up when the Lakers run. He has trouble getting off his feet and has not displayed the vision that used to result in bigger assist numbers.

Analysis: Thompson is a pleasure to have around, but his ability to contribute has dwindled with the emergence of Divac as the Lakers' center of the future. His defense and veteran leadership are probably enough to keep him on someone's roster for another year.

PLAYER SUMMARY

Will	play post defense
Can't	regain young legs
Expect	likeable personality
Don't Expect	increased minutes
Fantasy Value	$1-3
Card Value	5¢

COLLEGE STATISTICS

		G	FGP	FTP	RPG	PPG
74-75	MINN	23	.530	.756	7.7	12.5
75-76	MINN	25	.573	.696	12.5	25.9
76-77	MINN	27	.606	.705	8.9	22.0
77-78	MINN	21	.536	.630	10.9	22.0
Totals		96	.567	.692	10.0	20.8

NBA REGULAR-SEASON STATISTICS

		G	MIN	FGs FG	PCT	3-PT FGs FG	PCT	FTs FT	PCT	Rebounds OFF	TOT	AST	STL	BLK	PTS	PPG
78-79	POR	73	2144	460	.490	0	.000	154	.572	198	604	176	67	134	1074	14.7
80-81	POR	79	2790	569	.494	0	.000	207	.641	223	686	284	62	170	1345	17.0
81-82	POR	79	3129	681	.523	0	.000	280	.628	258	921	319	69	107	1642	20.8
82-83	POR	80	3017	505	.489	0	.000	249	.621	183	753	380	68	110	1259	15.7
83-84	POR	79	2648	487	.524	0	.000	266	.667	235	688	308	84	108	1240	15.7
84-85	POR	79	2616	572	.515	0	.000	307	.684	211	618	205	78	104	1451	18.4
85-86	POR	82	2569	503	.498	0	.000	198	.641	181	608	176	76	35	1204	14.7
86-87	SA/LAL	82	1890	359	.450	1	.500	219	.737	138	412	115	45	71	938	11.4
87-88	LAL	80	2007	370	.512	0	.000	185	.634	198	489	66	38	79	925	11.6
88-89	LAL	80	1994	291	.559	0	.000	156	.678	157	467	48	58	59	738	9.2
89-90	LAL	70	1883	281	.500	0	.000	144	.706	173	477	43	33	73	706	10.1
90-91	LAL	72	1077	113	.496	0	.000	62	.705	74	228	21	23	23	288	4.0
Totals		935	27764	5191	.504	1	.083	2427	.655	2229	6951	2141	701	1073	12810	13.7

OTIS THORPE

Team: Houston Rockets
Position: Forward
Height: 6'10" **Weight:** 246
Birthdate: August 5, 1962
NBA Experience: 7 years

College: Providence
Acquired: Traded from Kings for Rodney McCray and Jim Petersen, 10/88

Background: Thorpe left Providence with the all-time Big East record for rebounds and was a consensus all-conference selection as a senior. He started his pro career with the Kings, where he began an amazing streak of games started that has carried through his three years with Houston. Thorpe has started 411 straight games, leading the closest active player (Michael Jordan) by 223. His 460 straight appearances also leads all active players. In 1990-91, Thorpe ranked seventh in the NBA in field goal accuracy and ninth in rebounding.

Strengths: Thorpe gives a team steady rebounding. He has bulked up over the past couple of seasons and is better able to bang in the post. The same goes for his interior defense. Thorpe runs the floor, handles the ball well in transition, dunks, and does not take unwise shots. His percentage is consistently high.

Weaknesses: What Thorpe boasts in athletic ability he lacks in low-post moves. He gets his points off the pick-and-roll and by going to the offensive boards, but he does not own a vast collection of shots from the interior.

Analysis: Those who knocked Thorpe for his inability to step forward in big situations should take note of his 1990-91 accomplishments. When Hakeem Olajuwon was injured, Thorpe averaged 21.1 points, 11.7 rebounds, and 3.7 assists in 25 games, shooting 57 percent from the field. When Olajuwon is on the floor, Thorpe does not need to be an offensive force. He does his job well.

PLAYER SUMMARY

Will	rebound
Can't	shoot FTs
Expect	10 RPG
Don't Expect	missed starts
Fantasy Value	$38-42
Card Value	10-15¢

COLLEGE STATISTICS

		G	FGP	FTP	RPG	PPG
80-81	PROV	26	.515	.658	5.3	9.6
81-82	PROV	27	.541	.643	8.0	14.1
82-83	PROV	31	.636	.659	8.0	16.1
83-84	PROV	29	.580	.653	10.3	17.1
Totals		113	.575	.653	8.0	14.4

NBA REGULAR-SEASON STATISTICS

		G	MIN	FGs FG	FGs PCT	3-PT FGs FG	3-PT FGs PCT	FTs FT	FTs PCT	Rebounds OFF	Rebounds TOT	AST	STL	BLK	PTS	PPG
84-85	KC	82	1918	411	.600	0	.000	230	.620	187	556	111	34	37	1052	12.8
85-86	SAC	75	1675	289	.587	0	.000	164	.661	137	420	84	35	34	742	9.9
86-87	SAC	82	2956	567	.540	0	.000	413	.761	259	819	201	46	60	1547	18.9
87-88	SAC	82	3072	622	.507	0	.000	460	.755	279	837	266	62	56	1704	20.8
88-89	HOU	82	3135	521	.542	0	.000	328	.729	272	787	202	82	37	1370	16.7
89-90	HOU	82	2947	547	.548	0	.000	307	.688	258	734	261	66	24	1401	17.1
90-91	HOU	82	3039	549	.556	3	.429	334	.696	287	846	197	73	20	1435	17.5
Totals		567	18742	3506	.548	3	.100	2236	.711	1679	4999	1322	398	268	9251	16.3

SEDALE THREATT

Team: Seattle SuperSonics
Position: Guard
Height: 6'2" **Weight:** 177
Birthdate: October 10, 1961

NBA Experience: 8 years
College: West Virginia Tech
Acquired: Traded from Bulls for Sam Vincent, 2/88

Background: Threatt was an NAIA All-American at West Virginia Tech, where he finished his career as the school's all-time scoring leader. Originally a sixth-round draft pick by Philadelphia, he entered the 1990-91 season as the lowest draft choice still active in the NBA. He had never averaged double figures in scoring until his second full season in Seattle in 1989-90. He put up the biggest numbers of his career in 1990-91, when he started 57 games for the Sonics.

Strengths: Threatt is regarded as one of the league's purest shooters and has earned that billing by connecting on well over 50 percent of his attempts over the last two years. He is at his best when spotting up off the break. Blessed with great lateral quickness, Threatt can defend virtually any guard.

Weaknesses: Although his passing is decent and his ball-handling good, Threatt is not a team-oriented point man when asked to play that role. He is much better at off guard, where he spent the 1990-91 campaign. He does not dribble and shoot as well as he catches and shoots. His 3-point range is questionable.

Analysis: After years of bouncing around in various roles, Threatt seems to have found his calling. With Gary Payton their point guard of the future, the Sonics have been able to keep Threatt at off guard, allowing him to bury those pull-up jumpers and not worry about running the offense. As either a starter or a reserve, Threatt's shooting and defense will keep him on the floor.

PLAYER SUMMARY

Will ....spot up for jumpers
Can't ....excel at point
Expect ....a quick defender
Don't Expect ....a 3-point title
Fantasy Value $4-6
Card Value...5¢

COLLEGE STATISTICS

		G	FGP	FTP	RPG	PPG
79-80	WVAT	28	.481	.714	3.5	17.8
80-81	WVAT	31	.452	.712	3.9	17.7
81-82	WVAT	34	.500	.729	3.5	22.2
82-83	WVAT	27	.557	.732	3.9	25.5
Totals		120	.498	.724	3.7	20.7

NBA REGULAR-SEASON STATISTICS

				FGs		3-PT FGs		FTs		Rebounds						
		G	MIN	FG	PCT	FG	PCT	FT	PCT	OFF	TOT	AST	STL	BLK	PTS	PPG
83-84	PHI	45	464	62	.419	1	.125	23	.821	17	40	41	13	2	148	3.3
84-85	PHI	82	1304	188	.452	4	.182	66	.733	21	99	175	80	16	446	5.4
85-86	PHI	70	1754	310	.453	1	.042	75	.833	21	121	193	93	5	696	9.9
86-87	PHI/CHI	68	1446	239	.448	7	.219	95	.798	26	108	259	74	13	580	8.5
87-88	CHI/SEA	71	1055	216	.508	3	.111	57	.803	23	88	160	60	8	492	6.9
88-89	SEA	63	1220	235	.494	11	.367	63	.818	31	117	238	81	4	544	8.6
89-90	SEA	65	1481	303	.506	8	.250	130	.828	43	115	216	65	8	744	11.4
90-91	SEA	80	2066	433	.519	10	.286	137	.792	25	99	273	113	8	1013	12.7
Totals		544	10790	1986	.482	45	.214	646	.802	207	787	1555	581	64	4663	8.6

WAYMAN TISDALE

Team: Sacramento Kings
Position: Forward
Height: 6'9" **Weight:** 260
Birthdate: June 9, 1964
NBA Experience: 6 years

College: Oklahoma
Acquired: Traded from Pacers with a 1990 2nd-round pick for LaSalle Thompson and Randy Wittman, 2/89

Background: At Oklahoma, Tisdale became the first player in college basketball history to be named first-team All-America in his first three seasons. He led the 1984 gold medal-winning U.S. Olympic team in rebounds and finished his college career with 17 school records and nine Big Eight marks. He was an All-Rookie selection with Indiana and was a big scorer off the bench before coming into his own as Sacramento's top scorer in 1989-90. He was again leading the Kings in 1990-91 when a ruptured tendon in his right foot limited him to 33 games.

Strengths: Tisdale is a big-time low-post scorer who gets his shots off despite his relatively small size. His offensive arsenal includes a variety of twisting moves in the lane and a consistent short-range jumper. He has improved his rebounding and was leading the Kings in that department before the injury. He is a hard worker and is well liked by teammates and community.

Weaknesses: Defense is not in Tisdale's vocabulary. His size (or lack of it) does not serve him well on that end of the court and he expends a lot of energy on offense. Constantly double-teamed, he needs to become a better passer.

Analysis: Tisdale was on his way to a second great season when the January injury pretty much ended it. He tried coming back, playing two games in March, before sitting out the rest of the year. If he can return at his previous level of play, he could be making an All-Star trip before long.

PLAYER SUMMARY

Will ....work for inside shots
Can't.................................play defense
Expect..........................a return to form
Don't Expect ....great passing
Fantasy Value $18-21
Card Value...8¢

COLLEGE STATISTICS

		G	FGP	FTP	RPG	PPG
82-83	OKLA	33	.580	.635	10.3	24.5
83-84	OKLA	34	.577	.640	9.7	27.0
84-85	OKLA	37	.578	.703	10.2	25.2
Totals		104	.578	.661	10.1	25.6

NBA REGULAR-SEASON STATISTICS

		G	MIN	FGs FG	FGs PCT	3-PT FGs FG	3-PT FGs PCT	FTs FT	FTs PCT	Rebounds OFF	Rebounds TOT	AST	STL	BLK	PTS	PPG
85-86	IND	81	2277	516	.515	0	.000	160	.684	191	584	79	32	44	1192	14.7
86-87	IND	81	2159	458	.513	0	.000	258	.709	217	475	117	50	26	1174	14.5
87-88	IND	79	2378	511	.512	0	.000	246	.783	168	491	103	54	34	1268	16.1
88-89	IND/SAC	79	2434	532	.514	0	.000	317	.773	187	609	128	55	52	1381	17.5
89-90	SAC	79	2937	726	.525	0	.000	306	.783	185	595	108	54	54	1758	22.3
90-91	SAC	33	1116	262	.483	0	.000	136	.800	75	253	66	23	28	660	20.0
Totals		432	13301	3005	.513	0	.000	1423	.756	1023	3007	601	268	238	7433	17.2

TOM TOLBERT

Team: Golden State Warriors
Position: Forward
Height: 6'8" **Weight:** 240
Birthdate: October 16, 1965
NBA Experience: 3 years

College: Cal.-Irvine; Cerritos; Arizona
Acquired: Signed as a free agent, 11/89

Background: Tolbert played college basketball at Cal.-Irvine (ten games), Cerritos College, and finally the University of Arizona, where he teamed with fellow NBA players Sean Elliott, Steve Kerr, and Jud Buechler on a Final Four squad. He played 14 games with Charlotte as a rookie before spending the rest of 1988-89 playing in the Canary Islands. He landed with the Warriors in 1989-90 and has become a key player over the last two years. In 1990-91, Tolbert was fifth on the team in rebounding and sixth in scoring.

Strengths: Tolbert is aggressive on the boards and owns a decent perimeter game, although an arch injury limited his 1990-91 numbers. He is not afraid to go after the ball and plays physical defense against bigger men. He handles the ball well for his size. A flake with a goofy haircut, teammates and fans love him.

Weaknesses: You would never imagine Tolbert could make it in the NBA judging solely on athletic ability. He is not quick, does not jump to the moon, and is undersized for the small forward position he usually plays. The latter deficiency pretty much rules out low-post offense.

Analysis: Tolbert went from "happy to be in the league" to legitimate weapon during the 1991 playoffs, when the Warriors used him to run the offense against San Antonio, pulling the Spurs' David Robinson away from the hoop. Golden State won the series. That sums up what Tolbert can do—nothing spectacular, but whatever it takes.

PLAYER SUMMARY

Will ....play many roles
Can't ....shoot over big men
Expect ....great work ethic
Don't Expect ....any backing down
Fantasy Value $1-2
Card Value..10¢

COLLEGE STATISTICS

		G	FGP	FTP	RPG	PPG
83-84	C-I	4	.750	.000	0.3	1.5
84-85	C-I	6	.316	.800	2.0	2.7
85-86	CERR	32	.613	.680	7.8	16.2
86-87	ARIZ	30	.511	.705	6.2	13.9
87-88	ARIZ	38	.547	.812	5.8	14.1
Totals		110	.556	.743	6.1	13.6

NBA REGULAR-SEASON STATISTICS

				FGs		3-PT FGs		FTs		Rebounds						
		G	MIN	FG	PCT	FG	PCT	FT	PCT	OFF	TOT	AST	STL	BLK	PTS	PPG
88-89	CHA	14	117	17	.459	0	.000	6	.500	7	21	7	2	4	40	2.9
89-90	GS	70	1347	218	.493	5	.278	175	.726	122	363	58	23	25	616	8.8
90-91	GS	62	1371	183	.423	7	.333	127	.738	87	275	76	35	38	500	8.1
Totals		146	2835	418	.458	12	.286	308	.725	216	659	141	60	67	1156	7.9

ANDY TOOLSON

Team: Utah Jazz
Position: Forward
Height: 6'6" **Weight:** 210
Birthdate: January 19, 1966
NBA Experience: 1 year

College: Brigham Young
Acquired: Signed as a free agent, 10/90

Background: Toolson was an Academic All-American at Brigham Young and shot 49 percent from 3-point range during his senior season. He made the Utah roster as an undrafted free agent in 1990-91 and was the team leader in 3-point accuracy. He saw action in 47 games and started 15, helping the Jazz compile a 12-3 record in those contests.

Strengths: Toolson shoots from long range with great accuracy and confidence. Is it coincidence that his cousin is married to another BYU product named Danny Ainge? Toolson has good size to shoot over guards and is quick enough to beat forwards to the spot. He is smart, a decent passer, and can get off his feet. He competes.

Weaknesses: While Toolson hit at an impressive rate from behind the 3-point line, his overall field goal percentage was barely above 40. Get him inside the line with a hand in his face and he becomes much less effective. The biggest problem is his inability to get his own shot off the dribble. Although he uses his head on the defensive end, he can be beaten in the post.

Analysis: Making an NBA roster and earning 15 starts is enough to convince anyone of Toolson's competitiveness. You can put him on the court and be sure he will not hurt the team. In fact, he made some crucial shots in Utah wins this season. Despite his long-range gun, Toolson does not yet have the all-around tools to become a regular starter. At small forward, you have to be able to do some creating on your own.

PLAYER SUMMARY

Will ....launch 3's
Can't ....improvise
Expect..........................nothing foolish
Don't Expect ....many more starts
Fantasy Value $1-2
Card Value......................................5¢

COLLEGE STATISTICS

		G	FGP	FTP	RPG	PPG
84-85	BYU	29	.503	.726	2.7	8.5
87-88	BYU	32	.430	.736	2.8	6.0
88-89	BYU	26	.475	.833	6.6	15.3
89-90	BYU	30	.510	.766	6.6	18.3
Totals		117	.487	.766	4.6	11.9

NBA REGULAR-SEASON STATISTICS

			FGs		3-PT FGs		FTs		Rebounds						
	G	MIN	FG	PCT	FG	PCT	FT	PCT	OFF	TOT	AST	STL	BLK	PTS	PPG
90-91 UTA	47	470	50	.403	12	.375	25	.758	32	67	31	14	2	137	2.9
Totals	47	470	50	.403	12	.375	25	.758	32	67	31	14	2	137	2.9

TRENT TUCKER

Team: New York Knicks   **NBA Experience:** 9 years
Position: Guard   **College:** Minnesota
Height: 6'5" **Weight:** 190 **Acquired:** 1st-round pick in 1982 draft
Birthdate: December 20, 1959 (6th overall)

Background: A standout at the University of Minnesota, Tucker teamed with Kevin McHale for two seasons. After being drafted by the Knicks in 1982, he opted for uniform No. 6 because he was the sixth player chosen. Tucker's most productive year came in 1986-87 (11.4 PPG). He made a whopping 118 treys in 1988-89. Last year, he shot less than 45 percent from the field for the second straight season.

Strengths: While his bread-and-butter, perimeter shooting, has failed him of late, Tucker still contributes as a tough, underrated defender. He knows exactly what every opposing big guard can and can't do, and he doesn't take chances. Tucker sees the whole floor and handles the ball with confidence.

Weaknesses: A spot-up perimeter jumper is the only shot left in Tucker's limited arsenal. He drives to the basket about as often as the Knicks win championships. As solid as he is defensively, he doesn't rebound. When his shot's not falling, he doesn't belong on the floor.

Analysis: The Knicks' elder statesman, Tucker remains valuable as a team leader. Regardless, his career's nearing an end. When you're a team's designated 3-point shooter off the bench and you averaged only 7.1 PPG last year, your future isn't real bright.

PLAYER SUMMARY

Will ....overachieve on defense
Can't ....drive the lane
Expect ....fewer minutes
Don't Expect ....rebounds
Fantasy Value $1-2
Card Value.......................................5¢

COLLEGE STATISTICS

		G	FGP	FTP	RPG	PPG
78-79	MINN	25	.477	.594	3.4	9.9
79-80	MINN	32	.490	.739	3.2	10.6
80-81	MINN	29	.517	.812	3.5	14.8
81-82	MINN	29	.504	.822	3.6	14.8
Totals		115	.499	.772	3.4	12.6

NBA REGULAR-SEASON STATISTICS

				FGs		3-PT FGs		FTs		Rebounds						
		G	MIN	FG	PCT	FG	PCT	FT	PCT	OFF	TOT	AST	STL	BLK	PTS	PPG
82-83	NY	78	1830	299	.462	14	.467	43	.672	75	216	195	56	6	655	8.4
83-84	NY	63	1228	225	.500	6	.375	25	.758	43	130	138	63	8	481	7.6
84-85	NY	77	1819	293	.483	29	.403	38	.792	74	188	199	75	15	653	8.5
85-86	NY	77	1788	349	.472	41	.451	79	.790	70	169	192	65	8	818	10.6
86-87	NY	70	1691	325	.470	68	.422	77	.762	49	135	166	116	13	795	11.4
87-88	NY	71	1248	193	.424	69	.413	51	.718	32	119	117	53	6	506	7.1
88-89	NY	81	1824	263	.454	118	.399	55	.782	55	176	132	88	6	687	8.5
89-90	NY	81	1725	253	.417	95	.388	66	.767	57	174	173	74	8	667	8.2
90-91	NY	65	1194	191	.440	64	.418	17	.630	33	105	111	44	9	463	7.1
Totals		663	14347	2391	.459	504	.409	439	.750	488	1412	1423	634	79	5725	8.6

ANDRE TURNER

Team: Philadelphia 76ers
Position: Guard
Height: 5'11" **Weight:** 160
Birthdate: March 13, 1964
NBA Experience: 5 years

College: Memphis St.
Acquired: Signed as a free agent, 11/90

Background: Turner graduated from Memphis State as the school's assists and steals leader. Drafted by the Lakers in 1986, he has played for nine pro teams in the NBA, CBA, and WBL and has gone to training camp with two others. He enjoyed his most productive season in 1989-90 with the CBA's LaCrosse Catbirds. The 1990-91 season was, by far, his best in the NBA. In 70 games, he posted career highs in points, assists, and rebounds.

Strengths: Turner's a mighty-mite playmaker who possesses lightning-quick speed and a knack for feeding open teammates. His three-to-one assist-to-turnover ratio should keep him in the league a little bit longer.

Weaknesses: Not much of a shooter, opponents are more than happy to leave him open outside. He's often out of control when leading the break. Despite his quickness, Turner's diminutive size makes him a defensive liability. He doesn't get his hands on as many loose balls as he should.

Analysis: Rarely will you find a player who has been rejected as much as Turner. The Lakers, Celtics, Rockets, Heat, Hornets, and Clippers all let him go within a span of three years. After last season's success, he should find a home in the NBA. However, things are going to get crowded at the Philly point position this year when Johnny Dawkins returns from injury. The Sixers would be wise to keep Turner over Rickey Green, who turned 37 in August.

PLAYER SUMMARY	
Will	find the open man
Can't	shoot from outside
Expect	the unexpected
Don't Expect	defensive stopper
Fantasy Value	$1-2
Card Value	5¢

COLLEGE STATISTICS

		G	FGP	FTP	RPG	PPG
82-83	MSU	31	.518	.806	1.1	9.9
83-84	MSU	33	.457	.667	1.4	8.2
84-85	MSU	34	.498	.714	2.3	11.4
85-86	MSU	34	.478	.854	2.0	13.9
Totals		132	.487	.757	1.7	10.9

NBA REGULAR-SEASON STATISTICS

		G	MIN	FGs FG	FGs PCT	3-PT FGs FG	3-PT FGs PCT	FTs FT	FTs PCT	Rebounds OFF	Rebounds TOT	AST	STL	BLK	PTS	PPG
86-87	BOS	3	18	2	.400	0	.000	0	.000	1	2	1	0	0	4	1.3
87-88	HOU	12	99	12	.353	1	.143	10	.714	4	8	23	7	1	35	2.9
88-89	MIL	4	13	3	.500	0	.000	0	.000	0	3	0	2	0	6	1.5
89-90	LAC/CHA	11	115	11	.289	0	.000	4	1.000	4	8	23	8	0	26	2.4
90-91	PHI	70	1407	168	.439	12	.364	64	.736	36	152	311	63	0	412	5.9
Totals		100	1652	196	.421	13	.302	78	.743	45	173	358	80	1	483	4.8

JEFF TURNER

Team: Orlando Magic
Position: Forward/Center
Height: 6'9" **Weight:** 240
Birthdate: April 9, 1962

NBA Experience: 5 years
College: Vanderbilt
Acquired: Signed as a free agent, 7/89

Background: Turner was a two-time SEC All-Academic selection at Vanderbilt, where he finished as the tenth-leading scorer in school history. He played for the 1984 gold medal-winning U.S. Olympic team. Turner saw limited action with New Jersey in his first three NBA seasons before opting to play professionally in Europe for two years. He returned to the NBA with Orlando, where he was primarily a back-up in 1989-90 but made 43 starts in 1990-91. In the last 40 games (all starts), Turner averaged 11.2 points and six rebounds.

Strengths: A perimeter-oriented forward, Turner has a soft touch and good range (6-of-15 on 3-pointers) with his lefty jump shot. He uses his head and does not try to do too much offensively. He is unselfish and works hard in all aspects of the game.

Weaknesses: Turner can do little offensively other than shoot. He cannot put the ball on the floor and does not possess an inside game to bail him out. He lacks quickness for the perimeter and muscle in the paint. The same dilemma haunts him on defense, where he often resorts to fouling both bigger and quicker players.

Analysis: Turner enjoyed his best NBA season in 1990-91, but there were still enough holes in his game to make one wonder how he could be starting. With a non-expansion team, he would spend most of his time on the bench. Turner makes a decent reserve if only because of his jumper. The rest of his game remains questionable.

PLAYER SUMMARY

Will	score from outside
Can't	do much off dribble
Expect	defensive problems
Don't Expect	all-around ability
Fantasy Value	$2-4
Card Value	5¢

COLLEGE STATISTICS

		G	FGP	FTP	RPG	PPG
80-81	VAND	28	.417	.645	3.0	3.6
81-82	VAND	27	.524	.732	5.4	9.3
82-83	VAND	33	.492	.765	5.5	13.2
83-84	VAND	29	.533	.843	7.3	16.8
Totals		117	.506	.772	5.3	10.9

NBA REGULAR-SEASON STATISTICS

				FGs		3-PT FGs		FTs		Rebounds						
		G	MIN	FG	PCT	FG	PCT	FT	PCT	OFF	TOT	AST	STL	BLK	PTS	PPG
84-85	NJ	72	1429	171	.454	0	.000	79	.859	88	218	108	29	7	421	5.8
85-86	NJ	53	650	84	.491	0	.000	58	.744	45	137	14	21	3	226	4.3
86-87	NJ	76	1003	151	.465	0	.000	76	.731	80	197	60	33	13	378	5.0
89-90	ORL	60	1105	132	.429	2	.200	42	.778	52	227	53	23	12	308	5.1
90-91	ORL	71	1683	259	.487	6	.400	85	.759	108	363	97	29	10	609	8.6
Totals		332	5870	797	.465	8	.267	340	.773	373	1142	332	135	45	1942	5.8

KELVIN UPSHAW

Team: Dallas Mavericks
Position: Guard
Height: 6'2" **Weight:** 180
Birthdate: January 24, 1963

NBA Experience: 3 years
College: N.E. Oklahoma A&M; Utah
Acquired: Signed as a free agent, 11/90

Background: Upshaw played one year at Northeastern Oklahoma A&M before transferring to Utah, where he led the Utes in scoring as a junior and in assists, steals, and free throw percentage as a senior. He was never selected in the NBA draft, but he has played with Miami, Boston, Dallas, and Golden State in his three-year pro career, in addition to tours in the CBA and Italy. Upshaw appeared in 35 of the Mavericks' 38 games after the 1990-91 All-Star break, scoring 6.2 PPG in those contests.

Strengths: As one glance at his travel log suggests, Upshaw loves to play basketball and plans to stick with it, no matter where it may take him. He works hard on defense and does an admirable job against more talented point guards. He has become a good free throw shooter.

Weaknesses: Upshaw plays the point with scoring in mind, yet is not consistent from the perimeter. His career field goal percentage is 45 and his 3-point percentage is less than 25, though he does shoot it well in streaks. Unfortunately, his playmaking is the same way. He makes a great pass every so often but does not make the routine ones every time down the floor.

Analysis: If Upshaw has anything, he has persistence. He plays hard and is determined to stick around on someone's NBA roster. Chances are, he will. He has proven he can handle the ball against pressure and he works harder at the defensive end than the average NBA player. Although he has not shown the skills that would earn a more permanent home in the league, determination has to count for something.

PLAYER SUMMARY

Will ....work defensively
Can't..................find permanent home
Expect ....a scoring bent
Don't Expect..................a starting job
Fantasy Value $1-2
Card Value..................................5¢

COLLEGE STATISTICS

		G	FGP	FTP	RPG	PPG
81-82	NEOK	31	.488	.737	2.9	19.3
83-84	UTA	30	.517	.832	3.0	14.6
84-85	UTA	28	.503	.786	3.6	17.4
85-86	UTA	26	.487	.830	2.2	11.7
Totals		115	.498	.794	3.0	15.9

NBA REGULAR-SEASON STATISTICS

		G	MIN	FGs FG	FGs PCT	3-PT FGs FG	3-PT FGs PCT	FTs FT	FTs PCT	Rebounds OFF	Rebounds TOT	AST	STL	BLK	PTS	PPG
88-89	MIA/BOS	32	617	99	.467	3	.200	18	.692	10	49	117	26	3	219	6.8
89-90	BOS/DAL/GS	40	387	64	.438	4	.267	28	.757	9	41	54	27	1	160	4.0
90-91	DAL	48	514	104	.450	7	.241	55	.859	20	55	86	28	5	270	5.6
Totals		120	1518	267	.453	14	.237	101	.795	39	145	257	81	9	649	5.4

DARNELL VALENTINE

Team: Cleveland Cavaliers
Position: Guard
Height: 6'1" **Weight:** 183
Birthdate: February 3, 1959

NBA Experience: 9 years
College: Kansas
Acquired: Signed as a free agent, 12/90

Background: A member of the 1980 U.S. Olympic Team, Valentine was an All-American at the University of Kansas. He was selected in the first round by Portland in 1981. Valentine also played for the Clippers before being nabbed by Miami in the '88 expansion draft. Days later, he was dealt to the Cavs. Out of basketball in 1989-90, he was playing in Mexico when the Cavs summoned him to replace Mark Price in early December. He led Cleveland in assists a team-high 29 times.

Strengths: Steady but unspectacular, Valentine went from figuring his NBA career was over to starting and playing nearly 30 minutes per night. He's not the all-around player he once was, but he can run a halfcourt offense. You can usually count the bad decisions he makes in a game on one hand. He shot 83 percent from the line last season.

Weaknesses: He doesn't get up and down the floor as well as Price did. Valentine doesn't possess sufficient natural ability when trying to guard some of the younger point guards. He gets beat on a lot of switches. Valentine's muscular thighs, his trademark, are losing their tone.

Analysis: When Price returns from the injured list, Valentine may well be out of a job. Cleveland drafted two guards and signed John Battle. Valentine played well enough last season to receive another offer somewhere.

PLAYER SUMMARY

Will ....make few mistakes
Can't.................defend like he used to
Expect..........................a battle for a job
Don't Expect ....expanded role
Fantasy Value $2-4
Card Value..5¢

COLLEGE STATISTICS

		G	FGP	FTP	RPG	PPG
77-78	KAN	29	.481	.741	2.8	13.5
78-79	KAN	29	.443	.680	4.6	16.1
80-81	KAN	28	.481	.777	3.2	16.5
81-82	KAN	32	.503	.682	3.7	15.6
Totals		118	.476	.718	3.6	15.4

NBA REGULAR-SEASON STATISTICS

		G	MIN	FGs FG	FGs PCT	3-PT FGs FG	3-PT FGs PCT	FTs FT	FTs PCT	Rebounds OFF	Rebounds TOT	AST	STL	BLK	PTS	PPG
81-82	POR	82	1387	187	.413	0	.000	152	.760	48	149	270	94	3	526	6.4
82-83	POR	47	1298	209	.454	0	.000	169	.793	34	117	293	101	5	587	12.5
83-84	POR	68	1893	251	.447	0	.000	194	.789	49	127	395	107	6	696	10.2
84-85	POR	75	2278	321	.473	0	.000	230	.793	54	219	522	143	5	872	11.6
85-86	POR/LAC	62	1217	161	.415	4	.286	130	.743	32	125	246	72	2	456	7.4
86-87	LAC	65	1759	275	.410	13	.232	163	.815	38	150	447	116	10	726	11.2
87-88	LAC	79	1636	223	.418	15	.455	101	.743	37	156	382	122	8	562	7.1
88-89	CLE	77	1086	136	.426	3	.214	91	.813	22	103	174	57	7	366	4.8
90-91	CLE	65	1841	230	.464	6	.240	143	.831	37	172	351	98	12	609	9.4
Totals		620	14395	1993	.437	41	.261	1373	.787	351	1318	3080	910	58	5400	8.7

KIKI VANDEWEGHE

Team: New York Knicks
Position: Forward
Height: 6'8" **Weight:** 220
Birthdate: August 1, 1958

NBA Experience: 11 years
College: UCLA
Acquired: Traded from Trail Blazers for a 1989 1st-round pick, 2/89

Background: Vandeweghe led UCLA to the NCAA title game vs. Louisville in 1980. Unable to come to terms with Dallas that same year, he was sent to Denver for draft choices. After four years with the Nuggets, which included two All-Star Game invites, he went to Portland in a multi-player trade. The Blazers shipped him to New York in 1989 for a first-round draft choice. Between 1981-82 and 1987-88, Vandeweghe averaged more than 20 PPG each year. He played in more games last season (75) than he had since 1986-87.

Strengths: When healthy, Vandeweghe's made a career out of his ability to put the ball in the basket. Behind Patrick Ewing, he's the Knicks' second option offensively. A great first step (his trademark) enables Kiki to get off a lot of uncontested shots. He's one of the best foul shooters in the league.

Weaknesses: He gets slower defensively every year. There's not a small forward in the league who can't beat Vandeweghe off the dribble. He's a lousy rebounder. Frequent back and foot problems have taken their toll on his stamina.

Analysis: A defensive liability, Vandeweghe must put the ball in the basket to justify his presence on the court. Until the Knicks acquire a small forward who excels at both ends, Vandeweghe will be Pat Riley's starter by default.

PLAYER SUMMARY

Will..........................shoot the lights out
Can't...rebound
Expect ....more back problems
Don't Expect...........improved defense
Fantasy Value............................$19-22
Card Value..8¢

COLLEGE STATISTICS

		G	FGP	FTP	RPG	PPG
76-77	UCLA	23	.500	.706	1.8	3.6
77-78	UCLA	28	.549	.687	4.4	8.9
78-79	UCLA	30	.622	.812	6.3	14.2
79-80	UCLA	32	.557	.791	6.8	19.5
Totals		113	.570	.776	5.0	12.2

NBA REGULAR-SEASON STATISTICS

			FGs		3-PT FGs		FTs		Rebounds						
	G	MIN	FG	PCT	FG	PCT	FT	PCT	OFF	TOT	AST	STL	BLK	PTS	PPG
80-81 DEN	51	1376	229	.426	0	.000	130	.818	86	270	94	29	24	588	11.5
81-82 DEN	82	2775	706	.560	1	.077	347	.857	149	461	247	52	29	1760	21.5
82-83 DEN	82	2909	841	.547	15	.294	489	.875	124	437	203	66	38	2186	26.7
83-84 DEN	78	2734	895	.558	11	.367	494	.852	84	373	238	53	50	2295	29.4
84-85 POR	72	2502	618	.534	11	.333	369	.896	74	228	106	37	22	1616	22.4
85-86 POR	79	2791	719	.540	1	.125	523	.869	92	216	187	54	17	1962	24.8
86-87 POR	79	3029	808	.523	39	.481	467	.886	86	251	220	52	17	2122	26.9
87-88 POR	37	1038	283	.508	22	.379	159	.878	36	109	71	21	7	747	20.2
88-89 POR/NY	45	934	200	.469	19	.396	80	.899	26	71	69	19	11	499	11.1
89-90 NY	22	563	102	.442	10	.526	44	.917	15	53	41	15	3	258	11.7
90-91 NY	75	2420	458	.494	51	.362	259	.899	78	180	110	42	10	1226	16.3
Totals	702	23071	5859	.527	180	.368	3361	.873	850	2649	1586	440	228	15259	21.7

LOY VAUGHT

Team: Los Angeles Clippers
Position: Forward/Center
Height: 6'9" **Weight:** 235
Birthdate: February 27, 1967
NBA Experience: 1 year

College: Michigan
Acquired: 1st-round pick in 1990 draft (13th overall)

Background: Vaught led the Big Ten in field goal percentage as a junior and senior and was the first Michigan player since Roy Tarpley to average double-figure points and rebounds. He also paced the conference in rebounding as a senior. He saw action in 73 games as a rookie, leading the Clippers in rebounding five times.

Strengths: Vaught is a relentless rebounder who approaches basketball in workmanlike fashion. Coaches love his desire to hit the boards on both ends. Equally as impressive is his muscular frame. He gets up and down the floor, finishes plays, hits the jumper from short-to-medium range, and rarely puts up a bad shot. He plays within himself. On defense, Vaught gets up to block and alter shots.

Weaknesses: Vaught is not a reliable shooter outside of 16 feet and the verdict is still out on his low-post offense. Most of his points come off rebounds, fastbreaks, or are of the garbage variety. He does not pass the ball well, amassing a higher number of turnovers (49) than assists (40) as a rookie. He lacks finesse.

Analysis: Vaught was never as highly acclaimed as fellow Michigan big man Terry Mills, but pro scouts fell in love with his work ethic. Vaught says he admires players who do the dirty work but do not get a lot of credit, and that is exactly how he plays. When he learns to score out of halfcourt sets and refines his court awareness, Vaught's rebounding prowess could carry him a long way.

PLAYER SUMMARY

Will ....chase rebounds
Can't ....be a scorer
Expect.............................all-out effort
Don't Expect............................10 PPG
Fantasy Value $2-4
Card Value...5¢

COLLEGE STATISTICS

		G	FGP	FTP	RPG	PPG
86-87	MICH	32	.557	.500	3.9	4.6
87-88	MICH	34	.621	.724	4.4	10.5
88-89	MICH	37	.661	.778	8.0	12.6
89-90	MICH	31	.595	.804	11.2	15.5
Totals		134	.617	.752	6.8	10.8

NBA REGULAR-SEASON STATISTICS

				FGs		3-PT FGs		FTs		Rebounds						
		G	MIN	FG	PCT	FG	PCT	FT	PCT	OFF	TOT	AST	STL	BLK	PTS	PPG
90-91	LAC	73	1178	175	.487	0	.000	49	.662	124	349	40	20	23	399	5.5
Totals		73	1178	175	.487	0	.000	49	.662	124	349	40	20	23	399	5.5

SAM VINCENT

Team: Orlando Magic
Position: Guard
Height: 6'2" **Weight:** 185
Birthdate: May 18, 1963

NBA Experience: 6 years
College: Michigan St.
Acquired: Selected from Bulls in 1989 expansion draft

Background: Vincent led the Big Ten in scoring as a senior at Michigan State, where he combined with brother Jay to form the highest scoring brother duo in conference history. He also played college ball with Orlando guard Scott Skiles. Vincent was the lone rookie on Boston's 1985-86 championship team, then played in Seattle and Chicago before becoming a starter for 45 games with the Magic in 1989-90. That starting spot was taken by Skiles for all but 17 games in 1990-91. Vincent did not get off the bench in 14 of the season's last 17 games.

Strengths: In terms of raw speed, few players can compare. Vincent races the ball up-court on the break and can penetrate from the halfcourt set. He handles it well and gets his shots off the dribble. Vincent is also a fine free throw shooter. He averaged 12.6 PPG in his 1990-91 starts.

Weaknesses: Vincent thinks to score first and pass second, which is not good for a point guard. He takes a lot of ill-advised shots, like pull-up jumpers off the break when there are three defenders and no teammates back. His percentage is not high enough to allow that. Although his speed makes him a good penetrator, Vincent is not the drive-and-dish type. He plays virtually no defense.

Analysis: Vincent is the type of player who will perform better when guaranteed playing time, but he does not run the point well enough to warrant many minutes in light of Skiles's recent emergence. He prefers shooting to passing yet has never been great from the outside. He will get his points; however, he needs to become more unselfish.

PLAYER SUMMARY

Will .... get his shots
Can't .... play defense
Expect .... blinding speed
Don't Expect .... unselfishness
Fantasy Value $5-8
Card Value .... 10¢

COLLEGE STATISTICS

		G	FGP	FTP	RPG	PPG
81-82	MSU	28	.461	.747	2.8	11.7
82-83	MSU	30	.449	.773	2.6	16.6
83-84	MSU	23	.498	.811	2.7	15.6
84-85	MSU	29	.544	.846	3.9	23.0
Totals		110	.491	.803	3.0	16.8

NBA REGULAR-SEASON STATISTICS

				FGs		3-PT FGs		FTs		Rebounds						
		G	MIN	FG	PCT	FG	PCT	FT	PCT	OFF	TOT	AST	STL	BLK	PTS	PPG
85-86	BOS	57	432	59	.364	1	.250	65	.929	11	48	69	17	4	184	3.2
86-87	BOS	46	374	60	.441	0	.000	51	.927	5	27	59	13	1	171	3.7
87-88	SEA/CHI	72	1501	210	.456	8	.381	145	.868	35	152	381	55	16	573	8.0
88-89	CHI	70	1703	274	.484	2	.118	106	.822	34	190	335	53	10	656	9.4
89-90	ORL	63	1657	258	.457	1	.071	188	.879	37	194	354	65	20	705	11.2
90-91	ORL	49	975	152	.431	3	.158	99	.825	17	107	197	30	5	406	8.3
Totals		357	6642	1013	.452	15	.200	654	.866	139	718	1395	233	56	2695	7.5

DARRELL WALKER

Team: Washington Bullets
Position: Guard
Height: 6'4" **Weight:** 180
Birthdate: March 9, 1961
NBA Experience: 8 years

College: Westark; Arkansas
Acquired: Traded from Nuggets with Mark Alarie for Jay Vincent and Michael Adams, 11/87

Background: Following college days at Arkansas, Walker made the NBA All-Rookie Team in 1984 as a member of the Knicks. He missed only one game with New York in three seasons. Walker was traded to Denver for a No. 1 draft choice in 1986. After one season with the Nuggets, he was dealt along with Mark Alarie to the Bullets. Washington's leading rebounder in 1989-90, Walker paced the team in assists and ranked third in boards last season.

Strengths: Blessed with an uncanny nose for the ball and tremendous leaping ability, Walker grabs more offensive rebounds than any other guard in the league. Long arms, quickness, and aggressiveness make Walker one of the top half-dozen defensive point guards in the NBA.

Weaknesses: His jumper's erratic, he can't shoot treys, and his marksmanship from the line is an embarrassment (60 percent last year). He's not a true playmaking point guard, but he played the position before Michael Adams arrived because no one else could.

Analysis: One of the league's premier jack-of-all-trade guards, Walker registered four triple-doubles last year and nine in 1989-90. Although he can't shoot a lick, he's creative enough to occasionally find ways to score and talented enough defensively to play in the league another three or four seasons.

PLAYER SUMMARY

Will ....play tough defense
Can't ....shoot FTs
Expect ....more triple-doubles
Don't Expect ....increased PPG
Fantasy Value $14-17
Card Value.....................................8¢

COLLEGE STATISTICS

		G	FGP	FTP	RPG	PPG
79-80	WEST	37	.540	.657	7.0	16.9
80-81	ARK	31	.509	.600	4.5	11.3
81-82	ARK	29	.513	.658	5.2	14.8
82-83	ARK	30	.527	.639	5.7	18.2
Totals		127	.525	.641	5.7	15.4

NBA REGULAR-SEASON STATISTICS

		G	MIN	FGs FG	FGs PCT	3-PT FGs FG	3-PT FGs PCT	FTs FT	FTs PCT	Rebounds OFF	Rebounds TOT	AST	STL	BLK	PTS	PPG
83-84	NY	82	1324	216	.417	4	.267	208	.791	74	167	284	127	15	644	7.9
84-85	NY	82	2489	430	.435	0	.000	243	.700	128	278	408	167	21	1103	13.5
85-86	NY	81	2023	324	.430	0	.000	190	.686	100	220	337	146	36	838	10.3
86-87	DEN	81	2020	358	.482	0	.000	272	.745	157	327	282	129	37	988	12.2
87-88	WAS	52	940	114	.392	0	.000	82	.781	43	127	100	62	10	310	6.0
88-89	WAS	79	2565	286	.420	0	.000	142	.772	135	507	496	155	23	714	9.0
89-90	WAS	81	2883	316	.454	2	.095	138	.687	173	714	652	139	30	772	9.5
90-91	WAS	71	2305	230	.430	0	.000	93	.604	140	498	459	78	33	553	7.8
Totals		609	16549	2274	.437	6	.066	1368	.722	950	2838	3018	1003	205	5922	9.7

KENNY WALKER

Team: New York Knicks
Position: Forward
Height: 6'8" **Weight:** 217
Birthdate: August 18, 1964
NBA Experience: 5 years

College: Kentucky
Acquired: 1st-round pick in 1986 draft
(5th overall)

Background: An All-American at Kentucky in 1985-86, Walker finished third on the Wildcats' all-time scoring list. "Sky Walker" captured the NBA Slam Dunk Contest in 1989, just days after the death of his father. Walker was sidelined for the first 21 games of the 1990-91 season with a sprained left knee. His 4.3 PPG were a career low. New York renounced his rights at season's end.

Strengths: A great leaper with speed and quickness, Walker plays above the rim. He takes high-percentage shots, but just not enough of them. Walker plays with more defensive intensity than any other Knick (sorry, Patrick). He's extremely tough to beat off the dribble.

Weaknesses: Walker's a power forward in a small forward's body who doesn't dribble well and can't create scoring chances for himself. His offense seems to tail off with each passing season. Defensively, he's not big and physical enough to match up with the other teams' power forwards for very long. Always plagued by injuries, Walker's failed to appear in 82 games in a season four times in five years.

Analysis: Realizing that he'll never become the player the Knicks thought he'd be when they drafted him, Walker is a spirited reserve who knows his limitations. It's his play at the defensive end that will keep him in the league.

PLAYER SUMMARY

Will ....go all out defensively
Can't..score
Expect ....spirited play
Don't Expect ....good health
Fantasy Value $1-3
Card Value...5¢

COLLEGE STATISTICS

		G	FGP	FTP	RPG	PPG
82-83	KEN	31	.611	.662	4.9	7.3
83-84	KEN	34	.555	.734	5.9	12.4
84-85	KEN	31	.559	.768	10.2	22.9
85-86	KEN	36	.582	.764	7.7	20.0
Totals		132	.571	.750	7.1	15.8

NBA REGULAR-SEASON STATISTICS

				FGs		3-PT FGs		FTs		Rebounds						
		G	MIN	FG	PCT	FG	PCT	FT	PCT	OFF	TOT	AST	STL	BLK	PTS	PPG
86-87	NY	68	1719	285	.491	0	.000	140	.757	118	338	75	49	49	710	10.4
87-88	NY	82	2139	344	.473	0	.000	138	.775	192	389	86	63	59	826	10.1
88-89	NY	79	1163	174	.489	5	.250	66	.776	101	230	36	41	45	419	5.3
89-90	NY	68	1595	204	.531	2	.400	125	.723	131	343	49	33	52	535	7.9
90-91	NY	54	771	83	.435	0	.000	64	.780	63	157	13	18	30	230	4.3
Totals		351	7387	1090	.487	7	.226	533	.758	605	1457	259	204	235	2720	7.7

SPUD WEBB

Team: Sacramento Kings
Position: Guard
Height: 5'7" **Weight:** 135
Birthdate: July 13, 1963
NBA Experience: 6 years

College: Midland; North Carolina St.
Acquired: Traded from Hawks with a 1994 2nd-round pick for Travis Mays, 7/91

Background: Originally drafted by Detroit in 1985 after pacing North Carolina State in assists for two straight seasons, Webb was a free agent signee with Atlanta three months later. He briefly teamed with 7'7" Manute Bol in the USBL. As a Hawks rookie, he won the 1986 NBA Slam Dunk Contest in his hometown of Dallas. Webb started 64 ballgames last season, after taking over for first-year flop Rumeal Robinson, and led the Hawks in assists. He was traded to Sacramento over the summer.

Strengths: His incredible quickness is the primary reason Webb's playing in the league. When teams double down in the paint, he can nail the 18- to 21-footer with regularity. A great leaper, the 5'7" Webb blocked six shots last winter. No other player under 6'0" plays as well as Webb.

Weaknesses: He's always going to be susceptible to being posted up since every player in the league besides Muggsy Bogues stands taller. Although his decision-making is greatly improved, he still has a ways to go, particularly in a halfcourt set.

Analysis: Webb will split point-guard duties with veteran Rory Sparrow. Although he's still mistaken for a ball boy on occasion, inch-for-inch Webb is the best player in the NBA. He needs minutes to be effective.

PLAYER SUMMARY

Will ....blow by defenders
Can't............................walk the ball up
Expect ....occasional dunks
Don't Expect......................missed FTs
Fantasy Value $5-7
Card Value.......................................10¢

COLLEGE STATISTICS

		G	FGP	FTP	RPG	PPG
81-82	MID	38	.515	.781	2.0	20.8
82-83	MID	35	.445	.774	3.0	14.6
83-84	NCST	33	.459	.761	1.8	9.8
84-85	NCST	33	.481	.761	2.0	11.1
Totals		139	.479	.773	2.2	14.3

NBA REGULAR-SEASON STATISTICS

			FGs		3-PT FGs		FTs		Rebounds						
	G	MIN	FG	PCT	FG	PCT	FT	PCT	OFF	TOT	AST	STL	BLK	PTS	PPG
85-86 ATL	79	1229	199	.483	2	.182	216	.785	27	123	337	82	5	616	7.8
86-87 ATL	33	532	71	.438	1	.167	80	.762	6	60	167	34	2	223	6.8
87-88 ATL	82	1347	191	.475	1	.053	107	.817	16	146	337	63	11	490	6.0
88-89 ATL	81	1219	133	.459	1	.045	52	.867	21	123	284	70	6	319	3.9
89-90 ATL	82	2184	294	.477	1	.053	162	.871	38	201	477	105	12	751	9.2
90-91 ATL	75	2197	359	.447	54	.321	231	.868	41	174	417	118	6	1003	13.4
Totals	432	8708	1247	.464	60	.245	848	.829	149	827	2019	472	42	3402	7.9

BILL WENNINGTON

Team: Sacramento Kings
Position: Center
Height: 7'0" **Weight:** 257
Birthdate: April 26, 1963
NBA Experience: 6 years

College: St. John's
Acquired: Traded from Mavericks with two 1990 1st-round picks for Rodney McCray and 1990 and 1991 2nd-round picks, 6/90

Background: Wennington improved his scoring and rebounding numbers in each of his four seasons at St. John's, where he teamed with Chris Mullin and Walter Berry in posting a 31-4 record in his senior year. The Montreal native spent the first five years of his pro career in a back-up role with Dallas, his biggest moment coming when he hit an unlikely 3-pointer at the third-quarter buzzer of a 1986 playoff win over the Lakers. He enjoyed his best season in 1990-91 in Sacramento, recording career highs in almost all categories.

Strengths: Wennington stands tall but prefers the perimeter, where he possesses a fairly accurate mid-range shot. He runs the floor quite well for a big man and is a capable finisher. Coaches are sold on his attitude and effort.

Weaknesses: For low-post play, Wennington is not blessed with great skill on either end of the court. He coughs up the ball on offense and does not have a variety of shots in the paint. Defensively, he gets pushed around in the post and does not keep his man away from the hoop. He has made rebounding strides but is still below average for a seven-footer.

Analysis: Wennington is a capable back-up center. He makes a few shots, grabs a few rebounds, and keeps up in transition. For defensive purposes, however, he is best left on the bench. He has never been a physical player but is skilled enough in other areas to get his minutes. He has helped the Kings.

PLAYER SUMMARY

Will ....run the floor
Can't ....play much defense
Expect.....................modest numbers
Don't Expect.............low-post offense
Fantasy Value $1-2
Card Value..............................8¢

COLLEGE STATISTICS

		G	FGP	FTP	RPG	PPG
81-82	STJ	30	.435	.676	4.2	3.2
82-83	STJ	33	.605	.698	4.4	5.5
83-84	STJ	26	.593	.675	5.7	11.7
84-85	STJ	35	.602	.816	6.4	12.5
Totals		124	.579	.738	5.2	8.2

NBA REGULAR-SEASON STATISTICS

		G	MIN	FGs FG	FGs PCT	3-PT FGs FG	3-PT FGs PCT	FTs FT	FTs PCT	Rebounds OFF	Rebounds TOT	AST	STL	BLK	PTS	PPG
85-86	DAL	56	562	72	.471	0	.000	45	.726	32	132	21	11	22	189	3.4
86-87	DAL	58	560	56	.424	0	.000	45	.750	53	129	24	13	10	157	2.7
87-88	DAL	30	125	25	.510	1	.500	12	.632	14	39	4	5	9	63	2.1
88-89	DAL	65	1074	119	.433	1	.111	61	.744	82	286	46	16	35	300	4.6
89-90	DAL	60	814	105	.449	0	.000	60	.800	64	198	41	20	21	270	4.5
90-91	SAC	77	1455	181	.436	1	.200	74	.787	101	340	69	46	59	437	5.7
Totals		346	4590	558	.444	3	.115	297	.758	346	1124	205	111	156	1416	4.1

DOUG WEST

Team: Minnesota Timberwolves
Position: Guard
Height: 6'6" **Weight:** 200
Birthdate: May 27, 1967
NBA Experience: 2 years

College: Villanova
Acquired: 2nd-round pick in 1989 draft (38th overall)

Background: West was a four-year starter at Villanova, finishing his career third on the school's all-time scoring list and seventh in steals. He has served as a reserve for Minnesota in each of his two pro seasons. West averaged 15.1 minutes per game over the final quarter of the 1990-91 campaign and scored a season-high 17 points April 14 at Philadelphia.

Strengths: West has good size and a sweet jumper. He improved his field goal percentage by nearly 90 points between his first and second years, although that is somewhat misleading since he rarely played in 1989-90. He is much better than his rookie numbers. West is athletic, a good finisher, and strong on the boards. He averaged 8.5 rebounds per 48 minutes during April. He works hard in both games and practices.

Weaknesses: Perhaps in an effort to impress coaches and secure more playing time, West occasionally exceeds his limits. His shot selection has become much better, but his turnover total (41 last year) is nearly as high as his assists (48). He can use the dribble to get his shot but is not an NBA-caliber playmaker. West's free throw shooting must improve and he is still learning on defense.

Analysis: West has had the dilemma of playing behind Tony Campbell, who averaged more than 37 minutes per game in 1990-91. When given the chance, he can spark a team with his jump shot, hustle, and work on the glass. He shows a strong desire to improve, which makes him a promising prospect entering his third NBA season.

PLAYER SUMMARY

Will ....hustle
Can't..........................displace starters
Expect.....................more playing time
Don't Expect 3-pointers
Fantasy Value $1-2
Card Value...8¢

COLLEGE STATISTICS

		G	FGP	FTP	RPG	PPG
85-86	VILL	37	.515	.682	3.7	10.2
86-87	VILL	31	.479	.729	4.9	15.2
87-88	VILL	37	.497	.724	4.9	15.8
88-89	VILL	33	.463	.720	4.9	18.4
Totals		138	.486	.716	4.6	14.8

NBA REGULAR-SEASON STATISTICS

				FGs		3-PT FGs		FTs		Rebounds						
		G	MIN	FG	PCT	FG	PCT	FT	PCT	OFF	TOT	AST	STL	BLK	PTS	PPG
89-90	MIN	52	378	53	.393	3	.273	26	.813	24	70	18	10	6	135	2.6
90-91	MIN	75	824	118	.480	0	.000	58	.690	56	136	48	35	23	294	3.9
Totals		127	1202	171	.449	3	.250	84	.724	80	206	66	45	29	429	3.4

MARK WEST

Team: Phoenix Suns
Position: Center
Height: 6'10" **Weight:** 246
Birthdate: November 5, 1960
NBA Experience: 8 years
College: Old Dominion

Acquired: Traded from Cavaliers with Kevin Johnson, Tyrone Corbin, 1988 1st- and 2nd-round picks, and a 1989 2nd-round pick for Larry Nance, Mike Sanders, and a 1988 2nd-round pick, 2/88

Background: West ended his college career at Old Dominion as the third-leading shot-blocker in NCAA history. He was cast off by Dallas and Milwaukee in his first two seasons before landing with Cleveland in 1984-85. A 1988 trade to Phoenix gave him a chance to start. West led the league in field goal accuracy in 1989-90. He has led the Suns in rebounding and blocked shots each of the past two years.

Strengths: West is a workhorse who has made himself one of the NBA's better shot-blockers and interior defenders. He attacks both boards. West has made huge strides with his low-post offense and rarely takes a bad shot.

Weaknesses: Foul trouble traditionally plagues West, although he has improved greatly in that area. He becomes completely ineffective offensively when outside the paint. West does not possess any of the perimeter skills like ball-handling and passing. His free throw shooting has "improved" to around 65 percent.

Analysis: West's game is completely motored by physical strength and hard work. He is a power player all the way. While his scoring average has reached double figures only once in his career (1989-90), teams can no longer afford to ignore his offense altogether. Ignoring West's defense is impossible.

PLAYER SUMMARY

Will ....excel on defense
Can't ....score outside
Expect ....a physical style
Don't Expect ....bad shots
Fantasy Value $14-17
Card Value..8¢

COLLEGE STATISTICS

		G	FGP	FTP	RPG	PPG
79-80	OD	30	.475	.370	7.1	4.8
80-81	OD	28	.527	.578	10.3	10.9
81-82	OD	30	.610	.531	10.0	15.7
82-83	OD	29	.569	.491	10.8	14.4
Totals		117	.559	.514	9.5	11.4

NBA REGULAR-SEASON STATISTICS

		G	MIN	FGs FG	FGs PCT	3-PT FGs FG	3-PT FGs PCT	FTs FT	FTs PCT	Rebounds OFF	Rebounds TOT	AST	STL	BLK	PTS	PPG
83-84	DAL	34	202	15	.357	0	.000	7	.318	19	46	13	1	15	37	1.1
84-85	MIL/CLE	66	888	106	.546	0	.000	43	.494	90	251	15	13	49	255	3.9
85-86	CLE	67	1172	113	.541	0	.000	54	.524	97	322	20	27	62	280	4.2
86-87	CLE	78	1333	209	.543	0	.000	89	.514	126	339	41	22	81	507	6.5
87-88	CLE/PHO	83	2098	316	.551	0	.000	170	.596	165	523	74	47	147	802	9.7
88-89	PHO	82	2019	243	.653	0	.000	108	.535	167	551	39	35	187	594	7.2
89-90	PHO	82	2399	331	.625	0	.000	199	.691	212	728	45	36	184	861	10.5
90-91	PHO	82	1957	247	.647	0	.000	135	.655	171	564	37	32	161	629	7.7
Totals		574	12068	1580	.588	0	.000	805	.589	1047	3324	284	213	886	3965	6.9

RANDY WHITE

Team: Dallas Mavericks
Position: Forward
Height: 6'8" **Weight:** 249
Birthdate: November 4, 1967
NBA Experience: 2 years

College: Louisiana Tech
Acquired: 1st-round pick in 1989 draft
(8th overall)

Background: White was named American South Player of the Year as a senior at Louisiana Tech, where he drew comparisons to former Bulldog standout Karl Malone. Those comparisons began to cease in White's rookie year with Dallas, as he struggled to a .369 shooting campaign in which he did not get off the bench for 26 of the last 55 games. The 1990-91 season was much better for White, who nearly tripled his scoring and rebounding numbers and started 29 times.

Strengths: White is strong, athletic, and hits the boards. A former college center, he is willing to bang. He shows good range on his jump shot, although he has not hit it with any regularity. He runs the floor aggressively and finishes well on the break.

Weaknesses: The transition from inside to outside is taking longer than the Mavericks had hoped. White has yet to hit 40 percent from the field and is much worse from 3-point range. Defensively, he is not quick enough to guard the league's explosive small forwards and often picks up fouls. He accounted for six of the Mavs' 14 foul-outs in 1990-91.

Analysis: As much as White has improved, the advantages of having an inside-outside player are nullified when he connects on less than four out of every ten shots and commits a lot of fouls. White played with his back to the basket in college and has much to learn about facing the hoop on the NBA level.

PLAYER SUMMARY

Will ....play physically
Can't.............................shoot straight
Expect ....more improvement
Don't Expect..............50-pct. shooting
Fantasy Value $1-2
Card Value...8¢

COLLEGE STATISTICS

		G	FGP	FTP	RPG	PPG
85-86	LAT	34	.520	.667	4.6	9.2
86-87	LAT	30	.575	.677	6.5	12.6
87-88	LAT	31	.638	.640	11.6	18.6
88-89	LAT	32	.600	.747	10.5	21.2
Totals		127	.592	.689	8.3	15.3

NBA REGULAR-SEASON STATISTICS

		G	MIN	FGs FG	FGs PCT	3-PT FGs FG	3-PT FGs PCT	FTs FT	FTs PCT	Rebounds OFF	Rebounds TOT	AST	STL	BLK	PTS	PPG
89-90	DAL	55	707	93	.369	1	.071	50	.562	78	173	21	24	6	237	4.3
90-91	DAL	79	1901	265	.398	6	.162	159	.707	173	504	63	81	44	695	8.8
Totals		134	2608	358	.390	7	.137	209	.666	251	677	84	105	50	932	7.0

DOMINIQUE WILKINS

Team: Atlanta Hawks
Position: Forward
Height: 6'8" **Weight:** 200
Birthdate: January 12, 1960
NBA Experience: 9 years

College: Georgia
Acquired: Draft rights traded from
Jazz for John Drew, Freeman
Williams, and cash, 9/82

Background: Born in France while his father was stationed in the Air Force, Wilkins was a first-team All-American at Georgia in 1982. He left college following his junior year. A six-time NBA All-Star, Wilkins led the league in scoring in 1986. 'Nique received league MVP consideration last season for the first time. Although he averaged less than 26 PPG (25.9) for the first time since 1983-84, Wilkins registered career highs in rebounds, assists, and treys.

Strengths: One of the NBA's all-time great scorers, he became more of a team player last season and the Hawks became a much better club. He still relies on his offense to turn a game around in a hurry. "The Human Highlight Film" can still dunk with more authority than anyone else in the league.

Weaknesses: He's never been able to use his left hand and he takes as many ill-advised shots as ever. Rather than going all out on defense and saving energy on offense, Dominique does just the opposite. He gets by on defense with athletic ability, not effort and intensity.

Analysis: Realizing that he's at least two-thirds of the way through his career and no closer to a championship than ever, Wilkins surprisingly changed his game last season. He's more interested in wins and losses than individual statistics. It's about time.

PLAYER SUMMARY
Will ....play team ball
Can't..........................focus on defense
Expect.....................better overall play
Don't Expect.............increased points
Fantasy Value $48-52
Card Value.......................................20¢

COLLEGE STATISTICS

		G	FGP	FTP	RPG	PPG
79-80	GA	16	.525	.730	6.5	18.6
80-81	GA	31	.533	.752	7.5	23.6
81-82	GA	31	.529	.644	8.1	21.3
Totals		78	.530	.699	7.5	21.6

NBA REGULAR-SEASON STATISTICS

				FGs		3-PT FGs		FTs		Rebounds						
		G	MIN	FG	PCT	FG	PCT	FT	PCT	OFF	TOT	AST	STL	BLK	PTS	PPG
82-83	ATL	82	2697	601	.493	2	.182	230	.682	226	478	129	84	63	1434	17.5
83-84	ATL	81	2961	684	.479	0	.000	382	.770	254	582	126	117	87	1750	21.6
84-85	ATL	81	3023	853	.451	25	.309	486	.806	226	557	200	135	54	2217	27.4
85-86	ATL	78	3049	888	.468	13	.186	577	.818	261	618	206	138	49	2366	30.3
86-87	ATL	79	2969	828	.463	31	.292	607	.818	210	494	261	117	51	2294	29.0
87-88	ATL	78	2948	909	.464	38	.295	541	.826	211	502	224	103	47	2397	30.7
88-89	ATL	80	2997	814	.464	29	.276	442	.844	256	553	211	117	52	2099	26.2
89-90	ATL	80	2888	810	.484	59	.322	459	.807	217	521	200	126	47	2138	26.7
90-91	ATL	81	3078	770	.470	85	.341	476	.829	261	732	265	123	65	2101	25.9
Totals		720	26610	7157	.469	282	.298	4200	.807	2122	5037	1822	1060	515	18796	26.1

EDDIE LEE WILKINS

Team: New York Knicks
Position: Forward/Center
Height: 6'10" **Weight:** 220
Birthdate: May 7, 1962
NBA Experience: 5 years

College: Gardner-Webb
Acquired: 6th-round pick in 1984 draft
(133rd overall)

Background: Wilkins set the school record for rebounds at Gardner-Webb College. Drafted on the sixth round by the Knicks in 1984, he collected a career-high 24 points in his first pro game. He sat out the 1985-86 season with a badly injured knee. Wilkins spent the 1987-88 campaign in the CBA. Last season's highlight was his 20-point performance at Portland. He missed a couple of weeks in January with a hyperextended elbow.

Strengths: He's not shy about shooting the ball, even in heavy traffic. To his credit, Wilkins has developed an effective jump hook and a fadeaway jumper. Both shots are nearly impossible to defend. He gets good position under the offensive glass.

Weaknesses: Wilkins couldn't dish out an assist if his life depended on it. He's a terrible passer and he can't dribble and chew gum at the same time. He'll bang you but do little else at the defensive end. Wilkins doesn't jump well and he's a miserable free throw shooter.

Analysis: Don't be surprised to see Pat Riley try and replace Wilkins with a younger, more effective low-post defender. Although he may stick for one more season, his days in New York appear numbered. Wilkins is a marginal player who wouldn't even be in the league if not for hard work and perseverance.

PLAYER SUMMARY

Will.............................score in a crowd
Can't ....pass
Expect ....competition for job
Don't Expect ....high FT pct.
Fantasy Value $1-3
Card Value...8¢

COLLEGE STATISTICS

		G	FGP	FTP	RPG	PPG
80-81	GW	36	.561	.638	6.7	12.1
81-82	GW	29	.620	.673	8.9	19.9
82-83	GW	32	.637	.715	10.6	24.8
83-84	GW	29	.569	.612	9.1	19.2
Totals		126	.601	.666	8.8	18.7

NBA REGULAR-SEASON STATISTICS

			FGs		3-PT FGs		FTs		Rebounds						
	G	MIN	FG	PCT	FG	PCT	FT	PCT	OFF	TOT	AST	STL	BLK	PTS	PPG
84-85 NY	54	917	116	.498	0	.000	66	.541	86	262	16	21	16	298	5.5
86-87 NY	24	454	56	.441	0	.000	27	.466	45	107	6	9	2	139	5.8
88-89 NY	71	584	114	.465	0	.000	61	.550	72	148	7	10	16	289	4.1
89-90 NY	79	972	141	.455	0	.000	89	.605	114	265	16	18	18	371	4.7
90-91 NY	68	668	114	.447	0	.000	51	.567	69	180	15	17	7	279	4.1
Totals	296	3595	541	.462	0	.000	294	.557	386	962	60	75	59	1376	4.6

GERALD WILKINS

Team: New York Knicks
Position: Guard
Height: 6'6" **Weight:** 195
Birthdate: September 11, 1963
NBA Experience: 6 years

College: Moberly Area; Tennessee-Chattanooga
Acquired: 2nd-round pick in 1985 draft (47th overall)

Background: Dominique's little brother, Gerald slam-dunked his way to three outstanding collegiate seasons at Tennessee-Chattanooga. His second pro season (1986-87) was his best. After missing just five games in his first five pro seasons, Wilkins missed 14 last year with a severely sprained ankle. Last year's scoring output was his lowest since his rookie campaign. He was the Knicks' Player of the Month for February.

Strengths: A super athlete who lets it all hang out in the open court, Wilkins can dominate a game for four or five minutes at a crack with his explosive style. He drives the entire lane with a single stride. He's a much better rebounder than he was earlier in his career and he handles the ball better.

Weaknesses: His flair for the dramatic often results in forced shots and bad passes. He's a streaky shooter who displays very average 3-point range. The halfcourt game's not his specialty. Defensively, he has a hard time staying focused against mediocre competition.

Analysis: Not a consistent enough perimeter shooter to start for a lot of teams, Wilkins may be most effective as a sixth man. More often than not, teams take their chances by packing their defense inside around Patrick Ewing and giving Wilkins the wide-open perimeter jumper.

PLAYER SUMMARY

Will ....score in the teens
Can't ....shoot treys
Expect..............crowd-pleasing dunks
Don't Expect ....intense defense
Fantasy Value $5-7
Card Value.......................................10¢

COLLEGE STATISTICS

		G	FGP	FTP	RPG	PPG
81-82	MA	39	.551	.770	5.9	18.5
82-83	T-C	30	.483	.661	3.8	12.6
83-84	T-C	23	.542	.695	4.0	17.3
84-85	T-C	32	.519	.632	4.6	21.0
Totals		124	.526	.685	4.7	17.5

NBA REGULAR-SEASON STATISTICS

				FGs		3-PT FGs		FTs		Rebounds						
		G	MIN	FG	PCT	FG	PCT	FT	PCT	OFF	TOT	AST	STL	BLK	PTS	PPG
85-86	NY	81	2025	437	.468	7	.280	132	.557	92	208	161	68	9	1013	12.5
86-87	NY	80	2758	633	.486	26	.351	235	.701	120	294	354	88	18	1527	19.1
87-88	NY	81	2703	591	.446	39	.302	191	.786	106	270	326	90	22	1412	17.4
88-89	NY	81	2414	462	.451	51	.297	186	.756	95	244	274	115	22	1161	14.3
89-90	NY	82	2609	472	.457	39	.312	208	.803	133	371	330	95	21	1191	14.5
90-91	NY	68	2164	380	.473	9	.209	169	.820	78	207	275	82	23	938	13.8
Totals		473	14673	2975	.463	171	.301	1121	.735	624	1594	1720	538	115	7242	15.3

BUCK WILLIAMS

Team: Portland Trail Blazers
Position: Forward
Height: 6'8" **Weight:** 225
Birthdate: March 8, 1960

NBA Experience: 10 years
College: Maryland
Acquired: Traded from Nets for Sam Bowie and a 1989 1st-round pick, 6/89

Background: Williams turned pro after his junior season at Maryland, where he ended his career ranked second on the school's all-time rebounding chart. He was named 1982 NBA Rookie of the Year and played in three All-Star Games as a New Jersey Net. He remains New Jersey's all-time leader in nine categories, including games, minutes, points, and rebounds. Williams helped lead Portland to the championship series after the 1989-90 season and made the NBA All-Defensive Team. He won the field goal percentage crown in 1990-91.

Strengths: Williams's calling card is rebounding, a trade he has mastered through the years. He also ranks among the very best low-post defenders. He denies his man inside position and forces him to play to his weaknesses. Offensively, Williams converts short jumpers and hooks and beats his man off the dribble. Williams brings a great attitude to work.

Weaknesses: Williams is a below-average passer who can be forced into turnovers. He does not handle the ball well in the open court, but rarely has to.

Analysis: Williams, one of the hardest working men the game has known, continues to lead by example. His business-like approach is contagious. Not by coincidence, Portland made the NBA Finals the year he arrived. Though most of his career has been spent with poor New Jersey teams, Williams is a winner.

PLAYER SUMMARY

Will	rebound, defend
Can't	pass well
Expect	high FG pct.
Don't Expect	lack of effort
Fantasy Value	$10-12
Card Value	8¢

COLLEGE STATISTICS

		G	FGP	FTP	RPG	PPG
78-79	MD	30	.583	.550	10.8	10.0
79-80	MD	24	.606	.664	10.1	15.5
80-81	MD	31	.647	.637	11.7	15.5
Totals		85	.615	.623	10.9	13.6

NBA REGULAR-SEASON STATISTICS

				FGs		3-PT FGs		FTs		Rebounds						
		G	MIN	FG	PCT	FG	PCT	FT	PCT	OFF	TOT	AST	STL	BLK	PTS	PPG
81-82	NJ	82	2825	513	.582	0	.000	242	.624	347	1005	107	84	84	1268	15.5
82-83	NJ	82	2961	536	.588	0	.000	324	.620	365	1027	125	91	110	1396	17.0
83-84	NJ	81	3003	495	.535	0	.000	284	.570	355	1000	130	81	125	1274	15.7
84-85	NJ	82	3182	577	.530	1	.250	336	.625	323	1005	167	63	110	1491	18.2
85-86	NJ	82	3070	500	.523	0	.000	301	.676	329	986	131	73	96	1301	15.9
86-87	NJ	82	2976	521	.557	0	.000	430	.731	322	1023	129	78	91	1472	18.0
87-88	NJ	70	2637	466	.560	1	1.000	346	.668	298	834	109	68	44	1279	18.3
88-89	NJ	74	2446	373	.531	0	.000	213	.666	249	696	78	61	36	959	13.0
89-90	POR	82	2801	413	.548	0	.000	288	.706	250	800	116	69	39	1114	13.6
90-91	POR	80	2582	358	.602	0	.000	217	.705	227	751	97	47	47	933	11.7
Totals		797	28483	4752	.554	2	.095	2981	.657	3065	9127	1189	715	782	12487	15.7

HERB WILLIAMS

Team: Dallas Mavericks
Position: Forward/Center
Height: 6'11" **Weight:** 242
Birthdate: February 16, 1958
NBA Experience: 10 years

College: Ohio St.
Acquired: Traded from Pacers for Detlef Schrempf and a 1990 or 1991 2nd-round pick, 2/89

Background: Williams left Ohio State as the school's all-time scoring leader. He spent his first seven-plus NBA seasons with Indiana, where he was a double-figure scorer every season. When he joined Dallas in 1988-89, he did so as the Pacers' career leader in 12 categories, including points, rebounds, minutes, and blocked shots. He led the Mavericks in blocks in 1989-90, but his 1990-91 season was cut 22 games short by bursitis in his right knee.

Strengths: Williams's main weapon is his defense, which the Mavericks sorely missed when he was injured. He is active on the interior—note his shot-blocking—and hustles back in transition. He can stick with both centers and power forwards.

Weaknesses: While defense is a strength, offense is not. His inside moves are predictable, although he will hit the short turnaround with regularity. In fact, the 1990-91 season was one of his better ones on the offensive end. He is not a good ball-handler and will not win awards for intensity.

Analysis: Williams meant a great deal to the Mavericks in 1990-91. Without him, they struggled to stop opposing big men from tearing them apart. His offense has become more a matter of opportunity than skill, but his defense remains solid.

PLAYER SUMMARY

Will ....play defense
Can't ....handle the ball
Expect ....decreased scoring
Don't Expect ....non-stop intensity
Fantasy Value $4-6
Card Value...5¢

COLLEGE STATISTICS

		G	FGP	FTP	RPG	PPG
77-78	OSU	27	.482	.659	11.4	16.7
78-79	OSU	31	.524	.669	10.5	19.9
79-80	OSU	29	.496	.660	9.1	17.6
80-81	OSU	27	.486	.688	8.0	16.0
Totals		114	.499	.669	9.7	17.6

NBA REGULAR-SEASON STATISTICS

				FGs		3-PT FGs		FTs		Rebounds						
		G	MIN	FG	PCT	FG	PCT	FT	PCT	OFF	TOT	AST	STL	BLK	PTS	PPG
81-82	IND	82	2277	407	.477	2	.286	126	.670	175	605	139	53	178	942	11.5
82-83	IND	78	2513	580	.499	0	.000	155	.705	151	583	262	54	171	1315	16.9
83-84	IND	69	2279	411	.478	0	.000	207	.702	154	554	215	60	108	1029	14.9
84-85	IND	75	2557	575	.475	1	.111	224	.657	154	634	252	54	134	1375	18.3
85-86	IND	78	2770	627	.492	1	.083	294	.730	172	710	174	50	184	1549	19.9
86-87	IND	74	2526	451	.480	0	.000	199	.740	143	543	174	59	93	1101	14.9
87-88	IND	75	1966	311	.425	0	.000	126	.737	116	469	98	37	146	748	10.0
88-89	IND/DAL	76	2470	322	.436	0	.000	133	.686	135	593	124	46	134	777	10.2
89-90	DAL	81	2199	295	.444	2	.222	108	.679	76	391	119	51	106	700	8.6
90-91	DAL	60	1832	332	.507	0	.000	83	.638	86	357	95	30	88	747	12.4
Totals		748	23389	4311	.474	6	.083	1655	.698	1362	5439	1652	494	1342	10283	13.7

JAYSON WILLIAMS

Team: Philadelphia 76ers
Position: Forward
Height: 6'10" **Weight:** 240
Birthdate: February 22, 1968
NBA Experience: 1 year

College: St. John's
Acquired: Traded from Suns for a
1993 1st-round pick, 10/90

Background: After guiding St. John's to an NIT title in 1989 as a junior (he was tourney MVP), Williams broke his foot halfway through his senior year. Originally drafted by Phoenix on the first round in 1990, Williams was dealt to the Sixers four months later in exchange for their top draft pick in 1993. He averaged almost ten minutes per game and recorded a double-double (points, rebounds) last April vs. the Pacers.

Strengths: Williams can put his head down and power his way inside or rely on his agility and smooth shooting stroke to nail a 15-foot turnaround jumper. He plays taller than 6'10" and loves to force contact.

Weaknesses: He tries so hard to impress Sixers coach Jim Lynam while he's in the game that he takes bad shots, turns the ball over, and takes too many chances on defense. Williams has to learn to settle down and get into the flow. He doesn't pass real well and he lost confidence in his shot late last season.

Analysis: He may never get the minutes he needs in Philly to move his game to the next level. Missing half of his senior season at St. John's and riding pine for much of his rookie season has adversely affected his game. This isn't the same player we saw three years ago at St. John's.

PLAYER SUMMARY

Will ....play more minutes
Can't ....go with the flow
Expect ....greater confidence
Don't Expect ....improved play
Fantasy Value $2-4
Card Value...10¢

COLLEGE STATISTICS

		G	FGP	FTP	RPG	PPG
87-88	STJ	28	.513	.600	5.1	9.9
88-89	STJ	31	.573	.702	7.9	19.5
89-90	STJ	13	.534	.613	7.8	14.6
Totals		72	.550	.652	6.8	14.9

NBA REGULAR-SEASON STATISTICS

			FGs		3-PT FGs		FTs		Rebounds						
		G	MIN	FG	PCT	FG	PCT	FT	PCT	OFF	TOT	AST	STL	BLK	PTS	PPG
90-91	PHI	52	508	72	.447	1	.500| 37	.661	41	111	16	9	6	182	3.5
Totals		52	508	72	.447	1	.500| 37	.661	41	111	16	9	6	182	3.5

JOHN WILLIAMS

Team: Cleveland Cavaliers
Position: Forward/Center
Height: 6'11" **Weight:** 238
Birthdate: August 9, 1961
NBA Experience: 5 years

College: Tulane
Acquired: 2nd-round pick in 1985
draft (45th overall)

Background: His involvement in an alleged point-fixing scandal at Tulane rocked the basketball world in the mid-1980s. He paced the Green Wave in scoring three of his four years. Williams was named to the NBA All-Rookie Team in 1987. A stress fracture in his foot shelved "Hot Rod" for nearly half of the 1990-91 season. He acquired his nickname as a baby for his habit of scooting across the floor backward.

Strengths: He can shoot, go hard to the basket, draw fouls, block shots, crash the boards, and muscle people off the ball. What more could you ask for in a power forward? Even with his high price tag, there's not a team in the league that doesn't covet him. Whether he starts or comes off the bench, plays 40 minutes or 25, he never complains. A clutch performer, the fourth quarter is often his best.

Weaknesses: He doesn't pass well, can barely put the ball on the floor, and commits too many turnovers in the open court. The 12- to 15-foot jumper he knocked down so regularly in 1989-90 disappeared last season.

Analysis: One of the highest paid players in the game today, Williams has the potential to justify earning those big bucks when healthy. His added bulk and long arms make him an opposing force in the paint. Hot Rod's best days are still ahead of him.

PLAYER SUMMARY

Will	cash big paychecks
Can't	play small forward
Expect	best year yet
Don't Expect	more injuries
Fantasy Value	$7-10
Card Value	5¢

COLLEGE STATISTICS

		G	FGP	FTP	RPG	PPG
81-82	TUL	28	.584	.662	7.2	14.8
82-83	TUL	31	.476	.703	5.4	12.4
83-84	TUL	28	.569	.761	7.9	19.4
84-85	TUL	28	.566	.774	7.8	17.8
Totals		115	.549	.731	7.0	16.0

NBA REGULAR-SEASON STATISTICS

			FGs		3-PT FGs		FTs		Rebounds						
	G	MIN	FG	PCT	FG	PCT	FT	PCT	OFF	TOT	AST	STL	BLK	PTS	PPG
86-87 CLE	80	2714	435	.485	0	.000	298	.745	222	629	154	58	167	1168	14.6
87-88 CLE	77	2106	316	.477	0	.000	211	.756	159	506	103	61	145	843	10.9
88-89 CLE	82	2125	356	.509	1	.250	235	.748	173	477	108	77	134	948	11.6
89-90 CLE	82	2776	528	.493	0	.000	325	.739	220	663	168	86	167	1381	16.8
90-91 CLE	43	1293	199	.463	0	.000	107	.652	111	290	100	36	69	505	11.7
Totals	364	11014	1834	.488	1	.143	1176	.736	885	2565	633	318	682	4845	13.3

JOHN WILLIAMS

Team: Washington Bullets
Position: Forward
Height: 6'9" **Weight:** 255
Birthdate: October 26, 1966
NBA Experience: 5 years

College: Louisiana St.
Acquired: 1st-round pick in 1986 draft
(12th overall)

Background: A product of the streets of Los Angeles, Williams played only two years of college ball at LSU. He was the SEC's top freshman in 1984-85 and a unanimous All-SEC pick in 1985-86. The past two years have been complete washouts for Williams. Eighteen games into the 1989-90 campaign, he severely injured his right knee and hasn't been the same since. He appeared in only 33 games last year after prolonging his rehab.

Strengths: When healthy, he can play all five positions—yes, even point guard. Few NBA players (not named Magic) can make that claim. He handles the ball, runs the floor, goes to the glass hard, and shoots a smooth mid-range jumper. His big, quick hands can make him deceivingly tough defensively.

Weaknesses: He doesn't know what the word "work" means. While supposedly rehabilitating his knee, he got lazy and let his weight balloon to well over 300 pounds. He doesn't realize that natural ability will take even the great ones only so far.

Analysis: This will be a make-or-break year for Williams. Hiding somewhere inside his oversized body is bona fide All-Star potential. Someone must try to squeeze it out of him. Although Williams is inconsistent and reluctant about his knee, it's not too late for him to become a star.

PLAYER SUMMARY

Will ....break coach's heart
Can't.............................avoid fast food
Expect .... make-or-break year
Don't Expect.................quick success
Fantasy Value $20-22
Card Value..8¢

COLLEGE STATISTICS

		G	FGP	FTP	RPG	PPG
84-85	LSU	29	.534	.765	6.6	13.4
85-86	LSU	37	.498	.774	8.5	17.8
Totals		66	.511	.771	7.6	15.8

NBA REGULAR-SEASON STATISTICS

				FGs		3-PT FGs		FTs		Rebounds						
		G	MIN	FG	PCT	FG	PCT	FT	PCT	OFF	TOT	AST	STL	BLK	PTS	PPG
86-87	WAS	78	1773	283	.454	8	.222	144	.646	130	366	191	129	30	718	9.2
87-88	WAS	82	2428	427	.469	5	.132	188	.734	127	444	232	117	34	1047	12.8
88-89	WAS	82	2413	438	.466	19	.268	225	.776	158	573	356	142	70	1120	13.7
89-90	WAS	18	632	130	.474	2	.111	65	.774	27	136	84	21	9	327	18.2
90-91	WAS	33	941	164	.417	10	.244	73	.753	42	177	133	39	6	411	12.5
Totals		293	8187	1442	.459	44	.216	695	.732	484	1696	996	448	149	3623	12.4

KEN WILLIAMS

Team: Indiana Pacers
Position: Forward
Height: 6'9" **Weight:** 205
Birthdate: June 9, 1969
NBA Experience: 1 year

College: Barton County
Acquired: 2nd-round pick in 1990 draft (46th overall)

Background: Recognized as one of the top five high school players in America in 1988, Williams was recruited by North Carolina but never enrolled due to poor grades. He played one year of junior college ball in Kansas. The Pacers were impressed enough with his Chicago pre-draft camp showing to select him in 1990. Despite averaging only seven minutes per game as a rookie, he was third on the team in blocks.

Strengths: An excellent athlete who can run the floor all day long, Williams knows how to score when given the chance (which isn't often). He passes and jumps exceptionally well and he's better defensively than a lot of players his age. Williams grabbed a lot of offensive rebounds in limited minutes last year. He doesn't turn 23 until June.

Weaknesses: He's a big forward playing in a small forward's body. Rather than shoot from the wing, he'd rather post up inside. Problem is, he's not big enough (205 pounds) to operate in the paint. Although he shows an occasional glimmer of brilliance, Williams is plagued by his lack of all-around basketball knowledge.

Analysis: He has a lot to learn. He needs to mature on and off the court. Had he stayed in college for four years, he'd be in this coming year's draft class. Williams's future could ultimately depend on how patient the Pacers can afford to be. He really needs a year of seasoning in Europe or the CBA.

PLAYER SUMMARY

Will...........................have his moments
Can't...........................play big forward
Expect...............gradual improvement
Don't Expect.......................heady play
Fantasy Value.................................$1-3
Card Value..8¢

COLLEGE STATISTICS

		G	FGP	FTP	RPG	PPG
88-89	BC	31	—	—	9.0	20.5
Totals		31	—	—	9.0	20.5

NBA REGULAR-SEASON STATISTICS

				FGs		3-PT FGs		FTs		Rebounds						
		G	MIN	FG	PCT	FG	PCT	FT	PCT	OFF	TOT	AST	STL	BLK	PTS	PPG
90-91	IND	75	527	93	.520	0	.000	34	.680	56	131	31	11	31	220	2.9
Totals		75	527	93	.520	0	.000	34	.680	56	131	31	11	31	220	2.9

MICHEAL WILLIAMS

Team: Indiana Pacers
Position: Guard
Height: 6'2" **Weight:** 175
Birthdate: July 23, 1966
NBA Experience: 3 years

College: Baylor
Acquired: Signed as a free agent, 8/90

Background: A two-time all-league selection at Baylor, Williams has been around. A member of Detroit's world-championship team in 1988-89, he spent the following season with Phoenix, Dallas, Charlotte, and the CBA's Rapid City Thrillers. He was signed as a free agent by Indiana in August 1990. Williams displaced Vern Fleming as the Pacers' starting point guard last season (37 starts). He led the team in steals and ranked second in assists. Until last season, his name had always been spelled M-I-C-H-A-E-L.

Strengths: His blistering speed and tough defense have won him over with coach Bob Hill and the Pacer fans. He's the most well-liked guy on the Indiana team. Williams possesses a lightning-quick first step and an above-average pull-up jumper. He shoots 88 percent from the line.

Weaknesses: Williams is a scorer trapped in a point guard's body. He does a nice job of pushing the ball up the floor, but his entry passes too often result in turnovers. Simply put, he's not accustomed to quarterbacking a club for 30-to-35 minutes a game.

Analysis: Nothing more than a journeyman at this time last year, the 1990-91 season was a very good one for Williams. With a little added seasoning, he could handle the point for the Pacers for many years to come.

PLAYER SUMMARY

Will ....start full-time
Can't ....see the entire floor
Expect............................added maturity
Don't Expect.............................10 APG
Fantasy Value $4-6
Card Value......................................10¢

COLLEGE STATISTICS

		G	FGP	FTP	RPG	PPG
84-85	BAY	28	.487	.793	2.4	14.6
85-86	BAY	22	.462	.806	2.9	13.0
86-87	BAY	31	.475	.714	3.0	17.2
87-88	BAY	34	.505	.697	3.2	18.4
Totals		115	.485	.738	2.9	16.1

NBA REGULAR-SEASON STATISTICS

		G	MIN	FGs		3-PT FGs		FTs		Rebounds		AST	STL	BLK	PTS	PPG
				FG	PCT	FG	PCT	FT	PCT	OFF	TOT					
88-89	DET	49	358	47	.364	2	.222	31	.660	9	27	70	13	3	127	2.6
89-90	PHO/CHA	28	329	60	.504	0	.000	36	.783	12	32	81	22	1	156	5.6
90-91	IND	73	1706	261	.499	1	.143	290	.879	49	176	348	150	17	813	11.1
Totals		150	2393	368	.477	3	.158	357	.844	70	235	499	185	21	1096	7.3

REGGIE WILLIAMS

Team: Denver Nuggets
Position: Guard
Height: 6'7" **Weight:** 195
Birthdate: March 5, 1964

NBA Experience: 4 years
College: Georgetown
Acquired: Signed as a free agent, 1/91

Background: Williams was a consensus All-American and Big East Player of the Year as a senior at Georgetown. He was named NCAA tournament MVP when the Hoyas won the title in 1984. He has not been nearly as successful as a pro. He was a letdown in L.A. (with the Clippers), Cleveland, and San Antonio, and was released by the Spurs in 1990-91. After being signed by Denver two weeks later, Williams went on to average 16.1 PPG for the Nuggets. He finished 15th in the league in 3-point accuracy (.363).

Strengths: Williams is as his best in a racehorse game, which explains his resurrection as a Denver Nugget. He runs the floor and finishes well. He has 3-point range on his jumper and a scorer's mentality.

Weaknesses: Erratic shooting has hurt Williams throughout his NBA career. His biggest problem, however, has come from within. He lost confidence in himself early on; his shooting accuracy was less than 36 percent in his rookie year. Williams does not handle the ball well for a guard and is too frail and uninterested to play good defense.

Analysis: Many thought Williams was a sure-fire star coming out of college, but it never came close to happening. Some of the skills were there, but not the effort or the intensity. Williams should continue to score in Denver, where the talent is thin and the pace quick. Whether he will ever reach his expectations is doubtful.

PLAYER SUMMARY

Will ....run the court
Can't ....fulfill expectations
Expect ....streaky shooting
Don't Expect ....adequate defense
Fantasy Value $1-2
Card Value...5¢

COLLEGE STATISTICS

		G	FGP	FTP	RPG	PPG
83-84	GEOR	37	.433	.768	3.5	9.1
84-85	GEOR	35	.506	.755	5.7	11.9
85-86	GEOR	32	.528	.732	8.2	17.6
86-87	GEOR	34	.482	.804	8.6	23.6
Totals		138	.490	.768	6.4	15.3

NBA REGULAR-SEASON STATISTICS

		G	MIN	FGs FG	FGs PCT	3-PT FGs FG	3-PT FGs PCT	FTs FT	FTs PCT	Rebounds OFF	Rebounds TOT	AST	STL	BLK	PTS	PPG
87-88	LAC	35	857	152	.356	13	.224	48	.727	55	118	58	29	21	365	10.4
88-89	LAC	63	1303	260	.438	30	.288	92	.754	70	179	103	81	29	642	10.2
89-90	LAC/CLE/SA															
		47	743	131	.388	6	.162	52	.765	28	83	53	32	14	320	6.8
90-91	SA/DEN	73	1896	384	.449	57	.363	166	.843	133	306	133	113	41	991	13.6
Totals		218	4799	927	.419	106	.298	358	.790	286	686	347	255	105	2318	10.6

SCOTT WILLIAMS

Team: Chicago Bulls
Position: Center
Height: 6'10" **Weight:** 230
Birthdate: August 21, 1968
NBA Experience: 1 year

College: North Carolina
Acquired: Signed as a free agent, 7/90

Background: Dean Smith's first West Coast recruit, Williams paced Carolina in rebounding and blocked shots as a senior. Great personal tragedy affected his early development at UNC. After being bypassed in the 1990 NBA draft, Williams was signed by the Bulls as a free agent. He was the only rookie on the NBA champs' squad. Williams appeared in 51 regular-season games and logged a career-high ten points at Denver in November.

Strengths: He gives the Bulls size, shot-blocking ability, and gutty low-post defense. Williams is very agile and he possesses a nice shooting touch. His big, strong hands bolster his game under the boards. He's rarely caught out of position.

Weaknesses: Williams needs to develop more effective post moves and better overall knowledge of the pro game. While sitting on the Bulls' bench last season, his mind often wandered. When he does play, he's inconsistent and foul-prone. He's been plagued by shoulder separations throughout his career.

Analysis: He solidified a spot on last year's team with a decent post-season effort. Williams's rare combination of strength and quickness make him one of the game's more intriguing young defensive stoppers. He'll take a championship ring any day over seeing more minutes on a lesser team.

PLAYER SUMMARY

Will ....play low-post defense
Can't.....................create his own shot
Expect ....further development
Don't Expect ....much more PT
Fantasy Value $4-6
Card Value...5¢

COLLEGE STATISTICS

		G	FGP	FTP	RPG	PPG
86-87	NC	36	.497	.558	4.2	5.5
87-88	NC	34	.572	.673	6.4	12.8
88-89	NC	35	.556	.654	7.3	11.4
89-90	NC	33	.554	.615	7.3	14.5
Totals		138	.551	.636	6.2	10.9

NBA REGULAR-SEASON STATISTICS

			FGs		3-PT FGs		FTs		Rebounds						
	G	MIN	FG	PCT	FG	PCT	FT	PCT	OFF	TOT	AST	STL	BLK	PTS	PPG
90-91 CHI	51	337	53	.510	1	.500	20	.714	42	98	16	12	13	127	2.5
Totals	51	337	53	.510	1	.500	20	.714	42	98	16	12	13	127	2.5

KEVIN WILLIS

Team: Atlanta Hawks
Position: Forward/Center
Height: 7'0" **Weight:** 235
Birthdate: September 6, 1962
NBA Experience: 6 years

College: Michigan St.
Acquired: 1st-round pick in 1984 draft (11th overall)

Background: Tops in the Big Ten in rebounding and field goal percentage as a junior at Michigan State, Willis received all-league mention as a senior. He also played in the 1983 World University Games. Willis sat out the 1988-89 season with a broken left foot. Last year, he ranked second on the team in rebounds and fifth in scoring. He co-owns Atlanta's most popular leather store.

Strengths: Willis is a definite asset offensively. He runs the floor exceptionally well for a seven-footer, and he goes to the offensive glass hard. A quick, little jump hook is his best shot. He's developed a useful medium-range baseline jumper.

Weaknesses: Added muscle makes him look good in a tank top but it hasn't helped his shooting touch. Willis's hands are small and his arms are short. He doesn't block as many shots as he should. He's got no business putting the ball on the floor as often as he does. During his 1988-89 layoff, he fell out of favor with management by failing to adhere to his rehab program and not attending games.

Analysis: Willis never has been able to duplicate his 1986-87 success, when he was on the verge of becoming an NBA All-Star. When he's not feeling too sorry for himself, he still enjoys his moments, but they're far too sporadic. A change of scenery could be what he needs.

PLAYER SUMMARY

Will..........................have his moments
Can't.................make the logical pass
Expect...............................selfish play
Don't Expect.......................an All-Star
Fantasy Value................................$6-8
Card Value..5¢

COLLEGE STATISTICS

		G	FGP	FTP	RPG	PPG
81-82	MSU	27	.474	.567	4.2	6.0
82-83	MSU	27	.596	.514	9.6	13.3
83-84	MSU	25	.492	.661	7.7	11.0
Totals		79	.530	.579	7.1	10.1

NBA REGULAR-SEASON STATISTICS

				FGs		3-PT FGs		FTs		Rebounds						
		G	MIN	FG	PCT	FG	PCT	FT	PCT	OFF	TOT	AST	STL	BLK	PTS	PPG
84-85	ATL	82	1785	322	.467	2	.222	119	.657	177	522	36	31	49	765	9.3
85-86	ATL	82	2300	419	.517	0	.000	172	.654	243	704	45	66	44	1010	12.3
86-87	ATL	81	2626	538	.536	1	.250	227	.709	321	849	62	65	61	1304	16.1
87-88	ATL	75	2091	356	.518	0	.000	159	.649	235	547	28	68	42	871	11.6
89-90	ATL	81	2273	418	.519	2	.286	168	.683	253	645	57	63	47	1006	12.4
90-91	ATL	80	2373	444	.504	4	.400	159	.668	259	704	99	60	40	1051	13.1
Totals		481	13448	2497	.512	9	.237	1004	.672	1488	3971	327	353	283	6007	12.5

KENNARD WINCHESTER

Team: Houston Rockets
Position: Guard
Height: 6'5" **Weight:** 212
Birthdate: September 3, 1966
NBA Experience: 1 year

College: James Madison; Averett
Acquired: Signed as a free agent, 9/90

Background: Winchester attended James Madison before transferring to Division III Averett College in Virginia and averaging more than 20 points and nine rebounds per game as a senior. He was bypassed in the NBA draft and spent a year playing pro ball in Argentina before earning a chance with Houston in 1990 training camp. He stuck with the Rockets and played in 64 games as a rookie.

Strengths: Winchester brings great size and strength to the backcourt and can post up smaller defenders for easy buckets. He can get his shot off the dribble and possesses 3-point range (8-for-20 as a rookie). Winchester's size and good leaping ability give him rebounding potential. His work ethic is exemplary.

Weaknesses: Although teammates were calling him "Winchester Rifle" in the preseason, Kennard was terribly inconsistent from the perimeter, as his 40-percent shooting attests. A forward in college, he is not a steady playmaker and is prone to coughing up the ball (more turnovers than assists in 1990-91). His size helps on defense, but quick guards pose big problems.

Analysis: Winchester was determined to make the most of his shot at the NBA, and he did just that. Coaches like his ability to get his own shots and his size in the post. To stick around, he must prove he can hit the outside shot with some degree of consistency.

PLAYER SUMMARY

Will......................post up small guards
Can't.......................pose as playmaker
Expect..................improved accuracy
Don't Expect.......national recognition
Fantasy Value..............................$1-2
Card Value...5¢

COLLEGE STATISTICS

		G	FGP	FTP	RPG	PPG
84-85	JM	20	.455	.278	1.0	3.3
85-86	JM	30	.508	.763	5.7	13.6
86-87	JM	28	.461	.767	6.4	16.1
88-89	AVER	17	.569	.716	9.1	20.2
Totals		95	.502	.714	5.5	13.3

NBA REGULAR-SEASON STATISTICS

			FGs		3-PT FGs		FTs		Rebounds						
		G	MIN	FG	PCT	FG	PCT	FT	PCT	OFF	TOT	AST	STL	BLK	PTS	PPG
90-91	HOU	64	607	98	.400	8	.400	35	.778	34	67	25	16	13	239	3.7
Totals		64	607	98	.400	8	.400	35	.778	34	67	25	16	13	239	3.7

JOE WOLF

Team: Denver Nuggets
Position: Center
Height: 6'11" **Weight:** 230
Birthdate: December 17, 1964
NBA Experience: 4 years

College: North Carolina
Acquired: Signed as a free agent, 10/90

Background: Wolf earned All-Atlantic Coast Conference honors as a senior at North Carolina and left as the Tar Heels' 12th-leading career rebounder. The first three years of his pro career were spent with the Clippers, where he served mostly as back-up center and forward. He started 32 of his last 33 games with Denver in 1990-91, averaging 12.8 points and 8.5 rebounds over the last four games.

Strengths: Wolf has nice touch and good range, though he hasn't been steady from the perimeter since college. His .451 accuracy in 1990-91 was his best. Wolf has developed a decent hook shot and passes well for a big man.

Weaknesses: Intensity has been a career-long struggle for Wolf, who seemed comfortable in his back-up role until he started turning it up near the end of his first year in Denver. He plays with minimal power, which clearly hurts him on defense and under the boards.

Analysis: If Wolf could not contribute much with the Clippers, where can he contribute? In 1990-91, the answer was Denver. He enjoyed his best year, which does not really say much. Wolf must take his success from late in the 1990-91 season and continue playing well when it counts. There is offensive potential, but his production and motivation have not been reliable.

PLAYER SUMMARY

Will ....shoot from 20
Can't ....maintain intensity
Expect ....better rebounding
Don't Expect..................assertiveness
Fantasy Value $1-2
Card Value..5¢

COLLEGE STATISTICS

		G	FGP	FTP	RPG	PPG
83-84	NC	30	.481	.758	2.8	3.4
84-85	NC	30	.566	.781	5.3	9.1
85-86	NC	34	.532	.712	6.6	10.0
86-87	NC	34	.571	.793	7.1	15.2
Totals		128	.551	.765	5.5	9.6

NBA REGULAR-SEASON STATISTICS

				FGs		3-PT FGs		FTs		Rebounds							
		G	MIN	FG	PCT	FG	PCT	FT	PCT	OFF	TOT	AST	STL	BLK	PTS	PPG
87-88	LAC	42	1137	136	.407	3	.200	45	.833	51	187	98	38	16	320	7.6
88-89	LAC	66	1450	170	.423	2	.143	44	.688	83	271	113	32	16	386	5.8
89-90	LAC	77	1325	155	.395	5	.200	55	.775	63	232	62	30	24	370	4.8
90-91	DEN	74	1593	234	.451	2	.133	69	.831	136	400	107	60	31	539	7.3
Totals		259	5505	695	.422	12	.174	213	.783	333	1090	380	160	87	1615	6.2

DAVID WOOD

Team: Houston Rockets
Position: Forward
Height: 6'9" **Weight:** 230
Birthdate: November 30, 1964
NBA Experience: 2 years

College: Skagit Valley; Nevada-Reno
Acquired: Signed as a free agent, 8/90

Background: Wood was a center at Nevada-Reno, where he transferred after beginning his college career at Skagit Valley Junior College. He played two games with Chicago in 1989, but most of his pro career has been logged in the CBA and in Europe, where he was nicknamed "The Gladiator." Wood signed with Houston in 1990-91, saw action in all 82 games, and made 13 starts.

Strengths: Wood does little that stands out to the casual observer, but he plays the game with heart and helps make his team better. He makes sound decisions. He is not afraid to mix it up, play defense, or take the big shot. He uses his strength on the boards. The best aspect of Wood's game is that he gives 100 percent every night.

Weaknesses: Wood has not shown his best jump shot and is not able to get it off as easily as he did in Europe, where he was a clutch performer. He lacks the great physical skills like speed, quickness, and leaping ability. Wood plays physical post defense but is much less effective on the perimeter.

Analysis: Wood's raw ability may not impress, but his heart does. The teams he played for in Europe were struggling when he joined them but wound up with championships. Though he will not post big numbers in the NBA, he does things to help his team win.

PLAYER SUMMARY

Will ....help win games
Can't......................shoot consistently
Expect............................all-out effort
Don't Expect............................10 PPG
Fantasy Value $2-4
Card Value...5¢

COLLEGE STATISTICS

		G	FGP	FTP	RPG	PPG
83-84	SV	29	.546	.704	7.3	9.7
84-85	SV	26	.609	.719	11.6	18.2
86-87	UNR	28	.511	.662	6.0	9.0
87-88	UNR	30	.472	.726	9.4	12.1
Totals		113	.538	.709	8.5	12.1

NBA REGULAR-SEASON STATISTICS

				FGs		3-PT FGs		FTs		Rebounds						
		G	MIN	FG	PCT	FG	PCT	FT	PCT	OFF	TOT	AST	STL	BLK	PTS	PPG
88-89	CHI	2	2	0	.000	0	.000	0	.000	0	0	0	0	0	0	0.0
90-91	HOU	82	1421	148	.424	28	.311	108	.812	107	246	94	58	16	432	5.3
Totals		84	1423	148	.424	28	.311	108	.812	107	246	94	58	16	432	5.1

ORLANDO WOOLRIDGE

Team: Detroit Pistons
Position: Forward
Height: 6'9" **Weight:** 215
Birthdate: December 16, 1959

NBA Experience: 10 years
College: Notre Dame
Acquired: Traded from Nuggets for
Scott Hastings, 8/91

Background: Woolridge ranked third in the nation in field goal percentage in his senior year at Notre Dame. He averaged more than 20 PPG for three straight years with Chicago and New Jersey. Woolridge entered a drug treatment center in February 1988, and he returned with the Lakers to become one of the top scorers off the bench in 1989-90. He was in the hunt for the 1991 scoring title with Denver, but he was dealt to Detroit after the season.

Strengths: Woolridge remains one of the NBA's most explosive and productive scorers, having recorded his 10,000th point in 1990-91. Few are willing to stand in front of his muscular frame when he puts the ball on the floor. He is a tremendous finisher who runs the floor well and has developed his jump shot.

Weaknesses: For his size, Woolridge should be a better rebounder. He likes to get out on the break rather than hitting the defensive glass. Some have knocked his attitude, but there were seemingly few problems during his last year in L.A. and his first in Denver.

Analysis: Woolridge is a natural scorer. There are few who beat their men off the dribble like he can, and the up-tempo game allows him plenty of chances for thunderous dunks. The Pistons need a frontcourt player who can score, and Woolridge fits the bill.

PLAYER SUMMARY	
Will	score off drives
Can't	focus on boards
Expect	20-plus PPG
Don't Expect	10 RPG
Fantasy Value	$8-10
Card Value	15-25¢

COLLEGE STATISTICS

		G	FGP	FTP	RPG	PPG
77-78	ND	24	.526	.485	2.1	4.1
78-79	ND	30	.573	.732	4.8	11.0
79-80	ND	27	.585	.692	6.9	12.2
80-81	ND	28	.650	.667	6.0	14.4
Totals		109	.595	.669	5.0	10.6

NBA REGULAR-SEASON STATISTICS

				FGs		3-PT FGs		FTs		Rebounds						
		G	MIN	FG	PCT	FG	PCT	FT	PCT	OFF	TOT	AST	STL	BLK	PTS	PPG
81-82	CHI	75	1188	202	.513	0	.000	144	.699	82	227	81	23	24	548	7.3
82-83	CHI	57	1627	361	.580	0	.000	217	.638	122	298	97	38	44	939	16.5
83-84	CHI	75	2544	570	.525	1	.500	303	.715	130	369	136	71	60	1444	19.3
84-85	CHI	77	2816	679	.554	0	.000	409	.785	158	435	135	58	38	1767	22.9
85-86	CHI	70	2248	540	.495	4	.174	364	.788	150	350	213	49	47	1448	20.7
86-87	NJ	75	2638	556	.521	1	.125	438	.777	118	367	261	54	86	1551	20.7
87-88	NJ	19	622	110	.445	0	.000	92	.708	31	91	71	13	20	312	16.4
88-89	LAL	74	1491	231	.468	0	.000	253	.738	81	270	58	30	65	715	9.7
89-90	LAL	62	1421	306	.556	0	.000	176	.733	49	185	96	39	46	788	12.7
90-91	DEN	53	1823	490	.498	0	.000	350	.797	141	361	119	69	23	1330	25.1
Totals		637	18418	4045	.521	6	.107	2746	.748	1062	2953	1267	444	453	10842	17.0

JAMES WORTHY

Team: Los Angeles Lakers
Position: Forward
Height: 6'9" **Weight:** 225
Birthdate: February 27, 1961

NBA Experience: 9 years
College: North Carolina
Acquired: 1st-round pick in 1982 draft
(1st overall)

Background: Worthy passed up his senior year at North Carolina after leading the Tar Heels to the 1982 NCAA championship. He was named MVP of the Final Four after his All-America junior campaign. The top overall draft choice in 1982, Worthy has shot above 53 percent in eight of his nine pro seasons. He has won NBA titles with the Lakers in 1985, 1987, and 1988, and was named MVP of the 1988 championship series. Worthy played in his sixth All-Star Game in 1990-91 and led the Lakers in scoring for the first time in his career.

Strengths: Worthy remains one of the NBA's best small forwards when it comes to putting the ball in the hoop. His baseline spin move is lethally quick and usually ends with a patented one-handed dunk. He sticks the baseline jumper as well, forcing defenders to play close. Worthy runs the floor well, is a fine passer when doubled, and is known for coming up big in the playoffs.

Weaknesses: The most troubling aspect of Worthy's game is a pair of knees which have a tendency to cause him pain. When his quickness is affected, he is not nearly the offensive force he is otherwise.

Analysis: Without Worthy, the Lakers would not have been the juggernaut they were during the 1980s. He has continued his big-time scoring in the 1990s and remains virtually impossible to stop (when healthy) in a one-on-one situation. Notice, the Lakers almost always go his way after a timeout.

PLAYER SUMMARY

Will	explode to the hoop
Can't	be stopped on spin move
Expect	20 PPG
Don't Expect	young knees
Fantasy Value	$27-30
Card Value	15¢

COLLEGE STATISTICS

		G	FGP	FTP	RPG	PPG
79-80	NC	14	.587	.600	7.4	12.5
80-81	NC	36	.500	.640	8.4	14.2
81-82	NC	34	.573	.674	6.3	15.6
Totals		84	.541	.652	7.4	14.5

NBA REGULAR-SEASON STATISTICS

				FGs		3-PT FGs		FTs		Rebounds						
		G	MIN	FG	PCT	FG	PCT	FT	PCT	OFF	TOT	AST	STL	BLK	PTS	PPG
82-83	LAL	77	1970	447	.579	1	.250	138	.624	157	399	132	91	64	1033	13.4
83-84	LAL	82	2415	495	.556	0	.000	195	.759	157	515	207	77	70	1185	14.5
84-85	LAL	80	2696	610	.572	0	.000	190	.776	169	511	201	87	67	1410	17.6
85-86	LAL	75	2454	629	.579	0	.000	242	.771	136	387	201	82	77	1500	20.0
86-87	LAL	82	2819	651	.539	0	.000	292	.751	158	466	226	108	83	1594	19.4
87-88	LAL	75	2655	617	.531	2	.125	242	.796	129	374	289	72	55	1478	19.7
88-89	LAL	81	2960	702	.548	2	.087	251	.782	169	489	288	108	56	1657	20.5
89-90	LAL	80	2960	711	.548	15	.306	248	.782	160	478	288	99	49	1685	21.1
90-91	LAL	78	3008	716	.492	26	.289	212	.797	107	356	275	104	35	1670	21.4
Totals		710	23937	5578	.546	46	.208	2010	.763	1342	3975	2107	828	556	13212	18.6

DANNY YOUNG

Team: Portland Trail Blazers
Position: Guard
Height: 6'4" **Weight:** 175
Birthdate: July 26, 1962
NBA Experience: 7 years

College: Wake Forest
Acquired: Signed as a free agent, 11/88

Background: Young graduated as Wake Forest's career leader in games played and was third on the all-time assists list. He was waived twice in his four-year stint in Seattle and spent time in the CBA during the 1984-85 season. He has served primarily as back-up point guard in his three years with Portland and stands seventh on the team's all-time list for 3-pointers made and attempted. He shot a career-low 38 percent from the field in 1990-91.

Strengths: Young is reliable with the ball, refraining from forcing plays when nothing is there. He is a decent 3-point shooter and an excellent free throw shooter (career-high .911 in 1990-91). He plays solid man-to-man defense and stays within his limitations in all areas.

Weaknesses: Normally a decent shooter, Young's percentage fell off a cliff in 1990-91. Less than 40-percent shooting does not give an NBA player much job security. While he is a steady passer and ball-handler, Young does not possess the quickness to create much offense on his own. He goes with what's there.

Analysis: Young has been a capable back-up who does not hurt his team, but his declining shooting eye is a source of concern. If he continues to struggle when left open on the outside, he will not warrant much playing time for a contending team. Otherwise, he is adequate but unspectacular.

PLAYER SUMMARY

Will ....run the offense
Can't ....show much creativity
Expect ....limited minutes
Don't Expect ....the spectacular
Fantasy Value $1-3
Card Value...........................5¢

COLLEGE STATISTICS

		G	FGP	FTP	RPG	PPG
80-81	WF	29	.496	.688	1.3	5.1
81-82	WF	30	.508	.714	2.5	10.6
82-83	WF	31	.457	.713	2.1	12.8
83-84	WF	32	.456	.707	1.8	9.6
Totals		122	.475	.708	1.9	9.6

NBA REGULAR-SEASON STATISTICS

		G	MIN	FGs FG	FGs PCT	3-PT FGs FG	3-PT FGs PCT	FTs FT	FTs PCT	Rebounds OFF	Rebounds TOT	AST	STL	BLK	PTS	PPG
84-85	SEA	3	26	2	.200	0	.000	0	.000	0	3	2	3	0	4	1.3
85-86	SEA	82	1901	227	.506	24	.324	90	.849	29	120	303	110	9	568	6.9
86-87	SEA	73	1482	132	.458	29	.367	59	.813	23	113	353	74	3	352	4.8
87-88	SEA	77	949	89	.408	22	.286	43	.811	18	75	218	52	2	243	3.2
88-89	POR	48	952	115	.460	17	.340	50	.781	17	74	123	55	3	297	6.2
89-90	POR	82	1393	138	.421	16	.271	91	.813	29	122	231	82	4	383	4.7
90-91	POR	75	897	103	.380	36	.346	41	.911	22	75	141	50	7	283	3.8
Totals		440	7600	806	.444	144	.324	374	.829	138	582	1371	426	28	2130	4.8

1991 NBA Draft

FIRST ROUND

	Player	College	Team
1)	Larry Johnson	UNLV	Charlotte
2)	Kenny Anderson	Georgia Tech	New Jersey
3)	Billy Owens	Syracuse	Sacramento
4)	Dikembe Mutombo	Georgetown	Denver
5)	Steve Smith	Michigan St.	Miami
6)	Doug Smith	Missouri	Dallas
7)	Luc Longley	New Mexico	Minnesota
8)	Mark Macon	Temple	Denver
9)	Stacey Augmon	UNLV	Atlanta
10)	Brian Williams	Arizona	Orlando
11)	Terrell Brandon	Oregon	Cleveland
12)	Greg Anthony	UNLV	New York
13)	Dale Davis	Clemson	Indiana
14)	Rich King	Nebraska	Seattle
15)	Anthony Avent	Seton Hall	Atlanta
16)	Chris Gatling	Old Dominion	Golden State
17)	Victor Alexander	Iowa St.	Golden State
18)	Kevin Brooks	S.W. Louisiana	Milwaukee
19)	LaBradford Smith	Louisville	Washington
20)	John Turner	Phillips	Houston
21)	Eric Murdock	Providence	Utah
22)	LeRon Ellis	Syracuse	L.A. Clippers
23)	Stanley Roberts	Real Madrid	Orlando
24)	Rick Fox	North Carolina	Boston
25)	Shaun Vandiver	Colorado	Golden State
26)	Mark Randall	Kansas	Chicago
27)	Pete Chilcutt	North Carolina	Sacramento

SECOND ROUND

	Player	College	Team
28)	Kevin Lynch	Minnesota	Charlotte
29)	George Ackles	UNLV	Miami
30)	Rodney Monroe	N. Carolina St.	Atlanta
31)	Randy Brown	New Mexico St.	Sacramento
32)	Chad Gallagher	Creighton	Phoenix
33)	Donald Hodge	Temple	Dallas
34)	Myron Brown	Slippery Rock	Minnesota
35)	Mike Iuzzolino	St. Francis (PA)	Dallas
36)	Chris Corchiani	N. Carolina St.	Orlando
37)	Elliot Perry	Memphis St.	L.A. Clippers
38)	Joe Wylie	Miami (FL)	L.A. Clippers
39)	Jimmy Oliver	Purdue	Cleveland
40)	Doug Overton	La Salle	Detroit
41)	Sean Green	Iona	Indiana
42)	Steve Hood	James Madison	Sacramento
43)	Lamont Strothers	Chris. Newport	Golden State
44)	Alvaro Teheran	Houston	Philadelphia
45)	Bobby Phills	Southern	Milwaukee
46)	Richard Dumas	Israel	Phoenix
47)	Keith Hughes	Rutgers	Houston
48)	Isaac Austin	Arizona St.	Utah
49)	Greg Sutton	Oral Roberts	San Antonio
50)	Joey Wright	Texas	Phoenix
51)	Zan Tabak	Yugoslavia	Houston
52)	Anthony Jones	Oral Roberts	L.A. Lakers
53)	Von McDade	Wisconsin-Milwaukee	New Jersey
54)	Marcus Kennedy	Eastern Michigan	Portland

GEORGE ACKLES

Team: Miami Heat
Position: Forward/Center
Height: 6'9"
Weight: 215

Birthdate: July 4, 1967
College: Nevada-Las Vegas
Acquired: 2nd-round pick in 1991
draft (29th overall)

Background: Ackles, one of four Nevada-Las Vegas players taken in the 1991 draft, had a quiet, unspectacular career at UNLV. After spending his first two collegiate seasons at Garden City (Kansas) Community College, Ackles joined the Rebels in 1988, starting 27 games as a junior. He broke his wrist in the summer of 1989, missing UNLV's championship season as a medical redshirt. Last season, he averaged fewer points than any other UNLV starter but set a school record for blocked shots in a season with 77, as the Rebels went 34-1.

Strengths: One of the most intriguing players in the 1991 NBA draft, Ackles, once a star soccer goalie, is a terrific athlete who still is developing as a player. He is explosive off his feet, can handle the ball and run the floor, and is an outstanding shot-blocker. He is a competent defender.

Weaknesses: Ackles does not yet have any special basketball skills. He has limited shooting range and is a poor passer and free throw shooter. He needs time to develop, especially if converted to power forward.

Analysis: Miami needed shooters and rebounders to go with its nucleus of Sherman Douglas, Rony Seikaly, and Glen Rice. Steve Smith (No. 5 pick) is the shooter, Ackles the rebounder. However, it will take time for him to adjust to playing power forward. Starter Grant Long and back-up Alec Kessler split time at the position last year. Miami has been pursuing Cleveland power forward John Williams. If Williams is acquired, Ackles could be out of a job.

PLAYER SUMMARY	
Will	block shots
Can't	drill the jumper
Expect	a long-term project
Don't Expect	much PT
Fantasy Value	$8-10
Card Value	50-65¢

COLLEGE HIGHLIGHTS
- Second-team All-Big West, 1991
- Big West All-Tournament Team, 1991
- AP Honorable-Mention All-American, 1991

COLLEGE STATISTICS

		G	FGM	FGA	PCT	FTM	FTA	PCT	REB	AST	PTS	PPG
UNLV	88-89	33	81	150	.540	38	74	.514	166	19	200	5.6
UNLV	90-91	35	125	232	.539	37	63	.587	201	28	288	8.2
Totals		68	206	383	.538	75	137	.547	367	47	488	7.2

VICTOR ALEXANDER

Team: Golden State Warriors
Position: Center/Forward
Height: 6'9"
Weight: 265

Birthdate: August 31, 1969
College: Iowa St.
Acquired: 1st-round pick in 1991 draft
(17th overall)

Background: Alexander, a Detroit product, played sparingly his freshman season at Iowa State while serving as a back-up to Lafester Rhodes. The Cyclones listed Alexander at 265 pounds, but he often played at closer to 300. "Pasta" was a laughingstock as a freshman but exploded as a sophomore, finishing third in the Big Eight in scoring and rebounding. He had an outstanding senior season, finishing second to Doug Smith in Big Eight scoring.

Strengths: Alexander is an outstanding offensive player. He has surprising mobility, advanced post-up skills, a soft shooting touch, and tremendous hands. When he gets the ball within ten feet of the hoop, he's likely to get a basket, draw a foul, or both.

Weaknesses: There are doubts about Alexander's ability to keep up with the NBA pace. While he averaged 32.7 minutes per game as a senior, his stamina is questionable. He is turnover prone and isn't a good passer. He showed improvement as a free throw shooter last season, but he remains below average.

Analysis: The second of three first-round picks for Golden State, Alexander will battle Tyrone Hill for the starting spot at power forward, and Alton Lister for time at center. The Warriors, who hoped to draft Dikembe Mutombo, Luc Longley, or Rich King, figure to be pleased with Alexander. If he can keep his weight (285 in June) under control, he will be one of the draft's bargains.

PLAYER SUMMARY	
Will	score in bunches
Can't	say "no" at dinner
Expect	a solid career
Don't Expect	many assists
Fantasy Value	$6-8
Card Value	50-65¢

COLLEGE HIGHLIGHTS
- All-Big Eight, 1989 and 1991
- United States Team, World University Games, 1989

COLLEGE STATISTICS

		G	FGM	FGA	PCT	FTM	FTA	PCT	REB	AST	PTS	PPG
ISU	87-88	23	18	30	.600	3	6	.500	32	4	39	1.7
ISU	88-89	29	240	412	.583	97	149	.651	255	35	577	19.9
ISU	89-90	28	226	386	.585	100	173	.578	243	43	552	19.7
ISU	90-91	31	294	446	.659	136	201	.677	280	37	724	23.4
Totals		111	778	1274	.538	336	529	.635	810	119	1892	17.0

KENNY ANDERSON

Team: New Jersey Nets
Position: Guard
Height: 6'2"
Weight: 166

Birthdate: October 9, 1970
College: Georgia Tech
Acquired: 1st-round pick in 1991 draft
(2nd overall)

Background: A legend at New York City's Archbishop Malloy High, Anderson was an instant hit at Georgia Tech. He led the ACC in assists as a freshman, was fifth in scoring, and recorded the only triple-double in ACC history. When teammates Dennis Scott and Brian Oliver left for the NBA in 1990, Anderson was forced to carry Tech on his back. He looked to shoot more and pass less last season, and he appeared very tired by season's end. In two years, Anderson established a reputation as perhaps the finest college point guard ever.

Strengths: The left-handed Anderson is a terrific ball-handler, passer, penetrator, and team leader. He has a special ability to see the floor and take advantage of match-ups. A point guard with a scorer's mentality, Anderson has good range with his awkward-looking jumper, and he's a very good free throw shooter. Defensively, he relies on quick hands and superior anticipation.

Weaknesses: Anderson may have became too self-indulgent on the court last season. He lacks the bulk to get physical with the NBA's stronger point guards, and he may not yet have the stamina to withstand an 82-game season.

Analysis: New Jersey, expected to select Syracuse's Billy Owens with the No. 2 pick, opted for hometown hero Anderson, who should help drive Nets ticket sales. New Jersey needed a scoring guard to replace Reggie Theus, but general manager Willis Reed and coach Bill Fitch considered Anderson too good to pass up. He will challenge Mookie Blaylock for the starting spot at point guard.

PLAYER SUMMARY
Will ....distribute the ball
Can't ....handle bigger guards
Expect ....a Nate Archibald type
Don't Expect ....rebounds
Fantasy Value $8-10
Card Value ....75¢ -$1.00

COLLEGE HIGHLIGHTS
• UPI National Freshman of the Year, 1990
• AP first-team All-American, 1991
• ACC Rookie of the Year, 1990
• United States National Team, 1990

COLLEGE STATISTICS

		G	FGM	FGA	PCT	FTM	FTA	PCT	REB	AST	PTS	PPG
GT	89-90	35	283	549	.515	107	146	.733	193	185	721	20.6
GT	90-91	30	278	636	.437	155	187	.829	171	169	776	25.9
Totals		65	561	1185	.473	262	333	.787	364	454	1497	23.0

GREG ANTHONY

Team: New York Knicks
Position: Guard
Height: 6'2"
Weight: 190

Birthdate: October 15, 1967
College: Portland; Nevada-Las Vegas
Acquired: 1st-round pick in 1991 draft
(12th overall)

Background: Anthony spent his first college season at Portland, where he played shooting guard. Jerry Tarkanian moved him to point guard at UNLV and, although the transition wasn't smooth, Anthony eventually became one of the nation's best lead guards. He directed the Rebels to the national title in 1990. Anthony fouled out of UNLV's loss to Duke in the 1991 NCAA Final Four, which ended the Rebels' 45-game winning streak.

Strengths: A tremendous leader, Anthony was the glue that held UNLV together. He loves to compete and is extremely confident. He is a competent scorer. He is adept at the running game and can make long, baseball-style passes with accuracy. Anthony is an outstanding defensive disrupter.

Weaknesses: Anthony isn't a great shooter or ball defender (he usually guarded the opponent's shooting guard while at UNLV). He tends to gamble too much on defense. Playing at UNLV may have inflated his value; certainly opponents would have played him tougher had he been his team's best player.

Analysis: New York, 10-16 in playoff games in the Patrick Ewing era, needed a leader, and it may have found one in Anthony. At the very least, the charismatic Anthony will be a hit in Madison Square Garden. He was drafted to displace Mark Jackson, whom the Knicks soured on two years ago. Anthony will receive his schooling from 13-year veteran Maurice Cheeks, one of the best in the business.

PLAYER SUMMARY	
Will	provide leadership
Can't	score consistently
Expect	a rocky first year
Don't Expect	a starter
Fantasy Value	$8-10
Card Value	75¢ -$1.00

COLLEGE HIGHLIGHTS
- AP Honorable-Mention All-American, 1990 and 1991
- UPI Honorable-Mention All-American, 1991
- WCAC Freshman of the Year, 1987
- All-Big West, 1991

COLLEGE STATISTICS

		G	FGM	FGA	PCT	FTM	FTA	PCT	REB	AST	PTS	PPG
PORT	86-87	28	147	369	.398	100	144	.694	121	112	429	15.3
UNLV	88-89	36	155	350	.443	107	153	.699	102	239	464	12.9
UNLV	89-90	39	145	317	.457	101	148	.682	116	289	436	11.2
UNLV	90-91	35	141	309	.456	79	102	.775	89	310	406	11.6
Totals		138	588	1345	.437	387	547	.707	428	950	1735	12.6

STACEY AUGMON

Team: Atlanta Hawks
Position: Forward
Height: 6'8"
Weight: 206

Birthdate: August 1, 1968
College: Nevada-Las Vegas
Acquired: 1st-round pick in 1991 draft
(9th overall)

Background: Augmon, who played four positions for UNLV, established a reputation as the nation's finest defensive player over the past four seasons. After his freshman season, that defensive prowess earned him a berth on the U.S. Olympic Team. Augmon was a key player in UNLV's run to the national title in 1990, but his career ended on a sour note, as he was a non-factor in the Rebels' loss to Duke in the 1991 NCAA Final Four semifinals.

Strengths: Augmon has been compared to Dennis Rodman for his defensive ability. He has excellent quickness, blocks shots, has a huge wingspan, and can shut down most opponents one-on-one. Augmon runs the floor well, fills the lanes, and finishes on the break. He is a hard worker, and coachable.

Weaknesses: His outside shot once was atrocious; it now is barely passable. He's not a good free throw shooter. Augmon is above average in every other area, although some scouts suggest his performance was enhanced by other great players at UNLV.

Analysis: Atlanta, in the midst of rebuilding, was lucky to find Augmon available at No. 9. He had slipped in the draft because of his poor showing in the NCAA tournament. However, several teams covet Augmon, and the Hawks could use him as trade bait to fill other needs. Otherwise, he provides depth up front as a back-up to Dominique Wilkins and as a designated defender.

PLAYER SUMMARY

Will..............................run the floor
Can't.......................shoot from outside
Expect........................a defensive whiz
Don't Expect.........................an All-Star
Fantasy Value.............................$12-15
Card Value.............................75¢-$1.00

COLLEGE HIGHLIGHTS

- AP first-team All-American, 1991
- United States Olympic Team, 1988
- Big West MVP, 1989
- Henry Iba Corinthian Award (defensive player of the year) 1989,1990, and 1991

COLLEGE STATISTICS

		G	FGM	FGA	PCT	FTM	FTA	PCT	REB	AST	PTS	PPG
UNLV	87-88	34	117	204	.574	75	116	.647	206	64	311	9.2
UNLV	88-89	37	210	405	.519	106	160	.663	274	101	567	15.3
UNLV	89-90	39	210	380	.553	118	176	.671	270	143	554	14.2
UNLV	90-91	35	220	375	.587	101	139	.727	255	125	579	16.5
Totals		145	757	1364	.555	400	591	.677	1005	433	2011	13.7

ISAAC AUSTIN

Team: Utah Jazz
Position: Center
Height: 6'10"
Weight: 255

Birthdate: August 18, 1969
College: Arizona St.
Acquired: 2nd-round pick in 1991 draft (48th overall)

Background: Austin originally attended Kings River Junior College near his hometown of Gridley, California. Austin, whose older brother Alex played at Arizona State from 1985-90, was ASU head coach Bill Frieder's first recruit, signing in the spring of 1989. Austin improved steadily during his two seasons, as did the Sun Devils, who reached the NCAA tournament last season for the first time since 1981. Austin scored 25 points in a first-round upset of Rutgers and played well in a second-round loss to Arkansas.

Strengths: Austin has the necessary bulk to bang with NBA power forwards. He's a good athlete with above-average agility and hands, and quick feet. He is an excellent shooter facing the basket, with 15-foot range.

Weaknesses: Austin's biggest drawback is his poor physical condition. He's always out of shape. Though he's a competent rebounder, Austin is slow off his feet. He can't block shots, doesn't run the floor well, and is a below-average free throw shooter.

Analysis: Utah, which gambled on 7'2" Dartmouth center Walter Palmer in the 1990 draft, took another long shot with Austin. They hope he becomes a capable back-up to center Mark Eaton and power forward Karl Malone, who was second in the NBA in minutes played last season. Eaton's shot-blocking keys Utah's fastbreak, but Austin has far better offensive skills. He should make the team.

PLAYER SUMMARY

Will ....provide offense
Can't...................................stay in shape
Expect ....a battle to make it
Don't Expect ....great defense
Fantasy Value $4-6
Card Value ....35-50¢

COLLEGE HIGHLIGHTS

- All-Pac-10, 1991
- *Basketball Times* Honorable-Mention All-West, 1991
- *Basketball Weekly* Honorable-Mention All-Far West, 1991

COLLEGE STATISTICS

		G	FGM	FGA	PCT	FTM	FTA	PCT	REB	AST	PTS	PPG
ASU	89-90	31	164	300	.547	97	150	.647	192	27	425	13.7
ASU	90-91	30	189	331	.571	112	178	.629	262	57	490	16.3
Totals		61	353	631	.559	209	328	.637	454	84	915	15.0

ANTHONY AVENT

Team: Milwaukee Bucks
Position: Forward/Center
Height: 6'10"
Weight: 235
Birthdate: October 18, 1969

College: Seton Hall
Acquired: Draft rights traded from Nuggets for draft rights to Kevin Brooks, a 1994 2nd-round pick, and other considerations, 7/91

Background: Avent was forced to sit out his freshman season at Seton Hall under Prop 48 guidelines. He was Ramon Ramos's back-up as a sophomore, as The Hall went 31-7 and advanced to the NCAA title game, where it lost to Michigan. Avent moved into a starting role as a junior. He recorded 22 double-doubles last season as Seton Hall went 25-9 and advanced to the NCAA West Regional final, where it lost to UNLV. Avent was drafted 15th overall by Atlanta this summer, but his rights were traded to Milwaukee in a three-team deal.

Strengths: Avent's strengths are rebounding and defense. He is a very strong low-post defender, always plays hard, and has a good understanding of the team concept. He can score on the low blocks. Avent has shown continued improvement and could be a better pro than college player. He has a great work ethic.

Weaknesses: Avent isn't very instinctive; he's more of a self-made player. He's a below-average shooter who can't score facing the basket. He's a poor passer, especially in a fullcourt game, and is not particularly quick with his first step.

Analysis: Milwaukee acquired Avent in a three-way trade that sent the Bucks' first-round pick, small forward Kevin Brooks, to Denver, and Denver center Blair Rasmussen to Atlanta. Milwaukee's frontcourt—forwards Fred Roberts and Frank Brickowski, centers Danny Schayes and Moses Malone—is weak, so Avent should make the team. He has a chance to start by 1993.

PLAYER SUMMARY

Will ....make the team
Can't..........................score in bunches
Expect ....consistent effort
Don't Expect ....much flash
Fantasy Value $9-11
Card Value ....75¢-$1.00

COLLEGE HIGHLIGHTS

- Second-team All-Big East, 1991
- Big East All-Tournament Team, 1991
- AP Honorable-Mention All-American, 1991

COLLEGE STATISTICS

		G	FGM	FGA	PCT	FTM	FTA	PCT	REB	AST	PTS	PPG
SH	88-89	38	68	142	.456	32	49	.653	114	12	168	4.4
SH	89-90	28	119	244	.488	55	89	.618	262	47	293	10.5
SH	90-91	34	228	395	.577	150	200	.750	335	53	606	17.8
Totals		100	415	781	.531	237	338	.701	711	112	1067	10.7

TERRELL BRANDON

Team: Cleveland Cavaliers
Position: Guard
Height: 6'0"
Weight: 180

Birthdate: May 20, 1970
College: Oregon
Acquired: 1st-round pick in 1991 draft
(11th overall)

Background: Brandon led Portland's Grant High to the 1988 Oregon state championship, and he also won the state title in the triple-jump. He sat out his freshman year at Oregon under Prop 40 guidelines, then had two terrific seasons at point guard, during which time the Ducks went 28-29. Brandon opted to enter this year's NBA draft even though many basketball people advised him to stay at Oregon. Last season, Brandon led the Pac-10 in scoring and steals, was second in free throw percentage, and finished fifth in assists.

Strengths: Brandon is a terrific offensive player. He has good vision and court sense, is an excellent leaper with superb hang time, and is explosive with the ball. He has a quick release and a pull-up jump shot. He's strong for his size, charismatic, and loves to play the game.

Weaknesses: Brandon lacks experience and maturity and is shorter than the 6'0" Oregon listed him at. He's not a good defender, lacking intensity on the defensive end.

Analysis: Cleveland pulled the first big surprise of the draft, taking point guard Brandon despite its big need for a shooting guard. Brandon provides the Cavs with insurance should Mark Price not make it back from a serious knee injury. Cleveland signed veteran guard John Battle in July, which could seriously hurt Brandon's playing time.

PLAYER SUMMARY	
Will	provide excitement
Can't	stop his man
Expect	a future star
Don't Expect	immediate stardom
Fantasy Value	$5-7
Card Value	50-65¢

COLLEGE HIGHLIGHTS
- Pac-10 Player of the Year, 1991
- All-Pac-10, 1990 and 1991
- AP Honorable-Mention All-American, 1991

COLLEGE STATISTICS

		G	FGM	FGA	PCT	FTM	FTA	PCT	REB	AST	PTS	PPG
ORE	89-90	29	190	401	.474	97	129	.752	106	174	518	17.9
ORE	90-91	28	273	556	.491	159	187	.850	101	141	745	26.6
Totals		57	463	957	.484	256	316	.810	207	315	1263	22.2

KEVIN BROOKS

Team: Denver Nuggets
Position: Forward
Height: 6'8"
Weight: 200
Birthdate: October 29, 1969

College: S.W. Louisiana
Acquired: Draft rights traded from Bucks with a 1994 2nd-round pick and other considerations for Anthony Avent, 7/91

Background: Perhaps the most heralded recruit in Southwestern Louisiana history, Brooks, from nearby White Castle, Louisiana, was an immediate hit for the run-and-gun Ragin' Cajuns. He finished third among the nation's freshmen in scoring in 1988, behind Mark Macon and Richard Dumas. USL, 12-17 that season, went 58-31 over the next three seasons. Brooks ranks third behind Bo Lamar and Andrew Toney on the USL's all-time scoring list. His stock rose with a good showing at the post-season Orlando Classic. He was drafted 18th overall by Milwaukee but his rights were traded to the Nuggets.

Strengths: Offense is the name of Brooks's game. He has been compared to George Gervin and Alex English. He has outstanding shooting range, is a good ball-handler and passer, and can run the floor. He is versatile, can play small forward or off guard, and has a good feel for the game.

Weaknesses: Brooks isn't strong enough to defend forwards or quick enough to handle most guards. He lacks the bulk to bang inside and is a poor rebounder.

Analysis: Atlanta and Denver made a pre-draft deal, the Hawks drafting Anthony Avent with the 15th pick, then trading him to the Nuggets for Blair Rasmussen. The Nuggets promptly shipped Avent to Milwaukee for Brooks, who should fit superbly in coach Paul Westhead's up-tempo system. The Nuggets are weak at small forward, so Brooks should play a lot as a rookie.

PLAYER SUMMARY	
Will	score in bunches
Can't	clean offensive glass
Expect	a role player
Don't Expect	all-rookie season
Fantasy Value	$5-7
Card Value	35-50¢

COLLEGE HIGHLIGHTS
- American South Newcomer of the Year, 1988
- All-American South, 1989, 1990, and 1991
- AP Honorable-Mention All-American, 1991

COLLEGE STATISTICS

		G	FGM	FGA	PCT	FTM	FTA	PCT	REB	AST	PTS	PPG
SWL	87-88	27	179	317	.565	83	109	.761	170	42	453	16.8
SWL	88-89	29	218	418	.522	128	170	.753	158	48	600	20.7
SWL	89-90	29	225	451	.499	93	114	.816	204	61	583	20.1
SWL	90-91	31	261	507	.515	77	99	.778	187	47	658	21.2
Totals		116	883	1693	.522	381	492	.774	719	198	2294	19.8

MYRON BROWN

Team: Minnesota Timberwolves
Position: Guard
Height: 6'3"
Weight: 180

Birthdate: November 3, 1969
College: Slippery Rock
Acquired: 2nd-round pick in 1991 draft (34th overall)

Background: Ignored by Division I schools in his home state of Pennsylvania, "Flyin' Myron" went to Division II Slippery Rock, a school better known for its football team. Brown increased his scoring average in each of his four seasons, and averaged 25.1 points in 11 games vs. Division I competition. He was spectacular at the post-season Orlando Classic, winning a slam-dunk competition and finishing second to Rodney Monroe in a 3-point shooting contest.

Strengths: Brown has exciting physical attributes. He is quick, a terrific leaper, and runs the floor very well. He has a good all-around offensive game; he can shoot with range and direct an offense from the point. He is durable and an excellent free throw shooter.

Weaknesses: Brown lacks experience against top-level competition, and he'll have to show that he can defend NBA players. He's not aggressive and isn't a take-charge type. He lacks consistency with his outside shot.

Analysis: Brown is a scorer—he was called the Michael Jordan of Division II— but will fit best in the NBA as a point guard. Minnesota, with Pooh Richardson and Scott Brooks, can afford to bring him along slowly. The T-Wolves are thin in the backcourt, so Brown should make the team, though he won't make much of an impact this season.

PLAYER SUMMARY

Will ....provide excitement
Can't ....intimidate
Expect ....a back-up point guard
Don't Expect............an immediate star
Fantasy Value $2-4
Card Value ....25-35¢

COLLEGE HIGHLIGHTS

- Division II All-American, 1991
- Division II second-team All-American, 1990
- Pennsylvania State Athletic Conference Player of the Year, 1991

COLLEGE STATISTICS

		G	FGM	FGA	PCT	FTM	FTA	PCT	REB	AST	PTS	PPG
SR	87-88	28	196	395	.496	89	110	.809	150	55	516	18.4
SR	88-89	28	192	395	.486	131	159	.824	189	57	568	20.3
SR	89-90	29	246	522	.471	167	197	.848	189	88	709	24.4
SR	90-91	31	253	533	.475	251	306	.820	232	99	826	26.7
Totals		116	887	1845	.481	638	772	.826	760	299	2619	22.6

RANDY BROWN

Team: Sacramento Kings
Position: Guard
Height: 6'3"
Weight: 190

Birthdate: May 22, 1968
College: Houston; New Mexico St.
Acquired: 2nd-round pick in 1991 draft (31st overall)

Background: Brown, who wasn't highly recruited out of Chicago's Collins High, originally signed with Houston, where he was among the Southwest Conference leaders in assists as a sophomore. He left Houston in 1988, unhappy because the Cougars had signed prep star Derrick Daniels. Brown enrolled at Howard County (Texas) Junior College but didn't play basketball, then transferred to New Mexico State. He became one of the nation's top point guards, leading the Aggies to a 49-11 record in two seasons. He was the only non-UNLV player named first-team All-Big West in 1991.

Strengths: A good athlete, Brown was one of the quickest point guards in the 1991 NBA draft. He pushes the ball up the court, penetrates well, and is a good finisher. He's solid defensively. Brown is very aggressive and is outstanding pressuring the ball. He's an above-average rebounder and passer.

Weaknesses: His Achilles' heel is his outside shooting. He's very inconsistent, has poor mechanics, and lacks range. Brown struggles in halfcourt situations and is a below-average free throw shooter.

Analysis: Sacramento, undercut by New Jersey in its bid to draft point guard Kenny Anderson, may have found a diamond in the rough in Brown. He likely will back up incumbent starter Rory Sparrow and newcomer Spud Webb this year, but he could win the job outright by next season. Sparrow is entering his 12th NBA campaign; both he and Webb are best as reserves.

PLAYER SUMMARY

Will ....run and gun
Can't..........................score consistently
Expect......................an eventual starter
Don't Expect ....a Tim Hardaway
Fantasy Value $2-4
Card Value ....25-40¢

COLLEGE HIGHLIGHTS

- All-Big West, 1990 and 1991
- Finalist, United States National Team, 1990

COLLEGE STATISTICS

		G	FGM	FGA	PCT	FTM	FTA	PCT	REB	AST	PTS	PPG
HOU	86-87	28	42	83	.506	21	36	.583	75	81	105	3.8
HOU	87-88	29	64	142	.450	75	100	.750	83	162	203	7.0
NMS	89-90	31	131	294	.445	131	184	.712	106	109	409	13.2
NMS	90-91	29	110	276	.398	121	175	.691	116	187	351	12.1
Totals		117	347	795	.436	348	495	.703	380	539	1068	9.1

DARRIN CHANCELLOR

Team: Undrafted
Position: Guard
Height: 6'5"
Weight: 185

Birthdate: June 25, 1969
College: Southern Mississippi

Background: Playing in the Metro Conference with LaBradford Smith, Bimbo Coles, and teammate Clarence Weatherspoon, Chancellor received little notoriety. After playing only 148 minutes as a freshman for coach M.K. Turk, Chancellor led the Golden Eagles in scoring in each of the next three seasons while playing full-time. He averaged about 38 minutes per game as a sophomore, junior, and senior. He was the "Lightning" and Weatherspoon the "Thunder" as Southern Miss went to the NCAA tournament in 1990 and 1991, its first NCAA appearances ever.

Strengths: Chancellor is a good all-around shooting guard. He can take the ball to the hoop, shoot with range, and handle it in transition. He is aggressive and likes a challenge. He doesn't make many mistakes.

Weaknesses: He has poor shooting mechanics, though he consistently puts the ball in the basket. Chancellor is a below-average defensive player and rebounder, and he lacks any skill that would separate him from other fringe NBA prospects.

Analysis: Chancellor was projected as a late-second-round draft pick, but he was not among the 24 guards selected in the draft. He participated in summer rookie camps for Boston and Milwaukee. If Chancellor works on his defense in the CBA or elsewhere, he may eventually catch on with an NBA club.

PLAYER SUMMARY

Will ....stick some 3's
Can't ....be a stopper
Expect.....................a struggle to stick
Don't Expect ....a long career
Fantasy Value $3-5
Card Value ....25-35¢

COLLEGE HIGHLIGHTS

* All-Metro, 1991
* Second-team All-Metro, 1989 and 1990
* Metro All-Tournament Team, 1990

COLLEGE STATISTICS

		G	FGM	FGA	PCT	FTM	FTA	PCT	REB	AST	PTS	PPG
SMIS	87-88	21	15	34	.441	6	9	.666	19	17	37	1.8
SMIS	88-89	27	211	400	.528	101	133	.759	81	89	555	20.6
SMIS	89-90	32	218	409	.533	110	154	.714	114	98	570	17.8
SMIS	90-91	29	185	375	.493	106	134	.791	90	76	508	18.8
Totals		109	629	1218	.516	323	430	.751	304	280	1670	15.3

MELVIN CHEATUM

Team: Undrafted
Position: Forward
Height: 6'8"
Weight: 200

Birthdate: April 17, 1968
College: Alabama

Background: Cheatum, from a small town in Louisiana, earned a starting spot as a freshman at Alabama. He played both forward positions for the Tide, leading Alabama to three consecutive SEC tournament championships. Last season, Cheatum averaged 19 points and ten rebounds in three NCAA tournament games as the Tide advanced to the Sweet 16 before losing to Arkansas in a Southeast Regional semifinal. He is one of nine players in Alabama history to score more than 1,400 points and grab more than 700 rebounds.

Strengths: Cheatum is a good offensive player inside 15 feet, capable of getting his own shot. He is effective with a turnaround jumper, goes to the offensive glass, has good quickness, and works hard. He is a leaper, moves well without the ball, and runs the floor very well.

Weaknesses: Cheatum lacks the bulk to sustain his inside production against bigger players. He is too small to be a power forward and lacks the perimeter shooting and passing skills to excel at small forward. He is turnover prone.

Analysis: Cheatum was not among the eight small forwards selected in this year's NBA draft, though many thought he would be taken. Cheatum, an inside player, just doesn't have enough body to compete with the NBA big boys. His strong work ethic, however, may enable him to catch on somewhere. He participated in several summer camps, including Milwaukee's and Philadelphia's.

PLAYER SUMMARY

Will ....stick the turnaround
Can't...................................pass the ball
Expect.......................a struggle to stick
Don't Expect ....an NBA starter
Fantasy Value $3-5
Card Value ....25-35¢

COLLEGE HIGHLIGHTS

- Coaches' All-SEC, 1990 and 1991
- SEC All-Tournament Team, 1991
- SEC Tournament MVP, 1990
- Coaches' SEC All-Freshman Team, 1988

COLLEGE STATISTICS

		G	FGM	FGA	PCT	FTM	FTA	PCT	REB	AST	PTS	PPG
ALA	87-88	31	112	258	.434	70	95	.737	196	12	294	9.5
ALA	88-89	28	75	157	.477	36	55	.655	98	9	188	6.7
ALA	89-90	35	215	415	.518	224	307	.730	235	28	548	15.7
ALA	90-91	33	217	450	.482	108	151	.715	256	24	545	16.5
Totals		127	619	1280	.484	438	608	.720	785	73	1575	12.4

PETE CHILCUTT

Team: Sacramento Kings
Position: Forward/Center
Height: 6'10"
Weight: 232

Birthdate: September 14, 1968
College: North Carolina
Acquired: 1st-round pick in 1991 draft (27th overall)

Background: Chilcutt was a solid complementary player for coach Dean Smith at North Carolina, but he was slow to reach his potential and never was named first- or second-team All-ACC. He sat out his first year as a redshirt, then played in every game over the next four seasons. UNC went 106-34 in that span. Chilcutt's stock rose rapidly late last season, when he played well in the ACC and NCAA tournaments. He was named to the all-tournament team at the post-season Orlando Classic, pulling down 21 rebounds in one game.

Strengths: Chilcutt was among the best shooting big men in the draft. His jumper is reliable to about 16 feet. He has good hands, is an above-average passer, runs the floor surprisingly well, and is hard-nosed. He has a good feel for the game and a great attitude. Scouts feel he still is improving.

Weaknesses: Scouts had trouble evaluating Chilcutt because of the Tar Heel system, which shuffles players in and out and narrowly defines their roles. Chilcutt has no ball-handling skills and isn't an accomplished post-up player.

Analysis: Sacramento, which selected Billy Owens with the No. 3 pick in the draft, took Chilcutt with the 27th pick, the last in the first round. The Kings, seeking a point guard, were shopping big forwards Wayman Tisdale and Antoine Carr this summer. If either is traded, Chilcutt provides insurance at the position. The Kings were a poor shooting and rebounding team last season; Chilcutt will help in both areas.

PLAYER SUMMARY	
Will	play hard
Can't	handle the rock
Expect	a solid career
Don't Expect	athletic talent
Fantasy Value	$3-5
Card Value	25-40¢

COLLEGE HIGHLIGHTS

- Third-team All-ACC, 1991
- Second-team ACC All-Tournament Team, 1991
- Orlando Classic All-Tournament Team, 1991

COLLEGE STATISTICS

		G	FGM	FGA	PCT	FTM	FTA	PCT	REB	AST	PTS	PPG
NC	87-88	34	66	117	.564	36	51	.706	110	43	168	4.9
NC	88-89	37	110	205	.537	33	53	.623	200	51	256	6.9
NC	89-90	34	132	257	.514	30	42	.714	225	47	306	9.0
NC	90-91	35	175	325	.538	65	85	.765	231	47	420	12.0
Totals		140	483	901	.536	164	231	.710	766	188	1154	8.2

CHRIS CORCHIANI

Team: Orlando Magic
Position: Guard
Height: 6'1"
Weight: 186

Birthdate: March 28, 1968
College: North Carolina St.
Acquired: 2nd-round pick in 1991 draft (36th overall)

Background: Corchiani, Florida's two-time Mr. Basketball as a prep player in Miami, was the fire in N.C. State's "Fire and Ice" duo; Rodney Monroe was the ice. One writer, alluding to Corchiani's love of the game, dubbed him the "Boss Hog of all gym rats." Corchiani, the first player in NCAA history with more than 1,000 assists, considered transferring to Florida State or New Orleans prior to last season after the Wolfpack was put on probation and head coach Jim Valvano was ousted. Corchiani elected to stay in Raleigh. He led depth-shy N.C. State to a 20-win season.

Strengths: Corchiani is a great quarterback. He has adequate quickness, excellent vision, can penetrate, and has a great feel for the game. He is tough, durable, and a winner.

Weaknesses: While Corchiani has good first-step quickness to penetrate, he has trouble finishing. His outside shot—an awkward standing push shot—needs work. Defensively, he projects as only adequate on the pro level.

Analysis: After choosing centers Brian Williams and Stanley Roberts with its two first-round picks, Orlando selected Corchiani with its final pick. The Magic already has a solid backcourt, with shooting guard Nick Anderson and point guard Scott Skiles. Corchiani will battle former starter Sam Vincent for the back-up role to Skiles. He will play 12 to 15 minutes per game if he beats out Vincent.

PLAYER SUMMARY	
Will	play with fire
Can't	dunk the ball
Expect	a back-up point guard
Don't Expect	a big scorer
Fantasy Value	$2-4
Card Value	25-35¢

COLLEGE HIGHLIGHTS
- Second-team All-ACC, 1989 and 1991
- AP All-ACC, 1989
- NABC third-team All-American, 1991
- AP Honorable-Mention All-American, 1991

COLLEGE STATISTICS

		G	FGM	FGA	PCT	FTM	FTA	PCT	REB	AST	PTS	PPG
NCST	87-88	32	61	120	.508	60	72	.833	44	235	202	6.3
NCST	88-89	31	101	204	.495	99	123	.805	78	266	324	10.5
NCST	89-90	30	131	311	.421	99	119	.832	63	238	394	13.1
NCST	90-91	31	160	343	.466	134	163	.822	78	299	505	16.3
Totals		124	453	978	.463	392	477	.822	263	1038	1425	11.5

DALE DAVIS

Team: Indiana Pacers
Position: Center
Height: 6'11"
Weight: 230

Birthdate: March 25, 1969
College: Clemson
Acquired: 1st-round pick in 1991 draft
(13th overall)

Background: Davis was a solid four-year contributor at Clemson, which produced NBA players Tree Rollins, Larry Nance, Horace Grant, and Elden Campbell. Davis teamed with Campbell for three seasons to form the "Duo of Doom." They led the Tigers of 1989-90 to a 26-9 record and their first ACC title. Clemson dipped to 11-17 last year, but Davis led the ACC in rebounding for the third consecutive season. He joined Mike Gminski and Ralph Sampson as the only ACC players with more than 1,500 points, 1,200 rebounds, and 200 blocked shots.

Strengths: Davis is strictly an effort guy. He is strong, an above-average rebounder and shot-blocker, and gets his share of garbage points off the offensive glass.

Weaknesses: A poor offensive player, Davis has virtually no post-up skills, very limited shooting range, and is a poor free throw shooter and passer. Some scouts feel he regressed as a senior, losing quickness to the ball.

Analysis: Indiana went 41-41 last season, then nearly upset Boston in the first round of the playoffs. But the Pacers were exposed as a weak rebounding team. Davis fills the need for board strength, but his limitations likely will prevent him from beating out veteran power forward LaSalle Thompson or centers Rik Smits and Greg Dreiling.

PLAYER SUMMARY

Will ....crash the glass
Can't ....shoot the ball
Expect ....a role player
Don't Expect ....any offense
Fantasy Value $11-13
Card Value $1.00-1.25

COLLEGE HIGHLIGHTS

- All-ACC, 1990
- AP Honorable-Mention All-American, 1990 and 1991
- UPI Honorable-Mention All-American, 1990 and 1991

COLLEGE STATISTICS

		G	FGM	FGA	PCT	FTM	FTA	PCT	REB	AST	PTS	PPG
CLEM	87-88	29	91	171	.532	45	89	.506	223	10	227	7.8
CLEM	88-89	29	146	218	.670	93	144	.646	258	16	385	13.3
CLEM	89-90	35	205	328	.625	127	213	.596	395	21	537	15.3
CLEM	90-91	28	191	359	.532	119	205	.580	340	37	501	17.9
Totals		121	633	1076	.588	384	651	.589	1216	84	1650	13.6

RICHARD DUMAS

Team: Phoenix Suns
Position: Forward
Height: 6'7"
Weight: 210

Birthdate: May 19, 1969
College: Oklahoma St.; Phillips
Acquired: 2nd-round pick in 1991 draft (46th overall)

Background: A high school All-American from Tulsa, Dumas was one of the nation's best freshmen at Oklahoma State in 1987-88. His career began to unravel following his sophomore season, when he was suspended for substance abuse, had knee surgery, and suffered an Achilles' tendon injury. He was suspended again early in his junior season, tried to revive his career at Phillips University, then signed with a pro team in Israel, where he played last season.

Strengths: Dumas has terrific small-forward skills. He shoots well from 18 to 20 feet, can put the ball on the floor, runs well, and is a sensational leaper. He's active defensively and has very good hands.

Weaknesses: Dumas's alcohol-related suspensions are cause for concern, but his game is NBA-caliber. Scouts consider him a solid individual with a problem, not a bad apple. Dumas is a bit thin; he eventually could be a power forward if he adds bulk. He is turnover prone but has few other on-court weaknesses.

Analysis: Phoenix gambled in drafting Dumas, who had a terrific year in Israel. Other NBA clubs had negative reports on Dumas's off-court behavior. The Suns are loaded at small forward with starter Xavier McDaniel and rising star Cedric Ceballos, so Dumas will struggle to make the club. If he fails, he likely will return to Israel.

PLAYER SUMMARY	
Will	dunk with style
Can't	intimidate inside
Expect	a terrific talent
Don't Expect	an instant star
Fantasy Value	$2-4
Card Value	15-25¢

COLLEGE HIGHLIGHTS

- UPI Big Eight All-Freshman Team, 1988
- Second-team All-Big Eight, 1988 and 1989
- USBWA All-District 5 Team, 1988

COLLEGE STATISTICS

		G	FGM	FGA	PCT	FTM	FTA	PCT	REB	AST	PTS	PPG
OSU	87-88	30	203	372	.546	115	154	.747	193	49	521	17.4
OSU	88-89	28	184	411	.448	66	107	.617	197	73	439	15.7
Totals		58	387	783	.494	181	261	.693	390	122	960	16.6

LeRON ELLIS

Team: Los Angeles Clippers
Position: Center/Forward
Height: 6'10"
Weight: 250

Birthdate: April 28, 1969
College: Kentucky; Syracuse
Acquired: 1st-round pick in 1991 draft
(22nd overall)

Background: Ellis, whose father Leroy played 14 NBA seasons with the Lakers, 76ers, and Bullets, was a rising star at Kentucky, but he left the program after it was placed on probation in 1989. He failed to progress at Syracuse, where he was forced to take a back seat to Derrick Coleman and Billy Owens. Ellis was inconsistent, often in foul trouble, and regularly in head coach Jim Boeheim's doghouse. He wasn't projected as a certain draft pick until his outstanding performance at the post-season Orlando Classic.

Strengths: Though Ellis was a disappointment at Syracuse, scouts love his athleticism and defensive ability. He can run and jump and has excellent quickness and hands. He was one of the top ten defensive players in the draft, offering shot-blocking ability and an aggressive approach.

Weaknesses: Ellis generally comes up short at the offensive end, where he lacks post-up skills and has trouble finishing plays inside. He has decent range but is streaky. He thinks like a small forward but has a center's body.

Analysis: The Clippers needed a center but feared Stanley Roberts would prove to be another Benoit Benjamin. Ellis played center in college but likely will back up at both forward positions. Minutes could be hard to come by as a rookie, because Los Angeles already has young talents Charles Smith, Danny Manning, Ken Norman, and Loy Vaught. Ellis could beat out Vaught.

PLAYER SUMMARY	
Will	make the team
Can't	dominate inside
Expect	early struggles
Don't Expect	3-pointers
Fantasy Value	$10-13
Card Value	50-75¢

COLLEGE HIGHLIGHTS
• Second-team All-SEC, 1989

COLLEGE STATISTICS

		G	FGM	FGA	PCT	FTM	FTA	PCT	REB	AST	PTS	PPG
KEN	87-88	28	49	106	.462	22	42	.524	83	13	120	4.3
KEN	88-89	32	200	385	.519	111	164	.677	177	65	511	16.0
SYR	89-90	32	79	175	.451	28	54	.519	129	24	192	6.0
SYR	90-91	32	142	280	.507	72	119	.605	246	43	356	11.1
Totals		124	470	946	.497	233	379	.615	635	145	1179	9.5

RICK FOX

Team: Boston Celtics
Position: Forward/Guard
Height: 6'7"
Weight: 231

Birthdate: July 24, 1969
College: North Carolina
Acquired: 1st-round pick in 1991 draft (24th overall)

Background: Fox, born in Canada, moved to the Bahamas when he was two years old. He had a very limited basketball background before playing high school ball in Warshaw, Indiana. He never was a marquee player at North Carolina, but he was consistent and had a knack for late-game heroics. He beat No. 1-ranked Oklahoma with a last-second basket in the 1990 NCAA tournament. Last season, he led the Tar Heels to the Final Four but played poorly in UNC's loss to Kansas.

Strengths: Fox has adequate skills and a great feel for the game. He is strong, an excellent passer, and a good inside/outside offensive threat who can stroke the jumper. He is a competent defender.

Weaknesses: Like many players attempting to make it in the NBA, Fox is a tweener because of his size. He is too slow to play with the better small forwards and lacks quickness. Scouts say he is too heavy at 231 pounds.

Analysis: The aging Celtics added another youngster to their future nucleus of Reggie Lewis and Dee Brown (and Brian Shaw, if he isn't traded). Boston's triumvirate of Larry Bird, Kevin McHale, and Robert Parish will be a combined 107 years old this season. Fox will get minutes backing up small forward Kevin Gamble and shooting guard Lewis. He could replace Gamble as the starter within the next two seasons.

PLAYER SUMMARY
Will ....score inside and out
Can't ....run the floor
Expect ....more improvement
Don't Expect ....many dunks
Fantasy Value $4-6
Card Value ....35-50¢

COLLEGE HIGHLIGHTS
- All-ACC, 1991
- AP Honorable-Mention All-American, 1991
- ACC Tournament MVP, 1991
- Canadian National Team, 1990

COLLEGE STATISTICS

		G	FGM	FGA	PCT	FTM	FTA	PCT	REB	AST	PTS	PPG
NC	87-88	34	59	94	.628	15	30	.500	63	32	136	4.0
NC	88-89	37	165	283	.583	83	105	.790	142	76	426	11.5
NC	89-90	34	203	389	.522	75	102	.735	157	84	551	16.2
NC	90-91	35	206	455	.453	111	138	.804	232	131	590	16.9
Totals		140	633	1221	.518	284	375	.757	594	323	1703	12.2

CHAD GALLAGHER

Team: Phoenix Suns
Position: Forward
Height: 6'10"
Weight: 245

Birthdate: May 30, 1969
College: Creighton
Acquired: 2nd-round pick in 1991
draft (32nd overall)

Background: Gallagher teamed with Bob Harstad to form Creighton's "Dynamic Duo." They led the Bluejays to a 65-31 record and two NCAA tournament appearances in the past three seasons. Gallagher began his career as a perimeter-oriented player, but he showed considerable improvement inside last season. He excelled in Creighton's NCAA tournament victory over New Mexico State, scoring 18 points and grabbing 13 rebounds. Gallagher disappointed NBA scouts with uninspired play at the post-season Orlando Classic.

Strengths: Gallagher has good shooting range and touch and outstanding mechanics. Last year, he showed the ability to score inside with hooks and drop-step moves. He runs the floor well and is a good passer and positional rebounder.

Weaknesses: He can't score consistently in the paint because he lacks strength and quickness and isn't explosive. Gallagher has improved defensively but is average at best. He lacks aggressiveness.

Analysis: Phoenix, without a first-round pick, used the first of its three second-round selections on Gallagher. He could back up center Mark West but figures more as a back-up to big forward Tom Chambers. There's little talent (Kurt Rambis, Tim Perry) behind Chambers, so Gallagher could stick.

PLAYER SUMMARY	
Will	score from perimeter
Can't	dominate inside
Expect	a Joe Wolf clone
Don't Expect	much PT
Fantasy Value	$6-8
Card Value	50-65¢

COLLEGE HIGHLIGHTS

- Missouri Valley Player of the Year, 1991
- All-MVC, 1990 and 1991
- UPI Honorable-Mention All-American, 1991
- MVC Tournament Most Outstanding Player, 1989

COLLEGE STATISTICS

		G	FGM	FGA	PCT	FTM	FTA	PCT	REB	AST	PTS	PPG
CRE	87-88	32	163	313	.521	39	65	.600	168	19	365	11.4
CRE	88-89	27	171	303	.564	70	105	.667	177	23	414	15.3
CRE	89-90	33	240	437	.549	99	140	.707	266	46	584	17.7
CRE	90-91	32	237	419	.566	141	175	.806	280	41	620	19.4
Totals		124	811	1472	.551	349	485	.720	891	129	1983	16.0

CHRIS GATLING

Team: Golden State Warriors
Position: Forward
Height: 6'10"
Weight: 220

Birthdate: September 2, 1967
College: Old Dominion
Acquired: 1st-round pick in 1991 draft (16th overall)

Background: Gatling, a high school star in Elizabeth City, New Jersey, did not play during his first two years in college. He originally signed with Pittsburgh but sat out the 1986-87 season because of Prop 48 restrictions. He then transferred to Old Dominion, where NCAA rules required him to sit out the 1987-88 season. Gatling led the Sun Belt Conference in field goal percentage as a sophomore. Though ODU was a disappointing 43-45 during his tenure, Gatling joined Terry Catledge as the only two-time Sun Belt Players of the Year.

Strengths: Gatling was as talented as any small forward in the 1991 NBA draft, with the exception of Billy Owens. He is an explosive jumper who can block shots and get to balls on the offensive glass. He has good quickness and runs the floor well. He is quick to the basket, relying on spin moves and reverses.

Weaknesses: A poor showing at the post-season Orlando Classic added credence to scouts' claims that Gatling doesn't want to succeed badly enough. He's average defensively and isn't very physical, though some scouts project him as a top defender. He's a streak shooter.

Analysis: Golden State selected Gatling with the first of its three first-round picks, then added big men Victor Alexander and Shaun Vandiver. The Warriors still need a center to replace Alton Lister; one or more of the draft picks could be packaged with a veteran in a trade for a center. If Gatling stays, he will get time at both forward spots.

PLAYER SUMMARY	
Will	excel on the break
Can't	be a stopper
Expect	an exciting player
Don't Expect	many assists
Fantasy Value	$8-10
Card Value	75¢-$1.00

COLLEGE HIGHLIGHTS

- Sun Belt Player of the Year, 1990 and 1991
- AP Honorable-Mention All-American, 1990 and 1991
- Virginia State Player of the Year, 1991

COLLEGE STATISTICS

		G	FGM	FGA	PCT	FTM	FTA	PCT	REB	AST	PTS	PPG
OD	88-89	27	239	388	.616	126	179	.704	244	26	604	22.4
OD	89-90	26	207	357	.580	120	170	.670	259	25	534	20.5
OD	90-91	32	251	405	.620	171	247	.692	356	24	673	21.0
Totals		85	697	1150	.606	417	605	.689	859	75	1811	21.3

SEAN GREEN

Team: Indiana Pacers
Position: Guard
Height: 6'5"
Weight: 210

Birthdate: February 2, 1970
College: Iona
Acquired: 2nd-round pick in 1991 draft (41st overall)

Background: Green, from Queens, New York, attended powerful Oak Hill Academy in Virginia, then signed with Jim Valvano at N.C. State. After a brief stay, he transferred to Iona to be closer to home. The move also allowed him to avoid competition with Rodney Monroe, who played the same position. Green, the most highly publicized player to sign with Iona since Jeff Ruland, had an exciting yet inconsistent career with the Gaels. Last season, he scored 43 points vs. Siena to lead Iona within a game of the NCAA tournament. He was limited to ten points in a loss to St. Peter's in the Metro Atlantic championship game.

Strengths: Green is an exciting athlete with tremendous size and strength and nearly a 40-inch vertical leap. He has good shooting range and can rebound with any guard when so inclined.

Weaknesses: Undisciplined at times, Green shot far too much in college. The result was a terrible field goal percentage. Though he has the tools to be a fine defender, he doesn't understand defensive theory and remains a liability.

Analysis: One publication listed Green as the 28th-best shooting guard available in the draft. That didn't stop Indiana, which drafted him to compete for a back-up role to starter Reggie Miller. Green could displace George McCloud, the seventh overall pick in the 1989 draft, who has been a big disappointment.

PLAYER SUMMARY

Will.................................shoot anytime
Can't.............................score every time
Expect..........................acrobatic dunks
Don't Expect......................any defense
Fantasy Value..................................$2-4
Card Value ....25-35¢

COLLEGE HIGHLIGHTS

- All-Metro Atlantic, 1991
- Second-team All-Metro Atlantic, 1990
- Metro Atlantic All-Tournament Team, 1991

COLLEGE STATISTICS

		G	FGM	FGA	PCT	FTM	FTA	PCT	REB	AST	PTS	PPG
IONA	88-89	23	119	291	.409	37	55	.673	93	14	301	13.1
IONA	89-90	28	215	508	.423	71	104	.683	139	26	553	19.8
IONA	90-91	30	265	550	.482	113	149	.758	157	41	696	23.2
Totals		81	599	1349	.444	221	308	.718	389	81	1550	19.1

CARL HERRERA

Team: Houston Rockets
Position: Forward/Center
Height: 6'9"
Weight: 215
Birthdate: December 14, 1966

College: Houston
Acquired: Draft rights traded from Heat with draft rights to Dave Jamerson for draft rights to Alec Kessler, 6/90

Background: Herrera, born in Trinidad and raised in Venezuela, did not play basketball until he was age 13. He was noticed by college coaches in 1983 when, as a 16-year-old, he played point guard for the Venezuelan National Team in the Pan American Games. Herrera spent his first two collegiate seasons at Jacksonville (Texas) Junior College, then one season at Houston. Herrera left the Cougars program early. Miami drafted him in the 1990 draft and then traded his rights to the Rockets. Herrera passed on the NBA altogether and signed a two-year contract with Real Madrid of the Spanish League. Late this summer, the Rockets were trying to buy out his contract from Real Madrid.

Strengths: Herrera's greatest attribute is his understanding of the team concept. He is a terrific athlete and was a standout volleyball player as a teenager. He is a good passer, has above-average quickness, has excellent hands, and can run the floor. He is mature, experienced, and motivated.

Weaknesses: Though he is a competent scorer, Herrera needs work on his perimeter game and more strength to defend and rebound with NBA centers and power forwards.

Analysis: Houston soon could have the NBA's best front line if Herrera joins the team and develops. He played center in college but projects as a forward in the NBA. He could supplant Buck Johnson at small forward within the next two seasons.

PLAYER SUMMARY	
Will	provide versatility
Can't	outmuscle anyone
Expect	an eventual star
Don't Expect	a lack of effort
Fantasy Value	$2-4
Card Value	25-35¢

COLLEGE HIGHLIGHTS

- All-SWC, 1990
- First-team Junior College All-American, 1989
- Venezuelan National Team, 1987

COLLEGE STATISTICS

		G	FGM	FGA	PCT	FTM	FTA	PCT	REB	AST	PTS	PPG
HOU	89-90	33	188	333	.565	172	214	.804	302	54	551	16.7
Totals		33	188	333	.565	172	214	.804	302	54	551	16.7

DONALD HODGE

Team: Dallas Mavericks
Position: Center
Height: 7'0"
Weight: 230

Birthdate: February 25, 1969
College: Temple
Acquired: 2nd-round pick in 1991 draft (33rd overall)

Background: Hodge had a brief career at Temple. He sat out his freshman year because of Prop 48 restrictions and forfeited his senior year to enter the NBA draft. As a sophomore, he led the Owls in rebounding and field goal percentage, scoring 31 points in a game vs. eventual national champion UNLV. He had a lackluster 1990-91 season, feuded with coach John Chaney, then came on strong in the post-season. Chaney and many NBA scouts felt Hodge made a poor decision entering the draft this year.

Strengths: Hodge has the size and skill to be an effective low-post offensive player. He has very good hands and a nice shooting touch around the key, is an excellent passer, moves fairly well, and has a good feel for the game.

Weaknesses: He isn't aggressive or physical enough to have an impact as a rebounder. He's especially weak on the defensive boards. Scouts have questioned Hodge's mental toughness and conditioning. He doesn't run the floor very well.

Analysis: Hodge lacks the experience to be an immediate factor in the NBA. Dallas, which starts 34-year-old James Donaldson at center, hopes Hodge can be ready in three years. With John Shasky as the Mavs' back-up center, Hodge should have little trouble making the team.

PLAYER SUMMARY

Will ....pass effectively
Can't ....rebound consistently
Expect ....a long-term project
Don't Expect...................physical play
Fantasy Value $5-7
Card Value ....35-50¢

COLLEGE HIGHLIGHTS

* Second-team All-Atlantic 10, 1990 and 1991

COLLEGE STATISTICS

		G	FGM	FGA	PCT	FTM	FTA	PCT	REB	AST	PTS	PPG
TEMP	89-90	31	164	303	.541	139	195	.713	253	22	467	15.1
TEMP	90-91	34	147	275	.535	101	141	.716	234	35	395	11.6
Totals		65	311	578	.538	240	336	.714	487	57	862	13.3

STEVE HOOD

Team: Sacramento Kings
Position: Guard
Height: 6'7"
Weight: 185

Birthdate: April 4, 1968
College: Maryland; James Madison
Acquired: 2nd-round pick in 1991 draft (42nd overall)

Background: Hood, from prep powerhouse DeMatha High in Hyattsville, Maryland, was recruited in 1986 by then-Maryland coach Lefty Driesell. However, he didn't play for Driesell until 1989, when the two were united at James Madison. The coach was forced out at Maryland after Len Bias's death in 1986, and Hood left in 1988 after Brian Williams became the focal point of the Terrapins offense. Hood established himself at JMU as one of the nation's best long-distance shooters. As a senior, he scored 32 points vs. UNLV, the most by any Rebels opponent last season.

Strengths: Hood has excellent size for an NBA off guard. His greatest strength is his shooting ability; he has outstanding range and can fill it up in a hurry. He handles the ball well. Though he played two seasons in a weak conference, Hood never had trouble with top-level competition.

Weaknesses: Hood isn't strong enough to handle the day-to-day banging in the NBA. He's a marginal defensive player and hasn't shown much skill as a rebounder or passer.

Analysis: Sacramento's backcourt will have a new look this season, with draft picks Hood and Randy Brown and point guard Spud Webb, acquired from Atlanta in a trade for Travis Mays. The Kings, held below 100 points 50 times last season, need scorers. If Hood makes the team, it will be for his ability to provide instant offense off the bench.

PLAYER SUMMARY	
Will	score in streaks
Can't	shut down his man
Expect	bench offense
Don't Expect	double-doubles
Fantasy Value	$2-4
Card Value	15-25¢

COLLEGE HIGHLIGHTS
- Colonial Athletic Association Player of the Year, 1990 and 1991
- All-CAA, 1990 and 1991

COLLEGE STATISTICS

		G	FGM	FGA	PCT	FTM	FTA	PCT	REB	AST	PTS	PPG
MD	86-87	26	136	290	.469	62	95	.653	101	56	369	14.2
MD	87-88	29	80	166	.482	40	54	.741	72	55	226	7.8
JM	89-90	31	233	477	.488	148	201	.736	125	42	682	22.0
JM	90-91	29	195	419	.465	156	215	.726	100	52	600	20.7
Totals		115	644	1352	.476	406	565	.718	398	205	1877	16.3

KEITH HUGHES

Team: Cleveland Cavaliers
Position: Forward
Height: 6'9"
Weight: 235
Birthdate: June 29, 1968

College: Syracuse; Rutgers
Acquired: Draft rights traded from Rockets for a 1996 2nd-round pick and future considerations, 6/91

Background: Hughes, a star high school center from Carteret, New Jersey, signed with Syracuse but quit the Orangemen midway through his sophomore season, frustrated by lack of playing time. He sat out the 1988-89 season after transferring to Rutgers, where he started every game as a junior. Hughes led the Scarlet Knights in scoring and rebounding in each of his two seasons, and he impressed pro scouts at the post-season Orlando Classic. Houston drafted him with the 47th pick but traded his rights to Cleveland.

Strengths: Rebounding is Hughes's greatest asset. He is especially adept on the offensive glass. He has a body like Jerome Kersey's, plays a physical game, and can run the floor. He has good shooting mechanics and range and can score posting up. He has excellent quickness.

Weaknesses: Hughes is a tweener, lacking the size to play power forward and the floor game to excel at small forward. He must improve his penetrating and his passing off the dribble. He is average defensively and he takes poor shots.

Analysis: Cleveland acquired Hughes to compete for a back-up role at both forward positions. Cleveland was shopping big forward John Williams this summer; if he goes, Hughes has a realistic chance to make the team. The Cavs have excellent talent up front with Williams, Larry Nance, and Danny Ferry, but little in reserve.

```
PLAYER SUMMARY
Will..............................go to the boards
Can't........................bang in the middle
Expect..................a good bench player
Don't Expect.....................many blocks
Fantasy Value ................................$2-4
Card Value ...................................15-25¢
```

COLLEGE HIGHLIGHTS
* Atlantic 10 Player of the Year, 1991
* All-Atlantic 10, 1991
* Second-team All-Atlantic 10, 1990

COLLEGE STATISTICS

		G	FGM	FGA	PCT	FTM	FTA	PCT	REB	AST	PTS	PPG
SYR	86-87	20	14	28	.500	9	12	.750	19	6	37	1.9
SYR	87-88	19	44	104	.423	14	25	.560	51	7	103	5.4
RUT	89-90	35	242	543	.446	130	193	.674	286	17	649	18.5
RUT	90-91	29	213	485	.439	144	221	.652	289	25	608	21.0
Totals		103	513	1160	.442	297	451	.659	645	55	1397	13.6

MARK HUGHES

Team: Detroit Pistons
Position: Forward
Height: 6'8"
Weight: 235

Birthdate: October 5, 1966
College: Michigan
Acquired: Signed as a free agent, 7/90

Background: Hughes, from Muskegon, Michigan, played four seasons at Michigan, where he started 47 games in his sophomore and junior seasons. He was the Wolverines' co-captain as a senior but was relegated to a back-up role, as Michigan–starting Loy Vaught, Terry Mills, and Glen Rice up front–won the national championship. He wasn't drafted in 1989 and was the Pistons' final cut as a free agent. Detroit kept him on its injured list last year, though some said he really wasn't hurt. Hughes has played in Europe the past two years.

Strengths: Hughes is an inside banger with strength, size, and a good work ethic. He is hard-nosed and consistent in his approach.

Weaknesses: He lacks shooting touch and range, and isn't a good ball-handler or free throw shooter. He is not a shot-blocker. Hughes lacks any superior skill that would separate him from other fringe NBA players.

Analysis: Detroit isn't nearly as strong as it was in 1989, when Hughes was cut for the first time. James Edwards is nearing retirement, as is Bill Laimbeer. The Pistons used their only 1991 draft pick on guard Doug Overton, so Hughes has a shot to make the team.

PLAYER SUMMARY

Will.............................pound the boards
Can't.................................shoot the 3
Expect.......................a struggle to stick
Don't Expect ....a key contributor
Fantasy Value...............................$1-3
Card Value ....15-25¢

COLLEGE HIGHLIGHTS

* Michigan Co-Captain, 1989
* Member of NCAA championship team, 1989

COLLEGE STATISTICS

		G	FGM	FGA	PCT	FTM	FTA	PCT	REB	AST	PTS	PPG
MICH	85-86	14	12	24	.500	7	9	.778	18	2	31	2.2
MICH	86-87	32	86	158	.544	22	29	.759	192	42	194	6.1
MICH	87-88	34	65	123	.526	26	43	.605	133	33	156	4.6
MICH	88-89	35	104	171	.608	29	48	.604	142	40	238	6.8
Totals		115	267	476	.560	84	129	.651	485	117	619	5.4

ANDERSON HUNT

Team: Undrafted
Position: Guard
Height: 6'1"
Weight: 176

Birthdate: May 5, 1969
College: Nevada-Las Vegas

Background: Hunt came to UNLV from renowned Southwestern High in Detroit. After sitting out the 1987-88 season as an academic redshirt, Hunt had a terrific three-year run with the Rebels, who went 98-14 during his stay. Hunt scored 29 points in UNLV's victory over Duke in the 1990 NCAA championship game. A shooting guard, he had an opportunity to learn to play the point this season, but he passed up his final year of eligibility to enter the NBA draft.

Strengths: Hunt is strictly a spot-up scorer, but he is a marvelous one. He is adept at getting to his spot, catching the ball, and shooting it quickly. He has outstanding range with his jumper. He is a fine ball defender; he usually would guard the opposing point guard. He is a good leaper and can run the floor.

Weaknesses: Hunt is too short to be an effective NBA shooting guard, and he lacks the ball-handling and passing skills, and the creative sense, to be a quality NBA point guard. He is a streaky shooter who often struggled when he missed his first few shots in a game.

Analysis: Hunt's decision to enter the draft a year early cost him dearly. Although many thought he would be drafted, he wasn't, and he ended up scrambling for a free agent tryout. NBA teams don't have much use for small, long-range shooters. Those who do make it, such as Jon Sundvold and Steve Alford, usually don't have much job security. Hunt wouldn't either.

PLAYER SUMMARY	
Will	shoot with range
Can't	play inside
Expect	a role player
Don't Expect	a long career
Fantasy Value	$5-7
Card Value	35-50¢

COLLEGE HIGHLIGHTS
- AP Honorable-Mention All-American, 1991
- All-Big West, 1991
- NCAA Final Four MVP, 1990

COLLEGE STATISTICS

		G	FGM	FGA	PCT	FTM	FTA	PCT	REB	AST	PTS	PPG
UNLV	88-89	37	158	396	.399	48	70	.686	64	134	443	12.0
UNLV	89-90	39	230	478	.481	61	92	.663	87	158	620	15.9
UNLV	90-91	33	218	455	.479	28	42	.667	53	95	569	17.2
Totals		109	606	1329	.456	137	204	.672	204	387	1632	14.8

MIKE IUZZOLINO

Team: Dallas Mavericks
Position: Guard
Height: 5'10"
Weight: 180

Birthdate: January 22, 1968
College: Penn St.; St. Francis (PA)
Acquired: 2nd-round pick in 1991 draft (35th overall)

Background: Iuzzolino, who scored below 700 on his first try at the SAT, enrolled at Penn State. Two years later, with his grade-point average higher than his scoring average, he transferred to St. Francis, sat out a year, and became a star. Last season, he finished in the top five nationally in free throw shooting and 3-point field goal percentage and led the Red Flash to the NCAA tournament, where he scored 20 points in a first-round loss to Arizona. He left St. Francis with a 3.8 GPA.

Strengths: Iuzzolino has been described as a "thinking man's guard" and a "coach's player." He is hard-nosed, tough mentally and physically, gives maximum effort defensively, and has a good feel for the game. He is a very good spot-up shooter with range.

Weaknesses: Iuzzolino is slow, short, and has limited quickness. He must show that he can create offensively against quicker players. He projects as a defensive liability.

Analysis: Dallas used the last of its three draft picks on Iuzzolino. With veteran point guard Brad Davis on his last legs, Iuzzolino will be given a chance to win a job backing up starter Derek Harper. The Mavs aren't deep in the backcourt, but Iuzzolino's physical limitations will make it difficult for him to make the team.

PLAYER SUMMARY

Will ....drill jumpers
Can't............................out-quick anyone
Expect ....a cerebral player
Don't Expect..........................any dunks
Fantasy Value $2-4
Card Value ....25-35¢

COLLEGE HIGHLIGHTS

- Northeast Conference Player of the Year, 1991
- NABC Scholar Athlete of the Year, 1991
- COSIDA/GTE Academic All-American, 1990 and 1991

COLLEGE STATISTICS

		G	FGM	FGA	PCT	FTM	FTA	PCT	REB	AST	PTS	PPG
PSU	86-87	27	13	46	.283	35	41	.854	32	30	64	2.4
PSU	87-88	26	26	55	.473	17	19	.895	15	31	83	3.2
STF	89-90	27	180	326	.552	135	155	.871	67	130	574	21.3
STF	90-91	32	227	419	.542	215	243	.885	71	127	772	24.1
Totals		112	446	846	.527	402	458	.877	185	318	1493	13.3

N B A ROOKIES
339

KEITH JENNINGS

Team: Undrafted
Position: Guard
Height: 5'7"
Weight: 160

Birthdate: November 2, 1968
College: East Tennessee St.

Background: "Mister" Jennings was not heavily recruited, but he was an immediate impact player at East Tennessee State for coach Les Robinson. The Bucs went 14-15 in Jennings's first season and 75-23 in his last three, winning three straight Southern Conference titles. Jennings is the NCAA's all-time leader in 3-point field goal percentage, is second in assists, and fourth in steals.

Strengths: Jennings, short but powerful, is the consummate playmaker. He is tough and intelligent and knows how to take advantage of match-ups. He has excellent quickness and hands and outstanding shooting range. He is adept at pulling up on the break and hurting opponents with his jumper. He is an excellent free throw shooter.

Weaknesses: His stature and lack of blazing speed are his biggest liabilities. Bigger guards have little problem taking him inside or posting him up, and he can't alter shots when he rotates out on defense. Opponents have little trouble passing the ball over him, and he can't double down defensively.

Analysis: Nine point guards were selected in the NBA draft, but Jennings wasn't among them after following up a poor NCAA tournament performance with poor showings in the NABC All-Star Game and the Portsmouth Invitational. He played this summer in the USBL. Jennings, a better scorer than Spud Webb and Muggsy Bogues, eventually should see time in the NBA.

PLAYER SUMMARY
Will ....excite the fans
Can't ....post up
Expect ....a deep reserve
Don't Expect ....blocked shots
Fantasy Value $3-5
Card Value ....25-35¢

COLLEGE HIGHLIGHTS
* Francis Naismith Award (best player under six feet), 1991
* Ed Steitz Award (best 3-point shooter), 1991
* AP third-team All-American, 1991

COLLEGE STATISTICS

		G	FGM	FGA	PCT	FTM	FTA	PCT	REB	AST	PTS	PPG
ETS	87-88	29	116	237	.489	109	132	.826	119	183	374	12.9
ETS	88-89	31	134	263	.510	138	163	.847	114	202	448	14.5
ETS	89-90	34	167	291	.575	107	122	.877	132	297	504	14.8
ETS	90-91	33	221	371	.596	136	152	.895	129	301	662	20.1
Totals		127	638	1162	.549	490	569	.861	494	983	1988	15.7

LARRY JOHNSON

Team: Charlotte Hornets
Position: Forward
Height: 6'7"
Weight: 250

Birthdate: March 14, 1969
College: Nevada-Las Vegas
Acquired: 1st-round pick in 1991 draft
(1st overall)

Background: The indomitable "L.J." originally signed with Southern Methodist, but he ended up at Odessa (Texas) Junior College after SMU officials questioned his score on a retake of the SAT. UNLV won the national championship in Johnson's first season (1989-90) and went 34-1 in 1990-91. Johnson's brilliant two-year run at UNLV ended on a down note: He was limited to 13 points, and passed up the potential game-winning shot, in the Rebels' 79-77 loss to Duke in an NCAA Final Four semifinal game.

Strengths: One of the strongest players in the game, Johnson can't be moved once he gets position on the low blocks. He has advanced post-up scoring skills, is a superb passer, rebounds with a vengeance, and is an outstanding defensive player. He is a terrific free throw shooter, despite horrible mechanics. His shooting range extends to 20 feet.

Weaknesses: Johnson's in-between height—he may be closer to 6'5" than his listed 6'7"—may hurt him in the NBA, because he will be matched up against either taller power forwards or quicker small forwards. Critics have questioned his ability to rebound in the NBA.

Analysis: Charlotte made Johnson the No. 1 pick in the draft despite concerns about his height. He measured 6'5 ½" at the NBA's Chicago camp. The Hornets did not decide on Johnson until the weekend before the draft. L.J. brings much-needed power to the Hornets, who finished 27th in the NBA in rebounding last year.

PLAYER SUMMARY
Will......................outmuscle opponents
Can't..............................outjump them
Expect ....a solid career
Don't Expect..................an instant star
Fantasy Value $14-17
Card Value $1.00-1.50

COLLEGE HIGHLIGHTS
- John Wooden Player of the Year, 1991
- James Naismith Player of the Year, 1991
- AP first-team All-American, 1990 and 1991
- Big West Player of the Year, 1990 and 1991

COLLEGE STATISTICS

		G	FGM	FGA	PCT	FTM	FTA	PCT	REB	AST	PTS	PPG
UNLV	89-90	40	304	487	.624	201	262	.767	457	84	822	20.6
UNLV	90-91	35	308	465	.662	162	198	.818	380	104	795	22.7
Totals		75	612	952	.643	363	460	.789	837	188	1617	21.6

ANTHONY JONES

Team: Los Angeles Lakers
Position: Forward/Guard
Height: 6'7"
Weight: 200

Birthdate: March 21, 1967
College: Union; Oral Roberts
Acquired: 2nd-round pick in 1991 draft (52nd overall)

Background: Jones, a high school teammate of Stacey King's in Lawton, Oklahoma, began his college career at Connors State Junior College. He signed with Oklahoma State in 1989 but was diverted to Union College because he lacked enough credits to play for the Cowboys. Jones played part of the 1988-89 season at Union, then transferred to Oral Roberts. There, he sat out the 1989-90 season before starring last year. He and ORU teammate Greg Sutton played this summer for Empire State in the USBL.

Strengths: Jones can play small forward but projects as a shooting guard in the NBA. He has NBA 3-point shooting range and is especially deadly from the corners. A good athlete, he runs the floor well and is a leaper. His is an above-average rebounder, especially at guard.

Weaknesses: Jones must work on his ball-handling skills to make it at shooting guard. He is small for a forward and isn't a banger. He tends to get down on himself.

Analysis: The Lakers used their only draft pick on Jones, who will be given a chance to win a back-up job to shooting guards Byron Scott and Terry Teagle. He also could earn limited minutes at small forward, where the Lakers have no depth behind starter James Worthy. If Jones sticks, he will be a deep reserve.

PLAYER SUMMARY

Will......................score from the corner
Can't ....mix it up inside
Expect ....a designated shooter
Don't Expect ....much PT
Fantasy Value $4-6
Card Value ....25-35¢

COLLEGE HIGHLIGHTS

- NAIA Honorable-Mention All-American, 1991

COLLEGE STATISTICS

		G	FGM	FGA	PCT	FTM	FTA	PCT	REB	AST	PTS	PPG
UC	88-89	10	85	149	.570	21	29	.724	44	33	197	19.7
OR	90-91	35	276	564	.489	73	106	.689	234	36	684	19.5
Totals		45	361	713	.506	94	135	.696	278	69	881	19.6

MARCUS KENNEDY

Team: Portland Trail Blazers
Position: Forward
Height: 6'6"
Weight: 235

Birthdate: January 29, 1967
College: Eastern Michigan
Acquired: 2nd-round pick in 1991 draft (54th overall)

Background: Kennedy, not heavily recruited out of Troy, Michigan, played three seasons at Division II Ferris State before transferring to Eastern Michigan, where last season he led the Hurons to a 26-7 record and two upset victories (vs. Mississippi State and Penn State) in the NCAA tournament. He finished fifth in the nation in field goal percentage and led EMU in scoring, rebounding, and blocked shots.

Strengths: Kennedy, a center at Eastern Michigan, is strong and tough. He plays bigger than his size because he has a seven-foot wingspan. He is a good inside scorer, with strong post-up moves and adequate quickness. He runs the floor well and is a capable defender.

Weaknesses: Kennedy projects as an NBA power forward but, despite his giant wingspan, is too small for the position. He has virtually no perimeter game (zero 3-point field goals in college), isn't a shot-blocker, and is an average rebounder. He is turnover prone.

Analysis: Portland had only one draft pick—the last one in the second round. The Blazers pulled a surprise in selecting Kennedy, who has little chance of making the team. Portland is loaded with power forwards, with Buck Williams, Cliff Robinson, Mark Bryant, and Alaa Abdelnaby all capable of playing the position.

PLAYER SUMMARY

Will..............................post up strongly
Can't......................shoot from outside
Expect ....a battle to stick
Don't Expect ....much dazzle
Fantasy Value $2-4
Card Value ....15-25¢

COLLEGE HIGHLIGHTS

- Mid-American Conference Player of the Year, 1991
- All-Mid-American, 1991
- All-Great Lakes Conference, 1988
- Second-team All-Great Lakes, 1989

COLLEGE STATISTICS

		G	FGM	FGA	PCT	FTM	FTA	PCT	REB	AST	PTS	PPG
EMU	90-91	33	240	352	.682	179	250	.716	266	42	659	20.0
Totals		33	240	352	.682	179	250	.716	266	42	659	20.0

RICH KING

Team: Seattle SuperSonics
Position: Center
Height: 7'2"
Weight: 245

Birthdate: April 4, 1969
College: Nebraska
Acquired: 1st-round pick in 1991 draft (14th overall)

Background: From Burke High in Omaha, King went to Nebraska as the tallest Cornhuskers player ever. Progress as a player came slowly. Even as a senior, King never was regarded as a franchise-type center, though he was the 'Huskers' go-to guy in 1991. His stock rose rapidly last season as Nebraska posted a surprising 26-8 record—its most victories ever.

Strengths: King's biggest asset is his size. He has the tools to be a good player, plus the intelligence and determination to reach that level. King catches the ball well, has a good touch around the basket, and runs the floor well. He will block shots if a smaller player foolishly ventures into his area.

Weaknesses: King lacks the necessary strength to bang with NBA-caliber players, and he's not aggressive enough pursuing rebounds. He was foul prone in college, although that doesn't figure to be much of a problem in the pros. He has good, not great, shooting range (one career 3-pointer).

Analysis: Seattle fans attending a Sonics draft-day party booed loudly when president Bob Whitsitt announced the selection of King, but the pick was a good one. King projects as a back-up for his first few seasons, but he could emerge as a solid starter if the Sonics tire of Benoit Benjamin. Whitsitt considered taking Stanley Roberts instead of King, but he backed off because of concerns about Roberts's weight and attitude.

PLAYER SUMMARY

Will...............................clog the middle
Can't........................outmuscle anyone
Expect ....a three-year project
Don't Expect..................much PT early
Fantasy Value $6-8
Card Value ....50-65¢

COLLEGE HIGHLIGHTS

- Academic All-Big Eight, 1990
- Honorable-Mention All-Big Eight, 1989 and 1990
- Second-team All-Big Eight, 1991
- UPI Honorable-Mention All-American, 1991

COLLEGE STATISTICS

		G	FGM	FGA	PCT	FTM	FTA	PCT	REB	AST	PTS	PPG
NEB	87-88	29	56	108	.519	24	34	.706	84	22	136	4.7
NEB	88-89	33	136	235	.579	91	139	.655	195	53	363	11.0
NEB	89-90	28	170	305	.557	110	158	.696	208	58	450	16.1
NEB	90-91	34	202	352	.574	120	179	.670	274	90	526	15.5
Totals		124	564	1000	.564	345	510	.676	761	223	1475	11.9

TREG LEE

Team: Undrafted
Position: Forward
Height: 6'8"
Weight: 235

Birthdate: February 26, 1968
College: Ohio St.

Background: Lee, one of the nation's most coveted prep players in 1987 while at Cleveland's St. Joseph High, sat out his freshman season at Ohio State under Prop 48 guidelines. He struggled as a sophomore and junior, starting just four games. Lee improved dramatically last season for the Buckeyes, who went 27-4 and won their first Big Ten championship since 1971. Lee hit the game-winning shot with two seconds left in OSU's 97-95 double-overtime victory over Indiana, which all but clinched the title.

Strengths: Lee has tremendous all-around skills. He is a very good passer and can shoot from about 20 feet out, handle the ball, rebound, and play good defense. He's still improving and could develop into a nice pro.

Weaknesses: Though Lee has few glaring weaknesses, he needs to be pushed to be motivated. He wasn't a productive college player and needs to show NBA people that he wants to be better. He's not a good post-up player.

Analysis: Eleven power forwards were among the 54 players taken in the draft. Despite interest from several teams, Lee was not one of them. If he doesn't stick as a free agent, he could play this season in the CBA. With his tremendous athleticism, Lee will get several chances to make an NBA team.

PLAYER SUMMARY	
Will	provide versatility
Can't	score on low blocks
Expect	rookie struggles
Don't Expect	great intensity
Fantasy Value	$4-6
Card Value	25-35¢

COLLEGE HIGHLIGHTS

- AP Honorable-Mention All-American, 1991
- Honorable-Mention All-Big Ten, 1991

COLLEGE STATISTICS

		G	FGM	FGA	PCT	FTM	FTA	PCT	REB	AST	PTS	PPG
OSU	88-89	32	58	108	.537	19	31	.613	72	40	141	4.4
OSU	89-90	29	67	144	.465	22	37	.595	100	51	156	5.4
OSU	90-91	32	140	244	.574	73	84	.869	179	43	350	10.9
Totals		93	265	496	.534	114	152	.750	351	134	647	7.0

LUC LONGLEY

Team: Minnesota Timberwolves
Position: Center
Height: 7'2"
Weight: 265

Birthdate: January 19, 1969
College: New Mexico
Acquired: 1st-round pick in 1991 draft (7th overall)

Background: Longley, from Perth, Australia, has been coveted by pro scouts since he arrived at New Mexico in 1987. He progressed slowly for the Lobos and never was a consistent force in his four seasons. It was written that Longley could play like Bill Walton one night and John Boy Walton the next. Last season, he led the Lobos to the NCAA tournament for the first time since 1978. He is New Mexico's all-time leading scorer and rebounder.

Strengths: Longley is as skilled as any college center in the past five seasons, and is far more advanced than Dikembe Mutombo. Longley is a great passer, is mobile, is an excellent free throw shooter, and can score in the paint. He has the size and intelligence NBA teams want.

Weaknesses: The rap on Longley is that he lacks intensity and the desire to dominate. He certainly could use more fire in his approach. He isn't physical and is prone to traveling violations and turnovers.

Analysis: Minnesota needed a big forward like Doug Smith to replace Sam Mitchell and Tod Murphy, but Smith was selected by Dallas with the No. 5 pick. The T-Wolves considered Longley more promising than Brian Williams, Dale Davis, and Anthony Avent. Minnesota may have long-range plans to move promising center Felton Spencer, the No. 6 pick in the 1990 draft, to power forward. Longley has potential to be a marquee center.

PLAYER SUMMARY

Will ....block shots
Can't.....................perform consistently
Expect ....a back-up pivot
Don't Expect..................great intensity
Fantasy Value $18-20
Card Value $1.00-1.25

COLLEGE HIGHLIGHTS

- AP Honorable-Mention All-American, 1990 and 1991
- All-WAC, 1990 and 1991
- Australian National Team, 1988 and 1990

COLLEGE STATISTICS

		G	FGM	FGA	PCT	FTM	FTA	PCT	REB	AST	PTS	PPG
NM	87-88	35	60	120	.500	20	51	.392	94	22	140	4.0
NM	88-89	33	174	301	.578	80	104	.769	223	78	428	13.0
NM	89-90	34	233	417	.559	161	196	.821	330	108	627	18.4
NM	90-91	30	229	349	.656	116	162	.716	275	109	574	19.1
Totals		132	696	1187	.586	377	513	.735	922	317	1769	13.4

KEVIN LYNCH

Team: Charlotte Hornets
Position: Guard
Height: 6'5"
Weight: 200

Birthdate: December 24, 1968
College: Minnesota
Acquired: 2nd-round pick in 1991 draft (28th overall)

Background: In his first three seasons at Minnesota, Lynch was a good player on an outstanding team. Last season, the Gophers slumped to 12-16, but Lynch, the only returning starter, had a chance to showcase his talents. He finished in the top seven in the Big Ten in five categories, including steals and 3-point field goal percentage. Lynch, who never missed a practice at Minnesota, played in a school-record 119 consecutive games.

Strengths: Lynch's biggest assets are his versatility and durability. He plays hard at both ends of the floor, is a quick leaper and effective rebounder, and has good ball-handling skills. He has above-average shooting range and the ideal size to play shooting guard. He also can fill in at the point.

Weaknesses: Lynch is a streak shooter who often succumbs to questionable shot selection. He lacks lateral quickness and is stiff defensively. He doesn't have the necessary one-on-one skills and feel for the game to be a prime-time NBA guard.

Analysis: After filling a need for frontcourt power with Larry Johnson, Charlotte used its second-round pick on Lynch. He should be an adequate back-up to shooting guards Rex Chapman and Dell Curry. The selection of Lynch also enables the Hornets to trade either Chapman or Curry for more help up front. If neither is traded, Lynch will ride the bench.

PLAYER SUMMARY

Will........................shoot from anywhere
Can't........................outmuscle anyone
Expect........................up-and-down play
Don't Expect....................great defense
Fantasy Value..................................$3-5
Card Value...............................15-25¢

COLLEGE HIGHLIGHTS

- AP Honorable-Mention All-American, 1991
- Finalist, United States National Team, 1990
- Second-team All-Big Ten, 1991

COLLEGE STATISTICS

		G	FGM	FGA	PCT	FTM	FTA	PCT	REB	AST	PTS	PPG
MINN	87-88	28	39	101	.386	15	19	.789	31	39	103	3.7
MINN	88-89	31	123	262	.469	48	64	.750	131	70	318	10.3
MINN	89-90	32	167	330	.506	53	71	.746	91	102	428	13.4
MINN	90-91	28	190	413	.460	84	101	.832	121	90	506	18.1
Totals		119	519	1106	.469	200	255	.784	374	301	1355	11.4

MARK MACON

Team: Denver Nuggets
Position: Guard
Height: 6'5"
Weight: 185

Birthdate: April 14, 1969
College: Temple
Acquired: 1st-round pick in 1991 draft
(8th overall)

Background: Macon's big mistake at Temple was being a superstar from Day One. He was the nation's top freshman scorer and led the Owls to a 32-2 record in 1987-88. After that, he bore the burden of unreasonable expectations. His shooting percentage never was impressive, but the rest of his game was. Macon, Temple's all-time leading scorer, went out with a flourish last season, scoring 31 points in a 75-72 loss to North Carolina in the NCAA East Regional finals.

Strengths: Macon's greatest strength is his defensive ability. He has superior lateral quickness, can blanket opponents one-on-one, is a good jumper, and loves to compete. His quickness also allows him to create his own shot in one-on-one situations. He is a competent rebounder.

Weaknesses: Macon tried to do too much at Temple, especially on the offensive end. His shot selection was horrible, and he endured a host of 4-for-16 and 5-for-20 shooting nights. He's an average passer at best.

Analysis: Denver yielded an NBA-high 130.8 points per game last season. It began rebuilding with defense, taking Dikembe Mutombo with the No. 4 pick and Macon at No. 8—a pick acquired from Washington in a trade for Michael Adams. Macon teams with Chris Jackson, Todd Lichti, and Reggie Williams, giving coach Paul Westhead a talented, young backcourt. Macon may not start right away, but he'll play a lot.

PLAYER SUMMARY	
Will	play defense
Can't	score consistently
Expect	a Dennis Johnson type
Don't Expect	lack of effort
Fantasy Value	$6-8
Card Value	60-75¢

COLLEGE HIGHLIGHTS

- AP Honorable-Mention All-American, 1991
- Atlantic 10 Player of the Year, 1989
- All-Atlantic 10, 1988, 1989, 1990, and 1991
- National Freshman of the Year, 1988

COLLEGE STATISTICS

		G	FGM	FGA	PCT	FTM	FTA	PCT	REB	AST	PTS	PPG
TEMP	87-88	34	280	617	.454	74	96	.771	192	98	699	20.6
TEMP	88-89	30	204	501	.407	97	125	.776	168	115	548	18.3
TEMP	89-90	31	242	622	.389	134	168	.798	187	68	679	21.9
TEMP	90-91	31	254	578	.440	98	128	.766	153	71	683	22.0
Totals		126	980	2318	.423	403	517	.780	700	352	2609	20.7

VON McDADE

Team: New Jersey Nets
Position: Guard
Height: 6'4"
Weight: 185
Birthdate: June 7, 1967

College: Oklahoma St.; Wisconsin-Milwaukee
Acquired: 2nd-round pick in 1991 draft (53rd overall)

Background: McDade played two seasons at Iowa Lakes Junior College, then transferred to Oklahoma State, where he was expected to be a key player. After averaging nine minutes in 14 games, McDade dropped out of OSU, transferring to his hometown Milwaukee to play for Wisconsin-Milwaukee. Last season, he led the Panthers to an 18-10 record in their first year in Division I. McDade, who lit up Illinois for 50 points and Utah for 38, finished third in the nation in scoring and fourth in steals per game (3.5).

Strengths: McDade is an athletic, all-around combination guard. He has outstanding shooting range, can get his shot off the dribble, and is a leaper. He's also a good ball-handler. He is active defensively, with a knack for getting to loose balls. Scouts like his cocky, emotional approach, comparing him to Dennis Rodman.

Weaknesses: McDade is too thin to match up with some NBA shooting guards. He tends to be selfish with the ball, not creating opportunities for his teammates. He is a streak shooter and a marginal rebounder.

Analysis: McDade should prove to be a good pick for New Jersey, which got additional guard help in the first round, taking Kenny Anderson. Reggie Theus, the Nets' starting off guard last season, will play this season in Italy; that opens a spot for McDade, who projects as a back-up to Drazen Petrovic.

PLAYER SUMMARY

Will ....fill it up
Can't...give it up
Expect ....instant bench scoring
Don't Expect.......................any muscle
Fantasy Value $2-4
Card Value ....15-25¢

COLLEGE HIGHLIGHTS

- USBWA All-District IV, 1991
- *Milwaukee Journal* Wisconsin Player of the Year, 1991
- Runner-up, NCAA Independents Player of the Year, 1991

COLLEGE STATISTICS

		G	FGM	FGA	PCT	FTM	FTA	PCT	REB	AST	PTS	PPG
OSU	88-89	14	20	55	.364	8	13	.660	23	11	50	3.6
W-M	90-91	28	274	633	.433	186	238	.782	152	103	830	29.6
Totals		42	294	688	.427	194	251	.773	175	114	880	21.0

RODNEY MONROE

Team: Atlanta Hawks
Position: Guard
Height: 6'3"
Weight: 181

Birthdate: April 16, 1968
College: North Carolina St.
Acquired: 2nd-round pick in 1991 draft (30th overall)

Background: Nicknamed "Ice" for his cool temperament, Monroe was the player North Carolina State looked to in clutch situations over the past three seasons. He led the Wolfpack in scoring in 69 of its 92 games during that span, and he had a penchant for late-game heroics. He's the third-leading scorer in ACC history. Last year, Monroe finished seventh in the nation in scoring.

Strengths: Monroe is a stone scorer. He has excellent shooting mechanics, can get his shot off in traffic, is an effective penetrator, and moves well without the ball. He has outstanding range spotting up with his jumper, and he's deadly from the foul line. He's tough and competitive.

Weaknesses: Monroe is average or below average in every area except scoring. He has good hands and will make an occasional steal, but otherwise he's a defensive liability. He's a bit undersized and lacks a good enough one-on-one game to be a big-time NBA scoring guard.

Analysis: Atlanta, mediocre last season, has begun a complete overhaul. Guards Doc Rivers and Spud Webb were traded, John Battle left as a free agent, and Monroe was drafted to fill a need at shooting guard. The Hawks were lucky to get Monroe, who had been projected as a mid- to late first-round selection until he measured 6'1" and 168 pounds at the NBA's Chicago camp. He should be among the highest scoring rookies this season.

PLAYER SUMMARY	
Will	score in bunches
Can't	stop anybody
Expect	an All-Rookie
Don't Expect	many assists
Fantasy Value	$5-7
Card Value	35-50¢

COLLEGE HIGHLIGHTS
- ACC Player of the Year, 1991
- AP third-team All-American, 1991
- All-ACC, 1991
- Second-team All-ACC, 1990

COLLEGE STATISTICS

		G	FGM	FGA	PCT	FTM	FTA	PCT	REB	AST	PTS	PPG
NCST	87-88	32	132	277	.477	42	51	.824	77	47	355	11.1
NCST	88-89	31	240	513	.468	98	123	.797	149	89	663	21.4
NCST	89-90	30	228	505	.451	157	192	.818	130	75	697	23.2
NCST	90-91	31	285	641	.445	162	183	.885	136	88	836	27.0
Totals		124	885	1936	.457	459	549	.836	492	299	2551	20.6

ERIC MURDOCK

Team: Utah Jazz
Position: Guard
Height: 6'2"
Weight: 189

Birthdate: June 14, 1968
College: Providence
Acquired: 1st-round pick in 1991 draft
(21st overall)

Background: Murdock struggled during his junior season at Providence. He suffered a stress fracture in his leg and was hospitalized in February 1990 because of an irregular heartbeat. Murdock, recruited by then-Friars coach Rick Pitino, had a terrific senior season. He set career scoring highs in four consecutive games, topped by a Big East single-game record 48 vs. Pittsburgh. He established the NCAA record for career steals, with 376.

Strengths: Murdock has the skills to play both guard positions. He's quick with the ball, can penetrate, creates off the dribble, and has good shooting range. He is an outstanding defensive player. He guards the ball well, is active, and has terrific hands.

Weaknesses: Murdock is an in-between guard. He lacks the speed to be a front-line NBA point guard and the size to be a standout off guard. He tends to float defensively when his man doesn't have the ball, and he tends to be selfish offensively.

Analysis: Utah, which made it past the first round of the NBA playoffs for the first time in four seasons, selected Murdock to back up John Stockton at the point and Jeff Malone at shooting guard. Utah lacks depth in the backcourt, so Murdock should play a lot this season. He could become a favorite of coach Jerry Sloan, who also was a terrific defensive player.

PLAYER SUMMARY

Will ....play defense
Can't ....out-quick anybody
Expect ....a bench player
Don't Expect ....an instant hit
Fantasy Value $8-10
Card Value ....35-50¢

COLLEGE HIGHLIGHTS

- AP second-team All-American, 1991
- All-Big East, 1991
- USBWA Most Courageous Award, 1991
- Big East All-Rookie Team, 1988

COLLEGE STATISTICS

		G	FGM	FGA	PCT	FTM	FTA	PCT	REB	AST	PTS	PPG
PROV	87-88	28	114	276	.413	45	61	.738	85	106	300	10.7
PROV	88-89	29	164	359	.457	99	130	.762	135	141	471	16.2
PROV	89-90	28	147	351	.419	96	126	.762	146	92	432	15.4
PROV	90-91	32	262	589	.445	238	293	.812	168	148	818	25.6
Totals		117	687	1575	.436	478	610	.783	504	487	2021	17.3

DIKEMBE MUTOMBO

Team: Denver Nuggets
Position: Center
Height: 7'2"
Weight: 240

Birthdate: June 25, 1966
College: Georgetown
Acquired: 1st-round pick in 1991 draft
(4th overall)

Background: Mutombo, who is 25 years old, was raised in Zaire, a French-speaking nation in central Africa. He was forced to sit out his freshman year at Georgetown because he was unable to take the SAT test; it wasn't offered in French. Mutombo, who entered college with a crude offensive game, always has been a shot-blocker. In his first season with the Hoyas, he and 6'10" Alonzo Mourning combined for 244 blocks as Georgetown set an NCAA record with 309 rejections.

Strengths: Mutombo has great size, including a giant wingspan, and quickness. He's a terrific defensive player. Though he's an effective rebounder, he's not yet a great one because he's not very physical and does not yet understand the nuances of positioning. His offensive game has improved significantly with the addition of a hook shot.

Weaknesses: Mutombo lacks shooting range and is a poor passer and ball-handler. He lacks the hands and feel for the game that would allow him to make more than a handful of steals per season.

Analysis: Denver, the NBA's worst team last season, had a terrific draft despite losing the league's lottery drawing. Mutombo projects as a dominating shot-blocker and a perfect fit in coach Paul Westhead's up-tempo system. He also brings charisma to a team that has fallen out of favor with fans in Denver. Mutombo displaces Blair Rasmussen, who was traded to Atlanta.

PLAYER SUMMARY	
Will	block shots
Can't	shoot the jumper
Expect	an immediate starter
Don't Expect	an instant star
Fantasy Value	$22-25
Card Value	$1.50-2.00

COLLEGE HIGHLIGHTS
* Big East Defensive Player of the Year, 1990 and 1991
* All-Big East, 1991
* AP third-team All-American, 1991

COLLEGE STATISTICS

		G	FGM	FGA	PCT	FTM	FTA	PCT	REB	AST	PTS	PPG
GEOR	88-89	33	53	75	.707	23	48	.479	109	5	129	3.9
GEOR	89-90	31	129	182	.709	73	122	.598	325	18	331	10.7
GEOR	90-91	32	170	290	.586	147	209	.703	389	52	487	15.2
Totals		96	352	547	.644	243	379	.641	823	75	947	9.9

JIMMY OLIVER

Team: Cleveland Cavaliers
Position: Guard/Forward
Height: 6'6"
Weight: 208

Birthdate: July 12, 1969
College: Purdue
Acquired: 2nd-round pick in 1991 draft (39th overall)

Background: Oliver, Arkansas' Mr. Basketball in 1987, wasn't heavily recruited because of poor grades. He sat out his freshman season at Purdue to work on academics. Oliver was a part-time starter as a sophomore, the Boilermakers' "super sub" as a junior, and their main weapon as a senior. He finished the 1990-91 season strongly, then was outstanding in post-season all-star competition. He scored 25 points, on 9-for-13 shooting, in the NABC All-Star Game in Indianapolis.

Strengths: Oliver can play shooting guard or small forward. He has a great stroke and good range with his jumper and can create his own shot. He's tough and aggressive on defense. He has good leadership qualities.

Weaknesses: Oliver is a poor ball-handler and can't do anything with the ball in the open court. He can be streaky and is inconsistent defensively. Scouts rate him average or below in every area except shooting.

Analysis: Cleveland, which selected guard Terrell Brandon in the first round, drafted another guard, Oliver, in the second. The Cavs then went out and signed free agent guard John Battle. Mark Price may still be recovering from injury, but Cleveland now has a roomful of bodies to compete for his playing time. Oliver may become an odd man out.

PLAYER SUMMARY
Will ....be better as a pro
Can't ....dribble the ball
Expect ....points off the bench
Don't Expect ....an All-Rookie
Fantasy Value $4-6
Card Value ....25-35¢

COLLEGE HIGHLIGHTS
- All-Big Ten, 1991
- NABC All-Star Game MVP, 1991
- Japan Classic MVP, 1991

COLLEGE STATISTICS

		G	FGM	FGA	PCT	FTM	FTA	PCT	REB	AST	PTS	PPG
PURD	88-89	31	60	138	.435	18	31	.581	74	73	164	5.3
PURD	89-90	30	88	180	.489	43	67	.642	76	59	239	8.0
PURD	90-91	29	189	406	.466	99	115	.861	133	89	556	19.2
Totals		90	337	724	.466	160	213	.751	283	221	959	10.7

DOUG OVERTON

Team: Detroit Pistons
Position: Guard
Height: 6'3"
Weight: 190

Birthdate: August 3, 1969
College: La Salle
Acquired: 2nd-round pick in 1991
draft (40th overall)

Background: Overton, a high school teammate of Hank Gathers and Bo Kimble at Philadelphia's Dobbins Tech, dedicated his career to Gathers, who died in 1990. A point guard for most of his career at La Salle, Overton was a solid complementary player to All-American Lionel Simmons from 1987-90. When Simmons joined the NBA, however, Overton struggled with increased scoring responsibilities and a nagging ankle injury. The Explorers went 19-10 last year, missing the NCAA tournament for the first time in four years.

Strengths: Overton can play both guard positions but is best at the point. He's a decent shooter, despite his poor percentage as a senior, and dependable with the ball. He's an outstanding defensive player, having physical toughness and a desire to compete. Scouts have compared him to Joe Dumars.

Weaknesses: Though he played well in the NBA's post-season Chicago camp, Overton looked much slower than he appeared earlier in his career. He lacks top-level point-guard quickness and tends to overhandle the ball.

Analysis: With Isiah Thomas aging, Vinnie Johnson seeking a large contract, and Lance Blanks a disappointment, Detroit felt it was time to draft for guard depth. Overton should fit in well with the Pistons' aggressive defensive approach. He could supplant Gerald Henderson as Thomas's back-up, though rookies have played very little for coach Chuck Daly.

PLAYER SUMMARY	
Will	provide defense
Can't	out-quick anybody
Expect	a bench player
Don't Expect	a long career
Fantasy Value	$2-4
Card Value	25-35¢

COLLEGE HIGHLIGHTS
* All-Metro Atlantic, 1989, 1990, and 1991
* AP Honorable-Mention All-American, 1990 and 1991
* Metro Atlantic All-Tournament Team, 1989 and 1990

COLLEGE STATISTICS

		G	FGM	FGA	PCT	FTM	FTA	PCT	REB	AST	PTS	PPG
LaS	87-88	34	110	221	.498	37	44	.841	81	91	265	7.8
LaS	88-89	32	174	352	.494	47	59	.787	101	244	421	13.2
LaS	89-90	32	201	387	.519	95	119	.798	133	212	551	17.2
LaS	90-91	25	199	447	.445	106	128	.818	103	124	558	22.3
Totals		123	684	1407	.486	285	350	.814	418	671	1795	14.6

BILLY OWENS

Team: Sacramento Kings
Position: Forward/Guard
Height: 6'9"
Weight: 225

Birthdate: May 1, 1969
College: Syracuse
Acquired: 1st-round pick in 1991 draft (3rd overall)

Background: Owens, the 1988 AP High School Player of the Year at Carlisle (Pennsylvania) High, was Syracuse coach Jim Boeheim's prize recruit, and Owens didn't disappoint the coach. Owens finished his three years at Syracuse ranked in the school's top seven in career scoring, rebounds, blocked shots, steals, and assists. He started all 103 games in his career, recorded 36 double-doubles, and last season became the first player to average more than 20 PPG under Boeheim. Last year, Owens pulled down more offensive rebounds than Dikembe Mutombo.

Strengths: As his statistics suggest, Owens is incredibly versatile. He can play every position but center, passes the ball extremely well, runs the floor, and has great quickness. He has good shooting range, is adept at using the backboard, and can score on the low blocks. He works hard and plays defense.

Weaknesses: Critics suggest that Owens rarely is at his best in big games. Otherwise, there's little not to like about his game.

Analysis: Despite getting a great talent in Owens, Sacramento was devastated when New Jersey took point guard Kenny Anderson with the No. 2 pick. Owens also was disappointed, because he had hoped to be reunited in New Jersey with former Syracuse teammate Derrick Coleman. Owens will be an immediate starter, probably at small forward, with Lionel Simmons moving to off guard to replace Travis Mays, who was traded to Atlanta for Spud Webb.

PLAYER SUMMARY	
Will	be Rookie of the Year
Can't	miss as a pro
Expect	triple-doubles
Don't Expect	blocked shots
Fantasy Value	$10-12
Card Value	75¢-$1.00

COLLEGE HIGHLIGHTS
* AP first-team All-American, 1991
* All-Big East, 1990 and 1991
* Big East Player of the Year, 1991
* United States National Team, 1990

COLLEGE STATISTICS

		G	FGM	FGA	PCT	FTM	FTA	PCT	REB	AST	PTS	PPG
SYR	88-89	38	196	376	.521	94	145	.648	263	119	494	13.0
SYR	89-90	33	228	469	.486	127	176	.722	276	151	602	18.2
SYR	90-91	32	282	554	.509	157	233	.674	371	111	744	23.3
Totals		103	706	1399	.505	378	554	.682	910	381	1840	17.7

ELLIOT PERRY

Team: Los Angeles Clippers
Position: Guard
Height: 6'0"
Weight: 155

Birthdate: March 28, 1969
College: Memphis St.
Acquired: 2nd-round pick in 1991 draft (37th overall)

Background: The diminutive, be-goggled Perry was a familiar sight in college hoops for the past four seasons, during which time he led Memphis State to a 76-50 record. A product of the fertile Memphis prep ranks, Perry was an instant hit for the Tigers, playing well as a freshman and sophomore. He tailed off badly as a junior, struggling with inconsistency and poor outside shooting. Though Memphis State was 17-15 last season, Perry had a solid campaign. He scored 42 points in a match-up with East Tennessee State's Keith Jennings.

Strengths: Perry has great quickness and the speed to blow by defenders in the open court. He's an adequate shooter within 17 feet, but is better penetrating than spotting up. He works very hard defensively and has a terrific attitude. He was versatile enough to play both guard positions in college.

Weaknesses: As one scout said, "The problem is, he has no body." Perry is too small and weak to withstand the NBA grind, and he projects as a defensive liability in halfcourt situations. He lacks a true point-guard mentality, partly because he was counted on to score so much at Memphis State.

Analysis: The Clippers, desperate for a point guard, traded the No. 9 pick in the draft to Atlanta for Doc Rivers, then drafted Perry. They expect him to compete with incumbent starter Gary Grant for the back-up role to Rivers. The Clippers will bring lots of bodies to training camp; Perry may not make the team.

PLAYER SUMMARY	
Will	disrupt defensively
Can't	bury the 3
Expect	a struggle to stick
Don't Expect	much PT
Fantasy Value	$3-5
Card Value	25-35¢

COLLEGE HIGHLIGHTS

• All-Metro, 1989 and 1991
• Second-team All-Metro, 1990
• Metro Conference Freshman of the Year, 1988

COLLEGE STATISTICS

		G	FGM	FGA	PCT	FTM	FTA	PCT	REB	AST	PTS	PPG
MSU	87-88	32	140	336	.417	87	108	.806	113	130	420	13.1
MSU	88-89	32	202	437	.462	192	234	.821	109	118	620	19.3
MSU	89-90	30	175	419	.418	137	182	.753	110	150	504	16.8
MSU	90-91	32	235	507	.464	146	184	.793	111	148	665	20.8
Totals		126	752	1699	.443	562	707	.795	443	546	2209	17.5

BOBBY PHILLS

Team: Milwaukee Bucks
Position: Guard
Height: 6'5"
Weight: 210

Birthdate: December 20, 1969
College: Southern
Acquired: 2nd-round pick in 1991 draft (45th overall)

Background: Phills, the son of a college dean, stayed home in Baton Rouge, Louisiana, to attend Southern, where he was head coach Ben Jobe's first recruit. After a quiet freshman season, Phills exploded as a scorer and 3-point bomber. He fired up 788 3-point attempts during his career. Last season, he led the nation in 3-pointers per game (4.4). He finished sixth the country in scoring and ninth in steals (3.2 per game), as Southern led the nation in scoring with 104.4 PPG

Strengths: Phills is a good all-around player. He has NBA 3-point shooting range and is smart, competitive, and aggressive. He is quick, an above-average rebounder and ball-handler, and runs the floor well. Scouts like his strength and intensity.

Weaknesses: Though he has no glaring weakness, Phills may not be good enough to make it in the NBA. He has no superior skills to separate him from other fringe players. His college shooting percentage was poor because of poor shot selection.

Analysis: Milwaukee satisfied a big need for front-line help by trading first-round pick Kevin Brooks to Denver for Anthony Avent. It then took a flyer on Phills, who goes into training camp as the fourth shooting guard behind Alvin Robertson, Dale Ellis, and Jeff Grayer. The Bucks won't carry four players at the position. Barring a trade, Phills will be a likely cut.

PLAYER SUMMARY

Will ....shoot with range
Can't ....score inside
Expect ....a battle to make it
Don't Expect ....great talent
Fantasy Value $2-4
Card Value ....15-35¢

COLLEGE HIGHLIGHTS

• All-Southwestern Athletic Conference, 1991

COLLEGE STATISTICS

		G	FGM	FGA	PCT	FTM	FTA	PCT	REB	AST	PTS	PPG
SU	87-88	23	25	53	.491	30	42	.714	41	8	85	3.7
SU	88-89	31	166	385	.431	44	60	.733	142	55	420	13.5
SU	89-90	31	232	574	.451	46	70	.657	132	89	622	20.1
SU	90-91	28	260	641	.407	152	211	.720	132	52	795	28.4
Totals		113	683	1653	.413	272	383	.710	447	204	1922	17.0

MARK RANDALL

Team: Chicago Bulls
Position: Forward
Height: 6'9"
Weight: 230

Birthdate: September 30, 1967
College: Kansas
Acquired: 1st-round pick in 1991 draft
(26th overall)

Background: Randall, from Englewood, Colorado, had a tremendous five-year run at Kansas. He started four games as a freshman, finished eighth in the Big Eight in scoring as a sophomore, led the conference in field goal percentage as a junior, and, as the Jayhawks' only returning starter, led Kansas to the national title game as a senior. Randall missed the 1987-88 season—the team's national-championship year—as a medical redshirt (jaw surgery).

Strengths: Randall is versatile; he played both forward and center at Kansas. He always is around the ball, has a good feel for the game, and is an outstanding passer. He runs the floor well and has good hands. He's well versed in fundamentals and has the special ability to make teammates better.

Weaknesses: Randall is not a go-to offensive weapon, doesn't have great shooting range, and is only adequate from the foul line. Randall is not very athletic; he's not a leaper and rarely blocks shots.

Analysis: Chicago has not had a good draft since 1987, when it acquired starting forwards Horace Grant and Scottie Pippen. Randall eventually may be a good pro. For now, he projects as a bench-warmer. The Bulls sought to upgrade their rebounding but were stymied when Dale Davis, Anthony Avent, John Turner, and Stanley Roberts were selected before Chicago's pick at No. 26.

PLAYER SUMMARY	
Will	play with intensity
Can't	shoot the 3
Expect	a role player
Don't Expect	an athlete
Fantasy Value	$2-4
Card Value	25-40¢

COLLEGE HIGHLIGHTS

* AP Honorable-Mention All-American, 1991
* World University Games, 1989
* All-Big Eight, 1991
* Academic All-Big Eight, 1990

COLLEGE STATISTICS

		G	FGM	FGA	PCT	FTM	FTA	PCT	REB	AST	PTS	PPG
KAN	86-87	31	54	102	.529	32	51	.627	83	19	140	4.5
KAN	88-89	31	201	311	.646	95	145	.655	208	53	497	16.0
KAN	89-90	35	183	305	.600	100	148	.676	216	65	466	13.3
KAN	90-91	35	205	319	.643	113	178	.635	216	80	524	15.0
Totals		132	643	1037	.620	340	522	.651	723	217	1627	12.1

STANLEY ROBERTS

Team: Orlando Magic
Position: Center
Height: 7'0"
Weight: 288

Birthdate: February 7, 1970
College: Louisiana St.
Acquired: 1st-round pick in 1991 draft (23rd overall)

Background: After sitting out his freshman season at LSU because of academic shortcomings, Roberts teamed with All-America center Shaquille O'Neal for one season (1989-90), forming the "Twin Towers." In his 32-game college career, Roberts had 14 double-doubles, but he fouled out eight times. He continued to struggle academically and was declared ineligible in August 1990. He promptly signed a contract with Real Madrid, a professional team in Spain.

Strengths: Roberts is a force within ten feet of the basket. He has a decent turnaround jumper, is effective on the offensive boards, and is nearly impossible to move once he gets position on the low blocks. His hands are adequate (O'Neal had nearly twice as many turnovers in their season together), and he can block shots.

Weaknesses: Roberts doesn't have a great feel for the game, doesn't run the floor very well, is a terrible free throw shooter, and isn't a good passer. His work ethic also has been questioned, and he is a bit overweight.

Analysis: With Brian Williams already in tow with the No. 10 pick, Orlando selected Roberts after several teams, including Seattle and Golden State, passed on him because of his weight problem (304 pounds on draft day) and questionable attitude. "When Roberts was here, we had to remove an obstruction from his throat," said Orlando GM Pat Williams. "It was a pizza." Roberts eventually could be great, or a gigantic bust.

PLAYER SUMMARY	
Will	score in the paint
Can't	shoot FTs
Expect	an eventual force
Don't Expect	an All-Rookie
Fantasy Value	$3-5
Card Value	25-40¢

COLLEGE HIGHLIGHTS
• Third-team All-SEC, 1990

COLLEGE STATISTICS

		G	FGM	FGA	PCT	FTM	FTA	PCT	REB	AST	PTS	PPG
LSU	89-90	32	200	347	.576	51	111	.460	315	40	451	14.1
Totals		32	200	347	.576	51	111	.460	315	40	451	14.1

DOUG SMITH

Team: Dallas Mavericks
Position: Forward
Height: 6'10"
Weight: 220

Birthdate: September 17, 1969
College: Missouri
Acquired: 1st-round pick in 1991 draft
(6th overall)

Background: Smith went from Detroit's MacKenzie High to immediate stardom at Missouri. He was named first-team Freshman All-American in 1988, and the Tigers went 94-35 in his four seasons. Missouri was placed on NCAA probation last year, and rumors had Smith leaving early for the NBA or to play in Europe. He started last season slowly, but he eventually carried a young and injury-depleted Missouri team to the Big Eight tournament championship.

Strengths: Smith is a terrific open-court player. He runs the floor as well as any player his size and he finishes fastbreaks with authority. He's an adequate ball-handler and a very good passer. His shooting range extends to about 15 feet. He's most effective around the basket, especially from the baseline.

Weaknesses: Smith hasn't added any bulk, and that will hurt him if he has to play power forward in the NBA. His post-up skills need work, as does his shooting range (he had four career 3-pointers). Defensively, he made strides last season and stayed out of foul trouble, but he remains a liability.

Analysis: Dallas was in desperate need of frontcourt help last year. The Mavericks lost free agent Sam Perkins to the Lakers before the season and Roy Tarpley to a knee injury after five games. Dallas' recent draft picks (Randy White, Phil Henderson) have been disappointing, but Smith looks like a perfect fit. He should be an immediate starter and a Rookie of the Year candidate.

PLAYER SUMMARY	
Will	make an early impact
Can't	shoot from outside
Expect	highlight-film jams
Don't Expect	much defense
Fantasy Value	$11-14
Card Value	75¢ -$1.00

COLLEGE HIGHLIGHTS
* Big Eight Player of the Year, 1990 and 1991
* Big Eight Male Athlete of the Year, 1991
* United States National Team, 1990
* AP Second-team All-American, 1990

COLLEGE STATISTICS

		G	FGM	FGA	PCT	FTM	FTA	PCT	REB	AST	PTS	PPG
MO	87-88	30	145	288	.504	48	75	.640	197	72	338	11.3
MO	88-89	36	217	455	.477	67	91	.736	250	88	502	13.9
MO	89-90	32	260	462	.563	115	161	.714	295	64	635	19.8
MO	90-91	30	275	553	.497	156	190	.821	311	96	709	23.6
Totals		128	897	1758	.510	386	517	.747	1053	320	2184	17.1

LaBRADFORD SMITH

Team: Washington Bullets
Position: Guard
Height: 6'3"
Weight: 200

Birthdate: April 3, 1969
College: Louisville
Acquired: 1st-round pick in 1991 draft
(19th overall)

Background: A tremendous athlete, Smith has high-jumped 6'10" and was drafted in 1990 by the Toronto Blue Jays as a pitching prospect. He was expected to be the next Darrell Griffith at Louisville, but he never lived up to those expectations. Nonetheless, Smith had a solid, sometimes spectacular, four-year career for the Cardinals. He is Louisville's all-time leader in assists, and he was one of the greatest free throw shooters in NCAA history.

Strengths: Smith is a good all-around player. He is a good, not great, passer, can score inside or from the perimeter, and contributes defensively, on the boards, and from the foul line. He's a terrific leaper and dunker. He's versatile enough to play both guard spots, and he'll play hurt.

Weaknesses: Smith has the potential to be an NBA point guard, but at this point he lacks great point-guard skills. He isn't consistent in his approach and production, and he didn't improve significantly from his freshman season at Louisville. He has a bad attitude, will sulk, and lacks composure.

Analysis: Washington, with a passable front line of Pervis Ellison, Bernard King, John Williams, and Harvey Grant, needed backcourt help, and may have found it in Smith. He likely will play both guard spots, backing up Darrell Walker at the point and providing an occasional 3-pointer (Washington made a league-low 55 treys last season).

PLAYER SUMMARY	
Will	dunk with flair
Can't	play consistently
Expect	a good career
Don't Expect	a great career
Fantasy Value	$6-8
Card Value	50-65¢

COLLEGE HIGHLIGHTS
- All-Metro, 1990 and 1991
- Metro Tournament Most Outstanding Player, 1990 and 1991
- Metro All-Freshman Team, 1988

COLLEGE STATISTICS

		G	FGM	FGA	PCT	FTM	FTA	PCT	REB	AST	PTS	PPG
LOU	87-88	35	136	285	.477	143	158	.905	88	156	443	12.7
LOU	88-89	33	125	269	.465	112	129	.868	75	184	394	11.9
LOU	89-90	35	158	318	.497	123	143	.860	117	226	471	13.5
LOU	90-91	30	173	359	.482	113	137	.825	110	147	498	16.6
Totals		133	592	1231	.481	491	567	.866	390	713	1806	13.6

STEVE SMITH

Team: Miami Heat
Position: Guard
Height: 6'6"
Weight: 195

Birthdate: March 31, 1969
College: Michigan St.
Acquired: 1st-round pick in 1991 draft
(5th overall)

Background: Smith, a Detroit product, was an immediate star at Michigan State, where he led the Spartans to a 28-6 record and the Big Ten title in 1989-90. Last year, Smith led the league in scoring for the second straight season and he finished in the top 11 in six other categories, including rebounds and assists. He set a Big Ten record by hitting 45 consecutive free throws, and he finished his career as the Spartans' all-time leading scorer, ahead of Scott Skiles.

Strengths: Smith has more offensive talent than any other shooting guard taken in the 1991 NBA draft. He has great shooting range, can create shots one-on-one, can pass off the dribble, and has a nice feel for the game. Smith is an outstanding rebounder for a guard, and a very good passer. He's a clutch player who loves to have the ball late in the game.

Weaknesses: Smith has a fragile body. He'll have to learn how to play NBA-style defense or he will be punished running into picks. In any event, he's liable to give up as many points as he scores. He needs more mental toughness to handle the NBA grind.

Analysis: Miami selected Steve Smith instead of Doug Smith, who might have filled a bigger need. Steve should quickly emerge as Miami's shooting guard, joining Sherman Douglas in a terrific, young backcourt, and allowing Glen Rice to move to small forward. Smith could be the Rookie of the Year.

PLAYER SUMMARY

Will.....................................be a fine pro
Can't..............................guard anyone
Expect..........................30-point nights
Don't Expect....................physical play
Fantasy Value..............................$8-10
Card Value............................75¢ -$1.00

COLLEGE HIGHLIGHTS

- AP second-team All-American, 1991
- *Sporting News* first-team All-American, 1990
- Big Ten MVP, 1990
- World University Games, 1989

COLLEGE STATISTICS

		G	FGM	FGA	PCT	FTM	FTA	PCT	REB	AST	PTS	PPG
MSU	87-88	28	108	232	.466	69	91	.758	112	82	299	10.7
MSU	88-89	33	217	454	.478	129	169	.763	229	112	585	17.7
MSU	89-90	31	233	443	.526	116	167	.695	216	150	627	20.2
MSU	90-91	30	268	566	.474	150	187	.802	183	109	752	25.1
Totals		122	826	1695	.487	464	614	.756	740	453	2263	18.5

LaMONT STROTHERS

Team: Portland Trail Blazers
Position: Guard
Height: 6'4"
Weight: 192
Birthdate: May 10, 1968

College: Christopher Newport
Acquired: Draft rights traded from Warriors for 2nd-round picks in 1995 and 1999, 6/91

Background: Strothers, a year out of high school, was working in a meat-packing plant when an assistant coach at Division III Christopher Newport College noticed him in a pick-up game. Strothers enrolled at the school in Newport News, Virginia, and was an immediate star. He broke Lionel Simmons's NCAA record for consecutive games in double figures, with 116. Strothers is the third-leading scorer in Division III history. He was drafted 43rd overall by Golden State but his rights were dealt to Portland.

Strengths: A strong 6'4", Strothers has the physical tools to make it as an NBA shooting guard. He has terrific shooting mechanics and good range, moves well without the ball, can penetrate, and is a good ball-handler. He loves to compete, challenging opponents at both ends of the floor.

Weaknesses: Strothers lacks experience against quality competition. He must show that he can finish inside against bigger players. He needs to refine his passing, rebounding, and defense.

Analysis: Strothers earned rave reviews at the post-season Portsmouth Invitational. Unfortunately for him, the Blazers were among the most impressed. Portland has more depth than any other NBA club. Strothers has an outside shot to make the team, backing up Clyde Drexler and Danny Ainge.

PLAYER SUMMARY	
Will	go toe-to-toe
Can't	reject shots
Expect	a battle to make it
Don't Expect	much finesse
Fantasy Value	$1-3
Card Value	15-25¢

COLLEGE HIGHLIGHTS
- Division III All-American, 1991
- Dixie Conference Player of the Year, 1989 and 1991
- Dixie Conference Tournament MVP, 1988, 1990, and 1991

COLLEGE STATISTICS

		G	FGM	FGA	PCT	FTM	FTA	PCT	REB	AST	PTS	PPG
CN	87-88	30	250	531	.471	125	168	.744	191	42	652	21.7
CN	88-89	29	255	549	.465	124	181	.685	158	43	695	24.0
CN	89-90	28	232	491	.473	92	129	.713	166	69	603	21.5
CN	90-91	29	279	578	.483	146	195	.749	202	69	759	26.2
Totals		116	1016	2149	.473	487	673	.724	717	225	2709	23.4

GREG SUTTON

Team: San Antonio Spurs
Position: Guard
Height: 6'2"
Weight: 170

Birthdate: December 3, 1967
College: Langston; Oral Roberts
Acquired: 2nd-round pick in 1991
draft (49th overall)

Background: Sutton, from Oklahoma City, played one season at NAIA Langston University before transferring to Division I Oral Roberts, which downgraded its program to NAIA after his sophomore season. Sutton promptly emerged as a prolific scorer. Last season, he scored a school-record 68 points in a game vs. Oklahoma City. Sutton, who scored 19 points in the post-season NABC All-Star Game, scored in double figures in all 104 games he played at Oral Roberts. He spent this summer terrorizing USBL opponents with 3-pointers.

Strengths: Sutton is a pure offensive talent with a terrific shooting stroke, a quick release, and excellent range. He has quickness to penetrate and shoots well off the dribble. He is a good passer. Defensively, he is quick and aggressive.

Weaknesses: Despite great mechanics, Sutton is an inconsistent shooter, capable of missing several in a row. He suffers from poor shot selection and occasionally plays out of control. He is closer to 6'0" than the 6'2" he was listed at in college, making him a defensive liability against most NBA guards.

Analysis: The Spurs, with only one draft pick to work with, gambled on Sutton. He never will be a starting off guard because of his size, but he could establish himself as a viable reserve, providing instant offense off the bench. The Spurs have little depth at guard.

PLAYER SUMMARY
Will ....fill it up
Can't...................................play it cool
Expect.................a struggle to make it
Don't Expect..........................any dunks
Fantasy Value $1-3
Card Value ....15-25¢

COLLEGE HIGHLIGHTS
- NAIA Player of the Year, 1991
- NAIA All-American, 1990 and 1991

COLLEGE STATISTICS

		G	FGM	FGA	PCT	FTM	FTA	PCT	REB	AST	PTS	PPG
LANG	87-88	29	198	487	.406	93	124	.750	90	61	536	18.4
OR	88-89	28	214	564	.379	103	157	.656	121	89	614	21.9
OR	89-90	41	417	976	.427	252	328	.768	205	249	1256	30.6
OR	90-91	35	393	585	.458	229	280	.818	168	152	1200	34.3
Totals		133	1222	2885	.424	677	889	.750	584	551	3606	27.1

ALVARO TEHERAN

Team: Philadelphia 76ers
Position: Center
Height: 7'1"
Weight: 235

Birthdate: January 6, 1966
College: Houston Baptist; Houston
Acquired: 2nd-round pick in 1991 draft (44th overall)

Background: Teheran, from Colombia, did not play basketball until he was age 19. He was recruited to Houston Baptist by then-coach Tommy Jones, who noticed Teheran when in Colombia scouting another prospect. Houston Baptist dropped its program after the 1988-89 season, with Jones taking an assistant's job at Houston. Teheran followed, seeing limited action as a junior before blossoming last season, when he recorded eight double-doubles. After the season, Teheran signed a two-year contract with a pro team in Malaga, Spain.

Strengths: Teheran has improved significantly in the past year. He gained 15 pounds between his junior and senior seasons, developed an effective hook shot, and emerged as an effective shot-blocker. He has very good quickness and can run the floor.

Weaknesses: Teheran needs lots of work. His low-post game is unrefined, he doesn't move well without the ball, and he's a below-average passer and man-to-man defender. His shooting range is limited.

Analysis: Philadelphia had little to lose by drafting Teheran, who already had signed to play in Spain. He only has been playing for six years and will benefit by playing, rather than riding the bench. The 76ers, who renounced their rights to Rick Mahorn, will be hurting at center this season. If Teheran continues to develop, he could be the starter by 1995.

PLAYER SUMMARY	
Will	block shots
Can't	dominate physically
Expect	a three-year project
Don't Expect	to see him soon
Fantasy Value	$1-3
Card Value	35-50¢

COLLEGE HIGHLIGHTS

- Second-team All-Southwest Conference, 1991
- Southwest Conference All-Defensive Team, 1991
- Honorable-Mention All-Trans America Conference, 1989

COLLEGE STATISTICS

		G	FGM	FGA	PCT	FTM	FTA	PCT	REB	AST	PTS	PPG
HB	87-88	27	119	230	.517	71	111	.640	155	16	309	11.4
HB	88-89	27	163	307	.531	69	103	.670	146	14	395	14.6
HOU	89-90	33	61	131	.466	55	85	.647	113	12	177	5.4
HOU	90-91	29	155	291	.433	104	157	.662	245	32	414	14.3
Totals		116	498	959	.519	299	456	.656	659	74	1295	11.2

JOHN TURNER

Team: Houston Rockets
Position: Forward
Height: 6'9"
Weight: 245

Birthdate: November 30, 1967
College: Georgetown; Phillips
Acquired: 1st-round pick in 1991 draft (20th overall)

Background: Turner made three collegiate stops in five years. He attended Allegany (Maryland) Community College as a freshman, then sat out a season after transferring to Georgetown. He started 27 games for the Hoyas his first year there, pulling down ten or more rebounds seven times. Turner then transferred to Phillips University, an NAIA school in Enid, Oklahoma, where he played under head coach Denny Price, Mark Price's father. Turner's stock rose rapidly in 1991 with outstanding performances at the post-season Portsmouth Invitational and Orlando Classic.

Strengths: Turner has impressive strength in his chiseled body. He does a lot of things well—he's an adequate shooter, penetrator, jumper, and rebounder— though is not outstanding in any area. He has good court presence. His game is intimidation, and he was able to back it up in college.

Weaknesses: Though his long arms enable him to play bigger than his height, Turner remains too small to handle NBA power forwards, and he lacks the skills to compete with the league's small forwards. He doesn't work hard defensively.

Analysis: Turner was advertised as 6'9", but measured 6'5 ½" at the NBA's pre-draft camp in Chicago. Houston drafted him to compete for a back-up role to power forward Otis Thorpe and small forward Buck Johnson. The Rockets, 3-12 in playoff games the past four seasons, need toughness. Turner figures to be a good fit. He looks like a two- to three-year project.

PLAYER SUMMARY	
Will	hammer on people
Can't	run the floor
Expect	early struggles
Don't Expect	Mr. Congeniality
Fantasy Value	$8-10
Card Value	60-75¢

COLLEGE HIGHLIGHTS
- NAIA All-American, 1991
- Sooner Athletic Conference Player of the Year, 1991
- All-SAC, 1990 and 1991
- Portsmouth Invitational MVP, 1991

COLLEGE STATISTICS

		G	FGM	FGA	PCT	FTM	FTA	PCT	REB	AST	PTS	PPG
GEOR	88-89	32	73	156	.468	64	116	.552	199	30	210	6.6
PHIL	89-90	18	152	310	.490	80	142	.543	243	46	414	23.0
PHIL	90-91	27	242	422	.574	119	190	.627	370	89	644	23.9
Totals		77	467	888	.526	263	448	.587	812	165	1268	16.5

SHAUN VANDIVER

Team: Golden State Warriors
Position: Center/Forward
Height: 6'10"
Weight: 220

Birthdate: June 15, 1968
College: Colorado
Acquired: 1st-round pick in 1991 draft
(25th overall)

Background: Vandiver, a Chicago product, was a redshirt his first year at Hutchinson (Kansas) Community College, after suffering a severe knee injury. He was a sixth man for Hutchinson in 1988, averaging nine points per game, as the Dragons went 34-2 and won the NJCAA national championship. Vandiver was an instant star at Colorado. As a junior, he led the Big Eight in both scoring and rebounding. Vandiver went out with a flourish last season, playing very impressively in the postseason NIT tournament. This summer, he signed a two-year contract to play in Italy.

Strengths: His greatest attribute is consistency. Predominantly an inside player, Vandiver has good shooting range, outstanding touch around the basket, and refined post-up moves. He is a tenacious rebounder.

Weaknesses: The knee injury robbed Vandiver of mobility. He can't run the floor and he isn't particularly quick in halfcourt sets or playing defense. A mediocre passer, he had more turnovers than assists during his college career.

Analysis: In desperate need for size, Golden State spent three first-round draft picks on big people. The other two, Chris Gatling and Victor Alexander, were selected No. 16 and No. 17, respectively. Vandiver, at No. 25, would have had a harder time to make his mark. The seasoning in Italy will do him good. If or when he comes back, he should be able to contribute some solid minutes.

PLAYER SUMMARY	
Will	clean the boards
Can't	run the floor
Expect	a solid reserve
Don't Expect	an All-Rookie
Fantasy Value	$1-3
Card Value	50-75¢

COLLEGE HIGHLIGHTS
- All-Big Eight, 1990 and 1991
- Big Eight Newcomer of the Year, 1989
- Orlando All-Star Classic MVP, 1991
- Big Eight Tournament MVP, 1991

COLLEGE STATISTICS

		G	FGM	FGA	PCT	FTM	FTA	PCT	REB	AST	PTS	PPG
COLO	88-89	28	198	367	.540	112	146	.767	295	56	509	18.2
COLO	89-90	30	274	462	.593	117	171	.684	336	62	668	22.3
COLO	90-91	33	278	478	.582	137	182	.753	331	65	699	21.2
Totals		91	750	1307	.574	366	499	.733	962	183	1876	20.6

BRIAN WILLIAMS

Team: Orlando Magic
Position: Center/Forward
Height: 6'11"
Weight: 242

Birthdate: April 6, 1969
College: Maryland; Arizona
Acquired: 1st-round pick in 1991 draft
(10th overall)

Background: Williams, who played at three different high schools, originally signed with Maryland. He had a tremendous freshman season for the Terrapins but decided to transfer to Arizona, citing "philosophical differences" with then-Maryland coach Bob Wade. Williams, who sat out the 1988-89 season, teamed with 7'0" Ed Stokes and 6'11" Sean Rooks to form the "Tucson Skyline," and Arizona went 53-14 in his two seasons. Williams, whose career was marked by inconsistency, passed up a year of eligibility to enter the NBA draft.

Strengths: Williams is a fine athlete. He has good quickness and jumping ability and he runs the floor well. He's an effective scorer along the baseline and has a soft touch on his jumper. When motivated, he is a force rebounding, blocking shots, and playing defense. In his final season at Arizona, he had a penchant for playing best in big games.

Weaknesses: Williams has been criticized for not being "focused" on the game. He is a poor passer and rarely gives up the ball once he touches it. His low-post game is unrefined, and he hasn't shown mental or physical toughness.

Analysis: Orlando, in dire need of frontcourt help, took Williams with the No. 10 pick. Williams shouldn't take long to supplant Greg Kite, perhaps the NBA's worst starting center. Williams also can provide quality minutes at power forward, substituting for Terry Catledge and Jeff Turner. The Magic drafted another center, Stanley Roberts, with the 23rd pick.

PLAYER SUMMARY	
Will	score in the paint
Can't	perform consistently
Expect	a productive career
Don't Expect	an instant hit
Fantasy Value	$8-10
Card Value	60-75¢

COLLEGE HIGHLIGHTS
- All-Pac-10, 1991
- AP Honorable-Mention All-American, 1991
- ACC Newcomer of the Year, 1988

COLLEGE STATISTICS

		G	FGM	FGA	PCT	FTM	FTA	PCT	REB	AST	PTS	PPG
MD	87-88	29	156	260	.600	51	76	.671	176	22	363	12.5
ARIZ	89-90	32	130	235	.553	80	110	.727	181	14	340	10.6
ARIZ	90-91	35	195	315	.619	99	147	.673	273	21	489	14.0
Totals		96	481	810	.594	230	333	.691	630	57	1192	12.4

JOEY WRIGHT

Team: Phoenix Suns
Position: Guard
Height: 6'3"
Weight: 185

Birthdate: September 4, 1968
College: Drake; Texas
Acquired: 2nd-round pick in 1991 draft (50th overall)

Background: Wright, a high school star in Hammond, Indiana, was snubbed in-state by Bob Knight and Gene Keady. He enrolled at Drake but left after one season, frustrated by then-coach Gary Garner's down-tempo approach. Wright proved to be a perfect fit in Texas coach Tom Penders's run-and-gun offense. He teamed for two seasons with current NBA players Lance Blanks and Travis Mays to form the Longhorns' "BMW" backcourt. Last year, Wright was the go-to guy for Texas, which went 72-27 in his three seasons.

Strengths: Wright has limited athletic tools but a burning desire to make it. He is tough both mentally and physically, with excellent strength. He's an adequate mid-range shooter and a good ball-handler. He has a penchant for late-game heroics.

Weaknesses: He's an in-between guard, with point-guard size and skills more suited to off guard. Wright is a poor passer and has below-average quickness and speed. He is an erratic outside shooter without great range, and he lacks defensive intensity. Scouts have called him a poor man's Doc Rivers.

Analysis: Phoenix used the last of its three draft picks on Wright, who is a long shot to make the team. The Suns have the deepest backcourt in the NBA, with starters Kevin Johnson and Jeff Hornacek and reserves Negele Knight and Dan Majerle.

PLAYER SUMMARY

Will..............................challenge anyone
Can't..........................score consistently
Expect.........................a fight to make it
Don't Expect...................any quickness
Fantasy Value..................................$1-3
Card Value....................................15-25¢

COLLEGE HIGHLIGHTS

- AP Honorable-Mention All-American, 1991
- All-Southwest Conference, 1991
- GTE Southwest Conference All-Academic Team, 1990 and 1991

COLLEGE STATISTICS

		G	FGM	FGA	PCT	FTM	FTA	PCT	REB	AST	PTS	PPG
DRAK	86-87	16	15	29	.517	7	11	.636	11	10	38	2.4
TEX	88-89	33	173	345	.501	49	116	.674	105	96	519	15.7
TEX	89-90	33	209	455	.459	160	206	.777	149	126	644	19.5
TEX	90-91	31	207	481	.430	182	239	.762	134	113	656	21.2
Totals		113	604	1310	.461	473	640	.739	399	345	1857	16.4

JOE WYLIE

Team: New York Knicks
Position: Forward
Height: 6'9"
Weight: 210
Birthdate: February 10, 1968

College: Miami (FL)
Acquired: Draft rights traded from Clippers for a 1993 2nd-round pick, 7/91

Background: Wylie, from Wilson High in Washington, D.C., sat out his freshman season under Prop 48 guidelines. He progressed in each of the three seasons he played, leading Miami in scoring, rebounding, and blocked shots as a junior and senior. Wylie was a virtual one-man team last season as the 'Canes struggled to a 9-19 record under new coach Leonard Hamilton. His NBA stock rose with a terrific showing at the post-season Orlando Classic. He was drafted No. 38 overall by the Clippers but was traded to the Knicks.

Strengths: Wylie was a center in college, but he has the tools to be a quality small forward. He is an NBA-caliber athlete with speed, quickness, and jumping ability. He has good shooting range. He passes the ball well and is an adequate rebounder. His quickness helps him defensively, though he will have to learn NBA defense at a new position.

Weaknesses: Wylie was inconsistent at Miami, especially with his shot. He tends to lose concentration or play out of control at times, and he's a poor free throw shooter. His floor game needs work, especially his ball-handling.

Analysis: The Knicks expect Wylie to compete with Brian Quinnett for the back-up role to small forward Kiki Vandeweghe. Wylie's chances of making the team were enhanced in July when New York renounced its rights to small forward Kenny Walker. Progress may come slowly as Wylie learns a new position.

PLAYER SUMMARY

Will.....................................run the floor
Can't........................shoot consistently
Expect.......................a two-year project
Don't Expect ....much PT
Fantasy Value.................................$5-7
Card Value ....35-50¢

COLLEGE HIGHLIGHTS
* Miami team MVP, 1990 and 1991
* NCAA Independent All-American, 1991

COLLEGE STATISTICS

		G	FGM	FGA	PCT	FTM	FTA	PCT	REB	AST	PTS	PPG
MIA	88-89	25	105	202	.520	55	104	.529	213	44	268	10.7
MIA	89-90	28	210	430	.488	91	153	.595	266	38	514	18.4
MIA	90-91	28	186	400	.465	143	194	.737	279	42	515	18.4
Totals		81	501	1032	.485	289	451	.640	758	124	1297	16.0

NBA Team Overviews

This section evaluates all 27 NBA teams, sectioning them off by their divisions. (Note that the Orlando Magic have moved from the Midwest Division to the Atlantic Division.) For each team, you'll find:

- the club's address and phone number
- arena information
- a listing of the team's owner, general manager (or equivalent thereof), and coaches
- the head coach's record (lifetime and with team)
- a review of the team's history
- team finishes over the last five years
- a review of the team's 1990-91 season
- the club's 1991-92 roster
- a preview of the 1991-92 season

The team rosters include players who were drafted in June. The rosters include each player's 1990-91 statistics. Stats include points per game (PPG), rebounds per game (RPG), and assists per game (APG). The category "EXP" (experience) indicates the number of years the player has played in the NBA.

Each 1991-92 season preview tips off with an "opening line," which looks at the players the team lost and those that are coming in. The preview then examines the team at each position, including guard, forward, center, and coaching. "Analysis" evaluates the team's strengths and weaknesses and puts it all into perspective. The preview ends with a prediction, stating where the club will finish within its division.

BOSTON CELTICS

Division: Atlantic
Home: Boston Garden
Capacity: 14,890
Year Built: 1928

Address
151 Merrimac St.
Boston, MA 02114
(617) 523-6050

Chairman of the Board:
Don F. Gaston
Executive V.P./General Manager:
Jan Volk
Head Coach: Chris Ford
Assistant Coach: Don Casey
Assistant Coach: Jon Jennings

Coach Chris Ford			
	W	L	Pct.
NBA Record	56	26	.683
W/Celtics	56	26	.683
1990-91 Record	56	26	.683

Celtics History

The history of the Boston Celtics drips with tradition. The Celtics have won 16 world championships, and must be listed with baseball's Yankees, football's Packers, and hockey's Canadiens as one of the greatest teams in sports history.

Boston began as a member of the old BAA in 1946-47 and joined the NBA at its inception. Red Auerbach took over as coach of the team in 1950-51 and began assembling the pieces of the Celtic machine. He started with guard Bob Cousy, added Bill Sharman, and in 1956 bagged the big one—Bill Russell.

Boston won its first championship in 1956-57, then won every title from 1958-59 through 1965-66, thoroughly dominating pro basketball. Russell, famous for his battles with Wilt Chamberlain, redefined post defense. His supporting cast included Sam and K.C. Jones, Tom Heinsohn, Frank Ramsey, and John Havlicek. Auerbach moved to the front office in 1966 and Russell took over as player/coach, but the Celtics didn't falter, winning championships in 1968 and '69. Heinsohn assumed control of the bench in 1969 and won titles in 1974 and '76 with stars like Havlicek, center Dave Cowens, and guard Jo Jo White.

The Celtics' modern era dawned in 1979, when the team drafted forward Larry Bird. Behind Bird and frontcourt partners Robert Parish and Kevin McHale, Boston shared the 1980s spotlight with the Los Angeles Lakers, taking world championships in 1981, '84, and '86.

Last Five Years

Season	W	L	Pct.	Place	Playoffs	Coach
1986-87	59	23	.720	First	L-NBA Finals	K.C. Jones
1987-88	57	25	.695	First	L-East Finals	K.C. Jones
1988-89	42	40	.512	Third	L-Round One	Jimmy Rodgers
1989-90	52	30	.634	Second	L-Round One	Jimmy Rodgers
1990-91	56	26	.683	First	L-East Semis	Chris Ford

1990-91 Recap

While Boston fans thrilled to the exploits of a new generation of Celtic heroes during 1990-91, their primary focus was on the old-timers. For as exciting as youngsters Brian Shaw, Reggie Lewis, Kevin Gamble, and Dee Brown proved to be, the aging frontcourt of Larry Bird, Robert Parish, and Kevin McHale would have to stand up to the rigors of the grueling NBA schedule.

Instead of succumbing to Father Time, the Celts thrived. Shaw came back from Italy to team with Lewis and give Boston a backcourt for the next decade. Brown, a little-known first-round draft selection from Jacksonville, proved adroit at turbocharging the fastbreak, and Gamble proved solid enough at forward to send McHale back to his traditional sixth-man spot.

The young talent rejuvenated Boston. The Celtics stormed to the Atlantic title, rolling up a 56-26 record and dusting second-place Philadelphia by 12 games. They were one of only two teams to shoot better than 50 percent from the field, and six Celtics scored in double figures. They withstood a spirited challenge by Chuck Person and the Pacers in the first round of the playoffs and stretched Detroit to six games before falling in the conference semifinals.

But despite the renaissance, the same questions continued to haunt the Celtics. Bird's back forced him to miss 22 regular-season games and limited his playoff performance–although he became the fifth player in history to collect 20,000 points, 5,000 rebounds, and 5,000 assists in a career. Parish, the oldest NBA player at 38, and McHale (33) weren't getting any younger, and the Celtic bench was inconsistent after McHale and Brown.

1991-92 Roster

No.	Player	Pos.	Ht.	Wt.	Exp.	College	1990-91 PPG	RPG	APG
5	John Bagley	G	6'0"	205	9	Boston College	—	—	—
33	Larry Bird	F	6'9"	220	12	Indiana St.	19.4	8.5	6.1
7	Dee Brown	G	6'1"	161	1	Jacksonville	8.7	2.2	4.2
44	Rick Fox	F/G	6'7"	231	R	North Carolina	—	—	—
34	Kevin Gamble	G/F	6'5"	210	4	Iowa	15.6	3.3	3.1
53	Joe Kleine	C	7'0"	271	6	Arkansas	3.6	3.4	0.3
35	Reggie Lewis	G/F	6'7"	195	4	Northeastern	18.7	5.2	2.5
32	Kevin McHale	F/C	6'10"	225	11	Minnesota	18.4	7.1	1.9
00	Robert Parish	C	7'0"	230	15	Centenary	14.9	10.6	0.8
54	Ed Pinckney	F	6'9"	215	6	Villanova	5.2	4.9	0.6
20	Brian Shaw	G	6'6"	190	2	Cal.-Santa Bar.	13.8	4.7	7.6
43	Derek Smith	G/F	6'6"	218	9	Louisville	2.5	0.0	2.5
11	Michael Smith	F	6'10"	225	2	Brigham Young	4.6	1.2	0.9
52	Stojko Vrankovic	C	7'2"	260	1	None	1.9	1.6	0.1
12	A.J. Wynder	G	6'2"	180	1	Fairfield	2.0	0.5	1.3

Boston Celtics
1991-92 Season Preview

Opening Line: The Celtics are a curious mix of old (*very* old) and new. The Hall of Fame front line of Larry Bird, Kevin McHale, and Robert Parish is 105 years of age. But then there are the smaller young bloods—Reggie Lewis, Kevin Gamble, Brian Shaw, and Dee Brown. Coach Chris Ford molded this team into a division winner last year and, if the aching old-timers can make it to the floor, he could do it again this season. With the 24th pick in the draft, Boston added Rick Fox, a 6'7" small forward from North Carolina.

Guard: Shaw, Lewis, and Brown give the Celtics a young but talented guard trio. The point guard is Shaw (13.8 PPG, 7.6 APG), a speedster who has the advantage of being 6'6". Given time, he could develop into an All-Star. Lewis (18.7 PPG) is a prime-time scorer. He can race it down the court, take it to the hole, or pull up for an 18-footer. At 6'7", he also has a height advantage. Little Brown won last year's NBA Slam Dunk title and made the All-Rookie Team. He's a runner and a jumper who can push the ball up-court in a flash. These three still must prove they can win in the playoffs.

Forward: Despite age (34), surgically repaired heels, and back problems, Bird remains an outstanding small forward, as last year's numbers indicate (19.4 PPG, 8.4 RPG, 7.2 APG). He remains the heart of this team. McHale is still a force both offensively and defensively in the low post, but injuries are reducing his minutes. Gamble has come out of nowhere to earn a starting spot. He's a 6'5" runner who can score; he canned 59 percent of his shots last year. Ed Pinckney is a lanky wing player who is ineffective in a halfcourt offense. Lewis can also play small forward.

Center: Robert Parish, age 38, continues to amaze the basketball world with his All-Star level of play (14.9 PPG, 10.6 RPG). He'll continue to rebound as long as he can stand up. Back-up Joe Kleine is a bruiser who's effective in his limited role. McHale also spends time at the pivot.

Coaching: Ford has served as a teammate, assistant coach, and head coach of Boston's Bird-McHale-Parish front line. In 1990-91, his first year, Ford did an commendable job of meshing the old-timers with younger players. Ever since his playing days, he's been known as heady basketball man. Ford is assisted by Don Casey, the former head coach of the Los Angeles Clippers, and Jon Jennings.

Analysis: While the aging frontcourt is losing a step, the younger players are picking one up. If the Big Three can avoid any serious injuries, Boston should win the Atlantic one more time. The problem comes when the old guys retire. Boston has no big men to take their place.

Prediction: 1st place, Atlantic

MIAMI HEAT

Division: Atlantic
Home: Miami Arena
Capacity: 15,008
Year Built: 1988

Address
Miami Arena
Miami, FL 33136
(305) 577-4328

Partners: Ted Arison, Zev Bufman, Billy Cunningham, Lewis Schaffel
Managing Partner: Lewis Schaffel
Head Coach: Kevin Loughery
Assistant Coach: Bob Staak

	Coach Kevin Loughery		
	W	L	Pct.
NBA Record	341	503	.404
W/Heat	0	0	.000
1990-91 Record	0	0	.000

Heat History

Although it has spent three seasons dwelling in various divisional basements, Miami has stood fast on its commitment to building through the draft. The city was awarded a franchise in April 1987 and entered the league in 1988-89 under the direction of coach Ron Rothstein.

The team had few recognizable players at its inception, but it certainly had some ownership clout in the form of Billy Cunningham, a former All-Star forward and the coach of the 1982-83 champion Philadelphia 76ers. The Heat stumbled to a 15-67 record in its inaugural campaign, relying on rookies Rony Seikaly and Kevin Edwards and a collection of NBA castaways. One of the definite highlights of the first year was the sharp shooting of guard Jon

Sundvold, who led the league in 3-point shooting with a remarkable 52 percent average.

The following year brought rookies Glen Rice and Sherman Douglas to the Heat, along with three more wins. But there was even bigger news for Miami fans. The city hosted the 1990 All-Star Game and found a hated rival in the expansion Orlando Magic. Magic president Pat Williams, formerly GM in Philadelphia when Cunningham coached there, fueled the competition with several anti-Miami remarks, and soon the two teams thirsted to defeat each other.

Unfortunately, that desire didn't translate into too many wins. After Miami posted a 24-58 record in 1990-91, Rothstein resigned under pressure.

Last Three Years

Season	W	L	Pct.	Place	Playoffs	Coach
1988-89	15	67	.183	Sixth	DNQ	Ron Rothstein
1989-90	18	64	.220	Fifth	DNQ	Ron Rothstein
1990-91	24	58	.293	Sixth	DNQ	Ron Rothstein

1990-91 Recap

Things warmed up a little bit for Miami in 1990-91, but not enough to save coach Ron Rothstein, who "resigned" following a 24-58 performance. Sure, the Heat showed a six-game improvement over the previous year, but that's hardly an occasion for hurrahs. The cold facts were that only Denver, the NBA's version of a carnival freak show, had a worse record than the Heat.

Though the blame fell upon Rothstein, it must be said that only guard Sherman Douglas (8.5 assists) appeared among the league leaders in any positive statistical category. The Heat had the worst assist-to-turnover ratio in the league and had one of the worst shooting percentages. Not even Red Auerbach could have won with this club.

Miami's commitment to building with youth has been noble, but outside of a small nucleus of talent, the team was overmatched in 1990-91. Had Cleveland not matched the huge offer sheet Miami tendered forward John Williams in 1990, things could have been different, but the Cavs did, and Miami's fortunes sagged.

Douglas was solid at the point, adding a team-high 18.5 points a game to his assist total. Forward Glen Rice reaped the benefits of his off-season shooting diligence by averaging 17.4 a game and hitting 38.6 percent from 3-point range.

Injuries hampered the effectiveness of center Rony Seikaly (16.4 points, 11.1 rebounds), while forward Grant Long slipped to 9.2 PPG. Rookie swing man Willie Burton (12.0 points) showed promise, and guard Kevin Edwards (12.1 points) scored some but shot only 41 percent from the field.

1991-92 Roster

No.	Player	Pos.	Ht.	Wt.	Exp.	College	1990-91 PPG	RPG	APG
45	George Ackles	F/C	6'9"	215	R	UNLV	—	—	—
2	Keith Askins	G/F	6'8"	197	1	Alabama	2.2	1.7	0.5
34	Willie Burton	G/F	6'7"	219	1	Minnesota	12.0	3.4	1.4
12	Bimbo Coles	G	6'1"	182	1	Virginia Tech	4.9	1.9	2.8
11	Sherman Douglas	G	6'0"	180	2	Syracuse	18.5	2.9	8.5
21	Kevin Edwards	G	6'3"	197	3	DePaul	12.1	2.6	3.0
33	Alec Kessler	F/C	6'11"	245	1	Georgia	6.2	4.3	0.4
43	Grant Long	F	6'8"	230	3	E. Michigan	9.2	7.1	2.2
53	Alan Ogg	C	7'2"	235	1	Ala.-Birmingham	1.7	1.6	0.1
41	Glen Rice	F	6'7"	220	2	Michigan	17.4	4.9	2.5
4	Rony Seikaly	C	6'11"	252	3	Syracuse	16.4	11.1	1.5
3	Steve Smith	G	6'6"	195	R	Michigan St.	—	—	—
20	Jon Sundvold	G	6'2"	175	8	Missouri	4.7	0.4	1.0

Miami Heat
1991-92 Season Preview

Opening Line: After three years as Heat coach, Ron Rothstein is out. In is Kevin Loughery, a veteran who has coached five other NBA clubs. Despite the coaching change, the team is committed to the same philosophy—building through the draft. That philosophy has brought the Heat Rony Seikaly, Sherman Douglas, Kevin Edwards, Glen Rice, and Willie Burton. And in June, Miami selected Michigan State shooting guard Steve Smith with the fifth pick in the draft. The Heat also chose George Ackles, UNLV's 6'9" center, with the 29th pick. Miami did not re-sign part-timers Billy Thompson and Terry Davis.

Guard: Point guard Douglas is the man who runs this team. He's an outstanding penetrator who led Miami in both scoring (18.5 PPG) and assists (8.5 APG) last season. Back-up Bimbo Coles can handle the ball but has trouble shooting it. After struggling to find a dependable shooting guard, the Heat are now overloaded at the position. Edwards, who has had trouble canning his shots, will probably lose his job to rookie Smith, a do-it-all 6'6" guard. Shooting star Rice excelled in the big-guard position late last year, but he'll probably be moved back to forward. Burton provides athletic skills at both big guard and small forward.

Forward: Rice (17.4 PPG) is starting to sink his feathery jumpers on a regular basis, though he doesn't provide much else at the forward position. Grant Long offers few skills, but he has muscled and hustled his way into the starting lineup. He'll commit as many fouls as any man in the league. Miami's power forward of the future may be sophomore Alec Kessler, who can shoot from outside and possesses some unrefined inside skills. Burton will see plenty of minutes at small forward.

Center: Young Rony Seikaly (16.4 PPG, 11.1 RPG) is one of the top ten centers in the NBA. He possesses both speed and strength and has exceptional coordination for an NBA pivot man. Seikaly is backed up by Kessler and Alan Ogg, a 7'2" project. Ackles is a low-risk gamble.

Coaching: Though his lifetime record is only 341-503, Loughery is a respected coach who has had to deal with some talent-poor ballclubs. Loughery knows the league and brings a different perspective to a team that had experienced the high-strung, demanding tactics of Rothstein. Loughery is assisted by Bob Staak.

Analysis: Miami has accumulated so much young talent that it's only a matter of time before Heat fans see the payoff. Every player on this team—Douglas, Seikaly, Rice, etc.—will only get better, and Smith will solidify the troubled off-guard position. The Heat is perhaps a power forward away from reaching the playoffs.

Prediction: 5th Place, Atlantic

NEW JERSEY NETS

Division: Atlantic
Home: Brendan Byrne Arena
Capacity: 20,039
Year Built: 1981

Address
Brendan Byrne Arena
East Rutherford, NJ 07073
(201) 935-8888

Chairman of the Board:
Alan L. Aufzien
Senior V.P./Basketball Operations:
Willis Reed
Head Coach: Bill Fitch
Assistant Coach: Tom Newell
Assistant Coach: Rick Carlisle

Coach Fill Fitch			
	W	L	Pct
NBA Record	805	835	.491
W/Nets	43	121	.262
1990-91 Record	26	56	.317

Nets History

Basketball fans can choose from two images of the Nets. The first comes from the mid-1970s, back in the days of the ABA, when the team was still based on Long Island. Back then, the team featured skywalking forward Julius Erving, the man who carried the Nets to the 1976 league title. The second image is that of the current club, one that has posted five straight depressing seasons in the New Jersey Meadowlands.

The franchise was born in 1967 as the New Jersey Americans, a charter member of the ABA. The team moved to Long Island the next year, became the New York Nets, and acquired high-scoring Rick Barry for the 1970-71 season. The Nets made it to the ABA finals the next year, but they lost Barry to the NBA. Erving came aboard in

1973-74 and led the team to the league title in 1975-76. When the Nets became one of four teams to merge with the NBA, they appeared to be in great shape.

Then the problems started. Erving had a contract dispute with owner Roy Boe, who sold him to Philadelphia. The Nets made the playoffs six of the next ten years but won only one series, beating Philadelphia in 1983-84. That team featured an impressive frontcourt of Buck Williams, Albert King, and Darryl Dawkins.

The past five years have been dismal, as management has made some questionable draft decisions. New Jersey's Derrick Coleman did win the Rookie of the Year Award in 1990-91, but that hardly guarantees that a renaissance is at hand.

Last Five Years

Season	W	L	Pct.	Place	Playoffs	Coach
1986-87	24	58	.293	Fourth	DNQ	Dave Wohl
1987-88	19	63	.232	Fifth	DNQ	D. Wohl/B. MacKinnon/W. Reed
1988-89	26	56	.317	Fifth	DNQ	Willis Reed
1989-90	17	65	.207	Sixth	DNQ	Bill Fitch
1990-91	26	56	.317	Fifth	DNQ	Bill Fitch

1990-91 Recap

When Derrick Coleman accepted his award as the 1990-91 NBA Rookie of the Year, Nets officials probably had to search for the key to the trophy case. It had been so long since someone had won anything in North Jersey that the cobwebs in the case were probably as big as fishing nets.

Coleman lived up to his No. 1-pick status, not to mention his huge contract, by leading all rookies in scoring (18.4) and rebounding (10.3) and establishing himself as one of the league's top power forwards. And while Coleman was taking his bows and collecting the headlines, the Nets quietly improved.

Of course, there was still a long way to go. With a 26-56 record, the Nets barely escaped the Atlantic Division cellar—thanks to Miami—and were near the bottom of several statistical categories. A couple more

Colemans would come in handy.

Coleman's rebounding passion was shared by his teammates, however, and the Nets led the Eastern Conference with an average of 54.5 boards a game. Forward Chris Morris, known primarily for his penchant for shooting, pulled down 6.6 rebounds a game, to go with his 13.2 points, and fragile center Sam Bowie claimed 7.7 RPG during his 62 games of action.

Veteran guard Reggie Theus again led the Nets in scoring, pumping in 18.6 PPG. Backcourt mate Mookie Blaylock showed signs of maturing with 14.1 points, 6.1 assists, and 2.35 steals a game. There were other encouraging statistics, like center Chris Dudley's 2.51 blocks a game— good for fifth in the league—and the offense provided off the bench by Drazen Petrovic (12.6 PPG in 43 games), who was a mid-season acquisition from Portland.

1991-92 Roster

No.	Player	Pos.	Ht.	Wt.	Exp.	College	1990-91 PPG	1990-91 RPG	1990-91 APG
7	Kenny Anderson	G	6'2"	166	R	Georgia Tech	—	—	—
10	Mookie Blaylock	G	6'1"	185	2	Oklahoma	14.1	3.5	6.1
31	Sam Bowie	C	7'1"	240	6	Kentucky	12.9	7.7	2.4
21	Stanley Brundy	F	6'7"	215	2	DePaul	—	—	—
35	Jud Buechler	F	6'6"	220	1	Arizona	3.1	1.9	0.7
44	Derrick Coleman	F	6'10"	230	1	Syracuse	18.4	10.3	2.2
22	Chris Dudley	C	6'11"	240	4	Yale	7.1	8.4	0.6
12	Tate George	G	6'5"	190	1	Connecticut	3.4	0.8	1.9
54	Jack Haley	F	6'10"	240	3	UCLA	5.6	4.6	0.4
6	Roy Hinson	F	6'9"	215	8	Rutgers	4.6	2.1	0.4
11	Von McDade	G	6'4"	185	R	Wis.-Milwaukee	—	—	—
5	Terry Mills	F	6'10"	230	1	Michigan	5.7	4.2	0.6
34	Chris Morris	F	6'8"	210	3	Auburn	13.2	6.6	2.8
3	Drazen Petrovic	G	6'5"	195	2	Zagreb	10.2	1.8	1.4

New Jersey Nets
1991-92 Season Preview

Opening Line: The New Jersey Nets, perennial poor souls of the East, found a savior last season and may have found another this year. Derrick Coleman, last season's NBA Rookie of the Year, gave coach Bill Fitch a take-charge, multi-talented power forward. Now comes rookie point guard Kenny Anderson, chosen out of Georgia Tech with the No. 2 overall pick, who has been compared to Isiah Thomas and Nate Archibald. The Nets also chose Von McDade, a 6'4" guard from Wisconsin-Milwaukee, with the 53rd pick. The team did lose leading scorer Reggie Theus to Europe, and back-up gunner Derrick Gervin became an unrestricted free agent.

Guard: Anderson possesses brilliant playmaking skills and also has the shooting ability to light it up. He's a future All-Star who could step right into the starting lineup. Incumbent point guard Mookie Blaylock is super-quick and a great pickpocket, but he's been too erratic, especially with his shooting, to lead the team. Drazen Petrovic can drain shots from the perimeter, but he's too slow to take over the starting off-guard slot. New Jersey desperately needs a starting shooting guard.

Forward: Coleman, a fast, agile big man, can do it all, from hitting the medium-range jumper (18.4 PPG) to cleaning the boards (10.3 RPG). He'll be an All-Star throughout the 1990s. Small forward Chris Morris has outstanding talent, but his up-and-down play and poor attitude has caused Fitch fits. Power forward Terry Mills offers a big body and a soft touch, but he too has trouble with his intensity. Jud Buechler is a heady, fundamentally sound player with little talent, while Jack Haley is nothing more than a tough guy who likes to bang.

Center: After years of leg injuries, Sam Bowie is finally playing legitimate minutes. Bowie, a respectable NBA center, provides strong rebounding and even some scoring and shot-blocking. Chris Dudley, a notoriously terrible free throw shooter, offers great rebounding for a back-up (8.4 RPG).

Coaching: Fitch has coached in the NBA for 19 years, has won 805 games (fourth on the all-time list), has been named Coach of the Year twice, and won a world title with Boston in 1981. He turned both Cleveland and Houston into winning teams, so he can do it in New Jersey too. He is assisted by Rick Carlisle and Tom Newell.

Analysis: The Nets are too young and talent-poor to do anything this year, but Coleman and Anderson give the team a great foundation for the future. If the talented Morris and Mills tune up their intensity—and if Bowie's legs hold up—then New Jersey could be a solid playoff team within a couple years. But of course, Nets fans have learned not to get too optimistic.

Prediction: 6th Place, Atlantic

NEW YORK KNICKS

Division: Atlantic
Home: Madison Square Garden
Capacity: 19,081
Year Built: 1968

Address
Four Pennsylvania Plaza
New York, NY 10001
(212) 465-6000

Chief Executive Officer:
Richard H. Evans
President: Dave Checketts
Head Coach: Pat Riley
Assistant Coach: Dick Harter
Assistant Coach: Paul Silas
Assistant Coach: Jeff Van Gundy

Coach Pat Riley			
	W	L	Pct.
NBA Record	533	194	.733
W/Knicks	0	0	.000
1990-91 Record	0	0	.000

Knicks History

Despite playing in the nation's media capital, the Knicks have spent much of their existence in the shadow of their rival to the north—Boston.

Soon after the franchise's inception as a BAA member, the Knicks made trips to the league finals in 1951, '52, and '53. Hall of Fame coach Joe Lapchick molded forward Carl Braun with Harry Gallatin, Dick McGuire, and Nat "Sweetwater" Clifton and reached the playoffs nine years straight (1947-55).

The following ten years were not so kind. The Knicks wandered through six coaches and made the playoffs only once—1958-59. But fortunes changed quickly when Red Holzman took over in 1967-68. The Knicks built a powerhouse on the backs of center Willis Reed, forwards Bill Bradley and Dave DeBusschere, and guards Walt "Clyde" Frazier and Dick Barnett. In 1969-70, they defeated the Lakers in seven games for the title.

Jerry Lucas replaced Reed in the middle, and flashy Earl Monroe joined Frazier to form one of the game's best-ever backcourts. Together, they won the NBA championship in 1973.

The subsequent 18 seasons have featured few peaks. High-scoring Bernard King provided some thrills in the mid-1980s, but a serious knee injury cut short his run with the Knicks. Star center Patrick Ewing arrived in 1985 and he sparked the team to the Atlantic Division title in 1988-89, but they have accomplished little else.

Last Five Years

Season	W	L	Pct.	Place	Playoffs	Coach
1986-87	24	58	.293	Fourth	DNQ	Hubie Brown/Bob Hill
1987-88	38	44	.463	Second	L-Round One	Rick Pitino
1988-89	52	30	.634	First	L-East Semis	Rick Pitino
1989-90	45	37	.549	Third	L-East Semis	Stu Jackson
1990-91	39	43	.476	Third	L-Round One	S. Jackson/John MacLeod

1990-91 Recap

While the Knicks spent most of 1990-91 trying to decide on the right combination of management personnel, they paid little attention to the people they put on the court. That neglect resulted in a 39-43 record and some serious questions for a team that two years earlier appeared close to the NBA elite.

The Knicks fired Stu Jackson early in the season and replaced him with John MacLeod, who left town for the Notre Dame job following New York's three-game playoff drubbing at the hands of Chicago. Meanwhile, president Jack Diller and GM Al Bianchi were deposed in mid-season, and the resulting power base of president Dave Checketts and vice-president Ernie Grunfeld embarked on a whirlwind courtship of ex-Lakers coach Pat Riley.

While the parents bickered, the children suffered. Center Patrick Ewing was again a tower of strength (26.6 points, 11.2 rebounds), though some thought he was more interested in securing a huge contract extension than winning. Power forward Charles Oakley was a beast on the boards (12.1 average) and an adequate scorer (11.2 average). But even with those two, the Knicks were still a poor rebounding team; their next highest rebounder averaged 3.0 a game.

Forwards Kiki Vandeweghe (16.3 PPG) and Gerald Wilkins (13.8 PPG) proved once again that they could score, but neither showed an affection for mixing it up inside. Veteran point guard Maurice Cheeks (7.8 points, 5.7 assists) continued to keep the starting job warm for talented but immature Mark Jackson (8.8 points, 6.3 assists). Off guard Trent Tucker's numbers slipped (7.1 points), and the Knicks had little to try in his place.

1991-92 Roster

No.	Player	Pos.	Ht.	Wt.	Exp.	College	PPG	RPG	APG
—	Greg Anthony	G	6'2"	190	R	UNLV	—	—	—
1	Maurice Cheeks	G	6'1"	180	13	West Texas St.	7.8	2.3	5.7
33	Patrick Ewing	C	7'0"	240	6	Georgetown	26.6	11.2	3.0
13	Mark Jackson	G	6'3"	205	4	St. John's	8.8	2.7	6.3
32	Jerrod Mustaf	F	6'10"	244	1	Maryland	4.3	2.7	0.6
34	Charles Oakley	F	6'9"	245	6	Virginia Union	11.2	12.1	2.7
23	Brian Quinnett	F	6'8"	236	2	Washington St.	4.7	2.1	0.8
3	John Starks	G	6'5"	180	1	Oklahoma St.	7.6	2.1	3.3
6	Trent Tucker	G	6'5"	190	9	Minnesota	7.1	1.6	1.7
55	Kiki Vandeweghe	F	6'8"	220	11	UCLA	16.3	2.4	1.5
7	Kenny Walker	F	6'8"	217	5	Kentucky	4.3	2.9	0.2
45	Eddie Lee Wilkins	F/C	6'10"	220	5	Gardner-Webb	4.1	2.6	0.2
21	Gerald Wilkins	G	6'6"	195	6	Tenn.-Chattanooga	13.8	3.0	4.0
—	Joe Wylie	F	6'9"	210	R	Miami (FL)	—	—	—

New York Knicks
1991-92 Season Preview

Opening Line: After a disastrous season, New York was able to lure Pat Riley out of retirement. Now that the Knicks have a marquee coach in place, they have to do something about the team's miserable chemistry. Even though they have the dominating Patrick Ewing, they have to put other players around him who work as a compatible unit. Mark Jackson, the club's erratic and trouble-making point guard, is Riley's biggest concern. Rookie Greg Anthony, a 6'2" guard from UNLV (12th pick in the draft), may take his place. Kenny Walker and Eddie Lee Wilkins were unrestricted free agents.

Guard: When he's not bad-mouthing management and playing out of control, Jackson can be an explosive NBA playmaker. The Big Apple waits to see how he'll perform under Riley. Maurice Cheeks has long been one of the league's steadiest, most respected point guards, but he's growing old (age 35). Anthony, a strong leader and open-court player, piloted the great UNLV clubs. He won't need much time to develop. Starting off guard Gerald Wilkins (13.8 PPG) can explode to the hoop, but he's too inconsistent to be a starter. Trent Tucker will shoot the 3-pointer and play defense, while John Starks is a spark plug off the bench.

Forward: Kiki Vandeweghe (16.3 PPG) has long been one of the league's premier scorers. However, a bad back, horrible defense, and poor rebounding cancel out the positives. Charles Oakley (12.1 RPG) continues to reign as the NBA's "Chairman of the Boards." Jerrod Mustaf, age 22, is a power forward with finesse. Given time, he'll develop into a heck of player. Brian Quinnett has some offensive talent but is basically a fringe player.

Center: Ewing is a throwback to the great low-post centers of old, a la Bill Russell. As evident by his numbers (26.6 PPG, 11.2 RPG, 3.2 BPG), Patrick is clearly a dominant, franchise player. All he needs is a competent point guard to feed him the ball.

Coaching: Riley proved he was one of basketball's all-time great coaches by leading the Lakers to four NBA titles in the 1980s and nine first-place finishes in nine seasons. Riley is also the NBA's all-time leader in playoff victories (102-47). Expect him to rework the Knicks to fit his style. Several players may go. Riley's assistants are Dick Harter, Paul Silas, and Jeff Van Gundy.

Analysis: With the Knicks, expect Riley to use Ewing in the same manner he utilized Kareem Abdul-Jabbar in Los Angeles. Riley will use Ewing as a go-to threat underneath, while Patrick's rebounding will trigger the fastbreak. Riley's philosophy will work better once he gets the right type of players to fit into his system. This will be a transition year.

Prediction: 3rd Place, Atlantic

ORLANDO MAGIC

Division: Atlantic
Home: Orlando Arena
Capacity: 15,077
Year Built: 1989

General Partner: William duPont III
President/General Manager:
 Pat Williams
Head Coach: Matt Guokas
Assistant Coach: Brian Hill
Assistant Coach: John Gabriel
Assistant Coach: George Scholz

Address
One Magic Place
Orlando Arena
Orlando, FL 32801
(407) 649-3200

Coach Matt Guokas			
	W	L	Pct.
NBA Record	168	203	.453
W/Magic	49	115	.299
1990-91 Record	31	51	.378

Magic History

It's surprising that the Magic is not owned by a consortium of Mickey Mouse, Donald Duck, and Pluto. After all, the team has worked hard to tie itself to the Disney World image of Orlando. When the team presented its franchise application check to David Stern on July 2, 1986, it also handed the NBA commissioner a set of Mickey Mouse ears. Even the team's nickname conjures up an image of the Magic Kingdom.

In its two years of existence, the team has built an identity of its own. After a predictably dreadful 18-64 debut in 1989-90, the Magic improved to 31-51 in 1990-91 and showed some signs of progress.

The inaugural season was noteworthy for style, if not substance. The Magic became the second team in NBA history to wear pinstriped uniforms (Charlotte was the first), and Orlando Arena's playing surface paid parquet homage to venerable Boston Garden. But the play on that hardwood was not reminiscent of the old Celtics. Coach Matt Guokas blended expansion-draft acquisitions Reggie Theus, Sam Vincent, Otis Smith, and Scott Skiles with rookies Nick Anderson and Michael Ansley into a team that was exciting, though not very successful.

Things improved in 1990-91. Orlando drafted sharp-shooter Dennis Scott, and Skiles developed into one of the league's top point guards (setting a single-game assist record in the process). Orlando played .500 ball after the All-Star break and had a 24-17 home record.

Last Two Years

Season	W	L	Pct.	Place	Playoffs	Coach
1989-90	18	64	.220	Seventh	DNQ	Matt Guokas
1990-91	31	51	.378	Fourth	DNQ	Matt Guokas

1990-91 Recap

No team improved more during the 1990-91 season than the Magic. Its final record of 31-51 represented a 13-game advance on the previous year's mark and caused some big smiles around central Florida. Though Orlando did not qualify for the playoffs, it came closer than any of the four recent expansion teams and inched its way toward NBA respectability.

One of the biggest reasons for the Magic's jump in stature was the play of point guard Scott Skiles. Skiles, who averaged just 7.7 PPG in 1989-90, bulked his total up to a team-leading 17.2; he also increased his assist average to 8.4 per game. One of the biggest highlights of the season was his NBA-record-setting 30 assists against Denver on December 30. Skiles's radical improvement not only keyed the Magic's improvement but

earned him a huge new contract in mid-season.

Rookie Dennis Scott was another key. The long-bomber from Georgia Tech averaged 15.7 PPG and shot 37.4 percent from 3-point range. Though he struggled with bouts of inconsistency, Scott proved he had the talent to be a big scorer.

Up front, the Magic played to mixed reviews. Nick Anderson (14.1 points, 5.5 rebounds), Otis Smith (13.9 points, 5.2 rebounds), and Terry Catledge (14.6 points, 7.0 rebounds) gave coach Matt Guokas a steady rotation, with Jeff Turner (8.6 points, 5.1 rebounds) in reserve. But there were serious problems at center. Greg Kite was an okay rebounder (7.2 average), but he could score only 4.8 per game. Back-up Mark Acres (4.2 points, 5.3 rebounds) gave Guokas more of the same.

1991-92 Roster

No.	Player	Pos.	Ht.	Wt.	Exp.	College	1990-91		
							PPG	RPG	APG
42	Mark Acres	F/C	6'11"	225	4	Oral Roberts	4.2	5.3	0.4
25	Nick Anderson	G/F	6'6"	205	2	Illinois	14.1	5.5	1.5
33	Terry Catledge	F	6'8"	230	6	South Alabama	14.6	7.0	1.1
—	Chris Corchiani	G	6'1"	186	R	N. Carolina St.	—	—	—
34	Greg Kite	C	6'11"	260	8	Brigham Young	4.8	7.2	0.7
35	Jerry Reynolds	G/F	6'8"	206	6	Louisiana St.	12.9	3.7	2.5
—	Stanley Roberts	C	7'0"	288	R	Louisiana St.	—	—	—
3	Dennis Scott	G/F	6'8"	229	1	Georgia Tech	8.6	5.1	1.4
4	Scott Skiles	G	6'1"	180	5	Michigan St.	17.2	3.4	8.4
32	Otis Smith	G/F	6'5"	210	5	Jacksonville	13.9	5.2	2.3
31	Jeff Turner	F/C	6'9"	240	5	Vanderbilt	15.7	2.9	1.6
11	Sam Vincent	G	6'2"	185	6	Michigan St.	8.3	2.2	4.0
20	Morlon Wiley	G	6'4"	192	3	Long Beach St.	3.3	0.5	2.1
—	Brian Williams	C/F	6'11"	242	R	Arizona	—	—	—

Orlando Magic
1991-92 Season Preview

Opening Line: The Magic is coming off a 31-win season—darn good for a second-year expansion team—but now must complement its fine perimeter play with a strong inside game. Orlando got a good start in the draft by taking two centers—Arizona's Brian Williams (tenth pick) and Louisiana State's Stanley Roberts (No. 23). The Magic took playmaker Chris Corchiani, a point guard out of North Carolina State, with the 36th pick. Free agent forward Michael Ansley was not re-signed.

Guard: Scott Skiles sparks the Magic with fiery leadership, precision passing (8.4 APG), and long-range shooting (17.2 PPG). He's the soul of this ballclub. Nick Anderson doesn't have the outside shot for a two guard, but he's strong, can sky, and can take it to the hole with authority (14.1 PPG). Otis Smith is a similar player with similar numbers (13.9 PPG). Both will also play the small-forward position. Sam Vincent has great speed for a point guard, but he takes so many ill-advised shots and plays such poor defense that he's becoming a liability to have on the floor.

Forward: Sophomore Dennis Scott, another forward/guard, can fill it up from the nacho stand (125 3-pointers). He offers few other skills, but his outside bombs make him a force. Jeff Turner earned a starting job last year, but he gives you little except for a medium-range jumper. Jerry "Ice" Reynolds is a talented playground player. Though he'll often play out of control, he'll wow the crowd with his moves to the basket. Terry Catledge possesses good strength and rebounding for a 6'8" forward, but he worked his way out of the lineup last year because of his selfish shooting habits. In desperate need of a power forward, the Heat may turn to Williams, an agile 6'11" big man who can shoot and rebound but has trouble staying focused.

Center: Williams may wind up at center, which is even a worse disaster area for Orlando. Last year's starter, Greg Kite, was considered the worst starting center in the NBA, while back-up Mark Acres wasn't any better. Rookie Roberts is a talented seven-footer with weight problems.

Coaching: Matt Guokas has done a creditable job in Orlando, winning 31 games with a hodge-podge expansion team. However, too many of his players play out of control (Catledge, Vincent, Reynolds), and the coach needs to take at least some responsibility for that. Guokas is assisted by John Gabriel, Brian Hill, and George Scholz.

Analysis: Orlando has had serious problems up front—guys like Turner and Kite should not be starting. In time, Williams and Roberts could solidify the inside positions, but they won't make a major difference this year. Skiles will keep this team competitive, but it won't win more than 30 games.

Prediction: 7th Place, Atlantic

PHILADELPHIA 76ERS

Division: Atlantic
Home: The Spectrum
Capacity: 18,168
Year Built: 1967

Owner: Harold Katz
General Manager: Gene Shue
Head Coach: Jim Lynam
Assistant Coach: Fred Carter
Assistant Coach: Buzz Braman

Address
Veterans Stadium
P.O. Box 25040
Philadelphia, PA 19147
(215) 339-7600

Coach Jim Lynam			
	W	L	Pct.
NBA Record	211	217	.493
W/76ers	159	126	.558
1990-91 Record	44	38	.537

Sixers History

The 76ers own the distinction of having the Alpha and the Omega of NBA basketball history. The 1966-67 Sixers thrashed the league with a 68-13 record and a world title. On the other hand, the 1972-73 Sixers posted the worst-ever mark of 9-73.

The Sixers began in 1949-50 as the Syracuse Nationals and reached the first NBA Finals series, losing in six games to Minneapolis. Hall of Fame center Dolph Schayes was the big gun on both that team and the 1953-54 squad that fell again in the NBA Finals to the Lakers.

The team moved to Philadelphia in 1963-64 and acquired Wilt Chamberlain in a trade in early 1965. They moved onto a level with the dominating Boston Celtics and began to challenge them for league supremacy. In fact,

the Nationals/ Sixers have met the Celtics in 17 playoff series, winning seven. Philadelphia beat Boston in the 1967 East finals on the way to the NBA title.

The Sixers nosedived in the early 1970s, but the arrival of coach Gene Shue and ABA imports George McGinnis and Julius Erving signaled a renaissance. Philadelphia advanced to the NBA Finals in 1976-77 but lost to Portland. Similar excursions were made in 1979-80 and 1981-82, thanks to Erving, Bobby Jones, Maurice Cheeks, and Andrew Toney.

Moses Malone arrived for the 1982-83 season, and the Sixers blitzed to another NBA title. In 1984, Philly drafted super-forward Charles Barkley, who led the team to the 1989-90 Atlantic Division title.

Last Five Years

Season	W	L	Pct.	Place	Playoffs	Coach
1986-87	45	37	.549	Second	L-Round One	Matt Guokas
1987-88	36	46	.439	Fourth	DNQ	Matt Guokas/Jim Lynam
1988-89	46	36	.561	Second	L-Round One	Jim Lynam
1989-90	53	29	.646	First	L-East Semis	Jim Lynam
1990-91	44	38	.537	Second	L-East Semis	Jim Lynam

1990-91 Recap

Those who wondered just how far Charles Barkley could carry the 76ers got their answer in 1990-91. The Sixers slipped from Atlantic Division champions the previous season to the middle of the Eastern Conference playoff pack thanks to injuries and questionable trades. Not even Barkley, the team's undeniable leader and catalyst, was immune. He suffered a sprained left knee late in the season.

That Philadelphia advanced to the Eastern semifinals (losing in five games to Chicago) was a testimony to Barkley and the skill of coach Jimmy Lynam, who kept the team together throughout an odd year.

Trouble started in November when point guard Johnny Dawkins tore up his knee. Though veteran Rickey Green (10.0 points, 5.2 assists) and quick reserve Andre Turner (5.9 points, 4.4 assists) were above-average replacements, the Sixer offense suffered. The mid-season trade of center Mike Gminski to Charlotte for Armon Gilliam left a hole in the middle that aging Rick Mahorn (a natural power forward) couldn't fill. Off-season acquisition Manute Bol (4.3 rebounds, 3.0 blocks) was inconsistent and no threat to score.

Barkley was again awesome, averaging 27.6 points and 10.1 rebounds a game. Guard Hersey Hawkins was also a potent offensive weapon, averaging 22.1 points and flashing the scoring mentality the Sixers expected when they drafted him.

Veteran swing man Ron Anderson was again formidable off the bench, averaging 14.6 points a game, but Gilliam was disappointing. He averaged 16.6 PPG and 8.0 RPG but was soft inside, something the center-less Sixers couldn't afford.

1991-92 Roster

No.	Player	Pos.	Ht.	Wt.	Exp.	College	PPG	1990-91 RPG	APG
20	Ron Anderson	F	6'7"	215	7	Fresno St.	14.6	4.5	1.4
34	Charles Barkley	F	6'6"	250	7	Auburn	27.6	10.1	4.2
11	Manute Bol	C	7'7"	225	6	Bridgeport	1.9	4.3	0.2
12	Johnny Dawkins	G	6'2"	170	5	Duke	15.8	4.0	7.0
35	Armon Gilliam	F	6'9"	245	4	UNLV	16.6	8.0	1.4
14	Rickey Green	G	6'0"	172	13	Michigan	10.0	1.7	5.2
33	Hersey Hawkins	G	6'3"	190	3	Bradley	22.1	3.9	3.7
40	Dave Hoppen	C	6'11"	240	4	Nebraska	2.1	1.3	0.1
31	Brian Oliver	G	6'4"	210	1	Georgia Tech	3.8	1.1	1.2
21	Kenny Payne	F	6'8"	220	2	Louisville	3.5	1.4	0.3
50	Charles Shackleford	C/F	6'10"	225	2	N. Carolina St.	—	—	—
4	Andre Turner	G	5'11"	160	6	Memphis St.	5.9	2.2	4.4
23	Mitchell Wiggins	G	6'4"	185	5	Clemson	—	—	—
55	Jayson Williams	F	6'10"	240	1	St. John's	3.5	2.1	0.3

Philadelphia 76ers
1991-92 Season Preview

Opening Line: The Sixers may boast Charles Barkley, but they need the return of point guard Johnny Dawkins (torn anterior cruciate ligament) to lift them from a good team to a title contender. Philadelphia renounced its rights to Rick Mahorn, but it brought in power forward/center Charles Shackleford from Europe. It also signed guard Mitchell Wiggins, a solid NBA vet whose career has been crippled by drugs. Philly's only draft pick, second-rounder Alvaro Teheran, bolted to Europe.

Guard: Hersey Hawkins (22.1 PPG) has emerged as one of the game's best shooting guards. He canned 108 treys and was an All-Star last season. Before the torn ACL, the super-quick Dawkins was coming into his own at the point. The injury could hamper his speed, which is his greatest asset. With Dawkins sidelined, the Sixers backcourt was piloted by 36-year-old Rickey Green last year. Despite his age, Green is still capable of running an NBA team. Andre Turner struck out in four previous tries at the NBA but found a home in Philadelphia as the back-up point guard. Sophomore Brian Oliver, a reserve two guard, provides decent defense but little else. Wiggins, if right, can score and play strong defense. There's a lot of uncertainty in this backcourt.

Forward: The presence of Barkley makes this a strong front line. The "Round Mound of Rebound" can board (10.1 RPG), score (27.6 PPG), and single-handedly dominate. Power forward Armon Gilliam has a repertoire of inside scoring moves, but his soft defense will allow the other team right back in the game. Small forward Ron Anderson is a premier sixth man who can fill it up in a hurry with his feathery jump shots. Philly needs more depth here.

Center: After trading Mike Gminski for Gilliam, the Sixers were left very vulnerable at the center position. Shackleford, a former Nets semi-regular, is a great athlete who will serve as a competent board man. Manute Bol, the 7'7" wonder, provides intimidating shot-blocking but absolutely nothing else.

Coaching: Jim Lynam should have gotten some consideration as NBA Coach of the Year last season. The Sixers won 44 games despite losing Dawkins to injury, using 19 different players, losing Barkley for 15 games, and making a major trade in the middle of the season. The team still made it to the second round of the NBA playoffs. Lynam is assisted by Fred Carter and Buzz Braman.

Analysis: If Dawkins comes back healthy, and if Barkley is able to play in all 82 games, and if there are no major injuries to other important players, then there is no reason why this team can't win 50 games this season. But then, "if" is always a big word. Philly could also use another big man.

Prediction: 2nd Place, Atlantic

WASHINGTON BULLETS

Division: Atlantic
Home: Capital Centre
Capacity: 18,756
Year Built: 1973

Address
One Harry S. Truman Dr.
Landover, MD 20785
(301) 773-2255

Chairman of the Board: Abe Pollin
V.P./General Manager: John Nash
Head Coach: Wes Unseld
Assistant Coach: Bill Blair
Assistant Coach: Jeff Bzdelik

Coach Wes Unseld			
	W	L	Pct.
NBA Record	131	170	.435
W/Bullets	131	170	.435
1990-91 Record	30	52	.366

Bullets History

The Bullets' greatest years came in the 1970s, but the franchise rolled off the assembly line in 1961-62 as the Chicago Packers. In 1963, it blew the Windy City, moved to Baltimore, and adopted its current nickname.

In 1964-65, the Bullets advanced to the Western finals behind center Walt Bellamy and forward Bailey Howell. Prior to the 1968-69 season, Baltimore drafted huge Wes Unseld, and he went on to win the MVP Award in his first season. Unseld teamed with bruising Gus Johnson and slick Earl "The Pearl" Monroe to help the Bullets win the Eastern Division.

The Bullets made their first trip to the league finals in 1970-71, but they were dispatched in four games by Milwaukee. They made it back in 1974-75, this time as Washington, but

Golden State swept them 4-0. Dick Motta took over the Bullets in 1976-77 and led them to the finals the following year. This time, Unseld, Elvin Hayes, Bob Dandridge, and company whipped Seattle in seven games. The Sonics got revenge in the finals the next year, winning in five games and closing out the Bullets' big decade.

The 1980s featured some talented players (Jeff Ruland, Rick Mahorn, Greg Ballard, Jeff Malone) but few highlights. The Bullets won just one playoff series during the whole decade, and by its end, they were a lottery team. Unseld took over as coach in 1987-88 and tried to revive the franchise with youth and a few veterans, like high-scoring All-Star forward Bernard King.

Last Five Years

Season	W	L	Pct.	Place	Playoffs	Coach
1986-87	42	40	.512	Third	L-Round One	Kevin Loughery
1987-88	38	44	.463	Second	L-Round One	K. Loughery/W. Unseld
1988-89	40	42	.488	Fourth	DNQ	Wes Unseld
1989-90	31	51	.378	Fourth	DNQ	Wes Unseld
1990-91	30	52	.366	Fourth	DNQ	Wes Unseld

1990-91 Recap

While Bernard King proved to the NBA during the 1990-91 season that he could still score in buckets, the rest of the Bullets proved they still had some major problems. Washington failed to qualify for the playoffs for the third straight year, and its total of 30 wins was even worse than 1989-90's 31-win debacle. You can't fault coach Wes Unseld, who coaxed that many victories out of what amounted to an expansion team, but you may want to question the front office's personnel decisions.

The choice to keep King paid off big. The former Knick star made good on his vow to become the first person to play in the NBA All-Star Game without a medial collateral knee ligament. He tormented opponents for 28.4 points a night, and though he shot only 47.2 percent from the field, it was still higher than the rest of the team.

Power forward Harvey Grant (18.2 points, 7.2 rebounds) was effective opposite King, but the Bullets could have used more from John Williams (12.5 points, 5.4 rebounds), whose off-season weight gain/holdout/injury soap opera limited him to just 33 games. Second-year center Pervis Ellison made strides following an injury-plagued rookie season. He averaged 10.4 points and 7.7 rebounds but still needed to work on his moves around the basket.

Off guard Ledell Eackles lived up to his reputation as a no-conscious gunner and scored 13.0 PPG, though he shot a mediocre 45.3 percent from the field. Rookie A.J. English (8.8 points) was an inconsistent back-up. Point guard Darrell Walker continued to play good defense and contributed 7.8 points, 7.0 rebounds, and 6.5 assists per game.

1991-92 Roster

No.	Player	Pos.	Ht.	Wt.	Exp.	College	1990-91 PPG	RPG	APG
1	Michael Adams	G	5'10"	165	6	Boston College	26.5	3.9	10.5
31	Mark Alarie	F	6'8"	225	5	Duke	5.8	2.8	1.1
21	Ledell Eackles	G	6'5"	215	3	New Orleans	13.0	1.9	2.0
43	Pervis Ellison	F/C	6'10"	225	2	Louisville	10.4	7.7	1.3
14	A.J. English	G	6'3"	180	1	Virginia Union	8.8	2.1	2.5
42	Greg Foster	C	6'11"	240	1	Texas-El Paso	4.4	2.8	0.7
44	Harvey Grant	F	6'9"	215	3	Oklahoma	18.2	7.2	2.6
12	Tom Hammonds	F	6'9"	225	2	Georgia Tech	5.2	2.9	0.6
32	Byron Irvin	G	6'5"	190	2	Missouri	5.2	1.4	0.7
23	Charles Jones	F	6'9"	225	8	Albany St.	2.6	5.8	0.8
30	Bernard King	F	6'7"	205	13	Tennessee	28.4	5.0	4.6
2	Larry Robinson	G	6'5"	185	1	Centenary	6.9	2.3	1.8
22	LaBradford Smith	G	6'3"	200	R	Louisville	—	—	—
5	Darrell Walker	G	6'4"	180	8	Arkansas	7.8	7.0	6.5
34	John Williams	F	6'9"	255	5	Louisiana St.	12.5	5.4	4.0

Washington Bullets
1991-92 Season Preview

Opening Line: The Bullets needed help in the backcourt and they think they found it in 5'10" Michael Adams, who averaged 26.5 PPG in Denver's high-octane offense last year. He'll team with veteran forward Bernard King (28.4 PPG) to give Washington two explosive scorers. To obtain Adams, the Bullets traded the No. 8 pick in the 1991 draft. But they did retain the No. 19 selection and they spent it on another guard, LaBradford Smith of Louisville. Guard Haywoode Workman, a semi-regular, jumped to Italy.

Guard: Adams possesses the quickness to fly to the hoop for lay-ups and the shooting ability to launch from 3-point land—which he did 564 times last year. Coach Wes Unseld will have to put the reigns on him a little bit. Team captain Darrell Walker can't shoot at all, but he'll dish off (6.5 APG) and rebound relentlessly (7.0 RPG). Both Ledell Eackles and A.J. English are talented, young scorers who need to improve their consistency. Rookie Smith is a solid all-around guard who can play both positions, though he has to work on his attitude.

Forward: King has recovered from a horrible knee injury to become one of the game's top scorers. Nevertheless, age (34) and a bad back will likely curtail his output this year. Though still too lean to play power forward, Harvey Grant has a nice outside shot and has developed into a fine scorer (18.2 PPG). John Williams, a remarkably well-rounded talent, has suffered from a bad knee injury and terrible work habits. Tom Hammonds, a scorer in college, isn't big, strong, or quick enough to do it in the pros. Mark Alarie, a reliable team player, provides steady but unexciting minutes. Power forward Charles Jones is a designated shot-blocker (2.00 BPG).

Center: Pervis Ellison, the first man taken in the 1989 draft, has not quite lived up to his billing. Still, he's a tremendous leaper who can rebound (7.7 RPG) and swat shots (2.07 BPG). Back-up Greg Foster is a big, physical player with few skills.

Coaching: Unseld, bullish and determined as a player, tries to get his men to play the same way. The Bullets' team motto last year was, "We've Got a Few Scores to Settle." Most NBA coaches agree that Unseld has gotten the most out of the little talent he's had. He is assisted by Bill Blair and Jeff Bzdelik.

Analysis: Inserting the run-and-gunning Adams into Washington's conservative offense is like inviting Pee Wee Herman to a black-tie dinner party; it's hard to tell if he'll ruin the affair or liven it up. Williams is another question mark. He's an All-Star talent, but will he ever put his game together? King's age and health are another concern. On the whole, this a mediocre ballclub that probably won't make the playoffs.

Prediction: 4th Place, Atlantic

ATLANTA HAWKS

Division: Central
Home: The Omni
Capacity: 16,371
Year Built: 1972

Owner: Ted Turner
V.P./General Manager: Pete Babcock
Head Coach: Bob Weiss
Assistant Coach: Johnny Davis
Assistant Coach: Bob Weinhauer

Address
One CNN Center
Suite 405, South Tower
Atlanta, GA 30303
(404) 827-3800

Coach Bob Weiss			
	W	L	Pct.
NBA Record	102	144	.415
W/Hawks	43	39	.524
1990-91 Record	43	39	.524

Hawks History

Few teams have had as many different addresses as the Hawks. Before settling in Georgia, the franchise roamed the Midwest, calling Moline, Rock Island, Davenport, Milwaukee, and St. Louis home.

An original member of the NBA, the franchise was first known as the Tri-City (Moline, Rock Island, and Davenport) Blackhawks. Two years later, it moved to Milwaukee and shortened its nickname to its current form. Though active off the court, it wasn't until the team drafted Bob Pettit in 1954 that it started to show some life on it.

The Hawks moved to St. Louis in 1955, won consecutive Western Conference championships from 1957-61, and defeated Boston in 1958 for the franchise's lone NBA title. Pettit,

Cliff Hagan, Ed Macauley, Charlie Share, and Slater Martin formed the nucleus of those teams. In the title win over Boston, Pettit played with his broken left wrist in a cast, and Share played with his busted jaw wired shut.

The 1960s featured talented players like Lou Hudson, Joe Caldwell, and Zelmo Beatty, but the Hawks could not get back to the NBA Finals. The team moved to Atlanta for the 1968-69 season and staggered through the next decade as a .500 team.

Things started to change in 1982, when Atlanta drafted exciting forward Dominique Wilkins. The Hawks won the NBA Central Division title in 1986-87 and recorded a franchise-record 57 wins. Despite the improvement, the Hawks never advanced past the Eastern Conference semifinals.

Last Five Years

Season	W	L	Pct.	Place	Playoffs	Coach
1986-87	57	25	.695	First	L-East Semis	Mike Fratello
1987-88	50	32	.610	Second	L-East Semis	Mike Fratello
1988-89	52	30	.634	Third	L-Round One	Mike Fratello
1989-90	41	41	.500	Sixth	DNQ	Mike Fratello
1990-91	43	39	.524	Fourth	L-Round One	Bob Weiss

1990-91 Recap

Few people could be blamed for laughing when Bob Weiss assumed control of the Hawk bench at the start of 1990-91 and announced his intention to install a motion offense. After all, Atlanta had spent most of the last seven years under Mike Fratello standing around, waiting for Dominique Wilkins to add another few frames to his highlight reel.

But Weiss was adamant, and after some early problems, the Hawks actually started passing the ball around a bit. The results were encouraging. Though their 43-39 record—good for fourth place in the Central Division—was but a two-game improvement on the 1989-90 mark that had earned Mike Fratello a shot at a broadcasting career, the Hawks did improve. They returned to the playoffs after a one-year hiatus and extended Detroit to game five of their first-round mini-series.

At the forefront of the progression was Wilkins. The acrobatic forward had his best all-around season, averaging 25.9 points and 9.0 rebounds a game. Pint-sized Spud Webb emerged as a quality point guard (13.4 points, 5.6 assists), allowing Weiss to move Doc Rivers (15.2 PPG) to off guard and use dangerous John Battle (13.6 PPG) off the bench.

Wilkins and the backcourt were solid all year, but the Hawks were weak up front. Jon Koncak continued to disappoint at center, averaging but 4.1 points and 4.9 rebounds a game and again doing little to justify his huge contract. Kevin Willis (13.1 points, 8.8 rebounds) was a little more consistent at power forward, and aging Moses Malone was quite productive (10.6 points, 8.1 rebounds) in limited duty.

1991-92 Roster

No.	Player	Pos.	Ht.	Wt.	Exp.	College	1990-91 PPG	1990-91 RPG	1990-91 APG
2	Stacey Augmon	F	6'8"	206	R	UNLV	—	—	—
33	Duane Ferrell	F	6'7"	210	3	Georgia Tech	6.1	2.3	0.7
32	Jon Koncak	C	7'0"	260	6	Southern Meth.	4.1	4.9	1.6
34	Gary Leonard	C	7'1"	240	2	Missouri	0.5	0.5	0.0
1	Travis Mays	G	6'2"	190	1	Texas	14.3	2.8	4.0
40	Tim McCormick	C	7'0"	240	7	Michigan	4.5	2.9	0.6
15	Sidney Moncrief	G	6'3"	181	11	Arkansas	4.7	1.8	1.4
12	Rodney Monroe	G	6'3"	181	R	N. Carolina St.	—	—	—
24	Dave Popson	F	6'10"	230	2	North Carolina	1.8	0.7	0.1
41	Blair Rasmussen	C	7'0"	260	6	Oregon	12.5	9.7	1.0
22	Rumeal Robinson	G	6'2"	195	1	Michigan	5.6	1.5	2.8
8	Alexander Volkov	F	6'10"	218	2	Kiev Institute	—	—	—
21	Dominique Wilkins	F	6'8"	200	9	Georgia	25.9	9.0	3.3
42	Kevin Willis	F/C	7'0"	235	6	Michigan St.	13.1	8.8	1.2

Atlanta Hawks
1991-92 Season Preview

Opening Line: The Hawks were busy bees over the summer, revamping half their team. Center Moses Malone and guard John Battle left as free agents, while two other guards were traded. Spud Webb went to Sacramento for young guard Travis Mays, and Doc Rivers went to the Clippers for the No. 9 pick in the 1991 draft. The Hawks used that pick to draft UNLV defensive ace Stacey Augmon, and then grabbed North Carolina State guard Rodney Monroe with the 30th selection. The Hawks drafted Seton Hall's Anthony Avent with the No. 15 pick, but they traded him away in a three-team deal, ending up with Denver center Blair Rasmussen.

Guard: Though small at 6'2", sophomore Mays is a true NBA talent who can score from 3-point land, take it to the hole, and play aggressive defense. Second-year point guard Rumeal Robinson, a strong, physical competitor, will get a chance to rebound from a turnover-prone rookie season. Rookie Monroe can flat-out score, but he needs work in all other areas of his game. The great Sidney Moncrief has lost nearly everything except his leadership skills. Atlanta is painfully raw at this position.

Forward: Small forwards are paid to score, and Dominique Wilkins does it better than anyone. Wilkins (25.9 PPG, 9.0 RPG) also shed his selfish label last year with more team-oriented play. He'll be backed up by Augmon. Stacey, a three-time national defensive player of the year in college, will provide more of the same in the NBA. Small forward Duane Ferrell, a borderline NBA talent who played in 78 games last season, will see fewer minutes this year. Starting power forward Kevin Willis is a seven-footer who can run and crash the boards (8.8 RPG), but he has never lived up to his All-Star potential.

Center: Jon Koncak is a strong inside defender but his offense is dwindling out of existence (4.1 PPG). He may lose his starting job to Rasmussen, a fine shooter (12.5 PPG) and rebounder (9.7 RPG) who is soft defensively.

Coaching: The Hawks had a history of playing individual basketball, but coach Bob Weiss, in his first year with the Hawks last season, got the club to work as a unit. Even Wilkins took to the team approach. Atlanta looks like it finally has a coach who has the respect and control of his ballclub. He's assisted by Johnny Davis and Bob Weinhauer.

Analysis: The trades and free agent losses seriously depleted this team. Though dominantly strong at small forward, the Hawks are mediocre at center, thin at power forward, and terribly inexperienced at guard. Of the guards, only Mays deserves to play 20 minutes a game. The new youth movement may help the club in the long run, but it will cripple the team this year.

Prediction: 6th place, Central

CHARLOTTE HORNETS

Division: Central
Home: Charlotte Coliseum
Capacity: 23,901
Year Built: 1988

Address
Hive Drive
Charlotte, NC 28217
(704) 357-0252

Owner: George Shinn
Vice President: Gene Littles
Head Coach: Allan Bristow
Assistant Coach: Mike Pratt

Coach Allan Bristow			
	W	L	Pct.
NBA Record	0	0	.000
W/Hornets	0	0	.000
1990-91 Record	0	0	.000

Hornets History

They've always loved college basketball down on Tobacco Road, so it was a natural for the NBA to try and tap into that market. And though huge crowds have filled Charlotte Coliseum to back the Hornets since their inception, the level of play has sometimes been below the high expectations of spoiled Carolina fans.

The city was awarded a franchise in April 1987, and it created an immediate stir by commissioning renowned clothing designer Alexander Julian to create the uniforms. The Hornets may have looked sharp in their teal-and-blue pinstriped duds, but their 20-62 record in 1988-89, their initial season, wasn't as fashionable.

Among the highlights of that first season were the play of veterans Kelly Tripucka and 5'3" Muggsy Bogues and the exciting, though inconsistent, performance of rookie guard Rex Chapman. Charlotte also led the league in attendance.

Charlotte took a step backward in 1989-90, winning only 19 games, and coach Dick Harter was replaced by Gene Littles. Rookie J.R. Reid, a star at North Carolina, was a crowd favorite, though his 6'9" frame seemed too small for the center spot.

Littles boosted the team's production to 26 wins in 1990-91, as the team moved from the Midwest to the Central Division. Rookie guard Kendall Gill showed flashes of a brilliant future, Reid and Chapman displayed more consistency, and the addition of center Mike Gminski stabilized the pivot.

Last Three Years

Season	W	L	Pct.	Place	Playoffs	Coach
1988-89	20	62	.244	Sixth	DNQ	Dick Harter
1989-90	19	63	.232	Seventh	DNQ	Dick Harter/Gene Littles
1990-91	26	56	.317	Seventh	DNQ	Gene Littles

1990-91 Recap

The Hornets' 1990-91 highlight film will no doubt begin in New York, though not with clips of anything like a scintillating win over the Knicks. The undisputed zenith of Charlotte's season came on May 19, when NBA commissioner David Stern revealed that the Hornets had won the first pick in the league's upcoming draft.

Other than that bit of excitement, it was another tough year in Charlotte. Sure, the fans still came out in droves—the Hornets led the league in attendance (23,906 average) for the second time in their three years—but for the first time, they began to voice their displeasure with the quality of play. Charlotte settled at the bottom of the Central Division standings, and though their 26-56 record was a seven-game improvement over the previous season, it was still fourth-worst in the league.

There was some good news. Rookie guard Kendall Gill averaged 11.0 PPG and showed flashes of brilliance. Forward Johnny Newman (16.9 PPG) and guard Rex Chapman (15.7 PPG) continued to be potent weapons, and 5'3" guard Muggsy Bogues was an adept playmaker, averaging 8.3 assists per game.

But the Hornets continued to struggle up front. Charlotte dealt soft forward Armon Gilliam and bench-warming center Dave Hoppen to Philadelphia in mid-season for veteran center Mike Gminski, whose propensity for jump-shooting didn't do much for the team's rebounding needs underneath the basket. Power forward J.R. Reid (11.3 points, 6.3 rebounds) was again inconsistent, and Hornet coaches and fans wondered if he would ever deliver on his promise.

1991-92 Roster

No.	Player	Pos.	Ht.	Wt.	Exp.	College	1990-91 PPG	RPG	APG
1	Muggsy Bogues	G	5'3"	140	4	Wake Forest	7.0	2.7	8.3
3	Rex Chapman	G	6'4"	195	3	Kentucky	15.7	2.7	3.6
30	Dell Curry	G	6'5"	200	5	Virginia Tech	10.6	2.6	2.2
44	Kenny Gattison	F	6'8"	252	5	Old Dominion	9.0	5.3	0.6
13	Kendall Gill	G	6'5"	200	1	Illinois	11.0	3.2	3.7
42	Mike Gminski	C	6'11"	260	11	Duke	10.6	7.3	1.2
4	Scott Haffner	G	6'3"	180	2	Evansville	2.4	0.6	1.3
2	Larry Johnson	F	6'7"	250	R	UNLV	—	—	—
45	Eric Leckner	C	6'11"	265	3	Wyoming	4.5	4.1	0.5
33	Kevin Lynch	G	6'5"	200	R	Minnesota	—	—	—
22	Johnny Newman	F	6'7"	190	5	Richmond	16.9	3.1	2.3
34	J.R. Reid	F/C	6'9"	256	2	North Carolina	11.3	6.3	1.1

Charlotte Hornets
1991-92 Season Preview

Opening Line: The big trade in Charlotte this summer occurred within the organization. Allan Bristow, the team's vice-president of basketball operations, took over as head coach, while bench leader Gene Littles assumed Bristow's position. The Hornets, the worst rebounding team in the league last year, will welcome UNLV board man Larry Johnson, the No. 1 pick in the 1991 draft. Charlotte also nabbed Minnesota guard Kevin Lynch with the No. 28 pick. The team chose not to re-sign Kelly Tripucka.

Guard: Rex Chapman (15.7 PPG) is a tremendous leaper with a fine outside shot. His poor passing and decision-making, though, are preventing him from stardom. Second-year guard Kendall Gill hits from the perimeter, plays tough defense, and possesses good size and intelligence. In time, he'll be a good one. Off the bench comes 5'3" Muggsy Bogues, a blazingly quick waterbug who excels in an up-tempo offense (8.3 APG). His size, of course, can be a problem. Dell Curry is one of the best pure shooters in basketball, but his defense and attitude have limited his minutes. Lynch provides good size, but he isn't talented enough to become a regular.

Forward: Johnny Newman is the top scorer (16.9 PPG) on a poor-scoring club. Though a fine player, Newman is rather streaky and has had squabbles with the coaching staff. Young J.R. Reid brings good size and speed to the power-forward spot. However, his inexperience and lackadaisical play have brought out the boo birds in Charlotte. Johnson may edge Reid out of the picture. A 6'7" power forward, L.J. is amazingly strong, rebounds like a madman, and can score in the post or from the perimeter. The hard-working Kenny Gattison does whatever's asked of him.

Center: Mike Gminski provides excellent outside shooting, solid defense, and veteran leadership. He won't earn an All-Star trip, but he'll definitely pull his weight. Eric Leckner's only talent is his shooting touch, although even that betrayed him last year.

Coaching: Bristow has never been a head coach on any level, yet he does boast legitimate credentials. He spent ten years in the NBA as a scrappy, heady player, and then served seven years as an NBA assistant coach—he was Doug Moe's top aide in Denver. Bristow is assisted by Mike Pratt.

Analysis: Despite better experience and the addition of Johnson, this is below-average team. The young backcourt of Chapman and Gill still has a lot to learn, starters Newman and Gminski are just average at their positions, and Johnson (probably the starting power forward) is only a rookie. Johnson will help solve the rebounding problem, but at 6'7" he won't make a major impact. Expect 30 wins, tops.

Prediction: 7th Place, Central

CHICAGO BULLS

Division: Central
Home: Chicago Stadium
Capacity: 17,339
Year Built: 1929

Chairman: Jerry Reinsdorf
V.P./Basketball Operations:
Jerry Krause
Head Coach: Phil Jackson
Assistant Coach: John Bach
Assistant Coach: Jim Cleamons
Assistant Coach: Tex Winter

Address
One Magnificent Mile
980 N. Michigan Ave, Suite 1600
Chicago, IL 60611
(312) 943-5800

Coach Phil Jackson			
	W	L	Pct.
NBA Record	116	48	.707
W/Bulls	116	48	.707
1990-91 Record	61	21	.744

Bulls History

The Bulls are defined today by the atmospheric antics of all-world Michael Jordan, but the team's 25-year history has not always been so spectacular. Until 1991, Chicago never advanced to the NBA Finals, joining the Cubs, White Sox, and Blackhawks as examples of futility in the Second City.

Chicago joined the league in 1966 as a lone expansion club. After four losing seasons, the Bulls enjoyed regular-season success during their next five. Coach Dick Motta pulled together Chet Walker, Bob Love, Jerry Sloan, and Norm Van Lier to form a quick team that advanced to the West finals in 1973-74, losing in four games to Milwaukee. The following year, the Bulls acquired Nate Thurmond from Golden State and won the Midwest Division, only to drop a disappointing 4-3 decision to the Warriors in the West finals.

Chicago managed only two winning seasons during the next 12 and won just one playoff series, but the Bulls' fortunes changed radically in 1984 when they selected Jordan with the third pick in the draft. Almost instantly, Jordan became a high-flying ambassador for basketball everywhere.

By 1987, the results matched the enthusiasm. Chicago surrounded Jordan with young talents like Scottie Pippen, John Paxson, and Horace Grant and advanced to the Eastern Conference finals in 1988-89 and 1989-90, losing both times to Detroit. The Bulls matured in 1990-91 and breezed to the NBA championship.

Last Five Years

Season	W	L	Pct.	Place	Playoffs	Coach
1986-87	40	42	.488	Fifth	L-Round One	Doug Collins
1987-88	50	32	.610	Second	L-East Semis	Doug Collins
1988-89	47	35	.573	Fifth	L-East Finals	Doug Collins
1989-90	55	27	.671	Second	L-East Finals	Phil Jackson
1990-91	61	21	.744	First	NBA Champs	Phil Jackson

1990-91 Recap

After 25 years in the NBA, the Bulls claimed their first NBA title in 1991. Chicago won a team-record 61 games during the regular season and then turned it up one more notch in the playoffs. Led by Michael Jordan, the Bulls swept New York, beat Philadelphia in five, and then broomed Detroit (which had eliminated Chicago from the playoffs the previous three years). After losing game one of the NBA Finals to the Lakers, the Bulls took the next four for the world crown.

Jordan was again spectacular, winning his second MVP Award and his fifth straight scoring championship. He averaged 31.5 points, 6.0 rebounds, and 5.5 assists and made the All-Defensive Team. But Jordan had starred before, and the Bulls didn't advance very far in the playoffs. As marvelous as Jordan was, the story of the Bulls' success was his teammates.

The Bulls were only one of two teams to shoot better than 50 percent for the year, and their aggressive, trapping team defense was truly outstanding, particularly in the playoffs. Forward Scottie Pippen (17.8 points, 7.3 rebounds) teamed with Jordan to provide a lethal scoring punch and a bevy of fastbreak highlights. Horace Grant finally asserted himself at power forward, scoring 12.8 points and pulling down 8.4 rebounds a night, while shooting 54.7 percent.

Aging center Bill Cartwright was again steady (9.6 points, 6.2 rebounds), and point guard John Paxson provided outside shooting accuracy (8.7 points, 43.8 percent from 3-point range). Bench players B.J. Armstrong (8.8 points), Stacey King (5.5 points), and Craig Hodges (5.0 points) formed the remainder of a solid rotation.

1991-92 Roster

| No. | Player | Pos. | Ht. | Wt. | Exp. | College | 1990-91 | | |
							PPG	RPG	APG
10	B.J. Armstrong	G	6'2"	175	2	Iowa	8.8	1.8	3.7
24	Bill Cartwright	C	7'1"	245	11	San Francisco	9.6	6.2	1.6
54	Horace Grant	F	6'10"	220	4	Clemson	12.8	8.4	2.3
14	Craig Hodges	G	6'2"	190	9	Long Beach St.	5.0	0.6	1.3
2	Dennis Hopson	G	6'5"	195	4	Ohio St.	4.3	1.8	1.1
23	Michael Jordan	G	6'6"	198	7	North Carolina	31.5	6.0	5.5
34	Stacey King	F/C	6'11"	230	2	Oklahoma	5.5	2.7	0.6
53	Cliff Levingston	F	6'8"	210	9	Wichita St.	4.0	2.9	0.7
5	John Paxson	G	6'2"	185	8	Notre Dame	8.7	1.1	3.6
32	Will Perdue	C	7'0"	240	3	Vanderbilt	4.1	4.5	0.6
33	Scottie Pippen	F	6'7"	210	4	Cent. Arkansas	17.8	7.3	6.2
52	Mark Randall	F	6'9"	230	R	Kansas	—	—	—
42	Scott Williams	C	6'10"	230	1	North Carolina	2.5	1.9	0.3

Chicago Bulls
1991-92 Season Preview

Opening Line: The Bulls were clicking on all cylinders last year, winning 61 regular-season games and storming to the NBA championship with a 15-2 playoff record. Now they're primed to repeat, as they return the same talented cast including the god of basketball, Michael Jordan. Only center Bill Cartwright, at age 34, appears on the downswing. In the draft, they picked up Mark Randall near the end of the first round. He's a 6'9" forward from Kansas.

Guard: Jordan reigns as the biggest sports superstar in the world. Not only can he score better than anyone else (31.5 PPG), but he can dish off (5.5 APG), rebound (19 in a playoff game last year), play defense, and pick your pocket (2.7 SPG). He gives the Bulls at least 20 wins a year. Backcourt mate John Paxson isn't very talented, but he will bury nearly 100 percent of his open jumpers. Waterbug B.J. Armstrong gets wiser and more confident each season, and he'll play at least as much as Paxson this year. Craig Hodges will only be used as a designated 3-point shooter.

Forward: Scottie Pippen is emerging as one of the best small forwards in the NBA. Pippen can score inside and out (17.8 PPG), rebound (7.3 RPG), and find the open man (6.2 APG). He also made 193 steals last year and impressed the basketball world with his cool, confident play in the playoffs. Horace Grant is an athletic power forward who can score some (12.8

PPG), run the floor, and crash the offensive boards. Though not a scorer, Levingston is an active body and an intimidating defensive player. Randall will probably never be a starter and will see limited minutes this year.

Center: The aging Bill Cartwright, a classic low-post pivot man, gives the Bulls steady play in the middle. However, he's rather slow and doesn't rebound as well as you'd like (6.2 RPG). Will Perdue is emerging as a respectable back-up center. He pulled down 336 boards in just 972 minutes last year. The Bulls have spotted some talent in sophomore Scott Williams, but he still won't play very much.

Coaching: Phil Jackson did a superb job of keeping the Bulls focused for the drive to the NBA title. He knew he had a shaky bench and did an outstanding job of juggling his roster to disguise the holes. Jackson is an astute coach who understands both strategy and motivation. He is ably assisted by John Bach, Tex Winter, and Jim Cleamons.

Analysis: The heart of the Bulls—Jordan, Pippen, Grant, Armstrong—is in its prime, and there's no reason this team can't repeat. Don't expect a letdown. Under Jackson's leadership, this club is too mature, professional, and focused for that. The only thing that could hurt the Bulls would be injuries to either Pippen or (God forbid) Jordan.

Prediction: 1st place, Central

CLEVELAND CAVALIERS

Division: Central
Home: The Coliseum
Capacity: 20,273
Year Built: 1974

Address
The Coliseum
2923 Streetsboro Rd.
Richfield, OH 44286
(216) 659-9100

Co-Chairmen of the Board:
George Gund III, Gordon Gund
Executive V.P./General Manager:
Wayne Embry
Head Coach: Lenny Wilkens
Assistant Coach: Dick Helm
Assistant Coach: Brian Winters

Coach Lenny Wilkens			
	W	L	Pct.
NBA Record	758	839	.475
W/Cavaliers	205	205	.500
1990-91 Record	33	49	.402

Cavaliers History

Since their debut in 1970, the Cavaliers have been one of the NBA's most disappointing teams, winning only one playoff series in their history. Until recently, the Cavs haven't had many marquee players—the result of some poor drafting and questionable trades during the 1970s. Things changed in the late 1980s thanks to smarter drafting and the stewardship of coach Lenny Wilkens.

The early years were tough, as Cleveland spent its first four seasons in the Central basement. In 1975-76, coach Bill Fitch was rewarded for his patience with a division title, as well as the team's only playoff series win. They beat Washington in seven games in the Eastern Conference semis. Center Jim Chones, forwards Campy Russell and Jim Brewer, and guard

Bobby "Bingo" Smith were the main performers on that team, but the good times ended soon thereafter. Cleveland qualified for the playoffs the next two seasons but made it back only once (1984-85) in the ensuing nine years.

In 1986, the Cavs began their renaissance by drafting center Brad Daugherty. Daugherty, guards Ron Harper and Mark Price, and forward Larry Nance led the Cavs to a 42-40 record in 1987-88, and a 57-25 mark the next year. In 1989-90, Cleveland dealt Harper to the Clippers for the rights to former Duke star Danny Ferry. However, the team's high expectations were dashed by injuries in 1990-91; Price missed most of the year due to knee problems.

Last Five Years

Season	W	L	Pct.	Place	Playoffs	Coach
1986-87	31	51	.378	Sixth	DNQ	Lenny Wilkens
1987-88	42	40	.512	Fourth	L-Round One	Lenny Wilkens
1988-89	57	25	.695	Second	L-Round One	Lenny Wilkens
1989-90	42	40	.512	Fourth	L-Round One	Lenny Wilkens
1990-91	33	49	.402	Sixth	DNQ	Lenny Wilkens

1990-91 Recap

Instead of 1990-91 being the year Cleveland finally snapped its string of first-round playoff exits, it developed into a nightmare. Injuries, inconsistency, and some questionable front-office dealings haunted the Cavaliers, and they slipped into the draft lottery with a 33-49 record, nine games off the previous year's pace.

The undeniable lowlight was the knee injury to point guard Mark Price just 16 games into the season. The departure of Price, one of the league's top playmakers and the leader of the Cavs, proved to be devastating. Though veteran Darnell Valentine (9.4 points, 5.4 assists) was steady as a fill-in, Cleveland's offense sputtered without its chief.

Cleveland's off-guard situation wasn't much better. Craig Ehlo (10.1 points) shot only 44.5 percent from the field, and it was obvious that the Cavs missed Ron Harper, whom they dealt in 1989-90 to the Clippers for the rights to Danny Ferry. Ferry did not impress either. He averaged 8.6 points and 3.5 rebounds in a reserve role and was criticized for his lack of speed and unfamiliarity with the intense NBA game.

A few things did go as expected for Cleveland. Center Brad Daugherty was again outstanding, averaging 21.6 points and 10.9 rebounds per game, and high-flying Larry Nance contributed 19.2 points and 8.6 boards per contest. Forward John Williams, sidelined for half the year with injuries, contributed 11.7 points and 6.7 rebounds as a sixth man. These three comprised one of the most talented frontcourts in the league, but they couldn't overcome the team's injuries and poor guard play.

1991-92 Roster

No.	Player	Pos.	Ht.	Wt.	Exp.	College	1990-91 PPG	RPG	APG
10	John Battle	G	6'2"	175	6	Rutgers	13.6	2.0	2.7
20	Winston Bennett	F	6'7"	210	2	Kentucky	4.3	2.4	1.0
—	Terrell Brandon	G	6'0"	180	R	Oregon	—	—	—
52	Chucky Brown	F	6'8"	214	2	N. Carolina St.	8.5	2.9	1.1
43	Brad Daugherty	C	7'0"	263	5	North Carolina	21.6	10.9	3.3
3	Craig Ehlo	G/F	6'7"	205	8	Washington St.	10.1	4.7	4.6
35	Danny Ferry	F	6'10"	230	1	Duke	8.6	3.5	1.8
31	Keith Hughes	F	6'9"	235	R	Rutgers	—	—	—
32	Henry James	F	6'9"	220	1	St. Mary's (TX)	8.1	2.1	0.9
4	Steve Kerr	G	6'3"	180	3	Arizona	4.8	0.6	2.3
23	John Morton	G	6'3"	183	2	Seton Hall	5.4	1.6	3.7
22	Larry Nance	F/C	6'10"	235	10	Clemson	19.2	8.6	3.0
21	Jimmy Oliver	G/F	6'6"	208	R	Purdue	—	—	—
25	Mark Price	G	6'0"	178	5	Georgia Tech	16.9	2.8	10.4
18	John Williams	F/C	6'11"	238	5	Tulane	11.7	6.7	2.3

Cleveland Cavaliers
1991-92 Season Preview

Opening Line: If the Cavaliers could ever make it through a season healthy, they could be legitimate division contenders. But All-Star guard Mark Price is still limping after missing most of last season with a torn anterior cruciate ligament, and John "Hot Rod" Williams is coming off an injury-plagued year. The additions of No. 11 pick Terrell Brandon, a 6'0" point guard from Oregon, and No. 39 pick Jimmy Oliver, a 6'6" forward from Purdue, should help. The Cavs also traded for Keith Hughes, a 6'9" forward from Rutgers who was the 47th player chosen. Guard John Battle was signed as a free agent.

Guard: Price won't be healed when the season starts. When healthy, he's a brilliant outside shooter, a big assist man, and the team's leader. Many felt the Cavs drafted Brandon because they didn't feel Price would be ready. Brandon is an explosive little point guard but needs a lot of work defensively. Darnell Valentine, who started at the point last year, is solid but unspectacular. Off guard Craig Ehlo is a good team player who can shoot from outside or drive into traffic. Battle will provide solid depth, while Steve Kerr is deadly from 3-point land.

Forward: Larry Nance continues to prove he can compete at a near-All-Star level. He can score, rebound, and block shots (19.2 PPG, 8.6 RPG, 2.5 BPG). Williams, one of the NBA's highest paid players, is also one of its best young power forwards. Like Nance, he's a great athlete and a triple threat. Danny Ferry, a major bust last year after coming over from Europe, was supposed to be a Larry Bird-type player. His confidence improved at the end of last season and he should be better this year. Henry James, pulled from the CBA, is a streaky scorer off the bench. Sophomore back-up Chucky Brown is most comfortable in a running game.

Center: Brad Daugherty has established himself as an All-Star center. Though not a dominant pivot man, Daugherty can score (21.6 PPG) and rebound (10.9 RPG). He's a classic low-post center who's strong and quick enough to handle almost anybody. He's a terrific passer. Nance can also move over to the center position.

Coaching: When his team was healthy, Lenny Wilkens guided this club to 57 wins (1988-89). Cavs management realized Wilkens could not be blamed for last year's injuries and rewarded him with a contract extension. Wilkens, a Hall of Fame guard, is assisted by Brian Winters and Dick Helm.

Analysis: If Price comes back soon, expect the Cavaliers to win 50 games. The starting frontcourt is extremely talented, and a backcourt of Price and Ehlo is heady and productive. Ferry can only get better. Don't be surprised if Cleveland trades Williams and his huge salary.

Prediction: 2nd Place, Central

DETROIT PISTONS

Division: Central
Home: The Palace
Capacity: 21,454
Year Built: 1988

Managing Partner: William Davidson
General Manager: Jack McCloskey
Head Coach: Chuck Daly
Assistant Coach: Brendan Suhr
Assistant Coach: Brendan Malone

Address
The Palace
Two Championship Dr.
Auburn Hills, MI 48057
(313) 377-0100

Coach Chuck Daly			
	W	L	Pct.
NBA Record	428	269	.614
W/Pistons	419	237	.639
1990-91 Record	50	32	.610

Pistons History

Any discussion of Pistons history is bound to be a little heavy on recent events. After three fruitless decades, the Pistons won back-to-back NBA titles in 1988-89 and 1989-90.

The franchise was established in Fort Wayne, Indiana, in 1941 as a member of the old National Basketball League. It joined the BAA in 1948 and became a charter NBA club in 1949. The Fort Wayne Pistons, led by high-scoring George Yardley, advanced to the NBA Finals twice during the 1950s, losing to Syracuse in 1954-55 and Philadelphia in 1955-56.

The Pistons moved to Detroit in 1957 but began to falter, finishing below .500 for the next 13 seasons. Detroit made some news during the period, naming 24-year old Dave DeBusschere player/coach in 1964

and drafting hot-shot guard Dave Bing in 1966. Things got a little better in the mid-1970s. Detroit posted a 52-30 record in 1973-74, due largely to the play of Bing and center Bob Lanier. But the Pistons were eliminated in the Western semis and had to wait another nine seasons for a strong team.

That came in 1983-84 when Chuck Daly took over as coach. Daly, building his team around point guard Isiah Thomas, won the Central Division title in 1987-88. They advanced to the NBA Finals that season, losing to Los Angeles in seven games. Thomas, Bill Laimbeer, Dennis Rodman, and Joe Dumars were not denied the next two years, sweeping the Lakers in 1988-89 and whipping Portland in 1989-90.

Last Five Years

Season	W	L	Pct.	Place	Playoffs	Coach
1986-87	52	30	.634	Second	L-East Finals	Chuck Daly
1987-88	54	28	.650	First	L-NBA Finals	Chuck Daly
1988-89	63	19	.768	First	NBA Champs	Chuck Daly
1989-90	59	23	.720	First	NBA Champs	Chuck Daly
1990-91	50	32	.610	Second	L-East Finals	Chuck Daly

1990-91 Recap

The "Bad Boys" are dead. Though the Pistons had won back-to-back NBA championships, age, injuries, and the Chicago Bulls conspired to rob Detroit of its much-desired "three-peat" in 1990-91. The same cast that blitzed to titles in 1988-89 and 1989-90 returned to bully the NBA, and a 13-1 start made the Pistons appear still invulnerable. As the season wore on, some weaknesses were discovered. And when the Bulls swept Detroit in the Eastern Conference finals, it appeared a team shake-up was imminent.

Isiah Thomas's late-season wrist injury nearly paralyzed the Piston offense down the stretch, and Detroit staggered to a 50-32 record and a second-place finish in the Central Division. Age was also a factor in the demise—nine Pistons were 30 or older.

Though Thomas returned in time for the playoffs, his effectiveness was diminished greatly. The Pistons needed five games to dispose of the Hawks in their first-round playoff series and slugged it out with Boston for six contests in the Eastern semifinals. By the time it got to Chicago, weary Detroit was no match for the quicker, hungrier Bulls, who whipped the Pistons in four straight.

Guard Joe Dumars was his usual outstanding self all year, averaging 20.4 PPG and taking a turn at the point when Thomas went down with the injury. But there were problems up front, as Detroit's age started to show. Center James "Buddha" Edwards (13.6 points) and reserve forward Mark Aguirre (14.2) suffered from sore backs much of the year. Bill Laimbeer (11.0 points, 9.0 rebounds) was sturdy during the season but disappeared against the Bulls.

Detroit's physical style made it the league's top defensive team again. Opponents could score only 96.5 points a game against John Salley, Dennis Rodman (12.5 rebounds), and company, who proved they could still intimidate.

1991-92 Roster

No.	Player	Pos.	Ht.	Wt.	Exp.	College	1990-91 PPG	RPG	APG
23	Mark Aguirre	F	6'6"	232	10	DePaul	14.2	4.8	1.8
00	William Bedford	C	7'1"	235	4	Memphis St.	4.5	2.2	0.5
32	Lance Blanks	G	6'4"	195	1	Texas	1.7	0.5	0.7
4	Joe Dumars	G	6'3"	195	6	McNeese St.	20.4	2.3	5.5
31	Mark Hughes	F/C	6'8"	235	R	Michigan	—	—	—
40	Bill Laimbeer	C	6'11"	260	11	Notre Dame	11.0	9.0	1.9
—	Jeff Martin	G	6'5"	195	2	Murray St.	7.1	1.8	0.9
—	Jimmy Overton	G	6'3"	190	R	La Salle	—	—	—
10	Dennis Rodman	F	6'8"	210	5	S.E. Okla. St.	8.2	12.5	1.0
22	John Salley	F/C	6'11"	244	5	Georgia Tech	7.4	4.4	0.9
—	Brad Sellers	F	7'0"	227	4	Ohio St.	—	—	—
11	Isiah Thomas	G	6'1"	182	10	Indiana	16.2	3.3	9.3
—	Orlando Woolridge	F	6'9"	215	10	Notre Dame	25.1	6.8	2.2

Detroit Pistons
1991-92 Season Preview

Opening Line: After being whipped by the Bulls in the 1991 Eastern Conference finals, GM Jack McCloskey began to rebuild this aging team over the summer. Veteran guard Vinnie Johnson was waived, while 7'0" forward Brad Sellers was brought in from Europe. In a three-way deal with Denver and the Clippers, Detroit traded big men James Edwards and Scott Hastings and ended up with forward Orlando Woolridge and guard Jeff Martin. Detroit drafted La Salle guard Doug Overton with the No. 40 pick.

Guard: All-Stars Isiah Thomas and Joe Dumars are so talented that they can interchange at both guard positions. Thomas (9.3 APG) is a gutsy leader who still runs the show. Dumars (20.4 PPG) will quietly kill you with his near-perfect shooting and his stifling defense. Jeff Martin, a fine driver and defensive player, will be a solid but mediocre back-up at big guard. Lance Blanks, a long-range bomber who saw limited action as a rookie last year, could be part of the rebuilding plan. Overton is similar in style to Dumars.

Forward: Woolridge (25.1 PPG) is a muscular, explosive scorer. Though his numbers were inflated in Denver, he'll still be an offensive force with Detroit. Not only was Dennis Rodman voted Defensive Player of the Year the last two seasons, but he pulled down 12.5 rebounds last year—the second-best mark in the league. Mark Aguirre can still provide lethal scoring off the bench (14.2 PPG), though

coach Chuck Daly has never been happy with his defense. The sinewy John Salley, another key reserve, can run the floor and block shots. Sellers, a good outside shooter, is very soft inside.

Center: The NBA's No. 1 villain, Bill Laimbeer, is still a factor at age 34. He can rebound on defense (9.0 RPG) and hit the outside shot on offense—although his perimeter shooting disappeared in last year's playoffs. He's close to retiring. William Bedford, a nimble seven-footer, has been groomed for the pivot, but Bedford, a four-year veteran, is still considered a project player.

Coaching: Daly is easily one of the NBA's best coaches, having led Detroit to two straight NBA championships. His teams play hard, tough, and physical, and he's perhaps the game's greatest defensive coach. He'll coach the U.S. team in the 1992 Olympics. Daly is assisted by a pair of Brendans—Suhr and Malone. Suhr may become Daly's heir apparent.

Analysis: As evidenced by their off-season moves, it's pretty clear that the Pistons have opted for a youth movement. It's a good decision, considering the team was very old and could no longer beat the young, hungry Bulls. The Pistons will make the playoffs, but each round will be a struggle. Woolridge should provide a little more offense than the aging Edwards.

Prediction: 3rd place, Central

INDIANA PACERS

Division: Central
Home: Market Square Arena
Capacity: 16,912
Year Built: 1974

Address
300 E. Market St.
Indianapolis, IN 46204
(317) 263-2100

Owners: Melvin Simon, Herbert Simon
President: Don Walsh
Head Coach: Bob Hill
Assistant Coach: Bob Ociepka
Assistant Coach: Billy Knight

Coach Bob Hill	W	L	Pct.
NBA Record	52	71	.423
W/Pacers	32	25	.561
1990-91 Record	32	25	.561

Pacers History

If there can be such a thing as the "Boston Celtics of the ABA," it would definitely be the Indiana Pacers. The Pacers won three ABA titles and finished second twice between 1968-69 and 1974-75.

But the Pacers were sorry to see the old league die. Since joining the NBA, the Pacers have been nearly moribund, reaching the playoffs only four times during their 15 years in the league. Despite playing in a basketball-crazed state, the Pacers have never won an NBA playoff series.

But the old days were something in Indianapolis. Led by Mel Daniels, a 6'9" bull of a center, the early Pacers featured a lineup that was equal to many NBA teams. Guard Freddie Lewis and forward Roger Brown were deadly scorers, and power forward Bob Netolicky was a bruiser. In 1971, Indiana signed forward George McGinnis from Indiana University. It later added guard Bill Keller and forward Billy Knight to a potent rotation.

Yet the same penchant for accumulating talented personnel has not carried over to Indiana's years in the NBA. The Pacers have had only two winning seasons since the merger, though the last two years have given fans a hint of promise. Forward Chuck Person and do-everything sixth man Detlef Schrempf have teamed with long-range bomber Reggie Miller to make things exciting, as evidenced by their thrilling, five-game loss to Boston in the 1991 playoffs.

Last Five Years

Season	W	L	Pct.	Place	Playoffs	Coach
1986-87	41	41	.500	Fourth	L-Round One	Jack Ramsay
1987-88	38	44	.463	Sixth	DNQ	Jack Ramsay
1988-89	28	54	.341	Sixth	DNQ	J. Ramsay/G. Irvine/D. Versace
1989-90	42	40	.512	Fourth	L-Round One	Dick Versace
1990-91	41	41	.500	Fifth	L-Round One	Dick Versace/Bob Hill

1990-91 Recap

The enduring image of the 1990-91 Pacers will be Chuck Person's rapid-fire shooting—of the basketball and his mouth—in the scintillating five-game, first-round playoff series with Boston. Sure, Indiana lost to the Celtics (it has never won an NBA playoff series), but it went down in style.

With the cocky Person lighting it up from all regions of the court, the Pacers took the highly regarded Atlantic Division champs down to the final seconds in Boston Garden (and even won one in Boston along the way). It was only after Person's turnaround 3-pointer fell short that Indiana went away.

Still, Pacers fans have a lot to be happy about. Indiana closed the year 32-25 under coach Bob Hill, who replaced unpopular Dick Versace, to finish at 41-41. The late-season emergence of point guard Micheal Williams complemented gunner Reggie Miller and helped the Pacers average 111.7 PPG—fifth in the league.

Miller continued to be one of the league's top shooters, averaging 22.6 points a game while shooting 51.2 percent. He also led the NBA in free throw shooting, converting on 91.8 percent of his attempts. Person was another marksman, averaging 18.4 a night and shooting 50.4 percent from the field. Detlef Schrempf was named the league's top sixth man, thanks to another great all-around year (16.1 points, 8.0 rebounds, 3.7 assists).

The Pacers struggled up front once again. Centers LaSalle Thompson (7.6 points, 6.9 rebounds) and Rik Smits (10.9 points, 4.7 rebounds) were inconsistent, and Greg Dreiling (3.5 points, 3.5 rebounds) was inadequate.

1991-92 Roster

| No. | Player | Pos. | Ht. | Wt. | Exp. | College | 1990-91 | | |
							PPG	RPG	APG
32	Dale Davis	C	6'11"	230	R	Clemson	—	—	—
54	Greg Dreiling	C	7'1"	250	5	Kansas	3.5	3.5	0.7
10	Vern Fleming	G	6'5"	185	7	Georgia	12.7	3.1	5.3
12	Sean Green	G	6'5"	210	R	Iona	—	—	—
20	George McCloud	G/F	6'8"	215	2	Florida St.	4.6	1.6	2.0
31	Reggie Miller	G	6'7"	185	4	UCLA	22.6	3.4	4.0
45	Chuck Person	F	6'8"	225	5	Auburn	18.4	5.2	3.0
33	Mike Sanders	F	6'6"	215	9	UCLA	5.8	2.3.	1.3
11	Detlef Schrempf	F	6'10"	230	6	Washington	16.1	8.0	3.7
24	Rik Smits	C	7'4"	265	3	Marist	10.9	4.7	1.1
41	LaSalle Thompson	F/C	6'10"	260	9	Texas	7.6	6.9	1.8
44	Ken Williams	F	6'9"	205	1	Elizabeth City	2.9	1.7	0.4
4	Micheal Williams	G	6'2"	175	3	Baylor	11.1	2.4	4.8
14	Randy Wittman	G	6'6"	210	8	Indiana	1.8	0.8	0.6

Indiana Pacers
1991-92 Season Preview

Opening Line: Led by perimeter stars Reggie Miller (22.6 PPG) and Chuck Person (18.4 PPG), the Pacers will try to win their first-ever post-season series in 1992. Though this team can score, it has troubles defensively and on the boards. Indiana hopes 6'10" rookie Dale Davis, the 13th pick out of Clemson, will help. The Pacers also selected Sean Green, a 6'5" guard out of Iona, with the 41st pick.

Guard: Miller has blossomed into one of the most feared shooters on the planet. The man who calls himself "Hollywood" not only buries the jumper but is lethal from 3-point land (112-of-322 last year) and at the line (92 percent). He's a certified All-Star. Micheal Williams, a little point guard who's been banished from four NBA teams in his young career, blossomed into a starter last season. Vern Fleming, a steady but mediocre Pacers starter since 1984, will get substantial minutes off the bench. George McCloud (37 percent from the floor) has failed to live up to his seventh selection in the 1989 draft. The brilliance of Miller and the solid play of Williams and Fleming makes this a decent backcourt.

Forward: Person is more famous for his trash talking than for his outstanding scoring. By challenging Larry Bird in last season's playoffs, he proved he could back up his words. Person has a fine outside touch and can also drive to the basket with power. Detlef Schrempf, last year's Sixth Man Award winner, will play 30 quality minutes a night. He'll play all along the front line and score inside and out. No other Pacer forward knows how to score. LaSalle Thompson (6'10") crashes the boards (6.9 RPG) but doesn't look to shoot. Mike Sanders provides blue-collar defense as Person's back-up. And rookie Davis offers boards and blocks but no offensive skills.

Center: For three years, the Pacers have been waiting for 7'4" Rik Smits to develop into a dominating NBA center. Smits possesses amazing mobility and touch for his monstrous size, but his timid play cost him a starting job last year. Coach Bob Hill replaced him with Greg Dreiling, whose only talent is throwing his 7'1" body around.

Coaching: Despite little NBA coaching experience, Hill enjoys an outstanding relationship with his players and was able to get far more out of them than his predecessor, Dick Versace. Hill is assisted by former ABA and NBA star Billy Knight and Bob Ociepka.

Analysis: The Pacers are as average as last year's .500 record indicates. Person showed signs of maturity last year, and Indiana will need more of that this season. If Smits lives up to his enormous potential, it could elevate this team to another level—but that's not likely to happen. Indiana may exceed the .500 mark in 1991-92, but it won't be by much.

Prediction: 5th Place, Central

MILWAUKEE BUCKS

Division: Central
Home: The Bradley Center
Capacity: 18,633
Year Built: 1988

Owner: Herb Kohl
V.P./Basketball Operations:
 Del Harris
Head Coach: Del Harris
Assistant Coach: Frank Hamblen
Assistant Coach: Mack Calvin
Assistant Coach: Larry Riley

Address
The Bradley Center
1001 N. Fourth St.
Milwaukee, WI 53203
(414) 227-0500

Coach Del Harris			
	W	L	Pct.
NBA Record	324	322	.502
W/Bucks	183	145	.558
1990-91 Record	48	34	.585

Bucks History

During their 23 years of existence, the Bucks have missed out on post-season play only five times. But despite that gleaming record, the franchise's glory period is long past.

Milwaukee stumbled through its rookie season in 1968-69, but the Bucks won the coin toss with Phoenix for the rights to UCLA star Lew Alcindor. The Bucks signed the big rookie and embarked on a five-year run of success. In 1969-70, Milwaukee reached the Eastern finals, and the arrival of guard Oscar Robertson during the off-season was the final piece in coach Larry Costello's puzzle. In 1970-71, Alcindor, Robertson, Bob Dandridge, Greg Smith, and Jon McGlocklin led the Bucks to a 66-16 record and the NBA championship.

Alcindor changed his name to Kareem Abdul-Jabbar, and in 1973-74 the Bucks made it back to the title series. However, they lost to Boston in seven games. Jabbar was dealt to Los Angeles for four players following the 1974-75 season, and the Bucks floundered for the next four years, finishing over .500 just once.

Don Nelson took over as coach in 1976-77 and directed the team back into the playoffs on a regular basis. But although the nucleus of Sidney Moncrief, Junior Bridgeman, Marques Johnson, and Terry Cummings was strong enough to win 50-plus games each year from 1980-81 to 1986-87, it couldn't get back to the NBA Finals. The Bucks replaced Nelson with Del Harris for 1987-88 and continued their playoff-appearance run.

Last Five Years

Season	W	L	Pct.	Place	Playoffs	Coach
1986-87	50	32	.610	Third	L-East Semis	Don Nelson
1987-88	42	40	.512	Fourth	L-Round One	Del Harris
1988-89	49	33	.598	Fourth	L-East Semis	Del Harris
1989-90	44	38	.537	Third	L-Round One	Del Harris
1990-91	48	34	.585	Third	L-Round One	Del Harris

1990-91 Recap

The Bucks' mixture of quick guards and plodding frontcourt players once again carried them into the playoffs in 1990-91, but did little else. Milwaukee's abrupt three-game exit from the post-season, courtesy of Philadelphia, was further proof of the team's lack of overall quickness. Milwaukee turtled its way to a 48-34 record and a third-place finish in the Central Division, though it slumped to 18-15 after the All-Star break.

Some may argue that the Bucks' sluggish ways carried over to the front office, which decided to deal sixth-man scoring machine Ricky Pierce to Seattle for terminal malcontent and highway hazard Dale Ellis. When Ellis (bad back) came up lame late in the season, Milwaukee was forced to sign Adrian Dantley as a bench scorer. It didn't work. In the playoffs, the quicker Sixers ran through the Bucks, who didn't have the firepower to keep up with Philly.

The Buck backcourt of Jay Humphries (15.2 points, 6.7 assists) and all-world defensive star Alvin Robertson (13.6 points, 5.7 rebounds, 5.5 assists, 3.04 steals) was again strong, though Ellis (19.3 points in 21 games with the Bucks) will have to stay out of trouble to replace Pierce adequately.

Up front, the big, slow guys were solid. Forwards Frank Brickowski (12.6 points, 5.7 rebounds) and Fred Roberts (10.8 points) teamed with center Danny Schayes (10.6 points, 6.5 rebounds) in the starting rotation, while veteran Jack Sikma (10.4 points) and Brad Lohaus (5.3 points) came off the bench.

1991-92 Roster

No.	Player	Pos.	Ht.	Wt.	Exp.	College	PPG	1990-91 RPG	APG
—	Anthony Avent	F/C	6'10"	235	R	Seton Hall	—	—	—
40	Frank Brickowski	F/C	6'10"	240	7	Penn St.	12.6	5.7	1.7
15	Lester Conner	G	6'4"	213	8	Oregon St.	3.5	1.5	2.2
7	Adrian Dantley	F	6'5"	210	15	Notre Dame	5.7	1.3	0.9
3	Dale Ellis	G	6'7"	213	8	Tennessee	16.8	3.4	1.9
20	Jeff Grayer	G/F	6'5"	213	3	Iowa St.	6.4	3.0	1.5
12	Steve Henson	G	5'11"	177	1	Kansas St.	3.1	0.8	1.9
24	Jay Humphries	G	6'3"	185	7	Colorado	15.2	2.8	6.7
42	Larry Krystkowiak	F	6'10"	240	5	Montana	—	—	—
54	Brad Lohaus	F/C	6'11"	235	4	Iowa	5.3	2.7	0.9
8	Moses Malone	C	6'10"	255	15	None	10.6	8.1	0.8
34	Bobby Phills	G	6'5"	210	R	Southern	—	—	—
44	Fred Roberts	F	6'10"	245	8	Brigham Young	10.8	3.4	1.6
21	Alvin Robertson	G	6'4"	202	7	Arkansas	13.6	5.7	5.5
10	Dan Schayes	C	6'11"	250	10	Syracuse	10.6	6.5	1.2

Milwaukee Bucks
1991-92 Season Preview

Opening Line: Once again, coach Del Harris will attempt to take an apparently mediocre team and lead it to the playoffs—where the Bucks have been the past 12 years. This year, Milwaukee features several new faces. Dale Ellis and Adrian Dantley were acquired at the end of last season, while Larry Krystkowiak returns after missing nearly two seasons with a knee injury. The Bucks let Jack Sikma go but signed the legendary Moses Malone as a free agent. Milwaukee drafted Kevin Brooks with the 18th choice and then traded him to Denver for Anthony Avent, a 6'10" rookie from Seton Hall. The Bucks also chose Bobby Phills, a 6'5" guard from Southern University, with the 45th pick.

Guard: Jay Humphries (15.2 PPG, 6.7 APG) is not the most spectacular point guard around, but he's solid in every phase of the game. For an off guard, Alvin Robertson can't shoot very well, but his defense is second to none—he led the league in steals last year. If Ellis doesn't crack the starting lineup, he'll be one of the scariest sixth men in the league. Ellis, who averaged 27.5 PPG three years ago, will kill you with his long-range jumpers. Sophomore Steve Henson is a smart, sound playmaker but lacks size (5'11"). Lester Conner is a defensive role player, while Jeff Grayer's career has been retarded by knee problems.

Forward: Power forward Frank Brickowski is a big body who will surprise you with some inside scoring

skills. Still, he would be better suited as a part-time role player. Ditto for starting small forward Fred Roberts, a fine team player who lacks the talent and consistency to justify his starting spot. Krystkowiak, a hard-working 6'10" forward, may fight his way back into the starting lineup. Avent is a strong rebounder and defender who should join the front-line rotation. The ancient Dantley could provide some offense from the low post.

Center: Danny Schayes offers few offensive or defensive skills but knows what to do to get by. Brad Lohaus is a 6'11" perimeter shooter who does nothing inside. Malone still knows how to rebound. He'll be an effective reserve.

Coaching: Critics like to laugh at Harris and his frontcourt, but they keep winning. The credit goes to Harris who, in his four seasons in Milwaukee, has posted four winning records while playing in a brutal division. Harris is assisted by Frank Hamblen, Mack Calvin, and Larry Riley.

Analysis: The trade of Ricky Pierce for Ellis figures to be a an even deal, as does the replacement of Sikma with Malone. The return of Krystkowiak will help some, but the Bucks probably won't be much better than last year. They'll play sound, team-oriented ball and win 45-50 games. They won't challenge the Bulls for the Central title.

Prediction: 4th Place, Central

DALLAS MAVERICKS

Division: Midwest
Home: Reunion Arena
Capacity: 17,007
Year Built: 1980

Owner: Donald Carter
General Manager: Norm Sonju
Head Coach: Richie Adubato
Assistant Coach: Gar Heard
Assistant Coach: Bob Zuffelato

Address
Reunion Arena
777 Sports St.
Dallas, TX 75207
(214) 748-1808

Coach Richie Adubato			
	W	L	Pct.
NBA Record	82	141	.368
W/Mavericks	70	83	.458
1990-91 Record	28	54	.341

Mavericks History

Few teams in NBA history have experienced so much success as quickly as the Mavericks. Through intelligent drafting and the old-school tactics of coach Dick Motta, Dallas finished with a winning record in only its fourth year of existence.

Dallas entered the league in 1980 and soon made its mark. In the 1981 draft, the Mavs selected Mark Aguirre, Rolando Blackman, and Jay Vincent. In 1983, they brought in standout guards Dale Ellis and Derek Harper. That high-scoring nucleus won 43 games in 1983-84, finishing second in the Midwest and advancing to the West semifinals.

Dallas won the Midwest in 1986-87, buoyed by the addition of mammoth center James Donaldson and rookie forward Roy Tarpley, but the Mavs bowed out in the first round of the playoffs. The excitement really ran high the next season. Motta was replaced by former Phoenix coach John MacLeod, and Dallas stretched eventual champion Los Angeles to seven games in the Western finals.

Things started to sour in 1988-89. Aguirre was traded in mid-season to Detroit for the mercurial Adrian Dantley, and Tarpley—now the league's premier sixth man—played only 19 games due to alcohol abuse problems. The Mavericks fell to 38-44 in 1988-89, and though they rebounded to 47-35 the next season, MacLeod was fired and Dallas lost in the first round of the 1990 playoffs. A knee injury to Tarpley early in 1990-91 contributed to a 28-54 record.

Last Five Years

Season	W	L	Pct.	Place	Playoffs	Coach
1986-87	55	27	.671	First	L-Round One	Dick Motta
1987-88	53	29	.646	Second	L-West Finals	John MacLeod
1988-89	38	44	.463	Fourth	DNQ	John MacLeod
1989-90	47	35	.573	Third	L-Round One	J. Macleod/R. Adubato
1990-91	28	54	.341	Sixth	DNQ	Richie Adubato

1990-91 Recap

Any hopes that the Mavs would continue their progress under coach Richie Adubato were eliminated five games into the 1990-91 season when center Roy Tarpley tore apart his knee. Dallas had already lost versatile forward Sam Perkins to free agency during the off-season, and Tarpley's injury depleted its frontcourt. Moreover, the Mavericks waited all season for the recovery of do-everything guard Fat Lever, who missed 78 games with a knee injury.

With the loss of those three key performers, Dallas didn't have a chance. In fact, the Mavs' 28-54 record landed them in sixth place in the Midwest Division, behind second-year franchises Orlando and Minnesota. And since Dallas sported the league's oldest roster, the future didn't look very bright.

Though Tarpley was through on the court, he did seek action elsewhere and was arrested for driving while intoxicated and violating his parole. His NBA future was left in doubt.

As expected, the Mavericks' strength was their guards—despite the absence of Lever. Rolando Blackman continued to score in bunches, averaging 19.9 a game, and Derek Harper set an NBA record by increasing his scoring average (19.7) for the eighth consecutive season.

Up front, mammoth center James Donaldson was his usual self, averaging 10.0 points and 8.9 boards a contest. In Tarpley's absence, the Mavs used a four-man forward rotation with mixed results. Herb Williams (12.5 points, 6.0 boards) was the top scorer on the front line, while Rodney McCray (11.4, 7.6), Alex English (9.7 points), and Randy White (8.8 points, 6.4 rebounds) were adequate.

1991-92 Roster

No.	Player	Pos.	Ht.	Wt.	Exp.	College	1990-91 PPG	1990-91 RPG	1990-91 APG
22	Rolando Blackman	G	6'6"	206	10	Kansas St.	19.9	3.2	3.8
15	Brad Davis	G	6'3"	183	14	Maryland	5.4	1.5	2.9
—	Terry Davis	F	6'9"	236	2	Virginia Union	4.5	4.8	0.7
40	James Donaldson	C	7'2"	280	11	Washington St.	10.0	8.9	0.8
50	Jim Grandholm	C	7'0"	235	1	South Florida	3.0	1.9	0.3
12	Derek Harper	G	6'4"	200	8	Illinois	19.7	3.0	7.1
—	Donald Hodge	C	7'0"	230	R	Temple	—	—	—
—	Mike Iuzzolino	G	5'10"	180	R	St. Francis (PA)	—	—	—
21	Lafayette Lever	G	6'3"	175	9	Arizona St.	7.3	3.8	3.0
1	Rodney McCray	F	6'8"	235	8	Louisville	11.4	7.6	3.5
55	John Shasky	C	6'11"	240	3	Minnesota	2.6	2.4	0.2
34	Doug Smith	F	6'10"	220	R	Missouri	—	—	—
42	Roy Tarpley	F	6'11"	250	5	Michigan	20.4	11.0	2.4
5	Kelvin Upshaw	G	6'2"	180	3	Utah	5.6	1.1	1.8
33	Randy White	F	6'8"	249	2	Louisiana Tech	8.8	6.4	0.8
32	Herb Williams	F/C	6'11"	242	10	Ohio St.	12.5	6.0	1.6

Dallas Mavericks
1991-92 Season Preview

Opening Line: The Mavericks can improve on their 28-54 record if they regain star talents Lafayette Lever and Roy Tarpley, both of whom missed last season with knee injuries. The Mavs never know about Tarpley, a noted substance abuser who's had run-ins with the law. Dallas used the No. 6 pick in the draft on the highly regarded Doug Smith, a 6'10" power forward from Missouri. The Mavs also drafted Donald Hodge, a 7'0" center from Temple, with the 33rd pick, and grabbed heady guard Mike Iuzzolino from St. Francis with the 35th. Dallas released the legendary Alex English but signed free agent forward Terry Davis.

Guard: With a healthy Lever, Dallas would have the best guard trio in the NBA. Rolando Blackman is a big-time scorer (19.9 PPG), a strong defender, and one of the most respected guards in the league. Point guard Derek Harper is equally esteemed. Harper can score (19.7 PPG), run the offense (7.1 APG), and go nose to nose defensively with any point guard in the NBA. Lever, a former All-Star with Denver, was known for his triple-doubles (points, assists, and rebounds). Brad Davis, a 14-year veteran, provides leadership off the bench.

Forward: When clean and injury-free, the 6'11" Tarpley can practically dominate a game. However, he's rarely clean and injury-free, and Dallas can no longer depend on his presence. His fill-in, veteran Herb Williams, gives the Mavs sound defense but little offensive ability. Rookie Smith, an open-court player with some offensive skills, may start at power forward. Rodney McCray (11.4 PPG, 7.6 RPG) can play both forward positions and displays speed, strength, and quickness. Randy White clearly hasn't lived up to his Karl Malone comparisons, while Terry Davis is still a project player. Dallas needs Smith to boost this troublesome position.

Center: At 7'2", James Donaldson fits the mold of the classic journeyman center. Although Donaldson will never be a dominant scorer, he is an immovable object in the paint. Williams is the back-up center.

Coaching: Richie Adubato has been unable to keep this sinking team afloat. After weathering a 28-54 campaign, he may not have much time left at the helm, even though poor front-office decisions and injuries can't be blamed on Adubato. The Dallas assistants include Gar Heard and Bob Zuffelato.

Analysis: Maybe the best thing this team could do is throw away some of its pieces and start over. As long as Dallas puts its hopes in the hands of Tarpley, Mavericks fans should always be prepared for disappointment. After several major front-office blunders, including the decision to trade draft picks for players past their prime (such as Alex English), the future looks bleak for Dallas.

Prediction: 4th Place, Midwest

DENVER NUGGETS

Division: Midwest
Home: McNichols Sports Arena
Capacity: 17,022
Year Built: 1975

Address
1635 Clay St.
Denver, CO 80204
(303) 893-6700

Owners: Peter C.B. Bynoe, Bertram M. Lee, Robert J. Wussler
General Manager: Bernie Bickerstaff
Head Coach: Paul Westhead
Assistant Coach: Jim Boyle
Assistant Coach: Mike Evans
Assistant Coach: Judas Prada

Coach Paul Westhead			
	W	L	Pct.
NBA Record	159	166	.489
W/Nuggets	20	62	.244
1990-91 Record	20	62	.244

Nuggets History

The Nuggets were one of the rarities of the old ABA—a team that stayed in the same place throughout the league's tumultuous nine-year history. A charter ABA member, the Denver Rockets were one of the league's strongest franchises.

Early on, Rocket fans were thrilled by the high-flying exploits of forward Spencer Haywood, who led Denver to the Western Conference finals in 1969-70, where it lost to Los Angeles. But Haywood soon left and the franchise's fortunes dimmed until 1974, when GM Carl Scheer and coach Larry Brown came to the Rockies from the Carolina Cougars. Scheer immediately changed the team nickname to the Nuggets. Denver won 65 games in 1974-75 but lost in the Western finals to Indiana.

The next season, the Nuggets acquired guard David Thompson and made it to the championship series.

The Nuggets were one of four ABA teams to merge with the NBA in 1976, and they won the Midwest Division in their first two seasons. Denver won Midwest titles in 1984-85 and 1987-88 under Doug Moe and made it to the Western finals in 1985, but they failed in their bid for the elusive NBA championship.

Following the 1989-90 season, Denver fired Moe and hired Paul Westhead, who had led the Lakers to the NBA championship in 1980. Westhead's high-octane running game recalled the wild ABA days but didn't bring too many results, as Denver registered the league's worst record.

Last Five Years

Season	W	L	Pct.	Place	Playoffs	Coach
1986-87	37	45	.451	Fourth	L-Round One	Doug Moe
1987-88	54	28	.659	First	L-West Semis	Doug Moe
1988-89	44	38	.537	Third	L-Round One	Doug Moe
1989-90	43	39	.524	Fourth	L-Round One	Doug Moe
1990-91	20	62	.244	Seventh	DNQ	Paul Westhead

1990-91 Recap

If Denver was anything during the 1990-91 season, it was sincere. The Nuggets delivered on their promise to build a high-scoring, fuel-injected team around new coach Paul Westhead's radical shoot-'em-up philosophy. In the process, they proved that collegiate novelty acts don't work in the NBA.

Westhead wowed NCAA fans with his scoreboard-spinning Loyola-Marymount teams and convinced the Nugget brass that his system was universal. In a way, it was. Denver led the NBA in scoring with 119.8 PPG, but it surrendered a league-record 130.8 a night. The Nuggets made just 44 percent of their shots, while opponents converted at a 51.2-percent clip. It's little wonder that Denver's 20-62 mark was the worst in the league, not to mention the franchise's history.

Denver's racehorse philosophy made for some pretty interesting evenings. The Nuggets and Warriors combined on opening night to set an NBA record for most points (320) in a non-overtime game. On November 10, Phoenix tied Boston's record for most points scored in a 173-143 drubbing of Denver. What was thought to be a difficult adjustment for opponents turned out to be a run-and-gun festival for all.

Of course, certain Nuggets thrived in Westhead's system. Michael Adams (26.5 points, 10.5 assists) launched 3-pointers at will, and Orlando Woolridge (25.1 points) revived his dormant career thanks to the high-speed offense. Rookie guard Chris Jackson struggled early but still averaged 14.1 PPG. Forward Jerome Lane pulled down 9.3 rebounds a game, and Blair Rasmussen (9.7 RPG) was productive in the middle.

1991-92 Roster

No.	Player	Pos.	Ht.	Wt.	Exp.	College	1990-91 PPG	RPG	APG
33	Greg Anderson	F/C	6'10"	230	4	Houston	4.3	4.7	0.2
43	Kevin Brooks	F	6'8"	200	R	S.W. Louisiana	—	—	—
45	Anthony Cook	F/C	6'9"	215	1	Arizona	5.3	5.6	0.4
11	Winston Garland	G	6'2"	175	4	S.W. Misso. St.	8.2	2.9	4.6
—	Scott Hastings	F	6'11"	245	9	Arkansas	1.8	1.0	0.3
3	Chris Jackson	G	6'1"	168	1	Louisiana St.	14.1	1.8	3.1
35	Jerome Lane	F	6'6"	232	3	Pittsburgh	7.5	9.3	2.0
30	Marcus Liberty	F	6'8"	205	1	Illinois	6.7	2.9	0.8
21	Todd Lichti	G	6'4"	205	2	Stanford	14.0	3.9	2.5
12	Mark Macon	G	6'5"	185	R	Temple	—	—	—
55	Dikembe Mutombo	C	7'2"	240	R	Georgetown	—	—	—
34	Reggie Williams	G/F	6'7"	195	4	Georgetown	13.6	4.2	1.8
42	Joe Wolf	C	6'11"	230	4	North Carolina	7.3	5.4	1.4

Denver Nuggets
1991-92 Season Preview

Opening Line: The runnin'-and-gunnin' Nuggets had one of the league's best drafts. They used the No. 4 pick on Georgetown shot-blocker Dikembe Mutombo, and spent the No. 8 choice on star Temple guard Mark Macon. In a three-way trade, Denver dealt center Blair Rasmussen and ended up with rookie forward Kevin Brooks, the No. 18 pick. The Nuggets traded Michael Adams for the Macon pick, and sent draft picks to the Clippers for guard Winston Garland. High-scoring Orlando Woolridge was traded to Detroit for bit player Scott Hastings.

Guard: Sophomore Chris Jackson (14.1 PPG) has had trouble scoring in the NBA because of his size (6'1"), though he should improve some this season. Todd Lichti will drive the lane and play defense. If his bum knee holds up, he could be a solid starter at off guard. Macon, a 20-PPG scorer in college and a renowned defender, will get plenty of PT as a rookie. The 6'7" Reggie Williams (13.6 PPG) loves to play racehorse ball, though his defense and intensity are lacking. Garland is a mediocre back-up at both guard spots.

Forward: Newcomer Hastings is a banger with little talent. The rest of this crew has serious problems. Jerome Lane possesses brilliant rebounding skills (9.3 RPG), but he's so inconsistent and so bad offensively that you can't play him for extended minutes. Small forward Marcus Liberty is great on the fastbreak, but his shooting, defense, and intensity need work. Anthony Cook is a shot-blocker who needs more polish. Forward/center Greg Anderson, a skilled scorer and rebounder, has gone to pot since 1989 knee surgery. Rookie Brooks, an outstanding shooter, could leap-frog a couple of these guys.

Center: With Rasmussen gone, the 7'2" Mutombo will inherit the center position. Mutombo, a tremendous athlete and dominating shot-blocker, will fit nicely into Coach Paul Westhead's system. Joe Wolf, who has a nice touch for a big man, has also had problems with motivation.

Coaching: Westhead won at Loyola Marymount with his shoot-'em-up approach, but he has not—and *can* not—do it in the big show. NBA players are just too talented and experienced to get burned up and down the floor. Westhead, a Shakespearean scholar, better brush up on his Macbeth, because he may not last the season. Westhead is assisted by Mike Boyle, Jim Evans, and Judas Prada.

Analysis: Regardless of system, Denver wouldn't win more than 25 games. Though the Nuggets boast three talented young guards and a potentially dominating center, they're still too inexperienced to be considered factors. The rest of the team is a mix of fringe players.

Prediction: 6th place, Midwest

HOUSTON ROCKETS

Division: Midwest
Home: The Summit
Capacity: 16,279
Year Built: 1975

Address
Ten Greenway Plaza
Houston, TX 77046
(713) 627-0600

Chairman of the Board:
Charlie Thomas
General Manager: Steve Patterson
Head Coach: Don Chaney
Assistant Coach: Carroll Dawson
Assistant Coach: Rudy Tomjanovich
Assistant Coach: John Killilea

Coach Don Chaney			
	W	L	Pct.
NBA Record	191	240	.443
W/Rockets	138	108	.561
1990-91 Record	52	30	.634

Rockets History

Throughout their 24 seasons in San Diego and Houston, the Rockets have featured some of the NBA's finest big men. The tradition began during the team's second year when it drafted Elvin Hayes. Behind Hayes, the league's leading scorer and Rookie of the Year, San Diego advanced to the 1968-69 Western Conference semis, losing to Atlanta.

The Rockets moved to Houston in 1971, but Hayes spent only one season there before being dealt to Baltimore. Houston then built its team around considerably shorter players like 5'11" guard Calvin Murphy and forwards Mike Newlin and Rudy Tomjanovich.

Star center No. 2 came in 1976, when Moses Malone moved over from the defunct ABA. Houston won the Central Division crown in 1976-77 and advanced to the NBA Finals in 1980-81, losing in six games to Boston. In 1983, Houston drafted 7'4" Ralph Sampson from Virginia; one year later, they selected the dominating Akeem Olajuwon. In 1985-86, the Rockets made it back to the NBA Finals behind their "Twin Towers," only to lose to Boston in six.

Trouble hit the next season when guards Lewis Lloyd and Mitchell Wiggins were banned for two years for violating the league's drug-abuse policy. Injuries crippled Sampson's career and coach Bill Fitch was fired following the 1987-88 season. Don Chaney took over in 1988-89, and though the Rockets showed some spunk in 1990-91, they again fizzled in the playoffs.

Last Five Years

Season	W	L	Pct.	Place	Playoffs	Coach
1986-87	42	40	.512	Third	L-West Semis	Bill Fitch
1987-88	46	36	.561	Fourth	L-Round One	Bill Fitch
1988-89	45	37	.549	Second	L-Round One	Don Chaney
1989-90	41	41	.500	Fifth	L-Round One	Don Chaney
1990-91	52	30	.634	Third	L-Round One	Don Chaney

1990-91 Recap

Rocket fans pulled out their rosaries on January 3, the day center Hakeem Olajuwon suffered a broken eye socket courtesy of a stray Bill Cartwright elbow. For a while, it seemed like The Summit was going to be a pretty lonely place.

But what happened? The Rockets banded together and enjoyed one of the finest stretches in franchise history. By the time Olajuwon returned, fans were wondering whether they needed the big guy at all. Very strange.

But that's the kind of year it was in Houston. It began with Olajuwon complaining about the lack of support he received from his teammates and ended with the Rockets on a 29-9 tear. In between were Olajuwon's injury and subsequent 26-game hiatus, and the emergence of Larry and Kenny Smith as vital cogs in the Houston machine.

It all added up to a franchise-record 52 wins for Houston and Coach of the Year honors for Don Chaney. And even though it fell in the first round of the playoffs (for the fourth straight year), it appeared Houston finally had an adequate supporting cast for its All-Star center.

Kenny Smith went from disappointment to revelation at point guard, averaging 17.7 points and 7.1 assists per game. Larry Smith, a 6'8" veteran forward, filled in at center for Olajuwon and became a rebounding machine, racking up several 20-plus performances on the boards. Ever-improving banger Otis Thorpe (17.5 points, 10.3 rebounds) joined Olajuwon (21.2 points, 13.8 rebounds, 3.95 blocks) to form a powerful inside combination. And guards Vernon Maxwell (17.0 points) and Sleepy Floyd (12.3 points) provided outside firepower.

1991-92 Roster

No.	Player	Pos.	Ht.	Wt.	Exp.	College	1990-91 PPG	1990-91 RPG	1990-91 APG
50	Matt Bullard	F	6'10"	225	1	Iowa	2.2	0.8	0.1
44	Adrian Caldwell	F	6'8"	266	2	Lamar	1.8	2.4	0.2
21	Sleepy Floyd	G	6'3"	183	9	Georgetown	12.3	1.9	3.9
32	Dave Jamerson	G	6'5"	192	1	Ohio	3.1	0.8	0.7
1	Buck Johnson	F	6'7"	206	5	Alabama	13.6	4.5	1.9
11	Vernon Maxwell	G	6'4"	190	3	Florida	17.0	2.9	3.7
34	Hakeem Olajuwon	C	7'0"	258	7	Houston	21.2	13.8	2.3
30	Kenny Smith	G	6'3"	170	4	North Carolina	17.7	2.1	7.1
13	Larry Smith	F/C	6'8"	251	11	Alcorn St.	3.3	8.8	1.1
33	Otis Thorpe	F	6'10"	246	7	Providence	17.5	10.3	2.4
40	John Turner	F	6'7"	245	R	Phillips	—	—	—
20	Kennard Winchester	G	6'5"	212	1	Averett	3.7	1.0	0.4
10	David Wood	F	6'9"	230	2	Nevada-Reno	5.3	3.0	1.1

Houston Rockets
1991-92 Season Preview

Opening Line: Don Chaney, last year's NBA Coach of the Year, has turned a pool of mediocrity into a winning ballclub. The team pulled together last year when superstar center Hakeem Olajuwon went down with an eye injury and they were even better upon his return—winning 13 in a row. The Rockets will try to ride that winning magic into this season. Houston drafted a project player with its 20th pick, signing John Turner of Phillips University, an NAIA school.

Guard: Kenny Smith, considered an underachiever with Sacramento, has come alive with the Rockets (17.7 PPG). He's a cat-quick point guard with a remarkably high shooting average (52 percent). Vernon Maxwell, another castoff, fires 3-pointers from sunrise to sundown (172-of-510 last year). Besides the scoring (17.0 PPG), he'll give you competent defense too. Sleepy Floyd is a strong penetrator who has always been hot-and-cold with his shot. He was too inconsistent as a starter, but now he's an ideal No. 3 guard, one who can come in and either run the offense or (if he's hot) provide instant scoring. Chaney has turned a trio of disappointments into a quality three-guard rotation.

Forward: Power forward Otis Thorpe played perhaps the best ball of his career last year (17.5 PPG, 10.3 RPG), especially when Olajuwon went down with the eye injury. Small forward Buck Johnson isn't much of a shooter, but he's a hard worker who will hold his own and play strong defense. Larry Smith, a physical 6'8" veteran, has made a living cleaning the boards. David Wood is a talentless player who gives it his all. Rookie Turner, a rather smallish forward, has decent all-around skills that need refining.

Center: Olajuwon ranks with David Robinson as the best centers in the game. The strong, quick, tenacious Olajuwon can flat out dominate. He'll score (21.2 PPG), rebound better than anyone in the world (13.8 RPG), and block everything in sight (3.95 BPG). Smith, the respected board man, proved last year that he could fill in for Olajuwon, should he go down.

Coaching: Patience and understanding have always been the trademarks of Don Chaney. After manipulating his lineup following Olajuwon's injury—using mediocre NBA vets and even CBA products—Chaney began to look like a coaching genius. The trick will be to do it again. He is assisted by Rudy Tomjanovich, Carroll Dawson, and John Killilea.

Analysis: This team has the potential to win the NBA's Midwest Division, or finish below .500. If Chaney can keep the Rockets focussed the way he did last year, look out. However, it's doubtful the club can sustain that intensity over 82 games. Expect a winning record, but don't expect more than 50 wins.

Prediction: 3rd Place, Midwest

MINNESOTA TIMBERWOLVES

Division: Midwest
Home: Target Center
Capacity: 18,200
Year Built: 1990

Address
600 First Ave. North
Minneapolis, MN 55403
(612) 673-1600

Owners: Harvey Ratner,
Marv Wolfenson
President: Bob Stein
Head Coach: Jimmy Rodgers
Assistant Coach: Jim Brewer
Assistant Coach: Sidney Lowe

Coach Jimmy Rodgers			
	W	L	Pct.
NBA Record	94	70	.573
W/Wolves	0	0	.000
1990-91 Record	0	0	.000

Timberwolves History

Minnesota is one of the few teams in sports history to fire a head coach for trying to win too hard. After enduring two seasons of Bill Musselman's frenetic commitment to winning games—often at the expense of developing young talent—the Timberwolf management decided to move on.

Musselman's game was defense, and the T-Wolves were one of the league's best at maintaining tempo and stopping opponents from scoring. Unfortunately, the team's slow pace sometimes stopped it from scoring as well and shackled some of its younger, more free-wheeling players.

After being awarded the franchise in 1987, the Timberwolves had to wait two years before finally taking the floor. The first year's results were predictable—22-60 in 1989-90. But the poor record did nothing to stem the enthusiasm of the Twin Cities faithful, who packed the Metrodome with 26,000-plus fans per night, establishing a season attendance record of more than one-million patrons.

On the floor, forward Tony Campbell emerged as a top scoring threat, and rookie guard Pooh Richardson was an adroit playmaker and scorer. Minnesota added 7'0" center Felton Spencer and forward Gerald Glass for the 1990-91 season and moved into the brand new Target Center in downtown Minneapolis. The team improved to 29-53, good for fifth in the Midwest Division. But despite the six-game improvement, the players rebelled against Musselman's structured approach and he was fired.

Last Two Years

Season	W	L	Pct.	Place	Playoffs	Coach
1989-90	22	60	.268	Sixth	DNQ	Bill Musselman
1990-91	29	53	.354	Fifth	DNQ	Bill Musselman

1990-91 Recap

In May, Minnesota coach Bill Musselman stood in the NBA's unemployment line, scratching his head, wondering why he had been fired. After sweating blood all year to lift the T-Wolves to a 29-53 record and a fifth-place finish in the Midwest Division—the best of the young franchise's history—Musselman was canned for trying too hard to win.

In fact, there was grousing in the front office that Minnesota's season-ending 6-4 spurt robbed the team of a higher spot in the subsequent draft by limiting its chances in the lottery. It would have been easy for Musselman to have slouched his way to fewer victories but that wasn't in his fiery nature, so he was fired. The players, who blanched at his defensive philosophy—only the Sacramento Kings averaged fewer points—were happy to see him go.

Most relieved was point guard Pooh Richardson, who increased his personal output to 17.1 points and 9.0 assists per game, but longed to cut loose. Chances are, he'll get the opportunity in 1991-92. Tony Campbell continued his high-scoring ways by leading the team with 21.8 points a game, though he contributed little else.

Forwards Tyrone Corbin (18.0 points, 7.2 rebounds) and Sam Mitchell (14.6 points, 6.3 rebounds) were steady, and rookie center Felton Spencer (7.1 points, 7.9 rebounds) showed promise. Mitchell and Spencer finished one-two in the NBA in personal fouls.

1991-92 Roster

No.	Player	Pos.	Ht.	Wt.	Exp.	College	PPG	1990-91 RPG	APG
45	Randy Breuer	C	7'3"	258	8	Minnesota	5.9	4.7	1.0
1	Scott Brooks	G	5'11"	165	3	California-Irvine	5.3	0.9	2.6
—	Myron Brown	G	6'3"	180	R	Slippery Rock	—	—	—
19	Tony Campbell	G/F	6'7"	215	7	Ohio St.	21.8	4.5	2.8
23	Tyrone Corbin	F	6'6"	222	6	DePaul	18.0	7.2	4.2
22	Gerald Glass	G/F	6'6"	221	1	Mississippi	6.9	2.0	0.8
52	Dan Godfread	F	6'10"	250	1	Evansville	1.3	0.2	0.0
—	Luc Longley	C	7'2"	265	R	New Mexico	—	—	—
42	Sam Mitchell	F	6'7"	210	2	Mercer	14.6	6.3	1.6
4	Tod Murphy	F	6'10"	220	3	California-Irvine	4.8	4.9	1.2
24	Pooh Richardson	G	6'1"	180	2	UCLA	17.1	3.5	9.0
50	Felton Spencer	C	7'0"	265	1	Louisville	7.1	7.9	0.3
25	Bob Thornton	F/C	6'10"	225	6	California-Irvine	1.3	1.3	0.1
5	Doug West	G	6'6"	200	2	Villanova	3.9	1.8	0.6

Minnesota Timberwolves
1991-92 Season Preview

Opening Line: The Wolves, tired of coach Bill Musselman's win-at-all-costs approach, told him to take a hike after the season. Management is more interested in developing its young players, not burning them out (three Wolves played more than 3,100 minutes apiece last year). The club will be much more relaxed under new coach Jimmy Rodgers. Minnesota spent the No. 7 pick on Luc Longley, a 7'2" center from New Mexico. With the 34th pick, it selected Myron Brown, a guard from Slippery Rock.

Guard: Sophomore Pooh Richardson already ranks among the NBA's top ten point guards. Richardson is known for his smart passing (9.0 APG), but he can also hit his shots (17.1 PPG). Though a big scorer (21.8 PPG), Tony Campbell has long been accused of firing up too many shots, and his defense leaves much to be desired. Gerald Glass is a methodical scorer who loves to hit the fadeaway, but he lacks the quickness and aggressiveness to earn quality minutes. Scott Brooks, just 5'11", is a hustling defensive specialist who's best used as a role player. Big guard Doug West, a hard worker with a nice jumper, is another part-timer.

Forward: Sam Mitchell (14.6 PPG) clawed out of the USBL and CBA and into the Timberwolves' starting lineup. Though a fine defender with a nice shot, Mitchell is not a legitimate NBA starter. Starter Tyrone Corbin, only 6'6", is a physical inside grinder who fights for rebounds (7.2 RPG) and finds a way to score (18.0 PPG). Tod Murphy is another hard worker who likes to battle inside. Murphy lacks NBA talent, but he's the team's only regular forward over 6'7". Campbell and Glass can also play the small-forward position.

Center: Second-year man Felton Spencer has already proven he can rebound (7.9 RPG) and block shots. Now he must continue to develop his offensive game. In time, he'll be a good one. Randy Breuer offers a 7'3" frame but not much more. Though 7'2", rookie Longley is a remarkably skilled center who's a potential star.

Coaching: Rodgers coached the Celtics for two years and went 94-71, though he was fired after losing in the first round of the 1990 playoffs. He may not squeeze as many wins out of this club as Musselman did, but he'll be more of a steadying influence. He's assisted by Jim Brewer and Sidney Lowe.

Analysis: The Timberwolves are undermanned and undersized at forward, but overloaded at the center position. Perhaps Spencer will be moved to power forward. By starting twin towers Longley and Spencer, as well as point guard Richardson, Minnesota would at least have some groundwork for the future. As for 1991-92, the Wolves simply lack the talent (they were 26th in the NBA in scoring last year) to win 30 games.

Prediction: 5th Place, Midwest

SAN ANTONIO SPURS

Division: Midwest
Home: HemisFair Arena
Capacity: 15,910
Year Built: 1968

Address
600 E. Market, Suite 102
San Antonio, TX 78205
(512) 554-7787

Owner: Red McCombs
V.P./Basketball Operations:
Bob Bass
Head Coach: Larry Brown
Assistant Coach: Gregg Popovich
Assistant Coach: R.C. Buford
Assistant Coach: Ed Manning

Coach Larry Brown			
	W	L	Pct.
NBA Record	349	272	.562
W/Spurs	132	114	.537
1990-91 Record	55	27	.671

Spurs History

This Texas franchise was born in Dallas in 1967 as a charter member of the ABA. Its name? The Dallas Chaparrals. The stay in Dallas was a haphazard one, featuring six coaches in six years, low attendance, and little playoff fortunes.

Angelo Drossos brought the team to the home of the Alamo in 1973, and the team was renamed the Spurs. It was an exciting squad that fans embraced immediately. The Spurs had 50-plus-win seasons in 1974-75 and 1975-76 and moved into the NBA at full gallop.

Led by unstoppable guard George Gervin, mammoth center Artis Gilmore, and a talented supporting cast that included Johnny Moore, Larry Kenon, and James Silas, the Spurs won two Central and three Midwest Division championships in six years. Gervin was the NBA scoring champ four times. However, San Antonio could not make it to the NBA Finals, as it fell in the conference finals three times.

The Spurs' nucleus began to age in the mid-1980s, and the team fell from its lofty status. But the collapse did lead to something worthwhile. In 1987, the Spurs drafted David Robinson of Navy. The team continued to sag in the next two seasons while Robinson completed his military obligation, but he joined the Spurs in 1989-90. Robinson immediately emerged as one of the NBA's best centers. He teamed with Terry Cummings, Sean Elliott, and Vernon Maxwell to help San Antonio win the Midwest title the following two years.

Last Five Years

Season	W	L	Pct.	Place	Playoffs	Coach
1986-87	28	54	.341	Sixth	DNQ	Bob Weiss
1987-88	31	51	.378	Fifth	L-Round One	Bob Weiss
1988-89	21	61	.256	Fifth	DNQ	Larry Brown
1989-90	56	26	.683	First	L-West Semis	Larry Brown
1990-91	55	27	.671	First	L-Round One	Larry Brown

1990-91 Recap

Mr. Robinson's Neighborhood was a pretty neat place to be in 1990-91—until playoff time, that is. The Spurs rode the "Admiral" to their second consecutive Midwest Division title and looked ready to do some serious post-season damage. Then came Don Nelson and his dwarfish Golden State Warriors. The Warriors bounced Robinson and San Antonio from the playoffs in the first round, stopping the fun deep in the heart of Texas and raising some questions about the Spurs' age and depth.

Once again, Robinson was remarkable, averaging 25.6 points, 13.0 rebounds, 3.9 blocks and generally producing highlights wherever he went. He finished the fastbreak, was deadly in the set offense, and formed the last line of a defense that limited opponents to just 44.8-percent shooting.

His supporting cast was once again sound—at least as far as the starting five was concerned. Forward Terry Cummings (17.6 points, 7.8 rebounds) was productive, but he missed 15 games with injuries and was on the downside of a great career. Young Sean Elliott (15.9 PPG, 5.6 RPG) made great strides at the other forward position.

The backcourt of Willie Anderson (14.4 points, only 45.7-percent shooting) and Rod Strickland (13.8 points, 8.0 assists) had flash but was inconsistent at times. San Antonio's biggest problem was depth. Paul Pressey (7.5 PPG) and Sidney Green (6.7 points, 4.7 rebounds) were mediocre replacements. Guard David Wingate was a defensive specialist, but legal problems robbed him of all but 25 games.

1991-92 Roster

No.	Player	Pos.	Ht.	Wt.	Exp.	College	1990-91 PPG	1990-91 RPG	1990-91 APG
40	Willie Anderson	G/F	6'8"	185	3	Georgia	14.4	4.7	4.8
34	Terry Cummings	F	6'9"	235	9	DePaul	17.6	7.8	2.3
32	Sean Elliott	F	6'8"	205	2	Arizona	15.9	5.6	2.9
21	Sidney Green	F	6'9"	230	8	UNLV	6.7	4.7	0.8
3	Sean Higgins	F	6'9"	195	1	Michigan	4.5	1.3	0.7
15	Avery Johnson	G	5'11"	175	3	Southern	4.7	1.1	3.4
45	Tony Massenburg	F	6'9"	230	1	Maryland	2.3	1.7	0.1
8	Paul Pressey	G/F	6'5"	203	9	Tulsa	7.5	2.5	3.9
14	Kevin Pritchard	G	6'3"	185	1	Kansas	3.9	1.0	1.3
50	David Robinson	C	7'1"	235	2	Navy	25.6	13.0	2.5
24	Dwayne Schintzius	C	7'1"	260	1	Florida	3.8	2.9	0.4
1	Rod Strickland	G	6'3"	175	3	DePaul	13.8	3.8	8.0
—	Greg Sutton	G	6'2"	170	R	Oral Roberts	—	—	—

San Antonio Spurs
1991-92 Season Preview

Opening Line: For two years in a row, the Spurs have won the Midwest Division with impressive records, only to fall early in the playoffs. With the dominating David Robinson leading the way, San Antonio will again field one of the NBA's elite teams. Coach Larry Brown hopes another year of experience will push this team to the conference finals and beyond. The Spurs' only draft choice was Greg Sutton, a 6'2" guard from Oral Roberts chosen with the 49th pick. Part-timers David Greenwood and David Wingate were let go.

Guard: Rod Strickland (13.8 PPG, 8.0 APG) is a fast, sleek playmaker who has the potential to become one of the best point guards in the NBA. Maturity is his problem. Last season, he broke his hand in a fight in the parking lot of a San Antonio nightclub. Willie Anderson (14.4 PPG) stands 6'8" but spends most of his time in the backcourt. Anderson knows how to score, but he has trouble getting along with Brown. Veteran Paul Pressey, a versatile, long-armed swing man, specializes in defense. Avery Johnson is a quick, little point guard who needs to work on his shot.

Forward: Veteran power forward Terry Cummings (17.6 PPG, 7.8 RPG) earns A's across the board. Cummings provides points, rebounds, defense, and strength—all on a remarkably consistent level. Sean Elliott, the No. 3 pick in the 1989 draft, is another all-around talent. He can pass, rebound, hit the 3-pointer, and drive the lane. And he's only getting better. Vagabond Sidney Green is a snarling rebounder with a lot of holes in his game.

Center: Robinson has established himself as one of the best, if not *the* best, center in the NBA. Consider his scoring (25.6 PPG), rebounding (13.0 RPG), and shot-blocking (3.90 BPG). Besides awesome inside play, Mr. Robinson has the agility and speed of a small forward. Robinson's back-up is enigmatic sophomore Dwayne Schintzius, who started slowly last season but improved near the end.

Coaching: In 19 years of coaching—in the ABA, in college, and in the NBA—Brown has gone 757-444. He won the NCAA title with Kansas in 1988. Brown is a hard-driving, demanding coach who will inevitably push this club to the NBA Finals. Brown's assistants are Gregg Popovich, R.C. Buford, and Ed Manning, Danny Manning's father.

Analysis: With a little more maturity, this young team could win 60 games and an NBA title this season. The starting front line is brilliant and nearly flawless. The only thing that could tear this team apart is dissension between Brown and two players, Cummings and Anderson. They'd be wise to listen to their coach. With 18 winning seasons in 19 years, he's proven that he knows what he's doing.

Prediction: 1st Place, Midwest

UTAH JAZZ

Division: Midwest
Home: Salt Palace
Capacity: 12,616
Year Built: 1969

Address
5 Triad Center, Fifth Floor
Salt Lake City, UT 84180
(801) 575-7800

Owner: Larry H. Miller
General Manager: Tim Howells
Head Coach: Jerry Sloan
Assistant Coach: Phil Johnson
Assistant Coach: Gordon Chiesa
Assistant Coach: David Fredman

Coach Jerry Sloan			
	W	L	Pct.
NBA Record	243	201	.547
W/Jazz	149	80	.651
1990-91 Record	54	28	.659

Jazz History

About the last city you'd expect to find a team named the Jazz would be in puritan Salt Lake City, Utah. However, the name comes with an easy explanation. When the franchise was born back in 1974, its hometown was New Orleans, a jazzy place if ever there was one. When it moved west in 1979, it decided to hold onto the name.

The early days did have their moments. In the mid-1970s, Louisiana native "Pistol" Pete Maravich lit up the Bayou, scoring baskets in bushels and once torching the Knicks for 68. Maravich's knee went out in 1977-78 and, despite the emergence of all-world rebounder Leonard "Truck" Robinson, the Jazz limped along.

Coach Frank Layden was hired in 1981-82 and was immediately popular for his sense of humor and regular-guy charm. The Jazz captured the Midwest Division crown in 1983-84 and advanced to the conference semi-finals, relying on league scoring leader Adrian Dantley, quick backcourt men Darrell Griffith and Ricky Green, and mammoth, 7'4" center Mark Eaton.

The Jazz selected power forward Karl Malone in the 1985 draft, and he was an immediate sensation, teaming with assist machine John Stockton to form a solid nucleus. Utah won the 1988-89 Midwest title under new coach Jerry Sloan but fell in the first round of the playoffs. Utah was eliminated again in the first round the following year and advanced to the conference semis in 1990-91.

Last Five Years

Season	W	L	Pct.	Place	Playoffs	Coach
1986-87	44	38	.537	Second	L-Round One	Frank Layden
1987-88	47	35	.573	Third	L-West Semis	Frank Layden
1988-89	51	31	.622	First	L-Round One	Frank Layden/Jerry Sloan
1989-90	55	27	.671	Second	L-Round One	Jerry Sloan
1990-91	54	28	.659	Second	L-West Semis	Jerry Sloan

1990-91 Recap

Cynics will probably say that the Jazz went from a two-man to a three-man team in 1990-91, thanks to the off-season acquisition of shooting guard Jeff Malone. But those same folks can't deny that Utah also won its first playoff series in three years, whipping the favored Phoenix Suns in the first round and making a strong argument for its trifecta philosophy.

The Jazz racked up its third consecutive 50-plus-win season (54-28) and just missed the Midwest Division title when it lost to Golden State on the season's last day. Utah finished third in the league in defense, holding opponents to 45.7-percent shooting and just 100.7 points per game.

Jeff Malone (18.6 PPG, 50.8-percent shooting) was the perfect outside complement to behemoth power forward Karl Malone. The "Mailman" was again spectacular (29.0 points, 11.8 rebounds), finishing the break with authority and continuing to improve in the set offense. The two Malones gave passing machine John Stockton (17.2 points, league-record 1,164 assists) easy targets.

It was a lack of depth that ultimately hurt the Jazz in the Western Conference semifinals against the deep Trail Blazers. No one could stop the Malone-Malone-Stockton trio, but there was a big drop-off after them. Center Mark Eaton (5.1 points, 8.3 rebounds, 2.35 blocks) continued to be invisible on offense, and forward Blue Edwards (9.3 PPG) couldn't develop into a consistent threat. Off the bench, only Thurl Bailey (12.4 points, 5.0 rebounds) provided punch. Forward Mike Brown (4.8 points, 4.1 rebounds) and guard Delaney Rudd (4.0 points) could not produce during long stretches.

1991-92 Roster

No.	Player	Pos.	Ht.	Wt.	Exp.	College	1990-91 PPG	RPG	APG
—	Isaac Austin	C	6'10"	255	R	Arizona St.	—	—	—
41	Thurl Bailey	F	6'11"	232	8	N. Carolina St.	12.4	5.0	1.5
54	Alan Bannister	C	7'5"	300	1	Arkansas St.	—	—	—
40	Mike Brown	F/C	6'9"	260	5	George Wash.	4.8	4.1	0.6
21	Tony Brown	F	6'6"	195	6	Arkansas	2.8	1.4	0.5
53	Mark Eaton	C	7'4"	290	9	UCLA	5.1	8.3	0.6
30	Blue Edwards	G	6'5"	200	2	East Carolina	9.3	3.2	1.7
35	Darrell Griffith	G	6'4"	195	10	Louisville	5.7	1.2	0.5
24	Jeff Malone	G	6'4"	205	8	Mississippi St.	18.6	3.0	2.1
32	Karl Malone	F	6'9"	256	6	Louisiana Tech	29.0	11.8	3.3
—	Eric Murdock	G	6'2"	189	R	Providence	—	—	—
33	Walter Palmer	C	7'1"	215	1	Dartmouth	1.4	0.8	0.2
11	Delaney Rudd	G	6'2"	195	2	Wake Forest	4.0	0.8	2.6
12	John Stockton	G	6'1"	175	7	Gonzaga	17.2	2.9	14.2
5	Andy Toolson	F	6'6"	210	1	Brigham Young	2.9	1.4	0.7

Utah Jazz
1991-92 Season Preview

Opening Line: Critics still call coach Jerry Sloan's team "too thin," but he continues to win 50 games a season. Led by the game's greatest power forward, Karl Malone, and its best assist man, John Stockton, the Jazz should again join the exclusive 50-win club. Eric Murdock, the 21st pick out of Providence, will serve as a back-up to Stockton. Utah also chose Isaac Austin, a 6'10" center from Arizona State, with the 48th choice.

Guard: Stockton, the NBA's most phenomenal assist man of all time, is a lightning-quick, masterful playmaker (14.2 APG). And when he's not setting up teammates for easy buckets, he'll hit the jumper or take it inside himself (17.2 PPG). Jeff Malone has earned two All-Star berths with his blistering shooting (18.6 PPG). He doesn't do much else, but nearly 20 PPG is enough for Sloan. Delaney Rudd has been a steady back-up to Stockton, but his lack of playmaking skills prompted the drafting of Murdock. Murdock will provide the point-guard ability and will also give the Jazz sound defense. Darrell Griffith is a veteran long-range bomber, but injuries have taken a toll on his career.

Forward: Karl Malone, a perennial MVP candidate, may be the best power forward of all time. Malone (29.0 PPG, 11.8 RPG) is quick, extremely strong, and destroys opponents with his inside moves. No one can handle him alone. Young Blue Edwards (6'5") starts at small forward but often plays at big guard. Edwards is an explosive open-court player who needs work on his shooting and ball-handling. Sixth man Thurl Bailey is respected for his consistency and his ability to get off his shots down low. Mike Brown offers versatility—he rebounds from both the forward and center positions—but he remains inconsistent.

Center: Shot-blocker Mark Eaton, 7'4" is such an intimidating force in the middle that he has twice been named Defensive Player of the Year. Eaton's blocks are starting to dwindle however, and his offense is non existent. Brown spends time at center but he's only 6'9".

Coaching: Sloan spent three years in the early 1980s coaching the Bulls and now enters his fourth year with Utah Sloan is well respected among the Jazz and has earned a reputation as a player's coach. He has won at least 50 games in his three years in Utah. He is assisted by Gordon Chiesa, David Fredman, and Phil Johnson.

Analysis: With Karl Malone, Jeff Malone, and Stockton providing the firepower, the Jazz should once again challenge the Spurs for the Midwest Division title. The continued development of Edwards should make the team a touch better. However, Utah still doesn't have enough horses to make it all the way to the NBA Finals It's perhaps one player away.

Prediction: 2nd Place, Midwest

GOLDEN STATE WARRIORS

Division: Pacific
Home: Oakland Coliseum Arena
Capacity: 15,025
Year Built: 1966

Chairman: Jim Fitzgerald
General Manager: Don Nelson
Head Coach: Don Nelson
Assistant Coach: Garry St. Jean
Assistant Coach: Donn Nelson

Address
Oakland Coliseum Arena
Oakland, CA 94621
(415) 638-6300

Coach Don Nelson			
	W	L	Pct.
NBA Record	664	466	.588
W/Warriors	124	122	.504
1990-91 Record	44	38	.537

Warriors History

Present-day Warrior fans may find it difficult to identify with the team's East Coast roots. For 16 seasons, the Philadelphia Warriors enjoyed success in the old BAA and as a charter member of the NBA. Philadelphia won the first BAA championship in 1946-47 behind scoring machine Joe Fulks.

The Warriors advanced to the BAA finals in 1948, losing to Baltimore. But they defeated Fort Wayne in 1956 to win the NBA title behind Paul Arizin, Neil Johnston, and Tom Gola. In 1959, Wilt Chamberlain joined the team and was an immediate sensation, winning the MVP Award in his rookie season. The team moved to San Francisco in 1962 and lost to Boston in the NBA Finals in 1963-64. The Warriors traded Chamberlain to the new Philadelphia

76ers in 1964-65, but lost to the Sixers in the NBA Finals two years later.

The Warriors changed their name to Golden State in 1971 and moved across the bay to Oakland, but the futility continued until 1974-75. That year, coach Al Attles incorporated a ten-man rotation around Rick Barry and took the Warriors to the NBA title.

The Warriors didn't rebound again until 1988, when Don Nelson took over as coach. Using a small lineup built around Chris Mullin and Mitch Richmond, the Warriors made it to the Western semis in 1988-89. Point guard Tim Hardaway was added for the 1989-90 season, and in 1990-91, Golden State again advanced to the West semis, losing to Los Angeles.

Last Five Years

Season	W	L	Pct.	Place	Playoffs	Coach
1986-87	42	40	.512	Third	L-West Semis	George Karl
1987-88	20	62	.244	Fifth	DNQ	George Karl/Ed Gregory
1988-89	43	39	.524	Fourth	L-West Semis	Don Nelson
1989-90	37	45	.451	Fifth	DNQ	Don Nelson
1990-91	44	38	.537	Fourth	L-West Semis	Don Nelson

1990-91 Recap

Don Nelson retained his title as the NBA's chief sorcerer in 1990-91 when the small-fry Warriors advanced to the Western Conference semifinals. Nelson used creative lineups and attempted to accelerate the tempo to benefit his shorter team. His experiments led to a first-round playoff upset of San Antonio and a semifinal scare of the Lakers.

Of course, Nelson wasn't completely responsible for Golden State's 44 regular-season wins. The high-scoring triumvirate of guard Tim Hardaway (22.9 points, 9.7 assists), guard Mitch Richmond (23.9 points), and forward Chris Mullin (25.7 points) gave the Warriors enough firepower to stay close with anyone. The trio, nicknamed "Run-TMC," increased its joint output nearly 11 points from the previous season and took the pressure off Golden State's weaker inside game.

But the NBA is five-on-five, not three-on-three, and that's where Golden State had its problems. Reserve guard Sarunas Marciulionis (10.9 points) was the only other Warrior to average in double figures, though Rod Higgins (9.5 points) was dangerous off the bench as well. Too often, the Warriors were content to let the big guns do all the work.

Golden State was hurt in the middle. Veteran centers Alton Lister and Jim Petersen were never confused with David Robinson or Hakeem Olajuwon, and power forwards Tom Tolbert and rookie Tyrone Hill had trouble matching up with the league's elite at that position. Nelson was candid throughout the year, emphasizing that it was never his preference to rely solely on his three stars and that he was searching for help inside. The search continues.

1991-92 Roster

No.	Player	Pos.	Ht.	Wt.	Exp.	College	1990-91		
							PPG	RPG	APG
52	Victor Alexander	C/F	6'9"	265	R	Iowa St.	—	—	—
4	Vincent Askew	G	6'6"	226	2	Memphis St.	4.7	1.6	1.9
20	Mario Elie	G	6'5"	210	1	American Inter.	7.2	3.3	1.4
25	Chris Gatling	F	6'10"	220	R	Old Dominion	—	—	—
10	Tim Hardaway	G	6'0"	175	2	Texas-El Paso	22.9	4.0	9.7
22	Rod Higgins	F	6'7"	205	9	Fresno St.	9.5	4.3	1.4
32	Tyrone Hill	F	6'9"	243	1	Xavier (OH)	5.3	5.2	0.3
51	Les Jepsen	C	7'0"	237	1	Iowa	1.3	1.8	0.0
53	Alton Lister	F/C	7'0"	240	10	Arizona St.	6.4	6.3	1.2
13	S. Marciulionis	G	6'5"	200	2	Lithuania	10.9	2.4	1.7
17	Chris Mullin	F	6'7"	215	6	St. John's	25.7	5.4	4.0
43	Jim Petersen	F/C	6'10"	235	7	Minnesota	4.5	3.2	0.4
23	Mitch Richmond	G	6'5"	215	3	Kansas St.	23.9	5.9	3.1
34	Tom Tolbert	F	6'7"	240	3	Arizona	8.1	4.4	1.2

Golden State Warriors
1991-92 Season Preview

Opening Line: Coach Don Nelson has been remarkably successful with his pint-sized lineup. Little men Tim Hardaway, Mitch Richmond, and Chris Mullin are the highest-scoring trio in the league. But Nelson needs a big fellow in the middle, and he went whole hog to find him in the 1991 draft. The Warriors had three picks in the first round, and they chose 6'10" forward Chris Gatling of Old Dominion (No. 16), 6'9" center Victor Alexander of Iowa State (No. 17), and 6'10" center Shaun Vandiver of Colorado (No. 25). Golden State traded its second-round choice, LaMont Strothers of Christopher Newport, to Portland for two second-round picks. Vandiver will play in Europe this year.

Guard: All-Star Hardaway, the 14th player selected in the 1989 draft, has proven to be the best of that group. Hardaway is a master ball-handler who can score (22.9 PPG), shoot from long range, and dish off (9.7 APG). Richmond, the 1989 NBA Rookie of the Year, is a muscular kid who can score from anywhere (23.9 PPG). Soviet Sarunas Marciu-lionis can reach double figures off the bench thanks to his long-range jumper. Mario Elie, a CBA product, is a versatile role player whose skills are unrefined.

Forward: Despite a dumpy physique, 6'7" Mullin has emerged as a certified superstar. He's a remarkable shooter who can score from all over the floor (25.7 PPG). A la Larry Bird, he can also pass and rebound and is a noted team leader. Rod Higgins is a fine team player and a 3-point shooter. He has played all three frontcourt positions, but at 6'7" is obviously undersized. The 6'9" Tyrone Hill is a strong board man (5.2 RPG as a reserve). Tom Tolbert doesn't have much talent, but he's enthusiastic and gets the job done at every frontcourt position. Gatling is an explosive forward who will swat shots and clean the offensive glass.

Center: Alton Lister, 7'0", gives the Warriors strong interior defense but not much offense. Nelson hopes Alexander can make a difference. Though overweight, Alexander is a mobile power forward/center with a soft touch and strong post-up skills.

Coaching: No other coach gets so much out of so little as Nelson. Some of his coaching tactics have been revolutionary, such as using Mullin as a "point forward." Nelson is assisted by Garry St. Jean and Donn Nelson, the coach's son.

Analysis: As long as Don Nelson is coaching this team, and he has Hardaway, Richmond, and Mullin to shoot the basketball, the Warriors will be competitive. But until this team gets a legitimate center, it will struggle to advance past the first round of the playoffs. Barring a trade, Golden State will have to wait for its young big men to develop.

Prediction: 5th Place, Pacific

LOS ANGELES CLIPPERS

Division: Pacific
Home: L.A. Memorial Sports Arena
Capacity: 15,350
Year Built: 1959

Owner: Donald T. Sterling
Executive V.P./General Manager:
Elgin Baylor
Head Coach: Mike Schuler
Assistant Coach: John Hammond
Assistant Coach: Alvin Gentry

Address
Los Angeles Sports Arena
3939 S. Figueroa St.
Los Angeles, CA 90037
(213) 748-8000

Coach Mike Schuler			
	W	L	Pct.
NBA Record	158	135	.539
W/Clippers	31	51	.378
1990-91 Record	31	51	.378

Clippers History

Except for a brief, three-year run of moderate success in the mid-1970s, the Clippers have been the league's weakest and, at times, most poorly managed team.

Born the Buffalo Braves in 1970, the team flourished briefly under the direction of Jack Ramsay. The Braves crept above the .500 mark (42-40) in 1973-74, behind NBA scoring leader Bob McAdoo, slick playmaker Ernie DiGregorio, and sharp-shooting forward Jim McMillian. The Braves improved to 49-33 the next season with MVP McAdoo again leading the way. Washington bounced the Braves from the 1975 Eastern semifinals, but the Braves persevered and whipped Philadelphia in the first round of the 1976 playoffs, before succumbing to Boston in the semis.

Thus ended the good times for Braves/Clippers fans. Prior to the 1978-79 season, Braves owner John Y. Brown traded the team to Irving Levin in return for control of the Celtics. Levin moved the club to San Diego, renamed it the Clippers, and watched it register an abysmal 17-65 mark in 1981-82. The Clippers moved north to L.A. for the 1984-85 season and were an immediate poor cousin to the flourishing Lakers.

Though it won 30-plus games in 1984-85 and 1985-86, Los Angeles embarked on three consecutive miserable seasons, with the lowlight being a 12-70 mark in 1986-87. A 31-51 record in 1990-91 and young talent like Ron Harper, Danny Manning, and Charles Smith provide some hope for the future.

Last Five Years

Season	W	L	Pct.	Place	Playoffs	Coach
1986-87	12	70	.146	Sixth	DNQ	Don Chaney
1987-88	17	65	.207	Sixth	DNQ	Gene Shue
1988-89	21	61	.256	Seventh	DNQ	Gene Shue/Don Casey
1989-90	30	52	.366	Sixth	DNQ	Don Casey
1990-91	31	51	.378	Sixth	DNQ	Mike Schuler

1990-91 Recap

As has been the case for the past 15 seasons, the Clippers entered 1990-91 with high hopes and exited with many questions. You have to go back to the days of the old Buffalo Braves to find the last time the franchise qualified for the playoffs, and there are Clippers fans who wish the team would shuffle off to Buffalo as well.

About the best thing that happened to the Clippers in 1990-91 was that someone relieved them of the onus of center Benoit Benjamin, a long-time attitude problem and a mountain of unrealized potential. Dealing the enigmatic Benjamin to Seattle not only saved piles of money, but it also may have preserved the sanity of coach Mike Schuler. Replacement Olden Polynice didn't exactly shine (12.3 points, 9.1 rebounds) during his 31 games in L.A., but he worked hard, something alien to Benjamin.

The Clippers' 31-51 record earned them a spot in the draft lottery (they practically have reserved seats) and allowed them the chance to add yet another talented rookie to their burgeoning stable of first-round draft choices. Forward Charles Smith, a former lottery pick, was the premier Clipper, averaging 20.0 points and 8.2 rebounds. Guard Ron Harper came back from knee surgery to average 19.6 points in 39 games, and forwards Ken Norman (17.4 points) and Danny Manning (15.9 points) were steady.

But a lot went wrong. The Clippers made only 46.4 percent of their shots, and they developed a glaring deficiency at point guard. Winston Garland (8.2 points, 4.6 assists) had to replace turnover-prone Gary Grant, though neither gave Schuler the floor leadership he needed. The Clippers committed the third most turnovers in the NBA.

1991-92 Roster

No.	Player	Pos.	Ht.	Wt.	Exp.	College	1990-91		
							PPG	RPG	APG
—	James Edwards	F/C	7'1"	252	14	Washington	13.6	3.8	0.9
22	LeRon Ellis	C/F	6'10"	250	R	Syracuse	—	—	—
1	Gary Grant	G	6'3"	195	3	Michigan	8.7	3.1	8.6
4	Ron Harper	G	6'6"	198	5	Miami (OH)	19.6	4.8	5.4
30	Bo Kimble	G	6'4"	190	1	Loyola Mary.	6.9	1.9	1.2
5	Danny Manning	F	6'10"	230	3	Kansas	15.9	5.8	2.7
3	Ken Norman	F	6'8"	219	4	Illinois	17.4	7.1	2.3
34	Elliot Perry	G	6'0"	155	R	Memphis St.	—	—	—
0	Olden Polynice	C	7'0"	245	4	Virginia	9.8	7.0	0.5
25	Doc Rivers	G	6'4"	185	8	Marquette	15.2	3.2	4.3
54	Charles Smith	F	6'10"	238	3	Pittsburgh	20.0	8.2	1.8
35	Loy Vaught	C	6'9"	240	1	Michigan	5.5	4.8	0.5

Los Angeles Clippers
1991-92 Season Preview

Opening Line: The L.A. Clippers, that perennial collection of wasted lottery picks, will try it again this year. L.A., desperate for leadership at the point, traded its 1991 lottery pick to Atlanta for lead guard Doc Rivers. The Clippers did have the 22nd choice and they spent it on Syracuse center LeRon Ellis. In the second round, they landed Elliot Perry, a string-bean guard from Memphis State, and Joe Wylie, a 6'9" forward from Miami (FL). Wylie and guard Winston Garland were traded for draft picks. Guard Jeff Martin was dealt to Detroit for center James Edwards. Part-timers Tom Garrick, Ken Bannister, and Mike Smrek were all let go.

Guard: The spirited Ron Harper (19.6 PPG) is full-strength after missing half of last season with an injury. Harper, a legitimate All-Star contender, is an electric open-court player who can beat anybody one-on-one. Rivers will provide solid playmaking skills and veteran leadership—two things the Clippers haven't received from Gary Grant. Despite impressive assist totals (8.6 APG), Grant has become notorious for his poor shot selection and bad judgment. Bo Kimble, a phenomenal long-range scorer in college, must improve on a horrible rookie year (38-percent shooting).

Forward: Charles Smith ranks as one of the most talented power forwards this side of Karl Malone. A mixture of power and finesse, Smith scores (20.0 PPG), rebounds (8.2 RPG), and blocks shots (1.96 BPG). Ken Norman is a strong open-court player who loves to score in the paint (17.4 PPG), though his intensity has been a concern. Danny Manning, still not 100 percent after a 1988-89 knee injury, plays like a 6'10" point guard. He's a brilliant passer who can score inside and out (15.9 PPG). Loy Vaught is a young rebounder who needs to develop.

Center: Olden Polynice is a strong defender, but his poor offensive skills would prevent him from starting on most clubs. The aging Edwards still knows how to score down low. Rookie Ellis, another defensive specialist, may play both forward and center.

Coaching: Mike Schuler has gained a reputation as a tough taskmaster— he was a head coach at Virginia Military Institute and an assistant to Bobby Knight at Army. He's also known as a top offensive strategist. In his first year as an NBA coach— 1986-87—he was named Coach of the Year. Schuler is assisted by John Hammond and Alvin Gentry.

Analysis: This team has outstanding young talent, and with Harper around all year and Manning coming into his own, it can only get better. Moreover, the addition of Rivers will stabilize the troubled guard position and improve the club's poor chemistry. Though they play in a rough division, L.A. should challenge for a playoff spot.

Prediction: 6th Place, Pacific

LOS ANGELES LAKERS

Division: Pacific
Home: The Great Western Forum
Capacity: 17,505
Year Built: 1967

Address
3900 W. Manchester Blvd
Inglewood, CA 90306
(213) 419-3100

Owner: Dr. Jerry Buss
General Manager: Jerry West
Head Coach: Mike Dunleavy
Assistant Coach: Bill Bertka
Assistant Coach: Randy Pfund
Assistant Coach: Jim Eyen

Coach Mike Dunleavy			
	W	L	Pct.
NBA Record	58	24	.707
W/Lakers	58	24	.707
1990-91 Record	58	24	.707

Lakers History

No team has equaled the tradition and success of the Boston Celtics, but the Lakers have come close. During the franchise's 43 years of existence, it has put a dazzling array of talent onto NBA courts. Along the way, it has won 11 world championships.

The Laker magic began in Minneapolis and was built around 6'10" center George Mikan, clearly the premier player of his day. With Mikan, Bob Pollard, Vern Mikkelsen, and Slater Martin, the Minneapolis Lakers won five championships in six years from 1949-54.

In 1960, the team moved to Los Angeles, keeping its Minnesota-style nickname. But the early years in L.A. led to heartbreak, as the Lakers lost in the NBA Finals to the Celtics six times, despite the heroics of guard Jerry West and forward Elgin Baylor.

Even the arrival of Wilt Chamberlain in 1968-69 couldn't stop the string of runner-up finishes. The Lakers dropped the 1968-69 series to the Celtics and the 1969-70 title series to the Knicks. The Lakers gained revenge two years later by going 69-13 (including a 33-game winning streak) and beating New York 4-1 in the finals.

Kareem Abdul-Jabbar continued the tradition of Hall of Fame pivot men for the Lakers when he was acquired from Milwaukee in 1975. But it wasn't until Magic Johnson was drafted in 1979 that the Lakers truly began to shine. The team won five titles in the 1980s, including two over Boston, and assumed the "Showtime" image that predominated its home city.

Last Five Years

Season	W	L	Pct.	Place	Playoffs	Coach
1986-87	65	17	.793	First	NBA Champs	Pat Riley
1987-88	62	20	.756	First	NBA Champs	Pat Riley
1988-89	57	25	.695	First	L-NBA Finals	Pat Riley
1989-90	63	19	.768	First	L-West Semis	Pat Riley
1990-91	58	24	.707	Second	L-NBA Finals	Mike Dunleavy

1990-91 Recap

It can be said that the 1990-91 season was the one in which "Showtime" became "Slowtime." After wowing the NBA world with a lethal fastbreak that yielded five league championships during the 1980s, the Lakers started the first full season in the '90s with a new coach and a new philosophy.

Mike Dunleavy brought his corporate look to the spot occupied for so many years by the flashy Pat Riley, and with his conservative attire came a new, slowdown approach to success.

All five Laker starters averaged double figures in points, giving the team a bevy of options. Of course, Magic Johnson (19.4 points, 12.5 assists, 7.0 rebounds) was again spectacular, and in mid-season he surpassed Oscar Robertson's career assist record. His usual cast of cronies was joined by free agent newcomer Sam Perkins (13.5 points, 7.4 rebounds), who gave L.A. a new dimension underneath.

James Worthy (21.4 points) was his usual outstanding self, and second-year center Vlade Divac (11.2 points, 8.1 rebounds) began to assert himself more as the season progressed. Guard Byron Scott (14.5 points) scored from outside, and off-season acquisition Terry Teagle (9.9 points) joined A.C. Green (9.1 points, 6.3 rebounds) as a key bench performer.

Portland broke L.A.'s nine-year stranglehold on the Pacific Division regular-season title, but the Lakers got revenge in the Western Conference finals, setting up the league's dream championship series of Magic vs. Michael. However, Worthy and Scott suffered injuries in the finals, and the powerful Bulls simply overwhelmed L.A. The Lakers won game one on a Perkins 3-pointer, but Chicago took the next four.

1991-92 Roster

No.	Player	Pos.	Ht.	Wt.	Exp.	College	1990-91 PPG	RPG	APG
41	Elden Campbell	F/C	6'11"	215	1	Clemson	2.8	1.8	0.2
12	Vlade Divac	C	7'1"	248	2	None	11.2	8.1	1.1
10	Larry Drew	G	6'2"	190	10	Missouri	2.9	0.7	2.5
45	A.C. Green	F	6'9"	224	6	Oregon St.	9.1	6.3	0.9
32	Magic Johnson	G	6'9"	220	12	Michigan St.	19.4	7.0	12.5
—	Anthony Jones	F/G	6'7"	200	R	Oral Roberts	—	—	—
14	Sam Perkins	F/C	6'9"	257	7	North Carolina	13.5	7.4	1.5
4	Byron Scott	G	6'4"	193	8	Arizona St.	14.5	3.0	2.2
34	Tony Smith	G	6'4"	195	1	Marquette	3.7	1.1	2.1
20	Terry Teagle	G/F	6'5"	195	9	Baylor	9.9	2.2	1.0
30	Irving Thomas	F	6'8"	225	1	Florida St.	1.8	1.2	0.4
43	Mychal Thompson	F/C	6'10"	235	12	Minnesota	4.0	3.2	0.3
42	James Worthy	F	6'9"	225	9	North Carolina	21.4	4.6	3.5

Los Angeles Lakers
1991-92 Season Preview

Opening Line: As long as Magic Johnson puts on his Laker tank top, L.A. will always be a championship contender. Magic appeared in his tenth NBA Finals last year. The Lakers had just one pick in the draft, choosing Anthony Jones of Oral Roberts, a 6'7" forward, with the 52nd pick.

Guard: Johnson (19.4 PPG, 12.5 APG) owns virtually every record a point guard can accumulate. Last season, he broke Oscar Robertson's all-time assists record. But what sets Johnson apart from other NBA players is his five NBA championship rings. Though age 32, Magic still racks up triple-doubles on a regular basis. Byron Scott (14.5 PPG) is a long-range bomber, but he couldn't buy a basket in last year's NBA Finals. In fact, claimed comedian Arsenio Hall, Scott went into Kentucky Fried Chicken and even *the Colonel* wouldn't sell him a bucket. Terry Teagle is a potent scorer off the bench but is rather streaky. Tony Smith, a young, well-rounded point guard, backs up Magic.

Forward: James Worthy (21.4 PPG) is without a doubt one of the NBA's best small forwards. His outstanding speed has made him the key to the Lakers' fastbreak—although aching knees may start to limit his effectiveness. The addition of Sam Perkins, Worthy's teammate at North Carolina, proved to be a major boost to the Lakers in 1990-91. Although Perkins's sleepy eyes give fans the impression that he is going through the motions, his production (13.5 PPG, 7.4 RPG) proves otherwise. When Perkins needs a rest, A.C. Green comes off the bench and crashes boards. Sophomore string bean Elden Campbell has shown signs of becoming a potent power forward. He'll get more minutes this year.

Center: Yugoslavian Vlade Divac is developing into a heck of a player. Though not an intimidator, Divac has the agility, passing skills, and ball-handling ability of a small forward. The ancient Mychal Thompson, a strong rebounder, barely makes it off the bench anymore.

Coaching: Mike Dunleavy made a smashing debut as an NBA head coach last season, taking the pieces that were already in place from the Pat Riley era and forming an NBA title contender. But as long as Dunleavy has Johnson on his team, that may be enough to make him look like a coaching genius. Dunleavy's assistants include Bill Bertka, Jim Eyen, and Randy Pfund.

Analysis: Every season, the Lakers get older; but every season, they remain one of the top teams in the NBA. This year, they'll battle Portland and Phoenix for the top spot in the Pacific. One of these days, the Lakers will fall from their lofty perch. But that day probably won't come until after Magic Johnson and James Worthy retire.

Prediction: 3rd Place, Pacific

PHOENIX SUNS

Division: Pacific
Home: Veterans' Memorial Coliseum
Capacity: 14,487
Year Built: 1965

Address
2910 N. Central Ave.
Phoenix, AZ 85012
(602) 266-5753

Chief Executive Officer:
Jerry Colangelo
Director of Player Personnel:
Cotton Fitzsimmons
Head Coach: Cotton Fitzsimmons
Assistant Coach: Paul Westphal
Assistant Coach: Lionel Hollins

Coach Cotton Fitzsimmons			
	W	L	Pct.
NBA Record	752	716	.512
W/Suns	261	149	.624
1990-91 Record	55	27	.671

Suns History

If there is one team in the NBA synonymous with the term "near miss," it is the Suns. Throughout its 23-year history, Phoenix has missed out on superstars and championships by the narrowest of margins.

The team's destiny was shaped by a coin toss following the 1968-69 season, when the Suns lost the draft rights to Lew Alcindor to the Milwaukee Bucks. Instead, the Suns chose journeyman-to-be Neal Walk and continued a seven-year run of mediocrity. Players like Connie Hawkins and Dick Van Arsdale made things exciting, but the Suns could only make the playoffs once during the period.

The next close call came during the 1976 playoffs, when underdog Phoenix advanced to the NBA Finals against Boston. With the series tied 2-2, the Suns lost Game Five in a triple-overtime heart-stopper, 128-126. In 1978-79, center Alvan Adams, Truck Robinson, and superb guard Paul Westphal formed a solid nucleus that again fell just short, losing to Seattle in a seven-game Western Conference finals.

The Suns enjoyed some success in the early 1980s and won the Pacific Division in 1980-81, but they dropped off in the middle of the decade. It wasn't until Cotton Fitzsimmons took over in 1988 that the Suns began to shine again. Tom Chambers and Kevin Johnson led Phoenix to three straight 50-plus-win seasons and an appearance in the 1989-90 Western finals, where they dropped a tight series to Portland.

Last Five Years

Season	W	L	Pct.	Place	Playoffs	Coach
1986-87	36	46	.439	Fifth	DNQ	J. MacLeod/D. Van Arsdale
1987-88	28	54	.341	Fourth	DNQ	John Wetzel
1988-89	55	27	.671	Second	L-West Finals	Cotton Fitzsimmons
1989-90	54	28	.659	Third	L-West Finals	Cotton Fitzsimmons
1990-91	55	27	.671	Third	L-Round One	Cotton Fitzsimmons

1990-91 Recap

Before their abrupt, first-round dismissal from the 1991 playoffs, the Suns were looked at as one of the league's best teams. Their 1989-90 advancement to the Western Conference finals was thought to be just a precursor to their membership among the league's elite.

Throughout 1990-91, Phoenix made good on the promise, and its 55-27 record in the rugged Western Conference was an indication of its potential. But Phoenix couldn't translate its regular-season success into post-season results, and its first-round loss to Utah left some questions.

Perhaps the biggest concern was whether high-scoring forwards Tom Chambers and Xavier McDaniel could co-exist with only one basketball. McDaniel, acquired early in the season from Seattle for Eddie Johnson, averaged 17.0 points and 6.9 rebounds, both down from his 1989-90 numbers. Chambers's scoring fell significantly, from 27.2 to 19.9.

One person who continued to perform at his usual high level was ultra-quick point guard Kevin Johnson (22.2 points, 10.1 assists), who was practically unstoppable all year. Backcourt mate Jeff Hornacek (16.9 PPG) was again a valuable weapon outside and a good target on the fastbreak. Sixth man Dan Majerle (13.6 PPG, 5.4 RPG) continued to set a league standard for hustle and desire.

With the arrival of McDaniel, center Mark West's offensive responsibilities were diminished even more, and he averaged 7.7 points and 6.9 rebounds a game. Late-season acquisition Joe Barry Carroll didn't have time to blend in, but he could be a factor in the future.

1991-92 Roster

No.	Player	Pos.	Ht.	Wt.	Exp.	College	1990-91 PPG	1990-91 RPG	1990-91 APG
2	Joe Barry Carroll	C	7'1"	255	10	Purdue	3.4	2.2	1.0
23	Cedric Ceballos	F	6'6"	210	1	Cal. St. Fuller.	8.2	2.4	0.6
24	Tom Chambers	F	6'10"	230	10	Utah	19.9	6.4	2.6
—	Richard Dumas	F	6'7"	210	R	Oklahoma St.	—	—	—
—	Chad Gallagher	F	6'10"	245	R	Creighton	—	—	—
14	Jeff Hornacek	G	6'4"	190	5	Iowa St.	16.9	4.0	5.1
7	Kevin Johnson	G	6'1"	190	4	California	22.2	3.5	10.1
32	Negele Knight	G	6'1"	182	1	Dayton	5.3	1.1	3.0
28	Andrew Lang	C	6'11"	250	3	Arkansas	4.9	4.8	0.4
9	Dan Majerle	G/F	6'6"	220	3	Cent. Michigan	13.6	5.4	2.8
35	Xavier McDaniel	F	6'8"	205	6	Wichita St.	17.0	6.9	2.3
45	Ed Nealy	F	6'7"	240	8	Kansas St.	2.2	2.7	0.7
34	Tim Perry	F	6'9"	220	3	Temple	4.2	2.7	0.6
31	Kurt Rambis	F	6'8"	213	10	Santa Clara	3.6	4.3	1.0
41	Mark West	C	6'10"	246	8	Old Dominion	7.7	6.9	0.5
—	Joey Wright	G	6'3"	185	R	Texas	—	—	—

Phoenix Suns
1991-92 Season Preview

Opening Line: Over the last three seasons, the Suns have won twice as many games as they've lost. The problem is they keep getting knocked off by Western Conference superpowers in the playoffs. This year, Cotton Fitzsimmons's club is brimming with tough, talented, championship-style ballplayers. The Suns didn't have a first-round draft pick, but they chose 6'10" center Chad Gallagher of Creighton with the 32nd overall pick. They also grabbed 6'6" forward Richard Dumas of Oklahoma State with the 46th selection and Joey Wright, a 6'3" guard from Texas, with the 50th pick.

Guard: Point guard Kevin Johnson, perhaps the best point guard in basketball behind Magic Johnson, leads this four-star group. K.J.'s unbelievable quickness allows him to penetrate and dish off (10.1 APG), while his outside touch makes him a dangerous scorer (22.2 PPG). Jeff Hornacek (16.9 PPG) isn't nearly as quick, but he's a well-schooled off guard who's fundamentally strong in all areas. He'll hit from anywhere if left open. Dan Majerle, one of the NBA's top sixth men, is an intense defender and a tenacious board-crasher. Negele Knight, a highly regarded sophomore point guard, is nearly ready for a starting spot—though that won't happen in Phoenix as long as Johnson remains.

Forward: Tom Chambers is a perennial 20-PPG scorer who will fill it up every which way. At 6'10", he's difficult to defend. Small forward Xavier McDaniel, who like Chambers is a borderline All-Star, will score (17.0 PPG), rebound (6.9 RPG), and play his man tooth-and-nail. Veteran Kurt Rambis is the classic lunch-bucket player who does whatever it takes. Young Cedric Ceballos, who scored 34 in a game last year, is an encouraging talent who needs some experience.

Center: Mark West can't do much offensively, but he provides powerful defense and major-league shot-blocking. The same can be said for back-up Andrew Lang. Phoenix could use a more offensive post-up center.

Coaching: In his 18 seasons, Cotton Fitzsimmons has won 752 games—seventh most in NBA history. The Suns were 28-54 in 1987-88, but when Cotton took over the next season they went 55-27. Fitzsimmons is an up-beat guy, but he isn't afraid to get on his players from time to time. He is assisted by Paul Westphal and Lionel Hollins.

Analysis: This is one of the premier teams in the NBA. It's hard-nosed, well coached, and has what it takes to win the title. In the last couple of years, Phoenix has been a little short in the talent department, but it's getting stronger and stronger. Expect the Suns to reach the Western Conference semifinals and then duke it out with the Lakers, Trail Blazers, and/or Spurs for a spot in the NBA Finals.

Prediction: 2nd Place, Pacific

PORTLAND TRAIL BLAZERS

Division: Pacific
Home: Memorial Coliseum
Capacity: 12,884
Year Built: 1960

Governor: Paul Allen
V.P./Basketball Operations:
Bucky Buckwalter
Head Coach: Rick Adelman
Assistant Coach: Jack Schalow
Assistant Coach: John Wetzel

Address
Suite 950, Lloyd Building
700 N.E. Multnomah St.
Portland, OR 97232
(503) 234-9291

Coach Rick Adelman			
	W	L	Pct.
NBA Record	136	63	.683
W/Blazers	136	63	.683
1990-91 Record	63	19	.768

Trail Blazers History

Few teams in sports can boast of fan loyalty the way Portland can. The Blazers have sold out Memorial Coliseum 632 consecutive times, believed to be a record for any sport.

Portland was a typical expansion team in the early 1970s, losing far more than it won and shuttling players and coaches in and out. Early stars included Geoff Petrie, Sidney Wicks, and future Blazers coach Rick Adelman.

Things began to change in 1974 when the Blazers drafted UCLA center Bill Walton. Two years later, Jack Ramsay became coach and led the team to its only NBA title. With Walton serving as a do-everything high-post in Ramsay's motion offense, Portland upset Philadelphia in the 1977 finals, 4-2. Bob Gross, Maurice Lucas, Dave Twardzik, and Lionel Hollins comprised the rest of that starting unit.

The Blazers appeared primed to repeat in 1977-78, but Walton injured his foot and Portland was eliminated by Seattle in the West semifinals. Walton never returned to form, and the Blazers fell behind Los Angeles and Seattle as the top team in the Pacific Division.

In the 1980s, management drafted star guards Clyde Drexler and Terry Porter, and in 1989 Portland traded for rebounding forward Buck Williams. The Blazers advanced to the 1990 NBA Finals, where they lost to Detroit. In 1990-91, Portland broke L.A.'s nine-year stranglehold on the Pacific Division title, though it fell to the Lakers in the West finals.

Last Five Years

Season	W	L	Pct.	Place	Playoffs	Coach
1986-87	49	33	.598	Second	L-Round One	Mike Schuler
1987-88	53	29	.646	Second	L-Round One	Mike Schuler
1988-89	39	43	.476	Fifth	L-Round One	M. Schuler/R. Adelman
1989-90	59	23	.720	Second	L-NBA Finals	Rick Adelman
1990-91	63	19	.768	First	L-West Finals	Rick Adelman

1990-91 Recap

After advancing to the NBA Finals in 1989-90, the Blazers were looked at as the heirs to the Pistons' throne. Their blend of speed, finesse, and power appeared to be too much for anyone else, and the additions of Danny Ainge and Walter Davis to their bench made them appear even more invincible. So, when they were whipped by the resurgent Lakers in the Western Conference finals, Portland fans were left open-mouthed. All of a sudden, the Blazers were exposed as susceptible to a team with several post-up weapons and an ability to slow the game's pace.

The Blazers' regular-season performance left little doubts about their potential to win it all. Portland opened the year with an 11-game winning streak and closed it with a 16-1 spurt. The Blazers set a franchise record with 63 wins, had the league's best home and road records, and accumulated another paragraph of team superlatives.

Portland's starting five was once again spectacular. Off guard Clyde Drexler zipped, floated, and dashed his way to 21.5 points, 6.7 rebounds, and 6.0 assists per game. Speedy point guard Terry Porter (17.0 points, 8.0 assists) was again masterful on the break, and the forward tandem of Jerome Kersey (14.8 points, 6.6 rebounds) and Buck Williams (11.7 points, 9.4 rebounds, league-leading 60.2 shooting percentage) was among the league's finest.

Center Kevin Duckworth (15.8 points, 6.6 rebounds) was a force in the middle, though he sagged against the Lakers. Forward Cliff Robinson (11.7 PPG, 4.3 RPG) and Davis (13.0 PPG) and Ainge (11.1 PPG) rounded out a potent rotation.

1991-92 Roster

No.	Player	Pos.	Ht.	Wt.	Exp.	College	PPG	1990-91 RPG	APG
31	Alaa Abdelnaby	F	6'10"	240	1	Duke	3.1	2.1	0.3
9	Danny Ainge	G	6'5"	185	10	Brigham Young	11.1	2.6	3.6
2	Mark Bryant	F	6'9"	245	3	Seton Hall	5.1	3.6	0.5
42	Wayne Cooper	C	6'10"	220	13	New Orleans	2.2	2.8	0.3
6	Walter Davis	G/F	6'6"	207	14	North Carolina	13.0	2.5	1.8
22	Clyde Drexler	G	6'7"	222	8	Houston	21.5	6.7	6.0
00	Kevin Duckworth	C	7'0"	270	5	Eastern Illinois	15.8	6.6	1.1
—	Marcus Kennedy	F	6'6"	235	R	E. Michigan	—	—	—
25	Jerome Kersey	F	6'7"	225	7	Longwood Coll.	14.8	6.6	3.1
30	Terry Porter	G	6'3"	195	6	Wisc. Stevens Pt.	17.0	3.5	8.0
3	Cliff Robinson	F	6'10"	225	2	Connecticut	11.7	4.3	1.8
—	LaMont Strothers	G	6'4"	192	R	Chris. Newport	—	—	—
52	Buck Williams	F	6'8"	225	10	Maryland	11.7	9.4	1.2
21	Danny Young	G	6'4"	175	7	Wake Forest	3.8	1.0	1.9

Portland Trail Blazers
1991-92 Season Preview

Opening Line: After pacing the NBA with a 63-19 record last season, the Trail Blazers will try to recover from their discouraging Western Conference Finals loss to the Lakers. Though the Blazers may have the most complete team in basketball, several players are getting along in years; if Portland is to win a world title, it's going to be now or never. The Blazers drafted Eastern Michigan forward Marcus Kennedy with the 54th pick in the draft. They also traded for rookie guard Lamont Strothers, a second-round pick by Golden State.

Guard: Portland features a super backcourt of point guard Terry Porter and Clyde Drexler. Porter (17.0 PPG, 8.0 APG) is a strong all-around playmaker who can also kill you with his 3-point shooting. Clyde "The Glide" does it all at off guard. This extraordinary leaper scores (21.5 PPG), rebounds (6.7 RPG), and creates (6.0 APG), and has become one of top superstars in the game. Veteran Danny Ainge provides fiery leadership and a winning attitude, not to mention a great 3-point shot. Walter Davis is one of the greatest jump-shooters of all time, though he's 37 years old. Danny Young is an adequate back-up guard, but he needs to improve his shooting.

Forward: The revered Buck Williams will rebound relentlessly (9.4 RPG) and play tenacious low-post defense. He's one of the best at power forward. Jerome Kersey is a fine small forward who will run the floor and play strong defense, though his shooting is rather mediocre. Back-up Cliff Robinson, a remarkably versatile 6'10" reserve, can drive to the whole like a guard and swat away shots like a center. Mark Bryant is a physical, inside forward who needs more development.

Center: Kevin Duckworth is a massive 7'0", 275 pounds, yet he's remarkably agile with a repertoire of inside scoring moves. Though not a dominating center, he's certainly above average. Thirteen-year vet Wayne Cooper is known for his shot-blocking.

Coaching: Rick Adelman has taken a team that was in turmoil under Mike Schuler and turned it into a prime-time winner. Though a journeyman as a player, Adelman has earned the respect of his players and peers as a coach. His three-year record with Portland, 136-63, speaks for itself. He's assisted by Jack Schalow and John Wetzel.

Analysis: The Blazers have it all—All-Star starters, a deep bench (eight men averaged in double figures last year), and loads of experience. The problem is, several other clubs are nearly as good or *as* good as the Blazers, and all have the ability to knock them off in the playoffs. That happened the last two years and could easily happen again this year. Nevertheless, jot down Portland as the No. 1 favorite to win the West.

Prediction: 1st Place, Pacific

SACRAMENTO KINGS

Division: Pacific
Home: ARCO Arena
Capacity: 17,014
Year Built: 1988

Address
One Sports Parkway
Sacramento, CA 95834
(916) 928-0000

Managing General Partner:
Gregg Lukenbill
President: Rick Benner
Head Coach: Dick Motta
Assistant Coach: Rex Hughes

Coach Dick Motta			
	W	L	Pct.
NBA Record	849	845	.501
W/Kings	41	95	.301
1990-91 Record	25	57	.305

Kings History

Like the sun rises in the East and sets in the West, so has the Royals/Kings franchise. The Rochester (New York) Royals, a charter member of the NBA, won the franchise's only league title in 1950-51. But cross-country franchise moves, ending in Sacramento, have only led to futility.

That Rochester championship team featured a slick backcourt of Bob Davies, Bobby Wanzer, and Red Holzman, with Arnie Risen in the middle. Rochester advanced to the West finals in 1951-52, but it lost to Minneapolis. The Royals made the playoffs only once from 1956-61, though they featured a potent forecourt of Maurice Stokes, Jack Twyman, and Clyde Lovellette.

The team moved to Cincinnati for the 1957-58 season and added

exciting rookie Oscar Robertson in 1960. The Royals advanced to the Eastern finals in 1962-63 and 1963-64, thanks to Robertson, Twyman, and 1963-64 Rookie of the Year Jerry Lucas, but the success was short-lived. The team didn't have a winning season from 1966-67 to 1973-74 and moved again in 1972, splitting time between Kansas City and Omaha as the Kings.

In 1974-75, the team won 44 games and featured brilliant point guard Nate "Tiny" Archibald. The 1980-81 edition lost to Houston in the conference finals. The most recent move came in 1985, when the franchise landed in Sacramento. Aside from a brief playoff appearance that season, the team has been a perennial lottery team ever since.

Last Five Years

Season	W	L	Pct.	Place	Playoffs	Coach
1986-87	29	53	.354	Fifth	DNQ	Phil Johnson/Jerry Reynolds
1987-88	24	58	.293	Sixth	DNQ	Bill Russell/Jerry Reynolds
1988-89	27	55	.329	Sixth	DNQ	Jerry Reynolds
1989-90	23	59	.280	Seventh	DNQ	Jerry Reynolds/Dick Motta
1990-91	25	57	.305	Seventh	DNQ	Dick Motta

1990-91 Recap

It can be said with assurance that Sacramento was hardly the "Kings of the Road" during the 1990-91 season. No team in the history of the NBA proved to be as inept in visiting uniforms as Sacramento was last season. The Kings' 122-94 loss in Minnesota set a new record for road futility—35 consecutive losses. In all, the Kings dropped 37 straight—a streak they'll lug into the 1991-92 campaign—and compiled a nightmarish 1-40 record as visitors. Only an early season win in Philadelphia prevented the Kings from going 0-for-the-road.

Since the Kings finished 25-57, they had to have a pretty good record in the friendlier confines of the ARCO Arena, but that is little solace. In order to make the playoffs in the NBA, you have to win at least two games on the road. Part of the inability to adjust to hostile arenas (and teams) was Sacramento's young club. Four rookies—Lionel Simmons, Duane Causwell, Travis Mays, and Anthony Bonner—saw considerable time for the Kings in 1990-91, with Simmons finishing second in the Rookie of the Year balloting to New Jersey's Derrick Coleman.

From his small-forward spot, Simmons averaged 18.0 points and 8.8 rebounds per games, both second among rookies. Veterans Antoine Carr (20.1 points, 5.5 rebounds) and Wayman Tisdale (20.0 points, 7.7 rebounds) split time opposite him. Causwell started much of the year at center, and while his offensive skills (6.9 points) were weak, he was strong defensively (5.1 rebounds, 1.95 blocks).

Mays averaged 14.3 points a game from his shooting-guard spot, and veteran Rory Sparrow (10.4 PPG, 4.5 APG) was steady at the point. Reserve guard Jim Les led the NBA in 3-point shooting (.461).

1991-92 Roster

No.	Player	Pos.	Ht.	Wt.	Exp.	College	PPG	RPG	APG
								1990-91	
24	Anthony Bonner	F	6'8"	225	1	St. Louis	7.4	4.7	1.4
3	Randy Brown	G	6'3"	190	R	New Mexico St.	—	—	—
—	Rick Calloway	G	6'6"	180	1	Kansas	3.2	1.2	1.0
35	Antoine Carr	F	6'8"	265	7	Wichita St.	20.1	5.5	2.5
31	Duane Causwell	C	7'0"	240	1	Temple	6.9	5.1	0.9
32	Pete Chilcutt	F/C	6'10"	232	R	North Carolina	—	—	—
20	Bob Hansen	G	6'6"	195	8	Iowa	6.4	2.7	2.5
—	Steve Hood	G	6'7"	185	R	James Madison	—	—	—
33	Jim Les	G	5'11"	165	3	Bradley	7.2	2.0	5.4
30	Billy Owens	F/G	6'9"	225	R	Syracuse	—	—	—
50	Ralph Sampson	C	7'4"	250	8	Virginia	3.0	4.4	0.7
22	Lionel Simmons	F	6'7"	210	1	La Salle	18.0	8.8	4.0
23	Wayman Tisdale	F	6'9"	260	6	Oklahoma	20.0	7.7	2.0
4	Spud Webb	G	5'7"	135	6	N. Carolina St.	13.4	2.3	5.6
34	Bill Wennington	C	7'0"	260	6	St. John's	5.7	4.4	0.9

Sacramento Kings
1991-92 Season Preview

Opening Line: The Kings, hoping to improve on their 1-40 road record, landed four players in the draft for the second straight year. The big catch was the multi-talented Billy Owens of Syracuse, chosen with the No. 3 pick. Sacramento also selected 6'10" Pete Chilcutt of North Carolina (No. 27), guard Randy Brown of New Mexico St. (No. 31), and guard Steve Hood of James Madison (No. 42). Guard Travis Mays, one of four first-rounders taken last year, was dealt to Atlanta for the tiny Spud Webb.

Guard: Webb earned a starting job with Atlanta last year thanks to his incredible quickness and long-range jumper. Still, he's only 5'7. Veteran Rory Sparrow is a reliable, old point guard who does nothing exceptional. His leadership is his biggest asset. Though small and slow, Jim Les has earned quality reserve minutes thanks to the best 3-point shooting in the league (71-154, .461). Veteran Bobby Hansen is known for his defense and outside shot.

Forward: Despite having the league's worst offense last year, the Kings boast three high-scoring forwards. Antoine Carr (20.1 PPG) does all of his scoring damage inside, though his rebounding could be better. Wayman Tisdale (20.0 PPG in 33 games) is another close-in scorer with a repertoire of inside shots. Defense is his flaw. Young Lionel Simmons (18.0 PPG) is a well-rounded offensive player with a terrific future. Rookie Owens can do literally everything well. Although 6'9", Owens is versatile

enough to play guard. (Actually, given the glut of talented forwards on this team, either Owens or Simmons will likely become the starting off guard.) Anthony Bonner specializes in rebounding, while rookie Chilcutt could become a steady reserve.

Center: Sophomore Duane Causwell is a project player with enormous shot-blocking ability. Bill Wennington, a perimeter player, serves as an adequate back-up, though his defense remains a problem. Sacramento does not have a legitimate starting center.

Coaching: Dick Motta has coached 21 years in the NBA—in Chicago, Washington, Dallas, and Sacramento—and has racked up 849 wins, third most in league history. He needs 16 victories to move into second place. Motta has become known as a rebuilder of bad teams. With the Kings, he's found his biggest challenge yet. Motta is assisted by Rex Hughes.

Analysis: With Carr, Tisdale, Simmons, and Owens, Sacramento boasts four outstanding forwards. Unfortunately, this is the team's only strength. The backcourt is below average and the center position is in bad shape. Moving Simmons to the starting off-guard spot would help some. The addition of Owens, plus a healthy Tisdale, will spark this team to a few more wins, but it won't make it out of the cellar in the tough Pacific.

Prediction: 7th Place, Pacific

SEATTLE SUPERSONICS

Division: Pacific
Home: The Coliseum
Capacity: 14,132
Year Built: 1962

Address
190 Queen Anne Ave. N.
Seattle, WA 98109
(206) 281-5850

Owner: Barry Ackerley
President: Bob Whitsitt
Head Coach: K.C. Jones
Assistant Coach: Bob Kloppenburg
Assistant Coach: Kip Motta
Assistant Coach: Gary Wortman

Coach K.C. Jones			
	W	L	Pct.
NBA Record	504	234	.683
W/Sonics	41	41	.500
1990-91 Record	41	41	.500

SuperSonics History

Though Seattle has been in the league for 24 years, there has been only one Sonic boom. It came in the late 1970s.

Seattle's 1977-78 team featured rookie center Jack Sikma, rebounding machine Paul Silas, and the guard triumvirate of Gus Johnson, Dennis Johnson, and "Downtown" Fred Brown. They fell in seven games to Washington in the NBA championship. The team was not denied the following season. The Sonics roared to the Pacific Division championship and dispatched Los Angeles and Phoenix in the playoffs. The Sonics won the title in five games over the Bullets.

That two-year period stands in stark contrast to the rest of the franchise's history. Born in 1967, the team failed to qualify for the playoffs for seven seasons and boasted few stars, other than powerful Bob Rule and highly talented but enigmatic Spencer Haywood. Seattle made it to the Western semifinals in 1974-75 and 1975-76, setting the stage for its runs to the finals. But aside from big years in 1979-80 (56 wins, loss to L.A. in the West finals) and 1981-82 (52 wins), Seattle has enjoyed little success.

There have been some moments. Despite finishing with a losing record in 1986-87, the Sonics advanced to the Western finals, thanks to a high-scoring trio of Xavier McDaniel, Dale Ellis, and Tom Chambers. But Chambers left via free agency in 1988, and McDaniel and Ellis were traded away during the 1990-91 season as part of the team's commitment to youth.

Last Five Years

Season	W	L	Pct.	Place	Playoffs	Coach
1986-87	39	43	.476	Fourth	L-West Finals	Bernie Bickerstaff
1987-88	44	38	.537	Third	L-Round One	Bernie Bickerstaff
1988-89	47	35	.573	Third	L-West Semis	Bernie Bickerstaff
1989-90	41	41	.500	Fourth	DNQ	Bernie Bickerstaff
1990-91	41	41	.500	Fifth	L-Round One	K.C. Jones

1990-91 Recap

If the Sonics led the league in any category during the 1990-91 season, it was probably media guide revisions. Seattle shook up its team with three major trades during the year, and the resulting combination got the Sonics back to the playoffs after a one-year hiatus. Though Seattle stretched Portland to the fifth game of their first-round series, the wisdom of the deals can still be questioned.

The year started with Seattle dealing brutish forward Xavier McDaniel to Phoenix for sharp-shooting forward Eddie Johnson and draft picks. Johnson averaged 16.7 PPG but couldn't match McDaniel's strength under the boards. The next two deals came rapid-fire. The Sonics shipped mercurial guard Dale Ellis to Milwaukee for sixth man Ricky Pierce, who averaged 20.5 a game but didn't help solve the team's guard backlog, which included disgruntled vets Dana Barros and Nate McMillan, plus Quintin Dailey.

The biggie came just days later when Seattle acquired talented but terminally inconsistent center Benoit Benjamin from the Clippers, along with his fright-wigged agent Don King and a huge contract demand. Benjamin gave the Sonics a legitimate center (14.0 points, 10.3 rebounds)—when he decided to show up.

Though there were plenty of questions, the Sonics seemed to find some answers elsewhere. Young dunking machine Shawn Kemp (15.0 points, 8.4 rebounds) arrived at power forward, while Sedale Threatt (12.7 PPG, 51.9-percent shooting) stepped up and played well at off guard. Reserve forward Derrick McKey (15.3 PPG, 5.8 RPG) continued to shine, but rookie point guard Gary Payton (7.2 points, 6.4 assists) was inconsistent.

1991-92 Roster

No.	Player	Pos.	Ht.	Wt.	Exp.	College	PPG	1990-91 RPG	APG
11	Dana Barros	G	5'11"	163	2	Boston College	6.3	1.1	1.7
00	Benoit Benjamin	C	7'0"	260	6	Creighton	14.0	10.3	1.7
44	Michael Cage	F	6'9"	230	7	San Diego St.	6.4	6.8	1.1
20	Quintin Dailey	G	6'2"	180	9	San Francisco	6.1	1.1	0.5
22	Eddie Johnson	F	6'7"	215	10	Illinois	16.7	3.3	1.4
40	Shawn Kemp	F	6'10"	240	2	None	15.0	8.4	1.8
25	Rich King	C	7'2"	245	R	Nebraska	—	—	—
31	Derrick McKey	F	6'9"	210	4	Alabama	15.3	5.8	2.3
10	Nate McMillan	G	6'5"	197	5	N. Carolina St.	4.3	3.2	4.8
8	Scott Meents	F	6'10"	235	2	Illinois	1.3	0.8	0.6
2	Gary Payton	G	6'4"	190	1	Oregon St.	7.2	3.0	6.4
21	Ricky Pierce	G	6'4"	210	9	Rice	20.5	2.4	2.2
4	Sedale Threatt	G	6'2"	177	8	W. Virg. Tech	12.7	1.2	3.4

Seattle SuperSonics
1991-92 Season Preview

Opening Line: Last year, Seattle finished in the middle of the pack in scoring and defense and ended the season at 41-41. The Sonics have some rising, young talent—notably Gary Payton and Shawn Kemp—who could push the team over .500. Coach K.C. Jones hopes that 7'2" Nebraska center Rich King, chosen 14th overall in the draft, will help strengthen the troubled center position.

Guard: Sophomore Payton is a pure point guard known for his stifling defense. Though a trash talker, Payton backs up his words with quality play. Off guard Sedale Threatt owns a beautiful jump shot and also possesses the quickness to defend any guard in the league. Ricky Pierce (20.5 PPG), one of the greatest sixth men of our generation, will come off the bench and score from everywhere. Nate McMillan is a role player who specializes in defense and rebounding, while Dana Barros is a fine, young point guard who needs a little more development.

Forward: Though just 21 years old, power forward Kemp is on the verge of superstardom. Kemp (15.0 PPG, 8.4 RPG) is quick and powerful and can rattle the roof with one of his awesome dunks. Starting small forward Eddie Johnson is a softer player with rebounding and defensive deficiencies, but his sweet jumper is a sight to behold (16.7 PPG). The talented Derrick McKey knows how to score in the NBA (15.3 PPG), but he's been criticized for his laid-back attitude.

Aging veteran Michael Cage has always been known for his outstanding rebounding.

Center: After six years in the league, the enigmatic Benoit Benjamin (14.0 PPG, 10.3 RPG) is finally approaching his star potential. Benjamin has the all-around skills to be a dominating center, but his lackadaisical attitude has given coaches fits. He's getting better but still has a ways to go. King has fine all-around tools and should eventually develop into a solid NBA center.

Coaching: Jones, one of the most revered coaches in the league, has an NBA championship ring for all ten fingers. He won eight world titles as a player with Boston and coached the Celtics to two more. In nine NBA seasons as a coach, he has never had a losing record. If he's given the talent, he will win in Seattle. He is assisted by Bob Kloppenburg, Kip Motta, and Gary Wortman.

Analysis: Seattle certainly has the potential to be a winning ballclub. Quarterback Payton will surely be better in his sophomore year, while the young Kemp continues to grow by leaps and bounds. The rest of the guards and forwards are proven NBA talents. If Benjamin can bear down and play up to his capacity, then this could be a heck of club. But that, of course, is a big "if."

Prediction: 4th Place, Pacific

NBA Awards and Records

This section showcases the NBA's champions, award-winners, and record-setters. Here is a breakdown of what you'll find:

- NBA champions

- Most Valuable Players
- Rookies of the Year
- NBA Finals MVPs
- Coaches of the Year
- Defensive Players of the Year
- Sixth Man Award winners

- All-NBA Teams
- All-Rookie Teams
- All-Defensive Teams

- All-Star Game results

- career leaders
- active career leaders
- regular-season records
- game records
- team records
- playoff records—career
- playoff records—series
- playoff records—game
- playoff records—team

WORLD CHAMPIONS

	CHAMPION	FINALIST	RESULT		CHAMPION	FINALIST	RESULT
1946-47	Philadelphia	Chicago	4-1	1969-70	New York	Los Angeles	4-3
1947-48	Baltimore	Philadelphia	4-2	1970-71	Milwaukee	Baltimore	4-0
1948-49	Minneapolis	Washington	4-2	1971-72	Los Angeles	New York	4-1
1949-50	Minneapolis	Syracuse	4-2	1972-73	New York	Los Angeles	4-1
1950-51	Rochester	New York	4-3	1973-74	Boston	Milwaukee	4-3
1951-52	Minneapolis	New York	4-3	1974-75	Golden State	Washington	4-0
1952-53	Minneapolis	New York	4-1	1975-76	Boston	Phoenix	4-2
1953-54	Minneapolis	Syracuse	4-3	1976-77	Portland	Philadelphia	4-2
1954-55	Syracuse	Fort Wayne	4-3	1977-78	Washington	Seattle	4-3
1955-56	Philadelphia	Fort Wayne	4-1	1978-79	Seattle	Washington	4-1
1956-57	Boston	St. Louis	4-3	1979-80	Los Angeles	Philadelphia	4-2
1957-58	St. Louis	Boston	4-2	1980-81	Boston	Houston	4-2
1958-59	Boston	Minneapolis	4-0	1981-82	Los Angeles	Philadelphia	4-2
1959-60	Boston	St. Louis	4-3	1982-83	Philadelphia	Los Angeles	4-0
1960-61	Boston	St. Louis	4-1	1983-84	Boston	Los Angeles	4-3
1961-62	Boston	Los Angeles	4-3	1984-85	L.A. Lakers	Boston	4-2
1962-63	Boston	Los Angeles	4-2	1985-86	Boston	Houston	4-2
1963-64	Boston	San Francisco	4-1	1986-87	L.A. Lakers	Boston	4-2
1964-65	Boston	Los Angeles	4-1	1987-88	L.A. Lakers	Detroit	4-3
1965-66	Boston	Los Angeles	4-3	1988-89	Detroit	L.A. Lakers	4-0
1966-67	Philadelphia	San Francisco	4-2	1989-90	Detroit	Portland	4-1
1967-68	Boston	Los Angeles	4-2	1990-91	Chicago	L.A. Lakers	4-1
1968-69	Boston	Los Angeles	4-3				

MOST VALUABLE PLAYERS

	PLAYER	PPG		PLAYER	PPG
1955-56	Bob Pettit, St. Louis	25.7	1973-74	Kareem Abdul-Jabbar, Mil.	27.0
1956-57	Bob Cousy, Boston	20.6	1974-75	Bob McAdoo, Buffalo	34.5
1957-58	Bill Russell, Boston	16.6	1975-76	Kareem Abdul-Jabbar, L.A.	27.7
1958-59	Bob Pettit, St. Louis	29.2	1976-77	Kareem Abdul-Jabbar, L.A.	26.2
1959-60	Wilt Chamberlain, Phil.	37.6	1977-78	Bill Walton, Portland	18.9
1960-61	Bill Russell, Boston	16.9	1978-79	Moses Malone, Houston	24.8
1961-62	Bill Russell, Boston	18.9	1979-80	Kareem Abdul-Jabbar, L.A.	24.8
1962-63	Bill Russell, Boston	16.8	1980-81	Julius Erving, Philadelphia	24.6
1963-64	Oscar Robertson, Cincinnati	31.4	1981-82	Moses Malone, Houston	31.1
1964-65	Bill Russell, Boston	14.1	1982-83	Moses Malone, Philadelphia	24.5
1965-66	Wilt Chamberlain, Phil.	33.5	1983-84	Larry Bird, Boston	24.2
1966-67	Wilt Chamberlain, Phil.	24.1	1984-85	Larry Bird, Boston	28.7
1967-68	Wilt Chamberlain, Phil.	24.3	1985-86	Larry Bird, Boston	25.8
1968-69	Wes Unseld, Baltimore	.13.8	1986-87	Magic Johnson, L.A. Lakers	23.9
1969-70	Willis Reed, New York	21.7	1987-88	Michael Jordan, Chicago	35.0
1970-71	Lew Alcindor, Milwaukee	31.7	1988-89	Magic Johnson, L.A. Lakers	22.5
1971-72	Kareem Abdul-Jabbar, Mil.	34.8	1989-90	Magic Johnson, L.A. Lakers	22.3
1972-73	Dave Cowens, Boston	20.5	1990-91	Michael Jordan, Chicago	31.5

ROOKIES OF THE YEAR

1952-53	Don Meineke, Fort Wayne	1971-72	Sidney Wicks, Portland
1953-54	Ray Felix, Baltimore	1972-73	Bob McAdoo, Buffalo
1954-55	Bob Pettit, Milwaukee	1973-74	Ernie DiGregorio, Buffalo
1955-56	Maurice Stokes, Rochester	1974-75	Keith Wilkes, Golden State
1956-57	Tom Heinsohn, Boston	1975-76	Alvan Adams, Phoenix
1957-58	Woody Sauldsberry, Philadelphia	1976-77	Adrian Dantley, Buffalo
1958-59	Elgin Baylor, Minneapolis	1977-78	Walter Davis, Phoenix
1959-60	Wilt Chamberlain, Philadelphia	1978-79	Phil Ford, Kansas City
1960-61	Oscar Robertson, Cincinnati	1979-80	Larry Bird, Boston
1961-62	Walt Bellamy, Chicago	1980-81	Darrell Griffith, Utah
1962-63	Terry Dischinger, Chicago	1981-82	Buck Williams, New Jersey
1963-64	Jerry Lucas, Cincinnati	1982-83	Terry Cummings, San Diego
1964-65	Willis Reed, New York	1983-84	Ralph Sampson, Houston
1965-66	Rick Barry, San Francisco	1984-85	Michael Jordan, Chicago
1966-67	Dave Bing, Detroit	1985-86	Patrick Ewing, New York
1967-68	Earl Monroe, Baltimore	1986-87	Chuck Person, Indiana
1968-69	Wes Unseld, Baltimore	1987-88	Mark Jackson, New York
1969-70	Lew Alcindor, Milwaukee	1988-89	Mitch Richmond, Golden State
1970-71	Dave Cowens, Boston	1989-90	David Robinson, San Antonio
	Geoff Petrie, Portland	1990-91	Derrick Coleman, New Jersey

NBA FINALS MVPS

1969	Jerry West, Los Angeles	1981	Cedric Maxwell, Boston
1970	Willis Reed, New York	1982	Magic Johnson, Los Angeles
1971	Lew Alcindor, Milwaukee	1983	Moses Malone, Philadelphia
1972	Wilt Chamberlain, Los Angeles	1984	Larry Bird, Boston
1973	Willis Reed, New York	1985	Kareem Abdul-Jabbar, L.A. Lakers
1974	John Havlicek, Boston	1986	Larry Bird, Boston
1975	Rick Barry, Golden State	1987	Magic Johnson, L.A. Lakers
1976	Jo Jo White, Boston	1988	James Worthy, L.A. Lakers
1977	Bill Walton, Portland	1989	Joe Dumars, Detroit
1978	Wes Unseld, Washington	1990	Isiah Thomas, Detroit
1979	Dennis Johnson, Seattle	1991	Michael Jordan, Chicago
1980	Magic Johnson, Los Angeles		

DEFENSIVE PLAYERS OF THE YEAR

1982-83	Sidney Moncrief, Milwaukee	1987-88	Michael Jordan, Chicago
1983-84	Sidney Moncrief, Milwaukee	1988-89	Mark Eaton, Utah
1984-85	Mark Eaton, Utah	1989-90	Dennis Rodman, Detroit
1985-86	Alvin Robertson, San Antonio	1990-91	Dennis Rodman, Detroit
1986-87	Michael Cooper, L.A. Lakers		

SIXTH MAN AWARD WINNERS

1982-83	Bobby Jones, Philadelphia	1987-88	Roy Tarpley, Dallas
1983-84	Kevin McHale, Boston	1988-89	Eddie Johnson, Phoenix
1984-85	Kevin McHale, Boston	1989-90	Ricky Pierce, Milwaukee
1985-86	Bill Walton, Boston	1990-91	Detlef Schrempf, Milwaukee
1986-87	Ricky Pierce, Milwaukee		

COACHES OF THE YEAR

1962-63	Harry Gallatin, St. Louis	1977-78	Hubie Brown, Atlanta
1963-64	Alex Hannum, San Francisco	1978-79	Cotton Fitzsimmons, Kansas City
1964-65	Red Auerbach, Boston	1979-80	Bill Fitch, Boston
1965-66	Dolph Schayes, Philadelphia	1980-81	Jack McKinney, Indiana
1966-67	Johnny Kerr, Chicago	1981-82	Gene Shue, Washington
1967-68	Richie Guerin, St. Louis	1982-83	Don Nelson, Milwaukee
1968-69	Gene Shue, Baltimore	1983-84	Frank Layden, Utah
1969-70	Red Holzman, New York	1984-85	Don Nelson, Milwaukee
1970-71	Dick Motta, Chicago	1985-86	Mike Fratello, Atlanta
1971-72	Bill Sharman, Los Angeles	1986-87	Mike Schuler, Portland
1972-73	Tom Heinsohn, Boston	1987-88	Doug Moe, Denver
1973-74	Ray Scott, Detroit	1988-89	Cotton Fitzsimmons, Phoenix
1974-75	Phil Johnson, K.C.-Omaha	1989-90	Pat Riley, L.A. Lakers
1975-76	Bill Fitch, Cleveland	1990-91	Don Chaney, Houston
1976-77	Tom Nissalke, Houston		

ALL-NBA TEAMS

1946-47
Joe Fulks, Philadelphia
Bob Feerick, Washington
Stan Miasek, Detroit
Bones McKinney, Washington
Max Zaslofsky, Chicago

1947-48
Joe Fulks, Philadelphia
Max Zaslofsky, Chicago
Ed Sadowski, Boston
Howie Dallmar, Philadelphia
Bob Feerick, Washington

1948-49
George Mikan, Minneapolis
Joe Fulks, Philadelphia
Bob Davies, Rochester
Max Zaslofsky, Chicago
Jim Pollard, Minneapolis

1949-50
George Mikan, Minneapolis
Jim Pollard, Minneapolis
Alex Groza, Indianapolis
Bob Davies, Rochester
Max Zaslofsky, Chicago

1950-51
George Mikan, Minneapolis
Alex Groza, Indianapolis
Ed Macauley, Boston
Bob Davies, Rochester
Ralph Beard, Indianapolis

1951-52
George Mikan, Minneapolis
Ed Macauley, Boston
Paul Arizin, Philadelphia
Bob Cousy, Boston
Bob Davies, Rochester
Dolph Schayes, Syracuse

1952-53
George Mikan, Minneapolis
Bob Cousy, Boston
Neil Johnston, Philadelphia
Ed Macauley, Boston
Dolph Schayes, Syracuse

1953-54
Bob Cousy, Boston
Neil Johnston, Philadelphia
George Mikan, Minneapolis
Dolph Schayes, Syracuse
Harry Gallatin, New York

1954-55
Neil Johnston, Philadelphia
Bob Cousy, Boston
Dolph Schayes, Syracuse
Bob Pettit, Milwaukee
Larry Foust, Fort Wayne

1955-56
Bob Pettit, St. Louis
Paul Arizin, Philadelphia
Neil Johnston, Philadelphia
Bob Cousy, Boston
Bill Sharman, Boston

1956-57
Paul Arizin, Philadelphia
Dolph Schayes, Syracuse
Bob Pettit, St. Louis
Bob Cousy, Boston
Bill Sharman, Boston

1957-58
Dolph Schayes, Syracuse
George Yardley, Detroit
Bob Pettit, St. Louis
Bob Cousy, Boston
Bill Sharman, Boston

1958-59
Bob Pettit, St. Louis
Elgin Baylor, Minneapolis
Bill Russell, Boston
Bob Cousy, Boston
Bill Sharman, Boston

1959-60
Bob Pettit, St. Louis
Elgin Baylor, Minneapolis
Wilt Chamberlain, Philadelphia
Bob Cousy, Boston
Gene Shue, Detroit

1960-61
Elgin Baylor, Los Angeles
Bob Pettit, St. Louis
Wilt Chamberlain, Philadelphia
Bob Cousy, Boston
Oscar Robertson, Cincinnati

1961-62
Bob Pettit, St. Louis
Elgin Baylor, Los Angeles
Wilt Chamberlain, Philadelphia
Jerry West, Los Angeles
Oscar Robertson, Cincinnati

1962-63
Elgin Baylor, Los Angeles
Bob Pettit, St. Louis
Bill Russell, Boston
Oscar Robertson, Cincinnati
Jerry West, Los Angeles

1963-64
Bob Pettit, St. Louis
Elgin Baylor, Los Angeles

Wilt Chamberlain, San Francisco
Oscar Robertson, Cincinnati
Jerry West, Los Angeles

1964-65
Elgin Baylor, Los Angeles
Jerry Lucas, Cincinnati
Bill Russell, Boston
Oscar Robertson, Cincinnati
Jerry West, Los Angeles

1965-66
Rick Barry, San Francisco
Jerry Lucas, Cincinnati
Wilt Chamberlain, Philadelphia
Oscar Robertson, Cincinnati
Jerry West, Los Angeles

1966-67
Rick Barry, San Francisco
Elgin Baylor, Los Angeles
Wilt Chamberlain, Philadelphia
Jerry West, Los Angeles
Oscar Robertson, Cincinnati

1967-68
Elgin Baylor, Los Angeles
Jerry Lucas, Cincinnati
Wilt Chamberlain, Philadelphia
Dave Bing, Detroit
Oscar Robertson, Cincinnati

1968-69
Billy Cunningham, Philadelphia
Elgin Baylor, Los Angeles
Wes Unseld, Baltimore
Earl Monroe, Baltimore
Oscar Robertson, Cincinnati

1969-70
Billy Cunningham, Philadelphia
Connie Hawkins, Phoenix
Willis Reed, New York
Jerry West, Los Angeles
Walt Frazier, New York

1970-71
John Havlicek, Boston
Billy Cunningham, Philadelphia
Lew Alcindor, Milwaukee
Jerry West, Los Angeles
Dave Bing, Detroit

1971-72
John Havlicek, Boston
Spencer Haywood, Seattle
Kareem Abdul-Jabbar, Milwaukee
Jerry West, Los Angeles
Walt Frazier, New York

1972-73
John Havlicek, Boston
Spencer Haywood, Seattle
Kareem Abdul-Jabbar, Milwaukee
Nate Archibald, K.C.-Omaha
Jerry West, Los Angeles

1973-74
John Havlicek, Boston
Rick Barry, Golden State
Kareem Abdul-Jabbar, Milwaukee
Walt Frazier, New York
Gail Goodrich, Los Angeles

1974-75
Rick Barry, Golden State
Elvin Hayes, Washington
Bob McAdoo, Buffalo
Nate Archibald, K.C.-Omaha
Walt Frazier, New York

1975-76
Rick Barry, Golden State
George McGinnis, Philadelphia
Kareem Abdul-Jabbar, Los Angeles
Nate Archibald, Kansas City
Pete Maravich, New Orleans

1976-77
Elvin Hayes, Washington
David Thompson, Denver
Kareem Abdul-Jabbar, Los Angeles
Pete Maravich, New Orleans
Paul Westphal, Phoenix

1977-78
Truck Robinson, New Orleans
Julius Erving, Philadelphia
Bill Walton, Portland
George Gervin, San Antonio
David Thompson, Denver

1978-79
Marques Johnson, Milwaukee
Elvin Hayes, Washington
Moses Malone, Houston

George Gervin, San Antonio
Paul Westphal, Phoenix

1979-80
Julius Erving, Philadelphia
Larry Bird, Boston
Kareem Abdul-Jabbar, Los Angeles
George Gervin, San Antonio
Paul Westphal, Phoenix

1980-81
Julius Erving, Philadelphia
Larry Bird, Boston
Kareem Abdul-Jabbar, Los Angeles
George Gervin, San Antonio
Dennis Johnson, Phoenix

1981-82
Larry Bird, Boston
Julius Erving, Philadelphia
Moses Malone, Houston
George Gervin, San Antonio
Gus Williams, Seattle

1982-83
Larry Bird, Boston
Julius Erving, Philadelphia
Moses Malone, Philadelphia
Magic Johnson, Los Angeles
Sidney Moncrief, Milwaukee

1983-84
Larry Bird, Boston
Bernard King, New York
Kareem Abdul-Jabbar, Los Angeles
Magic Johnson, Los Angeles
Isiah Thomas, Detroit

1984-85
Larry Bird, Boston
Bernard King, New York
Moses Malone, Philadelphia
Magic Johnson, L.A. Lakers
Isiah Thomas, Detroit

1985-86
Larry Bird, Boston
Dominique Wilkins, Atlanta
Kareem Abdul-Jabbar, L.A. Lakers
Magic Johnson, L.A. Lakers
Isiah Thomas, Detroit

1986-87
Larry Bird, Boston
Kevin McHale, Boston
Akeem Olajuwon, Houston
Magic Johnson, L.A. Lakers
Michael Jordan, Chicago

1987-88
Larry Bird, Boston
Charles Barkley, Philadelphia
Akeem Olajuwon, Houston
Michael Jordan, Chicago
Magic Johnson, L.A. Lakers

1988-89
Karl Malone, Utah
Charles Barkley, Philadelphia
Akeem Olajuwon, Houston
Magic Johnson, L.A. Lakers
Michael Jordan, Chicago

1989-90
Karl Malone, Utah
Charles Barkley, Philadelphia
Patrick Ewing, New York

Magic Johnson, L.A. Lakers
Michael Jordan, Chicago

1990-91
FIRST
Karl Malone, Utah
Charles Barkley, Philadelphia
David Robinson, San Antonio
Michael Jordan, Chicago
Magic Johnson, L.A. Lakers

SECOND
Dominique Wilkins, Atlanta
Chris Mullin, Golden State
Patrick Ewing, New York
Kevin Johnson, Phoenix
Clyde Drexler, Portland

THIRD
James Worthy, L.A. Lakers
Bernard King, Washington
Hakeem Olajuwon, Houston
John Stockton, Utah
Joe Dumars, Detroit

ALL-ROOKIE TEAMS

1962-63
Terry Dischinger, Chicago
Chet Walker, Syracuse
Zelmo Beaty, St. Louis
John Havlicek, Boston
Dave DeBusschere, Detroit

1963-64
Jerry Lucas, Cincinnati
Gus Johnson, Baltimore
Nate Thurmond, San Francisco
Art Heyman, New York
Rod Thorn, Baltimore

1964-65
Willis Reed, New York
Jim Barnes, New York
Howard Komives, New York
Lucious Jackson, Philadelphia
Wally Jones, Baltimore
Joe Caldwell, Detroit

1965-66
Rick Barry, San Francisco
Billy Cunningham, Philadelphia

Tom Van Arsdale, Detroit
Dick Van Arsdale, New York
Fred Hetzel, San Francisco

1966-67
Lou Hudson, St. Louis
Jack Marin, Baltimore
Erwin Mueller, Chicago
Cazzie Russell, New York
Dave Bing, Detroit

1967-68
Earl Monroe, Baltimore
Bob Rule, Seattle
Walt Frazier, New York
Al Tucker, Seattle
Phil Jackson, New York

1968-69
Wes Unseld, Baltimore
Elvin Hayes, San Diego
Bill Hewitt, Los Angeles
Art Harris, Seattle
Gary Gregor, Phoenix

1969-70
Lew Alcindor, Milwaukee
Bob Dandridge, Milwaukee
Jo Jo White, Boston
Mike Davis, Baltimore
Dick Garrett, Los Angeles

1970-71
Geoff Petrie, Portland
Dave Cowens, Boston
Pete Maravich, Atlanta
Calvin Murphy, San Diego
Bob Lanier, Detroit

1971-72
Elmore Smith, Buffalo
Sidney Wicks, Portland
Austin Carr, Cleveland
Phil Chenier, Baltimore
Clifford Ray, Chicago

1972-73
Bob McAdoo, Buffalo
Lloyd Neal, Portland
Fred Boyd, Philadelphia
Dwight Davis, Cleveland
Jim Price, Los Angeles

1973-74
Ernie DiGregorio, Buffalo
Ron Behagen, K.C.-Omaha
Mike Bantom, Phoenix
John Brown, Atlanta
Nick Weatherspoon, Capital

1974-75
Keith Wilkes, Golden State
John Drew, Atlanta
Scott Wedman, K.C.-Omaha
Tom Burleson, Seattle
Brian Winters, Los Angeles

1975-76
Alvan Adams, Phoenix
Gus Williams, Golden State
Joe Meriweather, Houston
John Shumate, Phoe./Buff.
Lionel Hollins, Portland

1976-77
Adrian Dantley, Buffalo
Scott May, Chicago
Mitch Kupchak, Washington

John Lucas, Houston
Ron Lee, Phoenix

1977-78
Walter Davis, Phoenix
Marques Johnson, Milwaukee
Bernard King, New Jersey
Jack Sikma, Seattle
Norm Nixon, Los Angeles

1978-79
Phil Ford, Kansas City
Mychal Thompson, Portland
Ron Brewer, Portland
Reggie Theus, Chicago
Terry Tyler, Detroit

1979-80
Larry Bird, Boston
Magic Johnson, Los Angeles
Bill Cartwright, New York
Calvin Natt, Portland
David Greenwood, Chicago

1980-81
Joe Barry Carroll, Golden State
Darrell Griffith, Utah
Larry Smith, Golden State
Kevin McHale, Boston
Kelvin Ransey, Portland

1981-82
Kelly Tripucka, Detroit
Jay Vincent, Dallas
Isiah Thomas, Detroit
Buck Williams, New Jersey
Jeff Ruland, Washington

1982-83
Terry Cummings, San Diego
Clark Kellogg, Indiana
Dominique Wilkins, Atlanta
James Worthy, Los Angeles
Quintin Dailey, Chicago

1983-84
Ralph Sampson, Houston
Steve Stipanovich, Indiana
Byron Scott, Los Angeles
Jeff Malone, Washington
Thurl Bailey, Utah
Darrell Walker, New York

1984-85
Michael Jordan, Chicago
Akeem Olajuwon, Houston
Sam Bowie, Portland
Charles Barkley, Philadelphia
Sam Perkins, Dallas

1985-86
Xavier McDaniel, Seattle
Patrick Ewing, New York
Karl Malone, Utah
Joe Dumars, Detroit
Charles Oakley, Chicago

1986-87
Brad Daugherty, Cleveland
Ron Harper, Cleveland
Chuck Person, Indiana
Roy Tarpley, Dallas
John Williams, Cleveland

1987-88
Mark Jackson, New York
Armon Gilliam, Phoenix
Kenny Smith, Sacramento
Greg Anderson, San Antonio
Derrick McKey, Seattle

1988-89
Mitch Richmond, Golden State
Willie Anderson, San Antonio
Hersey Hawkins, Philadelphia
Rik Smits, Indiana
Charles Smith, L.A. Clippers

1989-90
David Robinson, San Antonio
Tim Hardaway, Golden State
Vlade Divac, L.A. Lakers
Sherman Douglas, Miami
Pooh Richardson, Minnesota

1990-91
Derrick Coleman, New Jersey
Lionel Simmons, Sacramento
Dee Brown, Boston
Kendall Gill, Charlotte
Dennis Scott, Orlando

SECOND
Felton Spencer, Minnesota
Willie Burton, Miami
Travis Mays, Sacramento
Gary Payton, Seattle
Chris Jackson, Denver

ALL-DEFENSIVE TEAMS

1968-69
Dave DeBusschere, New York
Nate Thurmond, San Francisco
Bill Russell, Boston
Walt Frazier, New York
Jerry Sloan, Chicago

1969-70
Dave DeBusschere, New York
Gus Johnson, Baltimore
Willis Reed, New York
Walt Frazier, New York
Jerry West, Los Angeles

1970-71
Dave DeBusschere, New York
Gus Johnson, Baltimore
Nate Thurmond, San Francisco
Walt Frazier, New York
Jerry West, Los Angeles

1971-72
Dave DeBusschere, New York
John Havlicek, Boston
Wilt Chamberlain, Los Angeles
Jerry West, Los Angeles
Walt Frazier, New York
Jerry Sloan, Chicago

1972-73
Dave DeBusschere, New York
John Havlicek, Boston
Wilt Chamberlain, Los Angeles
Jerry West, Los Angeles
Walt Frazier, New York

1973-74
Dave DeBusschere, New York
John Havlicek, Boston
Kareem Abdul-Jabbar, Milwaukee
Norm Van Lier, Chicago
Walt Frazier, New York
Jerry Sloan, Chicago

1974-75
John Havlicek, Boston
Paul Silas, Boston
Kareem Abdul-Jabbar, Milwaukee
Jerry Sloan, Chicago
Walt Frazier, New York

1975-76
Paul Silas, Boston
John Havlicek, Boston
Dave Cowens, Boston
Norm Van Lier, Chicago
Don Watts, Seattle

1976-77
Bobby Jones, Denver
E.C. Coleman, New Orleans
Bill Walton, Portland
Don Buse, Indiana
Norm Van Lier, Chicago

1977-78
Bobby Jones, Denver
Maurice Lucas, Portland
Bill Walton, Portland
Lionel Hollins, Portland
Don Buse, Phoenix

1978-79
Bobby Jones, Philadelphia
Bobby Dandridge, Washington
Kareem Abdul-Jabbar, Los Angeles
Dennis Johnson, Seattle
Don Buse, Phoenix

1979-80
Bobby Jones, Philadelphia
Dan Roundfield, Atlanta
Kareem Abdul-Jabbar, Los Angeles
Dennis Johnson, Seattle
Don Buse, Phoenix
Michael Ray Richardson, New York

1980-81
Bobby Jones, Philadelphia
Caldwell Jones, Philadelphia
Kareem Abdul-Jabbar, Los Angeles
Dennis Johnson, Phoenix
Michael Ray Richardson, New York

1981-82
Bobby Jones, Philadelphia
Dan Roundfield, Atlanta

Caldwell Jones, Philadelphia
Michael Cooper, Los Angeles
Dennis Johnson, Phoenix

1982-83
Bobby Jones, Philadelphia
Dan Roundfield, Atlanta
Moses Malone, Philadelphia
Sidney Moncrief, Milwaukee
Dennis Johnson, Phoenix
Maurice Cheeks, Philadelphia

1983-84
Bobby Jones, Philadelphia
Michael Cooper, Los Angeles
Tree Rollins, Atlanta
Maurice Cheeks, Philadelphia
Sidney Moncrief, Milwaukee

1984-85
Sidney Moncrief, Milwaukee
Paul Pressey, Milwaukee
Mark Eaton, Utah
Michael Cooper, L.A. Lakers
Maurice Cheeks, Philadelphia

1985-86
Paul Pressey, Milwaukee
Kevin McHale, Boston
Mark Eaton, Utah
Sidney Moncrief, Milwaukee
Maurice Cheeks, Philadelphia

1986-87
Kevin McHale, Boston
Michael Cooper, L.A. Lakers
Akeem Olajuwon, Houston
Alvin Robertson, San Antonio
Dennis Johnson, Boston

1987-88
Kevin McHale, Boston
Rodney McCray, Houston
Akeem Olajuwon, Houston
Michael Cooper, L.A. Lakers
Michael Jordan, Chicago

1988-89
Dennis Rodman, Detroit
Larry Nance, Cleveland
Mark Eaton, Utah
Michael Jordan, Chicago
Joe Dumars, Detroit

1989-90
Dennis Rodman, Detroit
Buck Williams, Portland
Akeem Olajuwon, Houston
Michael Jordan, Chicago
Joe Dumars, Detroit

1990-91
Dennis Rodman, Detroit
Buck Williams, Portland

David Robinson, San Antonio
Michael Jordan, Chicago
Alvin Robertson, Milwaukee

SECOND
Scottie Pippen, Chicago
Dan Majerle, Phoenix
Hakeem Olajuwon, Houston
Joe Dumars, Detroit
John Stockton, Utah

ALL-STAR GAMES

	RESULT	SITE	MVP
1950-51	East 111, West 94	Boston	Ed Macauley, Boston
1951-52	East 108, West 91	Boston	Paul Arizin, Philadelphia
1952-53	West 79, East 75	Fort Wayne	George Mikan, Minneapolis
1953-54	East 98, West 93 (OT)	New York	Bob Cousy, Boston
1954-55	East 100, West 91	New York	Bill Sharman, Boston
1955-56	West 108, East 94	Rochester	Bob Pettit, St. Louis
1956-57	East 109, West 97	Boston	Bob Cousy, Boston
1957-58	East 130, West 118	St. Louis	Bob Pettit, St. Louis
1958-59	West 124, East 108	Detroit	E. Baylor, Minn./B. Pettit,St. L.
1959-60	East 125, West 115	Philadelphia	Wilt Chamberlain, Philadelphia
1960-61	West 153, East 131	Syracuse	Oscar Robertson, Cincinnati
1961-62	West 150, East 130	St. Louis	Bob Pettit, St. Louis
1962-63	East 115, West 108	Los Angeles	Bill Russell, Boston
1963-64	East 111, West 107	Boston	Oscar Robertson, Cincinnati
1964-65	East 124, West 123	St. Louis	Jerry Lucas, Cincinnati
1965-66	East 137, West 94	Cincinnati	Adrian Smith, Cincinnati
1966-67	West 135, East 120	San Francisco	Rick Barry, San Francisco
1967-68	East 144, West 124	New York	Hal Greer, Philadelphia
1968-69	East 123, West 112	Baltimore	Oscar Robertson, Cincinnati
1969-70	East 142, West 135	Philadelphia	Willis Reed, New York
1970-71	West 108, East 107	San Diego	Lenny Wilkens, Seattle
1971-72	West 112, East 110	Los Angeles	Jerry West, Los Angeles
1972-73	East 104, West 84	Chicago	Dave Cowens, Boston
1973-74	West 134, East 123	Seattle	Bob Lanier, Detroit
1974-75	East 108, West 102	Phoenix	Walt Frazier, New York
1975-76	East 123, West 109	Philadelphia	Dave Bing, Washington
1976-77	West 125, East 124	Milwaukee	Julius Erving, Philadelphia
1977-78	East 133, West 125	Atlanta	Randy Smith, Buffalo
1978-79	West 134, East 129	Detroit	David Thompson, Denver
1979-80	East 144, West 135 (OT)	Washington	George Gervin, San Antonio
1980-81	East 123, West 120	Cleveland	Nate Archibald, Boston
1981-82	East 120, West 118	E. Rutherford	Larry Bird, Boston
1982-83	East 132, West 123	Los Angeles	Julius Erving, Philadelphia
1983-84	East 154, West 145 (OT)	Denver	Isiah Thomas, Detroit
1984-85	West 140, East 129	Indianapolis	Ralph Sampson, Houston
1985-86	East 139, West 132	Dallas	Isiah Thomas, Detroit
1986-87	West 154, East 149 (OT)	Seattle	Tom Chambers, Seattle
1987-88	East 138, West 133	Chicago	Michael Jordan, Chicago
1988-89	West 143, East 134	Houston	Karl Malone, Utah
1989-90	East 130, West 113	Miami	Magic Johnson, L.A. Lakers
1990-91	East 116, West 114	Charlotte	Charles Barkley, Philadelphia

CAREER LEADERS

(Players active at the close of 1990-91
are listed in bold)

POINTS

Kareem Abdul-Jabbar	38,387
Wilt Chamberlain	31,419
Elvin Hayes	27,313
Oscar Robertson	26,710
John Havlicek	26,395
Moses Malone	**25,737**
Alex English	**25,613**
Jerry West	25,192
Adrian Dantley	**23,177**
Elgin Baylor	23,149
Hal Greer	21,586
Walt Bellamy	20,941
Larry Bird	**20,883**
Bob Pettit	20,880
George Gervin	20,708
Robert Parish	**19,519**
Bernard King	**19,432**
Dolph Schayes	19,249
Bob Lanier	19,248
Gail Goodrich	19,181

GAMES

Kareem Abdul-Jabbar	1,560
Elvin Hayes	1,303
John Havlicek	1,270
Paul Silas	1,254
Alex English	**1,193**
Robert Parish	**1,181**
Moses Malone	**1,164**
Hal Greer	1,122
Jack Sikma	**1,107**
Dennis Johnson	1,100
Lenny Wilkens	1,077

MINUTES

Kareem Abdul-Jabbar	57,446
Elvin Hayes	50,000
Wilt Chamberlain	47,859
John Havlicek	46,471
Oscar Robertson	43,886
Moses Malone	**41,689**
Rill Russell	40,726
Hal Greer	39,788
Walt Bellamy	38,940
Lenny Wilkens	38,064

SCORING AVERAGE

(Minimum 400 Games or 10,000 Points)

Michael Jordan	**32.6**
Wilt Chamberlain	30.1
Elgin Baylor	27.4
Jerry West	27.0
Bob Pettit	26.4
George Gervin	26.2
Dominique Wilkins	**26.1**
Oscar Robinson	25.7
Karl Malone	**25.6**
Kareem Abdul-Jabbar	24.6

REBOUNDS

Wilt Chamberlain	23,924
Bill Russell	21,620
Kareem Abdul-Jabbar	17,440
Elvin Hayes	16,279
Moses Malone	**15,150**
Nate Thurmond	14,464
Walt Bellamy	14,241
Wes Unseld	13,769
Jerry Lucas	12,942
Bob Pettit	12,849

ASSISTS

Magic Johnson	**9,921**
Oscar Robertson	9,887
Isiah Thomas	**7,431**
Lenny Wilkens	7,211
Maurice Cheeks	**7,100**
Bob Cousy	6,955
Guy Rodgers	6,917
Nate Archibald	6,476
John Lucas	6,454
Reggie Theus	**6,453**

STEALS

Maurice Cheeks	**2,194**
Magic Johnson	**1,698**
Gus Williams	1,638
Alvin Robertson	**1,581**
Isiah Thomas	**1,552**
Larry Bird	**1,514**
Julius Erving	1,508
Dennis Johnson	1,477
Michael Richardson	1,463
Lafayette Lever	**1,461**
Randy Smith	1,403

BLOCKED SHOTS

Kareem Abdul-Jabbar	3,189
Mark Eaton	**2,780**
Tree Rollins	**2,394**
George T. Johnson	2,082
Robert Parish	**1,952**
Hakeem Olajuwon	**1,798**
Elvin Hayes	1,771
Artis Gilmore	1,747
Manute Bol	**1,737**
Moses Malone	**1,641**

PERSONAL FOULS

Kareem Abdul-Jabbar	4,657
Elvin Hayes	4,193
Jack Sikma	**3,879**
Hal Greer	3,855
Dolph Schayes	3,664
Robert Parish	**3,628**
Walt Bellamy	3,536
Caldwell Jones	3,527
Bailey Howell	3,498
James Edwards	**3,489**

DISQUALIFICATIONS

Vern Mikkelsen	127
Walter Dukes	121
Charlie Share	105
Paul Arizin	101
Darryl Dawkins	100
James Edwards	**94**
Tom Gola	94
Tom Sanders	94
Steve Johnson	92
Tree Rollins	**91**

FIELD GOALS ATTEMPTED

Kareem Abdul-Jabbar	28,307
Elvin Hayes	24,272
John Havlicek	23,930
Wilt Chamberlain	23,497
Alex English	**21,036**
Elgin Baylor	20,171
Oscar Robertson	19,620
Jerry West	19,032
Hal Greer	18,811
Moses Malone	**17,987**

FIELD GOALS MADE

Kareem Abdul-Jabbar	15,837
Wilt Chamberlain	12,681
Elvin Hayes	10,976
Alex English	**10,659**
John Havlicek	10,513

Oscar Robertson	9,508
Jerry West	9,016
Moses Malone	**8,867**
Elgin Baylor	8,693
Hal Greer	8,504

FIELD GOAL PCT.
(Minimum 2,000 FGM)

Artis Gilmore	599
Charles Barkley	**580**
James Donaldson	**576**
Steve Johnson	572
Darryl Dawkins	572
Jeff Ruland	564
Kevin McHale	**562**
Kareem Abdul-Jabbar	559
Buck Williams	**554**
Larry Nance	**549**

FREE THROWS ATTEMPTED

Wilt Chamberlain	11,862
Moses Malone	**10,406**
Kareem Abdul-Jabbar	9,304
Oscar Robertson	9,185
Jerry West	8,801
Adrian Dantley	**8,351**
Dolph Schayes	8,273
Bob Pettit	8,119
Walt Bellamy	8,088
Elvin Hayes	7,999

FREE THROWS MADE

Moses Malone	**7,999**
Oscar Robertson	7,694
Jerry West	7,160
Dolph Schayes	6,979
Adrian Dantley	**6,832**
Kareem Abdul-Jabbar	6,712
Bob Pettit	6,182
Wilt Chamberlain	6,057
Elgin Baylor	5,763
Lenny Wilkens	5,394

FREE THROW PCT.
(Minimum 1,200 FTM)

Rick Barry	900
Calvin Murphy	892
Larry Bird	**884**
Bill Sharman	883
Chris Mullin	**880**
Jeff Malone	**874**
Reggie Miller	**873**
Kiki Vandeweghe	**873**
Mike Newlin	870

3-PT. FIELD GOALS ATTEMPTED
Michael Adams	1,946
Larry Bird	1,599
Darrell Griffith	1,596
Danny Ainge	1,591
Dale Ellis	1,562
Craig Hodges	1,312
Derek Harper	1,306
Sleepy Floyd	1,296
Michael Cooper	1,260
Trent Tucker	1,231

3-PT. FIELD GOALS MADE
Michael Adams	658
Dale Ellis	625
Danny Ainge	616
Larry Bird	597
Darrell Griffith	530
Craig Hodges	527
Trent Tucker	504
Derek Harper	449
Sleepy Floyd	432
Michael Cooper	428

3-PT. FIELD GOAL PCT.
(Minimum 100 made)
Steve Kerr	489
Mark Price	418
Hersey Hawkins	414
Trent Tucker	409
Craig Hodges	402
Dale Ellis	400
Dana Barros	398
Jon Sundvold	391
Danny Ainge	387
Reggie Miller	383

MOST VICTORIES, COACH
Red Auerbach	938
Jack Ramsay	864
Dick Motta	849
Bill Fitch	805
Gene Shue	784
Lenny Wilkens	758
Cotton Fitzsimmons	752
John MacLeod	707
Red Holzman	696
Don Nelson	664

ACTIVE CAREER LEADERS

(Includes players active at the close
of the 1990-91 season)

POINTS
Moses Malone	25,737
Alex English	25,613
Adrian Dantley	23,177
Larry Bird	20,883
Robert Parish	19,519
Bernard King	19,432
Walter Davis	19,064
Reggie Theus	19,015
Dominique Wilkins	18,796
Jack Sikma	17,287

GAMES
Alex English	1,193
Robert Parish	1,181
Moses Malone	1,164
Jack Sikma	1,107
Reggie Theus	1,026
Maurice Cheeks	1,010
Walter Davis	987
Wayne Cooper	959
Tree Rollins	959
Adrian Dantley	955

MINUTES
Moses Malone	41,689
Alex English	38,063
Jack Sikma	36,943
Robert Parish	36,442
Reggie Theus	34,603
Adrian Dantley	34,151
Maurice Cheeks	33,249
Larry Bird	32,781
Magic Johnson	32,287
Bill Laimbeer	29,541

SCORING AVERAGE
(Minimum 400 Games or 10,000 Points)
Michael Jordan	32.6
Dominique Wilkins	26.1
Karl Malone	25.6
Larry Bird	24.5
Adrian Dantley	24.3
Charles Barkley	23.7
Patrick Ewing	23.6
Hakeem Olajuwon	23.0
Bernard King	22.9
Moses Malone	22.1

REBOUNDS

Moses Malone 15,150
Robert Parish.......................................11,995
Jack Sikma..10,816
Bill Laimbeer...9,474
Buck Williams 9,127
Larry Bird...8,540
Larry Smith 7,601
James Donaldson 7,067
Mychal Thompson 6,951
Hakeem Olajuwon 6,596

ASSISTS

Magic Johnson 9,921
Isiah Thomas 7,431
Maurice Cheeks......................................7,100
Reggie Theus 6,453
John Stockton...6,239
Larry Bird...5,389
Rickey Green..5,153
Brad Davis 4,643
Sleepy Floyd 4,577
Lafayette Lever.......................................4,376

STEALS

Maurice Cheeks......................................2,194
Magic Johnson 1,698
Alvin Robertson 1,581
Isiah Thomas..1,552
Larry Bird...1,514
Lafayette Lever.......................................1,461
Michael Jordan 1,412
Clyde Drexler 1,390
John Stockton...1,389
Rickey Green..1,331

BLOCKED SHOTS

Mark Eaton 2,780
Tree Rollins 2,394
Robert Parish...1,952
Hakeem Olajuwon 1,798
Manute Bol 1,737
Moses Malone 1,641
Kevin McHale 1,572
Larry Nance 1,531
Wayne Cooper 1,508
Patrick Ewing 1,361

PERSONAL FOULS

Jack Sikma 3,879
Robert Parish...3,628
James Edwards 3,489
Bill Laimbeer..3,166
Tree Rollins 3,131

Wayne Cooper..3,087
Alex English...3,027
Reggie Theus 3,008
Rick Mahorn 2,961
Tom Chambers..2,913

DISQUALIFICATIONS

James Edwards 94
Tree Rollins 91
Jack Sikma 80
Robert Parish...78
Rick Mahorn 74
Alton Lister 72
Tom Chambers..69
Bill Laimbeer..59
Danny Schayes 59
Larry Smith 59

FIELD GOALS ATTEMPTED

Alex English...21,036
Moses Malone 17,987
Larry Bird...16,576
Walter Davis 15,468
Dominique Wilkins 15,249
Adrian Dantley 15,121
Reggie Theus 14,973
Bernard King...14,932
Robert Parish..14,791
Jack Sikma...13,792

FIELD GOALS MADE

(Minimum 2,000 FGM)
Alex English...10,659
Moses Malone 8,867
Larry Bird...8,238
Adrian Dantley 8,169
Robert Parish..8,025
Walter Davis 7,933
Bernard King...7,739
Dominique Wilkins 7,157
Reggie Theus 7,057
Mark Aguirre...6,512

FIELD GOAL PCT.

Charles Barkley 580
James Donaldson.......................................576
Kevin McHale 562
Buck Williams 554
Larry Nance 549
Otis Thorpe...548
James Worthy..546
Robert Parish..543
Adrian Dantley 540
Bill Cartwright 535

FREE THROWS ATTEMPTED

Moses Malone	10,406
Adrian Dantley	8,351
Magic Johnson	5,649
Reggie Theus	5,644
Bernard King	5,387
Tom Chambers	5,253
Dominique Wilkins	5,205
Alex English	5,141
Jack Sikma	5,053
Michael Jordan	4,866

FREE THROWS MADE

Moses Malone	7,999
Adrian Dantley	6,832
Magic Johnson	4,788
Reggie Theus	4,663
Jack Sikma	4,292
Alex English	4,277
Tom Chambers	4,232
Dominique Wilkins	4,200
Michael Jordan	4,129
Bernard King	3,933

FREE THROW PCT.
(Minimum 1,200 FTM)

Larry Bird	884
Chris Mullin	880
Jeff Malone	874
Reggie Miller	873
Kiki Vandeweghe	873
Ricky Pierce	866
Danny Ainge	853
Kevin Johnson	852
Walter Davis	850
Jack Sikma	849

3-PT FIELD GOALS ATTEMPTED

Michael Adams	1,946
Larry Bird	1,599
Darrell Griffith	1,596
Danny Ainge	1,591
Dale Ellis	1,562
Craig Hodges	1,312
Derek Harper	1,306
Sleepy Floyd	1,296
Trent Tucker	1,231

3-PT. FIELD GOALS MADE

Michael Adams	658
Dale Ellis	625
Danny Ainge	616
Larry Bird	597
Darrell Griffith	530
Craig Hodges	527
Trent Tucker	504
Derek Harper	449
Sleepy Floyd	432

3-PT. FIELD GOAL PCT.
(Minimum 100 Made)

Steve Kerr	489
Mark Price	418
Hersey Hawkins	414
Trent Tucker	409
Craig Hodges	402
Dale Ellis	400
Dana Barros	398
Jon Sundvold	391
Danny Ainge	387
Reggie Miller	383

MOST VICTORIES, COACH

Dick Motta	849
Bill Fitch	805
Lenny Wilkens	758
Cotton Fitzsimmons	752
Don Nelson	664
K.C. Jones	504
Chuck Daly	428
Larry Brown	349
Kevin Loughery	341
Del Harris	324

REGULAR-SEASON RECORDS

MINUTES
(First Kept in 1951-52)

3,882	Wilt Chamberlain, PHI	1961-62
3,836	Wilt Chamberlain, PHI	1967-68
3,806	Wilt Chamberlain, SF	1962-63
3,773	Wilt Chamberlain, PHI	1960-61
3,737	Wilt Chamberlain, PHI	1965-66
3,698	John Havlicek, BOS	1971-72
3,689	Wilt Chamberlain, SF	1963-64
3,682	Wilt Chamberlain, PHI	1966-67
3,681	Nate Archibald, KCO	1972-73
3,678	John Havlicek, BOS	1970-71

POINTS

4,029	Wilt Chamberlain, PHI	1961-62
3,586	Wilt Chamberlain, SF	1962-63
3,041	Michael Jordan, CHI	1986-87
3,033	Wilt Chamberlain, PHI	1960-61

2,948 ......Wilt Chamberlain, SF...........1963-64
2,868 ......Michael Jordan, CHI 1987-88
2,831 ......Bob McAdoo, BUF...............1974-75
2,822 ......Kareem Abdul-Jabbar, MIL..1971-72
2,775 ......Rick Barry, SF 1966-67
2,753 ......Michael Jordan, CHI 1989-90

SCORING AVERAGE
(Minimum 70 Games or 1400 Points)
50.4 ....Wilt Chamberlain, PHI 1961-62
44.8 ....Wilt Chamberlain, SF............1962-63
38.4 ....Wilt Chamberlain, PHI 1960-61
37.6 ....Wilt Chamberlain, PHI 1959-60
37.1 ....Michael Jordan, CHI 1986-87
36.9 ....Wilt Chamberlain, SF............1963-64
35.6 ....Rick Barry, SF 1966-67
35.0 ....Michael Jordan, CHI 1987-88
34.8 ....Kareem Abdul-Jabbar, MIL..1971-72
34.7 ....Wilt Chamberlain, SF/PHI....1964-65

REBOUNDS
(First Kept in 1950-51)
2,149 ......Wilt Chamberlain, PHI 1960-61
2,052 ......Wilt Chamberlain, PHI 1961-62
1,957 ......Wilt Chamberlain, PHI 1966-67
1,952 ......Wilt Chamberlain, PHI 1967-68
1,946 ......Wilt Chamberlain, SF............1962-63
1,943 ......Wilt Chamberlain, PHI 1965-66
1,941 ......Wilt Chamberlain, PHI 1959-60
1,930 ......Bill Russell, BOS 1963-64
1,878 ......Bill Russell, BOS 1964-65
1,868 ......Bill Russell, BOS 1960-61

ASSISTS
1,164 ......John Stockton, UTA..............1990-91
1,134 ......John Stockton, UTA..............1989-90
1,128 ......John Stockton, UTA..............1987-88
1,123 ......Isiah Thomas, DET...............1984-85
1,118 ......John Stockton, UTA..............1988-89
1,099 ......Kevin Porter, DET................1978-79
991 ....Kevin Johnson, PHO 1988-89
989 ....Magic Johnson, LAL.............1990-91
988 ....Magic Johnson, LAL.............1988-89
977 ....Magic Johnson, LAL.............1986-87

STEALS
(First Kept in 1973-74)
301 ....Alvin Robertson, SA 1985-86
281 ....Don Buse, IND.....................1976-77
265 ....Michael Richardson, NY 1979-80
263 ....John Stockton, UTA..............1988-89
261 ....Slick Watts, SEA..................1975-76
260 ....Alvin Robertson, SA 1986-87

259 ....Michael Jordan, CHI 1987-88
246 ....Alvin Robertson, MIL 1990-91
243 ....Michael Richardson, NJ.......1984-85
243 ....Alvin Robertson, SA 1987-88

BLOCKED SHOTS
(First Kept in 1973-74)
456 ....Mark Eaton, UTA.................1984-85
397 ....Manute Bol, WAS 1985-86
393 ....Elmore Smith, LA 1973-74
376 ....Akeem Olajuwon, HOU 1989-90
369 ....Mark Eaton, UTA.................1985-86
351 ....Mark Eaton, UTA.................1982-83
345 ....Manute Bol, GS 1988-89
343 ....Tree Rollins, ATL.................1982-83
338 ....Kareem Abdul-Jabbar, LA ...1975-76
327 ....Patrick Ewing, NY...............1989-90

PERSONAL FOULS
386 ....Darryl Dawkins, NJ..............1983-84
382 ....Darryl Dawkins, NJ..............1982-83
372 ....Steve Johnson, KC...............1981-82
367 ....Bill Robinzine, KC................1978-79
366 ....Bill Bridges, STL..................1967-68
363 ....Lonnie Shelton, NY..............1976-77
363 ....James Edwards, IND...........1978-79
361 ....Kevin Kunnert, HOU 1976-77
358 ....Dan Roundfield, ATL 1978-79
358 ....Rick Mahorn, WAS 1983-84

DISQUALIFICATIONS
(First Kept in 1950-51)
26 ....Don Meineke, FTW...............1952-53
25 ....Steve Johnson, KC...............1981-82
23 ....Darryl Dawkins, NJ..............1982-83
22 ....Walter Dukes, DET...............1958-59
22 ....Darryl Dawkins, NJ..............1983-84
21 ....Joe Meriweather, ATL 1976-77
20 ....Joe Fulks, PHI 1952-53
20 ....Vern Mikkelsen, MIN 1957-58
20 ....Walter Dukes, DET...............1959-60
20 ....Walter Dukes, DET...............1961-62
20 ....George Johnson, NJ.............1977-78

FIELD GOALS ATTEMPTED
3,159 ......Wilt Chamberlain, PHI 1961-62
2,770 ......Wilt Chamberlain, SF............1962-63
2,457 ......Wilt Chamberlain, PHI 1960-61
2,311 ......Wilt Chamberlain, PHI 1959-60
2,298 ......Wilt Chamberlain, SF............1963-64
2,279 ......Michael Jordan, CHI 1986-87
2,273 ......Elgin Baylor, LA 1962-63
2,217 ......Rick Barry, GS....................1974-75
2,215 ......Elvin Hayes, SD..................1970-71
2,166 ......Elgin Baylor, LA 1960-61

FIELD GOALS MADE

1,597	Wilt Chamberlain, PHI	1961-62
1,463	Wilt Chamberlain, SF	1962-63
1,251	Wilt Chamberlain, PHI	1960-61
1,204	Wilt Chamberlain, SF	1963-64
1,159	Kareem Abdul-Jabbar, MIL	1971-72
1,098	Michael Jordan, CHI	1986-87
1,095	Bob McAdoo, BUF	1974-75
1,074	Wilt Chamberlain, PHI	1965-66
1,069	Michael Jordan, CHI	1987-88
1,065	Wilt Chamberlain, PHI	1959-60

FIELD GOAL PCT.
(Minimum 300 FGM)

.727	Wilt Chamberlain, LA	1972-73
.683	Wilt Chamberlain, PHI	1966-67
.670	Artis Gilmore, CHI	1980-81
.652	Artis Gilmore, CHI	1981-82
.649	Wilt Chamberlain, LA	1971-72
.637	James Donaldson, LAC	1984-85
.632	Steve Johnson, SA	1985-86
.626	Artis Gilmore, SA	1982-83
.625	Mark West, PHO	1989-90
.623	Artis Gilmore, SA	1984-85

FREE THROWS ATTEMPTED

1,363	Wilt Chamberlain, PHI	1961-62
1,113	Wilt Chamberlain, SF	1962-63
1,054	Wilt Chamberlain, PHI	1960-61
1,016	Wilt Chamberlain, SF	1963-64
991	Wilt Chamberlain, SF	1959-60
977	Jerry West, LA	1965-66
976	Wilt Chamberlain, PHI	1965-66
972	Michael Jordan, CHI	1986-87
951	Charles Barkley, PHI	1987-88
946	Adrian Dantley, UTA	1983-84

FREE THROWS MADE

840	Jerry West, LA	1965-66
835	Wilt Chamberlain, PHI	1961-62
833	Michael Jordan, CHI	1986-87
813	Adrian Dantley, UTA	1983-84
800	Oscar Robertson, CIN	1963-64
753	Rick Barry, SF	1966-67
742	Oscar Robertson, CIN	1965-66
737	Moses Malone, PHI	1984-85
736	Oscar Robertson, CIN	1966-67
723	Michael Jordan, CHI	1987-88

FREE THROW PCT.
(Minimum 125 FTM)

.958	Calvin Murphy, HOU	1980-81
.947	Rick Barry, HOU	1978-79
.945	Ernie DiGregorio, BUF	1976-77
.935	Ricky Sobers, CHI	1980-81
.935	Rick Barry, HOU	1979-80
.932	Bill Sharman, BOS	1958-59
.930	Larry Bird, BOS	1989-90
.928	Calvin Murphy, HOU	1978-79
.924	Rick Barry, GS	1977-78
.923	Rick Barry, GS	1975-76

3-PT FIELD GOALS ATTEMPTED
(Rule went into effect in 1979-80)

564	Michael Adams, DEN	1990-91
510	Vernon Maxwell, HOU	1990-91
466	Michael Adams, DEN	1988-89
432	Michael Adams, DEN	1989-90
379	Michael Adams, DEN	1987-88
374	Mark Price, CLE	1989-90
362	Reggie Miller, IND	1989-90
357	Danny Ainge, BOS	1987-88
339	Dale Ellis, SEA	1988-89
334	Dennis Scott, ORL	1990-91

3-PT FIELD GOALS MADE

172	Vernon Maxwell, HOU	1990-91
167	Michael Adams, DEN	1990-91
166	Michael Adams, DEN	1988-89
162	Dale Ellis, SEA	1988-89
158	Michael Adams, DEN	1989-90
152	Mark Price, CLE	1989-90
150	Reggie Miller, IND	1989-90
148	Danny Ainge, BOS	1987-88
139	Michael Adams, DEN	1987-88
130	Terry Porter, POR	1990-91

3-PT FIELD GOAL PCT.
(Minimum 25 Made)

.522	Jon Sundvold, MIA	1988-89
.507	Steve Kerr, CLE	1989-90
.491	Craig Hodges, MIL/PHO	1987-88
.486	Mark Price, CLE	1987-88
.481	Kiki Vandeweghe, POR	1986-87
.481	Craig Hodges, CHI	1989-90
.478	Detlef Schrempf, DAL	1986-87
.478	Dale Ellis, SEA	1988-89
.461	Jim Les, SAC	1990-91
.459	Drazen Petrovic, POR	1989-90

GAME RECORDS

POINTS
100 ...Wilt Chamberlain, PHI vs. NY, March 2, 1962
78 .....Wilt Chamberlain, PHI vs. LA, Dec. 8, 1961 (3 OT)
73 .....Wilt Chamberlain, PHI vs. CHI, Jan. 13, 1962
73 .....Wilt Chamberlain, SF vs. NY, Nov. 6, 1962
73 .....David Thompson, DEN vs. DET, April 9, 1978
72 .....Wilt Chamberlain, SF vs. LA, Nov. 3, 1962
71 .....Elgin Baylor, LA vs. NY, Nov. 15, 1960
70 .....Wilt Chamberlain, SF vs. SYR, March 10, 1963
69 .....Michael Jordan, CHI vs. CLE, March 28, 1990 (OT)
68 .....Wilt Chamberlain, PHI vs. CHI, Dec. 16, 1967
68 .....Pete Maravich, NO vs. NY, Feb. 25, 1977

REBOUNDS
55 .....Wilt Chamberlain, PHI vs. BOS, Nov. 24, 1960
51 .....Bill Russell, BOS vs. SYR, Feb. 5, 1960
49 .....Bill Russell, BOS vs. PHI, Nov. 16, 1957
49 .....Bill Russell, BOS vs. DET, March 11, 1965
45 .....Wilt Chamberlain, PHI vs. SYR, Feb. 6, 1960
45 .....Wilt Chamberlain, PHI vs. LA, Jan. 21, 1961

ASSISTS
30 .....Scott Skiles, ORL vs. DEN, Dec. 30, 1990
29 .....Kevin Porter, NJ vs. HOU, Feb. 24, 1978
28 .....Bob Cousy, BOS vs. MIN, Feb., 27, 1959
28 .....Guy Rodgers, SF vs. STL, March 14, 1963
28 .....John Stockton, UTA vs. SA, Jan. 15, 1991

STEALS
11 .....Larry Kenon, SA vs. KC, Dec. 26, 1976
10 .....Jerry West, LA vs. SEA, Dec. 7, 1973
10 .....Larry Steele, POR vs. L.A., Nov. 16, 1974
10 .....Fred Brown, SEA vs. PHI, Dec. 3, 1976
10 .....Gus Williams, SEA vs. NJ, Feb. 22, 1978
10 .....Eddie Jordan, NJ vs. PHI, March 23, 1979
10 .....Johnny Moore, SA vs. IND, March 6, 1985
10 .....Lafayette Lever, DEN vs. IND, March 9, 1985
10 ......Clyde Drexler, POR vs. MIL, Jan. 10, 1986

10 .....Alvin Robertson, SA vs. PHO, Feb. 18, 1986
10 .....Ron Harper, CLE vs. PHI, March 10, 1987
10 .....Michael Jordan, CHI vs. NJ, Jan. 29, 1988
10 .....Alvin Robertson, SA vs. HOU, Jan. 11, 1989 (OT)
10 .....Alvin Robertson, MIL vs UTA, Nov. 19, 1990

BLOCKED SHOTS
17 .....Elmore Smith, LA vs. POR, Oct. 28, 1973
15 .....Manute Bol, WAS vs. ATL, Jan. 25, 1986
15 .....Manute Bol, WAS vs. IND, Feb. 26, 1987
14 .....Elmore Smith, LA vs. DET, Oct. 26, 1973
14 .....Elmore Smith, LA vs. HOU, Nov. 4, 1973
14 .....Mark Eaton, UTA vs. POR, Jan. 18, 1985
14 .....Mark Eaton, UTA vs. SA, Feb. 18, 1989

FIELD GOALS ATTEMPTED
63 .....Wilt Chamberlain, PHI vs. NY, March 2, 1962
62 .....Wilt Chamberlain, PHI vs. LA, Dec. 8, 1961 (3 OT)
60 .....Wilt Chamberlain, SF vs. CIN, Oct. 28, 1962 (OT)
58 .....Wilt Chamberlain, SF vs. PHI, Nov. 26, 1964
57 .....Wilt Chamberlain, SF vs. SYR, Dec. 11, 1962

FIELD GOALS MADE
36 .....Wilt Chamberlain, PHI vs. NY, March 2, 1962
31 .....Wilt Chamberlain, PHI vs. LA, Dec. 8, 1961 (3 OT)
30 .....Wilt Chamberlain, PHI vs. CHI, Dec. 16, 1967
30 .....Rick Barry, GS vs. POR, March 26, 1974
29 .....Wilt Chamberlain, PHI vs. CHI, Jan. 13, 1962
29 .....Wilt Chamberlain, SF vs. LA, Nov. 3, 1962
29 .....Wilt Chamberlain, SF vs. NY, Nov. 16, 1962
29 .....Wilt Chamberlain, LA vs. PHO, Feb. 9, 1969

FIELD GOAL PCT.
(Minimum 15 Attempts)
1.000.Wilt Chamberlain, PHI vs. BAL, Feb. 24, 1967 (18/18)
1.000.Wilt Chamberlain, PHI vs. BAL, March 19, 1967 (16/16)

1.000.Wilt Chamberlain, PHI vs. LA, Jan. 20,
    1967(15/15)
.947 ..Wilt Chamberlain, SF vs. NY, Nov. 27,
    1963 (18/19)
.941 ..Wilt Chamberlain, PHI vs. BAL, Nov. 25,
    1966 (16/17)

FREE THROWS ATTEMPTED
34 .....Wilt Chamberlain, PHI vs. STL, Feb. 22,
    1962
32 .....Wilt Chamberlain, PHI vs. NY, March 2,
    1962
31 .....Adrian Dantley, UTA vs. DEN, Nov. 25,
    1983
29 .....Lloyd Free, SD vs. ATL, Jan. 13, 1979
29 .....Adrian Dantley, UTA vs. DAL, Oct. 31,
    1980
29 .....Adrian Dantley, UTA vs. HOU, Jan. 4,
    1984

FREE THROWS MADE
28 .....Wilt Chamberlain, PHI vs. NY, March 2,
    1962
28 .....Adrian Dantley, UTA vs. HOU, Jan. 4,
    1984
27 .....Adrian Dantley, UTA vs. DEN, Nov. 25,
    1983
26 .....Adrian Dantley, UTA vs. DAL, Oct. 31,
    1980
26 .....Michael Jordan, CHI vs. NJ, Feb. 26,
    1987

FREE THROW PCT.
(Most with No Misses)
1.000.Bob Pettit, STL vs. BOS, Nov. 22, 1961
    (19/19)
1.000.Bill Cartwright, NY vs. KC, Nov. 17, 1981
    (19/19)
1.000 Adrian Dantley, DET vs. CHI, Dec. 15, 1987
    (19/19) (OT)
1.000.14 players with 18 free throws and no
    misses

3-PT FIELD GOALS ATTEMPTED
20 .....Michael Adams, DEN vs. LAC, April 12,
    1991
16 .....Michael Adams, DEN vs. MIL, March 23,
    1991 (OT)
15 .....Michael Adams, DEN vs. UTA, March 14,
    1988
14 .....Ricky Berry, SAC vs. GS, Feb. 9, 1989

3-PT FIELD GOALS MADE
9 ....Dale Ellis, SEA vs. LAC, April 20, 1990
9 ....Michael Adams, DEN vs. LAC, April 12,
    1991
8 ....Rick Barry, HOU vs. UTA, Feb. 9, 1980
8 ....John Roche, DEN vs. SEA, Jan. 9, 1982
8 ....Michael Adams, DEN vs. MIL, Jan. 21,
    1989
8 ....Vernon Maxwell, HOU vs. DEN, April 5,
    1991

TEAM RECORDS—SEASON

HIGHEST WINNING PCT.
.841 .....69-13 Los Angeles, 1971-72
.840 .....68-13 Philadelphia, 1966-67
.829 .....68-14 Boston, 1972-73

LOWEST WINNING PCT.
.110 ..... 9-73 Philadelphia, 1972-73
.125 ..... 6-42 Providence, 1947-48
.146 .....12-70 L.A. Clippers, 1986-87

HIGHEST WINNING PCT., HOME
.976 .....40-1 Boston, 1985-86
.971 .....33-1 Rochester, 1949-50
.969 .....31-1 Syracuse, 1949-50

HIGHEST WINNING PCT., ROAD
.816 .....31-7 Los Angeles, 1971-72
.800 .....32-8 Boston, 1972-73
.780 .....32-9 Boston, 1974-75

CONSECUTIVE WINS
33 ....Los Angeles, Nov. 5, 1971-Jan. 7, 1972
20 ....Milwaukee, Feb. 6-March 8, 1971
20 ....Washington, March 13-Dec. 4, 1948
    (overlapping seasons)

CONSECUTIVE WINS
(Start of Season)
15 ....Washington, Nov. 3-Dec. 4, 1948
14 ....Boston, Oct. 22-Nov. 27, 1957
12 ....Seattle, Oct. 29-Nov. 19, 1982

CONSECUTIVE LOSSES
24 ....Cleveland, March 19-Nov. 5, 1982
    (overlapping seasons)
21 ....Detroit, March 7-Oct. 22, 1980
    (overlapping seasons)
20 ....Philadelphia, Jan. 9-Feb. 11, 1973

CONSECUTIVE WINS, HOME
38 ....Boston, Dec. 10, 1985-Nov. 28, 1986
          (overlapping seasons)
36 ....Philadelphia, Jan. 14, 1966-Jan. 20,
          1967 (overlapping seasons)
34 ....Portland, March 5, 1977-Feb. 3, 1978
          (overlapping seasons)

CONSECUTIVE WINS, ROAD
16 ....Los Angeles, Nov. 6, 1971-Jan 7, 1972
12 ....New York, Oct. 14-Dec. 10, 1969
12 ....Los Angeles, Oct. 15-Dec. 20, 1972

HIGHEST SCORING AVERAGE
126.5 ...Denver, 1981-82
125.4 ...Philadelphia, 1961-62
125.2 ...Philadelphia, 1966-67

LOWEST SCORING AVERAGE
(Since 1954-55, first year of the 24-second clock)
87.4 .....Milwaukee, 1954-55
90.8 .....Rochester, 1954-55
91.1 .....Syracuse, 1954-55

FEWEST POINTS ALLOWED PER GAME
(Since 1954-55, first year of the 24-second clock)
89.9 .....Syracuse, 1954-55
90.0 .....Ft. Wayne, 1954-55
90.4 .....Milwaukee, 1954-55

MOST POINTS ALLOWED PER GAME
130.8 ...Denver, 1990-91
126.0 ...Denver, 1981-82
125.1 ...Seattle, 1967-68

TEAM RECORDS—GAME

MOST POINTS
186 ......Detroit vs. Denver, Dec. 13, 1983 (3
          OT)
184 ......Denver vs. Detroit, Dec. 13, 1983 (3
          OT)
173 ......Boston vs. Minneapolis, Feb. 27, 1959
173 ......Phoenix vs. Denver, Nov. 10, 1990
171 ......San Antonio vs. Milwaukee, March 6,
          1982 (3 OT)
169 ......Philadelphia vs. New York, March 2,
          1962

FEWEST POINTS
(Since 1954-55, first year of the 24-second clock)
57 ....Milwaukee vs. Boston, Feb. 27, 1955
59 ....Sacramento vs. Charlotte, Jan. 10, 1991
62 ....Boston vs. Milwaukee, Feb. 27, 1955

MOST POINTS, BOTH TEAMS
370 ...Detroit (186) vs. Denver (184), Dec. 13,
      1983 (3 OT)
337 ...San Antonio (171) vs. Milwaukee (166),
      March 6, 1982 (3 OT)
318 ...Denver (163) vs. San Antonio (155), Jan.
      11, 1984

316 ...Philadelphia (169) vs. New York (147),
      March 2, 1962
316 ...Cincinnati (165) vs. San Diego (151),
      March 12, 1970
316 ...Phoenix (173) vs. Denver (143), Nov. 10,
      1990

FEWEST POINTS, BOTH TEAMS
(Since 1954-55, first year of the 24-second clock)
119 ...Milwaukee (57) vs. Boston (62), Feb. 27,
      1955
135 ...Syracuse (66) vs. Ft. Wayne (69), Jan. 25,
      1955
142 ...Syracuse (70) vs. Philadelphia (72), Dec.
      29, 1954

LARGEST MARGIN OF VICTORY
63 .....Los Angeles (162) vs. Golden State (99),
      March 19, 1972
62 .....Syracuse (162) vs. New York (100), Dec.
      25, 1960
59 .....Golden State (150) vs. Indiana (91),
      March 19, 1977
59 .....Milwaukee (143) vs. Detroit (84), Dec. 26,
      1978

PLAYOFF RECORDS—CAREER

POINTS
5,762 ...Kareem Abdul-Jabbar
4,457 ...Jerry West
3,852 ...Larry Bird

SCORING AVERAGE
(Minimum 25 Games)
34.6 .....Michael Jordan
29.1 .....Jerry West
27.2 .....Bernard King

REBOUNDS
4,104 ...Bill Russell
3,913 ...Wilt Chamberlain
2,481 ...Kareem Abdul-Jabbar

REBOUNDS PER GAME
(Minimum 25 Games)
24.9 .....Bill Russell
24.5 .....Wilt Chamberlain
14.9 .....Wes Unseld

ASSISTS
2,320 ...Magic Johnson
1,041 ...Larry Bird
1,006 ...Dennis Johnson

ASSISTS PER GAME
(Minimum 25 games)
12.5 .....Magic Johnson
10.6 .....John Stockton
 9.0 ......Isiah Thomas

PLAYOFF RECORDS—SERIES

POINTS
2-Game Series
68 ....Bob McAdoo, NY vs. CLE, 1978
3-Game Series
131 ......Michael Jordan, CHI vs. BOS, 1986
4-Game Series
150 ......Akeem Olajuwon, HOU vs. DAL, 1988
5-Game Series
226 ......Michael Jordan, CHI vs. CLE, 1988
6-Game Series
278 ......Jerry West, LA vs. BAL, 1965
7-Game Series
284 ......Elgin Baylor, LA vs. BOS, 1962

REBOUNDS
2-Game Series
41 ....Moses Malone, HOU vs. ATL, 1979
3-Game Series
84 ....Bill Russell, BOS vs. SYR, 1957
4-Game Series
118 ......Bill Russell, BOS vs. MIN, 1959

5-Game Series
160 ......Wilt Chamberlain, PHI vs. BOS, 1967
6-Game Series
171 ......Wilt Chamberlain, PHI vs. SF, 1967
7-Game Series
220 ......Wilt Chamberlain, PHI vs. BOS, 1965

ASSISTS
2-Game Series
20 ....Frank Johnson, WAS vs. NJ, 1982
3-Game Series
48 ....Magic Johnson, LAL vs. SA, 1986
4-Game Series
57 ....Magic Johnson, LAL vs. PHO, 1989
5-Game Series
85 ....Magic Johnson, LAL vs. POR, 1985
6-Game Series
90 ....Johnny Moore, SA vs. LA, 1983
7-Game Series
115 ......John Stockton, UTA vs. LAL, 1988

PLAYOFF RECORDS—GAME

POINTS
63 .....Michael Jordan, CHI vs. BOS, April 20, 1986 (2 OT)
61 .....Elgin Baylor, LA vs. BOS, April 14, 1962
56 .....Wilt Chamberlain, PHI vs. SYR, March 22, 1962

REBOUNDS
41 .....Wilt Chamberlain, PHI vs. BOS, April 5, 1967
40 .....Bill Russell, BOS vs. PHI, March 23, 1958
40 .....Bill Russell, BOS vs. STL, March 29, 1960
40 .....Bill Russell, BOS vs. LA, April 18, 1962 (OT)

ASSISTS
24 .....Magic Johnson, LA vs. PHO, May 15, 1984
24 .....John Stockton, UTA vs. LAL, May 17, 1988
23 .....Magic Johnson, LAL vs. POR, May 3, 1985

STEALS
8 ....Rick Barry, GS vs. SEA, April 14, 1975
8 ....Lionel Hollins, POR vs. LA, May 8, 1977
8 ....Maurice Cheeks, PHI vs. NJ, April 11, 1979
8 ....Craig Hodges, MIL vs. PHI, May 9, 1986

BLOCKED SHOTS
10 .....Mark Eaton, UTA vs. HOU, April 26, 1985
10 .....Akeem Olajuwon, HOU vs. LAL, April 29, 1990
9 ......Kareem Abdul-Jabbar, LA vs. GS, April 22, 1977
9 ......Manute Bol, WAS vs. PHI, April 18, 1986

PLAYOFF RECORDS—TEAM

CONSECUTIVE GAMES WON
13 .....L.A. Lakers, 1988-89
12 .....Detroit, 1989-90
9 .....Los Angeles, 1982

CONSECUTIVE GAMES LOST
11 .....Baltimore, 1965-66 and 1969-70
9 .....New York, 1953-55
9 .....Denver, 1988-90 (still active)

CONSECUTIVE SERIES WON
18 .....Boston 1959-1967
11 .....L.A. Lakers 1987-89
10 .....Minneapolis 1952-55
10 .....Detroit 1989-91

MOST POINTS, GAME
157 ...Boston vs. New York, April 28, 1990
156 ...Milwaukee vs. Philadelphia, March 30, 1970
153 ...L.A. Lakers vs. Denver, May 22, 1985

FEWEST POINTS, GAME
(Since 1954-55, first year of the 24-second clock)
70 .....Golden State vs. Los Angeles, April 21, 1973
70 .....Seattle vs. Houston, April 23, 1982
71 .....Syracuse vs. Ft. Wayne, April 7, 1955
71 .....Houston vs. Boston, May 5, 1981

MOST POINTS, BOTH TEAMS, GAME
285 ...San Antonio (152) vs. Denver (133), April 26, 1983
285 ...Boston (157) vs. New York (128), April 28, 1990
280 ...Dallas (151) vs. Seattle (129), April 23, 1987

FEWEST POINTS, BOTH TEAMS, GAME
145 ...Syracuse (71) vs. Ft. Wayne (74), March 24, 1956
157 ...Kansas City (76) vs. Phoenix (81), April 17, 1981
157 ...Detroit (78) vs. Boston (79), May 30, 1988

LARGEST MARGIN OF VICTORY, GAME
58 .....Minneapolis (133) vs. St. Louis (75), March 19, 1956
56 .....Los Angeles (126) vs. Golden State (70), April 21, 1973
50 .....Milwaukee (136) vs. San Francisco (86), April 4, 1971

NBA Year-By-Year Results

In this section, you'll find the final standings of every NBA season since its inception in 1946-47. Actually, in its first three years of existence, the league was called the BAA (Basketball Association of America), but it is still considered part of NBA history.

This section also includes league leaders in every major category since 1946-47. In its first three years of existence, the league kept track of only four statistics—scoring, assists, field goal percentage, and free throw percentage. In 1950-51, it began keeping track of rebounds. In 1973-74, the league added blocked shots and steals to the stat sheets. In 1979-80, the three-point shot arrived in the NBA.

Because most statistical categories are based on averages, the NBA has had to establish qualifying criteria (e.g., a player can only qualify for the scoring championship if he appears in at least 70 games). Through the years, the league has frequently changed its qualifying criteria. These are the standards that players have had to meet in order to qualify:

Scoring
1946-47 to 1968-69: Based on total points, not on an average.
1969-70 to 1973-74: Minimum 70 games.
1974-75 to present: Minimum 70 games or 1400 points.

Rebounds
1950-51 to 1968-69: Based on total rebounds, not on an average.
1969-70 to 1973-74: Minimum 70 games.
1974-75 to present: Minimum 70 games or 800 rebounds.

Assists
1946-47 to 1968-69: Based on total assists, not on an average.
1969-70 to 1973-74: Minimum 70 games.
1974-75 to present: Minimum 70 games or 400 assists.

Steals
1973-74: Minimum 70 games.
1974-75 to present: Minimum 70 games or 125 steals.

Blocked Shots
1973-74: Minimum 70 games.
1974-75 to present: Minimum 70 games or 100 blocks.

Field Goal Pct.
Over the years, the NBA has changed the qualifications for field goal percentage 14 times. Since 1974-75, a player has needed to make 300 field goals in order to qualify.

Free Throw Pct.
Since its inception, the league has changed the qualifications for free throw percentage 13 times. Since 1974-75, a player has needed to make 125 free throws in order to qualify.

3-Point Field Goal Pct.
1979-80 to 1989-90: Minimum 25 3-point field goals made.
1990-91: Minimum 50 3-point field goals made.

Besides standings and statistics, this section contains results of every playoff series of every season. This includes game-by-game scores of all of the NBA Finals series. The last year of this section, 1990-91, has been expanded to include more statistical information.

1946-47
FINAL STANDINGS

Eastern Division

	W	L	PCT	GB
Washington	49	11	.817	
Philadelphia	35	25	.583	14
New York	33	27	.550	16
Providence	28	32	.467	21
Toronto	22	38	.367	27
Boston	22	38	.367	27

Western Division

	W	L	PCT	GB
Chicago	39	22	.639	
St. Louis	38	23	.623	1
Cleveland	30	30	.500	8.5
Detroit	20	40	.333	18.5
Pittsburgh	15	45	.250	23.5

POINTS

	AVG	NO.
J. Fulks, PHI	23.2	1389
B. Feerick, WAS	16.3	926
S. Miasek, DET	14.9	895
E. Sadowski, TOR/CLE	16.5	877
M. Zaslofsky, CHI	14.4	877
E. Calverley, PRO	14.3	845
C. Halbert, CHI	12.7	773
J. Logan, STL	12.6	770
L. Mogus, CLE/TOR	13.0	753
C. Gunther, PIT	14.1	734
D. Martin, PRO	12.2	733
F. Scolari, WAS	12.6	728
H. Beenders, PRO	12.3	713
J. Janisch, DET	11.6	697
H. McKinney, WAS	12.0	695
E. Shannon, PRO	12.1	687
M. Riebe, CLE	12.1	663
M. McCarron, TOR	10.8	649
F. Baumholtz, CLE	14.0	631
D. Carlson, CHI	10.7	630

ASSISTS

	AVG	NO.
E. Calverley, PRO	3.4	202
K. Sailors, CLE	2.3	134
O. Schectman, NY	2.0	109
H. Dallmar, PHI	1.7	104
M. Rottner, CHI	1.7	93
S. Miasek, DET	1.6	93

E. Shannon, PRO	1.5	84
L. Mogus, CLE/TOR	1.4	84
J. Logan, STL	1.3	78
B. Feerick, WAS	1.3	69

FIELD GOAL PCT

Bob Feerick, WAS	.401
Ed Sadowski, TOR/CLE	.369
Earl Shannon, PRO	.339
Coulby Gunther, PIT	.336
Max Zaslofsky, CHI	.329
Don Carlson, CHI	.322
Connie Simmons, BOS	.320
John Norlander, WAS	.319
Ken Sailors, CLE	.309
Mel Riebe, CLE	.307

FREE THROW PCT

Fred Scolari, WAS	.811
Tony Kapper, PIT/BOS	.795
Stan Stutz, NY	.782
Bob Feerick, WAS	.762
John Logan, STL	.748
Max Zaslofsky, CHI	.737
Joe Fulks, PHI	.730
Leo Mogus, CLE/TOR	.723
George Mearns, PRO	.720
Tony Jaros, CHI	.707

QUARTERFINALS

Philadelphia 2, St. Louis 1
New York 2, Cleveland 1

SEMIFINALS

Chicago 4, Washington 2
Philadelphia 2, New York 0

FINALS

Philadelphia 84, Chicago 71
Philadelphia 85, Chicago 74
Philadelphia 75, Chicago 72
Chicago 74, Philadelphia 73
Philadelphia 83, Chicago 80

1947-48
FINAL STANDINGS

Eastern Division

	W	L	PCT	GB
Philadelphia	27	21	.563	
New York	26	22	.542	1
Boston	20	28	.417	7
Providence	6	42	.125	21

Western Division

	W	L	PCT	GB
St. Louis	29	19	.604	
Baltimore	28	20	.583	1
Chicago	28	20	.583	1
Washington	28	20	.583	1

POINTS

	AVG	NO.
M. Zaslofsky, CHI	21.0	1007
J. Fulks, PHI	22.1	949
E. Sadowski, BOS	19.4	910
B. Feerick, WAS	16.1	775
S. Miasek, CHI	14.9	716
C. Braun, NY	14.3	671
J. Logan, STL	13.4	644
J. Palmer, NY	13.0	622
R. Rocha, STL	12.7	611
F. Scolari, WAS	12.5	589
H. Dallmar, PHI	12.2	587
K. Hermsen, BAL	12.0	575
E. Calverley, PRO	11.9	559
J. Reiser, BAL	11.5	541
B. Smawley, STL	11.1	535
K. Sailors, PRO	11.9	524
G. Nostrand, PRO	11.6	521
M. Bloom, BAL/BOS	10.6	508
D. Holub, NY	10.5	504
B. Jeannette, BAL	10.7	491

ASSISTS

	AVG	NO.
H. Dallmar, PHI	2.5	120
E. Calverley, PRO	2.5	119
J. Seminoff, CHI	1.8	89
C. Gilmur, CHI	1.6	77
A. Phillip, CHI	2.3	74
E. Sadowski, BOS	1.6	74

B. Jeannette, BAL	1.5	70
J. Logan, STL	1.3	62
C. Braun, NY	1.3	61
S. Mariaschin, BOS	1.4	60

FIELD GOAL PCT

Bob Feerick, WAS	.340
Ed Sadowski, BOS	.323
Carl Braun, NY	.323
Max Zaslofsky, CHI	.323
Chick Reiser, BAL	.322
John Palmer, NY	.315
Red Rocha, STL	.314
Mel Riebe, BOS	.309
Belus Smawley, STL	.308
Stan Miasek, CHI	.303

FREE THROW PCT

Bob Feerick, WAS	.788
Max Zaslofsky, CHI	.784
Joe Fulks, PHI	.762
Buddy Jeannette, BAL	.758
Howie Dallmar, PHI	.744
John Palmer, NY	.744
John Logan, STL	.743
John Norlander, WAS	.742
Chick Reiser, BAL	.741
Fred Scolari, WAS	.732

QUARTERFINALS
Baltimore 2, New York 1
Chicago 2, Boston 1

SEMIFINALS
Philadelphia 4, St. Louis 3
Baltimore 2, Chicago 0

FINALS
Philadelphia 71, Baltimore 60
Baltimore 66, Philadelphia 63
Baltimore 72, Philadelphia 70
Baltimore 78, Philadelphia 75
Philadelphia 91, Baltimore 82
Baltimore 88, Philadelphia 73

1948-49
FINAL STANDINGS

Eastern Division

	W	L	PCT	GB
Washington	38	22	.633	
New York	32	28	.533	6
Baltimore	29	31	.483	9
Philadelphia	28	32	.467	10
Boston	25	35	.417	13
Providence	12	48	.200	26

Western Division

	W	L	PCT	GB
Rochester	45	15	.750	
Minneapolis	44	16	.733	1
Chicago	38	22	.633	7
St. Louis	29	31	.483	16
Fort Wayne	22	38	.367	23
Indianapolis	18	42	.300	27

POINTS

	AVG.	NO.
G Mikan, MIN	28.3	1698
J. Fulks, PHI	26.0	1560
M. Zaslofsky, CHI	20.6	1197
A. Risen, ROC	16.6	995
E. Sadowski, PHI	15.3	920
B. Smawley, STL	15.5	914
B. Davies, ROC	15.1	904
K. Sailors, PRO	15.8	899
C. Braun, NY	14.2	810
J. Logan, STL	14.1	803
J. Pollard, MIN	14.8	784
C. Simmons, BAL	13.0	779
R. Lumpp, IND/NY	12.7	777
B. Feerick, WAS	13.0	752
H. Shannon, PRO	13.4	736
H. McKinney, WAS	12.7	723
A. Phillip, CHI	12.0	718
J. Palmer, NY	12.3	714
K. Hermsen, WAS	11.8	708
W. Budko, BAL	11.5	692

ASSISTS

	AVG	NO.
B. Davies, ROC	5.4	321
A. Phillip, CHI	5.3	319
J. Logan, STL	4.8	276
E. Calverley, PRO	4.3	251
G. Senesky, PHI	3.9	233
J. Seminoff, BOS	3.9	229

G. Mikan, MIN	3.6	218
K. Sailors, PRO	3.7	209
B. Feerick, WAS	3.2	188
B. Wanzer, ROC	3.1	186

FIELD GOAL PCT

Arnie Risen, ROC	.423
George Mikan, MIN	.416
Ed Sadowski, PHI	.405
Jim Pollard, MIN	.396
Red Rocha, STL	.389
Bob Wanzer, ROC	.379
Connie Simmons, BAL	.377
Herm Schaefer, MIN	.374
Belus Smawley, STL	.372
Howie Shannon, PRO	.364

FREE THROW PCT

Bob Feerick, WAS	.859
Max Zaslofsky, CHI	.840
Bob Wanzer, ROC	.823
Herm Schaefer, MIN	.817
Howie Shannon, PRO	.804
Harold Tidrick, IND/BAL	.800
John Logan, STL	.791
John Pelkington, FTW/BAL	.790
Walter Budko, BAL	.790
Joe Fulks, PHI	.787

EAST SEMIFINALS
Washington 2, Philadelphia 0
New York 2, Baltimore 1

EAST FINALS
Washington 2, New York 1

WEST SEMIFINALS
Rochester 2, St. Louis 0
Minneapolis 2, Chicago 0

WEST FINALS
Minneapolis 2, Rochester 0

FINALS
Minneapolis 88, Washington 84
Minneapolis 76, Washington 62
Minneapolis 94, Washington 74
Washington 83, Minneapolis 71
Washington 74, Minneapolis 65
Minneapolis 77, Washington 56

1949-50
FINAL STANDINGS

Eastern Division

	W	L	PCT	GB
Syracuse	51	13	.797	
New York	40	28	.588	13
Washington	32	36	.471	21
Philadelphia	26	42	.382	27
Baltimore	25	43	.368	28
Boston	22	46	.324	31

Western Division

	W	L	PCT	GB
Indianapolis	39	25	.609	
Anderson	37	27	.578	2
Tri-Cities	29	35	.453	10
Sheboygan	22	40	.355	16
Waterloo	19	43	.306	19
Denver	11	51	.177	27

Central Division

	W	L	PCT	GB
Minneapolis	51	17	.750	
Rochester	51	17	.750	
Fort Wayne	40	28	.588	11
Chicago	40	28	.588	11
St. Louis	26	42	.382	25

POINTS

	AVG	NO.
G. Mikan, MIN	27.4	1865
A. Groza, IND	23.4	1496
F. Brian, AND	17.8	1138
M. Zaslofsky, CHI	16.4	1115
E. Macauley, STL	16.1	1081
D. Schayes, SYR	16.8	1072
C. Braun, NY	15.4	1031
K. Sailors, DEN	17.3	987
J. Pollard, MIN	14.7	973
F. Schaus, FTW	14.3	972
J. Fulks, PHI	14.2	965
R. Beard, IND	14.9	895
B. Davies, ROC	14.0	895
D. Mehen, WAT	14.4	892
J. Nichols, WAS/TC	13.1	879
E. Sadowski, PHI/BAL	12.6	872
P. Hoffman, BAL	14.4	866
F. Scolari, WAS	13.0	860
V. Gardner, PHI	13.5	853
B. Smawley, STL	13.7	834

ASSISTS

	AVG	NO.
D. McGuire, NY	5.7	386
A. Phillip, CHI	5.8	377
B. Davies, ROC	4.6	294
A. Cervi, SYR	4.7	264
G. Senesky, PHI	3.9	264

D. Schayes, SYR	4.0	259
J. Pollard, MIN	3.8	252
J. Seminoff, BOS	3.8	249
C. Braun, NY	3.7	247
J. Logan, STL	3.9	240

FIELD GOAL PCT

Alex Groza, IND	.478
Dick Mehen, WAT	.420
Bob Wanzer, ROC	.414
George Mikan, MIN	.407
John Hargis, AND	.405
Red Rocha, STL	.405
Vern Mikkelsen, MIN	.399
Ed Macauley, STL	.398
Jack Toomay, DEN	.397
Harry Gallatin, NY	.396

FREE THROW PCT

Max Zaslofsky, CHI	.843
Chick Reiser, WAS	.835
Al Cervi, SYR	.829
Belus Smawley, STL	.828
Frank Brian, AND	.824
Fred Scolari, WAS	.822
Fred Schaus, FTW	.818
Leo Kubiak, WAT	.814
Bob Wanzer, ROC	.806
John Logan, STL	.783

EAST SEMIFINALS
Syracuse 2, Philadelphia 0
New York 2, Washington 0

EAST FINALS
Syracuse 2, New York 1

CENTRAL SEMIFINALS
Minneapolis 2, Chicago 0
Fort Wayne 2, Rochester 0

CENTRAL FINALS
Minneapolis 2, Fort Wayne 0

WEST SEMIFINALS
Indianapolis 2, Sheboygan 1
Anderson 2, Tri-Cities 1

WEST FINALS
Anderson 2, Indianapolis 1

NBA SEMIFINALS
Minneapolis 2, Anderson 0

NBA FINALS
Minneapolis 68, Syracuse 66
Syracuse 91, Minneapolis 85
Minneapolis 91, Syracuse 77
Minneapolis 77, Syracuse 69
Syracuse 83, Minneapolis 76
Minneapolis 110, Syracuse 95

1950-51
FINAL STANDINGS

Eastern Division

	W	L	PCT	GB
Philadelphia	40	26	.606	
Boston	39	30	.565	2.5
New York	36	30	.545	4
Syracuse	32	34	.485	8
Baltimore	24	42	.364	16
Washington*	10	25	.286	14.5

*Folded on Jan. 9, 1951

Western Division

	W	L	PCT	GB
Minneapolis	44	24	.647	
Rochester	41	27	.603	3
Fort Wayne	32	36	.471	12
Indianapolis	31	37	.456	13
Tri-Cities	25	43	.368	19

POINTS

	AVG	NO.
G. Mikan, MIN	28.4	1932
A. Groza, IND	21.7	1429
E. Macauley, BOS	20.4	1384
J. Fulks, PHI	18.7	1236
F. Brian, TC	16.8	1144
P. Arizin, PHI	17.2	1121
D. Schayes, SYR	17.0	1121
R. Beard, IND	16.8	1111
B. Cousy, BOS	15.6	1078
A. Risen, ROC	16.3	1077
D. Eddleman, TC	15.3	1040
F. Schaus, FTW	15.1	1028
V. Boryla, NY	14.9	982
B. Davies, ROC	13.5	955
L. Foust, FTW	13.5	915
V. Mikkelsen, MIN	14.1	904
F. Scolari, WAS/SYR	13.4	883
K. Murray, BAL/FTW	12.9	850
G. Ratkovicz, SYR	12.9	849
H. Gallatin, NY	12.8	845

REBOUNDS

	AVG	NO.
D. Schayes, SYR	16.4	1080
G. Mikan, MIN	14.1	958
H. Gallatin, NY	12.1	800
A. Risen, ROC	12.0	795
A. Groza, IND	10.7	709
L. Foust, FTW	10.0	681
V. Mikkelsen, MIN	10.2	655
P. Arizin, PHI	9.8	640
E. Macauley, BOS	9.1	616
J. Coleman, ROC	8.7	584

ASSISTS

	AVG	NO.
A. Phillip, PHI	6.3	414
D. McGuire, NY	6.3	400
G. Senesky, PHI	5.3	342
B. Cousy, BOS	4.9	341
R. Beard, IND	4.8	318
B. Davies, ROC	4.6	287
F. Brian, TC	3.9	266
F. Scolari, WAS/SYR	3.9	255
E. Macauley, BOS	3.7	252
D. Schayes, SYR	3.8	251

FIELD GOAL PCT

Alex Groza, IND	.470
Ed Macauley, BOS	.466
George Mikan, MIN	.428
Jack Coleman, ROC	.421
Harry Gallatin, NY	.416
George Ratkovicz, SYR	.415
Paul Arizin, PHI	.407
Vince Boryla, NY	.406
Vern Mikkelsen, MIN	.402
Robert Wanzer, ROC	.401

FREE THROW PCT

Joe Fulks, PHI	.855
Belus Smawley, SYR/BAL	.850
Bob Wanzer, ROC	.850
Fred Scolari, WAS/SYR	.843
Vince Boryla, NY	.837
Fred Schaus, FTW	.835
Sonny Hertzberg, BOS	.826
Frank Brian, TC	.823

EAST SEMIFINALS
Syracuse 2, Philadelphia 0
New York 2, Boston 0

EAST FINALS
New York 3, Syracuse 2

WEST SEMIFINALS
Minneapolis 2, Indianapolis 1
Rochester 2, Fort Wayne 1

WEST FINALS
Rochester 3, Minneapolis 1

NBA FINALS
Rochester 92, New York 65
Rochester 99, New York 84
Rochester 78, New York 71
New York 79, Rochester 73
New York 92, Rochester 89
New York 80, Rochester 73
Rochester 79, New York 75

1951-52
FINAL STANDINGS

Eastern Division	W	L	PCT	GB
Syracuse	40	26	.606	
Boston	39	27	.591	1
New York	37	29	.561	3
Philadelphia	33	33	.500	7
Boston	20	46	.303	20

Western Division	W	L	PCT	GB
Rochester	41	25	.621	
Minneapolis	40	26	.606	1
Indianapolis	34	32	.515	7
Fort Wayne	29	37	.439	12
Milwaukee	17	49	.258	24

POINTS	AVG	NO.
P. Arizin, PHI	25.4	1674
G. Mikan, MIN	23.8	1523
B. Cousy, BOS	21.7	1433
E. Macauley, BOS	19.2	1264
B. Davies, ROC	16.2	1052
F. Brian, FTW	15.9	1051
L. Foust, FTW	15.9	1047
B. Wanzer, ROC	15.7	1033
A. Risen, ROC	15.6	1032
V. Mikkelsen, MIN	15.3	1009
J. Pollard, MIN	15.5	1005
F. Scolari, BAL	14.6	933
M. Zaslofsky, NY	14.1	931
J. Fulks, PHI	15.1	922
J. Graboski, IND	13.7	904
F. Schaus, FTW	14.1	872
D. Schayes, SYR	13.8	868
R. Rocha, SYR	12.9	854
L. Barnhorst, IND	12.4	820
A. Phillip, PHI	12.0	790

REBOUNDS	AVG	NO.
L. Foust, FTW	13.3	880
M. Hutchins, MIL	13.3	880
G. Mikan, MIN	13.5	866
A. Risen, ROC	12.7	841
D. Schayes, SYR	12.3	773
P. Arizin, PHI	11.3	745
N. Clifton, NY	11.8	731
J. Coleman, ROC	10.5	692
V. Mikkelsen, MIN	10.3	681
H. Gallatin, NY	10.0	661

ASSISTS	AVG	NO.
A. Phillip, PHI	8.2	539
B. Cousy, BOS	6.7	441
B. Davies, ROC	6.0	390
D. McGuire, NY	6.1	388
F. Scolari, BAL	4.7	303
G. Senesky, PHI	4.9	280
B. Wanzer, ROC	4.0	262
L. Barnhorst, IND	3.9	255
S. Martin, MIN	3.8	249
F. Schaus, FTW	4.0	247

FIELD GOAL PCT
Paul Arizin, PHI	.448
Harry Gallatin, NY	.442
Ed Macauley, BOS	.432
Bob Wanzer, ROC	.425
Vern Mikkelsen, MIN	.419
Jack Coleman, ROC	.415
George King, SYR	.406
Paul Walther, IND	.401
Red Rocha, SYR	.401
Bob Lavoy, IND	.397

FREE THROW PCT
Bob Wanzer, ROC	.904
Al Cervi, SYR	.883
Bill Sharman, BOS	.859
Frank Brian, FTW	.848
Fred Scolari, BAL	.835
Fred Schaus, FTW	.833
Joe Fulks, PHI	.825
Bill Tosheff, IND	.824

EAST SEMIFINALS
Syracuse 2, Philadelphia 1
New York 2, Boston 1

EAST FINALS
New York 3, Syracuse 1

WEST SEMIFINALS
Rochester 2, Fort Wayne 0
Minneapolis 2, Indianapolis 0

WEST FINALS
Minneapolis 3, Rochester 1

NBA FINALS
Minneapolis 83, New York 79 (OT)
New York 80, Minneapolis 72
Minneapolis 82, New York 77
New York 90, Minneapolis 89 (OT)
Minneapolis 102, New York 89
New York 76, Minneapolis 68
Minneapolis 82, New York 65

1952-53
FINAL STANDINGS

Eastern Division

	W	L	PCT	GB
New York	47	23	.671	
Syracuse	47	24	.662	.5
Boston	46	25	.648	1.5
Baltimore	16	54	.229	31
Philadelphia	12	57	.174	34.5

Western Division

	W	L	PCT	GB
Minneapolis	48	22	.686	
Rochester	44	26	.629	4
Fort Wayne	36	33	.522	11.5
Indianapolis	28	43	.394	20.5
Milwaukee	27	44	.380	21.5

POINTS

	AVG	NO.
N. Johnston, PHI	22.3	1564
G. Mikan, MIN	20.6	1442
B. Cousy, BOS	19.8	1407
E. Macauley, BOS	20.3	1402
D. Schayes, SYR	17.8	1262
B. Sharman, BOS	16.2	1147
J. Nichols, MIL	15.8	1090
V. Mikkelsen, MIN	15.0	1047
B. Davies, ROC	15.6	1029
B. Wanzer, ROC	14.6	1020
C. Braun, NY	14.0	977
L. Barnhorst, IND	13.6	967
L. Foust, FTW	14.3	958
P. Seymour, SYR	14.2	952
D. Barksdale, BAL	13.8	899
J. Graboski, IND	13.0	894
A. Risen, ROC	13.0	884
H. Gallatin, NY	12.4	865
J. Pollard, MIN	13.0	859
J. Fulks, PHI	11.9	832

REBOUNDS

	AVG	NO.
G. Mikan, MIN	14.4	1007
N. Johnston, PHI	13.9	979
D. Schayes, SYR	13.0	920
H. Gallatin, NY	13.1	916
M. Hutchins, MIL	11.2	793
J. Coleman, ROC	11.1	774
L. Foust, FTW	11.5	769
N. Clifton, NY	10.9	761
A. Risen, ROC	11.0	745
J. Graboski, IND	10.0	687

ASSISTS

	AVG	NO.
B. Cousy, BOS	7.7	547
A. Phillip, PHI/FTW	5.7	397
G. King, SYR	5.1	364
D. McGuire, NY	4.9	296
P. Seymour, SYR	4.4	294
B. Davies, ROC	4.2	280
E. Macauley, BOS	4.1	280
L. Barnhorst, IND	3.9	277
G. Senesky, PHI	3.8	264
B. Wanzer, ROC	3.6	252

FIELD GOAL PCT

Neil Johnston, PHI	.45242
Ed Macauley, BOS	.45236
Harry Gallatin, NY	.444
Bill Sharman, BOS	.436
Vern Mikkelsen, MIN	.435
Ernie Vandeweghe, NY	.435
Jack Coleman, ROC	.420
Slater Martin, MIN	.410
Bob Lavoy, IND	.402
George King, SYR	.402

FREE THROW PCT

Bill Sharman, BOS	.850
Fred Scolari, FTW	.844
Dolph Schayes, SYR	.827
Carl Braun, NY	.825
Fred Schaus, FTW	.821
Odie Spears, ROC	.819
Paul Seymour, SYR	.817
Bob Cousy, BOS	.816

EAST SEMIFINALS
New York 2, Baltimore 0
Boston 2, Syracuse 0

EAST FINALS
New York 3, Boston 1

WEST SEMIFINALS
Minneapolis 2, Indianapolis 0
Fort Wayne 2, Rochester 1

WEST FINALS
Minneapolis 3, Fort Wayne 2

NBA FINALS
New York 96, Minneapolis 88
Minneapolis 73, New York 71
Minneapolis 90, New York 75
Minneapolis 71, New York 69
Minneapolis 91, New York 84

1953-54
FINAL STANDINGS

Eastern Division

	W	L	PCT	GB
New York	44	28	.611	
Boston	42	30	.583	2
Syracuse	42	30	.583	2
Philadelphia	29	43	.403	15
Baltimore	16	56	.222	28

Western Division

	W	L	PCT	GB
Minneapolis	46	26	.639	
Rochester	44	28	.611	2
Fort Wayne	40	32	.556	6
Milwaukee	21	51	.292	25

POINTS

	AVG	NO.
N. Johnston, PHI	24.4	1759
B. Cousy, BOS	19.2	1383
E. Macauley, BOS	18.9	1344
G. Mikan, MIN	18.1	1306
R. Felix, BAL	17.6	1269
D. Schayes, SYR	17.1	1228
B. Sharman, BOS	16.0	1155
L. Foust, FTW	15.1	1090
C. Braun, NY	14.8	1062
B. Wanzer, ROC	13.3	958
H. Gallatin, NY	13.2	949
A. Risen, ROC	13.2	949
J. Graboski, PHI	13.3	944
P. Seymour, SYR	13.1	931
B. Davies, ROC	12.3	887
J. Pollard, MIN	11.7	831
G. King, SYR	11.3	817
M. Zaslofsky, FTW	12.5	811
V. Mikkelsen, MIN	11.1	797
D. Sunderlage, MIL	11.2	760

REBOUNDS

	AVG	NO.
H. Gallatin, NY	15.3	1098
G. Mikan, MIN	14.3	1028
L. Foust, FTW	13.4	967
R. Felix, BAL	13.3	958
D. Schayes, SYR	12.1	870
N. Johnston, PHI	11.1	797
A. Risen, ROC	10.1	728
M. Hutchins, FTW	9.7	695
L. Hitch, MIL	9.6	691
J. Graboski, PHI	9.4	670

ASSISTS

	AVG	NO.
B. Cousy, BOS	7.2	518
A. Phillip, FTW	6.3	449
P. Seymour, SYR	5.1	364
D. McGuire, NY	5.2	354
B. Davies, ROC	4.5	323
J. George, PHI	4.4	312
P. Hoffman, BAL	4.0	285
G. King, SYR	3.8	272
E. Macauley, BOS	3.8	271
D. Finn, PHI	3.9	265

FIELD GOAL PCT

Ed Macauley, BOS	.486
Bill Sharman, BOS	.450
Neil Johnston, PHI	.449
Clyde Lovellette, MIN	.423
Ray Felix, BAL	.411
Larry Foust, FTW	.409
Eddie Miller, BAL	.407
Jack Coleman, ROC	.405
Harry Gallatin, NY	.404
Mel Hutchins, FTW	.401

FREE THROW PCT

Bill Sharman, BOS	.844
Dolph Schayes, SYR	.827
Carl Braun, NY	.825
Paul Seymour, SYR	.813
Bob Zawoluk, PHI	.809
Bob Cousy, BOS	.787
Harry Gallatin, NY	.784
George Mikan, MIN	.777

EAST ROUND ROBIN
Syracuse 4-0
Boston 2-2
New York 0-4

EAST FINALS
Syracuse 2, Boston 0

WEST ROUND ROBIN
Minneapolis 3-0
Rochester 2-1
Fort Wayne 0-4

WEST FINALS
Minneapolis 2, Rochester 1

NBA FINALS
Minneapolis 79, Syracuse 68
Syracuse 62, Minneapolis 60
Minneapolis 81, Syracuse 67
Syracuse 80, Minneapolis 69
Minneapolis 84, Syracuse 73
Syracuse 65, Minneapolis 63
Minneapolis 87, Syracuse 80

1945-55
FINAL STANDINGS

Eastern Division

	W	L	PCT	GB
Syracuse	43	29	.597	
New York	38	34	.528	5
Boston	36	36	.500	7
Philadelphia	33	39	.458	10

Western Division

	W	L	PCT	GB
Fort Wayne	43	29	.597	
Minneapolis	40	32	.556	3
Rochester	29	43	.403	14
Milwaukee	26	46	.361	17

POINTS AVG NO.
N. Johnston, PHI 22.7 1631
P. Arizin, PHI 21.0 1512
B. Cousy, BOS 21.2 1504
B. Pettit, MIL.............20.4 1466
F. Selvy, BAL/MIL....19.0 1348
D. Schayes, SYR.....18.8 1333
V. Mikkelsen, MIN ..18.4 1327
C. Lovellette, MIN...18.7 1311
B. Sharman, BOS.....18.4 1253
E. Macauley, BOS...17.6 1248
L. Foust, FTW..........17.0 1189
C. Braun, NY 15.1 1074
H. Gallatin, NY........14.6 1053
P. Seymour, SYR 14.6 1050
R. Felix, NY 14.4 1038
G. Yardley, FTW......17.3 1036
J. Baechtold, NY......13.9 1003
S. Martin, MIN 13.6 976
J. Graboski, PHI.......13.6 954
N. Clifton, NY...........13.1 944

REBOUNDS AVG NO.
N. Johnston, PHI ...15.1 1085
H. Gallatin, NY........13.8 995
B. Pettit, MIL............13.8 994
D. Schayes, SYR.....12.3 887
R. Felix, NY 11.4 818
C. Lovellette, MIN....11.5 802
J. Coleman, ROC 10.1 729
V. Mikkelsen, MIN ..10.2 722
A. Risen, ROC.........10.2 703
L. Foust, FTW..........10.0 700

ASSISTS AVG NO.
B. Cousy, BOS 7.8 557
D. McGuire, NY 7.6 542
A. Phillip, FTW..........7.7 491
P. Seymour, SYR 6.7 483
S. Martin, MIN 5.9 427
J. George, PHI..........5.3 359
G. King, SYR.............4.9 331
B. Sharman, BOS.....4.1 280
E. Macauley, BOS....3.9 275
C. Braun, NY 3.9 274

FIELD GOAL PCT
Larry Foust, FTW 487
Jack Coleman, ROC.........462
Neil Johnston, PHI.............440
Ray Felix, NY 438
Clyde Lovellette, MIN 435
Bill Sharman, BOS 427
Ed Macauley, BOS............424
Vern Mikkelsen, MIN 422
John Kerr, SYR 419
George Yardley, FTW 418

FREE THROW PCT
Bill Sharman, BOS 897
Frank Brian, FTW..............851
Dolph Schayes, SYR.........833
Dick Schnittker, MIN..........823
Jim Baechtold, NY.............823
Harry Gallatin, NY 814
Odie Spears, ROC 812
Paul Seymour, SYR 811

EAST SEMIFINALS
Boston 2, New York 1

EAST FINALS
Syracuse 3, Boston 1

WEST SEMIFINALS
Minneapolis 2, Rochester 1

WEST FINALS
Fort Wayne 3, Minneapolis 1

NBA FINALS
Syracuse 86, Fort Wayne 82
Syracuse 87, Fort Wayne 84
Fort Wayne 96, Syracuse 89
Fort Wayne 109, Syracuse 102
Fort Wayne 74, Syracuse 71
Syracuse 109, Fort Wayne 104
Syracuse 92, Fort Wayne 91

1955-56
FINAL STANDINGS

Eastern Division

	W	L	PCT	GB
Philadelphia	45	27	.625	
Boston	39	33	.542	6
Syracuse	35	37	.486	10
New York	35	37	.486	10

Western Division

	W	L	PCT	GB
Fort Wayne	37	35	.514	
Minneapolis	33	39	.458	4
St. Louis	33	39	.458	4
Rochester	31	41	.431	6

POINTS

	AVG	NO.
B. Pettit, STL	25.7	1849
P. Arizin, PHI	24.2	1741
N. Johnston, PHI	22.1	1547
C. Lovellette, MIN	21.5	1526
D. Schayes, SYR	20.4	1472
B. Sharman, BOS	19.9	1434
B. Cousy, BOS	18.8	1356
E. Macauley, BOS	17.5	1240
G. Yardley, FTW	17.4	1233
L. Foust, FTW	16.2	1166
M. Stokes, ROC	16.8	1125
C. Braun, NY	15.4	1112
J. Twyman, ROC	14.4	1038
J. Graboski, PHI	14.4	1034
H. Gallatin, NY	13.9	1002
J. George, PHI	13.9	1000
C. Share, STL	13.6	976
V. Mikkelsen, MIN	13.4	962
J. Kerr, SYR	13.3	961
J. Coleman, ROC/STL	12.8	957

REBOUNDS

	AVG	NO.
B. Pettit, STL	16.2	1164
M. Stokes, ROC	16.3	1094
C. Lovellette, MIN	14.0	992
D. Schayes, SYR	12.4	891
N. Johnston, PHI	12.5	872
C. Share, STL	10.8	774
H. Gallatin, NY	10.3	740
J. Coleman, ROC/STL	9.2	688
G. Yardley, FTW	9.7	686
L. Foust, FTW	9.0	648

ASSISTS

	AVG	NO.
B. Cousy, BOS	8.9	642
J. George, PHI	6.3	457
S. Martin, MIN	6.2	445
A. Phillip, FTW	5.9	410
G. King, SYR	5.7	410
T. Gola, PHI	5.9	404
D. McGuire, NY	5.8	362
B. Sharman, BOS	4.7	339
M. Stokes, ROC	4.9	328
C. Braun, NY	4.1	298

FIELD GOAL PCT

Neil Johnston, PHI	.457
Paul Arizin, PHI	.448
Larry Foust, FTW	.447
Ken Sears, NY	.438
Bill Sharman, BOS	.438
Clyde Lovellette, MIN	.434
Charles Share, STL	.430
Bob Houbregs, FTW	.430
Bob Pettit, STL	.429
Mel Hutchins, FTW	.425

FREE THROW PCT

Bill Sharman, BOS	.867
Dolph Schayes, SYR	.858
Dick Schnittker, MIN	.856
Bob Cousy, BOS	.844
Carl Braun, NY	.838
Slater Martin, MIN	.833
Paul Arizin, PHI	.810
Vern Mikkelsen, MIN	.804

EAST SEMIFINALS
Syracuse 2, Boston 1

EAST FINALS
Philadelphia 3, Syracuse 2

WEST SEMIFINALS
St. Louis 2, Minneapolis 1

WEST FINALS
Fort Wayne 3, St. Louis 2

NBA FINALS
Philadelphia 98, Fort Wayne 94
Fort Wayne 84, Philadelphia 83
Philadelphia 100, Fort Wayne 96
Philadelphia 107, Fort Wayne 105
Philadelphia 99, Fort Wayne 88

1956-57
FINAL STANDINGS

Eastern Division

	W	L	PCT	GB
Boston	44	28	.611	
Syracuse	38	34	.528	6
Philadelphia	37	35	.514	7
New York	36	36	.500	8

Western Division

	W	L	PCT	GB
St. Louis	34	38	.472	
Minneapolis	34	38	.472	
Fort Wayne	34	38	.472	
Rochester	31	41	.431	3

POINTS

	AVG	NO.
P. Arizin, PHI	25.6	1817
B. Pettit, STL	24.7	1755
D. Schayes, SYR	22.5	1617
N. Johnston, PHI	22.8	1575
G. Yardley, FTW	21.5	1547
C. Lovellette, MIN	20.8	1434
B. Sharman, BOS	21.1	1413
B. Cousy, BOS	20.6	1319
E. Macauley, STL	16.5	1187
D. Garmaker, MIN	16.3	1177
J. Twyman, ROC	16.3	1174
T. Heinsohn, BOS	16.2	1163
M. Stokes, ROC	15.6	1124
H. Gallatin, NY	15.0	1079
K. Sears, NY	14.8	1069
J. Graboski, PHI	14.3	1032
C. Braun, NY	13.9	1001
V. Mikkelsen, MIN	13.7	986
E. Conlin, SYR	13.4	953
J. Kerr, SYR	12.4	891

REBOUNDS

	AVG	NO.
M. Stokes, ROC	17.4	1256
B. Pettit, STL	14.6	1037
D. Schayes, SYR	14.0	1008
B. Russell, BOS	19.6	943
C. Lovellette, MIN	13.5	932
N. Johnston, PHI	12.4	855
J. Kerr, SYR	11.2	807
W. Dukes, MIN	11.2	794
G. Yardley, FTW	10.5	755
J. Loscutoff, BOS	10.4	730

ASSISTS

	AVG	NO.
B. Cousy, BOS	7.5	478
J. McMahon, STL	5.1	367
M. Stokes, ROC	4.6	331
J. George, PHI	4.6	307
S. Martin, NY/STL	4.1	269
C. Braun, NY	3.6	256
G. Shue, FTW	3.3	238
B. Sharman, BOS	3.5	236
L. Costello, PHI	3.3	236
D. Schayes, SYR	3.2	229

FIELD GOAL PCT

Neil Johnston, PHI	.447
Charles Share, STL	.439
Jack Twyman, ROC	.439
Bob Houbregs, FTW	.432
Bill Russell, BOS	.427
Clyde Lovellette, MIN	.426
Paul Arizin, PHI	.422
Ed Macauley, STL	.419
Ken Sears, NY	.418
Ray Felix, NY	.416

FREE THROW PCT

Bill Sharman, BOS	.905
Dolph Schayes, SYR	.904
Dick Garmaker, MIN	.839
Paul Arizin, PHI	.829
Neil Johnston, PHI	.826
Bob Cousy, BOS	.821
Carl Braun, NY	.809
Vern Mikkelsen, MIN	.807

EAST SEMIFINALS
Syracuse 2, Philadelphia 0

EAST FINALS
Boston 3, Syracuse 0

WEST SEMIFINALS
Minneapolis 2, Fort Wayne 0

WEST FINALS
St. Louis 3, Minneapolis 0

NBA FINALS
St. Louis 125, Boston 123 (OT)
Boston 119, St. Louis 99
St. Louis 100, Boston 98
Boston 123, St. Louis 118
Boston 124, St. Louis 109
St. Louis 96, Boston 94
Boston 125, St. Louis 123 (2 OT)

1957-58
FINAL STANDINGS

Eastern Division

	W	L	PCT	GB
Boston	49	23	.681	
Syracuse	41	31	.569	8
Philadelphia	37	35	.514	12
New York	35	37	.486	14

Western Division

	W	L	PCT	GB
St. Louis	41	31	.569	
Detroit	33	39	.458	8
Cincinnati	33	39	.458	8
Minneapolis	19	53	.264	22

POINTS

	AVG	NO.
G. Yardley, DET	27.8	2001
D. Schayes, SYR	24.9	1791
B. Pettit, STL	24.6	1719
C. Lovellette, CIN	23.4	1659
P. Arizin, PHI	20.7	1406
B. Sharman, BOS	22.3	1402
C. Hagan, STL	19.9	1391
N. Johnston, PHI	19.5	1388
K. Sears, NY	18.6	1342
V. Mikkelsen, MIN	17.3	1248
J. Twyman, CIN	17.2	1237
T. Heinsohn, BOS	17.8	1230
W. Naulls, NY	18.1	1228
L. Foust, MIN	16.8	1210
C. Braun, NY	16.5	1173
B. Cousy, BOS	18.0	1167
B. Russell, BOS	16.6	1142
F. Ramsey, BOS	16.5	1137
D. Garmaker, MIN	16.1	1094
J. Kerr, SYR	15.2	1094

REBOUNDS

	AVG	NO.
B. Russell, BOS	22.7	1564
B. Pettit, STL	17.4	1216
M. Stokes, CIN	18.1	1142
D. Schayes, SYR	14.2	1022
J. Kerr, SYR	13.4	963
W. Dukes, DET	13.3	954
L. Foust, MIN	12.2	876
C. Lovellette, CIN	12.1	862
V. Mikkelsen, MIN	11.2	805
W. Naulls, NY	11.8	799

ASSISTS

	AVG	NO.
B. Cousy, BOS	7.1	463
D. McGuire, DET	6.6	454
M. Stokes, CIN	6.4	403
C. Braun, NY	5.5	393
G. King, CIN	5.3	337
J. McMahon, STL	4.6	333
T. Gola, PHI	5.5	327
R. Guerin, NY	5.0	317
L. Costello, SYR	4.4	317
J. George, PHI	3.3	234

FIELD GOAL PCT

Jack Twyman, CIN	.452
Cliff Hagan, STL	.443
Bill Russell, BOS	.442
Ray Felix, NY	.442
Clyde Lovellette, CIN	.441
Ken Sears, NY	.439
Neil Johnston, PHI	.429
Ed Macauley, STL	.428
Larry Costello, SYR	.426
Bill Sharman, BOS	.424

FREE THROW PCT

Dolph Schayes, SYR	.904
Bill Sharman, BOS	.893
Bob Cousy, BOS	.850
Carl Braun, NY	.849
Dick Schnittker, MIN	.848
Larry Costello, SYR	.847
Gene Shue, DET	.844
Willie Naulls, NY	.826

EAST SEMIFINALS
Philadelphia 2, Syracuse 1

EAST FINALS
Boston 4, Philadelphia 1

WEST SEMIFINALS
Detroit 2, Cincinnati 0

WEST FINALS
St. Louis 4, Detroit 1

NBA FINALS
St. Louis 104, Boston 102
Boston 136, St. Louis 112
St. Louis 111, Boston 108
Boston 109, St. Louis 98
St. Louis 102, Boston 100
St. Louis 110, Boston 109

1958-59
FINAL STANDINGS

Eastern Division

	W	L	PCT	GB
Boston	52	20	.722	
New York	40	32	.556	12
Syracuse	35	37	.486	17
Philadelphia	32	40	.444	20

Western Division

	W	L	PCT	GB
St. Louis	49	23	.681	
Minneapolis	33	39	.458	16
Detroit	28	44	.389	21
Cincinnati	19	53	.264	30

POINTS	AVG	NO.
B. Pettit, STL	29.2	2105
J. Twyman, CIN	25.8	1857
P. Arizin, PHI	26.4	1851
E. Baylor, MIN	24.9	1742
C. Hagan, STL	23.7	1707
D. Schayes, SYR	21.3	1534
K. Sears, NY	21.0	1488
B. Sharman, BOS	20.4	1466
B. Cousy, BOS	20.0	1297
R. Guerin, NY	18.2	1291
J. Kerr, SYR	17.8	1285
G. Shue, DET	17.6	1266
T. Heinsohn, BOS	18.8	1242
G. Yardley, DET/SYR	19.8	1209
B. Russell, BOS	16.7	1168
W. Sauldsberry, PHI	15.4	1112
L. Costello, SYR	15.8	1108
F. Ramsey, BOS	15.4	1107
W. Naulls, NY	15.7	1068
J. Graboski, PHI	14.7	1058

REBOUNDS	AVG	NO.
B. Russell, BOS	23.0	1612
B. Pettit, STL	16.4	1182
E. Baylor, MIN	15.0	1050
J. Kerr, SYR	14.0	1008
D. Schayes, SYR	13.4	962
W. Dukes, DET	13.3	958
W. Sauldsberry, PHI	11.5	826
C. Hagan, STL	10.9	783
J. Graboski, PHI	10.4	751
W. Naulls, NY	10.6	723

ASSISTS	AVG	NO.
B. Cousy, BOS	8.6	557
D. McGuire, DET	6.2	443
L. Costello, SYR	5.4	379
R. Guerin, NY	5.1	364
C. Braun, NY	4.8	349
S. Martin, STL	4.7	336
J. McMahon, STL	4.1	298
B. Sharman, BOS	4.1	292
E. Baylor, MIN	4.1	287
T. Gola, PHI	4.2	269

FIELD GOAL PCT	
Ken Sears, NY	.490
Bill Russell, BOS	.457
Cliff Hagan, STL	.456
Clyde Lovellette, STL	.454
Hal Greer, SYR	.454
John Kerr, SYR	.441
Bob Pettit, STL	.438
Larry Costello, SYR	.437
Sam Jones, BOS	.434
Paul Arizin, PHI	.431

FREE THROW PCT	
Bill Sharman, BOS	.932
Dolph Schayes, SYR	.864
Ken Sears, NY	.861
Bob Cousy, BOS	.855
Willie Naulls, NY	.830
Clyde Lovellette, STL	.820
Paul Arizin, PHI	.813
Vern Mikkelsen, MIN	.806

EAST SEMIFINALS
Syracuse 2, New York 0

EAST FINALS
Boston 4, Syracuse 3

WEST SEMIFINALS
Minneapolis 2, Detroit 1

WEST FINALS
Minneapolis 4, St. Louis 2

NBA FINALS
Boston 118, Minneapolis 115
Boston 128, Minneapolis 108
Boston 123, Minneapolis 120
Boston 118, Minneapolis 113

1959-60
FINAL STANDINGS

Eastern Division

	W	L	PCT	GB
Boston	59	16	.787	
Philadelphia	49	26	.653	10
Syracuse	45	30	.600	14
New York	27	48	.360	32

Western Division

	W	L	PCT	GB
St. Louis	46	29	.613	
Detroit	30	45	.400	16
Minneapolis	25	50	.333	21
Cincinnati	19	56	.253	27

POINTS	AVG	NO.
W. Chamberlain, PHI	37.6	2707
J. Twyman, CIN	31.2	2338
E. Baylor, MIN	29.6	2074
B. Pettit, STL	26.1	1882
C. Hagan, STL	24.8	1859
G. Shue, DET	22.8	1712
D. Schayes, SYR	22.5	1689
T. Heinsohn, BOS	21.7	1629
R. Guerin, NY	21.8	1615
P. Arizin, PHI	22.3	1606
G. Yardley, SYR	20.2	1473
B. Cousy, BOS	19.4	1455
C. Lovellette, STL	20.8	1416
W. Naulls, NY	21.4	1388
B. Sharman, BOS	19.3	1370
B. Russell, BOS	18.2	1350
B. Howell, DET	17.8	1332
K. Sears, NY	18.5	1187
T. Gola, PHI	15.0	1122
F. Ramsey, BOS	15.3	1117

REBOUNDS	AVG	NO.
W. Chamberlain, PHI	27.0	1941
B. Russell, BOS	24.0	1778
B. Pettit, STL	17.0	1221
E. Baylor, MIN	16.4	1150
D. Schayes, SYR	12.8	959
W. Naulls, NY	14.2	921
J. Kerr, SYR	12.2	913
W. Dukes, DET	13.4	883
K. Sears, NY	13.7	876
C. Hagan, STL	10.7	803

ASSISTS	AVG	NO.
B. Cousy, BOS	9.5	715
G. Rodgers, PHI	7.1	482
R. Guerin, NY	6.3	468
L. Costello, SYR	6.3	449
T. Gola, PHI	5.5	409
D. McGuire, DET	5.3	358
R. Hundley, MIN	4.6	338
S. Martin, STL	5.2	330
J. McCarthy, STL	4.4	328
C. Hagan, STL	4.0	299

FIELD GOAL PCT	
Ken Sears, NY	.477
Hal Greer, SYR	.476
Clyde Lovellette, STL	.468
Bill Russell, BOS	.467
Cliff Hagan, STL	.464
Wilt Chamberlain, PHI	.461
Bill Sharman, BOS	.456
Bailey Howell, DET	.456
Sam Jones, BOS	.454
George Yardley, SYR	.453

FREE THROW PCT	
Dolph Schayes, SYR	.893
Gene Shue, DET	.872
Ken Sears, NY	.868
Bill Sharman, BOS	.866
Larry Costello, SYR	.862
Willie Naulls, NY	.836
Clyde Lovellette, STL	.821
George Yardley, SYR	.816

EAST SEMIFINALS
Philadelphia 2, Syracuse 1

EAST FINALS
Boston 4, Philadelphia 2

WEST SEMIFINALS
Minneapolis 2, Detroit 0

WEST FINALS
St. Louis 4, Minneapolis 3

NBA FINALS
Boston 140, St. Louis 122
St. Louis 113, Boston 103
Boston 102, St. Louis 86
St. Louis 106, Boston 96
Boston 127, St. Louis 102
St. Louis 105, Boston 102
Boston 122, St. Louis 103

1960-61
FINAL STANDINGS

Eastern Division

	W	L	PCT	GB
Boston	57	22	.722	
Philadelphia	46	33	.582	11
Syracuse	38	41	.481	19
New York	21	58	.266	36

Western Division

	W	L	PCT	GB
St. Louis	51	28	.646	
Los Angeles	36	43	.456	15
Detroit	34	45	.430	17
Cincinnati	33	46	.418	18

POINTS

	AVG	NO.
W. Chamberlain, PHI.	38.4	3033
E. Baylor, LA	34.8	2538
O. Robertson, CIN	30.5	2165
B. Pettit, STL	27.9	2120
J. Twyman, CIN	25.3	1997
D. Schayes, SYR	23.6	1868
W. Naulls, NY	23.4	1846
P. Arizin, PHI	23.2	1832
B. Howell, DET	23.6	1815
G. Shue, DET	22.6	1765
R. Guerin, NY	21.8	1720
C. Hagan, STL	21.9	1705
T. Heinsohn, BOS	21.3	1579
H. Greer, SYR	19.6	1551
C. Lovellette, STL	22.0	1471
J. West, LA	17.6	1389
B. Cousy, BOS	18.1	1378
B. Russell, BOS	16.9	1322
D. Barnett, SYR	16.9	1320
F. Ramsey, BOS	15.1	1191

REBOUNDS

	AVG	NO.
W. Chamberlain, PHI	27.2	2149
B. Russell, BOS	23.9	1868
B. Pettit, STL	20.3	1540
E. Baylor, LA	19.8	1447
B. Howell, DET	14.4	1111
W. Naulls, NY	13.4	1055
W. Dukes, DET	14.1	1028
D. Schayes, SYR	12.2	960
J. Kerr, SYR	12.0	951
W. Embry, CIN	10.9	864

ASSISTS

	AVG	NO.
O. Robertson, CIN	9.7	690
G. Rodgers, PHI	8.7	677
B. Cousy, BOS	7.7	587
G. Shue, DET	6.8	530
R. Guerin, NY	6.4	503
J. McCarthy, STL	5.4	430
L. Costello, SYR	5.5	413
C. Hagan, STL	4.9	381
E. Baylor, LA	5.1	371
R. Hundley, LA	4.4	350

FIELD GOAL PCT

Wilt Chamberlain, PHI	.509
Jack Twyman, CIN	.488
Larry Costello, SYR	.482
Oscar Robertson, CIN	.473
Barney Cable, SYR	.472
Bailey Howell, DET	.469
Clyde Lovellette, STL	.453
Dick Barnett, SYR	.452
Wayne Embry, CIN	.451
Hal Greer, SYR	.451

FREE THROW PCT

Bill Sharman, BOS	.921
Dolph Schayes, SYR	.868
Gene Shue, DET	.856
Frank Ramsey, BOS	.833
Paul Arizin, PHI	.833
Dave Gambee, SYR	.831
Clyde Lovellette, STL	.830
Ken Sears, NY	.830

EAST SEMIFINALS
Syracuse 3, Philadelphia 0

EAST FINALS
Boston 4, Syracuse 1

WEST SEMIFINALS
Los Angeles 3, Detroit 2

WEST FINALS
St. Louis 4, Los Angeles 3

NBA FINALS
Boston 129, St. Louis 95
Boston 116, St. Louis 108
St. Louis 124, Boston 120
Boston 119, St. Louis 104
Boston 121, St. Louis 112

1961-62
FINAL STANDINGS

Eastern Division

	W	L	PCT	GB
Boston	60	20	.750	
Philadelphia	49	31	.613	11
Syracuse	41	39	.513	19
New York	29	51	.363	31

Western Division

	W	L	PCT	GB
Los Angeles	54	26	.675	
Cincinnati	43	37	.538	11
Detroit	37	43	.463	17
St. Louis	29	51	.363	25
Chicago	18	62	.225	36

POINTS

	AVG	NO.
W. Chamberlain, PHI	50.4	4029
W. Bellamy, CHI	31.6	2495
O. Robertson, CIN	30.8	2432
B. Pettit, STL	31.1	2429
J. West, LA	30.8	2310
R. Guerin, NY	29.5	2303
W. Naulls, NY	25.0	1877
E. Baylor, LA	38.3	1836
J. Twyman, CIN	22.9	1831
C. Hagan, STL	22.9	1764
T. Heinsohn, BOS	22.1	1742
P. Arizin, PHI	21.9	1706
H. Greer, SYR	22.8	1619
B. Howell, DET	19.9	1576
G. Shue, DET	19.0	1522
W. Embry, CIN	19.8	1484
B. Russell, BOS	18.9	1436
S. Jones, BOS	18.4	1435
R. LaRusso, LA	17.2	1374
D. Gambee, SYR	16.7	1338

REBOUNDS

	AVG	NO.
W. Chamberlain, PHI	25.7	2052
B. Russell, BOS	23.6	1790
W. Bellamy, CHI	19.0	1500
B. Pettit, STL	18.7	1459
J. Kerr, SYR	14.7	1176
J. Green, NY	13.3	1066
B. Howell, DET	12.6	996
O. Robertson, CIN	12.5	985
W. Embry, CIN	13.0	977
E. Baylor, LA	18.6	892

ASSISTS

	AVG	NO.
O. Robertson, CIN	11.4	899
G. Rodgers, PHI	7.9	663
B. Cousy, BOS	7.8	584
R. Guerin, NY	6.9	539
G. Shue, DET	5.8	465
J. West, LA	5.4	402
F. Selvy, LA	4.8	381
B. Leonard, CHI	5.4	378
C. Hagan, STL	4.8	370
A. Bockhorn, CIN	4.6	366

FIELD GOAL PCT

Walt Bellamy, CHI	.519
Wilt Chamberlain, PHI	.506
Jack Twyman, CIN	.479
Oscar Robertson, CIN	.478
Al Attles, PHI	.474
Larry Foust, STL	.471
Clyde Lovellette, STL	.471
Cliff Hagan, STL	.470
Wayne Embry, CIN	.466
Rudy LaRusso, LA	.466

FREE THROW PCT

Dolph Schayes, SYR	.896
Willie Naulls, NY	.842
Larry Costello, SYR	.837
Frank Ramsey, BOS	.825
Cliff Hagan, STL	.825
Tom Meschery, PHI	.824
Richie Guerin, NY	.820
Hal Greer, SYR	.819

EAST SEMIFINALS
Philadelphia 3, Syracuse 2

EAST FINALS
Boston 4, Philadelphia 3

WEST SEMIFINALS
Detroit 3, Cincinnati 1

WEST FINALS
Los Angeles 4 Detroit 2

NBA FINALS
Boston 122, Los Angeles 108
Los Angeles 129, Boston 122
Los Angeles 117, Boston 115
Boston 115, Los Angeles 103
Los Angeles 126, Boston 121
Boston 119, Los Angeles 105
Boston 110, Los Angeles 107 (OT)

1962-63
FINAL STANDINGS

Eastern Division	W	L	PCT	GB	Western Division	W	L	PCT	GB
Boston	58	22	.725		Los Angeles	53	27	.663	
Syracuse	48	32	.600	10	St. Louis	48	32	.600	5
Cincinnati	42	38	.525	16	Detroit	34	46	.425	19
New York	21	59	.263	37	San Francisco	31	49	.388	22
					Chicago	25	55	.313	28

POINTS	AVG	NO.
W. Chamberlain, SF	44.8	3586
E. Baylor, LA	34.0	2719
O. Robertson, CIN	28.3	2264
B. Pettit, STL	28.4	2241
W. Bellamy, CHI	27.9	2233
B. Howell, DET	22.7	1793
R. Guerin, NY	21.5	1701
J. Twyman, CIN	19.8	1586
H. Greer, SYR	19.5	1562
D. Ohl, DET	19.3	1547
S. Jones, BOS	19.7	1499
J. West, LA	27.1	1489
L. Shaffer, SYR	18.6	1488
T. Dischinger, CHI	25.5	1452
J. Green, NY	18.1	1444
T. Heinsohn, BOS	18.9	1440
D. Barnett, LA	18.0	1437
W. Embry, CIN	18.6	1411
B. Russell, BOS	16.8	1309
J. Kerr, SYR	15.7	1255

REBOUNDS	AVG	NO.
W. Chamberlain, SF	24.3	1946
B. Russell, BOS	23.0	1843
W. Bellamy, CHI	16.4	1309
B. Pettit, STL	15.1	1191
E. Baylor, LA	14.3	1146
J. Kerr, SYR	13.1	1049
J. Green, NY	12.1	964
W. Embry, CIN	12.3	936
B. Howell, DET	11.5	910
B. Boozer, CIN	11.1	878

ASSISTS	AVG	NO.
G. Rodgers, SF	10.4	825
O. Robertson, CIN	9.5	758
B. Cousy, BOS	6.8	515
S. Green, CHI	5.8	422
E. Baylor, LA	4.8	386
L. Wilkens, STL	5.1	381
B. Russell, BOS	4.5	348
R. Guerin, NY	4.4	348
L. Costello, SYR	4.3	334
J. Barnhill, STL	4.2	322

FIELD GOAL PCT

Wilt Chamberlain, SF	.528
Walt Bellamy, CHI	.527
Oscar Robertson, CIN	.518
Bailey Howell, DET	.516
Terry Dischinger, CHI	.512
Dave Budd, NY	.502
Jack Twyman, CIN	.480
Al Attles, SF	.478
Sam Jones, BOS	.476
John Kerr, SYR	.474

FREE THROW PCT

Larry Costello, SYR	.881
Richie Guerin, NY	.848
Elgin Baylor, LA	.837
Tom Heinsohn, BOS	.835
Hal Greer, SYR	.834
Frank Ramsey, BOS	.816
Dick Barnett, LA	.815
Adrian Smith, CIN	.811

EAST SEMIFINALS
Cincinnati 3, Syracuse 2

EAST FINALS
Boston 4, Cincinnati 3

WEST SEMIFINALS
St. Louis 3, Detroit 1

WEST FINALS
Los Angeles 4, St. Louis 3

NBA FINALS
Boston 117, Los Angeles 114
Boston 113, Los Angeles 106
Los Angeles 119, Boston 99
Boston 108, Los Angeles 105
Los Angeles 126, Boston 119
Boston 112, Los Angeles 109

1963-64
FINAL STANDINGS

Eastern Division

	W	L	PCT	GB
Boston	59	21	.738	
Cincinnati	55	25	.688	4
Philadelphia	34	46	.425	25
New York	22	58	.275	37

Western Division

	W	L	PCT	GB
San Francisco	48	32	.600	
St. Louis	46	34	.575	2
Los Angeles	42	38	.525	6
Baltimore	31	49	.388	17
Detroit	23	57	.288	25

POINTS

	AVG	NO.
W. Chamberlain, SF	36.9	2948
O. Robertson, CIN	31.4	2480
B. Pettit, ST	27.4	2190
W. Bellamy, BAL	27.0	2159
J. West, LA	28.7	2064
E. Baylor, LA	25.4	1983
H. Greer, PHI	23.3	1865
B. Howell, DET	21.6	1666
T. Dischinger, BAL	20.8	1662
J. Havlicek, BOS	19.9	1595
S. Jones, BOS	19.4	1473
D. Barnett, LA	18.4	1433
C. Hagan, STL	18.4	1413
R. Scott, DET	17.6	1406
J. Lucas, CIN	17.7	1400
W. Embry, CIN	17.3	1383
G. Johnson, BAL	17.3	1352
L. Chappell, PHI/NY	17.1	1350
J. Kerr, PHI	16.8	1340
C. Walker, PHI	17.3	1314

REBOUNDS

	AVG	NO.
B. Russell, BOS	24.7	1930
W. Chamberlain, SF	22.3	1787
J. Lucas, CIN	17.4	1375
W. Bellamy, BAL	17.0	1361
B. Pettit, STL	15.3	1224
R. Scott, DET	13.5	1078
G. Johnson, BAL	13.6	1064
J. Kerr, PHI	12.7	1018
E. Baylor, LA	12.0	936
W. Embry, CIN	11.6	925

ASSISTS

	AVG	NO.
O. Robertson, CIN	11.0	868
G. Rodgers, SF	7.0	556
K. Jones, BOS	5.1	407
J. West, LA	5.6	403
W. Chamberlain, SF	5.0	403
R. Guerin, NY/STL	4.7	375
H. Greer, PHI	4.7	374
B. Russell, BOS	4.7	370
L. Wilkens, STL	4.6	359
J. Egan, DET/NY	5.4	358

FIELD GOAL PCT

Jerry Lucas, CIN	.527
Wilt Chamberlain, SF	.524
Walt Bellamy, BAL	.513
Terry Dischinger, BAL	.496
Bill McGill, NY	.487
Jerry West, LA	.484
Oscar Robertson, CIN	.483
Bailey Howell, DET	.472
John Green, NY	.470
Bob Pettit, STL	.463

FREE THROW PCT

Oscar Robertson, CIN	.853
Jerry West, LA	.832
Hal Greer, PHI	.829
Tom Heinsohn, BOS	.827
Richie Guerin, NY/STL	.818
Cliff Hagan, STL	.813
Bailey Howell, DET	.809
Elgin Baylor, LA	.804

EAST SEMIFINALS
Cincinnati 3, Philadelphia 2

EAST FINALS
Boston 4, Cincinnati 1

WEST SEMIFINALS
St. Louis 3, Los Angeles 2

WEST FINALS
San Francisco 4, St. Louis 3

NBA FINALS
Boston 108, San Francisco 96
Boston 124, San Francisco 101
San Francisco 115, Boston 91
Boston 98, San Francisco 95
Boston 105, San Francisco 99

1964-65
FINAL STANDINGS

Eastern Division

	W	L	PCT	GB
Boston	62	18	.715	
Cincinnati	48	32	.600	14
Philadelphia	40	40	.500	22
New York	31	49	.388	31

Western Division

	W	L	PCT	GB
Los Angeles	49	31	.613	
St. Louis	45	35	.563	4
Baltimore	37	43	.463	12
Detroit	31	49	.388	18
San Francisco	17	63	.213	32

POINTS

	AVG	NO.
W. Chamber., SF/PHI	34.7	2534
J. West, LA	31.0	2292
O. Robertson, CIN	30.4	2279
S. Jones, BOS	25.9	2070
E. Baylor, LA	27.1	2009
W. Bellamy, BAL	24.8	1981
W. Reed, NY	19.5	1560
B. Howell, BAL	19.2	1534
T. Dichinger, DET	18.2	1456
D. Ohl, BAL	18.4	1420
G. Johnson, BAL	18.6	1415
J. Lucas, CIN	21.4	1414
H. Greer, PHI	20.2	1413
J. Havlicek, BOS	18.3	1375
Z. Beaty, STL	16.9	1351
D. DeBusschere, DET	16.7	1322
L. Wilkens, STL	16.5	1284
N. Thurmond, SF	16.5	1273
A. Smith, CIN	15.1	1210
J. Barnes, NY	15.5	1159

REBOUNDS

	AVG	NO.
B. Russell, BOS	24.1	1878
W. Chamber., SF/PHI	22.9	1673
N. Thurmond, SF	18.1	1395
J. Lucas, CIN	20.0	1321
W. Reed, NY	14.7	1175
W. Bellamy, BAL	14.6	1166
G. Johnson, BAL	13.0	988
L. Jackson, PHI	12.9	980
Z. Beaty, STL	12.1	966
E. Baylor, LA	12.8	950

ASSISTS

	AVG	NO.
O. Robertson, CIN	11.5	861
G. Rodgers, SF	7.3	565
K. Jones, BOS	5.6	437
L. Wilkens, STL	5.5	431
B. Russell, BOS	5.3	410
J. West, LA	4.9	364
H. Greer, PHI	4.5	313
K. Loughery, BAL	3.7	296
E. Baylor, LA	3.8	280
L. Costello, PHI	4.3	275

FIELD GOAL PCT

Wilt Chamberlain, SF/PHI	.510
Walt Bellamy, BAL	.509
Jerry Lucas, CIN	.498
Jerry West, LA	.497
Bailey Howell, BAL	.495
Terry Dischinger, DET	.493
John Egan, NY	.488
Zelmo Beaty, STL	.482
Oscar Robertson, CIN	.480
Paul Neumann, PHI/SF	.473

FREE THROW PCT

Larry Costello, PHI	.877
Oscar Robertson, CIN	.839
Howard Komives, NY	.835
Adrian Smith, CIN	.830
Jerry West, LA	.821
Sam Jones, BOS	.820
Bob Pettit, STL	.820
Jerry Lucas, CIN	.814

EAST SEMIFINALS
Philadelphia 3, Cincinnati 1

EAST FINALS
Boston 4, Philadelphia 3

WEST SEMIFINALS
Baltimore 3, St. Louis 1

WEST FINALS
Los Angeles 4, Baltimore 2

NBA FINALS
Boston 142, Los Angeles 110
Boston 129, Los Angeles 123
Los Angeles 126, Boston 105
Boston 112, Los Angeles 99
Boston 129, Los Angeles 96

1965-66
FINAL STANDINGS

Eastern Division

	W	L	PCT	GB
Philadelphia	55	25	.688	
Boston	54	26	.675	1
Cincinnati	45	35	.563	10
New York	30	50	.375	25

Western Division

	W	L	PCT	GB
Los Angeles	45	35	.563	
Baltimore	38	42	.475	7
St. Louis	36	44	.450	9
San Francisco	35	45	.438	10
Detroit	22	58	.275	23

POINTS

	AVG	NO.
W. Chamberlain, PHI	33.5	2649
J. West, LA	31.3	2476
O. Robertson, CIN	31.3	2378
R. Barry, SF	25.7	2059
W. Bellamy, BAL/NY	22.8	1820
H. Greer, PHI	22.7	1819
D. Barnett, NY	23.1	1729
J. Lucas, CIN	21.5	1697
Z. Beaty, STL	20.7	1656
S. Jones, BOS	23.5	1577
E. Miles, DET	19.6	1566
D. Ohl, BAL	20.6	1502
A. Smith, CIN	18.4	1470
G. Rodgers, SF	18.6	1468
R. Scott, DET	17.9	1411
B. Howell, BAL	17.3	1364
K. Loughery, BAL	18.2	1349
J. Havlicek, BOS	18.8	1334
D. DeBusschere, DET	16.4	1297
L. Wilkens, STL	18.0	1244

REBOUNDS

	AVG	NO.
W. Chamberlain, PHI	24.6	1943
B. Russell, BOS	22.8	1779
J. Lucas, CIN	21.1	1668
N. Thurmond, SF	18.0	1312
W. Bellamy, BAL/NY	15.7	1254
Z. Beaty, STL	13.6	1086
B. Bridges, STL	12.2	951
D. DeBusschere, DET	11.6	916
W. Reed, NY	11.6	883
R. Barry, SF	10.6	850

ASSISTS

	AVG	NO.
O. Robertson, CIN	11.1	847
G. Rodgers, SF	10:7	846
K. Jones, BOS	6.3	503
J. West, LA	6.1	480
L. Wilkens, STL	6.2	429
H. Komives, NY	5.3	425
W. Chamberlain, PHI	5.2	414
W. Hazzard, LA	4.9	393
R. Guerin, STL	4.9	388
H. Greer, PHI	4.8	384

FIELD GOAL PCT

Wilt Chamberlain, PHI	.540
John Green, NY/BAL	.536
Walt Bellamy, BAL/NY	.506
Al Attles, SF	.503
Happy Hairston, CIN	.489
Bailey Howell, BAL	.488
Bob Boozer, LA	.484
Oscar, Robertson, CIN	.475
Zelmo Beaty, STL	.473
Jerry West, LA	.473

FREE THROW PCT

Larry Siegfried, BOS	.881
Rick Barry, SF	.862
Howard Komives, NY	.861
Jerry West, LA	.860
Adrian Smith, CIN	.850
Oscar Robertson, CIN	.842
Paul Neumann, SF	.836
Kevin Loughery, BAL	.830

EAST SEMIFINALS
Boston 3, Cincinnati 2

EAST FINALS
Boston 4, Philadelphia 1

WEST SEMIFINALS
St. Louis 3, Baltimore 0

WEST FINALS
Los Angeles 4, St. Louis 3

NBA FINALS
Los Angeles 133, Boston 129 (OT)
Boston 129, Los Angeles 109
Boston 120, Los Angeles 106
Boston 122, Los Angeles 117
Los Angeles 121, Boston 117
Los Angeles 123, Boston 115
Boston 95, Los Angeles 93

1966-67
FINAL STANDINGS

Eastern Division

	W	L	PCT	GB
Philadelphia	68	13	.840	
Boston	60	21	.741	8
Cincinnati	39	42	.481	29
New York	36	45	.444	32
Baltimore	20	61	.247	48

Western Division

	W	L	PCT	GB
San Francisco	44	37	.543	
St. Louis	39	42	.481	5
Los Angeles	36	45	.444	8
Chicago	33	48	.407	11
Detroit	30	51	.370	14

POINTS

	AVG	NO.
R. Barry, SF	35.6	2775
O. Robertson, CIN	30.5	2412
W. Chamberlain, PHI	24.1	1956
J. West, LA	28.7	1892
E. Baylor, LA	26.6	1862
H. Greer, PHI	22.1	1765
J. Havlicek, BOS	21.4	1733
W. Reed, NY	20.9	1628
B. Howell, BOS	20.0	1621
D. Bing, DET	20.0	1601
S. Jones, BOS	22.1	1594
C. Walker, PHI	19.3	1567
G. Johnson, BAL	20.7	1511
W. Bellamy, NY	19.0	1499
B. Cunningham, PHI	18.5	1495
L. Hudson, STL	18.4	1471
G. Rodgers, CHI	18.0	1459
J. Lucas, CIN	17.8	1438
B. Boozer, CHI	18.0	1436
E. Miles, DET	17.6	1425

REBOUNDS

	AVG	NO.
W. Chamberlain, PHI	24.2	1957
B. Russell, BOS	21.0	1700
J. Lucas, CIN	19.1	1547
N. Thurmond, SF	21.3	1382
B. Bridges, STL	15.1	1190
W. Reed, NY	14.6	1136
D. Imhoff, LA	13.3	1080
W. Bellamy, NY	13.5	1064
L. Ellis, BAL	12.0	970
D. DeBusschere, DET	11.8	924

ASSISTS

	AVG	NO.
G. Rodgers, CHI	11.2	908
O. Robertson, CIN	10.7	845
W. Chamberlain, PHI	7.8	630
B. Russell, BOS	5.8	472
J. West, LA	6.8	447
L. Wilkens, STL	5.7	442
H. Komives, NY	6.2	401
K. Jones, BOS	5.0	389
R. Guerin, STL	4.4	345
P. Neumann, SF	4.4	342

FIELD GOAL PCT

Wilt Chamberlain, PHI	.683
Walt Bellamy, NY	.521
Bailey Howell, BOS	.512
Oscar Robertson, CIN	.493
Willis Reed, NY	.490
Chet Walker, PHI	.488
Bob Boozer, CHI	.487
Tom Hawkins, LA	.481
Happy Hairston, CIN	.479
Dick Barnett, NY	.478

FREE THROW PCT

Adrian Smith, CIN	.903
Rick Barry, SF	.884
Jerry West, LA	.878
Oscar Robertson, CIN	.873
Sam Jones, BOS	.857
Larry Siegfried, BOS	.847
Wally Jones, PHI	.838
John Havlicek, BOS	.828

EAST SEMIFINALS
Philadelphia 3, Cincinnati 1
Boston 3, New York 1

EAST FINALS
Philadelphia 4, Boston 1

WEST SEMIFINALS
San Francisco 3, Los Angeles 0
St. Louis 3, Chicago 0

WEST FINALS
San Francisco 4, St. Louis 2

NBA FINALS
Philadelphia 141, S.F. 135 (OT)
Philadelphia 126, S.F. 95
San Francisco 130, Phil. 124
Philadelphia 122, S.F. 108
San Francisco 117, Phil. 109
Philadelphia 125, S.F. 122

1967-68
FINAL STANDINGS

Eastern Division

	W	L	PCT	GB
Philadelphia	62	20	.756	
Boston	54	28	.659	8
New York	43	39	.524	19
Detroit	40	42	.488	22
Cincinnati	39	43	.476	23
Baltimore	36	46	.439	26

Western Division

	W	L	PCT	GB
St. Louis	56	26	.683	
Los Angeles	52	30	.634	4
San Francisco	43	39	.524	13
Chicago	29	53	.354	27
Seattle	23	59	.280	33
San Diego	15	67	.183	41

POINTS

	AVG	NO.
D. Bing, DET	27.1	2142
E. Baylor, LA	26.0	2002
W. Chamberlain, PHI	24.3	1992
E. Monroe, BAL	24.3	1991
H. Greer, PHI	24.1	1976
O. Robertson, CIN	29.2	1896
W. Hazzard, SEA	23.9	1894
J. Lucas, CIN	21.4	1760
Z. Beaty, STL	21.1	1733
R. LaRusso, SF	21.8	1726
J. Havlicek, BOS	20.7	1700
W. Reed, NY	20.8	1685
B. Boozer, CHI	21.5	1655
L. Wilkens, STL	20.0	1638
B. Howell, BOS	19.8	1621
A. Clark, LA	19.9	1612
S. Jones, BOS	21.3	1553
J. Mullins, SF	18.9	1493
B. Rule, SEA	18.1	1484
C. Walker, PHI	17.9	1465

REBOUNDS

	AVG	NO.
W. Chamberlain, PHI	23.8	1952
J. Lucas, CIN	19.0	1560
B. Russell, BOS	18.6	1451
C. Lee, SF	13.9	1141
N. Thurmond, SF	22.0	1121
R. Scott, BAL	13.7	1111
B. Bridges, STL	13.4	1102
D. DeBusschere, DET	13.5	1081
W. Reed, NY	13.2	1073
W. Bellamy, NY	11.7	961

ASSISTS

	AVG	NO.
W. Chamberlain, PHI	8.6	702
L. Wilkens, STL	8.3	679
O. Robertson, CIN	9.7	633
D. Bing, DET	6.4	509
W. Hazzard, SEA	6.2	493
A. Williams, SD	4.9	391
A. Attles, SF	5.8	390
J. Havlicek, BOS	4.7	384
G. Rodgers, CHI/CIN	4.8	380
H. Greer, PHI	4.5	372

FIELD GOAL PCT

Wilt Chamberlain, PHI	.595
Walt Bellamy, NY	.541
Jerry Lucas, CIN	.519
Jerry West, LA	.514
Len Chappell, CIN/DET	.513
Oscar Robertson, CIN	.500
Tom Hawkins, LA	.499
Terry Dischinger, DET	.494
Don Nelson, BOS	.494
Henry Finkel, SD	.492

FREE THROW PCT

Oscar Robertson, CIN	.873
Larry Siegfried, BOS	.868
Dave Gambee, SD	.847
Fred Hetzel, SF	.833
Adrian Smith, CIN	.829
Sam Jones, BOS	.827
Flynn Robinson, CIN/CHI	.821
John Havlicek, BOS	.812

EAST SEMIFINALS
Philadelphia 4, New York 2
Boston 4, Detroit 2

EAST FINALS
Boston 4, Philadelphia 3

WEST SEMIFINALS
San Francisco 4, St. Louis 2
Los Angeles 4, Chicago 1

WEST FINALS
Los Angeles 4, San Francisco 0

NBA FINALS
Boston 107, Los Angeles 101
Los Angeles 123, Boston 113
Boston 127, Los Angeles 119
Los Angeles 119, Boston 105
Boston 120, Los Angeles 117 (OT)
Boston 124, Los Angeles 109

1968-69
FINAL STANDINGS

Eastern Division

	W	L	PCT	GB
Baltimore	57	25	.695	
Philadelphia	55	27	.671	2
New York	54	28	.659	3
Boston	48	34	.585	9
Cincinnati	41	41	.500	16
Detroit	32	50	.390	25
Milwaukee	27	55	.329	30

Western Division

	W	L	PCT	GB
Los Angeles	55	27	.671	
Atlanta	48	34	.585	7
San Francisco	41	41	.500	14
San Diego	37	45	.451	18
Chicago	33	49	.402	22
Seattle	30	52	.366	25
Phoenix	16	66	.195	39

POINTS

	AVG	NO.
E. Hayes, SD	28.4	2327
E. Monroe, BAL	25.8	2065
B. Cunningham, PHI.	24.8	2034
B. Rule, SEA	24.0	1965
O. Robertson, CIN	24.7	1955
G. Goodrich, PHO	23.8	1931
H. Greer, PHI	23.1	1896
E. Baylor, LA	24.8	1881
L. Wilkens, SEA	22.4	1835
D. Kojis, SD	22.5	1820
K. Loughery, BAL	22.6	1806
D. Bing, DET	23.4	1800
J. Mullins, SF	22.8	1775
J. Havlicek, BOS	21.6	1771
L. Hudson, ATL	21.9	1770
W. Reed, NY	21.1	1733
B. Boozer, CHI	21.7	1716
D. Van Arsdale, PHO	21.0	1678
W. Chamberlain, LA	20.5	1664
F. Robinson, CHI/MIL	20.0	1662

REBOUNDS

	AVG	NO.
W. Chamberlain, LA	21.1	1712
W. Unseld, BAL	18.2	1491
B. Russell, BOS	19.3	1484
E. Hayes, SD	17.1	1406
N. Thurmond, SF	19.7	1402
J. Lucas, CIN	18.4	1360
W. Reed, NY	14.5	1191
B. Bridges, ATL	14.2	1132
W. Bellamy, NY/DET	12.5	1101
B. Cunningham, PHI	12.8	1050

ASSISTS

	AVG	NO.
O. Robertson, CIN	9.8	772
L. Wilkens, SEA	8.2	674
W. Frazier, NY	7.9	635
G. Rodgers, MIL	6.9	561
D. Bing, DET	7.1	546
A. Williams, SD	6.6	524
G. Goodrich, PHO	6.4	518
W. Hazzard, ATL	5.9	474
J. Havlicek, BOS	5.4	441
J. West, LA	6.9	423

FIELD GOAL PCT

Wilt Chamberlain, LA	.583
Jerry Lucas, CIN	.551
Willis Reed, NY	.521
Terry Dischinger, DET	.515
Walt Bellamy, NY/DET	.510
Joe Caldwell, ATL	.507
Walt Frazier, NY	.505
Tom Hawkins, LA	.499
Lou Hudson, ATL	.492
Jon McGlocklin, MIL	.487

FREE THROW PCT

Larry Siegfried, BOS	.864
Jeff Mullins, SF	.843
Jon McGlocklin, MIL	.842
Flynn Robinson, CHI/MIL	.839
Oscar Robertson, CIN	.838
Fred Hetzel, MIL/CIN	.838
Jack Marin, BAL	.830
Jerry West, LA	.821

EAST SEMIFINALS

New York 4, Baltimore 0
Boston 4, Philadelphia 1

EAST FINALS

Boston 4, New York 2

WEST SEMIFINALS

Los Angeles 4, San Francisco 2
Atlanta 4, San Diego 2

WEST FINALS

Los Angeles 4, Atlanta 1

NBA FINALS

Los Angeles 120, Boston 118
Los Angeles 118, Boston 112
Boston 111, Los Angeles 105
Boston 89, Los Angeles 88
Los Angeles 117, Boston 104
Boston 99, Los Angeles 90
Boston 108, Los Angeles 106

1969-70
FINAL STANDINGS

Eastern Division	W	L	PCT	GB
New York	60	22	.732	
Milwaukee	56	26	.683	4
Baltimore	50	32	.610	10
Philadelphia	42	40	.512	18
Cincinnati	36	46	.439	24
Boston	34	48	.415	26
Detroit	31	51	.378	29

Western Division	W	L	PCT	GB
Atlanta	48	34	.585	
Los Angeles	46	36	.561	2
Chicago	39	43	.476	9
Phoenix	39	43	.476	9
Seattle	36	46	.439	12
San Francisco	30	52	.366	18
San Diego	27	55	.329	21

SCORING
Jerry West, LA	31.2
Lew Alcindor, MIL	28.8
Elvin Hayes, SD	27.5
Billy Cunningham, PHI	26.1
Lou Hudson, ATL	25.4
Connie Hawkins, PHO	24.6
Bob Rule, SEA	24.6
John Havlicek, BOS	24.2
Earl Monroe, BAL	23.4
Dave Bing, DET	22.9
Tom Van Arsdale, CIN	22.8
Jeff Mullins, SF	22.1
Hal Greer, PHI	22.0
Flynn Robinson, MIL	21.8
Willis Reed, NY	21.7
Chet Walker, CHI	21.5
Dick Van Arsdale, PHO	21.3
Joe Caldwell, ATL	21.1
Bob Love, CHI	21.0
Walt Frazier, NY	20.9

REBOUNDS
Elvin Hayes, SD	16.9
Wes Unseld, BAL	16.7
Lew Alcindor, MIL	14.5
Bill Bridges, ATL	14.4
Gus Johnson, BAL	13.9
Willie Reed, NY	13.9
Billy Cunningham, PHI	13.6
Tom Boerwinkle, CHI	12.5
Paul Silas, PHO	11.7
Clyde Lee, SF	11.3

ASSISTS
Len Wilkens, SEA	9.1
Walt Frazier, NY	8.2
Clem Haskins, CHI	7.6
Jerry West, LA	7.5
Gail Goodrich, PHO	7.5
Walt Hazzard, ATL	6.8
John Havlicek, BOS	6.8
Art Williams, SD	6.3
Norm Van Lier, CIN	6.2
Dave Bing, DET	6.0

FIELD GOAL PCT
Johnny Green, CIN	.559
Darrall Imhoff, PHI	.540
Lou Hudson, ATL	.531
Jon McGlocklin, MIL	.530
Dick Snyder, SEA	.528
Jim Fox, PHO	.524
Lew Alcindor, MIL	.518
Wes Unseld, BAL	.518
Walt Frazier, NY	.518
Dick Van Arsdale, PHO	.508

FREE THROW PCT
Flynn Robinson, MIL	.898
Chet Walker, CHI	.850
Jeff Mullins, SF	.847
John Havlicek, BOS	.844
Bob Love, CHI	.842
Earl Monroe, BAL	.830
Lou Hudson, ATL	.824
Jerry West, LA	.824

EAST SEMIFINALS
New York 4, Baltimore 3
Milwaukee 4, Philadelphia 1

EAST FINALS
New York 4, Milwaukee 1

WEST SEMIFINALS
Atlanta 4, Chicago 1
Los Angeles 4, Phoenix 3

WEST FINALS
Los Angeles 4, Atlanta 0

NBA FINALS
New York 124, Los Angeles 112
Los Angeles 105, New York 103
New York 111, Los Angeles 108 (OT)
Los Angeles 121, New York 115 (OT)
New York 107, Los Angeles 100
Los Angeles 135, New York 113
New York 113, Los Angeles 99

1970-71
FINAL STANDINGS

Eastern Conference
Atlantic Division

	W	L	PCT	GB
New York	52	30	.634	
Philadelphia	47	35	.573	5
Boston	44	38	.537	8
Buffalo	22	60	.268	30

Central Division

	W	L	PCT	GB
Baltimore	42	40	.512	
Atlanta	36	46	.439	6
Cincinnati	33	49	.402	9
Cleveland	15	67	.183	27

Western Conference
Midwest Division

	W	L	PCT	GB
Milwaukee	66	16	.805	
Chicago	51	31	.622	5
Phoenix	48	34	.585	18
Detroit	45	37	.549	21

Pacific Division

	W	L	PCT	GB
Los Angeles	48	34	.585	
San Francisco	41	41	.500	7
San Diego	40	42	.488	8
Seattle	38	44	.463	10
Portland	29	53	.354	19

SCORING
Lew Alcindor, MIL 31.7
John Havlicek, BOS 28.9
Elvin Hayes, SD 28.7
Dave Bing, DET 27.0
Lou Hudson, ATL 26.8
Bob Love, CHI....................25.2
Geoff Petrie, POR.............24.8
Pete Maravich, ATL 23.2
Billy Cunningham, PHI.......23.0
Tom Van Arsdale, CIN 22.9
Chet Walker, CHI................22.0
Dick Van Arsdale, PHO......21.9
Walt Frazier, NY.................21.7
Earl Monroe, BAL..............21.4
Jo Jo White, BOS...............21.3
Archie Clark, PHI 21.3
Willis Reed, NY 20.9
Connie Hawkins, PHO 20.9
Jeff Mullins, SF 20.8

REBOUNDS
Wilt Chamberlain, LA 18.2
Wes Unseld, BAL...............16.9
Elvin Hayes, SD 16.6
Lew Alcindor, MIL 16.0
Jerry Lucas, SF..................15.8
Bill Bridges, ATL 15.0
Dave Cowens, BOS...........15.0
Tom Boerwinkle, CHI..........13.8
Nate Thurmond, SF 13.8
Willis Reed, NY 13.7

ASSISTS
Norm Van Lier, CIN...........10.1
Len Wilkens, SEA.............. 9.2
Oscar Robertson, MIL 8.2
John Havlicek, BOS 7.5
Walt Frazier, NY 6.7
Walt Hazzard, ATL 6.3
Ron Williams, SF............... 5.9
Nate Archibald, CIN........... 5.5
Archie Clark, PHI............... 5.4
Dave Bing, DET................. 5.0

FIELD GOAL PCT
Johnny Green, CIN............ .587
Lew Alcindor, MIL.............. .577
Wilt Chamberlain, LA......... .545
Jon McGlocklin, MIL.......... .535
Dick Snyder, SEA.............. .531
Greg Smith, MIL .... .512
Bob Dandridge, MIL .... .509
Wes Unseld, BAL .... .501
Jerry Lucas, SF .... .498

FREE THROW PCT
Chet Walker, CHI .... .859
Oscar Robertson, MIL .... .850
Ron Williams, SF............... .844
Jeff Mullins, SF................. .844
Dick Snyder, SEA.............. .837
Stan McKenzie, POR .... .836
Jerry West, LA................... .832
Jimmy Walker, DET.......... .831

EAST SEMIFINALS
New York 4, Atlanta 1
Baltimore 4, Philadelphia 3

EAST FINALS
Baltimore 4, New York 3

WEST SEMIFINALS
Milwaukee 4, San Francisco 1
Los Angeles 4, Chicago 3

WEST FINALS
Milwaukee 4, Los Angeles 1

NBA FINALS
Milwaukee 98, Baltimore 88
Milwaukee 102, Baltimore 83
Milwaukee 107, Baltimore 99
Milwaukee 118, Baltimore 106

1971-72
FINAL STANDINGS

Eastern Conference
Atlantic Division

	W	L	PCT	GB
Boston	56	26	.683	
New York	48	34	.585	8
Philadelphia	30	52	.366	26
Buffalo	22	60	.268	34

Central Division

	W	L	PCT	GB
Baltimore	38	44	.463	
Atlanta	36	46	.439	2
Cincinnati	30	52	.366	8
Cleveland	23	59	.280	25

Western Conference
Midwest Division

	W	L	PCT	GB
Milwaukee	63	19	.768	
Chicago	57	25	.695	6
Phoenix	49	33	.598	14
Detroit	26	56	.317	37

Pacific Division

	W	L	PCT	GB
Los Angeles	69	13	.841	
Golden State	51	31	.622	18
Seattle	47	35	.573	22
Houston	34	48	.415	35
Portland	18	64	.220	51

SCORING

Kareem Abdul-Jabbar, MIL 34.8
Nate Archibald, CIN 28.2
John Havlicek, BOS 27.5
Spencer Haywood, SEA ...26.2
Gail Goodrich, LA..............25.9
Bob Love, CHI...................25.8
Jerry West, LA 25.8
Bob Lanier, DET 25.7
Archie Clark, BAL..............25.2
Elvin Hayes, HOU 25.2
Lou Hudson, ATL...............24.7
Sidney Wicks, POR...........24.5
Billy Cunningham, PHI.......23.3
Walt Frazier, NY................23.2
Jo Jo White, BOS..............23.1
Jack Marin, BAL.................22.3
Chet Walker, CHI..............22.0
Jeff Mullins, GS.................21.5
Nate Thurmond, GS..........21.4
Cazzie Russell, GS...........21.4

REBOUNDS

Wilt Chamberlain, LA 19.2
Wes Unseld, BAL...............17.6
Kareem Abdul-Jabbar, MIL...16.6
Nate Thurmond, GS..........16.1
Dave Cowens, BOS...........15.2
Elmore Smith, BUF 15.2
Elvin Hayes, HOU 14.6
Clyde Lee, GS...................14.5
Bob Lanier, DET 14.2
Bill Bridges, PHI................13.5

ASSISTS

Jerry West, LA...................9.7
Len Wilkens, SEA..............9.6
Nate Archibald, CIN...........9.2
Archie Clark, BAL..............8.0
John Havlicek, BOS 7.5
Norm Van Lier, CIN/CHI 6.9
Billy Cunningham, PHI 5.9
Jeff Mullins, GS.................5.9
Walt Frazier, NY................5.8
Walt Hazzard, BUF............5.6

FIELD GOAL PCT

Wilt Chamberlain, LA.........649
Kareem Abdul-Jabbar, MIL....574
Walt Bellamy, ATL.............545
Dick Snyder, SEA.............529
Jerry Lucas, NY................512
Walt Frazier, NY 512
Jon McGlocklin, MIL..........510
Chet Walker, CHI 505
Lucius Allen, MIL...............505

FREE THROW PCT

Jack Marin, BAL 894
Calvin Murphy, HOU 890
Gail Goodrich, LA 850
Chet Walker, CHI 847
Dick Van Arsdale, PHO....845
Stu Lantz, HOU.................838
John Havlicek, BOS 834
Cazzie Russell, GS 833

EAST SEMIFINALS

Boston 4, Atlanta 2
New York 4, Baltimore 2

EAST FINALS

New York 4, Boston 1

WEST SEMIFINALS

Los Angeles 4, Chicago 0
Milwaukee 4, Golden State 1

WEST FINALS

Los Angeles 4, Milwaukee 2

NBA FINALS

New York 114, Los Angeles 92
Los Angeles 106, New York 92
Los Angeles 107, New York 96
Los Angeles 116, New York 111 (OT)
Los Angeles 114, New York 100

1972-73
FINAL STANDINGS

Eastern Conference
Atlantic Division

	W	L	PCT	GB
Boston	68	14	.829	
New York	57	25	.695	11
Buffalo	21	61	.256	47
Philadelphia	9	73	.110	59

Central Division

	W	L	PCT	GB
Baltimore	52	30	.634	
Atlanta	46	36	.561	6
Houston	33	49	.402	19
Cleveland	32	50	.390	20

Western Conference
Midwest Division

	W	L	PCT	GB
Milwaukee	60	22	.732	
Chicago	51	31	.622	9
Detroit	40	42	.488	20
K.C.-Omaha	36	46	.439	24

Pacific Division

	W	L	PCT	GB
Los Angeles	60	22	.732	
Golden State	47	35	.573	13
Phoenix	38	44	.463	22
Seattle	26	56	.317	34
Portland	21	61	.256	39

SCORING
Nate Archibald, KCO.........34.0
Kareem Abdul-Jabbar, MIL......30.2
Spencer Haywood, SEA ...29.2
Lou Hudson, ATL..............27.1
Pete Maravich, ATL..........26.1
Charlie Scott, PHO...........25.3
Geoff Petrie, POR.............24.9
Gail Goodrich, LA..............23.9
Sidney Wicks, POR...........23.8
Bob Lanier, DET 23.8
John Havlicek, BOS..........23.8
Bob Love, CHI................23.1
Dave Bing, DET 22.4
Rick Barry, GS 22.3
Elvin Hayes, BAL 21.2
Walt Frazier, NY................21.1
Austin Carr, CLE 20.5
Dave Cowens, BOS..........20.5
Len Wilkens, CLE 20.5

REBOUNDS
Wilt Chamberlain, LA 18.6
Nate Thurmond, GS..........17.1
Dave Cowens, BOS..........16.2
Kareem Abdul-Jabbar, MIL...16.1
Wes Unseld, BAL..............15.9
Bob Lanier, DET 14.9
Elvin Hayes, BAL 14.5
Walt Bellamy, ATL 13.0
Paul Silas, BOS 13.0
Spencer Haywood, SEA ...12.9

ASSISTS
Nate Archibald, KCO.........11.4
Len Wilkens, CLE 8.4
Dave Bing, DET 7.8
Oscar Robertson, MIL. 7.5
Norm Van Lier, CHI............7.1
Pete Maravich, ATL 6.9
John Havlicek, BOS..........6.6
Herm Gilliam, ATL..............6.3
Charlie Scott, PHO............6.1
Jo Jo White, BOS..............6.1

FIELD GOAL PCT
Wilt Chamberlain, LA......... .727
Matt Guokas, KCO .... .570
Kareem Abdul-Jabbar, MIL... .554
Curtis Rowe, DET............. .519
Jim Fox, SEA.................... .515
Jerry Lucas, NY................ .513
Mike Riordan, BAL .... .510
Archie Clark, BAL .... .507
Bob Kauffman, BUF .... .505

FREE THROW PCT
Rick Barry, GS.................. .902
Calvin Murphy, HOU .... .888
Mike Newlin, HOU .... .886
Jimmy Walker, HOU.......... .884
Bill Bradley, NY .... .871
Cazzie Russell, GS .... .864
Dick Snyder, SEA............. .861
Dick Van Arsdale, PHO .... .859

EAST SEMIFINALS
Boston 4, Atlanta 2
New York 4, Baltimore 1

EAST FINALS
New York 4, Boston 3

WEST SEMIFINALS
Los Angeles 4, Chicago 3
Golden State 4, Milwaukee 2

WEST FINALS
Los Angeles 4, Golden State 1

NBA FINALS
Los Angeles 115, New York 112
New York 99, Los Angeles 95
New York 87, Los Angeles 83
New York 103, Los Angeles 98
New York 102, Los Angeles 93

1973-74
FINAL STANDINGS

Eastern Conference
Atlantic Division

	W	L	PCT	GB
Boston	56	26	.683	
New York	49	33	.598	7
Buffalo	42	40	.512	14
Philadelphia	25	57	.305	31

Central Division

	W	L	PCT	GB
Capital	47	35	.573	
Atlanta	35	47	.427	12
Houston	32	50	.390	15
Cleveland	29	53	.354	18

Western Conference
Midwest Division

	W	L	PCT	GB
Milwaukee	59	23	.720	
Chicago	54	28	.659	5
Detroit	52	30	.634	7
K.C.-Omaha	33	49	.402	26

Pacific Division

	W	L	PCT	GB
Los Angeles	47	35	.573	
Golden State	44	38	.537	3
Seattle	36	46	.439	11
Phoenix	30	52	.366	17
Portland	27	55	.329	20

SCORING
Bob McAdoo, BUF 30.6
Pete Maravich, ATL 27.7
Kareem Abdul-Jabbar, MIL 27.0
Gail Goodrich, LA..............25.3
Rick Barry, GS 25.1
Rudy Tomjanovich, HOU ..24.5
Geoff Petrie, POR.............24.3
Spencer Haywood, SEA ...23.5
John Havlicek, BOS..........22.6
Bob Lanier, DET 22.5

REBOUNDS
Elvin Hayes, CAP..............18.1
Dave Cowens, BOS..........15.7
Bob McAdoo, BUF 15.1
Kareem Abdul-Jabbar, MIL.....14.5
Happy Hairston, LA...........13.5
Spencer Haywood, SEA ...13.4
Sam Lacey, KCO..............13.4
Bob Lanier, DET 13.3
Clifford Ray, CHI..............12.2

ASSISTS
Ernie DiGregorio, BUF 8.2
Calvin Murphy, HOU 7.4
Len Wilkens, CLE.............. 7.1
Walt Frazier, NY................ 6.9
Dave Bing, DET................. 6.9
Norm Van Lier, CHI........... 6.9
Oscar Robertson, MIL. 6.4
Rick Barry, GS.................. 6.1

STEALS
Larry Steele, POR.............2.68
Steve Mix, PHI 2.59
Randy Smith, BUF 2.48
Jerry Sloan, CHI................2.38
Rick Barry, GS 2.11
Phil Chenier, CAP.............2.04

BLOCKED SHOTS
Elmore Smith, LA..............4.85
Kareem Abdul-Jabbar, MIL 3.49
Bob McAdoo, BUF 3.32
Bob Lanier, DET 3.04
Elvin Hayes, CAP..............2.96
Garfield Heard, BUF 2.84

FIELD GOAL PCT
Bob McAdoo, BUF............. .547
Kareem Abdul-Jabbar, MIL...... .539
Rudy Tomjanovich, HOU.. .536
Calvin Murphy, HOU .... .522
Butch Beard, GS .... .512
Clifford Ray, CHI .... .511

FREE THROW PCT
Ernie DiGregorio, BUF ..... .902
Rick Barry, GS.................. .899
Jeff Mullins, GS .... .875
Chet Walker, CHI .... .875
Bill Bradley, NY .... .874
Calvin Murphy, HOU .... .868

EAST SEMIFINALS
Boston 4, Buffalo 2
New York 4, Capital 3

EAST FINALS
Boston 4, New York 1

WEST SEMIFINALS
Milwaukee 4, Los Angeles 1
Chicago 4, Detroit 3

WEST FINALS
Milwaukee 4, Chicago 0

NBA FINALS
Boston 98, Milwaukee 83
Milwaukee 105, Boston 96 (OT)
Boston 95, Milwaukee 83
Milwaukee 97, Boston 89
Boston 96, Milwaukee 87
Milwaukee 102, Boston 101 (OT)
Boston 102, Milwaukee 87

1974-75
FINAL STANDINGS

Eastern Conference
Atlantic Division

	W	L	PCT	GB
Boston	60	22	.732	
Buffalo	49	33	.598	11
New York	40	42	.488	20
Philadelphia	34	48	.415	26

Central Division

	W	L	PCT	GB
Washington	60	22	.732	
Houston	41	41	.500	19
Cleveland	40	42	.488	20
Atlanta	31	61	.378	29
New Orleans	23	59	.280	37

Western Conference
Midwest Division

	W	L	PCT	GB
Chicago	47	35	.573	
K.C.-Omaha	44	38	.537	3
Detroit	40	42	.488	7
Milwaukee	38	44	.463	9

Pacific Division

	W	L	PCT	GB
Golden State	48	34	.585	
Seattle	43	39	.524	5
Portland	38	44	.463	10
Phoenix	32	50	.390	16
Los Angeles	30	52	.366	18

SCORING
Bob McAdoo, BUF	34.5
Rick Barry, GS	30.6
Kareem Abdul-Jabbar, MIL	30.0
Nate Archibald, KCO	26.5
Charlie Scott, PHO	24.3
Bob Lanier, DET	24.0
Elvin Hayes, WAS	23.0
Gail Goodrich, LA	22.6
Spencer Haywood, SEA	22.4
Fred Carter, PHI	21.9

REBOUNDS
Wes Unseld, WAS	14.8
Dave Cowens, BOS	14.7
Sam Lacey, KCO	14.2
Bob McAdoo, BUF	14.1
Kareem Abdul-Jabbar, MIL	14.0
Happy Hairston, LA	12.8
Paul Silas, BOS	12.5
Elvin Hayes, WAS	12.2
Bob Lanier, DET	12.0

ASSISTS
Kevin Porter, WAS	8.0
Dave Bing, DET	7.7
Nate Archibald, KCO	6.8
Randy Smith, BUF	6.5
Pete Maravich, NO	6.2
Rick Barry, GS	6.2
Slick Watts, SEA	6.1
Walt Frazier, NY	6.1

STEALS
Rick Barry, GS	2.85
Walt Frazier, NY	2.44
Larry Steele, POR	2.41
Slick Watts, SEA	2.32
Fred Brown, SEA	2.31
Phil Chenier, WAS	2.29

BLOCKED SHOTS
Kareem Abdul-Jabbar, MIL	3.26
Elmore Smith, LA	2.92
Nate Thurmond, CHI	2.44
Elvin Hayes, WAS	2.28
Bob Lanier, DET	2.26
Bob McAdoo, BUF	2.12

FIELD GOAL PCT
Don Nelson, BOS	.539
Butch Beard, GS	.528
Rudy Tomjanovich, HOU	.525
Kareem Abdul-Jabbar, MIL	.513
Bob McAdoo, BUF	.512
Kevin Kunnert, HOU	.512

FREE THROW PCT
Rick Barry, GS	.904
Calvin Murphy, HOU	.883
Bill Bradley, NY	.873
Nate Archibald, KCO	.872
Jim Price, LA/MIL	.871
John Havlicek, BOS	.870

EAST FIRST ROUND
Houston 2, New York 1

EAST SEMIFINALS
Washington 4, Buffalo 3
Boston 4, Houston 1

EAST FINALS
Washington 4, Boston 2

WEST FIRST ROUND
Seattle 2, Detroit 1

WEST SEMIFINALS
Golden State 4, Seattle 2
Chicago 4, K.C.-Omaha 2

WEST FINALS
Golden State 4, Chicago 3

NBA FINALS
Golden State 101, Wash. 95
Golden State 92, Wash. 91
Golden State 109, Wash. 101
Golden State 96, Wash. 95

1975-76
FINAL STANDINGS

Eastern Conference
Atlantic Division

	W	L	PCT	GB
Boston	54	28	.659	
Buffalo	46	36	.561	8
Philadelphia	46	36	.561	8
New York	38	44	.463	16

Central Division

	W	L	PCT	GB
Cleveland	49	33	.598	
Washington	48	34	.585	1
Houston	40	42	.488	9
New Orleans	38	44	.463	11
Atlanta	29	53	.354	20

Western Conference
Midwest Division

	W	L	PCT	GB
Milwaukee	38	44	.463	
Detroit	36	46	.439	2
Kansas City	31	51	.378	7
Chicago	24	58	.293	14

Pacific Division

	W	L	PCT	GB
Golden State	59	23	.720	
Seattle	43	39	.524	16
Phoenix	42	40	.512	17
Los Angeles	40	42	.488	19
Portland	37	45	.451	22

SCORING
Bob McAdoo, BUF	31.1
Kareem Abdul-Jabbar, LA	27.7
Pete Maravich, NO	25.9
Nate Archibald, KC	24.8
Fred Brown, SEA	23.1
George McGinnis, PHI	23.0
Randy Smith, BUF	21.8
John Drew, ATL	21.6
Bob Dandridge, MIL	21.5
Rick Barry, GS	21.0

REBOUNDS
Kareem Abdul-Jabbar, LA	16.9
Dave Cowens, BOS	16.0
Wes Unseld, WAS	13.3
Paul Silas, BOS	12.7
Sam Lacey, KC	12.6
George McGinnis, PHI	12.6
Bob McAdoo, BUF	12.4
Elmore Smith, MIL	11.4
Spencer Haywood, NY	11.3

ASSISTS
Slick Watts, SEA	8.1
Nate Archibald, KC	7.9
Calvin Murphy, HOU	7.3
Norm Van Lier, CHI	6.6
Rick Barry, GS	6.1
Dave Bing, WAS	6.0
Randy Smith, BUF	5.9
Alvan Adams, PHO	5.6

STEALS
Slick Watts, SEA	3.18
George McGinnis, PHI	2.57
Paul Westphal, PHO	2.56
Rick Barry, GS	2.49
Chris Ford, DET	2.17
Larry Steele, POR	2.10

BLOCKED SHOTS
Kareem Abdul-Jabbar, LA	4.12
Elmore Smith, MIL	3.05
Elvin Hayes, WAS	2.53
Harvey Catchings, PHI	2.19
George Johnson, GS	2.12
Bob McAdoo, BUF	2.05

FIELD GOAL PCT
Wes Unseld, WAS	.56085
John Shumate, BUF	.56081
Jim McMillian, BUF	.536
Bob Lanier, DET	.532
Kareem Abdul-Jabbar, LA	.529
Elmore Smith, MIL	.518

FREE THROW PCT
Rick Barry, GS	.923
Calvin Murphy, HOU	.907
Cazzie Russell, LA	.892
Bill Bradley, NY	.878
Fred Brown, SEA	.869
Mike Newlin, HOU	.865

EAST FIRST ROUND
Buffalo 2, Philadelphia 1

EAST SEMIFINALS
Boston 4, Buffalo 2
Cleveland 4, Washington 3

EAST FINALS
Boston 4, Cleveland 2

WEST FIRST ROUND
Detroit 2, Milwaukee 1

WEST SEMIFINALS
Golden State 4, Detroit 2
Phoenix 4, Seattle 2

WEST FINALS
Phoenix 4, Golden State 3

NBA FINALS
Boston 98, Phoenix 87
Boston 105, Phoenix 90
Phoenix 105, Boston 98
Phoenix 109, Boston 107
Boston 128, Phoenix 126 (3 OT)
Boston 87, Phoenix 80

1976-77
FINAL STANDINGS

Eastern Conference
Atlantic Division

	W	L	PCT	GB
Philadelphia	50	32	.610	
Boston	44	38	.537	6
N.Y. Knicks	40	42	.488	10
Buffalo	30	52	.366	20
N.Y. Nets	22	60	.288	28

Central Division

	W	L	PCT	GB
Houston	49	33	.598	
Washington	48	34	.585	1
San Antonio	44	38	.537	5
Cleveland	43	39	.524	6
New Orleans	35	47	.427	14
Atlanta	31	51	.378	18

Western Conference
Midwest Division

	W	L	PCT	GB
Denver	50	32	.610	
Detroit	44	38	.537	6
Chicago	44	38	.537	6
Kansas City	40	42	.488	10
Indiana	36	46	.439	14
Milwaukee	30	52	.366	20

Pacific Division

	W	L	PCT	GB
Los Angeles	53	29	.646	
Portland	49	33	.598	4
Golden State	46	36	.561	7
Seattle	40	42	.488	13
Phoenix	34	48	.415	19

SCORING
Pete Maravich, NO............31.1
Billy Knight, IND 26.6
Kareem Abdul-Jabbar, LA.26.2
David Thompson, DEN 25.9
Bob McAdoo, BUF/KYK.......25.8
Bob Lanier, DET 25.3
John Drew, ATL 24.2
Elvin Hayes, WAS.............23.7
George Gervin, SA............23.1
Dan Issel, DEN 22.3

REBOUNDS
Bill Walton, POR 14.4
Kareem Abdul-Jabbar, LA.13.3
Moses Malone, BUF/HOU 13.1
Artis Gilmore, CHI.............13.0
Bob McAdoo, BUF/KYK.......12.9
Elvin Hayes, WAS.............12.5
Swen Nater, MIL 12.0
George McGinnis, PHI......11.5

ASSISTS
Don Buse, IND 8.5
Slick Watts, SEA 8.0
Norm Van Lier, CHI 7.8
Kevin Porter, DET 7.3
Tom Henderson, ATL/WAS... 6.9
Rick Barry, GS.................. 6.0
Jo Jo White, BOS.............. 6.0

STEALS
Don Buse, IND 3.47
Brian Taylor, KC................2.76
Slick Watts, SEA 2.71
Quinn Buckner, MIL 2.43
Mike Gale, SA...................2.33
Bobby Jones, DEN............2.27

BLOCKED SHOTS
Bill Walton, POR 3.25
Kareem Abdul-Jabbar, LA.3.18
Elvin Hayes, WAS.............2.68
Artis Gilmore, CHI.............2.48
Caldwell Jones, PHI...........2.44
George Johnson, GS/BUF ...2.27

FIELD GOAL PCT
Kareem Abdul-Jabbar, LA..... .579
Mitch Kupchak, WAS......... .572
Bobby Jones, DEN............ .570
George Gervin, SA .... .544
Bob Lanier, DET............... .534
Bob Gross, POR............... .529

FREE THROW PCT
Ernie DiGregorio, BUF ..... .945
Rick Barry, GS................. .916
Calvin Murphy, HOU .... .886
Mike Newlin, HOU .... .885
Fred Brown, SEA.............. .884
Dick Van Arsdale, PHO.... .873

EAST FIRST ROUND
Washington 2, Cleveland 1
Boston 2, San Antonio 0

EAST SEMIFINALS
Philadelphia 4, Boston 3
Houston 4, Washington 2

EAST FINALS
Philadelphia 4, Houston 2

WEST FIRST ROUND
Portland 2, Chicago 1
Golden State 2, Detroit 1

WEST SEMIFINALS
Los Angeles 4, Golden State 3
Portland 4, Denver 2

WEST FINALS
Portland 4, Los Angeles 0

NBA FINALS
Philadelphia 107, Portland 101
Philadelphia 107, Portland 89
Portland 129, Philadelphia 107
Portland 130, Philadelphia 98
Portland 110, Philadelphia 104
Portland 109, Philadelphia 107

1977-78
FINAL STANDINGS

Eastern Conference
Atlantic Division

	W	L	PCT	GB
Philadelphia	55	27	.671	
New York	43	39	.524	12
Boston	32	50	.390	23
Buffalo	27	55	.329	28
New Jersey	24	58	.293	31

Central Division

	W	L	PCT	GB
San Antonio	52	30	.634	
Washington	44	38	.537	8
Cleveland	43	39	.524	9
Atlanta	41	41	.500	11
New Orleans	39	43	.476	13
Houston	28	54	.341	24

Western Conference
Midwest Division

	W	L	PCT	GB
Denver	48	34	.585	
Milwaukee	44	38	.537	4
Chicago	40	42	.488	8
Detroit	38	44	.463	10
Indiana	31	51	.378	17
Kansas City	31	51	.378	17

Pacific Division

	W	L	PCT	GB
Portland	58	24	.707	
Phoenix	49	33	.598	9
Seattle	47	35	.573	11
Los Angeles	45	37	.549	13
Golden State	43	39	.524	15

SCORING
George Gervin, SA...........27.22
David Thompson, DEN ...27.15
Bob McAdoo, NY 26.5
Kareem Abdul-Jabbar, LA....25.8
Calvin Murphy, HOU 25.6
Paul Westphal, PHO 25.2
Randy Smith, BUF 24.6
Bob Lanier, DET 24.5
Walter Davis, PHO.............24.2
Bernard King, NJ...............24.2

REBOUNDS
Truck Robinson, NO 15.7
Moses Malone, HOU.........15.0
Dave Cowens, BOS...........14.0
Elvin Hayes, WAS.............13.3
Swen Nater, BUF...............13.2
Artis Gilmore, CHI 13.1
Kareem Abdul-Jabbar, LA......12.9
Bob McAdoo, NY 12.8

ASSISTS
Kevin Porter, DET/NJ...........10.2
John Lucas, HOU 9.4
Ricky Sobers, IND 7.4
Norm Nixon, LA 6.8
Norm Van Lier, CHI 6.8
Henry Bibby, PHI............... 5.7
Foots Walker, CLE 5.6

STEALS
Ron Lee, PHO....................2.74
Gus Williams, SEA............2.34
Quinn Buckner, MIL 2.29
Mike Gale, SA 2.27
Don Buse, PHO 2.26
Foots Walker, CLE............2.17

BLOCKED SHOTS
George Johnson, NJ.........3.38
Kareem Abdul-Jabbar, LA......2.98
Tree Rollins, ATL 2.73
Bill Walton, POR 2.52
Billy Paultz, SA..................2.43
Artis Gilmore, CHI.............2.21

FIELD GOAL PCT
Bobby Jones, DEN .... .578
Darryl Dawkins, PHI .... .575
Artis Gilmore, CHI .... .559
Kareem Abdul-Jabbar, LA...... .550
Alex English, MIL............... .542
Bob Lanier, DET .... .537

FREE THROW PCT
Rick Barry, GS.................. .924
Calvin Murphy, HOU .... .918
Fred Brown, SEA.............. .898
Mike Newlin, HOU .... .874
Scott Wedman, KC........... .870

EAST FIRST ROUND
Washington 2, Atlanta 0
New York 2, Cleveland 0

EAST SEMIFINALS
Philadelphia 4, New York 0
Washington 4, San Antonio 2

EAST FINALS
Washington 4, Philadelphia 2

WEST FIRST ROUND
Seattle 2, Los Angeles 1
Milwaukee 2, Phoenix 0

WEST SEMIFINALS
Seattle 4, Portland 2
Denver 4, Milwaukee 3

WEST FINALS
Seattle 4, Denver 2

NBA FINALS
Seattle 106, Washington 102
Washington 106, Seattle 98
Seattle 93, Washington 92
Washington 120, Seattle 116 (OT)
Seattle 98, Washington 94
Washington 117, Seattle 82
Washington 105, Seattle 99

1978-79
FINAL STANDINGS

Eastern Conference
Atlantic Division

	W	L	PCT	GB
Washington	54	28	.659	
Philadelphia	47	35	.573	7
New Jersey	37	45	.451	17
New York	31	51	.378	23
Boston	29	53	.354	25

Central Division

	W	L	PCT	GB
San Antonio	48	34	.585	
Houston	47	35	.573	1
Atlanta	46	36	.561	2
Cleveland	30	52	.366	18
Detroit	30	52	.366	18
New Orleans	26	56	.317	22

Western Conference
Midwest Division

	W	L	PCT	GB
Kansas City	48	34	.585	
Denver	47	35	.573	1
Indiana	38	44	.463	10
Milwaukee	38	44	.463	10
Chicago	31	51	.378	17

Pacific Division

	W	L	PCT	GB
Seattle	52	30	.634	
Phoenix	50	32	.610	2
Los Angeles	47	35	.573	5
Portland	45	37	.549	7
San Diego	43	39	.524	9
Golden State	38	44	.463	14

SCORING
George Gervin, SA.............29.6
Lloyd Free, SD 28.8
Marques Johnson, MIL 25.6
Bob McAdoo, NY/BOS 24.8
Moses Malone, HOU.........24.8
David Thompson, DEN 24.0
Paul Westphal, PHO.........24.0
Kareem Abdul-Jabbar, LA......23.8
Artis Gilmore, CHI 23.7
Walter Davis, PHO............23.6

REBOUNDS
Moses Malone, HOU.........17.6
Rich Kelley, NO.................12.8
Kareem Abdul-Jabbar, LA 12.8
Artis Gilmore, CHI 12.7
Jack Sikma, SEA 12.4
Elvin Hayes, WAS.............12.1
Robert Parish, GS.............12.1

ASSISTS
Kevin Porter, DET 13.4
John Lucas, GS................. 9.3
Norm Nixon, LA 9.0
Phil Ford, KC 8.6
Paul Westphal, PHO 6.5
Rick Barry, HOU................ 6.3
Ray Williams, NY 6.2

STEALS
M.L. Carr, DET 2.46
Ed Jordan, NJ 2.45
Norm Nixon, LA................2.45
Foots Walker, CLE............2.36
Phil Ford, KC 2.20
Randy Smith, SD 2.16

BLOCKED SHOTS
Kareem Abdul-Jabbar, LA......3.95
George Johnson, NJ.........3.24
Tree Rollins, ATL 3.14
Robert Parish, GS.............2.86
Terry Tyler, DET 2.45

FIELD GOAL PCT
Cedric Maxwell, BOS .... .584
Kareem Abdul-Jabbar, LA...... .577
Wes Unseld, WAS............ .577
Artis Gilmore, CHI .... .575
Swen Nater, SD................ .569

FREE THROW PCT
Rick Barry, HOU............... .947
Calvin Murphy, HOU .... .928
Fred Brown, SEA.............. .888
Robert Smith, DEN........... .883
Ricky Sobers, IND .... .882

EAST FIRST ROUND
Philadelphia 4, New Jersey 0
Atlanta 2, Houston 0

EAST SEMIFINALS
Washington 4, Atlanta 3
San Antonio 4, Philadelphia 3

EAST FINALS
Washington 4, San Antonio 3

WEST FIRST ROUND
Phoenix 2, Portland 1
Los Angeles 2, Denver 1

WEST SEMIFINALS
Seattle 4, Los Angeles 1
Phoenix 4, Kansas City 1

WEST FINALS
Seattle 4, Phoenix 3

NBA FINALS
Washington 99, Seattle 97
Seattle 92, Washington 82
Seattle 105, Washington 95
Seattle 114, Washington 112 (OT)
Seattle 97, Washington 93

1979-80
FINAL STANDINGS

Eastern Conference
Atlantic Division

	W	L	PCT	GB
Boston	61	21	.744	
Philadelphia	59	23	.720	2
Washington	39	43	.476	22
New York	39	43	.476	22
New Jersey	34	48	.415	27

Central Division

	W	L	PCT	GB
Atlanta	50	32	.610	
Houston	41	41	.500	9
San Antonio	41	41	.500	9
Indiana	37	45	.451	13
Cleveland	37	45	.451	13
Detroit	16	66	.195	34

Western Conference
Midwest Division

	W	L	PCT	GB
Milwaukee	49	33	.598	
Kansas City	47	35	.573	2
Denver	30	52	.366	19
Chicago	30	52	.366	19
Utah	24	58	.293	25

Pacific Division

	W	L	PCT	GB
Los Angeles	60	22	.732	
Seattle	56	26	.683	4
Phoenix	55	27	.671	5
Portland	38	44	.463	22
San Diego	35	47	.427	25
Golden State	24	58	.293	36

SCORING
George Gervin, SA............33.1
Lloyd Free, SD.................30.2
Adrian Dantley, UTA.........28.0
Julius Erving, PHI.............26.9
Moses Malone, HOU.........25.8
Kareem Abdul-Jabbar, LA.....24.8
Dan Issel, DEN 23.8
Elvin Hayes, WAS.............23.0
Otis Birdsong, KC............22.7
Mike Mitchell, CLE 22.2

REBOUNDS
Swen Nater, SD 15.0
Moses Malone, HOU.......14.5
Wes Unseld, WAS 13.3
Caldwell Jones, PHI..........11.9
Jack Sikma, SEA 11.1

ASSISTS
Michael Richardson, NY ...10.1
Nate Archibald, BOS 8.4
Foots Walker, CLE 8.0
Norm Nixon, LA 7.8
John Lucas, GS................ 7.5

STEALS
Michael Richardson, NY ...3.23
Ed Jordan, NJ 2.72

Dudley Bradley, IND 2.57
Gus Williams, SEA............2.44
Magic Johnson, LA 2.43

BLOCKED SHOTS
Kareem Abdul-Jabbar, LA..3.41
George Johnson, NJ.........3.19
Tree Rollins, ATL 2.98
Terry Tyler, DET 2.68
Elvin Hayes, WAS............2.33

FIELD GOAL PCT
Cedric Maxwell, BOS .... .609
Kareem Abdul-Jabbar, LA...... .604
Artis Gilmore, CHI .... .595
Adrian Dantley, UTA......... .576
Tom Boswell, DEN/UTA...... .564

FREE THROW PCT
Rick Barry, HOU............... .935
Calvin Murphy, HOU .... .897
Ron Boone, UTA .... .893
Paul Silas, SA.................. .887

3-PT. FIELD GOAL PCT
Fred Brown, SEA.............. .443
Chris Ford, BOS............... .427
Larry Bird, BOS .... .406
John Roche, DEN............. .380

EAST FIRST ROUND
Philadelphia 2, Washington 0
Houston 2, San Antonio 1

EAST SEMIFINALS
Boston 4, Houston 0
Philadelphia 4, Atlanta 1

EAST FINALS
Philadelphia 4, Boston 1

WEST FIRST ROUND
Seattle 2, Portland 1
Phoenix 2, Kansas City 1

WEST SEMIFINALS
Los Angeles 4, Phoenix 1
Seattle 4, Milwaukee 3

WEST FINALS
Los Angeles 4, Seattle 1

NBA FINALS
Los Angeles 109, Philadelphia 102
Philadelphia 107, Los Angeles 104
Los Angeles 111, Philadelphia 101
Philadelphia 105, Los Angeles 102
Los Angeles 108, Philadelphia 103
Los Angeles 123, Philadelphia 107

1980-81
FINAL STANDINGS

Eastern Conference
Atlantic Division

	W	L	PCT	GB
Boston	62	20	.756	
Philadelphia	62	20	.756	
New York	50	32	.610	12
Washington	39	43	.476	23
New Jersey	24	58	.293	38

Central Division

	W	L	PCT	GB
Milwaukee	60	22	.732	
Chicago	45	37	.549	15
Indiana	44	38	.537	16
Atlanta	31	51	.378	29
Cleveland	28	54	.341	32
Detroit	21	61	.256	39

Western Conference
Midwest Division

	W	L	PCT	GB
San Antonio	52	30	.634	
Kansas City	40	42	.488	12
Houston	40	42	.488	12
Denver	37	45	.451	15
Utah	28	54	.341	24
Dallas	15	67	.183	37

Pacific Division

	W	L	PCT	GB
Phoenix	57	25	.695	
Los Angeles	54	28	.659	3
Portland	45	37	.549	12
Golden State	39	43	.476	18
San Diego	36	46	.439	21
Seattle	34	48	.415	23

SCORING
Adrian Dantley, UTA 30.7
Moses Malone, HOU........27.8
George Gervin, SA............27.1
Kareem Abdul-Jabbar, LA.26.2
David Thompson, DEN 25.5
Otis Birdsong, KC 24.6
Julius Erving, PHI..............24.6
Mike Mitchell, CLE 24.5
Lloyd Free, GS..................24.1
Alex English, DEN.............23.8

REBOUNDS
Moses Malone, HOU........14.8
Swen Nater, SD 12.4
Larry Smith, GS 12.1
Larry Bird, BOS.................10.9
Jack Sikma, SEA..............10.4

ASSISTS
Kevin Porter, WAS 9.1
Norm Nixon, LA 8.8
Phil Ford, KC 8.8
Michael Richardson, NY.... 7.9
Nate Archibald, BOS 7.7

STEALS
Magic Johnson, LA 3.43
Michael Richardson, NY ...2.94
Quinn Buckner, MIL 2.40
Maurice Cheeks, PHI........2.38
Ray Williams, NY 2.34

BLOCKED SHOTS
George Johnson, SA.........3.39
Tree Rollins, ATL 2.93
Kareem Abdul-Jabbar, LA.2.85
Robert Parish, BOS 2.61
Artis Gilmore, CHI 2.41

FIELD GOAL PCT
Artis Gilmore, CHI .... .670
Darryl Dawkins, PHI .... .607
Cedric Maxwell, BOS .... .588
Bernard King, GS .... .588
Kareem Abdul-Jabbar, LA .574

FREE THROW PCT
Calvin Murphy, HOU .... .958
Ricky Sobers, CHI .... .935
Mike Newlin, NJ................ .888
Jim Spanarkel, DAL.......... .887

3-PT. FIELD GOAL PCT
Brian Taylor, SD .... .383
Freeman Williams, SD...... .340
Joe Hassett, DAL/GS............ .340
Mike Bratz, CLE .... .337

EAST FIRST ROUND
Philadelphia 2, Indiana 0
Chicago 2, New York 0

EAST SEMIFINALS
Boston 4, Chicago 0
Philadelphia 4, Milwaukee 3

EAST FINALS
Boston 4, Philadelphia 3

WEST FIRST ROUND
Houston 2, Los Angeles 1
Kansas City 2, Portland 1

WEST SEMIFINALS
Kansas City 4, Phoenix 3
Houston 4, San Antonio 3

WEST FINALS
Houston 4, Kansas City 1

NBA FINALS
Boston 98, Houston 95
Houston 92, Boston 90
Boston 94, Houston 71
Houston 91, Boston 86
Boston 109, Houston 80
Boston 102, Houston 91

1981-82
FINAL STANDINGS

Eastern Conference
Atlantic Division

	W	L	PCT	GB
Boston	63	19	.768	
Philadelphia	58	24	.707	5
New Jersey	44	38	.537	19
Washington	43	39	.524	20
New York	33	49	.402	30

Central Division

	W	L	PCT	GB
Milwaukee	55	27	.671	
Atlanta	42	40	.512	13
Detroit	39	43	.476	16
Indiana	35	47	.427	20
Chicago	34	48	.415	21
Cleveland	15	67	.183	40

Western Conference
Midwest Division

	W	L	PCT	GB
San Antonio	48	34	.585	
Denver	46	36	.561	2
Houston	46	36	.561	2
Kansas City	30	52	.366	18
Dallas	28	54	.341	20
Utah	25	57	.305	23

Pacific Division

	W	L	PCT	GB
Los Angeles	57	25	.695	
Seattle	52	30	.634	5
Phoenix	46	36	.561	11
Golden State	45	37	.549	12
Portland	42	40	.512	15
San Diego	17	65	.207	40

SCORING
George Gervin, SA............32.3
Moses Malone, HOU.........31.1
Adrian Dantley, UTA 30.3
Alex English, DEN.............25.4
Julius Erving, PHI..............24.4
Kareem Abdul-Jabbar, LA...23.9
Gus Williams, SEA.............23.4
Bernard King, GS..............23.2
World B. Free, GS..............22.9
Larry Bird, BOS.................22.9

REBOUNDS
Moses Malone, HOU.........14.7
Jack Sikma, SEA 12.7
Buck Williams, NJ 12.3
Mychal Thompson, POR...11.7
Maurice Lucas, NY............11.3

ASSISTS
Johnny Moore, SA.............. 9.6
Magic Johnson, LA............. 9.5
Maurice Cheeks, PHI 8.4
Nate Archibald, BOS 8.0
Norm Nixon, LA 8.0

STEALS
Magic Johnson, LA 2.67
Maurice Cheeks, PHI........2.65
Michael Richardson, NY ...2.60
Quinn Buckner, MIL 2.49
Ray Williams, NJ...............2.43

BLOCKED SHOTS
George Johnson, SA.........3.12
Tree Rollins, ATL 2.84
Kareem Abdul-Jabbar, LA.......2.72
Artis Gilmore, CHI 2.70
Robert Parish, BOS 2.40

FIELD GOAL PCT
Artis Gilmore, CHI .... .652
Steve Johnson, KC............ .613
Buck Williams, NJ............. .582
Kareem Abdul-Jabbar, LA...... .579
Calvin Natt, POR.............. .576

FREE THROW PCT
Kyle Macy, PHO................ .899
Charlie Criss, SD.............. .887
John Long, DET .... .865
George Gervin, SA........... .864

3-PT. FIELD GOAL PCT
Campy Russell, NY .... .439
Andrew Toney, PHI .... .424
Kyle Macy, PHO .... .390
Brian Winters, MIL............ .387

EAST FIRST ROUND
Philadelphia 2, Atlanta 0
Washington 2, New Jersey 0

EAST SEMIFINALS
Boston 4, Washington 1
Philadelphia 4, Milwaukee 2

EAST FINALS
Philadelphia 4, Boston 3

WEST FIRST ROUND
Seattle 2, Houston 1
Phoenix 2, Denver 1

WEST SEMIFINALS
Los Angeles 4, Phoenix 0
San Antonio 4, Seattle 1

WEST FINALS
Los Angeles 4, San Antonio 0

NBA FINALS
Los Angeles 124, Philadelphia 117
Philadelphia 110, Los Angeles 94
Los Angeles 129, Philadelphia 108
Los Angeles 111, Philadelphia 101
Philadelphia 135, Los Angeles 102
Los Angeles 114, Philadelphia 104

1982-83
FINAL STANDINGS

Eastern Conference
Atlantic Division

	W	L	PCT	GB
Philadelphia	65	17	.793	
Boston	56	26	.683	11
New Jersey	49	33	.598	16
New York	44	38	.537	21
Washington	42	40	.512	23

Central Division

	W	L	PCT	GB
Milwaukee	51	31	.622	
Atlanta	43	39	.524	8
Detroit	37	45	.451	14
Chicago	28	54	.341	23
Cleveland	23	59	.280	28
Indiana	20	62	.244	31

Western Conference
Midwest Division

	W	L	PCT	GB
San Antonio	53	29	.646	
Denver	45	37	.549	8
Kansas City	45	37	.549	8
Dallas	38	44	.463	15
Utah	30	52	.366	23
Houston	14	68	.171	39

Pacific Division

	W	L	PCT	GB
Los Angeles	58	24	.707	
Phoenix	53	29	.646	5
Seattle	48	34	.585	10
Portland	46	36	.561	12
Golden State	30	52	.366	28
San Diego	25	57	.305	33

SCORING

Alex English, DEN	28.4
Kiki Vandeweghe, DEN	26.7
Kelly Tripucka, DET	26.5
George Gervin, SA	26.2
Moses Malone, PHI	24.5
Mark Aguirre, DAL	24.4
Joe Barry Carroll, GS	24.1
World B. Free, GS/CLE	23.9
Reggie Theus, CHI	23.8
Terry Cummings, SD	23.7

REBOUNDS

Moses Malone, PHI	15.3
Buck Williams, NJ	12.5
Bill Laimbeer, DET	12.1
Artis Gilmore, SA	12.0
Jack Sikma, SEA	11.4

ASSISTS

Magic Johnson, LA	10.5
Johnny Moore, SA	9.8
Rickey Green, UTA	8.9
Larry Drew, KC	8.1
Frank Johnson, WAS	8.1

STEALS

Michael Richardson GS/NJ	2.84
Rickey Green, UTA	2.82
Johnny Moore, SA	2.52
Isiah Thomas, DET	2.46
Darwin Cook, NJ	2.37

BLOCKED SHOTS

Tree Rollins, ATL	4.29
Bill Walton, POR	3.61
Mark Eaton, UTA	3.40
Larry Nance, PHO	2.65
Artis Gilmore, CHI	2.34

FIELD GOAL PCT

Artis Gilmore, SA	.626
Steve Johnson, KC	.624
Darryl Dawkins, NJ	.599
Kareem Abdul-Jabbar, LA	.588
Buck Williams, NJ	.588

FREE THROW PCT

Calvin Murphy, HOU	.920
Kiki Vandeweghe, DEN	.875
Kyle Macy, PHO	.872
George Gervin, SA	.853

3-PT. FIELD GOAL PCT

Mike Dunleavy, SA	.345
Isiah Thomas, DET	.288
Darrell Griffith, UTA	.288
Allen Leavell, HOU	.240

EAST FIRST ROUND
Boston 2, Atlanta 1
New York 2, New Jersey 0

EAST SEMIFINALS
Philadelphia 4, New York 0
Milwaukee 4, Boston 0

EAST FINALS
Philadelphia 4, Milwaukee 1

WEST FIRST ROUND
Denver 2, Phoenix 1
Portland 2, Seattle 0

WEST SEMIFINALS
Los Angeles 4, Portland 1
San Antonio 4, Denver 1

WEST FINALS
Los Angeles 4, San Antonio 2

NBA FINALS
Philadelphia 113, Los Angeles 107
Philadelphia 103, Los Angeles 93
Philadelphia 111, Los Angeles 94
Philadelphia 115, Los Angeles 108

1983-84
FINAL STANDINGS

Eastern Conference
Atlantic Division

	W	L	PCT	GB
Boston	62	20	.756	
Philadelphia	52	30	.634	10
New York	47	35	.573	15
New Jersey	45	37	.549	17
Washington	35	47	.427	27

Central Division

	W	L	PCT	GB
Milwaukee	50	32	.610	
Detroit	49	33	.598	1
Atlanta	40	42	.488	10
Cleveland	28	54	.341	22
Chicago	27	55	.329	23
Indiana	26	56	.317	24

Western Conference
Midwest Division

	W	L	PCT	GB
Utah	45	37	.549	
Dallas	43	39	.524	2
Denver	38	44	.463	7
Kansas City	38	44	.463	7
San Antonio	37	45	.451	8
Houston	29	53	.354	16

Pacific Division

	W	L	PCT	GB
Los Angeles	54	28	.659	
Portland	48	34	.585	6
Seattle	42	40	.512	12
Phoenix	41	41	.500	13
Golden State	37	45	.451	17
San Diego	30	52	.366	24

SCORING
Adrian Dantley, UTA 30.6
Mark Aguirre, DAL 29.5
Kiki Vandeweghe, DEN.....29.4
Alex English, DEN.............26.4
Bernard King, NY 26.3
George Gervin, SA............25.9
Larry Bird, BOS 24.2
Mike Mitchell, SA 23.3
Terry Cummings, SD 22.9
Purvis Short, GS 22.8

REBOUNDS
Moses Malone, PHI..........13.4
Buck Williams, NJ 12.3
Jeff Ruland, WAS..............12.3
Bill Laimbeer, DET 12.2
Ralph Sampson, HOU 11.1

ASSISTS
Magic Johnson, LA 13.1
Norm Nixon, SD 11.1
Isiah Thomas, DET 11.1
John Lucas, SA.................10.7
Johnny Moore, SA............. 9.6

STEALS
Rickey Green, UTA...,.......2.65
Isiah Thomas, DET 2.49

Gus Williams, SEA............2.36
Maurice Cheeks, PHI.......2.28
Magic Johnson, LA 2.24

BLOCKED SHOTS
Mark Eaton, UTA 4.28
Tree Rollins, ATL 3.60
Ralph Sampson, HOU 2.40
Larry Nance, PHO.............2.11
Artis Gilmore, SA 2.06

FIELD GOAL PCT
Artis Gilmore, SA............... .631
James Donaldson, SD...... .596
Mike McGee, LA................ .594
Darryl Dawkins, NJ........... .593
Calvin Natt, POR .... .583

FREE THROW PCT
Larry Bird, BOS .... .888
John Long, DET .... .884
Bill Laimbeer, DET .... .866
Walter Davis, PHO .... .863

3-PT. FIELD GOAL PCT
Darrell Griffith, UTA .... .361
Mike Evans, DEN .... .360
Johnny Moore, SA............ .322
Michael Cooper, LA.......... .314

East First Round
Boston 3, Washington 1
Milwaukee 3, Atlanta 2
New Jersey 3 Philadelphia 2
New York 3, Detroit 2

East Semifinals
Boston 4, New York 3
Milwaukee 4, New Jersey 2

East Finals
Boston 4, Milwaukee 1

West First Round
Los Angeles 3, Kansas City 0
Utah 3, Denver 2
Phoenix 3, Portland 2
Dallas 3, Seattle 2

West Semifinals
Los Angeles 4, Dallas 1
Phoenix 4, Utah 2

West Finals
Los Angeles 4, Phoenix 2

NBA Finals
Los Angeles 115, Boston 109
Boston 124, Los Angeles 121 (OT)
Los Angeles 137, Boston 104
Boston 129, Los Angeles 125 (OT)
Boston 121, Los Angeles 103
Los Angeles 119, Boston 108
Boston 111, Los Angeles 102

1984-85
FINAL STANDINGS

Eastern Conference
Atlantic Division

	W	L	PCT	GB
Boston	63	19	.768	
Philadelphia	58	24	.707	5
New Jersey	42	40	.512	21
Washington	40	42	.488	23
New York	24	58	.293	29

Central Division

	W	L	PCT	GB
Milwaukee	59	23	.720	
Detroit	46	36	.561	13
Chicago	38	44	.463	21
Cleveland	36	46	.439	23
Atlanta	34	48	.415	25
Indiana	22	60	.268	37

Western Conference
Midwest Division

	W	L	PCT	GB
Denver	52	30	.634	
Houston	48	34	.585	4
Dallas	44	38	.537	8
San Antonio	41	41	.500	11
Utah	41	41	.500	11
Kansas City	31	51	.378	21

Pacific Division

	W	L	PCT	GB
L.A. Lakers	62	20	.756	
Portland	42	40	.512	20
Phoenix	36	46	.439	26
L.A. Clippers	31	51	.378	31
Seattle	31	51	.378	31
Golden State	22	60	.268	40

SCORING
Bernard King, NY 32.9
Larry Bird, BOS 28.7
Michael Jordan, CHI 28.2
Purvis Short, GS 28.0
Alex English, DEN.............27.9
Dominique Wilkins, ATL....27.4
Adrian Dantley, UTA 26.6
Mark Aguirre, DAL 25.7
Moses Malone, PHI...........24.6
Terry Cummings, MIL 23.6

REBOUNDS
Moses Malone, PHI...........13.1
Bill Laimbeer, DET 12.4
Buck Williams, NJ 12.3
Akeem Olajuwon, HOU.....11.9
Mark Eaton, UTA 11.3

ASSISTS
Isiah Thomas, DET 13.9
Magic Johnson, LAL 12.6
Johnny Moore, SA 10.0
Norm Nixon, LAC 8.8
John Bagley, CLE.............. 8.6

STEALS
Michael Richardson, NJ....2.96
Johnny Moore, SA 2.79
Lafayette Lever, DEN........2.46
Michael Jordan, CHI 2.39
Doc Rivers, ATL................2.36

BLOCKED SHOTS
Mark Eaton, UTA 5.56
Akeem Olajuwon, HOU.....2.68
Sam Bowie, POR 2.67
Wayne Cooper, DEN 2.46
Tree Rollins, ATL 2.39

FIELD GOAL PCT
James Donaldson, LAC..... .637
Artis Gilmore, SA.............. .623
Otis Thorpe, KC................ .600
Kareem Abdul-Jabbar, LAL .. .599
Larry Nance, PHO .... .587

FREE THROW PCT
Kyle Macy, PHO................ .907
Kiki Vandeweghe, POR..... .896
Brad Davis, DAL............... .888
Kelly Tripucka, DET.......... .885

3-PT. FIELD GOAL PCT
Byron Scott, LAL .... .433
Larry Bird, BOS .... .427
Brad Davis, DAL................ .409
Trent Tucker, NY .... .403

East First Round
Boston 3, Cleveland 1
Milwaukee 3, Chicago 1
Philadelphia 3, Washington 1
Detroit 3, New Jersey 0

East Semifinals
Boston 4, Detroit 2
Philadelphia 4, Milwaukee 0

East Finals
Boston 4, Philadelphia 1

West First Round
L.A. Lakers 3, Phoenix 0
Denver 3, San Antonio 2
Utah 3, Houston 2
Portland 3, Dallas 1

West Semifinals
L.A. Lakers 4, Portland 1
Denver 4, Utah 1

West Finals
L.A. Lakers 4, Denver 1

NBA Finals
Boston 148, L.A. Lakers 114
L.A. Lakers 109, Boston 102
L.A. Lakers 136, Boston 111
Boston 107, L.A. Lakers 105
L.A. Lakers 120, Boston 111
L.A. Lakers 111, Boston 100

1985-86
FINAL STANDINGS

Eastern Conference
Atlantic Division

	W	L	PCT	GB
Boston	67	15	.817	
Philadelphia	54	28	.659	13
Washington	39	43	.476	28
New Jersey	39	43	.476	28
New York	23	59	.280	44

Central Division

	W	L	PCT	GB
Milwaukee	57	25	.695	
Atlanta	50	32	.610	7
Detroit	46	36	.561	11
Chicago	30	52	.366	27
Cleveland	29	53	.354	28
Indiana	26	56	.317	31

Western Conference
Midwest Division

	W	L	PCT	GB
Houston	51	31	.622	
Denver	47	35	.573	4
Dallas	44	38	.537	7
Utah	42	40	.512	9
Sacramento	37	45	.451	14
San Antonio	35	47	.427	16

Pacific Division

	W	L	PCT	GB
L.A. Lakers	62	20	.756	
Portland	40	42	.488	22
L.A. Clippers	32	50	.390	30
Phoenix	32	50	.390	30
Seattle	31	51	.378	31
Golden State	30	52	.366	32

SCORING
Dominique Wilkins, ATL....30.3
Adrian Dantley, UTA 29.8
Alex English, DEN.............29.8
Larry Bird, BOS.................25.8
Purvis Short, GS 25.5
Kiki Vandeweghe, POR ...24.8
Moses Malone, PHI...........23.8
Akeem Olajuwon, HOU.....23.5
Mike Mitchell, SA 23.4
World B. Free, CLE...........23.4

REBOUNDS
Bill Laimbeer, DET............13.1
Charles Barkley, PHI.........12.8
Buck Williams, NJ 12.0
Moses Malone, PHI...........11.8
Ralph Sampson, HOU 11.1

ASSISTS
Magic Johnson, LAL 12.6
Isiah Thomas, DET 10.8
Reggie Theus, SAC........... 9.6
John Bagley, CLE.............. 9.4
Maurice Cheeks, PHI 9.2

STEALS
Alvin Robertson, SA..........3.67
Michael Richardson, NJ....2.66

Clyde Drexler, POR 2.63
Maurice Cheeks, PHI 2.52
Lafayette Lever, DEN........2.28

BLOCKED SHOTS
Manute Bol, WAS..............4.96
Mark Eaton, UTA 4.61
Akeem Olajuwon, HOU.....3.40
Wayne Cooper, DEN 2.91
Benoit Benjamin, LAC.......2.61

FIELD GOAL PCT
Steve Johnson, SA .... .632
Artis Gilmore, SA .... .618
Larry Nance, PHO............ .581
James Worthy, LAL........... .579
Kevin McHale, BOS .... .574

FREE THROW PCT
Larry Bird, BOS............... .8963
Chris Mullin, GS .... .8957
Mike Gminski, NJ............. .893
Jim Paxson, POR............. .889

3-PT. FIELD GOAL PCT
Craig Hodges, MIL .... .4506
Trent Tucker, NY............. .4505
Ernie Grunfeld, NY........... .426
Larry Bird, BOS................ .423

East First Round
Boston 3, Chicago 0
Milwaukee 3, New Jersey 0
Philadelphia 3, Washington 2
Atlanta 3, Detroit 1

East Semifinals
Boston 4, Atlanta 1
Milwaukee 4, Philadelphia 3

East Finals
Boston 4, Milwaukee 0

West First Round
L.A. Lakers 3, San Antonio 0
Houston 3, Sacramento 0
Denver 3, Portland 1
Dallas 3, Utah 1

West Semifinals
L.A. Lakers 4, Dallas 2
Houston 4, Denver 2

West Finals
Houston 4, L.A. Lakers 1

NBA Finals
Boston 112, Houston 100
Boston 117, Houston 95
Houston 106, Boston 104
Boston 106, Houston 103
Houston 111, Boston 96
Boston 114, Houston 97

1986-87
FINAL STANDINGS

Eastern Conference
Atlantic Division

	W	L	PCT	GB
Boston	59	23	.720	
Philadelphia	45	37	.549	14
Washington	42	40	.512	17
New Jersey	24	58	.293	35
New York	24	58	.293	35

Central Division

	W	L	PCT	GB
Atlanta	57	25	.695	
Detroit	52	30	.634	5
Milwaukee	50	32	.610	7
Indiana	41	41	.500	16
Chicago	40	42	.488	17
Cleveland	31	51	.378	26

Western Conference
Midwest Division

	W	L	PCT	GB
Dallas	55	27	.671	
Utah	44	38	.537	11
Houston	42	40	.512	13
Denver	37	45	.451	18
Sacramento	29	53	.354	26
San Antonio	28	54	.341	27

Pacific Division

	W	L	PCT	GB
L.A. Lakers	65	17	.793	
Portland	49	33	.598	16
Golden State	42	40	.512	23
Seattle	39	43	.476	26
Phoenix	36	46	.439	29
L.A. Clippers	12	70	.146	53

SCORING
Michael Jordan, CHI 37.1
Dominique Wilkins, ATL....29.0
Alex English, DEN.............28.6
Larry Bird, BOS.................28.1
Kiki Vandeweghe, POR ...26.9
Kevin McHale, BOS 26.1
Mark Aguirre, DAL 25.7
Dale Ellis, SEA..................24.9
Moses Malone, WAS 24.1
Magic Johnson, LAL 23.9

REBOUNDS
Charles Barkley, PHI.........14.6
Charles Oakley, CHI 13.1
Buck Williams, NJ 12.5
James Donaldson, DAL....11.9
Bill Laimbeer, DET............11.6

ASSISTS
Magic Johnson, LAL 12.2
Sleepy Floyd, GS..............10.3
Isiah Thomas, DET 10.0
Doc Rivers, ATL.................10.0
Terry Porter, POR 8.9

STEALS
Alvin Robertson, SA...........3.21
Michael Jordan, CHI 2.88

Maurice Cheeks, PHI 2.65
Ron Harper, CLE 2.55
Clyde Drexler, POR 2.49

BLOCKED SHOTS
Mark Eaton, UTA 4.06
Manute Bol, WAS..............3.68
Akeem Olajuwon, HOU....3.39
Benoit Benjamin, LAC.......2.60
Alton Lister, SEA...............2.40

FIELD GOAL PCT
Kevin McHale, BOS.......... .604
Artis Gilmore, SA.............. .597
Charles Barkley, PHI........ .594
James Donaldson, DAL.... .586
Kareem Abdul-Jabbar, LAL... .564

FREE THROW PCT
Larry Bird, BOS .... .910
Danny Ainge, BOS .... .897
Bill Laimbeer, DET .... .894
Byron Scott, LAL .... .892

3-PT. FIELD GOAL PCT
Kiki Vandeweghe, POR.... .481
Detlef Schrempf, DAL....... .478
Danny Ainge, BOS .... .443
Byron Scott, LAL .... .436

East First Round
Boston 3, Chicago 0
Atlanta 3, Indiana 1
Detroit 3, Washington 0
Milwaukee 3, Philadelphia 2

East Semifinals
Boston 4, Milwaukee 3
Detroit 4, Atlanta 1

East Finals
Boston 4, Detroit 3

West First Round
L.A. Lakers 3, Denver 0
Seattle 3, Dallas 1
Houston 3, Portland 1
Golden State 3, Utah 2

West Semifinals
L.A. Lakers 4, Golden State 1
Seattle 4, Houston 2

West Finals
L.A. Lakers 4, Seattle 0

NBA Finals
L.A. Lakers 126, Boston 113
L.A. Lakers 141, Boston 122
Boston 109, L.A. Lakers 103
L.A. Lakers 107, Boston 106
Boston 123, L.A. Lakers 108
L.A. Lakers 106, Boston 93

1987-88 FINAL STANDINGS

Eastern Conference

Atlantic Division

	W	L	PCT	GB
Boston	57	25	.695	
Washington	38	44	.463	19
New York	38	44	.463	19
Philadelphia	36	46	.439	21
New Jersey	19	63	.232	38

Central Division

	W	L	PCT	GB
Detroit	54	28	.659	
Atlanta	50	32	.610	4
Chicago	50	32	.610	4
Cleveland	42	40	.512	12
Milwaukee	42	40	.512	12
Indiana	38	44	.463	16

Western Conference

Midwest Division

	W	L	PCT	GB
Denver	54	28	.659	
Dallas	53	29	.646	1
Utah	47	35	.573	7
Houston	46	36	.561	8
San Antonio	31	51	.378	23
Sacramento	24	58	.293	30

Pacific Division

	W	L	PCT	GB
L.A. Lakers	62	20	.756	
Portland	53	29	.646	9
Seattle	44	38	.537	18
Phoenix	28	54	.341	34
Golden State	20	62	.244	42
L.A. Clippers	17	65	.207	45

SCORING

Michael Jordan, CHI	35.0
Dominique Wilkins, ATL	30.7
Larry Bird, BOS	29.9
Charles Barkley, PHI	28.3
Karl Malone, UTA	27.7
Clyde Drexler, POR	27.0
Dale Ellis, SEA	25.8
Mark Aguirre, DAL	25.1
Alex English, DEN	25.0
Akeem Olajuwon, HOU	22.8

REBOUNDS

Michael Cage, LAC	13.03
Charles Oakley, CHI	13.00
Akeem Olajuwon, HOU	12.1
Karl Malone, UTA	12.0
Buck Williams, NJ	11.9

ASSISTS

John Stockton, UTA	13.8
Magic Johnson, LAL	11.9
Mark Jackson, NY	10.6
Terry Porter, POR	10.1
Doc Rivers, ATL	9.3

STEALS

Michael Jordan, CHI	3.16
Alvin Robertson, SA	2.96

John Stockton, UTA	2.95
Lafayette Lever, DEN	2.72
Clyde Drexler, POR	2.51

BLOCKED SHOTS

Mark Eaton, UTA	3.71
Benoit Benjamin, LAC	3.41
Patrick Ewing, NY	2.99
Akeem Olajuwon, HOU	2.71
Manute Bol, WAS	2.70

FIELD GOAL PCT

Kevin McHale, BOS	.604
Robert Parish, BOS	.589
Charles Barkley, PHI	.587
John Stockton, UTA	.574
Walter Berry, SA	.563

FREE THROW PCT

Jack Sikma, MIL	.922
Larry Bird, BOS	.916
John Long, IND	.907
Mike Gminski, NJ/PHI	.906

3-PT. FIELD GOAL PCT

Craig Hodges, MIL/PHO.	.491
Mark Price, CLE	.486
John Long, IND	.442
Gerald Henderson, NY/PHI	.423

East First Round
Boston 3, New York 1
Detroit 3, Washington 2
Atlanta 3, Milwaukee 2
Chicago 3, Cleveland 2

East Semifinals
Boston 4, Atlanta 3
Detroit 4, Chicago 1

East Finals
Detroit 4, Boston 2

West First Round
L.A. Lakers 3, San Antonio 0
Denver 3, Seattle 2
Utah 3, Portland 1
Dallas 3, Houston 1

West Semifinals
L.A. Lakers 4, Utah 3
Dallas 4, Denver 2

West Finals
L.A. Lakers 4, Dallas 3

NBA Finals
Detroit 105, L.A. Lakers 93
L.A. Lakers 108, Detroit 96
L.A. Lakers 99, Detroit 86
Detroit 111, L.A. Lakers 86
Detroit 104, L.A. Lakers 94
L.A. Lakers 103, Detroit 102
L.A. Lakers 108, Detroit 105

1988-89 FINAL STANDINGS

Eastern Conference
Atlantic Division

	W	L	PCT	GB
New York	52	30	.634	
Philadelphia	46	36	.561	6
Boston	42	40	.512	10
Washington	40	42	.488	12
New Jersey	26	56	.317	26
Charlotte	20	62	.244	32

Central Division

	W	L	PCT	GB
Detroit	63	19	.768	
Cleveland	57	25	.695	6
Atlanta	52	30	.634	11
Milwaukee	49	33	.598	14
Chicago	47	35	.573	16
Indiana	28	54	.341	35

Western Conference
Midwest Division

	W	L	PCT	GB
Utah	51	31	.622	
Houston	45	37	.549	6
Denver	44	38	.537	7
Dallas	38	44	.463	13
San Antonio	21	61	.256	30
Miami	15	67	.183	36

Pacific Division

	W	L	PCT	GB
L.A. Lakers	57	25	.695	
Phoenix	55	27	.671	2
Seattle	47	35	.573	10
Golden State	43	39	.524	14
Portland	39	43	.476	18
Sacramento	27	55	.329	30
L.A. Clippers	21	61	.256	36

SCORING
Michael Jordan, CHI 32.5
Karl Malone, UTA..............29.1
Dale Ellis, SEA...................27.5
Clyde Drexler, POR 27.2
Chris Mullin, GS................26.5
Alex English, DEN.............26.5
Dominique Wilkins, ATL....26.2
Charles Barkley, PHI.........25.8
Tom Chambers, PHO 25.7
Akeem Olajuwon, HOU.....24.8

REBOUNDS
Akeem Olajuwon, HOU.....13.5
Charles Barkley, PHI.........12.5
Robert Parish, BOS 12.5
Moses Malone, ATL..........11.8
Karl Malone, UTA..............10.7

ASSISTS
John Stockton, UTA..........13.6
Magic Johnson, LAL 12.8
Kevin Johnson, PHO.........12.2
Terry Porter, POR 9.5
Nate McMillan, SEA 9.3

STEALS
John Stockton, UTA..........3.21
Alvin Robertson, SA..........3.03

Michael Jordan, CHI 2.89
Lafayette Lever, DEN........2.75
Clyde Drexler, POR 2.73

BLOCKED SHOTS
Manute Bol, GS.................4.31
Mark Eaton, UTA 3.84
Patrick Ewing, NY 3.51
Akeem Olajuwon, HOU.....3.44
Larry Nance, CLE 2.82

FIELD GOAL PCT
Dennis Rodman, DET .... .595
Charles Barkley, PHI......... .579
Robert Parish, BOS.......... .570
Patrick Ewing, BOS .... .567
James Worthy, LAL .... .548

FREE THROW PCT
Magic Johnson, LAL.......... .911
Jack Sikma, MIL................ .905
Scott Skiles, IND .... .903
Mark Price, CLE .... .901

3-PT. FIELD GOAL PCT
Jon Sundvold, MIA .... .522
Dale Ellis, SEA .... .478
Mark Price, CLE .... .441
Hersey Hawkins, PHI .... .428

East First Round
Detroit 3, Boston 0
New York 3, Philadelphia 0
Chicago 3, Cleveland 2
Milwaukee 3, Atlanta 2

East Semifinals
Detroit 4, Milwaukee 0
Chicago 4, New York 2

East Finals
Detroit 4, Chicago 2

West First Round
L.A. Lakers 3, Portland 0
Golden State 3, Utah 0
Phoenix 3, Denver 0
Seattle 3, Houston 1

West Semifinals
L.A. Lakers 4, Seattle 0
Phoenix 4, Golden State 1

West Finals
L.A. Lakers 4, Phoenix 0

NBA Finals
Detroit 109, L.A. Lakers 97
Detroit 108, L.A. Lakers 105
Detroit 114, L.A. Lakers 110
Detroit 105, L.A. Lakers 97

1989-90 FINAL STANDINGS

Eastern Conference

Atlantic Division

	W	L	PCT	GB
Philadelphia	53	29	.646	
Boston	52	30	.634	1
New York	45	37	.549	8
Washington	31	51	.378	22
Miami	18	64	.220	35
New Jersey	17	65	.207	36

Central Division

	W	L	PCT	GB
Detroit	59	23	.720	
Chicago	55	27	.671	4
Milwaukee	44	38	.537	15
Cleveland	42	40	.512	17
Indiana	42	40	.512	17
Atlanta	41	41	.500	18
Orlando	18	64	.220	41

Western Conference

Midwest Division

	W	L	PCT	GB
San Antonio	56	26	.683	
Utah	55	27	.671	1
Dallas	47	35	.573	9
Denver	43	39	.524	13
Houston	41	41	.500	15
Minnesota	22	60	.268	34
Charlotte	19	63	.232	37

Pacific Division

	W	L	PCT	GB
L.A. Lakers	63	19	.768	
Portland	59	23	.720	4
Phoenix	54	28	.659	9
Seattle	41	41	.500	22
Golden State	37	45	.451	26
L.A. Clippers	30	52	.366	33
Sacramento	23	59	.280	40

SCORING
Michael Jordan, CHI 33.6
Karl Malone, UTA.............31.0
Patrick Ewing, NY 28.6
Tom Chambers, PHO 27.2
Dominique Wilkins, ATL....26.7
Charles Barkley, PHI.........25.2
Chris Mullin, GS 25.1
Reggie Miller, IND..............24.6
Akeem Olajuwon, HOU.....24.3
David Robinson, SA...........24.3

REBOUNDS
Akeem Olajuwon, HOU.....14.0
David Robinson, SA...........12.0
Charles Barkley, PHI.........11.5
Karl Malone, UTA..............11.1
Patrick Ewing, NY 10.9

ASSISTS
John Stockton, UTA..........14.5
Magic Johnson, LAL 11.5
Kevin Johnson, PHO.........11.4
Tyrone Bogues, CHA........10.7

STEALS
Michael Jordan, CHI 2.77
John Stockton, UTA...........2.65

Scottie Pippen, CHI...........2.57
Alvin Robertson, MIL.........2.56
Derek Harper, DAL 2.28

BLOCKED SHOTS
Akeem Olajuwon, HOU.....4.59
Patrick Ewing, NY 3.99
David Robinson, SA...........3.89
Manute Bol, GS..................3.17
Benoit Benjamin, LAC.......2.63

FIELD GOAL PCT
Mark West, PHO .... .625
Charles Barkley, PHI .... .600
Robert Parish, BOS........... .580
Karl Malone, UTA .... .562

FREE THROW PCT
Larry Bird, BOS .... .930
Eddie Johnson, PHO........ .917
Walter Davis, DEN .... .912
Joe Dumars, DET.............. .900

3-PT. FIELD GOAL PCT
Steve Kerr, CLE .... .507
Craig Hodges, CHI .... .481
Drazen Petrovic, POR....... .459
Jon Sundvold, MIA .... .440

East First Round
Detroit 3, Indiana 0
Philadelphia 3, Cleveland 2
Chicago 3, Milwaukee 1
New York 3, Boston 2

East Semifinals
Detroit 4, New York 1
Chicago 4, Philadelphia 1

East Finals
Detroit 4, Chicago 3

West First Round
L.A. Lakers 3, Houston 1
San Antonio 3, Denver 0
Portland 3, Dallas 0
Phoenix 3, Utah 2

West Semifinals
Phoenix 4, L.A. Lakers 1
Portland 4, San Antonio 3

West Finals
Portland 4, Phoenix 2

NBA Finals
Detroit 105, Portland 99
Portland 106, Detroit 105 (OT)
Detroit 121, Portland 106
Detroit 112, Portland 109
Detroit 92, Portland 90

1990-91 FINAL STANDINGS

Eastern Conference
Atlantic Division

	W	L	PCT	GB
Boston	56	26	.683	
Philadelphia	44	38	.537	12
New York	39	43	.476	17
Washington	30	52	.366	26
New Jersey	26	56	.317	30
Miami	24	58	.293	32

Central Division

	W	L	PCT	GB
Chicago	61	21	.744	
Detroit	50	32	.610	11
Milwaukee	48	34	.585	13
Atlanta	43	39	.524	18
Indiana	41	41	.500	20
Cleveland	33	49	.402	28
Charlotte	26	56	.317	35

Western Conference
Midwest Division

	W	L	PCT	GB
San Antonio	55	27	.671	
Utah	54	28	.659	1
Houston	52	30	.634	3
Orlando	31	51	.378	24
Minnesota	29	53	.354	26
Dallas	28	54	.341	27
Denver	20	62	.244	35

Pacific Division

	W	L	PCT	GB
Portland	63	19	.768	
L.A. Lakers	58	24	.707	5
Phoenix	55	27	.671	8
Golden State	44	38	.537	19
Seattle	41	41	.500	22
L.A. Clippers	31	51	.378	32
Sacramento	25	57	.305	38

SCORING
Michael Jordan, CHI	31.5
Karl Malone, UTA	29.0
Bernard King, WAS	28.4
Charles Barkley, PHI	27.6
Patrick Ewing, NY	26.6
Michael Adams, DEN	26.5
Dominique Wilkins, ATL	25.9
Chris Mullin, GS	25.7
David Robinson, SA	25.6
Mitch Richmond, GS	23.9
Tim Hardaway, GS	22.9
Reggie Miller, IND	22.6
Kevin Johnson, PHO	22.2
Hersey Hawkins, PHI	22.1
Tony Campbell, MIN	21.8
Brad Daugherty, CLE	21.6
Clyde Drexler, POR	21.5
James Worthy, LAL	21.4

REBOUNDS
David Robinson, SA	13.0
Dennis Rodman, DET	12.5
Charles Oakley, NY	12.1
Karl Malone, UTA	11.8
Patrick Ewing, NY	11.2
Brad Daugherty, CLE	10.9
Robert Parish, BOS	10.6
Benoit Benjamin, SEA	10.3

ASSISTS
John Stockton, UTA	14.2
Magic Johnson, LAL	12.6
Michael Adams, DEN	10.5
Kevin Johnson, PHO	10.1
Tim Hardaway, GS	9.7
Isiah Thomas, DET	9.3
Pooh Richardson, MIN	9.0
Gary Grant, LAC	8.6

STEALS
Alvin Robertson, MIL	3.04
John Stockton, UTA	2.85
Michael Jordan, CHI	2.72
Tim Hardaway, GS	2.61
Scottie Pippen, CHI	2.35
Mookie Blaylock, NJ	2.35
Michael Adams, DEN	2.23
Hersey Hawkins, PHI	2.23

BLOCKED SHOTS
Hakeem Olajuwon, HOU	3.95
David Robinson, SA	3.90
Patrick Ewing, NY	3.19
Manute Bol, PHI	3.01
Chris Dudley, NJ	2.51
Larry Nance, CLE	2.50
Mark Eaton, UTA	2.35
Kevin McHale, BOS	2.15

FIELD GOAL PCT
Buck Williams, POR	.602
Robert Parish, BOS	.598
Kevin Gamble, BOS	.587
Charles Barkley, PHI	.570
Vlade Divac, LAL	.565
Olden Polynice, SEA/LAC	.560
Otis Thorpe, HOU	.556
Kevin McHale, BOS	.553

FREE THROW PCT
Reggie Miller, IND	.918
Jeff Malone, UTA	.917
Kelly Tripucka, CHA	.910
Ricky Pierce, MIL/SEA	.907
Magic Johnson, LAL	.906
Scott Skiles, ORL	.902
Kiki Vandeweghe, NY	.899
Jeff Hornacek, PHO	.897

3-PT. FIELD GOAL PCT
Jim Les, SAC	.461
Trent Tucker, NY	.418
Jeff Hornacek, PHO	.418
Terry Porter, POR	.415
Scott Skiles, ORL	.408
Danny Ainge, POR	.406
Hersey Hawkins, PHI	.400
Larry Bird, BOS	.389

1990-91 OFFENSIVE TEAM STATISTICS

	FIELD GOALS			FREE THROWS			REBOUNDS				MISCELLANEOUS					SCORING	
TEAM	ATT	FGs	PCT	ATT	FTs	PCT	OFF	DEF	TOT	AST	PFs	DQ	STL	TO	BLK	PTS	AVG
Denver	8868	3901	.440	2263	1726	.763	1520	2530	4050	2005	2235	46	856	1332	406	9828	119.9
Golden State	7346	3566	.485	2761	2162	.783	1113	2306	3419	1954	2207	37	803	1359	378	9564	116.6
Portland	7369	3577	.485	2538	1912	.753	1202	2561	3763	2254	1975	19	724	1309	410	9407	114.7
Phoenix	7199	3573	.496	2680	2064	.770	1132	2598	3730	2209	1850	12	687	1302	535	9348	114.0
Indiana	6994	3450	.493	2479	2010	.811	1018	2376	3394	2181	2088	16	658	1355	357	9159	111.7
Boston	7214	3695	.512	1997	1646	.824	1088	2697	3785	2160	1695	12	672	1320	565	9145	111.5
Chicago	7125	3632	.510	2111	1605	.760	1148	2342	3490	2212	1751	7	822	1184	438	9024	110.0
Atlanta	7223	3349	.464	2544	2034	.800	1235	2420	3655	1864	1768	14	729	1231	374	9003	109.8
San Antonio	6988	3409	.488	2459	1883	.766	1131	2657	3788	2140	1896	22	670	1445	571	8782	107.1
Houston	7287	3403	.467	2200	1631	.741	1275	2508	3783	1906	1874	32	796	1402	409	8753	106.7
Seattle	7117	3500	.492	2143	1608	.750	1222	2173	3395	2042	1973	23	861	1404	380	8744	106.6
Milwaukee	6948	3337	.480	2241	1796	.801	1079	2162	3241	2075	2033	25	894	1321	330	8727	106.4
L.A. Lakers	6911	3343	.484	2261	1805	.798	1078	2440	3518	2091	1524	7	642	1203	384	8717	106.3
Orlando	7256	3298	.455	2447	1818	.743	1233	2429	3662	1809	1976	20	602	1391	306	8684	105.9
Philadelphia	6925	3289	.475	2366	1868	.790	984	2496	3480	1824	1629	11	678	1230	479	8641	105.4
Utah	6537	3214	.492	2472	1951	.789	867	2474	3341	2217	1796	14	652	1305	451	8527	104.0
L.A. Clippers	7315	3391	.464	2273	1596	.702	1246	2500	3746	2119	2043	23	725	1438	507	8491	103.5
New York	6822	3308	.485	2147	1654	.770	1053	2436	3489	2172	1764	8	638	1379	418	8455	103.1
New Jersey	7459	3311	.444	2245	1658	.739	1400	2348	3748	1782	1954	18	748	1423	600	8441	102.9
Charlotte	7033	3286	.467	2214	1725	.779	1027	2200	3227	2019	1946	23	759	1290	304	8428	102.8
Miami	7139	3280	.459	2307	1649	.715	1232	2302	3534	1904	2080	29	757	1551	387	8349	101.8
Cleveland	6857	3259	.475	2176	1665	.765	1011	2329	3340	2240	1672	12	643	1281	450	8343	101.7
Washington	7268	3390	.466	2028	1478	.729	1173	2390	3563	2081	1927	17	588	1360	468	8313	101.4
Detroit	6875	3194	.465	2211	1686	.763	1206	2452	3658	1825	1869	27	487	1181	367	8205	100.1
Dallas	6890	3245	.471	1986	1512	.761	984	2360	3344	1821	1840	14	581	1186	397	8195	99.9
Minnesota	7276	3265	.449	2082	1531	.735	1275	2112	3387	1885	1864	35	712	1062	440	8169	99.6
Sacramento	6818	3086	.453	2105	1540	.732	1027	2218	3245	1991	2075	28	631	1272	513	7928	96.7

1990-91 DEFENSIVE TEAM STATISTICS

	FIELD GOALS			FREE THROWS			REBOUNDS				MISCELLANEOUS					SCORING		
TEAM	ATT	FGs	PCT	ATT	FTs	PCT	OFF	DEF	TOT	AST	PFs	DQ	STL	TO	BLK	PTS	AVG	DIF
Detroit	6743	3053	.453	2173	1674	.770	1002	2274	3276	1736	1987	24	581	1127	289	7937	96.8	+3.3
L.A. Lakers	7262	3354	.462	1700	1278	.752	1131	2187	3318	1998	1823	19	668	1175	334	8164	99.6	+6.7
Utah	7011	3217	.459	2090	1615	.773	1101	2278	3379	1858	1995	17	686	1254	409	8254	100.7	+3.3
Chicago	6884	3267	.475	2017	1554	.770	1062	2162	3224	2016	1826	17	633	1402	348	8278	101.0	+9.1
San Antonio	7289	3265	.448	2187	1664	.761	1122	2270	3392	1928	2008	31	801	1260	437	8412	102.6	+4.5
Houston	7316	3337	.456	2088	1609	.771	1242	2431	3673	1965	1786	20	711	1415	357	8466	103.2	+3.5
New York	7162	3410	.476	1903	1471	.773	1119	2336	3455	1999	1813	19	724	1239	368	8474	103.3	-0.2
Sacramento	6687	3142	.470	2686	2045	.761	1164	2542	3706	1912	1847	17	699	1312	448	8484	103.5	-6.8
Minnesota	6778	3320	.490	2219	1680	.757	1094	2379	3473	2142	1692	16	512	1238	511	8491	103.5	-3.9
Milwaukee	6775	3290	.486	2312	1755	.759	1108	2315	3423	2023	1912	17	704	1531	461	8524	104.0	+2.5
Cleveland	7117	3459	.486	1916	1464	.764	1097	2398	3495	2150	1895	20	710	1226	394	8545	104.2	-2.5
Dallas	6945	3346	.482	2296	1700	.740	1116	2489	3605	2025	1778	10	650	1147	400	8570	104.5	-4.6
Seattle	6738	3285	.488	2459	1866	.759	1107	2149	3256	1851	1820	20	729	1485	446	8643	105.4	+1.2
Philadelphia	7432	3536	.476	1794	1388	.774	1156	2519	3675	2220	1862	23	691	1177	391	8656	105.6	-0.2
Boston	7559	3419	.452	2084	1639	.786	1192	2204	3396	2052	1660	7	738	1127	381	8668	105.7	+5.8
Portland	7275	3320	.456	2341	1819	.777	1079	2354	3433	2048	2075	40	630	1397	352	8695	106.0	+8.7
Washington	7280	3396	.466	2288	1763	.771	1232	2473	3705	1861	1778	19	728	1254	492	8721	106.4	-5.0
L.A. Clippers	7151	3337	.467	2529	1901	.752	1115	2494	3609	1982	1887	23	773	1316	491	8774	107.0	-3.5
New Jersey	7206	3374	.468	2493	1927	.773	1287	2527	3814	1737	1896	18	831	1452	540	8811	107.5	-4.5
Phoenix	7499	3462	.462	2244	1705	.760	1195	2298	3493	1972	2059	24	682	1282	463	8811	107.5	+6.5
Miami	6974	3335	.478	2603	1997	.767	1176	2364	3540	2006	1960	13	853	1467	502	8840	107.8	-6.0
Charlotte	6915	3408	.493	2441	1884	.772	1151	2514	3665	2144	1841	19	675	1406	480	8858	108.0	-5.2
Atlanta	7219	3568	.494	2069	1587	.767	1080	2499	3579	2320	2034	29	668	1291	361	8940	109.0	+0.8
Orlando	7232	3454	.478	2451	1879	.767	1095	2500	3595	2118	1983	18	706	1215	654	9010	109.9	-4.0
Indiana	7299	3577	.490	2490	1851	.743	1202	2313	3515	2063	2037	21	729	1260	353	9191	112.1	-0.4
Golden State	7349	3544	.482	2797	2121	.758	1292	2480	3772	2164	2206	36	726	1534	437	9430	115.0	+1.6
Denver	7962	4076	.512	3068	2377	.775	1242	3067	4309	2492	1844	14	757	1527	525	10723	130.8	-10.9

1990-91 HOME-ROAD RECORDS

	Home	Road	Total		Home	Road	Total
Portland	36-5	27-14	63-19	Seattle	28-13	13-28	41-41
Chicago	35-6	26-15	61-21	New York	21-20	18-23	39-43
L.A. Lakers	33-8	25-16	58-24	Cleveland	23-18	10-31	33-49
Boston	35-6	21-20	56-26	L.A. Clippers	23-18	8-33	31-51
Phoenix	32-9	23-18	55-27	Orlando	24-17	7-34	31-51
San Antonio	33-8	22-19	55-27	Washington	21-20	9-32	30-52
Utah	36-5	18-23	54-28	Minnesota	21-20	8-33	29-53
Houston	31-10	21-20	52-30	Dallas	20-21	8-33	28-54
Detroit	32-9	18-23	50-32	Charlotte	17-24	9-32	26-56
Milwaukee	33-8	15-26	48-34	New Jersey	20-21	6-35	26-56
Golden State	30-11	14-27	44-38	Sacramento	24-17	1-40	25-57
Philadelphia	29-12	15-26	44-38	Miami	18-23	6-35	24-58
Atlanta	29-12	14-27	43-39	Denver	17-24	3-38	20-62
Indiana	29-12	12-29	41-41				

1990-91 PLAYOFFS

EAST FIRST ROUND
Chicago 126, New York 85
Chicago 89, New York 79
Chicago 103, New York 94

Boston 127, Indiana 120
Indiana 130, Boston 118
Boston 112, Indiana 105
Indiana 116, Boston 113
Boston 124, Indiana 121

Atlanta 103, Detroit 98
Detroit 101, Atlanta 88
Detroit 103, Atlanta 91
Atlanta 123, Detroit 111
Detroit 113, Atlanta 81

Phil. 99, Milwaukee 90
Phil.116, Milwaukee 112 (OT)
Phil. 121, Milwaukee 100

EAST SEMIFINALS
Chicago 105, Philadelphia 92
Chicago 112, Philadelphia 100
Philadelphia 99, Chicago 97
Chicago 101, Philadelphia 85
Chicago 100, Philadelphia 95

Detroit 86, Boston 75
Boston 109, Detroit 103
Boston 115, Detroit 83

Detroit 104, Boston 97
Detroit 116, Boston 111
Detroit 117, Boston 113 (OT)

EAST FINALS
Chicago 94, Detroit 83
Chicago 105, Detroit 97
Chicago 113, Detroit 107
Chicago 115, Detroit 94

WEST FIRST ROUND
Portland 110, Seattle 102
Portland 115, Seattle 106
Seattle 102, Portland 99
Seattle 101, Portland 89
Portland 119, Seattle 107

San Ant. 130, Golden St. 121
Golden St. 111, San Ant. 98
Golden St. 109, San Ant. 106
Golden St. 110, San Ant. 97

L.A. Lakers 94, Houston 92
L.A. Lakers 109, Houston 98
L.A. Lakers 94, Houston 90

Utah 129, Phoenix 90
Phoenix 102, Utah 92
Utah 107, Phoenix 98
Utah 101, Phoenix 93

WEST SEMIFINALS
Portland 117, Utah 97
Portland 118, Utah 116
Utah 107, Portland 101
Portland 104, Utah 101
Portland 103, Utah 96

LAL 126, Golden St. 116
Golden St. 125, LAL 124
LAL 115, Golden St. 112
LAL 123, Golden St. 107
LAL 124, Golden St. 119 (OT)

WEST FINALS
L.A. Lakers 111, Portland 106
Portland 109, L.A. Lakers 98
L.A. Lakers 106, Portland 92
Portland 95, L.A. Lakers 84
L.A. Lakers 91, Portland 90

NBA FINALS
L.A. Lakers 93, Chicago 91
Chicago 107, L.A. Lakers 86
Chicago 104, LAL 96 (OT)
Chicago 97, L.A. Lakers 82
Chicago 108, L.A. Lakers 101

BASKETBALL HALL OF FAME

This section honors the 178 people— and four teams—that are enshrined in the Naismith Memorial Basketball Hall of Fame in Springfield, Massachusetts. Like the Hall of Fame, this section is divided into five categories— "players," "coaches," "contributors," "referees," and "teams." The section includes bios on each member of the Hall. At the end of each bio is a date in parentheses; this is the year the member was enshrined into the Hall.

Abbreviations include BAA (Basketball Association of America), NBL (National Basketball League), ABA (American Basketball Association), and AAU (American Athletic Union). Others include NAIA (National Association of Intercollegiate Athletics), NIT (National Invitational Tournament), NABC (National Association of Basketball Coaches), and USBWA (United States Basketball Writers Association).

PLAYERS

NATE ARCHIBALD
Guard: Small in stature at 6'1", "Tiny" Archibald was a giant on the court. After starring at Texas-El Paso, he began his pro career in Cincinnati in 1970-71. In 1972-73, he led the NBA in assists (11.4) and scoring (34.0). In 1980-81, he helped the Celtics win the NBA title. Archibald played in six All-Star Games and was league MVP in 1981. (1991)

PAUL ARIZIN
Forward: A star at Villanova, where he was college Player of the Year in 1950, the sharp-shooting Arizin averaged better than 22 PPG over his ten-year NBA career in Philadelphia. Known for his deadly jump shot, Arizin led the league in scoring in 1952 and '57 and led the Warriors to the NBA title in 1956. He retired with 16,266 points and ten All-Star Game appearances. (1977)

TOM BARLOW
Forward: In the early years of this century, when the Eastern League was popular, "Babe" Barlow was among the game's most exciting players. A pro at age 16, Babe enjoyed 20 seasons of roundball (from 1912-32). Barlow was known as much for his defensive skills as for his scoring. (1980)

RICK BARRY
Forward: One of the game's most accurate shooters, Barry starred at Miami of Florida. In 1965, Rick led the NCAA with an average of 37.4 PPG. As a pro, he played in both the ABA and NBA and is the only player to lead both leagues in scoring. His career NBA free throw pct. was .900—the best mark in league history. In 1975, he led the Golden State Warriors to the NBA title. (1986)

ELGIN BAYLOR
Forward: Baylor was considered the most devastating, artistic forward of his era. After a spectacular college career in which he led Seattle to the NCAA finals in 1958, Baylor debuted in the NBA in 1958-59. He averaged 24.9 PPG as a rookie for Minneapolis and won Rookie of the Year honors. Over his 14-year career, he netted 23,149 points, averaging 27.4 per game. (1976)

JOHNNY BECKMAN

Forward: From 1910 until the 1940s, "Becky" Beckman was often referred to as the Babe Ruth of basketball. A star in the Interstate, New York State, and Eastern Leagues, Beckman eventually joined the Original Celtics. As their captain, he led them to some of their greatest years. In 1935, he was selected by Nat Holman as "Basketball's Finest Competitive Athlete." (1972)

BENNIE BORGMANN

Guard: Though only 5'8", Borgmann was one of the most popular touring pros on the East Coast in the early years. His pro career spanned over 2,500 games in various Eastern leagues. It wasn't unusual for Borgmann to score half of his team's points during any given game. He later coached both at the college and professional level. (1961)

BILL BRADLEY

Forward: "Dollar Bill" Bradley was an intelligent player with a graceful, deadly shooting touch. As a three-time All-American at Princeton, he averaged 30 PPG and was the 1965 college Player of the Year. In 1964, he helped the U.S. win the Olympic gold medal. A Rhodes Scholar, Bradley played ten seasons with the New York Knicks, amassing 9,217 points, 2,533 assists, and two NBA championship rings. He is currently a U.S. senator in New Jersey. (1982)

JOE BRENNAN

Forward: "Poison Joe" Brennan enjoyed a 17-year pro career, starting at age 19 when he joined the Brooklyn Visitation and led them to their greatest years. In 1950, the New York Basketball Old-Timers voted Brennan second only to Johnny Beckman as the greatest player of his era. (1974)

AL CERVI

Guard: An outstanding clutch performer, Cervi was an immediate star with the NBL's Buffalo Bisons. His pro career was interrupted by a five-year stint in World War II, but he resumed his career in 1945, playing for the Rochester Royals. In 1948, he became a player/coach for the Syracuse Nats. He was named Coach of the Year five times in the next eight seasons. (1984)

WILT CHAMBERLAIN

Center: At 7'1", Wilt "The Stilt" Chamberlain was an awesome, dominant figure on the court. After two All-America years at Kansas, Wilt spent a year with the Harlem Globetrotters before entering the NBA in 1959. In just his first year, he was named the NBA's MVP. During 14 years, he was the league MVP four times (1960, 1966-68). He still holds NBA records for career rebounds (23,924), season scoring average (50.4 in 1961-62), and most points in a game (100). He won world titles with Philadelphia (1967) and Los Angeles ('72). (1978)

CHARLES COOPER

Center: In his day, "Tarzan" Cooper was a giant among men. The 6'4", 214-pound Cooper was a consistent winner for 20 years of pro basketball. In 11 years with the New York Renaissance, his teams compiled a record of 1303-203. In 1932-33, the club won 88 straight games. He has been called the greatest center of his day. (1976)

BOB COUSY

Guard: At 6'1", Cousy made his name as the most sensational passer the game had ever known. After three All-America years at Holy Cross, "Mr. Basketball" joined the Boston Celtics in 1950. Eventually, he led them to six NBA titles, including five in a row (1959-63). He led the league in assists for eight straight years (1953-60) and played in 13 consecutive All-Star Games. (1970)

DAVE COWENS

Center: Cowens was a tough, physical player. "The Redhead" starred at Florida State, where he averaged 19 points and 17 rebounds per game. In his first NBA season with Boston, he was Co-Rookie of the Year. In ten seasons with the Celtics, he won two championships (1974 and '76) and was player/coach for a year. In his career, Cowens averaged 17.6 PPG and collected 10,444 rebounds. (1991)

BILLY CUNNINGHAM

Guard: A scrappy playmaker at North Carolina, Cunningham debuted in the NBA with the Philadelphia 76ers in 1965. In 11 pro seasons (including two with the ABA Carolina Cougars), Cunningham made the All-NBA First Team three times and was named ABA MVP in 1973. In 770 pro games, he averaged 21.8 PPG. He became the 76ers' coach in 1978, bringing them a 454-196 record over eight seasons, including a league title in 1983. (1985)

BOB DAVIES

Guard: Davies has been called the "first superstar of modern pro basketball." A two-time All-American at Seton Hall, Davies turned pro in 1945 with Rochester. In ten BAA and NBA seasons, he was all-league seven times. He led the Royals to league titles in 1946, '47, and '51. His patented behind-the-back dribble made him popular with fans. (1969)

FORREST DeBERNARDI

Forward/Guard/Center: DeBernardi's career revolved around AAU tournaments. He was an AAU All-American in 1921, '22, and '23 and won four AAU titles. In 11 AAU tournaments, "De" was all-tournament seven times. He starred at three different positions. (1961)

DAVE DeBUSSCHERE

Forward: DeBusschere was one of the game's great defensive forwards. After three All-America years at the University of Detroit, DeBusschere debuted with his hometown Pistons in 1962. Two years later at age 24, he became the Pistons' player/coach. He was traded to the Knicks in 1969 and helped them to two championships (1970 and '73). In 875 games, he amassed 14,053 points and 9,618 rebounds. (1982)

DUTCH DEHNERT

Guard: Without Henry "Dutch" Dehnert, there might never have been a three-second rule in basketball. Back in the 1920s, playing for the powerful Celtics, Dehnert inadvertently invented the pivot play when he routinely stationed himself at the foul line to relay passes back and forth to weaving teammates. Though he didn't play either high school or college ball, Dehnert honed his skills in Eastern pro leagues. He joined the Celts at age 22. (1968)

PAUL ENDACOTT

Guard: Endacott attended Kansas, where he achieved status as "the greatest player ever coached" by Kansas' Phog Allen. Endacott was selected as Player of the Year in 1923. In 1969, he received the Sportsmen's World Award in basketball, because his "exemplary personal conduct has made him an outstanding inspiration for youth to emulate." (1971)

BUD FOSTER

Guard: Harold "Bud" Foster, a star player in college, also excelled as a coach. As a senior at Wisconsin in 1930, he earned All-America honors. Foster played briefly as a pro before embarking on a glorious 25-year career as a coach. He guided Wisconsin to three Big Ten titles (1935, '41, and '47) and the NCAA championship (1941). (1964)

WALT FRAZIER

Guard: A smooth backcourt specialist known for sleek passing and laser-accurate shooting, "Clyde" Frazier played 13 seasons in the NBA, including ten with the New York Knicks. Frazier helped the Knicks to league titles in 1970 and 1973, played in seven All-Star Games, was a celebrated defensive wizard, and finished his career with an average of 18.9 PPG. (1986)

MARTY FRIEDMAN

Guard: A turn-of-the-century hero, Max "Marty" Friedman was one of a pair of hoops stars known as the "Heavenly Twins" (his counterpart was longtime buddy Barney Sedran). Friedman was one of the great defensive players of his era. He played in six Eastern leagues and, in 1915, helped Carbondale win 35 straight games. He later won accolades as well as championships as a coach. (1971)

JOE FULKS

Forward: "Jumping Joe" Fulks was one of the first scoring superstars of the BAA and NBA. An ambidextrous jump-shot artist, Fulks shocked the BAA in 1946-47 by scoring 23.2 PPG for Philadelphia. Two years later, he averaged 26.0 PPG and was named *The Sporting News* Athlete of the Year for 1949. (1977)

LADDIE GALE

Forward: Lauren "Laddie" Gale's excellence on the court helped bring recognition to the basketball programs in the Pacific Northwest. Gale was an All-American at Oregon, and in 1939 he led his school to the NCAA title. Gale played professionally and was also a successful coach. (1976)

HARRY GALLATIN

Center: A large center for his time (6'6"), Harry "The Horse" Gallatin was the centerpiece of the New York Knicks for nine years. Gallatin established a consecutive-games-played record (746) that included regular-season, playoff, All-Star, and exhibition contests. In 1953-54, Gallatin led the NBA in rebounds (1,098). He later went on to a successful coaching career both at the pro and college levels. (1991)

WILLIAM GATES

Guard: "Pop" Gates went from a championship high school team to a champion pro team in consecutive seasons. In 1938, he led Benjamin Franklin (New York) to a high school title. In 1939, he helped the New York Renaissance to 68 straight victories and a World Professional Championship. Throughout his 12-year career, he played for many outstanding teams, including the Harlem Globetrotters, where he was a player/coach from 1950-55. (1988)

TOM GOLA

Forward: Tom Gola combined outstanding scoring prowess with defensive wizardry to become one of the most respected all-around players in the game. At La Salle in the mid-1950s, Gola was a four-year All-American, averaging 21 points and 20 rebounds per game. He played ten years professionally with Philadelphia, San Francisco, and New York, scoring 7,871 points. He was often high in assists and rebounds. (1975)

HAL GREER

Guard: Greer was the first black scholarship athlete to attend Marshall (1955-59) and earned All-America status in 1958. He played five years with the Syracuse Nationals before joining the powerful Philadelphia 76ers for another ten seasons. He recorded 21,586 career points, was named to ten All-Star Games, and won a world title with Philly in 1967. (1981)

ROBERT GRUENIG

Center: A 6'8" center with a shooter's touch, "Ace" Gruenig was a brilliant AAU performer. He shined in the AAU from 1931 until he retired in the late 1940s. From 1937-48, he was the annual choice as first-team all-tournament center. In 1943, he received the Los Angeles Sports Award Medallion as the nation's greatest player. (1963)

CLIFF HAGAN

Forward: At Kentucky, Hagan was a two-time All-American (1952 and '54) who led his Wildcats to an NCAA title in 1951 and a perfect 25-0 record in 1954. During ten years in the NBA with the St. Louis Hawks, he scored 13,447 points, relying heavily on his amazingly accurate hook shot. He appeared in four All-Star Games and helped the Hawks win the league title in 1958. He also played three years in the ABA, serving as player/coach for the Dallas Chaparrals. (1977)

VICTOR HANSON

Guard: Hanson starred at Syracuse in basketball, football, and baseball. He was a three-time All-American in hoops (1925-27), winning a national championship in 1926. In his senior campaign, Hanson was the college Player of the Year. He later played pro ball with the Cleveland Rosenblums, and he also played minor-league baseball in the New York Yankees farm system. (1960)

JOHN HAVLICEK

Forward: After leading Ohio State to three NCAA finals and one championship, "Hondo" Havlicek embarked on a 16-year NBA career with Boston. Havlicek began as the Celts' sixth man, ultimately earned a starting spot, and was later named team captain. In his career, he scored 26,395 points, appeared in 13 All-Star Games, and was an eight-time member of the NBA All-Defensive Team. (1983)

ELVIN HAYES

Forward: The 6'9" Hayes used strength, speed, and grace to achieve amazing results. At Houston, "The Big E." was a three-time All-American and 1968 college Player of the Year. Hayes led the NBA in scoring as a rookie and went on to play 16 years with San Diego, the Bullets, and Houston. In 1977-78, he led the Bullets to the NBA title. He played exactly 50,000 NBA minutes--second most in league history. He scored 27,313 points in his career. (1989)

TOMMY HEINSOHN

Forward: A two-time All-American at Holy Cross, Heinsohn became the NBA Rookie of the Year for Boston in 1957 and started for the champion Celtics for the next eight seasons. Heinsohn, who was named to six All-Star Games, averaged 18.6 PPG over his career. In 1970, he took over as coach. He guided Boston to a 427-263 record and two NBA titles, in 1974 and '76. (1985)

NAT HOLMAN

Guard: Holman, who gained fame as coach of the City College of New York Beavers, was also a player of note from 1916-33. Holman joined the Original Celtics in 1920, stayed nine seasons, and was one of their greatest players, exploiting his skills as a passer, shooter, and strategist. In 1933, he retired from playing to concentrate on coaching. In 1950, his Beavers won both the NIT and NCAA titles, which no team had ever done before. Holman retired from coaching in 1960. (1964)

BOB HOUBREGS

Center: A superb collegian, Houbregs was an All-American with Washington in 1953, leading the Huskies to a third-place finish in the '53 NCAA tournament. Houbregs held the second highest scoring average in NCAA tournament history

(34.8 PPG) before being drafted by
Milwaukee. He played five years in the
NBA and later served as GM of the
Seattle SuperSonics from 1970-73.
(1986)

CHUCK HYATT

Forward: One of the finest amateur
players of the century, Hyatt starred at the
University of Pittsburgh from 1927-30 and
was a three-time All-American. He was
the top scorer in the nation in 1930. The
Panthers were 60-7 during Hyatt's career,
winning national titles in 1928 and '30. He
later joined the Phillips 66 Oilers and
became a legend of the AAU circuit,
earning All-America honors nine times.
(1959)

WILLIAM JOHNSON

Center: Tall and lanky, "Skinny" Johnson
was a dominant center for Kansas from
1930-33, earning All-America honors in
his senior year. He guided his squad to a
record of 42-11 and three Big Six
championships. In 1934, as an AAU star,
he was the top scorer in the Missouri
Valley. In 1975, he was named an All-
Time Great in Oklahoma, his home state.
(1976)

NEIL JOHNSTON

Center: After two years at Ohio State, the
6'8" Johnston tried his luck as a pitcher,
signing a pro baseball contract. A sore
arm turned him back to basketball, where
he joined the Philadelphia Warriors in
1951. In eight seasons, he led the NBA in
scoring and field goal percentage three
times, led in rebounding once, and helped
the Warriors win the title in 1956. A knee
injury ended his playing career, but he
stayed in the game as a coach, a scout,
and an athletic director. (1989)

K.C. JONES

Guard: After starring in college at San
Francisco, Jones joined the Boston

Celtics in 1958 and stayed for nine years,
where he was a dependable guard on
their championship teams. As a coach,
Jones has won more than 500 NBA
games, including 308 with the Celts. He
has been involved in 11 titles in Boston—
eight as a player, one as an assistant
coach, and two more as head coach
(1984 and '86). He currently coaches the
Seattle SuperSonics. (1988)

SAM JONES

Guard: After playing brilliantly at tiny
North Carolina College, Jones cracked
the Celtics lineup in 1958 and became
part of ten championship teams. He led
the club in scoring three times and
averaged 25.9 PPG in 1964-65. His
patented jump shot off the glass, his most
effective weapon, was feared around the
NBA. (1983)

EDWARD KRAUSE

Center: A star at Notre Dame in the early
1930s, Krause was a three-time All-
American in two sports—basketball and
football. At 6'3", 215 pounds, he was
considered the first "agile" center, setting
many scoring records for the Irish.
"Moose" later played professionally in the
Midwest and New England before
returning to the college scene as a coach
and athletic director. (1975)

BOB KURLAND

Center: The first of the truly great
seven-foot centers, Kurland carved out
one of the most impressive amateur
careers ever. At Oklahoma State, he
led his squad to NCAA titles in 1945
and '46, leading the nation in scoring
the latter year. He later played six
seasons of AAU ball with the Phillips 66
Oilers, where he was All-AAU each
year and an Olympian in 1948 and '52.
(1961)

JOE LAPCHICK

Center: The son of poor, immigrant parents, Lapchick began playing pro basketball at age 17 without a high school education. The 6'5" center played in several leagues and centered the Original Celtics from 1923-27. Later, he became a great coach, leading St. John's to four NIT titles. He also coached the New York Knicks for nine seasons. (1966)

CLYDE LOVELLETTE

Center: Lovellette was a winner wherever he played. As a college star at Kansas, he was a three-time All-American (1950-52) and the Big Seven scoring champion each year. In 1952, he led the nation in scoring and guided the Jayhawks to the NCAA title. He played for the 1952 gold-medal Olympic team before starting an 11-year NBA career. He played with the champion Minneapolis Lakers in 1954 and later won titles with the 1963 and '64 Boston Celtics. (1987)

JERRY LUCAS

Forward: A fine shooter, passer, and defensive ace, Lucas was a two-time college Player of the Year at Ohio State, where his team captured one NCAA title and three Big Ten titles. He also helped the U.S. win the gold in the 1960 Olympics. In 1963-64 with Cincinnati, Lucas was the NBA's Rookie of the Year. He went on to play in seven All-Star Games and was part of the New York Knicks' 1973 championship team. He finished his career with 14,053 points and 12,942 rebounds. (1979)

HANK LUISETTI

Forward: Luisetti was a revolutionary who broke old standards by developing a one-handed shot. In three seasons at Stanford, Hank led his squad to successive Pacific Coast Conference titles. An All-American in 1937 and '38, Luisetti was the first college player ever to

score 50 points in a game. He later starred on the AAU scene, twice more earning All-America honors. (1959)

ED MACAULEY

Forward: "Easy Ed" Macauley was a four-time All-American at St. Louis (1946-49). In 1947, he led the nation with a .524 shooting percentage, and was MVP of the NIT tournament the following year. Professionally, Macauley played ten NBA seasons, earning seven All-Star Game appearances and netting 11,234 career points. (1960)

PETE MARAVICH

Forward: Maravich, one of the great gunners in basketball history, shattered many NCAA records, including highest career scoring average (44.2). Maravich starred at Louisiana State, earning three All-America berths and college Player of the Year honors in 1970. "Pistol Pete" played NBA ball with Atlanta, the Jazz, and Boston. In 658 NBA games, he averaged 24.2 PPG. In 1976-77, he led the league in scoring with a 31.1 average. (1986)

SLATER MARTIN

Guard: At 5'10", "Dugie" Martin was the first "small superstar" of the NBA, playing throughout the 1950s. After three outstanding years at Texas, Martin joined the NBA. He played for four league championship teams in Minneapolis before moving to St. Louis, where he helped the Hawks win the 1958 title. In 11 seasons, he tallied 7,337 points and 3,160 assists and earned a reputation as a defensive genius. (1981)

BRANCH McCRACKEN

Forward: One of Indiana's great amateurs, McCracken starred for three years at Indiana University, winning the conference MVP Award in 1928. During his career, he scored nearly one-third of all the points recorded by the Hoosiers. He later had great success as a coach, winning four Big Ten and two NCAA titles at Indiana. (1960)

JACK McCRACKEN
Center: A two-time All-American at N.W. Missouri State (1931-32), McCracken was known for his outstanding passing and domination of the backboards. As a star of the AAU circuit, he was an eight-time All-American between 1932 and 1945 and won two AAU championships. (1962)

BOBBY McDERMOTT
Forward: McDermott turned pro after his freshman year of high school and played for 17 years. According to coaches and managers of the NBL in 1945, McDermott was "the greatest professional basketball player of all time." He was a seven-time NBL All-Star, won five straight MVP Awards, and led the league twice in scoring. He was a champion with Brooklyn, Fort Wayne, Chicago, and the Original Celtics. (1987)

GEORGE MIKAN
Center: The game's first dominating big man, the 6'10" Mikan was a three-time NBA scoring leader and played in the first four NBA All-Star Games. Previously, he was a three-time All-American at DePaul and twice was named college Player of the Year (1945 and '46), leading the nation in scoring in both of those years. Mikan played on five NBA title teams in Minneapolis. (1959)

EARL MONROE
Guard: Earl "The Pearl" Monroe's slick ball-handling and dead-eye shooting made him a prolific scorer and crowd-pleaser. A two-time All-American at Winston-Salem State, he was drafted by Baltimore and was the NBA Rookie of the Year in 1968. He spent 13 years in the NBA and helped the New York Knicks win the 1973 league title. An amazing clutch player, Monroe set an NBA record for most points (13) in a single overtime period. (1989)

STRETCH MURPHY
Center: "Stretch" Murphy was one of the most feared big men of his time, as he helped Purdue to a Big Ten championship in 1928. A two-time All-American, Murphy set a Western Conference and Big Ten scoring mark when he netted 143 points in 1929. In his senior year, 1930, he captained Purdue to an undefeated record. (1960)

PAT PAGE
Forward: An outstanding defensive player and a star in three sports, Page led his University of Chicago squad to Western Conference titles in 1907, 1909 (when they were undefeated), and 1910. In 1910, Page was named college Player of the Year. He later coached at Chicago, Butler, and the College of Idaho. (1962)

BOB PETTIT
Forward: A three-time All-American at Louisiana State (1952-54), Pettit played ten NBA seasons with the St. Louis Hawks. He was named NBA Rookie of the Year in 1955 and league MVP in 1956 and '59. He led the Hawks to the league title in 1958. He finished as the greatest scorer in league history with 20,880 points. (1970)

ANDY PHILLIP
Guard: One of the stars of the University of Illinois "Whiz Kids," Phillip set Big Ten scoring marks in 1942 and '43 and once scored 40 points in a game. Phillip's college career was disrupted by three years in World War II. However, he returned to Illinois and enjoyed an All-America year in 1947. He later played in the BAA and NBA for more than a decade. (1961)

JIM POLLARD

Forward: After earning All-America status at Stanford, Pollard entered the military, where he was a Service All-Star. He led Stanford to an NCAA championship in 1942 and later starred in the AAU circuit, winning MVP honors in 1947 and '48. He joined the Minneapolis Lakers in 1949 and helped them to five league championships. (1977)

FRANK RAMSEY

Guard: A two-time All-American while playing at Kentucky (1952 and '54), Ramsey joined the Boston Celtics and revolutionized the game by "inventing" the sixth-man position. Ramsey won seven titles in nine NBA seasons. He was called "the most versatile player in the NBA" by his longtime coach, Red Auerbach. (1981)

WILLIS REED

Center: One of the most intense competitors of his time, Reed began as a two-time All-American at Grambling. In ten pro seasons with the New York Knicks, he won two NBA titles (1970 and '73), was Rookie of the Year (1964-65), and played in seven All-Star Games. He averaged 18.7 PPG in his career and grabbed 8,414 boards. (1981)

OSCAR ROBERTSON

Guard: One of the greatest all-around players ever, "The Big O." starred at the University of Cincinnati, where he was a two-time college Player of the Year and a three-time scoring leader among major-college players. He set 14 NCAA scoring marks. As a pro for Cincinnati, he was league MVP in 1964. Later, he led the Milwaukee Bucks to the 1971 NBA title. He finished his career with 26,710 points (25.7 PPG) and set an NBA record with 9,887 assists. (1979)

JOHN ROOSMA

Forward: Roosma made his mark on the game as a member of the U.S. Army squad. In his Army career, he scored more than 1,000 points, including 354 in one season. Roosma, whose Army team went 70-3 during his tenure, served in the military for 30 years and retired as an Army colonel in 1956. (1961)

BILL RUSSELL

Center: Russell reigns as one of the great winners and rebounders of all time. As a collegian, he was Player of the Year in 1956 for San Francisco and also led his school to two NCAA titles. He then led the U.S. to gold in the 1956 Olympic Games. As a pro, he helped the Celtics to eight straight NBA crowns (1959-66) and 11 in his 13-year career. He collected 21,620 rebounds, averaged 15.1 PPG, and was league MVP five times. As player/coach, he led the Celts to titles in 1968 and '69. (1974)

HONEY RUSSELL

Guard: A great defensive player, John "Honey" Russell played against the best players in virtually every professional league during his 28-year career. He led the Cleveland Rosenblums to five straight championships (1925-29) and later coached his alma mater, Seton Hall, to nearly 300 victories, including a string of 44 straight. In 1946-47, he became the first coach of the NBA Boston Celtics. (1964)

DOLPH SCHAYES

Forward: Schayes played his college ball at New York University, where he was an All-American in 1948. In 15 seasons with the Syracuse Nationals, he was one of the game's great scorers, chalking up 19,249 points (18.2 per game). From February 1952 to December 1961, he played in a record 765 straight games. Later, he was named Coach of the Year in 1966 when he guided the Philadelphia 76ers to a division title. His son Danny plays for the Milwuakee Bucks. (1972)

ERNEST SCHMIDT

Forward: Schmidt was known as "One Grand Schmidt" after scoring 1,000 career points in his Kansas State Teachers College days. He was a four-time conference all-star in the early 1930s and was widely recognized as the greatest player ever to come out of the Missouri Valley. Later, he suited up for three seasons on the AAU circuit, playing for Denver and Reno. (1973)

JOHN SCHOMMER

Center: A star in basketball, football, baseball, and track, Schommer led the Chicago Maroon basketball squad to three straight Big Ten titles (1907-09) and was the conference scoring leader all three years. He also enjoyed a 47-year career as athletic director, coach, and teacher at Illinois Institute of Technology. In 1949, the Helms Foundation named him a center on its All-Time All-America Team. (1959)

BARNEY SEDRAN

Guard: At 5'4", Sedran proved that size truly wasn't everything. Despite being banished from high school basketball, Sedran starred at City College of New York and was his team's leading scorer three years in a row. Upon his graduation in 1911, he embarked on a 15-year pro career that included ten championships. He helped Carbondale to 35 straight victories in 1914-15 and later was a coach for another 20 years. (1962)

BILL SHARMAN

Guard: After two All-America years at Southern California, the sharp-shooting Sharman enjoyed an 11-year stint in the NBA, where he played on four championship Boston Celtics teams in the

1950s and early 1960s. Sharman's secret weapon was free throw shooting. His career 88-percent mark is among the best ever. After retiring with 12,665 points, he won titles as a coach in the ABA and NBA. (1975)

CHRISTIAN STEINMETZ

Guard: The "father of Wisconsin basketball," Christian Steinmetz turned basketball into a recognized sport at the University of Wisconsin. As a senior in 1905, he set school scoring records (some of which would stand for the next 50 years) including: most points in a game (50), most free throws in a game (26), and most points in a season (462). (1961)

JOHN THOMPSON

Guard: A star at Montana State, John "Cat" Thompson was selected to All-Rocky Mountain Conference teams for four years in a row. In 1929, they were the Helms national champions and the Cat was named Player of the Year. Thompson eventually became a coach, where he remained for 14 years. (1962)

NATE THURMOND

Center: An All-American at Bowling Green, Thurmond was a defensive genius with strong shooting skills. In his 14-year NBA career, he averaged 15 points and 15 rebounds per game. In a 1974 game, he became the first to record a "quadruple-double." Playing for several NBA teams, Thurmond was named to seven All-Star Games and finished his career with 14,464 boards. (1984)

JACK TWYMAN

Forward: An All-American at Cincinnati, Jack Twyman joined the Rochester Royals in 1955-56. In 11 NBA seasons, he scored 15,840 points. A durable forward with precision shooting skills, Twyman played 823 games (including a stretch of 609 consecutively) and averaged 19.2 PPG. He also played on six All-Star teams. (1982)

WES UNSELD

Center: After an explosive career at Louisville, where he was an All-American in 1967 and '68, Unseld entered the NBA with an equally loud bang in 1968-69, when he was the NBA's MVP for the Baltimore Bullets. Unseld led the Bullets to an NBA championship in 1978. In his career, he averaged 14 rebounds a game and played in five All-Star Games. He's currently coach of the Washington Bullets. (1987)

FUZZY VANDIVIER

Guard: Robert "Fuzzy" Vandivier was a high school superstar who became one of the greatest players in the history of Indiana basketball. He took his perennial-champion Franklin High School team directly to Franklin College in 1922 and helped establish a legendary squad. He is a member of the All-Time All-Star Five of Indiana. (1974)

ED WACHTER

Center: As a turn-of-the-century player, Wachter starred on nearly every team in the Eastern circuit. He was an annual scoring champion and a member of more title-winning clubs than anyone else of his time. Later, as a coach at Harvard, he founded the New England Basketball Association and struggled to gain national uniformity of rules and regulations. (1961)

BOBBY WANZER

Guard: An All-American at Seton Hall in 1946, Wanzer played professionally for ten seasons with the Rochester Royals, appearing in five All-Star Games. He was the NBA's MVP in 1952-53, two years after helping the Royals win the 1951 NBA title. An outstanding shooter, Wanzer led the league in free throw accuracy (90 percent) in 1951-52. Later, he coached the Royals for three years. (1986)

JERRY WEST

Guard: One of the greatest high-pressure performers of all time, Jerry West earned his nickname "Mr. Clutch" during 14 seasons with the Los Angeles Lakers. A former two-time All-American while at West Virginia, and a gold medalist at the 1960 Olympic Games, West averaged 27.0 PPG in the NBA. He was also named to 14 All-Star Games and helped the Lakers win the 1972 NBA title. (1979)

LENNY WILKENS

Guard: A leader and a winner, Lenny Wilkens enjoyed success at every level of the game. As an All-American at Providence College, he was the 1960 NIT tournament's MVP. Wilkens, a 6'1" guard, went on to play 15 seasons in the NBA, averaging 16.5 PPG and making nine All-Star teams. He later coached the Seattle SuperSonics, one of his former teams, to the 1979 NBA championship. He currently coaches the Cleveland Cavaliers. (1988)

JOHN WOODEN

Forward: Before becoming one of basketball's greatest coaches, Wooden was an outstanding player. A three-time All-American at Purdue (1930-32) and college Player of the Year (1932), he set a Big Ten scoring record in his senior year and led his team to the national title. Wooden later starred as a pro for Indianapolis' Kautsky Grocers, where he once hit 138 straight free throws. (1960)

COACHES

PHOG ALLEN

A Doctor of Osteopathy, Forrest "Phog" Allen was one of the game's greatest coaches. In nearly 40 years of coaching, much of it at his alma mater (Kansas), Allen's teams won 31 championships, three national titles, and 746 games. He co-founded the National Association of Basketball Coaches in 1927, and in 1950 was given the prestigious NABC/MIBA/NIT Award in recognition of his basketball excellence. (1959)

HAROLD ANDERSON

Anderson was a star athlete in college, earning 11 letters in three sports before turning to coaching at age 23. After nine successful years coaching high school ball, he moved to the University of Toledo in 1934. There, he went 142-41. In more than 20 years at Bowling Green, he made several trips to NIT and NCAA tournaments. His college coaching record was 504-226. (1984)

RED AUERBACH

Called by many "the greatest coach in the history of the NBA," Red Auerbach is the only coach ever to win more than 1,000 games in pro basketball. A player at George Washington, Auerbach joined the burgeoning NBA as a coach in 1946. He took the job at Boston in 1950 and led the Celtics to nine NBA titles, including eight straight from 1959-66. He has been a part of the Celtic front office ever since. (1968)

SAM BARRY

A graduate of Wisconsin, Justin "Sam" Barry coached at Iowa for seven years, where he won the Big Ten title in 1923 and shared it in 1926. His greatest years came when he moved to

Southern California, where he coached for 17 years. There, he won three conference championships and seven division titles. (1978)

ERNEST BLOOD

Blood enjoyed a high school coaching career that was simply mind-boggling. From 1906-15, his Potsdam (New York) High School squad never lost a game. From 1915-24 at Passaic (New Jersey) High School, his team won 200 games, lost just once, and claimed seven state titles. He later coached at St. Benedict's Prep, winning another five state crowns. He also coached at West Point and Clarkson. (1960)

HOWARD CANN

A three-sport athlete while at New York University, Cann led NYU to the 1920 AAU title. He was a shot-putter on the 1920 Olympic team before becoming a coach at NYU for 35 years. His record was 409-232, which included an undefeated season in 1933-34. (1967)

H. CLIFFORD CARLSON

Two years after earning a medical degree, Dr. Carlson began coaching the University of Pittsburgh and remained a coach for more than 30 years. He led Pitt to a pair of national championships (1928 and '30) and is credited with inventing the "Figure Eight" offense. A founder of the National Association of Basketball Coaches, he was given the NABC/MIBA/NIT Award in 1948 for his contributions to the game. (1959)

BEN CARNEVALE

A graduate of New York University, Bernard Carnevale became a great teacher and coach. He earned his greatest honors during a 20-year stay with the U.S. Naval Academy, where he coached the Middies to 257 wins between 1946 and 1966. He also managed the 1968 U.S. Olympic team in Mexico City. (1969)

EVERETT CASE

A graduate of Wisconsin, Case enjoyed a 40-year coaching career. In 21 years of high school coaching, he won 467 games and four Indiana state championships (1925, '29, '36, and '39). He later went to coach at North Carolina State (1946-65), where he won 377 games and six straight Southern Conference titles. He finished his career with 844 wins and 258 losses. (1981)

EVERETT DEAN

An All-American at Indiana in 1921, Dean went to Carleton College after graduation and coached his way to a 48-4 record. He returned to Indiana and won 163 games over the next 14 years, tying for three Big Ten titles. He joined Stanford as a coach in 1938 and led the school to the 1942 NCAA title. He retired from coaching in 1955. (1966)

ED DIDDLE

A Kentucky product, Diddle was a successful high school coach before joining Western Kentucky in 1922. He stayed at WKU for the next 42 years, guiding the famous "fastbreak" Hilltoppers to 32 conference titles. He also took them to three NCAA and eight NIT tournaments. Diddle was the first coach ever to coach 1,000 games at the same school. (1971)

BRUCE DRAKE

An accomplished college athlete while attending Oklahoma, Drake later coached the Sooners, starting in 1939. In 17 years, his club won 200 games and captured six Big Six or Big Seven titles. Drake also served as chairman of the National Rules Committee and president of the NABC. (1972)

CLARENCE GAINES

In 1947, "Big House" Gaines was named athletic director and head coach of all sports at Winston-Salem State College. Five decades later, he was still at Winston-Salem and had become only the second college basketball coach to win 800 games. In 1967, his Rams, led by future NBA superstar Earl Monroe, won the NCAA College Division title with a 30-2 record. (1981)

JACK GARDNER

James "Jack" Gardner is the only college coach to lead two different schools to the Final Four twice apiece. At Kansas State, he won three Big Seven titles and got to the Final Four in 1948 and '51. At Utah, Gardner guided his squad to the 1961 and '66 Final Four. In 36 years of coaching, he posted a 70-percent winning mark and 649 victories. (1983)

SLATS GILL

An All-American at Oregon State, Amory "Slats" Gill eventually coached his alma mater for 35 years, until 1964. His Beavers won 599 games, five Pacific Coast Conference titles, nine Northern Division titles, and eight straight Far West Classics. Under Gill, the Beavers were ranked in the top five nationally in 1947, '49, and '55. (1967)

MARV HARSHMAN

An outstanding all-around athlete, Harshman captured 13 letters at Pacific Lutheran and was a two-time All-American in basketball. He began his coaching career in the mid-1940s at Lutheran, then coached at Washington State and Washington during the next four decades. His teams won 642 games. (1984)

EDDIE HICKEY

Besides being a prolific writer and researcher, Hickey was a successful coach. He enjoyed success at three universities—Creighton, St. Louis (where he won the 1948 NIT title), and Marquette (where he was named USBWA Coach of the Year in 1959). Over 35 years, his teams won 436 games and were participants in countless NCAA and NIT tournaments. (1978)

HOWARD HOBSON

Hobson was the first coach to win major championships on the West Coast *and* the East Coast. "Hobby" took Oregon to three conference titles (1937-39) and the first NCAA crown (1939), and he later guided Yale to five Big Three titles. His basketball teams won 400 games during his 28-year tenure. With an advanced degree in education, Hobson used his vast intellect to advance the game strategically and tactically. (1965)

RED HOLZMAN

Holzman was a collegiate star at the City College of New York, where he was a two-time All-American. Later, during his eight years as a player with NBL Rochester, he guided the club to the 1951 league title. He coached the New York Knicks for 14 years, winning NBA titles in 1970 and '73. He was the NBA's Coach of the Year in 1970. In 1981, Holzman became the first man to receive the NBA Coaches Achievement Award. (1985)

HENRY IBA

Iba was a fine player and an even better coach. He took over at Oklahoma State in 1934 and led the Aggies to 14 Missouri Valley championships, the 1965 Big Eight crown, and the 1945 and '46 NCAA titles. Iba then coached the U.S. Olympic team to gold medals in 1964 and 1968. He won 767 Division I games—second on the all-time list. (1968)

DOGGIE JULIAN

An accomplished athlete who played pro baseball and football, Alvin "Doggie" Julian won ten letters as a college star. He then became a solid coach for 41 years. His basketball teams won 381 games and made several trips to NCAA and NIT tournaments. In 1947, his Holy Cross club won the NCAA crown. At Dartmouth, his squad was a three-time Ivy League champ (1956, '58, and '59). He received the NABC/MIBA/NIT Award in 1967. (1967)

FRANK KEANEY

Keaney was instrumental in changing the face of basketball at the University of Rhode Island. Named athletic director at the school in 1920, Keaney instituted the fastbreak, "point-per-minute" offense that eventually led his teams to four NIT tournaments and 403 victories over 27 seasons. (1960)

GEORGE KEOGAN

Keogan took over as coach of Notre Dame in 1923 and led the Irish to 327 wins in the next two decades. During one stretch, his team lost only five of 61 games. His greatest claim to fame was creating a shifting man-to-man defense. After his death at age 52, he was posthumously bestowed the NABC/MIBA/NIT Award in 1943. (1961)

BOB KNIGHT

His practices may come under fire, but no one has ever questioned Knight's ability to get the most from his players. He has coached 20 years at Indiana, where he has won three NCAA crowns (1976, '81, and '87) and has never had a losing season. Knight also coached successfully at Army, where he led the

Cadets to a 102-52 record over six years. He is a three-time USBWA Coach of the Year. (1991)

WARD LAMBERT

A trained chemist, Ward "Piggy" Lambert also coached at Purdue, where he won 11 Big Ten titles and 371 games over 30 years. Among his more famous players were Charlie Murphy and John Wooden, both of whom executed Lambert's fastbreak style to near perfection. Lambert was given the NABC/MIBA/NIT Award in 1954. (1960)

HARRY LITWACK

Though rarely blessed with great talent, Litwack coached 21 years at Temple, his alma mater. At Temple, Litwack earned the reputation for "doing more with less than any coach in basketball history." Litwack's Owls won 373 games (losing 193) and went to 13 postseason tournaments. In 1969, they captured the NIT title. (1975)

KENNETH LOEFFLER

Loeffler played and coached the game and also earned a degree in law. He led La Salle to the 1952 NIT title and the 1954 NCAA crown. He also guided the NBA St. Louis Bombers to a 1948 division title. Loeffler also coached at Yale and Texas A&M and served as a representative of the U.S. State Department and the Armed Services. (1964)

DUTCH LONBORG

A star at Kansas, Arthur "Dutch" Lonborg took to coaching in 1922. Dutch won 323 games at McPherson College, Washburn, and Northwestern. Later, he served as chairman of the NCAA tournament committee and the U.S. Olympic basketball committee, and was manager of the 1960 U.S. Olympic basketball team. (1972)

ARAD McCUTCHAN

A graduate of Evansville College, McCutchan returned to his alma mater in 1946 and began a remarkable coaching career. He won five NCAA College Division championships and 514 games. In 1964 and '65, Arad was NCAA College Division Coach of the Year. McCutchan is one of only two college basketball coaches to win at least five NCAA titles. (1980)

JOHN McLENDON

McLendon began his long coaching career while still a student at Kansas. He coached high school, college, AAU, and pro basketball, winning 522 total games. He was the first coach to win three straight national titles, as he led Tennessee State to NAIA crowns in 1957-59. He also coached the Denver Rockets of the fledgling ABA and received the NABC/MIBA/NIT Award in 1976. (1978)

FRANK McGUIRE

McGuire is the only coach to win at least 100 games at three different colleges: St. John's (103), North Carolina (164), and South Carolina (283). He also is the only coach to reach the NCAA finals at two schools, winning it all with the 32-0 North Carolina Tar Heels in 1957, and losing it with St. John's in '52. McGuire also coached a season in the NBA, leading the 1962 Philadelphia Warriors to 49 wins. At the time of his induction into the Hall of Fame, McGuire had 675 career wins. (1976)

WALTER MEANWELL

A doctor of public health medicine, Dr. Meanwell coached basketball at Wisconsin for two decades and also coached Missouri for a couple years. During that time, he won 290 games and six conference titles. He later authored a book (with Knute Rockne) on training, conditioning, and injury care. Meanwell received the NABC/MIBA/NIT Award in 1953. (1959)

RAY MEYER

A coaching legend at DePaul, Meyer started out as captain of the Notre Dame basketball team. He eventually spent 42 years as leader of the Blue Demons (1943-84), guiding them to 724 victories and 22 NCAA and NIT tournaments. His Demons captured the NIT title in 1945. With his 724 victories, Meyer is fifth on the all-time Division I win list. (1978)

RALPH MILLER

A star player under Phog Allen at Kansas, "Cappy" Miller began a 38-year college coaching career in 1951. He coached at Wichita State (13 years), Iowa (six years), and Oregon State (19 years). He enjoyed 33 winning seasons and was the USBWA Coach of the Year in 1981 and '82. In all, his teams won 657 games. (1987)

PETE NEWELL

A 1939 graduate of Loyola, Newell coached at the University of San Francisco, Michigan State, and Cal.-Berkeley. As a coach, Newell won the 1949 NIT title with USF, the 1959 NCAA crown with Cal.-Berkeley, and the 1960 Olympic gold medal. In 1960, he was elected USBWA Coach of the Year. Newell's instructional programs have helped develop countless NBA stars. He received the NABC/MIBA/NIT Award in 1968. (1978)

ADOLPH RUPP

After a championship career at Kansas, Rupp coached Kentucky from 1931-72 and became the winningest coach in college history. Along the way, he won 875 games. His teams advanced to 24

Southeast Conference titles, won four NCAA crowns, and nabbed one NIT championship. He was co-coach of the 1948 gold-medal Olympic team, and he received the NABC/MIBA/NIT Award in 1966. (1968)

LEONARD SACHS

When he was 19 years old, Sachs was the star of the Illinois A.C., which won the national AAU championship in 1917. Sachs became the coach at Loyola of Chicago in 1924. Over the next 19 years, his teams won 224 games. His use of the 2-2-1 zone defense, in which the center was used as a blocker, was responsible for a growing trend toward big men in the game. (1961)

EVERETT SHELTON

A coach and clinician, Shelton won 850 games in his 46-year career. Shelton coached two national title-winning teams—the AAU Denver Safeways in 1937 and the NCAA champion Wyoming team in 1943. He was a successful teaching coach in high school, college, and amateur basketball, and was recognized for his contributions by receiving the NABC/MIBA/NIT Award in 1969. (1979)

DEAN SMITH

A successful player in Phog Allen's program at Kansas, Smith became coach of North Carolina in 1962. He's still there. Smith has won 717 games, has a winning pct. of .774, and has appeared in an all-time record 21 NCAA tournaments. He won the NCAA title in 1982 and copped a gold medal in the 1976 Olympics. (1982)

FRED TAYLOR

The Ohio-born Taylor starred on Ohio State's 1950 Big Ten championship team. After a brief pro baseball career in the Washington Senators system, Taylor eventually became head coach of Ohio State in 1959. Over the next 18 years, the Buckeyes won 297 games, took the 1960 NCAA title, and were runners-up in 1961 and '62. He was named the USBWA Coach of the Year in 1961 and '62. (1985)

MARGARET WADE

Wade coached girls high school basketball in Mississippi, going 453-89 over 19 years. She returned to her alma mater, Delta State, in 1973 and led it to three straight national championships. Wade retired in 1979 with a career record of 633-117. (1984)

STANLEY WATTS

A graduate of Brigham Young, Watts became coach of the BYU varsity in 1949. During his 23 years in that post, the Cougars won 433 games and two NIT crowns (1951 and '66). In 1970, he was given the NABC/MIBA/NIT Award. Two years later, he left coaching to become BYU's athletic director. (1985)

JOHN WOODEN

One of the greatest coaches of all time, Wooden coached 13 years of ball in high schools and at Indiana State, before arriving at UCLA in 1948. From 1964-75, UCLA won ten NCAA titles, including seven straight from 1967-73. He was UPI Coach of the Year six times and twice (1970 and 1972) swept all four Coach of the Year polls (NABC, USBWA, AP, and UPI). Wooden is the only person to be voted into the Hall of Fame twice—as both a player and a coach. (1972)

CONTRIBUTORS

SENDA ABBOTT

The "mother of women's basketball," Senda Berenson Abbott read of the "invention" of basketball by Dr. James Naismith, contacted him, and subsequently adapted a set of rules for women. Abbott's guidelines remained in effect for 75 years. (1984)

CLAIR BEE

A coach for 29 years, Bee's Long Island University teams (1931-51) won an astonishing 95 percent of their games. In 1939, they won the NIT championship. Bee later coached Baltimore in the NBA (1952-54) and was the inventor of the 1-3-1 zone defense. Bee wrote more than 20 instructional and non-fiction sports books. (1967)

WALTER BROWN

In 1946, Brown spearheaded the movement to organize the BAA. As president of the Boston Garden Arena Corporation, he was able to house one of the first BAA franchises—the Celtics. From 1961-64, Brown served as chairman of the Basketball Hall of Fame's board of trustees. (1965)

JOHN BUNN

An all-around athlete at Kansas, Bunn coached 25 years at Stanford, Springfield, and Colorado State, winning 321 games. Bunn wrote several textbooks on basketball and, in 1961, received the NABC/MIBA/NIT Award. (1964)

BOB DOUGLAS

Douglas organized the famous all-black Renaissance Five in 1922. A road club facing racism and discrimination wherever they went, the Rens won 2,318 games in 22 years, including 88 straight in 1933, another 128 total in 1934, and the World Professional Championship in 1939. (1971)

AL DUER

Duer helped establish and develop the NAIA, formerly the National Association of Intercollegiate Basketball. He served as its executive secretary from 1949-1971. He supervised the 1955 tournament, which was the first national basketball tourney to include black institutions. (1981)

CLIFFORD FAGAN

A tireless administrator, Fagan became executive director of the National Federation of High School Athletic Associations in 1959. He held the post for 18 years and expanded the organization to include all 50 states. He also was co-editor of *Basketball Rules Simplified*. (1983)

HARRY FISHER

Fisher led Columbia in scoring four years straight and guided them to undefeated seasons in 1904 and '05. He also coached for 11 years at Columbia. Later, Fisher was hand-picked by General Douglas MacArthur to guide the U.S. Military Academy. He led the Academy to a 46-5 record. (1973)

LARRY FLEISHER

Fleisher founded and led the National Basketball Players Association from 1962-88. Schooled at Harvard Law, Fleisher introduced collective bargaining to pro sports. Through his negotiations, players obtained benefits such as pension plans and minimum-salary levels. Fleisher also helped established free agency in sports. (1991)

EDDIE GOTTLIEB

A Russian-born immigrant and an adroit promoter, Gottlieb helped organize the BAA in 1946. He coached the Philadelphia Warriors team that won the first BAA title (1947). Gottlieb served as chairman of the NBA Rules Committee for 25 years. (1971)

LUTHER GULICK

As physical training chairman at Springfield College, Dr. Gulick asked James Naismith to create "an indoor game." The game Naismith created, of course, was basketball. Gulick helped create the Public School League of New York City, the Camp Fire Girls, and the Boy Scouts of America. (1959)

LESTER HARRISON

As owner of the Rochester Royals for 13 years, Harrison won an NBL title in 1946 and an NBA crown in 1951. Harrison was a proponent of the time clock and many other game innovations. (1979)

FERENC HEPP

The "father of basketball in Hungary," Dr. Hepp was the first director of Hungary's National School of Physical Education and Sports. Hepp was associated with basketball in Hungary from the 1930s on, and he wrote an important multi-language dictionary of basketball terminology. (1980)

EDWARD HICKOX

Hickox spent four decades as a coach and was the first executive secretary of the NABC. He served as president from 1944-46. Hickox also was a resident historian for two decades. (1959)

TONY HINKLE

Paul "Tony" Hinkle coached Butler University in his native Indiana, where he won 560 games and a national title in 1929. He became known as the "dean of Indiana coaches;" at one point, 55 of his charges held coaching positions in Indiana. He received the NABC/MIBA/NIT Award in 1962. (1965)

NED IRISH

Irish was a master promoter who, as basketball director at Madison Square Garden, instituted college doubleheaders. In 1946, he helped organize the BAA and also formed the New York Knickerbockers. Irish received the first NABC/MIBA/NIT Award, in 1942. (1964)

R. WILLIAM JONES

Jones was a British subject born and educated in Rome, Italy. In 1929, he brought basketball to Switzerland, and three years later he co-founded the International Amateur Basketball Federation. Ultimately, Jones helped spread the game to 130 nations. (1964)

J. WALTER KENNEDY

Kennedy was a scorekeeper, coach, referee, and publicity director for the NBA. More importantly, he served as NBA commissioner from 1963-75. Under Kennedy's caring and watchful leadership, the NBA boomed in TV revenue, in attendance, and in the number of teams competing. (1980)

EMIL LISTON

Besides coaching Baker University for 25 years, Liston organized the National Association of Intercollegiate Basketball and became its executive director in 1940. It has since grown to 500 members and is now known as the National Association of Intercollegiate Athletics (NAIA). (1974)

BILL MOKRAY

A superstar among basketball publicists, Mokray spent 21 years with the Boston Celtics. He compiled statistics for the *Converse Basketball Yearbook,* wrote a basketball history for the 1957 *Encyclopedia Britannica,* and edited an award-winning basketball encyclopedia in 1963. (1965)

RALPH MORGAN

As a student at Pennsylvania, Morgan called for the formation of the Collegiate Basketball Rules Committee. He remained an active member of the committee for more than a quarter-century. In 1910, at age 26, he formed the Eastern Intercollegiate Basketball League, currently known as the Ivy League. (1959)

FRANK MORGENWECK

"Pop" Morgenweck began his pro basketball career in 1901 as a 26-year-old manager in the NBL. In 1925, his Kingston (New York) squad played a six-game championship series with the New York Celtics, splitting it 3-3. From 1912 to his retirement in 1931, Morgenweck won various championship titles. (1962)

JAMES NAISMITH

Naismith is universally recognized at the "father of basketball." While serving as an instructor at the Springfield YMCA in 1891, Prof. Naismith searched for an indoor game that his boys could enjoy during the winter. He asked a custodian to nail two peach baskets to the gymnasium balcony, and the rest is history. (1959)

JOHN O'BRIEN

Besides playing pro basketball and serving as a referee, O'Brien formed the Metropolitan Basketball League in 1921. He served as president and treasurer of the MBL for seven years. He then reorganized the American Basketball League and served as president until 1953. (1961)

LARRY O'BRIEN

O'Brien spent many years in politics as advisor to Presidents John Kennedy and Lyndon Johnson. He was named commissioner of the NBA in 1975.

During his nine-year tenure, a collective-bargaining agreement was reached and the league expanded to 23 teams. (1991)

HAROLD OLSEN

Olsen coached for 23 years at Ohio State, winning five conference titles. Later, as chairman of the National Rules Committee, he helped pass the adoption of the ten-second rule. In 1938-39, he chaired the NABC study of an NCAA tournament, which eventually became a huge national event. (1959)

MAURICE PODOLOFF

Born in Russia, Podoloff assumed the leadership of the BAA in June 1946. Through his sensitivity and high standards, he was able to lead a merger between the BAA and the NBL, thus creating the NBA in 1949. He served as NBA president and, in 1954, secured the league's first TV contract. Podoloff retired in 1963. (1973)

HENRY PORTER

Porter invented the "molded" basketball, the fan-shaped backboard, and the 29 ½-inch ball. He also served on the National Rules Committee for three decades. Later, he wrote a handbook and developed the use of instructional films. (1960)

WILLIAM REID

A 1918 graduate of Colgate, Reid later coached his alma mater to 151 wins in ten years. He also served as manager and athletic director at Colgate for 36 years. Reid presided over the Eastern Collegiate Athletic Conference (1944-45) and was vice-president of the NCAA (1942-46). (1963)

ELMER RIPLEY

A star pro player in the 1910s, Ripley later coached at Wagner, Yale,

Georgetown, Columbia, Notre Dame, John Carroll, West Point, and Regis, accumulating nearly 300 victories. He also guided the Harlem Globetrotters (1953-56) and the 1960 Canadian Olympic team. (1972)

LYNN ST. JOHN

A star athlete in four sports and a successful college coach in Ohio, St. John served as Ohio State's athletic director from 1915-47. He was chairman of the NCAA Rules Committee for 18 years, and he helped form the National Basketball Committee of United States and Canada. (1962)

ABE SAPERSTEIN

The "father of the Harlem Globetrotters," Saperstein originally was asked to coach the Negro American Legion Team in 1926. It was from this team that the famous Globetrotters were born. Saperstein served the team as owner, manager, coach, and sometimes player. (1970)

ARTHUR SCHABINGER

A four-sport college star, Schabinger coached two decades and won 80 percent of his games at Ottawa University, Emporia State, and Creighton. Schabinger helped conceive the NABC and wrote its bylaws. He won the NABC/MIBA/NIT Award in 1955. (1961)

AMOS ALONZO STAGG

Besides becoming a great college football coach, Stagg played in the first public basketball game, held on March 11, 1892. Stagg also led the University of Chicago's first basketball team, back in 1896. (1959)

EDWARD STEITZ

Steitz coached Springfield College and also served as the school's athletic director. Steitz wrote more than 300 articles and 60 books and conducted hundreds of rules clinics around the world. In 1974, he received the NABC/MIBA/NIT Award. (1983)

CHUCK TAYLOR

Following an 11-year pro career, Charles Taylor became well known for several other basketball achievements. He produced the first *Converse Basketball Yearbook* and, in 1931, designed the famous Converse Chuck Taylor basketball sneaker. (1968)

BERTHA TEAGUE

Teague coached girls basketball at Cairo (Oklahoma) High School in 1926, then moved to Byng High and stayed for 42 years (1927-69). Her teams won 38 conference titles and eight state championships, winning 1,152 games while losing 115. (1984)

OSWALD TOWER

Tower remained in basketball for more than 60 years. As a member of the Rules Committee (1910-1959), he edited the *Official Guide* from 1915-59 and was official rules interpreter during the same period. He was given the NABC/MIBA/NIT Award in 1944. (1959)

ARTHUR TRESTER

Trester was brought in to save the struggling Indiana High School Athletic Association in 1913. Over time, he helped the IHSAA stabilize and grow. In the meantime, he built Indiana's annual basketball tournament, which became known as a model of efficiency. (1961)

CLIFFORD WELLS

A 1920 graduate of Indiana University, Wells won 617 games during 29 years of high school coaching in Indiana. In 1945, he became head coach at Tulane, where he stayed for 18 years. Wells conducted more than 100 clinics worldwide and received the NABC/MIBA/NIT Award in 1963. (1971)

LOU WILKE

In three years as coach of the Phillips 66 Oilers, Wilke won two AAU titles. He later served as president of the National AAU, and he chaired the AAU Basketball Committee for seven terms. Wilke was manager of the 1948 U.S. Olympic basketball team. (1982)

REFEREES

JIM ENRIGHT

During his 24-year career, Enright was a respected referee in the Big Ten, Big Eight, and Missouri Valley. He was also a clinician and a sports writer and served as president of the USBWA in 1967. (1978)

GEORGE HEPBRON

A friend of Dr. James Naismith, Hepbron was a pioneer of basketball rules. Hepbron helped draft the first guide book on how to play the game. He also refereed the first AAU tournament at Bay Ridge Athletic Club. (1960)

GEORGE HOYT

An early pioneer of the game, Hoyt traveled the Northeast introducing the principles of officiating to coaches and referees. He coached many teams and refereed many games during the first half of this century. (1961)

PAT KENNEDY

The colorful Kennedy officiated for 18 years at the high school, college, and pro level. He was the NBA's supervisor of officials from 1946-50, and he also toured with the Harlem Globetrotters for seven years. (1959)

LLOYD LEITH

Leith began a coaching career in 1927 and won 207 games at three California high schools. For 25 years, he was the top referee in the Pacific Coast Conference. He officiated in numerous NCAA tournaments. (1982)

RED MIHALIK

Mihalik began refereeing in the mid-1930s, and by 1951 he was voted the "best referee in the United States." An official at the amateur, collegiate, and pro levels, Mihalik also refereed at the 1964 and '68 Olympic Games. (1985)

JOHN NUCATOLA

Nucatola played ten years of pro basketball before starting his officiating career. Over the years, he called more than 2,000 games, including games in the NCAA and NIT tournaments. He worked the NBA as well. (1977)

ERNEST QUIGLEY

Quigley, a four-sport star at Kansas at the turn of the century, became a multisport official too. For three decades, he was a National League umpire, a football official, and a respected basketball referee. (1961)

J. DALLAS SHIRLEY

Shirley presented countless papers and clinics worldwide addressing development and improvement of rules interpretation. Shirley spent 32 years as an official in various college conferences and international tournaments—including the 1960 Olympics. (1979)

DAVID TOBEY

After a successful pro career as a player, Tobey turned to coaching, winning 367 high school games and 348 college games. From 1918-25, he refereed all vital pro games and was considered one of the best. (1961)

DAVID WALSH

Walsh enjoyed a 45-year career as a teacher, coach, and official in high school, college, and pro basketball. Walsh went on to conduct many clinics and rules-interpretation conferences to create uniformity in rules. (1961)

TEAMS

FIRST TEAM

Under the direction of James Naismith, the first game was played in 1891 at the Springfield (Massachusetts) YMCA Training School. The game was played with a peach basket and a soccer ball, and legend has it that only one basket was scored in the contest. (1959)

ORIGINAL CELTICS

Founded by promoters Jim and Tom Furey after World War I, the Original Celtics were a sensational barnstorming team. The Celts were known for their innovative strategies and brilliant passing. Johnny Beckman and Joe Lapchick were among the stars. (1959)

BUFFALO GERMANS

The Germans were a touring team from Buffalo that played from 1895-1929. The Germans played against amateurs and pros and compiled an all-time record of 792-86. At one point, they won 111 straight games. (1961)

NEW YORK RENS

Founded by Bob Douglas in 1922, the all-black Renaissance Five was a brilliant barnstorming club. Though they often encountered racism, the Rens won 2,318 games in 22 years, including 88 straight in 1933. Charles "Tarzan" Cooper starred in the middle. (1963)

100 Top College Stars & 64 Top College Teams

The following two sections evaluate the top players and teams in college basketball. Of the thousands of players in the college ranks, you'll read about the 100 that are expected to make the biggest impact in 1991-92. You'll also find season previews on the top 64 teams in the country.

Each player's scouting report begins with his vital stats, such as school, position, and height. Next comes a four-part evaluation of the player. "Background" reviews the player's career, starting with high school and continuing up through the 1990-91 season. "Strengths" examines his best assets, and "weaknesses" pinpoints his significant flaws. "Analysis" tries to put the player's whole game into perspective.

For a quick run-down on each player, you'll find a "player summary" box. You'll also find the player's career statistics. The stats include games (G), field goal percentage (FGP), free throw percentage (FTP), rebounds per game (RPG), assists per game (APG), and points per game (PPG).

Each of the 64 teams receives a one-page season preview. It begins with the basics, including 1990-91 overall record (this record includes NCAA or NIT games). It also lists the team's record in 1991 tournament play ("NCAA 2-1" means the team won two NCAA tournament games and then lost the third). The coach's career Division I record is also listed.

Each season preview begins with an "opening line," which discusses the players it lost and the freshmen that are coming in. The preview then rates the team at each position—guard, forward, and center. "Analysis" evaluates the team's strengths and weaknesses and puts it all into perspective.

Finally, each preview contains the team's 1991-92 roster, which includes the team's top 12 players. The roster includes each player's 1990-91 statistics. The stats include field goal percentage (FGP), free throw percentage (FTP), 3-point field goals/attempts (3-PT), rebounds per game (RPG), assists per game (APG), and points per game (PPG).

CORY ALEXANDER
School: Virginia
Year: Freshman
Position: Guard
Height: 6'1" **Weight:** 175
Birthdate: June 22, 1973
Birthplace: Waynesboro, VA

PLAYER SUMMARY	
Will	start
Can't	post up inside
Expect	immediate impact
Don't Expect	inconsistency

Background: Alexander attended three different high schools in three years. He averaged nearly 16 points and ten assists a game for national powerhouse Oak Hill Academy (Virginia) last winter and accepted invitations to play in the McDonald's All-American Game and the Dapper Dan Roundball Classic.

Strengths: He's an outstanding shooter and penetrator who excels at creating his own shot. Alexander's 3-point range is lethal, as are many of his pinpoint passes and dunks. He displays a lot of poise for a youngster his age.

Weaknesses: Inexperience at this level is Alexander's only major shortcoming. Defending ACC guards isn't like defending a bunch of high school kids. When his shot's not falling, it tends to impact his entire game.

Analysis: John Crotty's graduation creates an immediate opening. Point guard's a very difficult position for a young player to master, but Alexander's a very special player. Expect him to play in the NBA one day.

ERIC ANDERSON
School: Indiana
Year: Senior
Position: Forward/Center
Height: 6'9" **Weight:** 229
Birthdate: May 26, 1970
Birthplace: Chicago, IL

PLAYER SUMMARY	
Will	earn All-America votes
Can't	play above the rim
Expect	strong fundamentals
Don't Expect	foul problems

Background: Anderson was named first-team All-Big Ten by the league's coaches last season. Two years ago, Anderson was a second-team pick, while in 1988-89 he was Big Ten Freshman of the Year. He was Illinois' Mr. Basketball in 1987-88.

Strengths: He's the Hoosiers' only consistent inside threat as he shifts between forward and center. He likes to mix it up inside and relies on superb positioning for many of his rebounds. Anderson's a much better shooter than most guys his size and actually displays impressive range.

Weaknesses: His vertical jump isn't exactly dazzling. At times, Anderson struggles defensively because he's overmatched by taller and stronger low-post players. He can still be a little too passive against weaker opponents.

Analysis: While Hoosier stars Calbert Cheaney and Damon Bailey get most of the headlines, Anderson's inside presence may be even more important. He shows up every day ready to go to work with his lunch pail in hand.

COLLEGE STATISTICS

	G	FGP	FTP	RPG	APG	PPG
IND 88-89	34	.545	.726	6.1	0.3	11.9
IND 89-90	29	.537	.728	7.0	0.8	16.3
IND 90-91	34	.507	.697	7.1	1.1	13.7
Totals	97	.528	.716	6.7	0.7	13.8

DARIN ARCHBOLD

School: Butler
Year: Senior
Position: Guard
Height: 6'4" **Weight:** 190
Birthdate: July 11, 1969
Birthplace: Markle, IN

```
PLAYER SUMMARY
Will ............................pour in points
Can't..........................shoot in traffic
Expect.................great FT shooting
Don't Expect .............great defense
```

Background: A virtual no-name heading into 1990-91, Archbold walked away with Midwestern Collegiate Conference Player of the Year honors. He scored 20 or more points 15 times and 30 or more on six occasions.

Strengths: A self-made shooter, Archbold rarely takes a bad shot. Butler's go-to guy, he can take over a game down the stretch with his perimeter shooting. There's not a better free throw shooter in the land. His .912 mark last year was tops in the nation.

Weaknesses: Suspect lateral speed makes him a defensive liability at times. With the exception of scoring, Archbold's mediocre in all other phases. Primarily a stand-still jump-shooter, he has a hard time getting his shot off in traffic.

Analysis: Archbold has come out of nowhere to become one of the nation's top scoring threats. When you watch him, you don't think he's doing much; but in the end, he has 25 points and seven or eight boards. Though a solid college player, he's not athletic enough to play in the pros.

COLLEGE STATISTICS

	G	FGP	FTP	RPG	APG	PPG
BUTL 88-89	8	—	.875	0.9	—	0.9
BUTL 89-90	28	.513	.850	3.8	1.4	11.9
BUTL 90-91	29	.494	.912	4.4	2.1	21.8
Totals	65	.495	.892	3.7	1.6	15.0

DAMON BAILEY

School: Indiana
Year: Sophomore
Position: Guard
Height: 6'3" **Weight:** 192
Birthdate: October 21, 1971
Birthplace: Heltonville, IN

```
PLAYER SUMMARY
Will ..................continue to improve
Can't ....................................sky high
Expect .......................more minutes
Don't Expect......sophomore slump
```

Background: A storybook high school career in Indiana makes Bailey one of the most recognized players in the state's history. The state of Indiana's all-time leading scorer, he was honored as *USA Today's* Prep Player of the Year in 1989-90. He was named Big Ten Freshman of the Year last winter.

Strengths: Bailey performs as if he's a seasoned veteran. He's an extraordinary shooter and passer who makes his teammates better players. By the end of the season, he was Indiana's best all-around guard.

Weaknesses: It's no secret that Bailey lacks the athletic ability many of the great ones have. Of course, they said the same thing about fellow Indiana native Larry Bird. He could stand to look for his shot more often, but that will come in time.

Analysis: If Bob Knight could build a perfect player from scratch, he would make Bailey. Despite unbelievably high expectations, the "All-American Boy" has been able to keep his cool and play his game.

COLLEGE STATISTICS

		G	FGP	FTP	RPG	APG	PPG
IND	90-91	33	.506	.692	2.9	2.9	11.4
Totals		33	.506	.692	2.9	2.9	11.4

MARK BAKER

School: Ohio St.
Year: Senior
Position: Guard
Height: 6'1" **Weight:** 180
Birthdate: November 11, 1969
Birthplace: Dayton, OH

PLAYER SUMMARY	
Will	earn All-Big Ten votes
Can't	drill the 3
Expect	sticky defense
Don't Expect	an FT title

Background: A two-time all-state high school player, Baker led his Dayton Dunbar team to a state title as a junior. Baker sat out his freshman season at Ohio State due to Prop 48. He started 30 games last season and led the Buckeyes in assists.

Strengths: Equally adept at passing and shooting, Baker's the Big Ten's best all-around point guard. He's very difficult to defend one-on-one and he's a superb decision-maker on the break. A great leaper, he loves challenging bigger defenders.

Weaknesses: He doesn't possess great shooting range. As a result, defenders often lay off him a step or two and dare him to shoot from outside. His 71-percent marksmanship from the line needs improvement.

Analysis: He'd be an NBA prospect if he improved his perimeter shooting. Baker's at his best driving the lane, forcing contact, and dishing to the open man. Ohio State's Big Ten title chances will depend largely on his all-around play.

COLLEGE STATISTICS

	G	FGP	FTP	RPG	APG	PPG
OSU	89-90	30	.530	.614	2.4	3.6	9.1
OSU	90-91	30	.518	.711	2.4	5.0	10.9
Totals		60	.524	.665	2.4	4.3	10.0

VAL BARNES

School: Iowa
Year: Junior
Position: Guard
Height: 6'2" **Weight:** 195
Birthdate: February 14, 1971
Birthplace: Wichita, KS

PLAYER SUMMARY	
Will	improve FG pct.
Can't	become pure playmaker
Expect	nearly 20 PPG
Don't Expect	many rebounds

Background: Kansas' 1989 high school player of the year, Barnes spent one year at Butler County (Kansas) Junior College. He received juco All-America honors from *Basketball Weekly*. Iowa coach Tom Davis employed a three-guard offense last season in order to get Barnes in the starting lineup.

Strengths: Barnes brings a lot of speed and athleticism to a team that's most effective in the open court. A pure shooter, he can play either backcourt position. He digs in defensively with more intensity than any of his teammates.

Weaknesses: Does he think shot then pass, or vice versa? Barnes never seems too sure. Such suspect decision-making is a sin for a point guard. A lack of confidence late last year contributed to a woeful .396 field goal mark.

Analysis: Sure to regain his confidence offensively, Barnes should emerge as one of the bright new stars of the Big Ten. He's a big-time scorer who's darn near unstoppable when he finds his rhythm.

COLLEGE STATISTICS

		G	FGP	FTP	RPG	APG	PPG
IOWA	90-91	32	.396	.736	2.5	1.8	11.5
Totals		32	.396	.736	2.5	1.8	11.5

JON BARRY

School: Georgia Tech
Year: Senior
Position: Guard
Height: 6'5" **Weight:** 189
Birthdate: July 25, 1969
Birthplace: Oakland, CA

PLAYER SUMMARY	
Will	shoot the lights out
Can't	pass up open shots
Expect	comparisons to Dad
Don't Expect	less than 20 PPG

Background: Former NBA star Rick Barry's son, Jon spent one year at Pacific and a year at Paris (Texas) Junior College before arriving at Georgia Tech. He was a huge surprise last season. Expected to fill a reserve role, he started every game and was named *Basketball Weekly's* Juco Transfer of the Year.

Strengths: Like his dad, he's at his best with the ball in his hands. He has tremendous shooting range. Contrary to some public perception, he also displays decent passing skills and good anticipation, plus solid defense.

Weaknesses: At times, he's a little more interested in his own numbers than the team's—another trait passed along by Papa Rick. His shot selection is suspect on occasion and he commits too many needless fouls on the perimeter.

Analysis: Regardless of how many shots he has to take, Barry will get his points. He'll be a big-time scorer unless Dad's constant meddling damages his confidence.

COLLEGE STATISTICS

	G	FGP	FTP	RPG	APG	PPG
GT	90-91	30	.444	.732	3.7	3.7	15.9
Totals		30	.444	.732	3.7	3.7	15.9

ELMER BENNETT

School: Notre Dame
Year: Senior
Position: Guard
Height: 6'1" **Weight:** 165
Birthdate: February 13, 1970
Birthplace: Evanston, IL

PLAYER SUMMARY	
Will	lead Irish to NCAAs
Can't	muscle inside
Expect	more assists
Don't Expect	as many turnovers

Background: Named Mr. Basketball in Texas as a high school senior, Bennett averaged 35.8 PPG. He topped the Irish last season in steals, 3-point shooting, and minutes played. He moved into the starting lineup for good halfway through his sophomore season.

Strengths: Bennett's a solid mid-range jump-shooter who can be an effective scorer when the Irish run—something new coach John MacLeod plans to do a lot this season. He's at his best when the game's on the line.

Weaknesses: He plays out of control a little too often. Bennett's come a long way defensively, but he still has some improving to do. He could stand to add some weight and strength.

Analysis: Lightning fast, Bennett should prove to be a vital cog in MacLeod's new offense. More Irish points should mean more Bennett assists. When his shot's not falling, he can't let it affect the rest of his game.

COLLEGE STATISTICS

	G	FGP	FTP	RPG	APG	PPG
ND	88-89	30	.459	.641	1.2	2.0	5.5
ND	89-90	29	.481	.737	1.6	3.7	10.9
ND	90-91	32	.414	.736	3.0	4.6	14.4
Totals		91	.443	.724	1.9	3.4	10.4

TONY BENNETT

School: Wisconsin-Green Bay
Year: Senior
Position: Guard
Height: 6'0" **Weight:** 175
Birthdate: June 1, 1969
Birthplace: Clintonville, WI

PLAYER SUMMARY	
Will	approach 25 PPG
Can't	avoid injuries
Expect	a John Stockton type
Don't Expect	lazy play

Background: The driving force in the Fighting Phoenix's journey to the NCAA tournament, Bennett was the Mid-Continent Player of the Year last winter. He was also an honorable-mention All-American and an Academic All-American. His dad, Dick, is his coach.

Strengths: Bennett is deceivingly quick and, like most coaches' sons, possesses great court awareness. He makes very few mistakes and shoots as well from 3-point range (53 percent) as any player in the country. Few players are their team's primary scorer and playmaker. Bennett's one of the few.

Weaknesses: He does lack stamina at times. More physical guards prevent him from taking his usual shots. Bennett can't shoot as well off the drive as when he squares up from the perimeter.

Analysis: Remember the name. You'll be hearing about Tony Bennett (no, he doesn't sing) in the future. NBA star Terry Porter, a close family friend, swears he'll play in the NBA.

COLLEGE STATISTICS

	G	FGP	FTP	RPG	APG	PPG
WGB	88-89	27	.522	.847	2.0	5.1	19.1
WGB	89-90	30	.504	.859	2.2	5.2	16.6
WGB	90-91	31	.547	.836	2.4	5.0	21.5
Totals		88	.525	.845	2.2	5.1	19.1

TRAVIS BEST

School: Georgia Tech
Year: Freshman
Position: Guard
Height: 5'11" **Weight:** 175
Birthdate: July 12, 1972
Birthplace: Springfield, MA

PLAYER SUMMARY	
Will	make all-frosh teams
Can't	defend taller guards
Expect	outstanding debut
Don't Expect	Kenny Anderson

Background: Best capped a brilliant prep career by being named to *Basketball Weekly's* 1990-91 high school All-America first team. He played very well in last spring's McDonald's All-Star Game, which was held in his hometown. He exploded for 81 points in a game last February.

Strengths: Although his high school statistics were out of this world, Best's high school coach believes his leadership ability is his single greatest asset. He's a scoring whiz who also does a superb job of directing traffic and pushing the ball up the floor.

Weaknesses: Like any college freshman, inexperience can prove to be a major stumbling block. At this point in his career, help defense and shot selection are the two areas that need the most work.

Analysis: He's no Kenny Anderson, but he's darn close. Best is being billed as the finest freshman point guard in the country. He appears mature enough to take such lofty praise in stride.

BERNARD BLUNT
School: St. Joseph's (PA)
Year: Sophomore
Position: Guard
Height: 6'3" **Weight:** 200
Birthdate: November 21, 1971
Birthplace: Syracuse, NY

PLAYER SUMMARY	
Will	singe the nets
Can't	feed open teammates
Expect	another Microwave
Don't Expect	drop-off in points

Background: Blunt concluded his high school career as the third-leading scorer in New York state history. His decision to attend St. Joseph's rather than hometown Syracuse was a huge surprise. He garnered first-team frosh All-America accolades from *Basketball Times*.

Strengths: A deadly streak shooter, Blunt plays with a lot of poise, power, and strength. He's the college equivalent of Vinnie Johnson. NBA people rave about his scoring ability in the prestigious Sonny Hill summer leagues in Philadelphia. Quick feet contribute largely to his aggressive defense.

Weaknesses: When his shooting touch is off, the rest of his game suffers. He'll never be the team leader coach John Griffin expects unless he stops his occasional pouting about not getting enough shots.

Analysis: To be Blunt, he's a big-time talent. Griffin's first recruit at St Joe's, he's well on his way to becoming the best guard this program has produced since Matt Guokas in the mid-1960s.

COLLEGE STATISTICS

		G	FGP	FTP	RPG	APG	PPG
STJ	90-91	30	.418	.708	6.5	2.6	18.8
Totals		30	.418	.708	6.5	2.6	18.8

DAVID BOOTH
School: DePaul
Year: Senior
Position: Forward
Height: 6'7" **Weight:** 190
Birthdate: May 28, 1970
Birthplace: Peoria, IL

PLAYER SUMMARY	
Will	add more weight
Can't	make 3's consistently
Expect	2,000 career points
Don't Expect	shooting slumps

Background: Booth finished his prep career as one of the top 60 players in the country. An honorable-mention frosh All-American and an All-Independent selection as a sophomore, he received All-America consideration this past year. Booth's on pace to join Mark Aguirre as the only Blue Demons with more than 2,000 career points.

Strengths: An excellent shooter with good range, Booth can be counted on for 20 or more points nearly every time out. He's a slasher who's just as likely to take the ball to the hole as he is to fire from outside. Despite his slender build, he can rebound.

Weaknesses: He can come up flat in big games, as his five-point effort vs. Georgia Tech in last year's NCAA tournament would attest. Booth doesn't dribble real well with his left hand and he has trouble spotting up in traffic.

Analysis: DePaul's top gun, he's one of the most talented small forwards in the country today. Don't let his seemingly effortless style of play fool you. He's a hard worker.

COLLEGE STATISTICS

		G	FGP	FTP	RPG	APG	PPG
DeP	88-89	33	.471	.733	4.4	1.5	9.9
DeP	89-90	35	.441	.767	6.1	1.9	16.9
DeP	90-91	29	.509	.757	6.8	1.7	18.7
Totals		97	.471	.756	5.7	1.7	15.1

DEVIN BOYD

School: Towson St.
Year: Senior
Position: Guard
Height: 6'2" **Weight:** 180
Birthdate: September 13, 1970
Birthplace: Baltimore, MD

```
PLAYER SUMMARY
Will.....................thrive as a senior
Can't...............get his shot blocked
Expect....................fewer turnovers
Don't Expect.......defensive awards
```

Background: The East Coast Conference Player of the Year this past season, Boyd's been a starter since the first game of his freshman year. He paced the ECC in scoring and steals in 1990-91. He's helped lead the Tigers to two straight NCAA tourney appearances.

Strengths: A gifted scorer, he displays an effective outside-inside game. Boyd rarely turns the ball over and ranks as one of the premier passers off the dribble in the East. He makes a lot of big plays that win ballgames.

Weaknesses: He doesn't finish plays as well as he should, sometimes making an extra pass when he doesn't have to. He commits too many senseless fouls and is often caught out of position on defense.

Analysis: If there was ever an underrated player at the Division I level, Boyd's the guy. Towson State's best-ever player, he has all the tools to become the Tigers' second NBA product in the past three years (Kurk Lee was the other). He needs to improve his defense.

COLLEGE STATISTICS

		G	FGP	FTP	RPG	APG	PPG
TSU	88-89	29	.443	.789	2.0	4.8	13.7
TSU	89-90	30	.415	.814	2.8	3.9	11.7
TSU	90-91	29	.445	.804	3.1	3.4	20.7
Totals		88	.436	.802	2.6	4.1	15.3

JASON BUCHANAN

School: St. John's
Year: Senior
Position: Guard
Height: 6'0" **Weight:** 155
Birthdate: April 25, 1971
Birthplace: Syracuse, NY

```
PLAYER SUMMARY
Will.....................get tons of assists
Can't...........................score 20 PPG
Expect........................best year yet
Don't Expect.........poor confidence
```

Background: As a freshman, Buchanan was the point guard on the Redmen's 1989 NIT championship team. He was moved to off guard the following year to make room for Boo Harvey. Back at the point last winter, he became one of the East's premier playmakers.

Strengths: An adept penetrator, Buchanan does an outstanding job of taking it himself or dishing off to an open teammate in scoring position. His assist-to-turnover ratio sparkles. Though not a pure shooter, he can be a creative scorer.

Weaknesses: Although he possesses good foot speed and quickness, defense isn't one of his strong suits. It's his effort that's sometimes lacking. At times, he takes too many chances offensively.

Analysis: If Buchanan continues to make the kind of improvement he's shown the past two seasons, and gets a little help from his friends, the Redmen could be Final Four bound. He emerged as a much more confident player late last year.

COLLEGE STATISTICS

		G	FGP	FTP	RPG	APG	PPG
STJ	88-89	33	.507	.778	2.0	4.8	9.2
STJ	89-90	34	.349	.753	2.1	3.7	6.5
STJ	90-91	32	.412	.788	2.7	5.9	12.0
Totals		99	.424	.776	2.5	4.8	9.2

SCOTT BURRELL

School: Connecticut
Year: Junior
Position: Forward
Height: 6'7" **Weight:** 209
Birthdate: January 12, 1971
Birthplace: Hamden, CT

PLAYER SUMMARY	
Will	lead nation in steals
Can't	sit still
Expect	pro baseball career
Don't Expect	defensive lapses

Background: Burrell garnered third-team All-Big East honors this past season. He rifled the full-court inbound pass to Tate George which resulted in "The Shot" to beat Clemson in the 1990 NCAA tournament. He pitches in the Toronto Blue Jays' organization. Burrell was Connecticut's high school basketball and baseball player of the year during his senior season.

Strengths: His long arms and incredible quickness are responsible for nearly four steals a game, tops in the country. Burrell's a pure shooter who possesses good range. He's the best defensive small forward in the Big East.

Weaknesses: Due to his baseball career, he doesn't pick up a basketball from April until October. Burrell's ball-handling is a bit suspect. He committed more fouls than any other Husky last winter.

Analysis: Burrell's a very good player who'd be one of the game's greats if he worked at it year-round. His versatility is what sets him apart from most players.

COLLEGE STATISTICS

	G	FGP	FTP	RPG	APG	PPG
CONN 89-90	32	.386	.623	5.5	4.9	8.2
CONN 90-91	31	.440	.592	7.5	3.1	12.7
Totals	63	.417	.605	6.5	4.0	10.4

CALBERT CHEANEY

School: Indiana
Year: Junior
Position: Forward
Height: 6'6" **Weight:** 204
Birthdate: July 17, 1971
Birthplace: Evansville, IN

PLAYER SUMMARY	
Will	sink his shots
Can't	outmuscle opponents
Expect	All-America honors
Don't Expect	many assists

Background: Cheaney emerged as one of nation's premier players last season. He was All-Big Ten and a third-team All-American (AP and UPI). He was a frosh All-American in 1989-90. He's the first left-handed shooter to play for Bob Knight at Indiana. A broken foot ended Cheaney's final high school season prematurely.

Strengths: You won't find a more accurate shooter at any position. He shot 60 percent from the field last year, with many of his attempts from the 15- to 20-foot range (47 percent from 3). He works for the open shot and creates his own offense as well as anyone in the country.

Weaknesses: This is a very difficult question. Cheaney doesn't pass the ball often enough (1.4 APG) and he could do a better job of drawing fouls.

Analysis: He'll challenge Ohio State's Jim Jackson for Big Ten Player of the Year honors. Although he's adamant about staying at Indiana for four years, Cheaney has the skills and the maturity to play in the NBA today.

COLLEGE STATISTICS

	G	FGP	FTP	RPG	APG	PPG
IND 89-90	29	.572	.750	4.6	1.7	17.1
IND 90-91	34	.596	.801	5.5	1.4	21.6
Totals	63	.586	.781	5.1	1.5	19.5

DOUG CHRISTIE

School: Pepperdine
Year: Senior
Position: Guard
Height: 6'6" **Weight:** 200
Birthdate: May 9, 1970
Birthplace: Seattle, WA

PLAYER SUMMARY	
Will	ride Waves to NCAAs
Can't	excel on defense
Expect	more of the same
Don't Expect	fewer dunks

Background: Named West Coast Conference Player of the Year last season, Christie topped the Waves in scoring, assists, and steals. He missed the Waves' NCAA tourney game with Seton Hall after tearing cartilage in his right knee. He sat out his first year as a Prop 48.

Strengths: A scoring threat from anywhere inside the gym, Christie's at his best driving toward the basket. He has tremendous body control in traffic. His assortment of slam dunks rivals Mr. Jordan's. Defensively, he bothers shooters with his long arms and quickness.

Weaknesses: He has occasional trouble with opponents taking him off the dribble. He still gets by on defense with great athletic ability. It's about time he learns some technique.

Analysis: If you haven't had the chance to see him play, you're missing a great one. Calling him underrated is a colossal understatement. He has an NBA body and plenty of NBA moves. Christie is Pepperdine's best player since Dennis Johnson.

COLLEGE STATISTICS

	G	FGP	FTP	RPG	APG	PPG
PEP	89-90	28	.503	.714	4.1	4.0	8.9
PEP	90-91	28	.469	.765	5.2	4.8	19.1
Totals		56	.479	.747	4.6	4.4	14.0

JAMAL COLEMAN

School: Missouri
Year: Senior
Position: Forward
Height: 6'5" **Weight:** 199
Birthdate: December 3, 1969
Birthplace: San Antonio, TX

PLAYER SUMMARY	
Will	score more points
Can't	play a better defense
Expect	a much larger role
Don't Expect	many 3-pointers

Background: Coleman was an All-Big Eight honorable-mention selection last season while playing second fiddle to All-American Doug Smith. He started only three games in his first two years. NFL star Ronnie Lott is Coleman's cousin.

Strengths: A defensive stalwart, Coleman will rank among the league leaders in rebounds and steals. He's a pure athlete who can crash the boards like a center and run the floor like a point guard. A quick first step is the key to his rebounding prowess.

Weaknesses: Although he possesses solid shooting range, Coleman has always been hesitant to shoot from long distance. He needs to develop a 12- to 15-foot baseline jumper and more confidence in his offensive game.

Analysis: With Smith now in the NBA, Coleman must step his game up to the next level. He'll get as many minutes and as many shots as he wants. He must become more assertive with the ball in his hands.

COLLEGE STATISTICS

		G	FGP	FTP	RPG	APG	PPG
MO	88-89	16	.643	.563	0.8	0.3	1.7
MO	89-90	29	.500	.783	3.1	0.7	3.8
MO	90-91	30	.492	.714	6.5	2.0	10.8
Totals		75	.500	.708	4.0	1.1	6.2

ANTHONY DADE

School: Louisiana Tech
Year: Senior
Position: Forward
Height: 6'6" **Weight:** 240
Birthdate: August 7, 1970
Birthplace: Ruston, LA

PLAYER SUMMARY	
Will	lead by example
Can't	shoot FTs
Expect	league MVP honors
Don't Expect	any 3-pointers

Background: A second-team All-American South pick, Dade took center stage late in the 1990-91 season. His play fueled the Bulldogs' impressive post-season run. He led Tech in scoring in 1989-90 and ranked second as a freshman.

Strengths: Dade's combination of strength and quickness makes him a special player. He has a natural feel for the game that can't be coached. A deceiving leaper, he plays much taller than 6'6". He uses his wide frame to his advantage inside, a la Charles Barkley.

Weaknesses: Dade shoots better from the field than the free throw line (54 percent). Most of his shots are from ten feet and in. Dribbling seems to be a chore, as does defending more athletic opponents.

Analysis: Dade compensates for his shortcomings with a winner's mentality. Following in the footsteps of Karl Malone and Randy White, he could be the next Bulldog forward to play in the NBA. He wants to become a coach someday.

COLLEGE STATISTICS

		G	FGP	FTP	RPG	APG	PPG
LAT	88-89	32	.549	.573	7.3	1.7	14.0
LAT	89-90	27	.564	.615	7.4	1.4	18.1
LAT	90-91	31	.584	.535	5.9	1.3	14.4
Totals		90	.565	.576	6.8	1.5	15.4

HUBERT DAVIS

School: North Carolina
Year: Senior
Position: Guard
Height: 6'4" **Weight:** 177
Birthdate: May 17, 1970
Birthplace: Winston-Salem, NC

PLAYER SUMMARY	
Will	lead Heels in scoring
Can't	do damage inside
Expect	All-ACC mention
Don't Expect	many turnovers

Background: Only Rick Fox (graduated) scored more Carolina points than Davis last season. Formerly a reserve, he blossomed into a key starter at off guard. He's the nephew of former Tar Heel great Walter Davis. An average high school player, he was recruited as a favor to Walter.

Strengths: Davis has a scorer's mentality. He's a streak shooter who becomes more accurate the further away from the basket he gets. He shoots a blistering 84 percent from the line. His long arms and quick feet make him a solid defender.

Weaknesses: Overall consistency is Davis's chief drawback. Some added muscle would make him a much better rebounder. He needs to improve his offensive moves off the dribble.

Analysis: Davis is anxious to assume the role as UNC's primary go-to guy this season. If he can continue to nail treys like he did last year (49 percent), it'll really open things up for the big people inside. Coach Dean Smith's expectations are understandably high.

COLLEGE STATISTICS

		G	FGP	FTP	RPG	APG	PPG
NC	88-89	35	.512	.774	0.8	0.3	3.3
NC	89-90	34	.446	.797	1.8	1.5	9.6
NC	90-91	35	.521	.835	2.4	1.9	13.3
Totals		104	.491	.812	1.7	1.2	8.7

TODD DAY

School: Arkansas
Year: Senior
Position: Guard/Forward
Height: 6'8" **Weight:** 200
Birthdate: January 7, 1970
Birthplace: Memphis, TN

PLAYER SUMMARY	
Will	be NBA lottery pick
Can't	keep his mouth shut
Expect	first-team All-American
Don't Expect	off-court problems

Background: Day received All-America consideration in 1990-91 and also received SEC Player of the Year honors. He was suspended by the university for his involvement in an alleged sex violation but was later reinstated. As a sophomore, he led the Razorbacks in ten statistical categories.

Strengths: Day's a silky-smooth shooter who possesses unlimited range. He's an outstanding ball-handler who can run the floor, pass, score, and either rebound inside or bomb away from the perimeter. Day can play as many as four positions. He's come a long way defensively.

Weaknesses: He doesn't appear to have the stamina to sustain his shooting touch over the course of an entire season. A very emotional young man, Day runs his mouth and hot-dogs on the court a little too often.

Analysis: After giving serious consideration to the NBA last spring, Day will contend for first-team All-America honors at off guard. To reach his full potential, he must put his off-court problems behind him.

COLLEGE STATISTICS

	G	FGP	FTP	RPG	APG	PPG
ARK	88-89	32	.451	.715	4.0	1.5	13.3
ARK	89-90	35	.491	.760	5.4	2.5	19.5
ARK	90-91	38	.473	.747	5.3	2.9	20.7
Totals		105	.474	.743	4.9	2.4	18.1

TERRY DEHERE

School: Seton Hall
Year: Junior
Position: Guard
Height: 6'4" **Weight:** 175
Birthdate: September 12, 1971
Birthplace: Jersey City, NJ

PLAYER SUMMARY	
Will	launch from downtown
Can't	bench press 200 pounds
Expect	pretty 3-pointers
Don't Expect	fewer minutes

Background: Dehere was named to the All-Big East first team last winter—the only sophomore on the squad. In 1989-90, he became only the fifth frosh in Big East history to lead his team in scoring (16.1). Dehere was a high school teammate of Bobby Hurley's at famed St. Anthony's in Jersey City.

Strengths: The sharp-shooting Dehere is deadly from long range. More than half of his field goal attempts are from behind the 3-point arc. He's one of the prettiest pure shooters to watch in the country. At times, Dehere's the best defender on the floor.

Weaknesses: Shot selection and consistent defense are the only areas of Dehere's game that still need work. He could stand to spend a little more time in the weight room.

Analysis: The Pirates' Big East title hopes will fall largely on Dehere's slender shoulders. A can't-miss pro, he'll conclude his collegiate career as one of the greatest players in Seton Hall history.

COLLEGE STATISTICS

		G	FGP	FTP	RPG	APG	PPG
SH	89-90	28	.402	.747	3.4	2.1	16.1
SH	90-91	34	.460	.839	3.0	2.2	19.8
Totals		62	.438	.820	3.1	2.2	18.1

DELL DEMPS

School: Pacific
Year: Senior
Position: Guard
Height: 6'4" **Weight:** 205
Birthdate: February 12, 1970
Birthplace: Long Beach, CA

PLAYER SUMMARY	
Will	be All-Big West
Can't	shoot FTs
Expect	more alert play
Don't Expect	inside scoring

Background: A second-team All-Big West pick, Demps has led the Tigers in scoring the past two seasons. He topped Pacific in six offensive categories in 1990-91. Demps led his high school team to a three-year record of 91-11. He's a scholar athlete.

Strengths: Noted primarily as an offensive machine, Demps actually does a little bit of everything. He ranked second on last year's team in assists, steals, and offensive rebounds. When the game's on the line, Demps is at his best.

Weaknesses: An unusually short attention span hurts his defense, as does his lack of lateral speed. Demps shoots only 67 percent from the line. Coach Bob Thomason is convinced that he'd score another six points a game if he'd go inside.

Analysis: Demps is the best player you've never heard of. Along with everyone else in the Big West, he's played in UNLV's long shadow for the past two seasons. When the subject turns to the game's premier off guards, don't forget Demps's name.

COLLEGE STATISTICS

	G	FGP	FTP	RPG	APG	PPG
PAC	88-89	28	.374	.743	3.7	2.5	6.6
PAC	89-90	29	.488	.707	4.7	3.3	15.9
PAC	90-91	28	.455	.669	5.5	3.3	18.8
Totals		85	.451	.695	4.7	3.0	13.8

GREG DENNIS

School: East Tennessee St.
Year: Senior
Position: Center
Height: 6'11" **Weight:** 208
Birthdate: March 28, 1969
Birthplace: Charleston, WV

PLAYER SUMMARY	
Will	come back strong
Can't	rule the lane
Expect	a John Salley type
Don't Expect	a heavy eater

Background: Dennis broke his foot two games into the 1990-91 season and never returned. He was the Southern Conference's Freshman of the Year in 1987-88 and an all-league pick as a sophomore and junior.

Strengths: Unusually agile for a big man, Dennis gets up and down the court real well. His soft shooting touch enables him to move outside for plenty of treys. He blocks a lot of shots, passes well, and has good hands.

Weaknesses: From head to toe, he's too darn skinny. Opposing centers beat him up inside. Mostly a finesse player, he rarely takes the ball hard to the basket. He's not known for his man-to-man defense.

Analysis: If Dennis can regain his 1989-90 form, an average ETSU team becomes very good. His inside presence will help immensely. He'll get a shot in the NBA, although he won't last long unless they put him on a cheeseburgers-and-milk shakes diet.

COLLEGE STATISTICS

		G	FGP	FTP	RPG	APG	PPG
ETS	87-88	29	.543	.729	7.6	1.5	16.4
ETS	88-89	31	.513	.781	7.8	1.4	17.3
ETS	89-90	34	.494	.812	6.5	1.5	19.7
ETS	90-91	2	.303	.400	6.0	2.0	11.5
Totals		96	.508	.778	7.2	1.5	17.7

RADENKO DOBRAS

School: South Florida
Year: Senior
Position: Guard
Height: 6'7" **Weight:** 185
Birthdate: January 31, 1968
Birthplace: Banja Luka, Yugoslavia

PLAYER SUMMARY	
Will	be drafted
Can't	play man-to-man
Expect	higher-pct. shots
Don't Expect	many rebounds

Background: An All-Sun Belt performer last season, Dobras has led the Bulls in scoring all three years. Dobras originally planned to attend Kansas before Larry Brown bolted for the NBA. He's a close friend of fellow Yugoslav Vlade Divac. He first attracted interest from U.S. coaches while playing for the Yugoslavian Junior National Team.

Strengths: Putting the ball in the basket from anywhere on the court is Dobras's strong suit. He possesses an incredibly quick release. Due to his ball-handling and creative passing, he sees a lot of minutes at both backcourt positions.

Weaknesses: He played very little man-to-man defense in Yugoslavia and it shows. His 3-point production has decreased since his freshman season, while his turnovers have increased. He forgets to box out.

Analysis: His game draws comparisons to Drazen Petrovic of the New Jersey Nets. Some scouts think he's even better. A very heady and mature player, Dobras turns 24 in January.

COLLEGE STATISTICS

	G	FGP	FTP	RPG	APG	PPG
SFL	88-89	28	.435	.836	3.8	4.5	16.2
SFL	89-90	31	.458	.680	3.1	3.9	16.7
SFL	90-91	30	.418	.785	3.1	4.6	16.7
Totals		89	.437	.759	3.3	4.3	16.5

TONY DUNKIN

School: Coastal Carolina
Year: Junior
Position: Forward
Height: 6'7" **Weight:** 205
Birthdate: February 16, 1970
Birthplace: Rains, SC

PLAYER SUMMARY	
Will	dominate league
Can't	bury clutch FTs
Expect	lots of dunkin'
Don't Expect	3-point range

Background: Dunkin has been selected Big South Player of the Year in each of his two seasons at Coastal Carolina. He carried the Chanticleers to last year's NCAA tournament. He sat out the 1988-89 season after transferring from Jacksonville.

Strengths: Dunkin is a superb athlete who gets up and down the floor like a greyhound. He finishes plays as well as any small forward in the country. Nicknamed "Slam" Dunkin, he's a Dominique Wilkins-like leaper who loves to dunk. He has 61 career jams.

Weaknesses: He doesn't always work as hard as he should when matched against inferior opponents. Dunkin needs to extend his scoring range and improve his free throw percentage (.686). Defensively, he takes too many chances.

Analysis: Dunkin's immense talents coupled with his flamboyant style have begun to turn a lot of heads in the South. Due to mediocre conference competition, it's tough to really gauge how good he is.

COLLEGE STATISTICS

		G	FGP	FTP	RPG	APG	PPG
CC	89-90	23	.525	.754	6.6	0.7	18.1
CC	90-91	28	.523	.686	7.1	0.8	18.0
Totals		51	.524	.718	6.9	0.7	18.1

ACIE EARL

School: Iowa
Year: Junior
Position: Center
Height: 6'10" **Weight:** 225
Birthdate: June 23, 1970
Birthplace: Moline, IL

PLAYER SUMMARY	
Will	be All-Big Ten
Can't	handle the ball
Expect	boatload of blocks
Don't Expect	foul trouble

Background: Earl was redshirted in 1988-89. Although he averaged only 16 minutes per game as a freshman, he led the Big Ten in blocked shots. He swatted away eight Northern Iowa shots in a game last December and went on to lead the Hawkeyes in such categories as points, rebounds, and minutes played.

Strengths: He possesses quickness, coordination, and defensive instincts. Earl's 3.3 blocks per game ranked him among the national leaders. He's a decent shooter. He didn't foul out once last season.

Weaknesses: Outside of the lane, his offense is nonexistent. Earl will play outstanding defense for five or six minutes, then go into hiding the next few times down the floor. Many of his blocks go out of bounds.

Analysis: Earl was the most improved player in the Big Ten last season. His defensive presence is irreplaceable. Still raw offensively, he'll get better in time. Added maturity will help.

COLLEGE STATISTICS

	G	FGP	FTP	RPG	APG	PPG
IOWA 89-90	22	.440	.739	3.6	1.0	6.0
IOWA 90-91	32	.503	.665	6.7	1.5	16.3
Totals	54	.488	.677	5.4	1.3	12.1

DOUG EDWARDS

School: Florida St.
Year: Junior
Position: Forward
Height: 6'9" **Weight:** 220
Birthdate: January 21, 1971
Birthplace: Miami, FL

PLAYER SUMMARY	
Will	drive the ACC crazy
Can't	be called a ball hog
Expect	All-America mention
Don't Expect	any let-up

Background: Arguably the best recruit in school history, Edwards sat out his freshman year after failing to qualify academically. He was a consensus first-team prep All-American in 1988-89. Last season, he paced the Seminoles in points and minutes played. He sparkled in the NCAA tournament with a two-game effort of 42 points and 23 rebounds.

Strengths: An awesome combination of skill, power, and savvy, Edwards can score from anywhere on the floor. He's versatile enough to play all five positions. His aggressive style makes him a factor on the boards.

Weaknesses: A real likeable youngster, he needs to develop more of a mean streak on the court. Edwards is almost too selfless at times, trying too hard to get his teammates involved.

Analysis: Sitting out a year certainly hasn't harmed Edwards's game. Although the competition's much tougher in the ACC than in the Metro, this future pro will be hard to leave off the all-league first team.

COLLEGE STATISTICS

	G	FGP	FTP	RPG	APG	PPG
FSU 90-91	32	.519	.709	7.1	1.9	16.4
Totals	32	.519	.709	7.1	1.9	16.4

LaPHONSO ELLIS

School: Notre Dame
Year: Senior
Position: Forward
Height: 6'9" **Weight:** 245
Birthdate: May 5, 1970
Birthplace: East St. Louis, IL

PLAYER SUMMARY	
Will ....impress new coach	
Can't ....be sure about grades	
Expect.............best all-around year	
Don't Expect........less than 20 PPG	

Background: Ellis arrived as one of the nation's top half-dozen recruits in the star-studded Class of '88. Poor grades limited him to 15 games last winter. He missed seven for the same reason in 1989-90. He ranked third nationally in rebounding two years ago (12.6).

Strengths: He can dominate when he feels like it. Very quick and agile for someone his size, Ellis is an outstanding rebounder who also does an above-average job of shooting, passing, blocking shots, and running the floor.

Weaknesses: Academic woes, foul trouble, and inconsistency have transformed this potential superstar into far less. Never one to take the ball strong to the basket, he appears to be a finesse player in a big man's body.

Analysis: Ellis has the potential to make a major impact under John MacLeod if he can remain eligible. He could be an NBA draft lottery pick next spring if he's willing to work harder than he ever has before. It's put-up or shut-up time for the big fella.

COLLEGE STATISTICS

	G	FGP	FTP	RPG	APG	PPG
ND	88-89 27	.563	.684	9.4	1.1	15.4
ND	89-90 22	.511	.675	12.6	1.1	15.4
ND	90-91 15	.573	.716	10.5	1.2	18.9
Totals	64	.548	.690	10.8	1.4	14.4

JAMAL FAULKNER

School: Arizona St.
Year: Sophomore
Position: Forward
Height: 6'7" **Weight:** 200
Birthdate: July 3, 1971
Birthplace: Middle Village, NY

PLAYER SUMMARY	
Will ....give opponents fits	
Can't ....throw a bounce pass	
Expect.................points, rebounds	
Don't Expect ....sophomore jinx	

Background: One of the top 20 players in the nation as a high school senior, Faulkner spent the next year at Cheshire Academy in Connecticut after backing out of a commitment to Pitt. He was named last season's Pac-10 Freshman of the Year—the Sun Devils' first such honoree since Byron Scott (1979-80).

Strengths: His ability to play inside or out makes him double trouble. Faulkner possesses the strength to score and rebound in the paint and the shooting range and ball-handling skills to be just as effective from the perimeter. Defensively, he's better than most sophomores.

Weaknesses: Greater concentration and an improved work ethic would do wonders. Like most young players, Faulkner has trouble getting up for every game. A below-average passer, he turns the ball over too often.

Analysis: Before his ASU career is over, he'll rank among the school's all-time greats. Although he'll admit he still needsplenty of polish, Faulkner's clearly the much-improved Sun Devils' best player.

COLLEGE STATISTICS

	G	FGP	FTP	RPG	APG	PPG
ASU	90-91 30	.492	.699	6.2	1.2	15.4
Totals	30	.492	.699	6.2	1.2	15.4

ALPHONSO FORD

School: Mississippi Valley St.
Year: Junior
Position: Guard
Height: 6'4" **Weight:** 190
Birthdate: October 31, 1971
Birthplace: Greenwood, MS

PLAYER SUMMARY	
Will	lead nation in PPG
Can't	pass up open jumpers
Expect	ton of triple tries
Don't Expect	low FG pct.

Background: A two-time all-league performer in the Southwestern Athletic Conference, Ford ranked second nationally in scoring last season with 32.7 PPG. A Black College All-American, he averaged an amazing 24 shots per game. In 1989-90, Ford was named SWAC Freshman of the Year (29.9 PPG).

Strengths: Ford's incredibly quick first step and picturesque jumper make him a bona fide scoring machine. Incredibly, many of his points come with two or three defenders draped all over him. An underrated defender himself, he averaged 2.2 steals a game last winter.

Weaknesses: Because his team is so lousy (9-19), Ford is accustomed to trying to do too much. He sometimes lets the pressure get to him. Mediocre competition prevents his game from improving.

Analysis: Ford truly is the Cadillac of the SWAC. Called "Mr. Do It All" by Devils coach Lafayette Stribling, he's the most dominant scorer in the country. Adored by NBA scouts, he could leave school early.

COLLEGE STATISTICS

	G	FGP	FTP	RPG	APG	PPG
MVS 89-90	27	.441	.737	4.9	3.3	29.9
MVS 90-91	28	.487	.765	6.0	1.4	32.7
Totals	55	.464	.753	5.5	2.3	31.3

JOSH GRANT

School: Utah
Year: Senior
Position: Forward
Height: 6'10" **Weight:** 216
Birthdate: August 7, 1967
Birthplace: Salt Lake City, UT

PLAYER SUMMARY	
Will	dominate WAC
Can't	play above rim
Expect	great versatility
Don't Expect	lazy play

Background: Named Western Athletic Conference Player of the Year last season, Grant topped the 30-4 Utes in scoring, rebounding, blocks, steals, and minutes played. He was second-team All-WAC as a sophomore. Grant went on a church mission before signing at Utah. His dad also played for the Utes, while two older brothers played at Utah State.

Strengths: He's as versatile as a 6'10" player gets. One time down the floor, he's posting up inside. The next, he's swishing 3-pointers. Perhaps only UCLA's Don MacLean is a superior shooting big man. Quite mature, Grant turned 24 last summer.

Weaknesses: Not terribly athletic, Grant's not going to finish first in too many 100-yard dashes. He's not exactly a skywalker either. Coach Rick Majerus would like to see him work harder for good shots.

Analysis: A more modern hairstyle is about the only thing the multi-talented Grant is lacking. No one else in the WAC is in his league. A future pro, Grant is one of the top half-dozen senior forwards in the game today.

COLLEGE STATISTICS

	G	FGP	FTP	RPG	APG	PPG
UTAH 88-89	33	.461	.754	7.2	3.5	10.4
UTAH 89-90	30	.511	.783	7.0	2.8	16.5
UTAH 90-91	33	.472	.823	7.9	2.7	17.5
Totals	96	.482	.798	7.4	3.0	14.8

LITTERIAL GREEN
School: Georgia
Year: Senior
Position: Guard
Height: 6'1" **Weight:** 185
Birthdate: March 7, 1970
Birthplace: Pescagoula, MS

PLAYER SUMMARY	
Will	score often
Can't	shy away from contact
Expect	greater consistency
Don't Expect	team leadership

Background: Green's brilliant prep career was overshadowed by high school chum Chris Jackson. Green scored nearly 40 PPG as a prep senior. Only Dominique Wilkins scored more points as a Bulldog freshman. Green earned All-SEC honors last season for the second straight year.

Strengths: He's an explosive scorer who doesn't think twice about challenging bigger and stronger players inside. Although he's played off guard the past two seasons, he handles the ball and sees the court well enough to also excel at the point (his frosh position).

Weaknesses: Consistency stands between Green and All-America contention. His frequent indifference can affect the entire team. A streaky shooter, his shot always seems to disappear when the 'Dawgs need it most.

Analysis: While Green is probably the premier guard in the SEC not named Allan Houston, he's yet to achieve the stardom everyone predicted he would three years ago. With the proper attitude, his best basketball is still ahead of him.

COLLEGE STATISTICS

	G	FGP	FTP	RPG	APG	PPG
GA	88-89	31	.405	.775	1.8	4.3	15.5
GA	89-90	28	.417	.708	2.7	4.3	17.5
GA	90-91	28	.442	.777	2.5	3.5	20.6
Totals		87	.422	.755	2.4	4.0	17.8

TOM GUGLIOTTA
School: North Carolina St.
Year: Senior
Position: Forward
Height: 6'9" **Weight:** 230
Birthdate: December 19, 1969
Birthplace: Huntington Station, NY

PLAYER SUMMARY	
Will	be all-conference
Can't	shoot in traffic
Expect	a Jeff Ruland type
Don't Expect	less than 10 RPG

Background: Gugliotta's solid but unspectacular play earned him second-team All-ACC honors last winter. In his first season as a starter (1989-90), he led the Wolfpack in rebounds. A knee injury ended his freshman season prematurely.

Strengths: Other than Christian Laettner, Gugliotta is the best passing big man in the ACC. His 3-point shooting proficiency is unheard-of for a guy his size. Very mobile, he runs the break exceptionally well. He makes very few bad decisions.

Weaknesses: His increased upper-body strength is having an adverse effect on his perimeter shooting. Gugliotta gets flustered when he tries to shoot in a crowd. His shot's a little flat and tends to be blocked easily.

Analysis: Although it's tough to get noticed in a conference that features frontcourters like Laettner, Bryant Stith, and Rodney Rogers, Gugliotta has quietly become one of the finest all-around players in the ACC. Without Rodney Monroe and Chris Corchiani, he'll have to shoulder a huge load.

COLLEGE STATISTICS

	G	FGP	FTP	RPG	APG	PPG
NCST	88-89	21	.429	.655	1.7	0.2	2.7
NCST	89-90	30	.504	.672	7.0	1.6	11.1
NCST	90-91	31	.500	.644	6.5	2.8	15.2
Totals		82	.497	.654	6.5	1.7	10.6

MIKE HANSEN

School: Louisiana St.
Year: Junior
Position: Guard
Height: 6'1" **Weight:** 175
Birthdate: April 17, 1970
Birthplace: Madrid, Spain

PLAYER SUMMARY	
Will	shoot more
Can't	play intense defense
Expect	a team-leader role
Don't Expect	less than 16 PPG

Background: Hansen sat out the 1989-90 season after transferring from Tennessee-Martin (where he averaged 20 PPG). He caught Dale Brown's eye when he scored 40 against the Tigers in December 1988. He started 24 games for LSU last season. For three seasons, Hansen was one of Spain's best teenage players.

Strengths: A natural leader, Hansen is one of the SEC's top 3-point threats. He has the green light once he gets past the halfcourt stripe. A more comfortable shooter when he plays off guard, Hansen also does a nice enough job at the point.

Weaknesses: He has trouble distinguishing good shots from bad shots. His rebounding needs a lot of work, as does his defensive intensity. He hardly ever commits a foul and he rarely shoots free throws.

Analysis: The Tigers desperately need his perimeter scoring to help prevent defenses from sagging on Shaquille O'Neal. Although he had his moments last year, Hansen's yet to live up to his lofty expectations.

COLLEGE STATISTICS

	G	FGP	FTP	RPG	APG	PPG
LSU	90-91 27	.428	.857	2.2	2.4	12.7
Totals	27	.428	.857	2.2	2.4	12.7

ANFERNEE HARDAWAY

School: Memphis St.
Year: Sophomore
Position: Guard
Height: 6'7" **Weight:** 185
Birthdate: July 18, 1971
Birthplace: Memphis, TN

PLAYER SUMMARY	
Will	turn a lot of heads
Can't	get well fast enough
Expect	nights of magic
Don't Expect	instant success

Background: Recognized by *Parade* magazine as the prep player of the year in 1989-90, Hardaway sat out last season under Prop 48 requirements. He averaged nearly 37 points, ten rebounds, and five assists per game as a senior at Memphis Treadwell High. Hardaway was shot in the right foot during an altercation this past spring. He's no relation to Tim Hardaway.

Strengths: Hardaway possesses an incredible amount of natural ability. A bona fide point guard, his size (6'7") is a huge advantage. He's a crowd-pleasing passer who can penetrate any defense. Hardaway's shooting stroke is a sight to behold.

Weaknesses: Sitting out a year can do nothing but hurt a player. The gunshot wound in his foot is healing slowly. He's picked up some selfish playground-ball habits that he'll have to break in a hurry.

Analysis: Before he has even stepped onto the court, Hardaway has been billed by some talent scouts as one of the game's all-time greats. Memphis State fans shouldn't expect too much too soon. By 1997, he'll be an NBA All-Star.

BRIAN HENDRICK

School: California
Year: Junior
Position: Forward/Center
Height: 6'8" **Weight:** 225
Birthdate: September 9, 1970
Birthplace: Los Angeles, CA

PLAYER SUMMARY	
Will	play taller than 6'8"
Can't	resist forcing shots
Expect	double-figure RPG
Don't Expect	any home runs

Background: An All-Pac-10 performer, Hendrick was Cal's top scorer and rebounder last season. As a freshman, he led the Bears in rebounds and blocked shots. He was redshirted in 1988-89 after starring in basketball and baseball in high school. His father George was a major-league baseball star.

Strengths: A physical force to be reckoned with under the basket, he possesses a plethora of offensive moves and good quickness at the defensive end. Hendrick has an extremely soft shooting touch for a big man. He snared ten or more rebounds 14 times last winter.

Weaknesses: Rather than pass the ball to an open teammate, he often forces difficult shots. After receiving an entry pass, Hendrick puts the ball on the floor too often in the paint.

Analysis: Although opponents attempt to neutralize his dominant presence underneath with virtually every defensive scheme known to man, Hendrick still gets his points. He'll push UCLA's Don MacLean for Pac-10 Player of the Year honors this season.

COLLEGE STATISTICS

	G	FGP	FTP	RPG	APG	PPG
CAL	89-90	32	.593	.681	7.6	1.2	14.9
CAL	90-91	28	.556	.757	9.0	1.4	17.6
Totals		60	.573	.715	8.2	1.3	16.2

RIC HERRIN

School: Nevada
Year: Junior
Position: Center
Height: 6'10" **Weight:** 250
Birthdate: October 14, 1971
Birthplace: Rio Linda, CA

PLAYER SUMMARY	
Will	pound the boards
Can't	shoot 3-pointers
Expect	a Big Sky MVP
Don't Expect	good hands

Background: The top scorer and rebounder in the Big Sky last season, Herrin garnered all-league honors and just missed Player of the Year recognition. A former McDonald's High School All-American, Herrin started every game as a true freshman—the only player on the Nevada team to do so.

Strengths: Herrin runs the floor real well and he's become a lot more physical inside. Through hard work, he's developed numerous effective low-post moves. He's very consistent and mature for a youngster who has played only two college seasons.

Weaknesses: Passing and catching the ball are his two biggest problems. Herrin's shooting range doesn't extend much beyond 12 feet. He fouled out of six ballgames last winter.

Analysis: If he continues to improve at his present pace, Herrin will be employed by an NBA team by 1993. Even if his play regresses slightly, he's still good enough to earn Big Sky Player of the Year honors and guide the Wolf Pack to the NCAA tournament.

COLLEGE STATISTICS

	G	FGP	FTP	RPG	APG	PPG
NEV	89-90	28	.512	.594	5.7	0.6	9.8
NEV	90-91	31	.498	.664	9.8	0.7	18.2
Totals		59	.502	.641	7.9	0.7	14.2

GRANT HILL

School: Duke
Year: Sophomore
Position: Guard/Forward
Height: 6'7" **Weight:** 205
Birthdate: November 5, 1972
Birthplace: Reston, VA

PLAYER SUMMARY	
Will	take more shots
Can't	hit from outside
Expect	aggressive defense
Don't Expect	sophomore jinx

Background: A *Parade* All-American as a high school senior, Hill was his class valedictorian. His father Calvin was a former NFL star. Despite missing three games and parts of five others with a broken nose and a painful hip-pointer, Hill was an impact player last season. He received third-team *Basketball Weekly* Freshman All-America honors.

Strengths: An outstanding finisher on the break, Hill gets up and down the floor like a racehorse. He rebounds well and isn't hesitant about handling the ball. It's not often that a true freshman starts 31 games for a national champion. It's even rarer for one to show so much maturity.

Weaknesses: After displaying good range in high school, Hill's perimeter jumper went into hiding last season. He made only one trey. Hill shoots only 61 percent from the line.

Analysis: Not since Johnny Dawkins in 1982-83 have the Blue Devils gotten so much offense out of a freshman. And like Dawkins, Hill's numbers should continue to grow each season.

COLLEGE STATISTICS

	G	FGP	FTP	RPG	APG	PPG
DUKE 90-91	36	.516	.609	5.1	2.2	11.2
Totals	36	.516	.609	5.1	2.2	11.2

ROBERT HORRY

School: Alabama
Year: Senior
Position: Forward
Height: 6'9" **Weight:** 210
Birthdate: August 25, 1970
Birthplace: Memphis, TN

PLAYER SUMMARY	
Will	grab loose balls
Can't	find consistency
Expect	boards and blocks
Don't Expect	tough play

Background: Alabama's top high school player as a senior, Horry received Converse All-America honors. He became a full-time Crimson Tide starter as a sophomore. After pacing the team in rebounds and blocks last winter, Horry was an All-Deep South selection by *Basketball Weekly*.

Strengths: A very smooth and versatile player with sticky fingers, Horry totals more rebounds, blocks, and steals than any other small forward in the SEC. He can play both forward positions and big guard. His shooting range extends beyond the 3-point arc.

Weaknesses: He was suspended from the team for disciplinary reasons last March. Despite his rebounding numbers, he's not mean enough inside. He's also too inconsistent for a senior.

Analysis: Though compared favorably to former Alabama standout Derrick McKey, Horry has one final chance to impress NBA scouts. Coach Wimp Sanderson won't tolerate a repeat of last year's suspension. Instead, he expects Horry to be the team leader.

COLLEGE STATISTICS

	G	FGP	FTP	RPG	APG	PPG
ALA 88-89	31	.427	.644	5.0	1.1	6.5
ALA 89-90	35	.467	.760	6.2	1.9	13.1
ALA 90-91	32	.449	.804	8.1	1.8	11.9
Totals	98	.452	.751	6.5	1.6	10.6

ALLAN HOUSTON

School: Tennessee
Year: Junior
Position: Guard
Height: 6'6" **Weight:** 185
Birthdate: April 4, 1971
Birthplace: Louisville, KY

PLAYER SUMMARY	
Will	rewrite record books
Can't	rebound consistently
Expect	an MVP season
Don't Expect	inside points

Background: Houston was a unanimous All-SEC performer in 1990-91 for the second straight season. He was MVP of the '91 SEC tournament. The son of Vols coach Wade Houston, Allan originally signed a letter of intent to attend Louisville, where his father was an assistant at the time.

Strengths: One of the most consistent scorers in the country, Houston tallied 20 or more points in 27 games last winter. As his .429 mark from 3-point land would attest, he's a brilliant perimeter shooter. Houston's an unselfish passer and very versatile too. He can play both guard positions and small forward.

Weaknesses: Wade Houston will tell you that Allan's defense, offensive rebounding, and overall consistency need work. You know how tough fathers can be. Realistically, rebounding is his only major flaw.

Analysis: By the time he graduates, Houston figures to be the greatest player in Tennessee history not named Bernard King. With continued defensive improvement, he'll become an NBA All-Star.

COLLEGE STATISTICS

	G	FGP	FTP	RPG	APG	PPG
TENN 89-90	30	.437	.805	2.9	4.2	20.3
TENN 90-91	34	.482	.863	3.1	3.9	23.7
Totals	64	.461	.839	3.0	4.0	22.1

BYRON HOUSTON

School: Oklahoma St.
Year: Senior
Position: Forward/Center
Height: 6'7" **Weight:** 235
Birthdate: November 22, 1969
Birthplace: Watonga, KS

PLAYER SUMMARY	
Will	be a lottery pick
Can't	shoot from outside
Expect	a Big Eight MVP
Don't Expect	passive defense

Background: The highest scoring frosh in the Big Eight in 1988-89, Houston earned first-team all-conference accolades each of the past two seasons. He shared Big Eight MVP honors with Missouri's Doug Smith last year. Houston rejected offers from Arkansas and UCLA to attend OSU.

Strengths: Born to crash the boards, Houston is on the verge of becoming a bona fide superstar. He'd rather rebound than score. His brute strength and quickness, combined with some exceptional low-post moves, make him unstoppable when he gets the ball in the paint.

Weaknesses: Houston's shooting range is very limited, his ball-handling's suspect, and he's not the fastest guy in the world. He is working hard to develop a much-needed mid-range jumper.

Analysis: Houston is clearly the best player in the Big Eight. By season's end, he could become one of the top five players in the country. He's an awesome talent who could carry the Cowboys a long way in the NCAA tournament.

COLLEGE STATISTICS

	G	FGP	FTP	RPG	APG	PPG
OSU 88-89	30	.583	.745	8.4	1.1	13.0
OSU 89-90	31	.528	.731	10.0	1.5	18.5
OSU 90-91	32	.573	.743	10.5	2.1	22.7
Totals	93	.560	.739	9.6	1.6	18.2

BOBBY HURLEY

School: Duke
Year: Junior
Position: Guard
Height: 6'0" **Weight:** 160
Birthdate: June 28, 1971
Birthplace: Jersey City, NJ

PLAYER SUMMARY	
Will	be first-team All-ACC
Can't	rest on laurels
Expect	all the right moves
Don't Expect	any letdown

Background: Named MVP of last spring's Midwest Regional, this droopy-eyed city kid deserved similar Final Four honors. Handed the starting point-guard job the minute he arrived on the Duke campus, Hurley finished second to Kenny Anderson for ACC Rookie of the Year honors.

Strengths: By adding increased offense to a sparkling all-around floor game, Hurley's emerged as one of the ACC's premier point guards. He's a talented trigger man who doesn't make many poor decisions. Deceivingly fast, Hurley's rarely beaten off the dribble.

Weaknesses: Other than his diminutive size, he's not lacking in too many areas. Hurley does foul a little too much and sometimes doesn't react quick enough to obvious steal opportunities. He's still too unselfish.

Analysis: He looks like the kid next door, but he plays like a seasoned pro. Hurley took his game to the next level during last year's NCAA tournament, particularly with his shooting. He turned in an almost perfect game vs. UNLV.

COLLEGE STATISTICS

	G	FGP	FTP	RPG	APG	PPG
DUKE 89-90	38	.351	.769	1.8	7.6	8.8
DUKE 90-91	39	.423	.728	2.4	7.4	11.3
Totals	77	.386	.751	2.1	7.5	10.1

JIM JACKSON

School: Ohio St.
Year: Junior
Position: Forward/Guard
Height: 6'6" **Weight:** 210
Birthdate: October 14, 1970
Birthplace: Toledo, OH

PLAYER SUMMARY	
Will	be an All-American
Can't	be labeled selfish
Expect	him to go pro early
Don't Expect	him to panic

Background: Jackson was the Big Ten Player of the Year last season and, in 1989-90, he was voted Big Ten Freshman of the Year. As a prepster, Jackson established himself as one of Ohio's greatest all-time players. He suffered a stress fracture in his left foot at last summer's Pan Am Games.

Strengths: As complete a package as you'll find at this level, Jackson can hold his own at every position but center. He can hit from inside, outside, or the third row of the stands. Jackson seems to score or be involved in every critical basket when the game's on the line.

Weaknesses: Jackson is still selfless to a fault. Passing up the number of high-percentage shots he does, just to get his teammates more involved, doesn't make much sense. To become a true superstar, he must look to score more early in the game.

Analysis: When the game's on the line, Jackson's your man. A mentally tough kid, he's truly got ice water in his veins. Like all the great players, he never gets too excited when he plays well or too depressed when he doesn't.

COLLEGE STATISTICS

	G	FGP	FTP	RPG	APG	PPG
OSU 89-90	30	.499	.785	5.5	3.7	16.1
OSU 90-91	31	.517	.752	5.5	4.3	18.9
Totals	61	.508	.764	5.5	4.0	17.5

ALONZO JAMISON

School: Kansas
Year: Senior
Position: Forward
Height: 6'6" **Weight:** 225
Birthdate: July 22, 1968
Birthplace: Orange, CA

PLAYER SUMMARY	
Will	give it his all
Can't	hit his FTs
Expect	more points, boards
Don't Expect	perimeter play

Background: A star prepster in Santa Ana, California, Jamison spent a year at nearby Rancho Santiago Junior College before enrolling at Kansas. An honorable-mention All-Big Eight selection last year, Jamison burst onto the national scene after being named MVP of the Southeast Regional.

Strengths: A terrific low-post defender, Jamison takes full advantage of his bulk and quick hands and feet. He's the strongest guy on the team. His leaping ability and dominating defense make Jamison seem much taller than 6'6". A 60-percent shooter, he's allergic to bad shots.

Weaknesses: Often plagued by foul problems, Jamison fouled out of seven games last season. He misses more free throws than he makes. "Perimeter game" isn't in his vocabulary.

Analysis: Jamison's outstanding play in last year's NCAA tournament was responsible for nationwide notoriety. He's not going to sneak up on anyone this time around. He plays only one way—all out, all the time.

COLLEGE STATISTICS

	G	FGP	FTP	RPG	APG	PPG
KAN 89-90	17	.614	.500	2.0	1.5	4.9
KAN 90-91	35	.595	.497	6.4	3.6	10.4
Totals	52	.599	.497	4.9	2.9	8.6

DAVE JOHNSON

School: Syracuse
Year: Senior
Position: Forward
Height: 6'6" **Weight:** 210
Birthdate: November 16, 1970
Birthplace: Morgan City, LA

PLAYER SUMMARY	
Will	face gimmick defenses
Can't	clear his mind
Expect	late-game heroics
Don't Expect	lack of effort

Background: A second-team All-Big East pick last season, Johnson was arguably the most improved player in the country. He went from being a bench-warmer to an All-America candidate, while increasing his scoring output by 13 PPG.

Strengths: Johnson has always been a tremendous all-around athlete who could pass well, finish the break, force turnovers, and play tenacious defense. Now, he has broken through in the all-important scoring column. A great second-half player, he does a lot of damage when it means the most.

Weaknesses: A late-season shooting slump has weighed heavily on his mind during the off-season, as have numerous allegations against himself and the Syracuse program. Like most Orangemen, free throw shooting isn't Johnson's strong suit.

Analysis: This season will tell us just how good of a player Johnson really is. Without Billy Owens, defenses will give him their full attention. A smart, classy kid, he's anxious to meet the challenge.

COLLEGE STATISTICS

	G	FGP	FTP	RPG	APG	PPG
SYR 88-89	37	.457	.515	2.0	1.0	4.2
SYR 89-90	31	.400	.611	2.4	1.1	6.5
SYR 90-91	32	.499	.658	6.3	2.3	19.4
Totals	100	.468	.619	3.5	1.5	9.8

ERVIN JOHNSON

School: New Orleans
Year: Junior
Position: Center
Height: 6'11" **Weight:** 213
Birthdate: December 21, 1967
Birthplace: New Orleans, LA

PLAYER SUMMARY
Will ....jump through the gym
Can't..................be Earvin Johnson
Expect..........................12-plus RPG
Don't Expect..............polished play

Background: A supermarket employee for four years after high school, Johnson suddenly walked into coach Tim Floyd's office and told him he wanted a tryout. Floyd thought he was joking. Two years later, he's the game's second-best rebounder and shot-blocker (behind Shaquille O'Neal). While Earvin answers to the nickname "Magic," Ervin prefers "Slim."

Strengths: His great anticipation, quickness, and leaping ability make Johnson an awesome force defensively. He rebounds like Magic Johnson chalks up assists. A great practice player, he never stops working to improve.

Weaknesses: Still raw and unproven in a lot of areas, he drifts in and out of the action at times. He's still not real comfortable offensively. Johnson still has a lot to learn about the intricacies of the game.

Analysis: Johnson is truly one of the most amazing college basketball success stories in recent years. He won't be satisfied until he leads the nation in rebounding. It may happen. His potential is limitless.

COLLEGE STATISTICS

	G	FGP	FTP	RPG	APG	PPG
NO	89-90	32	.579	.561	6.8	0.9	6.3
NO	90-91	30	.572	.537	12.2	1.1	12.7
Totals		62	.575	.546	9.4	1.0	9.4

POPEYE JONES

School: Murray St.
Year: Senior
Position: Center
Height: 6'8" **Weight:** 260
Birthdate: June 17, 1970
Birthplace: Dresden, TN

PLAYER SUMMARY
Will...........................rebound all day
Can't...........................jump too high
Expect............overall improvement
Don't Expect..............Charles Atlas

Background: Ron Jones was named Ohio Valley Player of the Year for the second time in as many seasons in 1990-91. Fat in high school (315 pounds), Jones shed 60 pounds between his freshman and sophomore seasons at Murray. He acquired his nickname when his mother brought him home from the hospital and the popular cartoon was on TV at the time.

Strengths: Popeye gobbles up rebounds to the tune of more than 14 per game. He passes surprisingly well and doesn't commit many turnovers. He's a dependable shooter from 15 feet and in.

Weaknesses: Jones is not as strong as he should be. Keeping his weight down will always be a problem. Not much of a vertical leaper, he relies on positioning for many of his rebounds.

Analysis: There's not another 6'8" player in the country who can do so much damage on the glass. He almost appears bored with the college game at times. With a little more discipline and conditioning, he could play in the NBA right now.

COLLEGE STATISTICS

	G	FGP	FTP	RPG	APG	PPG
MSU	88-89	30	.489	.754	4.6	0.7	5.8
MSU	89-90	30	.500	.757	11.2	2.0	19.5
MSU	90-91	33	.493	.711	14.2	2.1	20.2
Totals		93	.495	.737	10.1	1.6	15.3

ADONIS JORDAN

School: Kansas
Year: Junior
Position: Guard
Height: 5'11" **Weight:** 170
Birthdate: August 21, 1970
Birthplace: Brooklyn, NY

PLAYER SUMMARY	
Will	..........................be team leader
Can't	...............think shot then pass
Expect	........................more scoring
Don't Expect	........Final Four repeat

Background: Jordan exceeded all expectations after taking over for Kevin Pritchard at the point last season. A second-team All-Big Eight selection, his playmaking was a vital factor in the Jayhawks' unexpected Final Four march. A capable back-up in 1989-90, Jordan was named to the freshman all-conference team.

Strengths: A talented penetrator and passer, Jordan can supply offensive punch of his own when needed. He shot better than 50 percent from the field last season. Defensively, he doesn't give you much room to operate.

Weaknesses: He gets so caught up in getting the club in the right offensive and defensive sets that he goes long stretches without even thinking about shooting. Coach Roy Williams would like him to shoot between 12 and 15 times a game. He averaged only eight shots last season.

Analysis: An unsung hero in the eyes of some, Jordan can drop the word "unsung" with another solid season. He quarterbacks a team as well as any point guard in the Midwest. He'll have to adjust to a lot of new faces.

COLLEGE STATISTICS

	G	FGP	FTP	RPG	APG	PPG
KAN	89-90	35	.340	.694	1.2	3.1	3.0
KAN	90-91	34	.507	.765	3.0	4.5	12.5
Totals		69	.463	.750	2.1	3.8	7.6

ANDY KAUFMANN

School: Illinois
Year: Senior
Position: Guard/Forward
Height: 6'6" **Weight:** 218
Birthdate: November 17, 1969
Birthplace: Jacksonville, IL

PLAYER SUMMARY	
Will	...................lead league in shots
Can't	..........................jump real well
Expect	............better shot selection
Don't Expect	...................fewer PPG

Background: Kaufmann topped the state of Illinois in scoring as a high school junior and senior. A blood clot in his shoulder cut his freshman season short. As a sophomore, he shot better beyond the 3-point stripe. Last season, he ranked among the league leaders in scoring and was second-team All-Big Ten.

Strengths: A natural small forward, he's versatile enough to move to shooting guard when necessary. Kaufmann displays great shooting range, and he deserves more credit than he gets for his ball-handling and defense. He gets to the free throw line a lot.

Weaknesses: Kaufmann was benched briefly last season for taking too many bad shots. At times, he has no conscience. His unwillingness to pass has upset some of his teammates. He doesn't jump real well.

Analysis: Though not the prettiest player in the world to watch, Kaufmann gets the job done. Bad shots aside, he's the Illini's go-to guy when the game's on the line. He's an aggressive scorer, not a pure shooter.

COLLEGE STATISTICS

	G	FGP	FTP	RPG	APG	PPG
ILL	88-89	12	.360	.700	1.7	0.7	4.3
ILL	89-90	29	.450	.800	3.2	1.9	9.8
ILL	90-91	31	.467	.833	5.0	2.2	21.3
Totals		72	.455	.815	3.7	1.8	13.8

ADAM KEEFE

School: Stanford
Year: Senior
Position: Center
Height: 6'9" **Weight:** 230
Birthdate: February 22, 1970
Birthplace: Irvine, CA

PLAYER SUMMARY	
Will	earn national acclaim
Can't	reject many shots
Expect	a Dave Cowens type
Don't Expect	a volleyball career

Background: Keefe established himself as the best big man on the West Coast last season while leading the Cardinal to the NIT championship. Named NIT tourney MVP, Keefe averaged 23 points and nine rebounds per game. He's also a key member of Stanford's nationally-ranked volleyball team.

Strengths: Keefe's an outstanding offensive rebounder. He's a physical kid who plays center or big forward with great intensity. The big redhead understands positioning, knows how to seal people off, and takes the ball strong to the basket.

Weaknesses: He'd be even better if he worked on his game during the off-season. Instead, he's at the beach playing volleyball. He actually prefers it over basketball. Keefe's not as strong as he should be.

Analysis: Although he lost almost his entire supporting cast, Keefe is talented enough to keep this team respectable. An NBA team will grab him early in next year's draft, unless he turns his full attention to a spot on the 1992 U.S. Olympic volleyball team.

COLLEGE STATISTICS

	G	FGP	FTP	RPG	APG	PPG
STAN 88-89	33	.633	.689	5.4	0.7	8.4
STAN 89-90	30	.627	.725	9.1	1.4	20.0
STAN 90-91	33	.609	.760	9.5	1.8	21.5
Totals	96	.619	.732	8.0	1.3	16.5

MIK KILGORE

School: Temple
Year: Senior
Position: Forward
Height: 6'8" **Weight:** 210
Birthdate: April 28, 1970
Birthplace: Philadelphia, PA

PLAYER SUMMARY	
Will	be team's top star
Can't	concentrate
Expect	expanded role
Don't Expect	many water breaks

Background: Kilgore hasn't missed a start in his three seasons at Temple. He led the club in minutes last winter and ranked second in scoring and assists. He quietly averaged nearly 20 PPG, five RPG, and four APG in last spring's NCAA tournament. Kilgore was the top player in Philadelphia as a high school senior.

Strengths: He's played every position but center for the Owls. An effective baseline performer, he's probably best suited for small forward. A hard worker under the basket at both ends, Kilgore adds an extra dimension on the perimeter with his shooting and defense.

Weaknesses: Kilgore can be bothered by a lack of concentration at times—the sin of sins in coach John Chaney's eyes. He needs to improve his .411 mark from the field. He led last year's team in turnovers.

Analysis: Minus top guns Mark Macon and Donald Hodge, Kilgore becomes the Owls' primary offensive threat. Can a guy who has always been a nice complementary player now adjust to top billing? Chaney thinks Kilgore can.

COLLEGE STATISTICS

	G	FGP	FTP	RPG	APG	PPG
TEMP 88-89	30	.394	.672	2.7	2.7	8.0
TEMP 89-90	31	.382	.722	5.7	3.3	10.8
TEMP 90-91	34	.411	.744	5.8	3.3	14.0
Totals	95	.397	.726	4.8	3.1	11.1

CHRIS KING

School: Wake Forest
Year: Senior
Position: Forward
Height: 6'8" **Weight:** 225
Birthdate: July 24, 1969
Birthplace: Newton Grove, CA

PLAYER SUMMARY	
Will	lead by example
Can't	be denied on break
Expect	fine all-around play
Don't Expect	a ball-handler

Background: King moved from power forward to small forward last season to make room for the nation's premier freshman, Rodney Rogers. King led the team in minutes and blocked shots and finished second to Rogers in scoring and rebounding. He topped Wake in scoring and rebounding as a freshman and a sophomore.

Strengths: An exceptionally quick player who runs the break like a guard, King can score facing the basket or with his back to the goal. He broadened his overall game significantly last season, concentrating more on assists and perimeter shooting.

Weaknesses: He's still working on his ball-handling, passing, and perimeter shooting—three things he wasn't asked to do too often as a power forward. King must maintain proper work habits and desire.

Analysis: Last year, he helped lead the Demon Deacons to their first winning season since 1985. The unsung star they can't do without, King will again be the guy this young, hungry squad will look to in a pinch.

COLLEGE STATISTICS

	G	FGP	FTP	RPG	APG	PPG
WF	88-89	28	.540	.654	6.1	0.8	14.4
WF	89-90	28	.546	.589	7.4	1.0	16.1
WF	90-91	30	.489	.636	5.7	2.1	15.1
Totals		86	.524	.625	6.4	1.3	15.2

CHRISTIAN LAETTNER

School: Duke
Year: Senior
Position: Center/Forward
Height: 6'11" **Weight:** 225
Birthdate: August 17, 1969
Birthplace: Angola, NY

PLAYER SUMMARY	
Will	push for ACC MVP
Can't	go to his left
Expect	an All-American
Don't Expect	great stamina

Background: Last year's Final Four MVP, Laettner was a consensus second-team All-American and an ACC selection. Duke's team leader in points, rebounds, steals, and blocks, he shot 58 percent from the field. He was second-team All-ACC as a sophomore.

Strengths: Laettner's strong inside game and outside shooting make him perhaps the most versatile big man in the game today. He's consistent too, scoring in double figures in 35 games in 1990-91. A tremendous passer, he's also very smart defensively.

Weaknesses: A lot of games tend to wear him out. He appeared tired during last year's NCAA tournament. An 82-game NBA schedule could really take its toll. He forces a few too many shots and passes.

Analysis: Laettner will see time at center and power forward this season after dispelling the notion last year that he wasn't physical enough. He's already more talented than his mentor, Danny Ferry. He'll be one of the first three players drafted next June.

COLLEGE STATISTICS

	G	FGP	FTP	RPG	APG	PPG
DUKE	88-89	36	.723	.727	4.7	1.2	8.9
DUKE	89-90	38	.511	.836	9.6	2.2	16.3
DUKE	90-91	39	.575	.802	8.7	1.9	19.8
Totals		113	.574	.802	7.7	1.8	15.1

JARVIS LANG
School: North Carolina-Charlotte
Year: Sophomore
Position: Forward
Height: 6'6" **Weight:** 210
Birthdate: June 25, 1972
Birthplace: Farmville, NC

PLAYER SUMMARY	
Will	continue to improve
Can't	defend big scorers
Expect	double-doubles
Don't Expect	erratic play

Background: Lang's one of the most highly regarded recruits to ever attend UNC-Charlotte. He earned second-team Freshman All-America honors from *Basketball Weekly* after leading the nation in rookie scoring and rebounding. Lang shattered a backboard in a recent slam-dunk contest.

Strengths: As consistent a player as you'll find, Lang established a UNCC record with 15 double-doubles (points and rebounds) last season. His deceiving strength and leaping ability makes him nearly impossible to box out, while his unique release makes his shot difficult to block.

Weaknesses: Lang's team defense and overall knowledge of the game need development. He must let the game come to him rather than forcing the action. He needs to develop more offensive moves.

Analysis: Although he was overshadowed last year by Sun Belt super frosh Kendrick Warren (VCU) and standout teammate Henry Williams, Lang is truly one of the best young power players in the nation. He should make the All-Metro first team.

COLLEGE STATISTICS
	G	FGP	FTP	RPG	APG	PPG
NCC	90-91	28	.474	.713	10.6	0.6	19.6
Totals		28	.474	.713	10.6	0.6	19.6

GEOFF LEAR
School: Pepperdine
Year: Senior
Position: Forward
Height: 6'8" **Weight:** 240
Birthdate: June 9, 1970
Birthplace: West Covina, CA

PLAYER SUMMARY	
Will	be unstoppable inside
Can't	go beyond the paint
Expect	him to draw fouls
Don't Expect	better FT pct.

Background: A two-time All-West Coast Conference selection, Lear was named MVP of last year's WCC tournament. He was the Waves' leading scorer in their NCAA tourney loss to Seton Hall. Lear was one of Southern California's finest players as a high school senior.

Strengths: Determined and instinctive, Lear won't be denied when he gets the ball within ten feet of the basket. He either scores, compliments of hard work and a soft shooting touch, or goes to the line. He fires length-of-the-floor outlet passes at the blink of an eye. He's also a skilled shot-blocker.

Weaknesses: The more free throws he shoots, the worse he seems to get. Lear's the guy the other team fouls when it's trying to get back into the game. He still can't knock down a medium-range jumper with any consistency.

Analysis: Lear teams with star guard Doug Christie to make Pepperdine one of the most dangerous teams in the West. With a few more rebounds and better shooting range, he could dethrone Christie as WCC Player of the Year.

COLLEGE STATISTICS
	G	FGP	FTP	RPG	APG	PPG
PEP 88-89	33	.456	.537	4.9	0.5	5.0
PEP 89-90	28	.571	.616	8.9	1.1	13.8
PEP 90-91	31	.563	.564	9.8	1.6	18.5
Totals	92	.558	.576	7.8	1.1	12.2

TERRELL LOWERY

School: Loyola Marymount
Year: Senior
Position: Guard
Height: 6'2" **Weight:** 170
Birthdate: October 25, 1970
Birthplace: Oakland, CA

PLAYER SUMMARY	
Will	do more than score
Can't	shoot in traffic
Expect	30-plus PPG
Don't Expect	tough defense

Background: An All-West Coast Conference first-teamer last season, Lowery burst onto the national scene in mid-December with back-to-back 41- and 40-point efforts against Oklahoma and LSU. His 28.5 PPG and 9.1 APG ranks him among the top half-dozen scorers and passers in the country. He never started a college game until last season.

Strengths: Known for his outstanding perimeter shooting, Lowery connected on 40 percent of his trey tries last winter. Like all Lions players, he thrives in the open court. More than just a scorer, he's developed into a consistent playmaker.

Weaknesses: Defense. At LMU, guards play defense by releasing to the other end of the floor as soon as the ball goes up. He does possess quick hands and speed, but it's technique he's lacking.

Analysis: Minus a combined 87 PPG from 1989-90 standouts Bo Kimble, Hanks Gathers, and Jeff Fryer, the entire offensive load fell squarely into Lowery's lap last season. He responded, and he will this winter too.

COLLEGE STATISTICS

	G	FGP	FTP	RPG	APG	PPG
LOY 88-89	30	.357	.816	1.6	3.1	5.9
LOY 89-90	32	.513	.738	2.6	6.3	14.5
LOY 90-91	31	.480	.801	4.5	9.1	28.5
Totals	93	.471	.781	2.9	6.2	16.4

GEORGE LYNCH

School: North Carolina
Year: Junior
Position: Forward
Height: 6'7" **Weight:** 214
Birthdate: September 3, 1970
Birthplace: Roanoke, VA

PLAYER SUMMARY	
Will	pace UNC in boards
Can't	shoot from the wing
Expect	more offense
Don't Expect	weak effort

Background: As a high school senior, Lynch attracted interest from college teams across the country at prep powerhouse Flint Hill (Virginia). If not for Kenny Anderson, he probably would have been named ACC Freshman of the Year in 1989-90. Last year, he paced the Tar Heels in rebounding.

Strengths: He's an exceptional rebounder for a youngster his size, particularly at the offensive end. His quick first step makes him a baseline scoring threat, as does a lethal turnaround jumper. Lynch loves contact and goes to the line often to convert 3-point plays.

Weaknesses: Instead of passing the ball back outside on occasion, he often forces up off-balance shots in a crowd. The experiment of moving him to the perimeter never really worked last season.

Analysis: Look for Lynch to assume more of a leadership role following the graduation of three senior starters. He's a blue-collar guy who'll always give a supreme effort. He should give his offensive game more attention.

COLLEGE STATISTICS

	G	FGP	FTP	RPG	APG	PPG
NC 89-90	34	.521	.663	5.4	1.0	8.6
NC 90-91	35	.523	.630	7.4	1.2	12.5
Totals	69	.522	.644	6.4	1.1	10.6

MALCOLM MACKEY

School: Georgia Tech
Year: Junior
Position: Forward
Height: 6'11" **Weight:** 248
Birthdate: July 11, 1970
Birthplace: Chattanooga, TN

```
PLAYER SUMMARY
Will..........................play in the NBA
Can't................escape the low post
Expect...............All-ACC accolades
Don't Expect...........many mistakes
```

Background: Talented but raw and indecisive as a freshman, Mackey emerged as one of the most improved players in the country last winter. He became the first Yellow Jacket since Rich Yunkus in 1971 to average double figures in rebounds. He pulled down 19 in NCAA tournament play vs. Ohio State.

Strengths: Big and strong, Mackey runs the court well and doesn't take a back seat to anybody inside. He's got quick feet and good hands and makes very few mistakes. When he gets the ball in the low post, he either scores or draws a foul.

Weaknesses: Mackey's shooting range doesn't extend beyond about eight feet. While he's become more of an offensive threat, he still can't produce on a consistent basis. When his shooting suffers early, it can affect his entire game.

Analysis: Mackey possesses the size, natural ability, and work ethic to develop into one of the game's most valuable big men. Last year's numbers were better than ex-Yellow Jacket John Salley's as a senior.

COLLEGE STATISTICS

		G	FGP	FTP	RPG	APG	PPG
GT	89-90	35	.559	.441	7.5	0.5	7.2
GT	90-91	30	.551	.597	10.7	1.0	15.3
Totals		65	.554	.549	9.0	0.7	11.0

DON MacLEAN

School: UCLA
Year: Senior
Position: Forward
Height: 6'10" **Weight:** 235
Birthdate: January 16, 1970
Birthplace: Palo Alto, CA

```
PLAYER SUMMARY
Will....................score from outside
Can't..............muscle to the basket
Expect..................................25 PPG
Don't Expect......as many tantrums
```

Background: After being named Pac-10 Freshman of the Year, MacLean has since earned All-Pac-10 honors twice. He was a John Wooden Award finalist last spring. MacLean's on pace to break Lew Alcindor's career scoring record at UCLA.

Strengths: Arguably the best shooting big man in America, MacLean's hit nearly 55 percent from the field and 85 percent from the line in his career. He possesses a deadly baseline stroke from both sides of the basket. A solid rebounder and top-notch defender, MacLean also runs the floor real well.

Weaknesses: MacLean's on-court tirades have infuriated opposing players, coaches, and fans. Shaun Vandiver got so upset with MacLean during the 1990 U.S. National Team trials that he punched him in the jaw.

Analysis: In MacLean's defense, he has toned down his act. In order to reach his full potential, it'll have to continue. He has an outside chance at national Player of the Year honors, while the Bruins may be headed to the Final Four.

COLLEGE STATISTICS

	G	FGP	FTP	RPG	APG	PPG
UCLA 88-89	31	.555	.816	7.5	1.2	18.6
UCLA 89-90	33	.516	.848	8.7	1.1	19.9
UCLA 90-91	31	.551	.846	7.3	2.0	23.0
Totals	95	.540	.838	7.8	1.4	20.5

DARRICK MARTIN

School: UCLA
Year: Senior
Position: Guard
Height: 6'0" **Weight:** 160
Birthdate: March 6, 1971
Birthplace: Denver, CO

PLAYER SUMMARY	
Will	whiz by defenders
Can't	shoot 3-pointers
Expect	best season yet
Don't Expect	late-season woes

Background: Martin led the Bruins in minutes played and assists last season. He's started 87 straight games since moving into the starting lineup as a freshman. After signing early with UCLA in November 1987, Martin tried to back out when Walt Hazzard was fired.

Strengths: A fine penetrator with blazing speed, Martin can be one of the premier playmakers in the West as long as he stays under control. A solid medium-range jumper has made him more of an offensive threat. Quick hands are his ticket to numerous steals.

Weaknesses: Unlike in the spring of 1990, when he led the Bruins to the Sweet 16, Martin had his problems late last season. His shots weren't falling and he was failing to make smart court decisions.

Analysis: A consistent perimeter shot is the only thing that prevents Martin from being one of the game's most dangerous point guards. He possesses all the other ingredients. Until he begins knocking down 18- to 22-footers, no one's going to come out and guard him.

COLLEGE STATISTICS

	G	FGP	FTP	RPG	APG	PPG
UCLA 88-89	31	.453	.747	1.9	2.9	8.5
UCLA 89-90	33	.466	.714	2.2	6.8	11.3
UCLA 90-91	32	.464	.750	2.4	6.8	11.6
Totals	96	.462	.736	2.2	5.3	10.5

JAMAL MASHBURN

School: Kentucky
Year: Sophomore
Position: Forward
Height: 6'9" **Weight:** 244
Birthdate: November 29, 1972
Birthplace: New York, NY

PLAYER SUMMARY	
Will	top 'Cats in boards
Can't	play hard each night
Expect	bigger numbers
Don't Expect	20 PPG, yet

Background: As a high school senior, Mashburn was the finest player in New York City—no small feat—and was voted Mr. Basketball in the state of New York. An impressive rookie season earned him SEC Freshman of the Year and national first-team Freshman All-America honors. Based on minutes played, he was the Wildcats' top rebounder.

Strengths: Unusually agile and quick for a guy his size, Mashburn can bang inside or pop out and nail the medium-range jumper. He's an outstanding rebounder with great hands who can put the ball on the floor on the break. He's perfected a sweet baseline turnaround jumper.

Weaknesses: He doesn't always play hard. For whatever reason, Mashburn ran out of steam during the final three weeks of the 1990-91 season. He's foul-prone and often out of position on defense.

Analysis: With added maturity, Mashburn's liable to become one of the top Kentucky players of all time. One of the top six forwards in the SEC last winter, he's just scratching the surface of his enormous potential.

COLLEGE STATISTICS

	G	FGP	FTP	RPG	APG	PPG
KEN 90-91	28	.518	.727	7.0	1.5	12.9
Totals	28	.518	.727	7.0	1.5	12.9

LEE MAYBERRY

School: Arkansas
Year: Senior
Position: Guard
Height: 6'2" **Weight:** 175
Birthdate: June 12, 1970
Birthplace: Tulsa, OK

PLAYER SUMMARY	
Will ....leave scouts drooling	
Can't ....find shooting stroke	
Expect ....calm, cool demeanor	
Don't Expect ....many turnovers	

Background: Named Oklahoma's Player of the Year as a high school senior, Mayberry was the Southwest Conference's co-MVP in 1989-90. He garnered All-SWC honors last season while leading the Razorbacks in minutes, assists, and steals. Coach Nolan Richardson is Mayberry's brother-in-law.

Strengths: Mayberry is one of the most complete all-around floor leaders in the business. For the second straight season, his three-to-one assist-to-turnover ratio was tops in the nation. He does a brilliant job of delivering the ball to his teammates in scoring position.

Weaknesses: Mayberry didn't shoot as well from the field last season as he did in 1989-90. He converts only 63 percent of his free throws. Quicker point guards can beat him off the dribble.

Analysis: With a little help from fellow All-America candidates Todd Day and Oliver Miller, Mayberry could drive his team to the Final Four. Describe the qualities that comprise the perfect point guard and you've described Lee Mayberry.

COLLEGE STATISTICS

	G	FGP	FTP	RPG	APG	PPG
ARK	88-89	32	.500	.736	3.2	4.2	12.9
ARK	89-90	35	.507	.792	2.9	5.2	14.5
ARK	90-91	38	.484	.634	3.4	5.5	13.2
Totals		105	.496	.715	3.2	5.0	13.5

JIM McCOY

School: Massachusetts
Year: Senior
Position: Guard
Height: 6'3" **Weight:** 175
Birthdate: December 1, 1969
Birthplace: Pittsburgh, PA

PLAYER SUMMARY	
Will ....create his own shots	
Can't ....play man-to-man	
Expect ....national acclaim	
Don't Expect ....3-point range	

Background: An NIT all-tourney selection last spring, McCoy was named to the All-Atlantic 10 first team for the second straight year. As a sophomore, McCoy became the first Massachusetts player since Julius Erving to average more than 20 PPG. He's the school's all-time scoring leader.

Strengths: A big-time scorer who works extremely hard to get good shots, McCoy's one of the premier clutch shooters in the country. After employing an unstoppable head fake and stutter step to get into the lane, McCoy does a masterful job of shooting the jumper off the dribble.

Weaknesses: His range stops at the 3-point stripe. He attempted only 14 treys all last year. McCoy turns the ball over too often and his idea of defense wouldn't be tolerated by some coaches.

Analysis: After shooting the surprising Minutemen all the way to the NIT Final Four last season, McCoy and Co. should be NCAA tournament-bound this year. He'll have to extend his shooting range before he plays in the NBA.

COLLEGE STATISTICS

	G	FGP	FTP	RPG	APG	PPG
MASS 88-89	28	.415	.724	3.5	2.0	19.8
MASS 89-90	31	.442	.764	3.3	1.0	20.7
MASS 90-91	33	.447	.703	3.5	1.6	18.9
Totals	92	.436	.731	3.4	1.5	19.8

OLIVER MILLER

School: Arkansas
Year: Senior
Position: Center
Height: 6'9" **Weight:** 290
Birthdate: June 12, 1970
Birthplace: Tulsa, OK

PLAYER SUMMARY

Will.................block over 100 shots
Can't...............take game seriously
Expect.....................high-pct. shots
Don't Expect..............added weight

Background: Last season, Miller was one of three Arkansas players on the All-SWC first team. He shot a blistering 70 percent from the field. He also blocked three shots per game, paced the Razorbacks in rebounding, and trailed only Todd Day in scoring. His .650 career field goal percentage is tops in school history.

Strengths: He shoots, catches, and passes the ball as well as any big man at any level. Great anticipation, quickness, and timing help explain his shot-blocking and rebounding dominance. He's an intimidating force at both ends.

Weaknesses: Miller's a fun-lover who rarely takes the game seriously. When he's in the mood, he's one of the best around. A thyroid problem makes it difficult for him to keep his weight under control.

Analysis: If he wants it bad enough, he could develop into a Wes Unseld type in the NBA. The only thing that could hold Miller back is himself. With the proper concentration and intensity, he could have a huge senior season.

COLLEGE STATISTICS

		G	FGP	FTP	RPG	APG	PPG
ARK	88-89	30	.547	.641	3.7	1.4	7.7
ARK	89-90	35	.639	.652	6.3	1.4	11.1
ARK	90-91	38	.704	.644	7.7	2.7	15.7
Totals		103	.650	.646	6.1	1.9	118

CHRIS MILLS

School: Arizona
Year: Junior
Position: Guard/Forward
Height: 6'6" **Weight:** 210
Birthdate: January 25, 1970
Birthplace: Los Angeles, CA

PLAYER SUMMARY

Will ....be team's go-to-guy
Can't ....avoid Kentucky incident
Expect ....all-league honors
Don't Expect ....great defense

Background: Mills topped the Wildcats in scoring last season, his first at Arizona. A transfer from Kentucky, Mills will forever be remembered for the alleged $1,000 package shipped to his home from the Kentucky basketball office. He paced Kentucky in rebounding in 1988-89.

Strengths: At Arizona, they spell versatile C-H-R-I-S M-I-L-L-S. He plays as many as four positions. Mills can shoot a trey or take the ball inside, handle the ball or pass off, and pull down his share of boards. He has a coach's knowledge of the game.

Weaknesses: Mills passes up a lot of open shots. Defensively, shorter, quicker guards can be too much for him to handle. He needs to move better without the ball.

Analysis: Before his Wildcat playing days are over, he'll be compared favorably to Sean Elliott. Mills's numbers should grow across the board this season. He'll likely be moved from small forward to big guard in order to give the 'Cats a bigger, quicker perimeter attack.

COLLEGE STATISTICS

	G	FGP	FTP	RPG	APG	PPG
KEN	88-89	32	.484	.713	8.7	2.9	14.3
ARIZ	90-91	35	.519	.746	6.2	1.9	15.6
Totals		67	.502	.730	7.4	2.4	15.0

HAROLD MINER

School: Southern California
Year: Junior
Position: Guard
Height: 6'5" **Weight:** 195
Birthdate: May 5, 1971
Birthplace: Inglewood, CA

PLAYER SUMMARY	
Will	eclipse 25 PPG
Can't	focus on defense
Expect	an All-American
Don't Expect	any less offense

Background: Miner eclipsed the 20-point barrier 24 times last season (including five 30-point games). He earned All-Pac-10 honors for the second year in a row. After two seasons, Miner has netted more points that any other sophomore in school history.

Strengths: There's not another guard in the country who consistently shoots as well as Miner. An outstanding long-range bomber, his leaping ability also makes him a solid inside threat. In short, his offensive game is next to impossible to defend.

Weaknesses: He must realize offense is just one facet of the game. Miner lacks focus on defense. From 3-point territory, his shooting mark dropped from 42 to 34 percent between his first and second seasons.

Analysis: With teams keying solely on Miner now that offensive minded Ronnie Coleman has graduated, he'll have to work twice as hard for good shots. A high-flying sharpshooter who regularly brings fans to their feet, Miner is the finest guard to play at USC since Paul Westphal.

COLLEGE STATISTICS

	G	FGP	FTP	RPG	APG	PPG
USC	89-90 28	.473	.841	3.6	2.1	20.6
USC	90-91 29	.453	.800	5.5	2.0	23.5
Totals	57	.464	.816	4.6	2.0	22.1

MARK MONTGOMERY

School: Michigan St.
Year: Senior
Position: Guard
Height: 6'2" **Weight:** 170
Birthdate: April 1, 1970
Birthplace: Inkster, MI

PLAYER SUMMARY	
Will	shine as a playmaker
Can't	shoot consistently
Expect	tons of assists
Don't Expect	bad decisions

Background: The 1990-91 Big Ten assists leader, Montgomery was an honorable-mention all-conference selection. He's also an academic All-American. He started in a combined 32 games his first two seasons.

Strengths: Montgomery's an outstanding playmaker who doesn't make nearly as many bad decision as he once did. At the defensive end, he takes full advantage of his impressive quickness. Montgomery is rarely beaten off the dribble.

Weaknesses: This seasoned southpaw can't shoot the ball with any consistency. Sure, he'll make a big shot or two to win a ballgame during the season, but he can't do it often enough. Montgomery's release is more of a push than a shot, and his perimeter jumper is very flat.

Analysis: He'd be one of the premier lead guards in the country if he learned how to shoot. He's going to have to contribute more points, somehow, now that Steve Smith has graduated to the NBA. A real outgoing and likeable youngster, Montgomery is the team leader on and off the court.

COLLEGE STATISTICS

	G	FGP	FTP	RPG	APG	PPG
MSU	88-89 33	.363	.698	1.9	3.2	3.7
MSU	89-90 34	.436	.550	2.0	2.9	3.6
MSU	90-91 29	.403	.606	3.4	5.8	7.5
Totals	96	.400	.617	2.4	3.9	4.8

ERIC MONTROSS
School: North Carolina
Year: Sophomore
Position: Center
Height: 7'0" **Weight:** 251
Birthdate: September 23, 1971
Birthplace: Indianapolis, IN

```
PLAYER SUMMARY
Will.....................enjoy a bigger year
Can't................hit FTs consistently
Expect ........................a lot more PT
Don't Expect..........All-ACC honors
```

Background: *Basketball Weekly* made Montross a sixth-team Freshman All-American last spring. Coming out of high school as the No. 1 center in the nation, he offended a lot of Hoosiers by opting for North Carolina instead of Indiana. His father and grandfather both played at Michigan.

Strengths: He possesses just about everything you'd want in a center—strength, coordination, mobility, good hands, and a dominating presence. Montross's patented turnaround jumper is silky smooth. He runs the floor like a small forward.

Weaknesses: At the coaching staff's request, Montross spent the off-season working on the following areas—offensive positioning, defensive rebounding, outlet passing, and free throws. With only one season under his belt, he's still rough around the edges.

Analysis: The best is definitely yet to come. Sticking to his 13-man substitution pattern, Dean Smith brought Montross along slowly. With more minutes, look for him to be far more productive.

COLLEGE STATISTICS

	G	FGP	FTP	RPG	APG	PPG
NC	90-91 35	.587	.612	4.2	0.3	5.8
Totals	35	.587	.612	4.2	0.3	5.8

ALONZO MOURNING
School: Georgetown
Year: Senior
Position: Center/Forward
Height: 6'10" **Weight:** 240
Birthplace: Chesapeake, VA

```
PLAYER SUMMARY
Will .......................regain star status
Can't...................afford a slow start
Expect ............intimidating defense
Don't Expect............1990-91 repeat
```

Background: A strained left arch sidelined Mourning for nine games early last season. He garnered All-Big East accolades in 1989-90 and was named the Big East's best defender as a freshman. Coming out of high school, he inspired Patrick Ewing and Lew Alcindor comparisons.

Strengths: Active and quick for a big man, Mourning can do it all in the low post. A pure shooter, he shot 52 percent from the field and 79 percent from the stripe last winter. Defensively, his mere presence can turn a game around.

Weaknesses: After injuring his foot, Mourning never got back on track during the 1990-91 season. He's not as dominant in the paint as he was as a freshman. Mysteriously, his usual intensity and aggressiveness were missing last year.

Analysis: While it doesn't appear he'll ever become the can't-miss Hall of Famer everyone predicted, Mourning is still an outstanding player. Without Dikembe Mutombo, he'll have to assume more of the offensive load.

COLLEGE STATISTICS

	G	FGP	FTP	RPG	APG	PPG
GEOR 88-89	34	.527	.667	7.3	0.7	12.0
GEOR 89-90	31	.525	.783	8.5	1.2	16.5
GEOR 90-91	23	.522	.793	7.7	1.1	15.8
Totals	88	.525	.752	7.8	1.0	14.5

TRACY MURRAY

School: UCLA
Year: Junior
Position: Center
Height: 6'8" **Weight:** 210
Birthdate: July 25, 1971
Birthplace: Los Angeles, CA

PLAYER SUMMARY	
Will	grab offensive boards
Can't	defend bigger centers
Expect	versatile play
Don't Expect	position change

Background: As a high school senior, Murray was the No. 1 prep scorer in America with 44.3 PPG. He started 18 games for UCLA as a freshman in 1989-90. Last year, he was a first-team all-conference selection, as his 22.8 PPG topped the Bruins in Pac-10 play.

Strengths: An outstanding 3-point shooter, Murray's versatile enough to excel at any position on the floor. He plays out of position at center because he's the most consistent rebounder on the team. He passes and dribbles like a guard on the break.

Weaknesses: Since he has only played the low post for a little over a year, Murray is still trying to adjust to the inside game. Some opponents are just too big and strong for him to handle. He's too valuable to the team to commit so many silly fouls.

Analysis: While Don MacLean gets most of the individual attention on the UCLA team, Murray is just as deserving. Few players can do so many different things for a team. He handles the ball and shoots well enough to play big guard in the NBA.

COLLEGE STATISTICS

	G	FGP	FTP	RPG	APG	PPG
UCLA 89-90	33	.442	.767	5.5	1.2	12.3
UCLA 90-91	32	.503	.794	6.7	1.3	21.2
Totals	65	.479	.784	6.1	1.3	16.7

SHAQUILLE O'NEAL

School: Louisiana St.
Year: Junior
Position: Center
Height: 7'1" **Weight:** 295
Birthdate: March 6, 1972
Birthplace: Newark, NJ

PLAYER SUMMARY	
Will	be drafted No. 1
Can't	avoid triple-teams
Expect	a Player of the Year
Don't Expect	passive play

Background: In 1990-91, O'Neal led the nation in rebounding and was a consensus first-team All-American. He's the only player in SEC history to lead the league in scoring, rebounding, field goal percentage, and blocks in the same season. He finished second in national Freshman of the Year voting in 1989-90.

Strengths: "The Wheel" scores like David Robinson, rebounds like Patrick Ewing, and blocks shots like Hakeem Olajuwon. He's an awesome physical specimen who plays with great aggressiveness. He doesn't turn 20 until March.

Weaknesses: None. Okay, okay, so maybe he could cut down on his turnovers and fouls, shoot a little better from the line, and add a few more offensive moves. But that's about it.

Analysis: Truly in a class of his own at the collegiate level, O'Neal's a bona fide franchise player who'll make the kind of immediate impact Robinson and Ewing did as NBA rookies. By the middle of the decade, he'll be the NBA's best (and richest) player.

COLLEGE STATISTICS

	G	FGP	FTP	RPG	APG	PPG
LSU 89-90	32	.573	.556	12.0	1.9	13.9
LSU 90-91	28	.628	.638	14.7	1.6	27.6
Totals	60	.607	.606	13.3	1.8	20.3

CHEROKEE PARKS

School: Duke
Year: Freshman
Position: Center
Height: 6'11" **Weight:** 210
Birthdate: October 11, 1972
Birthplace: Huntington Beach, CA

PLAYER SUMMARY	
Will	contribute in a hurry
Can't	muscle with centers
Expect	growing pains
Don't Expect	lack of effort

Background: A consensus first-team All-American, Parks averaged more than 28 points and 13 rebounds per game last season. Parks has been compared favorably to Bill Walton. Nicknamed "Chief," he's one-sixteenth Cherokee Indian.

Strengths: Parks is a fierce competitor who plays with a lot of enthusiasm. He can shoot from inside or out, handle the ball, and pass the ball. At 6'11", his mobility and quickness allows him to do things players six inches shorter can't do. He possesses a lethal turnaround jumper from the baseline.

Weaknesses: Parks, a little on the thin side, isn't accustomed to banging bodies with some of the behemoths who roam free in the ACC. He has to learn to hold his ground defensively. A pre-law major and a fine student, Parks has plenty of other interests.

Analysis: Although Blue Devil coach Mike Krzyzewski prefers to bring freshmen along slowly, Parks is talented and mature enough to make an immediate impact. He's got a memorable name and an even more memorable game.

ANTHONY PEELER

School: Missouri
Year: Senior
Position: Guard
Height: 6'4" **Weight:** 203
Birthdate: November 25, 1969
Birthplace: Kansas City, MO

PLAYER SUMMARY	
Will	eclipse 20 PPG
Can't	play team ball
Expect	beautiful moves
Don't Expect	lots of desire

Background: Despite missing nine games last year due to grades, Peeler was named second-team All-Big Eight by AP. He posted career-best averages in points and rebounds. In 1989-90, Peeler became the first Missouri sophomore since 1953 to reap first-team all-conference honors.

Strengths: A sweet-shooting southpaw who can bury a trey or dart inside, Peeler is the best all-around athlete in the Big Eight. A fantastic leaper, he possesses Michael Jordan-like hang time. A gifted passer, he's dished out more than 100 assists in each of the past three years.

Weaknesses: Without the ball in his hands, he's not much of a factor. Peeler needs to grow up, become more of a team player, and maintain better focus on the floor. He hasn't improved since the midpoint of his sophomore season.

Analysis: Peeler has the raw ability to be a first-round NBA draft choice. Sadly, he doesn't have the heart or the desire. Until he stands back and takes a serious look at himself, his vast talents will be wasted.

COLLEGE STATISTICS

	G	FGP	FTP	RPG	APG	PPG
MO 88-89	36	.504	.754	3.7	2.8	10.1
MO 89-90	31	.446	.769	5.4	5.8	16.8
MO 90-91	21	.475	.768	6.2	5.0	19.4
Totals	88	.470	.765	4.9	4.4	14.7

WESLEY PERSON

School: Auburn
Year: Sophomore
Position: Guard/Forward
Height: 6'4" **Weight:** 170
Birthdate: March 28, 1971
Birthplace: Crenshaw, AL

PLAYER SUMMARY	
Will	run and gun
Can't	score consistently
Expect	gradual improvement
Don't Expect	great defense

Background: A *Basketball Weekly* first-team Freshman All-American last year, Person paced the Tigers in minutes, blocked shots, and dunks. He was the team's second-leading scorer. He chalked up three 50-point games in high school. His older brother Chuck stars for the Indiana Pacers.

Strengths: The best pure athlete on the roster, Person can play small forward or either guard slot. He's a superb ball-handler, an even better passer, and he loves the transition game. Person's a dynamite outside shooter who has the wiry toughness and leaping ability to score and rebound inside.

Weaknesses: Defending some of the SEC's top small forwards began to take its toll on Person late last year. Although his offense is far more refined than his defense, he's too inconsistent—31 points one game (Tulane) and 11 the next (Alabama).

Analysis: A la Chuck, you don't know which Wesley Person is going to show up on any given night. He's got oodles of talent. Now he has to learn how to use it properly over the course of an entire game.

COLLEGE STATISTICS

	G	FGP	FTP	RPG	APG	PPG
AUB 90-91	26	.471	.765	5.7	1.8	15.4
Totals	26	.471	.765	5.7	1.8	15.4

BRENT PRICE

School: Oklahoma
Year: Senior
Position: Guard
Height: 6'1" **Weight:** 175
Birthdate: December 9, 1968
Birthplace: Enid, OK

PLAYER SUMMARY	
Will	strip an opponent
Can't	play consistently
Expect	heady basketball
Don't Expect	bashful shooting

Background: Price led the Sooners last year in steals and assists and was second in scoring. It was his first season at Oklahoma after transferring from South Carolina, where he played for two years. His brother Mark is an All-Star guard for the Cleveland Cavaliers.

Strengths: Price is a dangerous 3-point shooter and almost automatic from the stripe. He's a good ball-handler whose deceiving quickness allows him to penetrate. He has a wealth of basketball smarts and is a good defender one-on-one.

Weaknesses: Sometimes he tries to do too much on both ends of the court, which leads to foul problems. That takes him out of his rhythm and is one reason why he tends to disappear for extended periods during some games.

Analysis: Price is one of the best pure shooters in the country. He possesses many of Mark's best attributes—shooting, distributing, and intelligence. If he can drain his perimeter jumper a little more consistently, he has an outside chance of joining his brother in the pros.

COLLEGE STATISTICS

	G	FGP	FTP	RPG	APG	PPG
SCAR 87-88	29	.460	.857	1.6	2.7	10.7
SCAR 88-89	30	.490	.844	2.5	4.3	14.4
OKLA 90-91	35	.416	.838	3.6	5.5	17.5
Totals	94	.449	.830	2.6	4.2	14.4

JOE RHETT
School: South Carolina
Year: Senior
Position: Forward
Height: 6'8" **Weight:** 205
Birthdate: May 2, 1970
Birthplace: Columbia, SC

PLAYER SUMMARY	
Will	take good shots
Can't	play rugged inside
Expect	15 PPG, 8 RPG
Don't Expect	a quitter

Background: Rhett managed nearly seven boards and 13 points per game as a junior. As a sophomore, his season was cut short because of a heart irregularity and a pacemaker was installed. He enjoyed a fine freshman campaign and became only the sixth frosh ever named to the Metro all-tournament team.

Strengths: He's very quick and is a good shooter facing the basket, a la Alex English. He has range up to 18 feet. Rhett is well versed in the fundamentals of the game, taking only high-percentage shots and rarely turning the ball over. His incredibly positive attitude has caught on with his teammates.

Weaknesses: He's still not a polished inside player. He needs to further develop his post-play and crash the boards harder. Last season, he struggled from the free throw line.

Analysis: Rhett continues to be one of the best comeback stories in sports. In his first season with the pacemaker, he was third on the team in minutes and tops in rebounding. You won't find a tougher competitor.

COLLEGE STATISTICS

	G	FGP	FTP	RPG	APG	PPG
SCAR 88-89	30	.563	.700	4.4	1.0	7.1
SCAR 89-90	22	.485	.687	7.9	2.0	11.0
SCAR 90-91	33	.538	.584	6.9	1.5	12.6
Totals	85	.526	.636	6.3	1.4	10.3

JAMES ROBINSON
School: Alabama
Year: Sophomore
Position: Guard
Height: 6'2" **Weight:** 175
Birthdate: August 31, 1970
Birthplace: Jackson, MS

PLAYER SUMMARY	
Will	score his points
Can't	pass up open shots
Expect	hard-nosed play
Don't Expect	assists

Background: A high school phenom who scored nearly 41 per game, Robinson sat out a year at 'Bama because of questions concerning his entrance-exam scores. He got a favorable ruling in arbitration and was given four years of eligibility. The Tide's leading scorer last season, Robinson earned *Basketball Weekly* first-team Freshman All-America honors.

Strengths: He's a gifted athlete who has NBA 3-point range on his jumper. Robinson's other assets are his cougar-like quickness, his toughness, and his jumping ability. A lethal offensive player, he's virtually unstoppable when he gets on a roll.

Weaknesses: Robinson missed a whole year of competitive basketball, so he fell behind from a maturity standpoint. At this stage, he's too prone to foul trouble.

Analysis: In many respects, he plays a lot like Hersey Hawkins. He's got the same shooting stroke and the ability to create his own shot. Robinson will be a big star for the Crimson Tide and a big headache for opposing teams.

COLLEGE STATISTICS

	G	FGP	FTP	RPG	APG	PPG
ALA 90-91	33	.470	.699	3.9	1.2	16.8
Totals	33	.470	.699	3.9	1.2	16.8

RODNEY ROGERS

School: Wake Forest
Year: Sophomore
Position: Forward
Height: 6'7" **Weight:** 235
Birthdate: June 20, 1971
Birthplace: Durham, NC

PLAYER SUMMARY	
Will	continue to improve
Can't	be pushed around
Expect	awesome dunks
Don't Expect	immaturity

Background: Rogers earned national Freshman of the Year honors from *Basketball Weekly* after a remarkable first season. He led the Deacons in scoring, rebounding, field goal percentage, and steals. Rogers was a second-team All-ACC selection. As a senior in high school, he was North Carolina's Player of the Year and a McDonald's All-American. He comes from a very poor family.

Strengths: Rogers plain outmuscles his opponents, and his spectacular dunks inspire his teammates. Rogers also has a feathery touch from outside. He's very mature for his age and has great court savvy.

Weaknesses: There aren't many. He did make some of the usual rookie mistakes: He didn't always protect the ball like he should, he often didn't switch fast enough on defense, and he committed some senseless fouls.

Analysis: The sky's the limit for Rogers. He's an unbelievable talent. Another year of experience will make him a legitimate All-America candidate. He might land in the NBA before his four years are up.

COLLEGE STATISTICS

	G	FGP	FTP	RPG	APG	PPG
WF	90-91	30	.570	.669	7.9	1.5	16.3
Totals		30	.570	.669	7.9	1.5	16.3

STEVE ROGERS

School: Alabama St.
Year: Senior
Position: Guard
Height: 6'5" **Weight:** 185
Birthdate: July 30, 1968
Birthplace: Montgomery, AL

PLAYER SUMMARY	
Will	score from everywhere
Can't	be covered one-on-one
Expect	close to 30 PPG
Don't Expect	great intensity

Background: Rogers averaged more than 29 points and seven boards a game last year while winning Southwestern Athletic Conference Player of the Year honors. After transferring from Middle Tennessee State following his freshman year, he was the SWAC's Newcomer of the Year in 1989-90 on the strength of nearly 30 PPG.

Strengths: He handles the ball well enough to play either guard slot. He's a good passer, plays tough defense, and is a student of the game. Mostly what he can do, though, is score, score, score.

Weaknesses: Sometimes, in the midst of the double- and triple-teams opponents throw at him, he'll try to force the action. Also, since he is so much better than most SWAC players, he suffers from occasional mental lapses.

Analysis: Rogers just loves to play ball, and it shows on the court. For someone who is always the opponents' focus, he is remarkably consistent. Expect him to be a first-round draft choice, thanks to his incredible scoring ability.

COLLEGE STATISTICS

	G	FGP	FTP	RPG	APG	PPG
ASU	89-90	28	.522	.732	6.6	3.8	29.7
ASU	90-91	29	.500	.753	7.1	4.2	29.4
Totals		57	.511	.743	6.9	4.0	29.5

SEAN ROOKS

School: Arizona
Year: Senior
Position: Center
Height: 6'11" **Weight:** 245
Birthdate: September 9, 1969
Birthplace: New York, NY

PLAYER SUMMARY	
Will	score inside
Can't	dominate the glass
Expect	dazzling post moves
Don't Expect	an intimidator

Background: One of the Wildcats' three towers along with Ed Stokes and Brian Williams last year, Rooks scored in double figures and led the team in blocks. A Pac-10 All-Freshman selection in 1988-89, Rooks has shot better than 53 percent in each of his three seasons. He was redshirted in 1987-88.

Strengths: Rooks is a very effective inside scorer thanks to a variety of low-post moves. He makes good decisions with the ball, taking the high-percentage shots when they're there and dishing off when they're not.

Weaknesses: He still isn't the consistent rebounding and defensive threat he should be. Rooks has been accused of having poor work habits for much of his career and a tendency to be in less than top physical condition.

Analysis: This will be a very important year for Rooks. His biggest obstacle is himself. He needs to step up his play on the boards and lose his reputation for being lazy if he's to become the lottery pick many believe he could be.

COLLEGE STATISTICS

	G	FGP	FTP	RPG	APG	PPG
ARIZ 88-89	32	.598	.615	2.8	0.6	5.6
ARIZ 89-90	31	.532	.708	4.9	1.0	12.7
ARIZ 90-91	35	.562	.658	5.7	1.2	11.9
Totals	98	.557	.672	4.5	0.9	10.1

BRENT SCOTT

School: Rice
Year: Junior
Position: Center
Height: 6'9" **Weight:** 245
Birthdate: June 15, 1971
Birthplace: Jackson, MI

PLAYER SUMMARY	
Will	bang inside
Can't	connect at the line
Expect	high FG pct.
Don't Expect	blocked shots

Background: Following up on his Southwest Conference Freshman of the Year season, Scott led the league in rebounding as a sophomore and earned second-team All-SWC honors. He was an important member of the gold-medal-winning U.S. Junior National Team in 1990. Scott starred at Everett High School in Lansing, Michigan—Magic Johnson's alma mater.

Strengths: He's a banger who's also displayed a soft shooting touch. An excellent passer, Scott usually makes the right decisions with the ball. He shoots for a high percentage and is a very good offensive rebounder.

Weaknesses: Scott's had some miserable stretches at the line, where he's streaky. He needs to turn more of his weight into muscle. He'll often wait until the second half to really get into the flow of a game.

Analysis: Scott was a very good freshman player, and he showed marked improvement as a sophomore. If he continues to progress at his current pace, he'll be the most dangerous inside player in the SWC this year.

COLLEGE STATISTICS

	G	FGP	FTP	RPG	APG	PPG
RICE 88-89	28	.502	.524	8.2	0.8	15.3
RICE 90-91	30	.580	.549	10.1	3.1	16.9
Totals	58	.541	.538	9.2	2.0	16.1

MALIK SEALY

School: St. John's
Year: Senior
Position: Forward
Height: 6'8" **Weight:** 195
Birthdate: February 1, 1970
Birthplace: Bronx, NY

PLAYER SUMMARY	
Will	be All-Big East
Can't	play half-speed
Expect	tenacious defense
Don't Expect	high 3-point pct.

Background: A superstar at powerhouse Tolentine High School in the Bronx, Sealy was named New York state's Mr. Basketball for 1987-88. He's scored more than 1,700 points in three years at St. John's and earned first-team All-Big East honors last year. He's started 97 straight games since enrolling at St. John's.

Strengths: Sealy is very quick and surprisingly strong for his thin frame. He's as complete a small forward as you'll find, with good hands and anticipation on defense and the ability to take a game over with his scoring and rebounding.

Weaknesses: His jumper still needs work, but it has improved slightly each year. Sealy needs to become a more consistent threat from outside. A few extra pounds couldn't hurt his inside game.

Analysis: Sealy is a top All-America candidate this year and the Redmen's best forward since Walter Berry. He's a pleasure to watch because he's so silky smooth. Check out his defense. He's one of the top pickpockets in the country.

COLLEGE STATISTICS

	G	FGP	FTP	RPG	APG	PPG
STJ	88-89	31	.489	.558	6.4	2.2	12.9
STJ	89-90	34	.525	.746	6.9	1.7	18.1
STJ	90-91	32	.492	.743	7.7	1.7	22.1
Totals		97	.502	.705	7.0	1.8	17.8

VERNEL SINGLETON

School: Louisiana St.
Year: Senior
Position: Forward
Height: 6'7" **Weight:** 202
Birthdate: May 11, 1970
Birthplace: Natchez, MS

PLAYER SUMMARY	
Will	drive the lane
Can't	avoid foul trouble
Expect	tough defense
Don't Expect	3-pointers

Background: Singleton was selected 1990-91 first-team All-SEC by the league's coaches on the strength of his solid but unspectacular scoring and rebounding. A starter in 27 games as a sophomore, Singleton earned a spot on the All-SEC freshman team while playing out of position at center.

Strengths: He's got great leaping ability and agility. He's also versatile, having started at center and forward. Singleton is a good defensive player thanks to his quickness, anticipation, and knowledge of the game. He will usually draw the opponent's top scorer.

Weaknesses: He does have a tendency to get into foul trouble. He has a big enough wing span to block more shots than he does. On offense, the range on his jumper is limited.

Analysis: One of the nation's more underrated players, Singleton complements superstar teammate Shaquille O'Neal very well. He can drive the lane like a guard and is a bankable second option inside. His play will only get better as a senior.

COLLEGE STATISTICS

	G	FGP	FTP	RPG	APG	PPG
LSU	88-89	32	.571	.780	7.8	0.8	10.8
LSU	89-90	32	.590	.584	4.8	0.8	8.4
LSU	90-91	30	.518	.729	5.9	1.6	15.2
Totals		94	.552	.703	6.2	1.1	11.4

REGINALD SLATER

School: Wyoming
Year: Senior
Position: Forward
Height: 6'7" **Weight:** 245
Birthdate: August 27, 1970
Birthplace: Houston, TX

PLAYER SUMMARY	
Will	get to the line
Can't	hit from outside
Expect	high FG pct.
Don't Expect	inconsistency

Background: Slater concluded his junior year as a member of the All-WAC first team—the second straight season he garnered such honors. Last winter, he broke his own school record for rebounds in a season with 331. Slater was the leading rebounder on a U.S. All-Star team that toured South America in 1990.

Strengths: Slater is the model of consistency. He's also a force inside who makes the most of his scoring opportunities. His wide body allows him to play bigger than his 6'7" frame, and he is extremely determined on the court.

Weaknesses: Being such an aggressive player, he has a penchant for foul trouble. He also needs to cut down on his turnovers and mental mistakes. He has a hard time staying focused.

Analysis: After playing on a sore left knee much of the year, Slater had it scoped in April. He should be even more dominant in 1991-92 with that problem resolved. WAC beware. This isn't a guy you want to mess with in a dark alley (or in the low post).

COLLEGE STATISTICS

	G	FGP	FTP	RPG	APG	PPG
WYO 88-89	31	.564	.598	6.8	0.2	6.2
WYO 89-90	29	.578	.732	11.3	1.0	16.7
WYO 90-91	32	.605	.760	10.3	1.2	19.2
Totals	92	.589	.718	9.5	0.8	14.0

CHRIS SMITH

School: Connecticut
Year: Senior
Position: Guard
Height: 6'2" **Weight:** 182
Birthdate: May 17, 1970
Birthplace: Bridgeport, CT

PLAYER SUMMARY	
Will	take a lot of shots
Can't	pass up bad ones
Expect	20-plus PPG
Don't Expect	much bench time

Background: A prep All-American who averaged more than 28 PPG, Smith gained national notoriety when the Huskies made the first of two consecutive Sweet 16 trips his sophomore season. A two-time second-team All-Big East selection, Smith was a key member of the 1990 U.S. National Team that competed in the Goodwill Games and World Championships.

Strengths: Smith's versatile enough to play either guard slot and he's a tireless workhorse. He can handle the ball well and is a deadly 3-point shooter. His quick hands collect a lot of steals.

Weaknesses: He's never seen a shot he didn't like. Simply put, Smith needs to show more discretion in his shot selection. He also needs to be more consistent from the stripe.

Analysis: Smith should earn plenty of All-America consideration. He'll be the sparkplug of a team that has a chance to win it all. Expect to see him on the floor almost every minute of every game and expect him to become more aware of his teammates.

COLLEGE STATISTICS

	G	FGP	FTP	RPG	APG	PPG
CONN 88-89	29	.405	.565	2.8	3.0	9.9
CONN 89-90	37	.417	.811	2.5	3.6	17.2
CONN 90-91	31	.439	.719	2.9	3.4	18.9
Totals	97	.423	.743	2.7	3.3	15.5

ELMORE SPENCER

School: UNLV
Year: Senior
Position: Center
Height: 7'0" **Weight:** 265
Birthdate: December 6, 1969
Birthplace: Atlanta, GA

PLAYER SUMMARY	
Will	block shots
Can't	shoot FTs
Expect	physical play
Don't Expect	outside shots

Background: A touted high school star, Spencer enrolled at Georgia, where he took a medical redshirt year after suffering symptoms of manic-depression. He played well in 11 games for the Bulldogs in 1988-89 before suffering a foot injury. He transferred to Connors State Junior College and promptly led the school to a 1989-90 national title. Spencer came off the bench to play in 31 of 35 games for UNLV last season.

Strengths: He's a man-child who can dominate in the paint. Spencer's impossible to move in the blocks and he has good touch in close. He's got a nice overall feel for the game.

Weaknesses: His Achilles' heel is free throw shooting, where he shot 47 percent last year. Spencer's shooting range is limited to about eight feet. He's a bit overweight.

Analysis: Spencer should improve his pro stock as UNLV's top inside force. If he stays in shape, improves his shooting, and polishes his raw low-post moves, he'll make some NBA team very happy.

COLLEGE STATISTICS

	G	FGP	FTP	RPG	APG	PPG
GEOR 88-89	11	.641	.500	5.3	1.9	12.0
UNLV 90-91	31	.522	.471	4.0	1.2	6.4
Totals	42	.566	.480	4.3	1.4	7.8

MATT STEIGENGA

School: Michigan St.
Year: Senior
Position: Forward
Height: 6'7" **Weight:** 225
Birthdate: March 27, 1970
Birthplace: Grand Rapids, MI

PLAYER SUMMARY	
Will	jump to the rafters
Can't	erase expectations
Expect	mispronounced name
Don't Expect	a banger

Background: Michigan's Mr. Basketball in high school, Steigenga won the slam-dunk contest at the McDonald's All-American Game in 1988. He has gone on to start all but one game in his three years in East Lansing. An academic All-American, he was an honorable-mention All-Big Ten performer last winter.

Strengths: Steigenga is a phenomenal athlete whose jumping ability gets him out of a lot of tough situations. He's at his best on the fastbreak, where he is one of the best finishers in basketball. He possesses a sweet shooting touch.

Weaknesses: He's often accused of not living up to his ability. He can disappear during a game, raising questions about his aggressiveness. He lacks consistency at both ends of the floor.

Analysis: Steigenga is a very good player, but numerous other interests make improving his game a low priority. Basketball comes so easy to him that he can rely on natural ability. If he gets serious, he can be one of the top players in the country.

COLLEGE STATISTICS

	G	FGP	FTP	RPG	APG	PPG
MSU 88-89	33	.558	.740	4.5	1.4	8.7
MSU 89-90	34	.587	.779	3.5	1.9	10.4
MSU 90-91	30	.525	.700	4.9	2.1	12.6
Totals	97	.555	.739	4.3	1.8	10.5

BRYANT STITH

School: Virginia
Year: Senior
Position: Forward
Height: 6'5" **Weight:** 204
Birthdate: December 10, 1970
Birthplace: Emporia, VA

PLAYER SUMMARY	
Will	find a way to score
Can't	always hit the 3
Expect	20 PPG; 7 RPG
Don't Expect	many assists

Background: In 1990-91, Stith was a first-team All-ACC selection for the second consecutive year. He also earned numerous honorable-mention All-America honors. In high school, he was Virginia's AA Player of the Year as a junior and senior.

Strengths: Stith is an accomplished scorer and rebounder. His athleticism and intelligence make him a good one-on-one defender against an opponent's top scoring small forward or big guard. He can score from inside or out and goes to the offensive glass as well as any small forward in the ACC.

Weaknesses: As the first option in the offense, Stith needs to make better decisions on when to shoot and when to give it up. He needs to distribute the ball better and be more consistent with his jumper.

Analysis: Stith enters 1991 as a legitimate All-America candidate. He has a nose for the ball and versatility that is rare among college players. Watch for him on TV games. That's when he performs his best late-game heroics.

COLLEGE STATISTICS

	G	FGP	FTP	RPG	APG	PPG
VA	88-89	33	.548	.769	6.5	1.5	15.5
VA	89-90	32	.481	.777	6.9	1.7	20.8
VA	90-91	33	.471	.791	6.2	1.2	19.8
Totals		98	.495	.779	6.5	1.5	18.7

ED STOKES

School: Arizona
Year: Junior
Position: Forward/Center
Height: 7'0" **Weight:** 245
Birthdate: September 3, 1971
Birthplace: Syracuse, NY

PLAYER SUMMARY	
Will	block shots
Can't	hit his FTs
Expect	improved numbers
Don't Expect	inside strength

Background: Stokes followed up a Pac-10 All-Freshman season by averaging less than a half-dozen points and rebounds in only 17 minutes per game last year. He started just 11 games and was the third member of Arizona's triple towers (along with Sean Rooks and Brian Williams). He was a dominant rebounder and shot-blocker as a high school senior. His father is an orthopedic surgeon.

Strengths: He's very quick for a big man and possesses outstanding athletic ability. He's been a consistently dependable back-up to Rooks and Williams. He's a skilled shot-blocker who shows an abundance of court smarts.

Weaknesses: Stokes needs to improve his inside game. He doesn't have enough moves around the basket and lacks great upper-body strength. He needs to be more aggressive and show more intensity.

Analysis: Stokes will become a full-time starter this year. Although he was a disappointment as a sophomore, he has all the tools needed to be a star. The only question is how badly he wants it.

COLLEGE STATISTICS

	G	FGP	FTP	RPG	APG	PPG
ARIZ	89-90	29	.599	.564	4.6	0.3	8.0
ARIZ	90-91	34	.470	.538	4.3	0.4	5.9
Totals		63	.532	.551	4.4	0.3	6.9

EVERICK SULLIVAN

School: Louisville
Year: Senior
Position: Guard/Forward
Height: 6'5" **Weight:** 190
Birthdate: July 25, 1970
Birthplace: Simpsonville, SC

PLAYER SUMMARY	
Will	light it up
Can't	resist a dunk
Expect	a team leader
Don't Expect	steady play

Background: Louisville's second-leading scorer last year, Sullivan led the team in 3-pointers (54, a school record) for the second straight season. He was the Cards' top reserve scorer as a frosh. As a high school senior, he was a *Parade* magazine All-American.

Strengths: Sullivan can light up the scoreboard. Versatile enough to play guard or forward, he can score by posting up smaller guards inside or burying the outside jumper. He's a gifted athlete with great leaping ability.

Weaknesses: He's too streaky with his scoring. While Sullivan has improved his assist-to-turnover ratio, he's still too careless with the ball. He's not well schooled defensively.

Analysis: Sullivan is a talented offensive player who needs to increase his focus at the other end of the floor. He's shown steady improvement in most phases of his game over the years. With LaBradford Smith graduated to the NBA, Sullivan will shoulder much of the Cards' scoring load.

COLLEGE STATISTICS

		G	FGP	FTP	RPG	APG	PPG
LOU	88-89	32	.462	.603	2.8	2.6	8.5
LOU	89-90	35	.458	.681	4.5	2.9	12.7
LOU	90-91	30	.450	.680	4.0	3.5	15.6
Totals		97	.456	.661	3.7	3.0	12.2

DEON THOMAS

School: Illinois
Year: Sophomore
Position: Forward
Height: 6'9" **Weight:** 213
Birthdate: February 24, 1971
Birthplace: Chicago, IL

PLAYER SUMMARY	
Will	control the boards
Can't	step outside
Expect	more improvement
Don't Expect	low FG pct.

Background: Thomas scored more points than any freshman in Illinois history last season and earned third-team All-Big Ten honors. Thomas, who was Illinois' Mr. Basketball in 1989, took a redshirt year while the NCAA probed allegations that the Illini used illegal inducements in his recruitment. While the school did go on probation, infractions did not involve Thomas.

Strengths: He's a great inside player who can score, rebound, and block shots. That's because he's exceptionally quick around the basket, has great leaping ability, and has a big wing span. He also runs the floor well.

Weaknesses: Thomas is still inexperienced and a little ragged from his redshirt year. He needs to get more aggressive and improve his shooting touch.

Analysis: Thomas's immediate impact surprised a lot of people last season. Considering what he'd been through off the court in the past year, he showed remarkable poise and maturity. There's no reason to expect a sophomore slump. An All-Big Ten berth is far more likely.

COLLEGE STATISTICS

		G	FGP	FTP	RPG	APG	PPG
ILL	90-91	30	.577	.643	6.8	0.6	15.1
Totals		30	.577	.643	6.8	0.6	15.1

CHANDLER THOMPSON
School: Ball St.
Year: Senior
Position: Guard
Height: 6'4" **Weight:** 220
Birthdate: February 2, 1970
Birthplace: Muncie, IN

PLAYER SUMMARY	
Will	get to the line
Can't	perfect his jumper
Expect	spectacular dunks
Don't Expect	slow feet

Background: The most consistent player in the Mid-American Conference, Thompson earned first-team all-league honors last season. He ranked among league leaders in almost every offensive category. A Prop 48 victim in 1988-89, he received All-MAC honorable mention as a sophomore. As a prep senior, Thompson finished third in the voting for Indiana's Mr. Basketball award.

Strengths: He's very quick and has great leaping ability. Thompson is a solid rebounder who creates points for himself off the offensive boards. He can also pick your pocket and get to the other end of the court in a hurry.

Weaknesses: He has to improve his jump shot, which was erratic last year. Also, his ability to draw fouls was negated somewhat by a mediocre free throw percentage.

Analysis: After shaking off all the Prop 48 rust, Thompson is becoming the player that prompted Rick Majerus (his former coach) to say: "He's the best player I've ever recruited, including Butch Lee or anybody else at Marquette."

COLLEGE STATISTICS
	G	FGP	FTP	RPG	APG	PPG
BALL 89-90	33	.488	.746	5.6	1.8	11.7
BALL 90-91	31	.449	.669	6.4	3.3	15.4
Totals	64	.466	.716	6.0	2.5	13.5

KENDRICK WARREN
School: Virginia Commonwealth
Year: Sophomore
Position: Forward
Height: 6'8" **Weight:** 215
Birthdate: May 27, 1971
Birthplace: Richmond, VA

PLAYER SUMMARY	
Will	dominate the paint
Can't	shoot FTs
Expect	double-doubles
Don't Expect	outside touch

Background: Last year's impressive scoring and rebounding totals earned Warren first-team All-Sun Belt honors and landed him on *Basketball Weekly's* All-Freshman second team. As a senior in high school, he was Virginia's Group AAA Player of the Year. Some say he's the best player to ever come out of Richmond.

Strengths: Warren brings powerful leaping ability and strong inside moves to the court. He's a good passer and tough on defense, where an opponent is likely to get a shot or two stuffed back in his face. Very mobile, he can also put the ball on the floor.

Weaknesses: Mostly because of inexperience, Warren turns the ball over too often while trying to make difficult plays. He commits a lot of fouls and can't shoot free throws (51 percent).

Analysis: With continued development in the next three years, Warren could end his career as the Rams' best all-time player. He's so skilled and aggressive inside that any sort of perimeter shot would make him nearly impossible to defend.

COLLEGE STATISTICS
	G	FGP	FTP	RPG	APG	PPG
VCOM 90-91	31	.541	.506	8.5	1.6	15.7
Totals	31	.541	.506	8.5	1.6	15.7

CLARENCE WEATHERSPOON

School: Southern Mississippi
Year: Senior
Position: Forward
Height: 6'7" **Weight:** 230
Birthdate: September 8, 1970
Birthplace: Crawford, MS

PLAYER SUMMARY	
Will	clean the glass
Can't	be pushed around
Expect	Charles Barkley type
Don't Expect	bad shots

Background: Weatherspoon won his second straight Metro Conference Player of the Year award in 1990-91 thanks to his dominant inside play. After three seasons, "Spoon" leads USM in career blocks and ranks No. 4 in rebounds.

Strengths: He's extremely strong and can bang inside with anybody, even seven-footers. His post defense is good and he plays much bigger than his 6'7" frame. Weatherspoon takes good, high-percentage shots and can even hit the occasional trey.

Weaknesses: The only thing his game needs is a little more refinement. A few more offensive moves and a better understanding of help defense would do wonders. He could also stand to be more surly on the court.

Analysis: You can't watch him without thinking of Charles Barkley. With the departure of three USM starters, Weatherspoon will have to carry more of the load offensively and will face more trick defenses. He should still come away with his third straight conference Player of the Year award.

COLLEGE STATISTICS

	G	FGP	FTP	RPG	APG	PPG
SMIS 88-89	27	.545	.590	10.7	1.1	14.7
SMIS 89-90	32	.605	.691	11.6	0.9	17.8
SMIS 90-91	29	.589	.745	12.2	2.3	17.8
Totals	88	.582	.678	11.5	1.4	16.9

CHRIS WEBBER

School: Michigan
Year: Freshman
Position: Center/Forward
Height: 6'9" **Weight:** 235
Birthdate: March 1, 1973
Birthplace: Detroit, MI

PLAYER SUMMARY	
Will	play with emotion
Can't	lead team to title
Expect	a well-rounded kid
Don't Expect	instant success

Background: Generally regarded as the nation's top high school player, Webber led Detroit Country Day to its third consecutive state title last season. He was named co-MVP of the McDonald's All-American Game. He's a four-time all-state performer who attracted more attention than any other Michigan prepster since Magic Johnson. An avid chess player, Webber's also an outstanding student.

Strengths: He dominates in the low blocks. Webber scores, rebounds, and blocks shots from the paint and shoots well enough from the perimeter to make an immediate impact. He will pass as well as any big man in the Big Ten.

Weaknesses: His folks sent him to Country Day (a prestigious, private, suburban school) to get a good education, not to hone his basketball skills. He hasn't faced top-flight competition on a regular basis.

Analysis: While Webber will step into a starting role as a freshman, Wolverine fans must be patient. He'll likely need a year or two of polish before his awesome physical skills command bona fide All-America consideration.

ROBERT WERDANN

School: St. John's
Year: Senior
Position: Center
Height: 6'11" **Weight:** 240
Birthdate: September 12, 1969
Birthplace: Queens, NY

PLAYER SUMMARY	
Will	pound the boards
Can't	avoid fouls
Expect	hard-nosed play
Don't Expect	finesse

Background: The Redmen's top rebounder and shot-blocker over the past two seasons, Werdann was a standout in last year's NCAA tournament. He toured Europe with the NIT All-Star Team in 1989. In high school, Werdann counted Kenny Anderson among his teammates at Archbishop Malloy in New York City.

Strengths: Werdann has become a very aggressive player, especially on the boards. His low-post moves have drawn Kevin McHale comparisons. He's also a capable shot-blocker. He played the best basketball of his career last March.

Weaknesses: He doesn't always channel his aggressiveness correctly. Werdann gets into early foul trouble too often. He's fouled out of 19 games in his career. He still needs work on his defensive footwork, and he could use more offensive moves.

Analysis: Werdann showed a lot of improvement late last season. If he can be a little more consistent, he can be the dominant big man the Redmen have seen flashes of during the last three years. He certainly has all the tools.

COLLEGE STATISTICS

	G	FGP	FTP	RPG	APG	PPG
STJ	88-89	29	.495	.667	6.6	1.3	7.9
STJ	89-90	34	.504	.667	7.6	0.8	9.7
STJ	90-91	32	.494	.724	7.1	1.4	11.3
Totals		95	.498	.723	7.1	1.2	9.7

HENRY WILLIAMS

School: North Carolina-Charlotte
Year: Senior
Position: Guard
Height: 6'1" **Weight:** 170
Birthdate: June 6, 1970
Birthplace: Indianapolis, IN

PLAYER SUMMARY	
Will	slam it home
Can't	post up
Expect	25 PPG
Don't Expect	high FG pct.

Background: Williams captured Sun Belt Junior of the Year honors last winter on the strength of his 21.6 PPG. That'll go in the trophy case next to his Sophomore and Freshman of the Year awards. He was the first UNCC player to compete in the Olympic Festival (1989). Williams garnered first-team Freshman All-America honors from UPI.

Strengths: He's a great scorer who can light it up from anywhere, including NBA 3-point territory. He takes pride in his leadership skills and possesses the unique ability of making his teammates better.

Weaknesses: Williams's decision-making is questionable at times. Because he is constantly double- and triple-teamed, he throws up some ill-advised shots and is prone to some bad shooting nights.

Analysis: In 1991-92, his name should become more familiar to people outside Charlotte as the star of a team on the rise. In the 49ers' first year in the Metro Conference, they'll go as far as he takes them. He'll take his multiple skills to the NBA in the fall.

COLLEGE STATISTICS

	G	FGP	FTP	RPG	APG	PPG
NCC	88-89	29	.495	.796	3.6	2.7	17.4
NCC	89-90	30	.414	.831	3.5	4.1	21.0
NCC	90-91	27	.426	.833	3.0	2.0	21.6
Totals		86	.441	.825	3.4	3.0	20.0

WALT WILLIAMS

School: Maryland
Year: Senior
Position: Guard
Height: 6'8" **Weight:** 203
Birthdate: April 16, 1970
Birthplace: Temple Hills, MD

PLAYER SUMMARY	
Will	pick your pocket
Can't	play center
Expect	an All-American
Don't Expect	selfish play

Background: Although Williams missed half the 1990-91 season with a broken leg, his scoring average was the highest for a Terp player in four years. As a sophomore, he was among the ACC leaders in assists, steals, and blocks. He worked his way into the starting lineup eight games into his freshman season.

Strengths: As a 6'8" point guard, size is his biggest weapon. He's also extremely versatile, having played four different positions at Maryland. Williams can rebound, defend, block shots, distribute, and nail the 3-pointer.

Weaknesses: The biggest concern is his durability. He has missed time because of injuries as a freshman and junior. Because of the extended layoff last year, he slumped as a shooter.

Analysis: Williams has pro scouts drooling, and has already drawn comparisons to Magic Johnson. He sees the floor well and his athleticism allows him to drive the lane and get the ball where it needs to be. If healthy, he could be the nation's premier point guard.

COLLEGE STATISTICS

	G	FGP	FTP	RPG	APG	PPG
MD	88-89 26	.441	.623	3.5	2.5	7.3
MD	89-90 33	.483	.776	4.2	4.5	12.7
MD	90-91 17	.449	.837	5.1	5.4	18.7
Totals	76	.461	.766	4.2	4.0	12.2

KENNY WOOD

School: Richmond
Year: Junior
Position: Forward
Height: 6'5" **Weight:** 230
Birthdate: March 27, 1971
Birthplace: Southampton, NY

PLAYER SUMMARY	
Will	keep improving
Can't	run the offense
Expect	points and boards
Don't Expect	blocked shots

Background: As a sophomore, Wood led the Spiders in rebounding and field goal percentage and made the All-Colonial Conference second team. In high school, he became New York's second-leading career scoring leader (behind Kenny Anderson) and the highest scorer in the state's public-school history. His brother Howard played for the Utah Jazz.

Strengths: Wood is a versatile performer who can either bang inside or stroke the outside jumper. Wood has good touch from the free throw line and doesn't force many bad shots.

Weaknesses: He doesn't run the floor well and lacks the ball-handling skills of many wing players. A lack of quickness occasionally gets him beat one-on-one.

Analysis: Like the team he plays for, Wood is a talented but little-known commodity. That should change when his name starts climbing the national scoring and rebounding charts. A bullish performer who never backs down, Wood possesses great all-around ability.

COLLEGE STATISTICS

	G	FGP	FTP	RPG	APG	PPG
RICH	89-90 29	.496	.581	3.9	0.6	5.1
RICH	90-91 32	.539	.792	7.0	1.3	14.3
Totals	61	.527	.732	5.6	1.0	10.0

ALABAMA

Conference: Southeastern
1990-91: 23-10, 4th SEC

1990-91 NCAAs: 2-1
Coach: Wimp Sanderson (241-110)

Opening Line: Despite catching fire in March and advancing to the Sweet 16 for the sixth time in Wimp Sanderson's 11 seasons, the Crimson Tide failed to live up to last year's lofty expectations. A lack of overall team chemistry resulted in an inconsistent regular season. The departure of forwards Melvin Cheatum (16.5 PPG) and Marcus Campbell and guards Gary Waites, Bryant Lancaster, and Marcus Jones leave some gaping holes for seven signees to fill.

Guard: After starting only four games a year ago, James Robinson (team-high 16.8 PPG) returns as the Tide's most potent perimeter scoring threat. Only a sophomore, he'll be an All-American before his college career is over. Juco transfers Dennis Miller and Elliot Washington will battle for Waites's lead-guard position.

Forward: Robert Horry and Latrell Sprewell give the Tide one of the SEC's top frontcourts. Horry is the team's top rebounder. In order to become a bona fide star, he needs to develop more of a mean streak. Sprewell is an explosive scorer. Juco transfer Andre Perry (remember the name) should help immediately, while freshman Jason Caffey needs some seasoning.

Center: Wide-body Marcus Webb (6'8", 268) will take up plenty of space in the middle. Consistency is his biggest problem. Limited offensively, his bulk alone makes him a better-than-average defender.

Analysis: The Crimson Tide never get the credit they rightfully deserve. Yet, every March they're in the thick of the NCAA tournament. Although Sanderson, "the man in plaid," has many questions to answer about the heavy turnover in personnel, Alabama shouldn't finish too far off the pace (maybe two or three games) in the SEC if Robinson and Horry play like they're capable.

1991-92 ROSTER

	POS	HT	YR	FGP	FTP	3-PT	RPG	APG	PPG
James Robinson	G	6'1"	So	.47	.70	64/153	3.9	1.2	16.8
Robert Horry	F	6'9"	Sr	.45	.80	33/98	8.1	1.8	11.9
Latrell Sprewell	G/F	6'4"	Sr	.51	.69	5/12	5.0	1.9	8.9
Marcus Webb	F/C	6'8"	Sr	.53	.59	—	4.8	0.6	5.5
Kenneth Rice	G	6'3"	Jr	.26	.75	2/9	0.3	—	1.8
Darby Rich	G/F	6'5"	Sr	.38	.25	0/1	1.0	0.1	0.5
Phillip Pearson	G	6'2"	So	.50	—	—	0.1	0.3	0.4
Jason Caffey	F	6'8"	Fr	—	—	—	—	—	—
Dennis Miller	G	5'11"	Jr	—	—	—	—	—	—
Bryan Passink	G	6'4"	Fr	—	—	—	—	—	—
Andre Perry	F	6'8"	Jr	—	—	—	—	—	—
Elliot Washington	G	6'0"	Jr	—	—	—	—	—	—

ARIZONA

Conference: Pac-10
1990-91: 28-7, 1st Pac-10

1990-91 NCAAs: 2-1
Coach: Lute Olson (371-162)

Opening Line: After advancing to the Sweet 16 in the NCAA tourney last year, Arizona has been struck with disasters. They've lost potential All-American Brian Williams (a junior entry in the NBA draft), sophomore guard Khalid Reeves (suspended for a year for alleged sexual misconduct), and junior guard Casey Schmidt (transfer). Their departures, along with that of senior Matt Muehlebach and disgruntled freshman Tony Clark, leaves Lute Olson with only nine scholarship players. Nonetheless, no one should shed any tears.

Guard: Although often outplayed by more athletic opponents, 6'2" Matt Othick is back to man the point. He's a coach on the floor. Swing man Chris Mills, a multi-dimensional threat, makes up for whatever Othick lacks in athletic ability. Kevin Dempsey's a slasher who should play a lot.

Forward: Wayne Womack and 7'0 Ed Stokes are the most likely starters.

Womack and this team's up-tempo offense are a perfect fit. Stokes detests the "soft" label he's acquired and has apparently vowed to do something about it. Swing man Deron Johnson and iron-pumping Kevin Flanagan will be counted on off the bench.

Center: Sean Rooks is the 'Cats' premier big man. Criticized for his lousy work habits early in his career, he's done an about-face. Ever since the coaching staff figured out how to tap into his vast potential, he's been a true force.

Analysis: Despite the absence of Williams and Reeves and an overall lack of depth, this club should finish on UCLA's heels in the Pac-10. Mills and Rooks will contend for All-America accolades. With Williams, a Final Four trek appeared possible. Without him, the Wildcats could still reach the round of eight.

1991-92 ROSTER

	POS	HT	YR	FGP	FTP	3-PT	RPG	APG	PPG
Chris Mills	G/F	6'6"	Jr	.52	.75	42/122	6.2	1.9	15.6
Sean Rooks	C/F	6'11"	Sr	.56	.66	2/4	5.7	1.2	11.9
Matt Othick	G	6'2"	Sr	.38	.79	48/134	2.4	5.2	7.8
Ed Stokes	C	7'0"	Jr	.47	.54	—	4.3	0.4	5.9
Wayne Womack	F	6'8"	Sr	.54	.62	0/1	2.8	0.7	5.8
Deron Johnson	G/F	6'6"	So	.52	.68	0/1	1.8	0.6	3.9
Kevin Flanagan	F	6'9"	So	.40	.39	—	1.2	0.3	1.5
Sean Allen	F	6'8"	Fr	—	—	—	—	—	—
Kevin Dempsey	G/F	6'6"	Fr	—	—	—	—	—	—
Ray Owes	F	6'8"	Fr	—	—	—	—	—	—
Damon Stoudamire	G	5'10"	Fr	—	—	—	—	—	—

ARIZONA STATE

Conference: Pac-10
1990-91: 20-10, T-3rd Pac-10

1990-91 NCAAs: 1-1
Coach: Bill Frieder (226-113)

Opening Line: A young team gets even younger with the departure of senior starters Isaac Austin (16.3 PPG) and Tarence Wheeler (12 PPG). Led by Austin's intense work ethic in the pivot, the Sun Devils were an overachieving bunch in 1990-91 that fell seven points short of upsetting Arkansas and advancing to the Sweet 16. It was ASU's first NCAA appearance in a decade.

Guard: Point guard Lynn Collins, the team's only senior, becomes the leader by default. His assist-to-turnover ratio is outstanding. The other starting job is up for grabs between sophomore Stevin Smith and juco transfers Wun Versher and Dave Anderson. Smith had an impressive NCAA tourney. Versher can also swing to small forward. Freshman Tes Whitlock averaged 33.5 PPG as a high school senior.

Forward: Jamal Faulkner and Dwayne Fontana both made the Pac-10 All-Freshman Team last spring. Faulkner was Freshman of the Year. He excels inside and out, on defense and on offense. Fontana goes hard to the offensive boards. Freshmen Ian Dale (redshirt) and Mario Bennett, and beefy juco transfer Lester Neal, are raw but talented.

Center: Recruiting fanatic Bill Frieder went down under to fill the hole left by Austin. Riki Strother (6'10") is from New Zealand, while Tony Ronaldson (6'9") is a native of Australia. Both need work.

Analysis: If Frieder's talented young newcomers can play the team's swarming style of man-to-man defense, ASU should win a lot of close ballgames. An All-Pac-10 season from Faulkner would help. If the Sun Devils can avoid an abundance of rookie mistakes, a fourth-place league finish is possible. This will be a better team in 1992-93.

1991-92 ROSTER

	POS	HT	YR	FGP	FTP	3-PT	RPG	APG	PPG
Jamal Faulkner	F	6'7"	So	.49	.70	26/86	6.2	1.2	15.4
Dwayne Fontana	F	6'4"	So	.57	.55	1/2	4.0	1.5	8.4
Stevin Smith	G	6'2"	So	.41	.65	40/119	2.0	2.7	8.2
Lynn Collins	G	6'1"	Sr	.37	.71	20/66	2.9	5.2	8.1
Dave Anderson	G	6'1"	Jr	—	—	—	—	—	—
Mario Bennett	F	6'9"	Fr	—	—	—	—	—	—
Ian Dale	F	6'8"	Fr	—	—	—	—	—	—
Lester Neal	F	6'6"	Jr	—	—	—	—	—	—
Tony Ronaldson	C/F	6'9"	Fr	—	—	—	—	—	—
Riki Strother	C	6'10"	Fr	—	—	—	—	—	—
Wun Versher	G/F	6'5"	Jr	—	—	—	—	—	—
Tes Whitlock	G	6'2"	Fr	—	—	—	—	—	—

ARKANSAS

Conference: Southeastern
1990-91: 34-4, 1st SWC

1990-91 NCAAs: 3-1
Coach: Nolan Richardson (260-92)

Opening Line: After being ranked second nationally for most of 1990-91 and falling one game short of their second straight Final Four appearance last spring, these SEC newcomers have their sights set on Minneapolis in April. The terrific trio of Todd Day, Lee Mayberry, and Oliver Miller—each an All-America candidate—will lead the charge. Starting guard Arlyn Bowers and reserve forward Ron Huery graduated.

Guard: Mayberry (13.2 PPG) is recognized as one of the most complete all-around lead guards in the nation. He's Arkansas' all-time assist leader. Day, who will miss part of the season due to a disciplinary suspension, will likely move from small forward to shooting guard. Juco transfer Robert Shepherd will be the Razorbacks' first guard off the bench.

Forward: There's plenty of depth with bulky rebounders Isaiah Morris and Roosevelt Wallace the probable starters (230 and 235 pounds, respectively). Back-ups include Ken Biley, Clyde Fletcher, and Darrell Hawkins. Morris's scoring output was a bit of a disappointment last winter. Wallace is Charles Oakley's cousin. Biley's the hardest worker on the squad.

Center: When he's in the mood, the fun-loving Miller can be one of the most dominant big men in the country at both ends of the floor. "The Big O" is an intimidating shot-blocker and a 70-percent shooter from the field. Unsung Shawn Davis and 6'10" frosh John Carter will play too.

Analysis: The Razorbacks won't win as many games as last year simply because teams like Kentucky, LSU, and Alabama make the SEC a far tougher conference than the SWC. But if Miller can stay out of foul trouble and Day can put his off-the-court problems behind him, the Final Four becomes a realistic goal.

1991-92 ROSTER

	POS	HT	YR	FGP	FTP	3-PT	RPG	APG	PPG
Todd Day	G/F	6'9"	Sr	.47	.75	67/189	5.3	2.9	20.7
Oliver Miller	C	6'9"	Sr	.70	.64	1/3	7.7	2.7	15.7
Lee Mayberry	G	6'2"	Sr	.48	.63	57/149	3.4	5.5	13.2
Roosevelt Wallace	F	6'7"	Sr	.45	.79	11/30	5.0	0.7	8.2
Isaiah Morris	F	6'8"	Sr	.50	.80	1/2	4.1	0.8	7.5
Ken Biley	F	6'6"	So	.43	.61	0/1	2.4	0.3	3.1
Clyde Fletcher	F	6'7"	Sr	.41	.67	0/2	1.7	0.4	2.6
Darrell Hawkins	F	6'5"	Jr	.36	—	—	2.0	1.0	2.5
Shawn Davis	C	6'9"	Sr	.32	.63	—	1.9	0.3	1.6
John Carter	C	6'10"	Fr	—	—	—	—	—	—
Elmer Martin	F	6'8"	Fr	—	—	—	—	—	—
Robert Sheperd	G	6'1"	Jr	—	—	—	—	—	—

BALL STATE

Conference: Mid-American
1990-91: 21-10, T-2nd MAC

1990-91 NIT: 0-1
Coach: Dick Hunsaker (47-17)

Opening Line: Dick Hunsaker proved he knows a thing or two about coaching last winter. He guided a team that lost nine seniors, including four starters, to a 21-win season. Last year's leading scorer, guard Emanuel Cross, was a big loss, as was Todd Jones, who transferred to another school. Hunsaker was able to stock up with seven new recruits, thanks in part to the school's brand-new 12,000-seat arena.

Guard: Versatile swing man Chandler Thompson, a strong scorer and rebounder, is the front-runner for MAC Player of the Year honors. He thrives on big-game pressure. Light-scoring point guard Mike Spicer is Thompson's running mate. Keith Stalling and Rodney Holmes are the first guards off the bench. Juco transfer Jamie Matthews replaces Cross as BSU's top 3-point threat. Freshman Marlon Fleming is an Indiana All-State selection.

Forward: MAC All-Freshman selection Jeermal Sylvester will be joined up front by Steve Jones (injured knee) and juco recruits Clint Bailey and Michael Harris. One of the three must step up offensively. Bailey likes to mix it up inside.

Center: David Broz was another All-MAC frosh a year ago. Thanks to discipline and hard work, he started ahead of Bill Gillis in the second half of the season. Newcomer William Berry could move ahead of Broz.

Analysis: Interior defense could be a problem, although the MAC as a whole isn't exactly loaded with many big people inside. With as many as four starting positions up for grabs, fall practice should be a war. Other than Thompson, this team has no real stars—just an abundance of decent players who know their roles. It's this unusual depth that'll carry the Cards back to the top of the MAC.

1991-92 ROSTER

	POS	HT	YR	FGP	FTP	3-PT	RPG	APG	PPG
Chandler Thompson	G	6'4"	Sr	.45	.67	17/60	6.4	3.3	15.4
Keith Stalling	G	6'3"	Sr	.53	.70	10/17	3.9	1.6	10.6
Bill Gillis	C	6'7"	Jr	.50	.57	—	4.3	0.1	5.0
Jeermal Sylvester	F	6'6"	So	.56	.71	—	2.4	0.3	4.4
Steve Turner	F	6'9"	Jr	.52	.56	—	3.4	0.1	4.3
Rodney Holmes	G	5'11"	Jr	.38	.71	13/42	1.4	2.6	3.8
Jeff Robbins	G	6'3"	Sr	.43	.69	24/48	1.0	1.2	3.6
Mike Spicer	G	5'11"	Sr	.40	.82	2/8	2.0	4.5	2.6
David Broz	C	6'9"	So	.50	.70	0/1	2.8	0.4	2.2
Clint Bailey	F	6'6"	Jr	—	—	—	—	—	—
William Berry	C	6'8"	Jr	—	—	—	—	—	—
Jamie Matthews	G	5'10"	Jr	—	—	—	—	—	—

CONNECTICUT

Conference: Big East
1990-91: 20-11, T-3rd Big East

1990-91 NCAAs: 2-1
Coach: Jim Calhoun (348-200)

Opening Line: Add one of the nation's top three recruiting classes to a Sweet 16 team that returns four starters and you've got the makings of an outstanding club. After inking five top recruits last November, including standouts Rudy Johnson and Brian Fair, Jim Calhoun saved the best for last when he inked Donyell Marshall in April. Gone from the lineup are starter Steve Pikiell, John Gwynn, Murray Williams, and Lyman DePriest (combined 22 PPG).

Guard: Everything Connecticut does begins with senior All-America candidate Chris Smith. A multi-talented floor general, he's the perfect point man for Calhoun's transition game. Israeli import Gilad Katz and 3-point specialist Fair are the Huskies' top big guards. Oliver Macklin backs up Smith. Sleeper prospect Richie Ashmeade returns after missing the 1990-91 season due to academics.

Forward: Scott Burrell is the best athlete on the team. Thanks to incredible quickness, he averaged nearly four steals per game last season. Don't be surprised to see Marshall (a shot-blocking specialist) swipe Toraino Walker's starting big-forward job. He's that good. Johnson will also see action, as should 6'6" newcomer Donny Marshall.

Center: Look for 6'9" Rod Sellers to continue to outplay much taller and heavier opponents. He sparkles defensively and continues to improve his shooting range. Reserve Dan Cyrulik is 7'1" but still lacks agility.

Analysis: Smith, Burrell, and Sellers will see to it that the Huskies finish no lower than third in the Big East. If they're to contend for the top spot, a couple freshmen must produce. Impressive team speed should compensate for a lack of height.

1991-92 ROSTER

	POS	HT	YR	FGP	FTP	3-PT	RPG	APG	PPG
Chris Smith	G	6'2"	Sr	.44	.72	46/117	2.9	3.4	18.9
Scott Burrell	F	6'7"	Jr	.44	.59	37/108	7.5	3.1	12.7
Rod Sellers	C	6'9"	Sr	.55	.57	—	8.0	1.1	11.7
Toraino Walker	F	6'7"	Jr	.54	.26	—	5.7	1.3	5.1
Dan Cyrulik	C	7'1"	Sr	.44	.63	0/1	2.3	0.5	3.0
Gilad Katz	G	6'3"	Sr	.55	.57	13/26	0.6	1.0	2.9
Oliver Macklin	G	6'3"	Jr	.31	.57	1/3	0.8	—	1.0
Richie Ashmeade	G	6'2"	So	—	—	—	—	—	—
Brian Fair	G	6'3"	Fr	—	—	—	—	—	—
Rudy Johnson	F	6'6"	Fr	—	—	—	—	—	—
Donny Marshall	F	6'7"	Fr	—	—	—	—	—	—
Donyell Marshall	F	6'9"	Fr	—	—	—	—	—	—

DePAUL

Conference: Great Midwest
1990-91: 20-9

1990-91 NCAAs: 0-1
Coach: Joey Meyer (148-70)

Opening Line: For the third straight season, DePaul got off to a painfully slow start last winter. Only 10-9 in January, the Blue Demons turned things around and won ten of their last 11 before bowing to Georgia Tech in the NCAAs. After years as one of the nation's top independents, the Blue Demons have joined the newly formed Great Midwest Conference. Guard Melvon Foster is the only starter who graduated.

Guard: This is a crowded, talented backcourt. Senior Joe Daughrity may have started his last game if newcomers Brandon Cole and Howard Nathan are as good as advertised. While Daughrity's more of a true point guard, the 3-point minded Cole (6'1") and Nathan (5'11") can play either backcourt position. Nathan earned Illinois Mr. Basketball honors this past season. Brad Niemann and Chuck Murphy can also stroke it from long range.

Forward: Slender David Booth returns as the team's top scorer and rebounder. An All-America candidate, he's made great strides defensively in the past year. Terry Davis swings between forward and guard and Stephen Howard between forward and center. Davis started 25 games last winter, Howard 14.

Center: Jeff Stern's defensive presence is critical. He runs and jumps very well for a 6'10", 230-pound youngster. He should be scoring more. Howard will spend a lot of time in the pivot.

Analysis: DePaul includes an interesting mix of six seniors and talented newcomers. Memphis State will pose the biggest challenge to the Blue Demons in a league that also includes Cincinnati, Marquette, St. Louis, and UAB. Historically slow starters, the Demons need a quick start in December.

1991-92 ROSTER

	POS	HT	YR	FGP	FTP	3-PT	RPG	APG	PPG
David Booth	F	6'7"	Sr	.51	.76	7/26	6.8	1.7	18.7
Stephen Howard	F/C	6'9"	Sr	.52	.72	11/33	6.3	1.5	15.3
Terry Davis	F/G	6'4"	Jr	.44	.78	11/41	2.4	1.4	10.4
Brad Niemann	G	6'3"	Sr	.39	.97	36/88	0.8	1.0	6.0
Jeff Stern	C	6'10"	Sr	.51	.43	—	4.1	0.3	5.1
Joe Daughrity	G	6'0"	Sr	.38	.78	10/38	2.8	4.6	5.1
Curtis Price	F	6'6"	Jr	.50	.61	0/1	3.8	0.6	3.6
Chuck Murphy	G	6'1"	Sr	.37	.88	14/32	0.6	1.0	3.2
Brandon Cole	G	6'1"	So	—	—	—	—	—	—
Tom Kleinschmidt	F	6'5"	Fr	—	—	—	—	—	—
Will Macon	F	6'7"	Fr	—	—	—	—	—	—
Howard Nathan	G	5'11"	Fr	—	—	—	—	—	—

DUKE

Conference: Atlantic Coast
1990-91: 32-7, 1st ACC

1990-91 NCAAs: 6-0
Coach: Mike Krzyzewski (336-167)

Opening Line: After years of runner-up finishes, the Blue Devils finally won the national title in 1991. Coach Mike Krzyzewski, Christian Laettner, and Bobby Hurley became household names during last year's tournament, particularly after their stirring 79-77 upset of UNLV. Bill McCaffrey, who scored 16 vs. Kansas in the title game, shocked everyone with his transfer to Vanderbilt. Greg Koubek graduated and back-up center Crawford Palmer transferred to Dartmouth.

Guard: Hurley took his game to a new level during the '91 NCAA tournament as the team's gutsy little point guard. He's added increased offensive production to a very solid floor game. Thomas Hill, a perimeter-defense whiz, can bury the outside jumper or take the ball to the hole with a variety of moves. Marty Clark and Kenny Blakeney are comers.

Forward: Laettner, a preseason All-American, is expected to move back to forward to make room for freshman sensation Cherokee Parks in the middle. Laettner's versatility is unmatched for a player his size. Like Thomas Hill, Grant Hill's a great finisher on the break. Brian Davis can mix it up inside or move out to either guard position.

Center: Parks is the best center prospect from California in nearly two decades. Some observers compare him to Bill Walton. To take some of the pressure off Parks, Coach K is wisely thinking about starting Laettner in the pivot early.

Analysis: Can tourney-tested Duke repeat in '92? Although a viable question, it's one this Blue Devil team is sick of hearing. Winning a title has as much to do with luck, avoiding injuries, and playing well in March as it does with having the most talent. Yes, they'll be in Minneapolis as a Final Four entry, but they won't win it all.

1991-92 ROSTER

	POS	HT	YR	FGP	FTP	3-PT	RPG	APG	PPG
Christian Laettner	C/F	6'11"	Sr	.58	.80	18/53	8.7	1.9	19.8
Thomas Hill	G/F	6'4"	Jr	.55	.74	21/52	3.6	1.3	11.5
Bobby Hurley	G	6'0"	Jr	.42	.73	76/188	2.4	7.4	11.3
Grant Hill	F/G	6'8"	So	.52	.61	1/2	5.1	2.2	11.2
Brian Davis	G/F	6'6"	Sr	.46	.73	1/5	4.1	1.6	7.6
Antonio Lang	F	6'8"	So	.61	.53	—	2.6	0.2	4.3
Marty Clark	G	6'6"	So	.45	.63	2/9	0.7	0.3	2.1
Christian Ast	F	6'8"	So	.67	.75	1/4	0.6	—	1.6
Kenny Blakeney	G	6'4"	So	—	—	—	—	—	—
Erik Meek	C	6'10"	Fr	—	—	—	—	—	—
Cherokee Parks	F	6'11"	Fr	—	—	—	—	—	—

EAST TENNESSEE STATE

Conference: Southern
1990-91: 28-5, T-1st Southern

1990-91 NCAAs: 0-1
Coach: Alan LeForce (28-5)

Opening Line: Alan LeForce's 32-year wait to become a Division I head coach proved to be well worth it, as he helped put the Buccaneers' program on the map with the most successful season in school history. And remarkably, they did it without 6'11" All-America candidate Greg Dennis (broken foot) in the middle. This year's team will be without 5'7" Keith "Mister" Jennings (20 PPG, nine APG). Jennings's running mate, Major Geer, has also graduated, as has steady sixth man Alvin West.

Guard: While no one will ever be able to fill Jennings's shoes at the point, fellow mighty mites Eric Palmer (5'6") and Damian Hodge (5'10") show promise. Whether spunky Rodney English plays big guard or small forward, he'll be a regular. Improved Trazel Silvers and freshman Justin McClellan will also log big-guard minutes.

Forward: ETSU's starting forward tandem of 6'4" Calvin Talford and 6'3" Marty Story is one of the smallest in Division I—and one of the best. Both play much taller than their height. Talford missed last year's post-season after tearing up his knee. Jerry Pelphrey is a tough competitor off the pine.

Center: How important is Dennis's return? He transforms an average team into an NCAA tourney contender. Dennis gets up and down the floor real well, has a nice shot, and has loads of agility.

Analysis: The Bucs did a nice job last year of off-setting size mismatches with superior quickness. This time around, they'll at least have the luxury of Dennis's presence in the low post. If LeForce can get some steady point-guard play, the Bucs will stay alive a little longer at the NCAAs.

1991-92 ROSTER

	POS	HT	YR	FGP	FTP	3-PT	RPG	APG	PPG
Calvin Talford	F	6'4"	Sr	.54	.77	41/110	4.4	1.0	14.6
Rodney English	G/F	6'4"	Sr	.65	.66	1/3	5.8	1.2	13.8
Greg Dennis	C	6'11"	Sr	.30	.40	1/7	6.0	2.0	11.5
Marty Story	F	6'3"	Sr	.55	.62	9/25	3.8	1.0	9.1
Jerry Pelphrey	F	6'6"	Jr	.47	.77	36/82	2.5	1.6	6.8
Trazel Silvers	G/F	6'5"	So	.57	.76	—	2.6	0.4	5.0
Darell Jones	F	6'8"	Jr	.49	.38	—	3.5	0.8	3.6
Eric Palmer	G	5'6"	So	.33	.69	4/12	0.6	0.7	1.4
Moe Hayes	G	5'8"	Sr	—	.50	—	0.4	0.5	0.2
Junior Floyd	F	6'7"	Fr	—	—	—	—	—	—
Damian Hodge	G	5'10"	Fr	—	—	—	—	—	—
Justin McClellan	G/F	6'5"	Fr	—	—	—	—	—	—

FLORIDA STATE

Conference: Atlantic Coast
1990-91: 21-11, 2nd Metro

1990-91 NCAAs: 1-1
Coach: Pat Kennedy (221-116)

Opening Line: Last year's NCAA tourney invite was the Seminoles' third in four seasons. But despite the success, coach Pat Kennedy and his teams have failed to receive the respect they deserve. Until now. Since FSU has relocated to the hoop-crazed ACC, it won't have to worry about recognition. Kennedy made a top-notch recruiting haul in an attempt to fill the shoes of departed starters Michael Polite and Aubry Boyd (combined 25 PPG).

Guard: Football quarterback Charlie Ward gave basketball a try last winter and wound up starting 21 games at point guard and leading the team in assists. He'll share time at the point with court-smart Derrick Myers. Off guard is the deepest position on the team, with incumbent Chuck Graham (10.9 PPG), juco transfer Sam Cassell, and frosh Dwight Brown. Cassell's too good not to start somewhere.

Forward: Doug Edwards is the most talented player on this team. He can play all five positions. His brilliant NCAA tourney play vs. USC and Indiana (42 points, 23 rebounds) drew rave reviews from Bob Knight. Ray Donald joins Edwards up front. Donald likes to sneak inside. Forward Jesse Salters transfered to South Florida, leaving the team thin at the position.

Center: Rodney Dobard is an effective defender in the post. His long arms and quickness give opponents fits. With a little added strength, 7'0" Andre Reid could leap-frog past Dobard.

Analysis: One of the top two teams in the Metro, the Seminoles could easily plummet to fifth or sixth in the ACC. Kennedy will put a better team on the floor than he suited up last year, but their final record won't be as good. Edwards is sure to turn plenty of heads.

1991-92 ROSTER

	POS	HT	YR	FGP	FTP	3-PT	RPG	APG	PPG
Doug Edwards	F	6'9"	Jr	.52	.71	12/36	7.1	1.9	16.4
Chuck Graham	G	6'3"	Jr	.43	.71	36/104	2.7	0.9	10.9
Rodney Dobard	C	6'9"	Jr	.57	.54	—	5.2	0.9	8.5
Charlie Ward	G	6'1"	Jr	.46	.71	15/48	3.0	3.4	8.0
Lorenzo Hands	G	6'3"	Sr	.45	.54	2/6	1.0	0.5	2.8
Derrick Myers	G	6'1"	Sr	.45	.82	3/10	1.4	1.8	2.7
Andre Reid	C	7'0"	So	.34	.61	—	2.8	0.2	1.9
Dwight Brown	G	6'4"	Fr	—	—	—	—	—	—
Sam Cassell	G	6'3"	Sr	—	—	—	—	—	—
Ray Donald	F	6'8"	Fr	—	—	—	—	—	—
Bob Sura	G	6'5"	Fr	—	—	—	—	—	—
Byron Wells	F	6'8"	Sr	—	—	—	—	—	—

FRESNO STATE

Conference: Big West
1990-91: 14-16, T-6th Big West

1990-91 NCAAs: Not invited
Coach: Gary Colson (313-259)

Opening Line: Gary Colson's Bulldogs have the potential to be one of the nation's most improved teams this winter. Their new up-tempo, run-and-gun style is reminiscent of UNLV's. Players love it and so do the fans. Point guard Dave Barnett (15 PPG) is the only missing starter. Eight new recruits could make for some pretty competitive practices.

Guard: Juco transfer Steve Rankin (6'5") is Barnett's replacement. Rankin, one of the Big West's most talked-about newcomers, is a more complete player than Barnett. Leaping lizard Carl Ray Harris (14.7 PPG) is a fine outside shooter. Colson will have plenty of confidence in freshman substitute DeAndre Austin.

Forward: High-scoring Tod Bernard and team leader Wilbert Hooker are the most experienced returning forwards in the conference. They'll account for much of the Bulldogs' offense. Hooker will also see a lot of action at big guard, particularly if juco transfer Ted Bull proves to be as good as advertised in the paint. Pat Riddlesprigger can swish an open jumper faster than you can pronounce his name.

Center: Dimitri Lambrecht was a pleasant surprise last winter. Lambrecht, who can run up and down the court, gained a lot of confidence playing in Colson's run-and-gun system. Lambrecht had been ineffective in the halfcourt set that former FSU coach Ron Adams employed.

Analysis: The Bulldogs aren't going to turn things around overnight, but they are going to be a far more consistent team in Colson's second season. UNLV's still the class of the conference, but Fresno is slowly closing the gap. With a little added low-post defense, this team has an outside shot at the NCAAs.

1991-92 ROSTER

	POS	HT	YR	FGP	FTP	3-PT	RPG	APG	PPG
Tod Bernard	G/F	6'5"	Sr	.49	.70	25/61	7.5	1.9	19.2
Wilbert Hooker	F/G	6'3"	Sr	.47	.82	72/171	4.4	2.5	16.1
Carl Ray Harris	G	6'2"	Jr	.53	.69	15/43	2.9	3.1	14.7
Pat Riddlesprigger	F	6'6"	Sr	.53	.62	—	5.2	1.9	6.8
Dimitri Lambrecht	C	6'9"	Jr	.54	.61	3/6	4.8	1.2	6.2
Sammie Lindsey	F	6'8"	Sr	.47	.41	—	2.0	0.3	1.9
DeAndre Austin	G	6'3"	Fr	—	—	—	—	—	—
Brian Baumgartner	C	6'9"	So	—	—	—	—	—	—
Kevin Beal	F	6'4"	Fr	—	—	—	—	—	—
Ted Bull	F	6'7"	Jr	—	—	—	—	—	—
Lee Mayberry	C	6'9"	So	—	—	—	—	—	—
Steve Rankin	G	6'5"	Jr	—	—	—	—	—	—

GEORGETOWN

Conference: Big East
1990-91: 19-13, 6th Big East

1990-91 NCAAs: 1-1
Coach: John Thompson (442-155)

Opening Line: Now that Dikembe Mutombo's in the NBA, this is Alonzo Mourning's chance to shine. Simply put, 1990-91 was a disappointing year. Mutombo and Mourning had trouble playing together, injuries sidelined Mourning for nine games, and frosh point guard Joey Brown was plagued by indecisiveness. Many questions remain.

Guard: Freshman Brown was thrown to the wolves too soon last season and it cost the Hoyas on many occasions. Experience alone will make him a far better player this winter. Charles Harrison also started every game as a frosh in 1990-91. He must improve upon his .347 shooting or else Lamont Morgan and Ronny Thompson will scoot past him on the depth chart. Freshman Irvin Church could be a player to watch.

Forward: John Thompson will start Robert Churchwell, the third freshman to start every game last year, and hard-working Brian Kelly. While Churchwell must become more involved offensively, Kelly should repeat as the team leader in floor burns. Freshmen Lonnie Harrell and Kevin Millen provide the depth.

Center: When he's on his game, Mourning is the best big man in the country not named Shaquille. Too often last year, he appeared to lack confidence and aggressiveness. Look for him to return to the Alonzo of old and have a big, big year. Freshman Don Reid opted for Georgetown over Connecticut and Duke.

Analysis: This is a difficult team to figure. Although the Hoyas are a cinch to finish in the top half of the Big East, something—in addition to Mutombo—seems to be missing. Besides Kelly, there are too many passive players, and at times Thompson seems like a disinterested coach. It'll be Mourning's job to light the fire.

1991-92 ROSTER

	POS	HT	YR	FGP	FTP	3-PT	RPG	APG	PPG
Alonzo Mourning	C/F	6'10"	Sr	.52	.79	4/13	7.7	1.1	15.8
Charles Harrison	G	6'2"	So	.35	.78	25/94	2.8	2.0	11.7
Joey Brown	G	5'10"	So	.35	.72	18/78	4.2	3.6	9.1
Robert Churchwell	F	6'6"	So	.41	.62	3/12	4.8	1.6	8.4
Lamont Morgan	G	6'3"	So	.37	.69	13/35	2.3	1.5	4.4
Ronny Thompson	G	6'4"	Sr	.34	.79	4/22	1.5	0.5	3.1
Brian Kelly	F	6'6"	Sr	.32	.62	1/3	1.6	0.3	2.6
Irvin Church	G	6'1	Fr	—	—	—	—	—	—
Lonnie Harrell	G/F	6'6"	Fr	—	—	—	—	—	—
John Jacques	G	6'3"	Fr	—	—	—	—	—	—
Kevin Millen	F	6'7"	Fr	—	—	—	—	—	—
Don Reid	C/F	6'9"	Fr	—	—	—	—	—	—

GEORGIA

Conference: Southeastern
1990-91: 17-13, 6th SEC

1990-91 NCAAs: 0-1
Coach: Hugh Durham (466-257)

Opening Line: After being crowned SEC champs for the first time in 1989-90, the Bulldogs mysteriously lost their bite last season. Georgia faded all the way to the SEC's second division. It took a late-season five-game winning streak to salvage an NCAA tourney invite. Graduation losses Marshall Wilson (13.1 PPG), Rod Cole, and Neville Austin (5.3 RPG) started every game last winter.

Guard: In addition to Cole, backcourt graduation claimed extraordinary sixth man Jody Patton. As a result, more pressure than ever will be on All-SEC product Litterial Green (20.6 PPG). He'll vie for All-America honors while playing both guard positions. Two guard Shaun Golden is a strong defender who passes up too many open shots. Freshman Tyrone Wilson, the top guard in the state of South Carolina, should have an immediate impact.

Forward: Juco transfer Mike Green (6'9") is an aggressive player at the offensive end. The Bulldogs were counting heavily on 6'11" shot-blocker Antonio Harvey, but he has since left the school. Reggie Tinch and Kendall Rhine will be asked to contribute more.

Center: Arlando Bennett's not the best center in the SEC and he's not the worst. He's actually more skilled offensively than Austin. Bennett wears down when he plays a lot of minutes. Harvey and Green will play some pivot in order to keep him fresh.

Analysis: Although there was plenty of talent, the absence of true senior leadership hurt this team a year ago. That's Litterial Green's job this time around. If he can get his teammates to play up to their potential, the 'Dawgs could finish in the top third of the 12-team SEC.

1991-92 ROSTER

	POS	HT	YR	FGP	FTP	3-PT	RPG	APG	PPG
Litterial Green	G	6'1"	Sr	.44	.78	56/151	2.6	3.5	20.6
Reggie Tinch	F	6'5"	Sr	.57	.61	0/3	3.8	0.9	5.2
Arlando Bennett	C	6'10"	Jr	.51	.52	—	3.6	0.7	4.3
Kendall Rhine	F	6'6"	Jr	.43	.48	3/16	2.7	1.4	3.1
Shaun Golden	G	6'3"	Jr	.47	.57	—	1.2	1.3	2.5
Bernard Davis	G	5'11"	So	.40	.50	1/6	0.6	0.7	0.8
Dathon Brown	F	6'6"	Fr	—	—	—	—	—	—
Charles Claxton	C	7'1"	Fr	—	—	—	—	—	—
Mike Green	F	6'9"	Jr	—	—	—	—	—	—
Steve Jones	G/F	6'5"	Fr	—	—	—	—	—	—
Marcel Kon	F	6'10"	So	—	—	—	—	—	—
Tyrone Wilson	G	6'3"	Fr	—	—	—	—	—	—

GEORGIA TECH

Conference: Atlantic Coast
1990-91: 17-13, T-5th ACC

1990-91 NCAAs: 1-1
Coach: Bobby Cremins (298-182)

Opening Line: Drop a consensus All-American from a 17-13 team and watch it get better? Huh? Yep, that's right. Even without Kenny "The Wizard of Ahhs" Anderson, the Yellow Jackets should improve on a terribly inconsistent 1990-91 season. Every other starter is back, and newcomers Travis Best and James Forrest are two of the ten top freshmen in the nation.

Guard: Best is no Anderson, but he's close. Really. A gifted floor general, he'll start at the point. He scored 81 in a high school game last February. Shooting guard Jon Barry (15.9 PPG) was a huge surprise in his first season at Tech. A fine outside shooter, Barry was named *Basketball Weekly's* Juco Transfer of the Year. Reserves Rod Balanis and Greg White lack experience.

Forward: Malcolm Mackey (15.3 PPG, 10.7 RPG) was the team's most improved player a year ago. He's now one of the premier big men in the ACC. Either returning starter Bryan Hill or Forrest figure to get the call at small forward. Forrest is a boy in a man's body (6'7", 240). Improved Ivano Newbill is a solid rebounder and a defensive force.

Center: Matt Geiger's name should appear after the word "inconsistent" in the dictionary. This 7'0" ex-Auburn transfer suffered through a very mediocre 1990-91 season, although he did come on late in the year. Bobby Cremins is expecting far more this winter.

Analysis: The Yellow Jackets may be better off without their star player. Too often last year, Anderson's teammates stood around and expected him to shoulder much of the load. If Best is as good as advertised and Mackey and Barry perform as well as they did last season, Tech will finish as high as third in the ACC behind Duke and North Carolina.

1991-92 ROSTER

	POS	HT	YR	FGP	FTP	3-PT	RPG	APG	PPG
Jon Barry	G	6'5"	Sr	.44	.73	77/209	3.7	3.7	15.9
Malcolm Mackey	F	6'11"	Jr	.55	.60	0/1	10.7	1.0	15.3
Matt Geiger	C	7'0"	Sr	.55	.67	0/3	6.4	1.0	11.4
Bryan Hill	G/F	6'4"	Jr	.47	.53	24/50	3.9	3.0	6.5
Darryl Barnes	F	6'9"	Jr	.50	—	—	2.0	2.0	6.0
Ivano Newbill	F	6'9"	So	.53	.46	0/3	6.1	0.9	4.5
Rod Balanis	G	6'3"	So	.25	1.00	0/2	0.3	0.4	0.7
Greg White	G	6'2"	Sr	.25	.50	0/1	—	0.2	0.7
Drew Barry	G	6'4"	Fr	—	—	—	—	—	—
Travis Best	G	5'11"	Fr	—	—	—	—	—	—
Brian Black	G	6'1"	So	—	—	—	—	—	—
James Forrest	F	6'7"	Fr	—	—	—	—	—	—

ILLINOIS

Conference: Big Ten
1990-91: 21-10, T-3rd Big Ten

1990-91 NCAAs: Not eligible
Coach: Lou Henson (577-267)

Opening Line: Thanks to strong defensive play and hard work on the boards, the undermanned Illini stunned the basketball world with 21 wins last year. Lou Henson will miss graduated guard Larry Smith and center Andy Kpedi, particularly on the boards. Versatile freshman forward Robert Bennett has ability.

Guard: Sophomore point guard Rennie Clemons will run the offense. He's a talented distributor who topped the Illini in steals as a frosh. He'll be joined by either Andy Kaufmann, Brooks Taylor, or T.J. Wheeler. Taylor, who patterns his game after Kendall Gill, showed great improvement over the summer.

Forward: Rising star Deon Thomas (15 PPG) was remarkably consistent for a first-year player last winter, although he did break his left wrist during informal summer workouts. Kaufmann returns as the team's leader and top scorer with more than 21 PPG. Although he played forward last year, Kauffmann may be moved to shooting guard. Frontcourt subs Scott Pierce, Tom Michael, and Tim Geers will be pressed for minutes by Bennett and Marc Davidson. Bennett reminds Henson of Nick Anderson.

Center: Now that Kpedi is gone, Thomas is probably the closest thing the Illini have to a center. Actually, Henson will employ more of a three-forward attack. Although Thomas is expected to see action at all three frontcourt positions, he'll do the bulk of his work inside.

Analysis: Due to probation, the Illini were all dressed up with nowhere to go last March. This time around, they're eligible. And although it's not in Indiana's or Ohio State's class, Illinois is NCAA tourney-bound. The continued improvement of youngsters Thomas and Clemons will largely determine just how far Illinois goes.

1991-92 ROSTER

	POS	HT	YR	FGP	FTP	3-PT	RPG	APG	PPG
Andy Kaufmann	F/G	6'6"	Sr	.47	.83	41/104	5.0	2.2	21.3
Deon Thomas	F/C	6'9"	So	.58	.64	—	6.8	0.6	15.3
Rennie Clemons	G	6'0"	So	.45	.63	8/18	3.2	3.1	8.5
T.J. Wheeler	G	6'4"	So	.47	.79	4/13	2.2	1.5	4.5
Scott Pierce	F	6'8"	So	.50	.75	0/1	3.1	0.6	4.4
Tom Michael	F	6'8"	So	.43	.47	18/44	2.7	1.0	4.2
Brooks Taylor	G	6'4"	Jr	.42	.46	1/6	2.0	1.0	2.1
Tim Geers	F	6'5"	Jr	.35	.84	5/16	0.8	0.4	1.9
Robert Bennett	F	6'7"	Fr	—	—	—	—	—	—
Marc Davidson	F	6'7"	Fr	—	—	—	—	—	—

INDIANA

Conference: Big Ten
1990-91: 29-5, T-1st Big Ten

1990-91 NCAAs: 2-1
Coach: Bob Knight (561-203)

Opening Line: With every regular but Lyndon Jones back from an extremely young and talented squad, Indiana will contend for Bob Knight's fourth national championship. The Hoosier frontcourt will be bolstered by the addition of freshmen forwards Alan Henderson and Brian Evans and 7'0" frosh center Todd Lindeman.

Guard: Knight gets solid play and leadership at the point from Jamal Meeks. He doesn't score a lot, but that's not necessary with Damon Bailey, Calbert Cheaney, and Eric Anderson around. Meeks is a super defender. Bailey, an Indiana schoolboy legend, enjoyed a solid first year in Bloomington. He was Big Ten Freshman of the Year. The bench is well stocked with Greg Graham, Pat Graham, and Chris Reynolds. They would start for most teams.

Forward: Super-smooth Cheaney is the most talented player in the program. He'll contend for national Player of the Year accolades. Without Cheaney's offense, the Hoosiers would be in big trouble. No one knows for sure who'll start at the other forward. Muscular junior Matt Nover will compete with Henderson and Evans, two youngsters who aren't real physical.

Center: Although the hard-working Anderson (6'9") doesn't get many headlines, he can be as dangerous as anybody. He likes to mix it up inside. Lindeman is Indiana's first seven-footer since Uwe Blab. Chris Lawson transferred to Vanderbilt.

Analysis: Give Knight practically any 15 kids and he can win 20. Give him an 11- or 12-deep cast that includes guys like Cheaney, Anderson, and Bailey and things could get real interesting. How important is Meeks? The Hoosiers will not advance to the Final Four unless he continues to play up to Knight's lofty expectations.

1991-92 ROSTER

	POS	HT	YR	FGP	FTP	3-PT	RPG	APG	PPG
Calbert Cheaney	F	6'6"	Jr	.60	.80	43/91	5.5	1.4	21.6
Eric Anderson	F/C	6'9"	Sr	.51	.70	1/4	7.1	1.1	13.7
Damon Bailey	G	6'3"	So	.51	.69	33/76	2.9	2.9	11.4
Greg Graham	G	6'4"	Jr	.51	.69	7/29	2.6	1.6	8.7
Pat Graham	G	6'5"	Jr	.50	.85	13/38	1.6	1.6	7.4
Matt Nover	C/F	6'8"	Sr	.54	.68	—	3.9	0.4	6.9
Chris Reynolds	G	6'1"	Jr	.54	.68	—	1.7	2.2	4.1
Jamal Meeks	G	6'0"	Sr	.51	.75	5/15	2.0	4.9	3.5
Pat Knight	F	6'6"	So	.41	.70	0/2	1.0	0.9	1.8
Brian Evans	F	6'7"	Fr	—	—	—	—	—	—
Alan Henderson	F	6'9"	Fr	—	—	—	—	—	—
Todd Lindeman	C	7'0"	Fr	—	—	—	—	—	—

IOWA

Conference: Big Ten
1990-91: 21-11, T-5th Big Ten

1990-91 NCAAs: 1-1
Coach: Tom Davis (384-202)

Opening Line: Had you predicted a year ago that the 1990-91 Hawkeyes would finish with 21 wins, you would have been laughed out of Iowa City. But Dr. Tom Davis promptly went to work like a master surgeon and transformed an incredibly inexperienced, senior-less team into a Big Ten title contender.

Guard: After plugging in juco transfer Val Barnes at lead guard and giving inconsistent shooting guard James Moses the green light, the Hawkeyes had themselves a pretty solid backcourt. Barnes is an adequate scorer who does a nice job of distributing the ball. Moses is a superb standstill jump-shooter. Senior leader Troy Skinner is probably the team's best pure playmaker. He started 19 games a year ago as part of a three-guard offense.

Forward: The foursome of Rodell Davis, Chris Street, James Winters, and Jay Webb will evenly divide time in the Iowa frontcourt. Davis, plagued throughout his career by knee problems, and Street, a solid rebounder, will likely start. Keep an eye on Winters, a physical kid who can score when needed. Davis is looking for the healthy return of consummate team player Wade Lookingbill. Freshman Russ Millard is another big power player.

Center: As 6'10" junior Acie Earl goes, so go the Hawkeyes. The conference's top shot-blocker last year, Earl (16.3 PPG) possesses limitless potential. He's perfectly suited to Iowa's up-tempo style, as is substitute Brig Tubbs.

Analysis: Earl's continued development will affect this team more than anything else. With a little added seasoning and some tighter defense, this talented cast could finish as high as third in the Big Ten. Iowa's 12th NCAA tourney invite in the past 14 years is a given.

1991-92 ROSTER

	POS	HT	YR	FGP	FTP	3-PT	RPG	APG	PPG
Acie Earl	C	6'10"	Jr	.50	.67	1/1	6.7	1.5	16.3
James Moses	G	6'4"	Sr	.47	.69	34/92	3.2	1.3	12.0
Val Barnes	G	6'2"	Jr	.40	.74	38/93	2.5	1.8	11.5
Rodell Davis	F/G	6'3"	Sr	.59	.55	2/5	3.0	0.6	7.9
Troy Skinner	G	6'0"	Sr	.45	.84	42/89	1.4	3.4	7.7
Kevin Smith	G	5'11"	So	.42	.42	14/39	2.1	3.2	5.0
Chris Street	F	6'8"	So	.50	.65	1/2	5.1	1.1	5.0
Jay Webb	F	6'8"	Jr	.54	.62	—	4.2	0.5	4.8
James Winters	G/F	6'5"	So	.55	.51	1/3	3.6	0.7	4.3
Brig Tubbs	F	6'9"	Sr	.47	.69	—	1.5	0.2	2.0
Wade Lookingbill	F	6'5"	Jr	.00	1.00	0/1	1.0	1.0	2.0
Russ Millard	F	6'8"	Fr	—	—	—	—	—	—

KANSAS

Conference: Big Eight
1990-91: 27-8, T-1st Big Eight

1990-91 NCAAs: 5-1
Coach: Roy Williams (76-25)

Opening Line: While teams like UNLV, Duke, and Arkansas grabbed most of the national headlines last year, the Jayhawks quietly won 27 games and came within six points of beating Duke in the national championship game. Minus key starters Mark Randall, Terry Brown, and Mike Maddox, Kansas won't be as formidable a foe in 1992. But if a solid returning cast blends well with seven newcomers, you never know where Roy Williams could have these guys by season's end.

Guard: Though Adonis Jordan is no Michael, you can't help but be impressed by his ability to quarterback a team. He's the catalyst. Cat-quick freshman Calvin Rayford is Jordan's back-up. Shooting guard Sean Tunstall and versatile Steve Woodberry will have a tough time keeping Northwestern transfer Rex Walters off the floor. Walters averaged nearly 18 PPG for the Wildcats in 1989-90.

Forward: Alonzo Jamison, a great low-post defender, became a household name during the NCAA tournament last March. Jamison's work ethic rubs off on his teammates. One day, frosh power forward Ben Davis will be even better than Adonis Jordan. Final Four vets Richard Scott and Patrick Richey can score from inside or out.

Center: Defensive minded senior David Johanning faces some stiff competition from 6'10" juco transfer Eric Pauley and 7'1" freshman Greg Ostertag. Pauley has definite star potential, while Ostertag draws comparisons to Greg Dreiling.

Analysis: Many of the names have changed but the final record may not. If guys like Walters and Davis fit in with the veterans, the end result could be just as impressive. Though they may need time to gel, the Jayhawks could be one of the nation's top dozen teams in March.

1991-92 ROSTER

	POS	HT	YR	FGP	FTP	3-PT	RPG	APG	PPG
Adonis Jordan	G	5'11"	Jr	.51	.77	47/115	3.0	4.5	12.5
Alonzo Jamison	F	6'6"	Sr	.60	.50	2/4	6.4	3.6	10.4
Richard Scott	F	6'7"	So	.56	.41	0/2	2.6	0.4	5.9
Sean Tunstall	G	6'2"	Sr	.42	.74	14/42	2.6	1.2	5.7
Patrick Richey	G/F	6'8"	So	.45	.70	17/41	1.9	1.1	4.2
Steve Woodberry	G/F	6'4"	So	.51	.78	5/11	1.9	1.5	3.0
David Johanning	C	6'10"	Sr	.57	.52	—	1.4	0.3	1.8
Ben Davis	F	6'8"	Fr	—	—	—	—	—	—
Greg Ostertag	C	7'1"	Fr	—	—	—	—	—	—
Eric Pauley	C	6'10"	Jr	—	—	—	—	—	—
Calvin Rayford	G	5'8"	Fr	—	—	—	—	—	—
Rex Walters	G	6'4"	Jr	—	—	—	—	—	—

KENTUCKY

Conference: Southeastern
1990-91: 22-6, 1st SEC

1990-91 NCAAs: Not eligible
Coach: Rick Pitino (169-94)

Opening Line: You get the feeling that master motivator Rick Pitino could mold the two of us and three nuns into a winner. With the likes of Jamal Mashburn, John Pelphrey, and Travis Ford, the guy can win 20 with his eyes closed. The recruiting class was good, but not as good as it should be under Pitino.

Guard: An average backcourt got a lot better when Pitino signed high-scoring shooting guards Dale Brown (juco) and Chris Harrison (frosh). While improved Sean Woods and Missouri transfer Ford will direct traffic from the point, Brown, Harrison, Richie Farmer, and Jeff Brassow will stage a 3-point shooting contest. Pitino will encourage all of them to shoot, shoot, and shoot some more.

Forward: Mashburn's the youngster Pitino's building the program around. Although he tailed off a bit late last season, this New York City product is by far the most talented player on the

team. He's very agile and deceivingly quick at 6'9", 244 pounds. What Pelphrey (a dynamite 3-point shooter) and Deron Feldhaus lack in physical skills, they make up for in court smarts. Both are overachievers.

Center: Unless disappointing sophomore Gimel Martinez or freshman string bean Andre Riddick can step forward, the pivot position will be the primary weakness now that Reggie Hanson has graduated. Riddick played in the New York summer leagues with Mashburn.

Analysis: The Kentucky faithful have taken to Pitino's high-octane offensive style and full-court defensive pressure. After last year's surprising success, they won't accept anything less. But that's being a little unrealistic. A lack of overall frontcourt talent means the 'Cats are NCAA-tourney material but still a year or two away from true greatness.

1991-92 ROSTER

	POS	HT	YR	FGP	FTP	3-PT	RPG	APG	PPG
John Pelphrey	F	6'7"	Sr	.43	.78	62/164	5.2	3.1	14.4
Jamal Mashburn	F	6'9"	So	.47	.73	24/82	7.0	1.5	12.9
Deron Feldhaus	F	6'7"	Sr	.52	.69	29/74	4.1	1.6	10.8
Richie Farmer	G	6'0"	Sr	.38	.84	46/130	1.8	1.8	10.1
Sean Woods	G	6'2"	Sr	.45	.65	6/20	2.6	5.6	9.7
Jeff Brassow	G	6'5"	Jr	.37	.82	46/147	3.2	1.1	8.1
Junior Braddy	G	6'2"	Jr	.34	.61	10/31	1.2	0.5	3.3
Gimel Martinez	C	6'9"	So	.41	.64	—	1.2	0.2	1.6
Dale Brown	G	6'4"	Jr	—	—	—	—	—	—
Travis Ford	G	5'10"	So	—	—	—	—	—	—
Chris Harrison	G	6'3"	Fr	—	—	—	—	—	—
Andre Riddick	C	6'9"	Fr	—	—	—	—	—	—

La SALLE

Conference: Metro Atlantic
1990-91: 19-10, T-1st MAAC

1990-91 NIT: 0-1
Coach: Speedy Morris (119-41)

Opening Line: For the past four seasons, Speedy Morris's Explorers have either won or shared the MAAC title. From 1987-90, All-American Lionel Simmons led the way. Last year, Doug Overton (22 PPG, five APG) was the star. This year? Senior starters Randy Woods, Jack Hurd, and Milko Lieverst will comprise the nucleus of a squad that has the talent to make it five straight titles.

Guard: Woods (21.6 PPG), an All-MAAC selection, takes over for Overton at the point. Woods is the team's top returning scorer and one of the finest defensive guards in the East. After playing a lot of small forward last year, Hurd figures to see more action at shooting guard. He's a hard worker with no respect for his body. He'll be encouraged to take 3-pointers. Lamont Carter and Jeff Neubauer are reliable reserves.

Forward: Burly Bron Holland, a one-time St. Bonaventure transfer, will start up front with either Hurd, Don Shelton, or Ray Schultz. Broderick President's graduation greatly expands Holland's role. He'll do most of his damage within five feet of the basket. Shelton and Schultz lack crunch-time experience.

Center: Lieverst, a Dutch import, has improved every year. Nicknamed "The Milkman," he needs to improve his shot selection and defensive positioning. He worked hard on his game during the off-season in the tough Philadelphia summer leagues.

Analysis: A little thin on reserves, Morris will have to get plenty of mileage out of Woods, Hurd, and Lieverst. All three could be all-league selections. Morris-coached teams are always aggressive and entertaining, and this year's unit is no exception. After settling for the NIT a year ago, it's back to the NCAA's party this spring.

1991-92 ROSTER

	POS	HT	YR	FGP	FTP	3-PT	RPG	APG	PPG
Randy Woods	G	6'0"	Sr	.43	.80	80/227	4.9	2.8	21.6
Jack Hurd	G	6'6"	Sr	.40	.67	64/193	5.6	2.3	15.9
Milko Lieverst	C	6'9"	Sr	.50	.50	0/1	8.0	1.3	7.4
Bron Holland	F	6'8"	Sr	.47	.71	1/6	3.2	0.8	5.1
Jeff Neubauer	G	6'4"	Jr	.41	.79	16/53	1.9	1.5	3.8
Lamont Carter	G	6'3"	So	.36	.75	3/13	1.0	0.1	2.9
Don Shelton	C	6'8"	Sr	.45	.47	—	2.0	0.4	2.3
Ray Schultz	F/C	6'9"	Jr	.48	.54	—	1.5	0.2	1.4
Mike Bergin	G	6'4"	Jr	.25	—	1/2	0.3	0.3	0.6
Keith Morris	G	5'10"	Sr	.33	.67	0/2	0.5	0.8	0.5
Blitz Wooten	F	6'7"	Fr	—	—	—	—	—	—

LEHIGH

Conference: Patriot
1990-91: 19-10, 2nd Patriot

1990-91 NCAAs: Not invited
Coach: Dave Duke (47-40)

Opening Line: If there was ever a team Rodney Dangerfield could empathize with, it would be the Engineers. They simply don't get any respect. Overshadowed by Fordham and Holy Cross in the underrated Patriot League, Lehigh returns four starters—two of which are all-league performers. Sweet-shooting guard Mike O'Hara was the only graduation loss.

Guard: Rich Hudock and Mike McKee give this team a pair of sound but unspectacular point guards who make very few mistakes. Hudock is more experienced; McKee is the better athlete. Big guard Steve Yaniga will rank among the league leaders in 3-point attempts. Multi-talented Chuck Penn will give Yaniga a breather off the bench.

Forward: Patriot Player of the Year candidate Bob Krizansky is a tough customer inside. He's the guts of the team and a pretty decent shooter for a brute. Jay Hipps is a double-figure scorer who does a lot of the little things. Little-used Stefan Falke had a productive summer.

Center: Dozie Mbonu's presence in the middle is one of the strengths of this team. A 6'6" jumping jack, he can post up, face the basket, block shots, clean the offensive glass, fire a letter-perfect outlet pass, and bring the ball up the court when needed. If he were three inches taller, he'd eventually play in the NBA.

Analysis: Due to a lack of size, quickness, and all-around athletic ability, the Engineers aren't on par with the top 30 or 40 teams in the country. However, they're certainly capable of pulling off an upset or two in December. Coach Dave Duke expects a lot from his youngsters and he gets a lot in return. As for their NCAA tourney chances, they'll likely have to face a team like Duke, Indiana, or Arkansas in the first round.

1991-92 ROSTER

	POS	HT	YR	FGP	FTP	3-PT	RPG	APG	PPG
Bob Krizansky	F	6'4"	Sr	.58	.71	17/37	6.9	4.5	16.9
Dozie Mbonu	C	6'6"	Sr	.59	.76	0/1	8.0	1.1	16.6
Jay Hipps	F	6'5"	Sr	.50	.76	0/1	4.0	1.1	11.7
Chuck Penn	G/F	6'4"	Jr	.48	.73	10/32	1.8	1.5	9.3
Steve Yaniga	F/G	6'5"	Sr	.51	.73	25/65	2.3	2.1	8.4
Rich Hudock	G	5'10"	Jr	.40	.69	12/27	0.9	3.5	2.9
Jason Kokoszka	F/C	6'6"	So	.67	1.00	1/1	0.3	—	2.3
Stefan Falke	F	6'6"	Sr	.50	.60	—	1.2	0.3	1.9
Allan Campbell	F/C	6'7"	So	.31	1.00	1/5	1.0	—	1.6
Mike McKee	G	5'11"	So	.57	.73	2/3	0.6	0.4	1.3
Jason Fichter	F	6'7"	Fr	—	—	—	—	—	—
Ivan Wilkins	G/F	6'5"	Fr	—	—	—	—	—	—

LOUISIANA STATE

Conference: Southeastern
1990-91: 20-10, T-2nd SEC

1990-91 NCAAs: 0-1
Coach: Dale Brown (360-212)

Opening Line: You can sum up Dale Brown's Tigers with two words—Shaquille O'Neal. LSU fans breathed a sigh of relief last spring when O'Neal (27.6 PPG, 14.7 RPG) announced he'd be returning for his junior season. Add ex-prep All-American Jamie Brandon to O'Neal and his solid supporting cast and Brown's first national title is no longer just a pipe dream.

Guard: Although he could stand to shoot a little more often, super-quick point man T.J. Pugh does an outstanding job of dictating tempo. Spaniard Mike Hansen is the Tigers' top 3-point threat. He can play either guard slot. Brandon has All-SEC potential.

Forward: Defensive stopper Vernel Singleton is Brown's most experienced forward. With little fanfare, Singleton has developed into a fine all-around player. Shawn Griggs probably would have started this year,

but he transferred to another school. Harold Boudreaux (8.4 PPG) will likely takes his spot in the lineup. Hometown freshmen Doug Annison and Clarence Ceasar could see some action. Brown could use more depth here.

Center: Despite constantly being double- and triple-teamed, O'Neal is the most dominant college player in the game today. He's sure to join David Robinson, Patrick Ewing, and Hakeem Olajuwon as one of the world's greatest centers. His free throw shooting and frequent fouls may be his only negatives. Geert Hammink is an adequate back-up.

Analysis: A kid like O'Neal can make Dale Brown look like a great coach. Heck, he'd make *you* look like a great coach. With O'Neal in the middle, there's no reason why LSU can't advance to the Final Four. Removing him from the lineup is the only way to tame these Tigers.

1991-92 ROSTER

	POS	HT	YR	FGP	FTP	3-PT	RPG	APG	PPG
Shaquille O'Neal	C	7'2"	Jr	.63	.64	—	14.7	1.6	27.6
Vernel Singleton	F	6'7"	Sr	.52	.73	0/6	5.9	1.6	15.2
Mike Hansen	G	6'0"	Jr	.43	.86	58/154	2.2	2.4	12.7
Harold Boudreaux	F	6'9"	Sr	.43	.60	21/69	4.0	1.0	8.4
T.J. Pugh	G	6'0"	Sr	.47	.73	15/44	3.7	6.5	6.6
Geert Hammink	C	7'0"	Jr	.42	.82	0/1	2.9	0.4	4.6
Lenear Burns	F	6'6"	So	.37	.70	8/26	1.7	0.6	3.1
John Picou	G	6'2"	So	.37	.64	3/14	0.4	1.1	1.4
Doug Annison	G/F	6'5"	Fr	—	—	—	—	—	—
Jamie Brandon	G	6'4"	So	—	—	—	—	—	—
Clarence Ceasar	F	6'7"	Fr	—	—	—	—	—	—
David Mascia	G	6'3"	Fr	—	—	—	—	—	—

LOUISIANA TECH

Conference: Sun Belt
1990-91: 21-10, 3rd American South

1990-91 NCAAs: 0-1
Coach: Jerry Loyd (41-18)

Opening Line: Jerry Loyd's team is overflowing with confidence after closing the 1990-91 season with 11 wins in its final 14 games, including seven straight heading into the NCAA tournament. Tech will play in the Sun Belt Conference in 1990-91. Three starters return, including a pair of potential professional prospects in P.J. Brown and Anthony Dade. With nine players back in the fold, many of the eight recruits Loyd brought in will be redshirted.

Guard: This has quickly turned into a problem area. Starting point guard Reni Mason recently left the team, creating a void at the point position. The 3-point-bombing Eric Brown and the streaky JoJo Goldsmith are best suited as shooting guards. Antuan Morris is a capable back-up.

Forward: Dade and Ron Ellis give Tech its best frontcourt combo since the Karl Malone-Robert Godbolt days. Dade's unique combination of strength and quickness makes him one of the most underrated forwards in the game today. Ellis looks more like a prize fighter than a basketball player. Mark Spradling and Antonio Robinson will be pushed for back-up duty by freshman Paul Seymore.

Center: P.J. Brown was a man possessed during last spring's American South tournament. If he can avoid early foul trouble, he'll have NBA scouts flocking to Ruston, Louisiana. They love his rebounding and shot-blocking. Dan Magett is Brown's back up.

Analysis: Few teams across the country possess this kind of frontcourt talent. The guards are more suspect, particularly if their perimeter shooting doesn't improve. Mason's departure only makes matters worse. Regardless of the guard play, seniors Dade, Ellis, and P.J. Brown will see to it that they close out their college careers in NCAA-tournament style.

1991-92 ROSTER

	POS	HT	YR	FGP	FTP	3-PT	RPG	APG	PPG
Anthony Dade	F	6'6"	Sr	.58	.54	0/1	5.9	1.3	14.4
P.J. Brown	C	6'11"	Sr	.54	.65	7/20	9.7	1.9	14.4
Ron Ellis	F	6'7"	Sr	.53	.75	10/24	7.4	1.5	13.4
Eric Brown	G	6'0"	Sr	.42	.82	48/133	1.1	1.6	10.0
JoJo Goldsmith	G	6'3"	Sr	.39	.75	16/45	2.8	1.0	9.6
Antuan Morris	G	6'4"	Jr	.46	.54	8/28	1.0	0.3	3.0
Mark Spradling	F	6'7"	Jr	.37	.58	2/7	2.0	0.5	2.1
Dan Magett	C	6'10"	So	.50	.59	—	1.1	0.2	1.7
Antonio Robinson	F	6'5"	So	.26	.71	0/2	1.1	0.1	1.2
Reggie Hill	G	6'3"	Fr	—	—	—	—	—	—
LaMont King	G	6'2"	Fr	—	—	—	—	—	—
Paul Seymore	F	6'8"	Fr	—	—	—	—	—	—

LOUISVILLE

Conference: Metro
1990-91: 14-16, 8th Metro

1990-91 NCAAs: Not invited
Coach: Denny Crum (477-172)

Opening Line: Not even a five-game winning streak in the final two weeks could prevent the Cardinals from finishing with their first losing season since 1944-45. To make matters worse, leading scorer LaBradford Smith has graduated. Every other starter does return, although they may not be starters for long thanks to four impressive newcomers.

Guard: The lack of a bona fide playmaking guard really hurt Louisville last season. Smith tried to play the point with limited success. This year, it's solidly built freshman Keith LeGree's job to lose. His game compares favorably to Rumeal Robinson's. Everick Sullivan is a gifted athlete who can pop from the perimeter or post up inside. He'll have to score on a more consistent basis. James Brewer and Derwin Webb both love the open court.

Forward: Rugged rebounder Cornelius Holden (8.2 RPG) will contend for All-Metro honors this season. In addition to doing much of the team's scoring and rebounding, he'll try to groom new additions Dwayne Morton and Greg Minor (ineligible in 1990-91). Tony Smith and Tremaine Wingfield also figure in coach Denny Crum's plans.

Center: Holden will likely see a lot of time in the low post while 6'10" newcomer Brian Hopgood is brought along slowly. Some observers believe Hopgood is already talented enough to become a starter as early as mid-season. He'll get the chance.

Analysis: Forget about another sub-.500 season. Crum is too good of a coach with too much talent. The won-loss record will depend largely on how quickly the youngsters can develop and the kind of leadership seniors Sullivan and Holden can provide. Southern Miss and UNC-Charlotte are the only real competition in the diluted Metro.

1991-92 ROSTER

	POS	HT	YR	FGP	FTP	3-PT	RPG	APG	PPG
Everick Sullivan	G/F	6'5"	Sr	.45	.68	54/140	4.0	3.5	15.6
Cornelius Holden	F/C	6'7"	Sr	.60	.68	1/4	8.2	1.1	12.5
James Brewer	G	6'3"	Jr	.43	.73	44/102	2.6	1.9	9.7
Troy Smith	F	6'8"	Jr	.55	.60	—	5.1	1.2	8.9
Derwin Webb	G/F	6'4"	Jr	.61	.65	0/1	3.5	1.2	7.0
Kip Stone	G	6'4"	So	.36	.76	1/11	1.5	1.7	3.4
Tremaine Wingfield	F	6'7"	So	.50	.59	—	3.2	0.4	2.3
Mike Case	F	6'6"	Jr	.28	.54	1/8	1.0	0.2	1.1
Brian Hopgood	C	6'10"	So	—	—	—	—	—	—
Keith LeGree	G	6'2"	Fr	—	—	—	—	—	—
Greg Minor	F	6'7"	So	—	—	—	—	—	—
Dwayne Morton	F/G	6'6"	So	—	—	—	—	—	—

MASSACHUSETTS

Conference: Atlantic 10
1990-91: 20-13, T-3rd A-10

1990-91 NIT: 3-2
Coach: John Calipari (47-45)

Opening Line: John Calipari. Remember the name. In three short seasons, this spirited young coach has transformed perennial Atlantic 10 also-ran Massachusetts (11 straight losing seasons) into one of the East's up-and-coming teams. He guided the Minutemen all the way to the NIT Final Four last spring. And the best news of all? All five starters return!

Guard: More than any other player, star shooting guard Jim McCoy is the guy who turned this program around. McCoy is the school's all-time leading scorer. A year from now, he'll be playing in the NBA. Anton Brown is back at the point after being slowed by torn knee ligaments last season. He managed to start 14 games and led the team in assists. Part-time starter Rafer Giles (10.2 PPG) graduated.

Forward: Tony Barbee and William Herndon averaged more than 27 points and ten rebounds per game a

year ago. Herndon shot 63 percent from the field. Only 6'3", he makes up for his lack of height with brute strength and quickness. Barbee struggled offensively late in the season. Sixth man John Tate's graduation leaves Kennard Robinson and talented freshman Scott Drapeau as the top reserves.

Center: Versatile Harper Williams (6'7") is actually more of a third forward. He prefers facing the basket. Although he can take the ball to the hole (13.9 PPG), rebounding is his No. 1 priority. Jeff Meyer is a 7'2" project who has a lot to learn.

Analysis: Last year's 20-13 record was Massachusetts' best since 1976-77. This season, they'll do even better. Only Temple stands between the Minutemen and their first Atlantic 10 title. An NCAA bid is a sure thing. McCoy's A-10 Player of the Year chances are just as strong.

1991-92 ROSTER

	POS	HT	YR	FGP	FTP	3-PT	RPG	APG	PPG
Jim McCoy	G	6'3"	Sr	.45	.70	4/14	3.5	1.6	18.9
Tony Barbee	F	6'6"	Jr	.45	.69	13/55	4.2	2.8	15.3
Harper Williams	C/F	6'7"	Jr	.56	.72	0/2	7.7	1.0	13.9
William Herndon	F	6'3"	Jr	.63	.68	0/1	6.0	2.4	11.9
Anton Brown	G	6'2"	Sr	.39	.78	8/21	2.9	4.1	4.8
Kennard Robinson	C	6'10"	Jr	.42	.50	0/1	0.8	0.2	1.1
Jeff Meyer	C	7'2"	So	.10	.67	—	1.0	—	0.2
Tommy Pace	F	6'5"	Jr	—	—	—	0.3	—	—
Ted Cottrell	C/F	6'9"	Fr	—	—	—	—	—	—
Scott Drapeau	F	6'8"	Fr	—	—	—	—	—	—
Jerome Malloy	G/F	6'4"	Fr	—	—	—	—	—	—
Louis Roe	F	6'7"	Fr	—	—	—	—	—	—

MEMPHIS STATE

Conference: Great Midwest
1990-91: 17-15, T-4th Metro

1990-91 NIT: 1-1
Coach: Larry Finch (102-58)

Opening Line: Bad news—the Tigers lose one star. Good news—they gain two. Point guard Elliot Perry and his trademark space goggles will long be remembered in Memphis State roundball annals. New pages in MSU history will be written by 6'7" point guard Anfernee Hardaway and 6'10" power forward David Vaughn, a pair of legitimate can't-miss prospects. Memphis State will play in the new Great Midwest Conference.

Guard: Senior Tony Madlock, Perry's unspectacular but steady backcourt mate, assumes the team-leader role. He started 31 games a year ago. Hardaway, a Prop 48 who sat out last season after garnering high school player of the year honors in 1989-90, is a potential superstar at either guard position. His career suffered a brief setback in April when he was shot in the foot after being robbed. Billy Smith and Russell Young come off the bench.

Forward: Vaughn, coach Larry Finch's nephew, was understandably assured of a starting job the day he signed. Similar in many ways to Pervis Ellison, Vaughn was one of the top five preps in the nation. Jumping jack Ernest Smith or Kelvin Allen will start alongside Vaughn. Muscular reserve Anthony Douglas tips the scales at a rock-solid 250 pounds.

Center: Seven-footer Todd Mundt is coming along slowly in the middle. He'll follow up an outstanding game with three mediocre ones. Finch remains patient with him.

Analysis: Hardaway and Vaughn will make immediate impacts. As good a player as Perry was, he often tried to assume too much of the offensive load himself. It hurt the whole team. The points will be more evenly distributed this year and the wins will be more frequent. A Great Midwest crown isn't out of the question.

1991-92 ROSTER

	POS	HT	YR	FGP	FTP	3-PT	RPG	APG	PPG
Tony Madlock	G	6'1"	Sr	.51	.80	2/9	2.4	3.4	9.8
Ernest Smith	F	6'5"	Sr	.51	.66	3/12	4.5	2.2	8.1
Kelvin Allen	F	6'7"	Jr	.53	.71	—	4.8	0.4	7.3
Todd Mundt	C	7'0"	Jr	.46	.68	0/1	4.3	1.3	6.8
Anthony Douglas	F/C	6'7"	Jr	.49	.51	—	4.9	0.5	6.3
Billy Smith	G	6'5"	Jr	.34	.75	13/49	0.9	0.6	5.1
Russell Young	F	6'5"	Sr	.39	.77	4/15	2.1	0.4	3.6
Tim Duncan	F/C	6'8"	Sr	.58	.74	—	2.9	0.3	3.1
Anfernee Hardaway	G	6'7"	So	—	—	—	—	—	—
Chris Haynes	G	6'4"	Fr	—	—	—	—	—	—
Marcus Nolan	G	6'2"	Fr	—	—	—	—	—	—
David Vaughn	F/C	6'10"	Fr	—	—	—	—	—	—

MICHIGAN

Conference: Big Ten
1990-91: 14-15, 8th Big Ten

1990-91 NIT: 0-1
Coach: Steve Fisher (43-23)

Opening Line: After finishing ahead of only Minnesota and Northwestern in the Big Ten standings last winter, Michigan should vault into the conference's upper division this year, thanks to the No. 1 recruiting class in America. Guard Demetrius Calip (20.5 PPG) is a significant loss. Tony Tolbert transferred to Detroit.

Guard: This is sassy junior Michael Talley's year to shine. As long as he doesn't try to force things, he's on pace to become one of the Big Ten's top point guards. Kirk Taylor played better than expected last year after coming back from a serious knee injury. He'll have to beat out super-frosh Jimmy King to keep his starting job. Rob Pelinka should supply some points off the bench.

Forward: In time, the Wolverines' frontcourt will be downright scary. Returning lettermen Sam Mitchell, Freddie Hunter, and James Voskuil figure to surrender their positions to freshmen Chris Webber, Juwan Howard, and multi-talented Jalen Rose. Webber, from nearby Detroit, was the nation's No. 1 prep. He's a can't-miss superstar who could play all three frontcourt positions. Howard was a second-team prep All-American.

Center: Pencil-thin Eric Riley is back after finishing the regular season as the Big Ten's second-leading rebounder. In NIT play vs. Colorado, he grabbed 14 boards. Riley possesses deceiving strength but never will be a force offensively.

Analysis: You've got to give Steve Fisher plenty of credit for being able to recruit superstars like Webber and Howard. It'll take time for the new kids to mature and grow as a team, but by March the Wolverines could be something special. Like any young team, they'll be awesome one night and mediocre the next.

1991-92 ROSTER

	POS	HT	YR	FGP	FTP	3-PT	RPG	APG	PPG
Michael Talley	G	6'1"	Jr	.44	.77	26/62	2.9	3.2	11.0
Eric Riley	C	6'11"	Jr	.45	.76	0/1	8.6	1.0	10.6
Kirk Taylor	G	6'3"	Sr	.49	.61	24/62	4.1	2.5	10.4
James Voskuil	G/F	6'7"	Jr	.47	.52	21/47	2.9	0.6	6.7
Sam Mitchell	F/C	6'9"	So	.41	.64	2/5	3.6	0.6	4.9
Freddie Hunter	F	6'5"	Sr	.51	.58	—	4.4	1.2	3.6
Bob Pelinka	G	6'5"	Sr	.29	.58	9/31	1.1	0.4	1.7
Juwan Howard	F/C	6'9"	Fr	—	—	—	—	—	—
Ray Jackson	F	6'6"	Fr	—	—	—	—	—	—
Jimmy King	G	6'3"	Fr	—	—	—	—	—	—
Jalen Rose	G/F	6'7"	Fr	—	—	—	—	—	—
Chris Webber	F/C	6'9"	Fr	—	—	—	—	—	—

MICHIGAN STATE

Conference: Big Ten
1990-91: 19-11, T-3rd Big Ten

1990-91 NCAAs: 1-1
Coach: Jud Heathcote (564-333)

Opening Line: After a disappointing 1990-91 season, things have gone from bad to worse for the Spartans. First, they lost All-America superstar Steve Smith to graduation. Then, tough-guy forward Parish Hickman was indicted on drug charges. The cupboard's by no means bare, but it could stand to be a little fuller.

Guard: Spirited senior playmaker Mark Montgomery led the Big Ten in assists last season. While he continues to improve defensively, Montgomery's a lousy shooter. Inconsistent Andy Penick and Kris Weshinskey and unproven Shawn Respert will share time at shooting guard. Freshman Eric Snow will also play.

Forward: At times, jumping jack Matt Steigenga looks like a future pro. Other times, you don't even realize he's on the court. He must become more aggressive offensively. After sitting out last year due to Prop 48, 6'9" Anthony Miller could play his way into the starting lineup. He's an outstanding prospect. Dwayne Stephens is MSU's best defensive forward. Jon Zulauf's another outstanding leaper.

Center: Jud Heathcote needs to get free-spirited, 6'10", 270-pound Mike Peplowski more involved in the MSU offense. Knee problems have prevented him from fulfilling his early promise. He's coming off two impressive NCAA tourney performances last March.

Analysis: Without a go-to guy on the team, someone's going to have to step forward on offense. Steigenga's the most likely candidate. If the Spartans aren't careful, they could finish in the Big Ten's second division. If Steigenga, Peplowski, and Montgomery flourish, the Sweet 16's possible.

1991-92 ROSTER

	POS	HT	YR	FGP	FTP	3-PT	RPG	APG	PPG
Matt Steigenga	F	6'7"	Sr	.53	.70	13/26	4.9	2.1	12.6
Mike Peplowski	C	6'10"	Jr	.63	.68	—	6.9	0.5	7.7
Mark Montgomery	G	6'2"	Sr	.40	.61	22/74	3.4	5.8	7.5
Dwayne Stephens	F	6'7"	Jr	.50	.67	0/1	4.2	1.4	5.3
Kris Weshinskey	G	6'3"	So	.39	.74	4/18	1.0	0.6	2.5
Jon Zulauf	F	6'6"	Jr	.37	.45	—	1.8	0.2	1.3
Andy Penick	G	6'2"	So	.42	.80	21/47	0.6	0.8	4.0
Daimon Beathea	F	6'7"	Fr	—	—	—	—	—	—
Anthony Miller	F	6'9"	So	—	—	—	—	—	—
Steve Nicodemus	G	6'4"	Fr	—	—	—	—	—	—
Shawn Respert	G	6'3"	So	—	—	—	—	—	—
Eric Snow	G	6'3"	Fr	—	—	—	—	—	—

MISSOURI

Conference: Big Eight
1990-91: 20-10, 4th Big Eight

1990-91 NCAAs: Not eligible
Coach: Norm Stewart (572-283)

Opening Line: Although they'll be without All-America forward Doug Smith (23.6 PPG, 10.4 RPG), the Tigers are plenty optimistic after closing last season with a six-game winning streak and the Big Eight tourney title. Everyone else returns, including two dynamic seniors—guard Anthony Peeler and forward Jamal Coleman. The cloud of uncertainty that hovered over the program for months is finally gone.

Guard: Peeler, a smooth-shooting southpaw, steps forward as the Tigers' next superstar. Despite missing nine games last year due to grades, his 19.4 PPG was a career best. Sophomore Melvin Booker starts at the point, while Reggie Smith and Jed Frost will be the first guards off the bench. Booker and Smith need to improve their shooting.

Forward: Without Smith, Mizzou is bound to suffer defensively. Coleman, only 6'5", becomes the most effective defensive stopper. He's the team's best pure athlete. After sitting out the second half of his frosh season with a broken wrist, Jevon Crudup (12 PPG) returns rested and ready to go. He'll make his presence felt inside immediately. Jeff Warren, Lamont Frazier, and freshman Steve Horton supply solid depth.

Center: Missouri's late-season resurgence coincided with the insertion of 6'10" Chris Heller into the starting lineup. As a starter, he averaged nearly ten points and six boards per game. Now he must concentrate on his defense.

Analysis: Coleman, Crudup, and Heller must all help pick up the slack now that Smith has moved on. Heller's improvement will be the key. Peeler and Booker can open things up inside by nailing their outside shots. More teams will finish below the Tigers in the Big Eight than above.

1991-92 ROSTER

	POS	HT	YR	FGP	FTP	3-PT	RPG	APG	PPG
Anthony Peeler	G	6'4"	Sr	.48	.77	24/58	6.2	5.0	19.4
Jevon Crudup	F	6'9"	So	.53	.57	0/1	7.1	1.3	12.0
Jamal Coleman	F	6'5"	Sr	.49	.71	7/15	6.5	2.0	10.8
Melvin Booker	G	6'1"	So	.43	.67	19/35	2.2	3.5	8.3
Jeff Warren	F	6'8"	Jr	.67	.45	—	3.5	1.2	6.2
Chris Heller	C	6'10"	Jr	.50	.56	—	4.1	1.0	5.8
Jim Horton	C	6'10"	Sr	.58	.67	0/1	2.3	0.3	3.4
Reggie Smith	G	6'1"	So	.36	.53	3/14	2.0	2.7	2.4
Jed Frost	G	6'1"	So	.38	.31	7/24	0.7	0.8	2.1
Lamont Frazier	G/F	6'4"	So	.30	.38	1/5	1.6	0.8	1.7
John Burns	G	6'6"	Jr	.27	1.00	3/8	0.9	0.2	0.9
Steve Horton	F	6'8"	Fr	—	—	—	—	—	—

MURRAY STATE

Conference: Ohio Valley
1990-91: 24-9, 1st OVC

1990-91 NCAAs: 0-1
Coach: Scott Edgar (0-0)

Opening Line: Led by two-time OVC Player of the Year Ron "Popeye" Jones, the Racers advanced to the NCAA tournament for the third time in four seasons last spring—although they fell to Alabama in the first round. The loss of All-OVC performers Greg Coble and Paul King (second team) certainly won't help this team's chances for a fifth consecutive OVC title. The defection of coach Steve Newton to South Carolina also hurts. Scott Edgar, an assistant at Arkansas, takes over. Two starters, including Popeye, do return and help's on the way with a solid recruiting class.

Guard: The addition of juco transfers Maurice Cannon and Darren Hill will help fill this position. Cannon was the No. 2 junior college scorer in America last year with 29 PPG. Returning starter Frank Allen (14.1 PPG) has been declared academically ineligible. He was the most complete guard Newton had ever coached.

Forward: Although more suited for center, Scott Adams started 23 games last winter at forward. A lack of able bodies means he'll probably be back at big forward. Reserves Jerry Wilson and Scott Sivills lack game experience and could slip behind juco transfers Keelon Lawson and Reggie Dupree in the rotation.

Center: Jones is clearly the Racers' go-to guy. With his 14.2 RPG, he trailed only Shaquille O'Neal nationally. There's not another 6'8" player in the country who can dominate a game like Popeye can.

Analysis: With newcomers as talented as Cannon and Lawson, the loss of Coble, King, and Allen isn't that traumatic. As long as Popeye's in the lineup, the Racers are the class of the OVC. But for the third straight season, their joy of winning the OVC will quickly turn to sorrow when they fall in the first round of the NCAAs.

1991-92 ROSTER

	POS	HT	YR	FGP	FTP	3-PT	RPG	APG	PPG
Popeye Jones	C	6'8"	Sr	.49	.71	7/32	14.2	2.1	20.2
Scott Adams	C	6'9"	Jr	.47	.62	—	3.0	0.5	3.6
Donnie Langhi	F	6'6"	Jr	.67	.33	2/2	0.3	—	2.7
Cedric Gumm	G	6'1"	So	.45	.73	4/7	0.9	0.6	2.1
Terry Birdsong	G	6'3"	Sr	.29	.73	0/5	1.0	0.2	1.5
Jerry Wilson	F	6'7"	So	.45	.42	—	0.7	0.2	1.0
Scott Sivills	F	6'7"	Jr	.21	.58	—	1.4	0.4	1.0
Maurice Cannon	G	6'4"	Jr	—	—	—	—	—	—
Reggie Dupree	F	6'6"	Jr	—	—	—	—	—	—
Darren Hill	G	6'4"	Jr	—	—	—	—	—	—
Keelon Lawson	F	6'6"	Jr	—	—	—	—	—	—
Doug Turner	C	7'0"	Jr	—	—	—	—	—	—

NEVADA

Conference: Big Sky
1990-91: 17-14, 2nd Big Sky

1990-91 NCAAs: Not invited
Coach: Len Stevens (164-163)

Opening Line: Times are changing in the Big Sky Conference these days. Not only did the University of Nevada drop Reno from its name last year, but the Wolf Pack have vaulted past long-time league heavyweights Montana, Idaho, and Boise State and into the driver's seat in this year's title chase. Six of eight regulars, including four starters, return for what should be a promising season. Ric Herrin and Kevin Soares are the best center and point guard, respectively, in the Big Sky.

Guard: Soares attracted some interest from pro scouts with a solid all-around 1990-91 season. He averaged six assists, five rebounds, and more than 11 points per game. His perimeter shooting remains his only real shortcoming. Bryan Thomasson will be counted on for long-range scoring. His perimeter defense is a bonus. Juco transfer Melvin Jones, Rod Brown, and Herb LeDee also fit into the backcourt

formula. Like Soares, Brown can't shoot the ball real well.

Forward: Jerry Hogan's a pure shooter who could see action at small forward and big guard. He possesses superb range. Jason Schmidt and Gary Scott will also be in the running for starting jobs, as will juco transfer Kasey Brown. Schmidt's the best rebounder of the bunch. Brown's the most developed.

Center: When the pro scouts are in town, they're also paying a lot of attention to Herrin (6'10", 240). He's the Big Sky's top NBA prospect. He runs the floor well and possesses effective low-post moves.

Analysis: The Wolf Pack's success will revolve around Herrin and Soares inside and out. Having four more experienced regulars doesn't hurt either. If Herrin can avoid injuries and foul trouble, Nevada's season will last longer than UNLV's.

1991-92 ROSTER

	POS	HT	YR	FGP	FTP	3-PT	RPG	APG	PPG
Ric Herrin	C	6'10"	Jr	.50	.67	—	9.8	0.7	18.2
Bryan Thomasson	G	6'3"	Jr	.36	.64	45/136	2.7	1.0	11.9
Kevin Soares	G	6'1"	Sr	.40	.60	27/91	4.8	5.8	11.4
Gary Scott	F	6'5"	Sr	.43	.67	12/30	4.0	0.4	7.9
Jerry Hogan	G/F	6'5"	So	.39	.81	56/136	2.3	1.1	6.6
Jason Schmidt	F	6'7"	Jr	.53	.67	0/1	3.0	0.2	4.1
Rod Brown	G	6'1"	Jr	.31	.50	21/75	1.0	1.1	3.4
Herb LeDee	G/F	6'4"	Jr	.42	.40	0/3	1.0	0.2	1.3
Kasey Brown	F	6'7"	Jr	—	—	—	—	—	—
Kirk Davidson	C	6'10"	So	—	—	—	—	—	—
Melvin Jones	G	6'3"	So	—	—	—	—	—	—
Dan Lomas	C	6'10"	Jr	—	—	—	—	—	—

NEVADA-LAS VEGAS

Conference: Big West
1990-91: 34-1, 1st Big West

1990-91 NCAAs: 4-1
Coach: Jerry Tarkanian (599-120)

Opening Line: The Runnin' Rebs couldn't produce back-to-back national titles, but they did stage one of the most memorable games in NCAA history last March in a national semifinal against Duke. Despite the loss, Vegas was clearly one of the finest teams ever assembled. But that's ancient history now. This year's version is without NBA talents Larry Johnson, Stacey Augmon, Greg Anthony, Anderson Hunt, and George Ackles. Talk about having holes to fill!

Guard: Before opting for the NBA, Hunt was going to be the cornerstone of this year's club. Now it's up to star juco transfers J.R. Rider and Dexter Boney to replace him. Rider may even play some small forward. Inexperienced but capable sophomore H Waldman figures to inherit Anthony's point-guard slot.

Forward: Evric Gray and Melvin Love, two more juco products, will be Jerry Tarkanian's starting forwards.

Both played well in limited minutes last year. Gray's a superb athlete who knows how to take the ball to the basket. Love (6'10") will be counted on for shot-blocking and rebounding. Bobby Joyce is a strong, young kid with pointed elbows.

Center: The Rebels' inside game will revolve around chunky 7'0" senior Elmore Spencer. If he wants it bad enough, he could emerge as one of the top half-dozen big men in the country. He can score down low, rebound, and block shots with the best of 'em. He could also stand to shed a pound or two.

Analysis: Although you won't know the players without a program, this remains a pretty decent squad. Don't ever underestimate a Tarkanian-coached team. Future NBAers Rider and Spencer alone are capable of leading UNLV into Big West title contention.

1991-92 ROSTER

	POS	HT	YR	FGP	FTP	3-PT	RPG	APG	PPG
Evric Gray	F	6'7"	Jr	.50	.61	18/41	3.7	1.4	6.8
Elmore Spencer	C	7'0"	Sr	.52	.47	—	4.0	1.2	6.4
Melvin Love	C	6'10"	Sr	.67	.40	—	1.8	—	2.5
Bobby Joyce	F	6'7"	Jr	.47	.33	0/2	1.9	0.3	2.3
H Waldman	G	6'3"	So	.51	.60	11/24	1.0	2.3	2.1
Bryan Emerzian	G	6'0"	Sr	.00	—	0/1	0.1	—	—
Dexter Boney	G/F	6'4"	Jr	—	—	—	—	—	—
Danny Griffin	F	6'8"	So	—	—	—	—	—	—
Reggie Manuel	G	6'3"	Fr	—	—	—	—	—	—
J.R. Rider	G	6'5"	Jr	—	—	—	—	—	—
Dedan Thomas	G	6'0"	So	—	—	—	—	—	—
Barry Young	G/F	6'7"	Sr	—	—	—	—	—	—

NEW ORLEANS

Conference: Sun Belt
1990-91: 23-8, T-1st American South

1990-91 NCAAs: 0-1
Coach: Tim Floyd (98-55)

Opening Line: As the Privateers continue to chalk up 20-win seasons (four in five years), the NFL's Saints could fast become New Orleans' other team. The Privateers won 17 in a row last season. With everyone back except starters Tank Collins and Cass Clarke, there's no reason to believe they won't win 20 again.

Guard: Louweegi Dyer takes over for Clarke on a full-time basis at the point. Dyer and Clarke actually split time at the position over the past two seasons. Dyer's a far better shooter. There's a logjam at shooting guard between undersized Dwight Myvett (6'0"), Leonard Bennett, and Darren Laiche. Juco transfer Reggie Smith could beat them all out.

Forward: Although Collins (17.3 PPG, 5.5 RPG) is the team's only frontcourt loss, it's a costly one. He was the American South Player of the Year in 1990-91. Either untested holdover Fred Hill or freshman

Barnabas James will take his place. James was chosen America's top eighth grader by *Sports Illustrated* in 1986-87. No one is going to take muscle-bound power forward Melvin Simon's job. He was a frosh All-American last winter.

Center: Ervin Johnson can't pass like the guy in L.A., but he can certainly play defense and rebound. He grabbed more than a dozen caroms a night last season. Johnson worked in a supermarket for four years after high school before even enrolling at UNO.

Analysis: After losing to Kansas by six in last year's NCAA tourney, this could be the season New Orleans breaks through and wins a post-season game. Outstanding young coach Tim Floyd is no longer satisfied with just making the tournament and neither are his players. Johnson, Simon, and Dyer are the guys who must produce.

1991-92 ROSTER

	POS	HT	YR	FGP	FTP	3-PT	RPG	APG	PPG
Ervin Johnson	C	6'11"	Jr	.57	.54	—	12.2	1.1	12.7
Melvin Simon	F	6'8"	So	.50	.60	2/2	6.6	1.7	11.6
Dwight Myvett	G	6'0"	Sr	.46	.85	14/42	2.8	2.8	8.6
Louweegi Dyer	G	6'0"	Sr	.50	.75	1/5	1.4	2.9	7.4
Leonard Bennett	G	6'1"	Sr	.43	.71	29/66	2.1	1.8	5.5
Sydney Rice	F/C	6'10"	Sr	.46	.56	0/1	4.4	0.3	5.1
Fred Hill	F	6'6"	Jr	.35	.55	0/1	0.9	0.1	1.4
Darren Laiche	F/G	6'4"	Jr	.57	.54	—	1.6	0.6	0.9
Levan Alston	G	6'3"	Fr	—	—	—	—	—	—
Reginald Garrett	G/F	6'4"	Fr	—	—	—	—	—	—
Barnabas James	F	6'6"	Fr	—	—	—	—	—	—
Reggie Smith	F	6'4"	Jr	—	—	—	—	—	—

NORTH CAROLINA

Conference: Atlantic Coast
1990-91: 29-6, 2nd ACC

1990-91 NCAAs: 4-1
Coach: Dean Smith (717-209)

Opening Line: Replacing three proven veterans like Rick Fox, Pete Chilcutt, and King Rice won't be easy. But at Carolina, the blow is softened by the fact that the ten returnees appeared in an average of 29 games each! Dean Smith's revolving-door tactic of shuttling players in and out promises to pay dividends this season. Although the Tar Heels are young, they do possess experience and depth.

Guard: Lone senior Hubert Davis (13.3 PPG) returns as UNC's go-to guy offensively. The nephew of Walter Davis, he's a streaky shooter who finished second in scoring to Fox last winter. His forte is the 3-pointer. Athletic swing man Brian Reese will often spell Davis. Derrick Phelps (a Kenny Smith clone) will handle the point. Phelps's presence made Rice a better player last season. Freshman Donald Williams will contend for playing time.

Forward: Like Davis, George Lynch also knows a thing or two about scoring. Smith will encourage him to shoot often. He plays much taller than 6'7". Big Clifford Rozier's decision to transfer to Louisville will affect Carolina on the boards. Swing man Henrik Rodl and Pat Sullivan both have a scorer's mentality.

Center: In Eric Montross, Kevin Salvadori, and Matt Wenstrom, Smith's got three seven-footers at his disposal. Montross should be ready to explode on the national scene as a sophomore. All he needs is more minutes.

Analysis: Without Fox, Chilcutt, and Rice, don't expect the Tar Heels to visit the Final Four until 1993. Although there's talent galore, it's going to take a while for it all to mesh. An ACC title appears possible, as does an incredible 12th straight Sweet 16 visit.

1991-92 ROSTER

	POS	HT	YR	FGP	FTP	3-PT	RPG	APG	PPG
Hubert Davis	G	6'4"	Sr	.52	.84	64/131	2.4	1.9	13.3
George Lynch	F	6'7"	Jr	.52	.63	7/10	7.4	1.2	12.5
Eric Montross	C	7'0"	So	.59	.61	—	4.2	0.3	5.8
Brian Reese	G	6'5"	So	.53	.55	3/5	1.6	0.5	4.0
Henrik Rodl	G/F	6'7"	Jr	.57	.62	12/27	1.5	1.8	3.6
Derrick Phelps	G	6'3"	So	.49	.76	2/9	1.1	1.9	2.3
Kevin Salvadori	C	7'0"	So	.51	.63	—	0.9	—	1.5
Scott Cherry	G	6'4"	Jr	.71	.69	1/1	0.4	0.6	1.5
Pat Sullivan	F	6'8"	So	.44	.65	1/5	0.6	0.5	1.0
Matt Wenstrom	C	7'1"	Jr	.33	.58	—	0.9	—	0.7
Larry Davis	G	6'3"	Fr	—	—	—	—	—	—
Donald Williams	G	6'3"	Fr	—	—	—	—	—	—

NORTH CAROLINA-CHARLOTTE

Conference: Metro
1990-91: 14-14, 6th Sun Belt

1990-91 NCAAs: Not invited
Coach: Jeff Mullins (95-83)

Opening Line: After hitting their stride in mid-January, the 49ers faded from 12-6 to a final mark of 14-14 last season. It was a terribly disappointing and unexpected ending for a promising young team that will now embark upon life in the new-look Metro Conference. With 12 of 13 lettermen returning, including all five starters, UNCC will be vastly improved in 1991-92.

Guard: Senior scoring whiz Henry Williams is one of the top half-dozen guards in the country. He's double- and tripled-teamed now on a regular basis. He's been selected Sun Belt Freshman, Sophomore, and Junior of the Year. Bershuan Thompson and Delano Johnson will share the point-guard duties. Johnson's 77 steals ranked him among the national leaders. Able reserves Cedrick Broadhurst and James Terrell averaged a combined 15 PPG last winter.

Forward: Freshman All-American Jarvis Lang became only the third frosh in NCAA history to lead all rookies in both scoring (19.6) and rebounding (10.6). Malru Dottin is a strong interior player who'll start the year ahead of offensive minded Daryl DeVaull.

Center: Hard-working senior Jack Bolly has experience going for him, but he'll have to contend with 6'11" newcomers Rodney Odom (formerly at UCLA) and Jermaine Parker (redshirt freshman). Odom should make an immediate impact. Improved low-post defense is a must.

Analysis: Last year's woes centered around inexperience. The 49ers simply couldn't make the big plays when they had to. Led by the one-two punch of Williams and Lang, their luck is bound to change in 1992. They'll make the Metro a three-team race with Southern Miss and Louisville.

1991-92 ROSTER

	POS	HT	YR	FGP	FTP	3-PT	RPG	APG	PPG
Henry Williams	G	6'2"	Sr	.43	.83	72/212	3.0	2.0	21.6
Jarvis Lang	F	6'6"	So	.47	.71	4/11	10.6	0.6	19.6
Delano Johnson	G	6'0"	Jr	.41	.56	6/27	4.0	5.3	8.6
Cedrick Broadhurst	G	6'3"	Jr	.37	.58	25/61	2.7	2.0	7.7
James Terrell	G	6'0"	So	.40	.57	30/77	1.2	1.3	7.0
Malru Dottin	F	6'6"	Jr	.50	.65	—	5.0	0.5	6.1
Daryl DeVaull	F	6'9"	Jr	.45	.71	2/14	4.9	0.5	5.9
Bershuan Thompson	G	6'3"	So	.38	.66	9/30	2.2	2.3	4.8
Benny Moss	F	6'8"	Jr	.33	.62	10/37	0.8	0.9	4.4
Jack Bolly	C	6'9"	Sr	.29	.50	—	4.3	1.3	1.8
Rodney Odom	C	6'11"	So	—	—	—	—	—	—
Jermaine Parker	C	6'11"	Fr	—	—	—	—	—	—

NOTRE DAME

Conference: Independent
1990-91: 12-20

1990-91 NCAAs: Not invited
Coach: John MacLeod (90-69)

Opening Line: Although he hasn't coached at the collegiate level since his days at Oklahoma in the early 1970s, John MacLeod is Digger Phelps's unexpected successor. Last year's collapse wasn't entirely Digger's fault. In his defense, highly regarded sophomore Monty Williams's career ended due to a heart defect, All-America candidate LaPhonso Ellis was declared ineligible, and point guard Tim Singleton missed time with a back injury. Singleton and part-time starter Kevin Ellery both graduated.

Guard: Cat-quick senior Elmer Bennett is a natural leader who, like many of his teammates, wasn't broken-hearted over Digger's decision to move on. When he stays under control, Bennett's as good as any point guard in the Midwest. Freshman Jason Williams is his protege. Although he's not much of a perimeter scorer, Daimon Sweet (16.3 PPG) should see a lot of time at shooting guard. Heady sophomore Brooks Boyer is the utility man.

Forward: Ellis's return is a real key. He's not the superstar many originally projected he'd be, but he is a true impact player when he's in the mood. Versatile Malik Russell or fellow frosh Billy Taylor could join Ellis in the starting frontcourt, as could improved Jon Ross.

Center: Keith Tower is a tough, physical kid (6'11", 252) who practices better than he plays. MacLeod needs to instill a more positive attitude in the big fella. Freshman Nathion Gilmore can also be counted on.

Analysis: MacLeod will no doubt open up the attack, something Phelps was always hesitant to do even though he stocked his team with quick, open-court players. If Ellis stays eligible, there's sufficient talent on this team to win 18 to 20 games.

1991-92 ROSTER

	POS	HT	YR	FGP	FTP	3-PT	RPG	APG	PPG
LaPhonso Ellis	F	6'9"	Sr	.57	.72	8/17	10.5	1.7	16.4
Daimon Sweet	F	6'5"	Sr	.57	.80	—	4.1	1.5	16.3
Elmer Bennett	G	6'1"	Sr	.41	.74	32/87	3.0	4.6	14.4
Keith Tower	C	6'11"	Sr	.46	.63	—	7.0	1.7	7.9
Brooks Boyer	G	6'2"	So	.35	.74	15/39	0.7	0.4	2.8
Jon Ross	F	6'9"	So	.46	.58	1/1	1.8	0.2	2.0
Joe Ross	F/C	6'10"	So	.46	.60	—	1.1	0.1	1.3
Nathion Gilmore	G	6'9"	Fr	—	—	—	—	—	—
Lamarr Justice	G	6'3"	Fr	—	—	—	—	—	—
Malik Russell	F	6'8"	Fr	—	—	—	—	—	—
Billy Taylor	F	6'6"	Fr	—	—	—	—	—	—
Jason Williams	G	6'3"	Fr	—	—	—	—	—	—

OHIO STATE

Conference: Big Ten
1990-91: 27-4, T-1st Big Ten

1990-91 NCAAs: 2-1
Coach: Randy Ayers (44-17)

Opening Line: Buckeye fans hadn't seen a team like they saw last year since the glory days of the early 1960s. Led by Big Ten Player of the Year Jim Jackson and national Coach of the Year Randy Ayers, Ohio State won its first 17 games last winter before losing at Michigan State on January 31. The loss of behemoths Perry Carter and Treg Lee means 23.5 PPG and 14 RPG will have to come from other sources.

Guard: Mark Baker returns as the Big Ten's best all-around point guard. Equally adept at passing and shooting, he's difficult to defend one-on-one. Jamaal Brown established himself as more than just a solid defender last season. He shot 40 percent from 3-point land and ranked third on the team in scoring (12 PPG). Alex Davis and Jamie Skelton return as key subs.

Forward: Jackson's one of those rare birds who makes better players out of those around him. The only knock on him is his unselfishness. Many of his points are scored in the game's closing minutes. Ayers would like to see him become a little more assertive offensively. Super-intense Chris Jent (former sixth man) and Tom Brandewie will see a lot of action. One-time Indiana recruit Lawrence Funderburke (6'8") could be eligible for the second semester.

Center: Bill Robinson (7'0", 240) still looks better in airports than he does on the court. He's yet to develop a mean streak. Freshman Antonio Watson has a great future.

Analysis: Despite the loss of Carter and Lee, the Buckeyes will again be in the running for a top-ten finish. Only Indiana can give them a run in the Big Ten. Jackson's a real gem. Ayers must devise a way for his team to get some rebounds. Robinson and Watson could really be a big help.

1991-92 ROSTER

	POS	HT	YR	FGP	FTP	3-PT	RPG	APG	PPG
Jim Jackson	F/G	6'6"	Jr	.52	.75	17/51	5.5	4.3	18.9
Jamaal Brown	G	6'4"	Sr	.46	.75	34/85	2.4	2.2	12.0
Mark Baker	G	6'1"	Sr	.52	.71	0/4	2.4	5.0	10.9
Chris Jent	F/G	6'7"	Sr	.47	.81	32/79	3.6	1.8	8.1
Jamie Skelton	G	6'2"	So	.38	.61	10/34	0.7	0.6	3.0
Jimmy Ratliff	F	6'8"	So	.44	.70	0/1	1.7	0.4	2.9
Bill Robinson	C	7'0"	Sr	.59	.64	—	3.4	0.2	2.7
Tom Brandewie	F	6'8"	Jr	.61	.62	1/2	1.9	0.2	2.4
Alex Davis	G	6'1"	Sr	.38	.88	3/18	0.6	0.9	2.3
Rickey Dudley	F	6'7"	Fr	—	—	—	—	—	—
Doug Etzler	G	6'0"	Fr	—	—	—	—	—	—
Antonio Watson	C/F	6'9"	Fr	—	—	—	—	—	—

OKLAHOMA

Conference: Big Eight
1990-91: 20-15, T-6th Big Eight

1990-91 NIT: 4-1
Coach: Billy Tubbs (352-144)

Opening Line: What was the problem with the Sooners last season? Injuries. After they claimed starters Kermit Holmes, Terry Evans, and Terrence Mullins, Oklahoma lost 11 of 14 games. Led by promising center Bryan Sallier, the Sooners did get things turned around during NIT play before succumbing to Stanford in the title game. Holmes and Mullins have graduated. Coach Billy Tubbs has brought in a half-dozen juco transfers.

Guard: South Carolina transfer Brent Price (Mark's brother) made a big splash last season while topping the team in steals and averaging 17.5 PPG. Valuable 3-point specialist Terry Evans can also handle the point. Juco transfer Angelo Hamilton and heralded freshman Shon Alexander will vie for time at big guard.

Forward: Jeff Webster ended the 1990-91 season as the second-highest freshman scorer in Big Eight history (behind Wayman Tisdale). He was named conference newcomer of the year. Joel Davis was considered the top small forward in the juco ranks last winter. He scored 54 in one game. Roland Ware is a gutsy rebounder who started 16 games a year ago. Damon Patterson, a 1989-90 all-conference honoree, could regain his eligibility.

Center: After appearing out of shape for much of the year, Sallier was unstoppable down the stretch. In his final six games, he averaged 18 points and nearly ten rebounds per game. His potential is limitless.

Analysis: Even with all the new faces, this remains a high-flying bunch that's liable to lead the nation in scoring. With no real defensive stoppers and a press that seems to get less effective every year, the Sooners may also finish first in points allowed. At the very least, a fourth-place finish is in the cards.

1991-92 ROSTER

	POS	HT	YR	FGP	FTP	3-PT	RPG	APG	PPG
Jeff Webster	F	6'8"	So	.57	.80	0/2	5.5	0.2	18.3
Brent Price	G	6'1"	Sr	.42	.84	91/244	3.6	5.5	17.5
Terry Evans	G	6'1"	Jr	.35	.79	65/192	3.0	6.2	11.1
Bryan Sallier	C	6'8"	So	.53	.54	0/1	5.6	0.9	10.2
Roland Ware	C	6'6"	So	.47	.69	9/22	5.0	1.9	7.5
Keke Hicks	G	6'1"	So	.33	.68	7/37	1.1	1.2	5.0
Shon Alexander	G/F	6'4"	Fr	—	—	—	—	—	—
Eric Coates	G/F	6'5"	Jr	—	—	—	—	—	—
Joel Davis	F	6'5"	Jr	—	—	—	—	—	—
Derrick Gallien	F	6'8"	Jr	—	—	—	—	—	—
Angelo Hamilton	G/F	6'5"	Jr	—	—	—	—	—	—
Damon Patterson	F	6'8"	Sr	—	—	—	—	—	—

OKLAHOMA STATE

Conference: Big Eight
1990-91: 24-8, T-1st Big Eight

1990-91 NCAAs: 2-1
Coach: Eddie Sutton (454-172)

Opening Line: New coach Eddie Sutton wasn't so sure he could chalk up 20 wins in his first year at his alma mater, let alone win 24 and advance to the Sweet 16. Yet after they proved they weren't afraid of a little defense and hard work, the 'Pokes make quick believers out of Sutton and their Big Eight foes. Two key starters, center Johnny Pittman and forward John Potter, must be replaced.

Guard: Darwyn Alexander, Sean Sutton (Eddie's son), and Corey Williams quietly comprise the top backcourt trio in the Big Eight. Sutton's the best passer of the bunch, while Alexander possesses blazing speed. Williams is probably the best pure shooter, although Sutton did nail 46 percent of his 3-point attempts. Defensively, Alexander's too quick to beat to the hole.

Forward: Mattias Sahlstrom and Milton Brown could be relegated to more bench duty if juco transfers Randy Davis and Jonathan Triplett live up to expectations. Although he's 6'10" and 220 pounds, Sahlstrom is more suited for the perimeter. Brown lacks experience, as does promising Cornell Hatcher. Davis is a player to watch.

Center: Co-Big Eight Player of the Year Byron Houston should have the award to himself this year. His exceptional low-post moves make him the team's most effective center, although big forward is his more natural position. A fierce competitor, he was born to rebound.

Analysis: Despite Houston's presence, this is basically a finesse team. Sutton is trying to change that with newcomers like Davis and Triplett. Led by Houston, a dynamite guard trio, and a veteran coach, anything less than first or second place in the Big Eight and another Sweet 16 performance would be a disappointment.

1991-92 ROSTER

	POS	HT	YR	FGP	FTP	3-PT	RPG	APG	PPG
Byron Houston	F/C	6'7"	Sr	.57	.74	3/4	10.5	2.1	22.7
Sean Sutton	G	6'1"	Sr	.47	.75	50/110	2.2	4.0	10.2
Darwyn Alexander	G	6'0"	Sr	.47	.90	9/26	2.3	3.0	9.2
Corey Williams	G	6'2"	Sr	.53	.70	16/40	2.1	2.3	8.3
Mattias Sahlstrom	F	6'10"	Sr	.42	.60	8/21	2.4	0.6	5.1
Milton Brown	F	6'4"	Jr	.47	.40	—	2.5	0.5	2.8
Cornell Hatcher	F	6'4"	Sr	.43	.64	0/5	2.2	1.7	2.5
Mike Philpott	F	6'6"	So	.46	.33	—	0.1	0.1	1.0
Terry Collins	G	6'5"	Fr	—	—	—	—	—	—
Randy Davis	C	6'9"	Jr	—	—	—	—	—	—
Sean Pell	F	6'9"	Fr	—	—	—	—	—	—
Jonathon Triplett	F	6'8"	Jr	—	—	—	—	—	—

PENN STATE

Conference: Independent
1990-91: 21-11, T-3rd A-10

1990-91 NCAAs: 1-1
Coach: Bruce Parkhill (208-191)

Opening Line: How unusual was it for the Nittany Lions to appear in last year's NCAA tournament? Very. They hadn't been in 26 years. Their tourney win, over UCLA, was their first in 36 years. With an average of 22 wins a season over the past three, Penn State backers are beginning to realize that football's no longer the only game in town. Power forward James Barnes (12.8 PPG, 7.5 RPG) is the only graduated starter. He's a key loss.

Guard: For the third straight year, the backcourt is in the capable hands of Freddie Barnes and Monroe Brown. They don't get the credit they deserve. Barnes is the playmaking trigger man who does a fine job of running Penn State's numerous halfcourt sets. Brown's an outstanding perimeter defender. Streak shooter Michael Jennings is the first man off the pine.

Forward: All-Atlantic 10 performer DeRon Hayes is the guy this team is built around. He's a big-time scorer who likes to take matters into his own hands when the game's on the line. Although Elton Carter, Jon Dietz, and Eric Carr will all play regularly, crashing the boards isn't their forte. Next to Hayes and center Dave Degitz, untested freshman Matt Gaudio may be the best rebounder on the team.

Center: Degitz gets the most out of his limited ability. A hard worker defensively, he's never really gotten into the flow on offense. Freshman Michael Joseph is a 6'10" project.

Analysis: With their Atlantic 10 days now history and Big Ten play still a year away, the Nittany Lions will compete as an independent. There will be more pressure than ever on Hayes now that James Barnes is no longer his running mate. With extraordinary guard play and a big year from Degitz, this club could return to the 20-win plateau.

1991-92 ROSTER

	POS	HT	YR	FGP	FTP	3-PT	RPG	APG	PPG
DeRon Hayes	F	6'6"	Jr	.51	.77	0/12	4.8	2.1	15.0
Freddie Barnes	G	6'0"	Sr	.37	.83	54/147	3.4	4.8	12.4
Monroe Brown	G	6'3"	Sr	.46	.68	23/59	3.6	4.7	9.8
Dave Degitz	C	6'9"	Sr	.47	.69	—	4.6	0.7	9.3
Michael Jennings	G	6'5"	Jr	.39	.63	13/38	1.2	0.9	3.8
Jon Dietz	F	6'8"	Jr	.36	.76	4/12	1.1	0.2	2.9
Elton Carter	F	6'7"	So	.36	.73	0/1	1.0	—	1.6
Eric Carr	F	6'6"	Jr	.12	.73	0/1	1.2	0.2	0.8
Greg Bartram	G	6'4"	Fr	—	—	—	—	—	—
Matt Gaudio	F	6'7"	Fr	—	—	—	—	—	—
Michael Joseph	C	6'10"	Fr	—	—	—	—	—	—
Donovan Williams	G	6'1"	Fr	—	—	—	—	—	—

PEPPERDINE

Conference: West Coast
1990-91: 22-9, 1st WCC

1990-91 NCAAs: 0-1
Coach: Tom Asbury (59-33)

Opening Line: After falling to San Diego on January 11 last season, the Waves didn't lose again until they met Seton Hall in the opening round of the NCAA tournament. In all, they reeled off an impressive 16-game winning streak. The outcome of the Seton Hall game may have been different had WCC Player of the Year Doug Christie been in the lineup. Christie tore cartilage in his knee on March 2. All five starters and two of the top three reserves are back.

Guard: Christie, now healthy, has an NBA career in his future. He topped the Waves in scoring, assists, and steals last year. Both graceful and versatile, he's a poor man's Steve Smith. Point guard Damin Lopez looks like the student manager, but get him on the floor and he does a fine job of executing the offense. Team leader Rick Welch is the top backcourt substitute.

Forward: Geoff Lear, a two-time All-WCC performer, is blessed with great instincts. He's a bulky power player who won't be denied down low. Dana Jones, the WCC Freshman of the Year last season, is the team's premier defender. Steve Guild and Byron Jenson come off the bench.

Center: Immobile Derek Noether started 29 games a year ago. Juco transfer Eric Bellamy or freshman LeRoi O'Brien could beat him out of a job. Ex-prep All-American Mark Georgeson hopes to rejoin the team after being seriously injured in 1989.

Analysis: The Waves should again roll through the WCC. But wait, that's not all. This is a talented and experienced group that is capable of a top-25 ranking and an NCAA tournament win or two. They excel in two vital areas—team defense and rebounding.

1991-92 ROSTER

	POS	HT	YR	FGP	FTP	3-PT	RPG	APG	PPG
Doug Christie	G/F	6'6"	Sr	.47	.77	17/65	5.2	4.8	19.1
Geoff Lear	F	6'8"	Sr	.56	.56	0/1	9.8	1.6	18.5
Dana Jones	F	6'6"	So	.58	.53	—	8.2	2.4	10.0
Rick Welch	G	6'0"	Sr	.44	.88	53/116	1.5	2.7	7.5
Steve Guild	G	6'6"	Jr	.41	.68	26/79	2.8	1.5	6.9
Derek Noether	C/F	6'8"	So	.54	.49	—	4.2	0.5	5.8
Damin Lopez	G	5'9"	So	.41	.85	25/69	0.8	2.2	3.8
Rodney Sanders	G	6'3"	So	.38	.63	6/18	0.3	0.3	1.5
Eric Bellamy	C	6'9"	Jr	—	—	—	—	—	—
Derric Croft	G	6'4"	Fr	—	—	—	—	—	—
Byron Jenson	F	6'7"	Jr	—	—	—	—	—	—
LeRoi O'Brien	F/C	6'8"	Fr	—	—	—	—	—	—

PRINCETON

Conference: Ivy League
1990-91: 24-3, 1st Ivy

1990-91 NCAAs: 0-1
Coach: Pete Carril (432-231)

Opening Line: Following near upsets of Georgetown and Arkansas in opening-round 1989 and 1990 NCAA tournament action, the Tigers lost a tourney game to Villanova they were actually supposed to win last spring. Princeton loses Kit Mueller, a two-time Ivy League Player of the Year. He was the team's best all-around frontcourter since Bill Bradley. The other four starters do return.

Guard: Shooting guard Sean Jackson inherits Mueller's role as the leader of the pack. He can nail 3-pointers with his eyes closed. Jackson and Mueller were the only double-figure scorers on last year's squad. Lead guard George Leftwich has committed only 75 turnovers in his 72-game career. Mike Brennan is being groomed as Leftwich's replacement.

Forward: Matt Eastwick and Chris Mooney return for their second season together as starters. A tough and intimidating defender, Eastwick is probably the flashiest player on a team that lacks flash. Mooney is the club's hardest worker. Able reserve Chris Marquardt shoots nearly 50 percent from 3-point land.

Center: How important was Mueller to this team? He led the Tigers in scoring, rebounding, and assists in each of the past three years. Michael Silas will be pressed for a starting job by freshman Rick Hielscher. Both need a lot of work defensively. Another potential starter, Jimmy Lane, quit the team.

Analysis: Carril's constant-motion, back-door offense is a basketball purist's delight, as is his high-intensity approach to defense. It's the system, not the players, that wins games for Princeton and that's why the Mueller-less Tigers will win the Ivy again. Despite their run of lousy post-season luck, they remain an extremely dangerous, deliberate team that no one wants to play.

1991-92 ROSTER

	POS	HT	YR	FGP	FTP	3-PT	RPG	APG	PPG
Sean Jackson	G	5'11"	Sr	.47	.83	95/198	1.9	1.0	12.7
Chris Marquardt	F	6'8"	Sr	.58	.68	41/86	1.9	1.7	7.9
George Leftwich	G	6'2"	Sr	.50	.67	6/22	2.3	2.3	5.0
Chris Mooney	F	6'5"	So	.45	.63	17/53	2.0	1.4	4.9
Matt Eastwick	F	6'8"	Sr	.54	.59	12/37	2.5	1.0	4.7
Mike Brennan	G	6'0"	So	.35	.81	6/20	1.3	0.3	2.6
Steve Eidle	G	5'11"	Fr	—	—	—	—	—	—
Rick Hielscher	C	6'8"	Fr	—	—	—	—	—	—
Peter LaMantia	G	6'1"	Fr	—	—	—	—	—	—
Brian Leftwich	G	6'2"	Fr	—	—	—	—	—	—
Brendan Pocock	C/F	6'7"	Fr	—	—	—	—	—	—
Michael Silas	C	6'9"	Jr	—	—	—	—	—	—

PURDUE

Conference: Big Ten
1990-91: 17-12, T-5th Big Ten

1990-91 NCAAs: 0-1
Coach: Gene Keady (270-124)

Opening Line: The better-than-expected Boilers succeeded a year ago by pounding the ball inside. Gene Keady's a big believer in high-percentage shots from the paint, outrebounding your opponent, and going to the line. The departure of solid senior forwards Jimmy Oliver (All-Big Ten) and Chuckie White (league's No. 1 rebounder) will force Keady to alter his game plan—unless freshman Cuonzo Martin is as good as his newspaper clippings say he is.

Guard: Senior Woody Austin scored 14.3 PPG last year, but as late as August he was scrambling to remain academically eligible. He's also had run-ins with Keady, so his status is shaky. Matt Painter (6'6") will play the point. He's an outstanding passer who rarely turns the ball over. Linc Darner, a 3-point threat, started 14 times last winter. Travis Trice is Purdue's quickest guard. In time, Herb Dove could be its best.

Forward: Ian Stanback gave the team a spark off the bench as a freshman last year. He's an aggressive offensive rebounder who shows loads of promise. He'll be joined up front by three very promising freshmen in Robinson, Martin, and Brandon Brantley. Glenn Robinson, a first-team high school All-American, would have made an impact if eligible (Prop 48). Todd Schoettelkotte transferred to Rice.

Center: Craig Riley's a solid 6'9" pivot man who can't jump a lick. He's trying to become more of an offensive threat. Cornelius McNary has settled into a valuable reserve role.

Analysis: The super-intense Keady seems to get more out of his players than any other coach. This year, he has a young team that will need a lot of teaching. Purdue's impressive recruiting class was ranked in the top ten by numerous scouting services.

1991-92 ROSTER

	POS	HT	YR	FGP	FTP	3-PT	RPG	APG	PPG
Woody Austin	G	6'2"	Sr	.46	.70	28/60	3.6	2.4	14.3
Craig Riley	C	6'9"	Sr	.52	.68	0/2	3.0	0.6	6.4
Ian Stanback	F	6'7"	So	.67	.45	1/1	3.9	0.4	5.8
Linc Darner	G	6'4"	So	.38	.82	32/84	2.0	1.3	5.4
Matt Painter	G	6'6"	Jr	.42	.63	15/42	1.9	3.0	4.2
Cornelius McNary	C	6'9"	Jr	.40	.71	—	2.0	0.2	3.8
Travis Trice	G	6'1"	So	.33	.73	4/24	1.2	2.6	2.2
Brandon Brantley	F	6'8"	Fr	—	—	—	—	—	—
Herb Dove	G	6'4"	Fr	—	—	—	—	—	—
Cuonzo Martin	F	6'6"	Fr	—	—	—	—	—	—
Matt Waddell	G	6'4"	So	—	—	—	—	—	—

RICE

Conference: Southwest
1990-91: 16-14, T-4th SWC

1990-91 NIT: 0-1
Coach: Scott Thompson (45-68)

Opening Line: Last year's winning record was the first for Rice since 1971. The Owls hadn't won as many as 16 games since 1957. Rice closed the season as one of the hottest teams in the nation with ten wins in its final 14 ballgames. Twelve lettermen—including all five starters—return, led by All-SWC candidates Brent Scott and Chase Maag.

Guard: Dana Hardy, a scoring point guard, was one of two Owls to start every game last season (along with Scott). He made a late-season run for All-SWC honors. Marvin Moore is a two guard trapped in a point guard's body. Tough defensively, he'll be pushed for minutes by Northwestern transfer David Holmes and inexperienced Will Strickland. Holmes, Scott's cousin, was a two-year Wildcat starter.

Forward: Maag was the league's newcomer of the year last season. A deadly shooter when he's given room, he exploded for 35 markers at Arkansas. He's a 42-percent shooter from 3-point territory, which takes a lot of pressure off Scott inside. Senior Kenneth Rourke is no slouch, but he hasn't been able to equal his big freshman season. Torrey Andrews and redshirt freshman Robert Glaze are players to watch.

Center: Scott is on pace to become the school's best-ever rebounder. This is the year he should make a name for himself nationally. He's got all the tools to be a great one by the time the NBA comes calling in 1993.

Analysis: With the eight players who played in the Owls' NIT loss to Arkansas State returning, Rice figures to join Texas at the top of the SWC. For the first time since he's been coach, Scott Thompson finally has some quality depth to work with. His motion offense could prove to be too much for the rest of the conference to handle.

1991-92 ROSTER

	POS	HT	YR	FGP	FTP	3-PT	RPG	APG	PPG
Brent Scott	C	6'9"	Jr	.58	.55	—	10.1	3.1	16.9
Chase Maag	F	6'4"	Sr	.42	.78	55/132	4.3	1.5	13.5
Dana Hardy	G	6'2"	Sr	.49	.69	51/118	3.3	4.5	12.1
Kenneth Rourke	F	6'10"	Sr	.51	.63	0/1	5.6	0.8	8.9
Marvin Moore	G	5'11"	Jr	.44	.64	16/55	2.5	3.1	8.3
Torrey Andrews	F	6'5"	So	.59	.82	3/6	3.5	0.6	6.8
Sam Campbell	G	6'2"	So	.40	.55	4/12	1.4	0.8	2.9
Will Strickland	G	6'5"	Sr	.34	.39	2/12	1.1	0.4	1.6
Hakim Ali Bell	F	6'7"	Fr	—	—	—	—	—	—
Robert Glaze	F/C	6'9"	Fr	—	—	—	—	—	—
David Holmes	G	6'5"	Fr	—	—	—	—	—	—
Scott Tynes	F	6'6"	So	—	—	—	—	—	—

RICHMOND

Conference: Colonial Athletic
1990-91: 22-10, 2nd CAA

1990-91 NCAAs: 1-1
Coach: Dick Tarrant (202-106)

Opening Line: Underrated coach Dick Tarrant's Spiders made NCAA tournament history last spring. When they shocked Syracuse in the opening round, it marked the first time a team seeded 15th or lower defeated a No. 2 or higher seed. In all, Tarrant's troops won 16 of their last 19 games. Everyone but starting forward Terry Connolly (8.2 PPG) returns.

Guard: While Gerald Jarmon and Eugene Burroughs do a commendable job of alternating at the point, All-CAA guard Curtis Blair is the team's most dangerous player. He's a strong, athletic shooting guard who can beat a team in a lot of ways. Jarmon and Burroughs both chalked up plenty of experience last year. Jarmon's a solid ball-handler, while Burroughs is a pickpocket.

Forward: Kenny Wood is on the verge of becoming a star. He began to assert himself in the middle of 1990-91 and went on to average 17 points and nearly eight rebounds a game in conference play. His older brother, Howard, played for the Utah Jazz (1981-82). Georgetown transfer Milton Bell or Jim Springer will join Wood in the starting lineup. A gifted scorer, Bell should make an immediate impact.

Center: Jim Shields is the team's premier low-post defender. Tarrant is hopeful that his 26-point, 11-rebound effort in a CAA title-game win over George Mason is a sign of things to come. Hot-shot freshman Jason Scott could see limited action.

Analysis: Led by a nucleus of Blair, Wood, and Shields, Richmond is a lock to finish on top of the CAA this season. A lack of proven depth, overall team speed, and consistency at point guard could prove to be the undoing of the Spiders' web. There's not a coach in the country who's a more astute student of the game than Tarrant.

1991-92 ROSTER

	POS	HT	YR	FGP	FTP	3-PT	RPG	APG	PPG
Curtis Blair	G	6'3"	Sr	.45	.74	33/96	4.1	3.2	16.1
Kenny Wood	F	6'5"	Jr	.54	.79	2/10	7.0	1.3	14.3
Jim Shields	C/F	6'10"	Sr	.52	.57	—	4.4	1.1	7.7
Chris Fleming	G/F	6'6"	Jr	.45	.64	44/99	1.6	0.6	7.4
Jim Springer	F	6'8"	Jr	.49	.73	—	3.9	0.7	5.9
Tim Weathers	F	6'6"	Jr	.41	.81	20/56	2.7	1.0	5.9
Gerald Jarmon	G	6'0"	So	.46	.63	11/29	1.3	2.4	3.7
Eugene Burroughs	G	6'1"	So	.39	.81	7/27	0.8	2.2	2.6
Michael Hodges	F	6'5"	So	.55	.50	1/4	1.3	0.2	2.4
Milton Bell	F	6'8"	Jr	—	—	—	—	—	—
Steve Belter	F	6'6"	Fr	—	—	—	—	—	—
Jason Scott	F	6'9"	Fr	—	—	—	—	—	—

ST. JOHN'S

Conference: Big East
1990-91: 23-9, 2nd Big East

1990-91 NCAAs: 3-1
Coach: Lou Carnesecca (507-189)

Opening Line: The Redmen's 1991 season finale was a carbon copy of 1990's—an NCAA tournament loss to Duke. They did manage to knock off Northern Illinois, Texas, and Ohio State prior to meeting the Blue Devils in the Midwest Regional Final. With everyone back but starting forward Billy Singleton and reserve center Sean Muto, the Redmen are primed to advance even further in '92.

Guard: Jason Buchanan can run a team as well as any guard in the East. His shooting and decision-making picked up during the Big East portion of the 1990-91 season. Athletic Chuck Sproling doesn't shoot as well as the coaches would like, but he does move well without the ball. His defense keeps him in the starting lineup. David Cain is Buchanan's caddie.

Forward: Malik Sealy is an All-Big East selection who'll push for first-team All-America mention this season. From 15 feet and in, there's nothing he can't do. Shawnelle Scott or juco transfer Mitchell Foster will start opposite Sealy. They both pack a powerful punch. Unsung Hartford transfer Lamont Middleton (6'6") averaged 19 PPG in 1989-90. Singleton was a hard worker who demanded the same from his teammates.

Center: Which Robert Werdann will show up on a given night? No one ever knows. Although he's foul-prone and terribly inconsistent, he's still one of the nation's top five centers. He played high school ball with Kenny Anderson.

Analysis: This is a very special team; one that conjures up memories of the club's 1985 Final Four entry. If Werdann plays as well this year as he did in last spring's NCAA tourney, the Redmen could be spending the first weekend in April in Minneapolis. They'll battle Seton Hall for Big East bragging rights.

1991-92 ROSTER

	POS	HT	YR	FGP	FTP	3-PT	RPG	APG	PPG
Malik Sealy	F	6'8"	Sr	.49	.74	16/53	7.7	1.7	22.1
Jason Buchanan	G	6'2"	Sr	.41	.79	39/108	2.7	5.9	12.0
Robert Werdann	C	6'11"	Sr	.49	.72	1/1	7.1	1.4	11.3
Chuck Sproling	G	6'6"	Sr	.42	.54	16/39	2.4	1.9	6.4
Shawnelle Scott	F/C	6'11"	So	.50	.53	—	3.6	0.2	5.2
Terrence Mullin	G	6'1"	Sr	.38	.70	11/32	0.7	0.7	3.1
David Cain	G	6'0"	Jr	.36	.63	1/4	1.3	1.7	2.6
Sergio Luyk	F	6'8"	So	.59	.17	5/10	0.8	0.2	2.1
Carl Beckett	G	6'4"	Jr	.55	.60	4/9	1.0	0.1	2.1
Mitchell Foster	F	6'9"	Jr	—	—	—	—	—	—
Lee Green	G	6'3"	So	—	—	—	—	—	—
Lamont Middleton	F	6'6"	Jr	—	—	—	—	—	—

SETON HALL

Conference: Big East
1990-91: 25-9, T-3rd Big East

1990-91 NCAAs: 3-1
Coach: P.J. Carlesimo (144-137)

Opening Line: Though inexperienced, the Pirates advanced to the round of eight in last year's NCAA tournament. A loser to UNLV in the West Regional finals, the Hall wound up only 12 points shy (77-65) of its second Final Four in three years. Graduates Anthony Avent and Oliver Taylor took with them nearly 30 points and 13 rebounds per game.

Guard: Terry Dehere has established himself as one of the game's greatest guards. A big-time scorer who doesn't shy away from in-your-face defense, he'll have to assume even more of the perimeter-scoring load now that Taylor is gone. Steady Bryan Caver and Daryl Crist may have a difficult time keeping freshman point guard Danny Hurley out of the starting lineup. He's a creative playmaker who has learned a few tricks from his older brother, Bobby.

Forward: Gordon Winchester and Arturas Karnishovas will quickly discover how much they miss Avent. It's time for Winchester to take his game to another level offensively. Super-sub Jerry Walker is a battler on the boards. Well built juco transfer Darrell Mims (6'8", 260) will help replace Avent's presence inside.

Center: After sitting out last year with academic woes, big Luther Wright (7'2", nearly 300 pounds) is itching to prove he's an impact player. Defense is his strength, motivation his weakness. In time, he'll be a great one. Jim Dickinson is his back-up.

Analysis: This is a squad that promises to play solid defense, shoot well, and rebound. The play of newcomers Hurley and Wright may prove to be the difference between a Big East title and a third-place finish.

1991-92 ROSTER

	POS	HT	YR	FGP	FTP	3-PT	RPG	APG	PPG
Terry Dehere	G	6'4"	Jr	.46	.84	105/245	3.0	2.2	19.8
Gordon Winchester	F	6'7"	Sr	.50	.67	0/1	4.7	2.3	7.4
Arturas Karnisovas	F	6'8"	So	.41	.84	33/89	4.6	1.2	7.3
Jerry Walker	F	6'7"	Jr	.52	.66	—	6.0	1.4	6.7
Bryan Caver	G	6'3"	So	.43	.77	4/16	1.7	2.3	4.6
Daryl Crist	G	6'0"	Jr	.58	.56	14/24	0.3	0.4	2.0
Chris Davis	F	6'8"	So	.47	.61	—	1.3	—	1.8
Jim Dickinson	C	7'0"	So	—	—	—	—	—	—
Danny Hurley	G	6'1"	Fr	—	—	—	—	—	—
John Leahy	F	6'7"	Fr	—	—	—	—	—	—
Darrell Mims	F	6'8"	Jr	—	—	—	—	—	—
Luther Wright	C	7'2"	So	—	—	—	—	—	—

SOUTH CAROLINA

Conference: Southeastern
1990-91: 20-13, 7th Metro

1990-91 NCAAs: Not invited
Coach: Steve Newton (116-65)

Opening Line: Before his stunning mid-May dismissal, George Felton quietly put together a top-flight program. Last year's 20-win season was the school's first since 1983. Now, Murray State's successful coach, Steve Newton, takes over. This season will be the Gamecocks' first in the SEC. Although four starters do return, they'll find out real fast that wins in the SEC are tougher to come by than in the Metro.

Guard: Barry Manning and Jo Jo English comprise one of the most underrated backcourt tandems in America. Manning's an unselfish distributor who has caught the eye of many NBA scouts, while English is a 42-percent shooter from 3-point land. Jamie Watson and Bojan Popovic also display adequate range.

Forward: Despite playing with a pacemaker, Alex English-clone Joe Rhett possesses All-SEC potential. He combines a fluid jumper with inside quickness and toughness. Michael Glover's loss will be felt at the defensive end. Chris Leso and Edmond Wilson will attempt to fill Glover's sneakers. Freshman Derrick Carroll is from the same Columbia, South Carolina, high school as Manning and Rhett.

Center: Big Jeff Roulston, 7'0," 250 and still growing, needs to increase his scoring (9.3 last year) and rebounding (6.7). He could be in a heap of trouble when matched against guys like Shaquille O'Neal and Oliver Miller.

Analysis: While the Gamecocks are one of the top 64 teams in the nation on paper, their record in the 12-team SEC may not be good enough to get a call from the NCAA. If the NCAA decides to take six or more teams from the SEC, the Gamecocks are in. English, Manning, and Rhett comprise the nucleus of a dark-horse club that deserves respect.

1991-92 ROSTER

	POS	HT	YR	FGP	FTP	3-PT	RPG	APG	PPG
Jo Jo English	G	6'4"	Sr	.46	.74	56/134	3.3	2.9	15.0
Barry Manning	G	6'4"	Sr	.45	.62	33/101	4.9	3.7	12.6
Joe Rhett	F	6'8"	Sr	.54	.58	1/3	6.9	1.5	12.6
Jeff Roulston	C	7'0"	Sr	.51	.62	—	6.7	1.3	9.3
Jamie Watson	G	6'5"	So	.42	.57	10/43	2.5	2.3	6.0
Chris Leso	F	6'8"	Jr	.45	.67	0/2	2.4	0.4	3.7
Bojan Popovic	G	6'3"	Sr	.33	.76	4/19	0.9	1.2	1.8
Edmond Wilson	F	6'9"	Jr	.48	.52	—	1.8	0.1	1.6
Obrad Ignjatovic	F	6'10"	Sr	.36	.58	2/10	0.7	0.3	1.4
Stefan Eggers	F	6'10"	Jr	.53	.33	—	0.7	0.1	1.3
Derrick Carroll	G/F	6'6"	Fr	—	—	—	—	—	—
Melvin Hartry	G	6'3"	Fr	—	—	—	—	—	—

SOUTHERN CALIFORNIA

Conference: Pac-10
1990-91: 19-10, T-3rd Pac-10

1990-91 NCAAs: 0-1
Coach: George Raveling (278-262)

Opening Line: Last year's 19-win season and NCAA tourney invite should serve as a stepping stone for the Trojans. While graduated starters Ronnie Coleman (four-time team MVP) and Robert Pack will be missed, All-America candidate Harold Miner will try to fill their shoes.

Guard: Miner's the best shooting guard in the country. A sizzling scorer, he can also do much more. Hard-working Duane Cooper, USC's top defender, returns to man the point. He and Miner comprise the most prolific backcourt in Trojan history. Highly regarded juco transfer Dwyane Hackett could possibly play Cooper out of a starting job, while Rodney Chatman and Phil Glenn can play either backcourt position.

Forward: There's not as much talent up front, where returnees Mark Boyd and Keith Greeley roam. Boyd displays a lot of potential, particularly on offense. He could be a pleasant surprise. Greeley will attempt to fend off newcomers Lorenzo Orr and Tremayne Anchrum for a starting berth. Orr was a McDonald's All-American following the 1989-90 season.

Center: Yamen Sanders started 15 games a year ago. While his mere presence bolsters USC's low-post defense, he needs to show improvement at both ends. If not, 6'10" Canadian Kirk Homenick could be pressed into action sooner than coach George Raveling would like.

Analysis: Without Coleman (17.3 PPG) and Pack (14.2 PPG) to help shoulder some of the scoring load, Miner will face defenses keying exclusively on him. That will be an adjustment. Raveling can't stop raving about Hackett and Boyd, two players who must have good years if USC is to continue its upward spiral. Another respectable third-place conference finish is within reach.

1991-92 ROSTER

	POS	HT	YR	FGP	FTP	3-PT	RPG	APG	PPG
Harold Miner	G	6'5"	Jr	.45	.80	59/175	5.5	2.0	23.5
Duane Cooper	G	6'1"	Sr	.45	.63	39/92	3.5	4.6	7.1
Mark Boyd	F	6'7"	So	.58	.55	—	3.9	0.2	5.0
Yamen Sanders	C	6'9"	Sr	.50	.52	—	4.4	0.1	4.9
Rodney Chatman	G	6'3"	Jr	.39	.52	7/23	1.3	1.5	2.4
Phil Glenn	G	6'2"	Jr	.37	.60	12/35	0.7	1.1	2.3
Keith Greeley	F/C	6'8"	Jr	.45	.63	0/2	2.1	0.1	2.3
Bosco Kante	G	6'2"	So	.50	—	—	0.3	0.3	0.5
Tremayne Anchrum	F	6'5"	Fr	—	—	—	—	—	—
Dwayne Hackett	G	6'1"	Jr	—	—	—	—	—	—
Kirk Homenick	C	6'11"	Fr	—	—	—	—	—	—
Lorenzo Orr	F	6'8"	Fr	—	—	—	—	—	—

SOUTHERN ILLINOIS

Conference: Missouri Valley
1990-91: 18-14, T-4th MVC

1990-91 NIT: 2-1
Coach: Rich Herrin (96-89)

Opening Line: Last year's 18-14 record was a bit deceiving, as 12 of the Salukis' losses were by six points or less. They never seemed to get the breaks they needed down the stretch. Losing point guard Sterling Mahan (17.2 PPG) and forward Rick Shipley to graduation is certainly no break. Three returning starters include all-league pick Ashraf Amaya.

Guard: It'll be a struggle without Mahan, the quarterback of past SIU teams. Untested frosh Mark Mosley figures to get first crack at his job. Returnees Chris Lowery and Matt Wynn aren't pure point guards, but they might have to do. Streak-shooting Tyrone Bell has first dibs on the other guard slot after starting there 30 times last winter. Highly regarded juco transfer Anthony Smith will play big guard and small forward.

Forward: Amaya could be the conference's premier player. A fast learner who has bulked up in the past year from 205 pounds to nearly 220, Amaya's 30-point outburst vs. Drake last winter could well be a preview of the kind of season he's going to have in 1991-92. Kelvan Lawrence has quietly made tremendous strides the past two seasons. Never too shy to shoot, his shot selection does need further improvement. So does his help defense.

Center: Talk about international flavor! Nigerian Emeka Okenwa will compete for minutes with 7'0" Brazilian Marcelo da Silva and Yugoslavian Mirko Pavlovic. Problem is, all three need a lot of work in all phases of the game.

Analysis: The slumping MVC is as weak and unpredictable as it's been in nearly two decades. As many as a half-dozen teams could be penciled into the top spot. Keyed by Amaya, the top-ranked Salukis have the most raw talent and arguably the league's best coach.

1991-92 ROSTER

	POS	HT	YR	FGP	FTP	3-PT	RPG	APG	PPG
Ashraf Amaya	F	6'8"	Jr	.60	.60	0/3	8.3	0.4	15.3
Kelvan Lawrence	F	6'8"	Sr	.43	.62	23/76	5.4	2.3	8.9
Tyrone Bell	G	6'3"	Jr	.41	.74	5/23	3.3	1.8	7.4
Chris Lowery	G	5'10"	So	.37	.75	17/62	0.9	1.6	4.2
Matt Wynn	G	6'0"	Sr	.48	.79	31/74	0.5	0.5	4.1
Mirko Pavlovic	C	6'8"	So	.36	.70	18/46	1.7	0.8	3.9
Emeka Okenwa	C	6'7"	Jr	.52	.67	—	2.4	—	3.7
Marcelo da Silva	C	7'0"	So	.44	.33	—	0.9	—	0.9
Mark Mosley	G	6'0"	Fr	—	—	—	—	—	—
Anthony Smith	G/F	6'5"	Jr	—	—	—	—	—	—
Ian Stewart	F	6'8"	Fr	—	—	—	—	—	—
Marcus Timmons	F	6'7"	Fr	—	—	—	—	—	—

SOUTHERN MISSISSIPPI

Conference: Metro
1990-91: 21-8, 1st Metro

1990-91 NCAAs: 0-1
Coach: M.K. Turk (233-191)

Opening Line: Sooner or later, someone has to take notice of this team. Led by Charles Barkley look-alike Clarence Weatherspoon, USM is in search of its third straight NCAA tourney appearance. The Eagles won 18 of their first 20 games last winter and cruised into the top ten in the polls. They did lose three talented starters (and more than 42 PPG) in forward Darrin Chancellor, center Daron Jenkins, and lead guard Russell Johnson.

Guard: Sophomore Bernard Haslett (9.5 PPG) shot his way into the starting lineup midway through last season and just missed being named Metro Freshman of the Year. Two promising newcomers, Avery Thomas and Terry Cameron, will push senior Dallas Dale for the point. Ron Rembert, a 14-game starter a year ago, will be a factor.

Forward: Although Weatherspoon's tired of the Barkley comparisons, there's no one else on the college level who can literally dominate a game like "Spoon" can. This two-time Metro Player of the Year could have been a lottery pick had he left school a year early. Untested juniors John Lacey and Newton Mealer take over for Chancellor.

Center: Freshman Glen Whisby gives the Eagles strength in the interior, something that was missing late last season. *Street & Smith* named him one of the top 20 preps in America. His all-out intensity is reminiscent of Weatherspoon's. Joe Courtney is a 6'8" banger who can play all three frontcourt positions.

Analysis: Whisby and Haslett need to produce enough offensively to keep defenses from keying on Weatherspoon. A prolonged injury to Weatherspoon or a subpar debut for Whisby is about the only thing that'll stop USM. It'll contend for one of the top two spots in the new-look Metro.

1991-92 ROSTER

	POS	HT	YR	FGP	FTP	3-PT	RPG	APG	PPG
Clarence Weatherspoon	F	6'7"	Sr	.59	.75	7/14	12.2	2.3	17.8
Bernard Haslett	G	6'3"	So	.47	.72	52/119	2.6	1.6	9.5
Ron Rembert	G/F	6'4"	Jr	.42	.58	18/51	2.3	1.3	6.1
Joe Courtney	F/C	6'8"	Sr	.46	.55	—	3.0	0.4	4.1
Dallas Dale	G	6'2"	Sr	.33	.85	14/40	0.7	2.3	2.9
John Lacey	F	6'7"	Jr	.45	.39	—	2.3	0.9	2.7
Newton Mealer	F	6'7"	Jr	.38	.57	1/5	0.8	0.2	1.7
Terry Cameron	G	6'1"	Jr	—	—	—	—	—	—
Donald Davenport	G/F	6'6"	Fr	—	—	—	—	—	—
Avery Thomas	G	6'1"	Fr	—	—	—	—	—	—
Glen Whisby	F/C	6'9"	Fr	—	—	—	—	—	—
Fred Williams	F	6'7"	Fr	—	—	—	—	—	—

SYRACUSE

Conference: Big East
1990-91: 26-6, 1st Big East

1990-91 NCAAs: 0-1
Coach: Jim Boeheim (395-119)

Opening Line: An opening-round NCAA tourney loss to 15th-seeded Richmond was a bitter pill for the Big East champion Orangemen to swallow, as was the announcement a few weeks later that consensus All-American Billy Owens was leaving school for the NBA. An NCAA investigation for possible recruiting violations continues to cast a shadow over this program.

Guard: This is the strength of the team, which isn't necessarily great news in the big-bruiser world of the Big East. Adrian Autry performed as well as any freshman lead guard in the country last year. He sees the floor well and is a better perimeter shooter than expected. Speedy Michael Edwards (5'11") is a shooting guard in a point guard's body. He'll play both positions. Heralded freshman Anthony Harris and junior Mike Hopkins add big-guard scoring punch.

Forward: Senior Dave Johnson came from nowhere a year ago to become an All-America candidate. He can score inside or out. Conrad McRae, 6'10" and growing, shows flashes of brilliance but disappears against top teams. It's his aggressive board play that keeps him in the lineup. Scott McCorkle does a little bit of everything.

Center: Knock underachiever LeRon Ellis all you want, but his 11 points and eight boards a game will be missed. Junior David Siock is as strong as an ox, but he'll never be mistaken for Ellis. McRae will also see time in the pivot.

Analysis: While opposing defenses made a habit of shadowing Owens last season, Johnson was often left wide open to can an easy 12- to 15-footer. His points will come much tougher this year. The Orange will finish fourth or fifth in the Big East.

1991-92 ROSTER

	POS	HT	YR	FGP	FTP	3-PT	RPG	APG	PPG
Dave Johnson	F	6'6"	Sr	.50	.66	38/100	6.3	2.3	19.4
Adrian Autry	G	6'4"	So	.40	.71	26/82	2.5	5.3	9.7
Michael Edwards	G	5'11"	Jr	.40	.66	33/99	1.5	2.6	7.9
Conrad McRae	F/C	6'10"	Jr	.54	.62	0/2	4.2	0.4	5.0
Scott McCorkle	G/F	6'5"	So	.52	.52	15/40	1.7	1.1	4.2
Mike Hopkins	G	6'5"	Jr	.51	.55	9/22	1.9	1.4	3.3
Dave Siock	F/C	6'10"	Jr	.50	.56	0/1	1.9	0.5	2.6
Anthony Harris	G	6'2"	Fr	—	—	—	—	—	—
Luke Jackson	F	6'6"	Fr	—	—	—	—	—	—
Lawrence Moten	G	6'4"	Fr	—	—	—	—	—	—
J.B. Reafsnyder	C	7'0"	Fr	—	—	—	—	—	—
Lazurus Sims	G/F	6'4"	Fr	—	—	—	—	—	—

TEMPLE

Conference: Atlantic 10
1990-91: 24-10, 2nd A-10

1990-91 NCAAs: 3-1
Coach: John Chaney (216-71)

Opening Line: While John Chaney lost a franchise player in Mark Macon, a dominant 7'0" big man in Donald Hodge, and a heady reserve guard in Michael Harden, life goes on. Sparked by Macon's MVP performance at the East Regional, the Owls came within three points of knocking off North Carolina and advancing to the Final Four. Macon had 31 points in a memorable final game. Three returning starters comprise this year's nucleus.

Guard: Cincinnati transfer Vic Carstarphen performed better than even he expected last season. A 32-game starter, he turned the ball over only once every 27 minutes and didn't commit a single turnover in seven games. Freshman Eric Brunson (East MVP at the McDonald's Classic) and Prop 48 victims Aaron McKie and Eddie Jones will compete for Macon's old job. Brunson can also play the point. McKie's a fabulous defender.

Forward: Returning starters Mik Kilgore and Mark Strickland make this the strongest position on the team. Kilgore's play intensified during the second half of the season and peaked in the NCAA tourney (nearly 20 PPG, five RPG, and four APG). He can play virtually any position but center. Strickland's high-wire athletic skills make him a fan's delight. He blocked eight Oklahoma State shots in tourney play. James Spears isn't afraid to mix things up inside.

Center: Hodge surprised everyone with his decision to jump to the NBA prematurely. His presence would have made a huge difference. Back-up Chris Lovelace is no longer with the team, leaving Temple with an empty space in the middle. Strickland will probably be a pseudo-center.

Analysis: The Owls can't possibly equal last year's success without Macon and Hodge, but they are talented enough to contend with Massachusetts for top honors in the A-10. Frontcourt depth is a serious concern. Brunson is a rising star.

1991-92 ROSTER

	POS	HT	YR	FGP	FTP	3-PT	RPG	APG	PPG
Mik Kilgore	F	6'8"	Sr	.41	.74	46/126	5.8	3.3	14.0
Vic Carstarphen	G	6'0"	Jr	.40	.73	79/214	2.2	3.5	10.4
Mark Strickland	F	6'9"	Sr	.49	.43	—	6.0	0.3	7.7
James Spears	F	6'6"	So	.43	.68	0/1	2.9	0.0	3.4
Johnnie Conic	G	6'5"	Jr	.29	.38	0/2	0.3	—	0.8
Anthony Battle	F	6'9"	Fr	—	—	—	—	—	—
Eric Brunson	G	6'3"	Fr	—	—	—	—	—	—
Eddie Jones	F/G	6'6"	So	—	—	—	—	—	—
Aaron McKie	G	6'5"	So	—	—	—	—	—	—

TEXAS

Conference: Southwest
1990-91: 23-9, 2nd SWC

1990-91 NCAAs: 1-1
Coach: Tom Penders (288-218)

Opening Line: Coach Tom Penders has led Texas to three straight NCAA tournaments, becoming the first Longhorn coach to do so. Now, however, he faces a horrifying rebuilding task. Seven seniors have departed, led by All-SWC selections Joey Wright (21.2 PPG) and Locksley Collie. Benford Williams is the lone returning starter.

Guard: DePaul transfer B.J. Tyler is no Joey Wright, but with a little work he's capable of becoming a superb penetrator and passer. Williams, the team's best all-around player, logged more minutes than anyone but Wright last winter. A bona fide scoring machine, Williams may be moved inside if freshman Terrence Rencher and juco transfer Michael Richardson can contribute. Rencher was New York's Mr. Basketball last season.

Forward: Dexter Cambridge must transform his enormous potential into production. He was the nation's leading juco scorer in 1989-90 (33.4 PPG). Inexperienced Albert Burditt shows as much potential as anyone on this team. He likes to play above the rim. Muscular Gerrald Houston will be a factor if his injured knee holds up.

Center: Corey Lockridge takes over here for Panama Myers. He's not really ready to assume a full-time role. At 6'10" and only 195 pounds, he gets pushed around a lot inside. If Lockridge struggles early, a three-forward frontcourt consisting of Williams, Cambridge, and Houston isn't out of the question.

Analysis: As long as Penders employs an up-tempo style and can continue to recruit via his New York City pipeline, the Longhorns will continue to be one of the top 30 programs in the country. Upstart Rice could give them problems in the SWC race. Youth could prevent the 'Horns from winning 20.

1991-92 ROSTER

	POS	HT	YR	FGP	FTP	3-PT	RPG	APG	PPG
Benford Williams	G/F	6'5"	Sr	.49	.65	0/4	6.0	2.4	13.4
Dexter Cambridge	F	6'7"	Sr	.47	.77	26/81	3.9	0.9	12.2
Albert Burditt	F	6'8"	So	.51	.43	—	4.0	0.5	3.2
Tony Watson	G	6'3"	So	.41	.40	1/6	1.1	0.2	1.8
Michael Chaplin	F	6'7"	Fr	—	—	—	—	—	—
Rob Garner	G	6'1"	Fr	—	—	—	—	—	—
Gerrald Houston	C/F	6'8"	So	—	—	—	—	—	—
Corey Lockridge	C/F	6'10"	So	—	—	—	—	—	—
Terrence Rencher	G	6'3"	Fr	—	—	—	—	—	—
Michael Richardson	G	6'4"	Jr	—	—	—	—	—	—
Al Segova	F	6'8"	Fr	—	—	—	—	—	—
B.J. Tyler	G	6'1"	So	—	—	—	—	—	—

UCLA

Conference: Pac-10
1990-91: 23-9, 2nd Pac-10

1990-91 NCAAs: 0-1
Coach: Jim Harrick (233-127)

Opening Line: With an outstanding coach like Jim Harrick and the surplus of talent the Bruins' possess, it's difficult to figure how they lost nine times last winter. A lack of senior leadership made a potentially great team settle for being good.

Guard: Point guard Darrick Martin is anxious to redeem himself after struggling a bit down the stretch last spring. He's added a solid medium-range jumper to his repertoire. Unselfish Gerald Madkins started every game at big guard last year. He's one of the Pac-10's most tenacious defenders. Super-soph Shon Tarver is an outstanding sixth man.

Forward: Now that the high-spirited Don MacLean is learning how to tone down his act on the court, the sweet-shooting big man can be considered a national Player of the Year front-runner. Ed O'Bannon may be the game's best freshman; he sat out the

entire 1990-91 season after tearing up his left knee in a pickup game last October. Flashy swing man Mitchell Butler started 28 games last year. Zan Mason transferred to Loyola Marymount.

Center: Although he prefers the perimeter, Tracy Murray is the closest thing to a center UCLA has in its three-forward offense. He's the team's most efficient offensive rebounder. Projects Rodney Zimmerman and 7'6" Mike Lanier still aren't ready to contribute on a full-time basis.

Analysis: This well-rounded team is clearly the class of the Pac-10. If MacLean doesn't let his quick temper get the best of him, he could lead the Bruins to their first national title since '75. Really. MacLean possesses that unique Larry Bird-like ability to make those around him even better. Rebounding remains a major concern.

1991-92 ROSTER

	POS	HT	YR	FGP	FTP	3-PT	RPG	APG	PPG
Don MacLean	F	6'10"	Sr	.55	.85	3/13	7.3	2.0	23.0
Tracy Murray	F/C	6'8"	Jr	.50	.79	73/189	6.7	1.3	21.2
Darrick Martin	G	5'11"	Sr	.46	.75	23/79	2.4	6.8	11.6
Gerald Madkins	G	6'4"	Sr	.52	.76	32/91	2.6	3.9	9.2
Shon Tarver	G	6'5"	So	.51	.53	15/42	3.0	2.1	9.0
Mitchell Butler	F/G	6'5"	Jr	.55	.51	6/25	4.2	1.5	7.9
Rodney Zimmerman	C/F	6'9"	So	.68	.58	—	1.7	0.3	1.9
Lou Richie	G	5'9"	So	.60	.56	2/3	0.5	0.7	1.0
Tyus Edney	G	5'10"	Fr	—	—	—	—	—	—
Mike Lanier	C	7'6"	Jr	—	—	—	—	—	—
Ed O'Bannon	F	6'8"	Fr	—	—	—	—	—	—
Jorge Zidek	C	7'1"	Fr	—	—	—	—	—	—

UTAH

Conference: Western Athletic
1990-91: 30-4, 1st WAC

1990-91 NCAAs: 2-1
Coach: Rick Majerus (133-58)

Opening Line: After missing all but six games of the 1989-90 season due to heart surgery, Rick Majerus came back stronger and healthier than ever to lead Utah to a WAC championship, a top-ten ranking, and its first Sweet 16 trip in eight years. The underrated Utes won 30 games. They win ugly, but they do win. Every starter's back except round mound Walter Watts (second-team All-WAC).

Guard: Playmaker Tyrone Tate is quicker than anyone else in the WAC. Though an average shooter, his great floor vision makes him an effective distributor. Byron Wilson possesses decent range, as does spark plug Craig Rydalch. Aggressive Jimmy Soto is a real crowd pleaser. Phil Dixon, a 3-point shooter, plays guard and forward.

Forward: WAC Player of the Year Josh Grant is probably the most versatile 6'10" player in the country. He'll do some dirty work inside for a while, then pop outside to can a few 3-pointers. Along with Grant, tough defender M'Kay McGrath started every game last season. Forming a line behind these two will be top-ranked freshman Silas Mills (if eligible), sophomore Thomas Wyatt, and juco transfer Antoine Davison.

Center: Improved Paul Afeaki, a dependable rebounder, takes over for Watts. He missed some time last season while recovering from a bullet wound in his shoulder. Prop 42 victim Deon Mims (6'11", 235) should help.

Analysis: Majerus, perhaps the most unsung bench coach in America, doesn't need much talent to transform a team into a winner. In this case, he's got an abundance of talent and depth. Although the team revolves around Grant, he's hardly the only weapon. Thirty wins is a bit much to ask, but another WAC title and an NCAA tournament win or two is not.

1991-92 ROSTER

	POS	HT	YR	FGP	FTP	3-PT	RPG	APG	PPG
Josh Grant	F	6'10"	Sr	.48	.83	47/130	8.0	2.7	17.5
Byron Wilson	G	6'3"	So	.43	.66	24/70	3.0	1.5	8.7
Phil Dixon	F/G	6'5"	So	.43	.68	49/114	2.9	1.0	7.0
Paul Afeaki	C	6'10"	Sr	.50	.69	0/1	3.5	0.3	6.5
Craig Rydalch	G/F	6'3"	Sr	.42	.72	36/104	1.9	1.6	6.3
Jimmy Soto	G	5'9"	Jr	.43	.81	23/52	1.6	2.6	6.1
M'Kay McGrath	F	6'5"	Sr	.50	.56	—	3.6	1.0	4.8
Tyrone Tate	G	6'1"	Jr	.34	.69	2/6	2.1	4.1	4.7
Antoine Davison	F	6'8"	Jr	—	—	—	—	—	—
Silas Mills	F	6'6"	Fr	—	—	—	—	—	—
Deon Mims	C	6'11"	So	—	—	—	—	—	—
Thomas Wyatt	F	6'7"	So	—	—	—	—	—	—

VILLANOVA

Conference: Big East
1990-91: 17-15, T-7th Big East

1990-91 NCAAs: 1-1
Coach: Rollie Massimino (343-226)

Opening Line: A disappointing 1990-91 season, which saw the Wildcats finish under .500 in conference play (7-9), was salvaged with a Big East tournament upset of Syracuse and an NCAA tournament victory over Princeton. In the Wildcats' defense, their schedule was one of the nation's toughest, as 16 of their 27 regular-season games were against top-25 opponents. All of the team's starters and key reserves return. Mysteriously, Rollie Massimino didn't recruit a single player.

Guard: Floor general Chris Walker and Greg Woodard are one of the most solid backcourt duos in the Big East. At his best when the game is on the line, Walker has amazingly won nearly a dozen games for the Wildcats with buzzer-beaters. Woodard is a big-time scorer who became more consistent in 1990-91. Gutsy defender David Miller can fill in at either spot.

Forward: Lance Miller is the best all-around player on this team. His quickness makes him tough to guard and box out on the glass. He needs to shoot more often. Arron Bain is a jack-of-all-trades type, while Calvin Byrd is a workhorse on the boards.

Center: If you could roll Marc Dowdell's shooting touch, Anthony Pelle's shot-blocking, James Bryson's rebounding, and Paul Vrind's defense into one player, you'd have yourself an All-American. Dowdell will play the most. Pelle, only a sophomore, could be the next Ed Pinckney.

Analysis: Rollie can no longer claim that the Wildcats are a young team that needs time to put the pieces together. The roster includes five seniors and four juniors. If Massimino gets better defense from his frontcourt, the Wildcats could be a big surprise. A fourth-place finish in the Big East is about right.

1991-92 ROSTER

	POS	HT	YR	FGP	FTP	3-PT	RPG	APG	PPG
Lance Miller	F	6'6"	Jr	.44	.73	17/76	6.8	2.7	15.0
Greg Woodard	G	6'6"	Sr	.45	.84	68/156	2.6	1.2	13.6
Arron Bain	F	6'7"	Jr	.49	.70	14/40	4.5	0.9	10.4
Marc Dowdell	F/C	6'9"	Sr	.45	.76	2/7	5.2	2.2	9.0
Chris Walker	G	5'11"	Sr	.38	.79	65/179	2.4	4.3	8.9
Calvin Byrd	F	6'6"	Jr	.48	.76	—	3.6	0.4	6.6
James Bryson	F/C	6'10"	Jr	.51	.50	—	2.0	0.2	3.8
Anthony Pelle	C	6'11"	So	.50	.63	—	1.7	0.1	2.0
Paul Vrind	C	7'2"	Sr	.33	.63	—	1.2	—	1.4
David Miller	G	6'1"	Sr	.46	.50	1/10	0.3	0.8	1.0
Ron Wilson	F	6'11"	Fr	—	—	—	—	—	—

VIRGINIA

Conference: Atlantic Coast
1990-91: 21-12, T-5th ACC

1990-91 NCAAs: 0-1
Coach: Jeff Jones (21-12)

Opening Line: If coach Jeff Jones's first year on the job is any indication of things to come in Charlottesville, the Cavs will continue to be a regular ACC title contender for years to come. Jones helped offset the loss of point guard John Crotty and forwards Kenny Turner and Matt Blundin by signing one of the nation's premier recruiting classes.

Guard: It shouldn't take the Cavs too long to get over Crotty's loss at the point. Freshman Cory Alexander was the second-best lead guard in the land as a high school senior. Shooting guard Anthony Oliver promises to be much more productive after breaking his hand halfway through the 1990-91 season. Football star Terry Kirby, Doug Smith, and freshman Jason Williford will be counted on off the bench.

Forward: Bryant Stith is going to need a moving van to cart home all the awards he'll receive this season.

There's not a more complete small forward in the game today. The Cavs' offense will revolve around him. He's joined by fabulous freshman Thomas Burrough, a high school teammate of Alexander's and one of the top 15 preps in America. Swing man Cornel Parker is a valuable utility player who can fill in at any one of four positions.

Center: Ted Jeffries overcomes numerous offensive weaknesses with dependable defense. He boxes out well and never stops hustling. Freshman Chris Alexander is already more developed offensively.

Analysis: Jones knows what to expect from Stith, Oliver, and Jeffries. What he doesn't know is how Cory Alexander and Burrough will react to starting and what kind of depth he'll receive from players like Kirby and Parker. Depending on the freshmen, the Cavaliers' ACC finish can be as high as third or as low as fifth.

1991-92 ROSTER

	POS	HT	YR	FGP	FTP	3-PT	RPG	APG	PPG
Bryant Stith	F/G	6'5"	Sr	.47	.79	38/125	6.2	1.2	19.8
Anthony Oliver	G	6'4"	Sr	.47	.82	1/8	2.5	1.2	8.7
Ted Jeffries	C/F	6'9"	Jr	.47	.64	—	5.5	0.8	6.2
Cornel Parker	G/F	6'7"	So	.43	.56	5/13	3.1	1.3	4.0
Terry Kirby	G	6'3"	Jr	.41	.40	1/3	1.1	0.2	2.1
Chris Havlicek	G	6'5"	So	.46	.50	0/1	0.1	0.1	1.7
Doug Smith	G	6'1"	Jr	.52	.90	1/4	0.9	1.5	1.6
Chris Alexander	F/C	6'10"	Fr	—	—	—	—	—	—
Cory Alexander	G	6'1"	Fr	—	—	—	—	—	—
Yuri Barnes	F	6'8"	Fr	—	—	—	—	—	—
Thomas Burrough	F	6'8"	Fr	—	—	—	—	—	—
Jason Williford	F/G	6'5"	Fr	—	—	—	—	—	—

WAKE FOREST

Conference: Atlantic Coast
1990-91: 19-11, T-3rd ACC

1990-91 NCAAs: 1-1
Coach: Dave Odom (69-69)

Opening Line: A long-time doormat in the ACC, Wake Forest is making the long trek back with one of the most exciting young teams in the country. The Demon Deacons are building on their first winning season since 1985 and their first NCAA tourney appearance since 1984. The only significant player to graduate was guard Robert Siler.

Guard: Wake's Derrick McQueen-Randolph Childress backcourt should emerge as one of the most respected in the ACC. McQueen's a steady playmaker who shines at the defensive end. Childress takes over for Siler as the starting big guard. He averaged 14 PPG last year as a freshman. Marc Blucas and Robert Doggett are untested reserves.

Forward: Man-child Rodney Rogers was arguably the best freshman in America last season, leading Wake Forest in both scoring and rebounding. He's a bull on the glass

and possesses a silky-smooth jumper. Chris King was also superb in 1990-91. A leader by example, he does much of his damage from the baseline. Hard-charging Anthony Tucker is a slasher who excels at getting shots off in traffic. Tough guy Trelonnie Owens's forte is rebounding.

Center: Other than Rogers, Phil Medlin and seven-footer Stan King are the team's only legitimate pivot men. It's unlikely that either will be more than bit players, as coach Dave Odom will attempt to keep Rogers, King, and Tucker on the floor together.

Analysis: Although the Demon Deacons' starting five can hold their own against any team in the ACC, a lack of quality depth could wear this bunch out by season's end. Another NCAA tournament bid is a given. An upper-division finish in the rugged ACC won't be as easy to come by.

1991-92 ROSTER

	POS	HT	YR	FGP	FTP	3-PT	RPG	APG	PPG
Rodney Rogers	F	6'7"	So	.57	.67	10/35	7.9	1.5	16.3
Chris King	F	6'8"	Sr	.49	.64	17/41	5.7	2.1	15.1
Randolph Childress	G	6'2"	So	.45	.77	64/166	2.1	2.2	14.0
Anthony Tucker	F	6'8"	Sr	.55	.67	4/12	5.1	2.2	11.4
Derrick McQueen	G	5'11"	Sr	.47	.82	19/48	2.3	4.9	6.7
Trelonnie Owens	F	6'8"	So	.40	.64	5/11	2.5	0.7	3.7
Phil Medlin	C	6'9"	Sr	.42	.33	—	2.7	0.4	1.3
Marc Blucas	G	6'3"	So	.39	.33	1/5	0.9	0.4	1.2
Robert Doggett	G	6'3"	So	.21	—	4/15	0.5	0.5	0.7
Stan King	C	7'0"	So	.25	.40	—	0.9	0.1	0.5
Scooter Banks	F	6'6"	Fr	—	—	—	—	—	—
David Rasmussen	F	6'7"	Jr	—	—	—	—	—	—

WASHINGTON STATE

Conference: Pac-10
1990-91: 16-12, T-5th Pac-10

1990-91 NCAAs: Not invited
Coach: Kelvin Sampson (46-69)

Opening Line: Kelvin Sampson was named Pac-10 Coach of the Year in 1990-91 after leading much-improved WSU to its first winning season in eight years. Four juco transfers and three freshmen paid immediate dividends for a club that finished 7-22 in 1989-90 and won only one Pac-10 game. All five starters return. Guard Reco Rowe was the biggest loss.

Guard: Prize playmaker Bennie Seltzer came alive late last season as he made fewer turnovers and handed out more assists. Too often, he thinks shot before pass. Tyrone Maxey, a suspect shooter, backs him up. Multi-talented Neil Derrick returns as Seltzer's running mate. He's more of a scorer than a pure shooter. Eddie Hill is the team's designated 3-point bomber. Iowa transfer Dale Reed will be eligible for the Pac-10 portion of the schedule.

Forward: Swing man Terrence Lewis is one of the most highly regarded players this program has ever landed. A juco All-American two years ago, he had his ups and downs last season as he often tried to do too much on his own. Hard work earned Rob Corkrum a starting job. He ranked among the Pac-10 leaders in blocked shots. David Vik is a big kid (6'11") who's too timid inside.

Center: Ken Critton is a bull who never stops working on defense. Underrated Brian Paine is now close to 100 percent after battling injuries for much of the 1990-91 season.

Analysis: Appearing in a post-season game is the team's motivation this season. Sampson's a fine coach who never had much talent to work with prior to last year. Barring major injuries to Seltzer, Derrick, or Lewis, WSU should improve its victory total by a game or two and sneak into the NCAA tournament for only the fourth time in school history.

1991-92 ROSTER

	POS	HT	YR	FGP	FTP	3-PT	RPG	APG	PPG
Terrence Lewis	G	6'4"	Sr	.47	.75	63/151	4.7	3.0	14.8
Neil Derrick	G	6'3"	Sr	.43	.66	31/96	2.4	2.0	14.7
Bennie Seltzer	G	6'0"	Jr	.44	.80	40/104	2.3	3.9	10.7
Ken Critton	C/F	6'8"	Sr	.57	.72	—	6.7	0.9	8.8
Eddie Hill	G	6'1"	So	.40	.81	31/77	1.7	0.9	6.8
Rob Corkrum	F	6'8"	So	.63	.71	—	3.9	1.0	6.0
Tyrone Maxey	G	5'10"	Sr	.35	.72	33/91	1.1	2.5	5.8
Brian Paine	C	6'10"	Sr	.50	.58	0/1	3.1	1.0	5.2
Sean Tresvant	G	5'11"	Jr	.57	.64	2/3	0.8	0.7	3.3
David Vik	F	6'11"	So	.42	.72	—	2.1	0.6	2.7
Tommie Oatis	C	6'8"	Jr	—	—	—	—	—	—
Dale Reed	G	6'4"	Jr	—	—	—	—	—	—

WISCONSIN-GREEN BAY

Conference: Mid-Continent
1990-91: 24-7, 2nd Mid-Continent

1990-91 NCAAs: 0-1
Coach: Dick Bennett (100-75)

Opening Line: The Packers aren't the only thing this town gets excited about these days. Led by John Stockton clone Tony Bennett (the coach's son), the Fighting Phoenix made their first NCAA tournament appearance last season. They fell in a two-point heartbreaker to Michigan State. UWGB's incredible 47-percent marksmanship from 3-point land was the team's secret weapon. The only personnel loss was a costly one—hard-working Dean Vander Plas, the squad's most reliable inside scorer and rebounder.

Guard: Bennett is coming off a Mid-Continent Player of the Year effort that saw him shoot a red-hot 53 percent from 3-point range. Bennett's deceiving quickness and uncanny court awareness make him an NBA prospect. Bennett's running mate, John Martinez, returns as the team's second-leading scorer. There's great chemistry between the two.

Forward: Ben Johnson is a tireless defender and the team's best athlete. He'll be expected to become more involved offensively. Swing man Dean Rondorf is the leading candidate to start across from Johnson. He does a lot of little things well. Army transfer Eric LeDuc will be worked into the lineup in time.

Center: Redshirted a year ago, Larry Hill (6'7") just might prove to be the most talented frontcourter on this team. He led the conference in blocked shots in 1989-90. He'll move to forward when unpolished Scott LeMoine comes off the bench.

Analysis: Due to a lack of backcourt depth, this team is sunk if Bennett or Martinez miss significant time with injuries. Although quicker and more athletic teams give the Phoenix fits, they can beat anyone on any given night thanks to Bennett and their 3-point shooting proficiency.

1991-92 ROSTER

	POS	HT	YR	FGP	FTP	3-PT	RPG	APG	PPG
Tony Bennett	G	6'0"	Sr	.55	.84	80/150	2.4	5.0	21.5
John Martinez	G	6'0"	Jr	.49	.79	36/81	2.6	4.4	11.0
Larry Hill	F/C	6'7"	Jr	.65	.75	—	4.6	1.0	8.6
Dean Rondorf	G/F	6'7"	Jr	.48	.77	38/88	2.3	1.2	7.2
Ben Johnson	F/G	6'3"	Sr	.45	.77	25/64	3.6	1.3	6.8
Jeremy Ludvigson	F	6'7"	So	.57	.50	—	3.3	0.3	3.4
Logan Vander Velden	F	6'9"	So	.54	.42	—	2.0	0.2	3.0
Scott LeMoine	C	6'9"	Sr	.46	.55	—	2.7	0.5	2.8
Gary Grzesk	G	6'3"	Fr	—	—	—	—	—	—
Eric LeDuc	F	6'7"	So	—	—	—	—	—	—
Jeff Nordgaard	F	6'6"	Fr	—	—	—	—	—	—
Chris Yates	F	6'5"	Sr	—	—	—	—	—	—

WRIGHT STATE

Conference: Mid-Continent
1990-91: 19-9

1990-91 NCAAs: Not invited
Coach: Ralph Underhill (73-38)

Opening Line: Who? Wright what? Wright State? That's right. Located in Dayton, Ohio, the Raiders are a sleeping giant. Housed in a brand-new, 10,600-seat arena, they also find themselves in a new conference—the Mid-Continent. For the past four season, Wright State competed as a Division I independent. The Raiders are a fun team to watch, as their 93-PPG average would attest. Part-time starter Scott Benton is the only player lost to graduation. Starting guard Mark Woods was charged with assault and was suspended by the school.

Guard: Marcus Mumphrey, who has played regularly for the past two seasons, is a dangerous streak shooter who plays strong man-to-man defense. Renaldo O'Neal, expected to be a reliable back-up, could take over for the suspended Woods. Home-grown freshman Chris McGuire spurned numerous Division I offers to play for the Raiders.

Forward: Bill Edwards is one of the finest forwards in the Midwest. Edwards is a silky smooth wing player who can go to the boards or fire away from the perimeter. His consistency is what makes him so special. Sean Hammonds is a rugged paint performer who relies on an effective jump hook. Jeff Unverferth is sound around the basket.

Center: Mike Haley's an outstanding inside scorer who gained some much-needed court maturity last season. He needs to pay more attention to his defensive game.

Analysis: You read it here first. Wright State is a top-flight team that deserves a shot at the NCAA tournament. On paper, the Raiders are probably more talented than defending Mid-Continent champ Wisconsin-Green Bay. With a supreme defensive effort from Haley in the low post, a conference title is within their grasp.

1991-92 ROSTER

	POS	HT	YR	FGP	FTP	3-PT	RPG	APG	PPG
Bill Edwards	F	6'8"	Jr	.55	.76	14/55	7.2	1.2	18.9
Marcus Mumphrey	G	6'1"	Sr	.48	.80	68/174	2.4	2.5	16.6
Sean Hammonds	F	6'5"	Jr	.54	.69	—	7.1	2.1	12.9
Mike Haley	F/C	6'9"	Jr	.49	.73	1/13	4.9	0.8	9.8
Jeff Unverferth	F	6'7"	Jr	.56	.76	—	2.5	0.5	6.4
Renaldo O'Neal	G	6'4"	Jr	.52	.60	0/1	2.1	2.9	4.1
Rob Haucke	G	6'5"	Sr	.33	.59	9/29	0.9	0.6	2.3
Andy Holderman	G	6'1"	So	.31	.67	7/25	0.4	0.8	1.6
Scott Blair	G	6'1"	So	.33	.50	0/1	0.3	0.6	1.1
Chris McGuire	G	5'11"	Fr	—	—	—	—	—	—
Jon Ramey	G	6'3"	Fr	—	—	—	—	—	—
Eric Wills	G	6'2"	Fr	—	—	—	—	—	—

WYOMING

Conference: Western Athletic
1990-91: 20-12, 4th WAC

1990-91 NIT: 1-1
Coach: Benny Dees (142-85)

Opening Line: Throw out the month of February and the 1990-91 season would have been one of the best in school history. Prior to a February swoon (3-7), the Cowboys were 15-3 and climbing rapidly in the national polls. The team's 20th victory finally came vs. Butler in the opening round of the NIT. The entire starting lineup returns. Forward Reginald Slater and guard Maurice Alexander each garnered All-WAC accolades.

Guard: After lacking a true point guard for two seasons, Alexander quickly established himself as one of the best in the West in 1990-91. The juco transfer is a fine perimeter shooter who can also thread a needle with his interior passes. Travis Butler and Paris Bryant will alternate at big guard. Butler creates a lot of havoc defensively. Bryant's range includes the parking lot.

Forward: Slater, the most consistent player on the Cowboy team, chipped in nearly 20 points and more than ten rebounds per game last winter. He'll battle Utah's Josh Grant for conference Player of the Year honors. Slater's rebounding prowess should land him an NBA job. Tim Breaux is the team's best defender. Injuries forced rising star Quein Higgins to the sidelines last year.

Center: Reggie Page is slowly developing into a quality big man. Originally an Arizona signee, Page began to master some effective low-post moves last winter. Good hands are his primary strength.

Analysis: The Cowboys simply ran out of gas too soon in 1990-91. With the exception of Slater, they didn't have anything left for the stretch drive. If Alexander and Page can play as consistently as Slater and the 'Pokes can improve upon last year's 0-3 record vs. league champ Utah, this bunch has the potential to rule the WAC.

1991-92 ROSTER

	POS	HT	YR	FGP	FTP	3-PT	RPG	APG	PPG
Reginald Slater	F	6'7"	Sr	.61	.76	—	10.3	1.2	19.2
Maurice Alexander	G	6'1"	Sr	.43	.86	69/183	3.2	3.9	15.2
Paris Bryant	G	6'2"	Sr	.41	.85	61/163	2.2	2.1	13.3
Tim Breaux	G/F	6'6"	Sr	.47	.77	15/61	4.5	1.5	12.5
Quein Higgins	F	6'9"	So	.62	.82	—	4.0	1.3	8.3
Reggie Page	C	6'11"	Jr	.54	.67	—	6.5	0.5	6.9
Travis Butler	G/F	6'5"	Sr	.45	.84	21/49	3.1	0.7	4.8
Rick Henry	G	6'4"	Sr	.45	.67	6/20	1.7	0.9	3.2
Brian Rewers	F/C	6'10"	Jr	.48	.69	—	2.2	0.1	2.7
Steve Gosar	G	6'0"	Sr	.20	.60	—	0.6	0.5	0.6
Hassan Sanders	G	6'2"	Fr	—	—	—	—	—	—
Bobby Taylor	F	6'7"	Fr	—	—	—	—	—	—

XAVIER

Conference: Midwestern Collegiate
1990-91: 22-10, 1st MCC

1990-91 NCAAs: 1-1
Coach: Pete Gillen (141-49)

Opening Line: Had he wanted the job, Pete Gillen would now be coaching at Notre Dame. But surprisingly, Gillen is so impressed with the program he's built on Xavier's Cincinnati campus that he'd rather stay put. Last year, he led the Musketeers to their sixth straight NCAA tourney appearance, where they upset Nebraska. All-MCC point guard Jamal Walker and forward Michael Davenport were a pair of costly graduation losses.

Guard: Leading scorer Jamie Gladden earned All-MCC honors last season while shooting a blistering 52 percent from the field (42 percent from 3-point territory). He'll struggle early without Walker, his usual running mate. Gladden will either be shifted to the point or newcomers Steve Gentry or Michael Hawkins will run the show. Although he's only 6'0", Gladden's a better two guard. Inexperienced shooting guard Tyrice Walker's role figures to expand.

Forward: Aaron Williams gives the Musketeers a solid shot-blocking threat. Though he's unrefined, his inside scoring improved late last year. Maurice Brantley is the team's most aggressive player. He's most valuable at the defensive end. Evansville transfer Chris Mack averaged ten PPG two years ago.

Center: As a frosh last year, Brian Grant started 31 games and averaged nearly nine rebounds and 12 points a game. He has as much potential as anyone on the squad. Freshman Larry Sykes will be brought along slowly.

Analysis: With St. Louis and Marquette bolting to the new Great Midwest Conference, there's not much competition left for the Musketeers in the six-team MCC. They're a major-league team playing in a minor-league conference. They'll walk away with the MCC by as many as six games.

1991-92 ROSTER

	POS	HT	YR	FGP	FTP	3-PT	RPG	APG	PPG
Jamie Gladden	G	6'0"	Jr	.52	.72	35/83	3.4	3.2	15.2
Brian Grant	F/C	6'8"	So	.57	.69	—	8.5	0.6	11.6
Aaron Williams	F	6'9"	Jr	.54	.71	—	6.5	1.0	9.7
Maurice Brantley	G/F	6'6"	Jr	.47	.57	14/42	2.9	2.0	7.0
Erik Edwards	F	6'8"	So	.49	.79	0/2	2.9	0.3	4.1
Dwayne Wilson	F	6'8"	Jr	.48	.71	—	1.5	0.2	2.1
Tyrice Walker	G/F	6'4"	So	.41	.47	0/1	1.1	0.3	1.9
DeWaun Rose	F	6'8"	So	.48	.75	—	0.9	—	1.5
Steve Gentry	G	6'0"	So	—	—	—	—	—	—
Michael Hawkins	G	6'0"	Fr	—	—	—	—	—	—
Chris Mack	F	6'5"	Jr	—	—	—	—	—	—
Larry Sykes	F/C	6'10"	Fr	—	—	—	—	—	—

College Basketball Review

The final section in the book reviews the 1990-91 college basketball season and lists important historical information.

First, you'll find the final 1990-91 standings of the 33 most significant conferences in Division I. Their conference records include regular-season conference games only. Their overall records include all post-season tournament games, including conference tournaments, the NCAA, and the NIT. The standings indicate the teams that made the NCAA tourney (*), those that won their conference tournaments (#), and those that were ineligible for post-season play (@).

The recap of the 1990-91 season also includes the following:

- final AP and UPI polls
- Division I statistical leaders

- NCAA tournament game-by-game results
- Final Four box scores

Finally, you'll find Division I historical information, including the following:

- national champions (1901-91)
- Final Four results (1939-91)
- Division I career leaders
- Division I season records
- Division I game records
- winningest Division I teams

The NCAA tournament didn't begin until 1939. Prior to that, there were no official national champions. However, the Helms Foundation selected national champs retroactively for the years 1901-38. These are the teams that are listed in the national champions chart.

DIVISION I FINAL STANDINGS, 1990-91

American South

	Conference			Overall		
	W	L	Pct.	W	L	Pct.
*New Orleans	9	3	.750	23	8	.742
Arkansas St.	9	3	.750	23	9	.719
*Louisiana Tech	8	4	.667	21	10	.677
S.W. Louisiana	6	6	.500	21	10	.677
Lamar	4	8	.333	15	13	.536
Central Florida	3	9	.250	10	17	.370
Texas-Pan Am	3	9	.250	7	21	.250

Atlantic Coast

	Conference			Overall		
	W	L	Pct.	W	L	Pct.
*Duke	11	3	.786	32	7	.821
*North Carolina	10	4	.714	29	6	.829
*N. Carolina St.	8	6	.571	20	11	.645
*Wake Forest	8	6	.571	19	11	.633
*Virginia	6	8	.429	21	12	.636
*Georgia Tech	6	8	.429	17	13	.567
Maryland	5	9	.357	16	12	.571
Clemson	2	12	.143	11	17	.393

Atlantic 10

	Conference			Overall		
	W	L	Pct.	W	L	Pct.
*Rutgers	14	4	.778	19	10	.655
*Temple	13	5	.722	24	10	.706
*Penn St.	10	8	.556	21	11	.656
George Wash.	10	8	.556	19	12	.613
Massachusetts	10	8	.556	20	13	.606
West Virginia	10	8	.556	17	14	.548
Duquesne	10	8	.556	13	15	.464
St. Joseph's	7	11	.389	13	17	.433
Rhode Island	6	12	.333	11	17	.393
St. Bonaventure	0	18	.000	5	23	.179

Big East

	Conference			Overall		
	W	L	Pct.	W	L	Pct.
*Syracuse	12	4	.750	26	6	.813
*St. John's	10	6	.625	23	9	.719
*Seton Hall	9	7	.563	25	9	.735
*Connecticut	9	7	.563	20	11	.645
*Pittsburgh	9	7	.563	21	12	.636
*Georgetown	8	8	.500	19	13	.594
Providence	7	9	.438	19	13	.594
*Villanova	7	9	.438	17	15	.531
Boston College	1	15	.063	11	19	.367

Big Eight

	Conference			Overall		
	W	L	Pct.	W	L	Pct.
*Kansas	10	4	.714	27	8	.771
*Oklahoma St.	10	4	.714	24	8	.750
*Nebraska	9	5	.643	26	8	.765
@Missouri	8	6	.571	20	10	.667
Iowa St.	6	8	.429	12	19	.387
Colorado	5	9	.357	19	14	.576
Oklahoma	5	9	.357	20	15	.571
Kansas St.	3	11	.214	13	15	.464

Big Sky

	Conference			Overall		
	W	L	Pct.	W	L	Pct.
*#Montana	13	3	.813	23	8	.742
Nevada	12	4	.750	17	14	.548
Idaho	11	5	.688	19	11	.633
Boise St.	10	6	.625	18	11	.621
Weber St.	7	9	.438	12	16	.429
Idaho St.	7	9	.438	11	18	.379
Montana St.	6	10	.375	12	16	.429
E. Washington	5	11	.313	11	16	.407
Northern Arizona	1	15	.063	4	23	.148

Big South

	Conference			Overall		
	W	L	Pct.	W	L	Pct.
*#Coastal Carol.	13	1	.929	24	8	.750
Radford	12	2	.857	22	7	.759
Augusta	9	5	.643	14	16	.467
Davidson	6	8	.429	10	19	.345
Winthrop	5	9	.357	8	20	.286
N.C.-Asheville	4	10	.286	8	20	.286
Charleston South.	4	10	.286	9	19	.321
Campbell	3	11	.214	9	19	.321

Big Ten

	Conference			Overall		
	W	L	Pct.	W	L	Pct.
*Ohio St.	15	3	.833	27	4	.871
*Indiana	15	3	.833	29	5	.853
@Illinois	11	7	.611	21	10	.677
*Michigan St.	11	7	.611	19	11	.633
*Iowa	9	9	.500	21	11	.656
*Purdue	9	9	.500	17	12	.586
Wisconsin	8	10	.444	15	15	.500
Michigan	7	11	.389	14	15	.483
Minnesota	5	13	.278	12	16	.429
Northwestern	0	18	.000	5	23	.179

Big West

	Conference			Overall		
	W	L	Pct.	W	L	Pct.
*#UNLV	18	0	1.000	34	1	.971
*New Mexico St.	15	3	.833	23	6	.793
Pacific	9	9	.500	14	15	.483
Cal.-Santa Barb.	8	10	.444	14	15	.483
Utah St.	8	10	.444	11	17	.393
Fullerton St.	7	11	.389	14	14	.500
Fresno St.	7	11	.389	14	16	.467
Long Beach St.	7	11	.389	11	17	.393
Cal.-Irvine	6	12	.333	11	19	.367
San Jose St.	5	13	.278	7	20	.259

Colonial Athletic Association

	Conference			Overall		
	W	L	Pct.	W	L	Pct.
James Madison	12	2	.857	19	10	.655
*#Richmond	10	4	.714	22	10	.688
American	8	6	.571	15	14	.517
George Mason	8	6	.571	14	16	.467

	W	L	Pct.	W	L	Pct.
William & Mary	6	8	.429	13	15	.464
N.C.-Wilmington	6	8	.429	11	17	.393
East Carolina	4	10	.286	12	16	.429
Navy	2	12	.143	8	21	.276

East Coast

	Conference			Overall		
	W	L	Pct.	W	L	Pct.
*#Towson St.	10	2	.833	19	11	.633
Delaware	8	4	.667	16	13	.552
Hofstra	7	5	.583	14	14	.500
Drexel	7	5	.583	12	16	.429
Rider	4	8	.333	14	16	.467
Maryl.-Balt. County	4	8	.333	7	22	.241
Central Conn.	2	10	.167	4	24	.143

Ivy League

	Conference			Overall		
	W	L	Pct.	W	L	Pct.
*Princeton	14	0	1.000	24	3	.889
Yale	9	5	.643	15	11	.577
Cornell	6	8	.429	13	13	.500
Brown	6	8	.429	11	15	.423
Harvard	6	8	.429	9	17	.346
Pennsylvania	6	8	.429	9	17	.346
Columbia	5	9	.357	7	19	.269
Dartmouth	4	10	.286	9	17	.346

Metro

	Conference			Overall		
	W	L	Pct.	W	L	Pct.
*S. Mississippi	10	4	.714	21	8	.724
*#Florida St.	9	5	.643	21	11	.656
Cincinnati	8	6	.571	18	12	.600
Tulane	7	7	.500	15	13	.536
Memphis St.	7	7	.500	17	15	.531
Virginia Tech	6	8	.429	13	16	.448
South Carolina	5	9	.357	20	13	.606
Louisville	4	10	.286	14	16	.467

Metro Atlantic Athletic

	Conference			Overall		
	W	L	Pct.	W	L	Pct.
Siena	12	4	.750	25	10	.714
La Salle	12	4	.750	19	10	.655
*#St. Peter's	11	5	.688	24	7	.774
Iona	11	5	.688	17	13	.567
Manhattan	8	8	.500	13	15	.464
Niagara	6	10	.375	8	20	.286
Loyola (MD)	5	11	.313	12	16	.429
Fairfield	4	12	.250	8	20	.286
Canisius	3	13	.188	10	19	.345

Mid-American

	Conference			Overall		
	W	L	Pct.	W	L	Pct.
*#E. Michigan	13	3	.813	26	7	.788
Ball St.	10	6	.625	21	10	.677
Miami (OH)	10	6	.625	16	12	.571
Bowling Green	9	7	.563	17	13	.567
Ohio	9	7	.563	16	12	.571
Central Michigan	8	8	.500	14	14	.500

	W	L	Pct.	W	L	Pct.
Toledo	7	9	.438	17	16	.515
Kent St.	4	12	.250	10	18	.357
Western Michigan	2	14	.125	5	22	.185

Mid-Continent

	Conference			Overall		
	W	L	Pct.	W	L	Pct.
*Northern Illinois	14	2	.875	25	6	.806
*#Wis.-Green Bay	13	3	.813	24	7	.774
Eastern Illinois	10	6	.625	17	12	.586
Cleveland St.	8	8	.500	12	16	.429
Northern Iowa	8	8	.500	13	19	.406
Akron	6	10	.375	15	13	.536
Western Illinois	6	10	.375	13	15	.464
Illinois-Chicago	5	11	.313	15	15	.500
Valparaiso	2	14	.125	5	22	.185

Mid-Eastern Athletic

	Conference			Overall		
	W	L	Pct.	W	L	Pct.
Coppin St.	14	2	.875	19	11	.633
Delaware St.	10	6	.625	19	11	.633
N. Carolina A&T	10	6	.625	17	10	.630
S. Carolina St.	10	6	.625	13	15	.464
#Florida A&M	9	7	.563	17	14	.548
Howard	7	9	.438	8	20	.286
Morgan St.	6	10	.375	7	22	.241
Maryland-E. Shore	3	13	.188	5	23	.179
Bethune-Cookman	3	13	.188	5	24	.172

Midwestern

	Conference			Overall		
	W	L	Pct.	W	L	Pct.
*#Xavier (OH)	11	3	.786	22	10	.688
Butler	10	4	.714	18	11	.621
St. Louis	8	6	.571	19	14	.576
Dayton	8	6	.571	14	15	.483
Evansville	7	7	.500	14	14	.500
Marquette	7	7	.500	11	18	.379
Loyola (IL)	3	11	.214	10	19	.345
Detroit	2	12	.143	9	19	.321

Missouri Valley

	Conference			Overall		
	W	L	Pct.	W	L	Pct.
*#Creighton	12	4	.750	24	8	.750
S.W. Missouri St.	11	5	.688	22	12	.647
Tulsa	10	6	.625	18	12	.600
Southern Illinois	9	7	.563	18	14	.563
Indiana St.	9	7	.563	14	14	.500
Wichita St.	7	9	.438	14	17	.452
Bradley	6	10	.375	8	20	.286
Drake	4	12	.250	8	21	.276
Illinois St.	4	12	.250	5	23	.179

North Atlantic

	Conference			Overall		
	W	L	Pct.	W	L	Pct.
*#Northeastern	8	2	.800	22	11	.667
Maine	7	3	.700	13	16	.448
Vermont	5	5	.500	15	13	.536
Hartford	5	5	.500	13	16	.448

	Conf W	L	Pct.	Ovr W	L	Pct.
Boston	5	5	.500	11	18	.379
New Hampshire	0	10	.000	3	25	.107

Northeast

	Conference			Overall		
	W	L	Pct.	W	L	Pct.
*#St. Francis (PA)	13	3	.813	24	8	.750
Fairleigh Dickin.	13	3	.813	22	9	.710
@Robert Morris	12	4	.750	17	11	.607
Monmouth	10	6	.625	19	10	.655
St. Francis (NY)	8	8	.500	15	14	.517
Mount St. Mary's	6	10	.375	8	19	.296
Long Island	4	12	.250	10	18	.357
Marist	4	12	.250	6	22	.214
Wagner	2	14	.125	4	26	.133

Ohio Valley

	Conference			Overall		
	W	L	Pct.	W	L	Pct.
*#Murray St.	10	2	.833	24	9	.727
Eastern Kentucky	9	3	.750	19	10	.655
Middle Tennessee	6	6	.500	21	9	.700
Austin Peay	6	6	.500	15	14	.517
Tennessee Tech	6	6	.500	12	16	.429
Morehead St.	4	8	.333	16	13	.552
Tennessee St.	1	11	.083	5	23	.179

Pacific-10

	Conference			Overall		
	W	L	Pct.	W	L	Pct.
*Arizona	14	4	.778	28	7	.800
*UCLA	11	7	.611	23	9	.719
*Arizona St.	10	8	.556	20	10	.667
*Southern Cal.	10	8	.556	19	10	.655
Stanford	8	10	.444	20	13	.606
Washington St.	8	10	.444	16	12	.571
Oregon St.	8	10	.444	14	14	.500
California	8	10	.444	13	15	.464
Oregon	8	10	.444	13	15	.464
Washington	5	13	.278	14	14	.500

Patriot League

	Conference			Overall		
	W	L	Pct.	W	L	Pct.
#Fordham	11	1	.917	25	8	.758
Lehigh	10	2	.833	19	10	.655
Holy Cross	8	4	.667	18	12	.600
Bucknell	7	5	.583	18	13	.581
Army	3	9	.250	6	22	.214
Colgate	2	10	.167	5	23	.179
Lafayette	1	11	.083	7	21	.250

Southeastern

	Conference			Overall		
	W	L	Pct.	W	L	Pct.
@Kentucky	14	4	.778	22	6	.786
*Mississippi St.	13	5	.722	20	9	.690
*Louisiana St.	13	5	.722	20	10	.667
*#Alabama	12	6	.667	23	10	.697
*Vanderbilt	11	7	.611	17	13	.567
*Georgia	9	9	.500	17	13	.567
Florida	7	11	.389	11	17	.393

	Conf W	L	Pct.	Ovr W	L	Pct.
Auburn	5	13	.278	13	16	.448
Tennessee	3	15	.167	12	22	.353
Mississippi	3	15	.167	9	19	.321

Southern

	Conference			Overall		
	W	L	Pct.	W	L	Pct.
Furman	11	3	.786	20	9	.690
*#E. Tenn. St.	11	3-	.786	28	5	.848
Tenn.-Chattan.	11	3	.786	19	10	.655
Appalachian St.	7	7	.500	16	14	.533
@Marshall	7	7	.500	14	14	.500
Virginia Military	5	9	.357	10	18	.357
Western Carolina	3	11	.214	11	17	.393
Citadel	1	13	.071	6	22	.214

Southland

	Conference			Overall		
	W	L	Pct.	W	L	Pct.
*#N.E. Louisiana	13	1	.929	25	8	.758
Texas-Arlington	11	3	.786	20	9	.690
North Texas	11	3	.786	17	13	.567
Stephen Austin	6	8	.429	11	17	.393
Sam Houston St.	5	9	.357	7	20	.259
S.W. Texas St.	4	10	.286	10	17	.370
@McNeese St.	4	10	.286	8	19	.296
N.W. Louisiana	2	12	.143	6	22	.214

Southwest

	Conference			Overall		
	W	L	Pct.	W	L	Pct.
*#Arkansas	15	1	.938	34	4	.895
*Texas	13	3	.813	23	9	.719
Houston	10	6	.625	18	11	.621
Texas Christian	9	7	.563	18	10	.643
Rice	9	7	.563	16	14	.533
SMU	6	10	.375	12	17	.414
Baylor	4	12	.250	12	15	.444
Texas Tech	4	12	.250	8	23	.258
Texas A&M	2	14	.125	8	21	.276

Southwestern Athletic

	Conference			Overall		
	W	L	Pct.	W	L	Pct.
#Jackson St.	10	2	.833	17	13	.567
Southern	8	4	.667	19	9	.679
Alabama St.	7	5	.583	18	11	.621
Texas Southern	7	5	.583	13	17	.433
Mississ. Valley St.	4	8	.333	9	19	.321
Alcorn St.	3	9	.250	8	21	.276
Grambling St.	3	9	.250	6	22	.214
Prairie View	0	0	.000	4	21	.160

Sun Belt

	Conference			Overall		
	W	L	Pct.	W	L	Pct.
*#South Alabama	11	3	.786	22	9	.710
Alabama-Birm.	9	5	.643	18	13	.581
South Florida	8	6	.571	19	11	.633
Western Kentucky	8	6	.571	14	14	.500
Virginia Common.	7	7	.500	14	17	.452
N.C.-Charlotte	6	8	.429	14	14	.500

	W	L	Pct.	W	L	Pct.
Old Dominion	5	9	.357	14	18	.438
Jacksonville	2	12	.143	6	22	.214

Trans America Athletic

	Conference			Overall		
	W	L	Pct.	W	L	Pct.
Texas-San Ant.	12	2	.857	21	8	.724
Centenary	10	4	.714	17	12	.586
Georgia Southern	9	5	.643	14	13	.519
Stetson	9	5	.643	15	16	.484
*#Georgia St.	7	7	.500	16	15	.516
Arkan.-Little Rock	6	8	.429	10	20	.333
Samford	2	12	.143	6	22	.214
Mercer	1	13	.071	2	25	.074

West Coast

	Conference			Overall		
	W	L	Pct.	W	L	Pct.
*#Pepperdine	13	1	.929	22	9	.710
Loyola Marymount	9	5	.643	16	15	.516
San Diego	8	6	.571	17	12	.586
Santa Clara	7	7	.500	16	13	.552
St. Mary's	7	7	.500	13	17	.433
Gonzaga	5	9	.357	14	14	.500
San Francisco	4	10	.286	12	17	.414
Portland	3	11	.214	5	23	.179

Western Athletic

	Conference			Overall		
	W	L	Pct.	W	L	Pct.
*Utah	15	1	.938	30	4	.882
*#Brigham Young	11	5	.688	21	13	.618
*New Mexico	10	6	.625	20	10	.667
Wyoming	8	8	.500	20	12	.625

	W	L	Pct.	W	L	Pct.
Hawaii	7	9	.438	16	13	.552
Texas-El Paso	7	9	.438	16	13	.552
Colorado St.	6	10	.375	15	14	.517
San Diego St.	6	10	.375	13	16	.448
Air Force	2	14	.125	9	20	.310

Division I Independents

	Overall		
	W	L	Pct.
*DePaul	20	9	.690
Wright St.	19	9	.679
Wisc.-Milwaukee	18	10	.643
Southern Utah St.	16	12	.571
Miss.-Kansas City	15	14	.517
Youngstown St.	12	16	.429
Brooklyn	11	16	.407
Notre Dame	12	20	.375
Miami (FL)	9	19	.321
S.E. Louisiana	9	19	.321
Cal. St.-Northridge	8	20	.286
Florida Intl.	6	22	.214
Liberty	5	25	.167
Chicago St.	4	24	.143
Nicholls St.	3	25	.107
N.E. Illinois	2	25	.074
U.S. International	2	26	.071

* Selected to the NCAA tournament.
\# Won post-season conference tournament. The Big Ten, Ivy League, and Pacific-10 did not hold tournaments.
@ Ineligible for both the NCAA tournament and the NIT.

FINAL AP POLL, 1990-91

	W-L	Points
1. UNLV (64)	30-0	1600
2. Arkansas	31-3	1490
3. Indiana	27-4	1446
4. North Carolina	25-5	1398
5. Ohio St.	25-3	1360
6. Duke	26-7	1234
7. Syracuse	26-5	1232
8. Arizona	26-6	1203
9. Kentucky	22-6	952
10. Utah	28-3	923
11. Nebraska	26-7	878
12. Kansas	22-7	796
13. Seton Hall	22-8	785
14. Oklahoma St.	22-7	691
15. New Mexico St.	23-5	687
16. UCLA	23-8	609
17. E. Tenn. St.	28-4	589
18. Princeton	24-2	517
19. Alabama	21-9	469
20. St. John's	20-8	364

FINAL UPI POLL, 1990-91

	W-L	Points
1. UNLV (35)	30-0	525
2. Arkansas	31-3	487
3. Indiana	27-4	446
4. North Carolina	25-5	438
5. Ohio St.	25-3	384
6. Duke	26-7	351
7. Arizona	26-6	342
8. Syracuse	26-5	285
9. Nebraska	26-7	187
10. Utah	28-3	156
11. Seton Hall	22-8	149
12. Kansas	22-7	135
13. Oklahoma St.	22-7	97
14. UCLA	23-8	81
15. E. Tenn. St.	28-4	51
16. Alabama	21-9	36
17. New Mexico St.	23-5	30
18. Mississippi St.	20-8	23
19. St. John's	20-8	20
20. Princeton	24-2	19

Polls taken prior to NCAA and NIT tournaments. Won-loss records reflect performances at the time the polls were taken. First-place votes in parentheses.

DIVISION I LEADERS, 1990-91

SCORING

Kevin Bradshaw, U.S. International	37.6
Alphonso Ford, Mississ. Valley St.	32.7
Von McDade, Wisconsin-Milwaukee	29.6
Steve Rogers, Alabama St.	29.4
Terrell Lowery, Loyola Marymount	28.5
Bobby Phills, Southern	28.4
Shaquille O'Neal, Louisiana St.	27.6
John Taft, Marshall	27.3
Rodney Monroe, North Carolina St.	27.0
Terrell Brandon, Oregon	26.6

REBOUNDS

Shaquille O'Neal, Louisiana St.	14.7
Popeye Jones, Murray St.	14.2
Larry Stewart, Coppin St.	13.4
Tim Burroughs, Jacksonville	13.0
Warren Kidd, Middle Tennessee St.	12.3
Clarence Weatherspoon, S. Mississ.	12.2
Ervin Johnson, New Orleans	12.2
Tom Davis, Delaware St.	12.2
Dikembe Mutombo, Georgetown	12.2
Dale Davis, Clemson	12.1

ASSISTS

Chris Corchiani, N. Carolina St.	9.6
Danny Tirado, Jacksonville	9.3
Terrell Lowery, Loyola Marymount	9.1
Keith Jennings, E. Tennessee St.	9.1
Greg Anthony, UNLV	8.9
Van Usher, Tennessee Tech	8.3
Orlando Smart, San Francisco	8.2
Ray Johnson, Sam Houston St.	8.0
Glover Cody, Texas-Arlington	7.9
Arnold Bernard, S.W. Missouri St.	7.6

STEALS

Van Usher, Tennessee Tech	3.7
Scott Burrell, Connecticut	3.6
Eric Murdock, Providence	3.5
Von McDade, Wisconsin-Milwaukee	3.5
Lynn Smith, St. Francis (NY)	3.4
Emmanual Davis, Delaware St.	3.4
Ronnie Ellison, Texas-San Antonio	3.3
Keith Jennings, E. Tennessee St.	3.3
Bobby Phills, Southern	3.2
Pat Baldwin, Northwestern	3.2

BLOCKED SHOTS

Shawn Bradley, Brigham Young	5.2
Cedric Lewis, Maryland	5.1
Shaquille O'Neal, Louisiana St.	5.0
Dikembe Mutombo, Georgetown	4.7
Kevin Robertson, Virginia Military	3.7
Lorenzo Williams, Stetson	3.6
Acie Earl, Iowa	3.3
Jim McIlvaine, Marquette	3.3
Luc Longley, New Mexico	3.2
Damon Lopez, Fordham	3.0

FIELD GOAL PCT.

Oliver Miller, Arkansas	70.4
Warren Kidd, Middle Tennessee St.	70.0
Pete Freeman, Akron	70.0
Lester James, St. Francis (NY)	69.3
Marcus Kennedy, Eastern Michigan	68.2
Allen Lightfoot, Montana St.	66.3
Chris Brooks, West Virginia	66.3
Larry Johnson, UNLV	66.2
Victor Alexander, Iowa St.	65.9
Luc Longley, New Mexico	65.6

FREE THROW PCT.

Darin Archbold, Butler	91.2
William Lewis, Monmouth	90.1
Darwyn Alexander, Oklahoma St.	89.7
Keith Jennings, E. Tennessee St.	89.5
Rodney Monroe, North Carolina St.	88.5
Mike Iuzzolino, St. Francis (PA)	88.5
Eddie Bird, Indiana St.	87.2
DaVor Marcelic, Southern Utah St.	87.1
Lewis Geter, Ohio	86.7
Andy Kennedy, Alabama-Birmingham	86.5

3-PT FIELD GOAL PCT.

Keith Jennings, E. Tennessee St.	59.2
Tony Bennett, Wisconsin-Green Bay	53.3
Mike Iuzzolino, St. Francis (PA)	52.8
Ross Richardson, Loyola Marymount	52.6
David Mitchell, Samford	52.6
Gary Waites, Alabama	51.5
Todd Leslie, Northwestern	51.2
Dave Olson, Eastern Illinois	50.0
Billy Dreher, California	50.0
Lance Vaughn, Boise St.	49.5

SCORING OFFENSE, TEAM

Southern	104.4
Loyola Marymount	103.6
Arkansas	99.6
UNLV	97.7
Oklahoma	96.1
Texas-Arlington	94.6
E. Tennessee St.	94.0
Southern Utah St.	93.0
Wright St.	92.6
UCLA	92.3

SCORING DEFENSE, TEAM

Princeton	48.9
Northern Illinois	57.5
Yale	58.0
Wisconsin-Green Bay	61.1
Georgetown	61.4
Colorado St.	61.5
St. Peter's	63.0
Monmouth	63.4
Temple	64.0
Utah	64.2

NCAA TOURNAMENT 1991

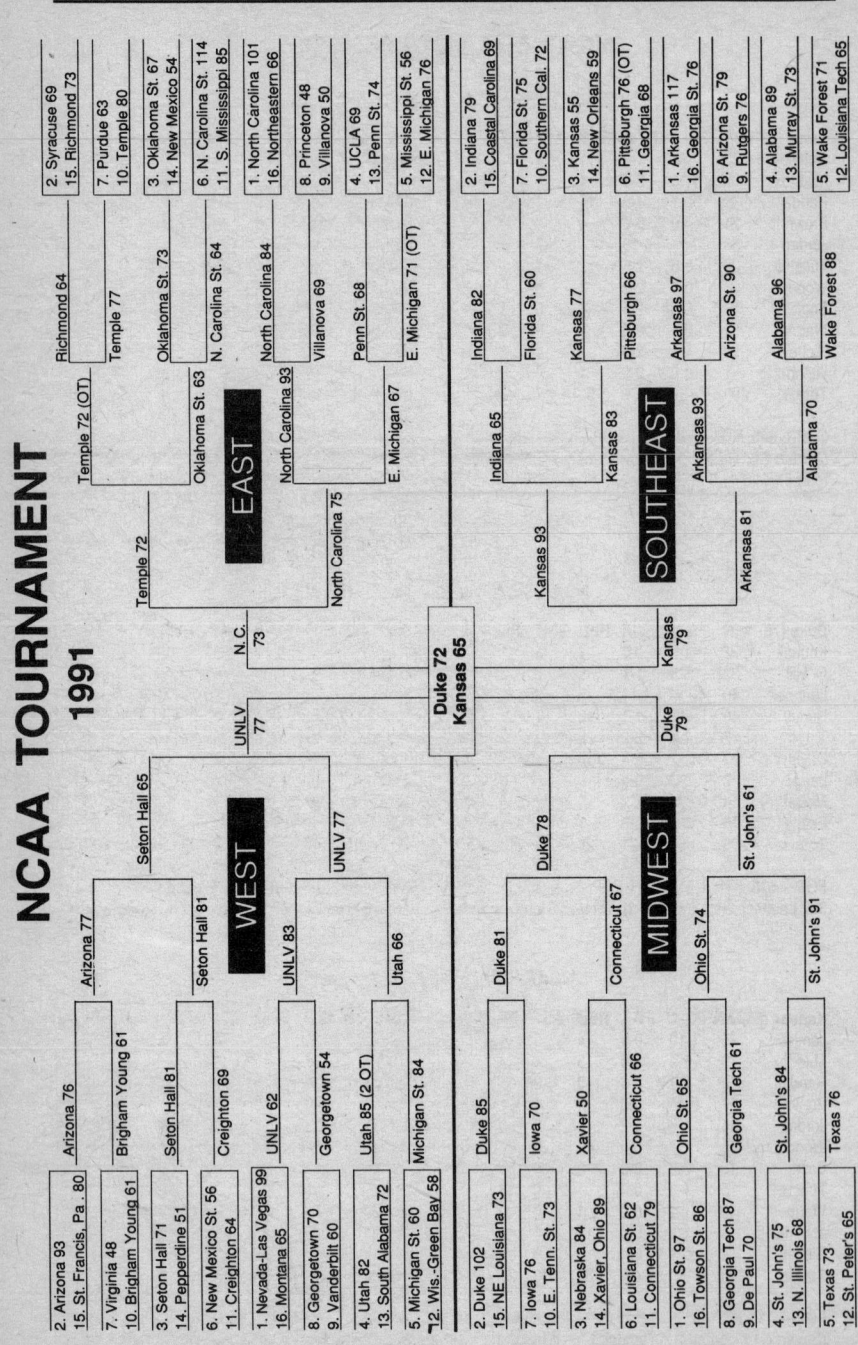

EAST

2. Syracuse 69
15. Richmond 73

Richmond 64

7. Purdue 63
10. Temple 80

Temple 77

Temple 72 (OT)

3. Oklahoma St. 67
14. New Mexico 54

Oklahoma St. 73

6. N. Carolina St. 114
11. S. Mississippi 85

N. Carolina St. 64

Oklahoma St. 63

Temple 72

1. North Carolina 101
16. Northeastern 66

North Carolina 84

North Carolina 93

8. Princeton 48
9. Villanova 50

Villanova 69

North Carolina 75

4. UCLA 69
13. Penn St. 74

Penn St. 68

5. Mississippi St. 56
12. E. Michigan 76

E. Michigan 71 (OT)

E. Michigan 67

N.C. 73

SOUTHEAST

2. Indiana 79
15. Coastal Carolina 69

Indiana 82

7. Florida St. 75
10. Southern Cal. 72

Florida St. 60

Indiana 65

3. Kansas 55
14. New Orleans 59

Kansas 77

Kansas 83

6. Pittsburgh 76 (OT)
11. Georgia 68

Pittsburgh 66

Kansas 93

1. Arkansas 117
16. Georgia St. 76

Arkansas 97

Arkansas 93

8. Arizona St. 79
9. Rutgers 76

Arizona St. 90

Arkansas 81

4. Alabama 89
13. Murray St. 73

Alabama 96

5. Wake Forest 71
12. Louisiana Tech 65

Wake Forest 88

Alabama 70

Kansas 79

Duke 72
Kansas 65

WEST

2. Arizona 93
15. St. Francis, Pa . 80

Arizona 76

7. Virginia 48
10. Brigham Young 61

Brigham Young 61

Arizona 77

3. Seton Hall 71
14. Pepperdine 51

Seton Hall 71

Seton Hall 81

6. New Mexico St. 56
11. Creighton 64

Creighton 69

Seton Hall 65

1. Nevada-Las Vegas 99
16. Montana 65

UNLV 62

UNLV 83

8. Georgetown 70
9. Vanderbilt 60

Georgetown 54

UNLV 77

4. Utah 82
13. South Alabama 72

Utah 85 (2 OT)

Utah 66

5. Michigan St. 60
12. Wis.-Green Bay 58

Michigan St. 84

UNLV 77

MIDWEST

2. Duke 102
15. NE Louisiana 73

Duke 85

7. Iowa 76
10. E. Tenn. St. 73

Iowa 70

Duke 81

3. Nebraska 84
14. Xavier, Ohio 89

Xavier 50

Connecticut 67

6. Louisiana St. 62
11. Connecticut 79

Connecticut 66

Duke 78

1. Ohio St. 97
16. Towson St. 86

Ohio St. 65

Ohio St. 74

8. Georgia Tech 87
9. De Paul 70

Georgia Tech 61

St. John's 61

4. St. John's 75
13. N. Illinois 68

St. John's 84

St. John's 91

5. Texas 73
12. St. Peter's 65

Texas 76

Duke 79

NCAA BOX SCORES 1990-91

NCAA SEMIFINAL: Kansas 79, North Carolina 73

Kans. (79)	MIN	FG-A	FT-A	REB	AST	PF	PTS
Jamison	25	4-8	1-3	11	2	4	9
Maddox	27	4-10	2-2	4	2	3	10
Randall	33	6-11	4-6	11	4	1	16
Brown	24	1-10	0-0	4	1	2	3
Jordan	36	4-11	6-13	4	7	2	16
Tunstall	20	1-5	2-5	2	1	2	5
Woodberry	6	0-0	2-2	1	0	1	2
Scott	16	6-9	2-3	6	0	3	14
Wagner	2	0-1	0-0	1	0	0	0
Richey	10	1-1	2-2	1	0	2	4
Johanning	1	0-0	0-0	1	0	0	0
Totals	200	27-66	21-36	51	17	20	79

FGP—.409. FTP—.583. 3-PT FGP—4-14, .286 (Jordan 2-6, Tunstall 1-2, Brown 1-6). Technical fouls—none.

N.C. (73)	MIN	FG-A	FT-A	REB	AST	PF	PTS
Lynch	30	5-8	3-6	5	2	5	13
Fox	29	5-22	3-3	9	7	5	13
Chilcutt	27	2-8	0-0	11	1	3	4
Rice	30	1-6	3-4	0	3	2	5
Davis	30	9-16	5-5	5	1	0	25
Rozier	3	0-0	0-0	0	0	0	0
Montross	19	3-4	0-1	3	1	4	6
Phelps	10	1-1	0-1	1	1	4	2
Rodl	8	0-1	0-0	2	0	1	0
Reese	11	2-5	0-3	2	0	0	5
Sullivan	1	0-0	0-0	0	0	3	0
Harris	2	0-2	0-0	0	0	0	0
Totals	200	28-73	14-23	42	16	27	73

FGP—.384. FTP—.609. 3-PT FGP—3-18, .167 (Davis 2-4, Reese 1-1, Chilcutt 0-1, Harris 0-2, Rice 0-3, Fox 0-7). Technical fouls—coach Smith 2 (ejected). Halftime—Kansas 43, North Carolina 34. Attendance—47,100 (Hoosier Dome, Indianapolis).

NCAA SEMIFINAL: Duke 79, UNLV 77

Duke (79)	MIN	FG-A	FT-A	REB	AST	PF	PTS
Koubek	22	1-6	0-0	1	3	1	2
G. Hill	33	5-8	1-1	5	5	2	11
Laettner	40	9-14	9-11	7	2	2	28
Hurley	40	4-7	1-1	2	7	3	12
T. Hill	22	2-6	2-2	2	1	2	6
Davis	21	6-12	3-4	4	1	1	15
Lang	2	0-0	0-0	0	0	0	0
McCaffrey	14	2-3	1-2	0	2	1	5
Palmer	6	0-0	0-0	1	0	1	0
Totals	200	29-56	17-21	26	21	13	79

FGP—.518. FTP—.810. 3-PT FGP—4-8, .500 (Hurley 3-4, Laettner 1-1, Koubek 0-3). Technical fouls—none.

UNLV (77)	MIN	FG-A	FT-A	REB	AST	PF	PTS
Johnson	39	5-10	3-4	13	2	3	13
Augmon	39	3-10	0-1	8	2	2	6
Ackles	25	3-6	1-2	5	0	4	7
Hunt	39	11-20	3-5	4	2	0	29
Anthony	35	8-18	1-1	5	6	5	19
Spencer	9	0-2	1-2	3	1	2	1
Gray	14	1-2	0-0	1	0	2	2
Totals	200	31-68	9-15	39	13	18	77

FGP—.456. FTP—.600. 3-PT FGP—6-15, .400 (Hunt 4-11, Anthony 2-2, Johnson 0-2). Technical fouls—Johnson. Halftime—UNLV 43, Duke 41. Attendance—47,100 (Hoosier Dome, Indianapolis).

NCAA FINAL: Duke 72, Kansas 65

Kansas (65)	MIN	FG-A	FT-A	REB	AST	PF	PTS
Jamison	25	1-10	0-0	4	5	4	2
Maddox	19	2-4	0-0	3	4	3	4
Randall	33	7-9	3-6	10	2	4	18
Brown	31	6-15	0-0	4	1	1	16
Jordan	34	4-6	1-2	0	3	0	11
Woodberry	18	1-4	0-0	4	0	4	2
Scott	15	3-9	0-0	2	0	1	6
Tunstall	15	1-5	0-0	1	0	3	2
Wagner	3	1-1	0-0	1	0	0	2
Johanning	3	1-1	0-0	2	1	1	2
Richey	4	0-1	0-0	1	0	0	0
Totals	200	27-65	4-8	32	16	21	65

FGP—.415. FTP—.500. 3-PT FGP—7-18, .389 (Brown 4-11, Jordan 2-2, Randall 1-1, Richey 0-1, Tunstall 0-1, Jamison 0-2). Technical fouls—none.

Duke (72)	MIN	FG-A	FT-A	REB	AST	PF	PTS
Koubek	17	2-4	0-0	4	0	1	5
G. Hill	28	4-6	2-8	8	3	1	10
Laettner	32	3-8	12-12	10	0	3	18
Hurley	40	3-5	4-4	1	9	1	12
T. Hill	23	1-5	0-0	4	1	2	3
Davis	24	4-5	0-2	2	1	4	8
Palmer	9	0-0	0-0	0	0	0	0
Lang	1	0-0	0-0	0	0	0	0
McCaffrey	26	6-8	2-2	1	0	1	16
Totals	200	23-41	20-28	31	14	13	72

FGP—.561. FTP—.714. 3-PT FGP—6-10, .600 (Hurley 2-4, McCaffrey 2-3, T. Hill 1-1, Koubek 1-2). Technical fouls—none. Halftime—Duke 42, Kansas 34. Attendance—47,100 (Hoosier Dome, Indianapolis).

NATIONAL CHAMPIONS

YEAR	CHAMPION	RECORD	COACH	YEAR	CHAMPION	RECORD	COACH
1901	Yale	10-4	No coach	1947	Holy Cross	27-3	Doggie Julian
1902	Minnesota	11-0	Louis Cooke	1948	Kentucky	36-3	Adolph Rupp
1903	Yale	15-1	W.H. Murphy	1949	Kentucky	32-2	Adolph Rupp
1904	Columbia	17-1	No coach	1950	CCNY	24-5	Nat Holman
1905	Columbia	19-1	No coach	1951	Kentucky	32-2	Adolph Rupp
1906	Dartmouth	16-2	No coach	1952	Kansas	28-3	Phog Allen
1907	Chicago	22-2	Joseph Raycroft	1953	Indiana	23-3	Branch McCracken
1908	Chicago	21-2	Joseph Raycroft	1954	La Salle	26-4	Ken Loeffler
1909	Chicago	12-0	Joseph Raycroft	1955	San Francisco	28-1	Phil Woolpert
1910	Columbia	11-1	Harry Fisher	1956	San Francisco	29-0	Phil Woolpert
1911	St. John's	14-0	Claude Allen	1957	North Carolina	32-0	Frank McGuire
1912	Wisconsin	15-0	Doc Meanwell	1958	Kentucky	23-6	Adolph Rupp
1913	Navy	9-0	Louis Wenzell	1959	California	25-4	Pete Newell
1914	Wisconsin	15-0	Doc Meanwell	1960	Ohio St.	25-3	Fred Taylor
1915	Illinois	16-0	Ralph Jones	1961	Cincinnati	27-3	Edwin Jucker
1916	Wisconsin	20-1	Doc Meanwell	1962	Cincinnati	29-2	Edwin Jucker
1917	Washington St.	25-1	Doc Bohler	1963	Loyola (IL)	29-2	George Ireland
1918	Syracuse	16-1	Edmund Dollard	1964	UCLA	30-0	John Wooden
1919	Minnesota	13-0	Louis Cooke	1965	UCLA	28-2	John Wooden
1920	Pennsylvania	22-1	Lon Jourdet	1966	Texas Western	28-1	Don Haskins
1921	Pennsylvania	21-2	Edward McNichol	1967	UCLA	30-0	John Wooden
1922	Kansas	16-2	Phog Allen	1968	UCLA	29-1	John Wooden
1923	Kansas	17-1	Phog Allen	1969	UCLA	29-1	John Wooden
1924	North Carolina	25-0	Bo Shepard	1970	UCLA	28-2	John Wooden
1925	Princeton	21-2	Al Wittmer	1971	UCLA	29-1	John Wooden
1926	Syracuse	19-1	Lew Andreas	1972	UCLA	30-0	John Wooden
1927	Notre Dame	19-1	George Keogan	1973	UCLA	30-0	John Wooden
1928	Pittsburgh	21-0	Doc Carlson	1974	N. Carol. St.	30-1	Norm Sloan
1929	Montana St.	36-2	Shubert Dyche	1975	UCLA	28-3	John Wooden
1930	Pittsburgh	23-2	Doc Carlson	1976	Indiana	32-0	Bobby Knight
1931	Northwestern	16-1	Dutch Lonborg	1977	Marquette	25-7	Al McGuire
1932	Purdue	17-1	Piggy Lambert	1978	Kentucky	30-2	Joe B. Hall
1933	Kentucky	20-3	Adolph Rupp	1979	Michigan St.	26-6	Jud Heathcote
1934	Wyoming	26-3	Dutch Witte	1980	Louisville	33-3	Denny Crum
1935	New York	18-1	Howard Cann	1981	Indiana	26-9	Bobby Knight
1936	Notre Dame	22-2-1	George Keogan	1982	North Carolina	32-2	Dean Smith
1937	Stanford	25-2	John Bunn	1983	N. Carol. St.	28-8	Jim Valvano
1938	Temple	23-2	James Usilton	1984	Georgetown	34-3	John Thompson
1939	Oregon	29-5	Howard Hobson	1985	Villanova	25-10	Rollie Massimino
1940	Indiana	20-3	Branch McCracken	1986	Louisville	32-7	Denny Crum
1941	Wisconsin	20-3	Bud Foster	1987	Indiana	30-4	Bobby Knight
1942	Stanford	28-4	Everett Dean	1988	Kansas	27-11	Larry Brown
1943	Wyoming	31-2	Everett Shelton	1989	Michigan	30-7	Steve Fisher
1944	Utah	22-4	Vadal Peterson	1990	UNLV	35-5	Jerry Tarkanian
1945	Oklahoma A&M	27-4	Hank Iba	1991	Duke	32-7	Mike Krzyzewski
1946	Oklahoma A&M	31-2	Hank Iba				

FINAL FOUR RESULTS

YEAR	CHAMPION	FINALS OPP.	SCORE	RUNNER-UP	RUNNER-UP
1939	Oregon	Ohio St.	46-33	Oklahoma	Villanova
1940	Indiana	Kansas	60-42	Duquesne	Southern Cal.
1941	Wisconsin	Washington St.	39-34	Arkansas	Pittsburgh
1942	Stanford	Dartmouth	53-38	Colorado	Kentucky
1943	Wyoming	Georgetown	46-34	DePaul	Texas
1944	Utah	Dartmouth	42-40 (OT)	Iowa St.	Ohio St.
1945	Oklahoma A&M	New York	49-45	Arkansas	Ohio St.
1946	Oklahoma A&M	North Carolina	43-40	Ohio St.	California
1947	Holy Cross	Oklahoma	58-47	Texas	CCNY
1948	Kentucky	Baylor	58-42	Holy Cross	Kansas St.
1949	Kentucky	Oklahoma A&M	46-36	Illinois	Oregon St.
1950	CCNY	Bradley	71-68	N. Carol. St.	Baylor
1951	Kentucky	Kansas St.	68-58	Illinois	Oklahoma A&M
1952	Kansas	St. John's	80-63	Illinois	Santa Clara
1953	Indiana	Kansas	69-68	Washington	Louisiana St.
1954	La Salle	Bradley	92-76	Penn St.	Southern Cal.
1955	San Francisco	La Salle	77-63	Colorado	Iowa
1956	San Francisco	Iowa	83-71	Temple	SMU
1957	North Carolina	Kansas	54-53 (3 OT)	San Francisco	Michigan St.
1958	Kentucky	Seattle	84-72	Temple	Kansas St.
1959	California	West Virginia	71-70	Cincinnati	Louisville
1960	Ohio St.	California	75-55	Cincinnati	New York
1961	Cincinnati	Ohio St.	70-65 (OT)	St. Joe's (PA)	Utah
1962	Cincinnati	Ohio St.	71-59	Wake Forest	UCLA
1963	Loyola (IL)	Cincinnati	60-58 (OT)	Duke	Oregon St.
1964	UCLA	Duke	98-83	Michigan	Kansas St.
1965	UCLA	Michigan	91-80	Princeton	Wichita St.
1966	Texas Western	Kentucky	72-65	Duke	Utah
1967	UCLA	Dayton	79-64	Houston	North Carolina
1968	UCLA	North Carolina	78-55	Ohio St.	Houston
1969	UCLA	Purdue	92-72	Drake	North Carolina
1970	UCLA	Jacksonville	80-69	New Mexico St.	St. Bonaventure
1971	UCLA	Villanova	68-62	W. Kentucky	Kansas
1972	UCLA	Florida St.	81-76	North Carolina	Louisville
1973	UCLA	Memphis St.	87-66	Indiana	Providence
1974	N. Carol. St.	Marquette	76-64	UCLA	Kansas
1975	UCLA	Kentucky	92-85	Louisville	Syracuse
1976	Indiana	Michigan	86-68	UCLA	Rutgers
1977	Marquette	North Carolina	67-59	UNLV	N.C.-Charlotte
1978	Kentucky	Duke	94-88	Arkansas	Notre Dame
1979	Michigan St.	Indiana St.	75-64	DePaul	Pennsylvania
1980	Louisville	UCLA	59-54	Purdue	Iowa
1981	Indiana	North Carolina	63-50	Virginia	Louisiana St.
1982	North Carolina	Georgetown	63-62	Houston	Louisville
1983	N. Carol. St.	Houston	54-52	Georgia	Louisville
1984	Georgetown	Houston	84-75	Kentucky	Virginia
1985	Villanova	Georgetown	66-64	Memphis St.	St. John's
1986	Louisville	Duke	72-69	Kansas	Louisiana St.
1987	Indiana	Syracuse	74-73	Providence	UNLV
1988	Kansas	Oklahoma	83-79	Arizona	Duke
1989	Michigan	Seton Hall	80-79 (OT)	Duke	Illinois
1990	UNLV	Duke	103-73	Arkansas	Georgia Tech
1991	Duke	Kansas	72-65	North Carolina	UNLV

DIVISION I CAREER LEADERS

POINTS
3,667................Pete Maravich, Louisiana St.
3,249................Freeman Williams, Portland St.
3,217................Lionel Simmons, La Salle
3,066................Harry Kelly, Texas Southern
3,008................Hersey Hawkins, Bradley
2,973................Oscar Robertson, Cincinnati
2,951................Danny Manning, Kansas
2,914................Alfredrick Hughes, Loyola (IL)
2,884................Elvin Hayes, Houston
2,850................Larry Bird, Indiana St.

SCORING AVERAGE
44.2................Pete Maravich, Louisiana St.
34.6................Austin Carr, Notre Dame
33.8................Oscar Robertson, Cincinnati
33.1................Calvin Murphy, Niagara
32.7................Dwight Lamar, S.W. Louisiana
32.5................Frank Selvy, Furman
32.3................Rick Mount, Purdue
32.1................Darrell Floyd, Furman
32.0................Nick Werkman, Seton Hall
31.5................Willie Humes, Idaho St.

REBOUNDS
2,201................Tom Gola, La Salle
2,030................Joe Holup, George Washington
1,916................Charlie Slack, Marshall
1,884................Ed Conlin, Fordham
1,802................Dickie Hemric, Wake Forest
1,751................Paul Silas, Creighton
1,716................Art Quimby, Connecticut
1,688................Jerry Harper, Alabama
1,679................Jeff Cohen, William & Mary
1,675................Steve Hamilton, Morehead St.

ASSISTS
960................Sherman Douglas, Syracuse
939................Gary Payton, Oregon St.
894................Andre LaFleur, Northeastern
884................Jim Les, Bradley
883................Frank Smith, Old Dominion
877................Taurence Chisholm, Delaware
857................Grayson Marshall, Clemson
855................Anthony Manuel, Bradley
838................Avery Johnson, Cameron & Southern
833................Pooh Richardson, UCLA

STEALS
341................Michael Anderson, Drexel
341................Kenny Robertson, New Mex., Clevel. St.
321................Gary Payton, Oregon St.
301................Aldwin Ware, Florida
301................Drafton Davis, Marist
300................Gary Grant, Michigan
298................Taurence Chisholm, Delaware
295................Frank Smith, Old Dominion
291................D'Wayne Tanner, Rice
282................Michael Williams, Baylor

BLOCKED SHOTS
399................Rodney Blake, St. Joseph's (PA)
392................Tim Perry, Temple
374................Pervis Ellison, Louisville
351................David Robinson, Navy
346................Charles Smith, Pittsburgh
345................Rik Smits, Marist
339................Derrick Lewis, Maryland
335................Kenny Green, Rhode Island
334................Elden Campbell, Clemson
319................Rony Seikaly, Syracuse

FIELD GOAL PCT.
68.5................Steve Scheffler, Purdue
67.8................Steve Johnson, Oregon St.
66.8................Murray Brown, Florida St
66.5................Lee Campbell, S.W. Missouri St
66.2................Joe Senser, West Chester
65.6................Kevin Magee, California-Irvine
65.4................Orlando Phillips, Pepperdine
65.1................Bill Walton, UCLA
63.9................Lew Alcindor, UCLA
63.9................Akeem Olajuwon, Houston

FREE THROW PCT.
90.9................Greg Starrick, Kentucky & S. Illinois
90.1................Jack Moore, Nebraska
90.0................Steve Henson, Kansas St.
89.8................Steve Alford, Indiana
89.8................Bob Lloyd, Rutgers
89.5................Jim Barton, Dartmouth
89.2................Tommy Boyer, Arkansas
89.0................Rick Park, Tulsa
88.8................Steve Kaplan, Rutgers
88.6................Don Smith, Dayton

3-PT FIELD GOAL PCT.
47.5................Kirk Manns, Michigan St.
46.0................Barry Booker, Vanderbilt
45.5................Jim Barton, Dartmouth
45.2................Charlton Becton, North Carolina A&T
44.7................Steve Henson, Kansas St.
44.7................Jeff McCool, New Mexico St.
43.6................Craig Davis, Pepperdine
43.2................Dana Barros, Boston College
43.1................Scott Haffner, Evansville
43.0................Sydney Grider, S.W. Louisiana
43.0................Dave Mooney, Coastal Carolina

MOST VICTORIES, COACH
875................Adolph Rupp
767................Hank Iba
759................Ed Diddle
746................Phog Allen
724................Ray Meyer
717................Dean Smith
664................John Wooden
657................Ralph Miller
642................Marv Harshman
627................Norm Sloan

DIVISION I SEASON RECORDS

POINTS

1,381 ....Pete Maravich, Louisiana St..................1970
1,214 ....Elvin Hayes, Houston 1968
1,209 ....Frank Selvy, Furman 1954
1,148 ....Pete Maravich, Louisiana St..................1969
1,138 ....Pete Maravich, Louisiana St..................1968
1,131 ....Bo Kimble, Loyola Marymount 1990
1,125 ....Hersey Hawkins, Bradley 1988
1,106 ....Austin Carr, Notre Dame 1970
1,101 ....Austin Carr, Notre Dame 1971
1,090 ....Otis Birdsong, Houston 1977

SCORING AVERAGE

44.5 ......Pete Maravich, Louisiana St..................1970
44.2 ......Pete Maravich, Louisiana St..................1969
43.8 ......Pete Maravich, Louisiana St..................1968
41.7 ......Frank Selvy, Furman 1954
40.1 ......Johnny Neumann, Mississippi...............1971
38.8 ......Freeman Williams, Portland St..............1977
38.8 ......Billy McGill, Utah 1962
38.2 ......Calvin Murphy, Niagara 1968
38.1 ......Austin Carr, Notre Dame 1970
38.0 ......Austin Carr, Notre Dame 1971

REBOUNDS

734 ....Walter Dukes, Seton Hall 1953
652 ....Leroy Wright, Pacific 1959
652 ....Tom Gola, La Salle 1954
645 ....Charlie Tyra, Louisville 1956
631 ....Paul Silas, Creighton 1964
624 ....Elvin Hayes, Houston 1968
621 ....Artis Gilmore, Jacksonville 1970
618 ....Tom Gola, La Salle 1955
612 ....Ed Conlin, Fordham 1953
611 ....Art Quimby, Connecticut 1955

ASSISTS

406 ....Mark Wade, Nevada-Las Vegas 1987
399 ....Avery Johnson, Southern 1988
373 ....Anthony Manuel, Bradley 1988
333 ....Avery Johnson, Southern 1987
328 ....Mark Jackson, St. John's 1986
326 ....Sherman Douglas, Syracuse..................1989
309 ....Reid Gettys, Houston 1984
305 ....Carl Golston, Loyola (IL) 1985
303 ....Craig Neal, Georgia Tech.......................1988
297 ....Keith Jennings, E. Tennessee St. 1990

STEALS

150 ....Mookie Blaylock, Oklahoma 1988
142 ....Aldwin Ware, Florida A&M 1988
139 ....Darron Bittman, Chicago St....................1986
138 ....Nadav Henefeld, Connecticut.................1990
131 ....Mookie Blaylock, Oklahoma 1989
130 ....Ronn McMahon, Eastern Washington...1990

124 ....Marty Johnson, Towson St....................1988
120 ....Jim Paguaga, St. Francis (NY)..............1986
114 ....Tony Fairly, Baptist...............................1987
111 ....Kenny Robertson, Cleveland St. 1989
111 ....Lance Blanks, Texas 1989

BLOCKED SHOTS

207 ....David Robinson, Navy 1986
169 ....Alonzo Mourning, Georgetown...............1989
144 ....David Robinson, Navy 1987
129 ....Alan Ogg, Alabama-Birmingham............1989
128 ....Dikembe Mutombo, Georgetown............1990
127 ....Derrick Coleman, Syracuse....................1989
124 ....Duane Causwell, Temple 1989
124 ....Kenny Green, Rhode Island 1990
123 ....Tim Perry, Temple.................................1986
121 ....Rodney Blake, St. Joseph's (PA) 1986
121 ....Lorenzo Williams, Stetson.....................1990

FIELD GOAL PCT.

74.6 ......Steve Johnson, Oregon St. 1981
72.2 ......Dwayne Davis, Florida 1989
71.3 ......Keith Walker, Utica...............................1985
71.0 ......Steve Johnson, Oregon St. 1980
70.3 ......Alan Williams, Princeton.......................1987
70.2 ......Mark McNamara, California....................1982
69.9 ......Joe Senser, West Chester 1977
69.8 ......Lee Campbell, S.W. Missouri St.............1990
69.8 ......Steve Scheffler, Purdue 1990
69.1 ......Murray Brown, Florida St........................1979

FREE THROW PCT.

95.9 ......Craig Collins, Penn St. 1985
95.0 ......Rod Foster, UCLA.................................1982
94.4 ......Carlos Gibson, Marshall 1978
94.2 ......Jim Barton, Dartmouth 1986
93.9 ......Jack Moore, Nebraska 1982
93.5 ......Rob Robbins, New Mexico 1990
93.3 ......Tommy Boyer, Arkansas 1962
93.1 ......Damon Goodwin, Dayton 1986
92.9 ......Brian Magid, George Washington 1980
92.9 ......Mike Joseph, Bucknell...........................1990

3-PT FIELD GOAL PCT.

63.4 ......Glenn Tropf, Holy Cross.........................1988
58.5 ......Dave Calloway, Monmouth 1989
57.3 ......Steve Kerr, Arizona 1988
57.1 ......Reginald Jones, Prairie View 1987
56.3 ......Joel Tribelhorn, Colorado St...................1989
56.0 ......Mike Joseph, Bucknell...........................1988
54.8 ......Reginald Jones, Prairie View 1988
54.7 ......Eric Rhodes, S.F. Austin St....................1987
54.5 ......Dave Orlandini, Princeton 1988
53.9 ......Mike Joseph, Bucknell...........................1989

DIVISION I GAME RECORDS

POINTS
72 Kevin Bradshaw, U.S. Intl. vs. Loyola Mary. 1991
69 Pete Maravich, Louisiana St. vs. Alabama   1970
68 Calvin Murphy, Niagara vs. Syracuse   1968
66 Jay Handlan, Washington & Lee vs. Furman   1951
66 Pete Maravich, Louisiana St. vs. Tulane   1969
66 Anthony Roberts, Oral Rob. vs. N.C. A&T   1977
65 Anthony Roberts, Oral Roberts vs. Oregon   1977
65 Scott Haffner, Evansville vs. Dayton   1989
64 Pete Maravich, Louisiana St. vs. Kentucky   1970
63 Johnny Neumann, Mississippi St. vs. LSU   1971
63 Hersey Hawkins, Bradley vs. Detroit   1988

REBOUNDS
51 Bill Chambers, William & Mary vs. Virginia   1953
43 Charlie Slack, Marshall vs. Morris Harvey   1954
42 Tom Heinsohn, Holy Cross vs. Boston Coll.   1955
40 Art Quimby, Connecticut vs. Boston U.   1955
39 Maurice Stokes, St. Fran. (PA) vs. J. Carroll 1955
39 Dave DeBusschere, Detroit vs. C. Michigan   1960
39 Keith Swagerty, Pacific vs. Cal.-Santa Barb.   1965

ASSISTS
22 Tony Fairly, Baptist vs. Armstrong St.   1987
22 Avery Johnson, Southern vs. Texas South.   1988

22 Sherman Douglas, Syracuse vs. Providence 1989
21 Mark Wade, Nevada-Las Vegas vs. Navy   1986
21 Kelvin Scarborough, New Mexico vs. Hawaii 1987
21 Anthony Manuel, Bradley vs. Cal.-Irvine   1987
21 Avery Johnson, Southern vs. Alabama St.   1988

STEALS
13 Mookie Blaylock, Oklahoma vs. Centenary   1987
13 Mookie Blaylock, Oklahoma vs. Loyola Mary. 1988
12 Kenny Robertson, Cleveland St. vs. Wagner 1988
11 Darron Bittman, Chicago St. vs. McKendree 1986
11 Darron Bittman, Chicago St. vs. St. Xavier 1986
11 Marty Johnson, Towson St. vs. Bucknell   1988
11 Aldwin Ware, Florida A&M vs. Tuskegee   1988
11 Mark Macon, Temple vs. Notre Dame   1989

BLOCKED SHOTS
14 David Robinson, Navy vs. N.C.-Wilmington   1987
12 David Robinson, Navy vs. James Madison   1986
12 Derrick Lewis, Maryland vs. James Madison 1987
12 Rodney Blake, St. Joseph's (PA) vs. Cle. St. 1987
12 Walter Palmer, Dartmouth vs. Harvard   1988
12 Alan Ogg, Alabama-Birm. vs. Florida A&M   1988
12 Dikembe Mutombo, Georget. vs. St. John's   1989
12 Shaquille O'Neal, LSU vs. Loyola Mary.   1990

DIVISION I WINNINGEST TEAMS

ALL-TIME WINS

	YRS	WINS
North Carolina	81	1508
Kentucky	88	1501
Kansas	93	1459
St. John's	84	1444
Oregon St.	90	1387
Duke	86	1377
Temple	95	1356
Notre Dame	86	1335
Pennsylvania	90	1324
Syracuse	90	1318
Washington	89	1294
Indiana	91	1271
UCLA	72	1243
Fordham	88	1242
Princeton	91	1242

ALL-TIME WINNING PCT.

	W	L	T	PCT
Kentucky	1501	495	1	.752
North Carolina	1508	550	0	.733
St. John's	1444	613	0	.702
UCLA	1244	561	0	.689
Kansas	1459	677	0	.683
Syracuse	1318	625	0	.678
Western Kentucky	1237	588	0	.678
DePaul	1098	533	0	.673
Notre Dame	1335	668	1	.667
Duke	1377	693	0	.665
La Salle	1009	534	0	.653
Louisville	1188	634	0	.652
North Carolina St.	1234	663	0	.650
Temple	1356	735	0	.648
Weber St.	528	288	0	.647